ASPEN PUBLISHE

Quick Reference to HIPAA Compliance
2009/2010 Edition

by Pamela Sande and Joan Vigliotta

Quick Reference to HIPAA Compliance is a guide for human resources managers and employee benefits professionals who administer employer-sponsored health plans, health care providers, and anyone who needs to understand and comply with all the regulations under the Health Insurance Portability and Accountability Act of 1996 (HIPAA). The book is designed to provide these individuals with essential information in an easy-to-use format, including checklists, forms, and other tools to facilitate compliance. A topical index is also provided.

Highlights of the 2009/2010 Edition

The 2009/2010 Edition has been revised significantly. This edition includes the following:

- Updates for changes to HIPAA imposed by the American Recovery and Reinvestment Act, an economic stimulus bill, including:
    - new rules for business associates;
    - more stringent notice requirements to protect patient information when security breaches occur;
    - expansion of the rights of individuals regarding the security and privacy of their health information; and
    - increased civil penalties for HIPAA security and privacy breaches.
- New requirements for Medicare Supplements to be considered excepted benefits under HIPAA.
- Updates for changes in other major laws affecting health plans, including the Mental Health Parity Act.
- The text of the American Recovery and Reinvestment Act of 2009 and associated regulations.

9/09

For questions concerning this shipment, billing, or other customer service matters, call our Customer Service Department at 1-800-234-1660.

For toll-free ordering, please call 1-800-638-8437.

ASPEN PUBLISHERS

QUICK REFERENCE TO

2009/ 2010

HIPAA
COMPLIANCE

Pamela Sande
Joan Vigliotta
Marcia S. Wagner, *Contributor*
Virginia S. Peabody, *Contributor*

 Wolters Kluwer

Law & Business

AUSTIN   BOSTON   CHICAGO   NEW YORK   THE NETHERLANDS

This publication is designed to provide accurate and authoritative information in regard to the subject matter covered. It is sold with the understanding that the publisher is not engaged in rendering legal, accounting, or other professional services. If legal advice or other professional assistance is required, the services of a competent professional person should be sought.

—From a *Declaration of Principles* jointly adopted by
a Committee of the American Bar Association and
a Committee of Publishers and Associations

Printed in the United States of America

ISBN 978-07355-8196-8

1 2 3 4 5 6 7 8 9 0

About Wolters Kluwer Law & Business

Wolters Kluwer Law & Business is a leading provider of research information and workflow solutions in key specialty areas. The strengths of the individual brands of Aspen Publishers, CCH, Kluwer Law International and Loislaw are aligned within Wolters Kluwer Law & Business to provide comprehensive, in-depth solutions and expert-authored content for the legal, professional and education markets.

CCH was founded in 1913 and has served more than four generations of business professionals and their clients. The CCH products in the Wolters Kluwer Law & Business group are highly regarded electronic and print resources for legal, securities, antitrust and trade regulation, government contracting, banking, pension, payroll, employment and labor, and healthcare reimbursement and compliance professionals.

Aspen Publishers is a leading information provider for attorneys, business professionals and law students. Written by preeminent authorities, Aspen products offer analytical and practical information in a range of specialty practice areas from securities law and intellectual property to mergers and acquisitions and pension/benefits. Aspen's trusted legal education resources provide professors and students with high-quality, up-to-date and effective resources for successful instruction and study in all areas of the law.

Kluwer Law International supplies the global business community with comprehensive English-language international legal information. Legal practitioners, corporate counsel and business executives around the world rely on the Kluwer Law International journals, loose-leafs, books and electronic products for authoritative information in many areas of international legal practice.

Loislaw is a premier provider of digitized legal content to small law firm practitioners of various specializations. Loislaw provides attorneys with the ability to quickly and efficiently find the necessary legal information they need, when and where they need it, by facilitating access to primary law as well as state-specific law, records, forms and treatises.

Wolters Kluwer Law & Business, a unit of Wolters Kluwer, is headquartered in New York and Riverwoods, Illinois. Wolters Kluwer is a leading multinational publisher and information services company.

ASPEN PUBLISHERS SUBSCRIPTION NOTICE

This Aspen Publishers product is updated on a periodic basis with supplements to reflect important changes in the subject matter. If you purchased this product directly from Aspen Publishers, we have already recorded your subscription for the update service.

   If, however, you purchased this product from a bookstore and wish to receive future updates and revised or related volumes billed separately with a 30-day examination review, please contact our Customer Service Department at 1-800-234-1660 or send your name, company name (if applicable), address, and the title of the product to:

ASPEN PUBLISHERS
7201 McKinney Circle
Frederick, MD 21704

Important Aspen Publishers Contact Information

- To order any Aspen Publishers title, go to *www.aspenpublishers.com* or call 1-800-638-8437.
- To reinstate your manual update service, call 1-800-638-8437.
- To contact Customer Care, e-mail *customer.care@aspenpublishers.com,* call 1-800-234-1660, fax 1-800-901-9075, or mail correspondence to Order Department, Aspen Publishers, PO Box 990, Frederick, MD 21705.
- To review your account history or pay an invoice online, visit *www.aspenpublishers.com/payinvoices*.

About the Authors

PAMELA SANDE, SPHR, is Managing Principal of HR Link, a human resources management consulting firm. Ms. Sande has more than 25 years of experience in Human Resources and employee benefits. She has authored several books on subjects of critical interest to employee benefits professionals, including the Family and Medical Leave Act and compliance with the Employee Retirement Income Security Act of 1974. She is the co-author with Joan Vigliotta of *Quick Reference to COBRA Compliance.* Ms. Sande received her master's degree in Management from Cambridge College and her undergraduate degree from Boston University.

JOAN VIGLIOTTA is Human Resources Director at Elite Detective Services, Inc., in Beverly, Massachusetts. Ms. Vigliotta has more than 20 years of experience in human resources and employee benefits. Her areas of expertise include retirement and welfare benefits consulting and compliance, development of employee communications, and researching technical compliance issues. Ms. Vigliotta has also designed various client reference materials. She is the co-author with Pamela Sande of *Quick Reference to COBRA Compliance.* In addition to a B.S., Ms. Vigliotta has received certification in legal studies from Northeastern University.

Acknowledgments

We wish to express our sincere gratitude to Marcia S. Wagner and Virginia S. Peabody of The Wagner Law Group, Boston, Massachusetts, for their work on the HIPAA privacy rules in Chapter 8 of this book.

We also wish to thank the editorial and production staff at Aspen Publishers for their guidance, support, assistance, and skills in the preparation of this book.

Table of Contents

Table of Contents

Chapter 1

About This Guide

Purpose of this guide

Quick Reference to HIPAA Compliance is a guide for human resources managers and employee benefits professionals who administer employer-sponsored health plans, health care providers, and anyone who needs to understand and comply with all the regulations under the Health Insurance Portability and Accountability Act of 1996 (HIPAA). The book is designed to provide these individuals with essential information in an easy-to-use format, including checklists, forms, and other tools to facilitate compliance.

HIPAA

The Health Insurance Portability and Accountability Act (HIPAA) was enacted on August 21, 1996. HIPAA amended the Internal Revenue Code of 1986 (IRC), the Employee Retirement Income Security Act of 1974 (ERISA), and the Public Health Service Act (PHSA). The main intent of HIPAA is to improve the portability and continuity of health care coverage in the group and individual insurance markets and group health plan coverage provided in connection with employment.

Rules imposed by HIPAA

The HIPAA provisions are designed to improve the availability and portability of health care coverage by:

- Limiting exclusions for preexisting medical conditions
- Providing credit for prior health coverage and a process for transmitting certificates and other information concerning prior coverage to a new group health plan or insurer
- Providing new rights that allow individuals to enroll for health coverage when they lose other health coverage or have a new dependent
- Prohibiting discrimination in enrollment and premiums against employees and their dependents based on health status
- Guaranteeing availability of health insurance coverage for small employers and renewability of health insurance in both the small and large group markets
- Preserving, through narrow preemption provisions, the states' traditional role in regulating health insurance, including state flexibility to provide greater protections

About This Guide, continued

In this guide

This edition contains 13 chapters:

The 2009/2010 Edition has been updated to include changes imposed by the American Recovery and Reinvestment Act (ARRA), an economic stimulus bill, signed into law by President Obama on February 17, 2009. ARRA imposes new requirements on covered entities and business associates. These rules also expand HIPAA's privacy and security regulations. In addition, this edition includes new requirements for Medicare supplements to be considered excepted benefits. Also, this edition has been updated for changes in other major laws affecting health plans, including the Mental Health Parity Act.

About This Guide, continued

Format

Within the chapters, information is presented in sections, each focusing on a topic or subtopic that relates to the heading printed at the top of the page. For ease of use, the subtopics are called out in the left margin. This format enables you to scan the pages and quickly locate the information you need.

Job aids

Many of the chapters include tools specifically designed to assist the benefits professional in HIPAA administration—charts, checklists, sample notices, worksheets, and flowcharts. A job aid is labeled as such and is identified by a heading or subtitle across the top of the page.

Legal and technical advice

Although the authors have made every effort to provide accurate and up-to-date information, this guide is not a substitute for legal or technical advice.

Chapter 2

Upcoming Requirements Imposed by the American Recovery and Reinvestment Act of 2009

Introduction President Barack Obama signed the American Recovery and Reinvestment Act (ARRA) (Pub. L. No. 111-5), an economic stimulus bill, into law on February 17, 2009. ARRA imposes new requirements on covered entities and business associates. These rules also expand HIPAA's privacy and security regulations.

Business Entities The new legislation requires that business associates be subject to the security and privacy requirements. Business associates are companies and consultants who provide services for covered entities such as health plans and providers.
Business Associates can include the following firms or businesses:

- Legal
- Actuarial
- Accounting
- Consulting
- Data aggregation
- Management
- Administrative
- Financial services

Previously, business associates were subject to the security and privacy rules through their contracts with the covered entities. Under ARRA, these business associates are directly subject to HIPAA.

Security Breach Notice Requirements ARRA imposes more stringent notice requirements to protect patient information. Covered entities and business associates must provide notification to any person whose protected health information was breached. Breach of security occurs when unsecured health information is acquired without the individual's authorization. Some examples of breach of security may be a laptop theft, theft of hard copy records, or unauthorized access by an employee or other person.

Upcoming Requirements Imposed by the American Recovery and Reinvestment Act of 2009, continued

Security Breach Notice Requirements (continued)

In general, these covered entities must notify affected persons by written notice within 60 days of discovery of the breach. The notices must include the following:

- A brief description of how the breach occurred, including the date of the breach and date of discovery of the breach.

- A description of the type of unsecured information that was involved (i.e, social security number, address, date of birth, etc.).

- Steps that individuals should take to protect themselves from harm.

- Contact procedures for individuals to ask questions or get additional information.

In addition, if over 500 individuals were affected by the breach, the covered entity may also have to notify the Federal Trade Commission of the breach.

Individuals' Rights

ARRA expands the rights of individuals regarding the security and privacy of his/her health information. Individuals may request certain disclosures in electronic format. For example, an individual may request information on treatment, payment, or health care operations.

Marketing

ARRA also includes strict prohibitions on the use of private health information for marketing purposes.

Increased Penalties

ARRA has increased the civil penalties for HIPAA security and privacy breaches. The penalties are as follows:

- Unknowing violations; at least $100 per violation, not to exceed $25,000 in a calendar year,

- Violation due to reasonable cause, not willful neglect; at least $1,000 per violation, not to exceed $100,000 in a calendar year, and

- Violation due to willful neglect; at least $10,000, not to exceed $250,000 in a calendar year.

However if the violation is not corrected within 30 days, the penalty increases to at least $50,000, not to exceed $1,500,000.

Upcoming Requirements Imposed by the American Recovery and Reinvestment Act of 2009, continued

Effective Dates

In general, the ARRA requirements will be effective on February 17, 2010, one year from the Act's enactment. However, notification of security breaches may be effective on September 18, 2009. Please refer to Chapter 8 of this Guide for details on all of these upcoming changes.

Chapter 3

Covered Plans

Introduction   This chapter discusses the rules for determining whether a group health plan is subject to the requirements of HIPAA, as well as the information needed to make that determination.

Most employers are required to meet the HIPAA requirements. Certain exemptions apply, however. This chapter discusses also exempt employers and exempt plans.

In this chapter   This chapter has three sections:

A. Group Health Plans

Plans subject to HIPAA
In general, all group health plans with two or more participants who are current employees, including partnerships and self-employed plans, are subject to HIPAA.[1] (See Sections B and C of this chapter for information on exempt plans and benefits.)

Group health plan, defined
A **group health plan** means an employee welfare benefit plan that provides medical care to employees or their dependents directly or through insurance, reimbursement, or otherwise.[2]

Medical care, defined
Medical care means the amount paid, including insurance, for the diagnosis, cure, mitigation, treatment, or prevention of disease, and any other undertaking that affects the structure or function of the human body. This definition also includes transportation used primarily for, and essential to, medical care.[3]

Health insurance coverage, defined
Health insurance coverage means the benefits consisting of medical care provided directly through insurance, reimbursement, or otherwise under any hospital or medical service policy or certificate, hospital or medical service plan contract, or health maintenance organization (HMO) contract offered by a health insurance issuer.[4]

---

[1] I.R.C. § 9831(a); ERISA § 732(a) and (d); PHSA 42 U.S.C.S. § 300gg-21(a).
[2] I.R.C. § 9832(a); ERISA § 733(a)(1); PHSA 42 U.S.C.S. § 300gg-91(a)(1).
[3] I.R.C. § 9832(d)(3) and § 213(d); ERISA § 733(a)(2); and PHSA 42 U.S.C.S. § 300gg-91(a)(2).
[4] I.R.C. § 9832(b)(1); ERISA § 733(b)(1); and PHSA 42 U.S.C.S. § 300gg-91(b)(1).

A. Group Health Plans, continued

Health insurance issuer, defined	The term **health insurance issuer** means an insurance company, insurance service, or insurance organization, including an HMO, that is licensed to engage in the business of insurance in a state and that is subject to state insurance regulation. This term does not include a group health plan.[5]
HMO, defined	In general, an **HMO** is an independent health care organization that consists of physicians, hospitals, and other medical professionals through which employers offer medical coverage to employees and their dependents who reside in the HMO's geographical service area. HIPAA defines an **HMO** as an organization recognized as such under state or federal law, or a similar organization recognized under state law.[6]
Group health insurance coverage, defined	**Group health insurance coverage** means health insurance coverage offered in connection with a group health plan.[7]
Dependent, defined	A **dependent** is any individual who is or may become eligible for coverage under the terms of the group health plan because of a relationship to the participant.[8]

---

[5] I.R.C. § 9832(b)(2); ERISA § 733(b)(2); and PHSA 42 U.S.C.S. § 300gg-91(b)(2).
[6] I.R.C. § 9832(b)(3); ERISA § 733(b)(3); and PHSA 42 U.S.C.S. § 300gg-91(b)(3).
[7] ERISA § 733(b)(4); PHSA 42 U.S.C.S. § 300gg-91(b)(4).
[8] I.R.S. Reg. § 54.9801-2.

B. Exempt Plans

Plans exempt from HIPAA

The following plans are exempt from the HIPAA requirements:

- Small plans[9]
- Certain state and local government plans[10]

Small plans

HIPAA does not apply to small group health plans that have fewer than two participants who are current employees on the first day of the plan year.[11]

State and local government plans

Some state and local government plans may elect not to be covered by HIPAA's portability, nondiscrimination, guaranteed availability, and guaranteed renewability provisions. However, these plans are not exempt from the certification requirements.[12]

When a state or local government plan opts not to be covered by HIPAA, it must notify enrollees annually of the election not to be covered and the facts and consequences of such an election.[13]

---

[9] I.R.C. § 9831(a)(2); ERISA § 732(a); and PHSA 42 U.S.C.S. § 300gg-21(a).
[10] PHSA 42 U.S.C.S. § 300gg-21(b).
[11] I.R.C. § 9831(a)(2); ERISA § 732(a); and PHSA 42 U.S.C.S. § 300gg-21(a).
[12] PHSA 42 U.S.C.S. § 300gg-21(b)(2)(A).
[13] PHSA 42 U.S.C.S. § 300gg-21(b)(2)(C).

C. Excepted Benefits

Excepted benefits, defined

Excepted benefits (i.e., benefits not subject to HIPAA) are the following:[14]

- Coverage only for accident or disability income insurance, or any combination thereof
- Liability insurance, including general liability and automobile liability insurance
- Coverage issued as a supplement to liability insurance
- Automobile medical payment insurance
- Workers' compensation or similar insurance
- Credit only insurance (i.e., mortgage insurance)
- Coverage for on-site medical clinics

In addition, health savings accounts (HSAs) and most health flexible spending accounts (FSAs) are excepted from the HIPAA requirements.[15]

Excepted benefits, if offered separately

The following benefits are excepted from HIPAA if they are provided under a separate policy, certificate, or insurance contract, or are otherwise not an integral part of the plan:[16]

- Limited scope dental benefits
- Limited scope vision benefits
- Long-term care benefits

Benefits are an integral part of the plan unless a participant has the right to elect not to receive coverage for the benefits. If the participant elects to receive coverage for excepted benefits, he or she would pay an additional premium or contribution for the coverage.

---

[14] I.R.C. § 9832(c)(1); ERISA § 733(c); and PHSA 42 U.S.C.S. § 300gg-21(c).
[15] I.R.S. Reg. §54.9831-1(c)(3)(v); DOL Reg. §2590.732(c)(3)(v); and HCFA Reg. § 146.145(c)(5),
[16] I.R.C. § 9832(c)(2); ERISA § 733(c)(2).

C. Excepted Benefits, continued

Limited scope dental benefits and limited scope vision benefits, defined

Limited scope dental benefits and **limited scope vision benefits** are dental benefits or vision benefits sold under a separate policy or rider and are not an integral part of the plan.[17]

Limited scope dental benefits are those which are substantially for treatment of the mouth, including the organs or structure of the mouth. Limited scope vision benefits are those which are substantially for treatment of the eye.[18]

Long-term care benefits, defined

Long-term care benefits are benefits that are:[19]

- Subject to state long-term care laws;
- Provided under a qualified long-term care insurance contract; and
- Based on cognitive impairment or a loss of functional capacity that is expected to be chronic.

Uncoordinated benefits

Specified disease coverage (e.g., cancer-only policies), hospital indemnity insurance, and other fixed-dollar indemnity insurance (e.g., $100 per day) are exempt from HIPAA if the following conditions are met:[20]

- Benefits are provided under a separate policy, certificate, or contract of insurance.
- No coordination exists between the benefits and an exclusion of benefits under any group health plan maintained by the same plan sponsor.
- Benefits are paid for an event without regard to whether benefits are provided for the event under any other covered group health plan maintained by the same plan sponsor.

---

[17] I.R.S. Reg. § 54.9804-1(b)(3)(iii); DOL Reg. § 2590.732(c)(3)(iii); and HCFA Reg. § 146.145(c)(3)(iii).

[18] I.R.S. Reg. § 54.9831-1(c)(3).

[19] I.R.S. Reg. § 54.9831-1(c)(3)(iv); DOL Reg. § 2590.732(c)(3)(iv); and HCFA Reg. § 146.145(c)(3)(iv).

[20] I.R.S. Reg. § 54.9831-1(c)(4); DOL Reg. § 2590.732(c)(4); and HCFA Reg. § 146.145(c)(4).

C. Excepted Benefits, continued

Medicare supplements

Medicare supplements and other similar group health plan supplements are excepted if offered under a separate policy, certificate, or contract of insurance.[21]

In addition, the supplement is required to satisfy all of the following rules:[22]

- Must be issued by an entity that does not provide the primary coverage under the plan;
- Must be specifically designed to fill gaps in primary coverage, such as coinsurance or deductibles, but does not include a policy, certificate, or contract of insurance that becomes secondary or supplements only under a coordination of benefits provision;
- Must not exceed 15 percent of the cost of primary coverage; and
- Must not differentiate among individuals in eligibility, benefits, or premiums based on any health fact of an individual or individual's dependent.

---

[21] I.R.S. Reg. § 54.9831-1(c)(5); DOL Reg. § 2590.732(c)(5); and HCFA Reg. § 146.145(c)(5).
[22] I.R.B. 2008-7.

Chapter 4

Limitations on Preexisting Condition Exclusions

Introduction   A primary purpose of HIPAA is to improve the availability and portability of group health plan coverage. This chapter addresses the three ways in which HIPAA accomplishes this purpose:

1. Limits exclusions for preexisting medical conditions
2. Gives credit for prior group health coverage and provides a procedure for certifying prior coverage
3. Provides individuals with the right to enroll in a group health plan if they lose other health coverage or acquire a new dependent

In this chapter   This chapter has 16 sections:

A. General Rules

Introduction   HIPAA places limits on group health plans with preexisting condition exclusions that limit or exclude benefits for new participants and beneficiaries with preexisting medical conditions before joining the plan.

Preexisting condition exclusion defined

A **preexisting condition exclusion** limits or excludes benefits for a participant or beneficiary with a medical condition that existed before the effective date of coverage under the plan (whether or not medical advice, diagnosis, care, or treatment for the condition was recommended or received before the coverage began).[1]

A preexisting condition exclusion includes any exclusion that applies to a participant or beneficiary as a result of information that was obtained about his or her health status before joining the plan, such as information obtained through a pre-enrollment questionnaire or pre-employment physical.

General requirements

Under HIPAA, a group health plan may impose a preexisting condition exclusion only if:[2]

- The exclusion relates to a physical or mental condition, regardless of cause, for which medical advice, diagnosis, care, or treatment has been recommended and received within the six-month period (or less if the plan so chooses) ending on the enrollment date. (This rule is referred to as the *six-month look-back rule*.)
- The exclusion cannot extend beyond 12 months (18 months in the case of a late enrollee) after the enrollment date. (This rule is referred to as the *maximum length of preexisting condition exclusion*.)
- The period of any exclusion is reduced by the aggregate periods of creditable coverage (if any) that apply to the participant or beneficiary as of the enrollment date. (This requirement is referred to as the *creditable coverage* rules.)

(See Sections B through G of this chapter for details on these rules.)

---

[1] I.R.S. Reg. § 54.9801-3(a)(1); PWBA Reg. § 2590.701-3(a)(1); and HCFA Reg. § 146.111(a)(1).
[2] I.R.S. Reg. § 54.9801-3(a)(2); PWBA Reg. § 2590.701-3(a)(2); and HCFA Reg. § 146.111(a)(2).

A. General Rules, continued

General notice of preexisting condition exclusion

If a plan imposes a preexisting exclusion, the plan must provide a written general notice of preexisting condition exclusion to plan participants.[3] The notice must be provided before the preexisting exclusion can be applied. The notice must be provided as part of any written application or enrollment materials. If no enrollment materials are provided, the notice must be provided as soon as possible following a request.

The notice must contain the following information:

- Existence and terms of any preexisting condition provision including the plan's look back period, maximum preexisting condition period, and how the plan will reduce the maximum exclusion period by creditable coverage
- Description of individual rights to demonstrate creditable coverage and any applicable waiting periods through a certificate of creditable coverage, including the right of an individual to request a certificate from a prior plan and that the plan will assist in obtaining the certificate from the prior plan
- Contact person, including address and telephone, for obtaining addition information and assistance regarding the preexisting condition exclusion

Individual notice of preexisting condition exclusion

Once an individual has presented evidence of creditable coverage and after the plan has made a determination of creditable coverage, the plan must provide the individual a written notice stating the length of the preexisting exclusion that remains after offsetting any prior creditable coverage.[4] This notice is not required to identify any specific medical conditions. A plan is not required to provide this notice if the plan does not impose any preexisting condition exclusion on the individual or if the exclusion is completely offset by the individual's prior creditable coverage.

The individual notice must be provided by the earliest date following a determination that the plan, acting in a reasonable and prompt fashion, can provide the notice.

---

[3] I.R.S. Reg. § 54.9801-3(c); PWBA Reg. § 2590.701-3(c); and HCFA Reg. § 146.111(c).
[4] I.R.S. Reg. § 54.9801-3(e); PWBA Reg. § 2590.701-3(e); and HCFA Reg. § 146.111(e).

A. General Rules, continued

Individual notice of preexisting condition exclusion (continued)

The notice must contain the following information:[5]

- The plan's determination of any preexisting condition exclusion, including the last day on which the preexisting condition exclusion applies
- The basis for such determination, including the source and substance of any information on which the plan relied
- Explanation of individual's right to submit additional evidence of creditable coverage
- Description of any applicable appeal procedures

USERRA

The final regulations, published in February 2005, provide that the Uniformed Services Employment and Reemployment Rights Act (USERRA) can affect how a preexisting condition exclusion applies to those employees returning to work following military leave.[6]

---

[5] I.R.S. Reg. § 54.9801-3(e); PWBA Reg. § 2590.701-3(e); and HCFA Reg. § 146.111(e).
[6] I.R.S. Reg. §54.9801-3(a)(2)(iv).

B. Six-Month Look-Back Rule

Compliance with six-month look-back rule

To comply with the six-month look-back rule, a plan's preexisting condition exclusion must relate to a participant's or beneficiary's physical or mental condition, regardless of cause, for which medical advice, diagnosis, care, or treatment was received within the six-month period (or shorter period if the plan provides) ending on the enrollment date.[7] (See Section D of this chapter for more information.) If a doctor recommends treatment before the six-month look-back period, a plan can impose a preexisting condition exclusion only if the participant actually receives the treatment within the six-month period.[8]

Medical advice and treatment

For purposes of the six-month look-back rule, medical advice, diagnosis, care, or treatment may be taken into account only if it is recommended by or received from an individual licensed or similarly authorized to provide the services under state law and operating within the scope of practice authorized by state law.[9]

When the six-month look-back period begins

The six-month look-back period ending on the enrollment date begins on the six-month anniversary date preceding the enrollment date.[10]

Example.

Ken enrolls in his employer's plan on August 1, 2009. The six-month look-back period begins February 1, 2009, and ends July 31, 2009.

---

[7] I.R.S. Reg. § 54.9801-3(a)(1)(i); PWBA Reg. § 2590.701-3(a)(1)(i); and HCFA Reg. § 146.111(a)(1)(i).

[8] I.R.S. Reg. §54.9801-3(a)(1).

[9] I.R.S. Reg. § 54.9801-3(a)(1)(i)(A); PWBA Reg. § 2590.701-3(a)(1)(i)(A); and HCFA Reg. § 146.111(a)(1)(i)(A).

[10] I.R.S. Reg. § 54.9801-3(a)(1)(i)(B); PWBA Reg. § 2590.701-3(a)(1)(i)(B); and HCFA Reg. § 146.111(a)(1)(i)(B).

B. Six-Month Look-Back Rule, continued

Applying the six-month look-back rule

The following examples, from the HIPAA Final Regulations, illustrate how to apply the six-month look-back rule.[11]

Example 1.

Jane Doe received treatment for a medical condition seven months before her enrollment date in her employer's group health plan. As part of her treatment, her physician recommended a follow-up exam for two months later. Ms. Doe did not return for the follow-up exam; nor did she receive any other medical advice, diagnosis, care, or treatment for her condition during the six-month look-back period.

The plan may not impose a preexisting medical condition exclusion period for the condition for which Ms. Doe received medical treatment seven months before her enrollment date.

Example 2.

The facts are the same as those in Example 1, except that the plan learns of Jane Doe's condition and attaches a rider to her policy excluding coverage for the condition. Three months after enrollment, Ms. Doe's medical condition recurs and the plan denies payment under the rider.

The rider is a preexisting condition exclusion and, therefore, cannot be imposed.

Example 3.

John Smith has asthma and is treated for his condition several times during the six-month look-back period before enrolling in his employer's group health plan. The plan imposes a 12-month preexisting condition exclusion. Mr. Smith has no prior creditable coverage to reduce the exclusion period. Three months after his enrollment date, Mr. Smith's coverage under the plan begins. Two months later, Mr. Smith is hospitalized for asthma.

---

[11] I.R.S. Reg. § 54.9801-3(a)(1)(i)(C); PWBA Reg. § 2590.701-3(a)(1)(i)(C); and HCFA Reg. § 146.111(a)(1)(i)(C).

B. Six-Month Look-Back Rule, continued

Applying the six-month look-back rule (continued)

Example 3 (cont'd).

The plan may exclude payment for John Smith's hospital stay, as well as for any physician services associated with his condition, because the care is for a medical condition (i.e., asthma) for which Mr. Smith received treatment during the six-month look-back period.

Example 4.

Mary Brown is a participant in her employer's group health plan, which has a preexisting condition exclusion. Ms. Brown has diabetes. In addition, she has a foot condition caused by poor circulation and retinal degeneration—both of which may be directly attributed to her diabetes. Shortly after enrolling in the plan, she falls and breaks her leg.

The leg fracture is not related to Ms. Brown's diabetes even though her poor circulation and vision may have contributed to causing the accident. Therefore, the plan's preexisting condition exclusion cannot be imposed for treatment for her fractured leg. However, any additional medical services that Mary Brown needs because of her preexisting diabetic condition that ordinarily would not be needed by another patient with a broken leg who does not have diabetes may be subject to the preexisting condition exclusion.

C. Maximum Length of Preexisting Condition Exclusion

Maximum length rule, defined

The **maximum length of preexisting condition rule** establishes the maximum duration of a preexisting condition exclusion period.

Under the rule, a preexisting condition exclusion period cannot extend for more than 12 months (or 18 months in the case of a *late enrollee*) after the enrollment date.[12] (See Section D of this chapter for enrollment definitions, including the definition of a late enrollee.)

The following examples illustrate the maximum length of preexisting condition exclusion rule:

Example 1.

Dave's enrollment date is August 1, 2009, and neither he nor his beneficiary is a late enrollee. Under the maximum length of preexisting condition rule, the preexisting condition period begins August 1, 2009, and ends July 31, 2010.

Example 2.

If Dave in Example 1 is a late enrollee, or his beneficiary is a late enrollee, the preexisting condition exclusion period would begin on his enrollment date, August 1, 2009, and end on January 31, 2011.

---

[12] I.R.S. Reg. § 54.9801-3(a)(1)(ii); PWBA Reg. § 2590.701-3(a)(1)(ii); and HCFA Reg. § 146.111(a)(1)(ii).

D. Enrollment Definitions

Introduction
The six-month look-back and maximum length of preexisting condition exclusion rules include enrollment terms. This section defines the terms.

Enrollment date, defined
Enrollment date is the first day of coverage or, if there is a waiting period, the first day of the waiting period.[13] The enrollment date does not change because of a plan participant changing coverage options (e.g., during open enrollment) or the insurer changes.[14]

First day of coverage, Defined
For an individual covered under a group health plan, the **first day of coverage** is the first day of coverage under the plan.[15]

Waiting period
The **waiting period** means the period that must pass before coverage for an employee or dependent who is otherwise eligible to enroll in a group health plan can become effective.[16] For late enrollees, any period before a late or special enrollment is not a waiting period.

The following example illustrates the terms *first day of coverage* and *enrollment date* as they apply to the six-month look back rule and the maximum length of preexisting condition exclusion. [17]

---

[13] I.R.S. Reg. § 54.9801-3(a)(3)(i); PWBA Reg. § 2590.701-3(a)(3)(i); and HCFA Reg. § 146.111(a)(3)(i).
[14] I.R.S. Reg. § 54.9801-3(a)(3).
[15] I.R.S. Reg. § 54.9801-3(a)(3)(ii); PWBA Reg. § 2590.701-3(a)(3)(ii); and HCFA Reg. § 146.111(a)(3)(ii).
[16] I.R.S. Reg. § 54.9801-3(a)(3)(iii); PWBA Reg. § 2590.701-3(a)(3)(iii); and HCFA Reg. § 146.111(a)(3)(iii).
[17] I.R.S. Reg. §54.9801-3(a)(3)(iv); PWBA Reg. § 2590.701-3(a)(2)(iv); and HCFA Reg. § 146.111(a)(2)(iv).

D. Enrollment Definitions, continued

> ### *Example.*
>
> The XYZ Company's health plan coverage begins on the first day of the first pay period following an employee's date of hire or on any subsequent January 1. The plan imposes a preexisting condition exclusion for 12 months (reduced by an individual's creditable coverage) following an individual's enrollment date. John Doe is hired on October 13, 2009. He has no creditable coverage.
>
> Mr. Doe's first day of coverage is October 25, 2009 (the first day of the pay period after his date of hire). His enrollment date is October 13, 2009, the first day of the waiting period for enrollment. The six-month look-back period begins April 13, 2009, and ends October 12, 2009. The maximum period during which the plan could apply a preexisting condition exclusion would be the period from October 13, 2009, through October 12, 2010.

Late enrollee, defined

A **late enrollee** is an individual whose enrollment in a plan is a *late enrollment*.[18]

Late enrollment, defined

Late enrollment is enrollment in a group health plan on a date other than:[19]

- The earliest date on which coverage can become effective under the plan's terms, or
- A special enrollment date for the individual.

---

[18] I.R.S. Reg. § 54.9801-3(a)(3)(v); PWBA Reg. § 2590.701-3(a)(3)(v); and HCFA Reg. § 146.111(a)(3)(v).
[19] I.R.S. Reg. § 54.9801-3(a)(3)(vi); PWBA Reg. § 2590.701-3(a)(3)(vi); and HCFA Reg. § 146.111(a)(3)(v).

D. Enrollment Definitions, continued

If an individual terminates employment (and, therefore, ceases to be eligible for plan coverage), then later is rehired and becomes eligible for coverage again, only eligibility during the most recent period of employment is taken into account in determining whether the individual is a late enrollee.[20] Similar rules apply if an individual again becomes eligible for coverage following a suspension of coverage that applied generally under the plan.

The following examples illustrate how to determine whether an individual is a late enrollee:[21]

Example 1.

Ann Jones first becomes eligible for coverage under her employer's group health plan on January 1, 2009. However, she does not elect to enroll in the plan until April 1, 2009. April 1 is not a special enrollment date for Ms. Jones. Ms. Jones is a late enrollee.

Example 2.

The facts are the same as those in Example 1, except that Ann Jones does not enroll in the plan on April 1, 2009, and terminates employment on July 1, 2009, without ever having enrolled in her employer's plan. Ms. Jones is rehired on January 1, 2009, and elects coverage under the plan, which is effective January 1. Ms. Jones is not a late enrollee.

---

[20] I.R.S. Reg. § 54.9801-3(a)(3)(vi)(B); PWBA Reg. § 2590.701-3(a)(3)(vi)(B); and HCFA Reg. § 146.111(a)(3)(vi)(B).
[21] I.R.S. Reg. § 54.9801-3(a)(3)(vii); PWBA Reg. § 2590.701-3(a)(3)(vii); and HCFA Reg. § 146.111(a)(3)(vii).

E. Creditable Coverage Rules

Creditable coverage rules

To comply with the creditable coverage rules, a plan must reduce a preexisting condition exclusion period by any aggregate periods of creditable coverage that apply to a participant or a beneficiary as of his or her enrollment date.[22]

Creditable coverage, defined

In general, **creditable coverage** is an individual's coverage under any of the following:[23]

- Group health plan
- Health insurance coverage
- Medicare Part A or B
- Medicaid (other than coverage consisting solely of benefits under Section 1928 of the Social Security Act, which is the program for distribution of pediatric vaccines)
- TRICARE (medical and dental coverage for members and former members of the military)
- Indian Health Service or tribal organization medical care program
- State health benefits risk pool
- Federal employees health benefits program
- Public health plan
- Peace Corps health plan
- S-CHIP (State children's health insurance program)[24]

---

[22] I.R.C. § 9801(a); ERISA § 701(a); and PHSA 42 U.S.C.S. § 300gg(a).
[23] I.R.S. Reg. § 54.9801-4(a)(1); PWBA Reg. § 2590.701-4(a)(1); and HCFA Reg. § 146.113(a)(1).
[24] I.R.S. Reg. § 54.9801-4(a).

E. Creditable Coverage Rules, continued

Methods of counting creditable coverage

In reducing a preexisting condition exclusion period for creditable coverage, a plan may use one of the following methods:[25]

- The standard method,
- The alternative method, or
- Any other counting method that is at least as favorable to the individual as either of the above.

(See Sections F and G of this chapter for details on the standard and alternative methods of counting creditable coverage.)

---

[25] I.R.S. Reg. § 54.9801-4(a)(3); PWBA Reg. § 2590.701-4(a)(3); and HCFA Reg. § 146.113(a)(3).

F. Standard Method

Standard method, defined

Under the **standard method**, a plan determines the amount of creditable coverage without regard to the type of benefits provided.[26] The amount of creditable coverage is based on days. To determine the amount, the plan must count every day the individual had creditable coverage.[27]

If the individual has creditable coverage from more than one source on a given day, the coverage is counted as one day.

Waiting period days are not counted as creditable coverage.

Days of creditable coverage before a significant break in coverage need not be counted.

Significant break in coverage, defined

A **significant break in coverage** is a period of at least 63 consecutive days during which an individual has no creditable coverage.[28] In determining whether an individual has had a significant break in coverage, waiting periods and affiliation periods may not be taken into account. In addition, if a state insurance law applies to a policy or contract for an ERISA-covered plan, and a law not preempted by ERISA from applying to the plan requires a break longer than 63 days before coverage can be disregarded, then the longer break applies.

---

[26] I.R.S. Reg. § 54.9801-4(b)(1); PWBA Reg. § 2590.701-4(b)(1); and HCFA Reg. § 146.113(b)(1).

[27] I.R.S. Reg. § 54.9801-4(b)(2); PWBA Reg. § 2590.701-4(b)(2); and HCFA Reg. § 146.113(b)(2).

[28] I.R.S. Reg. § 54.9801-4(b)(2)(iii); PWBA Reg. § 2590.701-4(b)(2)(iii); and HCFA Reg. § 146.113(b)(2)(iii).

F. Standard Method, continued

Examples   The following examples illustrate how to count creditable coverage using the standard method:[29]

> ### Example 1.
>
> Mary Ann worked for an employer and had creditable coverage for 18 months before she terminated employment. Sixty-four days after her coverage terminated, she accepted a new position and enrolled in her new employer's plan. Her new employer's plan has a 12-month preexisting condition exclusion period.
>
> Mary Ann had a significant break in coverage. Therefore, she is subject to the new employer's plan's 12-month preexisting condition exclusion.
>
> ### Example 2.
>
> The facts are the same as those in Example 1, except that Mary Ann starts her new job and is enrolled in her new employer's plan on the sixty-third day after her coverage under her former employer's plan terminated.
>
> Mary Ann has had a break in coverage of only 62 days. Therefore, her coverage under her former employer's plan must be counted for purposes of reducing the preexisting condition exclusion period under the new employer's plan.
>
> ### Example 3.
>
> The facts are the same as those in Example 1, except that the new employer's plan provides benefits through an insurance policy that, as required by state insurance laws, defines a significant break in coverage as 90 days. The new employer's plan must count Mary Ann's period of creditable coverage before the 62-day break.

---

[29] I.R.S. Reg. § 54.9801-4 (b)(2)(v); PWBA Reg. § 2590.701-4(b)(2)(v); and HCFA Reg. § 146.113(b)(2)(v).

F. Standard Method, continued

**Examples
(continued)**

Example 4.

The facts are the same as those in Example 3, except that the new employer's plan is self-insured and, therefore, not subject to state insurance laws. The plan is not governed by the longer break rules under state insurance law. Therefore, Mary Ann's previous coverage under her former employer's plan may be disregarded.

Example 5.

Roger begins employment with a new employer 45 days after terminating coverage under his former employer's group health plan. The new employer's plan has a 30-day waiting period before coverage begins. Roger enrolls in the plan when first eligible.

Roger has not had a significant break in coverage. Therefore, coverage under his prior employer's plan must be counted against the new employer's plan's preexisting condition exclusion period. Roger has had a break of only 44 days because the 30-day waiting period may not be counted in determining whether he had a significant break in coverage.

Example 6.

Ellen had 200 days of creditable coverage under her former employer's plan before she terminated employment and her coverage ceased. She was then unemployed for 51 days before accepting a new position with another employer. The second employer's plan has a three-month waiting period. However, Ellen worked for the second employer for only two months before terminating employment. Eleven days later, she accepted a new position with a third employer. The third employer's plan has no waiting period, but has a six-month preexisting condition exclusion period.

Ellen has not had a significant break in coverage because, after disregarding the waiting period in her second employer's plan, she had only a 62-day break in coverage. Therefore, Ellen has 200 days of creditable coverage. Consequently, the third employer's plan may not apply the six-month preexisting condition exclusion period to Ellen.

G. Alternative Method

Alternative method, defined

Under the **alternative method**, a plan may take into account specific types or categories of benefits to determine the amount of creditable coverage an individual has.[30] That is, a plan may determine creditable coverage based on whether the individual has creditable coverage in a particular category of benefits and not based on other coverage the individual may have had.

Categories of benefits

A plan may use the alternative method for counting creditable coverage for any of the following categories of benefits:[31]

- Mental health
- Substance abuse treatment
- Prescription drugs
- Dental care
- Vision care

Application of alternative method

In using the alternative method, the following rules apply:

- A plan may use the alternative method for any or all of the allowed benefits categories.[32]
- The plan may apply a different preexisting condition exclusion period for each category (and may apply a different preexisting condition exclusion period for benefits that are not within any category).[33]
- The creditable coverage determined for a category of benefits applies only for reducing the preexisting condition exclusion period for that category.[34]
- An individual's creditable coverage for benefits that are not in any category must be determined using the standard method.[35]

---

[30] I.R.S. Reg. § 54.9801-4(c)(1); PWBA § 2590.701(c)(1); and HCFA Reg. § 146.113(c)(1).
[31] I.R.S. Reg. § 54.9801-4(c)(3); PWBA § 2590.701(c)(3); and HCFA Reg. § 146.113(c)(3).
[32] I.R.S. Reg. § 54.9801-4(c)(1); PWBA § 2590.701(c)(1); and HCFA Reg. § 146.113(c)(1).
[33] *Id.*
[34] *Id.*
[35] *Id.*

G. Alternative Method, continued

Application of alternative method (continued)

- The plan must count creditable coverage within a category if any level of benefits is provided within the category.[36]
- Coverage under a reimbursement account or arrangement such as a flexible spending account is not considered to be coverage in any category of benefits.[37]

Counting creditable coverage

To count an individual's creditable coverage using the alternative method:[38]

- The plan first determines the amount of creditable coverage the individual has using the standard method up to a total of 365 days of the most recent creditable coverage (546 days for a late enrollee). (The period over which this creditable coverage is determined is called the **determination period**.)
- Next, for the category specified under the alternative method, the plan counts within the category all days of coverage that occurred during the determination period (whether or not a significant break in coverage for that category occurred).
- Then, the plan reduces the individual's preexisting condition exclusion period by that number of days.

The plan may count the amount of creditable coverage in any other reasonable manner, uniformly applied, that is at least as favorable to the individual.

---

[36] I.R.S. Reg. § 54.9801-4(c)(6)(i); PWBA Reg. § 2590.701-4(c)(6)(i); and HCFA Reg. § 146.113(c)(7)(i).

[37] *Id.*

[38] I.R.S. Reg. § 54.9801-4(c)(6)(ii); PWBA Reg. § 2590.701-4(c)(6)(ii); and HCFA Reg. § 146.113(c)(7)(ii).

G. Alternative Method, continued

Example
The following example illustrates how to count creditable coverage using the alternative method:[39]

> **Example.**
>
> Tom enrolls in his employer's plan on January 1, 2009. Plan coverage includes prescription drug benefits. On April 1, 2009, the plan ceases to provide prescription drug benefits. Tom terminates employment on January 1, 2010, after having had coverage for 365 days. He finds new employment and enrolls in his new employer's plan on February 2, 2009 (his enrollment date). His new employer's plan uses the alternative method of counting creditable coverage and has a 12-month preexisting condition exclusion on prescription drug benefits.
>
> The plan may impose a 275-day preexisting condition exclusion period on Tom for prescription drug benefits. This is because Tom had 90 days of creditable coverage for prescription drug benefits within his determination period.

Uniform application
A plan using the alternative method must apply it uniformly to all participants and beneficiaries in the plan.[40] If a plan provides benefits through one or more insurance policies, it will not fail to meet the uniform application requirement if the method is used (or not used) separately for participants and beneficiaries under any policy. However, the alternative method must be applied uniformly to all coverage under that policy.

---

[39] I.R.S. Reg. § 54.9801-4(c)(6)(iii); PWBA Reg. § 2590.701-4(c)(6)(iii), and HCFA Reg. § 146.113(c)(7)(iii).
[40] I.R.S. Reg. § 54.9801-4(c)(2); PWBA Reg. § 2590.701-4(c)(2); and HCFA Reg. § 146.113(c)(2).

G. Alternative Method, continued

Plan notice requirement

If the alternative method of counting creditable coverage is used, the plan must:[41]

- State prominently in disclosure statements that the plan is using the alternative method for counting creditable coverage;
- State prominently that the plan is using the alternative method of counting creditable coverage for each enrollee at the time the individual enrolls in the plan;
- Include in the statements a description of the effect of using the alternative method; and
- Identify the categories of benefits for which the alternative method is being used.

---

[41] I.R.S. Reg. § 54.9801-4(c)(4); PWBA Reg. § 2590.701-4(c)(4); and HCFA Reg. § 146.113(c)(4).

H. Certifying Coverage; General Rules

Certification requirement

In general, a group health plan or health insurance issuer (which includes health maintenance organizations and insurance companies) providing group health plan coverage must furnish certificates of creditable coverage.[42]

Special rule for group health plans

If coverage under a plan consists of group health insurance coverage, the plan will be treated as having satisfied the certification requirement if the issuer of the insurance instead of having provided the certificates under an agreement between the issuer and the employer sponsoring the plan.[43] If the issuer fails to provide a certificate to an individual when required, the plan will not be treated as having violated the certification requirements. Rather, the issuer will be treated as having violated the requirements.

Individuals for whom certificates must be provided

A group health plan (or the issuer) must automatically provide a certificate, without charge, to any participant or beneficiary (who is or was covered by the plan) under the following circumstances:[44]

- The participant or beneficiary has a COBRA qualifying event;
- The participant's or beneficiary's COBRA coverage ends; or
- The participant's or beneficiary's coverage ceases for a reason other than a COBRA qualifying event (e.g., the individual drops coverage).

In addition, a plan must provide certificates to individuals upon request.

---

[42] I.R.S. Reg. § 54.9801-5(a)(1)(i); PWBA Reg. § 2590.701-5(a)(1)(i); and HCFA Reg. § 146.115(a)(1)(i).
[43] I.R.S. Reg. § 54.9801-5(a)(1)(iii); PWBA Reg. § 2590.701-5(a)(1)(iii); and HCFA Reg. § 146.115(a)(1)(iii).
[44] I.R.S. Reg. § 54.9801-5(a)(2); PWBA Reg. § 2590.701-5(a)(2); and HCFA Reg. § 146.115(a)(2).

H. Certifying Coverage; General Rules, continued

Deadlines for providing automatic certificates

The deadlines for providing automatic certificates are as follows:

- For a participant or beneficiary who has a COBRA qualifying event, the plan must automatically provide a certificate at the time the participant or beneficiary would lose coverage under the plan in the absence of COBRA continuation coverage or alternative coverage elected instead of COBRA coverage.[45] A plan satisfies this requirement if it provides the automatic certificate no later than when it is required to notify the individual of his or her COBRA rights.

- For a qualified beneficiary who has elected COBRA continuation coverage, the plan must automatically provide the beneficiary a certificate when his or her COBRA coverage ends.[46] A plan satisfies this requirement if it provides the automatic certificate within a reasonable time after the coverage ends (or after the expiration of any grace period for nonpayment of premiums). This automatic certificate must be provided even though the individual previously received an automatic certificate at the time he or she would have otherwise lost coverage had he or she not elected COBRA coverage.

- For an individual whose coverage ends for reasons other than a COBRA qualifying event, the plan must automatically provide a certificate at the time the coverage ends.[47] A plan satisfies this requirement if it provides the automatic certificate within a reasonable time after the individual's coverage ends.

---

[45] I.R.S. Reg. § 54.9801-5(a)(2)(ii)(A); PWBA Reg. § 2590.701-5(a)(2)(ii)(A); and HCFA Reg. § 146.115(a)(2)(ii)(A).

[46] I.R.S. Reg. § 54.9801-5(a)(2)(ii)(C); PWBA Reg. § 2590.701-5(a)(2)(ii)(C); and HCFA Reg. § 146.115(a)(2)(ii)(C).

[47] I.R.S. Reg. § 54.9801-5(a)(2)(ii)(B); PWBA Reg. § 2590.701-5(a)(2)(ii)(B); and HCFA Reg. § 146.115(a)(2)(ii)(B).

H. Certifying Coverage; General Rules, continued

Deadline for providing certificates upon request

An individual (or another party authorized by the individual such as another group health plan) has the right to request a certificate at anytime within 24 months after the individual's coverage under the plan ends.[48] If the individual or other party requests a certificate, the plan or issuer must provide the certificate at the earliest date that the plan or issuer, acting in a reasonable and prompt fashion, can provide it. The plan or issuer is required to provide certificates on request, even if the plan previously provided the individual with a certificate.

---

[48] I.R.S. Reg. § 54.9801-5(a)(2)(iii); PWBA Reg. § 2590.701-5(a)(2)(iii); and HCFA Reg. § 146.115(a)(2)(iii).

Job Aid

Deadlines for Providing Certificates

Instructions: Use this table to determine the deadlines for providing certificates of creditable coverage.

If …	Then a certificate must be provided …	A plan satisfies this requirement if it provides a certificate …
A participant or beneficiary has a COBRA qualifying event	Automatically at the time coverage would otherwise end	No later than when it is required to notify the individual of his or her COBRA rights
A participant or beneficiary has COBRA coverage and the coverage ends	Automatically at the time COBRA coverage ends	Within a reasonable time after COBRA coverage ends (or after the expiration of any grace period for nonpayment of premiums)
A participant or beneficiary's coverage ends but a COBRA qualifying event has not occurred	Automatically at the time the coverage ends	Within a reasonable time after the coverage ends
An individual (or other party authorized by the individual) requests a certificate	At the earliest date that the plan, acting in a reasonable and prompt fashion, can provide the certificate	N/A

I. Certifying Coverage; Form and Content Requirements

Form requirements

In general, a certificate of creditable coverage must be provided in writing. However, a written certificate is not required if all of the following conditions are met:[49]

- The individual is entitled to receive a certificate.
- The individual requests that the certificate be sent to another plan or issuer instead of to the individual.
- The plan or issuer that would otherwise receive the certificate agrees to accept the information through a means other than a written certificate (e.g., by telephone).
- The receiving plan or issuer receives the information in such form within the time period required.

Content requirements

A certificate of creditable coverage must include all of the following information:[50]

- The date the certificate is issued.
- The name of the group health plan that provided the coverage described in the certificate.
- The name of the participant or beneficiary to whom the certificate applies, and any other information necessary for the plan providing the coverage specified in the certificate to identify the individual (e.g., the individual's identification number under the plan).
- The name, address, and telephone number of the plan administrator or issuer providing the certificate.
- The telephone number to call for further information about the certificate (if different from that of the plan administrator).

---

[49] I.R.S. Reg. § 54.9801-5(a)(3)(i); PWBA Reg. § 2590.701-5(a)(3)(i); and HCFA Reg. § 146.115(a)(3)(i).
[50] I.R.S. Reg. § 54.9801-5(a)(3)(ii); PWBA Reg. § 2590.701-5(a)(3)(ii); and HCFA Reg. § 146.115(a)(3)(ii).

I. Certifying Coverage; Form and Content Requirements, continued

Content requirements (continued)
- An educational statement on HIPAA portability rights[51]
- For individuals with at least 18 months of creditable coverage, a statement that the individual has at least 18 months of creditable coverage, disregarding days of creditable coverage before a significant break in coverage.
- For individuals with fewer than 18 months of creditable coverage, the date any waiting period (and affiliation period, if applicable) began, and the date creditable coverage began.
- The date creditable coverage ended, unless the certificate indicates that creditable coverage is continuing as of the date of the certificate.

Model certificate

A plan will be treated as satisfying the content requirements if it uses the model certificate.[52] (See the model certificate in the Job Aid at the end of this section.)

Periods of coverage under certificate

For certificates that must be provided automatically, the period of coverage that must be included on the certificate is the last period of continuous coverage ending on the date the individual's coverage ceased.[53]

For certificates that must be provided upon request, a certificate must be provided for each period of continuous coverage ending within the 24-month period that ends on the date of the request (or continuing on the date of the request). A separate certificate may be provided for each period of continuous coverage.

---

[51] I.R.S. Reg. §54.9801-5(a)(3).
[52] I.R.S. Reg. § 54.9801-5(a)(3)(v); PWBA Reg. § 2590.701-5(a)(3)(v); and HCFA Reg. § 146.115(a)(3)(v).
[53] I.R.S. Reg. § 54.9801-5(a)(3)(iii); PWBA Reg. § 2590.701-5(a)(3)(iii); and HCFA Reg. § 146.115(a)(3)(iii).

I. Certifying Coverage; Form and Content Requirements, continued

Combining information for families

A certificate of creditable coverage can combine and provide information for the participant and the participant's dependents if the information is:[54]

- Identical for each individual; or
- Not identical for each individual, but the certificate provides all the required information for each individual and separately states the information that is not identical.

Excepted benefits

Certificates are not required for excepted benefits.[55] However, if excepted benefits are provided with other creditable coverage so that the coverage in total does not consist solely of excepted benefits, information on the benefits may be required to be provided. (See Chapter 3 for information on excepted benefits.)

---

[54] I.R.S. Reg. § 54.9801-5(a)(3)(iv); PWBA Reg. § 2590.701-5(a)(3)(iv); and HCFA Reg. § 146.115(a)(3)(iv).

[55] I.R.S. Reg. § 54.9801-5T(a)(3)(vi); PWBA Reg. § 2590.701-5(a)(3)(vi); and HCFA Reg. § 146.115(a)(3)(vi).

Job Aid

Certificate Content Checklist

Instructions: Use this checklist to determine whether a certificate includes all of the information required.

Information Required	Check Here If Included
1. Date certificate is issued	☐
2. Name of group health plan that provided the coverage described in certificate	☐
3. Name of participant or beneficiary to whom certificate applies, and any other information necessary for the plan to identify the individual (e.g., the individual's identification number under the plan)	☐
4. Name, address, and telephone number of plan administrator or issuer required to provide certificate	☐
5. Telephone number to call for more information about certificate (if different from that of the plan administrator)	☐
6. For individuals with at least 18 months of creditable coverage, statement that individual has at least 18 months of creditable coverage, disregarding days of creditable coverage before significant break in coverage	☐
7. For individuals with fewer than 18 months of creditable coverage, date any waiting period (and affiliation period, if applicable) began, and the date creditable coverage began	☐
8. Date creditable coverage ended (unless the certificate indicates that creditable coverage is continuing as of the date of the certificate)	☐
9. If certificate is an automatic certificate, period of coverage on certificate is last period of continuous coverage ending on the date the individual's coverage ceased	☐
10. If certificate is being provided in response to a request, period of coverage on certificate includes each period of continuous coverage ending within the 24-month period that ends on the date of the request (or continuing on the date of the request)	☐
11. If combining information for a family, and the information is not identical for each family member, a statement that the information is not identical	☐
12. An educational statement regarding HIPAA portability rights	☐

Job Aid

Model Certificate of Group Health Plan Coverage

Instructions: You may use this model certificate to meet the certification requirements.

CERTIFICATE OF GROUP HEALTH PLAN COVERAGE

IMPORTANT. This certificate provides evidence of your prior health coverage. You may need to furnish this certificate if you become eligible under a group health plan that excludes coverage for certain medical conditions that are present before you enroll. This certificate may need to be provided if medical advice, diagnosis, care, or treatment was recommended or received for the condition within the six-month period before your enrollment in the new plan. If you become covered under another group health plan, check with the plan administrator to determine whether you need to provide this certificate. You may also need this certificate to buy, for yourself or your family, an insurance policy that does not exclude coverage for medical conditions that are present before you enroll.

1. Date of this certificate: _____

2. Name of group health plan: _____

3. Name of participant: _____

4. Identification number of participant: _____

5. Name of any individual(s) to whom this certificate applies: _____

6. Name, address, and telephone number of plan administrator or issuer responsible for providing this certificate:

    _____

    _____

7. For further information, call: _____

8. If the individual(s) identified in line 5 has (have) at least 18 months of creditable coverage (disregarding periods of coverage before a 63-day break), check here _____ and skip lines 9 and 10.

9. Date waiting period or affiliation period (if any) began:_____

10. Date coverage began:_____

11. Date coverage ended: _____ (if coverage has not ended, enter "continuing")

Note: Separate certificates will be furnished if information is not identical for the participant and each beneficiary.

Job Aid

Model Certificate of Group Health Plan Coverage

Statement of HIPAA Portability Rights

IMPORTANT—KEEP THIS CERTIFICATE. This certificate is evidence of your coverage under this plan. Under a federal law known as HIPAA, you may need evidence of your coverage to reduce a preexisting condition exclusion period under another plan, to help you get special enrollment in another plan, or to get certain types of individual health coverage even if you have health problems.

Preexisting condition exclusions. Some group health plans restrict coverage for medical conditions present before an individual's enrollment. These restrictions are known as "preexisting condition exclusions." A preexisting condition exclusion can apply only to conditions for which medical advice, diagnosis, care, or treatment was recommended or received within the 6 months before your "enrollment date." Your enrollment date is your first day of coverage under the plan, or, if there is a waiting period, the first day of your waiting period (typically, your first day of work). In addition, a preexisting condition exclusion cannot last for more than 12 months after your enrollment date (18 months if you are a late enrollee). Finally, a preexisting condition exclusion cannot apply to pregnancy and cannot apply to a child who is enrolled in health coverage within 30 days after birth, adoption, or placement for adoption.

If a plan imposes a preexisting condition exclusion, the length of the exclusion must be reduced by the amount of your prior creditable coverage. Most health coverage is creditable coverage, including group health plan coverage, COBRA continuation coverage, coverage under an individual health policy, Medicare, Medicaid, State Children's Health Insurance Program (SCHIP), and coverage through high-risk pools and the Peace Corps. Not all forms of creditable coverage are required to provide certificates like this one. If you do not receive a certificate for past coverage, talk to your new plan administrator.

You can add up any creditable coverage you have, including the coverage shown on this certificate. However, if at any time you went for 63 days or more without any coverage (called a break in coverage) a plan may not have to count the coverage you had before the break. Therefore, once your coverage ends, you should try to obtain alternative coverage as soon as possible to avoid a 63-day break. You may use this certificate as evidence of your creditable coverage to reduce the length of any preexisting condition exclusion if you enroll in another plan.

Right to get special enrollment in another plan. Under HIPAA, if you lose your group health plan coverage, you may be able to get into another group health plan for which you are eligible (such as a spouse's plan), even if the plan generally does not accept late enrollees, if you request enrollment within 30 days. (Additional special enrollment rights are triggered by marriage, birth, adoption, and placement for adoption.) Therefore, once your coverage ends, if you are eligible for coverage in another plan (such as a spouse's plan), you should request special enrollment as soon as possible.

Job Aid

Model Certificate of Group Health Plan Coverage

Prohibition against discrimination based on a health factor. Under HIPAA, a group health plan may not keep you (or your dependents) out of the plan based on anything related to your health. Also, a group health plan may not charge you (or your dependents) more for coverage, based on health, than the amount charged a similarly situated individual.

Right to individual health coverage. Under HIPAA, if you are an "eligible individual," you have a right to buy certain individual health policies (or in some states, to buy coverage through a high-risk pool) without a preexisting condition exclusion. To be an eligible individual, you must meet the following requirements:

- You have had coverage for at least 18 months without a break in coverage of 63 days or more;
- Your most recent coverage was under a group health plan (which can be shown by this certificate);
- Your group coverage was not terminated because of fraud or nonpayment of premiums;
- You are not eligible for COBRA continuation coverage or you have exhausted your COBRA benefits (or continuation coverage under a similar state provision); and
- You are not eligible for another group health plan, Medicare, or Medicaid, and do not have any other health insurance coverage.

The right to buy individual coverage is the same whether you are laid off, fired, or quit your job. Therefore, if you are interested in obtaining individual coverage and you meet the other criteria to be an eligible individual, you should apply for this coverage as soon as possible to avoid losing your eligible individual status due to a 63-day break.

State flexibility. This certificate describes minimum HIPAA protections under federal law. States may require insurers and HMOs to provide additional protections to individuals in that state.

For more information. If you have questions about your HIPAA rights, you may contact your state insurance department or the U.S. Department of Labor, Employee Benefits Security Administration (EBSA) toll-free at 1-866-444-3272 (for free HIPAA publications ask for publications concerning changes in health care laws). You may also contact the CMS publication hotline at 1-800-633-4227 (ask for "Protecting Your Health Insurance Coverage"). These publications and other useful information are also available on the Internet at: *http://www.dol.gov/ebsa*, the DOL's interactive web pages - Health *E*laws, or *http://www.cms.hhs.gov/hipaa1*.

Job Aid

Model Certificate for Categories of Benefits
(Alternative Method)

Instructions: A plan using the alternative method of determining creditable coverage may use this model certificate for categories of benefits.

INFORMATION ON CATEGORIES OF BENEFITS

1. Date of original certificate: _____

2. Name of group health plan providing the coverage: _____

3. Name of participant: _____

4. Identification number of participant: _____

5. Name of individual(s) to whom this information applies: _____

6. The following information applies to the coverage in the certificate that was provided to the individual(s) identified above[1]:

    a. Mental health: _____

    b. Substance abuse treatment: _____

    c. Prescription drugs: _____

    d. Dental care: _____

    e. Vision care: _____

[1]For categories a through e, enter "N/A" if the individual had no coverage within the category and either (i) enter both the date that the individual's coverage within the category began and the date that the individual's coverage within the category ended (or indicate if continuing), or (ii) enter "same" on the line if the beginning and ending dates for coverage within the category are the same as the beginning and ending dates for the coverage in the certificate.

J. Certifying Coverage; Procedural Requirements

Method of delivery

HIPAA established procedural requirements. The procedural requirements regarding delivery of certificates are as follows: [56]

- The plan may mail the certificate to an individual (or another party requesting a certificate on behalf of the individual) by first-class mail.
- If the plan mails the certificate to the participant and spouse at the participant's last known address, the plan satisfies the delivery requirement regarding all of the participant's dependents who live at the same address.
- If a dependent's last known address is different from the participant's, the plan must mail a separate certificate to the dependent at the dependent's last known address.
- If the plan is providing separate certificates to individuals who live at the same address, the plan can mail them in one envelope.

Procedure for requesting certificates

The procedural requirements also require plans and issuers to establish a procedure for individuals to request and receive certificates. [57]

---

[56] I.R.S. Reg. § 54.9801-5(a)(4)(i); PWBA Reg. § 2590.701-5(a)(4)(i); and HCFA Reg. § 146.115(a)(4)(i).
[57] I.R.S. Reg. § 54.9801-5(a)(4)(ii); PWBA Reg. § 2590.701-5(a)(4)(ii); and HCFA Reg. § 146.115(a)(4)(ii).

J. Certifying Coverage; Procedural Requirements, continued

Designated recipients

In addition, the procedural requirements establish rules for providing certificates to designated recipients. For automatic certificates, if an individual designates another person or entity to receive the certificate, the plan or issuer may provide it to the designated recipient, or the plan or issuer may choose instead to provide the certificate to the individual.[58]

For certificates that must be provided on request, if the individual designates another person or entity to receive the certificate, the plan must do as directed.

---

[58] I.R.S. Reg. § 54.9801-5(a)(4)(iii); PWBA Reg. § 2590.701-5(a)(4)(iii); and HCFA Reg. § 146.115(a)(4)(iii).

K. Demonstrating Creditable Coverage

Introduction

An employee can be required to present a certificate of creditable coverage before enrolling in a group health plan.[59] The rules for demonstrating creditable coverage were established for those instances in which an individual must establish creditable coverage through a means other than a certificate. Those instances might include:[60]

- An entity failing to provide a certificate within the required time period.
- The individual has creditable coverage but the entity is not required to provide a certificate.
- The coverage is for a period before July 1, 1996.
- The individual has an urgent medical condition and needs a determination before he or she can deliver a certificate to the plan.
- The individual has lost the certificate and cannot obtain another copy.
- The accuracy of the certificate is being contested.

Evidence of creditable coverage

To establish evidence of creditable coverage (and waiting or affiliation periods) in the absence of a certificate, an individual may provide the following documents:[61]

- Explanations of benefits (EOB) claims or other correspondence from the plan or issuer indicating coverage;
- Paycheck stubs showing payroll deductions for health coverage;
- Health insurance identification card;
- Certificate of coverage under a group health policy;
- Records from medical care providers indicating health coverage;

---

[59] I.R.C. § 9801(c)(4); ERISA § 701(c)(4); and PHSA 42 U.S.C.S. § 300gg(c)(4).
[60] I.R.S. Reg. § 54.9801-5(c)(1); PWBA Reg. § 2590.701-5(c)(1); and HCFA Reg. § 146.115(c)(1).
[61] I.R.S. Reg. § 54.9801-5(c)(2)(ii); PWBA Reg. § 2590.701-5(c)(2)(ii); and HCFA Reg. § 146.115(c)(2)(ii).

K. Demonstrating Creditable Coverage, continued

Evidence of creditable coverage (continued)

- Third-party statements verifying periods of coverage; or
- Any other relevant documents showing evidence of periods of health coverage

In addition, an individual may establish evidence of creditable coverage (and waiting or affiliation periods) through means such as a telephone call from the plan to another party to verify creditable coverage.[62]

Consideration of evidence

In determining how much creditable coverage an individual has, a plan must take into account all of the information it obtains or that is presented, based on facts and circumstances. A plan must treat the individual as having furnished a certificate if the individual:[63]

- Attests to the period of creditable coverage;
- Presents relevant corroborating evidence of some creditable coverage during the period; and
- Cooperates with the plan's efforts to verify the individual's coverage.

Cooperating with plan's efforts

Cooperating with the plan's efforts includes:[64]

- Giving the plan or issuer written authorization to request a certificate on the individual's behalf and
- Cooperating with the plan's efforts to determine the validity of the corroborating evidence and dates of creditable coverage.

A plan may refuse to credit coverage if an individual fails to cooperate. However, it cannot consider an individual's inability to obtain a certificate as evidence of no creditable coverage.

---

[62] I.R.S. Reg. § 54.9801-5(c)(2)(iii); PWBA Reg. § 2590.701-5(c)(2)(ii); and HCFA Reg. § 146.115(c)(2)(ii).
[63] I.R.S. Reg. § 54.9801-5(c)(2)(i); PWBA Reg. § 2590.701-5(c)(2)(i); and HCFA Reg. § 146.115(c)(2)(i).
[64] Id.

K. Demonstrating Creditable Coverage, continued

Demonstrating dependent status

If, in providing evidence (including a certificate) of creditable coverage, an individual must demonstrate dependent status, the group health plan or issuer must treat the individual as having furnished a certificate showing dependent status if the individual attests to the dependency status and cooperates with the plan's or issuer's efforts to verify the dependent status.[65]

---

[65] I.R.S. Reg. § 54.9801-5(c)(4); PWBA Reg. § 2590.701-5(c)(4); and HCFA Reg. § 146.115(c)(4).

L. Determination, Notice of Creditable Coverage

General rule
If a group health plan receives information concerning an individual's creditable coverage, the plan must determine the individual's creditable coverage and notify the individual of its determination within a reasonable time period.[66]

Reasonable time period
Whether a determination and notification of an individual's creditable coverage is made within a reasonable time period is based on the relevant facts and circumstances.[67] Relevant facts and circumstances include, for example, whether a plan's application of a preexisting condition exclusion period would prevent an individual from obtaining urgent medical care.

Altering initial decision of creditable coverage
A plan may alter its initial decision concerning an individual's creditable coverage if the plan determines that the individual did not have the claimed creditable coverage.[68] In altering a decision, the plan must

- Notify the individual in writing of its new decision, and
- Act in a manner consistent with its initial decision until the final determination is made with regard to approving access to medical services (e.g., presurgery authorization).

---

[66] I.R.S. Reg. § 54.9801-5(d)(1); PWBA Reg. § 2590.701-5(d)(1); and HCFA Reg. § 146.115(d)(1).
[67] *Id.*
[68] *Id.*

M. Exceptions to Preexisting Condition Exclusions

Introduction A plan cannot impose a preexisting existing exclusion period on newborns or adopted children, or for pregnancy.[69]

Newborns In general, a plan cannot impose a preexisting condition exclusion on a child who, within 30 days of birth, has creditable coverage.[70] The only exception to this is if the child has a significant break in coverage.

Example.

Ron Jamison's wife had a baby boy with a birth defect seven months after Ron enrolled in his employer's group health plan. Ron enrolled his son in the plan within 30 days of the child's birth; therefore, no preexisting condition exclusion period can be applied to the baby. Three months after his son's birth, Ron began working for a new employer and, 45 days after leaving his former employer, Ron enrolled his son in the new employer's plan. The new employer's plan has a 12-month preexisting condition exclusion.

The new plan cannot impose a preexisting condition exclusion on the baby, because the baby was covered within 30 days of birth and had no significant break in coverage. This is so whether Ron's baby is included in the certificate of creditable coverage indicating 30 days of dependent coverage or whether the child receives a separate certificate indicating 90 days of coverage. However, the new employer's plan may impose a preexisting condition exclusion on Ron for up to two months for any preexisting condition for which he sought medical advice, diagnosis, care, or treatment within the six-month period ending on his enrollment date in the new plan.

---

[69] I.R.S. Reg. § 54.9801-3(b)(1) and (2); PWBA Reg. § 2590.701-3(b)(1) and (2); and HCFA Reg. § 146.111(b)(1) and (2).
[70] I.R.S. Reg. § 54.9801-3(b)(1); PWBA Reg. § 2590.701-3(b)(1); and HCFA Reg. § 146.111(b)(1).

M. Exceptions to Preexisting Condition Exclusions, continued

Adopted children

A plan cannot impose a preexisting condition exclusion on a child who is adopted or placed for adoption before attaining 18 years of age and who, within 30 days of adoption or placement for adoption, has creditable coverage.[71] This rule does not apply to coverage before the adoption or placement for adoption.

Pregnancy

A group health plan may not impose a preexisting condition exclusion on an individual for pregnancy.[72]

Genetic information

HIPAA bars group health plans from treating genetic information as a preexisting condition absent a diagnosis of a condition related to the information.[73]

Special enrollment dates

See Section O of this chapter for special enrollment dates for new dependents.

---

[71] I.R.S. Reg. § 54.9801-3(b)(2); PWBA Reg. § 2590.701-3(b)(2); and HCFA Reg. § 146.111(b)(2).
[72] I.R.S. Reg. § 54.9801-3(b)(4); PWBA Reg. § 2590.701-3(b)(4); and HCFA Reg. § 146.111(b)(4).
[73] I.R.S. Reg. § 54.9801-3.

N. Special Enrollment Periods for Individuals Who Lose Other Coverage

Introduction

Special enrollment periods apply to employees and dependents who lose their coverage. Employees and dependents who enroll during special enrollment periods are not treated as late enrollees.[74]

Individuals who lose other coverage

A group health plan must allow employees and dependents who initially decline coverage to later enroll if the following conditions are met:[75]

- The employee and dependents are otherwise eligible to enroll in the benefit package
- When enrollment was previously offered and declined, the employee or dependent had other coverage.
- When enrollment was declined, the employee stated in writing that he or she was declining coverage because he or she or the dependent had other coverage.[76] This applies only if the plan:

  - Requires the statement at the time the employee declined the coverage
  - Notifies the employee of the requirement and the consequences of failing to provide the statement

- When enrollment was declined, the employee or dependent had COBRA coverage and that coverage has since been exhausted.[77]
- When enrollment was declined, the employee or dependent had other coverage that has since terminated due to loss of eligibility or because the employer ceased contributions to the plan.[78]

The final IRS regulations clarified that if an employee's spouse or dependent loses coverage creating special enrollment rights, the spouse (or dependent) and the employee may enroll in the plan.[79]

---

[74] I.R.C. § 9801(b)(3), ERISA § 701(b)(3); PHSA 42 U.S.C.S. § 300gg(b)(3).
[75] I.R.S. Reg. § 54.9801-6.
[76] I.R.S. Reg. § 54.9801-6(a)(5)(i); PWBA Reg. § 2590.701-5(a)(5)(i); and HCFA Reg. § 146.117(a)(5)(i).
[77] I.R.S. Reg. § 54.9801-6(a)(5)(ii)(A); PwWBA Reg. § 2590.701-5(a)(5)(ii)(A); and HCF Reg. § 146.117(a)(5)(ii)(A).
[78] I.R.S. Reg. § 54.9801-6(a)(5)(ii)(B); PWBA Reg. § 2590.701-6(a)(5)(ii)(B); and HCFA Reg. § 146.117(a)(5)(ii)(B).
[79] I.R.S. Reg.§ 54.9801-6.

N. Special Enrollment Periods for Individuals Who Lose Other Coverage, continued

Individuals who lose other coverage (continued)	In addition, if the employee is already enrolled in the plan, the employee may change benefit options if a spouse or dependent becomes eligible for special enrollment. The final regulations also clarify that an individual who initially declines coverage, even though he or she has no coverage, is eligible for special enrollment if, after later obtaining other coverage and again declining the employer's plan, he or she loses the other coverage. The final regulations also provide special enrollment rights for individuals who reach another plan's lifetime limit or if an individual moves out of an HMO's service area and no other coverage is available.
Loss of eligibility	Loss of eligibility for coverage includes loss of coverage as a result of a legal separation, divorce, death, termination of employment, reduction in hours, and any loss of eligibility after a period that is measured by reference to any of the foregoing.[80] For example, if an employee's coverage ceases after a termination of employment, and if the employee is eligible for, but fails to elect, COBRA coverage, a loss of eligibility has occurred. However, if the employee elects COBRA but later loses the coverage for cause or for nonpayment of premiums, a loss of eligibility has not occurred.
Length of special enrollment period	An employee must request enrollment for himself or herself or a dependent no later than 30 days after the employee's or dependent's COBRA coverage ends or other coverage terminates due to loss of eligibility or because an employer's contributions cease.[81] A plan may impose the same requirements that apply to other employees who are eligible for the plan concerning requesting enrollment (e.g., that the request be made in writing).

[80] *Id.*

[81] I.R.S. Reg. § 54.9801-6(a)(6); PWBA Reg. § 2590.701-6(a)(6); and HCFA Reg. § 146.117(a)(6).

N. Special Enrollment Periods for Individuals Who Lose Other Coverage, continued

Effective date	Enrollment must be effective no later than the first day of the first calendar month beginning after the date an employee requests enrollment.[82]
Notice of enrollment rights	A group health plan must notify an employee of his or her enrollment rights on or before the employee is offered enrollment in the plan.[83] (See the model description of the special enrollment rules in the Job Aid at the end of Section O of this chapter.)

---

[82] I.R.S. Reg. § 54.9801-6(a)(7); PWBA Reg. § 2590.701-6(a)(7); and HCFA Reg. § 146.117(a)(7).
[83] I.R.S. Reg. § 54.9801-6(c); PWBA Reg. § 2590.701-6(c); and HCFA Reg. § 146.117(c).

O. Special Enrollment Periods for Dependents

Introduction   Special enrollment periods apply to new dependents of employees and to employees who are not enrolled but who acquire new dependents. Employees and dependents enrolled during special enrollment periods are not treated as late enrollees.[84]

Employee   An employee may enroll in a plan if he or she[85]

- Is eligible for the plan;
- Is not enrolled because he or she previously declined enrollment; or
- Acquires a new dependent through marriage, birth, adoption, or placement for adoption.

Spouse of participant   A spouse of a participant may enroll in a plan if he or she either[86]

- Becomes the spouse of the participant; or
- Is the spouse of the participant, and they have a child who becomes a dependent through birth, adoption, or placement for adoption.

---

[84] I.R.S. Reg. § 54.9801-6(a)(2)(iv); PWBA Reg. § 2590.701-6(a)(2)(iv); and HCFA Reg. § 146.117(a)(2)(iv).
[85] I.R.S. Reg. § 54.9801-6(b)(2); PWBA Reg. § 2590.701-6(b)(2); and HCFA Reg. § 146.117(b)(2).
[86] I.R.S. Reg. § 54.9801-6(b)(3); PWBA Reg. § 2590.701-6(b)(3); and HCFA Reg. § 146.117(b)(3).

O. Special Enrollment Periods for Dependents, continued

Spouse and employee not enrolled	An employee and spouse may enroll in a plan if the following conditions are met:[87] • The employee is eligible for the plan. • The employee is not enrolled because he or she previously declined enrollment. • The employee takes a spouse, or the employee and spouse are married, and they have a child that becomes a dependent through birth, adoption, or placement for adoption.
Dependent of participant not enrolled	An individual may enroll in the plan if he or she becomes a dependent of a participant through marriage, birth, adoption, or placement for adoption.[88]
New dependent and employee not enrolled	An employee and his or her new dependent may enroll in a plan if the following conditions are met:[89] • The employee is eligible for the plan. • The employee is not enrolled because he or she previously declined enrollment. • The employee acquires the dependent through marriage, birth, adoption, or placement for adoption.

---

[87] I.R.S. Reg. § 54.9801-6(b)(4); PWBA Reg. § 2590.701-6(b)(4); and HCFA Reg. § 146.117(b)(4).
[88] I.R.S. Reg. § 54.9801-6(b)(5); PWBA Reg. § 2590.701-6(b)(5); and HCFA Reg. § 146.117(b)(5).
[89] I.R.S. Reg. § 54.9801-6(b)(6); PWBA Reg. § 2590.701-6(b)(6); and HCFA Reg. § 146.117(b)(6).

O. Special Enrollment Periods for Dependents, continued

Length of special enrollment period	The special enrollment period for dependents must last at least 30 days from the date of marriage, birth, adoption, or placement for adoption.[90]
Effective dates	The effective dates for special enrollment are as follows: • For marriage: Not later than the first day of the first calendar month beginning after the date the plan receives the enrollment request. • For birth: Date of dependent's birth. • For adoption or placement for adoption: Date of dependent's adoption or placement for adoption.
Notice of enrollment rights	A group health plan must notify an employee of his or her enrollment rights on or before the employee is offered enrollment in the plan.[91] (See the model description of special enrollment rules in the Job Aid at the end of this section.)

---

[90] I.R.S. Reg. § 54.9801-6(b)(7); PWBA Reg. § 2590.701-6(b)(7); and HCFA Reg. § 146.117(b)(7).
[91] I.R.S. Reg. § 54.9801-6(c); PWBA Reg. § 2590.701-6(c); and HCFA Reg. § 146.117(c).

Job Aid

Notice of Enrollment Rights; Model Description

Instructions: Employers may use this model description of special enrollment rights from the HIPAA Interim Rules to notify employees of their enrollment rights.

MODEL DESCRIPTION

If you are declining enrollment for yourself or your dependents (including your spouse) because of other health insurance coverage, you may in the future be able to enroll yourself or your dependents in this plan, provided that you request enrollment within 30 days after your other coverage ends. In addition, if you acquire a new dependent as a result of marriage, birth, adoption, or placement for adoption, you may be able to enroll yourself and your new dependent, provided that you request enrollment within 30 days after the marriage, birth, adoption, or placement for adoption.

P. HMO Affiliation Periods

General rule   A group health plan offering health insurance coverage through a health maintenance organization (HMO) or an HMO that offers health insurance coverage in connection with a group health plan may impose an affiliation period in lieu of a preexisting condition exclusion, but only if certain requirements are met.[92]

Affiliation period, defined   An **affiliation period** is a period of time that must expire before health insurance coverage provided by an HMO becomes effective and during which the HMO is not required to provide benefits.[93]

Requirements   To be able to impose an affiliation period, the HMO must meet the following requirements:[94]

- The HMO does not impose a preexisting condition exclusion for any coverage it offers in connection with the group health plan.
- The HMO does not charge the participant or beneficiary a premium for the affiliation period.
- The HMO applies the affiliation period uniformly without regard to an enrollee's health status.
- The affiliation period does not exceed two months (or three months in the case of a late enrollee).
- The affiliation period begins on the enrollment date.
- The affiliation period for enrollment in the HMO under a plan runs concurrently with any waiting period.

Alternatives   An HMO may use an alternative to an affiliation period to address adverse selection as approved by the state insurance commissioner or other official that regulates HMOs.[95] The HIPAA rules make it clear that the affiliation requirements do not require a state to receive proposals for or approve alternatives to affiliation periods.

---

[92] PWBA Reg. § 2590.701-7(a); HCFA Reg. § 146.119(a).
[93] I.R.S. Reg. § 54.9801-2; PWBA Reg. § 2590.701-2; and HCFA Reg. § 144.103.
[94] PWBA Reg. § 2590.701-7(b); HCFA Reg. § 146.119(b).
[95] PWBA Reg. § 2590.701-7(c); HCFA Reg. § 146.119(c).

Chapter 5

Nondiscrimination Rules

Introduction   HIPAA prohibits group health plans and group health insurance issuers from using health status to determine eligibility and premiums charged for coverage.

This chapter discusses the rules that prohibit plans and health insurance issuers from using health status in a discriminatory manner.

In this chapter   This chapter has five sections:

A. Nondiscrimination in Eligibility

General rule   A group health plan or group health issuer may not have eligibility rules, including waiting periods, that discriminate based on any of the following factors:[1]

- Health status
- Medical condition, including physical and mental illnesses
- Claims experience
- Receipt of health care
- Medical history
- Genetic information
- Evidence of insurability, including conditions arising out of acts of domestic violence and participation in activities such as snowmobiling, motorcycling, horseback riding, skiing, all-terrain driving, and other similar recreational activities
- Disability

Eligibility rules, defined   **Eligibility rules** include, but are not limited to:[2]

- Enrollment
- Coverage effective dates
- Waiting (or affiliation) periods
- Late and special enrollment
- Benefit package eligibility (including changing selections among benefit packages)
- Continued eligibility
- Coverage termination

The following examples illustrate the general eligibility rule:[3]

---

[1] I.R.S. Reg. § 54.9802-1(a)(1), (a)(2); and (a)(3); DOL Reg. § 2590.702(a)(1), (a)(2), and (a)(3); and HCFA Reg. § 146.121(a)(1), (a)(2), and (a)(3).
[2] I.R.S. Reg. § 54.9802-1(b)(1); DOL Reg. § 2590.702(b)(1); and HCFA Reg. §1 46.121(b)(1).
[3] I.R.S. Reg. § 54.9802-1(b)(1)(iii); DOL Reg. § 2590.702(b)(1)(iii); and HCFA Reg. § 146.121(b)(1)(iii).

A. Nondiscrimination in Eligibility, continued

Eligibility rules, defined (continued)

Example 1.

The ABC Company sponsors a group health plan that is available to all employees who enroll within the first 30 days of their employment. Employees who do not enroll within the first 30 days cannot later enroll unless they pass a physical examination. The plan discriminates on the basis of one or more health status-related factors.

Example 2.

The GBH Corporation sponsors a group health plan that allows employees who enroll during the first 30 days of employment (and during special enrollment periods) to choose between two benefit packages—an indemnity option and an HMO option. However, employees who enroll during late enrollment are permitted to enroll only in the HMO, and only if they provide evidence of good health.

The plan discriminates because it requires that employees provide evidence of good health. If the plan did not require evidence of good health but limited late enrollees to the HMO option, the rules for eligibility would not be discriminatory because the time an individual chooses to enroll is not a health status-related factor.

Example 3.

The NPR Organization sponsors a group health plan that allows employees to enroll within the first 30 days of employment. However, individuals who ride motorcycles are excluded from coverage. This plan discriminates on the basis of a health status-related factor.

Example 4.

As part of an employer's application for group health insurance, the issuer receives information about individuals who will be covered by the plan. The issuer learns that one of the employer's employees and the employee's dependents have a history of high health claims. Based on this information, the issuer excludes the said employee and his dependents from coverage in the plan. This plan violates the eligibility rules by excluding the employee and his dependents on the basis of health status-related factors.

B. Nondiscrimination in Benefits

General rule   The nondiscrimination requirements should not be construed as requiring a group health plan or group health issuer to provide any benefits other than those provided for under the terms of the plan or coverage. In addition, the plan or issuer may establish limitations or restrictions on the amount, level, extent, or nature of the benefits or coverage for similarly situated individuals enrolled in the plan or who are covered. However, benefits must be uniformly available to all similarly situated individuals, and any restriction on a benefit must be uniformly applied.

A plan may impose annual, lifetime, or other limits on benefits and may require satisfaction of a deductible, co-payment, coinsurance, or other cost-sharing requirement as long as the limits are applied uniformly to all similarly situated individuals.[4]

The following examples illustrate the general rule described above:[5]

Example 1.

A plan may limit or exclude benefits in relation to a specific disease or condition or limit benefits for certain types of treatments or drugs on the basis of whether the treatments or drugs are determined to be experimental or not medically necessary, only if the benefit limit or exclusion applies uniformly to all similarly situated individuals.

Example 2.

A plan may apply a $500,000 lifetime limit on all benefits to each participant or beneficiary under the plan when the limit is not directed at individual participants or beneficiaries.

---

[4] I.R.S. Reg. § 54.9802-1(b)(2); DOL Reg. § 2590.702(b)(2); and HCFA Reg. § 146.121(b)(2).
[5] I.R.S. Reg. § 54.9802-1(b)(2)(D); DOL Reg. § 2590.702(b)(2)(D); and HCFA Reg. § 146.121(b)(2)(D).

B. Nondiscrimination in Benefits, continued

General rule (continued)

> ### Example 3.
>
> A plan has a $2,000 lifetime limit for the treatment of temporomandibular joint (TMJ) syndrome. The limit is applied uniformly to all similarly situated individuals and is not directed at individual participants or beneficiaries.
>
> ### Example 4.
>
> A plan has a $2 million lifetime limit on all benefits. However, the $2 million lifetime limit is reduced to $10,000 for participants or beneficiaries with congenital heart defects. The lower lifetime limit for participants and beneficiaries with congenital heart defects violates the discrimination in eligibility rule because the limit does not apply uniformly to all similarly situated individuals.

Source of injury exclusions

Group heath plans may not deny benefits otherwise provided for treatment of an injury if the injury results from an act of domestic violence or a medical condition (including both physical and mental health conditions).[6]

> ### Example.
>
> A group health plan generally provides medical and surgical benefits, including benefits for hospital stays that are medically necessary. However, the plan excludes benefits for self-inflicted injuries or injuries sustained in connection with an attempted suicide. An individual enrolled in the plan suffers from depression and attempts suicide. As a result, he is hospitalized for treatment of the injuries. The plan denies benefits for treatment of injuries.
>
> The suicide attempt is the result of a medical condition and denial of benefits violates the nondiscrimination rules.

---

[6] I.R.S. Reg. § 54.9802-1(b)(2)(iii); DOL Reg. § 2590.702(b)(2)(iii); and HCFA Reg. § 146.121(b)(2)(iii).

B. Nondiscrimination in Benefits, continued

Plan amendments

Plan amendments may not be made effective earlier than the first day of the first plan year after the amendment is adopted. In addition, plan amendments must be applicable to all individuals in one or more groups of similarly situated individuals.[7]

> ### *Example.*
>
> An individual enrolled in an employer's plan has an adverse health condition. As part of the application, the insurer receives information about the individual. The policy offered by the insurer generally provides benefits for the adverse health condition from which the individual suffers. In this case, however, the insurer offers a modified plan that excludes benefits for that individual's condition. The amendment is made effective the first day of the next plan year.
>
> The amendment violates the nondiscrimination rules because it does not apply to all similarly situated individuals.

---

[7] I.R.S. Reg. § 54.9802-1(b)(2)(i)(C) and (D); DOL Reg. § 2590.702(b)(2)(i)(C) and (D); and HCFA Reg. § 146.121(b)(2)(i)(C) and (D).

B. Nondiscrimination in Benefits, continued

Preexisting condition exclusions

A preexisting condition exclusion that satisfies HIPAA (see Chapter 4), does not violate the nondiscrimination rules, provided that the exclusion[8]

- Applies uniformly to all similarly situated individuals and
- Is not directed at individual participants or beneficiaries based on any health factor.

Example 1.

A group health plan imposes a preexisting condition exclusion on all individuals enrolled in the plan. The exclusion applies to a condition for which medical advice, diagnosis, care, or treatment was recommended or received within the six-month period ending on an individual's enrollment date. In addition, the exclusion generally extends for 12 months after an individual's enrollment date. However, the 12-month period is offset by the number of days of an individual's creditable coverage.

Such a plan is not discriminatory, because the preexisting condition exclusion applies to all similarly situated individuals and is not directed at individual participants or beneficiaries.

Example 2.

The facts are the same as those in Example 1, except that the plan provides that if a participant has no claims within the first six months following enrollment, the remainder of the 12-month exclusion period is waived.

In this case, the plan's preexisting condition exclusion would be in violation of HIPAA's nondiscrimination rules because the exclusion does *not* apply uniformly to all similarly situated individuals.

---

[8] I.R.S. Reg. § 54.9802-1(b)(3); DOL Reg. § 2590.702(b)(3); and HCFA Reg. § 146.121(b)(3).

C. Nondiscrimination in Premiums or Contributions

General rule

A group health plan and a health insurance issuer offering health insurance coverage may not require, as a condition of enrollment or continued enrollment, an individual to pay a premium or contribution that is greater than the premium or contribution paid by similarly situated individuals enrolled in the plan. In addition, premiums or contributions cannot be based on an individual's or a dependent's health status.[9]

Discounts, rebates, payments in kind, and any other premium differential mechanisms are taken into account in determining an individual's premium or contribution rate.[10]

Premium rates

The above general rule does not restrict the aggregate amount an employer may be charged for a group health plan. However, a group health insurance issuer or group health plan may not quote or charge an employer (or an individual) a different premium for an individual in a group of similarly situated individuals based on a health factor.[11]

Cost-sharing mechanisms and wellness programs

A group health plan with a cost-sharing mechanism (i.e., a deductible, copayment, or coinsurance) that requires a higher payment from an individual based on a health factor (thus, not applying uniformly to all similarly situated individuals) does not violate the nondiscrimination rules if the cost differential is based on whether the individual complies with requirements of a wellness program.[12]

The above general rule should not be construed as prohibiting group health plans or insurance issuers from establishing premium discounts or rebates and/or modifying applicable copayments or deductibles in return for adherence to wellness programs.

---

[9] I.R.S. Reg. § 54.9802-1(c)(1); DOL Reg. § 2590.702(c)(1); and HCFA Reg. § 146.121(c)(1).
[10] *Id.*
[11] I.R.S. Reg. § 54.9802-1(c)(2); DOL Reg. § 2590.702(c)(2); and HCFA Reg. § 146.121(c)(2).
[12] I.R.S. Reg. § 54.9802-1(b)(2)(ii); DOL Reg. § 2590.702(b)(2)(ii); and HCFA Reg. § 146.121(b)(2)(ii).

C. Nondiscrimination in Premiums or Contributions, continued

Wellness defined

There are two kinds of wellness programs, one where the reward is **not conditioned** on the individual satisfying a standard relating to a health factor, and one where the reward **is conditioned** on satisfaction of a health-related standard. These types of wellness programs are excepted from the nondiscrimination rules as long as certain criteria are met.[13]

Wellness programs not conditioned on health standard

The following are examples of wellness programs that are **not** conditioned on satisfaction of a health-related standard:[14]

1. A program that reimbursed all or some of a fitness center membership.
2. A program that reimburses employees for smoking cessation programs without regard to whether the employee quits or not.
3. a diagnostic testing program that provides rewards based on participation rather than on test results.
4. A program that encourages preventative care based on waiver of the plan's co-payment or deductible (e.g., well-baby visits).
5. A program that provides a reward based on an employee attending a monthly health care seminar.

Wellness programs conditioned on health standard

If a wellness program conditions a reward on satisfaction of a health standard, the program must satisfy the following requirements:[15]

1. The reward may not exceed 20 percent of the total cost of coverage under the health plan.
2. The program must be available to all similarly situated individuals.
3. The program must also provide a reasonable alternative for obtaining the reward to individuals for which the standard is unreasonably difficult due to a medical condition. Plans may require a physician's statement that the individual's condition makes it unreasonably difficult or medically inadvisable to meet the health standard.
4. The program must give eligible individuals the opportunity to qualify for the reward at least once per year.
5. The plan must disclose the availability of a reasonable standard in all plan materials.

---

[13] I.R.S. Reg. § 54.9802-1(f); DOL Reg. § 2590.702(f); and HCFA Reg. § 146.121(f).
[14] *Id.*
[15] *Id.*

C. Nondiscrimination in Premiums or Contributions, continued

Wellness program checklist

The U.S. Department of Labor developed a Wellness Program Checklist that can be used to determine if an employer's wellness program is in compliance with HIPAA. A copy of the bulletin and checklist can be found at *http://www.dol.gov/ebsa/regs/fab2008-2.html*.

D. Special Rules and Exceptions

General rules for similarly situated participants and beneficiaries
A plan may establish rules for eligibility and set any individual's premium or contribution rate in accordance with the similarly situated participant and beneficiary rules. Accordingly, a plan may distinguish in rules for eligibility and premiums under the plan for full-time and part-time employees, current and former employees, or permanent and temporary employees.[16]

Similarly situated participants
A plan or issuer may treat participants as a group of similarly situated individuals separate from beneficiaries. In addition, participants may be treated as two or more distinct groups of similarly situated individuals.

If individuals have a choice of two or more benefit packages, individuals choosing one benefit package may be treated as a group of similarly situated individuals distinct from other individuals choosing another benefit package. However, the distinction between groups must be based on a bona fide employment-based classification consistent with the employer's usual business practice. These classifications may include full-time versus part-time status, different geographic locations, collective bargaining units, different occupations, and current versus former employment status.[17]

The following examples illustrate the rules for similarly situated participants:[18]

---

[16] I.R.S. Reg. § 54.9802-1(e)(3); DOL Reg. § 2590.702(e)(3); and HCFA Reg. § 146.121(e)(3).
[17] I.R.S. Reg. § 54.9802-1(d)(1); DOL Reg. § 2590.702(d)(1); and HCFA Reg. § 146.121(d)(1).
[18] I.R.S. Reg. § 54.9802-1(d)(4), DOL Reg. § 2590.702(d)(4), and HCFA Reg. § 146.121(d)(4).

D. Special Rules and Exceptions, continued

Similarly situated participants (continued)

> ### Example 1.
>
> An employer sponsors a group health plan for full-time employees only. Under the plan (consistent with the employer's usual business practice), employees who normally work at least 30 hours per week are considered full-time; other employees are considered part-time. There is no evidence to suggest that the classification is directed at individual participants.
>
> Treating the groups of full-time and part-time employees as separate groups of similarly situated individuals is permitted because the classification is bona fide and not directed at individual participants.
>
> ### Example 2.
>
> An employer sponsors a group health plan that provides the same benefit package to all of its seven employees. Six of the seven employees have the same job title and responsibilities, but Employee G has a different job title and responsibilities. After G files an expensive claim for benefits under the plan, coverage is modified so that employees with G's job title receive a different benefit package with lower lifetime dollar limits.
>
> Changing the coverage classification for G based on the existing employment classification is not permitted because the creation of new coverage for G is directed at G and based on one or more health factors.

Similarly situated beneficiaries

A plan or issuer may treat beneficiaries as a group of similarly situated individuals separate from beneficiaries. In addition, beneficiaries may be treated as two or more distinct groups of similarly situated beneficiaries.[19] However, the distinction between groups must be based on a bona fide employment-based classification based on the relationship between the beneficiary and the participant, such as:

- Relationship to the participant, (e.g., spouse, dependent child)
- Marital status
- Children classified according to age or student status

---

[19] I.R.S. Reg. § 54.9802-1(d)(2); DOL Reg. § 2590.702(d)(2); and HCFA Reg. § 146.121(d)(2).

D. Special Rules and Exceptions, continued

Similarly situated beneficiaries (continued)

The following example illustrates the aforementioned rule.[20]

> **Example.**
>
> Under a group health plan, coverage is made available to employees, spouses, and dependent children. However, coverage is made available to a dependent child only if he or she is under age 19 (or under age 25 if a full-time student at an institution of higher learning). There is no evidence to suggest that these classifications are aimed at individual beneficiaries or participants.
>
> Treating spouses and dependent children differently by imposing an age limit on a dependent child is permitted because the classification is not directed at an individual beneficiary.

Non-confinement and actively at work rules

Health plan eligibility and premium rates may not be based on whether an individual is confined to a hospital or other health care facility. Eligibility and rates may not be based on an individual's ability to engage in normal life activities. In addition, plans are prohibited from denying eligibility based on whether the employee is actively at work at the time coverage would normally become effective. However, plans can require that an individual begin work for the employer before coverage becomes effective.[21]

---

[20] I.R.S. Reg. § 54.9802-1(d)(4); DOL Reg. § 2590.702(d)(4); and HCFA Reg. § 146.121(d)(4).
[21] I.R.S. Reg. § 54.9802-1(e)(1) and (2); DOL Reg. § 2590.702(e)(1) and (2); and HCFA Reg. § 146.121(e)(1) and (2).

D. Special Rules and Exceptions, continued

Non-confinement and actively at work rules (continued)

The following examples illustrate the nonconfinement and actively at work rules.[22]

Example 1.

Under Employer A's group health plan, coverage for employees and their dependents generally becomes effective on the first day of employment. However, coverage for a dependent who is confined to a hospital does not become effective until the confinement ends.

Employer A's plan violates the rules because the effective date is delayed based on confinement to a health care facility.

Example 2.

Under Employer B's group health plan, coverage for an employee becomes effective after 90 days of continuous service. If an employee is absent from work (for any reason) before completing the 90 days of service, the beginning of the 90-day period is measured from the day the employee returns to work (without any credit for service before the absence).

Employer B's plan violates the rules because the 90-day continuous service rule is an eligibility requirement based on whether the individual is actively at work.

Example 3.

Under the eligibility requirements of Employer C's group health plan, coverage for new employees becomes effective on the first day that the employee reports to work. Henry is scheduled to begin work for Employer C on August 3; however, Henry is unable to begin work on that day because of illness. He begins working on August 4, and his coverage is effective on August 4.

Employer C's plan does not violate the rules because Henry did not report to work on his scheduled date.

---

[22] *Id.*

D. Special Rules and Exceptions, continued

Favorable treatment based on adverse health

A plan may treat individuals with adverse health factors (i.e., disability) more favorably under plan eligibility rules. In addition, a plan may charge individuals a smaller premium or contribution if the lower charge is based on an adverse health factor.[23]

---

[23] I.R.S. Reg. § 54.9802-1(g); DOL Reg. § 2590.702(g); and HCFA Reg. § 146.121(g).

E. Multiemployer and Multiple-Employer Plans

General rule   A group health plan that is a multiemployer or multiple-employer plan may not offer employees of different employers different coverage under the plan, except for the following reasons:[24]

- Nonpayment of contributions
- Fraud or other intentional misrepresentation of material fact by the employer
- Noncompliance with material plan provisions
- The plan is ceasing to offer any coverage in the geographic area
- For network plans, there is no longer any individual enrolled through the employer who lives, resides, or works in the service area, provided the plan applies this factor uniformly and without regard to claims experience or health status-related factors
- Failure to meet the terms of a collective bargaining agreement, to renew the agreement or other agreement authorizing contributions to the plan, or to employ employees covered by the agreement

---

[24] I.R.C. § 9803(a); ERISA § 703.

Chapter 6

Reporting and Disclosure Requirements

Introduction   This chapter discusses the special notice requirements imposed by HIPAA and explains information employers or plan sponsors must include in their summary plan descriptions (SPDs). Also discussed are the conditions that that must be met by employers providing information through electronic media.

In this chapter   This chapter has two sections:

Section	Title	Page
A	Notice to Employees	6:2
B	SPD Requirements	6:5

A. Notice to Employees

General rule
The employer must notify plan participants of any material reduction in covered services or benefits provided under a group health plan.[1]

Material reduction in covered services or benefits, defined
A **material reduction in covered services or benefits** means any modification to the plan or change in the information required to be included in the SPD that, independently or in conjunction with other changes or modifications, would be considered by the average plan participant to be an important reduction in covered services or benefits.[2]

Reduction in covered services or benefits
A reduction in covered services or benefits includes any plan modification or change that:[3]

- Eliminates benefits payable under a plan
- Reduces benefits payable under a plan, including a reduction occurring because of a change in formula, methodology, or schedules used for making benefit determinations
- Increases deductibles, copayments, or other amounts a participant or beneficiary must pay
- Reduces the service area covered by a health maintenance organization
- Establishes new conditions or requirements (e.g., pre-authorization requirements) for obtaining services or benefits under the plan

Due date
The plan must provide the notice of material reduction in covered services or benefits to participants and beneficiaries no later than 60 days after the date of adoption of the modification or change.[4]

---

[1] PWBA Reg. § 2520.104b-3(d)(1).
[2] PWBA Reg. § 2520.104b-3(d)(3)(i).
[3] PWBA Reg. § 2520.104b-3(d)(3)(ii).
[4] PWBA Reg. § 2520.104b-3(d)(1).

A. Notice to Employees, continued

Alternative due date

The aforementioned due date does not apply if the employer or plan sponsor provides a benefits summary in connection with a system of communication at regular intervals of not more than 90 days.

How to distribute notices

An employer or plan sponsor must distribute notices in a method that ensures that plan participants and beneficiaries will receive them.[5] Acceptable methods include:[6]

- Hand delivery to employees at their worksites
- Special inserts in employee periodicals, if the:
  - Distribution list is comprehensive, up-to-date, and accurate
  - Front page prominently states that the notice is inserted
- First-class mail
- Second- or third-class mail, if return and forwarding postage are guaranteed and address corrections are requested
- Electronic media

Special periodical inserts

If an employer distributes a notice by special insertion in an employee periodical, but some of the participants and beneficiaries are not on the mailing list, the employer may combine the periodical with another distribution method to ensure that participants and beneficiaries actually receive the notice.[7]

Second- or third-class mail

If an employer distributes notices by second- or third-class mail and later receives a returned notice with a corrected address, the employer must then distribute the notice by first-class mail or by personal delivery to the participant's worksite.[8]

---

[5] PWBA Reg. § 2520.104b-1.
[6] *Id.*
[7] *Id.*
[8] *Id.*

A. Notice to Employees, continued

Electronic media

If the employer furnishes the notice to employees through electronic media, the employer must:[9]

- Take appropriate measures to ensure that the system for furnishing notices results in actual receipt by participants (e.g., return receipt mail feature to confirm receipt of transmitted information)
- Prepare and furnish notices in a manner consistent with the applicable style, format, and content requirements
- Inform the participant through electronic means or in writing of the notice being electronically delivered, the significance of the notice, and the participant's right to request and receive, free of charge, a paper copy of the notice
- Upon a participant's request, furnish free of charge a paper copy of the notice originally delivered through electronic media

The furnishing of notices through electronic media satisfies the requirements only with respect to participants who have the ability to effectively access these notices at their worksites and who have the opportunity to readily convert notices from electronic to paper format free of charge.

---

[9] PWBA Reg. § 2520.104b-1(c).

B. SPD Requirements

General rule   HIPAA requires that employers include the following statement in their SPDs.[10]

Statement

If you have any questions about this statement or about your rights under ERISA, you should contact the nearest office of the Employee Benefits Security Administration, U.S. Department of Labor, listed in your telephone directory, or the Division of Technical Assistance and Inquiries, EBSA, U.S. Department of Labor, 200 Constitution Avenue, N.W., Washington, D.C. 20210.

* The Employee Benefits Security Administration (EBSA) was formerly the Pension Welfare Benefits Administration.

Health insurers   If a health insurance issuer is responsible in whole or in part for financing or administering a group health plan, the SPD must indicate the following:[11]

- Name and address of the issuer
- Whether and to what extent benefits under the plan are guaranteed under a contract or insurance policy
- The nature of any administrative services (e.g., claims payment) provided by the insurer

---

[10] PWBA Reg. § 2520.102-3(t)(2).
[11] PWBA Reg. § 2520.102-3(q).

Chapter 7

Rules for Group Health Insurers

Introduction

HIPAA limits the circumstances under which an insurer can refuse to renew a large or small employer's group health insurance policy. In addition, HIPAA requires insurers to make group health plans available to most small employers.

This chapter discusses the special requirements that apply to health insurers.

In this chapter

This chapter has three sections:

Section	Title	Page
A	Guaranteed Renewability Requirements	7:2
B	Guaranteed Availability Requirements	7:5
C	Disclosure Requirements	7:9

A. Guaranteed Renewability Requirements

General rule   An insurer that offers health insurance in the small- or large-group market must renew or continue coverage that is in force at the plan sponsor's option unless one of the exceptions described in the following subsection applies.[1]

Exceptions   An insurer is not required to renew or continue coverage if one or more of the following exceptions apply:[2]

Exception	Description
Nonpayment of premiums	The plan sponsor failed to pay premiums or contributions according to the plan's terms, including any timeliness requirements.
Fraud	The plan sponsor committed fraud or intentionally misrepresented a material fact in connection with the coverage.
Violation of participation or contribution rules	The plan sponsor failed to comply with a material plan provision concerning any employer contribution or group participation rules in the case of the small-group market or under applicable state law in the case of the large-group market.
Termination of plan	The insurer ceased to offer coverage in the market in compliance with the special rules for discontinuing products or coverage (see page 7:3).
Enrollees' movement outside service area	In the case of a network plan, there is no longer any enrollee in the group health plan who lives, resides, or works in the service area. In the case of the small-group market, the insurer applies the same criteria it would use in denying enrollment under the special rules for discontinuing products (see page 7:3).
Association membership ceases	Coverage was made available in the small- or large-group market only through one or more bona fide associations, and the employer's membership in the association(s) ceased. This exception applies only if the coverage is terminated uniformly without regard to the health status of any covered individual.

[1] HCFA Reg. § 146.152(a).
[2] HCFA Reg. § 146.152(b).

A. Guaranteed Renewability Requirements, continued

Product discontinued

An insurer may discontinue a product offered in the small- or large-group market only if the insurer meets the following requirements:[3]

- The insurer gives at least 90 days' advance written notice to each plan sponsor that has the product in that market (and to all covered participants and beneficiaries) that the product will be discontinued.
- The insurer offers each plan sponsor that has the product the option, on a guaranteed issue basis, of purchasing all (or, in the case of the large-group market, any) other health insurance coverage the insurer currently offers in that market.
- In discontinuing the product and offering the plan sponsor an alternative product, the insurer acts uniformly without regard to the plan's claims experience or any covered individual's health status.

Coverage discontinued

An insurer may discontinue offering all health insurance coverage in the small- or large-group market, or both, in a state in accordance with state law only if the insurer meets the following requirements:[4]

- The insurer gives at least 180 days' advance written notice to the appropriate state authority and each plan sponsor (and all covered participants and beneficiaries) that the coverage will be discontinued.
- All health insurance policies issued or delivered for issuance in the state in the market (or markets) are discontinued and not renewed.

---

[3] HCFA Reg. § 146.152(c).
[4] HCFA Reg. § 146.152(d).

A. Guaranteed Renewability Requirements, continued

Market reentry	If an insurer discontinues offering all health insurance in the large- and/or small-group market, the insurer may not offer health insurance in the market(s) and state involved for a five-year period that begins on the date the last coverage was discontinued and not renewed.[5]
Uniform modification of coverage exception	An insurer may modify a health insurance coverage product only at renewal.[6] In the case of the small-group market, the insurer may modify a product at renewal only if the modification is consistent with state law and uniform among group health plans with the product.

---

[5] HCFA Reg. § 146.152(e).
[6] HCFA Reg. § 146.152(f).

B. Guaranteed Availability Requirements

General rules An insurer that offers coverage a state's small-group market must

- Offer any small employer in the state all products that are approved for sale in the small-group market and that the insurer is actively marketing, and
- Accept any employer that applies for any of the products.[7]

(See Chapter 3 for a definition of a small employer.)

In addition, an insurer must accept all eligible individuals who apply for coverage during the period in which such individuals first become eligible to enroll in the group health plan or during a special enrollment period. The insurer may not impose any restrictions on an eligible individual that are inconsistent with HIPAA's nondiscrimination requirements.

Eligible individual, defined An **eligible individual** is an individual who[8]

- Is eligible under a small employer's group health plan's eligibility requirements;
- Is eligible for coverage under the health insurer's rules that uniformly apply in the state to small employers in the small-group market; or
- Is eligible for coverage under the state laws that govern the insurer and the small-group market.

Network plans An insurer that offers health insurance in the small-group health market through a network plan can limit coverage to employers with eligible individuals who live, work, or reside in the network plan's service area.[9]

---

[7] HCFA Reg. § 146.150(a).
[8] HCFA Reg. § 146.150(b).
[9] HCFA Reg. § 146.150(c)(1)(i).

B. Guaranteed Availability Requirements, continued

Network plans (continued)

In addition, an insurer can deny coverage to employers within the network plan's service area if the insurer demonstrates to the appropriate state authority (if required by the state authority) that it

- Will not have the capacity to deliver services adequately to enrollees of any additional groups because of its obligations to existing group contract holders and enrollees, and
- Is limiting coverage under the network plan uniformly to all employers without regard to their claims experience or the health status of any of their employees or dependents.[10]

If an insurer denies network plan coverage to an employer because of capacity, the insurer may not offer coverage in the small-group market within the service area to any employer for a period of 180 days after the date the coverage is denied.[11] This requirement does not limit an insurer's ability to renew coverage that is already in force; nor does it relieve the insurer of its responsibility for renewing coverage.

Financial capacity limits

An insurer may deny health insurance in the small-group market if it demonstrates to the appropriate state authority (if the state authority so requires) that it

- Does not have the financial reserves necessary to underwrite additional coverage, and
- Is denying coverage uniformly to all employers without regard to their claims experience or the health status of their employees or dependents.[12]

---

[10] HCFA Reg. § 146.150(c)(1)(ii).
[11] HCFA Reg. § 146.150(c)(2).
[12] HCFA Reg. § 146.150(d)(1).

B. Guaranteed Availability Requirements, continued

Financial capacity limits (continued)

If an insurer denies coverage based on insufficient financial reserves, the insurer may not offer group health insurance coverage in the small-group market in the state for at least 180 days after the later of

- The date the coverage is denied, or
- The date the insurer demonstrates to the appropriate state authority that it has sufficient financial reserves to underwrite additional coverage.[13]

This requirement does not limit an insurer's ability to renew coverage that is already in force; nor does it relieve the insurer of its responsibility for renewing coverage.[14]

Employer contribution rules or group participation rules

The requirement to make health insurance available to small employers does not preclude an insurer from establishing employer contribution rules or group participation rules as allowed by applicable state law.[15]

Employer contribution rules, defined

Employer contribution rules set the minimum level or amount an employer must contribute toward insurance premiums for a participant and/or his or her dependents.[16]

Group participation rules, defined

Group participation rules set the minimum number of participants or beneficiaries that must be enrolled in the plan. The minimum number usually relates to a specified percentage or number of eligible individuals or employees of the employer.[17]

---

[13] HCFA Reg. § 146.150(d)(2).
[14] HCFA Reg. § 146.150(d)(3).
[15] HCFA Reg. § 146.150(e)(1).
[16] HCFA Reg. § 146.150(e)(2)(i).
[17] HCFA Reg. § 146.150(e)(2)(ii).

B. Guaranteed Availability Requirements, continued

Association plans

The requirement to make health insurance available to small employers does not apply to health insurance coverage made available in the small-group market through one or more bona fide associations.[18]

---

[18] HCFA Reg. § 146.150(f).

C. Disclosure Requirements

Information that must be disclosed

In offering health insurance coverage to a small employer, the insurer must generally disclose the following information:[19]

- The insurer's right to change premium rates and the factors that may affect changes in premium rates
- Renewability of coverage
- Any preexisting condition exclusion, including use of the alternative method of counting creditable coverage
- Any affiliation periods applied by HMOs
- The geographic areas served by HMOs
- Benefits and premiums available under all health insurance coverage the employer qualifies for under applicable state law

An insurer is not required to disclose any information that is proprietary or trade secret information under applicable law.[20]

Disclosing information

In offering insurance to a small employer, the insurer must:[21]

- Make a reasonable disclosure to the employer in its solicitation and sales materials of the availability of the information listed directly above; and
- Upon an employer's request, provide the information listed directly above.

Form of information

Disclosed information must be understandable by the average small employer.[22] In addition, the description must provide enough details to reasonably inform small employers of their rights and obligations under the health insurance coverage. An insurer meets these requirements if it provides all of the following for each product offered:

---

[19] HCFA Reg. § 146.160(b).
[20] HCFA Reg. § 146.160(d).
[21] HCFA Reg. § 146.160(a).
[22] HCFA Reg. § 146.160(c).

C. Disclosure Requirements, continued

Form of information (continued)

- An outline of the coverage (i.e., a description of benefits in summary form);
- The rate or rating schedule that applies to the product (with and without the preexisting condition exclusion or affiliation period);
- The minimum employer contribution and group participation rules that apply to any particular type of coverage;
- For a network plan, a map or listing of counties served; and
- Any other information required by the state.

Chapter 8

HIPAA Privacy and Security Requirements

Introduction   This chapter focuses on the national standards for protecting the privacy of personal health information. It summarizes the HIPAA final rules issued by the U.S. Department of Health and Human Services and provides sample checklists that can be used to determine compliance.

This chapter is authored by Marcia S. Wagner and Virginia S. Peabody of The Wagner Law Group, located in Boston, Massachusetts.

Important reminder and tip   Employers must make sure that participants are informed every three years of the availability of the Privacy Notice and that the Privacy Notice is provided to a participant when the participant enrolls in a covered plan and if there are any material changes in the Privacy Notice, itself. To make sure the Privacy Notice requirement is met, consider including the notice in your open enrollment materials.

Also, it is important that the employee training requirements are met, including training new employees within a reasonable period of time after they are hired.

In this chapter   The discussion is organized by topic and subtopic. Sample checklists are presented as exhibits at the end of the chapter.

HIPAA Privacy and Security Requirements, continued

HIPAA Privacy and Security Requirements

By: Marcia S. Wagner, Esq.
Virginia S. Peabody
The Wagner Law Group
A Professional Corporation
Boston, Massachusetts

I.   Overview and Compliance Dates.

The Health Insurance Portability and Accountability Act of 1996 ("HIPAA") includes privacy requirements because Congress believed that the increased ease of transmitting and sharing individually identifiable health information posed an increasing threat to confidentiality. The United States Department of Health and Human Services ("HHS") issued comprehensive final privacy regulations in three parts: the Privacy Rule, EDI Rule, and the Security Rule. The Privacy Rule creates national standards to protect individuals' personal health information and gives patients increased access to their medical records. The EDI Rule establishes particular code sets that must be used to transmit electronic data, and the Security Rule establishes standards to protect the transmission and storage of electronic medical information. This chapter focuses on the Privacy Rule and the Security Rule.

The Privacy Rule established under the final regulation can generally be summarized as follows: "*Covered Entities*" may not use or disclose "*Protected Health Information*" ("PHI") except as authorized by the individual who is the subject of the information, or as explicitly required or permitted by the regulation. Even when the use or disclosure of PHI is permitted, only the "minimum necessary" amount of information to accomplish the intended purpose of the use, disclosure or request may be provided.

The American Recovery and Reinvestment Act of 2009 ("ARRA") made significant changes to the Privacy Rule and the Security Rule for both Covered Entities and Business Associates. Generally, the changes are effective as of February 17, 2010. Most of the security provisions, however, are effective 30 days after Health and Human Services ("HHS") issues regulations, and the changes affecting the enforcement provisions are effective for violations occurring after February 17, 2009.

II.   Covered Entities.

Covered Entities include: (i) health plans, (ii) health care clearinghouses, and (iii) health care providers who transmit PHI in electronic form.[1] While the Privacy Rule

---

[1] 45 C.F.R. §160.103.

directly regulates group health plans and not employers, given that a group health plan is usually nothing more than a plan document, it is the sponsor of the plan, the employer or the trustees who must comply. In addition, the companies and individuals who provide services to the health plan as "Business Associates" (see definition below under Section IV) must comply.

Health plans under the Privacy Rule include group health plans, health insurers, health maintenance organizations ("HMOs"), Medicare, Medicaid, issuers of Medicare supplemental policies, Medicare + Choice programs, issuers of long-term care policies (other than nursing home fixed indemnity policies), multiemployer health plans, multiple employer health plans, health care programs for active military personnel, veterans health care programs, the Civilian Health and Medical Program of the Uniformed Services ("CHAMPUS"), the Indian Health Service program under the Indian Health Care Improvement Act, the Federal Employees Health Benefits Program, an approved state child health plan providing benefits for child health assistance, a high risk pool established under state law to provide health insurance coverage or comparable coverage to eligible individuals, and any other individual and/or group plans providing or paying for the cost of medical care.[2] This definition includes medical, dental, vision, prescription drug, medical flexible spending account plans and employee assistance plans (except those that provide referral services only).

A group health plan that has less than 50 participants and that is administered solely by the employer that established and maintains the plan is not subject to the Privacy Rule.[3] For purposes of this exception, the ERISA definition of participant applies. Therefore, participant includes all employees or former employees of the employer who are or may become eligible to receive a benefit. As a result, if an employer maintains a medical flexible spending account and 50 or more employees are eligible to participate, then the plan must comply with the Privacy Rule even though only 25 employees are actually participating in the plan.

The following two types of government-funded programs are not health plans: (i) programs whose principal purpose is not providing or paying the cost of health care (*e.g.*, a food stamps program), and (ii) programs whose principal activity is directly providing health care (*e.g.*, certain community health centers), or the making of grants to

---

[2] 45 C.F.R. §160.103.
[3] 45 C.F.R. §160.103.

fund the direct provision of health care. The Privacy Rule does *not* cover worker's compensation, reinsurance (stop loss), accident insurance, disability insurance or liability insurance.

The Privacy Rule emphasizes that employers are not Covered Entities and, as such, employment records are specifically excluded from the definition of PHI. Records created, received or maintained by the employer in *its capacity as the employer* are not covered by the Privacy Rule.[4] For example, records maintained by the employer such as fitness-for-duty evaluations, drug screening results, sickness and disability leave requests and documents needed to comply with the Americans with Disabilities Act, worker's compensation laws, and the Family Medical Leave Act are employment records and are not subject to the Privacy Rule. It should be noted, however, that in order to obtain an employee's medical information from his health care providers, the employer will need the employee's written authorization. Therefore, while employers are not Covered Entities, they are affected by the Privacy Rule and need to understand its impact on their organizations. For example, employers may want to include written authorizations on their disability forms allowing health care providers to release PHI to the employer or the insurer in order to expedite processing disability claims. (See Authorizations below under Section VI.)

Any **PHI** created, received or maintained by the employer *acting on behalf of the group health plan*, however, remains subject to the Privacy Rule.

NOTE: While all of the rules discussed in this chapter apply to Covered Entities in general, the balance of this chapter will discuss these rules in the context of employer-sponsored group health plans.

III. **Effect of HIPAA on Fully Insured Plans.**

The applicability of certain HIPAA privacy protections with respect to the plan sponsor is a direct function of how involved the plan sponsor is in the maintenance of its fully insured plan. There are two operational modalities for fully insured plans, as follows:

A. **Operational Model 1: Fully Insured Employee Welfare Benefit Plan.**

An employer sponsors a group health plan that provides benefits solely through an insurance contract with a health insurance issuer. The group health plan and the plan sponsor do not create, maintain or receive PHI. The group health plan receives summary health information from the insurer and uses it to contract with the insurer (*e.g.*, evaluate premium costs, terms and conditions of insurance arrangement or perform "plan sponsor" activities such as plan amendment, modification or termination (see discussion below)). The employer collects information during an open enrollment period and passes that information on to the insurer.

---

[4] 45 C.F.R. §160.103.

The employer also retains benefits professionals, such as Human Resource personnel, who serve in an ombudsman-like role between employees and the insurer regarding health claims. These professionals assist employees with claims questions, disputes and appeals, but do not make any decisions regarding the outcome of claims payment questions. To the extent that these individuals assist employees, they require an authorization from the employees so that they may receive information from the insurer.

Neither the employer nor the group health plan is obligated to comply with most of the privacy rules under this scenario.[5] However, as discussed below, plan documents and summary plan descriptions must be amended to permit the exchange of anything other than summary or de-identified information between the plan and the insurer. The insurer takes on the compliance burden, including providing individuals with access and amendment rights to their PHI, providing a notice of privacy practices for PHI, appointing a privacy official and complying with any other administrative protections.

Note that all benefits must be insured for this example to be accurate. If the employer maintains any self-insured benefits or plans (*e.g.*, a medical flexible spending account plan or covered employee assistance plan) or engages in plan administration functions, it must fully and completely comply with the Privacy Rule with respect to such benefit plans.

Business Associates of the group health plan must be contracted to comply with the Privacy Rule. However, if the only Business Associate is also the insurer, a Business Associate agreement is not necessary because that insurer is obligated to comply as a covered entity in its own right.

B.   **Operational Model 2: Fully Insured Employee Welfare Benefit Plan with Employer that Engages in Plan Administration Function.**

An employer sponsors a group health plan that provides benefits solely through an insurance contract with a health insurance issuer (the "insurer"). However, unlike the plan discussed above, this plan and the employer are actively involved in monitoring benefit utilization. The employer also sponsors a wellness program and a medical flexible spending account ("FSA"), and requires information from the insurer to administer those benefits. Therefore, the group health plan creates, maintains and receives PHI and provides that information to the employer for plan administration purposes.

The group health plan receives summary health information from the insurer that is used to contract with the insurer (*e.g.*, evaluate premium costs, terms and conditions of insurance arrangement or perform "plan sponsor" activities such as plan amendment, modification or termination). It also receives PHI that may be

---

[5] 164.530(k).

individually identifiable (not summary or de-identified). The employer collects information during an open enrollment period and passes that enrollment and disenrollment information on to the insurer.

The employer retains benefits professionals who serve in an ombudsman-like role between employees and the insurer regarding health claims. These professionals also assist in quality evaluations of the group health plan and health outcomes. For purposes of the wellness program, the employees receive PHI related to diseases that the employer seeks to manage, such as asthma or diabetes. These benefit professionals also administer the medical FSA.

The group health plan contracts to provide pharmacy benefits through a discounted pharmacy network. It also contracts with a mental health network for mental health utilization review and provider services. All of these benefits are self-insured. The pharmacy and mental health network administer claims and the group health plan reimburses them for the cost of claims plus any administration fees.

This group health plan must take these steps to comply with the Privacy Rule:

- maintain plan documents that permit information sharing between the plan and the plan sponsor, and institute procedures to comply with the privacy provisions;
- obtain certification of compliance from the employer;
- comply with the Privacy Rule regarding PHI use and disclosure, including the consent and authorization requirements;
- enter into appropriate Business Associate agreements;
- provide plan participants with a notice of privacy practices for the self-insured portions/components of the group health plan;
- comply with provisions relating to individuals' rights to see and change their PHI; and
- comply with administrative requirements involving privacy procedures, safeguarding PHI, designating a privacy official, training, complaints and documentation.

IV.   Business Associates.

A Business Associate is a person or entity (other than a member of the group health plan's workforce) who:

(a)   on behalf of a group health plan, performs or assists in the performance of a function or activity involving the use or disclosure of PHI including claims processing or administration, data analysis, processing or administration, utilization review, quality assurance, billing, benefit management, practice management and repricing or any other activity regulated by the Privacy Rule; or

    (b)   provides legal, actuarial, accounting, consulting, data aggregation, management, administrative, accreditation, or financial services to or for the group health plan if the service involves the disclosure of individually identifiable health information from the group health plan or from another business associate of the group health plan. [6]

ARRA expands the definition of Business Associate to include organizations that provide data transmission of PHI to a Covered Entity or its Business Associate if the transactions routinely require access to PHI (*e.g.*, health information exchange organizations, regional health information organizations, e-prescribing gateways, or vendors that contract with a Covered Entity to allow that Covered Entity to offer a personal health record ("PHR") to patients).[7] PHR is an individual's electronic health record that (i) is created, gathered, managed, and consulted by authorized health care clinicians and staff, (ii) can be drawn from multiple sources, and (iii) is managed, shared, and controlled by or primarily for the individual.[8]

A Covered Entity can be the Business Associate of another Covered Entity. For example, a health insurer which is a Covered Entity would also be a Business Associate under (a) above for a group health plan.

Under ARRA, the Security Rule (discussed in detail in Section XII hereof) will apply directly to Business Associates. As a result, Business Associates must adopt administrative, physical and technical safeguards, and adopt security policies and procedures.[9] To comply with the Privacy Rule, Business Associates will need to develop written policies and procedures, workforce training and discipline, and periodic compliance reviews.[10] Violations of the Privacy Rule or the Security Rule may now be enforced directly against Business Associates rather than only against Covered Entities.[11] Furthermore, if a Business Associate knows of a violation of the Covered Entities' obligations under the Business Associate agreement, it must take steps to cure the breach. If steps to cure a breach are not successful and termination of the contract is not feasible, the Business Associate must report the problem to HHS.[12]

Group health plans may disclose PHI to a Business Associate only after receiving satisfactory assurance that the Business Associate will safeguard the information.[13] As such, group health plans must enter into contracts with its Business Associates which will protect the confidentiality of PHI when it is created, received, used by or disclosed by the Business Associates.[14]

---

[6] 45 C.F.R. §160.103.
[7] ARRA §13408.
[8] ARRA §13400.
[9] ARRA §13404(a).
[10] ARRA §13404(a).
[11] ARRA §13404(c).
[12] ARRA §13404(b).
[13] 45 C.F.R §164.502(e)(1).
[14] 45 C.F.R. §164.502(e)(2).

HIPAA Privacy and Security Requirements, continued

The contract between the group health plan and the Business Associate, otherwise known as a "Business Associate Agreement," must, among other requirements, establish the permitted and required uses and disclosures of PHI by the Business Associate and ensure that any agents and subcontractors to whom the Business Associate provides PHI on behalf of the group health plan also agree to the same restrictions and conditions that apply to the Business Associate with respect to the information.[15] These requirements help to ensure that group health plans do not avoid their HIPAA privacy responsibilities through "outsourcing."

ARRA states that Business Associate Agreements must clearly state that the Business Associate will comply with the Security Rule's administrative, physical, and technical safeguards and meet the Security Rule's policy and procedure (and other documentation) requirements.[16] (See Section XII hereof for a detailed discussion of the Security Rule.)

Note: Covered Entities and Business Associates should review and update all of their Business Associate Agreements to comply with ARRA's new requirements.

When a broker receives PHI directly from a group health plan and the broker then shares the PHI with a third party administrator ("TPA"), the broker is a Business Associate of the group health plan. As such, the group health plan must enter into a Business Associate Agreement with the broker. Plan sponsors will need to ensure such Agreements are in place. In the alternative, when a TPA provides PHI on behalf of the group health plan to a broker who is a subcontractor of the TPA and not a service provider for the group health plan, the broker is an agent for the TPA. As such, the TPA must enter into an agreement with the broker binding him to the same restrictions on PHI as contained in the Business Associate Agreement between the TPA and the plan.

V.   Protected Health Information.

Protected Health Information ("PHI") is all "individually identifiable health information" in any form or media, electronic or non-electronic, that is held or transmitted by a group health plan, including oral communication. PHI includes Electronic Protected Health Information ("ePHI") which is PHI that is transmitted or maintained in electronic media.

"Individually identifiable health information" is information, including demographic data, created or received by a health care provider, health plan, employer, or health care clearinghouse, that relates to the past, present, or future physical or mental health or condition of an individual, the provision of health care to an individual, or the past, present or future payment for health care to an individual, and that identifies an individual (or could reasonably be used to identify an individual).[17]

---

[15] 45 C.F.R. §164.504(e).
[16] ARRA §13401(a).
[17] 45 C.F.R. §160.103.

If information is "de-identified," then it is *not* covered by the Privacy Rule.[18] De-identified information is that which does not identify any individual and for which there is no reasonable basis to believe that the information can be used to identify an individual. In order to de-identify information, a group health plan must remove 19 factors concerning the individual, including names, birthdays, social security numbers, all geographic subdivisions smaller than a state, telephone numbers, fax numbers, e-mail addresses and more. The specific list of identifiers is generally as follows:

1. Names of individuals.
2. Geographic units – all geographic subdivisions smaller than a state, including street address, city, county, precinct, and zip code.
3. Dates – any month or day directly related to an individual, including birthdate, admission date, discharge date and date of death. However, listing an individual's age is broad enough to be allowed in de-identified information (subject to the exception for individuals age 90 or older described below).
4. Ages – all those over 89 and any combination of month, date or year that reveals an individual's age to be over 89, because nonagenarians are relatively rare. However, ages and identifying dates (month, day and year) or several individuals may be aggregated into a single category of age 90 or older.
5. Telephone numbers.
6. Fax numbers.
7. E-mail addresses.
8. Social Security numbers.
9. Medical record numbers.
10. Health plan beneficiary numbers.
11. Account numbers.
12. Certificate/license numbers.
13. Vehicle identifiers and serial numbers.
14. Device identifiers and serial numbers.
15. Web universal resource locators (URLs).
16. Internet protocol (IP) address numbers.
17. Biometric identifiers, including finger and voice prints.
18. Full face photographic images and any comparable images.
19. Any other unique identifying number, characteristic or code (except a code assigned by the covered entity to allow de-identified information to become re-identified).[19]

---

[18] 45 C.F.R. §164.502(d)((2).
[19] 45 C.F.R. §164.514(b)

In addition, even if all the listed identifiers have been removed, if the group health plan can identify an individual from the remaining information (alone or in combination with other reasonably available information), the information is not de-identified.[20]

VI. Disclosure of PHI.

A. General Rule.

Group health plans are prohibited from "using" or "disclosing" PHI except either:

- With an individual's written authorization; or
- As explicitly permitted or required by the Privacy Rule.

Health information is *"used"* when shared within the entity that holds the information (internal), while health information is *"disclosed"* when it is shared outside the entity (external).

B. Consents and Authorizations.

A "consent" and "authorization" are not the same and the Privacy Rule establishes an important distinction between them. A consent is a broad, general permission granted by the individual. An authorization is a specific and detailed permission granted by an individual.

C. Consents and TPO.

With the exception of psychotherapy notes, a group health plan does not need to obtain an individual's consent for the use and disclosure of PHI for routine health care delivery purposes, otherwise known as "treatment, payment or health care operations" ("TPO").

"Treatment" means the provision, coordination or management of health care and related services by one or more health care providers. It also includes coordination or management of health care by a health provider and a third party and consultation or referrals between one health care provider and another.[21]

"Payment" includes activities undertaken by the group health plan or health care provider to obtain or provide reimbursement or premiums for the provision of health care and other activities, such as determinations of eligibility of coverage (including coordination of benefits), adjudication or subrogation of claims, risk adjustments, billing, claims management, collections, medical necessity reviews and utilization reviews.[22]

---

[20] 45 C.F.R. §164.514(b)(1).
[21] 45 C.F.R. §164.501.
[22] 45 C.F.R. §164.501.

HIPAA Privacy and Security Requirements, continued

"Health Care Operations" includes certain services or activities necessary to carry out the covered functions of the group health plan with respect to treatment and payment such as quality assessment, case management, pre-certification and care coordination, contacting providers and patients with information about treatment alternatives, underwriting, premium rating and other activities relating to the creation, renewal or replacement of a contract of health insurance or health benefits, ceding, securing, or placing a contract for reinsurance of risk relating to claims for health care (including stop-loss insurance and excess loss insurance), deciding claim appeals, conducting or arranging for medical review and auditing functions, and business planning and development such as conducting cost-management and planning-related analyses related to managing and operating the plan.[23]

      D.   <u>**Consents and Enrollment.**</u>

A group health plan does not need to obtain consent from each plan participant to use and disclose his PHI to carry out TPO; however a plan may obtain such consent if the plan sponsor so chooses.

      E.   <u>**Authorization.**</u>

Authorizations from individuals are required in order to use PHI in most cases, *other than for carrying out TPO or as otherwise permitted or required by the Privacy Rule.*[24] Some cases where written individual authorizations are required include marketing of health and non-health items and services and the use of PHI by a non-health related division of the same corporation (*e.g.,* for use in marketing or underwriting life or casualty insurance). Employers may also need authorizations to obtain health information from health care providers for return to work certifications and medical certifications for family and medical leave. In addition, a covered entity must obtain authorization for any use or disclosure of psychotherapy notes including most uses or disclosures for TPO.[25]

Authorizations are <u>not</u> needed to use or disclose PHI for specified public health and public policy related purposes, including public health activities, research, health oversight, law enforcement and use by coroners. In addition, PHI may be used or disclosed when the group health plan is required to do so by law such as mandatory reporting under state law or pursuant to a search warrant.[26]

An authorization must be a written document that gives a Covered Entity permission to use or disclose PHI. The authorization must be specific in scope and limited in duration.

---

[23] 45 C.F.R. §164.501.
[24] 45 C.F.R. §164.508.
[25] 45 C.F.R. §164.508(a)(2)(i).
[26] 45 C.F.R. §512.

F.   **Plan Sponsor Actions Regarding Consents and Authorization.**

As noted above, a group health plan does not need to obtain an individual's consent for carrying out TPO (except for psychotherapy notes). Plan sponsors will need to keep in mind, however, that if the group health plan uses PHI for anything other than plan administration functions, the plan must first obtain an authorization from the individual whose information the plan seeks to view.

G.   **Personal Representatives.**

The Privacy Rule requires a Covered Entity to treat a Personal Representative as if the Personal Representative is the individual for purposes of HIPAA's privacy rule (*e.g.*, uses and disclosures of PHI and the individual's rights under the Privacy Rule). A Personal Representative is legally authorized to make health care decisions for the individual or to act for a deceased individual or an estate. A Covered Entity however, does not need to recognize a Personal Representative if it has a reasonable belief that the Personal Representative may be abusing or neglecting the individual or continuing to treat such person as the Personal Representative could endanger the individual.

H.   **Required Disclosures.**

The Privacy Rule requires group health plans to disclose PHI only in two instances:

1. to the individual who is the subject of the PHI when the individual requests it, and
2. to the Secretary of the Department of Health and Human Services when the Secretary is undertaking a compliance investigation or review or enforcement action.[27]

I.   **Permitted Uses and Disclosures.**

Plans are permitted to use and disclose PHI without consent or authorization, or without allowing the individual to agree to the use or disclosure if:

1. the PHI is used by or disclosed to the individual who is the subject of the PHI;
2. the PHI (other than psychotherapy notes) is used or disclosed to carry out TPO;
3. the PHI is used or disclosed with the individual's opportunity to agree or object (usually informal in nature by asking the individual outright or by circumstances that clearly give the individual the opportunity to agree acquiesce, or object) (*e.g.*, family member filling a prescription for a covered individual at the pharmacy);

---

[27] 45 C.F.R. §164.502(a)(2).

4. the use or disclosure of PHI is incidental to an otherwise permitted use or disclosure; and

5. the PHI is used or disclosed for one of 12 national activities of public interest and benefit.[28]

An "incidental use or disclosure" is a secondary use or disclosure that cannot reasonably be prevented, is limited in nature, and occurs as a by-product of an otherwise permitted use or disclosure of the Privacy Rule. For example, if employees of the group health plan are discussing a health claim in accordance with and as allowed by the plan's privacy policies, but a person who should not be privy to the information inadvertently overhears the discussion, this would be considered an incidental disclosure.

J. Plan Sponsor Actions Regarding Permitted Disclosures.

The plan sponsor will need to limit the employees who may access or use PHI to only those employees performing group health plan administrative functions (*i.e.*, payments and health care operations).[29] The plan sponsor may designate a class of employees (*e.g.*, all employees assigned to a particular department) or individual employees. The plan sponsor may identify these employees in whatever way best reflects the sponsor's business needs as long as participants can reasonably identify who will have access. For example, persons may be identified by naming individuals, job titles (*e.g.*, Director of Human Resources), functions (*e.g.*, employees with oversight responsibility for the TPA), divisions of the company (*e.g.*, Employee Benefits) or other entities related to the plan sponsor.

K. Minimum Necessary.

Even if the plan may use or disclose PHI in accordance with the Privacy Rule, the plan must make reasonable efforts to limit PHI to the "minimum necessary" to accomplish the intended purpose of use, disclosure, or the request for PHI.[30]

The minimum necessary standard is intended to make Covered Entities evaluate their practices and enhance protections as needed to prevent unnecessary or inappropriate access to PHI. The group health plan must develop and implement policies and procedures to reasonably limit uses and disclosures to the minimum necessary.

For routine uses of information, the Privacy Rule permits a group health plan to adopt general procedures for determining what the minimum necessary information is, then applying the general procedures. For example, a group health plan may take two steps:

---

[28] 45 C.F.R. §164.502(a)(1).
[29] 45 C.F.R. §164.504(f)(2)(iii)(A).
[30] 45 C.F.R. §164.502(b)(1).

First: identify persons or classes of persons in its workforce who need access to PHI to carry out their duties and job responsibilities; and

Second: for each person or classes of persons, identify the category or categories of PHI to which access is needed and any conditions appropriate to that access.

A group health plan could develop procedures that allow certain employees or classes of employees unrestricted access to aggregate claims information for rating/accounting/budgeting purposes. However, the procedures could require approval from the departmental manager to obtain an individual's specific identifiable claims records to determine the cause of the claims that can influence the rates/accounting/budgeting decisions.

ARRA modifies the minimum necessary rule by requiring a Covered Entity to limit the use, disclosure, or request of PHI, to the extent practicable, to the limited data set or, if the Covered Entity needs additional information, to the minimum necessary to accomplish the intended purpose of such use, disclosure, or request, respectively.[31] A limited data set excludes basic identifying information (*e.g.*, the covered individual's name, social security number, address, email address, telephone number and other similar identifiers).

Note: Currently, regulations do not define "minimum necessary." HHS will provide regulations providing guidance to comply with the minimum necessary requirement. At that time, plan sponsors will need to evaluate their procedures to ensure compliance with the minimum necessary rule.

The minimum necessary standards of the Privacy Rule do <u>not</u> apply to the following:

(a) Disclosures to or requests by a heath care provider for treatment purposes.

(b) Disclosures to the individual who is the subject of the information.

(c) Uses or disclosures made pursuant to an authorization.

(d) Uses or disclosures required for compliance with EDI transactions.

(e) Disclosures to the HHS when disclosure is required under the rule for investigation, compliance review or enforcement purposes.

(f) Uses or disclosures that are required by law.

(g) Uses or disclosures required to comply with the Privacy Rule.[32]

---

[31] ARRA §13405(b).
[32] 45 C.F.R. §164.502(b)(2).

VII. **Plan Document Requirements.**

In order for a group health plan to use and disclose PHI as permitted by the Privacy Rule, the plan sponsor must abide by specific requirements and amend the plan documents to include the following provisions:

(a) Explain the permitted and required uses and disclosures of PHI.

(b) Include a statement that group health will disclose protected health information to the plan sponsor only upon receipt of a certification by the plan sponsor that the plan document has been amended to incorporate and the plan sponsor agrees to:

(i) Not use or further disclose PHI other than as permitted or required by the plan documents or as required by law;

(ii) Ensure that any agents to whom it provides PHI agree to the same restrictions and conditions that apply to the plan sponsor;

(iii) Not use or disclose the information for employment-related actions and decisions or in connection with any other benefit plan of the plan sponsor;

(iv) Report to the group health plan any use or disclosure of PHI that is inconsistent with the permitted or required uses or disclosures.

(v) Provide individuals with the opportunity to inspect and copy their PHI;

(vi) Provide individuals with the opportunity to amend their PHI;

(vii) Provide individuals with an accounting of the disclosure of their PHI;

(viii) Make the plan's internal practices, books and records relating to the use and disclosure of PHI available to the Secretary of the Department of Health and Human Resources for compliance purposes; and

(ix) Ensure that adequate separation exists between employees who are authorized to use PHI and those who are not; describe those employees or classes of employees to be given access to the PHI; restrict the access to and use of PHI to these employees; provide an effective mechanism for resolving any issues of noncompliance by persons who have access to PHI.[33]

VIII. **Privacy Notice.**

The Privacy Rule provides that the individuals have a right to an adequate notice of the information practices of their group health plan. Group health plans must issue

---

[33] 45 C.F.R. §164.504((f)(2)(ii).

such Privacy Notices which are intended to inform individuals about what is done with their PHI and about any rights they may have with respect to that information.[34]

The Privacy Notice must be provided to new enrollees at the time of enrollment and within 60 days of a material revision to the notice to the individuals currently covered under the plan. No less frequently than once every three years, the plan must notify individuals covered by the plan of the availability of the Privacy Notice and how to obtain the Privacy Notice.[35] If the plan sponsor maintains a website that provides information about the group health plan, then the plan sponsor must post, in a prominent location, a copy of the Privacy Notice with the group health plan information.[36]

Note: Group health plans that provide a copy of the Privacy Notice annually in their open enrollment materials automatically comply with the three-year notice requirement.

IX. Individual's Rights to PHI.

A. Right to Request Restrictions of PHI.

Group health plans must permit individuals to request restrictions on (a) the uses and disclosures of their PHI for TPO and (b) certain disclosures to family members, other relatives, close personal friends or others identified by the individual.[37] For instance, an individual may request a restriction on information given to persons involved in the individual's care, or an individual may request a restriction regarding disclosures to family members. Group health plans are *not* required to agree to the requested restrictions, however, and may deny the request for any reason.[38]

If the group health plan agrees to a requested restriction, the group health plan may not use or disclose PHI in violation of the restriction, except in the case of emergency treatment where the restricted PHI is needed to provide the emergency treatment. If the restricted PHI is disclosed to a health care provider for emergency treatment, the group health plan must request that such health care provider not further use or disclose the information.[39]

In accordance with ARRA, a Covered Entity must comply with a requested restriction if: (a) the disclosure is to a health plan for purposes of carrying out payment or health care operations (and is not for purposes of carrying out treatment) unless otherwise required by law; and (b) the PHI relates solely to a health care item or service for which the health care provider involved has been paid out-of-pocket and in full.[40] For example, if a covered individual pays a healthcare provider for a service out-of-pocket

---

[34] 45 C.F.R. §164.520(a)(1).
[35] 45 C.F.R. §164.520(c)(1)(i).
[36] 45 C.F.R. §164.520(c)(3)(i).
[37] 45 C.F.R. §164.522(a)(1)(i).
[38] 45 C.F.R. §164.522(a)(1)(ii).
[39] 45 C.F.R. §164.522(a)(1)(iii) and (iv).
[40] ARRA §13405(a).

and in full, the healthcare provider may not release the information to a health plan if the covered individual has asked that the information be restricted.

B. **Right to Access PHI.**

Group health plans must give individuals the opportunity to inspect and/or obtain copies of their PHI. Only information held in the group health plan's "designated record set" must be made available. A "designated record set" includes information such as medical records, billing records, enrollment, payment, claims adjudication, case or medical management record systems or records used to make decisions about individuals. There are exceptions to this requirement, however, including information maintained in psychotherapy notes and information compiled for use in a civil, criminal, or administrative action. In the case of the exceptions, group health plans may deny individuals access to their PHI without providing the individual with an opportunity for review.[41]

Note: ARRA modifies the rule regarding an individual's right to access his or her own PHI. A Covered Entity that uses or maintains an electronic health record must allow the covered individual to obtain a copy of his or her PHI in an electronic format and, if the individual chooses, to direct the Covered Entity to transmit a copy of the information directly to an entity or person named by the individual, if the choice is clear, conspicuous, and specific. The Covered Entity may impose a fee for providing the individual with a copy of his or her information (or a summary or explanation of the information) if the copy (or summary or explanation) is in an electronic form. The fee may not exceed the Covered Entity's labor costs to respond to the request for the copy (or summary or explanation).[42]

C. **Right to Amend and Correct PHI.**

A group health plan must provide individuals with the opportunity to amend or correct their PHI held in the group health plan's designated record set for as long as the group health plan maintains the PHI. A group health plan may, however, deny an individual's request for amendment or correction if the information is accurate and complete or if the group health plan determines that the PHI was (a) not created by the group health plan, (b) is not part of the designated record set, or (c) not available for the individual's inspection.[43] Since medical records are not created by group health plans but, rather, are created by health care providers, the amendment process should not have a significant effect on group health plans.

D. **Right to Receive an Accounting of Disclosures.**

Upon request, individuals have a right to receive an accounting of instances where their PHI is disclosed by the group health plan or by one of the plan's Business Associates (such as the TPA). The Privacy Rule does not require accounting for certain disclosures, the more common of which are disclosures: *(a) for carrying out TPO, (b) to*

---

[41] 45 C.F.R. §164.524(a)(1) and (2).
[42] ARRA §13405(e).
[43] 45 C.F.R. §164.526(a).

the individual or the individual's personal representative, (c) pursuant to an authorization, and (d) for notification of or to persons involved in an individual's care or payment for health care. This right applies to disclosures made in the 6 years prior to the date on which the accounting of the disclosure is requested, but not before the group health plan's Privacy Rule compliance date. Group health plans must have procedures to give individuals an accurate accounting of the disclosures. Such accounting must include the following: (a) the date of each disclosure; (b) the name and address of the organization or person who received the PHI; (c) a brief description of the information disclosed; and (d) for disclosures other than those made at the request of the individual, the purpose for which the information was disclosed. The accounting must be provided as soon as possible, but no later than 60 days after receipt of the request.[44]

ARRA modifies this rule with respect to Covered Entities that use or maintain electronic health records for PHI. Each covered individual will have the right to receive an accounting of all disclosures of his or her electronic health records made by the Covered Entity during the three years before the date the accounting is requested.[45]

Note: Plan sponsors will need to review their procedures and modify them to ensure that they can provide an accounting of all disclosure of electronic health records upon request.

E.   Right to Request Confidentiality in Communications.

Individuals have the right to request that a group health plan communicate to them regarding their PHI either by an alternative means or at an alternative location, if such requests are reasonable.[46] "Reasonableness" is based upon the administrative difficulty in accommodating the request, not on the perceived merits of the request. A group health plan must accommodate such reasonable requests only if the individual clearly states that disclosing all or part of the information could put him or her in danger.

Health plans may require that the confidentiality request be in writing and may condition its accommodation on the individual specifying an alternative address or method of contact an individual wants to use. A group health plan can also require an explanation of how disclosure of all or part of the PHI could endanger the individual, but the group health plan cannot question the individual's explanation of the potential danger.[47]

X.   Administrative Requirements for Covered Entities to Ensure Privacy.

Covered Entities are required to develop and document policies and procedures relating to the use, disclosure and access to PHI.[48] This documentation should serve as

---

[44] 45 C.F.R. §164.528.
[45] ARRA § 13405(c).
[46] 45 C.F.R. §164.522(b)(1).
[47] 45 C.F.R. §164.522(b)(2).
[48] 45 C.F.R. §164.530(i)(1).

a tool for educating the Covered Entity's personnel about its policies and procedures and may also be a source of information for the Covered Entity's notice of privacy practices.

The Privacy Rule does not provide for all of the specific procedures that a group health plan must adopt. However, group health plans must abide by the following minimum administrative requirements:

1. **Privacy Official**: The group health plan must designate a privacy official who is responsible for the development and implementation of the privacy policies, as well as designate a contact person or office responsible for receiving complaints about privacy violations and providing individuals with information about the group health plan's privacy practices.[49] The privacy officer should have a sufficiently senior position with the organization such that he can impose sanctions for privacy violations and require training. The privacy officer should also review the uses and disclosures of PHI for compliance with the "minimum necessary" standard.

2. **Training**: The group health plan must train workforce members (*i.e.*, the employees of the plan sponsor) regarding its privacy requirements and document that the training has been provided. The initial training must be completed no later than the group health plan's Privacy Rule compliance date. Each new employee (including temporary employees) must be trained within a reasonable period of time after they are hired.[50]

3. **Data Safeguards**: The group health plan must have in place appropriate administrative, technical, and physical safeguards to protect PHI from intentional or accidental disclosure or misuse.[51]

4. **Complaints**: The group health plan must provide an avenue for individuals to make complaints concerning the group health plan's privacy policies and procedures regarding the use or disclosure of PHI and must document all complaints received and how they were handled.[52]

5. **Sanctions**: The group health plan must develop and apply appropriate sanctions against employees who fail to comply with the group health plan's

---

[49] 45 C.F.R. §164.530(a)(1).
[50] 45 C.F.R. §164.530(b)(1).
[51] 45 C.F.R. §164.530(c)(1). This requirement overlaps with the security rules. The security rules provide that security measures must include: administrative procedures to guard data integrity and confidentiality, including documented policies and procedures for the routine and non-routine receipt, manipulation, storage, dissemination, transmission and disposal of health information, as well as security procedures and awareness training for all personnel; physical safeguards to guard data integrity, including formal policies that govern the receipt and removal of hardware/software (such as diskettes and tapes) into and out of a facility, as well as secure workstations; technical security services including procedures to ensure that data has not been altered or destroyed in an unauthorized manner, entity authentication and mechanisms to protect data that is transmitted over a communications network.
[52] 45 C.F.R. §164.530(d)(1).

privacy policies and procedures, as well as document the sanctions that are applied. [53]

6. **Mitigation**: The group health plan must mitigate, to the extent practical, any harmful effect that is known from the use or disclosure of PHI in violation of its policies and procedures. [54]

7. **Retaliatory Actions**: The group health plan may not intimidate, threaten, coerce, discriminate against, or take retaliatory action against any individual who files a complaint with the Secretary of Health and Human Services. [55]

8. **Waiver of Rights**: The group health plan may not require individuals to waive their rights to complain to HHS as a condition of the provision of treatment, payment, enrollment in the group health plan, or eligibility for benefits. [56]

9. **Retention Period**: The plan must retain documentation of its policies and procedures, notices of privacy practices and disposition of complaints for 6 years from the later of the date they were created or the date last in effect. [57]

XI.   Enforcement and Penalties.

HHS can bring enforcement actions against group health plans. HIPAA establishes civil as well as criminal penalties for any person who knowingly uses a unique health identifier, or who obtains or discloses individually identifiable health information.

ARRA significantly increased the penalties for violations occurring after February 17, 2009. The increased civil monetary penalties are as follows: [58]

1. $100 per violation if the person did not know (and by exercising reasonable diligence would not have known) that a violation occurred up to a maximum of $25,000;

2. $1,000 per violation if the violation is due to reasonable cause and not willful neglect up to a maximum of $100,000;

3. $10,000 per violation if the violation is due to willful neglect and is corrected up to a maximum of $250,000; and

4. $50,000 per violation if the violation is due to willful neglect and is **not** corrected properly up to a maximum of $1,500,000 during a calendar year.

---

[53] 45 C.F.R. §164.530(e)(1).
[54] 45 C.F.R. §164.530(f)(1).
[55] 45 C.F.R. §164.530(g)(1).
[56] 45 C.F.R. §164.530(h)(1).
[57] 45 C.F.R. §164.530(j)(2).
[58] ARRA § 13410(d).

HHS shall determine the number of violations based on the nature of the group health plan's obligation that it violated (*e.g.*, obligation to act in a certain manner or within a particular time, or to act or not act with respect to certain individuals). In the case of a continuing violation, a separate violation occurs on each day the group health violates the provision.[59] These civil penalties are imposed by HHS.[60]

If a group health plan can establish an affirmative defense with respect to a violation, then HHS may not impose a civil penalty. Affirmative defenses include the group health plan demonstrates, to HHS's satisfaction, that it did not have knowledge of the violation and with reasonable diligence would not have known of the violation.[61] The final regulations also provide that civil penalties under HIPAA are not exclusive penalties where an act constitutes a violation of a state or other federal law.[62]

A group health plan is generally not liable for the privacy violations of its Business Associates; however, HHS regulations state that the plan will be held liable if it knew of a Business Associate's wrongful activity and failed to take action. If the plan "knew of a pattern of activity of practice of the Business Associate" that constituted a material breach of violation of the Business Associates obligation under the contact, then the plan is required to take action by implementing "reasonable steps" to cure the breach or to end the violation. If such steps are not successful, the plan must terminate the contract with the Business Associate, if feasible. If contract termination is not feasible, the plan must report the problem to HHS. While the plan is not required to actively monitor and ensure protection by its Business Associates, it must investigate credible evidence of a violation by a Business Associate and act upon any such knowledge.[63]

ARRA provides that state attorneys general can now bring a HIPAA enforcement action against a Covered Entity or Business Associate that violates the HIPAA Privacy Rules. A state attorney general can also obtain attorneys' fees.[64]

ARRA also provides that HHS will issue regulations during the next three years providing that individuals affected by a HIPAA violation may receive a percentage of any civil monetary penalty or monetary settlement.[65]

Note: This change will encourage individuals to file complaints with HHS. Therefore, Covered Entities should review their current practices for compliance with the HIPAA privacy and security rules.

The criminal provisions are enforced by the Department of Justice. The penalties include: (a) a fine of not more than $50,000 and/or imprisonment of not more than 1

---

[59] 45 C.F.R. §160.406.
[60] 45 C.F.R. §160.404(b)
[61] 45 C.F.R. §160.410 and ARRA § 13410(f).
[62] 45 C.F.R. §160.418.
[63] 45 C.F.R. §160.402(c).
[64] ARRA §13410(e).
[65] ARRA §13410(c)(3).

year; (b) if the offense is under false pretenses, a fine of not more than $100,000 and/or imprisonment of not more than 5 years; and (c) if the offense is with intent to sell, transfer, or use individually identifiable health information for commercial advantage, personal gain, or malicious harm, a fine of not more than $250,000 and/or imprisonment of not more than 10 years. The Secretary may conduct compliance reviews of Covered Entities. As such, group health plans will be subject to such reviews.[66]

XII.   The Security Rule.

HIPAA also contains security standards, which apply to electronic PHI ("ePHI"), which is PHI from the Privacy Rule that a group health plan maintains or transmits in electronic form. The Security Rule is intended to provide standards to assure the confidentiality, integrity, and limited availability of ePHI. These standards generally require Covered Entities to take steps to safeguard ePHI when it is stored or transmitted.

HHS focused on four goals/mandates when it developed the Security Rule. Generally, to be in compliance with the Security Rule, a group health plan must:

- ensure the confidentiality, integrity and availability of all ePHI that it creates, receives, maintains or transmits;
- protect against any reasonably anticipated threats or hazards to the security or integrity of the ePHI;
- protect against any reasonably anticipated uses or disclosures that are not permitted or required under the Privacy Rule; and
- ensure that its workforce complies with the Security Rule.[67]

As a result, each group health plan must safeguard the confidentiality, integrity and availability of all ePHI. Furthermore, plan sponsors must take steps to guard against reasonably anticipated threats or hazards and against reasonably anticipated uses or disclosures by unauthorized persons or by authorized employees in an unauthorized manner.

A.   Security Standards.

The Security Rule contains security standards, which are divided into the following categories:

- **Administrative safeguards**: In general, these are the administrative functions that should be implemented to meet the security standards. These include assignment or delegation of security responsibility to an individual and security training requirements.

- **Physical safeguards**: In general, these are the mechanisms required to protect electronic systems, equipment and the data they hold, from threats, environmental

---

[66] Pub. L. 104-191; 42 U.S.C. §1320d-6.
[67] 45 C.F.R. §164.306(a).

hazards and unauthorized intrusion. They include restricting access to ePHI and retaining off site computer backups.

• **Technical safeguards**: In general, these are primarily the automated processes used to protect data and control access to data. They include using authentication controls to verify that the person signing onto a computer is authorized to access that ePHI, or encrypting and decrypting data as it is being stored and/or transmitted.

Each category of safeguards is comprised of a number of standards, which, in turn, are generally comprised of a number of implementation specifications that are identified as either required or addressable. If an implementation specification is required, the group health plan must implement policies and/or procedures that satisfy the requirements for such specification. If an implementation specification is addressable, then the group health plan must assess whether it is a reasonable and appropriate safeguard in the group health plan's environment. This involves analyzing the specification in reference to the likelihood of protecting the group health plan's ePHI from reasonably anticipated threats and hazards. If the group health plan chooses not to implement an addressable specification based on its assessment, it must document the reason and, if reasonable and appropriate, implement an equivalent alternative measure.

HHS recognized that the security needs of group health plans could vary significantly. Therefore, the security standards are designed to be flexible and technology neutral. The Security Rule does not prescribe the use of specific technologies, systems and/or software that may become obsolete over time. Furthermore, group health plans may use appropriate security measures that reasonably enable them to implement a standard, taking into account its size, capabilities, the costs of the specific security measures and the operational impact.

B.   Reporting Security Breaches.

ARRA requires Covered Entities that access, maintain, retain, modify, record, store, destroy, or otherwise hold, use, or disclose "unsecured protected health information" ("Unsecured PHI") to notify each individual whose Unsecured PHI has been (or is reasonably believed to have been) accessed, acquired, or disclosed as a result of a security breach. A Business Associate that discovers a breach of Unsecured PHI that it accesses, maintains, retains, modifies, records, stores, destroys, or otherwise holds, uses, or discloses, must notify the Covered Entity.[68]

Note: If the PHI is secured in accordance with regulations to be issued by HHS, the Covered Entity does not need to report the security breach.

The notice must be in writing and must identify each individual whose Unsecured PHI has been, or is reasonably believed by the Business Associate to have been, accessed, acquired, or disclosed as a result of the breach. Unsecured PHI means PHI

---

[68] ARRA § 13407.

HIPAA Privacy and Security Requirements, continued

in any form that is not protected through technology or methods specified by the federal government.

Notifications must be made without unreasonable delay and in no case later than 60 calendar days after the Covered Entity of Business Associate discovers the breach. A breach is considered discovered as of the first day on which the Covered Entity or Business Associate (including any person, other than the individual committing the breach, that is an employee, officer, or other agent of the entity or associate) knows about the breach or should reasonably have known that a breach occurred. The Covered Entity (or Business Associate) required to provide the notice must be able to demonstrate that all notifications were sent (including evidence demonstrating the necessity of any delay).[69]

In the event that the Covered Entity or Business Associate determines that the situation is urgent based on the imminent misuse of the Unsecured PHI, the information in the notice must be communicated to affected individuals by phone and/or an employee meeting.[70]

The notice must contain the following information:[71]

- A brief description of the breach;
- Date of the breach;
- Date of the discovery;
- Descriptions of the types of PHI breached (*e.g.*, name, social security number, date of birth, home address, account number or disability code);
- Steps covered individuals need to take to protect themselves from potential harm resulting from the breach;
- A brief description of the investigation, efforts to minimize losses and prevent future breaches; and
- Contact information for covered individuals who wish to ask questions or learn more information, including a toll free number, e-mail address, website, or postal address.

The written notice must be sent to the affected individual (or next of kin if the covered individual is deceased) at the last known address. The notice must be sent by first-class mail, or electronically if specified by the Covered Individual (or next of kin). If there is insufficient or out of date contact information for ten or more covered individuals, a notice may be posted in a conspicuous location for a period determined by HHS.[72]

If a breach of Unsecured PHI involves more than 500 individuals, notice must be sent to HHS immediately. All other breaches of Unsecured PHI must be reported

---

[69] ARRA § 13402(d).
[70] ARRA §13402(e)(1)(C).
[71] ARRA § 13402(f).
[72] ARRA § 13402(e).

annually to HHS. If a breach of Unsecured PHI involves more than 500 residents of a state or jurisdiction, notice must be sent to prominent media outlets.[73]

C.   Steps to Comply With the Security Rule.

Plans must take the following steps to comply with the Security Rule:

- Ensure that plan documents and business associate agreements are compliant with HIPAA's Security Rule;[74]
- Appoint a Security Officer who is responsible for security of ePHI;[75]
- Establish limits on or restrict access to ePHI;[76]
- Implement procedures to report security violations;[77]
- Develop and implement written policies;[78]
- Provide security awareness training;[79]
- Develop a contingency plan;[80] and
- Establish sanctions against employees who fail to comply with the Security Rule.[81]

D.   Plan Documents and Business Associate Agreements.

A group health plan's documents must be updated to reasonably and appropriately safeguard all ePHI created, received, maintained or transmitted to or by the plan sponsor on behalf of the group health plan.

Business Associate agreements must be updated to require the Business Associate to: (i) implement administrative, physical and technical safeguards that reasonably and appropriately protect the confidentiality, integrity and availability of the ePHI that it creates, receives, maintains or transmits on behalf of the group health plan; (ii) ensure that any agent or subcontractor to whom it provides ePHI agrees to implement reasonable and appropriate safeguards to protect such ePHI; (iii) report to the group health plan any security incident of which it becomes aware; and (iv) authorize the termination of the contract by the plan sponsor on behalf of the group health plan if the plan sponsor determines that the Business Associate has violated a material term of the Business Associate agreement.

---

[73] ARRA § 13402(e)(2) and (3).
[74] 45 C.F.R. §§164.314(a) and (b).
[75] 45 C.F.R. §164.308(a)(2).
[76] 45 C.F.R. §164.308(a)(3)(i).
[77] 45 C.F.R. §164.308(a)(6).
[78] 45 C.F.R. §164.316(a).
[79] 45 C.F.R. §164.308(a)(5)(i).
[80] 45 C.F.R. §164.308(a)(7).
[81] 45 C.F.R. §164.308(a)(1)(ii)(C).

HIPAA Privacy and Security Requirements, continued

E.   Security Officer.

The group health plan must appoint a security officer to ensure compliance with the Security Rule.[82] The Security Officer should have an understanding of the technical issues and does not need to be the same person as the Privacy Officer.

F.   Controlling Access.

The group health plan must implement policies to ensure that employees who need to use or disclose ePHI have appropriate access to such information, and that prevent those employees who do not need access to ePHI from accessing it.[83] Therefore, ePHI needs to be catalogued (*i.e.*, divided into categories of ePHI stored and transmitted and how it is used and disclosed in the course of plan administration). Once the information is catalogued then the Security Officer needs to create lists of those who need access to the different categories of information. Access must be limited to those on the list who have a need for the information as part of their job function. For example, an individual in accounting who needs to access ePHI to reconcile the monthly premium bills should have access to ePHI limited to the minimum necessary information needed to reconcile the bills. The lists may change as job functions evolve, and temporary lists may need to be developed for special projects.

G.   Policies and Procedures.

In accordance with the Security Rule, written policies must be in place. These policies may be incorporated into the policies and procedures required by the Privacy Rule.[84] To comply with the Security Rule, the policies and procedures must provide for:

- Appropriate access to ePHI, including the proper handling of terminated employees;
- Training;
- Identifying reporting, investigating and responding to security incidents;
- Sanctioning employees for security violations;
- Proper data destruction.

H.   Security Awareness Training.

Group health plans must implement a security awareness and training program for all employees (including management).[85]

---

[82] 45 C.F.R. §164.308(a)(2).
[83] 45 C.F.R. §164.308(a)(3)(i).
[84] 45 C.F.R. §164.316(a).
[85] 45 C.F.R. §164.308(a)(5)(i).

I.   Sanctions.

The group health plan must establish sanctions against those employees who fail to comply with the Security Rule and the plan's policies and procedures implementing the Security Rule.[86]

J.   Contingency Planning.

The Security Rule requires planning for contingencies that might affect the integrity or availability of data (*e.g.*, flood, fire, vandalism, or a system crash).[87] Therefore, group health plans must:

- Create and maintain data back-ups;
- Be capable of restoring lost data; and
- Establish policies and procedures to safeguard information while ensuring access to ePHI while in emergency mode.

XIII.   How Does the Plan Sponsor Comply – A Practical Roadmap.

The Exhibits at the end of this chapter provide checklists for HIPAA compliance with the Privacy Rule and the Security Rule.

A.   Plan Document.

Under the Privacy Rule and the Security Rule, group health plan documents, including medical flexible spending arrangements, must contain provisions establishing the permitted and required uses and disclosures of PHI in accordance with the Privacy Rule and the Security Rule.

B.   Privacy Notice.

The privacy notice must be provided when plan participants enroll in the group health plan, and within 60 days of a material change in the privacy notice. Also, every three years the group health plan must remind existing plan participants about the privacy notice's availability. For the sake of efficiency and administrative ease, the group health plan may satisfy the three-year requirement by providing the notice annually with its open enrollment materials.

C.   Certification of Compliance.

In addition to HIPAA's requirement that group health plan documents contain HIPAA compliant language, the Privacy Rule also includes a certification requirement. Covered Entities may not release PHI to plan sponsors unless the plan sponsor provides

---

[86] 45 C.F.R. §164.308(a)(1)(ii)(C).
[87] 45 C.F.R. §164.308(a)(7)(i).

the Covered Entity with a certification of compliance. Certification is designed to ensure that plan sponsors will safeguard PHI.

D.   Employee Training and Confidentiality Agreement.

HIPAA's privacy rules require Covered Entities to train their "workforce" on policies and procedures regarding PHI. Although the final rules do not require workforce members to sign statements certifying that they completed privacy training, a group health plan still must prove that its workforce is trained. Employers may wish to require some certification from those who have completed the training. Furthermore, all employees with access to PHI should execute confidentiality agreements which shall be retained by the Director of Human Resources.

At a minimum, trainees should be employees who may have contact with PHI and who are identified in the group health plan documents. Plan sponsors may wish to include other employees who may not engage in plan functions but may have access to PHI for other reasons, such as human resource functions. Even employees who do not normally come into contact with PHI should be made aware, through training or other methods, of the group health plan's privacy policies.

The goals of training are to inform employees about HIPAA's technical requirements and raise general awareness about privacy issues.

Plan sponsors should provide detailed training to employees engaged in benefit administration – both health and other benefits, such as disability, flexible spending account administration and pension. Supervisors should receive training so they know how to handle inquiries from employees about health issues and to enforce the group health plan's privacy policies.

HHS has stated that training methods should be both flexible and manageable for the group health plan. For example, a small employer could satisfy the training requirements by providing each employee with access to PHI with a copy of its policies and requiring existing employees to acknowledge that they have reviewed the policies. A larger organization could have a training program with an instructor. In addition, one person (probably the privacy officer) should be identified as the contact for privacy questions and problems.

Regardless of the type of training, employees should receive information that applies the privacy rules to real situations at work. Training should include examples of possible privacy rule breaches, how breaches can be prevented and steps that employees should take if they become aware of a breach.

Security awareness training as required to comply with the Security Rule can be combined with the training for the Privacy Rule.

Note: Plan sponsors should consider conducting periodic training to remind employees of their responsibilities with respect to privacy and security. At a minimum, all employees who handle PHI or who might handle PHI should be advised of ARRA's changes and the impact, if any, on plan operations.

E.   Business Associate Contracts.

A group health plan is responsible for ensuring that all group health plan service providers (*i.e.*, Business Associates) take steps to avoid inappropriate uses and disclosures of PHI. The Privacy Rule requires these business associates to enter into written contracts stating that they will honor HIPAA's privacy policies and procedures. Business Associate agreements should be executed by all Business Associates and retained by an appropriate individual (*e.g.*, the Privacy Officer or the Director of Human Resources). All Business Associate agreements should comply with both the Privacy Rule and the Security Rule.

Note: Plan sponsors should review their Business Associate agreements and update them as needed to comply with ARRA. Updated Business Associate agreements should be executed before February 17, 2010.

F.   Authorization for Release of Health Information.

Under the Privacy Rule, an authorization allows the use and disclosure of PHI both by the group health plan requesting the authorization and a third party. It must be written in specific terms to allow PHI use and disclosure for purposes other than those of treatment, payment and health care operations, and is for a limited duration.

G.   Individual Rights Forms.

Under HIPAA's Privacy Rule, an individual can ask a group health plan's permission to see and copy his or her PHI. A group health plan does not have to give an individual all of the information; only information held in the group health plan's "designated record set" must be made available. A "designated record set" includes information such as medical records; billing records; enrollment, payment, claims adjudication; or records used to make decisions about individuals. Individuals have the right to see and obtain a copy of their PHI for as long as it is maintained in the designated record set. Individuals must request such access, which a group health plan can require to be in writing.

Furthermore, individuals can amend PHI. If their amendment request is denied, they can provide a "statement of disagreement" to the group health plan, which must be distributed with future PHI disclosures. Finally, individuals can request restrictions on PHI use and disclosure beyond basic protections already granted under the rules.

HIPAA Privacy and Security Requirements, continued

Note: In order to comply with ARRA, plan sponsors will need to review their procedures to record disclosures of PHI. Plan sponsors should also review their individual rights forms.

H. Appointment of Privacy Officer.

Oftentimes, there will be two (2) privacy officers, one for the group health plan and one for the medical FSA. Large organizations may wish to establish a privacy committee to handle the responsibilities of the privacy officer. Privacy committees should meet on a regular basis (*e.g.*, monthly or quarterly).

Plan sponsors have a fiduciary responsibility to ensure that their privacy officers have the appropriate skill sets to perform the functions of the job and are properly performing their responsibilities. In the event a privacy officer's performance is not adequate, the plan sponsor should take steps to replace (or retrain and monitor) the privacy officer.

I. Appointment of Security Officer.

The security officer should have an understanding of the technical issues involved with respect to the Security Rule. As a result, the security officer is often an individual in the IT department. The security officer is often not the same person as the privacy officer although the two officers should meet occasionally to ensure compliance with both the Privacy Rule and the Security Rule. If the plan decides to appoint a privacy committee, then the security officer should be member of the privacy committee.

Plan sponsors have a fiduciary responsibility to ensure that their security officers have the appropriate skill sets to perform the functions of the job and are properly performing their responsibilities. In the event a security officer's performance is not adequate, the plan sponsor should take steps to replace (or retrain and monitor) the security officer.

J. Board Votes.

The Board of Directors should vote to approve, authorize and adopt necessary group health plan amendments and appoint one or more privacy officers, and security officers. The Board may authorize an individual to take all steps described in this chapter to comply with the Privacy Rule and the Security Rule.

K. Safeguards to Protect PHI – Developing the Privacy Policy.

1. Firewalls and Access Controls.

Covered Entities are required to erect "*firewalls*" to prevent PHI from being accessed and used impermissibly. Group health plans and medical FSAs must therefore:

(1) Evaluate the roles of all employees to determine which employees are involved in the administration of such benefit plans.

(2) Implement procedures to ensure that only these designated employees have access to PHI, and even then, that they have access only to the minimum necessary amount of PHI to perform their duties.

(3) Implement a mechanism for ensuring that these employees do not use or disclose PHI in a way prohibited by the Privacy Rule. This might entail providing educational training for employees concerning the HIPAA Privacy Rule, the civil and criminal penalties associated with violations of the rules, and the plan sponsor's internal policies for dealing with such violations.

Access controls that restrict who can use PHI are key components of a firewall. The Privacy Rule requires that access controls be in place across the system – in administrative processes, technical systems and physical access. There are three types of access controls:

(1) *"Role-based"* access permits access to information based on an employee's role in the organization. Under this system, an organization must review the various roles in its system, assign a role to an individual employee and create authorization lists linked to those roles. For example, a benefits manager probably would have access to most PHI in his or her office. However, an individual who is responsible for processing claims from a medical flexible spending account would only have access to the FSA claims and coordinating group health plan materials (such as explanation-of-benefits ("EOB") forms related to those claims).

An access control system that includes role-based access could be set up so that the computer systems only recognize that type of access and only persons with certain roles can use certain offices.

(2) *"User-based"* access permits access to information based on the user's identity. This might be something an individual knows (a user ID or password), something a person is (biometric identifier or finger-print), or something a person has (a token, ID badge, or key).

(3) *"Context-based"* access is based on external factors related to a transaction's context, such as the time of day that an employee is working or the employee's location. For example, employees on duty on a certain shift will have access to a specific type of information.

The plan sponsor may find that _user-based access_ is the most efficient; if the benefits staff is limited, they may need access to any PHI that is used for plan administration purposes in that office. On the other hand, _role-based access_ may be easy to implement and potentially more secure due to the various tasks involved and potentially for personnel changes. The plan sponsor must document whichever system it chooses.

HIPAA Privacy and Security Requirements, continued

In addition, plan sponsors should implement physical access controls on information. Appropriate steps might include, but are not limited to, the following:

- Control physical access to the Human Resources Department.

- Ensure that a private space is available for employee discussions about benefit plan issues. While physically redesigning an office is not required, installing a separate cubicle for private conversations or erecting similar barriers may be reasonable.

- Shield computer monitors from the view of staff who do not need to know about the onscreen information. Make sure that monitors are not located in high traffic areas.

- Make sure that computers are turned off when an individual leaves for break, lunch or the end of the day. Place an automatic log-off in the system (for example, if no activity occurs, the computer logs off after 10 minutes).

- Protect hardware to ensure that only authorized personnel have access to the hardware, and that the hard drive is cleared of all data when the hardware is discarded.

- Implement facility safeguard plans, including the reasonable prevention of threats such as fire and burglary.

- Install backup systems for emergencies and consider off-site storage of backup data.

- Implement policies regarding telephone discussions of PHI with individuals, relatives and service providers (e.g., no using of cellular phones). Ensure that names are used as little as possible and that medical diagnoses are not discussed. Prohibit leaving voice-mail messages discussing PHI.

- Consider purchasing a dedicated fax machine for PHI transmissions. Place it in a secure location. In the alternative, ensure that a qualified individual monitors the fax for confidential transmissions. Eliminate or minimize the use of outbound faxing, or verify the fax number and request immediate pick-up if information is faxed.

- Consider implementing a policy to ensure that e-mail is confidential. Determine how and when e-mail and attachments will be encrypted.

Note: New regulations will be issued to comply with the changes ARRA made to the Security Rule. When the final regulations are released, plan sponsors will need to review their procedures to secure ePHI.

2. The Internal Complaint Process.

Covered entities must provide a complaint process for individuals regarding the entities' privacy policies, procedures and compliance efforts.

Under the complaint process, group health plans must:

(1) identify a contact person or office for receiving these complaints; and

(2) maintain a record of complaints and, if applicable, a brief explanation of their resolution.

The Privacy Rule does not dictate how the complaint process must be established or require a dedicated staff for this purpose. Therefore, a group health plan can establish a complaint process appropriate for its size and capabilities. The preamble to the Privacy Rule provided an example of a small medical practice that could assign:

(1) a clerk to log in written and/or verbal complaints; and

(2) an officer to review complaints monthly, address the situation and make any necessary changes to the privacy policies and procedures.

A larger plan or provider could have a more formal process with standard timeframes for responding to complaints.

Most group health plans should develop a complaint process somewhere between these two extremes. The complexity of the process will depend on the available resources. Plan sponsors may want to establish a process, supervised by the privacy official, in which all complaints are reviewed and resolved in a timely fashion. They also may consider using human resource professionals with expertise in resolving employee grievances.

Internal protocols should be developed for complaint investigations that include investigatory techniques such as interviews and reviews of relevant documents. Procedures can be borrowed from practices used to review and investigate discrimination complaints or denial-of-benefit claims.

The key is to establish a process that is fair, responsive, consistent, easy to use and confidential. Although an employee can file a complaint with HHS at any time, one of the goals of the complaint process should be to provide a resolution that avoids HHS involvement.

A complaint process should also include procedures for addressing breaches of privacy policy. Group health plans must mitigate, to the extent practicable, any damages that may result from a breach. Therefore, privacy policies and procedures should include specific actions that must be taken in response to a privacy breach. Different standards will apply depending on the type of breach. For example, discovering an improper disclosure to a third party may require, at a minimum, that the subject of the PHI be notified. The extent of the violation and the PHI's nature also may affect what type of corrective action is taken.

Note: Plan sponsors need to update their procedures in order to respond properly in the event of a breach of the privacy policy in compliance with ARRA.

3. Sanctions.

An attempt to resolve complaints is not legitimate unless it is combined with a policy of imposing *sanctions* against violators of the Privacy Rule. Employees must know that any breach of the privacy policies will be taken seriously. While the Privacy Rule requires group health plans to provide for sanctions, they do not give any examples of possible disciplinary action. Sanctions can range from an oral warning to temporary loss of privileges to termination of employment. Sanctions should be noted in employment policies and procedures, and standards should be established for first and subsequent offenses.

HIPAA Privacy and Security Requirements, continued

Exhibit A

Checklist to Determine Compliance with HIPAA Privacy Rule

INSTRUCTIONS: Use the checklist below to determine compliance with HIPAA's Privacy Rule.

The Privacy Rule imposes obligations on the use and disclosure of protected health information ("PHI"). This checklist is designed to help plan sponsors of covered group health plans determine their obligations under the Privacy Rule. Check an item as it is completed. Items left unchecked need to be addressed.

Determine If You Must Comply with the Privacy Rule

_____   Identify all health plans offered to employees (*e.g.*, medical, dental, vision, prescription, drug and health flexible spending account plans, certain employee assistance plans and on-site clinics). Workers' compensation, life insurance, accident only and disability plans are not health plans. Health plans generally must comply with the rules.

_____   Determine each plan that is self-administered and the number of participants. A health plan that is self-administered and has fewer than 50 participants is not a health plan for purposes of the privacy rule and does not need to comply.

Note: For flexible spending accounts, participant means eligible employee. Flexible spending accounts administered by a third party are not self-administered.

Determine the Extent to Which You Must Comply

_____   Identify each fully insured plan/contract and determine whether the plan sponsor receives PHI from the health plan. If the employer receives PHI, the health plan must complete the items listed under the "To Do List" below. If the employer does not receive PHI, the plan sponsor does not need to comply with all of the items listed under the "To Do List."

_____   Identify each self-funded health plan. All self-funded health plans must comply with all of the items listed under the "To Do List."

HIPAA Privacy and Security Requirements, continued

Exhibit A (*continued*)

<u>To Do List</u>

_____ Designate a privacy officer responsible for developing and administering privacy policies and procedures. The designation must be documented.

_____ Designate an individual to be responsible for handling complaints and responding to requests for additional information about the Privacy Notice. The contact person may be the privacy officer. The designation must be documented.

_____ Implement and maintain written policies and procedures to comply with the restrictions on use and disclosure of PHI.

_____ Provide privacy training for employees who handle PHI (including newly hired employees and temporary employees). The training must be documented.

_____ Prepare and distribute Privacy Notice as required.

_____ Amend plan documents to describe permitted and required uses and disclosures of PHI. Provide certification to the health plan that the documents have been amended.

_____ Implement "firewalls" to ensure adequate separation between the employer and the health plan. Firewalls include procedures limiting or restricting access to PHI as appropriate.

_____ Establish administrative, technical and physical safeguards to protect the privacy of PHI.

_____ Review relationships with any entity or person that receives PHI from the health plan and prepare Business Associate Agreements for each entity or person.

_____ Identify uses and disclosures of PHI for purposes other than treatment, payment or health care operations and prepare authorizations for such uses.

HIPAA Privacy and Security Requirements, continued

Exhibit B

Checklist to Determine Compliance with HIPAA Security Rule

This Checklist will be updated to reflect the changes imposed by ARRA when final regulations affecting the Security Rule are released.

INSTRUCTIONS: Use this checklist to determine compliance with HIPAA's Security Rule. The Security Rule establishes Implementation Specifications which are divided into two categories: "required" and "addressable." If an Implementation Specification is required it is labeled "Required" or "(R)." If an Implementation Specification is addressable, it is one of many options, none of which by itself is essential. An "addressable" Implementation Specification is not altogether discretionary. Rather, the plan must engage in a flexible approach and determine (1) if the addressable Implementation Specification is a reasonable and appropriate response to the risks under the Standard Rule, or (2) if an alternative is a reasonable and appropriate response. If the plan determines that an alternative is a reasonable and appropriate response, the decision and its basis must be documented in writing.

The following checklist specifies the Security Rule and corresponding Implementation Specifications, and indicates if they are Required ("R") or Addressable ("A").

_____ **Assign Security Official** (R). Identify the security official who is responsible for the development and implementation of the policies and procedures required by the Security Rule.

Security Management. The plan must implement policies and procedures to prevent, detect, contain and correct security violations.

_____ **Risk Analysis** (R). Conduct an "accurate and thorough" assessment of the potential risks and vulnerabilities to the confidentiality, integrity, and availability of the plan's ePHI.

_____ **Risk Management** (R). Implement security measures that reduce risk and vulnerabilities to a "reasonable and appropriate level."

_____ **Sanction Policy** (R). Apply "appropriate sanctions" against workforce employees who fail to comply with security policies and procedures.

_____ **Information System Activity Review** (R). Implement procedures to regularly review records of information system activity, such as audit logs, access reports and security incidence tracking reports.

HIPAA Privacy and Security Requirements, continued

Exhibit B (*continued*)

Workforce Security. Implement policies and procedures to ensure that all employees who need access to ePHI have the appropriate level of access and prevent those workforce members who should not have access from obtaining access to ePHI.

_____ **Authorization/Supervision Procedures** (A). Implement procedures to provide for the authorization and supervision of workforce employees who work with ePHI or who work in locations where it might be accessed.

_____ **Workforce Clearance Procedures** (A). Implement procedures to determine whether an employee's access to ePHI is appropriate.

_____ **Terminating Access Procedures** (A). Implement procedures to terminate an employee's access to ePHI when necessary or appropriate.

Information Access Management. Implement policies and procedures for authorizing access to ePHI that are consistent with the applicable requirements of the Privacy Rule.

_____ **Access Authorization** (A). Implement policies and procedures for granting access to ePHI (*e.g.*, through access to a workstation, transaction, program, process or other mechanism).

_____ **Access Establishment and Modification** (A). Implement policies and procedures that establish, document, review and modify a user's right to access a workstation, transaction, program or process.

Security Awareness and Training. Implement a security awareness and training program for all employees who need to have access to ePHI (including management).

_____ **Security Reminders** (A). Provide periodic security updates.

_____ **Protection from Malicious Software** (A). Implement procedures to guard against, detect, and report malicious software (*e.g.*, viruses).

_____ **Log-In Monitoring** (A). Implement procedures to monitor log-in attempts and reporting discrepancies.

_____ **Password Management** (A). Implement procedures for creating, changing and safeguarding passwords.

Security Incidents. Implement policies and procedures to address security incidents.

HIPAA Privacy and Security Requirements, continued

Exhibit B (*continued*)

_____ **Identify and Respond** (R). Implement policies and procedures to identify and respond to suspected or known security incidents.

_____ **Mitigate** (R). Implement policies and procedures to mitigate, to the extent practicable, harmful effects of any security incidents that are known to the plan.

_____ **Document** (R). Implement policies and procedures to document security incidents and their outcomes.

Contingency Plan. Establish (and implement as needed) policies and procedures for responding to an emergency or other occurrence (*e.g.*, fire, vandalism, system failure, and natural disaster) that damages systems containing ePHI.

_____ **Data Backup Plan** (R). Establish and implement procedures to create and maintain retrievable exact copies of ePHI.

_____ **Disaster Recovery Plan** (R). Establish (and implement as needed) procedures to restore any lost data.

_____ **Emergency Operation Plan** (R). Establish (and implement as needed) procedures to enable the continuation of critical business processes needed to protect the security of ePHI while operating in an emergency mode.

_____ **Testing and Revision Procedures** (A). Implement procedures for periodic testing and revision of contingency plans.

_____ **Applications and Data Criticality Analysis** (A). Assess the relative criticality of specific applications and data in support of other contingency plan components.

_____ **Evaluation** (R) Perform periodic technical and non-technical evaluations of the plan's security policies and procedures, based initially upon the standards implemented under the Security Rule and subsequently, in response to environmental or operational changes affecting the security of ePHI that establishes the extent to which the plan's security policies and procedures meet the requirements of the Security Rule.

Facility Access Controls. Implement policies and procedures to limit physical access to the electronic information systems and the facility or facilities in which they are housed, while ensuring that properly authorized access is allowed.

HIPAA Privacy and Security Requirements, continued

Exhibit B (*continued*)

_____ **Contingency Operations** (A). Establish (and implement as needed) procedures to allow access in support of the restoration of lost data under the disaster recovery plan and emergency mode operations plan in the event of an emergency.

_____ **Facility Security Plan** (A). Implement policies and procedures to safeguard the facility and equipment from unauthorized physical access, tampering and theft.

_____ **Access Control and Validation** (A). Implement procedures to control and validate a person's access to facilities based upon their role or function (including visitor control) and to control access to software programs for testing and revision.

_____ **Maintenance Records** (A). Implement policies and procedures to document repairs and modifications to the physical components of a facility which are related to security (*e.g.*, hardware, walls, doors, and locks).

_____ **Workstation Use** (R) Implement policies and procedures that specify the proper functions to be performed, the manner in which those functions are to be performed, and the physical attributes of the surroundings of the specific workstation or class of workstation that can access ePHI.

Workstation Security (R). Implement physical safeguards for all workstations that access ePHI, to restrict access to authorized users.

_____ **Device and Media Controls.** Implement policies and procedures that govern the receipt and removal of hardware and electronic media that contain ePHI into and out of a facility, and the movement of these items within the facility.

_____ **Disposal** (R). Implement policies and procedures to address the final disposition of ePHI and/or the hardware or electronic media on which ePHI has been stored.

_____ **Media Re-Use** (R). Implement procedures for removal of ePHI from electronic media before the media is made available for re-use.

_____ **Accountability** (A). Maintain a record of the movements of hardware and electronic media and any person responsible for such movements.

_____ **Data Backup and Storage** (A). Create a retrievable, exact copy of ePHI, when needed, before movement of equipment.

HIPAA Privacy and Security Requirements, continued

Access Control. Implement technical policies and procedures for electronic information systems that maintain ePHI to allow access only to those persons or software programs that have been granted access rights.

_____ **Unique User Identification** (R). Implement policies and procedures that assign a unique name and/or user number to identify and track user identity.

_____ **Emergency Access Procedure** (R). Establish (and implement as needed) procedures for obtaining ePHI in an emergency.

_____ **Automatic Log-Off** (A). Implement electronic procedures that terminate an electronic session after a pre-determined period of inactivity.

_____ **Encryption and Decryption** (A). Implement a mechanism to encrypt and decrypt ePHI.

Audit Controls (R).
_____ Implement hardware, software, and/or procedural mechanisms that record and examine activity on information systems that contain or use ePHI.

Integrity. Implement policies and procedures to protect ePHI from improper alteration or destruction.

_____ **Mechanism to Authenticate** (A). Implement electronic mechanisms to corroborate that ePHI has not been altered or destroyed in an unauthorized manner.

User Authentication (R)
_____ Implement procedures to verify that a person or entity seeking to access ePHI is the person or entity claimed.

Transmission Security. Implement technical security measures to guard against unauthorized access to ePHI that is being transmitted over an electronic communications network.

_____ **Integrity Controls** (A). Implement security measures to ensure that electronically transmitted ePHI is not improperly modified without detection until the ePHI is disposed of.

_____ **Encryption** (A). Implement a mechanism to encrypt ePHI whenever it is deemed appropriate.

Exhibit B (*continued*)

Policies and Procedures (R)

_____ Implement reasonable and appropriate policies and procedures to comply with the Security Rule. The plan may change its policies and procedures at any time, provided that the changes are documented and implemented in accordance with the Security Rule.

Documentation. Maintain the policies and procedures implemented to comply with the Security Rule in written (which may be electronic) form; and if an action, activity or assessment is required to be documented, maintain a written (which may be electronic) record of the action, activity or assessment.

_____ **Time Limits** (R). Retain all documentation for six years from the date of its creation or the date when it was last in effect, whichever is later.

_____ **Availability** (R). Make documentation available to those persons responsible for implementing the procedures to which the documentation pertains.

_____ **Updates** (R). Review documentation periodically and update that information as necessary to respond to environmental or operational changes that affect the security of ePHI.

HIPAA Privacy and Security Requirements (July 2009)
A0028021

Chapter 9

Penalties for Noncompliance

Introduction

If an employer or group health plan fails to comply with HIPAA, penalties may be imposed in accordance with the Internal Revenue Code (Code; I.R.C. in citations), the Employee Retirement Income Security Act of 1974 (ERISA), and the Public Health Service Act (PHSA).

In addition, the U.S. Department of Health and Human Services (HHS) imposes civil and criminal penalties for failure to comply with HIPAA's privacy protections.

This chapter discusses the various penalties for noncompliance.

In this chapter

This chapter has three sections:

A. General Information

Introduction   Efforts to fight fraud and abuse in health care programs have been stepped up. Fraud and abuse include, among other things, improper payments, unnecessary costs, and failure to provide needed care under contractual obligation. The DHHS is establishing a databank to identify health care providers that have been the subject of adverse actions as a result of illegal or abusive practices.

Individuals are rewarded for reporting fraud, and agencies and auditors will be awarded grants for investigating and prosecuting health care fraud.

ERISA penalties   The Department of Labor (DOL), the agency responsible for enforcing ERISA, may impose a $100 per day penalty for each participant the plan administrator fails to notify of his or her HIPAA rights.[1]

A participant or beneficiary may also sue a plan for HIPAA violations under ERISA. Courts may award civil penalties, including attorneys' fees.

PHSA penalties   Penalties under the PHSA apply to state and local government employers. The Centers for Medicare and Medicaid Services (CMS), formerly the Health Care Finance Administration (HCFA), is responsible for enforcing the PHSA. The CMS may impose a $100 per day penalty for each individual affected by the plan's failure to comply with HIPAA.[2]

In general, the states also enforce HIPAA requirements against insurers. If a state does not do so, however, the Secretary of Health and Human Services (HHS) has the authority to bring enforcement action.[3]

IRS penalties   The IRS may impose excise taxes on the liable party that fails to comply with HIPAA. The identity of the liable party is as follows:[4]

- For a multiemployer plan, the liable party is the plan.

---

[1] ERISA § 734(g).
[2] PHSA 42 U.S.C.S. § 300gg-6; HCFA Reg. § 146.180(d)(7).
[3] PHSA 42 U.S.C.S. § 300gg-61.
[4] I.R.C. § 4980D(e).

A. General Information, continued

IRS penalties (continued)

- For a multiple-employer welfare arrangement (MEWA) that violates the guaranteed renewability requirements, the liable party is the plan.
- In all other cases, the liable party is the employer.

The excise tax is $100 per day during the noncompliance period for each individual affected by a HIPAA violation.[5]

Civil and Criminal penalties

The American Recovery and Reinvestment Act significantly increased the penalties for civil violations of the HIPAA privacy rules occurring after February 17, 2009. The increased monetary penalties are as follows:[6]

Criteria	Penalty
Violator had no knowledge of violation and could not have been expected to know	$100 per violation up to $25,000 maximum
Violation is due to reasonable cause and not willful neglect	$1,000 per violation up to $100,000 maximum
Violation is due to willful neglect and is corrected	$10,000 per violation up to $250,000 maximum
Violation is due to willful neglect and is not corrected properly	$50,000 per violation up to $1,500,000 maximum

For criminal offenses related to knowingly obtaining protected health information (PHI), penalties can run up to $50,000 plus one year of imprisonment. For offenses related to false pretenses, criminal penalties can run up to $100,000 plus up to five years of imprisonment. For offenses related to the intent to sell or use PHI for commercial advantage, personal gain, or malicious harm, criminal penalties can run up to $250,000 plus up to 10 years of imprisonment.[7]

For additional details on these penalties, please refer to Chapter 8 of this Guide.

---

[5] I.R.C. § 4980D(b)(1).
[6] ARRA §13410.
[7] *Id.*

B. IRS Penalties; Corrections and Waivers

Introduction The IRS can impose a $100 per day penalty during the noncompliance period. However, the employer or other party may correct the violation and avoid some or all of the penalties.

Noncompliance period, defined The **noncompliance period** is the period generally beginning on the date the violation first occurs and ending on the date the violation is corrected.[8]

Corrections A failure to comply with HIPAA is considered corrected if the failure is retroactively undone to the extent possible and the affected individual is in as good a financial position as he or she would have been had the violation not occurred.[9]

Inadvertent violations An employer or other party may inadvertently violate the HIPAA rules. In this case, the excise tax generally will not be imposed if the employer or other party can show the IRS that no one knew or should have known that the violation occurred.[10]

Grace period The IRS will not assess an excise tax if[11]

- The violation is due to reasonable cause and not willful neglect or
- The violation is corrected within 30 days, beginning on the day any of the persons liable for the excise tax knew or should have known that the violation occurred.

Waiver of excise tax If a violation of HIPAA occurs because of a reasonable cause and not willful neglect, the IRS may waive all or part of the excise tax.[12]

---

[8] I.R.C. § 4980D(b)(2).
[9] I.R.C. § 4980D(f)(3).
[10] I.R.C. § 4980D(c)(1).
[11] I.R.C. § 4980D(c)(2).
[12] I.R.C. § 4980B(c)(4).

C. IRS Penalties; Minimum and Maximum Amounts

Introduction In general, the IRS imposes an excise tax of $100 per day during the noncompliance period for each individual affected by a HIPAA violation.[13]

Special audit rule For a HIPAA violation discovered after the IRS notifies an employer of an audit, a special audit rule applies. In this case, the IRS will impose a minimum excise tax, provided that:[14]

- One or more violations relating to the same individual are not corrected by the date the IRS sends the employer a notice of examination of income tax liability, or
- The violation occurred or continued during the tax period under examination.

(See Section B of this chapter for a discussion of the inadvertent violation and grace period rules that this special audit rule overrides.)

Minimum excise tax If the special audit rule applies, the minimum tax for each individual is the lesser of $2,500 or the amount that would have been imposed, disregarding the inadvertent violation and grace period rules.[15]

If an employer's violation is more than *de minimis*, however, the minimum excise tax can rise to $15,000.

---

[13] I.R.C. § 4980D(b)(1).
[14] I.R.C. § 4980D(b)(3).
[15] *Id.*

C. IRS Penalties; Minimum and Maximum Amounts, continued

Maximum excise tax

The maximum excise tax imposed for violations of HIPAA rules during an employer's tax year is $500,000, or, if less, 10 percent of the aggregate amount paid or incurred by the employer (or predecessor employer) during the prior tax year of the group health plan.[16]

If employers in the same controlled group do not all have the same tax year, a special rule applies to determine which tax year is to be used to determine the annual limit.[17]

---

[16] I.R.C. § 4980D(c)(3)(A).
[17] *Id.*

Chapter 10

HIPAA and Other Laws

Introduction   HIPAA has an impact on state insurance laws, the Consolidated Omnibus Budget Reconciliation Act of 1985 (COBRA), and health flexible spending accounts.

This chapter discusses HIPAA in relation to other laws.

In this chapter   This chapter has three sections:

A. State Insurance Laws and ERISA Preemption

General rule   In general, a state may continue to regulate the insurance business except when a state law conflicts with the requirements of HIPAA.[1]

In addition, ERISA will continue to preempt state insurance laws that affect group health plans subject to ERISA.[2]

State, defined   A **state** is any state of the United States, the District of Columbia, Puerto Rico, the Virgin Islands, Guam, American Samoa, and the Northern Mariana Islands, and any political subdivisions of a state or any agency or instrumentality of either.[3]

State law, defined   **State law** includes all laws, decisions, rules, regulations, or other state action having the effect of law of any state.[4] Federal law that applies only to the District of Columbia is considered to be a state law rather than a federal law.

Preexisting condition exclusions   In general, HIPAA supersedes any state law that establishes, implements, or continues in effect a standard or requirement concerning preexisting condition exclusions that differs from HIPAA's standards and requirements.[5]

---

[1] PWBA Reg. § 2590.731(a); HCFA Reg. § 146.143(a).
[2] PWBA Reg. § 2590.731(b); HCFA Reg. § 146.143(b).
[3] PWBA Reg. § 2590.731(d)(2); HCFA Reg. § 146.143(d)(2).
[4] PWBA Reg. § 2590.731(d)(1); HCFA Reg. § 146.143(d)(1).
[5] PWBA Reg. § 2590.731(c)(1); HCFA Reg. § 146.143(c)(1).

A. State Insurance Laws and ERISA Preemption, continued

Exceptions   HIPAA does not supersede a state law concerning preexisting condition exclusions to the extent that the state law satisfies one of the following conditions:[6]

- Shortens the six-month look-back period used to determine whether a preexisting condition exists
- Shortens the 12-month (or in the case of a late enrollee, the 18-month) maximum preexisting condition exclusion period
- Increases the 63-day threshold used to determine whether a significant break in coverage has occurred
- Lengthens the 30-day enrollment period for determining whether a preexisting condition exclusion or limitation can be applied to a newborn or child placed for adoption
- Expands the prohibitions on conditions and individuals to whom a preexisting condition exclusion period can be applied beyond HIPAA's exceptions
- Requires special enrollment periods in addition to the special enrollment periods for new dependents and individuals who lose other coverage
- Shortens the maximum affiliation period for HMOs that do not limit or exclude coverage for preexisting conditions

---

[6] PWBA Reg. § 2590.731(c)(2); HCFA Reg. § 146.143(c)(2).

B. Consolidated Omnibus Budget Reconciliation Act

HIPAA's impact on COBRA

HIPAA amended certain provisions under the Consolidated Omnibus Budget Reconciliation Act of 1985 (COBRA). HIPAA's creditable coverage and certification requirements impact COBRA administration. In addition, HIPAA has an impact on a qualified beneficiary's decision on whether to elect COBRA.

COBRA amendments

HIPAA amended the following three COBRA provisions:[7]

1. Disability extension;
2. Definition of qualified beneficiary; and
3. Maximum coverage period.

The changes were effective January 1, 1997, regardless of when a qualifying event occurred.

Disability extension

Under COBRA, when an employee's employment terminates or the hours of work are reduced, the employee may elect continuation coverage for 18 months (assuming the individual is eligible for COBRA coverage). Before HIPAA amended COBRA, the 18-month maximum coverage period was extended to 29 months for an individual who is disabled (as determined by the Social Security Administration) at the time of the qualifying event.[8]

HIPAA amended the disability extension provision to require that the 18-month period be extended to 29 months if an individual becomes disabled at any time during the first 60 days of COBRA continuation coverage. In addition, HIPAA clarified that the 29-month disability extension period also applies to an individual's nondisabled family members who are eligible for COBRA coverage.[9]

---

[7] PWBA Office of Regulations and Interpretations, Notice of Changes Under HIPAA to COBRA.
[8] *Id.*
[9] *Id.*

B. Consolidated Omnibus Budget Reconciliation Act, continued

Qualified beneficiaries, defined

Under COBRA, employees and their spouses and children who are eligible for continuation coverage are **qualified beneficiaries**.[10] To be a qualified beneficiary, the employee or spouse or child must be covered by the plan on the day before the qualifying event. HIPAA expanded this definition to require that a child born to a covered employee or placed for adoption with the employee during a period of COBRA coverage is also a qualified beneficiary.

Maximum coverage period

A group health plan may terminate an individual's COBRA coverage if the individual becomes covered by another group health plan that does not limit or exclude coverage for a preexisting medical condition of the individual.[11]

HIPAA limits the circumstances under which a plan may apply preexisting condition exclusions and limitations (see Chapter 4). HIPAA amended COBRA to make a coordinating change. The amendment provides that if a qualified beneficiary's other group health plan limits or excludes benefits for preexisting conditions and if the limits and exclusions do not apply to the beneficiary because of HIPAA's requirements, the COBRA plan may terminate the beneficiary's COBRA coverage.[12]

Notice requirement

In 1996, the Pension and Welfare Benefits Administration (PWBA), which is now known as the Employee Benefits Security Administration (EBSA), issued a release describing these changes and requiring that plans subject to COBRA notify qualified beneficiaries of the changes by November 1, 1996.

---

[10] *Id.*
[11] *Id.*
[12] *Id.*

B. Consolidated Omnibus Budget Reconciliation Act, continued

Creditable coverage

Under HIPAA, a plan must reduce a preexisting condition exclusion period by any aggregate periods of creditable coverage that apply to a participant or beneficiary at the time of enrollment.[13] Creditable coverage includes any COBRA coverage under a group health plan.[14] (See Chapter 4 for more details on creditable coverage.)

Certification requirements

A group health plan must automatically provide a certificate, without charge, to any participant or beneficiary who has a COBRA qualifying event or whose COBRA coverage ends.[15] (See Chapter 4 for more information on the certification requirements.)

Whether to elect COBRA

IRS Notice 98-12 [1998-15 I.R.B. 12] provides information to qualified beneficiaries about COBRA after the enactment of HIPAA. The notice provides information on the factors that qualified beneficiaries should consider when deciding whether to elect to continue coverage under COBRA. (See pages 10:7–10:22 for a copy of Notice 98-12 as it appears on the IRS's Web site.)

Life events checklist

At the end of this section is a Job Aid in the form of a checklist regarding COBRA and HIPAA and their application to major life events (e.g., marriage, birth of a child, and termination of employment). (See the Job Aid on pages 10:23–10:24.)

---

[13] I.R.C. § 9801(a); ERISA § 701(a); PHSA 42 U.S.C.S. § 300gg(a).
[14] I.R.S. Reg. § 54.9801-4(a)(1); PWBA Reg. § 2590.701-4(a)(1); HCFA Reg. § 146.113(a)(1); and *Questions & Answers: Recent Changes in Health Care Law*, p. 7.
[15] I.R.S. Reg. § 54.9801-5(a)(2); PWBA Reg. § 2590.701-5(a)(2); HCFA Reg. § 146.115(a)(2); and *Questions & Answers: Recent Changes in Health Care Law*, pp. 9-10.

B. Consolidated Omnibus Budget Reconciliation Act, continued

Deciding Whether to Elect COBRA Health Care Continuation Coverage After Enactment of HIPAA

Notice 98-12

INTRODUCTION

A key decision that millions of Americans face each year is whether to elect "COBRA[1]" health care continuation coverage. The purpose of this notice is to help people decide whether to elect COBRA coverage. In order to make that decision, they need to know about two laws, COBRA and HIPAA.[2] This notice provides information -- in the form of questions and answers -- about some factors that employees and their families should take into account in deciding whether to elect COBRA continuation coverage.

An employer maintaining a group health plan is not required to provide this notice. The information in this notice may be used by employers and plan administrators who want to supplement the information they are required to give to covered employees and beneficiaries. The notice may be modified to provide information specific to a plan. The information in this notice is not a substitute for any of the notices required to be furnished under COBRA or for any other information required by law to be furnished to participants or beneficiaries in employer group health plans.

---

[1] COBRA is the Consolidated Omnibus Budget Reconciliation Act of 1985, the law that added the health care continuation coverage requirements.

[2] HIPAA is the Health Insurance Portability and Accountability Act of 1996.

SHOULD I ELECT COBRA HEALTH CARE CONTINUATION COVERAGE?

Questions and Answers

If you lose or leave your job, or if another event occurs that would cause you to lose coverage under an employer's group health plan, you may have the right to elect COBRA[1] health care continuation coverage under the plan. In making this important decision, there are a number of considerations you should take into account, including:

- whether other group health coverage -- such as coverage under another employer's plan -- is available;

- whether any other available health coverage would exclude benefits for a medical condition that you or a family member has;

- when you will have the right to enroll in the other coverage;

- the cost, scope, and level of COBRA coverage compared with that of any other available group coverage or individual health coverage; and

- whether a guaranteed right to buy individual health coverage is important to you.

The following questions and answers are divided into three parts. Read Part I for background information about COBRA coverage and an important recent law, HIPAA[2], that might affect your COBRA decision. Read Part II if group health coverage other than COBRA coverage is available to you. Read Part III if you do not have other group health coverage available. These questions and answers reflect the law as in effect in January 1998.[3]

---

[1] COBRA is the Consolidated Omnibus Budget Reconciliation Act of 1985, the law that added the health care continuation coverage requirements.

[2] HIPAA is the Health Insurance Portability and Accountability Act of 1996.

[3] In most cases, HIPAA is effective by January 1998. However, a later effective date applies to certain employer group health plans and certain health coverage. The questions and

B. Consolidated Omnibus Budget Reconciliation Act, continued

These questions and answers are available at the IRS Internet site at:

http://www.irs.ustreas.gov

These questions and answers are also available at the Department of Labor (DOL) Internet site at:

http://www.dol.gov/dol/pwba

and at the Health Care Financing Administration (HCFA) Internet site at:

http://www.hcfa.gov

PART I: Overview of COBRA and HIPAA

COBRA

What rights to health care continuation coverage does COBRA provide?

If you are covered by an employer's group health plan, COBRA may give you the right to stay covered even if something happens, like losing your job, that would otherwise cause you to lose coverage. This continuation coverage under an employer's plan is called "COBRA coverage." COBRA coverage usually lasts only for a limited time, and you usually have to pay for it.

If you are covered by an employer's group health plan, and an event occurs that would otherwise cause you to lose that group health coverage, you need to understand whether COBRA applies to your specific situation and, if so, what your rights are under COBRA.

Which employer plans are subject to COBRA?

COBRA applies to most employer group health plans but not to all of them.

---

answers below assume that HIPAA is in effect.

B. Consolidated Omnibus Budget Reconciliation Act, continued

For example, it does not apply to plans of employers with fewer than 20 employees or to church plans. Many plans of small employers, though, are subject to State laws similar to COBRA. If you are covered under a plan of an employer with fewer than 20 employees, you can contact the department or commission of insurance in your State to find out if you have rights to continuation coverage under your State's insurance laws. (Federal employees, while not protected by COBRA, have similar continuation coverage rights under another federal law.)

What events result in COBRA rights and for how long is COBRA coverage available?

Even if COBRA applies to your group health plan, it gives rights only to certain people who would be losing health coverage for certain specific reasons. Some of the most common situations that give people COBRA rights are:

- *Loss of job.* If you are covered by your employer's group health plan and you lose or leave your job, COBRA generally gives you the right to stay in the employer's plan for up to 18 months. The same rights apply if you are the spouse or dependent child of an employee who loses his or her job. (The 18-month period can be increased to 29 months if someone in the family is disabled.)

- *Reduced hours.* If you are covered by your employer's group health plan and your hours are reduced, the employer's plan may provide that you lose coverage unless you elect COBRA. In this case, COBRA generally gives you the right to stay in the employer's plan for up to 18 months. The same rights apply if you are the spouse or dependent child of an employee whose hours are reduced. (The 18-month period can be increased to 29 months if someone in the family is disabled.)

- *Death or divorce of spouse.* You have the right to COBRA coverage if you are covered by a group health plan of your spouse's employer and you would lose coverage because your spouse dies or you and your spouse divorce or legally separate. In these cases, COBRA gives you the right to stay in the plan for up to 36 months.

- *Death or divorce of parent.* You have the right to COBRA coverage

B. Consolidated Omnibus Budget Reconciliation Act, continued

if you are a dependent child covered by a group health plan of your parent's employer and you would lose coverage because your parent dies or your parents divorce or legally separate. In these cases, COBRA gives you the right to stay in the plan for up to 36 months.

- *Change of Status as Dependent.* COBRA also gives you rights if you are a dependent child covered by a group health plan of your parent's employer and you would lose coverage because you reach an age or condition that causes you to no longer be covered as a dependent under the plan. In these cases, COBRA gives you the right to stay in the plan for up to 36 months.

If you become covered by another group health plan or by Medicare before your COBRA coverage would otherwise end, you usually lose the right to COBRA coverage. However, you do not lose the right to COBRA coverage if the new group health plan does not cover illnesses or conditions because you had them before you became covered under the plan.

What are the requirements for obtaining COBRA coverage?

If you want COBRA coverage, you can be required to elect it within 60 days after your coverage would otherwise end. If you elect COBRA coverage, the plan is required to continue the same coverage for you but can charge you for it.

- *Cost of COBRA coverage.* If you elect COBRA coverage, the plan can require you to pay for the entire cost of coverage, plus a small (2%) additional charge for administration. (If you are getting a longer period of coverage because of disability, you may have to pay more.) The cost of COBRA coverage will probably be more than what you were paying for coverage before. You can pay for COBRA coverage in monthly installments.

How can I get more information about COBRA ?

COBRA has a number of special rules, and the information above covers only basic points. The plan administrator of your group health plan is required to give you information about your COBRA rights. You should read that information

---

carefully. If you have any questions about your COBRA rights or would like additional information about COBRA and your group health plan, contact your plan administrator.

If you want to know more, the Department of Labor has a booklet called "Health Benefits under the Consolidated Omnibus Budget Reconciliation Act (COBRA)." You can request this booklet free of charge by calling 1-800-998-7542. The booklet is also available on the Internet at:

http://www.dol.gov/dol/pwba

HIPAA

What is HIPAA and why is it important in deciding whether to elect COBRA coverage?

HIPAA is a federal law that regulates employer group health plans and health insurance companies. HIPAA is important to your decision whether to elect COBRA coverage because HIPAA may affect when other coverage is available to you and the types of other coverage available to you, including the extent to which coverage can be restricted under a "preexisting condition exclusion."

What is a preexisting condition exclusion?

Some employer group health plans do not provide coverage for an illness or condition you had before you became covered under the plan. These illnesses or conditions are commonly called "preexisting conditions." A special limit on coverage for a preexisting condition is called a "preexisting condition exclusion."

How are preexisting condition exclusions limited by HIPAA?

HIPAA imposes the following limits on the situations in which employer group health plans may have preexisting condition exclusions and the length of time that such exclusions can apply:

- *Treatment or advice received in 6 months before enrollment.* An employer group health plan cannot exclude coverage for a preexisting condition you

B. Consolidated Omnibus Budget Reconciliation Act, continued

have unless medical advice, diagnosis, care, or treatment was received by you (or recommended to you) for the condition during a 6-month period. If there is a waiting period to get into the plan, the 6-month period is the 6 months before the start of the waiting period. If the plan has no waiting period, the 6-month period is the 6 months before you enter the plan.

- *Preexisting condition exclusion cannot last for more than 12 (or 18) months.* An employer group health plan cannot exclude coverage for a preexisting condition for more than 12 months after the start of the waiting period for coverage. If there is no waiting period, the plan cannot exclude coverage for a preexisting condition for more than 12 months after you enter the plan. However, if you do not enroll when you are first eligible and do not enroll when you have "special enrollment rights" (as described below), the plan can refuse to cover preexisting conditions for up to 18 months after you enter the plan.

- *Previous coverage reduces length of exclusion.* If you had other health coverage -- for example, under another group health plan (including COBRA coverage) or under an individual insurance policy, Medicare, or Medicaid -- your new plan's preexisting condition exclusion period generally must be reduced by the period of your other coverage. For example, if you were covered by your old employer's plan for 4 months and your new employer's plan has a 12-month preexisting condition exclusion, your new employer's plan cannot exclude coverage for you for any preexisting condition for more than 8 months. However, your new employer's plan does not have to count coverage before a 63-day break in coverage.

- *63-day break in coverage.* If there has been a break of 63 days or more during which you had no health coverage, then the plan can disregard your old coverage that preceded this break. Thus, if you had no coverage for at least 63 days just before you began working for your new employer, the new employer's plan can refuse to cover any preexisting conditions for up to 12 months (or 18 months, depending on when you enroll in the new plan). Time spent in any waiting period for coverage does not count toward the 63-day break.

- *No preexisting condition exclusion permitted for pregnancy, or for*

B. Consolidated Omnibus Budget Reconciliation Act, continued

newborn and adopted children. A plan cannot impose a preexisting condition exclusion relating to pregnancy. In addition, a plan cannot impose a preexisting condition exclusion on newborn children, adopted children, and children placed for adoption who are covered under a plan on the 30th day after their birth, adoption, or placement for adoption.

● *State insurance laws.* State insurance laws may further limit the extent to which insurance under an employer's plan can exclude coverage for preexisting conditions.

How does HIPAA affect my ability to enroll in an employer's plan?

● *Special enrollment rights.* HIPAA gives you and your family a special opportunity to enroll in your employer's plan in two situations: (1) if you lose other coverage (including COBRA coverage) or (2) if you have a new spouse or dependent. In these two situations, you (or your spouse or dependent) can be enrolled in your employer's plan even if the plan normally would not allow enrollment at that time.

  ● **Special enrollment because of loss of other coverage.** You (and your spouse and dependents) might have been eligible to enroll in your employer's plan at an earlier time but you decided not to because at that time you (or your family members) had other coverage (say, under the plan of your spouse's employer). In that case, if you (or your family members) later lose the other coverage, your employer's plan generally must allow you (and your family members) to enroll. The plan has to give you at least 30 days after that other coverage is lost to request enrollment, and must allow enrollment by the first day of the month after the plan receives your completed request.

    ● This special enrollment right generally is available only if the coverage is lost because it is no longer available (and not lost because of failure to pay for it or for cause, such as making a fraudulent claim). You are not required to elect COBRA coverage in order to have a special enrollment right; however, if you do elect COBRA coverage, you must continue it for the entire period it is available to you in order to preserve this

B. Consolidated Omnibus Budget Reconciliation Act, continued

special enrollment right.

- **Special enrollment because of a new spouse or dependent.** If you marry, then you, your spouse, and any new dependents you get as a result of the marriage have special rights to enroll. If a new child is born, you adopt a child, or a child is placed for adoption with you, then you, your spouse, and the new child also get special rights to enroll.

  - To be entitled to special enrollment on account of a new spouse or dependent, you must either be covered under the plan or be eligible to be covered under the plan. The plan has to give you at least 30 days after the marriage, birth, adoption, or placement for adoption to request enrollment.

  - If you get married, the plan must cover you, your spouse, and any new dependent by the first day of the month after the plan receives your completed request.

  - If you have a new child, the plan must cover you and your spouse and the child from the date of birth, adoption, or placement for adoption.

- *The plan cannot exclude you (or make you pay more) based on health status.* HIPAA prohibits employer group health plans from discriminating in their eligibility rules on the basis of your health.

  - For example, a plan cannot require you to pass a physical examination before you can enroll in the plan, or prevent you from enrolling because of your medical claims experience, medical history, genetic information, evidence of insurability, or disability.

In addition, a plan generally cannot require you to pay a higher contribution than similarly situated people covered under the plan due to your health or any of these other factors.

Which Employer Plans Are Subject to HIPAA?

10:15

B. Consolidated Omnibus Budget Reconciliation Act, continued

HIPAA's limits on preexisting condition exclusions, special enrollment rights, and restrictions on discrimination based on health status apply to most but not all employer group health plans. For example, HIPAA generally does not apply to plans where fewer than 2 of the participants are current employees. In addition, special exceptions apply to certain plans maintained by State or local governments and certain plans maintained by church organizations. Further, the HIPAA rules generally do not apply to coverage for certain types of excepted benefits.

Where can I get more information about HIPAA?

HIPAA has a number of special rules, and the information above covers only basic points. If you want to know more about how HIPAA applies to group health plans, the Department of Labor has a booklet called "Questions and Answers: Recent Changes in Health Care Law." You may request this booklet free of charge by calling 1-800-998-7542. The booklet is also available on the Internet at:

http://www.dol.gov/dol/pwba

More information about HIPAA is also available at the Health Care Financing Administration (HCFA) Internet site at:

http://www.hcfa.gov

PART II: Should I Elect COBRA Coverage If I Have Other Group Health Coverage Available?

The questions and answers in this Part are designed to assist you if you have group health coverage available in addition to COBRA coverage. In deciding whether to elect COBRA coverage, an important factor is whether the other group health coverage has a preexisting condition exclusion that applies to you.

How do I know if an employer group health plan has a preexisting condition exclusion that applies to me?

You should first determine whether you received medical advice, diagnosis, care, or treatment (or they were recommended to you) for a medical condition

B. Consolidated Omnibus Budget Reconciliation Act, continued

during the 6-month period before the start of the plan's waiting period (or before you enter the plan, if there is no waiting period). For this purpose, only medical advice, diagnosis, care, or treatment from a physician or other licensed or authorized person counts.

- If not, the employer's group health plan cannot apply a preexisting condition exclusion to you.

- If so, contact the plan administrator to find out whether and for how long the plan excludes your condition. Then, determine whether and to what extent your prior health coverage will reduce any preexisting condition exclusion period.

- While you must be notified if the plan has a preexisting condition exclusion before the exclusion can be applied to you, the plan is not required to give you this notice before your coverage begins. You have to ask for the information if you need it earlier.

How do I know how long I will be subject to the plan's preexisting condition exclusion?

A plan with a preexisting condition exclusion should specify the maximum period that the exclusion can apply. That period is reduced by your prior health coverage, so you will need to determine how much prior health coverage you had. Remember that if there has been a break of 63 days or more during which you had no health coverage, then the plan may be able to disregard your old coverage. Time spent in any waiting period for coverage does not count toward the 63-day break.

- ***Proof of Previous Health Coverage.*** Your old plan must give you a certificate showing how much coverage you had under that plan. The plan must give you the certificate shortly after you become eligible for COBRA coverage, shortly after your coverage ends, and at any other time you request it while you are covered or up to 24 months after your coverage ends. If you become covered by a plan that has a preexisting condition exclusion, you may use the certificate to show your new plan how long you had coverage under your old plan.

B. Consolidated Omnibus Budget Reconciliation Act, continued

- If you do not have a certificate, you can prove your prior coverage by producing documentation or other evidence.

- The new plan must notify you of any length of time that a preexisting condition exclusion may apply to you after counting your previous coverage.

What should I consider in deciding whether to elect COBRA coverage if I have other group health coverage available with a preexisting condition exclusion that applies to me?

If you have other group health coverage available, and that coverage has a preexisting condition exclusion that applies to you, your choices are to have (1) COBRA coverage instead of that other group coverage, (2) the other coverage instead of COBRA coverage (despite the preexisting condition exclusion), or (3) both COBRA coverage and the other coverage.

Your decision may depend on several factors, such as:

- how long your new coverage will be subject to the preexisting condition exclusion;

- how likely you are to need treatment for the preexisting condition before it is covered;

- the seriousness of your preexisting condition, how much the treatment would cost you in the absence of coverage, and the risks to you if treatment is delayed;

- the cost, level and scope of benefits of the COBRA coverage compared to the other coverage; and

- the HIPAA rules that require plans to offer special enrollment rights in certain cases and prohibit enrollment restrictions based on your health status (as discussed in Part I and below in this Part II).

What should I consider in deciding whether to elect COBRA coverage if

B. Consolidated Omnibus Budget Reconciliation Act, continued

I have other group health coverage available with no preexisting condition exclusion that applies to me?

If you have other group health coverage available that does not exclude coverage for a preexisting medical condition you have, your decision whether to elect COBRA coverage may be influenced by a variety of factors, including --

- *COBRA cut-off due to other coverage.* In general, if you get coverage from another employer's group health plan that is not subject to a preexisting condition exclusion, or from Medicare, your COBRA coverage can be cut off. This means that in most situations you would have to decline the other coverage if you decide you prefer the COBRA coverage. (Note that if you have been receiving disability payments from Social Security, you should not decline Medicare coverage without first consulting your Social Security office or the Medicare program.)

- *Cost, scope, and level of coverage.* Plans differ in their cost, and in the level and scope of benefits (such as particular medical services) they cover. You should take these differences into account in comparing the COBRA coverage with the other available coverage.

  - Employers often pay for a large portion of the cost of group health coverage for employees, while people on COBRA coverage typically have to pay for the entire cost of the coverage. This means it usually is cheaper to pay for the employee share of the cost of the other coverage than to pay for COBRA coverage. However, you might prefer more costly coverage if it provides more comprehensive benefits for treatment you may need.

- *Waiting period before other coverage begins.* If you (or your spouse or parent) get a new job that offers health coverage after some waiting period, you might want to elect to have COBRA coverage for that waiting period.

- *Special enrollment rights.* If you elect COBRA coverage instead of

10:19

taking other available group health plan coverage, HIPAA generally gives you the right to enroll in the new plan within 30 days after the COBRA coverage ends, or within 30 days after you get married or have a new dependent child -- even if the plan would not otherwise allow you to enroll at that time.

- But, once you have elected COBRA coverage, your special enrollment right for the loss of the coverage applies only if you keep the COBRA coverage for the entire period it is available to you. (Thus, this special enrollment right does not apply if the COBRA coverage ends because you stop paying for it.)

- *HIPAA Limits on Enrollment Restrictions Based on Health Status.* If you elect COBRA coverage instead of taking other group health plan coverage, but you later decide you want to enroll in the new plan, your new plan cannot exclude you (or charge you more) on the basis of your health.

PART III: Should I Elect COBRA Coverage If I Do Not Have Other Group Health Coverage Available?

The questions and answers in this Part are designed to assist you if you do not have other group health coverage available.

Why do I need health coverage?

You need health coverage to help pay for medical services for any health problems you might have after your current plan coverage ends.

Does HIPAA give me the right to buy individual health coverage?

If you meet certain requirements, HIPAA gives you the right to buy individual health coverage with no preexisting condition exclusion, without having to give evidence of good health. Depending on the State, the individual health coverage may be a policy issued by an insurance company, or coverage through a State high-risk pool or other governmental program. You must meet all of the following requirements to have this right:

B. Consolidated Omnibus Budget Reconciliation Act, continued

- Your most recent period of health coverage must have been under an employer group health plan.

- If you were eligible for COBRA coverage (or coverage due to a similar State provision) under that plan, you must have elected and continued that coverage for the entire period it was available to you.

  - You would not have to continue COBRA coverage for the entire period to maintain these rights if the only COBRA coverage available was in an HMO and you ceased to reside, live, or work in the HMO service area.

- You must have at least 18 months of prior health coverage, disregarding coverage before a break of 63 days or more during which you had no health coverage.

- You must not have lost your most recent health coverage because you failed to pay the premiums or because you committed fraud.

- You must not now be eligible for coverage under any employer group health plan, Medicare, or Medicaid.

- You must not now have any other health insurance coverage.

For more information on your right to buy individual health coverage, contact your State's department or commission of insurance.

What should I consider in deciding whether to elect COBRA coverage?

- *COBRA coverage compared to individual health coverage.* In comparing COBRA coverage with any individual coverage you have available, consider differences in cost and in the level and scope of benefits (such as particular medical services) covered.

- *COBRA coverage compared to no health coverage.* You may want to elect COBRA coverage to make sure you are covered for any medical services you need. Many people consider the benefits from having the protection that

---

15

COBRA coverage provides to be well worth the cost of COBRA coverage.

- You might also want to elect COBRA coverage because, in the future, you could become covered under an employer group health plan that has a preexisting condition exclusion. If you have a 63-day break in coverage, then your existing coverage may be disregarded. COBRA coverage can help you avoid having a 63-day break in coverage and also counts toward reducing any preexisting condition exclusion. See Part I for more information on these rules.

- *COBRA coverage to protect your right to buy individual health coverage with no preexisting condition exclusion.* As described above, if certain requirements are met, you and your family may have the right to buy individual health coverage with no preexisting condition exclusion, without having to give evidence of good health. These requirements include electing COBRA coverage as long as it is available to you. THUS, FAILURE TO ELECT COBRA COVERAGE MAY CAUSE YOU TO LOSE YOUR GUARANTEED RIGHTS TO PURCHASE INDIVIDUAL HEALTH COVERAGE.

Is there any State-sponsored coverage available to me?

Individuals in a family whose income is temporarily reduced (for example, due to loss of a job) may be eligible for low-cost or no-cost health insurance through public programs. Children are especially likely to be eligible for low-cost coverage. Eligibility for these programs varies by State and sometimes within a State. You can contact State government officials to find out if you are eligible.

CONCLUSION

There are many factors to consider in making the important decision whether to elect COBRA continuation coverage for you and each of the members of your family. The information above highlights factors that people in typical circumstances may want to take into account in deciding whether to elect COBRA coverage. You will need to consider your own family's circumstances in making your decision.

Job Aid

Life Events Compliance Checklist

	If Life Event Is:	Check Requirements of:	Description:
☐	Marriage	HIPAA and ERISA	• HIPAA gives employees and their spouses the right to enroll in a group health plan upon marriage. • HIPAA protects individuals who have preexisting conditions or who could suffer discrimination on the basis of health when they switch plans. • ERISA gives individuals the right to benefit information under their own employer's plan or their spouse's employer's plan.
☐	Divorce	HIPAA and COBRA	• HIPAA gives employees and dependents who were covered under a spouse's plan the special right to enroll under the employee's employer's plan upon divorce or legal separation if they are otherwise eligible. • COBRA gives spouses and dependent children the right to continue health coverage for a limited time upon divorce or legal separation.

☐	New baby (whether by birth or adoption)	HIPAA and Newborns' and Mothers' Health Protection Act	• HIPAA bars application of preexisting condition exclusions to:
			  ➢ Pregnancy regardless of whether the mother had previous health coverage and
			  ➢ Newborns and adopted children enrolled in a group health plan within 30 days of birth or adoption.
			• HIPAA gives employees, spouses, and new dependents special enrollment rights upon birth, adoption, or placement for adoption.
			• The Newborns' and Mothers' Health Protection Act gives mothers and newborns the right to stay in the hospital for a minimum period.

Job Aid

Life Events Compliance Checklist

	If Life Event Is:	Check Requirements of:	Description:
☐	Job termina-tion	HIPAA and COBRA	▪ HIPAA places limitations on the application of preexisting condition exclusions to employees and their dependents who have been covered by another group health plan. ▪ COBRA requires most employers to offer employees and their dependents up to 18 months of continuation coverage in the event of a termination of employment for any reason except gross misconduct.
☐	Retirement	HIPAA and COBRA	▪ HIPAA places limitations on the application of preexisting condition exclusions to employees and their dependents who have been covered by another group health plan. ▪ HIPAA protects individuals from being excluded from coverage under their group health plan and from being charged higher premiums based on health status. ▪ COBRA requires most employers to offer employees and their dependents up to 18 months of continuation coverage in the event of retirement.

C. Health Flexible Spending Accounts

Overview Flexible spending accounts (FSAs) are governed by the cafeteria plan rules of Code Section 125. In general, the rules permit employees to choose between health care benefits and other taxable or nontaxable benefits. FSAs enable employees to make pretax contributions, with which they can reimburse themselves, to an individual account for medical expenses that are not covered by a group health plan.

FSAs subject to COBRA Health FSAs are subject to COBRA unless they meet the exemptions described below. The IRS final regulations make it clear that COBRA applies only to a cafeteria plan or FSA that provides for health care.[16] In addition, the rules apply only to the type and level of coverage that a qualified beneficiary was actually receiving on the day before the qualifying event.[17]

FSAs exempt from COBRA The IRS final regulations provide that certain FSAs are exempt from COBRA. Under the regulations, if a health plan satisfies two conditions, it need not make COBRA coverage available after the first plan year during which the qualified beneficiary's qualifying event occurred.[18] The first condition is that the FSA is exempt from HIPAA. The second condition is that during the plan year in which the qualified beneficiary's qualifying event occurs, the maximum benefit amount that the FSA could require to be paid for a full plan year of COBRA coverage equals or exceeds the maximum benefit available under the FSA for the year.[19]

---

[16] I.R.S. Final Reg. § 54.4980B-2, Q&A 8.
[17] *Id.*
[18] I.R.S. Final Reg. § 54.4980B-2, Q&A-8(b), (c), and (d).
[19] I.R.S. Final Reg. § 54.4980B-2, Q&A-8(c).

C. Health Flexible Spending Accounts, continued

FSAs exempt from COBRA (continued)

In addition, if a third condition is satisfied, the FSA need not make COBRA coverage available to the qualified beneficiary at all.[20] An FSA satisfies the third condition if, as of the date of the qualifying event, the maximum benefit available to the qualified beneficiary for the remainder of the plan year is equal to or less than the maximum amount the plan could require as payment for the rest of the year to maintain the FSA coverage.

When a health FSA is excepted from HIPAA

Benefits provided by a health FSA are excepted from HIPAA if all of the following conditions are met:[21]

- The maximum benefit payable for an employee for the year does not exceed two times the employee's salary reduction election for the year (or if the maximum benefit is greater, the amount of the employee's salary reductions for the year plus $500).
- The employee has other coverage available under a group health plan of the employer for the year.
- The other coverage is not limited to benefits that are excepted benefits under HIPAA.

Certification not required

By treating health FSA benefits as excepted benefits, a health FSA is not subject to HIPAA's health coverage portability, nondiscrimination, and renewability requirements.[22] Therefore, a health FSA plan is not required to issue a certificate of creditable coverage. In addition, coverage under a health FSA plan is not considered creditable coverage.

FSAs and HHS rules

For purposes of the Department of Health and Human Services (DHHS) rules regarding privacy of personal health information, FSAs are considered covered entities and, therefore, subject to the rules.[23] (See Chapter 8 for detailed discussion of the HIPAA privacy rules.)

---

[20] I.R.S. Final Reg. § 54.4980B-2, Q&A-8(e).
[21] PWBA Reg. § 2590.732(c)(3)(v).
[22] PWBA Reg. § 2590.732(b).
[23] HCFA Reg. § 164.501

Chapter 11

Frequently Asked Questions

Introduction   Chapter 11 lists frequently asked questions about HIPAA and responses to the questions.

In this chapter   This chapter has four sections:

A. Covered Plans

Introduction	This Section A provides FAQs about covered plans and answers.

Covered group health plans

Question:

What group health plans are subject to HIPAA?

Answer:

In general, all group health plans with two or more participants who are current employees, including partnerships and self-employed plans, are subject to HIPAA. This includes group health plans that provide medical care to employees or their dependents directly or through insurance, reimbursement, or otherwise.

Plans exempt from HIPAA

Question:

What health plans are exempt from the HIPAA requirements?

Answer:

Small plans and certain state and local government plans are exempt from HIPAA. A small plan is a plan that covers fewer than two participants who are current employees on the first day of the plan year.

A. Covered Plans, continued

Benefits exempt from HIPAA

Question:

What benefits are exempt from HIPAA?

Answer:

Plans that provide only the following coverage are exempt from HIPAA:

- Accident and disability insurance
- Liability insurance
- Automobile medical payment insurance
- Workers' compensation or similar insurance
- Credit only insurance (e.g., mortgage insurance)
- Coverage for on-site medical clinics

In addition, health savings accounts (HSAs) and most health flexible spending accounts (FSAs) are exempt from the HIPAA requirements.

Health benefits exempt when offered separately

Question:

What health benefits are exempt from HIPAA when offered separately?

Answer:

The following benefits, when offered under a separate policy, certificate, or insurance contract are exempt from HIPAA:

- Limited scope dental benefits
- Limited scope vision benefits
- Long-term care benefits

Benefits are limited scope when limited in scope to a narrow range or type of benefits that are generally excluded from hospital, medical, or surgical benefits packages.

B. Portability Requirements

Introduction   The following FAQs are from the DOL's website at *http://www.dol.gov/ebsa/faqs/faq_consumer_hipaa.html*.

Purpose of HIPAA

Question:

What is the purpose of HIPAA?

Answer:

HIPAA provides rights and protections for participants and beneficiaries in group and individual health plans. HIPAA includes protections for coverage under group health plans that:

- Limit exclusions for preexisting conditions
- Prohibit discrimination against employees and dependents based on their health status
- Allow a special opportunity to enroll in a new plan to individuals in certain circumstances

Creditable coverage

Question:

What is creditable coverage?

Answer:

Most health coverage is creditable coverage, such as group health plan coverage (including COBRA coverage), HMO, individual health insurance, Medicaid, and Medicare. Creditable coverage is not coverage that consists solely of excepted benefits such as limited scope dental or vision benefits.

Days in a waiting period are not counted as creditable coverage nor are these days counted when determining if a significant break in coverage occurred (generally 63 days or more). This 63-day break period may be extended under state law if an individual's coverage is insured through an insurance company or offered through an HMO.

B. Portability Requirements, continued

Standard method for crediting prior coverage

Question:

How does crediting for prior coverage work under HIPAA?

Answer:

Most plans use the standard method of crediting coverage. Under the standard method, an individual receives credit for previous coverage that occurred without a significant break in coverage of 63 days or more. Any coverage occurring before the break in coverage of 63 days or more is not credited against a preexisting condition exclusion period.

Alternative method for crediting prior coverage

Question:

Is there another way a group health plan can credit coverage under HIPAA?

Answer:

Yes. A plan may elect the alternative method for crediting coverage for all employees. Under the alternative method, the plan determines the amount of an individual's creditable coverage for any of five specified categories of benefits, which are mental health, substance abuse treatment, prescription drugs, dental care, and vision care. The standard method is used to determine an individual's creditable coverage for benefits that are not within any of the five categories that a plan may use. (The plan may use some or all of these categories.)

When using the alternative method, the plan determines if an individual has coverage within a category of benefits (regardless of the specific level of benefits provided within that category). For example, if an individual who is a regular enrollee (not a late enrollee) has 12 months of creditable coverage, but coverage for only 6 of those months provided benefits for dental care, a preexisting condition exclusion period may be imposed with respect to that individual's dental care benefits for up to 6 months (irrespective of the level of dental care benefits).

If a plan requests information from a participant's former plan regarding any of the five categories of benefits under the alternative method, the former plan must provide the information regarding coverage under the categories of benefits. A plan can meet this requirement by using the Model for Categories of Benefits.

B. Portability Requirements, continued

Credit for COBRA coverage

Question:

Can an individual receive credit for previous COBRA coverage?

Answer:

Yes. Under HIPAA any period of time that an individual has COBRA continuation coverage is counted as previous health coverage as long as the coverage occurred without a break in coverage of 63 days or more. For example, if an individual was covered continuously for 5 months by a previous health plan and then received 7 months of COBRA continuation coverage, the individual would be entitled to receive credit for 12 months of coverage by the new group health plan.

Requirements for certificates of creditable coverage

Question:

What are the requirements regarding certificates of creditable coverage?

Answer:

Group health plans and health insurance issuers must furnish a certificate of coverage to an individual to provide documentation of the individual's prior creditable coverage. A certificate of creditable coverage:

- Must be provided automatically by the plan or issuer when an individual either loses coverage under the plan or becomes entitled to elect COBRA continuation coverage and when an individual's COBRA continuation coverage ceases
- Must be provided, if requested, before the individual loses coverage or within 24 months of losing coverage
- May be provided through the use of the Model Certificate of Creditable Coverage

C. Nondiscrimination Rules

Introduction   The following Q&As regarding HIPAA's nondiscrimination requirements are from the DOL's website at:

http://www.dol.gov/ebsa/faqs/faq_hipaa_ND.html.

Health factors

Question:

An individual cannot be denied eligibility for benefits or charged a higher premium based on a health factor. What are the health factors?

Answer:

The health factors are:

- Health status
- Medical condition (including both physical and mental illnesses)
- Claims experience
- Receipt of health care
- Medical history
- Genetic information
- Evidence of insurability
- Disability

The term "evidence of insurability" includes conditions arising out of acts of domestic violence, as well as participation in activities such as motorcycling, snowmobiling, all-terrain vehicle riding, horseback riding, skiing, and other similar activities.

C. Nondiscrimination Rules, continued

Whether plan can exclude coverage for health conditions

Question:

A group health plan excludes coverage for benefits for a certain health condition (without regard to whether it was preexisting in nature). Is the plan violating HIPAA's nondiscrimination provisions by imposing this exclusion?

Answer:

Group health plans may exclude coverage for a specific disease, limit or exclude benefits for certain types of treatments or drugs, or limit or exclude benefits based on a determination of whether the benefits are experimental or medically necessary, if the benefit restriction is applied uniformly to all similarly situated individuals and is not directed at any individual participants or beneficiaries based on a health factor. (Plan amendments applicable to all individuals in a group of similarly situated individuals and made effective no earlier than the first day of the next plan year after the amendment is adopted are not considered to be directed at individual participants and beneficiaries.)

Therefore, as long as the plan's condition-specific benefit exclusion is applied uniformly to all similarly situated individuals, and is not directed at individual participants or beneficiaries based on a health factor, the benefit exclusion is permissible under the HIPAA nondiscrimination provisions.

Lifetime limits on benefits

Question:

A health plan has a $500,000 lifetime limit on all benefits covered under the plan and a $2,000 lifetime limit on all benefits provided for one of an individual's health conditions. Are these limits permissible?

Answer:

A group health plan may apply lifetime limits generally or with respect to benefits for a specific disease or treatment, provided the limits are applied uniformly to all similarly situated individuals and are not directed at individual participants or beneficiaries based on a health factor.

Therefore, both the $500,000 lifetime limit and the $2,000 condition-specific lifetime limit are permissible if applied uniformly to all similarly situated individuals and not directed at any individual participants or beneficiaries based on a health factor.

C. Nondiscrimination Rules, continued

Whether insurers can charge higher premiums for one employer versus another

Question:

Is it permissible for a health insurance issuer to charge a higher premium to one group health plan that covers individuals, some of whom have adverse health factors, than it charges another group health plan comprised of fewer individuals with adverse health factors?

Answer:

Yes. HIPAA does not restrict a health insurance issuer from charging a higher rate to one group health plan (or employer) over another. An issuer may take health factors of individuals into account when establishing blended, aggregate rates for group health plans (or employers). This may result in one health plan (or employer) being charged a higher premium than another for the same coverage through the same issuer.

Wellness programs

Question:

Are wellness programs allowed under HIPAA's nondiscrimination rules?

Answer:

The HIPAA nondiscrimination provisions generally prohibit group health plans from charging similarly situated individuals different premiums or contributions or imposing different deductible, copayment or other cost sharing requirements based on a health factor. However, there is an exception that allows plans to offer wellness programs.

If none of the conditions for obtaining a reward under a wellness program are based on an individual satisfying a standard related to a health factor, or if no reward is offered, the program complies with the nondiscrimination requirements (assuming participation in the program is made available to all similarly situated individuals). For example:

1. A program that reimburses all or part of the cost of a fitness center.
2. A diagnostic testing program that provides a reward for participation rather than outcomes.
3. A program that encourages preventive care by waiving copayment or deductible requirement for the cost of, for example, prenatal care or well-baby visits.
4. A program that reimburses employees for the cost of smoking cessation programs without regard to whether the employee quits smoking.

C. Nondiscrimination Rules, continued

Wellness programs (continued)

5. A program that provides a reward to employees for attending a monthly health education seminar.

Wellness programs that condition a reward on an individual satisfying a standard related to a health factor must meet five requirements described in the final rules in order to comply with the nondiscrimination rules.

The wellness program rules are generally effective for the plan years starting on or after July 1, 2007

Wellness programs' standards

Question:

What are the five requirements for wellness programs that base a reward on satisfying a standard related to a health factor?

Answer:

The five requirements are as follows:

1. The total reward for all of the plan's wellness programs that require satisfaction of a standard related to a health factor is limited; generally, it must not exceed 20 percent of the cost of the employee-only coverage under the plan. If dependents (such as spouses and/or dependent children) may participate in the wellness program, the reward must not exceed 20 percent of the cost of the coverage in which an employee and any dependents are enrolled.
2. The program must be reasonably designed to promote health and prevent disease.
3. The program must give individuals eligible to participate the opportunity to qualify for the reward at least once per year.
4. The reward must be available to all similarly situated individuals. The program must allow a reasonable alternative standard (or waiver of initial standard) for obtaining the reward for any individual for whom it is unreasonably difficult due to a medical condition, or medically inadvisable, to satisfy the standard.
5. The plan must disclose in all materials describing the terms of the program the availability of a reasonable alternative standard (or the possibility of a waiver of the initial standard).

The wellness program rules are generally effective for the plan years starting on or after July 1, 2007.

C. Nondiscrimination Rules, continued

Wellness programs not conditioned on a health standard

Question:

How do the wellness program rules apply to a group program that offers a reward to individuals who participate in voluntary testing for early detection of health problems (the plan does not use the test results to determine whether an individual receives a reward or the amount of the reward)?

Answer:

The plan's program does not base any reward on the outcome of testing. Thus, it is allowed under the HIPAA nondiscrimination provisions without being subject to the five requirements for wellness programs that do require satisfaction of a standard related to a health factor.

Smoking cessation program

Question:

Can a plan provide a premium differential between smokers and nonsmokers?

Answer:

The plan is offering a reward based on an individual's ability to stop smoking.

Medical evidence suggests that smoking may be related to a health factor. *The Diagnostic and Statistical Manual of Mental Disorders,* which states that nicotine addiction is a medical condition, supports that position. In addition, a report of the Surgeon General adds that scientists in the field of drug addiction agree that nicotine, a substance common to all forms of tobacco, is a powerfully addictive drug.

For a group health plan to maintain the premium differential between smokers and nonsmokers and not be considered discriminatory, the plan's nonsmoking program would need to meet the five requirements for wellness programs that require satisfaction of a standard related to a health factor.

Accordingly, under the final rules, this wellness program would be permitted if:

C. Nondiscrimination Rules, continued

Smoking cessation program (continued)

- The premium differential is not more than 20 percent of the total cost of employee-only coverage (or 20 percent of the cost of coverage if dependents can participate in the program);
- The program is reasonably designed to promote health and prevent disease;
- Individuals eligible for the program are given an opportunity to qualify for the discount at least once per year.
- The program accommodates individuals for whom it is unreasonably difficult to quit using tobacco products due to addiction by providing a reasonable alternative standard (such as a discount in return for attending educational classes or for trying a nicotine patch); and
- All plan materials describing the terms of the premium differential describe the availability of a reasonable alternative standard to qualify for the lower premium.

Non-confine-ment provisions

Question:

My group health plan has a non-confinement provision, which states that if an individual is confined to a hospital at the time enrollment eligibility begins, such eligibility is postponed until that individual is no longer confined. Is this permissible?

Answer:

No. A group health plan may not restrict an individual's eligibility, benefits, or the effective date of coverage based on the individual's confinement in a hospital or other health care facility. Additionally, a health plan may not set an individual's premium rate based on the individual's confinement.

Waiting period provisions

Question:

A group health plan has a 90-day waiting period for enrollment. Under the terms of the plan, if an individual is actively at work on the 91st day, health coverage becomes effective on that day. If an individual is not actively at work on the 91st day, the effective date of coverage is delayed until the first day the individual is actively at work. If an employee misses work on the 91st day due to illness, can the employee be excluded from coverage under the plan's actively-at-work provision?

C. Nondiscrimination Rules, continued

Waiting period provisions (continued)

Answer:

No. A group health plan or issuer generally may not refuse to provide benefits because an individual is not actively at work on the day the

individual would otherwise become eligible for benefits. However, these actively-at-work clauses are permitted if the plan treats individuals who are absent from work due to a health factor (for example, individuals taking sick leave) as if they are actively at work for purposes of health coverage.

Nonetheless, a plan may require an individual to begin work before coverage may become effective. Additionally, plans may distinguish among groups of similarly situated individuals (for example, a plan may require an individual to work full time, such as 250 hours per quarter or 30 hours per week) in their eligibility provisions.

Age restrictions

Question:

A group health plan provides coverage for dependents generally only until age 25. This age restriction does not, however, apply to disabled dependents who may continue health coverage past age 25. Is this plan provision favoring disabled dependents permissible?

Answer:

Yes. It is permissible for a plan or issuer to treat an individual with an adverse health factor more favorably by offering extended coverage.

D. Privacy Rules

Introduction   The following FAQs are from the Q&As posted on The Department of Health and Human Services' website at: *http://www.hhs.gov./ocr/privacy/hipaa/faq/about/index.html*

When plan may disclose PHI

Question:

May a health plan disclose protected health information (PHI) to a person who calls the plan on the beneficiary's behalf?

Answer:

The privacy rules under HIPAA allow a health plan (or other covered entity) to disclose to a family member, relative, or close friend of an individual, the PHI that is directly relevant to that person's involvement with the individual's care or payment for care. A covered entity also may disclose PHI to persons who are not family members, relatives, or close friends of the individual, if the covered entity has obtained assurance that the person has been identified by the individual as being involved in his or her care or payment.

A covered entity may disclose relevant PHI to these persons only if the individual does not object or only if the covered entity can reasonably infer from the circumstances that the individual would not object to the disclosure. However, when the individual is not present or is incapacitated, the covered entity can make the disclosure if, in the exercise of professional judgment, it believes the disclosure is in the best interests of the individual.

The Department of Health and Human Services provided the following two examples of the circumstances under which a plan may disclose PHI:

- A health plan may disclose relevant PHI to a beneficiary's daughter who has called to assist her hospitalized, elderly mother in resolving a claim or other payment issue.
- A health plan may disclose relevant PHI to a human resources representative who has called the plan with the beneficiary also on the line, or who could turn the phone over to the beneficiary, who could then confirm for the plan that the representative calling is assisting the beneficiary.

D. Privacy Rules, continued

Notice of privacy practices

Question:

Must a health plan periodically notify enrollees about the availability of its Notice of Privacy Practices?

Answer:

Yes. Under the HIPAA privacy rules, a health plan must remind enrollees at least once every 3 years of the availability of its Notice of Privacy Practices, as well as how to obtain a copy. Health plans can satisfy this requirement in a number of ways, including:

- Sending a copy of their Notice of Privacy Practices
- Mailing only a reminder concerning the availability of the Notice of Privacy Practices and information on how to obtain a copy
- Including in a plan-produced newsletter or other publication information about the availability of the Notice of Privacy Practices and how to obtain a copy
- Sending the Notice of Privacy Practices to subscribers and enrollees annually

A health plan can satisfy the requirement by providing the reminder notice to the named insured of a policy under which coverage is provided to that named insured and one or more dependents.

D. Privacy Rules, continued

General requirements

Question:

Generally, what does the HIPAA Privacy Rule require the average health plan to do?

Answer:

For the average health plan, the Privacy Rule requires activities, such as:

- Notifying employees about their privacy rights and how their information can be used
- Adopting and implementing privacy procedures for the plan
- Training employees so that they understand the privacy procedures
- Designating an individual to be responsible for seeing that the privacy procedures are adopted and followed

Entities subject to HIPAA privacy rules

Question:

Who must comply with the HIPAA privacy rules?

Answer:

The following entities are subject to the HIPAA privacy rules:

- Health plans
- Health care clearinghouses
- Health care providers who conduct certain financial and administrative transactions electronically. (These electronic transactions are those for which standards have been adopted by the Secretary under HIPAA, such as electronic billing and fund transfers.)

The above entities are referred to as "covered entities." They are bound by the new privacy standards even if they contract with others (called "business associates") to perform some of their essential functions.

D. Privacy Rules, continued

Purpose of privacy rules

Question:

What is the purpose of the privacy rules?

Answer:

The HIPAA privacy rules create national standards to protect individuals' medical records and other personal health information:

- They give patients more control over their health information.
- They set boundaries on the use and release of health records.
- They establish appropriate safeguards that health care providers and others must achieve to protect the privacy of health information.
- They hold violators accountable, with civil and criminal penalties that can be imposed if they violate patients' privacy rights.
- They strike a balance when public responsibility supports disclosure of some forms of data, for example, to protect public health.

For patients, the rules mean being able to make informed choices when seeking care and reimbursement for care based on how personal health information may be used. The rules enable patients to find out how their information may be used and about certain disclosures of their information that have been made. The rules generally limit the release of information to the minimum reasonably needed for the purpose of the disclosure. The rules generally give patients the right to examine and obtain a copy of their own health records and request corrections, and the rules empower individuals to control certain uses and disclosures of their health information

Chapter 12

Regulations, Notices, and Other Government Publications

Introduction   This chapter provides copies of government laws, regulations, notices, and other information relating to HIPAA as of the publication of the 2009/2010 Edition.

In this chapter   This chapter has eight sections:

A. HIPAA Interim Final Rules and Proposed Rules

Summary The Internal Revenue Service, the Pension and Welfare Benefits Administration (now the Employee Benefits Security Administration), and the Health Care Financing Administration (now the Centers for Medicare and Medicaid Services) jointly published these regulations in the *Federal Register* on January 8, 2001.

A. HIPAA Interim Final Rules and Proposed Rules, continued

**Monday,
January 8, 2001**

Part II

Department of the Treasury
Internal Revenue Service
26 CFR Part 54

Department of Labor
Pension and Welfare Benefits Administration

29 CFR Part 2590

Department of Health and Human Services
Health Care Financing Administration

45 CFR Part 146

Nondiscrimination in Health Coverage in the Group Market; Interim Final Rules and Proposed Rules

A. HIPAA Interim Final Rules and Proposed Rules, continued

1378   Federal Register / Vol. 66, No. 5 / Monday, January 8, 2001 / Rules and Regulations

DEPARTMENT OF THE TREASURY

Internal Revenue Service

26 CFR Part 54

[TD 8931]

RIN 1545-AW02

DEPARTMENT OF LABOR

Pension and Welfare Benefits Administration

29 CFR Part 2590

RIN 1210-AA77

DEPARTMENT OF HEALTH AND HUMAN SERVICES

Health Care Financing Administration

45 CFR Part 146

RIN 0938-AI08

Interim Final Rules for Nondiscrimination in Health Coverage in the Group Market

AGENCIES: Internal Revenue Service, Department of the Treasury; Pension and Welfare Benefits Administration, Department of Labor; Health Care Financing Administration, Department of Health and Human Services.

ACTION: Interim final rules with request for comments.

SUMMARY: This document contains interim final rules governing the provisions prohibiting discrimination based on a health factor for group health plans and issuers of health insurance coverage offered in connection with a group health plan. The rules contained in this document implement changes made to the Internal Revenue Code of 1986 (Code), the Employee Retirement Income Security Act of 1974 (ERISA), and the Public Health Service Act (PHS Act) enacted as part of the Health Insurance Portability and Accountability Act of 1996 (HIPAA).

DATES: *Effective date.* The interim final rules are effective March 9, 2001.

Applicability dates. For rules describing when this section applies to group health plans and group health insurance issuers, see paragraph (i) of these interim regulations.[1]

Comment date. Written comments on these interim regulations are invited and

must be received by the Departments on or before April 9, 2001.

ADDRESSES: Written comments should be submitted with a signed original and three copies (except for electronic submissions to the Internal Revenue Service (IRS) or Department of Labor) to any of the addresses specified below. Any comment that is submitted to any Department will be shared with the other Departments.

Comments to the IRS can be addressed to: CC:M&SP:RU (REG–109707–97), Room 5226, Internal Revenue Service, POB 7604, Ben Franklin Station, Washington, DC 20044.

In the alternative, comments may be hand-delivered between the hours of 8 a.m. and 5 p.m. to: CC:M&SP:RU (REG–109707–97), Courier's Desk, Internal Revenue Service, 1111 Constitution Avenue, NW., Washington, DC 20224.

Alternatively, comments may be transmitted electronically via the IRS Internet site at: *http://www.irs.gov/tax regs/regslist.html.*

Comments to the Department of Labor can be addressed to: U.S. Department of Labor, Pension and Welfare Benefits Administration, 200 Constitution Avenue NW., Room C–5331, Washington, DC 20210, *Attention:* Nondiscrimination Comments.

Alternatively, comments may be hand-delivered between the hours of 9 a.m. and 5 p.m. to the same address. Comments may also be transmitted by e-mail to: HIPAA702@pwba.dol.gov.

Comments to HHS can be addressed to: Health Care Financing Administration, Department of Health and Human Services, Attention: HCFA–2022–IFC, P.O. Box 26688, Baltimore, MD 21207.

In the alternative, comments may be hand-delivered between the hours of 8:30 a.m. and 5 p.m. to either: Room 443–G, Hubert Humphrey Building, 200 Independence Avenue, SW., Washington, DC 20201 or Room C5–14–03, 7500 Security Boulevard, Baltimore, MD 21244–1850.

All submissions to the IRS will be open to public inspection and copying in room 1621, 1111 Constitution Avenue, NW., Washington, DC from 9 a.m. to 4 p.m.

All submissions to the Department of Labor will be open to public inspection and copying in the Public Documents Room, Pension and Welfare Benefits Administration, U.S. Department of Labor, Room N–1513, 200 Constitution Avenue, NW., Washington, DC from 8:30 a.m. to 5:30 p.m.

All submissions to HHS will be open to public inspection and copying in

room 309–G of the Department of Health and Human Services, 200 Independence Avenue, SW., Washington, DC from 8:30 a.m. to 5 p.m.

FOR FURTHER INFORMATION CONTACT: Russ Weinheimer, Internal Revenue Service, Department of the Treasury, at (202) 622–6080; Amy J. Turner, Pension and Welfare Benefits Administration, Department of Labor, at (202) 219–7006; or Ruth A. Bradford, Health Care Financing Administration, Department of Health and Human Services, at (410) 786–1565.

SUPPLEMENTARY INFORMATION:

Customer Service Information:

Individuals interested in obtaining additional information on HIPAA's nondiscrimination rules may request a copy of the Department of Labor's booklet entitled "Questions and Answers: Recent Changes in Health Care Law" by calling the PWBA Toll-Free Publication Hotline at 1–800–998–7542 or may request a copy of the Health Care Financing Administration's new publication entitled "Protecting Your Health Insurance Coverage" by calling (410) 786–1565. Information on HIPAA's nondiscrimination rules and other recent health care laws is also available on the Department of Labor's website (http://www.dol.gov/dol/pwba) and the Department of Health and Human Services' website (http://hipaa.hcfa.gov).

I. Background

The Health Insurance Portability and Accountability Act of 1996 (HIPAA), Public Law 104–191, was enacted on August 21, 1996. HIPAA amended the Internal Revenue Code of 1986 (Code), the Employee Retirement Income Security Act of 1974 (ERISA), and the Public Health Service Act (PHS Act) to provide for, among other things, improved portability and continuity of health coverage. HIPAA added section 9802 of the Code, section 702 of ERISA, and section 2702 of the PHS Act, which prohibit discrimination in health coverage. Interim final rules implementing the HIPAA provisions were first made available to the public on April 1, 1997 (published in the Federal Register on April 8, 1997, 62 FR 16894) (April 1997 interim rules). On December 29, 1997, the Departments published a clarification of the April 1997 interim rules as they relate to individuals who were denied coverage before the effective date of HIPAA on the basis of any health factor (62 FR 67689).

In the preamble to the April 1997 interim rules, the Departments invited

---

[1] References in this preamble to a specific paragraph in the interim regulations are to paragraphs in each of the three sets of regulations being published as part of this document. Specifically, references are to paragraphs in 26 CFR 54.9802–1 and 26 CFR 54.9802–1T (see discussion and table in "C. Format of Regulations" below), 29 CFR 2590.702, and 45 CFR 146.121.

A. HIPAA Interim Final Rules and Proposed Rules, continued

Federal Register / Vol. 66, No. 5 / Monday, January 8, 2001 / Rules and Regulations   1379

comments on whether additional guidance was needed concerning—
• The extent to which the statute prohibits discrimination against individuals in eligibility for particular benefits;
• The extent to which the statute may permit benefit limitations based on the source of an injury;
• The permissible standards for defining groups of similarly situated individuals;
• Application of the prohibitions on discrimination between groups of similarly situated individuals; and
• The permissible standards for determining bona fide wellness programs.

In the preamble to the April 1997 interim rules, the Departments stated that they intend to issue further regulations on the nondiscrimination rules and that in no event would the Departments take any enforcement action against a plan or issuer that had sought to comply in good faith with section 9802 of the Code, section 702 of ERISA, and section 2702 of the PHS Act before the additional guidance is provided. Accordingly, with the issuance of these interim regulations, the Departments have determined that the period for nonenforcement in cases of good faith compliance ends in accordance with the rules described in paragraph (i) of these interim regulations.[2] However, because the interim regulations do not include a discussion of bona fide wellness programs (see proposed rules relating to bona fide wellness programs published elsewhere in this issue of the **Federal Register**), the period for good faith compliance continues with respect to those provisions until further guidance is issued.

II. Overview of the Regulations

Section 9802 of the Code, section 702 of ERISA, and section 2702 of the PHS Act (the HIPAA nondiscrimination provisions) establish rules generally prohibiting group health plans and group health insurance issuers from discriminating against individual participants or beneficiaries based on any health factor of such participants or beneficiaries. These interim regulations interpret the HIPAA nondiscrimination provisions. Among other things, the interim regulations—
• Explain the application of these provisions to benefits;
• Clarify the relationship between the HIPAA nondiscrimination provisions and the HIPAA preexisting condition exclusion limitations;

[2] See footnote 1.

• Explain the application of these provisions to premiums;
• Describe similarly situated individuals;
• Explain the application of these provisions to actively-at-work and nonconfinement clauses; and
• Clarify that more favorable treatment of individuals with medical needs generally is permitted.

Described elsewhere in this issue of the **Federal Register** are proposed standards for defining bona fide wellness programs.

Of course, plans and benefits that are not subject to the HIPAA portability provisions (set forth in Chapter 100 of the Code, part 7 of subtitle B of title I of ERISA, and title XXVII of the PHS Act) are not subject to the HIPAA nondiscrimination requirements. Accordingly, the following plans and benefits are not subject to the HIPAA nondiscrimination requirements: benefits that qualify under the HIPAA portability provisions as excepted benefits; plans with fewer than two participants who are current employees on the first day of the plan year;[3] and self-funded non-Federal governmental plans that elect, under 45 CFR 146.180, to be exempt from these nondiscrimination requirements. In addition, under a proposed regulation published by the Department of the Treasury and described elsewhere in this issue of the **Federal Register**, certain church plans are treated as not violating the general HIPAA nondiscrimination provisions if the plan requires evidence of good health for the coverage of certain individuals.

Health Factors

The HIPAA nondiscrimination provisions set forth eight health status-related factors. The interim regulations refer to these as "health factors." The eight health factors are health status, medical condition (including both physical and mental illnesses), claims experience, receipt of health care, medical history, genetic information, evidence of insurability, and disability. These terms are largely overlapping and, in combination, include any factor related to an individual's health.

Evidence of insurability. Several commenters urged that the health factor "evidence of insurability" be interpreted to prohibit plans and issuers from denying coverage to individuals who engage in certain types of activities.

[3] However, a State may impose the requirements of the HIPAA portability provisions, in whole or in part, on health insurance coverage sold to groups that contain fewer than 2 current employees on the first day of the plan year. See sections 2723 and 2791(e) of the PHS Act.

Commenters cited language in the conference report that states, "The inclusion of evidence of insurability in the definition of health status is intended to ensure, among other things, that individuals are not excluded from health care coverage due to their participation in activities such as motorcycling, snowmobiling, all-terrain vehicle riding, horseback riding, skiing and other similar activities." H.R. Conf. Rep. No. 736, 104th Cong., 2d Sess. 186 (1996). The interim regulations clarify that evidence of insurability includes participation in activities listed in the conference report. In addition, the interim regulations incorporate the statutory clarification that evidence of insurability includes conditions arising out of acts of domestic violence. See also the discussion below concerning source-of-injury restrictions under the heading "Application to Benefits."

Late enrollees and special enrollees. Some commenters asked whether treating late enrollees differently from other enrollees is discrimination based on one or more health factors. HIPAA was designed to encourage individuals to enroll in health coverage when first eligible and to maintain coverage for as long as they continue to be eligible. Permitting plans and issuers to treat late enrollees less favorably than other enrollees is consistent with this objective. The interim regulations clarify that the decision whether to elect health coverage, including the time an individual chooses to enroll, such as late enrollment, is not itself within the scope of any health factor. Thus, the interim regulations permit plans and issuers to treat late enrollees differently from similarly situated individuals who enroll when first eligible.

Although the HIPAA nondiscrimination requirements do not prohibit different treatment of special enrollees, any differential treatment would violate the HIPAA special enrollment requirements. These interim regulations provide a cross-reference to the HIPAA regulations requiring special enrollees to be treated the same as individuals who enroll when first eligible.

Prohibited Discrimination in Rules for Eligibility

These interim regulations provide that group health plans and group health insurance issuers generally may not establish any rule for eligibility of any individual to enroll for benefits under the terms of the plan or group health insurance coverage that discriminates based on any health factor that relates to that individual or a dependent of that individual. Under these interim

A. HIPAA Interim Final Rules and Proposed Rules, continued

regulations, rules for eligibility include, but are not limited to, rules relating to enrollment; the effective date of coverage, waiting (or affiliation) periods, late and special enrollment, eligibility for benefit packages (including rules for individuals to change their selection among benefit packages), benefits (as described below under the heading "Application to Benefits"), continued eligibility, and terminating coverage of any individual under the plan.

The rules for eligibility apply in tandem with the rules describing similarly situated individuals (described below under the heading "Similarly Situated Individuals") to prevent discrimination in eligibility based on any health factor. Thus, while it is permissible for a plan or issuer to impose waiting periods of different lengths on different groups of similarly situated individuals, a plan or issuer would violate the interim regulations if it imposed a longer waiting period for individuals within the same group of similarly situated individuals based on the higher claims of those individuals (or based on any other adverse health factor of those individuals).

While the interim regulations clarify that late enrollment itself is not within the scope of any health factor, eligibility for late enrollment comes within the scope of rules for eligibility under which discrimination based on one or more health factors is prohibited. The effect of these rules is to permit plans or issuers to treat late enrollees differently from individuals who enroll when first eligible but to prohibit plans and issuers from distinguishing among applicants for late enrollment based on any health factor of the applicant. Thus, a plan could impose an 18-month preexisting condition exclusion on late enrollees while imposing no preexisting condition exclusion on individuals who enroll in the plan when first eligible, but a plan would violate the interim regulations if it conditioned the ability to enroll as a late enrollee on the passing of a physical examination (or on any other health factor of the individual, such as having incurred health claims during a past period below a certain dollar amount).

Application to Benefits

General rules. The extent to which the statutory language prohibits discrimination against individuals in eligibility for particular benefits is subject to a wide range of interpretations. At one extreme, the language could be interpreted as applying only to enrollment and to premiums. Under this interpretation, for example, it would be possible for a plan

or issuer to impose a $100 lifetime limit on a particular individual with a history of high health claims (provided that the individual is permitted to enroll in the plan and is charged the same premium as similarly situated individuals), while imposing a $1 million lifetime limit on all other participants in the plan.

At the other extreme, the statutory language could be interpreted to mandate parity in health benefits. This interpretation would prevent plans and issuers from designing benefit packages that control costs and are responsive to employees' preferences for balancing additional benefits with additional costs.

In the preamble to the April 1997 interim rules, the Departments specifically invited comments on whether guidance was needed concerning this issue. The comments received ranged between these two extremes. The approach in these interim regulations takes into account the concerns expressed by commenters, as well as the conference report. Specifically, the conference report states that:

> It is the intent of the conferees that a plan cannot knowingly be designed to exclude individuals and their dependents on the basis of health status. However, generally applicable terms of the plan may have a disparate impact on individual enrollees. For example, a plan may exclude all coverage of a specific condition, or may include a lifetime cap on all benefits, or a lifetime cap on specific benefits. Although individuals with the specific condition would be adversely affected by an exclusion of coverage for that condition * * * such plan characteristics would be permitted as long as they are not directed at individual sick employees or dependents.

H.R. Conf. Rep. No. 736, 104th Cong., 2d Sess. 186–187 (1996).

The interim regulations clarify that they do not require a plan or issuer to provide coverage for any particular benefit to any group of similarly situated individuals. However, benefits provided under a plan or group health insurance coverage must be uniformly available to all similarly situated individuals. Likewise, any restriction on a benefit or benefits must apply uniformly to all similarly situated individuals and must not be directed at individual participants or beneficiaries based on any health factor of the participants or beneficiaries (determined based on all the relevant facts and circumstances). Thus, for example, a plan or issuer may limit or exclude benefits in relation to a specific disease or condition, limit or exclude benefits for certain types of treatments or drugs, or limit or exclude benefits

based on a determination of whether the benefits are experimental or not medically necessary, but only if the benefit limitation or exclusion applies uniformly to all similarly situated individuals and is not directed at individual participants or beneficiaries based on any health factor of the participants or beneficiaries. In addition, a plan or issuer may impose annual, lifetime, or other limits on benefits and may require the satisfaction of a deductible, copayment, coinsurance, or other cost-sharing requirement in order to obtain a benefit if the limit or cost-sharing requirement applies uniformly to all similarly situated individuals and is not directed at individual participants or beneficiaries based on any health factor of the participants or beneficiaries.[4] These interim regulations clarify that whether any plan provision with respect to benefits complies with the interim regulations does not affect whether the provision is permitted under the Americans with Disabilities Act (ADA), or any other law, whether State or federal.[5]

Accordingly, for example, a group health plan may apply a lifetime limit on all benefits provided to each participant covered under the plan. While this limitation on all benefits may adversely impact individuals with serious medical conditions, the limitation is permitted provided that it applies to all similarly situated individuals and is not directed at individual participants or beneficiaries. Similarly, a plan or issuer may establish a specific lifetime limit on the treatment of a particular condition (such as the treatment of temporomandibular joint syndrome (TMJ)) for all similarly situated individuals in the plan. Although individuals with TMJ may be adversely affected by this limitation, because benefits for the treatment of TMJ are available uniformly to all similarly situated individuals and because the limit on benefits for TMJ applies to all similarly situated individuals, the limit is permissible.

Under these interim regulations, plans and issuers therefore have significant flexibility in designing benefits. However, to prevent plans and issuers from restricting benefits based on a

---

[4] For special rules that apply to cost-sharing mechanisms that are part of a bona fide wellness program, see the proposed regulations relating to bona fide wellness programs published elsewhere in this issue of the Federal Register.

[5] In this regard, the Equal Employment Opportunity Commission has commented, by letter of July 7, 1997, "Title I of the ADA prohibits disability-based employment discrimination, including discrimination in fringe benefits such as health insurance plans."

A. HIPAA Interim Final Rules and Proposed Rules, continued

specific health factor of an individual under the plan, the interim regulations prohibit benefit restrictions, even if applied uniformly to all similarly situated individuals, from being directed at individual participants or beneficiaries based on any health factor of the participants or beneficiaries. The interim regulations clarify that a plan amendment applicable to all individuals in one or more groups of similarly situated individuals under the plan and made effective no earlier than the first day of the first plan year after the amendment is adopted is not considered to be directed at individual participants and beneficiaries. This exception to the general facts and circumstances determination that a change is directed at an individual is necessary to preserve the flexibility of small employers that might otherwise be disproportionately affected and prevented from adopting changes in benefit design. If small employers are unable to modify future benefits to keep health coverage affordable, their alternative may be to eliminate health coverage entirely. At the same time, the exception reflects the common practice of modifying the terms of a plan on an annual basis. Finally, changes in benefit design that are effective earlier than the first day of the next plan year remain subject to a facts and circumstances determination regarding whether the change is directed at individual participants and beneficiaries.

An example illustrates that if an individual files a claim for the treatment of a condition, and shortly thereafter the plan is modified to restrict benefits for the treatment of the condition, effective before the beginning of the next plan year, the restriction would be directed at the individual based on a health factor (absent additional facts to indicate that the change was made independent of the claim) and the plan would violate these interim regulations.

Source-of-injury restrictions. While a person cannot be excluded from a plan for engaging in certain recreational activities (see previous discussion on evidence of insurability under the heading "Health Factors"), benefits for a particular injury can, in some cases, be excluded based on the source of an injury. These plan restrictions are known as source-of-injury restrictions.[6] Under these interim regulations, if a plan or group health insurance coverage

generally provides benefits for a type of injury, the plan or issuer may not use a source-of-injury restriction to deny benefits otherwise provided for treatment of the injury if it results from an act of domestic violence or a medical condition (including both physical and mental health conditions). An example in the interim regulations clarifies that benefits for injuries generally covered under the plan cannot be excluded merely because they were self-inflicted or were sustained in connection with a suicide or attempted suicide if the injuries resulted from a medical condition such as depression. Another example illustrates that a plan can nonetheless exclude benefits for injuries because they were sustained in connection with various recreational activities if the accident did not result from any medical condition (or from domestic violence).

The Relationship Between the HIPAA Nondiscrimination Provisions and the HIPAA Preexisting Condition Exclusion Provisions

Restrictions on benefits based on the fact that a medical condition was present before the first day of coverage discriminate against individuals based on one or more health factors. The statute nonetheless provides that the nondiscrimination provisions are intended to be construed in a manner consistent with the HIPAA provisions specifically allowing the application of preexisting condition exclusions. These latter provisions restrict the ability of a group health plan or group health insurance issuer to apply preexisting condition exclusions, both by restricting the circumstances under which an individual's condition is considered preexisting and by limiting the length of the exclusion period. The interim regulations clarify that a preexisting condition exclusion that satisfies the requirements of the HIPAA preexisting condition exclusion provisions is permitted under the HIPAA nondiscrimination requirements if the exclusion applies uniformly to individuals within the same group of similarly situated individuals and is not directed at individual participants or beneficiaries based on any health factor of the participants or beneficiaries. A plan amendment relating to a preexisting condition exclusion applicable to all individuals in one or more groups of similarly situated individuals under the plan and made effective no earlier than the first day of the first plan year after the amendment is adopted is not considered to be directed at individual participants or beneficiaries.

The examples illustrate that a typical preexisting condition exclusion permitted under the HIPAA preexisting condition exclusion requirements does not violate the HIPAA nondiscrimination requirements even though the exclusion inherently discriminates based on one or more health factors. The examples also illustrate that a plan nonetheless must apply the preexisting condition exclusion to similarly situated individuals in a uniform manner and cannot apply a longer preexisting condition exclusion period based on the submission of claims during the first part of the exclusion period.

Prohibited Discrimination in Premiums or Contributions

Under the interim regulations, a group health plan, and a health insurance issuer offering health insurance coverage in connection with a group health plan, may not require an individual, as a condition of enrollment or continued enrollment under the plan or group health insurance coverage, to pay a premium or contribution that is greater than the premium or contribution for a similarly situated individual enrolled in the plan or group health insurance coverage, based on any health factor that relates to that individual or a dependent of that individual. Under the interim regulations, when determining an individual's premium or contribution rate, discounts, rebates, payments in kind, or other premium differential mechanisms are taken into account.[7]

In general, the interim regulations do not restrict the amount that an employer may be quoted or charged by an issuer (or, in the case of a multiemployer plan, by the plan) for coverage of a group of similarly situated individuals. However, the interim regulations prohibit certain billing practices because in many instances they could directly or indirectly result in an individual's being charged more than a similarly situated individual based on a health factor.

Some health insurance issuers that offer health insurance coverage in connection with a group health plan use billing practices with separate individual rates that vary based, in part, on the health factors of the individuals who are eligible to participate in the plan. This practice is generally known as list billing. List billing based on a

---

[6] A commenter pointed out that this type of restriction is distinct from two other restrictions sometimes referred to as "source-of-injury restrictions"—(1) those based on the geographic location where the injury occurred, and (2) those based on when the injury occurred and whether other coverage was in effect.

[7] However, a group health plan or a health insurance issuer offering group health insurance coverage may establish premium or contribution differentials through a bona fide wellness program. (See proposed regulations relating to bona fide wellness programs published elsewhere in this issue of the Federal Register).

A. HIPAA Interim Final Rules and Proposed Rules, continued

1382   Federal Register / Vol. 66, No. 5 / Monday, January 8, 2001 / Rules and Regulations

health factor is prohibited under the interim regulations.

The HIPAA nondiscrimination requirements do not prohibit an issuer from considering all relevant health factors of individuals in order to establish aggregate rates for coverage provided under the group health plan. However, an individual may not be required to pay a higher premium based on any health factor of the individual. Under the interim regulations, an issuer (or a multiemployer plan) may not quote or charge an employer different premium rates on an individual-by-individual basis in a group of similarly situated individuals based on any health factor of the individuals, even if the employer does not pass the different rates through to the individuals. If an issuer wishes to increase rates to cover the additional exposure to expenses that may result from an individual's health factor, the issuer must blend the increase into an overall group rate and then quote or charge a higher per-participant rate. Nonetheless, the prohibition on the practice of list billing based on a health factor does not restrict communications between issuers and plans regarding rate calculations.

Similarly Situated Individuals

The statutory HIPAA nondiscrimination requirements clarify that the general rule prohibiting discrimination in eligibility does not prevent a group health plan or group health insurance coverage from establishing limitations or restrictions on the amount, level, extent, or nature of benefits for "similarly situated individuals" enrolled in the plan or coverage. The statutory rule prohibiting discrimination in charging individuals premiums or contributions prohibits a plan or issuer from requiring any individual, based on any health factor of that individual or a dependent of that individual, to pay a premium or contribution that is greater than the premium or contribution required of a "similarly situated individual." In the preamble to the April 1997 interim rules, the Departments requested comments both on the permissible standards for defining groups of similarly situated individuals and on the application of the prohibitions on discrimination between groups of similarly situated individuals.

Many commenters suggested that discrimination between groups of similarly situated individuals should be permitted, with the caveat that it should not be permissible to define a group based on a health factor. These interim regulations provide that the nondiscrimination rules apply only

within a group of similarly situated individuals. Thus, these interim regulations do not prohibit discrimination between or among groups of similarly situated individuals. However, these interim regulations also provide that if the creation or modification of an employment or coverage classification is directed at individual participants or beneficiaries based on any health factor of the participants or beneficiaries, the classification is not permitted. This is intended to be a broad anti-abuse standard that applies based on the relevant facts and circumstances of each case.

The permissibility of discrimination between or among groups of similarly situated individuals increases the possibility of abuse in establishing groups of similarly situated individuals. Most commenters addressing this issue focused on the classification of participants and suggested that classifications should be based on work activities and not on a health factor or on activities unrelated to employment. The interim regulations provide generally that participants may be treated as two or more groups of similarly situated individuals if the distinction between or among the groups is based on a bona fide employment-based classification consistent with the employer's usual business practice. The validity of a category as a bona fide employment-based classification is determined based on all the relevant facts and circumstances. Relevant facts and circumstances include whether the employer uses the classification for purposes independent of qualification for health coverage (for example, determining eligibility for other employee benefits or determining other terms of employment). Subject to the anti-abuse standard (described in the preceding paragraph), the interim regulations allow distinctions to be made based on full-time versus part-time status, different geographic location, membership in a collective bargaining unit, date of hire, length of service, current employee versus former employee status, and different occupations.

Some commenters expressed concern that allowing similarly situated individuals to be determined based on occupation or geographic location would allow plans and issuers to create artificial classifications, ostensibly based on occupation or geographic location, that are actually designed to discriminate based on a health factor of an individual or individuals. These interim regulations permit bona fide

classifications based on occupation or geographic location. In this connection, commenters had two principal concerns. First, there was a concern about reclassifications targeting unhealthy individuals. For example, a participant receiving expensive medical treatment might be reclassified to a separate employment category either with reduced health benefits or none at all. The broad anti-abuse standard of these interim regulations is intended, among other things, to prohibit reclassifications directed at individuals such as this.

A second concern that commenters had was that plans and issuers might design health benefits differently for employees in different occupations or geographic locations based, at least in part, on the health factors of these groups of individuals. One example is a plan that offers fewer benefits to employees in one occupation than to employees in another occupation at least in part because of the higher average historical claims of the employees in the first occupation. A second example is a plan that charges employees in one area more than employees in another area at least in part because the cost of medical care is generally higher in the first area. The statute and legislative history appear to allow this practice, and thus these interim regulations do not prohibit the provision of different health benefits for employees in different occupations or geographic locations, based at least in part on the health factors of the group as a whole, if the classifications are not directed at individual participants or beneficiaries based on a health factor of the participants or beneficiaries.

These interim regulations also permit plans and issuers, in certain circumstances, to treat beneficiaries as different groups of similarly situated individuals. Beneficiaries may be treated as a group of similarly situated individuals separate from participants, and different treatment is permitted among beneficiaries based on bona fide employment-based classifications of the participants through whom the beneficiaries are receiving coverage. Thus, if the plan provides different benefits to full-time employees than to part-time employees, then it may also provide different benefits to dependents of full-time employees than to dependents of part-time employees. Similarly, different treatment is permitted based on the beneficiary's relationship to the participant (for example, as a spouse or as a dependent child). Different treatment is also permitted based on the beneficiary's marital status, based on a dependent

A. HIPAA Interim Final Rules and Proposed Rules, continued

Federal Register / Vol. 66, No. 5 / Monday, January 8, 2001 / Rules and Regulations   1383

child's age or student status, or based on any other factor if the factor is not a health factor.

The rules in these interim regulations allowing the different treatment of individuals in different groups of similarly situated individuals are distinct from rules requiring that qualified beneficiaries under a COBRA continuation provision [a] have available the same coverage as similarly situated non-COBRA beneficiaries. Although these interim regulations would not prohibit making benefit packages available to non-COBRA beneficiaries (such as current employees) that are not made available to COBRA qualified beneficiaries (such as former employees), the COBRA continuation provisions prohibit such a difference.

Finally, all of the requirements relating to determining groups of similarly situated individuals are subject to other rules in these interim regulations permitting favorable treatment of individuals with certain adverse health factors (discussed below under the heading "More Favorable Treatment of Individuals with Adverse Health Factors Permitted").

Nonconfinement Provisions

Some group health plans and health insurance issuers refuse to provide benefits to an individual based on the individual's confinement to a hospital or other health care institution at the time coverage otherwise would become effective. Plan provisions like these are often called "nonconfinement clauses." Any reasonable interpretation or application of the statutory HIPAA nondiscrimination provisions prohibits a plan or issuer from imposing a nonconfinement clause.[9] Thus, a plan or issuer may not deny the eligibility of any individual to enroll for benefits or charge any individual a higher premium (or contribution) because the individual, or a dependent of the individual, is confined to a hospital or other health care institution. In addition, some plans and issuers refuse to provide benefits to an individual based on an individual's inability to engage in normal life activities. A plan or issuer generally may not deny the eligibility of any

individual to enroll for benefits or charge any individual a higher premium (or contribution) based on any individual's ability to engage in normal life activities. However, these interim regulations provide an exception that permits plans and issuers to distinguish among employees based on the performance of services. Although in practice nonconfinement clauses generally apply only to dependents, in some cases they apply also to employees. Thus, the interim regulations clarify that a nonconfinement clause would also be impermissible if applied to an employee.

These rules are of particular interest in the case of a group health plan switching coverage from one health insurance issuer to a succeeding health insurance issuer. In such a case, the HIPAA nondiscrimination provisions prohibit the succeeding issuer from denying eligibility to any individual due to confinement to a hospital or other health care institution because such a denial would discriminate in eligibility based on one or more health factors. The obligation of the succeeding issuer to provide coverage to such an individual does not preempt any obligation that the prior issuer may have under other applicable law, including State extension of benefits laws.

Actively-at-Work and Other Service Requirements

Some group health plans and health insurance issuers refuse to provide benefits to an individual if the individual is not actively at work on the day the individual would otherwise become eligible for benefits. Plan provisions like these are often called "actively-at-work clauses." These interim regulations provide that a plan or issuer generally may not impose an "actively-at-work clause." That is, these interim regulations prohibit a plan or issuer from denying the eligibility of any individual to enroll for benefits or charging any individual a higher premium or contribution based on whether an individual is actively at work (including whether an individual is continuously employed). However, an actively-at-work clause is permitted if individuals who are absent from work due to any health factor (for example, individuals taking sick leave) are treated, for purposes of health coverage, as if they are actively at work. Accordingly, plan provisions that delay enrollment until an individual is actively at work on a day following a waiting period (or for a continuous period) are prohibited unless absence

from work due to any health factor is considered being actively at work.

These interim regulations also provide an exception for the first day of work to the general prohibition against actively-at-work clauses. Under the exception, a plan or issuer may require an individual to begin work before coverage may become effective.

The interim regulations explain the relationship between the rules governing actively-at-work clauses and the rules describing similarly situated individuals. Under the interim regulations, a plan or issuer is generally permitted to distinguish between groups of similarly situated individuals (provided the distinction is not directed at individual participants or beneficiaries based on a health factor). Examples illustrate that a plan or issuer may condition coverage on an individual's meeting the plan's requirement of working full-time (such as a minimum of 250 hours in a three-month period or 30 hours per week). In addition, a plan or issuer may terminate coverage for former employees while providing coverage to current employees without violating the HIPAA nondiscrimination provisions if the rules describing similarly situated individuals are satisfied, even if the former employee is unable to work due to a health factor. Similarly, a plan or issuer may charge a higher premium to employees no longer performing services than to employees currently performing services without violating the HIPAA nondiscrimination provisions if the rules describing similarly situated individuals are met. An example illustrates that the interim regulations would not, however, permit a plan or issuer to treat individuals on annual or bereavement leave better than individuals on sick leave because groups of similarly situated individuals cannot be established based on any health factor (including the taking of sick leave).

In any case, other federal or State laws, including the COBRA continuation provisions and the Family and Medical Leave Act of 1993 (FMLA), may require individuals to be offered coverage and set limits on the premium or contribution rate.

Bona Fide Wellness Programs

The HIPAA nondiscrimination provisions do not prevent a plan or issuer from establishing premium discounts or rebates or modifying otherwise applicable copayments or deductibles in return for adherence to programs of health promotion and disease prevention. Thus, there is an exception to the general rule prohibiting

---

[a] The term COBRA continuation provision is defined in 26 CFR 54.9801–2T, 29 CFR 2590.701–2, and 45 CFR 144.103.

[9] For an example illustrating that the imposition of a nonconfinement clause is not a good faith interpretation of the HIPAA nondiscrimination provisions, and the rule requiring that individuals denied enrollment without a good faith interpretation of the law be provided an opportunity to enroll, see the discussion below under the heading "Transitional Rule for Individuals Previously Denied Coverage Based on a Health Factor."

A. HIPAA Interim Final Rules and Proposed Rules, continued

discrimination based on a health factor if the reward, such as a premium discount or waiver of a cost-sharing requirement, is based on participation in a program of health promotion or disease prevention. The April 1997 interim rules, these interim regulations, and proposed regulations published elsewhere in this issue of the Federal Register refer to programs of health promotion and disease prevention allowed under this exception as "bona fide wellness programs." For a discussion of bona fide wellness programs, see the preamble to proposed regulations published elsewhere in this issue of the Federal Register.

More Favorable Treatment of Individuals With Adverse Health Factors Permitted

Many group health plans make certain periods of extended coverage available to employees no longer performing services only if the employee is unable to work due to disability, and many plans make coverage available to dependent children past a certain age only if the child is disabled. Some plans waive or reduce the required employee contribution for coverage if the employee or a member of the employee's immediate family is in a critical medical condition for a prolonged period. Disability and medical condition are listed in the statute as health factors, and several commenters recognized that, under one possible interpretation of the HIPAA nondiscrimination requirements, plan provisions or practices such as these would be impermissible. These commenters asked for guidance clarifying that plan provisions and practices like these would be permissible. Other commenters cited the rule under the COBRA continuation provisions permitting plans to require payment of a higher amount during the disability extension than during other periods of COBRA coverage and asked whether following this COBRA rule is permissible under the HIPAA nondiscrimination requirements.

Eligibility. These interim regulations permit plans and issuers to establish rules for eligibility favoring individuals based on an adverse health factor, such as disability. Thus, a plan or issuer does not violate the HIPAA nondiscrimination requirements by making extended coverage available to employees no longer providing services only if the employee is unable to work due to disability nor by making coverage available to dependent children past a certain age only if the child is disabled. Examples clarify this rule.

Premiums. These interim regulations also address the circumstances under which differential premiums (or contributions) may be charged to an individual based on an adverse health factor. These interim regulations permit plans and issuers to charge a higher rate in some situations and also a lower rate to individuals based on an adverse health factor, such as disability. A higher rate may be charged only in situations where the individual with the adverse health factor would not have coverage were it not for the adverse health factor. Thus, in a case where a plan or issuer makes extended coverage available to employees no longer performing services only if the employee is unable to work due to disability, the plan could require a higher payment from the employee only while the employee is receiving coverage under that special eligibility provision. However, the plan could not charge a disabled employee a higher rate than nondisabled employees while the disabled employee was still eligible under a generally-applicable eligibility provision, rather than the special extended coverage provision. Accordingly, under the interim regulations, a plan or issuer could charge a higher rate for COBRA coverage during the disability extension than for COBRA coverage outside the disability extension (and the result is the same if the extended coverage for disability is provided pursuant to State law or plan provision rather than pursuant to a COBRA continuation provision).[10]

Although charging a higher rate based on an adverse health factor is limited to the situation in which coverage would not be available but for the adverse health factor, under these interim regulations a plan or issuer is always permitted to charge an individual a lower rate based on an adverse health factor. Thus, even though an employee is receiving coverage under the same eligibility provision as other employees who are required to pay the full employee share of the premium, under the interim regulations it is permissible to waive or reduce the employee share of the premium if the employee or a family member is in critical medical condition for a prolonged period.

---

[10] This result is consistent with the result under the COBRA continuation provisions. Under those provisions, plans are generally permitted to require payment of up to 102 percent of the applicable premium but are permitted to require payment for coverage of a disabled qualified beneficiary of up to 150 percent of the applicable premium during the disability extension period.

No Effect on Other Laws

Compliance with these interim regulations is not determinative of compliance with any other provision of ERISA, or any other State or federal law, including the Americans with Disabilities Act. Therefore, while these interim regulations generally do not impose any new disclosure requirements on plans or issuers, other applicable law continues to apply. For example, under Title I of ERISA, administrators of ERISA-covered group health plans are required to provide participants and beneficiaries with a summary plan description that is sufficiently accurate and comprehensive to reasonably apprise such participants and beneficiaries of their rights and obligations under the plan.[11] In addition, some courts have held that fiduciaries of ERISA-covered group health plans are obligated to ensure that plan documents and disclosures are consistent with applicable disclosure requirements and do not serve to mislead or misinform participants and beneficiaries concerning their rights and obligations under the plans in which they participate.[12] Fiduciaries are advised to take steps to ensure that plan disclosures are accurate and are not misleading.

These interim regulations are also not determinative of compliance with the COBRA continuation provisions, or any other State or federal law, such as the Americans with Disabilities Act.

Applicability Date

These interim regulations generally apply for plan years beginning on or after July 1, 2001 (although some provisions apply earlier, as discussed below under the heading "III. Format of Regulations"). As noted above, in the preamble to the April 1997 interim rules the Departments stated that they intended to issue further regulations on the statutory nondiscrimination rules. That preamble also stated that in no event would the Departments take any enforcement action against a plan or issuer that had sought to comply in good faith with the statutory nondiscrimination provisions before the additional guidance was issued. The Departments will not take any enforcement action against a plan or issuer with respect to efforts to comply in good faith with the statutory nondiscrimination provisions before the first plan year beginning on or after July 1, 2001. (See the description of

---

[11] See ERISA section 102, and the Department of Labor's regulations issued thereunder.

[12] See *Varity Corp* v. *Howe*, 516 U.S. 489, 506 (1996).

A. HIPAA Interim Final Rules and Proposed Rules, continued

transitional rules immediately below regarding certain interpretations that are not good faith interpretations of the statutory nondiscrimination requirements.) Upon the applicability of these regulations, however, good faith efforts to comply with the statutory provisions addressed by these interim regulations may not be sufficient to avoid adverse enforcement actions by the Departments. Therefore, for plan years beginning on or after July 1, 2001, plans and issuers must comply with the requirements of these regulations in order to avoid adverse enforcement actions. As discussed earlier, under the heading "Background," the period for good faith compliance continues with respect to bona fide wellness programs until further guidance is issued.

Transitional Rules for Individuals Previously Denied Coverage Based on a Health Factor

The April 1997 interim rules clarified that a plan or issuer violates the HIPAA nondiscrimination requirements if it requires an individual to pass a physical examination as a condition for enrollment, even if the condition is imposed only on late enrollees. The HIPAA nondiscrimination requirements apply both to eligibility and continued eligibility of any individual to enroll under a plan. Consequently, once HIPAA became effective with respect to a plan or health insurance issuer, it was a violation of the nondiscrimination requirements to continue to deny an individual eligibility to enroll if the reason the individual was denied enrollment previously was due to one or more health factors (such as requiring the individual to pass a physical examination).

On December 29, 1997, the Departments issued in the **Federal Register** a clarification of the April 1997 interim rules relating to individuals who were denied coverage due to a health factor before the effective date of HIPAA (62 FR 67689). The clarification restates the requirement of the April 1997 interim rules that an individual cannot be denied coverage based on a health factor on or after the effective date of HIPAA. The clarification then states that individuals to whom coverage had not been made available before the effective date of HIPAA based on a health factor and who enrolled when first eligible on or after the effective date of the HIPAA nondiscrimination provisions could not be treated as a late enrollee for purposes of the HIPAA preexisting condition exclusion provisions. Under the clarification, individuals to whom coverage had not been made available

include any individual who did not apply for coverage because it was reasonable to believe that the application would have been futile. The rules in the clarification apply whether or not the plan offered late enrollment.

Neither the April 1997 interim rules nor the December 1997 guidance clearly addressed the situation where an individual was denied only late enrollment based on a health factor prior to the effective date of HIPAA and, by the effective date of HIPAA, the plan eliminated late enrollment. For example, prior to HIPAA many plans and issuers allowed individuals to enroll when first eligible without regard to health status, but allowed late enrollees to enroll only if they could pass a physical examination (or present evidence of good health). Upon the effective date of HIPAA, some of these plans and issuers eliminated late enrollment.

Any plan or issuer that permitted these individuals to enroll once the HIPAA nondiscrimination provisions took effect, of course, is in compliance with this provision of the nondiscrimination rules. In contrast, a plan or issuer that continued to deny coverage to these individuals may have done so based on a good faith interpretation of the statute and the Departments' published guidance. For example, a plan or issuer might reasonably have thought that HIPAA did not require it to remedy pre-HIPAA denials of late enrollment based on a health factor for individuals who could have enrolled initially without regard to their health if the plan or issuer eliminated late enrollment by the effective date of HIPAA.

The interim regulations provide transitional rules for situations where coverage was denied to individuals based on one or more health factors, both where the denial was based on a good faith interpretation of the statute or the Departments' published guidance and where it was not. In either event, a safe harbor provides that the Departments will not take any enforcement action with respect to such a denial of coverage if the plan or issuer complies with the transitional rules.

Where the denial was not based on a good faith interpretation, the interim regulations provide that the plan or issuer is required to give the individual an opportunity to enroll (including notice of an opportunity to enroll) that continues for at least 30 days. This opportunity must be presented not later than March 9, 2001. If the opportunity is presented within the first plan year beginning on or after the effective date of the statutory HIPAA

nondiscrimination rules, the enrollment must be effective within that plan year. If this enrollment opportunity is presented after such plan year, the individual must be given an option to have coverage effective either (1) prospectively from the date the plan receives a request for enrollment in connection with the enrollment opportunity or (2) retroactively to the first day of the first plan year beginning on HIPAA's effective date for the plan (or, if the individual otherwise first became eligible to enroll for coverage after that date, on the date the individual was otherwise eligible to enroll in the plan).

The reason for giving the individual the opportunity to elect retroactive coverage is to make the individual whole; that is, to put the individual in the same financial condition that the individual would have been in had the individual not been denied enrollment. Thus, if the individual elects retroactive coverage, the plan or issuer may require the individual to pay premiums or contributions for the retroactive period (but the plan or issuer cannot charge interest on that amount).

The rule differs for situations where coverage was denied to individuals based on one or more health factors but where the denial was based on a good faith interpretation of the statute or the Departments' prior published guidance. In those situations, these interim regulations require plans and issuers to give the individuals an opportunity to enroll that continues for at least 30 days and with coverage effective not later than July 1, 2001.

In both situations (whether the denial of coverage was or was not based on a good faith interpretation), the interim regulations also clarify that, once enrolled, these individuals cannot be treated as late enrollees. The individual's enrollment date under the plan is the effective date of HIPAA (or, if later, the date the individual would have otherwise been eligible to enroll). In addition, any period between an individual's enrollment date and the effective date of coverage is treated as a waiting period. Thus, for example, with respect to a calendar year plan that is not collectively bargained, an individual who was previously denied late enrollment due to a health factor before the effective date of HIPAA has an enrollment date of January 1, 1998 (HIPAA's effective date for that plan) and a waiting period that begins on that date. Moreover, because any waiting period must begin on the individual's enrollment date, January 1, 1998, and the maximum preexisting exclusion period that can be applied is 12 months,

A. HIPAA Interim Final Rules and Proposed Rules, continued

individuals who enroll in the plan on July 1, 2001 cannot be subject to any preexisting condition exclusion period.

Special Transitional Rule for Self-Funded Non-Federal Governmental Plans Exempted Under 45 CFR 146.180

The sponsor of a self-funded non-Federal governmental plan may elect under section 2721(b)(2) of the PHS Act and 45 CFR 146.180 to exempt its group health plan from the nondiscrimination requirements of section 2702 of the PHS Act and 45 CFR 146.121. If the plan sponsor subsequently chooses to bring the plan into compliance with these nondiscrimination requirements, the plan must provide notice to that effect to individuals who were denied enrollment based on one or more health factors, and afford those individuals an opportunity, that continues for at least 30 days, to enroll in the plan. (An individual is considered to have been denied coverage if he or she failed to apply for coverage because, given an exemption election under 45 CFR 146.180, it was reasonable to believe

that an application for coverage would have been denied based on a health factor.) The notice must specify the effective date of compliance, and inform the individual regarding any enrollment restrictions that may apply under the terms of the plan once the plan comes into compliance. The plan may not treat the individual as a late enrollee or a special enrollee. Coverage must be effective no later than the date the exemption election under 45 CFR 146.180 (with regard to these nondiscrimination requirements) no longer applies, or July 1, 2001 (if later) and the plan was acting in accordance with a good faith interpretation of the statutory HIPAA nondiscrimination provisions and guidance published by the Health Care Financing Administration.

III. Format of Regulations

Final and Temporary Treasury Regulations

The Department of the Treasury is issuing a portion of these regulations as final regulations and a portion as

temporary and cross-referencing proposed regulations. The April 1997 interim rules were originally issued by Treasury in the form of temporary and cross-referencing proposed regulations. Under section 7805(e)(2) of the Code, however, any temporary regulation issued under the Code expires within three years after the date issued. Treasury is issuing final regulations that restate the rules relating to the HIPAA nondiscrimination requirements from the April 1997 regulations without significant modification. The final regulations apply March 9, 2001. Table 1 identifies which paragraphs of the final regulation issued today correspond to which paragraphs of the April 1997 regulation. New guidance being published today by Treasury is being issued as temporary and cross-referencing proposed regulations. This guidance will apply to group health plans beginning with the first plan year on or after July 1, 2001. (These new temporary regulations will also expire after three years pursuant to section 7805(e) of the Code.)

TABLE 1.—COMPARISON OF TREASURY'S APRIL 1997 REGULATIONS WITH TREASURY'S FINAL REGULATIONS

April 1997 regulations	Final regulation under § 9802
§ 54.9802–1T(a)(1)	§ 54.9802–1(a)(1),(2); (b)(1)
§ 54.9802–1T(a)(2)(i)	§ 54.9802–1(b)(2)(i)(A)
§ 54.9802–1T(a)(3)	[The corresponding provision is in the new temporary regulations.]
§ 54.9802–1T(a)(4)	§ 54.9802–1(b)(1)(iii)
§ 54.9802–1T(b)(1)	§ 54.9802–1(c)(1)(i)
§ 54.9802–1T(b)(2)(i)	§ 54.9802–1(c)(2)(i)
§ 54.9802–1T(b)(2)(ii)	§ 54.9802–1(b)(2)(i); (c)(3)
§ 54.9802–1T(b)(3)	[The corresponding provision is in the new proposed regulations for wellness programs.]

Interim Final Labor and HHS Regulations

The guidance issued by the Departments of Labor (Labor) and Health and Human Services (HHS) in April 1997 is not subject to a statutory expiration date. Accordingly, the Labor and HHS guidance is being published as interim final regulations. These regulations contain two applicability dates that parallel the two separate applicability dates in the Treasury guidance. Table 2 identifies which paragraphs of the interim final regulation issued today are applicable on March 9, 2001 and which paragraphs apply on or after July 1, 2001.

TABLE 2.—APPLICABILITY DATES FOR THE INTERIM FINAL REGULATIONS

Subject	Paragraph of the interim final regulations	Applies 3/9/01	Applies plan years beginning on or after 7/1/2001
Health factors	(a)(1)		
Health factors—Evidence of insurability—Conditions arising out of an act of domestic violence.	(a)(2)(i)	✔	
Health factors—Evidence of insurability—Participation in certain activities.	(a)(2)(ii)		✔
Health factors—The decision whether health coverage is elected	(a)(3)		✔
Prohibited discrimination in rules for eligibility—General rule	(b)(1)(i)	✔	
Prohibited discrimination in rules for eligibility—Rules for eligibility described.	(b)(1)(ii)		✔
Prohibited discrimination in eligibility—General rule—Example 1	(b)(1)(iii) Example 1	✔	
Prohibited discrimination in eligibility—General rule—Examples 2 through 4.	(b)(1)(iii) Examples 2 through 4		✔
Prohibited discrimination in eligibility—Application to benefits—No benefits mandated.	(b)(2)(i)(A)	✔	

A. HIPAA Interim Final Rules and Proposed Rules, continued

TABLE 2.—APPLICABILITY DATES FOR THE INTERIM FINAL REGULATIONS—Continued

Subject	Paragraph of the Interim final regulations	Applies 3/9/01	Applies plan years beginning on or after 7/1/2001
Prohibited discrimination in eligibility—Application to benefits—Nondiscriminatory benefit restrictions permitted.	(b)(2)(i)(B), (C), & (D)		✔
Prohibited discrimination in eligibility—Application to benefits—Certain cost-sharing mechanisms.	(b)(2)(ii)	✔	
Prohibited discrimination in eligibility—Application to benefits—Source-of-injury exclusions.	(b)(2)(iii)		✔
Prohibited discrimination in eligibility—Application to benefits—Relationship to HIPAA preexisting condition exclusion rules.	(b)(3)		✔
Prohibited discrimination in premiums or contributions—General rule	(c)(1)(i)	✔	
Prohibited discrimination in premiums or contributions—Determining an individual's premium rate.	(c)(1)(ii)		✔
Prohibited discrimination in premiums or contributions—Group rating on health factors not restricted.	(c)(2)(i)	✔	
Prohibited discrimination in premiums or contributions—List billing based on a health factor prohibited.	(c)(2)(ii) & (iii)		✔
Prohibited discrimination in premiums or contributions—Exception for bona fide wellness programs.	(c)(3)	✔	
Similarly situated individuals	(d)		✔
Nonconfinement and actively-at-work provisions	(e)		✔
Bona fide wellness programs	(f) [Reserved.]	See proposed regulations published elsewhere in this Federal Register.	
More favorable treatment of individuals with adverse health factors permitted.	(g)		✔
No effect on other laws	(h)		✔

IV. Interim Final Regulations With Request for Comments

The principal purpose of these interim final regulations is to provide additional guidance on how to comply with the HIPAA nondiscrimination provisions contained in section 9802 of the Code, section 702 of ERISA, and section 2702 of the PHS Act. Code section 9833, ERISA section 734, and PHS Act section 2792 authorize the Secretaries of the Treasury, Labor, and HHS to issue any interim final rules as the Secretaries deem are appropriate to carry out certain provisions of HIPAA, including the nondiscrimination provisions. As explained below, the Secretaries have determined that these regulations should be issued as interim final rules with requests for comments.

HIPAA was enacted in August of 1996. The Secretaries first issued interim final rules providing guidance on HIPAA's nondiscrimination provisions in April of 1997. In publishing this guidance, the Secretaries relied on the authority granted in section 9833 of the Code, section 734 of ERISA, and section 2792 of the PHS Act, as well as other authority including section 101(g)(4) of HIPAA and section 505 of ERISA. As part of the April 1997 rulemaking, the Secretaries requested comments on whether additional guidance was needed concerning the extent to which the statutory HIPAA nondiscrimination provisions prohibit discrimination against individuals in eligibility for particular benefits; the extent to which the statute may permit benefit limitations based on the source of an injury; the permissible standards for defining groups of similarly situated individuals; the application of the prohibitions on discrimination between groups of similarly situated individuals; and the permissible standards for determining bona fide wellness programs. Numerous comments were received in response to this request.

After evaluating all of the comments, and after speaking with various interested parties in the course of an extensive educational outreach campaign, the Departments have developed these comprehensive regulations. Among other things, the comments reflected the need for more comprehensive guidance on the application of the nondiscrimination provisions. In the period since HIPAA was enacted and the April 1997 regulations were issued, numerous issues have arisen concerning how plans and issuers should apply the nondiscrimination provisions. In addition, the number of comments and the breadth of issues raised demonstrates that these regulations should go into effect on an interim basis pending receipt of further comments. This need to act on an interim basis is also supported by the General Accounting Office's request that the Departments "promptly complete regulations related to HIPAA's non-discrimination provisions" (GAO/HEHS 00–85). Therefore, the Departments have determined that it is appropriate to issue the guidance on an interim final basis, with the exception of the bona fide wellness program provisions.[13] With respect to these last provisions, the Departments would like to better develop the administrative record before any provisions regarding such programs go into effect.

The Secretaries believe that this period of interim effectiveness will provide ample opportunity for the regulated community to comment specifically on this comprehensive guidance, providing a sound basis for developing final rules. The Departments are seeking comments from all those affected by these regulations, and the Departments will consider such comments and will reevaluate these regulations following the comment period in the same way that it would if the regulations had been published in proposed form. Based on such comments and other information obtained through the administration of the nondiscrimination requirements, the Departments will make any necessary modifications to the regulations when they are issued in final form.

[13] See proposed rules relating to bona fide wellness programs published elsewhere in this issue of the Federal Register.

A. HIPAA Interim Final Rules and Proposed Rules, continued

1388   Federal Register / Vol. 66, No. 5 / Monday, January 8, 2001 / Rules and Regulations

V. Economic Impact and Paperwork Burden

Summary—Department of Labor and Department of Health and Human Services

HIPAA's nondiscrimination provisions generally prohibit group health plans and group health plan issuers from discriminating against individuals in eligibility or premium on the basis of health status factors. The Departments crafted this regulation to secure these protections as intended by Congress in as economically efficient a manner as possible, and believe that the economic benefits of the regulation outweigh its costs.

The primary economic benefits associated with securing HIPAA's nondiscrimination provisions derive from increased access to affordable group health plan coverage for individuals with health problems. Increased access benefits both newly covered individuals and society at large. It fosters expanded insurance coverage, timelier and fuller medical care, better health outcomes, and improved productivity and quality of life. This is especially true for the individuals most affected by HIPAA's nondiscrimination provisions—those with adverse health conditions. Denied insurance, individuals in poorer health are more likely to suffer economic hardship, to forgo badly needed care for financial reasons, and to suffer adverse health outcomes as a result. For them, gaining insurance is more likely to mean gaining economic security, receiving timely, quality care, and living healthier, more productive lives.

Additional economic benefits derive directly from the improved clarity provided by the regulation. The regulation will reduce uncertainty and costly disputes and promote confidence in health benefits' value, thereby improving labor market efficiency and fostering the establishment and continuation of group health plans.

The Departments estimate that the cost of plans to implement amendments in order to comply with this regulation, revise materials accordingly, and provide notices of opportunities to enroll as required by the regulation will amount to less than $19 million. This is a one-time cost distinguishable from the transfer that will result from the self-implementing requirements of HIPAA's nondiscrimination provisions and the discretion exercised by the Departments in this regulation.

Such a transfer occurs when resources are redistributed without any direct change in aggregate social welfare. In this instance, the premium and claims cost incurred by group health plans to provide coverage under HIPAA's statutory nondiscrimination provisions to individuals previously denied coverage or offered restricted coverage based on health factors are offset by the commensurate or greater benefits realized by the newly eligible participants on whose behalf the premiums or claims are paid. Although the Departments are not aware of any published estimates of transfers attributable to HIPAA's statutory nondiscrimination provisions, a rough attempt to gauge the order of magnitude of this transfer suggests that it may amount to more than $400 million annually, which is a small fraction of 1 percent of total expenditures by group plans. The regulation clarifies at the margin exactly what practices are permitted or prohibited by these provisions, and may have the effect of slightly increasing the amount of this transfer.

Executive Order 12866—Department of Labor and Department of Health and Human Services

Under Executive Order 12866, the Departments must determine whether a regulatory action is "significant" and therefore subject to the requirements of the Executive Order and subject to review by the Office of Management and Budget (OMB). Under section 3(f), the order defines a "significant regulatory action" as an action that is likely to result in a rule (1) having an annual effect on the economy of $100 million or more, or adversely and materially affecting a sector of the economy, productivity, competition, jobs, the environment, public health or safety, or State, local or tribal governments or communities (also referred to as "economically significant"); (2) creating serious inconsistency or otherwise interfering with an action taken or planned by another agency; (3) materially altering the budgetary impacts of entitlement grants, user fees, or loan programs or the rights and obligations of recipients thereof; or (4) raising novel legal or policy issues arising out of legal mandates, the President's priorities, or the principles set forth in the Executive Order.

Pursuant to the terms of the Executive Order, it has been determined that this action raises novel policy issues arising out of legal mandates. In addition, the magnitude of the transfer that arises from the implementation of HIPAA's statutory nondiscrimination provisions is estimated to exceed $100 million. Therefore, this notice is "significant" and subject to OMB review under Sections 3(f)(1) and 3(f)(4) of the Executive Order. Consistent with the Executive Order, the Departments have assessed the costs and benefits of this regulatory action. The Departments' assessment, and the analysis underlying that assessment, is detailed below. The Departments performed a comprehensive, unified analysis to estimate the costs and benefits attributable to the interim regulation for purposes of compliance with the Executive Order 12866, the Regulatory Flexibility Act, and the Paperwork Reduction Act.

1. Statement of Need for Proposed Action

These interim regulations are needed to clarify and interpret the HIPAA nondiscrimination provisions (prohibiting discrimination against individual participants and beneficiaries based on health status) under section 702 of the Employee Retirement Income Security Act of 1974 (ERISA), section 2702 of the Public Health Service Act, and section 9802 of the Internal Revenue Code of 1986. The provisions are needed to ensure that group health plans and group health insurers and issuers do not discriminate against individuals, participants, and beneficiaries based on any health factors with respect to health care coverage and premiums. Additional guidance was required to explain the application of the statute to benefits, clarify the relationship between the HIPAA nondiscrimination provisions and the HIPAA preexisting condition exclusion limitations, explain the applications of these provisions to premiums, describe similarly situated individuals, explain the application of the provisions to actively-at-work and nonconfinement clauses, clarify that more favorable treatment of individuals with medical needs generally is permitted, and describe plans' and issuers' obligations with respect to plan amendments.

2. Costs and Benefits

The primary economic benefits associated with the HIPAA nondiscrimination provisions derive from increased access to affordable group health plan coverage for individuals with health problems. Expanding access benefits both newly covered individuals and society at large by fostering expanded insurance coverage, timelier and fuller medical care, better health outcomes, and improved productivity and quality of life. Additional economic benefits derive directly from the improved clarity provided by the regulation. By clarifying employees' rights and plan sponsors' obligations under HIPAA's

A. HIPAA Interim Final Rules and Proposed Rules, continued

nondiscrimination provisions, the regulation will reduce uncertainty and costly disputes and promote confidence in health benefits' value, thereby improving labor market efficiency and fostering the establishment and continuation of group health plans.

The Departments estimate that the cost to plans to implement amendments in order to comply with this regulation, revise materials accordingly, and provide notices of opportunities to enroll as required by the regulation will amount to less than $19 million. This is a one-time cost distinguishable from the transfer that will result from the self-implementing requirements of HIPAA's nondiscrimination provisions and the discretion exercised by the Departments in this regulation.

Such a transfer occurs when resources are redistributed without any direct change in aggregate social welfare. In this instance, the premium and claims cost incurred by group health plans to provide coverage under HIPAA's statutory nondiscrimination provisions to individuals previously denied coverage or offered restricted coverage based on health factors are offset by the commensurate or greater benefits realized by the newly eligible participants on whose behalf the premiums or claims are paid. Although the Departments are not aware of any published estimates of transfers attributable to HIPAA's statutory nondiscrimination provisions, a rough attempt to gauge the order of magnitude of this transfer suggests that it may amount to more than $400 million annually. The regulation clarifies at the margin exactly what practices are permitted or prohibited by these provisions, and may have the effect of slightly increasing the amount of this transfer. The Departments note that this transfer is the direct reflection of the intent and beneficial effect of HIPAA's nondiscrimination provisions: increasing access to affordable group health plan coverage for individuals with health problems. They also note that even the full transfer to plans attributable to HIPAA's statutory nondiscrimination provisions probably amounts to a small fraction of 1 percent of total expenditures by these plans.

The Departments believe that the benefits of the regulation outweigh its costs.

A fuller discussion of the Departments assessment of the costs and benefits of this regulation is provided below.

Regulatory Flexibility Act

The Regulatory Flexibility Act (5 U.S.C. 601 et seq.) (RFA) imposes certain requirements with respect to Federal rules that are subject to the notice and comment requirements of section 553(b) of the Administrative Procedure Act (5 U.S.C. 551 et seq.) and likely to have a significant economic impact on a substantial number of small entities. Unless an agency certifies that a proposed rule will not have a significant economic impact on a substantial number of small entities, section 603 of the RFA requires that the agency present an initial regulatory flexibility analysis at the time of the publication of the notice of proposed rule making describing the impact of the rule on small entities and seeking public comment on such impact. Small entities include small businesses, organizations, and governmental jurisdictions.

Because these rules are being issued as interim final rules and not as a notice of proposed rule making, the RFA does not apply and the Departments are not required to either certify that the rule will not have a significant impact on a substantial number of small businesses or conduct a regulatory flexibility analysis. The Departments nonetheless crafted this regulation in careful consideration of its effects on small entities, and have conducted an analysis of the likely impact of the rules on small entities.

For purposes of this discussion, the Departments consider a small entity to be an employee benefit plan with fewer than 100 participants. The basis of this definition is found in section 104(a)(2) of ERISA, which permits the Secretary of Labor to prescribe simplified annual reports for pension plans which cover fewer than 100 participants. The Departments believe that assessing the impact of this interim final rule on small plans is an appropriate substitute for evaluating the effect on small entities as that term is defined in the RFA.

Small plans in particular will benefit from the regulations' provisions that affirm and clarify the flexibility available to plans under HIPAA's nondiscrimination requirements. Consideration of small plans' needs and circumstances played an important part in the development of these provisions. These provisions are discussed in more detail below.

The Departments estimate that plans with 100 or fewer participants will incur costs of $4 million on aggregate to amend their provisions to comply with the regulation and revise their materials accordingly. These costs generally will fall directly to issuers who supply small group insurance products and stop-loss insurers who provide services to small self-insured plans, who will spread those costs across the much larger number of small plans that buy them. These same small plans will incur costs of $10 million to prepare and distribute notices of enrollment opportunities as required by the regulation, the Departments estimate. The total economic cost to small plans to comply with this regulation is estimated to be $14 million. This is a one-time cost distinguishable from the transfer that will result from the self-implementing requirements of HIPAA's nondiscrimination provisions and the discretion exercised by the Departments in this regulation.

Such a transfer occurs when resources are redistributed without any direct change in aggregate social welfare. In this instance, the premium and claims cost incurred by group health plans to provide coverage under HIPAA's statutory nondiscrimination provisions to individuals previously denied coverage or offered restricted coverage based on health factors are offset by the commensurate or greater benefits realized by the newly eligible participants on whose behalf the premiums or claims are paid. The Departments note that transfers to small plans attributable to HIPAA's statutory nondiscrimination provisions may amount to approximately $110 million. The regulation clarifies at the margin exactly what practices are permitted or prohibited by these provisions, and may have the effect of slightly increasing the amount of this transfer. The Departments note that this transfer is the direct reflection of the intent and beneficial effect of HIPAA's nondiscrimination provisions: increasing access to affordable group health plan coverage for individuals with health problems. They also note that even the full transfer to small plans attributable to HIPAA's statutory nondiscrimination provisions amounts to a small fraction of total expenditures by these plans.

Paperwork Reduction Act—Department of Labor and Department of the Treasury

1. Department of Labor

The Department of Labor, as part of its continuing effort to reduce paperwork and respondent burden, conducts a preclearance consultation program to provide the general public and federal agencies with an opportunity to comment on proposed and continuing collections of information in accordance with the Paperwork Reduction Act of 1995 (PRA 95), 44 U.S.C. 3506(c)(2)(A). This helps to ensure that requested data can be provided in the desired format,

A. HIPAA Interim Final Rules and Proposed Rules, continued

reporting burden (time and financial resources) is minimized, collection instruments are clearly understood, and the impact of collection requirements on respondents can be properly assessed.

Currently, the Pension and Welfare Benefits Administration (PWBA) is soliciting comments concerning the proposed information collection request (ICR) included in the Interim Final Rules for Nondiscrimination in Health Coverage in the Group Market.

The Department has submitted this ICR using emergency review procedures to the Office of Management and Budget (OMB) for its review and clearance in accordance with PRA 95. OMB approval has been requested by March 9, 2001. The Department and OMB are particularly interested in comments that:

• Evaluate whether the proposed collection of information is necessary for the proper performance of the functions of the agency, including whether the information will have practical utility;

• Evaluate the accuracy of the agency's estimate of the burden of the proposed collection of information, including the validity of the methodology and assumptions used;

• Enhance the quality, utility, and clarity of the information to be collected; and

• Minimize the burden of the collection of information on those who are to respond, including through the use of appropriate automated, electronic, mechanical, or other technological collection techniques or other forms of information technology, e.g., permitting electronic submission of the responses.

Comments on the collection of information should be sent to the Office of Information and Regulatory Affairs, Office of Management and Budget, Room 10235, New Executive Office Building, Washington DC 20503; Attention: Desk Officer for the Pension and Welfare Benefits Administration. Although comments may be submitted through March 9, 2001, OMB requests that comments be received within February 7, 2001 of the publication of the Interim Final Rule to ensure their consideration in OMB's review of the request for emergency approval. All comments will be shared among the Departments.

Requests for copies of the ICR may be addressed to: Gerald B. Lindrew, Office of Policy and Research, U.S. Department of Labor, Pension and Welfare Benefits Administration, 200 Constitution Avenue, NW, Room N–5647, Washington, DC, 20210. Telephone:

(202) 219–4782; Fax: (202) 219–4745 (these are not toll-free numbers).

2. Department of the Treasury

The collection of information is in 26 CFR 54.9802–1T(*i*)(3)(ii) and (iii). This information is required to be provided so that participants who have been denied group health plan coverage based on a health status factor may be made aware of the opportunity to enroll in the plan. The likely respondents are business or other for-profit institutions, non-profit institutions, small businesses or organizations, and Taft-Hartley trusts. Responses to this collection of information are mandatory for affected group health plans.

Books or records relating to a collection of information must be retained as long as their contents may become material in the administration of any internal revenue law. Generally, tax returns and tax return information are confidential, as required by 26 U.S.C. 6103.

Comments on the collection of information should be sent to the Office of Management and Budget, Attn: Desk Officer for the Department of the Treasury, Office of Information and Regulatory Affairs, Washington, DC, 20503, with copies to the Internal Revenue Service, Attn: IRS Reports Clearance Officer, T:FP, Washington, DC 20224. Comments on the collection of information should be received by February 7, 2001. In light of the request for OMB clearance by March 9, 2001, the early submission of comments is encouraged to ensure their consideration. Comments are specifically requested concerning:

• Whether the proposed collection of information is necessary for the proper performance of the functions of the Internal Revenue Service, including whether the information will have practical utility;

• How to enhance the quality, utility, and clarity of the information to be collected;

• How to minimize the burden of complying with the proposed collection of information, including the application of automated collection techniques or other forms of information technology; and

• Estimates of capital or start up costs and costs of operation, maintenance, and purchase of services to provide information.

3. Description of Collection of Information

29 CFR 2590.702(*i*)(3)(ii) and (iii) and 26 CFR 54.9802–1T(*i*)(3)(ii) and (iii) of these interim rules include information collection requests. Paragraphs (*i*)(3)(ii)

and (iii) describe the requirement that individuals previously denied coverage under a group health plan be provided with an opportunity to enroll in the plan, and a notice concerning this opportunity. Pursuant to paragraph (*i*)(3)(ii), where coverage denials were not based on a good faith interpretation of section 702 of the ERISA and section 9802 of the Code, notices of the opportunity for individuals previously denied coverage to enroll are required to be provided within 60 days of publication of this interim final rule. Where coverage was denied based on a good faith interpretation of section 702 of ERISA and section 9802 of the Code, the plan or issuer must provide notice of the opportunity to enroll that continues for at least 30 days, with coverage effective no later than July 1, 2001.

The method of estimating the hour and cost burdens of the information collection request is described in the section of this preamble appearing below entitled *Costs and Benefits of the Regulation*. Generally, the Departments have conservatively estimated that all group health plans that excluded individuals on the basis of health status factors prior to HIPAA's enactment will provide a notice of the opportunity to enroll to all participants. The total burden of providing notices to participants of private employers is divided equally between the Departments of Labor and Treasury.

Paragraph (h), *No effect on other laws*, is not considered to include an information collection request because the provision makes no substantive or material change to the Department of Labor's existing information collection request for the Summary Plan Description and Summary of Material Modifications currently approved under OMB control number 1210–0039.

Type of Review: New.

Agency: Pension and Welfare Benefits Administration, Department of Labor; U.S. Department of the Treasury, Internal Revenue Service.

Title: Notice of Opportunity To Enroll.

OMB Number: 1210–0NEW; 1545–0NEW.

Affected Public: Individuals or households; Business or other for-profit institutions; Not-for-profit institutions.

Total Respondents: 120,000.

Frequency of Response: One time.

Total Responses: 2.0 million.

Estimated Burden Hours: 5,950 (Pension and Welfare Benefits Administration); 5,950 (Internal Revenue Service).

Estimated Annual Costs (Operating and Maintenance): $5.1 million

A. HIPAA Interim Final Rules and Proposed Rules, continued

(Pension and Welfare Benefits Administration); $5.1 million (Internal Revenue Service).

Estimated Total Annual Costs: $5.1 million (Pension and Welfare Benefits Administration); $5.1 million (Internal Revenue Service).

Comments submitted in response to the information collection provisions of these Interim Final, final, and temporary rules will be shared among the Departments and summarized and/or included in the request for continuing OMB approval of the information collection request; they will also become a matter of public record.

Paperwork Reduction Act—Department of Health and Human Services

Under the Paperwork Reduction Act of 1995 (PRA), agencies are required to provide a 60-day notice in the **Federal Register** and solicit public comment before a collection of information requirement is submitted to the OMB for review and approval. In order to fairly evaluate whether an information collection should be approved by OMB, section 3506(c)(2)(A) of the PRA requires that we solicit comment on the following issues:

• Whether the information collection is necessary and useful to carry out the proper functions of the agency;

• The accuracy of the agency's estimate of the information collection burden;

• The quality, utility, and clarity of the information to be collected; and

• Recommendations to minimize the information collection burden on the affected public, including automated collection techniques.

We are, however, requesting an emergency review of this interim final rule with comment period. In compliance with section 3506(c)(2)(A) of the PRA, we are submitting to OMB the following requirements for emergency review. We are requesting an emergency review because the collection of this information is needed before the expiration of the normal time limits under OMB's regulations at 5 CFR Part 1320, to ensure compliance with section 2702 of the PHS Act. This section generally prohibits group health plans and group health insurance issuers from discriminating against individual participants or beneficiaries based on any health factor of such participants or beneficiaries. We cannot reasonably comply with normal clearance procedures because public harm is likely to result if the agency cannot enforce the requirements of this section 2702 of the PHS Act in order to ensure that individual participants or

beneficiaries are not subject to unfair discrimination.

HCFA is requesting OMB review and approval of this collection 60 working days after the publication of this rule, with a 180-day approval period. Written comments and recommendations will be accepted from the public if received by the individuals designated below within 30 working days after the publication of this rule.

During this 180-day period, we will publish a separate **Federal Register** notice announcing the initiation of an extensive 60-day agency review and public comment period on these requirements. We will submit the requirements for OMB review and an extension of this emergency approval.

We are soliciting public comment on each of the issues for the provisions summarized below that contain information collection requirements:

Section 146.121   Prohibiting Discrimination Against Participants and Beneficiaries Based on a Health Factor.

(h) *No effect on other laws.* Although this section generally does not impose new disclosure obligations on plans and issuers, this paragraph (h) states that this section does not affect any other laws, including those that require accurate disclosures and prohibit intentional misrepresentation. Therefore, plan documents (including, for example, group health insurance policies and certificates of insurance) must be amended if they do not accurately reflect the requirements set forth in this section, by the applicability date of this section.

The revisions to the plan documents are intended to eliminate provisions that do not comply with the HIPAA nondiscrimination statute and regulations. In particular, it is anticipated that changes will be required to the majority of actively-at-work provisions and nonconfinement clauses found in plan documents. The modifications are to be made by the applicability date of the regulation and the requirements do not impose any on-going burden. The revisions are anticipated to take 100 hours for state governmental plans and 4,900 hours for local governmental plans. The changes are expected to involve one hour of an attorney's time at a $72 hourly rate. The corresponding plan amendment cost to be performed by service providers who are acting on behalf of the plans, is $32,000 for State governmental plans and $1,311,000 for local governmental plans.

(i) *Special transitional rule for self-funded non-Federal governmental plans*

exempted under 45 CFR 146.180. Paragraph (4)(i) requires that if coverage has been denied to any individual because the sponsor of a self-funded non-Federal governmental plan has elected under § 146.180 of this part to exempt the plan from the requirements of this section, and the plan sponsor subsequently chooses to bring the plan into compliance with the requirements of this section, the plan must: notify the individual that the plan will be coming into compliance with the requirements of this section; afford the individual an opportunity that continues for at least 30 days, specify the effective date of compliance; and inform the individual regarding any enrollment restrictions that may apply under the terms of the plan once the plan is in compliance with this section (as a matter of administrative convenience; the notice may be disseminated to all employees).

The regulation clarifies that self-funded non-Federal governmental plans are required to give individuals who were previously discriminated against an opportunity to enroll, including notice of an opportunity to enroll. The development of the number of plans that are required to notify individuals were conservatively arrived at by assuming that all plans which have excluded individuals must notify all individuals who are eligible to participate in the plan. Development of the transitional notices are estimated to take 0 hours for State governmental plans and 200 hours for local governmental plans. The corresponding burden for work performed by service providers is anticipated to be $1,000 for State governmental plans and $535,000 for local governmental plans. The Department estimates that the burden to distribute transitional notices will require State governmental plans 800 hours and 1,400 hours for local governmental plans. The corresponding distribution burden performed by service providers is $72,000 for State governmental plans and $158,000 for local governmental plans.

The above costs will be reduced to the extent that State and local governmental plans have elected to opt out of the HIPAA requirements. As of the date of publishing, approximately 600 plans have opted out of the HIPAA statutory and regulatory requirements.

We have submitted a copy of this rule to OMB for its review of the information collection requirements. These requirements are not effective until they have been approved by OMB. A notice will be published in the **Federal Register** when approval is obtained.

If you comment on any of these information collection and record

A. HIPAA Interim Final Rules and Proposed Rules, continued

1392   Federal Register / Vol. 66, No. 5 / Monday, January 8, 2001 / Rules and Regulations

keeping requirements, please mail copies directly to the following:

Health Care Financing Administration, Office of Information Services, Information Technology Investment Management Group, Division of HCFA Enterprise Standards, Room C2–26–17, 7500 Security Boulevard, Baltimore, MD 21244–1850, Attn: John Burke HCFA–2022,

and

Office of Information and Regulatory Affairs, Office of Management and Budget, Room 10235, New Executive Office Building, Washington, DC 20503, Attn.: Allison Herron Eydt, HCFA–2022.

Small Business Regulatory Enforcement Fairness Act

This interim final rule is subject to the provisions of the Small Business Regulatory Enforcement Fairness Act of 1996 (5 U.S.C. 801 *et seq.*) and is being transmitted to Congress and the Comptroller General for review. The interim final rule, is a "major rule," as that term is defined in 5 U.S.C. 804, because it is likely to result in an annual effect on the economy of $100 million or more. As such, this interim final rule is being transmitted to Congress and the Comptroller General for review.

Unfunded Mandates Reform Act

For purposes of the Unfunded Mandates Reform Act of 1995 (Pub. L. 104–4), as well as Executive Order 12875, this interim final rule does not include any Federal mandate that may result in expenditures by State, local, or tribal governments, nor does it include mandates which may impose an annual burden of $100 million or more on the private sector.

Federalism Statement—Department of Labor and Department of Health and Human Services

Executive Order 13132 (August 4, 1999) outlines fundamental principles of federalism, and requires the adherence to specific criteria by federal agencies in the process of their formulation and implementation of policies that have substantial direct effects on the States, the relationship between the national government and States, or on the distribution of power and responsibilities among the various levels of government. Agencies promulgating regulations that have these federalism implications must consult with State and local officials, and describe the extent of their consultation and the nature of the concerns of State and local officials in the preamble to the regulation.

In the Departments' view, these interim final regulations do not have federalism implications, because they do not have substantial direct effects on the States, the relationship between the national government and States, or on the distribution of power and responsibilities among various levels of government. This is largely because, with respect to health insurance issuers, the vast majority of States have enacted laws which meet or exceed the federal standards in HIPAA prohibiting discrimination based on health factors. Therefore, the regulations are not likely to require substantial additional oversight of States by the Department of Health and Human Services.

In general, through section 514, ERISA supersedes State laws to the extent that they relate to any covered employee benefit plan, and preserves State laws that regulate insurance, banking, or securities. While ERISA prohibits States from regulating a plan as an insurance or investment company or bank, HIPAA added a new preemption provision to ERISA (as well as to the PHS Act) preserving the applicability of State laws establishing requirements for issuers of group health insurance coverage, except to the extent that these requirements prevent the application of the portability, access, and renewability requirements of HIPAA. The nondiscrimination provisions that are the subject of this rulemaking are included among those requirements.

In enacting these new preemption provisions, Congress indicated its intent to establish a preemption of State insurance requirements only to the extent that those requirements prevent the application of the basic protections set forth in HIPAA. HIPAA's Conference Report states that the conferees intended the narrowest preemption of State laws with regard to health insurance issuers. H.R. Conf. Rep. No. 736, 104th Cong. 2d Session 205 (1996). Consequently, under the statute and the Conference Report, State insurance laws that are more stringent than the federal requirements are unlikely to "prevent the application of" the HIPAA nondiscrimination provisions.

Accordingly, States are given significant latitude to impose requirements on health insurance issuers that are more restrictive than the federal law. In many cases, the federal law imposes minimum requirements which States are free to exceed. Guidance conveying this interpretation was published in the **Federal Register** on April 8, 1997 and these regulations do not reduce the discretion given to the States by the statute. It is the

Departments' understanding that the vast majority of States have in fact implemented provisions which meet or exceed the minimum requirements of the HIPAA non-discrimination provisions.

HIPAA provides that the States may enforce the provisions of HIPAA as they pertain to issuers, but that the Secretary of Health and Human Services must enforce any provisions that a State fails to substantially enforce. When exercising its responsibility to enforce the provisions of HIPAA, HCFA works cooperatively with the States for the purpose of addressing State concerns and avoiding conflicts with the exercise of State authority.[14] HCFA has developed procedures to implement its enforcement responsibilities, and to afford the States the maximum opportunity to enforce HIPAA's requirements in the first instance. HCFA's procedures address the handling of reports that States may not be enforcing HIPAA's requirements, and the mechanism for allocating enforcement responsibility between the States and HCFA. To date, HCFA has had occasion to enforce the HIPAA nondiscrimination provisions in only two States.

Although the Departments conclude that these interim final rules do not have federalism implications, in keeping with the spirit of the Executive Order that agencies closely examine any policies that may have federalism implications or limit the policy making discretion of the States, the Department of Labor and HCFA have engaged in numerous efforts to consult with and work cooperatively with affected State and local officials.

For example, the Departments were aware that some States commented on the way the federal provisions should be interpreted. Therefore, the Departments have sought and received input from State insurance regulators and the National Association of Insurance Commissioners (NAIC). The NAIC is a non-profit corporation established by the insurance commissioners of the 50 States, the District of Columbia, and the four U.S. territories, that among other

---

[14] This authority applies to insurance issued with respect to group health plans generally, including plans covering employees of church organizations. Thus, this discussion of federalism applies to all group health insurance coverage that is subject to the PHS Act, including those church plans that provide coverage through a health insurance issuer (but not to church plans that do not provide coverage through a health insurance issuer). For additional information relating to the application of these nondiscrimination rules to church plans, see the preamble to regulations being proposed elsewhere in this issue of the Federal Register regarding section 9802(c) of the Code relating to church plans.

A. HIPAA Interim Final Rules and Proposed Rules, continued

things provides a forum for the development of uniform policy when uniformity is appropriate. Its members meet, discuss, and offer solutions to mutual problems. The NAIC sponsors quarterly meetings to provide a forum for the exchange of ideas, and in-depth consideration of insurance issues by regulators, industry representatives, and consumers. HCFA and Department of Labor staff have attended the quarterly meetings consistently to listen to the concerns of the State Insurance Departments regarding HIPAA issues, including the nondiscrimination provisions. In addition to the general discussions, committee meetings and task groups, the NAIC sponsors the following two standing HIPAA meetings for members during the quarterly conferences:

• HCFA/DOL Meeting on HIPAA Issues (This meeting provides HCFA and Labor the opportunity to provide updates on regulations, bulletins, enforcement actions and outreach efforts regarding HIPAA.)

• The NAIC/HCFA Liaison Meeting (This meeting provides HCFA and the NAIC the opportunity to discuss HIPAA and other health care programs.)

In addition, in developing these interim final regulations, the Departments consulted with the NAIC and requested their assistance to obtain information from the State Insurance Departments. Specifically, we sought and received their input on certain insurance rating practices and late enrollment issues.

The Departments employed the States' insights on insurance rating practices in developing the provisions prohibiting "list-billing," and their experience with late enrollment in crafting the regulatory provision clarifying the relationship between the nondiscrimination provisions and late enrollment. Specifically, the regulations clarify that while late enrollment, if offered by a plan, must be available to all similarly situated individuals regardless of any health factor, an individual's status as a late enrollee is not itself within the scope of any health factor.

The Departments also cooperate with the States in several ongoing outreach initiatives, through which information on HIPAA is shared among federal regulators, State regulators, and the regulated community. In particular, the Department of Labor has established a Health Benefits Education Campaign with more than 70 partners, including HCFA, NAIC and many business and consumer groups. HCFA has sponsored four conferences with the States—the Consumer Outreach and Advocacy

conferences in March 1999 and June 2000, the Implementation and Enforcement of HIPAA National State-Federal Conferences in August 1999 and 2000. Furthermore, both the Department of Labor and HCFA websites offer links to important State websites and other resources, facilitating coordination between the State and federal regulators and the regulated community.

In conclusion, throughout the process of developing these regulations, to the extent feasible within the specific preemption provisions of HIPAA, the Departments have attempted to balance the States' interests in regulating health insurance issuers, and Congress's intent to provide uniform minimum protections to consumers in every State.

Unified Analysis of Costs and Benefits

1. Introduction

HIPAA's nondiscrimination provisions generally prohibit group health plans and group health plan issuers from discriminating against individuals on the basis of health status factors. The primary effect and intent of the provision is to increase access to affordable group health coverage for individuals with health problems. This effect, and the economic costs, benefits, and transfers attendant to it, generally flow directly from the HIPAA's statutory provisions, which are largely self-implementing. However, the statute alone leaves room for varying interpretations of exactly which practices are prohibited or permitted at the margin. This regulation draws on the Departments' authority to clarify and interpret HIPAA's statutory nondiscrimination provisions in order to secure the protections intended by Congress for plan participants and beneficiaries. The Departments crafted it to satisfy this mandate in as economically efficient a manner as possible, and believe that the economic benefits of the regulation outweigh its costs. The analysis underlying this conclusion takes into account both the effect of the statute and the impact of the discretion exercised in the regulation.

The nondiscrimination provisions of the HIPAA statute and of this regulation generally apply to both group health plans and to issuers of group health plan policies. Economic theory predicts that issuers will pass their costs of compliance back to plans, and that plans may pass some or all of issuers' and their own costs of compliance to participants. This analysis is carried out in light of this prediction.

2. Costs and Benefits of HIPAA's Statutory Nondiscrimination Provisions

As noted above, HIPAA's statutory nondiscrimination provisions are largely self-implementing even in the absence of interpretive guidance. It is the Departments' policy where practicable to evaluate such impacts separately from the impact of discretion exercised in regulation. The Departments provide qualitative assessments of the nature of the costs, benefits, and transfers that are expected to derive from statutory provisions, and provide summaries of any credible, empirical estimates of these effects that are available.

To the Departments' knowledge, there is no publicly available work that quantifies the magnitude or presents the nature of these benefits, costs, and transfers. In its initial scoring of the statute, the Congressional Budget Office did not separately quantify the costs of the nondiscrimination provisions. Therefore, this analysis considers the nature of anticipated costs, benefits, and transfers, and offers a basis for estimating separately the impacts of the statute and regulatory discretion, but does not present a detailed description of any other quantitative analysis of the statute's impact.

HIPAA's statutory nondiscrimination provisions entail new economic costs and benefits, as well as transfers of health care costs among plan sponsors and participants.

The primary statutory economic benefits associated with the HIPAA nondiscrimination provisions derive from increased access to affordable group health plan coverage for individuals with certain health status-related factors. Expanding access benefits both newly covered individuals and society at large. Individuals without health insurance are less likely to get preventive care and less likely to have a regular source of care.[15] A lack of health insurance generally increases the likelihood that needed medical treatment will be forgone or delayed. Forgoing or delaying care increases the risk of adverse health outcomes. These adverse outcomes in turn spawn higher medical costs which are often shifted to public funding sources (and therefore to taxpayers) or to other payers. They also erode productivity and the quality of life. Improved access to affordable group health coverage for individuals with health problems under HIPAA's

[15] Kaiser Family Foundation and the NewsHour. "Newshour/Kaiser Spotlights Misconceptions About the Medically Uninsured: Survey Examines Difficulties Faced by Those Without Health Coverage." News Release. May 18, 2000.

A. HIPAA Interim Final Rules and Proposed Rules, continued

1394   Federal Register / Vol. 66, No. 5 / Monday, January 8, 2001 / Rules and Regulations

nondiscrimination provisions will lead to more insurance coverage, timelier and fuller medical care, better health outcomes, and improved productivity and quality of life. This is especially true for the individuals most affected by HIPAA's nondiscrimination provisions—those with adverse health conditions. Denied insurance, individuals in poorer health are more likely to suffer economic hardship, to forgo badly needed care for financial reasons, and to suffer adverse health outcomes as a result. For them, gaining insurance is more likely to mean gaining economic security, receiving timely, quality care, and living healthier, more productive lives.

Plans and issuers will incur economic costs as a result of the law. These are generally limited to administrative costs, such as those incurred to change plan design and pricing structures and update plan materials.

The premiums and claims costs incurred by group health plans to provide coverage to individuals who were previously denied coverage or offered restricted coverage based on health factors are offset by the commensurate or greater benefits realized by the newly eligible participants on whose behalf the premiums or claims are paid. As such, these premiums and claims costs are properly characterized as transfers rather than as new economic costs. These transfers shift the burden of health care costs from one party to another without any direct change in aggregate social welfare. For example, as individuals' insurance status changes from insured through an individual policy to insured through an employment-based group health plan, health care costs are transferred from these individuals to their employers. Similarly, as individuals' insurance status changes from uninsured to insured through a group health plan, health care costs are transferred from the individuals and public funding sources to employers.

The HIPAA nondiscrimination statutory transfer is likely to be substantial. Annual per-participant group health plan costs average more than $4,000,[16] and it is likely that average costs would be higher for individuals who had faced discrimination due to health status factors. Prior to HIPAA's enactment approximately 106,000 employees were denied employment based coverage

[16] Gabel, Jon R. Job-based Health Insurance, 1977–1998: The Accidental System Under Scrutiny. *Health Affairs.* November/December 1999. Volume 18, Number 6.

because of health factors.[17] A simple assessment suggests that the total cost of coverage for such employees could exceed $400 million. However, this potential statutory transfer is small relative to the overall cost of employment-based health coverage. Group health plans will spend about $431 billion this year to cover approximately 77 million participants and their dependents. Transfers under HIPAA's nondiscrimination provision will represent a very small fraction of one percent of total group health plan expenditures.

3. Costs and Benefits of the Regulation

Prohibiting Discrimination—Many of the provisions of this regulation serve to specify more precisely than the statute alone exactly what practices are prohibited by HIPAA as unlawful discrimination in eligibility or employee premium among similarly situated employees. For example, under the regulation eligibility generally may not be restricted based on an individuals' participation in risky activities, confinement to an institution or absence from work on enrollment day due to illness, or status as a late enrollee. The regulation provides that various plan features including waiting periods and eligibility for certain benefits constitute rules for eligibility which may not vary across similarly situated employees based on health status factors. It provides that individuals who were previously denied eligibility based on health status factors (or who failed to enroll in anticipation of such denial) must be given an opportunity to enroll. It provides that plans may not reclassify employees based on health status factors in order to create separate groups of similarly situated employees among which discrimination would be permitted.

All of these provisions have the effect of clarifying and ensuring certain participants' right to freedom from discrimination in eligibility and premium amounts, thereby securing their access to affordable group health plan coverage. The costs and benefits attributable to these provisions resemble those attendant to HIPAA's statutory nondiscrimination provisions. Securing participants' access to affordable group coverage provides economic benefits by reducing uninsurance and thereby improving health outcomes. It entails transfers of costs from the employees whose rights are secured (and/or from other parties who would otherwise pay for their health care) to plan sponsors

[17] February 1997 Current Population Survey. Contingent Worker Supplement.

(or to other plan participants if sponsors pass those costs back evenly to them). And it imposes economic costs in the form of administrative burdens to design and implement necessary plan amendments.

The Departments lack any basis on which to distinguish these benefits, costs, and transfers from those of the statute itself. It is unclear how many plans might be engaging in the discriminatory practices targeted for prohibition by these regulatory provisions. Because these provisions operate largely at the margin of the statutory requirements, it is likely that the effects of these provisions will be far smaller than the similar statutory effects. The Departments are confident, however, that by securing employees' access to affordable coverage at the margin, the regulation, like the statute, will yield benefits in excess of costs.

Clarifying Requirements—Additional economic benefits derive directly from the improved clarity provided by the regulation. The regulation provides clarity through both its provisions and its examples of how those provisions apply in various circumstances. By clarifying employees' rights and plan sponsors' obligations under HIPAA's nondiscrimination provisions, the regulation will reduce uncertainty and costly disputes over these rights and obligations. It will promote employers' and employees' common understanding of the value of group health plan benefits and confidence in the security and predictability of those benefits, thereby improving labor market efficiency and fostering the establishment and continuation of group health plans by employers.[18]

[18] The voluntary nature of the employment-based health benefit system in conjunction with the open and dynamic character of labor markets make explicit as well as implicit negotiations on compensation a key determinant of the prevalence of employee benefits coverage. It is likely that 80% to 100% of the cost of employee benefits is borne by workers through reduced wages (see for example Jonathan Gruber and Alan B. Krueger. "The Incidence of Mandated Employer-Provided Insurance: Lessons from Workers Compensation Insurance," Tax Policy and Economy (1991); Jonathan Gruber. "The Incidence of Mandated Maternity Benefits," American Economic Review, Vol. 84 (June 1994), pp. 622–641; Lawrence H. Summers, "Some Simple Economics of Mandated Benefits," American Economic Review, Vol. 79, No. 2 (May 1989); Louise Sheiner, "Health Care Costs, Wages, and Aging," Federal Reserve Board of Governors working paper, April 1999; and Edward Montgomery, Kathryn Shaw, and Mary Ellen Benedict, "Pensions and Wages: An Hedonic Price Theory Approach," International Economic Review, Vol. 33 No. 1, Feb. 1992.) The prevalence of benefits is therefore largely dependent on the efficacy of this exchange. If workers perceive that there is the potential for inappropriate denial of benefits they will discount their value to adjust for this risk. This discount drives a wedge in the compensation

A. HIPAA Interim Final Rules and Proposed Rules, continued

Amending Plans—The regulation is expected to entail some new economic costs, in the form of two new administrative burdens, which are distinguishable from those attributable to the statute. First, it is likely that some of the regulation's nondiscrimination provisions will effectively require some plans to amend their terms and revise plan materials. Second, as noted above, the regulation requires that individuals who were previously denied eligibility based on health status factors (or who failed to enroll in anticipation of such denial) must be given an opportunity to enroll. It also requires that plans notify such individuals of their right enroll. Providing notices under these requirements will entail new administrative costs.

Plans that, prior to HIPAA's effective date, included provisions since prohibited by HIPAA's nondiscrimination requirements, were effectively required by HIPAA to implement conforming amendments and to revise plan materials accordingly. The costs associated with these actions generally are attributable to the HIPAA statute and not to this regulation. However, it is likely that some of the regulation's nondiscrimination provisions will effectively require some plans to amend their terms and revise their materials. For example, the Departments understand that plans commonly require employees to be actively at work on a designated enrollment day in order to qualify for enrollment. It is possible that some plans failed to interpret HIPAA's statutory provisions to prohibit this practice. Such plans will need to amend their terms and materials to provide that employees will not be denied enrollment solely because they were absent due to a health status factor. Such plans will incur administrative costs.

The Departments have no basis for estimating how many plans might need to implement amendments beyond those implemented in response to the HIPAA's statutory nondiscrimination provisions in order to comply with the regulation's corresponding provisions. They adopted conservative assumptions in order to develop an upper bound estimate of the cost to amend plans and materials to conform with the regulation. They assumed that all plans will require at least some amendment to conform with this regulation.

A large majority of fully insured plans do not have unique eligibility and

employee premium provisions but instead choose from a relatively small menu of standardized products offered by issuers. The Departments accordingly assumed that issuers will amend their standardized group insurance products, passing the associated cost back to the plans that buy them. They estimate that a total of approximately 33,000 group insurance products will be so amended, and that the cost of these amendments will be spread across a universe of approximately 2.6 million fully insured plans. The Departments assumed that small self-insured plans (which generally fall outside state regulation of insurance products) choose from a much larger menu of products and that large self-insured plans each have unique eligibility rules will need to be amended independently. This implies a total of approximately 76,000 self-insured plan configurations requiring amendment.

Assuming that each affected group insurance product and self-insured plan configuration would require 1 hour of professional time billed at $72 per hour to design and implement amendments, the aggregate cost to amend plans would be $8 million.

Separate from the cost to design and implement plan amendments is the cost to revise plan materials to reflect the amendments. The Departments note that the cost to revise plan materials can generally be attributed to legal requirements other than the HIPAA statute or this regulation. It is the policy of the Department of Labor to attribute the cost of revising private-sector group health plan materials to its regulation implementing ERISA's Summary Plan Description requirements. Various state laws compel issuers to provide accurate materials, and the Departments believe that State and local governmental plan sponsors and private plan sponsors routinely update plan materials as a matter of either law or compensation and employment policy.

Notifying Employees of Enrollment Opportunities—In estimating the costs associated with the notification requirements, the Departments separately considered the cost of preparing notices and the cost of distributing them.

Based on a 1993 Robert Wood Johnson Foundation survey of employers, the Departments estimate that 128,000 group health plans excluded individuals on the basis of health status factors prior to HIPAA's enactment and will therefore be

required by the regulation to prepare and distribute notices. The Departments assumed that preparing the notice will require one hour of time billed at a $72 hourly rate. The cost to develop notices is therefore estimated to be $9 million.

The Departments assumed that plans will distribute notices to all individuals who are eligible for coverage under the plan. It might be necessary to notify individuals who are currently enrolled because such individuals may have dependents for whom eligibility was denied based on a health status factor or may have failed to enroll dependents because they expected that eligibility would be so denied for them. This assumption probably results in an overestimate of the true cost. Some affected plans may already have notified affected individuals of their right to enroll under HIPAA. Others may have historical records of plan enrollment that are sufficiently detailed to allow for the notification of only specific individuals. Based on the 1997 Robert Wood Johnson Foundation survey, the Departments estimate that a total of 2.3 million employees are eligible for coverage under the 128,000 plans that are required to provide notices. The Departments assumed that distributing each notice costs $0.37 for mailing and materials plus 2 minutes of photocopying and mailing billed at a $15 per hour clerical rate for a total per-notice distribution cost of $0.87. The cost to distribute notices is therefore estimated to be $2 million.

The estimated combined cost to prepare and distribute notices therefore amounts to $11 million. The Departments note that this is a one-time cost which will be incurred concurrent with the regulation's applicability date.

The Department's note that the provision of notices will benefit employees who newly learn of opportunities to enroll themselves or their dependents. The result will be fuller realization of HIPAA's intent and employees' associated rights, as well as improved access to affordable group coverage and reduced rates of uninsurance for affected employees.

4. Summary of Cost Estimates

The cost estimates presented here are compiled in the table below. Upper bound cost estimates attributable to the regulation include $8 million to amend plans and revise documents and $11 million to prepare and distribute notices of enrollment opportunities, or a total of $19 million.

---

negotiation, limiting its efficiency. With workers unwilling to bear the full cost of the benefit, fewer benefits will be provided. The extent to which

workers perceive a federal regulation supported by enforcement authority to improve the security and quality of benefits, the differential between the

employers costs and workers willingness to accept wage offsets is minimized.

A. HIPAA Interim Final Rules and Proposed Rules, continued

1396   Federal Register / Vol. 66, No. 5 / Monday, January 8, 2001 / Rules and Regulations

Source of cost	$MM	Explanatory notes
Amending plans and revising materials	$8	Upper bound of new economic cost incurred as plans are amended to comply with the regulation. One-time cost.
Notifying employees of enrollment opportunities	$11	Upper bound of new economic cost to prepare and distribute notices. One-time cost.
Prohibiting discrimination	>$400	Transfer attributable to HIPAA's statutory nondiscriminatory provisions. Transfers attributable to the regulation were not estimated but are expected to be a very small fraction of this amount. Ongoing annual level.

5. Assessment of Likelihood of Adverse Secondary Effects

The Departments considered whether employers might reduce or eliminate health insurance benefits for all employees as a result of this regulation. They believe that this is highly unlikely because the regulation affirms and clarifies plan sponsors' flexibility and because its costs will be very small relative to group health plan expenditures.

The regulation affirms plan sponsors' flexibility to design plans and control plan costs in many ways. It affirms and clarifies plans' flexibility under HIPAA to exclude from coverage or limit coverage for certain conditions or services, to require employees to perform services before coverage becomes effective, and to provide different benefits or charge different premiums for employees in different bona fide employment classes. It also clarifies that more favorable treatment of individuals with adverse health factors is permitted, thereby allowing employers to assist employees and their families dealing with disabilities, medical conditions, or other health factors by extending coverage or lowering premiums.

Both the transfer of health insurance costs and the administrative costs generated by this regulation will be very small relative to total group health plan expenditures. The $19 million economic cost estimate attributed to this regulation amounts to a tiny fraction of one percent of the $431 billion that group health plans will spend this year. Even the more than $400 million transfer of cost attributed to HIPAA's statutory nondiscrimination provisions amount to a very small fraction of one percent of that spending. Plan sponsors wishing to do so generally can pass these costs back to participants with small, across the board changes to employee premiums or benefits.

Statutory Authority

The Department of the Treasury final and temporary rules are adopted pursuant to the authority contained in sections 7805 and 9833 of the Code (26 U.S.C. 7805, 9833).

The Department of Labor interim final rule is adopted pursuant to the authority contained in sections 107, 209, 505, 701–703, 711–713, and 731–734 of ERISA (29 U.S.C. 1027, 1059, 1135, 1171–1173, 1181, 1182, and 1191–1194), as amended by HIPAA (Public Law 104–191, 110 Stat. 1936), MHPA and NMHPA (Public Law 104–204, 110 Stat. 2935), and WHCRA (Public Law 105–277, 112 Stat. 2681–436), section 101(g)(4) of HIPAA, and Secretary of Labor's Order No. 1–87, 52 FR 13139, April 21, 1987.

The Department of HHS interim final rule is adopted pursuant to the authority contained in sections 2701 through 2763, 2791, and 2792 of the PHS Act (42 U.S.C. 300gg through 300gg–63, 300gg–91, and 300gg–92), as amended by HIPAA (Public Law 104–191, 110 Stat. 1936), MHPA and NMHPA (Public Law 104–204, 110 Stat. 2935), and WHCRA (Public Law 105–277, 112 Stat. 2681–436).

List of Subjects

26 CFR Part 54

Excise taxes, Health care, Health insurance, Pensions, Reporting and recordkeeping requirements.

29 CFR Part 2590

Employee benefit plans, Employee Retirement Income Security Act, Health care, Health insurance, Reporting and recordkeeping requirements.

45 CFR Part 146

Health care, Health insurance, Reporting and recordkeeping requirements, State regulation of health insurance.

Adoption of Amendments to the Regulations

Internal Revenue Service

26 CFR Chapter I

Accordingly, 26 CFR part 54 is amended as follows:

PART 54—PENSION EXCISE TAXES

Paragraph 1. The authority citation for part 54 continues to read in part as follows:

Authority: 26 U.S.C. 7805 * * *

Par. 2. Section 54.9802–1T is removed.

Par. 3. Section 54.9802–1 is added to read as follows:

§ 54.9802–1 Prohibiting discrimination against participants and beneficiaries based on a health factor.

(a) *Health factors.* (1) The term *health factor* means, in relation to an individual, any of the following health status-related factors:

(i) Health status;

(ii) Medical condition (including both physical and mental illnesses);

(iii) Claims experience;

(iv) Receipt of health care;

(v) Medical history;

(vi) Genetic information;

(vii) Evidence of insurability; or

(viii) Disability.

(2) Evidence of insurability includes—

(i) Conditions arising out of acts of domestic violence; and

(ii) [Reserved] For further guidance, see § 54.9802–1T(a)(2)(ii).

(b) *Prohibited discrimination in rules for eligibility*—(1) *In general*—(i) A group health plan may not establish any rule for eligibility (including continued eligibility) of any individual to enroll for benefits under the terms of the plan that discriminates based on any health factor that relates to that individual or a dependent of that individual. This rule is subject to the provisions of paragraph (b)(2) of this section (explaining how this rule applies to benefits), paragraph (b)(3) of this section (allowing plans to impose certain preexisting condition exclusions), paragraph (d) of this section (containing rules for establishing groups of similarly situated individuals), paragraph (e) of this section (relating to nonconfinement, actively-at-work, and other service requirements), paragraph (f) of this section (relating to bona fide wellness programs), and paragraph (g) of this section (permitting favorable treatment of individuals with adverse health factors).

(ii) [Reserved] For further guidance, see § 54.9802–1T(b)(1)(ii).

A. HIPAA Interim Final Rules and Proposed Rules, continued

(iii) The rules of this paragraph (b)(1) are illustrated by the following examples:

Example 1. (i) *Facts.* An employer sponsors a group health plan that is available to all employees who enroll within the first 30 days of their employment. However, employees who do not enroll within the first 30 days cannot enroll later unless they pass a physical examination.

(ii) *Conclusion.* In this *Example 1,* the requirement to pass a physical examination in order to enroll in the plan is a rule for eligibility that discriminates based on one or more health factors and thus violates this paragraph (b)(1).

Example 2. [Reserved]

(2) *Application to benefits*—(i) *General rule*—(A) Under this section, a group health plan is not required to provide coverage for any particular benefit to any group of similarly situated individuals.

(B) [Reserved] For further guidance, see § 54.9802–1T(b)(2)(i)(B).

(C) [Reserved] For further guidance, see § 54.9802–1T(b)(2)(i)(C).

(D) [Reserved] For further guidance, see § 54.9802–1T(b)(2)(i)(D).

(ii) *Cost-sharing mechanisms and wellness programs.* A group health plan with a cost-sharing mechanism (such as a deductible, copayment, or coinsurance) that requires a higher payment from an individual, based on a health factor of that individual or a dependent of that individual, than for a similarly situated individual under the plan (and thus does not apply uniformly to all similarly situated individuals) does not violate the requirements of this paragraph (b)(2) if the payment differential is based on whether an individual has complied with the requirements of a bona fide wellness program.

(iii) *Specific rule relating to source-of-injury exclusions.* [Reserved] For further guidance, see § 54.9802–1T(b)(2)(iii).

(3) *Relationship to section 9801(a), (b), and (d).* [Reserved] For further guidance, see § 54.9802–1T(b)(3).

(c) *Prohibited discrimination in premiums or contributions*—(1) *In general*—(i) A group health plan may not require an individual, as a condition of enrollment or continued enrollment under the plan, to pay a premium or contribution that is greater than the premium or contribution for a similarly situated individual (described in paragraph (d) of this section) enrolled in the plan based on any health factor that relates to the individual or a dependent of the individual.

(ii) [Reserved] For further guidance, see § 54.9802–1T(c)(1)(ii).

(2) *Rules relating to premium rates*—(i) *Group rating based on health factors* not restricted under this section. Nothing in this section restricts the aggregate amount that an employer may be charged for coverage under a group health plan.

(ii) *List billing based on a health factor prohibited.* [Reserved] For further guidance, see § 54.9802–1T(c)(2)(ii).

(3) *Exception for bona fide wellness programs.* Notwithstanding paragraphs (c)(1) and (2) of this section, a plan may establish a premium or contribution differential based on whether an individual has complied with the requirements of a bona fide wellness program.

(d) *Similarly situated individuals.* [Reserved] For further guidance, see § 54.9802–1T(d).

(e) *Nonconfinement and actively-at-work provisions.* [Reserved] For further guidance, see § 54.9802–1T(e).

(f) *Bona fide wellness programs.* [Reserved]

(g) *Benign discrimination permitted.* [Reserved] For further guidance, see § 54.9802–1T(g).

(h) *No effect on other laws.* [Reserved] For further guidance, see § 54.9802–1T(h).

(i) *Effective dates*—(1) Final rules apply March 9, 2001. This section applies March 9, 2001.

(2) *Cross-reference to temporary rules applicable for plan years beginning on or after July 1, 2001.* See § 54.9802–1T(i)(2), which makes the rules of that section applicable for plan years beginning on or after July 1, 2001.

(3) *Cross-reference to temporary transitional rules for individuals previously denied coverage based on a health factor.* See § 54.9802–1T(i)(3) for transitional rules that apply with respect to individuals previously denied coverage under a group health plan based on a health factor.

Par. 4. Section 54.9802–1T is added to read as follows:

§ 54.9802–1T Prohibiting discrimination against participants and beneficiaries based on a health factor (temporary).

(a) *Health factors.* (1) [Reserved] For further guidance, see § 54.9802–1(a).

(2) *Evidence of insurability includes*—

(i) [Reserved] For further guidance, see § 54.9802–1(a)(2)(i).

(ii) Participation in activities such as motorcycling, snowmobiling, all-terrain vehicle riding, horseback riding, skiing, and other similar activities.

(3) The decision whether health coverage is elected for an individual (including the time chosen to enroll, such as under special enrollment or late enrollment) is not, itself, within the scope of any health factor. (However, under section 9801(f) a plan must treat special enrollees the same as similarly situated individuals who are enrolled when first eligible.)

(b) *Prohibited discrimination in rules for eligibility*—(1) *In general*—(i) [Reserved] For further guidance, see § 54.9802–1(b)(1)(i).

(ii) For purposes of this section, rules for eligibility include, but are not limited to, rules relating to—

(A) Enrollment;

(B) The effective date of coverage;

(C) Waiting (or affiliation) periods;

(D) Late and special enrollment;

(E) Eligibility for benefit packages (including rules for individuals to change their selection among benefit packages);

(F) Benefits (including rules relating to covered benefits, benefit restrictions, and cost-sharing mechanisms such as coinsurance, copayments, and deductibles), as described in paragraphs (b) (2) and (3) of this section;

(G) Continued eligibility; and

(H) Terminating coverage (including disenrollment) of any individual under the plan.

(iii) The rules of this paragraph (b)(1) are illustrated by the following examples:

Example 1. [Reserved] For further guidance, see § 54.9802–1(b)(iii). *Example 1.*

Example 2. (i) *Facts.* Under an employer's group health plan, employees who enroll during the first 30 days of employment (and during special enrollment periods) may choose between two benefit packages: an indemnity option and an HMO option. However, employees who enroll during late enrollment are permitted to enroll only in the HMO option and only if they provide evidence of good health.

(ii) *Conclusion.* In this *Example 2,* the requirement to provide evidence of good health in order to be eligible for late enrollment in the HMO option is a rule for eligibility that discriminates based on one or more health factors and thus violates this paragraph (b)(1). However, if the plan did not require evidence of good health but limited late enrollees to the HMO option, the plan's rules for eligibility would not discriminate based on any health factor, and thus would not violate this paragraph (b)(1), because the time an individual chooses to enroll is not, itself, within the scope of any health factor.

Example 3. (i) *Facts.* Under an employer's group health plan, all employees generally may enroll within the first 30 days of employment. However, individuals who participate in certain recreational activities, including motorcycling, are excluded from coverage.

(ii) *Conclusion.* In this *Example 3,* excluding from the plan individuals who participate in recreational activities, such as motorcycling, is a rule for eligibility that discriminates based on one more health factors and thus violates this paragraph (b)(1).

Example 4. (i) *Facts.* A group health plan applies for a group health policy offered by

A. HIPAA Interim Final Rules and Proposed Rules, continued

an issuer. As part of the application, the issuer receives health information about individuals to be covered under the plan. Individual *A* is an employee of the employer maintaining the plan. *A* and *A*'s dependents have a history of high health claims. Based on the information about *A* and *A*'s dependents, the issuer excludes *A* and *A*'s dependents from the group policy it offers to the employer.

(ii) *Conclusion*. See *Example 4* in 29 CFR 2590.702(b)(1) and 45 CFR 146.121(b)(1) for a conclusion that the exclusion by the issuer of *A* and *A*'s dependents from coverage is a rule for eligibility that discriminates based on one or more health factors and violates rules under 29 CFR 2590.702(b)(1) and 45 CFR 146.121(b)(1) similar to the rules under this paragraph (b)(1). (If the employer is a small employer under 45 CFR 144.103 (generally, an employer with 50 or fewer employees), the issuer also may violate 45 CFR 146.150, which requires issuers to offer all the policies they sell in the small group market on a guaranteed available basis to all small employers and to accept every eligible individual in every small employer group.) If the plan provides coverage through this policy and does not provide equivalent coverage for *A* and *A*'s dependents through other means, the plan will also violate this paragraph (b)(1).

(2) *Application to benefits*—(i) *General rule*—(A) [Reserved] For further guidance, see § 54.9802–1(b)(2)(i)(A).

(B) However, benefits provided under a plan must be uniformly available to all similarly situated individuals (as described in paragraph (d) of this section). Likewise, any restriction on a benefit or benefits must apply uniformly to all similarly situated individuals and must not be directed at individual participants or beneficiaries based on any health factor of the participants or beneficiaries (determined based on all the relevant facts and circumstances). Thus, for example, a plan may limit or exclude benefits in relation to a specific disease or condition, limit or exclude benefits for certain types of treatments or drugs, or limit or exclude benefits based on a determination of whether the benefits are experimental or not medically necessary, but only if the benefit limitation or exclusion applies uniformly to all similarly situated individuals and is not directed at individual participants or beneficiaries based on any health factor of the participants or beneficiaries. In addition, a plan may impose annual, lifetime, or other limits on benefits and may require the satisfaction of a deductible, copayment, coinsurance, or other cost-sharing requirement in order to obtain a benefit if the limit or cost-sharing requirement applies uniformly to all similarly situated individuals and is not directed at individual participants or beneficiaries based on any health

factor of the participants or beneficiaries. In the case of a cost-sharing requirement, see also paragraph (b)(2)(ii) of this section, which permits variances in the application of a cost-sharing mechanism made available under a bona fide wellness program. (Whether any plan provision or practice with respect to benefits complies with this paragraph (b)(2)(i) does not affect whether the provision or practice is permitted under any other provision of the Code, the Americans with Disabilities Act, or any other law, whether State or federal.)

(C) For purposes of this paragraph (b)(2)(i), a plan amendment applicable to all individuals in one or more groups of similarly situated individuals under the plan and made effective no earlier than the first day of the first plan year after the amendment is adopted is not considered to be directed at any individual participants or beneficiaries.

(D) The rules of this paragraph (b)(2)(i) are illustrated by the following examples:

Example 1. (i) *Facts*. A group health plan applies a $500,000 lifetime limit on all benefits to each participant or beneficiary covered under the plan. The limit is not directed at individual participants or beneficiaries.

(ii) *Conclusion*. In this *Example 1*, the limit does not violate this paragraph (b)(2)(i) because $500,000 of benefits are available uniformly to each participant and beneficiary under the plan and because the limit is applied uniformly to all participants and beneficiaries and is not directed at individual participants or beneficiaries.

Example 2. (i) *Facts*. A group health plan has a $2 million lifetime limit on all benefits (and no other lifetime limits) for participants covered under the plan. Participant *B* files a claim for the treatment of AIDS. At the next corporate board meeting of the plan sponsor, the claim is discussed. Shortly thereafter, the plan is modified to impose a $10,000 lifetime limit on benefits for the treatment of AIDS, effective before the beginning of the next plan year.

(ii) *Conclusion*. Under the facts of this *Example 2*, the plan violates this paragraph (b)(2)(i) because the plan modification is directed at *B* based on *B*'s claim.

Example 3. (i) A group health plan applies for a group health policy offered by an issuer. Individual *C* is covered under the plan and has an adverse health condition. As part of the application, the issuer receives health information about the individuals to be covered, including information about *C*'s adverse health condition. The policy form offered by the issuer generally provides benefits for the adverse health condition that *C* has, but in this case the issuer offers the plan a policy modified by a rider that excludes benefits for *C* for that condition. The exclusionary rider is made effective the first day of the next plan year.

(ii) *Conclusion*. See *Example 3* in 29 CFR 2590.702(b)(2)(i) and 45 CFR 146.121(b)(2)(i)

for a conclusion that the issuer violates rules under 29 CFR 2590.702(b)(2)(i) and 45 CFR 146.121(b)(2)(i) similar to the rules under this paragraph (b)(2)(i) because the rider excluding benefits for the condition that *C* has is directed at *C* even though it applies by its terms to all participants and beneficiaries under the plan.

Example 4. (i) *Facts*. A group health plan has a $2,000 lifetime limit for the treatment of temporomandibular joint syndrome (TMJ). The limit is applied uniformly to all similarly situated individuals and is not directed at individual participants or beneficiaries.

(ii) *Conclusion*. In this *Example 4*, the limit does not violate this paragraph (b)(2)(i) because $2000 of benefits for the treatment of TMJ are available uniformly to all similarly situated individuals and a plan may limit benefits covered in relation to a specific disease or condition if the limit applies uniformly to all similarly situated individuals and is not directed at individual participants or beneficiaries.

Example 5. (i) *Facts*. A group health plan applies a $2 million lifetime limit on all benefits. However, the $2 million lifetime limit is reduced to $10,000 for any participant or beneficiary covered under the plan who has a congenital heart defect.

(ii) *Conclusion*. In this *Example 5*, the lower lifetime limit for participants and beneficiaries with a congenital heart defect violates this paragraph (b)(2)(i) because benefits under the plan are not uniformly available to all similarly situated individuals and the plan's lifetime limit on benefits does not apply uniformly to all similarly situated individuals.

Example 6. (i) *Facts*. A group health plan limits benefits for prescription drugs to those listed on a drug formulary. The limit is applied uniformly to all similarly situated individuals and is not directed at individual participants or beneficiaries.

(ii) *Conclusion*. In this *Example 6*, the exclusion from coverage of drugs not listed on the drug formulary does not violate this paragraph (b)(2)(i) because benefits for prescription drugs listed on the formulary are uniformly available to all similarly situated individuals and because the exclusion of drugs not listed on the formulary applies uniformly to all similarly situated individuals and is not directed at individual participants or beneficiaries.

Example 7. (i) *Facts*. Under a group health plan, doctor visits are generally subject to a $250 annual deductible and 20 percent coinsurance requirement. However, prenatal doctor visits are not subject to any deductible or coinsurance requirement. These rules are applied uniformly to all similarly situated individuals and are not directed at individual participants or beneficiaries.

(ii) *Conclusion*. In this *Example 7*, imposing different deductible and coinsurance requirements for prenatal doctor visits and other visits does not violate this paragraph (b)(2)(i) because a plan may establish different deductibles or coinsurance requirements for different services if the deductible or coinsurance requirement is applied uniformly to all similarly situated individuals and is not directed at individual participants or beneficiaries.

A. HIPAA Interim Final Rules and Proposed Rules, continued

(ii) *Cost-sharing mechanisms and wellness programs.* [Reserved] For further guidance, see § 54.9802–1(b)(2)(ii).

(iii) *Specific rule relating to source-of-injury exclusions*—(A) If a group health plan generally provides benefits for a type of injury, the plan may not deny benefits otherwise provided for treatment of the injury if the injury results from an act of domestic violence or a medical condition (including both physical and mental health conditions).

(B) The rules of this paragraph (b)(2)(iii) are illustrated by the following examples:

Example 1. (i) *Facts.* A group health plan generally provides medical/surgical benefits, including benefits for hospital stays, that are medically necessary. However, the plan excludes benefits for self-inflicted injuries or injuries sustained in connection with attempted suicide. Individual *D* suffers from depression and attempts suicide. As a result, *D* sustains injuries and is hospitalized for treatment of the injuries. Pursuant to the exclusion, the plan denies *D* benefits for treatment of the injuries.

(ii) *Conclusion.* In this *Example 1*, the suicide attempt is the result of a medical condition (depression). Accordingly, the denial of benefits for the treatments of *D*'s injuries violates the requirements of this paragraph (b)(2)(iii) because the plan provision excludes benefits for treatment of an injury resulting from a medical condition.

Example 2. (i) *Facts.* A group health plan provides benefits for head injuries generally. The plan also has a general exclusion for any injury sustained while participating in any of a number of recreational activities, including bungee jumping. However, this exclusion does not apply to any injury that results from a medical condition (nor from domestic violence). Participant *E* sustains a head injury while bungee jumping. The injury did not result from a medical condition (nor from domestic violence). Accordingly, the plan denies benefits for *E*'s head injury.

(ii) *Conclusion.* In this *Example 2*, the plan provision that denies benefits based on the source of an injury does not restrict benefits based on an act of domestic violence or any medical condition. Therefore, the provision is permissible under this paragraph (b)(2)(iii) and does not violate this section. (However, if the plan did not allow *E* to enroll in the plan (or applied different rules for eligibility to *E*) because *E* frequently participates in bungee jumping, the plan would violate paragraph (b)(1) of this section.)

(3) *Relationship to section 9801(a), (b), and (d).* (i) A preexisting condition exclusion is permitted under this section if it—

(A) Complies with section 9801(a), (b), and (d);

(B) Applies uniformly to all similarly situated individuals (as described in paragraph (d) of this section); and

(C) Is not directed at individual participants or beneficiaries based on any health factor of the participants or beneficiaries. For purposes of this paragraph (b)(3)(i)(C), a plan amendment relating to a preexisting condition exclusion applicable to all individuals in one or more groups of similarly situated individuals under the plan and made effective no earlier than the first day of the first plan year after the amendment is adopted is not considered to be directed at any individual participants or beneficiaries.

(ii) The rules of this paragraph (b)(3) are illustrated by the following examples:

Example 1. (i) *Facts.* A group health plan imposes a preexisting condition exclusion on all individuals enrolled in the plan. The exclusion applies to conditions for which medical advice, diagnosis, care, or treatment was recommended or received within the six-month period ending on an individual's enrollment date. In addition, the exclusion generally extends for 12 months after an individual's enrollment date, but this 12-month period is offset by the number of days of an individual's creditable coverage in accordance with section 9801(a). There is nothing to indicate that the exclusion is directed at individual participants or beneficiaries.

(ii) *Conclusion.* In this *Example 1*, even though the plan's preexisting condition exclusion discriminates against individuals based on one or more health factors, the preexisting condition exclusion does not violate this section because it applies uniformly to all similarly situated individuals, is not directed at individual participants or beneficiaries, and complies with section 9801(a), (b), and (d) (that is, the requirements relating to the six-month look-back period, the 12-month (or 18-month) maximum exclusion period, and the creditable coverage offset).

Example 2. (i) *Facts.* A group health plan excludes coverage for conditions with respect to which medical advice, diagnosis, care, or treatment was recommended or received within the six-month period ending on an individual's enrollment date. Under the plan, the preexisting condition exclusion generally extends for 12 months, offset by creditable coverage. However, if an individual has no claims in the first six months following enrollment, the remainder of the exclusion period is waived.

(ii) *Conclusion.* In this *Example 2*, the plan's preexisting condition exclusions violate this section because they do not meet the requirements of this paragraph (b)(3); specifically, they do not apply uniformly to all similarly situated individuals. The plan provisions do not apply uniformly to all similarly situated individuals because individuals who have medical claims during the first six months following enrollment are not treated the same as similarly situated individuals with no claims during that period. (Under paragraph (d) of this section, the groups cannot be treated as two separate groups of similarly situated individuals because the distinction is based on a health factor.)

(c) *Prohibited discrimination in premiums or contributions*—(1) *In general*—(i) [Reserved] For further guidance, see § 54.9802–1(c)(1)(i).

(ii) Discounts, rebates, payments in kind, and any other premium differential mechanisms are taken into account in determining an individual's premium or contribution rate. [For rules relating to cost-sharing mechanisms, see paragraph (b)(2) of this section (addressing benefits).]

(2) *Rules relating to premium rates*—(i) *Group rating based on health factors not restricted under this section.* [Reserved] For further guidance, see § 54.9802–1(c)(1)(i).

(ii) *List billing based on a health factor prohibited.* However, a group health plan may not quote or charge an employer (or an individual) a different premium for an individual in a group of similarly situated individuals based on a health factor. [But see paragraph (g) of this section permitting favorable treatment of individuals with adverse health factors.]

(iii) *Examples.* The rules of this paragraph (c)(2) are illustrated by the following examples:

Example 1. (i) *Facts.* An employer sponsors a group health plan and purchases coverage from a health insurance issuer. In order to determine the premium rate for the upcoming plan year, the issuer reviews the claims experience of individuals covered under the plan. The issuer finds that Individual F had significantly higher claims experience than similarly situated individuals in the plan. The issuer quotes the plan a higher per-participant rate because of *F*'s claims experience.

(ii) *Conclusion.* See *Example 1* in 29 CFR 2590.702(c)(2) and 45 CFR 146.121(c)(2) for a conclusion that the issuer does not violate the provisions of 29 CFR 2590.702(c)(2) and 45 CFR 146.121(c)(2) similar to the provisions of this paragraph (c)(2) because the issuer blends the rate so that the employer is not quoted a higher rate for *F* than for a similarly situated individual based on *F*'s claims experience.

Example 2. (i) *Facts.* Same facts as *Example 1*, except that the issuer quotes the employer a higher premium rate for *F*, because of *F*'s claims experience, than for a similarly situated individual.

(ii) *Conclusion.* See *Example 2* in 29 CFR 2590.702(c)(2) and 45 CFR 146.121(c)(2) for a conclusion that the issuer violates provisions of 29 CFR 2590.702(c)(2) and 45 CFR 146.121(c)(2) similar to the provisions of this paragraph (c)(2). Moreover, even if the plan purchased the policy based on the quote but did not require a higher participant contribution for *F* than for a similarly situated individual, see *Example 2* in 29 CFR 2590.702(c)(2) and 45 CFR 146.121(c)(2) for a conclusion that the issuer would still violate 29 CFR 2590.702(c)(2) and 45 CFR 146.121(c)(2) (but in such a case the plan would not violate this paragraph (c)(2)).

A. HIPAA Interim Final Rules and Proposed Rules, continued

1400   Federal Register / Vol. 66, No. 5 / Monday, January 8, 2001 / Rules and Regulations

(3) *Exception for bona fide wellness programs.* [Reserved] For further guidance, see § 54.9802–1(c)(3).

(d) *Similarly situated individuals.* The requirements of this section apply only within a group of individuals who are treated as similarly situated individuals. A plan may treat participants as a group of similarly situated individuals separate from beneficiaries. In addition, participants may be treated as two or more distinct groups of similarly situated individuals and beneficiaries may be treated as two or more distinct groups of similarly situated individuals in accordance with the rules of this paragraph (d). Moreover, if individuals have a choice of two or more benefit packages, individuals choosing one benefit package may be treated as one or more groups of similarly situated individuals distinct from individuals choosing another benefit package.

(1) *Participants.* Subject to paragraph (d)(3) of this section, a plan may treat participants as two or more distinct groups of similarly situated individuals if the distinction between or among the groups of participants is based on a bona fide employment-based classification consistent with the employer's usual business practice. Whether an employment-based classification is bona fide is determined on the basis of all the relevant facts and circumstances. Relevant facts and circumstances include whether the employer uses the classification for purposes independent of qualification for health coverage (for example, determining eligibility for other employee benefits or determining other terms of employment). Subject to paragraph (d)(3) of this section, examples of classifications that, based on all the relevant facts and circumstances, may be bona fide include full-time versus part-time status, different geographic location, membership in a collective bargaining unit, date of hire, length of service, current employee versus former employee status, and different occupations. However, a classification based on any health factor is not a bona fide employment-based classification, unless the requirements of paragraph (g) of this section are satisfied (permitting favorable treatment of individuals with adverse health factors).

(2) *Beneficiaries*—(i) Subject to paragraph (d)(3) of this section, a plan may treat beneficiaries as two or more distinct groups of similarly situated individuals if the distinction between or among the groups of beneficiaries is based on any of the following factors:

(A) A bona fide employment-based classification of the participant through

whom the beneficiary is receiving coverage;

(B) Relationship to the participant (e.g., as a spouse or as a dependent child);

(C) Marital status;

(D) With respect to children of a participant, age or student status; or

(E) Any other factor if the factor is not a health factor.

(ii) Paragraph (d)(2)(i) of this section does not prevent more favorable treatment of beneficiaries with adverse health factors in accordance with paragraph (g) of this section.

(3) *Discrimination directed at individuals.* Notwithstanding paragraphs (d)(1) and (2) of this section, if the creation or modification of an employment or coverage classification is directed at individual participants or beneficiaries based on any health factor of the participants or beneficiaries, the classification is not permitted under this paragraph (d), unless it is permitted under paragraph (g) of this section (permitting favorable treatment of individuals with adverse health factors). Thus, if an employer modified an employment-based classification to single out, based on a health factor, individual participants and beneficiaries and deny them health coverage, the new classification would not be permitted under this section.

(4) *Examples.* The rules of this paragraph (d) are illustrated by the following examples:

Example 1. (i) *Facts.* An employer sponsors a group health plan for full-time employees only. Under the plan (consistent with the employer's usual business practice), employees who normally work at least 30 hours per week are considered to be working full-time. Other employees are considered to be working part-time. There is no evidence to suggest that the classification is directed at individual participants or beneficiaries.

(ii) *Conclusion.* In this *Example 1*, treating the full-time and part-time employees as two separate groups of similarly situated individuals is permitted under this paragraph (d) because the classification is bona fide and is not directed at individual participants or beneficiaries.

Example 2. (i) *Facts.* Under a group health plan, coverage is made available to employees, their spouses, and their dependent children. However, coverage is made available to a dependent child only if the dependent child is under age 19 (or under age 25 if the child is continuously enrolled full-time in an institution of higher learning (full-time students)). There is no evidence to suggest that these classifications are directed at individual participants or beneficiaries.

(ii) *Conclusion.* In this *Example 2*, treating spouses and dependent children differently by imposing an age limitation on dependent children, but not on spouses, is permitted under this paragraph (d). Specifically, the

distinction between spouses and dependent children is permitted under paragraph (d)(2) of this section and is not prohibited under paragraph (d)(3) of this section because it is not directed at individual participants or beneficiaries. It is also permissible to treat dependent children who are under age 19 (or full-time students under age 25) as a group of similarly situated individuals separate from those who are age 25 or older (or age 19 or older if they are not full-time students) because the classification is permitted under paragraph (d)(2) of this section and is not directed at individual participants or beneficiaries.

Example 3. (i) *Facts.* A university sponsors a group health plan that provides one health benefit package to faculty and another health benefit package to other staff. Faculty and staff are treated differently with respect to other employee benefits such as retirement benefits and leaves of absence. There is no evidence to suggest that the distinction is directed at individual participants or beneficiaries.

(ii) *Conclusion.* In this *Example 3*, the classification is permitted under this paragraph (d) because there is a distinction based on a bona fide employment-based classification consistent with the employer's usual business practice and the distinction is not directed at individual participants and beneficiaries.

Example 4. (i) *Facts.* An employer sponsors a group health plan that is available to all current employees. Former employees may also be eligible, but only if they complete a specified number of years of service, are enrolled under the plan at the time of termination of employment, and are continuously enrolled from that date. There is no evidence to suggest that these distinctions are directed at individual participants or beneficiaries.

(ii) *Conclusion.* In this *Example 4*, imposing additional eligibility requirements on former employees is permitted because a classification that distinguishes between current and former employees is a bona fide employment-based classification that is permitted under this paragraph (d), provided that it is not directed at individual participants or beneficiaries. In addition, it is permissible to distinguish between former employees who satisfy the service requirement and those who do not, provided that the distinction is not directed at individual participants or beneficiaries. (However, former employees who do not satisfy the eligibility criteria may, nonetheless, be eligible for continued coverage pursuant to a COBRA continuation provision or similar State law.)

Example 5. (i) *Facts.* An employer sponsors a group health plan that provides the same benefit package to all seven employees of the employer. Six of the seven employees have the same job title and responsibilities, but Employee G has a different job title and different responsibilities. After G files an expensive claim for benefits under the plan, coverage under the plan is modified so that employees with G's job title receive a different benefit package that includes a lower lifetime dollar limit than in the benefit package made available to the other six employees.

A. HIPAA Interim Final Rules and Proposed Rules, continued

(ii) *Conclusion.* Under the facts of this *Example 5*, changing the coverage classification for *G* based on the existing employment classification for *G* is not permitted under this paragraph (d) because the creation of the new coverage classification for *G* is directed at *G* based on one or more health factors.

(e) *Nonconfinement and actively-at-work provisions*—(1) *Nonconfinement provisions*—(i) *General rule.* Under the rules of paragraphs (b) and (c) of this section, a plan may not establish a rule for eligibility (as described in paragraph (b)(1)(ii) of this section) or set any individual's premium or contribution rate based on whether an individual is confined to a hospital or other health care institution. In addition, under the rules of paragraphs (b) and (c) of this section, a plan may not establish a rule for eligibility or set any individual's premium or contribution rate based on an individual's ability to engage in normal life activities, except to the extent permitted under paragraphs (e)(2)(ii) and (3) of this section (permitting plans, under certain circumstances, to distinguish among employees based on the performance of services).

(ii) *Examples.* The rules of this paragraph (e)(1) are illustrated by the following examples:

Example 1. (i) *Facts.* Under a group health plan, coverage for employees and their dependents generally becomes effective on the first day of employment. However, coverage for a dependent who is confined to a hospital or other health care institution does not become effective until the confinement ends.

(ii) *Conclusion.* In this *Example 1*, the plan violates this paragraph (e)(1) because the plan delays the effective date of coverage for dependents based on confinement to a hospital or other health care institution.

Example 2. (i) *Facts.* In previous years, a group health plan has provided coverage through a group health insurance policy offered by Issuer *M*. However, for the current year, the plan provides coverage through a group health insurance policy offered by Issuer *N*. Under Issuer *N*'s policy, items and services provided in connection with the confinement of a dependent to a hospital or other health care institution are not covered if the confinement is covered under an extension of benefits clause from a previous health insurance issuer.

(ii) *Conclusion.* See *Example 2* in 29 CFR 2590.702(e)(1) and 45 CFR 146.121(e)(1) for a conclusion that Issuer *N* violates provisions of 29 CFR 2590.702(e)(1) and 45 CFR 146.121(e)(1) similar to the provisions of this paragraph (e)(1) because Issuer *N* restricts benefits based on whether a dependent is confined to a hospital or other health care institution that is covered under an extension of benefits from a previous issuer.

(2) *Actively-at-work and continuous service provisions*—(i) *General rule*—(A)

Under the rules of paragraphs (b) and (c) of this section and subject to the exception for the first day of work in paragraph (e)(2)(ii) of this section, a plan may not establish a rule for eligibility (as described in paragraph (b)(1)(ii) of this section) or set any individual's premium or contribution rate based on whether an individual is actively at work (including whether an individual is continuously employed), unless absence from work due to any health factor (such as being absent from work on sick leave) is treated, for purposes of the plan, as being actively at work.

(B) The rules of this paragraph (e)(2)(i) are illustrated by the following examples:

Example 1. (i) *Facts.* Under a group health plan, an employee generally becomes eligible to enroll 30 days after the first day of employment. However, if the employee is not actively at work on the first day after the end of the 30-day period, then eligibility for enrollment is delayed until the first day the employee is actively at work.

(ii) *Conclusion.* In this *Example 1*, the plan violates this paragraph (e)(2) (and thus also violates paragraph (b) of this section). However, the plan would not violate paragraph (e)(2) or (b) of this section if, under the plan, an absence due to any health factor is considered being actively at work.

Example 2. (i) *Facts.* Under a group health plan, coverage for an employee becomes effective after 90 days of continuous service; that is, if an employee is absent from work (for any reason) before completing 90 days of service, the beginning of the 90-day period is measured from the day the employee returns to work (without any credit for service before the absence).

(ii) *Conclusion.* In this *Example 2*, the plan violates this paragraph (e)(2) (and thus also violates paragraph (b) of this section) because the 90-day continuous service requirement is a rule for eligibility based on whether an individual is actively at work. However, the plan would not violate this paragraph (e)(2) or paragraph (b) of this section if, under the plan, an absence due to any health factor is not considered an absence for purposes of measuring 90 days of continuous service.

(ii) *Exception for the first day of work*—(A) Notwithstanding the general rule in paragraph (e)(2)(i) of this section, a plan may establish a rule for eligibility that requires an individual to begin work for the employer sponsoring the plan (or, in the case of a multiemployer plan, to begin a job in covered employment) before coverage becomes effective, provided that such a rule for eligibility applies regardless of the reason for the absence.

(B) The rules of this paragraph (e)(2)(ii) are illustrated by the following examples:

Example 1. (i) *Facts.* Under the eligibility provision of a group health plan, coverage for new employees becomes effective on the first

day that the employee reports to work. Individual *H* is scheduled to begin work on August 3. However, *H* is unable to begin work on that day because of illness. *H* begins working on August 4, and *H*'s coverage is effective on August 4.

(ii) *Conclusion.* In this *Example 1*, the plan provision does not violate this section. However, if coverage for individuals who do not report to work on the first day they were scheduled to work for a reason unrelated to a health factor (such as vacation or bereavement) becomes effective on the first day they were scheduled to work, then the plan would violate this section.

Example 2. (i) *Facts.* Under a group health plan, coverage for new employees becomes effective on the first day of the month following the employee's first day of work, regardless of whether the employee is actively at work on the first day of the month. Individual *J* is scheduled to begin work on March 24. However, *J* is unable to begin work on March 24 because of illness. *J* begins working on April 7 and *J*'s coverage is effective May 1.

(ii) *Conclusion.* In this *Example 2*, the plan provision does not violate this section. However, as in *Example 1*, if coverage for individuals absent from work for reasons unrelated to a health factor became effective despite their absence, then the plan would violate this section.

(3) *Relationship to plan provisions defining similarly situated individuals*—(i) Notwithstanding the rules of paragraphs (e)(1) and (2) of this section, a plan may establish rules for eligibility or set any individual's premium or contribution rate in accordance with the rules relating to similarly situated individuals in paragraph (d) of this section. Accordingly, a plan may distinguish in rules for eligibility under the plan between full-time and part-time employees, between permanent and temporary or seasonal employees, between current and former employees, and between employees currently performing services and employees no longer performing services for the employer, subject to paragraph (d) of this section. However, other federal or State laws (including the COBRA continuation provisions and the Family and Medical Leave Act of 1993) may require an employee or the employee's dependents to be offered coverage and set limits on the premium or contribution rate even though the employee is not performing services.

(ii) The rules of this paragraph (e)(3) are illustrated by the following examples:

Example 1. (i) *Facts.* Under a group health plan, employees are eligible for coverage if they perform services for the employer for 30 or more hours per week or if they are on paid leave (such as annual, sick, or bereavement leave). Employees on unpaid leave are treated as a separate group of similarly situated individuals in accordance with the rules of paragraph (d) of this section.

A. HIPAA Interim Final Rules and Proposed Rules, continued

(ii) *Conclusion.* In this *Example 1*, the plan provisions do not violate this section. However, if the plan treated individuals performing services for the employer for 30 or more hours per week, individuals on annual leave, and individuals on bereavement leave as a group of similarly situated individuals separate from individuals on sick leave, the plan would violate this paragraph (e) (and thus also would violate paragraph (b) of this section) because groups of similarly situated individuals cannot be established based on a health factor (including the taking of sick leave) under paragraph (d) of this section.

Example 2. (i) *Facts.* To be eligible for coverage under a bona fide collectively bargained group health plan in the current calendar quarter, the plan requires an individual to have worked 250 hours in covered employment during the three-month period that ends one month before the beginning of the current calendar quarter. The distinction between employees working at least 250 hours and those working less than 250 hours in the earlier three-month period is not directed at individual participants or beneficiaries based on any health factor of the participants or beneficiaries.

(ii) *Conclusion.* In this *Example 2*, the plan provision does not violate this section because, under the rules for similarly situated individuals allowing full-time employees to be treated differently than part-time employees, employees who work at least 250 hours in a three-month period can be treated differently than employees who fail to work 250 hours in that period. The result would be the same if the plan permitted individuals to apply excess hours from previous periods to satisfy the requirement for the current quarter.

Example 3. (i) *Facts.* Under a group health plan, coverage of an employee is terminated when the individual's employment is terminated, in accordance with the rules of paragraph (d) of this section. Employee B has been covered under the plan. B experiences a disabling illness that prevents B from working. B takes a leave of absence under the Family and Medical Leave Act of 1993. At the end of such leave, B terminates employment and consequently loses coverage under the plan. (This termination of coverage is without regard to whatever rights the employee (or members of the employee's family) may have for COBRA continuation coverage.)

(ii) *Conclusion.* In this *Example 3*, the plan provision terminating B's coverage upon B's termination of employment does not violate this section.

Example 4. (i) *Facts.* Under a group health plan, coverage of an employee is terminated when the employee ceases to perform services for the employer sponsoring the plan, in accordance with the rules of paragraph (d) of this section. Employee C is laid off for three months. When the layoff begins, C's coverage under the plan is terminated. (This termination of coverage is without regard to whatever rights the employee (or members of the employee's family) may have for COBRA continuation coverage.)

(ii) *Conclusion.* In this *Example 4*, the plan provision terminating C's coverage upon the cessation of C's performance of services does not violate this section.

(f) *Bona fide wellness programs.* [Reserved]

(g) *More favorable treatment of individuals with adverse health factors permitted*—(1) *In rules for eligibility*—(i) Nothing in this section prevents a group health plan from establishing more favorable rules for eligibility (described in paragraph (b)(1) of this section) for individuals with an adverse health factor, such as disability, than for individuals without the adverse health factor. Moreover, nothing in this section prevents a plan from charging a higher premium or contribution with respect to individuals with an adverse health factor if they would not be eligible for the coverage were it not for the adverse health factor. (However, other laws, including State insurance laws, may set or limit premium rates; these laws are not affected by this section.)

(ii) The rules of this paragraph (g)(1) are illustrated by the following examples:

Example 1. (i) *Facts.* An employer sponsors a group health plan that generally is available to employees, spouses of employees, and dependent children until age 23. However, dependent children who are disabled are eligible for coverage beyond age 23.

(ii) *Conclusion.* In this *Example 1*, the plan provision allowing coverage for disabled dependent children beyond age 23 satisfies this paragraph (g)(1) (and thus does not violate this section).

Example 2. (i) *Facts.* An employer sponsors a group health plan, which is generally available to employees (and members of the employee's family) until the last day of the month in which the employee ceases to perform services for the employer. The plan generally charges employees $50 per month for employee-only coverage and $125 per month for family coverage. However, an employee who ceases to perform services for the employer by reason of disability may remain covered under the plan until the last day of the month that is 12 months after the month in which the employee ceased to perform services for the employer. During this extended period of coverage, the plan charges the employee $100 per month for employee-only coverage and $250 per month for family coverage. (This extended period of coverage is without regard to whatever rights the employee (or members of the employee's family) may have for COBRA continuation coverage.)

(ii) *Conclusion.* In this *Example 2*, the plan provision allowing extended coverage for disabled employees and their families satisfies this paragraph (g)(1) (and thus does not violate this section). In addition, the plan is permitted, under this paragraph (g)(1), to charge the disabled employees a higher premium during the extended period of coverage.

Example 3. (i) *Facts.* To comply with the requirements of a COBRA continuation provision, a group health plan generally makes COBRA continuation coverage available for a maximum period of 18 months in connection with a termination of employment but makes the coverage available for a maximum period of 29 months to certain disabled individuals and certain members of the disabled individual's family. Although the plan generally requires payment of 102 percent of the applicable premium for the first 18 months of COBRA continuation coverage, the plan requires payment of 150 percent of the applicable premium for the disabled individual's COBRA continuation coverage during the disability extension if the disabled individual would not be entitled to COBRA continuation coverage but for the disability.

(ii) *Conclusion.* In this *Example 3*, the plan provision allowing extended COBRA continuation coverage for disabled individuals satisfies this paragraph (g)(1) (and thus does not violate this section). In addition, the plan is permitted, under this paragraph (g)(1), to charge the disabled individuals a higher premium for the extended coverage if the individuals would not be eligible for COBRA continuation coverage were it not for the disability. (Similarly, if the plan provided an extended period of coverage for disabled individuals pursuant to State law or plan provision rather than pursuant to a COBRA continuation coverage provision, the plan could likewise charge the disabled individuals a higher premium for the extended coverage.)

(2) *In premiums or contributions*—(i) Nothing in this section prevents a group health plan from charging individuals a premium or contribution that is less than the premium (or contribution) for similarly situated individuals if the lower charge is based on an adverse health factor, such as disability.

(ii) The rules of this paragraph (g)(2) are illustrated by the following example:

Example. (i) *Facts.* Under a group health plan, employees are generally required to pay $50 per month for employee-only coverage and $125 per month for family coverage under the plan. However, employees who are disabled receive coverage (whether employee-only or family coverage) under the plan free of charge.

(ii) *Conclusion.* In this *Example*, the plan provision waiving premium payment for disabled employees is permitted under this paragraph (g)(2) (and thus does not violate this section).

(h) *No effect on other laws.* Compliance with this section is not determinative of compliance with any other provision of the Code (including the COBRA continuation provisions) or any other State or federal law, such as the Americans with Disabilities Act. Therefore, although the rules of this section would not prohibit a plan or issuer from treating one group of similarly situated individuals differently from another (such as providing different benefit packages to current and former employees), other

A. HIPAA Interim Final Rules and Proposed Rules, continued

federal or State laws may require that two separate groups of similarly situated individuals be treated the same for certain purposes (such as making the same benefit package available to COBRA qualified beneficiaries as is made available to active employees). In addition, although this section generally does not impose new disclosure obligations on plans, this section does not affect any other laws, including those that require accurate disclosures and prohibit intentional misrepresentation.

(i) *Effective dates*—(1) Final rules apply March 9, 2001. [Reserved] For further guidance, see § 54.9802–1(i)(1).

(2) *This section applies for plan years beginning on or after July 1, 2001.* Except as provided in paragraph (i)(3) of this section, this section applies for plan years beginning on or after July 1, 2001. Except as provided in paragraph (i)(3) of this section, with respect to efforts to comply with section 9802 before the first plan year beginning on or after July 1, 2001, the Secretary will not take any enforcement action against a plan that has sought to comply in good faith with section 9802.

(3) *Transitional rules for individuals previously denied coverage based on a health factor.* This paragraph (i)(3) provides rules relating to individuals previously denied coverage under a group health plan based on a health factor of the individual. Paragraph (i)(3)(i) clarifies what constitutes a denial of coverage under this paragraph (i)(3). Paragraph (i)(3)(ii) of this section applies with respect to any individual who was denied coverage if the denial was not based on a good faith interpretation of section 9802 or the Secretary's published guidance. Under that paragraph, such an individual must be allowed to enroll retroactively to the effective date of section 9802, or, if later, the date the individual meets eligibility criteria under the plan that do not discriminate based on any health factor. Paragraph (i)(3)(iii) of this section applies with respect to any individual who was denied coverage based on a good faith interpretation of section 9802 or the Secretary's published guidance. Under that paragraph, such an individual must be given an opportunity to enroll effective July 1, 2001. In either event, whether under paragraph (i)(3)(ii) or (iii) of this section, the Secretary will not take any enforcement action with respect to denials of coverage addressed in this paragraph (i)(3) if the plan has complied with the transitional rules of this paragraph (i)(3).

(i) *Denial of coverage clarified.* For purposes of this paragraph (i)(3), an individual is considered to have been denied coverage if the individual—

(A) Failed to apply for coverage because it was reasonable to believe that an application for coverage would have been futile due to a plan provision that discriminated based on a health factor; or

(B) Was not offered an opportunity to enroll in the plan and the failure to give such an opportunity violates this section.

(ii) *Individuals denied coverage without a good faith interpretation of the law*—(A) *Opportunity to enroll required.* If a plan has denied coverage to any individual based on a health factor and that denial was not based on a good faith interpretation of section 9802 or any guidance published by the Secretary, the plan is required to give the individual an opportunity to enroll (including notice of an opportunity to enroll) that continues for at least 30 days. This opportunity must be presented not later than March 9, 2001.

(1) If this enrollment opportunity was presented before or within the first plan year beginning on or after July 1, 1997 (or in the case of a collectively bargained plan, before or within the first plan year beginning on the effective date for the plan described in section 401(c)(3) of the Health Insurance Portability and Accountability Act of 1996), the coverage must be effective within that first plan year.

(2) If this enrollment opportunity is presented after such plan year, the individual must be given the choice of having the coverage effective on either of the following two dates—

(i) The date the plan receives a request for enrollment in connection with the enrollment opportunity; or

(ii) Retroactively to the first day of the first plan year beginning on the effective date for the plan described in section 401(c)(1) or (3) of the Health Insurance Portability and Accountability Act of 1996 (or, if the individual otherwise first became eligible to enroll for coverage after that date, on the date the individual was otherwise eligible to enroll in the plan). If an individual elects retroactive coverage, the plan is required to provide the benefits it would have provided if the individual had been enrolled for coverage during that period (irrespective of any otherwise applicable plan provisions governing timing for the submission of claims). The plan may require the individual to pay whatever additional amount the individual would have been required to pay for the coverage (but the plan cannot charge interest on that amount).

(B) *Relation to preexisting condition rules.* For purposes of Chapter 100 of

Subtitle K, the individual may not be treated as a late enrollee or as a special enrollee. Moreover, the individual's enrollment date is the effective date for the plan described in section 401(c)(1) or (3) of the Health Insurance Portability and Accountability Act of 1996 (or, if the individual otherwise first became eligible to enroll for coverage after that date, on the date the individual was otherwise eligible to enroll in the plan), even if the individual chooses under paragraph (i)(3)(ii)(A) of this section to have coverage effective only prospectively. In addition, any period between the individual's enrollment date and the effective date of coverage is treated as a waiting period.

(C) *Examples.* The rules of this paragraph (i)(3)(ii) are illustrated by the following examples:

Example 1. (i) *Facts.* Employer X maintains a group health plan with a plan year beginning October 1 and ending September 30. Individual F was hired by Employer X before the effective date of section 9802. Before the effective date of section 9802 for this plan (October 1, 1997), the terms of the plan allowed employees and their dependents to enroll when the employee was first hired, and on each January 1 thereafter, but in either case, only if the individual could pass a physical examination. F's application to enroll when first hired was denied because F could not pass a physical examination. Upon the effective date of section 9802 for this plan (October 1, 1997), the plan is amended to delete the requirement to pass a physical examination. In November of 1997, the plan gives F an opportunity to enroll in the plan (including notice of the opportunity to enroll) without passing a physical examination, with coverage effective January 1, 1998.

(ii) *Conclusion.* In this *Example 1*, the plan complies with the requirements of this paragraph (i)(3)(ii).

Example 2. (i) *Facts.* The plan year of a group health plan begins January 1 and ends December 31. Under the plan, a dependent who is unable to engage in normal life activities on the date coverage would otherwise become effective is not enrolled until the dependent is able to engage in normal life activities. Individual G is a dependent who is otherwise eligible for coverage, but is unable to engage in normal life activities. The plan has not allowed G to enroll for coverage.

(ii) *Conclusion.* In this *Example 2*, beginning on the effective date of section 9802 for the plan (January 1, 1998), the plan provision is not permitted under any good faith interpretation of section 9802 or any guidance published by the Secretary. Therefore, the plan is required, not later than March 9, 2001, to give G an opportunity to enroll (including notice of the opportunity to enroll), with coverage effective, at G's option, either retroactively from January 1, 1998 or prospectively from the date G's request for enrollment is received by the plan. If G elects coverage to be effective beginning January 1,

A. HIPAA Interim Final Rules and Proposed Rules, continued

1998, the plan can require G to pay employee premiums for the retroactive coverage.

(iii) *Individuals denied coverage based on a good faith interpretation of the law*—(A) *Opportunity to enroll required.* If a plan has denied coverage to any individual before the first day of the first plan year beginning on or after July 1, 2001 based in part on a health factor and that denial was based on a good faith interpretation of section 9802 or guidance published by the Secretary, the plan is required to give the individual an opportunity to enroll (including notice of an opportunity to enroll) that continues for at least 30 days, with coverage effective no later than July 1, 2001. Individuals required to be offered an opportunity to enroll include individuals previously offered enrollment without regard to a health factor but subsequently denied enrollment due to a health factor.

(B) *Relation to preexisting condition rules.* For purposes of Chapter 100 of Subtitle K, the individual may not be treated as a late enrollee or as a special enrollee. Moreover, the individual's enrollment date under the plan is the effective date for the plan described in section 401(c)(1) or (3) of the Health Insurance Portability and Accountability Act of 1996 (or, if the individual otherwise first became eligible to enroll for coverage after that date, on the date the individual was otherwise eligible to enroll in the plan). In addition, any period between the individual's enrollment date and the effective date of coverage is treated as a waiting period.

(C) *Example.* The rules of this paragraph (i)(3)(iii) are illustrated by the following example:

Example. (i) *Facts.* Individual H was hired by Employer Y on May 3, 1995. Y maintains a group health plan with a plan year beginning on February 1. Under the terms of the plan, employees and their dependents are allowed to enroll when the employee is first hired (without a requirement to pass a physical examination), and on each February 1 thereafter if the individual can pass a physical examination. H chose not to enroll for coverage when hired in May of 1995. On February 1, 1997, H tried to enroll for coverage under the plan. However, H was denied coverage for failure to pass a physical examination. Shortly thereafter, Y's plan eliminated late enrollment, and H was not given another opportunity to enroll in the plan. There is no evidence to suggest that Y's plan was acting in bad faith in denying coverage under the plan beginning on the effective date of section 9802 (February 1, 1998).

(ii) *Conclusion.* In this *Example*, because coverage previously had been made available with respect to H without regard to any health factor of H and because Y's plan was acting in accordance with a good faith

interpretation of section 9802 (and guidance published by the Secretary), the failure of Y's plan to allow H to enroll effective February 1, 1998 was permissible on that date. However, under the transitional rules of this paragraph (i)(3)(iii), Y's plan must give H an opportunity to enroll that continues for at least 30 days, with coverage effective no later than July 1, 2001. (In addition, February 1, 1998 is H's enrollment date under the plan and the period between February 1, 1998 and July 1, 2001 is treated as a waiting period. Accordingly, any preexisting condition exclusion period permitted under section 9801 will have expired before July 1, 2001.)

Robert E. Wenzel,

Deputy Commissioner of Internal Revenue.

Approved:

Dated: August 8, 2000.

Jonathan Talisman,

Acting Assistant Secretary of the Treasury.

For the reasons set forth above, 29 CFR Part 2590 is amended as follows:

PART 2590 [AMENDED]—RULES AND REGULATIONS FOR HEALTH INSURANCE PORTABILITY AND RENEWABILITY FOR GROUP HEALTH PLANS

1. The authority citation for Part 2590 is revised to read as follows:

Authority: Secs. 107, 209, 505, 701–703, 711–713, and 731–734 of ERISA (29 U.S.C. 1027, 1059, 1135, 1171–1173, 1181–1183, and 1191–1194), as amended by HIPAA (Public Law 104–191, 110 Stat. 1936), MHPA and NMHPA (Public Law 104–204, 110 Stat. 2935), and WHCRA (Public Law 105–277, 112 Stat. 2681–436), section 101(g)(4) of HIPAA, and Secretary of Labor's Order No. 1–87, 52 FR 13139, April 21, 1987.

2. Section § 2590.702 is revised to read as follows:

§ 2590.702 Prohibiting discrimination against participants and beneficiaries based on a health factor.

(a) *Health factors.* (1) The term *health factor* means, in relation to an individual, any of the following health status-related factors:

(i) Health status;

(ii) Medical condition (including both physical and mental illnesses), as defined in § 2590.701–2;

(iii) Claims experience;

(iv) Receipt of health care;

(v) Medical history;

(vi) Genetic information, as defined in § 2590.701–2;

(vii) Evidence of insurability; or

(viii) Disability.

(2) Evidence of insurability includes—

(i) Conditions arising out of acts of domestic violence; and

(ii) Participation in activities such as motorcycling, snowmobiling, all-terrain vehicle riding, horseback riding, skiing, and other similar activities.

(3) The decision whether health coverage is elected for an individual (including the time chosen to enroll, such as under special enrollment or late enrollment) is not, itself, within the scope of any health factor. (However, under § 2590.701–6, a plan or issuer must treat special enrollees the same as similarly situated individuals who are enrolled when first eligible.)

(b) *Prohibited discrimination in rules for eligibility*—(1) *In general*—(i) A group health plan, and a health insurance issuer offering health insurance coverage in connection with a group health plan, may not establish any rule for eligibility (including continued eligibility) of any individual to enroll for benefits under the terms of the plan or group health insurance coverage that discriminates based on any health factor that relates to that individual or a dependent of that individual. This rule is subject to the provisions of paragraph (b)(2) of this section (explaining how this rule applies to benefits), paragraph (b)(3) of this section (allowing plans to impose certain preexisting condition exclusions), paragraph (d) of this section (containing rules for establishing groups of similarly situated individuals), paragraph (e) of this section (relating to nonconfinement, actively-at-work, and other service requirements), paragraph (f) of this section (relating to bona fide wellness programs), and paragraph (g) of this section (permitting favorable treatment of individuals with adverse health factors).

(ii) For purposes of this section, rules for eligibility include, but are not limited to, rules relating to—

(A) Enrollment;

(B) The effective date of coverage;

(C) Waiting (or affiliation) periods;

(D) Late and special enrollment;

(E) Eligibility for benefit packages (including rules for individuals to change their selection among benefit packages);

(F) Benefits (including rules relating to covered benefits, benefit restrictions, and cost-sharing mechanisms such as coinsurance, copayments, and deductibles), as described in paragraphs (b)(2) and (3) of this section;

(G) Continued eligibility; and

(H) Terminating coverage (including disenrollment) of any individual under the plan.

(iii) The rules of this paragraph (b)(1) are illustrated by the following examples:

Example 1. (i) *Facts.* An employer sponsors a group health plan that is available to all employees who enroll within the first 30 days of their employment. However, employees who do not enroll within the first

A. HIPAA Interim Final Rules and Proposed Rules, continued

30 days cannot enroll later unless they pass a physical examination.

(ii) *Conclusion.* In this *Example 1*, the requirement to pass a physical examination in order to enroll in the plan is a rule for eligibility that discriminates based on one or more health factors and thus violates this paragraph (b)(1).

Example 2. (i) *Facts.* Under an employer's group health plan, employees who enroll during the first 30 days of employment (and during special enrollment periods) may choose between two benefit packages: an indemnity option and an HMO option. However, employees who enroll during late enrollment are permitted to enroll only in the HMO option and only if they provide evidence of good health.

(ii) *Conclusion.* In this *Example 2*, the requirement to provide evidence of good health in order to be eligible for late enrollment in the HMO option is a rule for eligibility that discriminates based on one or more health factors and thus violates this paragraph (b)(1). However, if the plan did not require evidence of good health but limited late enrollees to the HMO option, the plan's rules for eligibility would not discriminate based on any health factor, and thus would not violate this paragraph (b)(1), because the time an individual chooses to enroll is not, itself, within the scope of any health factor.

Example 3. (i) *Facts.* Under an employer's group health plan, all employees generally may enroll within the first 30 days of employment. However, individuals who participate in certain recreational activities, including motorcycling, are excluded from coverage.

(ii) *Conclusion.* In this *Example 3*, excluding from the plan individuals who participate in recreational activities, such as motorcycling, is a rule for eligibility that discriminates based on one more health factors and thus violates this paragraph (b)(1).

Example 4. (i) *Facts.* A group health plan applies for a group health policy offered by an issuer. As part of the application, the issuer receives health information about individuals to be covered under the plan. Individual *A* is an employee of the employer maintaining the plan. *A* and *A*'s dependents have a history of high health claims. Based on the information about *A* and *A*'s dependents, the issuer excludes *A* and *A*'s dependents from the group policy it offers to the employer.

(ii) *Conclusion.* In this *Example 4*, the issuer's exclusion of *A* and *A*'s dependents from coverage is a rule for eligibility that discriminates based on one or more health factors, and thus violates this paragraph (b)(1). (If the employer is a small employer under 45 CFR 144.103 (generally, an employer with 50 or fewer employees), the issuer also may violate 45 CFR 146.150, which requires issuers to offer all the policies they sell in the small group market on a guaranteed available basis to all small employers and to accept every eligible individual in every small employer group.) If the plan provides coverage through this policy and does not provide equivalent coverage for *A* and *A*'s dependents through other means, the plan will also violate this paragraph (b)(1).

(2) *Application to benefits*—(i) *General rule*—(A) Under this section, a group health plan or group health insurance issuer is not required to provide coverage for any particular benefit to any group of similarly situated individuals.

(B) However, benefits provided under a plan or through group health insurance coverage must be uniformly available to all similarly situated individuals (as described in paragraph (d) of this section). Likewise, any restriction on a benefit or benefits must apply uniformly to all similarly situated individuals and must not be directed at individual participants or beneficiaries based on any health factor of the participants or beneficiaries (determined based on all the relevant facts and circumstances). Thus, for example, a plan or issuer may limit or exclude benefits in relation to a specific disease or condition, limit or exclude benefits for certain types of treatments or drugs, or limit or exclude benefits based on a determination of whether the benefits are experimental or not medically necessary, but only if the benefit limitation or exclusion applies uniformly to all similarly situated individuals and is not directed at individual participants or beneficiaries based on any health factor of the participants or beneficiaries. In addition, a plan or issuer may impose annual, lifetime, or other limits on benefits and may require the satisfaction of a deductible, copayment, coinsurance, or other cost-sharing requirement in order to obtain a benefit if the limit or cost-sharing requirement applies uniformly to all similarly situated individuals and is not directed at individual participants or beneficiaries based on any health factor of the participants or beneficiaries. In the case of a cost-sharing requirement, see also paragraph (b)(2)(ii) of this section, which permits variances in the application of a cost-sharing mechanism made available under a bona fide wellness program. (Whether any plan provision or practice with respect to benefits complies with this paragraph (b)(2)(i) does not affect whether the provision or practice is permitted under any other provision of the Act, the Americans with Disabilities Act, or any other law, whether State or federal.)

(C) For purposes of this paragraph (b)(2)(i), a plan amendment applicable to all individuals in one or more groups of similarly situated individuals under the plan and made effective no earlier than the first day of the first plan year after the amendment is adopted is not considered to be directed at any individual participants or beneficiaries.

(D) The rules of this paragraph (b)(2)(i) are illustrated by the following examples:

Example 1. (i) *Facts.* A group health plan applies a $500,000 lifetime limit on all benefits to each participant or beneficiary covered under the plan. The limit is not directed at individual participants or beneficiaries.

(ii) *Conclusion.* In this *Example 1*, the limit does not violate this paragraph (b)(2)(i) because $500,000 of benefits are available uniformly to each participant and beneficiary under the plan and because the limit is applied uniformly to all participants and beneficiaries and is not directed at individual participants or beneficiaries.

Example 2. (i) *Facts.* A group health plan has a $2 million lifetime limit on all benefits (and no other lifetime limits) for participants covered under the plan. Participant *B* files a claim for the treatment of AIDS. At the next corporate board meeting of the plan sponsor, the claim is discussed. Shortly thereafter, the plan is modified to impose a $10,000 lifetime limit on benefits for the treatment of AIDS, effective before the beginning of the next plan year.

(ii) *Conclusion.* Under the facts of this *Example 2*, the plan violates this paragraph (b)(2)(i) because the plan modification is directed at *B* based on *B*'s claim.

Example 3. (i) *Facts.* A group health plan applies for a group health policy offered by an issuer. Individual *C* is covered under the plan and has an adverse health condition. As part of the application, the issuer receives health information about the individuals to be covered, including information about *C*'s adverse health condition. The policy form offered by the issuer generally provides benefits for the adverse health condition that *C* has, but in this case the issuer offers the plan a policy modified by a rider that excludes benefits for *C* for that condition. The exclusionary rider is made effective the first day of the next plan year.

(ii) *Conclusion.* In this *Example 3*, the issuer violates this paragraph (b)(2)(i) because benefits for *C*'s condition are available to other individuals in the group of similarly situated individuals that includes *C* but are not available to *C*. Thus, the benefits are not uniformly available to all similarly situated individuals. Even though the exclusionary rider is made effective the first day of the next plan year, because the rider does not apply to all similarly situated individuals, the issuer violates this paragraph (b)(2)(i).

Example 4. (i) *Facts.* A group health plan has a $2,000 lifetime limit for the treatment of temporomandibular joint syndrome (TMJ). The limit is applied uniformly to all similarly situated individuals and is not directed at individual participants or beneficiaries.

(ii) *Conclusion.* In this *Example 4*, the limit does not violate this paragraph (b)(2)(i) because $2000 of benefits for the treatment of TMJ are available uniformly to all similarly situated individuals and a plan may limit benefits covered in relation to a specific disease or condition if the limit applies uniformly to all similarly situated individuals and is not directed at individual participants or beneficiaries.

A. HIPAA Interim Final Rules and Proposed Rules, continued

Example 5. (i) *Facts.* A group health plan applies a $2 million lifetime limit on all benefits. However, the $2 million lifetime limit is reduced to $10,000 for any participant or beneficiary covered under the plan who has a congenital heart defect.

(ii) *Conclusion.* In this *Example 5,* the lower lifetime limit for participants and beneficiaries with a congenital heart defect violates this paragraph (b)(2)(i) because benefits under the plan are not uniformly available to all similarly situated individuals and the plan's lifetime limit on benefits does not apply uniformly to all similarly situated individuals.

Example 6. (i) *Facts.* A group health plan limits benefits for prescription drugs to those listed on a drug formulary. The limit is applied uniformly to all similarly situated individuals and is not directed at individual participants or beneficiaries.

(ii) *Conclusion.* In this *Example 6,* the exclusion from coverage of drugs not listed on the drug formulary does not violate this paragraph (b)(2)(i) because benefits for prescription drugs listed on the formulary are uniformly available to all similarly situated individuals and because the exclusion of drugs not listed on the formulary applies uniformly to all similarly situated individuals and is not directed at individual participants or beneficiaries.

Example 7. (i) *Facts.* Under a group health plan, doctor visits are generally subject to a $250 annual deductible and 20 percent coinsurance requirement. However, prenatal doctor visits are not subject to any deductible or coinsurance requirement. These rules are applied uniformly to all similarly situated individuals and are not directed at individual participants or beneficiaries.

(ii) *Conclusion.* In this *Example 7,* imposing different deductible and coinsurance requirements for prenatal doctor visits and other visits does not violate this paragraph (b)(2)(i) because a plan may establish different deductibles or coinsurance requirements for different services if the deductible or coinsurance requirement is applied uniformly to all similarly situated individuals and is not directed at individual participants or beneficiaries.

(ii) *Cost-sharing mechanisms and wellness programs.* A group health plan or group health insurance coverage with a cost-sharing mechanism (such as a deductible, copayment, or coinsurance) that requires a higher payment from an individual, based on a health factor of that individual or a dependent of that individual, than for a similarly situated individual under the plan (and thus does not apply uniformly to all similarly situated individuals) does not violate the requirements of this paragraph (b)(2) if the payment differential is based on whether an individual has complied with the requirements of a bona fide wellness program.

(iii) *Specific rule relating to source-of-injury exclusions*—(A) If a group health plan or group health insurance coverage generally provides benefits for a type of injury, the plan or issuer may not deny

benefits otherwise provided for treatment of the injury if the injury results from an act of domestic violence or a medical condition (including both physical and mental health conditions).

(B) The rules of this paragraph (b)(2)(iii) are illustrated by the following examples:

Example 1. (i) *Facts.* A group health plan generally provides medical/surgical benefits, including benefits for hospital stays, that are medically necessary. However, the plan excludes benefits for self-inflicted injuries or injuries sustained in connection with attempted suicide. Individual *D* suffers from depression and attempts suicide. As a result, *D* sustains injuries and is hospitalized for treatment of the injuries. Pursuant to the exclusion, the plan denies *D* benefits for treatment of the injuries.

(ii) *Conclusion.* In this *Example 1,* the suicide attempt is the result of a medical condition (depression). Accordingly, the denial of benefits for the treatments of *D*'s injuries violates the requirements of this paragraph (b)(2)(iii) because the plan provision excludes benefits for treatment of an injury resulting from a medical condition.

Example 2. (i) *Facts.* A group health plan provides benefits for head injuries generally. The plan also has a general exclusion for any injury sustained while participating in any of a number of recreational activities, including bungee jumping. However, this exclusion does not apply to any injury that results from a medical condition (nor from domestic violence). Participant *E* sustains a head injury while bungee jumping. The injury did not result from a medical condition (nor from domestic violence). Accordingly, the plan denies benefits for *E*'s head injury.

(ii) *Conclusion.* In this *Example 2,* the plan provision that denies benefits based on the source of an injury does not restrict benefits based on an act of domestic violence or any medical condition. Therefore, the provision is permissible under this paragraph (b)(2)(iii) and does not violate this section. (However, if the plan did not allow *E* to enroll in the plan (or applied different rules for eligibility to *E*) because *E* frequently participates in bungee jumping, the plan would violate paragraph (b)(1) of this section.)

(3) *Relationship to § 2590.701–3.* (i) A preexisting condition exclusion is permitted under this section if it —

(A) Complies with § 2590.701–3;

(B) Applies uniformly to all similarly situated individuals (as described in paragraph (d) of this section); and

(C) Is not directed at individual participants or beneficiaries based on any health factor of the participants or beneficiaries. For purposes of this paragraph (b)(3)(i)(C), a plan amendment relating to a preexisting condition exclusion applicable to all individuals in one or more groups of similarly situated individuals under the plan and made effective no earlier than the first day of the first plan year after the amendment is adopted is not

considered to be directed at any individual participants or beneficiaries.

(ii) The rules of this paragraph (b)(3) are illustrated by the following examples:

Example 1. (i) *Facts.* A group health plan imposes a preexisting condition exclusion on all individuals enrolled in the plan. The exclusion applies to conditions for which medical advice, diagnosis, care, or treatment was recommended or received within the six-month period ending on an individual's enrollment date. In addition, the exclusion generally extends for 12 months after an individual's enrollment date, but this 12-month period is offset by the number of days of an individual's creditable coverage in accordance with § 2590.701–3. There is nothing to indicate that the exclusion is directed at individual participants or beneficiaries.

(ii) *Conclusion.* In this *Example 1,* even though the plan's preexisting condition exclusion discriminates against individuals based on one or more health factors, the preexisting condition exclusion does not violate this section because it applies uniformly to all similarly situated individuals, is not directed at individual participants or beneficiaries, and complies with § 2590.701–3 (that is, the requirements relating to the six-month look-back period, the 12-month (or 18-month) maximum exclusion period, and the creditable coverage offset).

Example 2. (i) *Facts.* A group health plan excludes coverage for conditions with respect to which medical advice, diagnosis, care, or treatment was recommended or received within the six-month period ending on an individual's enrollment date. Under the plan, the preexisting condition exclusion generally extends for 12 months, offset by creditable coverage. However, if an individual has no claims in the first six months following enrollment, the remainder of the exclusion period is waived.

(ii) *Conclusion.* In this *Example 2,* the plan's preexisting condition exclusions violate this section because they do not meet the requirements of this paragraph (b)(3); specifically, they do not apply uniformly to all similarly situated individuals. The plan provisions do not apply uniformly to all similarly situated individuals because individuals who have medical claims during the first six months following enrollment are not treated the same as similarly situated individuals with no claims during that period. (Under paragraph (d) of this section, the groups cannot be treated as two separate groups of similarly situated individuals because the distinction is based on a health factor.)

(c) *Prohibited discrimination in premiums or contributions*—(1) *In general*—(i) A group health plan, and a health insurance issuer offering health insurance coverage in connection with a group health plan, may not require an individual, as a condition of enrollment or continued enrollment under the plan or group health insurance coverage, to pay a premium or contribution that is

A. HIPAA Interim Final Rules and Proposed Rules, continued

greater than the premium or contribution for a similarly situated individual (described in paragraph (d) of this section) enrolled in the plan or group health insurance coverage based on any health factor that relates to the individual or a dependent of the individual.

(ii) Discounts, rebates, payments in kind, and any other premium differential mechanisms are taken into account in determining an individual's premium or contribution rate. (For rules relating to cost-sharing mechanisms, see paragraph (b)(2) of this section (addressing benefits).)

(2) *Rules relating to premium rates—* (i) *Group rating based on health factors not restricted under this section.* Nothing in this section restricts the aggregate amount that an employer may be charged for coverage under a group health plan.

(ii) *List billing based on a health factor prohibited.* However, a group health insurance issuer, or a group health plan, may not quote or charge an employer (or an individual) a different premium for an individual in a group of similarly situated individuals based on a health factor. (But see paragraph (g) of this section permitting favorable treatment of individuals with adverse health factors.)

(iii) *Examples.* The rules of this paragraph (c)(2) are illustrated by the following examples:

Example 1. (i) *Facts.* An employer sponsors a group health plan and purchases coverage from a health insurance issuer. In order to determine the premium rate for the upcoming plan year, the issuer reviews the claims experience of individuals covered under the plan. The issuer finds that Individual F had significantly higher claims experience than similarly situated individuals in the plan. The issuer quotes the plan a higher per-participant rate because of F's claims experience.

(ii) *Conclusion.* In this *Example 1*, the issuer does not violate the provisions of this paragraph (c)(2) because the issuer blends the rate so that the employer is not quoted a higher rate for F than for a similarly situated individual based on F's claims experience.

Example 2. (i) *Facts.* Same facts as *Example 1*, except that the issuer quotes the employer a higher premium rate for F, because of F's claims experience, than for a similarly situated individual.

(ii) *Conclusion.* In this *Example 2*, the issuer violates this paragraph (c)(2). Moreover, even if the plan purchased the policy based on the quote but did not require a higher participant contribution for F than for a similarly situated individual, the issuer would still violate this paragraph (c)(2) (but in such a case the plan would not violate this paragraph (c)(2)).

(3) *Exception for bona fide wellness programs.* Notwithstanding paragraphs (c)(1) and (2) of this section, a plan may establish a premium or contribution differential based on whether an individual has complied with the requirements of a bona fide wellness program.

(d) *Similarly situated individuals.* The requirements of this section apply only within a group of individuals who are treated as similarly situated individuals. A plan or issuer may treat participants as a group of similarly situated individuals separate from beneficiaries. In addition, participants may be treated as two or more distinct groups of similarly situated individuals and beneficiaries may be treated as two or more distinct groups of similarly situated individuals in accordance with the rules of this paragraph (d). Moreover, if individuals have a choice of two or more benefit packages, individuals choosing one benefit package may be treated as one or more groups of similarly situated individuals distinct from individuals choosing another benefit package.

(1) *Participants.* Subject to paragraph (d)(3) of this section, a plan or issuer may treat participants as two or more distinct groups of similarly situated individuals if the distinction between or among the groups of participants is based on a bona fide employment-based classification consistent with the employer's usual business practice. Whether an employment-based classification is bona fide is determined on the basis of all the relevant facts and circumstances. Relevant facts and circumstances include whether the employer uses the classification for purposes independent of qualification for health coverage (for example, determining eligibility for other employee benefits or determining other terms of employment). Subject to paragraph (d)(3) of this section, examples of classifications that, based on all the relevant facts and circumstances, may be bona fide include full-time versus part-time status, different geographic location, membership in a collective bargaining unit, date of hire, length of service, current employee versus former employee status, and different occupations. However, a classification based on any health factor is not a bona fide employment-based classification, unless the requirements of paragraph (g) of this section are satisfied (permitting favorable treatment of individuals with adverse health factors).

(2) *Beneficiaries*—(i) Subject to paragraph (d)(3) of this section, a plan or issuer may treat beneficiaries as two or more distinct groups of similarly situated individuals if the distinction between or among the groups of beneficiaries is based on any of the following factors:

(A) A bona fide employment-based classification of the participant through whom the beneficiary is receiving coverage;

(B) Relationship to the participant (e.g., as a spouse or as a dependent child);

(C) Marital status;

(D) With respect to children of a participant, age or student status; or

(E) Any other factor if the factor is not a health factor.

(ii) Paragraph (d)(2)(i) of this section does not prevent more favorable treatment of individuals with adverse health factors in accordance with paragraph (g) of this section.

(3) *Discrimination directed at individuals.* Notwithstanding paragraphs (d)(1) and (2) of this section, if the creation or modification of an employment or coverage classification is directed at individual participants or beneficiaries based on any health factor of the participants or beneficiaries, the classification is not permitted under this paragraph (d), unless it is permitted under paragraph (g) of this section (permitting favorable treatment of individuals with adverse health factors). Thus, if an employer modified an employment-based classification to single out, based on a health factor, individual participants and beneficiaries and deny them health coverage, the new classification would not be permitted under this section.

(4) *Examples.* The rules of this paragraph (d) are illustrated by the following examples:

Example 1. (i) *Facts.* An employer sponsors a group health plan for full-time employees only. Under the plan (consistent with the employer's usual business practice), employees who normally work at least 30 hours per week are considered to be working full-time. Other employees are considered to be working part-time. There is no evidence to suggest that the classification is directed at individual participants or beneficiaries.

(ii) *Conclusion.* In this *Example 1*, treating the full-time and part-time employees as two separate groups of similarly situated individuals is permitted under this paragraph (d) because the classification is bona fide and is not directed at individual participants or beneficiaries.

Example 2. (i) *Facts.* Under a group health plan, coverage is made available to employees, their spouses, and their dependent children. However, coverage is made available to a dependent child only if the dependent child is under age 19 (or under age 25 if the child is continuously enrolled full-time in an institution of higher learning (full-time students)). There is no evidence to suggest that these classifications are directed at individual participants or beneficiaries.

A. HIPAA Interim Final Rules and Proposed Rules, continued

(ii) *Conclusion.* In this *Example 2*, treating spouses and dependent children differently by imposing an age limitation on dependent children, but not on spouses, is permitted under this paragraph (d). Specifically, the distinction between spouses and dependent children is permitted under paragraph (d)(2) of this section and is not prohibited under paragraph (d)(3) of this section because it is not directed at individual participants or beneficiaries. It is also permissible to treat dependent children who are under age 19 (or full-time students under age 25) as a group of similarly situated individuals separate from those who are age 25 or older (or age 19 or older if they are not full-time students) because the classification is permitted under paragraph (d)(2) of this section and is not directed at individual participants or beneficiaries.

Example 3. (i) *Facts.* A university sponsors a group health plan that provides one health benefit package to faculty and another health benefit package to other staff. Faculty and staff are treated differently with respect to other employee benefits such as retirement benefits and leaves of absence. There is no evidence to suggest that the distinction is directed at individual participants or beneficiaries.

(ii) *Conclusion.* In this *Example 3*, the classification is permitted under this paragraph (d) because there is a distinction based on a bona fide employment-based classification consistent with the employer's usual business practice and the distinction is not directed at individual participants and beneficiaries.

Example 4. (i) *Facts.* An employer sponsors a group health plan that is available to all current employees. Former employees may also be eligible, but only if they complete a specified number of years of service, are enrolled under the plan at the time of termination of employment, and are continuously enrolled from that date. There is no evidence to suggest that these distinctions are directed at individual participants or beneficiaries.

(ii) *Conclusion.* In this *Example 4*, imposing additional eligibility requirements on former employees is permitted because a classification that distinguishes between current and former employees is a bona fide employment-based classification that is permitted under this paragraph (d), provided that it is not directed at individual participants or beneficiaries. In addition, it is permissible to distinguish between former employees who satisfy the service requirement and those who do not, provided that the distinction is not directed at individual participants or beneficiaries. (However, former employees who do not satisfy the eligibility criteria may, nonetheless, be eligible for continued coverage pursuant to a COBRA continuation provision or similar State law.)

Example 5. (i) *Facts.* An employer sponsors a group health plan that provides the same benefit package to all seven employees of the employer. Six of the seven employees have the same job title and responsibilities, but Employee G has a different job title and different responsibilities. After G files an expensive claim for benefits under the plan,

coverage under the plan is modified so that employees with G's job title receive a different benefit package that includes a lower lifetime dollar limit than in the benefit package made available to the other six employees.

(ii) *Conclusion.* Under the facts of this *Example 5*, changing the coverage classification for G based on the existing employment classification for G is not permitted under this paragraph (d) because the creation of the new coverage classification for G is directed at G based on one or more health factors.

(e) *Nonconfinement and actively-at-work provisions*—(1) *Nonconfinement provisions*—(i) *General rule.* Under the rules of paragraphs (b) and (c) of this section, a plan or issuer may not establish a rule for eligibility (as described in paragraph (b)(1)(ii) of this section) or set any individual's premium or contribution rate based on whether an individual is confined to a hospital or other health care institution. In addition, under the rules of paragraphs (b) and (c) of this section, a plan or issuer may not establish a rule for eligibility or set any individual's premium or contribution rate based on an individual's ability to engage in normal life activities, except to the extent permitted under paragraphs (e)(2)(ii) and (3) of this section (permitting plans and issuers, under certain circumstances, to distinguish among employees based on the performance of services).

(ii) *Examples.* The rules of this paragraph (e)(1) are illustrated by the following examples:

Example 1. (i) *Facts.* Under a group health plan, coverage for employees and their dependents generally becomes effective on the first day of employment. However, coverage for a dependent who is confined to a hospital or other health care institution does not become effective until the confinement ends.

(ii) *Conclusion.* In this *Example 1*, the plan violates this paragraph (e)(1) because the plan delays the effective date of coverage for dependents based on confinement to a hospital or other health care institution.

Example 2. (i) *Facts.* In previous years, a group health plan has provided coverage through a group health insurance policy offered by Issuer M. However, for the current year, the plan provides coverage through a group health insurance policy offered by Issuer N. Under Issuer N's policy, items and services provided in connection with the confinement of a dependent to a hospital or other health care institution are not covered if the confinement is covered under an extension of benefits clause from a previous health insurance issuer.

(ii) *Conclusion.* In this *Example 2*, Issuer N violates this paragraph (e)(1) because the group health insurance coverage restricts benefits (a rule for eligibility under paragraph (b)(1)) based on whether a dependent is confined to a hospital or other health care

institution that is covered under an extension of benefits clause from a previous issuer. This section does not affect any obligation Issuer M may have under applicable State law to provide any extension of benefits and does not affect any State law governing coordination of benefits.

(2) *Actively-at-work and continuous service provisions*—(i) *General rule*—(A) Under the rules of paragraphs (b) and (c) of this section and subject to the exception for the first day of work described in paragraph (e)(2)(ii) of this section, a plan or issuer may not establish a rule for eligibility (as described in paragraph (b)(1)(ii) of this section) or set any individual's premium or contribution rate based on whether an individual is actively at work (including whether an individual is continuously employed), unless absence from work due to any health factor (such as being absent from work on sick leave) is treated, for purposes of the plan or health insurance coverage, as being actively at work.

(B) The rules of this paragraph (e)(2)(i) are illustrated by the following examples:

Example 1. (i) *Facts.* Under a group health plan, an employee generally becomes eligible to enroll 30 days after the first day of employment. However, if the employee is not actively at work on the first day after the end of the 30-day period, then eligibility for enrollment is delayed until the first day the employee is actively at work.

(ii) *Conclusion.* In this *Example 1*, the plan violates this paragraph (e)(2) (and thus also violates paragraph (b) of this section). However, the plan would not violate paragraph (e)(2) or (b) of this section if, under the plan, an absence due to any health factor is considered being actively at work.

Example 2. (i) *Facts.* Under a group health plan, coverage for an employee becomes effective after 90 days of continuous service; that is, if an employee is absent from work (for any reason) before completing 90 days of service, the beginning of the 90-day period is measured from the day the employee returns to work (without any credit for service before the absence).

(ii) *Conclusion.* In this *Example 2*, the plan violates this paragraph (e)(2) (and thus also paragraph (b) of this section) because the 90-day continuous service requirement is a rule for eligibility based on whether an individual is actively at work. However, the plan would not violate this paragraph (e)(2) or paragraph (b) of this section if, under the plan, an absence due to any health factor is not considered an absence for purposes of measuring 90 days of continuous service.

(ii) *Exception for the first day of work*—(A) Notwithstanding the general rule in paragraph (e)(2)(i) of this section, a plan or issuer may establish a rule for eligibility that requires an individual to begin work for the employer sponsoring the plan (or, in the case of a multiemployer plan, to begin a job in

12:34

A. HIPAA Interim Final Rules and Proposed Rules, continued

covered employment) before coverage becomes effective, provided that such a rule for eligibility applies regardless of the reason for the absence.

(B) The rules of this paragraph (e)(2)(ii) are illustrated by the following examples:

Example 1. (i) *Facts.* Under the eligibility provision of a group health plan, coverage for new employees becomes effective on the first day that the employee reports to work. Individual *H* is scheduled to begin work on August 3. However, *H* is unable to begin work on that day because of illness. *H* begins working on August 4, and *H*'s coverage is effective on August 4.

(ii) *Conclusion.* In this *Example 1*, the plan provision does not violate this section. However, if coverage for individuals who do not report to work on the first day they were scheduled to work for a reason unrelated to a health factor (such as vacation or bereavement) becomes effective on the first day they were scheduled to work, then the plan would violate this section.

Example 2. (i) *Facts.* Under a group health plan, coverage for new employees becomes effective on the first day of the month following the employee's first day of work, regardless of whether the employee is actively at work on the first day of the month. Individual *J* is scheduled to begin work on March 24. However, *J* is unable to begin work on March 24 because of illness. *J* begins working on April 7 and *J*'s coverage is effective May 1.

(ii) *Conclusion.* In this *Example 2*, the plan provision does not violate this section. However, as in *Example 1*, if coverage for individuals absent from work for reasons unrelated to a health factor became effective despite their absence, then the plan would violate this section.

(3) *Relationship to plan provisions defining similarly situated individuals*—(i) Notwithstanding the rules of paragraphs (e)(1) and (2) of this section, a plan or issuer may establish rules for eligibility or set any individual's premium or contribution rate in accordance with the rules relating to similarly situated individuals in paragraph (d) of this section. Accordingly, a plan or issuer may distinguish in rules for eligibility under the plan between full-time and part-time employees, between permanent and temporary or seasonal employees, between current and former employees, and between employees currently performing services and employees no longer performing services for the employer, subject to paragraph (d) of this section. However, other federal or State laws (including the COBRA continuation provisions and the Family and Medical Leave Act of 1993) may require an employee or the employee's dependents to be offered coverage and set limits on the premium or contribution rate even though the employee is not performing services.

(ii) The rules of this paragraph (e)(3) are illustrated by the following examples:

Example 1. (i) *Facts.* Under a group health plan, employees are eligible for coverage if they perform services for the employer for 30 or more hours per week or if they are on paid leave (such as vacation, sick, or bereavement leave). Employees on unpaid leave are treated as a separate group of similarly situated individuals in accordance with the rules of paragraph (d) of this section.

(ii) *Conclusion.* In this *Example 1*, the plan provisions do not violate this section. However, if the plan treated individuals performing services for the employer for 30 or more hours per week, individuals on vacation leave, and individuals on bereavement leave as a group of similarly situated individuals separate from individuals on sick leave, the plan would violate this paragraph (e) (and thus also would violate paragraph (b) of this section) because groups of similarly situated individuals cannot be established based on a health factor (including the taking of sick leave) under paragraph (d) of this section.

Example 2. (i) *Facts.* To be eligible for coverage under a bona fide collectively bargained group health plan in the current calendar quarter, the plan requires an individual to have worked 250 hours in covered employment during the three-month period that ends one month before the beginning of the current calendar quarter. The distinction between employees working at least 250 hours and those working less than 250 hours in the earlier three-month period is not directed at individual participants or beneficiaries based on any health factor of the participants or beneficiaries.

(ii) *Conclusion.* In this *Example 2*, the plan provision does not violate this section because, under the rules for similarly situated individuals allowing full-time employees to be treated differently than part-time employees, employees who work at least 250 hours in a three-month period can be treated differently than employees who fail to work 250 hours in that period. The result would be the same if the plan permitted individuals to apply excess hours from previous periods to satisfy the requirement for the current quarter.

Example 3. (i) *Facts.* Under a group health plan, coverage of an employee is terminated when the individual's employment is terminated, in accordance with the rules of paragraph (d) of this section. Employee *B* has been covered under the plan. *B* experiences a disabling illness that prevents *B* from working. *B* takes a leave of absence under the Family and Medical Leave Act of 1993. At the end of such leave, *B* terminates employment and consequently loses coverage under the plan. (This termination of coverage is without regard to whatever rights the employee (or members of the employee's family) may have for COBRA continuation coverage.)

(ii) *Conclusion.* In this *Example 3*, the plan provision terminating *B*'s coverage upon *B*'s termination of employment does not violate this section.

Example 4. (i) *Facts.* Under a group health plan, coverage of an employee is terminated when the employee ceases to perform services for the employer sponsoring the plan, in accordance with the rules of paragraph (d) of this section. Employee *C* is laid off for three months. When the layoff begins, *C*'s coverage under the plan is terminated. (This termination of coverage is without regard to whatever rights the employee (or members of the employee's family) may have for COBRA continuation coverage.)

(ii) *Conclusion.* In this *Example 4*, the plan provision terminating *C*'s coverage upon the cessation of *C*'s performance of services does not violate this section.

(f) *Bona fide wellness programs.* [Reserved.]

(g) *More favorable treatment of individuals with adverse health factors permitted*—(1) *In rules for eligibility*—(i) Nothing in this section prevents a group health plan or group health insurance issuer from establishing more favorable rules for eligibility (described in paragraph (b)(1) of this section) for individuals with an adverse health factor, such as disability, than for individuals without the adverse health factor. Moreover, nothing in this section prevents a plan or issuer from charging a higher premium or contribution with respect to individuals with an adverse health factor if they would not be eligible for the coverage were it not for the adverse health factor. (However, other laws, including State insurance laws, may set or limit premium rates; these laws are not affected by this section.)

(ii) The rules of this paragraph (g)(1) are illustrated by the following examples:

Example 1. (i) *Facts.* An employer sponsors a group health plan that generally is available to employees, spouses of employees, and dependent children until age 23. However, dependent children who are disabled are eligible for coverage beyond age 23.

(ii) *Conclusion.* In this *Example 1*, the plan provision allowing coverage for disabled dependent children beyond age 23 satisfies this paragraph (g)(1) (and thus does not violate this section).

Example 2. (i) *Facts.* An employer sponsors a group health plan, which is generally available to employees (and members of the employee's family) until the last day of the month in which the employee ceases to perform services for the employer. The plan generally charges employees $50 per month for employee-only coverage and $125 per month for family coverage. However, an employee who ceases to perform services for the employer by reason of disability may remain covered under the plan until the last day of the month that is 12 months after the month in which the employee ceased to perform services for the employer. During this extended period of coverage, the plan charges the employee $100 per month for employee-only coverage and $250 per month

A. HIPAA Interim Final Rules and Proposed Rules, continued

for family coverage. (This extended period of coverage is without regard to whatever rights the employee (or members of the employee's family) may have for COBRA continuation coverage.)

(ii) *Conclusion.* In this *Example 2*, the plan provision allowing extended coverage for disabled employees and their families satisfies this paragraph (g)(1) (and thus does not violate this section). In addition, the plan is permitted, under this paragraph (g)(1), to charge the disabled employees a higher premium during the extended period of coverage.

Example 3. (i) *Facts.* To comply with the requirements of a COBRA continuation provision, a group health plan generally makes COBRA continuation coverage available for a maximum period of 18 months in connection with a termination of employment but makes the coverage available for a maximum period of 29 months to certain disabled individuals and certain members of the disabled individual's family. Although the plan generally requires payment of 102 percent of the applicable premium for the first 18 months of COBRA continuation coverage, the plan requires payment of 150 percent of the applicable premium for the disabled individual's COBRA continuation coverage during the disability extension if the disabled individual would not be entitled to COBRA continuation coverage but for the disability.

(ii) *Conclusion.* In this *Example 3*, the plan provision allowing extended COBRA continuation coverage for disabled individuals satisfies this paragraph (g)(1) (and thus does not violate this section). In addition, the plan is permitted, under this paragraph (g)(1), to charge the disabled individuals a higher premium for the extended coverage if the individuals would not be eligible for COBRA continuation coverage were it not for the disability. (Similarly, if the plan provided an extended period of coverage for disabled individuals pursuant to State law or plan provision rather than pursuant to a COBRA continuation coverage provision, the plan could likewise charge the disabled individuals a higher premium for the extended coverage.)

(2) *In premiums or contributions*—(i) Nothing in this section prevents a group health plan or group health insurance issuer from charging individuals a premium or contribution that is less than the premium (or contribution) for similarly situated individuals if the lower charge is based on an adverse health factor, such as disability.

(ii) The rules of this paragraph (g)(2) are illustrated by the following example:

Example. (i) *Facts.* Under a group health plan, employees are generally required to pay $50 per month for employee-only coverage and $125 per month for family coverage under the plan. However, employees who are disabled receive coverage (whether employee-only or family coverage) under the plan free of charge.

(ii) *Conclusion.* In this *Example*, the plan provision waiving premium payment for disabled employees is permitted under this

paragraph (g)(2) (and thus does not violate this section).

(h) *No effect on other laws.* Compliance with this section is not determinative of compliance with any other provision of the Act (including the COBRA continuation provisions) or any other State or federal law, such as the Americans with Disabilities Act. Therefore, although the rules of this section would not prohibit a plan or issuer from treating one group of similarly situated individuals differently from another (such as providing different benefit packages to current and former employees), other federal or State laws may require that two separate groups of similarly situated individuals be treated the same for certain purposes (such as making the same benefit package available to COBRA qualified beneficiaries as is made available to active employees). In addition, although this section generally does not impose new disclosure obligations on plans and issuers, this section does not affect any other laws, including those that require accurate disclosures and prohibit intentional misrepresentation.

(i) *Applicability dates*—(1) *Paragraphs applicable March 9, 2001.* Paragraphs (a)(1), (a)(2)(i), (b)(1)(i), (b)(1)(iii) *Example 1*, (b)(2)(i)(A), (b)(2)(ii), (c)(1)(i), (c)(2)(i), and (c)(3) of this section and this paragraph (i)(1) apply to group health plans and health insurance issuers offering group health insurance coverage March 9, 2001.

(2) *Paragraphs applicable for plan years beginning on or after July 1, 2001.* Except as provided in paragraph (i)(3) of this section, the provisions of this section not listed in paragraph (i)(1) of this section apply to group health plans and health insurance issuers offering group health insurance coverage for plan years beginning on or after July 1, 2001. Except as provided in paragraph (i)(3) of this section, with respect to efforts to comply with section 702 of the Act before the first plan year beginning on or after July 1, 2001, the Secretary will not take any enforcement action against a plan that has sought to comply in good faith with section 702 of the Act.

(3) *Transitional rules for individuals previously denied coverage based on a health factor.* This paragraph (i)(3) provides rules relating to individuals previously denied coverage under a group health plan or group health insurance coverage based on a health factor of the individual. Paragraph (i)(3)(i) clarifies what constitutes a denial of coverage under this paragraph (i)(3). Paragraph (i)(3)(ii) of this section applies with respect to any individual

who was denied coverage if the denial was not based on a good faith interpretation of section 702 of the Act or the Secretary's published guidance. Under that paragraph, such an individual must be allowed to enroll retroactively to the effective date of section 702 of the Act, or, if later, the date the individual meets eligibility criteria under the plan that do not discriminate based on any health factor. Paragraph (i)(3)(iii) of this section applies with respect to any individual who was denied coverage based on a good faith interpretation of section 702 of the Act or the Secretary's published guidance. Under that paragraph, such an individual must be given an opportunity to enroll effective July 1, 2001. In either event, whether under paragraph (i)(3)(ii) or (iii) of this section, the Secretary will not take any enforcement action with respect to denials of coverage addressed in this paragraph (i)(3) if the plan has complied with the transitional rules of this paragraph (i)(3).

(i) *Denial of coverage clarified.* For purposes of this paragraph (i)(3), an individual is considered to have been denied coverage if the individual—

(A) Failed to apply for coverage because it was reasonable to believe that an application for coverage would have been futile due to a plan provision that discriminated based on a health factor; or

(B) Was not offered an opportunity to enroll in the plan and the failure to give such an opportunity violates this section.

(ii) *Individuals denied coverage without a good faith interpretation of the law*—(A) *Opportunity to enroll required.* If a plan or issuer has denied coverage to any individual based on a health factor and that denial was not based on a good faith interpretation of section 702 of the Act or any guidance published by the Secretary, the plan or issuer is required to give the individual an opportunity to enroll (including notice of an opportunity to enroll) that continues for at least 30 days. This opportunity must be presented not later than March 9, 2001.

(*1*) If this enrollment opportunity was presented before or within the first plan year beginning on or after July 1, 1997 (or in the case of a collectively bargained plan, before or within the first plan year beginning on the effective date for the plan described in section 101(g)(3) of the Health Insurance Portability and Accountability Act of 1996), the coverage must be effective within that first plan year.

(*2*) If this enrollment opportunity is presented after such plan year, the individual must be given the choice of

A. HIPAA Interim Final Rules and Proposed Rules, continued

having the coverage effective on either of the following two dates—

(i) The date the plan receives a request for enrollment in connection with the enrollment opportunity; or

(ii) Retroactively to the first day of the first plan year beginning on the effective date for the plan described in sections 101(g)(1) and (3) of the Health Insurance Portability and Accountability Act of 1996 (or, if the individual otherwise first became eligible to enroll for coverage after that date, on the date the individual was otherwise eligible to enroll in the plan). If an individual elects retroactive coverage, the plan or issuer is required to provide the benefits it would have provided if the individual had been enrolled for coverage during that period (irrespective of any otherwise applicable plan provisions governing timing for the submission of claims). The plan or issuer may require the individual to pay whatever additional amount the individual would have been required to pay for the coverage (but the plan or issuer cannot charge interest on that amount).

(B) *Relation to preexisting condition rules.* For purposes of part 7 of subtitle B of title I of the Act, the individual may not be treated as a late enrollee or as a special enrollee. Moreover, the individual's enrollment date is the effective date for the plan described in sections 101(g)(1) and (3) of the Health Insurance Portability and Accountability Act (or, if the individual otherwise first became eligible to enroll for coverage after that date, on the date the individual was otherwise eligible to enroll in the plan), even if the individual chooses under paragraph (i)(3)(ii)(A) of this section to have coverage effective only prospectively. In addition, any period between the individual's enrollment date and the effective date of coverage is treated as a waiting period.

(C) *Examples.* The rules of this paragraph (i)(3)(ii) are illustrated by the following examples:

Example 1. (i) *Facts.* Employer *X* maintains a group health plan with a plan year beginning October 1 and ending September 30. Individual *F* was hired by Employer *X* before the effective date of section 702 of the Act. Before the effective date of section 702 of the Act for this plan (October 1, 1997), the terms of the plan allowed employees and their dependents to enroll when the employee was first hired, and on each January 1 thereafter, but in either case, only if the individual could pass a physical examination. *F*'s application to enroll when first hired was denied because *F* had diabetes and could not pass a physical examination. Upon the effective date of section 702 of the Act for this plan (October 1, 1997), the plan is amended to delete the requirement to pass

a physical examination. In November of 1997, the plan gives *F* an opportunity to enroll in the plan (including notice of the opportunity to enroll) without passing a physical examination, with coverage effective January 1, 1998.

(ii) *Conclusion.* In this *Example 1,* the plan complies with the requirements of this paragraph (i)(3)(ii).

Example 2. (i) *Facts.* The plan year of a group health plan begins January 1 and ends December 31. Under the plan, a dependent who is unable to engage in normal life activities on the date coverage would otherwise become effective is not enrolled until the dependent is able to engage in normal life activities. Individual *G* is a dependent who is otherwise eligible for coverage, but is unable to engage in normal life activities. The plan has not allowed *G* to enroll for coverage.

(ii) *Conclusion.* In this *Example 2,* beginning on the effective date of section 702 of the Act for the plan (January 1, 1998), the plan provision is not permitted under any good faith interpretation of section 702 of the Act or any guidance published by the Secretary. Therefore, the plan is required, not later than March 9, 2001, to give *G* an opportunity to enroll (including notice of the opportunity to enroll), with coverage effective, at *G*'s option, either retroactively from January 1, 1998 or prospectively from the date *G*'s request for enrollment is received by the plan. If *G* elects coverage to be effective beginning January 1, 1998, the plan can require G to pay any required employee premiums for the retroactive coverage.

(iii) *Individuals denied coverage based on a good faith interpretation of the law—*(A) *Opportunity to enroll required.* If a plan or issuer has denied coverage to any individual before the first day of the first plan year beginning on or after July 1, 2001 based in part on a health factor and that denial was based on a good faith interpretation of section 702 of the Act or guidance published by the Secretary, the plan or issuer is required to give the individual an opportunity to enroll (including notice of an opportunity to enroll) that continues for at least 30 days, with coverage effective no later than July 1, 2001. Individuals required to be offered an opportunity to enroll include' individuals previously offered enrollment without regard to a health factor but subsequently denied enrollment due to a health factor.

(B) *Relation to preexisting condition rules.* For purposes of Part 7 of Subtitle B of Title I of the Act, the individual may not be treated as a late enrollee or as a special enrollee. Moreover, the individual's enrollment date is the effective date for the plan described in sections 101(g)(1) and (3) of the Health Insurance Portability and Accountability Act (or, if the individual otherwise first became eligible to enroll

for coverage after that date, on the date the individual was otherwise eligible to enroll in the plan). In addition, any period between the individual's enrollment date and the effective date of coverage is treated as a waiting period.

(C) *Example.* The rules of this paragraph (i)(3)(iii) are illustrated by the following example:

Example. (i) *Facts.* Individual *H* was hired by Employer *Y* on May 3, 1995. *Y* maintains a group health plan with a plan year beginning on February 1. Under the terms of the plan, employees and their dependents are allowed to enroll when the employee is first hired (without a requirement to pass a physical examination), and on each February 1 thereafter if the individual can pass a physical examination. *H* chose not to enroll for coverage when hired in May of 1995. On February 1, 1997, *H* tried to enroll for coverage under the plan. However, *H* was denied coverage for failure to pass a physical examination. Shortly thereafter, *Y*'s plan eliminated late enrollment, and *H* was not given another opportunity to enroll in the plan. There is no evidence to suggest that *Y*'s plan was acting in bad faith in denying coverage under the plan beginning on the effective date of section 702 of the Act (February 1, 1998).

(ii) *Conclusion.* In this *Example,* because coverage previously had been made available with respect to *H* without regard to any health factor of *H* and because *Y*'s plan was acting in accordance with a good faith interpretation of section 702 (and guidance published by the Secretary), the failure of *Y*'s plan to allow *H* to enroll effective February 1, 1998 was permissible on that date. However, under the transitional rules of this paragraph (i)(3)(iii), *Y*'s plan must give *H* an opportunity to enroll that continues for at least 30 days, with coverage effective no later than July 1, 2001. (In addition, February 1, 1998 is *H*'s enrollment date under the plan and the period between February 1, 1998 and July 1, 2001 is treated as a waiting period. Accordingly, any preexisting condition exclusion period permitted under § 2590.701–3 will have expired before July 1, 2001.)

3. The heading, paragraph (a)(1), and the first sentence of paragraph (a)(2) of § 2590.736 are revised to read as follows:

§ 2590.736 Applicability dates.

(a) *General applicability dates—*(1) *Non-collectively bargained plans.* Part 7 of Subtitle B of Title I of the Act and §§ 2590.701–1 through 2590.701–7, 2590.703, 2590.731 through 2590.734, and this section apply with respect to group health plans, and health insurance coverage offered in connection with group health plans, for plan years beginning after June 30, 1997, except as otherwise provided in this section.

(2) *Collectively-bargained plans.* Except as otherwise provided in this section (other than in paragraph (a)(1) of

A. HIPAA Interim Final Rules and Proposed Rules, continued

this section), in the case of a group health plan maintained pursuant to one or more collective bargaining agreements between employee representatives and one or more employers ratified before August 21, 1996, Part 7 of Subtitle B of Title I of the Act and §§ 2590.701–1 through 2590.701–7, 2590.703, 2590.731 through 2590.734, and this section do not apply to plan years beginning before the later of July 1, 1997, or the date on which the last of the collective bargaining agreements relating to the plan terminates (determined without regard to any extension thereof agreed to after August 21, 1996). * * *

* * * * *

Signed at Washington, DC this 28th day of December, 2000.

Leslie B. Kramerich,

Assistant Secretary, Pension and Welfare Benefits Administration, U.S. Department of Labor.

For the reasons set forth above, 45 CFR Part 146 is amended as follows:

PART 146 [AMENDED]—RULES AND REGULATIONS FOR HEALTH INSURANCE PORTABILITY AND RENEWABILITY FOR GROUP HEALTH PLANS

1. The authority citation for Part 146 is revised to read as follows:

Authority: Secs. 2701 through 2763, 2791 and 2792 of the Public Health Service Act, 42 U.S.C. 300gg through 300gg–63, 300gg–91, 300gg–92 as amended by HIPAA (Public Law 104–191, 110 Stat. 1936), MHPA and NMHPA (Public Law 104–204, 110 Stat. 2935), and WHCRA (Public Law 105–277, 112 Stat. 2681–436), and section 102(c)(4) of HIPAA.

2. Section 146.121 is revised to read as follows:

§ 146.121   Prohibiting discrimination against participants and beneficiaries based on a health factor.

(a) *Health factors.* (1) The term *health factor* means, in relation to an individual, any of the following health status-related factors:

(i) Health status;

(ii) Medical condition (including both physical and mental illnesses), as defined in § 144.103;

(iii) Claims experience;

(iv) Receipt of health care;

(v) Medical history;

(vi) Genetic information, as defined in 45 CFR 144.103;

(vii) Evidence of insurability; or

(viii) Disability.

(2) Evidence of insurability includes—

(i) Conditions arising out of acts of domestic violence; and

(ii) Participation in activities such as motorcycling, snowmobiling, all-terrain vehicle riding, horseback riding, skiing, and other similar activities.

(3) The decision whether health coverage is elected for an individual (including the time chosen to enroll, such as under special enrollment or late enrollment) is not, itself, within the scope of any health factor. (However, under § 146.117, a plan or issuer must treat special enrollees the same as similarly situated individuals who are enrolled when first eligible.)

(b) *Prohibited discrimination in rules for eligibility*—(1) *In general*—(i) A group health plan, and a health insurance issuer offering health insurance coverage in connection with a group health plan, may not establish any rule for eligibility (including continued eligibility) of any individual to enroll for benefits under the terms of the plan or group health insurance coverage that discriminates based on any health factor that relates to that individual or a dependent of that individual. This rule is subject to the provisions of paragraph (b)(2) of this section (explaining how this rule applies to benefits), paragraph (b)(3) of this section (allowing plans to impose certain preexisting condition exclusions), paragraph (d) of this section (containing rules for establishing groups of similarly situated individuals), paragraph (e) of this section (relating to nonconfinement, actively-at-work, and other service requirements), paragraph (f) of this section (relating to bona fide wellness programs), and paragraph (g) of this section (permitting favorable treatment of individuals with adverse health factors).

(ii) For purposes of this section, rules for eligibility include, but are not limited to, rules relating to—

(A) Enrollment;

(B) The effective date of coverage;

(C) Waiting (or affiliation) periods;

(D) Late and special enrollment;

(E) Eligibility for benefit packages (including rules for individuals to change their selection among benefit packages);

(F) Benefits (including rules relating to covered benefits, benefit restrictions, and cost-sharing mechanisms such as coinsurance, copayments, and deductibles), as described in paragraphs (b) (2) and (3) of this section;

(G) Continued eligibility; and

(H) Terminating coverage (including disenrollment) of any individual under the plan.

(iii) The rules of this paragraph (b)(1) are illustrated by the following examples:

Example 1. (i) *Facts.* An employer sponsors a group health plan that is available to all employees who enroll within the first 30 days of their employment. However, employees who do not enroll within the first 30 days cannot enroll later unless they pass a physical examination.

(ii) *Conclusion.* In this *Example 1*, the requirement to pass a physical examination in order to enroll in the plan is a rule for eligibility that discriminates based on one or more health factors and thus violates this paragraph (b)(1).

Example 2. (i) *Facts.* Under an employer's group health plan, employees who enroll during the first 30 days of employment (and during special enrollment periods) may choose between two benefit packages: an indemnity option and an HMO option. However, employees who enroll during late enrollment are permitted to enroll only in the HMO option and only if they provide evidence of good health.

(ii) *Conclusion.* In this *Example 2*, the requirement to provide evidence of good health in order to be eligible for late enrollment in the HMO option is a rule for eligibility that discriminates based on one or more health factors and thus violates this paragraph (b)(1). However, if the plan did not require evidence of good health but limited late enrollees to the HMO option, the plan's rules for eligibility would not discriminate based on any health factor, and thus would not violate this paragraph (b)(1), because the time an individual chooses to enroll is not, itself, within the scope of any health factor.

Example 3. (i) *Facts.* Under an employer's group health plan, all employees generally may enroll within the first 30 days of employment. However, individuals who participate in certain recreational activities, including motorcycling, are excluded from coverage.

(ii) *Conclusion.* In this *Example 3*, excluding from the plan individuals who participate in recreational activities, such as motorcycling, is a rule for eligibility that discriminates based on one more health factors and thus violates this paragraph (b)(1).

Example 4. (i) *Facts.* A group health plan applies for a group health policy offered by an issuer. As part of the application, the issuer receives health information about individuals to be covered under the plan. Individual *A* is an employee of the employer maintaining the plan. *A* and *A*'s dependents have a history of high health claims. Based on the information about *A* and *A*'s dependents, the issuer excludes *A* and *A*'s dependents from the group policy it offers to the employer.

(ii) *Conclusion.* In this *Example 4*, the issuer's exclusion of *A* and *A*'s dependents from coverage is a rule for eligibility that discriminates based on one or more health factors, and thus violates this paragraph (b)(1). (If the employer is a small employer under 45 CFR 144.103 (generally, an employer with 50 or fewer employees), the issuer also may violate 45 CFR 146.150, which requires issuers to offer all the policies they sell in the small group market on a guaranteed available basis to all small employers and to accept every eligible

A. HIPAA Interim Final Rules and Proposed Rules, continued

Federal Register / Vol. 66, No. 5 / Monday, January 8, 2001 / Rules and Regulations 1413

individual in every small employer group.) If the plan provides coverage through this policy and does not provide equivalent coverage for A and A's dependents through other means, the plan will also violate this paragraph (b)(1).

(2) *Application to benefits*—(i) *General rule*—(A) Under this section, a group health plan or group health insurance issuer is not required to provide coverage for any particular benefit to any group of similarly situated individuals.

(B) However, benefits provided under a plan or through group health insurance coverage must be uniformly available to all similarly situated individuals (as described in paragraph (d) of this section). Likewise, any restriction on a benefit or benefits must apply uniformly to all similarly situated individuals and must not be directed at individual participants or beneficiaries based on any health factor of the participants or beneficiaries (determined based on all the relevant facts and circumstances). Thus, for example, a plan or issuer may limit or exclude benefits in relation to a specific disease or condition, limit or exclude benefits for certain types of treatments or drugs, or limit or exclude benefits based on a determination of whether the benefits are experimental or not medically necessary, but only if the benefit limitation or exclusion applies uniformly to all similarly situated individuals and is not directed at individual participants or beneficiaries based on any health factor of the participants or beneficiaries. In addition, a plan or issuer may impose annual, lifetime, or other limits on benefits and may require the satisfaction of a deductible, copayment, coinsurance, or other cost-sharing requirement in order to obtain a benefit if the limit or cost-sharing requirement applies uniformly to all similarly situated individuals and is not directed at individual participants or beneficiaries based on any health factor of the participants or beneficiaries. In the case of a cost-sharing requirement, see also paragraph (b)(2)(ii) of this section, which permits variances in the application of a cost-sharing mechanism made available under a bona fide wellness program. (Whether any plan provision or practice with respect to benefits complies with this paragraph (b)(2)(i) does not affect whether the provision or practice is permitted under any other provision of ERISA, the Americans with Disabilities Act, or any other law, whether State or federal.)

(C) For purposes of this paragraph (b)(2)(i), a plan amendment applicable to all individuals in one or more groups of similarly situated individuals under the plan and made effective no earlier than the first day of the first plan year after the amendment is adopted is not considered to be directed at any individual participants or beneficiaries.

(D) The rules of this paragraph (b)(2)(i) are illustrated by the following examples:

Example 1. (i) *Facts.* A group health plan applies a $500,000 lifetime limit on all benefits to each participant or beneficiary covered under the plan. The limit is not directed at individual participants or beneficiaries.

(ii) *Conclusion.* In this *Example 1*, the limit does not violate this paragraph (b)(2)(i) because $500,000 of benefits are available uniformly to each participant and beneficiary under the plan and because the limit is applied uniformly to all participants and beneficiaries and is not directed at individual participants or beneficiaries.

Example 2. (i) *Facts.* A group health plan has a $2 million lifetime limit on all benefits (and no other lifetime limits) for participants covered under the plan. Participant B files a claim for the treatment of AIDS. At the next corporate board meeting of the plan sponsor, the claim is discussed. Shortly thereafter, the plan is modified to impose a $10,000 lifetime limit on benefits for the treatment of AIDS, effective before the beginning of the next plan year.

(ii) *Conclusion.* Under the facts of this *Example 2*, the plan violates this paragraph (b)(2)(i) because the plan modification is directed at B based on B's claim.

Example 3. (i) A group health plan applies for a group health policy offered by an issuer. Individual C is covered under the plan and has an adverse health condition. As part of the application, the issuer receives health information about the individuals to be covered, including information about C's adverse health condition. The policy form offered by the issuer generally provides benefits for the adverse health condition that C has, but in this case the issuer offers the plan a policy modified by a rider that excludes benefits for C for that condition. The exclusionary rider is made effective the first day of the next plan year.

(ii) *Conclusion.* In this *Example 3*, the issuer violates this paragraph (b)(2)(i) because benefits for C's condition are available to other individuals in the group of similarly situated individuals that includes C but are not available to C. Thus, the benefits are not uniformly available to all similarly situated individuals. Even though the exclusionary rider is made effective the first day of the next plan year, because the rider does not apply to all similarly situated individuals, the issuer violates this paragraph (b)(2)(i).

Example 4. (i) *Facts.* A group health plan has a $2,000 lifetime limit for the treatment of temporomandibular joint syndrome (TMJ). The limit is applied uniformly to all similarly situated individuals and is not directed at individual participants or beneficiaries.

(ii) *Conclusion.* In this *Example 4*, the limit does not violate this paragraph (b)(2)(i) because $2,000 of benefits for the treatment of TMJ are available uniformly to all similarly situated individuals and a plan may limit benefits covered in relation to a specific disease or condition if the limit applies uniformly to all similarly situated individuals and is not directed at individual participants or beneficiaries.

Example 5. (i) *Facts.* A group health plan applies a $2 million lifetime limit on all benefits. However, the $2 million lifetime limit is reduced to $10,000 for any participant or beneficiary covered under the plan who has a congenital heart defect.

(ii) *Conclusion.* In this *Example 5*, the lower lifetime limit for participants and beneficiaries with a congenital heart defect violates this paragraph (b)(2)(i) because benefits under the plan are not uniformly available to all similarly situated individuals and the plan's lifetime limit on benefits does not apply uniformly to all similarly situated individuals.

Example 6. (i) *Facts.* A group health plan limits benefits for prescription drugs to those listed on a drug formulary. The limit is applied uniformly to all similarly situated individuals and is not directed at individual participants or beneficiaries.

(ii) *Conclusion.* In this *Example 6*, the exclusion from coverage of drugs not listed on the drug formulary does not violate this paragraph (b)(2)(i) because benefits for prescription drugs listed on the formulary are uniformly available to all similarly situated individuals and because the exclusion of drugs not listed on the formulary applies uniformly to all similarly situated individuals and is not directed at individual participants or beneficiaries.

Example 7. (i) *Facts.* Under a group health plan, doctor visits are generally subject to a $250 annual deductible and 20 percent coinsurance requirement. However, prenatal doctor visits are not subject to any deductible or coinsurance requirement. These rules are applied uniformly to all similarly situated individuals and are not directed at individual participants or beneficiaries.

(ii) *Conclusion.* In this *Example 7*, imposing different deductible and coinsurance requirements for prenatal doctor visits and other visits does not violate this paragraph (b)(2)(i) because a plan may establish different deductibles or coinsurance requirements for different services if the deductible or coinsurance requirement is applied uniformly to all similarly situated individuals and is not directed at individual participants or beneficiaries.

(ii) *Cost-sharing mechanisms and wellness programs.* A group health plan or group health insurance coverage with a cost-sharing mechanism (such as a deductible, copayment, or coinsurance) that requires a higher payment from an individual, based on a health factor of that individual or a dependent of that individual, than for a similarly situated individual under the plan (and thus does not apply uniformly to all similarly situated individuals) does not violate the requirements of this paragraph (b)(2) if the payment differential is based on whether an individual has complied

A. HIPAA Interim Final Rules and Proposed Rules, continued

with the requirements of a bona fide wellness program.

(iii) *Specific rule relating to source-of-injury exclusions*—(A) If a group health plan or group health insurance coverage generally provides benefits for a type of injury, the plan or issuer may not deny benefits otherwise provided for treatment of the injury if the injury results from an act of domestic violence or a medical condition (including both physical and mental health conditions).

(B) The rules of this paragraph (b)(2)(iii) are illustrated by the following examples:

Example 1. (i) *Facts.* A group health plan generally provides medical/surgical benefits, including benefits for hospital stays, that are medically necessary. However, the plan excludes benefits for self-inflicted injuries or injuries sustained in connection with attempted suicide. Individual *D* suffers from depression and attempts suicide. As a result, *D* sustains injuries and is hospitalized for treatment of the injuries. Pursuant to the exclusion, the plan denies *D* benefits for treatment of the injuries.

(ii) *Conclusion.* In this *Example 1*, the suicide attempt is the result of a medical condition (depression). Accordingly, the denial of benefits for the treatments of *D's* injuries violates the requirements of this paragraph (b)(2)(iii) because the plan provision excludes benefits for treatment of an injury resulting from a medical condition.

Example 2. (i) *Facts.* A group health plan provides benefits for head injuries generally. The plan also has a general exclusion for any injury sustained while participating in any of a number of recreational activities, including bungee jumping. However, this exclusion does not apply to any injury that results from a medical condition (nor from domestic violence). Participant *E* sustains a head injury while bungee jumping. The injury did not result from a medical condition (nor from domestic violence). Accordingly, the plan denies benefits for *E's* head injury.

(ii) *Conclusion.* In this *Example 2*, the plan provision that denies benefits based on the source of an injury does not restrict benefits based on an act of domestic violence or any medical condition. Therefore, the provision is permissible under this paragraph (b)(2)(iii) and does not violate this section. (However, if the plan did not allow *E* to enroll in the plan (or applied different rules for eligibility to *E*) because *E* frequently participates in bungee jumping, the plan would violate paragraph (b)(1) of this section.)

(3) *Relationship to § 146.111.* (i) A preexisting condition exclusion is permitted under this section if it—

(A) Complies with § 146.111;

(B) Applies uniformly to all similarly situated individuals (as described in paragraph (d) of this section); and

(C) Is not directed at individual participants or beneficiaries based on any health factor of the participants or beneficiaries. For purposes of this paragraph (b)(3)(i)(C), a plan

amendment relating to a preexisting condition exclusion applicable to all individuals in one or more groups of similarly situated individuals under the plan and made effective no earlier than the first day of the first plan year after the amendment is adopted is not considered to be directed at any individual participants or beneficiaries.

(ii) The rules of this paragraph (b)(3) are illustrated by the following examples:

Example 1. (i) *Facts.* A group health plan imposes a preexisting condition exclusion on all individuals enrolled in the plan. The exclusion applies to conditions for which medical advice, diagnosis, care, or treatment was recommended or received within the six-month period ending on an individual's enrollment date. In addition, the exclusion generally extends for 12 months after an individual's enrollment date, but this 12-month period is offset by the number of days of an individual's creditable coverage in accordance with § 146.111. There is nothing to indicate that the exclusion is directed at individual participants or beneficiaries.

(ii) *Conclusion.* In this *Example 1*, even though the plan's preexisting condition exclusion discriminates against individuals based on one or more health factors, the preexisting condition exclusion does not violate this section because it applies uniformly to all similarly situated individuals, is not directed at individual participants or beneficiaries, and complies with § 146.111 (that is, the requirements relating to the six-month look-back period, the 12-month (or 18-month) maximum exclusion period, and the creditable coverage offset).

Example 2. (i) *Facts.* A group health plan excludes coverage for conditions with respect to which medical advice, diagnosis, care, or treatment was recommended or received within the six-month period ending on an individual's enrollment date. Under the plan, the preexisting condition exclusion generally extends for 12 months, offset by creditable coverage. However, if an individual has no claims in the first six months following enrollment, the remainder of the exclusion period is waived.

(ii) *Conclusion.* In this *Example 2*, the plan's preexisting condition exclusions violate this section because they do not meet the requirements of this paragraph (b)(3); specifically, they do not apply uniformly to all similarly situated individuals. The plan provisions do not apply uniformly to all similarly situated individuals because individuals who have medical claims during the first six months following enrollment are not treated the same as similarly situated individuals with no claims during that period. (Under paragraph (d) of this section, the groups cannot be treated as two separate groups of similarly situated individuals because the distinction is based on a health factor.)

(c) *Prohibited discrimination in premiums or contributions*—(1) *In general*—(i) A group health plan, and a health insurance issuer offering health

insurance coverage in connection with a group health plan, may not require an individual, as a condition of enrollment or continued enrollment under the plan or group health insurance coverage, to pay a premium or contribution that is greater than the premium or contribution for a similarly situated individual (described in paragraph (d) of this section) enrolled in the plan or group health insurance coverage based on any health factor that relates to the individual or a dependent of the individual.

(ii) Discounts, rebates, payments in kind, and any other premium differential mechanisms are taken into account in determining an individual's premium or contribution rate. (For rules relating to cost-sharing mechanisms, see paragraph (b)(2) of this section (addressing benefits).)

(2) *Rules relating to premium rates*—(i) *Group rating based on health factors not restricted under this section.* Nothing in this section restricts the aggregate amount that an employer may be charged for coverage under a group health plan.

(ii) *List billing based on a health factor prohibited.* However, a group health insurance issuer, or a group health insurance issuer, or a group health insurance issuer, may not quote or charge an employer (or an individual) a different premium for an individual in a group of similarly situated individuals based on a health factor. (But see paragraph (g) of this section permitting favorable treatment of individuals with adverse health factors.)

(iii) *Examples.* The rules of this paragraph (c)(2) are illustrated by the following examples:

Example 1. (i) *Facts.* An employer sponsors a group health plan and purchases coverage from a health insurance issuer. In order to determine the premium rate for the upcoming plan year, the issuer reviews the claims experience of individuals covered under the plan. The issuer finds that Individual F had significantly higher claims experience than similarly situated individuals in the plan. The issuer quotes the plan a higher per-participant rate because of *F's* claims experience.

(ii) *Conclusion.* In this *Example 1*, the issuer does not violate the provisions of this paragraph (c)(2) because the issuer blends the rate so that the employer is not quoted a higher rate for *F* than for a similarly situated individual based on *F's* claims experience.

Example 2. (i) *Facts.* Same facts as *Example 1*, except that the issuer quotes the employer a higher premium rate for *F*, because of *F's* claims experience, than for a similarly situated individual.

(ii) *Conclusion.* In this *Example 2*, the issuer violates this paragraph (c)(2). Moreover, even if the plan purchased the policy based on the quote but did not require a higher participant contribution for *F* than

12:40

A. HIPAA Interim Final Rules and Proposed Rules, continued

for a similarly situated individual, the issuer would still violate this paragraph (c)(2) (but in such a case the plan would not violate this paragraph (c)(2)).

(3) *Exception for bona fide wellness programs.* Notwithstanding paragraphs (c)(1) and (2) of this section, a plan may establish a premium or contribution differential based on whether an individual has complied with the requirements of a bona fide wellness program.

(d) *Similarly situated individuals.* The requirements of this section apply only within a group of individuals who are treated as similarly situated individuals. A plan or issuer may treat participants as a group of similarly situated individuals separate from beneficiaries. In addition, participants may be treated as two or more distinct groups of similarly situated individuals and beneficiaries may be treated as two or more distinct groups of similarly situated individuals in accordance with the rules of this paragraph (d). Moreover, if individuals have a choice of two or more benefit packages, individuals choosing one benefit package may be treated as one or more groups of similarly situated individuals distinct from individuals choosing another benefit package.

(1) *Participants.* Subject to paragraph (d)(3) of this section, a plan or issuer may treat participants as two or more distinct groups of similarly situated individuals if the distinction between or among the groups of participants is based on a bona fide employment-based classification consistent with the employer's usual business practice. Whether an employment-based classification is bona fide is determined on the basis of all the relevant facts and circumstances. Relevant facts and circumstances include whether the employer uses the classification for purposes independent of qualification for health coverage (for example, determining eligibility for other employee benefits or determining other terms of employment). Subject to paragraph (d)(3) of this section, examples of classifications that, based on all the relevant facts and circumstances, may be bona fide include full-time versus part-time status, different geographic location, membership in a collective bargaining unit, date of hire, length of service, current employee versus former employee status, and different occupations. However, a classification based on any health factor is not a bona fide employment-based classification, unless the requirements of paragraph (g) of this section are satisfied (permitting

favorable treatment of individuals with adverse health factors).

(2) *Beneficiaries*—(i) Subject to paragraph (d)(3) of this section, a plan or issuer may treat beneficiaries as two or more distinct groups of similarly situated individuals if the distinction between or among the groups of beneficiaries is based on any of the following factors:

(A) A bona fide employment-based classification of the participant through whom the beneficiary is receiving coverage;

(B) Relationship to the participant (e.g., as a spouse or as a dependent child);

(C) Marital status;

(D) With respect to children of a participant, age or student status; or

(E) Any other factor if the factor is not a health factor.

(ii) Paragraph (d)(2)(i) of this section does not prevent more favorable treatment of individuals with adverse health factors in accordance with paragraph (g) of this section.

(3) *Discrimination directed at individuals.* Notwithstanding paragraphs (d)(1) and (2) of this section, if the creation or modification of an employment or coverage classification is directed at individual participants or beneficiaries based on any health factor of the participants or beneficiaries, the classification is not permitted under this paragraph (d), unless it is permitted under paragraph (g) of this section (permitting favorable treatment of individuals with adverse health factors). Thus, if an employer modified an employment-based classification to single out, based on a health factor, individual participants and beneficiaries and deny them health coverage, the new classification would not be permitted under this section.

(4) *Examples.* The rules of this paragraph (d) are illustrated by the following examples:

Example 1. (i) *Facts.* An employer sponsors a group health plan for full-time employees only. Under the plan (consistent with the employer's ususal business practice), employees who normally work at least 30 hours per week are considered to be working full-time. Other employees are considered to be working part-time. There is no evidence to suggest that the classification is directed at individual participants or beneficiaries.

(ii) *Conclusion.* In this *Example 1*, treating the full-time and part-time employees as two separate groups of similarly situated individuals is permitted under this paragraph (d) because the classification is bona fide and is not directed at individual participants or beneficiaries.

Example 2. (i) *Facts.* Under a group health plan, coverage is made available to employees, their spouses, and their

dependent children. However, coverage is made available to a dependent child only if the dependent child is under age 19 (or under age 25 if the child is continuously enrolled full-time in an institution of higher learning (full-time students)). There is no evidence to suggest that these classifications are directed at individual participants or beneficiaries.

(ii) *Conclusion.* In this *Example 2*, treating spouses and dependent children differently by imposing an age limitation on dependent children, but not on spouses, is permitted under this paragraph (d). Specifically, the distinction between spouses and dependent children is permitted under paragraph (d)(2) of this section and is not prohibited under paragraph (d)(3) of this section because it is not directed at individual participants or beneficiaries. It is also permissible to treat dependent children who are under age 19 (or full-time students under age 25) as a group of similarly situated individuals separate from those who are age 25 or older (or age 19 or older if they are not full-time students) because the classification is permitted under paragraph (d)(2) of this section and is not directed at individual participants or beneficiaries.

Example 3. (i) *Facts.* A university sponsors a group health plan that provides one health benefit package to faculty and another health benefit package to other staff. Faculty and staff are treated differently with respect to other employee benefits such as retirement benefits and leaves of absence. There is no evidence to suggest that the distinction is directed at individual participants or beneficiaries.

(ii) *Conclusion.* In this *Example 3*, the classification is permitted under this paragraph (d) because there is a distinction based on a bona fide employment-based classification consistent with the employer's usual business practice and the distinction is not directed at individual participants and beneficiaries.

Example 4. (i) *Facts.* An employer sponsors a group health plan that is available to all current employees. Former employees may also be eligible, but only if they complete a specified number of years of service, are enrolled under the plan at the time of termination of employment, and are continuously enrolled from that date. There is no evidence to suggest that these distinctions are directed at individual participants or beneficiaries.

(ii) *Conclusion.* In this *Example 4*, imposing additional eligibility requirements on former employees is permitted because a classification that distinguishes between current and former employees is a bona fide employment-based classification that is permitted under this paragraph (d), provided that it is not directed at individual participants or beneficiaries. In addition, it is permissible to distinguish between former employees who satisfy the service requirement and those who do not, provided that the distinction is not directed at individual participants or beneficiaries. (However, former employees who do not satisfy the eligibility criteria may, nonetheless, be eligible for continued coverage pursuant to a COBRA continuation provision or similar State law.)

12:41

A. HIPAA Interim Final Rules and Proposed Rules, continued

1416   Federal Register / Vol. 66, No. 5 / Monday, January 8, 2001 / Rules and Regulations

Example 5. (i) *Facts.* An employer sponsors a group health plan that provides the same benefit package to all seven employees of the employer. Six of the seven employees have the same job title and responsibilities, but Employee *G* has a different job title and different responsibilities. After *G* files an expensive claim for benefits under the plan, coverage under the plan is modified so that employees with *G*'s job title receive a different benefit package that includes a lower lifetime dollar limit than in the benefit package made available to the other six employees.

(ii) *Conclusion.* Under the facts of this *Example 5,* changing the coverage classification for *G* based on the existing employment classification for *G* is not permitted under this paragraph (d) because the creation of the new coverage classification for *G* is directed at *G* based on one or more health factors.

(e) *Nonconfinement and actively-at-work provisions*—(1) *Nonconfinement provisions*—(i) *General rule.* Under the rules of paragraphs (b) and (c) of this section, a plan or issuer may not establish a rule for eligibility (as described in paragraph (b)(1)(ii) of this section) or set any individual's premium or contribution rate based on whether an individual is confined to a hospital or other health care institution. In addition, under the rules of paragraphs (b) and (c) of this section, a plan or issuer may not establish a rule for eligibility or set any individual's premium or contribution rate based on an individual's ability to engage in normal life activities, except to the extent permitted under paragraphs (e)(2)(ii) and (3) of this section (permitting plans and issuers, under certain circumstances, to distinguish among employees based on the performance of services).

(ii) *Examples.* The rules of this paragraph (e)(1) are illustrated by the following examples:

Example 1. (i) *Facts.* Under a group health plan, coverage for employees and their dependents generally becomes effective on the first day of employment. However, coverage for a dependent who is confined to a hospital or other health care institution does not become effective until the confinement ends.

(ii) *Conclusion.* In this *Example 1,* the plan violates this paragraph (e)(1) because the plan delays the effective date of coverage for dependents based on confinement to a hospital or other health care institution.

Example 2. (i) *Facts.* In previous years, a group health plan has provided coverage through a group health insurance policy offered by Issuer *M.* However, for the current year, the plan provides coverage through a group health insurance policy offered by Issuer *N.* Under Issuer *N*'s policy, items and services provided in connection with the confinement of a dependent to a hospital or other health care institution are not covered if the confinement is covered under an

extension of benefits clause from a previous health insurance issuer.

(ii) *Conclusion.* In this *Example 2,* Issuer *N* violates this paragraph (e)(1) because the group health insurance coverage restricts benefits (a rule for eligibility under paragraph (b)(1)) based on whether a dependent is confined to a hospital or other health care institution that is covered under an extension of benefits clause from a previous issuer. This section does not affect any obligation Issuer *M* may have under applicable State law to provide any extension of benefits and does not affect any State law governing coordination of benefits.

(2) *Actively-at-work and continuous service provisions*—(i) *General rule*—(A) Under the rules of paragraphs (b) and (c) of this section and subject to the exception for the first day of work described in paragraph (e)(2)(ii) of this section, a plan or issuer may not establish a rule for eligibility (as described in paragraph (b)(1)(ii) of this section) or set any individual's premium or contribution rate based on whether an individual is actively at work (including whether an individual is continuously employed), unless absence from work due to any health factor (such as being absent from work on sick leave) is treated, for purposes of the plan or health insurance coverage, as being actively at work.

(B) The rules of this paragraph (e)(2)(i) are illustrated by the following examples:

Example 1. (i) *Facts.* Under a group health plan, an employee generally becomes eligible to enroll 30 days after the first day of employment. However, if the employee is not actively at work on the first day after the end of the 30-day period, then eligibility for enrollment is delayed until the first day the employee is actively at work.

(ii) *Conclusion.* In this *Example 1,* the plan violates this paragraph (e)(2) (and thus also violates paragraph (b) of this section). However, the plan would not violate paragraph (e)(2) or (b) of this section if, under the plan, an absence due to any health factor is considered being actively at work.

Example 2. (i) *Facts.* Under a group health plan, coverage for an employee becomes effective after 90 days of continuous service; that is, if an employee is absent from work (for any reason) before completing 90 days of service, the beginning of the 90-day period is measured from the day the employee returns to work (without any credit for service before the absence).

(ii) *Conclusion.* In this *Example 2,* the plan violates this paragraph (e)(2) (and thus also violates paragraph (b) of this section) because the 90-day continuous service requirement is a rule for eligibility based on whether an individual is actively at work. However, the plan would not violate this paragraph (e)(2) or paragraph (b) of this section if, under the plan, an absence due to any health factor is not considered an absence for purposes of measuring 90 days of continuous service.

(ii) *Exception for the first day of work*—(A) Notwithstanding the general rule in paragraph (e)(2)(i) of this section, a plan or issuer may establish a rule for eligibility that requires an individual to begin work for the employer sponsoring the plan (or, in the case of a multiemployer plan, to begin a job in covered employment) before coverage becomes effective, provided that such a rule for eligibility applies regardless of the reason for the absence.

(B) The rules of this paragraph (e)(2)(ii) are illustrated by the following examples:

Example 1. (i) *Facts.* Under the eligibility provision of a group health plan, coverage for new employees becomes effective on the first day that the employee reports to work. Individual *H* is scheduled to begin work on August 3. However, *H* is unable to begin work on that day because of illness. *H* begins working on August 4, and *H*'s coverage is effective August 4.

(ii) *Conclusion.* In this *Example 1,* the plan provision does not violate this section. However, if coverage for individuals who do not report to work on the first day they were scheduled to work for a reason unrelated to a health factor (such as vacation or bereavement) becomes effective on the first day they were scheduled to work, then the plan would violate this section.

Example 2. (i) *Facts.* Under a group health plan, coverage for new employees becomes effective on the first day of the month following the employee's first day of work, regardless of whether the employee is actively at work on the first day of the month. Individual *J* is scheduled to begin work on March 24. However, *J* is unable to begin work on March 24 because of illness. *J* begins working on April 7 and *J*'s coverage is effective May 1.

(ii) *Conclusion.* In this *Example 2,* the plan provision does not violate this section. However, as in *Example 1,* if coverage for individuals absent from work for reasons unrelated to a health factor became effective despite their absence, then the plan would violate this section.

(3) *Relationship to plan provisions defining similarly situated individuals*—(i) Notwithstanding the rules of paragraphs (e)(1) and (2) of this section, a plan or issuer may establish rules for eligibility or set any individual's premium or contribution rate in accordance with the rules relating to similarly situated individuals in paragraph (d) of this section. Accordingly, a plan or issuer may distinguish in rules for eligibility under the plan between full-time and part-time employees, between permanent and temporary or seasonal employees, between current and former employees, and between employees currently performing services and employees no longer performing services for the employer, subject to paragraph (d) of this section. However, other federal or

A. HIPAA Interim Final Rules and Proposed Rules, continued

State laws (including the COBRA continuation provisions and the Family and Medical Leave Act of 1993) may require an employee or the employee's dependents to be offered coverage and set limits on the premium or contribution rate even though the employee is not performing services.

(ii) The rules of this paragraph (e)(3) are illustrated by the following examples:

Example 1. (i) *Facts.* Under a group health plan, employees are eligible for coverage if they perform services for the employer for 30 or more hours per week or if they are on paid leave (such as vacation, sick, or bereavement leave). Employees on unpaid leave are treated as a separate group of similarly situated individuals in accordance with the rules of paragraph (d) of this section.

(ii) *Conclusion.* In this *Example 1,* the plan provisions do not violate this section. However, if the plan treated individuals performing services for the employer for 30 or more hours per week, individuals on vacation leave, and individuals on bereavement leave as a group of similarly situated individuals separate from individuals on sick leave, the plan would violate this paragraph (e) (and thus also would violate paragraph (b) of this section) because groups of similarly situated individuals cannot be established based on a health factor (including the taking of sick leave) under paragraph (d) of this section.

Example 2. (i) *Facts.* To be eligible for coverage under a bona fide collectively bargained group health plan in the current calendar quarter, the plan requires an individual to have worked 250 hours in covered employment during the three-month period that ends one month before the beginning of the current calendar quarter. The distinction between employees working at least 250 hours and those working less than 250 hours in the earlier three-month period is not directed at individual participants or beneficiaries based on any health factor of the participants or beneficiaries.

(ii) *Conclusion.* In this *Example 2,* the plan provision does not violate this section because, under the rules for similarly situated individuals allowing full-time employees to be treated differently than part-time employees, employees who work at least 250 hours in a three-month period can be treated differently than employees who fail to work 250 hours in that period. The result would be the same if the plan permitted individuals to apply excess hours from previous periods to satisfy the requirement for the current quarter.

Example 3. (i) *Facts.* Under a group health plan, coverage of an employee is terminated when the individual's employment is terminated, in accordance with the rules of paragraph (d) of this section. Employee *B* has been covered under the plan. *B* experiences a disabling illness that prevents *B* from working. *B* takes a leave of absence under the Family and Medical Leave Act of 1993. At the end of such leave, *B* terminates employment and consequently loses coverage under the plan. (This termination of coverage

is without regard to whatever rights the employee (or members of the employee's family) may have for COBRA continuation coverage.)

(ii) *Conclusion.* In this *Example 3,* the plan provision terminating *B's* coverage upon *B's* termination of employment does not violate this section.

Example 4. (i) *Facts.* Under a group health plan, coverage of an employee is terminated when the employee ceases to perform services for the employer sponsoring the plan, in accordance with the rules of paragraph (d) of this section. Employee *C* is laid off for three months. When the layoff begins, *C's* coverage under the plan is terminated. (This termination of coverage is without regard to whatever rights the employee (or members of the employee's family) may have for COBRA continuation coverage.)

(ii) *Conclusion.* In this *Example 4,* the plan provision terminating *C's* coverage upon the cessation of *C's* performance of services does not violate this section.

(f) *Bona fide wellness programs.* [Reserved.]

(g) *More favorable treatment of individuals with adverse health factors permitted*—(1) *In rules for eligibility*—(i) Nothing in this section prevents a group health plan or group health insurance issuer from establishing more favorable rules for eligibility (described in paragraph (b)(1) of this section) for individuals with an adverse health factor, such as a disability, than for individuals without the adverse health factor. Moreover, nothing in this section prevents a plan or issuer from charging a higher premium or contribution with respect to individuals with an adverse health factor if they would not be eligible for the coverage were it not for the adverse health factor. (However, other laws, including State insurance laws, may set or limit premium rates; these laws are not affected by this section.)

(ii) The rules of this paragraph (g)(1) are illustrated by the following examples:

Example 1. (i) *Facts.* An employer sponsors a group health plan that generally is available to employees, spouses of employees, and dependent children until age 23. However, dependent children who are disabled are eligible for coverage beyond age 23.

(ii) *Conclusion.* In this *Example 1,* the plan provision allowing coverage for disabled dependent children beyond age 23 satisfies this paragraph (g)(1) (and thus does not violate this section).

Example 2. (i) *Facts.* An employer sponsors a group health plan, which is generally available to employees (and members of the employee's family) until the last day of the month in which the employee ceases to perform services for the employer. The plan generally charges employees $50 per month for employee-only coverage and $125 per month for family coverage. However, an employee who ceases to perform services for

the employer by reason of disability may remain covered under the plan until the last day of the month that is 12 months after the month in which the employee ceased to perform services for the employer. During this extended period of coverage, the plan charges the employee $100 per month for employee-only coverage and $250 per month for family coverage. (This extended period of coverage is without regard to whatever rights the employee (or members of the employee's family) may have for COBRA continuation coverage.)

(ii) *Conclusion.* In this *Example 2,* the plan provision allowing extended coverage for disabled employees and their families satisfies this paragraph (g)(1) (and thus does not violate this section). In addition, the plan is permitted, under this paragraph (g)(1), to charge the disabled employees a higher premium during the extended period of coverage.

Example 3. (i) *Facts.* To comply with the requirements of a COBRA continuation provision, a group health plan generally makes COBRA continuation coverage available for a maximum period of 18 months in connection with a termination of employment but that makes the coverage available for a maximum period of 29 months to certain disabled individuals and certain members of the disabled individual's family. Although the plan generally requires payment of 102 percent of the applicable premium for the first 18 months of COBRA continuation coverage, the plan requires payment of 150 percent of the applicable premium for the disabled individual's COBRA continuation coverage during the disability extension if the disabled individual would not be entitled to COBRA continuation coverage but for the disability.

(ii) *Conclusion.* In this *Example 3,* the plan provision allowing extended COBRA continuation coverage for disabled individuals satisfies this paragraph (g)(1) (and thus does not violate this section). In addition, the plan is permitted, under this paragraph (g)(1), to charge the disabled individuals a higher premium for the extended coverage if the individuals would not be eligible for COBRA continuation coverage were it not for the disability. (Similarly, if the plan provided an extended period of coverage for disabled individuals pursuant to State law or plan provision rather than pursuant to a COBRA continuation coverage provision, the plan could likewise charge the disabled individuals a higher premium for the extended coverage.)

(2) *In premiums or contributions*—(i) Nothing in this section prevents a group health plan or group health insurance issuer from charging individuals a premium or contribution that is less than the premium (or contribution) for similarly situated individuals if the lower charge is based on an adverse health factor, such as disability.

(ii) The rules of this paragraph (g)(2) are illustrated by the following example:

Example. (i) *Facts.* Under a group health plan, employees are generally required to pay $50 per month for employee-only coverage and $125 per month for family coverage

A. HIPAA Interim Final Rules and Proposed Rules, continued

under the plan. However, employees who are disabled receive coverage (whether employee-only or family coverage) under the plan free of charge.

(ii) *Conclusion.* In this *Example,* the plan provision waiving premium payment for disabled employees is permitted under this paragraph (g)(2) (and thus does not violate this section).

(h) *No effect on other laws.* Compliance with this section is not determinative of compliance with any other provision of the PHS Act (including the COBRA continuation provisions) or any other State or federal law, such as the Americans with Disabilities Act. Therefore, although the rules of this section would not prohibit a plan or issuer from treating one group of similarly situated individuals differently from another (such as providing different benefit packages to current and former employees), other federal or State laws may require that two separate groups of similarly situated individuals be treated the same for certain purposes (such as making the same benefit package available to COBRA qualified beneficiaries as is made available to active employees). In addition, although this section generally does not impose new disclosure obligations on plans and issuers, this section does not affect any other laws, including those that require accurate disclosures and prohibit intentional misrepresentation.

(i) *Applicability dates*—(1) *Paragraphs applicable March 9, 2001.* Paragraphs (a)(1), (a)(2)(i), (b)(1)(i), (b)(1)(iii) *Example 1,* (b)(2)(i)(A), (b)(2)(ii), (c)(1)(i), (c)(2)(i), and (c)(3) of this section and this paragraph (i)(1) apply to group health plans and health insurance issuers offering group health insurance coverage March 9, 2001.

(2) *Paragraphs applicable for plan years beginning on or after July 1, 2001.* Except as provided in paragraph (i)(3) or (i)(4) of this section, the provisions of this section not listed in paragraph (i)(1) of this section apply to group health plans and health insurance issuers offering group health insurance coverage for plan years beginning on or after July 1, 2001. Except as provided in paragraph (i)(3) or (i)(4) of this section, with respect to efforts to comply with section 2702 of the PHS Act before the first plan year beginning on or after July 1, 2001, the Secretary will not take any enforcement action against an issuer or plan that has sought to comply in good faith with section 2702 of the PHS Act.

(3) *Transitional rules for individuals previously denied coverage based on a health factor.* This paragraph (i)(3) provides rules relating to individuals previously denied coverage under a

group health plan or group health insurance coverage based on a health factor of the individual. Paragraph (i)(3)(i) clarifies what constitutes a denial of coverage under this paragraph (i)(3). Paragraph (i)(3)(ii) of this section applies with respect to any individual who was denied coverage if the denial was not based on a good faith interpretation of section 2702 of the PHS Act or the Secretary's published guidance. Under that paragraph, such an individual must be allowed to enroll retroactively to the effective date of section 2702 of the PHS Act, or, if later, the date the individual meets eligibility criteria under the plan that do not discriminate based on any health factor. Paragraph (i)(3)(iii) of this section applies with respect to any individual who was denied coverage based on a good faith interpretation of section 2702 of the PHS Act or the Secretary's published guidance. Under that paragraph, such an individual must be given an opportunity to enroll effective July 1, 2001. In either event, whether under paragraph (i)(3)(ii) or (iii) of this section, the Secretary will not take any enforcement action with respect to denials of coverage addressed in this paragraph (i)(3) if the issuer or plan has complied with the transitional rules of this paragraph (i)(3).

(i) *Denial of coverage clarified.* For purposes of this paragraph (i)(3), an individual is considered to have been denied coverage if the individual—

(A) Failed to apply for coverage because it was reasonable to believe that an application for coverage would have been futile due to a plan provision that discriminated based on a health factor; or

(B) Was not offered an opportunity to enroll in the plan and the failure to give such an opportunity violates this section.

(ii) *Individuals denied coverage without a good faith interpretation of the law*—(A) *Opportunity to enroll required.* If a plan or issuer has denied coverage to any individual based on a health factor and that denial was not based on a good faith interpretation of section 2702 of the PHS Act or any guidance published by the Secretary, the plan or issuer is required to give the individual an opportunity to enroll (including notice of an opportunity to enroll) that continues for at least 30 days. This opportunity must be presented not later than March 9, 2001.

(1) If this enrollment opportunity was presented before or within the first plan year beginning on or after July 1, 1997 (or in the case of a collectively bargained plan, before or within the first plan year beginning on the effective date

for the plan described in section 102(c)(3) of the Health Insurance Portability and Accountability Act of 1996), the coverage must be effective within that first plan year.

(2) If this enrollment opportunity is presented after such plan year, the individual must be given the choice of having the coverage effective on either of the following two dates—

(i) The date the plan receives a request for enrollment in connection with the enrollment opportunity; or

(ii) Retroactively to the first day of the first plan year beginning on the effective date for the plan described in sections 102(c)(1) and (3) of the Health Insurance Portability and Accountability Act of 1996 (or, if the individual otherwise first became eligible to enroll for coverage after that date, on the date the individual was otherwise eligible to enroll in the plan). If an individual elects retroactive coverage, the plan or issuer is required to provide the benefits it would have provided if the individual had been enrolled for coverage during that period (irrespective of any otherwise applicable plan provisions governing timing for the submission of claims). The plan or issuer may require the individual to pay whatever additional amount the individual would have been required to pay for the coverage (but the plan or issuer cannot charge interest on that amount).

(B) *Relation to preexisting condition rules.* For purposes of section 2701 of the PHS Act, the individual may not be treated as a late enrollee or as a special enrollee. Moreover, the individual's enrollment date is the effective date for the plan described in sections 102(c)(1) and (3) of the Health Insurance Portability and Accountability Act (or, if the individual otherwise first became eligible to enroll for coverage after that date, on the date the individual was otherwise eligible to enroll in the plan), even if the individual chooses under paragraph (i)(3)(ii)(A) of this section to have coverage effective only prospectively. In addition, any period between the individual's enrollment date and the effective date of coverage is treated as a waiting period.

(C) *Examples.* The rules of this paragraph (i)(3)(ii) are illustrated by the following examples:

Example 1. (i) *Facts.* Employer X maintains a group health plan with a plan year beginning October 1 and ending September 30. Individual F was hired by Employer X before the effective date of section 2702 of the PHS Act. Before the effective date of section 2702 of the PHS Act for this plan (October 1, 1997), the terms of the plan allowed employees and their dependents to enroll when the employee was first hired.

A. HIPAA Interim Final Rules and Proposed Rules, continued

and on each January 1 thereafter, but in either case, only if the individual could pass a physical examination. F's application to enroll when first hired was denied because F had diabetes and could not pass a physical examination. Upon the effective date of section 2702 of the PHS Act for this plan (October 1, 1997), the plan is amended to delete the requirement to pass a physical examination. In November of 1997, the plan gives F an opportunity to enroll in the plan (including notice of the opportunity to enroll) without passing a physical examination, with coverage effective January 1, 1998.

(ii) *Conclusion.* In this *Example 1*, the plan complies with the requirements of this paragraph (i)(3)(ii).

Example 2. (i) *Facts.* The plan year of a group health plan begins January 1 and ends December 31. Under the plan, a dependent who is unable to engage in normal life activities on the date coverage would otherwise become effective is not enrolled until the dependent is able to engage in normal life activities. Individual G is a dependent who is otherwise eligible for coverage, but is unable to engage in normal life activities. The plan has not allowed G to enroll for coverage.

(ii) *Conclusion.* In this *Example 2*, beginning on the effective date of section 2702 of the PHS Act for the plan (January 1, 1998), the plan provision is not permitted under any good faith interpretation of section 2702 of the PHS Act or any guidance published by the Secretary. Therefore, the plan is required, not later than March 9, 2001, to give G an opportunity to enroll (including notice of the opportunity to enroll), with coverage effective, at G's option, either retroactively from January 1, 1998 or prospectively from the date G's request for enrollment is received by the plan. If G elects coverage to be effective beginning January 1, 1998, the plan can require G to pay any required employee premiums for the retroactive coverage.

(iii) *Individuals denied coverage based on a good faith interpretation of the law*—(A) *Opportunity to enroll required.* If a plan or issuer has denied coverage to any individual before the first day of the first plan year beginning on or after July 1, 2001 based in part on a health factor and that denial was based on a good faith interpretation of section 2702 of the PHS Act or guidance published by the Secretary, the plan or issuer is required to give the individual an opportunity to enroll (including notice of an opportunity to enroll) that continues for at least 30 days, with coverage effective no later than July 1, 2001. Individuals required to be offered an opportunity to enroll include individuals previously offered enrollment without regard to a health factor but subsequently denied enrollment due to a health factor.

(B) *Relation to preexisting condition rules.* For purposes of section 2701 of the PHS Act, the individual may not be treated as a late enrollee or as a special enrollee. Moreover, the individual's enrollment date is the effective date for the plan described in sections 102(c)(1) and (3) of the Health Insurance Portability and Accountability Act (or, if the individual otherwise first became eligible to enroll for coverage after that date, on the date the individual was otherwise eligible to enroll in the plan). In addition, any period between the individual's enrollment date and the effective date of coverage is treated as a waiting period.

(C) *Example.* The rules of this paragraph (i)(3)(iii) are illustrated by the following example:

Example. (i) *Facts.* Individual H was hired by Employer Y on May 3, 1995. Y maintains a group health plan with a plan year beginning on February 1. Under the terms of the plan, employees and their dependents are allowed to enroll when the employee is first hired (without a requirement to pass a physical examination), and on each February 1 thereafter if the individual can pass a physical examination. H chose not to enroll for coverage when hired in May of 1995. On February 1, 1997, H tried to enroll for coverage under the plan. However, H was denied coverage for failure to pass a physical examination. Shortly thereafter, Y's plan eliminated late enrollment, and H was not given another opportunity to enroll in the plan. There is no evidence to suggest that Y's plan was acting in bad faith in denying coverage under the plan beginning on the effective date of section 2702 of the PHS Act (February 1, 1998).

(ii) *Conclusion.* In this *Example*, because coverage previously had been made available with respect to H without regard to any health factor of H and because Y's plan was acting in accordance with a good faith interpretation of section 2702 of the PHS Act (and guidance published by the Secretary), the failure of Y's plan to allow H to enroll effective February 1, 1998 was permissible on that date. However, under the transitional rules of this paragraph (i)(3)(iii), Y's plan must give H an opportunity to enroll that continues for at least 30 days, with coverage effective no later than July 1, 2001. (In addition, February 1, 1998 is H's enrollment date under the plan and the period between February 1, 1998 and July 1, 2001 is treated as a waiting period. Accordingly, any preexisting condition exclusion period permitted under § 146.111 will have expired before July 1, 2001.)

(4) *Special transitional rule for self-funded non-Federal governmental plans exempted under 45 CFR 146.180*—(i) If coverage has been denied to any individual because the sponsor of a self-funded non-Federal governmental plan has elected under § 146.180 to exempt the plan from the requirements of this section, and the plan sponsor subsequently chooses to bring the plan into compliance with the requirements of this section, the plan—

(A) Must notify the individual that the plan will be coming into compliance with the requirements of this section, specify the effective date of compliance, and inform the individual regarding any enrollment restrictions that may apply under the terms of the plan once the plan is in compliance with this section (as a matter of administrative convenience, the notice may be disseminated to all employees);

(B) Must give the individual an opportunity to enroll that continues for at least 30 days;

(C) Must permit coverage to be effective as of the first day of plan coverage for which an exemption election under § 146.180 (with regard to this section) is no longer in effect (or July 1, 2001, if later, and the plan was acting in accordance with a good faith interpretation of section 2702 of the PHS Act and guidance published by HCFA); and

(D) May not treat the individual as a late enrollee or a special enrollee.

(ii) For purposes of this paragraph (i)(4), an individual is considered to have been denied coverage if the individual failed to apply for coverage because, given an exemption election under § 146.180, it was reasonable to believe that an application for coverage would have been denied based on a health factor.

(iii) The rules of this paragraph (i)(4) are illustrated by the following examples:

Example 1. (i) *Facts.* Individual D was hired by a non-Federal governmental employer in June 1996. The employer maintains a self-funded group health plan with a plan year beginning on October 1. Under the terms of the plan, employees and their dependents are allowed to enroll when the employee is first hired without regard to any health factor. If an individual declines to enroll when first eligible, the individual may enroll effective October 1 of any plan year if the individual can pass a physical examination. The plan sponsor elected under § 146.180 of this part to exempt the plan from the requirements of this section for the plan year beginning October 1, 1997, and renewed the exemption election for the plan year beginning October 1, 1998. That is, the plan sponsor elected to retain the evidence of good health requirement for late enrollees which, absent an exemption election under § 146.180 of this part, would have been in violation of this section as of October 1, 1997. D chose not to enroll for coverage when first hired. In February of 1998, D was treated for skin cancer but did not apply for coverage under the plan for the plan year beginning October 1, 1998, because D assumed D could not meet the evidence of good health requirement. With the plan year beginning October 1, 1999, the plan sponsor chose not to renew its exemption election and brought the plan into compliance with this section. However, the terms of the plan, effective

A. HIPAA Interim Final Rules and Proposed Rules, continued

October 1, 1999, were amended to permit enrollment only during the initial 30-day period of employment. The plan no longer permits late enrollment under any circumstances, including with respect to current employees not enrolled in the plan. Therefore, *D* was not given another opportunity to enroll in the plan. There is no evidence to suggest that the plan was acting in bad faith in denying *D* coverage under the plan beginning on the effective date of § 146.121 for the plan (October 1, 1999).

(ii) *Conclusion.* In this *Example 1*, because the plan under § 146.180 was previously excluded from the requirements of § 146.121 and thereafter was acting in accordance with a good faith interpretation of § 146.121 and guidance published by HCFA, the failure of the plan to give *D* an opportunity to enroll effective October 1, 1999 was permissible on that date. However, under the transitional rules of this paragraph (i)(4), the plan must give *D* an opportunity to enroll that continues for at least 30 days, with coverage effective no later than July 1, 2001. (Additionally, October 1, 1999 is *D's* enrollment date under the plan and the period between October 1, 1999 and July 1, 2001 is treated as a waiting period. Furthermore, if the plan sponsor has not elected to exempt the plan from limitations on preexisting condition exclusion periods, any preexisting condition exclusion period must be administered in accordance with § 146.111. Accordingly, any preexisting condition exclusion period permitted under § 146.111 will have expired before July 1, 2001.)

Example 2. (i) *Facts.* Individual *E* was hired by a non-Federal governmental employer in February 1995. The employer maintains a self-funded group health plan with a plan year beginning on September 1. Under the terms of the plan, employees and their dependents are allowed to enroll when the employee is first hired without regard to

any health factor. If an individual declines to enroll when first eligible, the individual may enroll effective September 1 of any plan year if the individual can pass a physical examination. All enrollees are subject to a 12-month preexisting condition exclusion period. The plan sponsor elected under § 146.180 of this part to exempt the plan from the requirements of this section and § 146.111 (limitations on preexisting condition exclusion periods) for the plan year beginning September 1, 1997, and renews the exemption election for the plan years beginning September 1, 1998, September 1, 1999, and September 1, 2000. *E* chose not to enroll for coverage when first hired. In June of 2001, *E* is diagnosed as having multiple sclerosis (MS). With the plan year beginning September 1, 2001, the plan sponsor chooses to bring the plan into compliance with this section, but renews its exemption election with regard to limitations on preexisting condition exclusion periods. The plan affords *E* an opportunity to enroll, without a physical examination, effective September 1, 2001. *E* is subject to a 12-month preexisting condition exclusion period with respect to any treatment *E* receives that is related to *E's* MS, without regard to any prior creditable coverage *E* may have. Beginning September 1, 2002, the plan will cover treatment of *E's* MS.

(ii) *Conclusion.* In this *Example 2*, the plan complies with the requirements of this section. (The plan is not required to comply with the requirements of § 146.111 because the plan continues to be exempted from those requirements in accordance with the plan sponsor's election under § 146.180.)

3. The heading, paragraph (a)(1), and the first sentence of paragraph (a)(2) of § 146.125 are revised to read as follows:

§ 146.125   Applicability dates.

(a) *General applicability dates—*(1) *Non-collectively bargained plans.* Part A

of title XXVII of the PHS Act and §§ 146.101 through 146.119, § 146.143, § 146.145, 45 CFR part 150, and this section apply with respect to group health plans, and health insurance coverage offered in connection with group health plans, for plan years beginning after June 30, 1997, except as otherwise provided in this section.

(2) *Collectively-bargained plans.* Except as otherwise provided in this section (other than paragraph (a)(1) of this section), in the case of a group health plan maintained pursuant to one or more collective bargaining agreements between employee representatives and one or more employers ratified before August 21, 1996, Part A of Title XXVII of the PHS Act and §§ 146.101 through 146.119, § 146.143, § 146.145, 45 CFR part 150, and this section do not apply to plan years beginning before the later of July 1, 1997, or the date on which the last of the collective bargaining agreements relating to the plan terminates (determined without regard to any extension thereof agreed to after August 21, 1996). * * *

*   *   *   *   *

Dated: June 22, 2000.

Nancy-Ann Min DeParle,

Administrator, Health Care Financing Administration.

Approved: August 29, 2000.

Donna E. Shalala,

Secretary.

[FR Doc. 01–106 Filed 1–5–01; 8:45 am]

BILLING CODE 4120-01-P; 4830-01-P; 4510-29-P

B. Notice of Changes Under HIPAA to COBRA

Summary
The DOL's Pension and Welfare Benefits Administration (now the Employee Benefits Security Administration) published a technical release regarding the changes to COBRA made by HIPAA. These changes affected:

- The disability extension
- The definition of qualified beneficiary
- The maximum coverage period

The release also notified employers and plan administrators of a onetime requirement to provide notice to qualified beneficiaries of the changes made to COBRA no later than November 1, 1996.

B. Notice of Changes Under HIPAA to COBRA, continued

PWBA Office of Regulations and Interpretations

NOTICE OF CHANGES UNDER HIPAA TO COBRA

CONTINUATION COVERAGE UNDER GROUP HEALTH PLANS

On August 21, 1996, the Health Insurance Portability and Accountability Act of 1996 (HIPAA) was signed into law (Pub. L. 104-191). HIPAA section 421 makes changes, described below, to three areas in the continuation coverage rules applicable to group health plans under the Consolidated Omnibus Budget Reconciliation Act of 1985 (COBRA), as amended. These three areas relate to the disability extension, the definition of qualified beneficiary and the duration of COBRA continuation coverage. These changes are effective beginning Jan. 1, 1997, regardless of when the event occurs that entitles an individual to COBRA continuation coverage.

Section 421(e) of HIPAA requires group health plans that are subject to COBRA to notify, by November 1, 1996, individuals who have elected COBRA continuation coverage of these changes. The Department is issuing this release to apprise employers and plan administrators of the changes in the continuation coverage rules made by HIPAA and to inform them of their obligation under HIPAA to notify qualified beneficiaries of such changes. Such notification must be given to qualified beneficiaries by Nov. 1, 1996. The following is a discussion of the specific changes in the continuation coverage rules made by HIPAA.

Disability Extension. Under current law, if an individual is entitled to COBRA continuation coverage because of a termination of employment or reduction in hours of employment, the plan generally is only required to make COBRA continuation coverage available to that individual for 18 months. However, if the individual entitled to the COBRA continuation coverage is disabled (as determined under the Social Security Act) and satisfies the applicable notice requirements, the plan must provide COBRA continuation coverage for 29 months, rather than 18 months. Under current law, the individual must be disabled at the time of the termination of employment or reduction in hours of employment. HIPAA makes changes to the current law to provide that, beginning Jan. 1, 1997, the disability extension will also apply if the individual becomes disabled at any time during the first 60 days of COBRA continuation coverage. HIPAA also makes it clear that, if the individual entitled to the disability extension has nondisabled family members who are entitled to COBRA continuation coverage, those nondisabled family members are also entitled to the 29 month disability extension.

Definition of Qualified Beneficiary. Individuals entitled to COBRA continuation coverage are called qualified beneficiaries. Individuals who may be qualified beneficiaries are the spouse and dependent children of a covered employee and, in certain cases, the covered employee. Under current law, in order to be a qualified beneficiary an individual must generally be covered under a group health plan on the day before the event that causes a loss of coverage (such as a termination of employment, or a divorce from or death of the covered employee). HIPAA changes this requirement so that a child who is born to the covered employee, or who is placed for adoption with the covered employee, during a

B. Notice of Changes Under HIPAA to COBRA, continued

period of COBRA continuation coverage is also a qualified beneficiary.

Duration of COBRA Continuation Coverage. Under the COBRA rules there are situations in which a group health plan may stop making COBRA continuation coverage available earlier than usually permitted. One of those situations is where the qualified beneficiary obtains coverage under another group health plan. Under current law, if the other group health plan limits or excludes coverage for any preexisting condition of the qualified beneficiary, the plan providing the COBRA continuation coverage cannot stop making the COBRA continuation coverage available merely because of the coverage under the other group health plan. HIPAA limits the circumstances in which plans can apply exclusions for preexisting conditions. HIPAA makes a coordinating change to the COBRA rules so that if a group health plan limits or excludes benefits for preexisting conditions but because of the new HIPAA rules those limits or exclusions would not apply to (or would be satisfied by) an individual receiving COBRA continuation coverage, then the plan providing the COBRA continuation coverage can stop making the COBRA continuation coverage available. The HIPAA rules limiting the applicability of exclusions for preexisting conditions become effective in plan years beginning on or after July 1, 1997 (or later for certain plans maintained pursuant to one or more collective bargaining agreements).

Effect of this Release. As noted above, the Department is issuing this release to advise employers and plan administrators of their obligation to notify, by Nov. 1, 1996, qualified beneficiaries of these statutory changes. The Department, as a matter of enforcement policy, will deem that supplying qualified beneficiaries with a written copy of the information described above (or with a copy of this release) constitutes compliance with the notice requirement in section 421(e) of HIPAA if this information is sent to each qualified beneficiary by first class mail at the last known address of the qualified beneficiary by Nov. 1, 1996.

---DISCLAIMER---

DOL Homepage | PWBA Homepage | Top of Document

C. HIPAA Final Rules, Privacy Standards

Summary   The U.S. Department of Health and Human Services (DHHS) initially published proposed regulations on the privacy standards in November 1999.[1] After an extended comment period, the DHHS published in December 2000 final rules that addressed the more than 52,000 comments it received. The final rules, which became effective on April 14, 2001, gave most covered entities until April 14, 2003, to comply. (Small health plans had until April 14, 2004, to comply.) After considering the comments on the final rules, the DHHS proposed some specific changes in March 2002 and a final set of modifications in August 2002.

---

[1] HHS Fact Sheet, May 9, 2001.

**Wednesday,
August 14, 2002**

Part V

Department of Health and Human Services

Office of the Secretary

45 CFR Parts 160 and 164
Standards for Privacy of Individually
Identifiable Health Information; Final
Rule

53182   Federal Register / Vol. 67, No. 157 / Wednesday, August 14, 2002 / Rules and Regulations

DEPARTMENT OF HEALTH AND HUMAN SERVICES

Office of the Secretary

45 CFR Parts 160 and 164

RIN 0991–AB14

Standards for Privacy of Individually Identifiable Health Information

AGENCY: Office for Civil Rights, HHS.
ACTION: Final rule.

SUMMARY: The Department of Health and Human Services ("HHS" or "Department") modifies certain standards in the Rule entitled "Standards for Privacy of Individually Identifiable Health Information" ("Privacy Rule"). The Privacy Rule implements the privacy requirements of the Administrative Simplification subtitle of the Health Insurance Portability and Accountability Act of 1996.

The purpose of these modifications is to maintain strong protections for the privacy of individually identifiable health information while clarifying certain of the Privacy Rule's provisions, addressing the unintended negative effects of the Privacy Rule on health care quality or access to health care, and relieving unintended administrative burdens created by the Privacy Rule.

DATES: This final rule is effective on October 15, 2002.

FOR FURTHER INFORMATION CONTACT: Felicia Farmer, 1–866–OCR–PRIV (1–866–627–7748) or TTY 1–866–788–4989.

SUPPLEMENTARY INFORMATION: Availability of copies, and electronic access.

Copies: To order copies of the **Federal Register** containing this document, send your request to: New Orders, Superintendent of Documents, P.O. Box 371954, Pittsburgh, PA 15250–7954. Specify the date of the issue requested and enclose a check or money order payable to the Superintendent of Documents, or enclose your Visa or Master Card number and expiration date. Credit card orders can also be placed by calling the order desk at (202) 512–1800 (or toll-free at 1–866–512–1800) or by fax to (202) 512–2250. The cost for each copy is $10.00. Alternatively, you may view and photocopy the **Federal Register** document at most libraries designated as Federal Depository Libraries and at many other public and academic libraries throughout the country that receive the **Federal Register**.

Electronic Access: This document is available electronically at the HHS Office for Civil Rights (OCR) Privacy Web site at *http://www.hhs.gov/ocr/ hipaa/*, as well as at the web site of the Government Printing Office at *http:// www.access.gpo.gov/su_docs/aces/ aces140.html*.

I. Background

A. Statutory Background

Congress recognized the importance of protecting the privacy of health information given the rapid evolution of health information systems in the Health Insurance Portability and Accountability Act of 1996 (HIPAA), Public Law 104–191, which became law on August 21, 1996. HIPAA's Administrative Simplification provisions, sections 261 through 264 of the statute, were designed to improve the efficiency and effectiveness of the health care system by facilitating the electronic exchange of information with respect to certain financial and administrative transactions carried out by health plans, health care clearinghouses, and health care providers who transmit information electronically in connection with such transactions. To implement these provisions, the statute directed HHS to adopt a suite of uniform, national standards for transactions, unique health identifiers, code sets for the data elements of the transactions, security of health information, and electronic signature.

At the same time, Congress recognized the challenges to the confidentiality of health information presented by the increasing complexity of the health care industry, and by advances in the health information systems technology and communications. Thus, the Administrative Simplification provisions of HIPAA authorized the Secretary to promulgate standards for the privacy of individually identifiable health information if Congress did not enact health care privacy legislation by August 21, 1999. HIPAA also required the Secretary of HHS to provide Congress with recommendations for legislating to protect the confidentiality of health care information. The Secretary submitted such recommendations to Congress on September 11, 1997, but Congress did not pass such legislation within its self-imposed deadline.

With respect to these regulations, HIPAA provided that the standards, implementation specifications, and requirements established by the Secretary not supersede any contrary State law that imposes more stringent privacy protections. Additionally,

Congress required that HHS consult with the National Committee on Vital and Health Statistics, a Federal advisory committee established pursuant to section 306(k) of the Public Health Service Act (42 U.S.C. 242k(k)), and the Attorney General in the development of HIPAA privacy standards.

After a set of HIPAA Administrative Simplification standards is adopted by the Department, HIPAA provides HHS with authority to modify the standards as deemed appropriate, but not more frequently than once every 12 months. However, modifications are permitted during the first year after adoption of the standards if the changes are necessary to permit compliance with the standards. HIPAA also provides that compliance with modifications to standards or implementation specifications must be accomplished by a date designated by the Secretary, which may not be earlier than 180 days after the adoption of the modification.

B. Regulatory and Other Actions to Date

HHS published a proposed Rule setting forth privacy standards for individually identifiable health information on November 3, 1999 (64 FR 59918). The Department received more than 52,000 public comments in response to the proposal. After reviewing and considering the public comments, HHS issued a final Rule (65 FR 82462) on December 28, 2000, establishing "Standards for Privacy of Individually Identifiable Health Information" ("Privacy Rule").

In an era where consumers are increasingly concerned about the privacy of their personal information, the Privacy Rule creates, for the first time, a floor of national protections for the privacy of their most sensitive information—health information. Congress has passed other laws to protect consumers' personal information contained in bank, credit card, other financial records, and even video rentals. These health privacy protections are intended to provide consumers with similar assurances that their health information, including genetic information, will be properly protected. Under the Privacy Rule, health plans, health care clearinghouses, and certain health care providers must guard against misuse of individuals' identifiable health information and limit the sharing of such information, and consumers are afforded significant new rights to enable them to understand and control how their health information is used and disclosed.

After publication of the Privacy Rule, HHS received many inquiries and unsolicited comments through

C. HIPAA Final Rules, Privacy Standards, continued

Federal Register / Vol. 67, No. 157 / Wednesday, August 14, 2002 / Rules and Regulations **53183**

telephone calls, e-mails, letters, and other contacts about the impact and operation of the Privacy Rule on numerous sectors of the health care industry. Many of these commenters exhibited substantial confusion and misunderstanding about how the Privacy Rule will operate; others expressed great concern over the complexity of the Privacy Rule. In response to these communications and to ensure that the provisions of the Privacy Rule would protect patients' privacy without creating unanticipated consequences that might harm patients' access to health care or quality of health care, the Secretary of HHS opened the Privacy Rule for additional public comment in March 2001 (66 FR 12738).

After an expedited review of the comments by the Department, the Secretary decided that it was appropriate for the Privacy Rule to become effective on April 14, 2001, as scheduled (65 FR 12433). At the same time, the Secretary directed the Department immediately to begin the process of developing guidelines on how the Privacy Rule should be implemented and to clarify the impact of the Privacy Rule on health care activities. In addition, the Secretary charged the Department with proposing appropriate changes to the Privacy Rule during the next year to clarify the requirements and correct potential problems that could threaten access to, or quality of, health care. The comments received during the comment period, as well as other communications from the public and all sectors of the health care industry, including letters, testimony at public hearings, and meetings requested by these parties, have helped to inform the Department's efforts to develop proposed modifications and guidance on the Privacy Rule.

On July 6, 2001, the Department issued its first guidance to answer common questions and clarify certain of the Privacy Rule's provisions. In the guidance, the Department also committed to proposing modifications to the Privacy Rule to address problems arising from unintended effects of the Privacy Rule on health care delivery and access. The guidance will soon be updated to reflect the modifications adopted in this final Rule. The revised guidance will be available on the HHS Office for Civil Rights (OCR) Privacy Web site at *http://www.hhs.gov/ocr/hipaa/*.

In addition, the National Committee for Vital and Health Statistics (NCVHS), Subcommittee on Privacy and Confidentiality, held public hearings on the implementation of the Privacy Rule on August 21–23, 2001, and January 24–

25, 2002, and provided recommendations to the Department based on these hearings. The NCVHS serves as the statutory advisory body to the Secretary of HHS with respect to the development and implementation of the Rules required by the Administrative Simplification provisions of HIPAA, including the privacy standards. Through the hearings, the NCVHS specifically solicited public input on issues related to certain key standards in the Privacy Rule: consent, minimum necessary, marketing, fundraising, and research. The resultant public testimony and subsequent recommendations submitted to the Department by the NCVHS also served to inform the development of these proposed modifications.

II. Overview of the March 2002 Notice of Proposed Rulemaking (NPRM)

As described above, through public comments, testimony at public hearings, meetings at the request of industry and other stakeholders, as well as other communications, the Department learned of a number of concerns about the potential unintended effects certain provisions would have on health care quality and access. On March 27, 2002, in response to these concerns, and pursuant to HIPAA's provisions for modifications to the standards, the Department proposed modifications to the Privacy Rule (67 FR 14776).

The Department proposed to modify the following areas or provisions of the Privacy Rule: consent; uses and disclosures for treatment, payment, and health care operations; notice of privacy practices; minimum necessary uses and disclosures, and oral communications; business associates; uses and disclosures for marketing; parents as the personal representatives of unemancipated minors; uses and disclosures for research purposes; uses and disclosures for which authorizations are required; and de-identification. In addition to these key areas, the proposal included changes to other provisions where necessary to clarify the Privacy Rule. The Department also included in the proposed Rule a list of technical corrections intended as editorial or typographical corrections to the Privacy Rule.

The proposed modifications collectively were designed to ensure that protections for patient privacy are implemented in a manner that maximizes the effectiveness of such protections while not compromising either the availability or the quality of medical care. They reflected a continuing commitment on the part of

the Department to strong privacy protections for medical records and the belief that privacy is most effectively protected by requirements that are not exceptionally difficult to implement. The Department welcomed comments and suggestions for alternative ways effectively to protect patient privacy without adversely affecting access to, or the quality of, health care.

Given that the compliance date of the Privacy Rule for most covered entities is April 14, 2003, and the Department's interest in having the compliance date for these revisions also be no later than April 14, 2003, the Department solicited public comment on the proposed modifications for only 30 days. As stated above, the proposed modifications addressed public concerns already communicated to the Department through a wide variety of sources since publication of the Privacy Rule in December 2000. For these reasons, the Department believed that 30 days should be sufficient for the public to state its views fully to the Department on the proposed modifications to the Privacy Rule. During the 30-day comment period, the Department received in excess of 11,400 comments.

III. Section-by-Section Description of Final Modifications and Response to Comments

A. Section 164.501—Definitions

1. Marketing

December 2000 Privacy Rule

The Privacy Rule defined "marketing" at § 164.501 as a communication about a product or service, a purpose of which is to encourage recipients of the communication to purchase or use the product or service, subject to certain limited exceptions. To avoid interfering with, or unnecessarily burdening communications about, treatment or about the benefits and services of health plans and health care providers, the Privacy Rule explicitly excluded two types of communications from the definition of "marketing:" (1) communications made by a covered entity for the purpose of describing the participating providers and health plans in a network, or describing the services offered by a provider or the benefits covered by a health plan; and (2) communications made by a health care provider as part of the treatment of a patient and for the purpose of furthering that treatment, or made by a provider or health plan in the course of managing an individual's treatment or recommending an alternative treatment. Thus, a health plan could send its

53184   Federal Register / Vol. 67, No. 157 / Wednesday, August 14, 2002 / Rules and Regulations

enrollees a listing of network providers, and a health care provider could refer a patient to a specialist without either an authorization under § 164.508 or having to meet the other special requirements in § 164.514(e) that attach to marketing communications. However, these communications qualified for the exception to the definition of "marketing" only if they were made orally or, if in writing, were made without remuneration from a third party. For example, it would not have been marketing for a pharmacy to call a patient about the need to refill a prescription, even if that refill reminder was subsidized by a third party; but it would have been marketing for that same, subsidized refill reminder to be sent to the patient in the mail.

Generally, if a communication was marketing, the Privacy Rule required the covered entity to obtain the individual's authorization to use or disclose protected health information to make the communication. However, the Privacy Rule, at § 164.514(e), permitted the covered entity to make health-related marketing communications without such authorization, provided it complied with certain conditions on the manner in which the communications were made. Specifically, the Privacy Rule permitted a covered entity to use or disclose protected health information to communicate to individuals about the health-related products or services of the covered entity or of a third party, without first obtaining an authorization for that use or disclosure of protected health information, if the communication: (1) Identified the covered entity as the party making the communication; (2) identified, if applicable, that the covered entity received direct or indirect remuneration from a third party for making the communication; (3) with the exception of general circulation materials, contained instructions describing how the individual could opt-out of receiving future marketing communications; and (4) where protected health information was used to target the communication about a product or service to individuals based on their health status or health condition, explained why the individual had been targeted and how the product or service related to the health of the individual.

For certain permissible marketing communications, however, the Department did not believe these conditions to be practicable. Therefore, § 164.514(e) also permitted a covered entity to make a marketing communication that occurred in a face-to-face encounter with the individual, or

that involved products or services of only nominal value, without meeting the above conditions or requiring an authorization. These provisions, for example, permitted a covered entity to provide sample products during a face-to-face communication, or to distribute calendars, pens, and the like, that displayed the name of a product or provider.

March 2002 NPRM

The Department received many complaints concerning the complexity and unworkability of the Privacy Rule's marketing requirements. Many entities expressed confusion over the Privacy Rule's distinction between health care communications that are excepted from the definition of "marketing" versus those that are marketing but permitted subject to the special conditions in § 164.514(e). For example, questions were raised as to whether disease management communications or refill reminders were "marketing" communications subject to the special disclosure and opt-out conditions in § 164.514(e). Others stated that it was unclear whether various health care operations activities, such as general health-related educational and wellness promotional activities, were to be treated as marketing under the Privacy Rule.

The Department also learned that consumers were generally dissatisfied with the conditions required by § 164.514(e). Many questioned the general effectiveness of the conditions and whether the conditions would properly protect consumers from unwanted disclosure of protected health information to commercial entities, and from the intrusion of unwanted solicitations. They expressed specific dissatisfaction with the provision at § 164.514(e)(3)(iii) for individuals to opt-out of future marketing communications. Many argued for the opportunity to opt-out of marketing communications before any marketing occurred. Others requested that the Department limit marketing communications to only those consumers who affirmatively chose to receive such communications.

In response to these concerns, the Department proposed to modify the Privacy Rule to make the marketing provisions clearer and simpler. First, the Department proposed to simplify the Privacy Rule by eliminating the special provisions for marketing health-related products and services at § 164.514(e). Instead, any use or disclosure of protected health information for a communication defined as "marketing" in § 164.501 would require an

authorization by the individual. Thus, covered entities would no longer be able to make any type of marketing communications that involved the use or disclosure of protected health information without authorization simply by meeting the disclosure and opt-out conditions in the Privacy Rule. The Department intended to effectuate greater consumer privacy protection by requiring authorization for all uses or disclosures of protected health information for marketing communications, as compared to the disclosure and opt-out conditions of § 164.514(e).

Second, the Department proposed minor clarifications to the Privacy Rule's definition of "marketing" at § 164.501. Specifically, the Department proposed to define "marketing" as "to make a communication about a product or service to encourage recipients of the communication to purchase or use the product or service." The proposed modification retained the substance of the "marketing" definition, but changed the language slightly to avoid the implication that in order for a communication to be marketing, the purpose or intent of the covered entity in making such a communication would have to be determined. The simplified language permits the Department to make the determination based on the communication itself.

Third, with respect to the exclusions from the definition of "marketing" in § 164.501, the Department proposed to simplify the language to avoid confusion and better conform to other sections of the regulation, particularly in the area of treatment communications. The proposal retained the exclusions for communications about a covered entity's own products and services and about the treatment of the individual. With respect to the exclusion for a communication made "in the course of managing the treatment of that individual," the Department proposed to modify the language to use the terms "case management" and "care coordination" for that individual. These terms are more consistent with the terms used in the definition of "health care operations," and were intended to clarify the Department's intent.

One substantive change to the definition proposed by the Department was to eliminate the condition on the above exclusions from the definition of "marketing" that the covered entity could not receive remuneration from a third party for any written communication. This limitation was not well understood and treated similar communications differently. For

Federal Register / Vol. 67, No. 157 / Wednesday, August 14, 2002 / Rules and Regulations   **53185**

example, a prescription refill reminder was marketing if it was in writing and paid for by a third party, while a refill reminder that was not subsidized, or was made orally, was not marketing. With the proposed elimination of the health-related marketing requirements in § 164.514(e) and the proposed requirement that any marketing communication require an individual's prior written authorization, retention of this condition would have adversely affected a health care provider's ability to make many common health-related communications. Therefore, the Department proposed to eliminate the remuneration prohibition to the exceptions to the definition so as not to interfere with necessary and important treatment and health-related communications between a health care provider and patient.

To reinforce the policy requiring an authorization for most marketing communications, the Department proposed to add a new marketing provision at § 164.508(a)(3) explicitly requiring an authorization for a use or disclosure of protected health information for marketing purposes. Additionally, if the marketing was expected to result in direct or indirect remuneration to the covered entity from a third party, the Department proposed that the authorization state this fact. As noted above, because a use or disclosure of protected health information for marketing communications required an authorization, the disclosure and opt-out provisions in § 164.514(e) no longer would be necessary and the Department proposed to eliminate them. As in the December 2000 Privacy Rule at § 164.514(e)(2), the proposed modifications at § 164.508(a)(3) excluded from the marketing authorization requirements face-to-face communications made by a covered entity to an individual. The Department proposed to retain this exception so that the marketing provisions would not interfere with the relationship and dialogue between health care providers and individuals. Similarly, the Department proposed to retain the exception to the authorization requirement for a marketing communication that involved products or services of nominal value, but proposed to replace the language with the common business term "promotional gift of nominal value."

As noted above, because some of the proposed simplifications were a substitute for § 164.514(e), the Department proposed to eliminate that section, and to make conforming changes to remove references to § 164.514(e) at § 164.502(a)(1)(vi) and in

paragraph (6)(v) of the definition of "health care operations" in § 164.501.

Overview of Public Comments

The following discussion provides an overview of the public comment received on this proposal. Additional comments received on this issue are discussed below in the section entitled, "Response to Other Public Comments."

The Department received generally favorable comment on its proposal to simplify the marketing provisions by requiring authorizations for uses or disclosures of protected health information for marketing communications, instead of the special provisions for health-related products and services at § 164.514(e). Many also supported the requirement that authorizations notify the individual of marketing that results in direct or indirect remuneration to the covered entity from a third party. They argued that for patients to make informed decisions, they must be notified of potential financial conflicts of interest. However, some commenters opposed the authorization requirement for marketing, arguing instead for the disclosure and opt-out requirements at § 164.514(e) or for a one-time, blanket authorization from an individual for their marketing activities.

Commenters were sharply divided on whether the Department had properly defined what is and what is not marketing. Most of those opposed to the Department's proposed definitions objected to the elimination of health-related communications for which the covered entity received remuneration from the definition of "marketing." They argued that these communications would have been subject to the consumer protections in § 164.514(e) but, under the proposal, could be made without any protections at all. The mere presence of remuneration raised conflict of interest concerns for these commenters, who feared patients would be misled into thinking the covered entity was acting solely in the patients' best interest when recommending an alternative medication or treatment. Of particular concern to these commenters was the possibility of a third party, such as a pharmaceutical company, obtaining a health care provider's patient list to market its own products or services directly to the patients under the guise of recommending an "alternative treatment" on behalf of the provider. Commenters argued that, even if the parties attempted to cloak the transaction in the trappings of a business associate relationship, when the remuneration flowed from the third party to the covered entity, the

transaction was tantamount to selling the patient lists and ought to be considered marketing.

On the other hand, many commenters urged the Department to broaden the categories of communications that are not marketing. Several expressed concern that, under the proposal, they would be unable to send newsletters and other general circulation materials with information about health-promoting activities (*e.g.*, screenings for certain diseases) to their patients or members without an authorization. Health plans were concerned that they would be unable to send information regarding enhancements to health insurance coverage to their members and beneficiaries. They argued, among other things, that they should be excluded from the definition of "marketing" because these communications would be based on limited, non-clinical protected health information, and because policyholders benefit and use such information to fully evaluate the mix of coverage most appropriate to their needs. They stated that providing such information is especially important given that individual and market-wide needs, as well as benefit offerings, change over time and by statute. For example, commenters informed the Department that some States now require long-term care insurers to offer new products to existing policyholders as they are brought to market and to allow policyholders to purchase the new benefits through a formal upgrade process. These health plans were concerned that an authorization requirement for routine communications about options and enhancements would take significant time and expense. Some insurers also urged that they be allowed to market other lines of insurance to their health plan enrollees.

A number of commenters urged the Department to exclude any activity that met the definitions of "treatment," "payment," or "health care operations" from the definition of "marketing" so that they could freely inform customers about prescription discount card and price subsidy programs. Still others wanted the Department to broaden the treatment exception to include all health-related communications between providers and patients.

Final Modifications. The Department adopts the modifications to marketing substantially as proposed in the NPRM, but makes changes to the proposed definition of "marketing" and further clarifies one of the exclusions from the definition of "marketing" in response to comments on the proposal. The

C. HIPAA Final Rules, Privacy Standards, continued

definition of "marketing" is modified to close what commenters characterized as a loophole, that is, the possibility that covered entities, for remuneration, could disclose protected health information to a third party that would then be able to market its own products and services directly to individuals. Also, in response to comments, the Department clarifies the language in the marketing exclusion for communications about a covered entity's own products and services.

As it proposed to do, the Department eliminates the special provisions for marketing health-related products and services at § 164.514(e). Except as provided for at § 164.508(a)(3), a covered entity must have the individual's prior written authorization to use or disclose protected health information for marketing communications and will no longer be able to do so simply by meeting the disclosure and opt-out provisions, previously set forth in § 164.514(e). The Department agrees with commenters that the authorization provides individuals with more control over whether they receive marketing communications and better privacy protections for such uses and disclosures of their health information. In response to commenters who opposed this proposal, the Department does not believe that an opt-out requirement for marketing communications would provide a sufficient level of control for patients regarding their health information. Nor does the Department believe that a blanket authorization provides sufficient privacy protections for individuals. Section 164.508(c) sets forth the core elements of an authorization necessary to give individuals control of their protected health information. Those requirements give individuals sufficient information and notice regarding the type of use or disclosure of their protected health information that they are authorizing. Without such specificity, an authorization would not have meaning. Indeed, blanket marketing authorizations would be considered defective under § 164.508(b)(2).

The Department adopts the general definition of "marketing" with one clarification. Thus, "marketing" means "to make a communication about a product or service that encourages the recipients of the communication to purchase or use the product or service." In removing the language referencing the purpose of the communication and substituting the term "that encourages" for the term "to encourage", the Department intends to simplify the

determination of whether a communication is marketing. If, on its face, the communication encourages recipients of the communication to purchase or use the product or service, the communication is marketing. A few commenters argued for retaining the purpose of the communication as part of the definition of "marketing" based on their belief that the intent of the communication was a clearer and more definitive standard than the effect of the communication. The Department disagrees with these commenters. Tying the definition of "marketing" to the purpose of the communication creates a subjective standard that would be difficult to enforce because the intent of the communicator rarely would be documented in advance. The definition adopted by the Secretary allows the communication to speak for itself.

The Department further adopts the three categories of communications that were proposed as exclusions from the definition of "marketing." Thus, the covered entity is not engaged in marketing when it communicates to individuals about: (1) The participating providers and health plans in a network, the services offered by a provider, or the benefits covered by a health plan; (2) the individual's treatment; or (3) case management or care coordination for that individual, or directions or recommendations for alternative treatments, therapies, health care providers, or settings of care to that individual. For example, a doctor that writes a prescription or refers an individual to a specialist for follow-up tests is engaging in a treatment communication and is not marketing a product or service. The Department continues to exempt from the "marketing" definition the same types of communications that were not marketing under the Privacy Rule as published in December 2000, but has modified some of the language to better track the terminology used in the definition of "health care operations." The commenters generally supported this clarification of the language.

The Department, however, does not agree with commenters that sought to expand the exceptions from marketing for all communications that fall within the definitions of "treatment," "payment," or "health care operations." The purpose of the exclusions from the definition of marketing is to facilitate those communications that enhance the individual's access to quality health care. Beyond these important communications, the public strongly objected to any commercial use of protected health information to attempt to sell products or services, even when

the product or service is arguably health related. In light of these strong public objections, ease of administration is an insufficient justification to categorically exempt all communications about payment and health care operations from the definition of "marketing."

However, in response to comments, the Department is clarifying the language that excludes from the definition of "marketing" those communications that describe network participants and the services or benefits of the covered entity. Several commenters, particularly insurers, were concerned that the reference to a "plan of benefits" was too limiting and would prevent them from sending information to their enrollees regarding enhancements or upgrades to their health insurance coverage. They inquired whether the following types of communications would be permissible: enhancements to existing products; changes in deductibles/copays and types of coverage (e.g., prescription drug); continuation products for students reaching the age of majority on parental policies; special programs such as guaranteed issue products and other conversion policies; and prescription drug card programs. Some health plans also inquired if they could communicate with beneficiaries about "one-stop shopping" with their companies to obtain long-term care, property, casualty, and life insurance products.

The Department understands the need for covered health care providers and health plans to be able to communicate freely to their patients or enrollees about their own products, services, or benefits. The Department also understands that some of these communications are required by State or other law. To ensure that such communications may continue, the Department is broadening its policy, both of the December 2000 Privacy Rule as well as proposed in the March 2002 NPRM, to allow covered entities to use protected health information to convey information to beneficiaries and members about health insurance products offered by the covered entity that could enhance or substitute for existing health plan coverage. Specifically, the Department modifies the relevant exemption from the definition of "marketing" to include communications that describe "a health-related product or service (or payment for such product or service) that is provided by, or included in a plan of benefits of, the covered entity making the communication, including communications about: the entities participating in a health care provider network or health plan network; replacement of, or enhancements to, a

C. HIPAA Final Rules, Privacy Standards, continued

Federal Register / Vol. 67, No. 157 / Wednesday, August 14, 2002 / Rules and Regulations 53187

health plan; and health-related products or services available only to a health plan enrollee that add value to, but are not part of, a plan of benefits." Thus, under this exemption, a health plan is not engaging in marketing when it advises its enrollees about other available health plan coverages that could enhance or substitute for existing health plan coverage. For example, if a child is about to age out of coverage under a family's policy, this provision will allow the plan to send the family information about continuation coverage for the child. This exception, however, does not extend to excepted benefits (described in section 2791(c)(1) of the Public Health Service Act, 42 U.S.C. 300gg–91(c)(1)), such as accident-only policies), nor to other lines of insurance (e.g., it is marketing for a multi-line insurer to promote its life insurance policies using protected health information).

Moreover, the expanded language makes clear that it is not marketing when a health plan communicates about health-related products and services available only to plan enrollees or members that add value to, but are not part of, a plan of benefits. The provision of value-added items or services (VAIS) is a common practice, particularly for managed care organizations. Communications about VAIS may qualify as a communication that is about a health plan's own products or services, even if VAIS are not considered plan benefits for the Adjusted Community Rate purposes. To qualify for this exclusion, however, the VAIS must meet two conditions. First, they must be health-related. Therefore, discounts offered by Medicare+Choice or other managed care organizations for eyeglasses may be considered part of the plan's benefits, whereas discounts to attend movie theaters will not. Second, such items and services must demonstrably "add value" to the plan's membership and not merely be a pass-through of a discount or item available to the public at large. Therefore, a Medicare+Choice or other managed care organization could, for example, offer its members a special discount opportunity for a health/fitness club without obtaining authorizations, but could not pass along to its members discounts to a health fitness club that the members would be able to obtain directly from the health/fitness clubs.

In further response to comments, the Department has added new language to the definition of "marketing" to close what commenters perceived as a loophole that a covered entity could sell protected health information to another company for the marketing of that company's products or services. For example, many were concerned that a pharmaceutical company could pay a provider for a list of patients with a particular condition or taking a particular medication and then use that list to market its own drug products directly to those patients. The commenters believed the proposal would permit this to happen under the guise of the pharmaceutical company acting as a business associate of the covered entity for the purpose of recommending an alternative treatment or therapy to the individual. The Department agrees with commenters that the potential for manipulating the business associate relationship in this fashion should be expressly prohibited. Therefore, the Department is adding language that would make clear that business associate transactions of this nature are marketing. Marketing is defined expressly to include "an arrangement between a covered entity and any other entity whereby the covered entity discloses protected health information to the other entity, in exchange for direct or indirect remuneration, for the other entity or its affiliate to make a communication about its own product or service that encourages recipients of the communication to purchase or use that product or service." These communications are marketing and can only occur if the covered entity obtains the individual's authorization pursuant to § 164.508. The Department believes that this provision will make express the fundamental prohibition against covered entities selling lists of patients or enrollees to third parties, or from disclosing protected health information to a third party for the marketing activities of the third party, without the written authorization of the individual. The Department further notes that manufacturers that receive identifiable health information and misuse it may be subject to action taken under other consumer protection statutes by other Federal agencies, such as the Federal Trade Commission.

The Department does not, however, agree with commenters who argued for retention of the provisions that would condition the exclusions from the "marketing" definition on the absence of remuneration. Except for the arrangements that are now expressly defined as "marketing," the Department eliminates the conditions that communications are excluded from the definition of "marketing" only if they are made orally, or, if in writing, are made without any direct or indirect remuneration. The Department does not

agree that the simple receipt of remuneration should transform a treatment communication into a commercial promotion of a product or service. For example, health care providers should be able to, and can, send patients prescription refill reminders regardless of whether a third party pays or subsidizes the communication. The covered entity also is able to engage a legitimate business associate to assist it in making these permissible communications. It is only in situations where, in the guise of a business associate, an entity other than the covered entity is promoting its own products using protected health information it has received from, and for which it has paid, the covered entity, that the remuneration will place the activity within the definition of "marketing."

In addition, the Department adopts the proposed marketing authorization provision at § 164.508(a)(3), with minor language changes to conform to the revised "marketing" definition. The Rule expressly requires an authorization for uses or disclosures of protected health information for marketing communications, except in two circumstances: (1) When the communication occurs in a face-to-face encounter between the covered entity and the individual; or (2) the communication involves a promotional gift of nominal value. A marketing authorization must include a statement about remuneration, if any. For ease of administration, the Department has changed the regulatory provision to require a statement on the authorization whenever the marketing "involves" direct or indirect remuneration to the covered entity from a third party, rather than requiring the covered entity to identify those situations where "the marketing is expected to result in" remuneration.

Finally, the Department clarifies that nothing in the marketing provisions of the Privacy Rule are to be construed as amending, modifying, or changing any rule or requirement related to any other Federal or State statutes or regulations, including specifically anti-kickback, fraud and abuse, or self-referral statutes or regulations, or to authorize or permit any activity or transaction currently proscribed by such statutes and regulations. Examples of such laws include the anti-kickback statute (section 1128B(b) of the Social Security Act), safe harbor regulations (42 CFR part 1001), Stark law (section 1877 of the Social Security Act) and regulations (42 CFR parts 411 and 424), and HIPAA statute on self-referral (section 1128C of the Social Security Act). The definition

C. HIPAA Final Rules, Privacy Standards, continued

53188   **Federal Register** / Vol. 67, No. 157 / Wednesday, August 14, 2002 / Rules and Regulations

of "marketing" is solely applicable to the Privacy Rule and the permissions granted by the Rule are only for a covered entity's use or disclosure of protected health information. In particular, although this regulation defines the term "marketing" to exclude communications to an individual to recommend, purchase, or use a product or service as part of the treatment of the individual or for case management or care coordination of that individual, such communication by a "white coat" health care professional may violate the anti-kickback statute. Similar examples for pharmacist communications with patients relating to the marketing of products on behalf of pharmaceutical companies were identified by the OIG as problematic in a 1994 Special Fraud Alert (December 19, 1994, 59 FR 65372). Other violations have involved home health care nurses and physical therapists acting as marketers for durable medical equipment companies. Although a particular communication under the Privacy Rule may not require patient authorization because it is not marketing, or may require patient authorization because it is "marketing" as the Rule defines it, the arrangement may nevertheless violate other statutes and regulations administered by HHS, the Department of Justice, or other Federal or State agency.

Response to Other Public Comments

Comment: Some commenters recommended that the definition of "marketing" be broadened to read as follows: "any communication about a product or service to encourage recipients of the communication to purchase or use the product or service or that will make the recipient aware of the product or service available for purchase or use by the recipient." According to these commenters, the additional language would capture marketing campaign activities to establish "brand recognition."

Response: The Department believes that marketing campaigns to establish brand name recognition of products is already encompassed within the general definition of "marketing" and that it is not necessary to add language to accomplish this purpose.

Comment: Some commenters opposed the proposed deletion of references to the covered entity as the source of the communications, in the definition of those communications that were excluded from the "marketing" definition. They objected to these non-marketing communications being made by unrelated third parties based on protected health information disclosed to these third parties by the covered

entity, without the individual's knowledge or authorization.

Response: These commenters appear to have misinterpreted the proposal as allowing third parties to obtain protected health information from covered entities for marketing or other purposes for which the Rule requires an individual's authorization. The deletion of the specific reference to the covered entity does not permit disclosures to a third party beyond the disclosures already permitted by the Rule. The change is intended to be purely editorial: since the Rule applies only to covered entities, the only entities whose communications can be governed by the Rule are covered entities, and thus the reference to covered entities there was redundant. Covered entities may not disclose protected health information to third parties for marketing purposes without authorization from the individual, even if the third party is acting as the business associate of the disclosing covered entity. Covered entities may, however, use protected health information to communicate with individuals about the covered entity's own health-related products or services, the individual's treatment, or case management or care coordination for the individual. The covered entity does not need an authorization for these types of communications and may make the communication itself or use a business associate to do so.

Comment: Some commenters advocated for reversion to the provision in § 164.514(e) that the marketing communication identify the covered entity responsible for the communication, and argued that the covered entity should be required to identify itself as the source of the protected health information.

Response: As modified, the Privacy Rule requires the individual's written authorization for the covered entity to use or disclose protected health information for marketing purposes, with limited exceptions. The Department believes that the authorization process itself will put the individual sufficiently on notice that the covered entity is the source of the protected health information. To the extent that the commenter suggests that these disclosures are necessary for communications that are not "marketing" as defined by the Rule, the Department disagrees because such a requirement would place an undue burden on necessary health-related communications.

Comment: Many commenters opposed the proposed elimination of the provision that would have transformed a communication exempted from

marketing into a marketing communication if it was in writing and paid for by a third party. They argued that marketing should include any activity in which a covered entity receives compensation, directly or indirectly, through such things as discounts from another provider, manufacturer, or service provider in exchange for providing information about the manufacturer or service provider's products to consumers, and that consumers should be advised whenever such remuneration is involved and allowed to opt-out of future communications.

Response: The Department considered whether remuneration should determine whether a given activity is marketing, but ultimately concluded that remuneration should not define whether a given activity is marketing or falls under an exception to marketing. In fact, the Department believes that the provision in the December 2000 Rule that transformed a treatment communication into a marketing communication if it was in writing and paid for by a third party blurred the line between treatment and marketing in ways that would have made the Privacy Rule difficult to implement. The Department believes that certain health care communications, such as refill reminders or informing patients about existing or new health care products or services, are appropriate, whether or not the covered entity receives remuneration from third parties to pay for them. The fact that remuneration is received for a marketing communication does not mean the communication is biased or inaccurate. For the same reasons, the Department does not believe that the communications that are exempt from the definition of "marketing" require any special conditions, based solely on direct or indirect remuneration received by the covered entity. Requiring disclosure and opt-out conditions on these communications, as § 164.514(e) had formerly imposed on health-related marketing communications, would add a layer of complexity to the Privacy Rule that the Department intended to eliminate. Individuals, of course, are free to negotiate with covered entities for limitations on such uses and disclosures, to which the entity may, but is not required to, agree.

The Department does agree with commenters that, in limited circumstances, abuses can occur. The Privacy Rule, both as published in December 2000 and as proposed to be modified in March 2002, has always prohibited covered entities from selling *protected health information to a third*

C. HIPAA Final Rules, Privacy Standards, continued

party for the marketing activities of the third party, without authorization. Nonetheless, in response to continued public concern, the Department has added a new provision to the definition of "marketing" to prevent situations in which a covered entity could take advantage of the business associate relationship to sell protected health information to another entity for that entity's commercial marketing purposes. The Department intends this prohibition to address the potential financial conflict of interest that would lead a covered entity to disclose protected health information to another entity under the guise of a treatment exemption.

Comment: Commenters argued that written authorizations (opt-ins) should be required for the use of clinical information in marketing. They stated that many consumers do not want covered entities to use information about specific clinical conditions that an individual has, such as AIDS or diabetes, to target them for marketing of services for such conditions.

Response: The Department does not intend to interfere with the ability of health care providers or health plans to deliver quality health care to individuals. The "marketing" definition excludes communications for the individual's treatment and for case management, care coordination or the recommendation of alternative therapies. Clinical information is critical for these communications and, hence, cannot be used to distinguish between communications that are or are not marketing. The covered entity needs the individual's authorization to use or disclose protected health information for marketing communications, regardless of whether clinical information is to be used.

Comment: The proposed modification eliminated the § 164.514 requirements that permitted the use of protected health information to market health-related products and services without an authorization. In response to that proposed modification, many commenters asked whether covered entities would be allowed to make communications about "health education" or "health promoting" materials or services without an authorization under the modified Rule. Examples included communications about health improvement or disease prevention, new developments in the diagnosis or treatment of disease, health fairs, health/wellness-oriented classes or support groups.

Response: The Department clarifies that a communication that merely promotes health in a general manner

and does not promote a specific product or service from a particular provider does not meet the general definition of "marketing." Such communications may include population-based activities to improve health or reduce health care costs as set forth in the definition of "health care operations" at § 164.501. Therefore, communications, such as mailings reminding women to get an annual mammogram, and mailings providing information about how to lower cholesterol, about new developments in health care (e.g., new diagnostic tools), about health or "wellness" classes, about support groups, and about health fairs are permitted, and are not considered marketing.

Comment: Some commenters asked whether they could communicate with beneficiaries about government programs or government-sponsored programs such as information about SCHIP; eligibility for Medicare/Medigap (e.g., eligibility for limited, six-month open enrollment period for Medicare supplemental benefits).

Response: The Department clarifies that communications about government and government-sponsored programs do not fall within the definition of "marketing." There is no commercial component to communications about benefits available through public programs. Therefore, a covered entity is permitted to use and disclose protected health information to communicate about eligibility for Medicare supplemental benefits, or SCHIP. As in our response above, these communications may reflect population-based activities to improve health or reduce health care costs as set forth in the definition of "health care operations" at § 164.501.

Comment: The proposed modification eliminated the § 164.514 requirements that allowed protected health information to be used and disclosed without authorization or the opportunity to opt-out, for communications contained in newsletters or similar general communication devices widely distributed to patients, enrollees, or other broad groups of individuals. Many commenters requested clarification as to whether various types of general circulation materials would be permitted under the proposed modification. Commenters argued that newsletters or similar general communication devices widely distributed to patients, enrollees, or other broad groups of individuals should be permitted without authorizations because they are "common" and "serve appropriate

information distribution purposes" and, based on their general circulation, are less intrusive than other forms of communication.

Response: Covered entities may make communications in newsletter format without authorization so long as the content of such communications is not "marketing," as defined by the Rule. The Department is not creating any special exemption for newsletters.

Comment: One commenter suggested that, even when authorizations are granted to disclose protected health information for a particular marketing purpose to a non-covered entity, there should also be an agreement by the third party not to re-disclose the protected health information. This same commenter also recommended that the Privacy Rule place restrictions on non-secure modes of making communications pursuant to an authorization. This commenter argued that protected health information should not be disclosed on the outside of mailings or through voice mail, unattended FAX, or other modes of communication that are not secure.

Response: Under the final Rule, a covered entity must obtain an individual's authorization to use or disclose protected health information for a marketing communication, with some exceptions. If an individual wanted an authorization to limit the use of the information by the covered entity, the individual could negotiate with the covered entity to make that clear in the authorization. Similarly, individuals can request confidential forms of communication, even with respect to authorized disclosures. See § 164.522(b).

Comment: Commenters requested that HHS provide clear guidance on what types of activities constitute a use or disclosure for marketing, and, therefore, require an authorization.

Response: The Department has modified the "marketing" definition to clarify the types of uses or disclosures of protected health information that are marketing, and, therefore, require prior authorization and those that are not marketing. The Department intends to update its guidance on this topic and address specific examples raised by commenters at that time.

Comment: A number of commenters wanted the Department to amend the face-to-face authorization exception. Some urged that it be broadened to include telephone, mail and other common carriers, fax machines, or the Internet so that the exception would cover communications between providers and patients that are not in person. For example, it was pointed out that some providers, such as home

C. HIPAA Final Rules, Privacy Standards, continued

delivery pharmacies, may have a direct treatment relationship, but communicate with patients through other channels. Some raised specific concerns about communicating with "shut-ins" and "persons living in rural areas." Other commenters asked the Department to make the exception more narrow to cover only those marketing communications made by a health care provider, as opposed to by a business associate, or to cover only those marketing communications of a provider that arise from a treatment or other essential health care communication.

Response: The Department believes that expanding the face-to-face authorization exception to include telephone, mail, and other common carriers, fax machines or the Internet would create an exception essentially for all types of marketing communications. All providers potentially use a variety of means to communicate with their patients. The authorization exclusion, however, is narrowly crafted to permit only face-to-face encounters between the covered entity and the individual.

The Department believes that further narrowing the exception to place conditions on such communications, other than that it be face-to-face, would neither be practical nor better serve the privacy interests of the individual. The Department does not intend to police communications between doctors and patients that take place in the doctor's office. Further limiting the exception would add a layer of complexity to the Rule, encumbering physicians and potentially causing them to second-guess themselves when making treatment or other essential health care communications. In this context, the individual can readily stop any unwanted communications, including any communications that may otherwise meet the definition of "marketing."

2. Health Care Operations: Changes of Legal Ownership

December 2000 Privacy Rule. The Rule's definition of "health care operations" included the disclosure of protected health information for the purposes of due diligence with respect to the contemplated sale or transfer of all or part of a covered entity's assets to a potential successor in interest who is a covered entity, or would become a covered entity as a result of the transaction.

The Department indicated in the December 2000 preamble of the Privacy Rule its intent to include in the definition of health care operations the actual transfer of protected health

information to a successor in interest upon a sale or transfer of its assets. (65 FR 82609.) However, the regulation itself did not expressly provide for the transfer of protected health information upon the sale or transfer of assets to a successor in interest. Instead, the definition of "health care operations" included uses or disclosures of protected health information only for due diligence purposes when a sale or transfer to a successor in interest is contemplated.

March 2002 NPRM. A number of entities expressed concern about the discrepancy between the intent as expressed in the preamble to the December 2000 Privacy Rule and the actual regulatory language. To address these concerns, the Department proposed to add language to paragraph (6) of the definition of "health care operations" to clarify its intent to permit the transfer of records to a covered entity upon a sale, transfer, merger, or consolidation. This proposed change would prevent the Privacy Rule from interfering with necessary treatment or payment activities upon the sale of a covered entity or its assets.

The Department also proposed to use the terms "sale, transfer, consolidation or merger" and to eliminate the term "successor in interest" from this paragraph. The Department intended this provision to apply to any sale, transfer, merger or consolidation and believed the current language may not accomplish this goal.

The Department proposed to retain the limitation that such disclosures are health care operations only to the extent the entity receiving the protected health information is a covered entity or would become a covered entity as a result of the transaction. The Department clarified that the proposed modification would not affect a covered entity's other legal or ethical obligation to notify individuals of a sale, transfer, merger, or consolidation.

Overview of Public Comments. The following discussion provides an overview of the public comment received on this proposal. Additional comments received on this issue are discussed below in the section entitled, "Response to Other Public Comments."

Numerous commenters supported the proposed modifications. Generally, these commenters claimed the modifications would prevent inconvenience to consumers, and facilitate timely access to health care. Specifically, these commenters indicated that health care would be delayed and consumers would be inconvenienced if covered entities were required to obtain individual consent or

authorization before they could access health records that are newly acquired assets resulting from the sale, transfer, merger, or consolidation of all or part of a covered entity. Commenters further claimed that the administrative burden of acquiring individual permission and culling records of consumers who do not give consent would be too great, and would cause some entities to simply store or destroy the records instead. Consequently, health information would be inaccessible, causing consumers to be inconvenienced and health care to be delayed. Some commenters noted that the proposed modifications recognize the realities of business without compromising the availability or quality of health care or diminishing privacy protections one would expect in the handling of protected health information during the course of such business transactions.

Opposition to the proposed modifications was limited, with commenters generally asserting that the transfer of records in such circumstances would not be in the best interests of individuals.

Final Modifications. The Department agrees with the commenters that supported the proposed modifications and, therefore, adopts the modifications to the definition of health care operations. Thus, "health care operations" includes the sale, transfer, merger, or consolidation of all or part of the covered entity to or with another covered entity, or an entity that will become a covered entity as a result of the transaction, as well as the due diligence activities in connection with such transaction. In response to a comment, the final Rule modifies the phrase "all or part of a covered entity" to read "all or part of the covered entity" to clarify that any disclosure for such activity must be by the covered entity that is a party to the transaction.

Under the final definition of "health care operations," a covered entity may use or disclose protected health information in connection with a sale or transfer of assets to, or a consolidation or merger with, an entity that is or will be a covered entity upon completion of the transaction; and to conduct due diligence in connection with such transaction. The modification makes clear it is also a health care operation to transfer records containing protected health information as part of the transaction. For example, if a pharmacy which is a covered entity buys another pharmacy which is also a covered entity, protected health information can be exchanged between the two entities for purposes of conducting due diligence, and the selling entity may

C. HIPAA Final Rules, Privacy Standards, continued

transfer any records containing protected health information to the new owner upon completion of the transaction. The new owner may then immediately use and disclose those records to provide health care services to the individuals, as well as for payment and health care operations purposes. Since the information would continue to be protected by the Privacy Rule, any other use or disclosure of the information would require an authorization unless otherwise permitted without authorization by the Rule, and the new owner would be obligated to observe the individual's rights of access, amendment, and accounting. The Privacy Rule would not interfere with other legal or ethical obligations of an entity that may arise out of the nature of its business or relationship with its customers or patients to provide such persons with notice of the transaction or an opportunity to agree to the transfer of records containing personal information to the new owner.

Response to Other Public Comments

Comment: One commenter was concerned about what obligations the parties to a transaction have regarding protected health information that was exchanged as part of a transaction if the transaction does not go through.

Response: The Department believes that other laws and standard business practices are adequate to address these situations and accordingly does not impose additional requirements of this type. It is standard practice for parties contemplating such transactions to enter into confidentiality agreements. In addition to exchanging protected health information, the parties to such transactions commonly exchange confidential proprietary information. It is a standard practice for the parties to these transaction to agree that the handling of all confidential information, such as proprietary information, will include ensuring that, in the event that the proposed transaction is not consummated, the information is either returned to its original owner or destroyed as appropriate. They may include protected health information in any such agreement, as they determine appropriate to the circumstances and applicable law.

3. Protected Health Information: Exclusion for Employment Records

December 2000 Privacy Rule. The Privacy Rule broadly defines "protected health information" as individually identifiable health information maintained or transmitted by a covered entity in any form or medium. The December 2000 Privacy Rule expressly excluded from the definition of "protected health information" only educational and other records that are covered by the Family Education Rights and Privacy Act of 1974, as amended, 20 U.S.C. 1232g. In addition, throughout the December 2000 preamble to the Privacy Rule, the Department repeatedly stated that the Privacy Rule does not apply to employers, nor does it apply to the employment functions of covered entities, that is, when they are acting in their role as employers. For example, the Department stated:

> Covered entities must comply with this regulation in their health care capacity, not in their capacity as employers. For example, information in hospital personnel files about a nurses' (sic) sick leave is not protected health information under this rule.

65 FR 82612. However, the definition of protected health information did not expressly exclude personnel or employment records of covered entities.

March 2002 NPRM. The Department understands that covered entities are also employers, and that this creates two potential sources of confusion about the status of health information. First, some employers are required or elect to obtain health information about their employees, as part of their routine employment activities [e.g., hiring, compliance with the Occupational Safety and Health Administration (OSHA) requirements]. Second, employees of covered health care providers or health plans sometimes seek treatment or reimbursement from that provider or health plan, unrelated to the employment relationship.

To avoid any confusion on the part of covered entities as to application of the Privacy Rule to the records they maintain as employers, the Department proposed to modify the definition of "protected health information" in § 164.501 to expressly exclude employment records held by a covered entity in its role as employer. The proposed modification also would alleviate the situation where a covered entity would feel compelled to elect to designate itself as a hybrid entity solely to carve out its employment functions. Individually identifiable health information maintained or transmitted by a covered entity in its health care capacity would, under the proposed modification, continue to be treated as protected health information.

The Department specifically solicited comments on whether the term "employment records" is clear and what types of records would be covered by the term.

In addition, as discussed in section III.C.1. below, the Department proposed to modify the definition of a hybrid entity to permit any covered entity that engaged in both covered and non-covered functions to elect to operate as a hybrid entity. Under the proposed modification, a covered entity that primarily engaged in covered functions, such as a hospital, would be allowed to elect hybrid entity status even if its only non-covered functions were those related to its capacity as an employer. Indeed, because of the absence of an express exclusion for employment records in the definition of protected health information, some covered entities may have elected hybrid entity status under the misconception that this was the only way to prevent their personnel information from being treated as protected health information under the Rule.

Overview of Public Comments. The following discussion provides an overview of the public comment received on this proposal. Additional comments received on this issue are discussed below in the section entitled, "Response to Other Public Comments."

The Department received comments both supporting and opposing the proposal to add an exemption for employment records to the definition of protected health information. Support for the proposal was based primarily on the need for clarity and certainty in this important area. Moreover, commenters supported the proposed exemption for employment records because it reinforced and clarified that the Privacy Rule does not conflict with an employer's obligation under numerous other laws, including OSHA, Family and Medical Leave Act (FMLA), workers' compensation, and alcohol and drug free workplace laws.

Those opposed to the modification were concerned that a covered entity may abuse its access to the individually identifiable health information in its employment records by using that information for discriminatory purposes. Many commenters expressed concern that an employee's health information created, maintained, or transmitted by the covered entity in its health care capacity would be considered an employment record and, therefore, would not be considered protected health information. Some of these commenters argued for the inclusion of special provisions, similar to the "adequate separation" requirements for disclosure of protected health information from group health plan to plan sponsor functions (§ 164.504(f)), to heighten the protection for an employee's individually identifiable health information when moving between a covered entity's

C. HIPAA Final Rules, Privacy Standards, continued

53192   Federal Register / Vol. 67, No. 157 / Wednesday, August 14, 2002 / Rules and Regulations

health care functions and its employer functions.

A number of commenters also suggested types of records that the Department should consider to be "employment records" and, therefore, excluded from the definition of "protected health information." The suggested records included records maintained under the FMLA or the Americans with Disabilities Act (ADA), as well as records relating to occupational injury, disability insurance eligibility, sick leave requests and justifications, drug screening results, workplace medical surveillance, and fitness-for-duty test results. One commenter suggested that health information related to professional athletes should qualify as an employment record.

Final Modifications. The Department adopts as final the proposed language excluding employment records maintained by a covered entity in its capacity as an employer from the definition of "protected health information." The Department agrees with commenters that the regulation should be explicit that it does not apply to a covered entity's employer functions and that the most effective means of accomplishing this is through the definition of "protected health information."

The Department is sensitive to the concerns of commenters that a covered entity not abuse its access to an employee's individually identifiable health information which it has created or maintains in its health care, not its employer, capacity. In responding to these concerns, the Department must remain within the boundaries set by the statute, which does not include employers per se as covered entities. Thus, we cannot regulate employers, even when it is a covered entity acting as an employer.

To address these concerns, the Department clarifies that a covered entity must remain cognizant of its dual roles as an employer and as a health care provider, health plan, or health care clearinghouse. Individually identifiable health information created, received, or maintained by a covered entity in its health care capacity is protected health information. It does not matter if the individual is a member of the covered entity's workforce or not. Thus, the medical record of a hospital employee who is receiving treatment at the hospital is protected health information and is covered by the Rule, just as the medical record of any other patient of that hospital is protected health information and covered by the Rule. The hospital may use that

information only as permitted by the Privacy Rule, and in most cases will need the employee's authorization to access or use the medical information for employment purposes. When the individual gives his or her medical information to the covered entity as the employer, such as when submitting a doctor's statement to document sick leave, or when the covered entity as employer obtains the employee's written authorization for disclosure of protected health information, such as an authorization to disclose the results of a fitness for duty examination, that medical information becomes part of the employment record, and, as such, is no longer protected health information. The covered entity as employer, however, may be subject to other laws and regulations applicable to the use or disclosure of information in an employee's employment record.

The Department has decided not to add a definition of the term "employment records" to the Rule. The comments indicate that the same individually identifiable health information about an individual may be maintained by the covered entity in both its employment records and the medical records it maintains as a health care provider or enrollment or claims records it maintains as a health plan. The Department therefore is concerned that a definition of "employment record" may lead to the misconception that certain types of information are never protected health information, and will put the focus incorrectly on the nature of the information rather than the reasons for which the covered entity obtained the information. For example, drug screening test results will be protected health information when the provider administers the test to the employee, but will not be protected health information when, pursuant to the employee's authorization, the test results are provided to the provider acting as employer and placed in the employee's employment record. Similarly, the results of a fitness for duty exam will be protected health information when the provider administers the test to one of its employees, but will not be protected health information when the results of the fitness for duty exam are turned over to the provider as employer pursuant to the employee's authorization.

Furthermore, while the examples provided by commenters represent typical files or records that may be maintained by employers, the Department does not believe that it has sufficient information to provide a complete definition of employment record. Therefore, the Department does

not adopt as part of this rulemaking a definition of employment record, but does clarify that medical information needed for an employer to carry out its obligations under FMLA, ADA, and similar laws, as well as files or records related to occupational injury, disability insurance eligibility, sick leave requests and justifications, drug screening results, workplace medical surveillance, and fitness-for-duty tests of employees, may be part of the employment records maintained by the covered entity in its role as an employer.

Response to Other Public Comments

Comment: One commenter requested clarification as to whether the term "employment record" included the following information that is either maintained or transmitted by a fully insured group health plan to an insurer or HMO for enrollment and/or disenrollment purposes: (a) the identity of an individual including name, address, birth date, marital status, dependent information and SSN; (b) the individual's choice of plan; (c) the amount of premiums/contributions for coverage of the individual; (d) whether the individual is an active employee or retired; (e) whether the individual is enrolled in Medicare.

Response: All of this information is protected health information when held by a fully insured group health plan and transmitted to an issuer or HMO, and the Privacy Rule applies when the group health plan discloses such information to any entity, including the plan sponsor. There are special rules in § 164.504(f) which describe the conditions for disclosure of protected health information to the plan sponsor. If the group health plan received the information from the plan sponsor, it becomes protected health information when received by the group health plan. The plan sponsor is not the covered entity, so this information will not be protected when held by a plan sponsor, whether or not it is part of the plan sponsor's "employment record."

Comment: One commenter asked for clarification as to how the Department would characterize the following items that a covered entity may have: (1) medical file kept separate from the rest of an employment record containing (a) doctor's notes; (b) leave requests; (c) physician certifications; and (d) positive hepatitis test results; (2) FMLA documentation including: (a) physician certification form; and (b) leave requests; (3) occupational injury files containing (a) drug screening; (b) exposure test results; (c) doctor's notes; and (d) medical director's notes.

C. HIPAA Final Rules, Privacy Standards, continued

Federal Register / Vol. 67, No. 157 / Wednesday, August 14, 2002 / Rules and Regulations   53193

Response: As explained above, the nature of the information does not determine whether it is an employment record. Rather, it depends on whether the covered entity obtains or creates the information in its capacity as employer or in its capacity as covered entity. An employment record may well contain some or all of the items mentioned by the commenter; but so too might a treatment record. The Department also recognizes that the employer may be required by law or sound business practice to treat such medical information as confidential and maintain it separate from other employment records. It is the function being performed by the covered entity and the purpose for which the covered entity has the medical information, not its record keeping practices, that determines whether the health information is part of an employment record or whether it is protected health information.

Comment: One commenter suggested that the health records of professional athletes should qualify as "employment records." As such, the records would not be subject to the protections of the Privacy Rule.

Response: Professional sports teams are unlikely to be covered entities. Even if a sports team were to be a covered entity, employment records of a covered entity are not covered by this Rule. If this comment is suggesting that the records of professional athletes should be deemed "employment records" even when created or maintained by health care providers and health plans, the Department disagrees. No class of individuals should be singled out for reduced privacy protections. As noted in the preamble to the December 2000 Rule, nothing in this Rule prevents an employer, such as a professional sports team, from making an employee's agreement to disclose health records a condition of employment. A covered entity, therefore, could disclose this information to an employer pursuant to an authorization.

B. Section 164.502—Uses and Disclosures of Protected Health Information: General Rules

1. Incidental Uses and Disclosures

December 2000 Privacy Rule. The December 2000 Rule did not explicitly address incidental uses and disclosures of protected health information. Rather, the Privacy Rule generally requires covered entities to make reasonable efforts to limit the use or disclosure of, and requests for, protected health information to the minimum necessary to accomplish the intended purpose.

See § 164.502(b). Additionally, § 164.530(c) of the Privacy Rule requires covered entities to implement appropriate administrative, technical, and physical safeguards to reasonably safeguard protected health information from any intentional or unintentional use or disclosure that violates the Rule.

Protected health information includes individually identifiable health information (with limited exceptions) in any form, including information transmitted orally, or in written or electronic form. See the definition of "protected health information" at § 164.501.

March 2002 NPRM. After publication of the Privacy Rule, the Department received a number of concerns and questions as to whether the Privacy Rule's restrictions on uses and disclosures will prohibit covered entities from engaging in certain common and essential health care communications and practices in use today. In particular, concern was expressed that the Privacy Rule establishes absolute, strict standards that would not allow for the incidental or unintentional disclosures that could occur as a by-product of engaging in these health care communications and practices. It was argued that the Privacy Rule would, in effect, prohibit such practices and, therefore, impede many activities and communications essential to effective and timely treatment of patients.

For example, some expressed concern that health care providers could no longer engage in confidential conversations with other providers or with patients, if there is a possibility that they could be overheard. Similarly, others questioned whether they would be prohibited from using sign-in sheets in waiting rooms or maintaining patient charts at bedside, or whether they would need to isolate X-ray lightboards or destroy empty prescription vials. These concerns seemed to stem from a perception that covered entities are required to prevent any incidental disclosure such as those that may occur when a visiting family member or other person not authorized to access protected health information happens to walk by medical equipment or other material containing individually identifiable health information, or when individuals in a waiting room sign their name on a log sheet and glimpse the names of other patients.

The Department, in its July 6 guidance, clarified that the Privacy Rule is not intended to impede customary and necessary health care communications or practices, nor to require that all risk of incidental use or

disclosure be eliminated to satisfy its standards. The guidance promised that the Department would propose modifications to the Privacy Rule to clarify that such communications and practices may continue, if reasonable safeguards are taken to minimize the chance of incidental disclosure to others.

Accordingly, the Department proposed to modify the Privacy Rule to add a new provision at § 164.502(a)(1)(iii) which would explicitly permit certain incidental uses and disclosures that occur as a result of a use or disclosure otherwise permitted by the Privacy Rule. The proposal described an incidental use or disclosure as a secondary use or disclosure that cannot reasonably be prevented, is limited in nature, and that occurs as a by-product of an otherwise permitted use or disclosure. The Department proposed that an incidental use or disclosure be permissible only to the extent that the covered entity had applied reasonable safeguards as required by § 164.530(c), and implemented the minimum necessary standard, where applicable, as required by §§ 164.502(b) and 164.514(d).

Overview of Public Comments. The following discussion provides an overview of the public comment received on this proposal. Additional comments received on this issue are discussed below in the section entitled, "Response to Other Public Comments."

The Department received many comments on its proposal to permit certain incidental uses and disclosures, the majority of which expressed strong support for the proposal. Many of these commenters indicated that such a policy would help to ensure that essential health care communications and practices are not chilled by the Privacy Rule. A few commenters opposed the Department's proposal to permit certain incidental uses and disclosures, one of whom asserted that the burden on medical staff to take precautions not to be overheard is minimal compared to the potential harm to patients if incidental disclosures were to be considered permissible.

Final Modifications. In response to the overwhelming support of commenters on this proposal, the Department adopts the proposed provision at § 164.502(a)(1)(iii), explicitly permitting certain incidental uses and disclosures that occur as a by-product of a use or disclosure otherwise permitted under the Privacy Rule. As in the proposal, an incidental use or disclosure is permissible only to the extent that the covered entity has applied reasonable safeguards as

53194 Federal Register / Vol. 67, No. 157 / Wednesday, August 14, 2002 / Rules and Regulations

required by § 164.530(c), and implemented the minimum necessary standard, where applicable, as required by §§ 164.502(b) and 164.514(d). The Department continues to believe, as was stated in the proposed Rule, that so long as reasonable safeguards are employed, the burden of impeding such communications is not outweighed by any benefits that may accrue to individuals' privacy interests.

However, an incidental use or disclosure that occurs as a result of a failure to apply reasonable safeguards or the minimum necessary standard, where required, is not a permissible use or disclosure and, therefore, is a violation of the Privacy Rule. For example, a hospital that permits an employee to have unimpeded access to patients' medical records, where such access is not necessary for the employee to do her job, is not applying the minimum necessary standard and, therefore, any incidental use or disclosure that results from this practice would be an unlawful use or disclosure under the Privacy Rule.

In response to the few comments that opposed the proposal to permit certain incidental uses and disclosures, the Department reiterates that the Privacy Rule must not impede essential health care communications and practices. Prohibiting all incidental uses and disclosures would have a chilling effect on normal and important communications among providers, and between providers and their patients, and, therefore, would negatively affect individuals' access to quality health care. The Department does not intend with this provision to obviate the need for medical staff to take precautions to avoid being overheard, but rather, will only allow incidental uses and disclosures where appropriate precautions have been taken.

The Department clarifies, in response to a comment, that this provision applies, subject to reasonable safeguards and the minimum necessary standard, to an incidental use or disclosure that occurs as a result of any permissible use or disclosure under the Privacy Rule made to any person, and not just to incidental uses and disclosures resulting from treatment communications or only to communications among health care providers or other medical staff. For example, a provider may instruct an administrative staff member to bill a patient for a particular procedure, and may be overheard by one or more persons in the waiting room. Assuming that the provider made reasonable efforts to avoid being overheard and reasonably limited the information

shared, an incidental disclosure resulting from such conversation is permissible under the Rule.

In the proposal, the Department did not address whether or not incidental disclosures would need to be included in the accounting of disclosures required by § 164.528. However, one commenter urged the Department to exclude incidental disclosures from the accounting. The Department agrees with this commenter and clarifies that covered entities are not required to include incidental disclosures in an accounting of disclosures provided to the individual pursuant to § 164.528. The Department does not believe such a requirement would be practicable; in many instances, the covered entity may not know that an incidental disclosure occurred. To make this policy clear, the Department includes an explicit exception for such disclosures to the accounting standard at § 164.528(a)(1).

Response to Other Public Comments

Comment: One commenter expressed concern that the requirement reasonably to safeguard protected health information would be problematic because any unintended use or disclosure could arguably demonstrate a failure to "reasonably safeguard." This commenter requested that the Department either delete the language in § 164.530(c)(2)(ii) or modify the language to make clear that the fact that an incidental use or disclosure occurs does not imply that safeguards were not reasonable.

Response: The Department clarifies that the fact that an incidental use or disclosure occurs does not by itself imply that safeguards were not reasonable. However, the Department does not believe that a modification to the proposed language is necessary to express this intent. The language proposed and now adopted at § 164.530(c)(2)(ii) requires only that the covered entity reasonably safeguard protected health information to limit incidental uses or disclosures, not that the covered entity prevent all incidental uses and disclosures. Thus, the Department expects that incidental uses and disclosures will occur and permits such uses and disclosures to the extent the covered entity has in place reasonable safeguards and has applied the minimum necessary standard, where applicable.

Comment: Another commenter requested that the Department clarify its proposal to assure that unintended disclosures will not result in civil penalties.

Response: The Department's authority to impose civil monetary penalties on

violations of the Privacy Rule is defined in HIPAA. Specifically, HIPAA added section 1176 to the Social Security Act, which prescribes the Secretary's authority to impose civil monetary penalties. Therefore, in the case of a violation of a disclosure provision in the Privacy Rule, a penalty may not be imposed, among other things, if the person liable for the penalty did not know and, by exercising reasonable diligence would not have known, that such person violated the provision. HIPAA also provides for criminal penalties under certain circumstances, but the Department of Justice, not this Department, has authority for criminal penalties.

Comment: One commenter requested that the Department clarify how covered entities should implement technical and physical safeguards when they do not yet know what safeguards the final Security Rule will require.

Response: Each covered entity should assess the nature of the protected health information it holds, and the nature and scope of its business, and implement safeguards that are reasonable for its particular circumstances. There should be no potential for conflict between the safeguards required by the Privacy Rule and the final Security Rule standards, for several reasons. First, while the Privacy Rule applies to protected health information in all forms, the Security Rule will apply only to electronic health information systems that maintain or transmit individually identifiable health information. Thus, all safeguards for protected health information in oral, written, or other non-electronic forms will be unaffected by the Security Rule. Second, in preparing the final Security Rule, the Department is working to ensure the Security Rule requirements for electronic information systems work "hand in glove" with any relevant requirements in the Privacy Rule, including § 164.530.

Comment: One commenter argued that while this new provision is helpful, it does not alleviate covered entities' concerns that routine practices, often beneficial for treatment, will be prohibited by the Privacy Rule. This commenter stated that, for example, specialists provide certain types of therapy to patients in a group setting, and, in some cases, where family members are also present.

Response: The Department reiterates that the Privacy Rule is not intended to impede common health care communications and practices that are essential in providing health care to the individual. Further, the Privacy Rule's new provision permitting certain incidental uses and disclosures is

C. HIPAA Final Rules, Privacy Standards, continued

intended to increase covered entities' confidence that such practices can continue even where an incidental use or disclosure may occur, provided that the covered entity has taken reasonable precautions to safeguard and limit the protected health information disclosed. For example, this provision should alleviate concerns that common practices, such as the use of sign-in sheets and calling out names in waiting rooms will not violate the Rule, so long as the information disclosed is appropriately limited. With regard to the commenters' specific example, disclosure of protected health information in a group therapy setting would be a treatment disclosure, and thus permissible without individual authorization. Further, § 164.510(b) generally permits a covered entity to disclose protected health information to a family member or other person involved in the individual's care. In fact, this section specifically provides that, where the individual is present during a disclosure, the covered entity may disclose protected health information if it is reasonable to infer from the circumstances that the individual does not object to the disclosure. Absent countervailing circumstances, the individual's agreement to participate in group therapy or family discussions is a good basis for such a reasonable inference. As such disclosures are permissible disclosures in and of themselves, they would not be incidental disclosures.

Comment: Some commenters, while in support of permitting incidental uses and disclosures, requested that the Department provide additional guidance in this area by providing additional examples of permitted incidental uses and disclosures and/or clarifying what would constitute "reasonable safeguards."

Response: The reasonable safeguards and minimum necessary standards are flexible and adaptable to the specific business needs and circumstances of the covered entity. Given the discretion covered entities have in implementing these standards, it is difficult for the Department to provide specific guidance in this area that is generally applicable to many covered entities. However, the Department intends to provide future guidance through frequently asked questions or other materials in response to specific scenarios that are raised by industry.

2. Minimum Necessary Standard

December 2000 Privacy Rule. The Privacy Rule generally requires covered entities to make reasonable efforts to limit the use or disclosure of, and

requests for, protected health information to the minimum necessary to accomplish the intended purpose. See § 164.502(b). Protected health information includes individually identifiable health information (with limited exceptions) in any form, including information transmitted orally, or in written or electronic form. See the definition of "protected health information" at § 164.501. The minimum necessary standard is intended to make covered entities evaluate their practices and enhance protections as needed to limit unnecessary or inappropriate access to, and disclosures of, protected health information.

The Privacy Rule contains some exceptions to the minimum necessary standard. The minimum necessary requirements do not apply to uses or disclosures that are required by law, disclosures made to the individual or pursuant to an authorization initiated by the individual, disclosures to or requests by a health care provider for treatment purposes, uses or disclosures that are required for compliance with the regulations implementing the other administrative simplification provisions of HIPAA, or disclosures to the Secretary of HHS for purposes of enforcing this Rule. See § 164.502(b)(2).

The Privacy Rule sets forth requirements for implementing the minimum necessary standard with regard to a covered entity's uses, disclosures, and requests at § 164.514(d). A covered entity is required to develop and implement policies and procedures appropriate to the entity's business practices and workforce that reasonably minimize the amount of protected health information used, disclosed, and requested. For uses of protected health information, the policies and procedures must identify the persons or classes of persons within the covered entity who need access to the information to carry out their job duties, the categories or types of protected health information needed, and the conditions appropriate to such access. For routine or recurring requests and disclosures, the policies and procedures may be standard protocols. Non-routine requests for, and disclosures of, protected health information must be reviewed individually.

With regard to disclosures, the Privacy Rule permits a covered entity to rely on the judgment of certain parties requesting the disclosure as to the minimum amount of information that is needed. For example, a covered entity is permitted reasonably to rely on representations from a public official,

such as a State workers' compensation official, that the information requested is the minimum necessary for the intended purpose. Similarly, a covered entity is permitted reasonably to rely on the judgment of another covered entity that the information requested is the minimum amount of information reasonably necessary to fulfill the purpose for which the request has been made. See § 164.514(d)(3)(iii).

March 2002 NPRM. The Department proposed a number of minor modifications to the minimum necessary standard to clarify the Department's intent or otherwise conform these provisions to other proposed modifications. First, the Department proposed to separate § 164.502(b)(2)(ii) into two subparagraphs (§ 164.502(b)(2)(ii) and (iii)) to eliminate confusion regarding the exception to the minimum necessary standard for uses or disclosures made pursuant to an authorization under § 164.508, and the separate exception for disclosures made to the individual. Second, to conform to the proposal to eliminate the special authorizations required by the Privacy Rule at § 164.508(d), (e), and (f), the Department proposed to exempt from the minimum necessary standard any uses or disclosures for which the covered entity had received an authorization that meets the requirements of § 164.508, rather than just those authorizations initiated by the individual.

Third, the Department proposed to modify § 164.514(d)(1) to delete the term "reasonably ensure" in response to concerns that the term connotes an absolute, strict standard and, therefore, is inconsistent with the Department's intent that the minimum necessary requirements be reasonable and flexible to the unique circumstances of the covered entity. In addition, the Department proposed to generally revise the language in § 164.514(d)(1) to be more consistent with the description of standards elsewhere in the Privacy Rule.

Fourth, so that the minimum necessary standard would be applied consistently to requests for, and disclosures of, protected health information, the Department proposed to add a provision to § 164.514(d)(4) to make the implementation specifications for applying the minimum necessary standard to requests for protected health information by a covered entity more consistent with the corresponding implementation specifications for disclosures. Specifically, for requests not made on a routine and recurring basis, the Department proposed to add the requirement that a covered entity must implement the minimum

C. HIPAA Final Rules, Privacy Standards, continued

53196 Federal Register / Vol. 67, No. 157 / Wednesday, August 14, 2002 / Rules and Regulations

necessary standard by developing and implementing criteria designed to limit its request for protected health information to the minimum necessary to accomplish the intended purpose.

Overview of Public Comments. The following discussion provides an overview of the public comment received on this proposal. Additional comments received on this issue are discussed below in the section entitled, "Response to Other Public Comments."

The Department received a number of comments on its proposal to exempt from the minimum necessary standard any use or disclosure of protected health information for which the covered entity has received an authorization that meets the requirements of § 164.508. Many commenters supported this proposal. A few commenters generally urged that the minimum necessary standard be applied to uses and disclosures pursuant to an authorization. A few other commenters appeared to misinterpret the policy in the December 2000 Rule and urged that the Department retain the minimum necessary standard for disclosures "pursuant to an authorization other than disclosures to an individual." Some commenters raised specific concerns about authorizations for psychotherapy notes and the particular need for minimum necessary to be applied in these cases.

A number of commenters expressed support for the Department's statements in the preamble to the proposed Rule reinforcing that the minimum necessary standard is intended to be flexible to account for the characteristics of the entity's business and workforce, and not intended to override the professional judgment of the covered entity. Similarly, some commenters expressed support for the Department's proposal to remove the term "reasonably ensure" from § 164.514(d)(1). However, a few commenters expressed concerns that the proposed alternative language actually would implement a stricter standard than that included in the December 2000 Privacy Rule.

Final Modifications. In this final Rule, the Department adopts the proposed policy to exempt from the minimum necessary standard any uses or disclosures for which the covered entity has received an authorization that meets the requirements of § 164.508. The final modification adopts the proposal to eliminate the special authorizations that were required by the December 2000 Privacy Rule at § 164.508(d), (e), and (f). (*See* section III.E.1. of the preamble for a detailed discussion of the modifications to the authorization requirements of the Privacy Rule.) Since

the only authorizations to which the minimum necessary standard applied are being eliminated in favor of a single consolidated authorization, the final Rule correspondingly eliminates the minimum necessary provisions that applied to the now-eliminated special authorizations. All uses and disclosures made pursuant to any authorization are exempt from the minimum necessary standard.

In response to commenters who opposed this proposal as a potential weakening of privacy protections or who wanted minimum necessary requirements to apply to authorizations other than disclosures to the individual, the Department notes that nothing in the final Rule eliminates an individual's control over his or her protected health information with respect to an authorization. All authorizations must include a description of the information to be used and disclosed that identifies the information in a specific and meaningful fashion as required by § 164.508(c)(1)(i). If the individual does not wish to release the information requested, the individual has the right to not sign the authorization or to negotiate a narrower authorization with the requestor.

Additionally, in response to those commenters who raised specific concerns with respect to authorizations which request release of psychotherapy notes, the Department clarifies that the final Rule does not require a covered entity to use and disclose protected health information pursuant to an authorization. Rather, as with most other uses and disclosures under the Privacy Rule, this is only a permissible use or disclosure. If a covered health care provider is concerned that a request for an individual's psychotherapy notes is not warranted or is excessive, the provider may consult with the individual to determine whether or not the authorization is consistent with the individual's wishes.

Further, the Privacy Rule does not permit a health plan to condition enrollment, eligibility for benefits, or payment of a claim on obtaining the individual's authorization to use or disclose psychotherapy notes. Nor may a health care provider condition treatment on an authorization for the use or disclosure of psychotherapy notes. Thus, the Department believes that these additional protections appropriately and effectively protect an individual's privacy with respect to psychotherapy notes.

The final Rule also retains for clarity the proposal to separate § 164.502(b)(2)(ii) into two subparagraphs (§ 164.502(b)(2)(ii) and

(iii)); commenters did not explicitly address or raise issues with this proposed clarification.

In response to concerns that the proposed language at § 164.514(d)(1) would implement a stricter standard, the Department disagrees and, therefore, adopts the proposed language. The language in § 164.514(d)(1) describes the standard: covered entities are required to meet the requirements in the implementation specifications of § 164.514(d)(2) through (d)(5). The implementation specifications describe what covered entities must do reasonably to limit uses, disclosures, and requests to the minimum necessary. Thus, the Department believes that the language in the implementation specifications is adequate to reflect the Department's intent that the minimum necessary standard is reasonable and flexible to accommodate the unique circumstances of the covered entity.

Commenters also generally did not address the Department's proposed clarification to make the implementation specifications for requests of protected health information consistent with those for disclosures of protected health information. Consequently, as commenters did not raise concerns with the proposal, this final Rule adopts the proposed provision at § 164.514(d)(4). For requests of protected health information not made on a routine and recurring basis, a covered entity must implement the minimum necessary standard by developing and implementing criteria designed to limit its request for protected health information to the minimum necessary to accomplish the intended purpose.

Response to Other Public Comments

Comment: Many commenters recommended changes to the minimum necessary standard unrelated to the proposed modifications. For example, some commenters urged that the Department exempt from the minimum necessary standard all uses of protected health information, or at least uses of protected health information for treatment purposes. Alternatively, one commenter urged that the minimum necessary standard be applied to disclosures for treatment purposes. Others requested that the Department exempt uses and disclosures for payment and health care operations from the standard, or exempt disclosures to another covered entity for such purposes. A few commenters argued that the minimum necessary standard should not apply to disclosures to another covered entity. Some urged that the minimum

C. HIPAA Final Rules, Privacy Standards, continued

necessary standard be eliminated entirely.

Response: The Department did not propose modifications relevant to these comments, nor did it seek comment on these issues. The proposed modifications generally were intended to address those problems or issues that presented workability problems for covered entities or otherwise had the potential to impede an individual's timely access to quality health care. Moreover, the proposed modifications to the minimum necessary standard were either minor clarifications of the Department's intent with respect to the standard or would conform the standard to other proposed modifications. The Department has, in previous guidance as well as in the preamble to the December 2000 Privacy Rule, explained its position with respect to the above concerns. The minimum necessary standard is derived from confidentiality codes and practices in common use today. We continue to believe that it is sound practice not to use or disclose private medical information that is not necessary to satisfy a request or effectively carry out a function. The privacy benefits of retaining the minimum necessary standard outweigh the burden involved with implementing the standard. The Department reiterates that position here.

Further, the Department designed the minimum necessary standard to be sufficiently flexible to accommodate the various circumstances of any covered entity. Covered entities will develop their own policies and procedures to meet this standard. A covered entity's policies and procedures may and should allow the appropriate individuals within an entity to have access to protected health information as necessary to perform their jobs with respect to the entity's covered functions. The Department is not aware of any workability issues with this standard.

With respect to disclosures to another covered entity, the Privacy Rule permits a covered entity reasonably to rely on another covered entity's request for protected health information as the minimum necessary for the intended disclosure. See § 164.514(d)(3)(iii). The Department does not believe, therefore, that a blanket exception for such disclosures is justified. The covered entity who holds the information always retains discretion to make its own minimum necessary determination.

Lastly, the Department continues to believe that the exception for disclosures to or requests by health care providers for treatment purposes is appropriate to ensure that access to

timely and quality treatment is not impeded.

As the Privacy Rule is implemented, the Department will monitor the workability of the minimum necessary standard and consider proposing revisions, where appropriate, to ensure that the Privacy Rule does not hinder timely access to quality health care.

Comment: One commenter requested that the Department state in the preamble that the minimum necessary standard may not be used to interfere with or obstruct essential health plan payment and health care operations activities, including quality assurance, disease management, and other activities. Another commenter asked that the final Rule's preamble acknowledge that, in some cases, the minimum protected health information necessary for payment or health care operations will be the entire record. One commenter urged that the Rule be modified to presume that disclosure of a patient's entire record is justified, and that such disclosure does not require individual review, when requested for disease management purposes.

Response: The minimum necessary standard is not intended to impede essential treatment, payment, or health care operations activities of covered entities. Nor is the Rule intended to change the way covered entities handle their differences with respect to disclosures of protected health information. The Department recognizes that, in some cases, an individual's entire medical record may be necessary for payment or health care operations purposes, including disease management purposes. However, the Department does not believe that disclosure of a patient's entire medical record is always justified for such purposes. The Privacy Rule does not prohibit the request for, or release of, entire medical records in such circumstances, provided that the covered entity has documented the specific justification for the request or disclosure of the entire record.

Comment: A few commenters requested that the Department add to the regulatory text some of the statements included in the preamble to the proposed modifications. For example, commenters asked that the final Rule state that the minimum necessary standard is "intended to be consistent with, and not override, professional judgement and standards." Similarly, others requested that the regulation specify that "covered entities must implement policies and procedures based on their own assessment of what protected health information is reasonably necessary for

a particular purpose, given the characteristics of their business and their workforce, and using their own professional judgment."

Response: It is the Department's policy that the minimum necessary standard is intended to be consistent with, and not override, professional judgment and standards, and that covered entities must implement policies and procedures based on their own assessment of what protected health information is reasonably necessary for a particular purpose, given the characteristics of their business and their workforce. However, the Department does not believe a regulatory modification is necessary because the Department has made its policy clear not only in the preamble to the proposed modifications but also in previous guidance and in this preamble.

Comment: A commenter argued that the Department should exempt disclosures for any of the standard transactions as required by the Transactions Rule, when information is requested by a health plan or its business associate.

Response: The Department disagrees. The Privacy Rule already exempts from the minimum necessary standard data elements that are required or situationally required in any of the standard transactions (§ 164.502(b)(2)(v)). If, however, a standard transaction permits the use of optional data elements, the minimum necessary standard applies. For example, the standard transactions adopted for the outpatient pharmacy sector use optional data elements. The payer currently specifies which of the optional data elements are needed for payment of its particular pharmacy claims. The minimum necessary standard applies to the payer's request for such information. A pharmacist is permitted to rely on the payer's request for information, if reasonable to do so, as the minimum necessary for the intended disclosure.

Comment: A few commenters expressed concerns with respect to a covered entity's disclosures for research purposes. Specifically, one commenter was concerned that a covered entity will not accept documentation of an external IRB's waiver of authorization for purposes of reasonably relying on the request as the minimum necessary. It was suggested that the Department deem that a disclosure to a researcher based on appropriate documentation from an IRB or Privacy Board meets the minimum necessary standard.

Response: The Department understands commenters' concerns that covered entities may decline to

C. HIPAA Final Rules, Privacy Standards, continued

53198 Federal Register / Vol. 67, No. 157 / Wednesday, August 14, 2002 / Rules and Regulations

participate in research studies, but believes that the Rule already addresses this concern. The Privacy Rule explicitly permits a covered entity reasonably to rely on a researcher's documentation or the representations of an IRB or Privacy Board pursuant to § 164.512(i) that the information requested is the minimum necessary for the research purpose. This is true regardless of whether the documentation is obtained from an external IRB or Privacy Board or one that is associated with the covered entity. The preamble to the March 2002 NPRM further reinforced this policy by stating that reasonable reliance on an IRB's documentation of approval of the waiver criteria and a description of the data needed for the research as required by § 164.512(i) would satisfy a covered entity's obligations with respect to limiting the disclosure to the minimum necessary. The Department reiterates this policy here and believes that this should give covered entities sufficient confidence in accepting IRB waivers of authorization.

Comment: A number of commenters requested that the Department limit the amount of information that pharmacy benefits managers (PBM) may demand from pharmacies as part of their claims payment activities.

Response: The health plan, as a covered entity, is obligated to instruct the PBM, as its business associate acting through the business associate contract, to request only the minimum amount of information necessary to pay a claim. The pharmacist may rely on this determination if reasonable to do so, and then does not need to engage in a separate minimum necessary assessment. If a pharmacist does not agree that the amount of information requested is reasonably necessary for the PBM to fulfill its obligations, it is up to the pharmacist and PBM to negotiate a resolution of the dispute as to the amount of information needed by the PBM to carry out its obligations and that the pharmacist is willing to provide, recognizing that the PBM is not required to pay claims if it has not received the information it believes is necessary to process the claim in accordance with its procedures, including fraud prevention procedures.

The standard for electronic pharmacy claims, adopted by the Secretary in the Transactions Rule, includes optional data elements and relies on each payer to specify the data elements required for payment of its claims. Understandably, the majority of health plans require some patient identification elements in order to adjudicate claims. As the National Council for Prescription Drug

Programs (NCPDP) moves from optional to required and situational data elements, the question of whether the specific element of "patient name" should be required or situational will be debated by the NCPDP, by the Designated Standards Maintenance Organizations, by the National Committee on Vital and Health Statistics, and ultimately will be decided in rulemaking by the Secretary.

Comment: One commenter requested that the minimum necessary standard be made an administrative requirement rather than a standard for uses and disclosures, to ease liability concerns with implementing the standard. The commenter stated that this change would mean that covered entities would be required to implement reasonable minimum necessary policies and procedures and would be liable if: (1) They fail to implement minimum necessary policies and procedures; (2) their policies and procedures are not reasonable; or (3) they fail to enforce their policies and procedures. The commenter further explained that health plans would be liable if their policies and procedures for requesting health information were unreasonable, but the burden of liability for the request shifts largely to the entity best suited to determine whether the amount of information requested is the minimum necessary.

Response: The Privacy Rule already requires covered entities to implement reasonable minimum necessary policies and procedures and to limit any use, disclosure, or request for protected health information in a manner consistent with its policies and procedures. The minimum necessary standard is an appropriate standard for uses and disclosures, and is not merely an administrative requirement. The Privacy Rule provides adequate flexibility to adopt minimum necessary policies and procedures that are workable for the covered entity, thereby minimizing a covered entity's liability concerns.

Comment: A number of commenters expressed concerns about application of the minimum necessary standard to disclosures for workers' compensation purposes. Commenters argued that the standard will prevent workers' compensation insurers and State administrators, as well as employers, from obtaining the information needed to pay injured workers the benefits guaranteed under the State workers' compensation system. They also argued that the minimum necessary standard could lead to fraudulent claims and unnecessary legal action in order to

obtain information needed for workers' compensation purposes.

Response: The Privacy Rule is not intended to disrupt existing workers' compensation systems as established by State law. In particular, the Rule is not intended to impede the flow of health information that is needed by employers, workers' compensation carriers, or State officials in order to process or adjudicate claims and/or coordinate care under the workers' compensation system. To this end, the Privacy Rule at § 164.512(l) explicitly permits a covered entity to disclose protected health information as authorized by, and to the extent necessary to comply with, workers' compensation or other similar programs established by law that provide benefits for work-related injuries or illnesses without regard to fault. The minimum necessary standard permits covered entities to disclose any protected health information under § 164.512(l) that is reasonably necessary for workers' compensation purposes and is intended to operate so as to permit information to be shared for such purposes to the full extent permitted by State or other law.

Additionally, where a State or other law requires a disclosure of protected health information for workers' compensation purposes, such disclosure is permitted under § 164.512(a). A covered entity also is permitted to disclose protected health information to a workers' compensation insurer where the insurer has obtained the individual's authorization pursuant to § 164.508 for the release of such information. The minimum necessary provisions do not apply to disclosures required by law or made pursuant to authorizations. See § 164.502(b), as modified herein.

Further, the Department notes that a covered entity is permitted to disclose information to any person or entity as necessary to obtain payment for health care services. The minimum necessary provisions apply to such disclosures but permit the covered entity to disclose the amount and types of information that are necessary to obtain payment.

The Department also notes that because the disclosures described above are permitted by the Privacy Rule, there is no potential for conflict with State workers' compensation laws, and, thus, no possibility of preemption of such laws by the Privacy Rule.

The Department's review of certain States workers' compensation laws demonstrates that many of these laws address the issue of the scope of information that is available to carriers and employers. The Privacy Rule's minimum necessary standard will not create an obstacle to the type and

C. HIPAA Final Rules, Privacy Standards, continued

Federal Register / Vol. 67, No. 157 / Wednesday, August 14, 2002 / Rules and Regulations   53199

amount of information that currently is provided to employers, workers' compensation carriers, and State administrative agencies under these State laws. In many cases, the minimum necessary standard will not apply to disclosures made pursuant to such laws. In other cases, the minimum necessary standard applies, but permits disclosures to the full extent authorized by the workers' compensation laws. For example, Texas workers' compensation law requires a health care provider, upon the request of the injured employee or insurance carrier, to furnish records relating to the treatment or hospitalization for which compensation is being sought. Since such disclosure is required by law, it also is permissible under the Privacy Rule at § 164.512(a) and exempt from the minimum necessary standard. The Texas law further provides that a health care provider is permitted to disclose to the insurance carrier records relating to the diagnosis or treatment of the injured employee without the authorization of the injured employee to determine the amount of payment or the entitlement to payment. Since the disclosure only is permitted and not required by Texas law, the provisions at § 164.512(l) would govern to permit such disclosure. In this case, the minimum necessary standard would apply to the disclosure but would allow for information to be disclosed as authorized by the statute, that is, as necessary to "determine the amount of payment or the entitlement to payment."

As another example, under Louisiana workers' compensation law, a health care provider who has treated an employee related to a workers' compensation claim is required to release any requested medical information and records relative to the employee's injury to the employer or the workers' compensation insurer. Again, since such disclosure is required by law, it is permissible under the Privacy Rule at § 164.512(a) and exempt from the minimum necessary standard. The Louisiana law further provides that any information relative to any other treatment or condition shall be available to the employer or workers' compensation insurer through a written release by the claimant. Such disclosure also would be permissible and exempt from the minimum necessary standard under the Privacy Rule if the individual's written authorization is obtained consistent with the requirements of § 164.508.

The Department understands concerns about the potential chilling effect of the Privacy Rule on the workers' compensation system.

Therefore, as the Privacy Rule is implemented, the Department will actively monitor the effects of the Rule on this industry to assure that the Privacy Rule does not have any unintended negative effects that disturb the existing workers' compensation systems. If the Department finds that, despite the above clarification of intent, the Privacy Rule is being misused and misapplied to interfere with the smooth operation of the workers' compensation systems, it will consider proposing modifications to the Rule to clarify the application of the minimum necessary standard to disclosures for workers' compensation purposes.

Comment: Another commenter urged the Department to clarify that a covered entity can reasonably rely on a determination made by a financial institution or credit card payment system regarding the minimum necessary information needed by that financial institution or payment system to complete a contemplated payment transaction.

Response: Except to the extent information is required or situationally required for a standard payment transaction (*see* 45 CFR 162.1601, 162.1602), the minimum necessary standard applies to a covered entity's disclosure of protected health information to a financial institution in order to process a payment transaction. With limited exceptions, the Privacy Rule does not allow a covered entity to substitute the judgment of a private, third party for its own assessment of the minimum necessary information for a disclosure. Under the exceptions in § 164.514(d)(3)(iii), a covered entity is permitted reasonably to rely on the request of another covered entity because, in this case, the requesting covered entity is itself subject to the minimum necessary standard and, therefore, required to limit its request to only that information that is reasonably necessary for the purpose. Thus, the Department does not agree that a covered entity should generally be permitted reasonably to rely on the request of a financial institution as the minimum necessary. However, the Department notes that where, for example, a financial institution is acting as a business associate of a covered entity, the disclosing covered entity may reasonably rely on a request from such financial institution, because in this situation, both the requesting and disclosing entity are subject to the minimum necessary standard.

Comment: A number of commenters continued to request additional guidance with respect to implementing this discretionary standard. Many

expressed support for the statement in the NPRM that HHS intends to issue further guidance to clarify issues causing confusion and concern in industry, as well as provide additional technical assistance materials to help covered entities implement the provisions.

Response: The Department is aware of the need for additional guidance in this area and intends to provide technical assistance and further clarifications as necessary to address these concerns and questions.

3. Parents as Personal Representatives of Unemancipated Minors [1]

December 2000 Privacy Rule. The Privacy Rule is intended to assure that parents have appropriate access to health information about their children. By creating new Federal protections and individual rights with respect to individually identifiable health information, parents will generally have new rights with respect to the health information about their minor children. In addition, the Department intended that the disclosure of health information about a minor child to a parent should be governed by State or other applicable law.

Under the Privacy Rule, parents are granted new rights as the personal representatives of their minor children. (*See* § 164.502(g).) Generally, parents will be able to access and control the health information about their minor children. (*See* § 164.502(g)(3).)

The Privacy Rule recognizes a limited number of exceptions to this general rule. These exceptions generally track the ability under State or other applicable laws of certain minors to obtain specified health care without parental consent. For example, every State has a law that permits adolescents to be tested for HIV without the consent of a parent. These laws are created to assure that adolescents will seek health care that is essential to their own health, as well as the public health. In these exceptional cases, where a minor can obtain a particular health care service without the consent of a parent under State or other applicable law, it is the minor, and not the parent, who may exercise the privacy rights afforded to individuals under the December 2000 Privacy Rule. (*See* § 164.502(g)(3)(i) and (ii), redesignated as § 164.502(g)(3)(i)(A) and (B)).

The December 2000 Privacy Rule also allows the minor to exercise control of

---

[1] Throughout this section of the preamble, "minor" refers to an unemancipated minor and "parent" refers to a parent, guardian, or other person acting *in loco parentis.*

C. HIPAA Final Rules, Privacy Standards, continued

protected health information when the parent has agreed to the minor obtaining confidential treatment (*see* § 164.502(g)(3)(iii), redesignated as § 164.502(g)(3)(i)(C) in this final Rule), and allows a covered health care provider to choose not to treat a parent as a personal representative of the minor when the provider is concerned about abuse or harm to the child. (*See* § 164.502(g)(5).)

Of course, a covered provider may disclose health information about a minor to a parent in the most critical situations, even if one of the limited exceptions discussed above apply. Disclosure of such information is always permitted as necessary to avert a serious and imminent threat to the health or safety of the minor. (See § 164.512(j).) The Privacy Rule adopted in December 2000 also states that disclosure of health information about a minor to a parent is permitted if State law authorizes disclosure to a parent, thereby allowing such disclosure where State law determines it is appropriate. (*See* § 160.202, definition of "more stringent.") Finally, health information about the minor may be disclosed to the parent if the minor involves the parent in his or her health care and does not object to such disclosure. (*See* § 164.502(g)(3)(i), redesignated as § 164.502(g)(3)(i)(A), and § 164.510(b)). The parent will retain all rights concerning any other health information about his or her minor child that does not meet one of the few exceptions listed above.

March 2002 NPRM. After reassessing the parents and minors provisions in the Privacy Rule, the Department identified two areas in which there were unintended consequences of the Rule. First, the language regarding deference to State law, which authorizes or prohibits disclosure of health information about a minor to a parent, fails to assure that State or other law governs when the law grants a provider discretion in certain circumstances to disclose protected health information to a parent. Second, the Privacy Rule may have prohibited parental access in certain situations in which State or other law may have permitted such access.

The Department proposed changes to these standards where they did not operate as intended and did not adequately defer to State or other applicable law with respect to parents and minors. First, in order to assure that State and other applicable laws that address disclosure of health information about a minor to his or her parent govern in all cases, the Department proposed to move the relevant language

about the disclosure of health information from the definition of "more stringent" (*see* § 160.202) to the standards regarding parents and minors (*see* § 164.502(g)(3)). This change would make it clear that State and other applicable law governs not only when a State explicitly addresses disclosure of protected health information to a parent but also when such law provides discretion to a provider. The language itself is also changed in the proposal to adapt it to the new section.

Second, the Department proposed to add a new paragraph (iii) to § 164.502(g)(3) to establish a neutral policy regarding the right of access of a parent to health information about his or her minor child under § 164.524, in the rare circumstance in which the parent is technically not the personal representative of his or her minor child under the Privacy Rule. This policy would apply particularly where State or other law is silent or unclear.

Overview of Public Comments. The following discussion provides an overview of the public comment received on this proposal. Additional comments received on this issue are discussed below in the section entitled, "Response to Other Public Comments."

The Department received a number of comments on the proposed changes to the parents and minors provisions of the Privacy Rule. Many commenters, particularly health care providers involved in provision of health care to minors, requested that the Department return to the approach under the Privacy Rule published in December 2000, because they believed that the proposed approach would discourage minors from seeking necessary health care. At a minimum, these commenters suggested that the Department clarify that discretion to grant a parent access under the proposal is limited to the covered health care provider that is providing treatment to the minor.

Supporters of the proposal asserted that the Department was moving in the right direction, but many also advocated for more parental rights. They asserted that parents have protected rights to act for their children and that the Privacy Rule interferes with these rights.

There were also some commenters that were confused by the new proposal and others that requested a Federal standard that would preempt all State laws.

Final Modifications. The Department will continue to defer to State or other applicable law and to remain neutral to the extent possible. However, the Department is adopting changes to the standards in the December 2000 Privacy Rule, where they do not operate as

intended and are inconsistent with the Department's underlying goals. These modifications are similar in approach to the NPRM and the rationale for these changes remains the same as was stated in the NPRM. However, the Department makes some changes from the language that was proposed, in order to simplify the provisions and clarify the Department's intent.

There are three goals with respect to the parents and minors provisions in the Privacy Rule. First, the Department wants to assure that parents have appropriate access to the health information about their minor children to make important health care decisions about them, while also making sure that the Privacy Rule does not interfere with a minor's ability to consent to and obtain health care under State or other applicable law. Second, the Department does not want to interfere with State or other applicable laws related to competency or parental rights, in general, or the role of parents in making health care decisions about their minor children, in particular. Third, the Department does not want to interfere with the professional requirements of State medical boards or other ethical codes of health care providers with respect to confidentiality of health information or with the health care practices of such providers with respect to adolescent health care.

In order to honor these differing goals, the Department has and continues to take the approach of deferring to State or other applicable law and professional practice with respect to parents and minors. Where State and other applicable law is silent or unclear, the Department has attempted to create standards, implementation specifications, and requirements that are consistent with such laws and that permit States the discretion to continue to define the rights of parents and minors with respect to health information without interference from the Federal Privacy Rule.

The Department adopts two changes to the provisions regarding parents and minors in order to address unintended consequences from the December 2000 Privacy Rule and to defer to State and other law. The first change is about disclosure of protected health information to a parent and the second is about access to the health information by the parent. Disclosure is about a covered entity providing individually identifiable information to persons outside the entity, either the individual or a third party. Access is a particular type of disclosure that is the right of an individual (directly or through a personal representative) to review or

C. HIPAA Final Rules, Privacy Standards, continued

obtain a copy of his or her health information under § 164.524. This modification treats both activities similarly by deferring to State or other applicable law.

The first change, regarding disclosure of protected health information to a parent, is the same as the change proposed in the NPRM. In order to assure that State and other applicable laws that address disclosure of health information about a minor to his or her parent govern in all cases, the language in the definition of "more stringent" (see § 160.202) that addresses the disclosure of protected health information about a minor to a parent has been moved to the standards regarding parents and minors (see § 164.502(g)(3)). The addition of paragraphs (g)(3)(ii)(A) and (B) of § 164.502, clarify that State and other applicable law governs when such law explicitly requires, permits, or prohibits disclosure of protected health information to a parent.

In connection with moving the language, the language is changed from the December 2000 Privacy Rule in order to adapt it to the new section. Section 164.502(g)(3)(ii)(A) states that a covered entity may disclose protected health information about a minor to a parent if an applicable provision of State or other law permits or requires such disclosure. By adopting this provision, the Department makes clear that nothing in the regulation prohibits disclosure of health information to a parent if, and to the extent that, State or other law permits or requires such disclosure. The Privacy Rule defers to such State or other law and permits covered entities to act in accordance to such law. Section 164.502(g)(3)(ii)(B) states that a covered entity may not disclose protected health information about a minor to a parent if an applicable provision of State or other law prohibits such disclosure. Again, regardless of how the Privacy Rule would operate in the absence of explicit State or other law, if such law prohibits the disclosure of protected health information about a minor to a parent, so does the Privacy Rule. The revision also clarifies that deference to State or other applicable law includes deference to established case law as well as explicit provisions in statutes or regulations that permit, require, or prohibit particular disclosures.

The second change, regarding access to protected health information, also reflects the same policy as proposed in the NPRM. There are two provisions that refer to access, in order to clarify the Department's intent in this area. The first is where there is an explicit State

or other law regarding parental access, and the second is where State or other law is silent or unclear, which is often the case with access.

Like the provisions regarding disclosure of protected health information to a parent, the final Rule defers to State or other applicable law regarding a parent's access to health information about a minor. The change assures that State or other applicable law governs when the law explicitly requires, permits, or prohibits access to protected health information about a minor to a parent. This includes deference to established case law as well as an explicit provision in a statute or regulation. This issue is addressed in paragraphs (g)(3)(ii)(A) and (B) of § 164.502 with the disclosure provisions discussed above.

In addition to the provision regarding explicit State access laws, the Department recognizes that the Privacy Rule creates a right of access that previously did not exist in most States. Most States do not have explicit laws in this area. In order to address the limited number of cases in which the parent is not the personal representative of the minor because one of the exceptions in the parents and minors provisions are met (see § 164.502(g)(3)(i)(A), (B), or (C)), the Department adds a provision, § 164.502(g)(3)(ii)(C), similar to a provision proposed in the NPRM, that addresses those situations in which State and other law about parental access is not explicit. Under this provision, a covered entity may provide or deny access to a parent provided that such discretion is permitted by State or other law. This new paragraph would assure that the Privacy Rule would not prevent a covered entity from providing access to a parent if the covered entity would have been able to provide this access under State or other applicable law. The new paragraph would also prohibit access by a parent if providing such access would violate State or other applicable law.

It is important to note that this provision regarding access to health information about a minor in cases in which State and other laws are silent or unclear will not apply in the majority of cases because, typically, the parent will be the personal representative of his or her minor child and will have a right of access to the medical records of his or her minor children under the Privacy Rule. This provision only applies in cases in which the parent is not the personal representative under the Privacy Rule.

In response to comments by health care providers, the final modifications also clarify that, the discretion to

provide or deny access to a parent under § 164.502(g)(3)(ii)(C) only may be exercised by a licensed health care professional, in the exercise of professional judgment. This is consistent with the policy described in the preamble to the NPRM, is similar to the approach in the access provisions in § 164.524(a)(3), and furthers the Department's interest in balancing the goals of providing appropriate information to parents and of assuring that minors obtain appropriate access to health care. This decision should be made by a health care professional, who is accustomed to exercising professional judgment. A health plan may also exercise such discretion if the decision is made by a licensed health care provider.

The Department takes no position on the ability of a minor to consent to treatment and no position on how State or other law affects privacy between the minor and parent. Where State or other law is unclear, covered entities should continue to conduct the same analysis of such law as they do now to determine if access is permissible or not. Because the Privacy Rule defers to State and other law in the area of parents and minors, the Department assumes that the current practices of health care providers with respect to access by parents and confidentiality of minor's records are consistent with State and other applicable law, and, therefore, can continue under the Privacy Rule.

Parental access under this section would continue to be subject to any limitations on activities of a personal representative in § 164.502(g)(5) and § 164.524(a)(2) and (3). In cases in which the parent is not the personal representative of the minor and State or other law does not require parental access, this provision does not provide a parent a right to demand access and does not require a covered entity to provide access to a parent. Furthermore, nothing in these modifications shall affect whether or not a minor would have a right to access his or her records. That is, a covered entity's exercise of discretion to not grant a parent access does not affect the right of access the minor may have under the Privacy Rule. A covered entity may deny a parent access in accordance with State or other law and may be required to provide access to the minor under the Privacy Rule.

These changes also do not affect the general provisions, explained in the section "December 2000 Privacy Rule" above, regarding parents as personal representatives of their minor children or the exceptions to this general rule, where parents would not be the

C. HIPAA Final Rules, Privacy Standards, continued

personal representatives of their minor children.

These changes adopted in this Rule provide States with the option of clarifying the interaction between their laws regarding consent to health care and the ability of parents to have access to the health information about the care received by their minor children in accordance with such laws. As such, this change should more accurately reflect current State and other laws and modifications to such laws.

Response to Other Public Comments

Comment: Some commenters urged the Department to retain the approach to parents and minors that was adopted in December 2000. They claimed that the NPRM approach would seriously undermine minors' willingness to seek necessary medical care. Other commenters advocated full parental access to health information about their minor children, claiming that the Privacy Rule interferes with parents' rights.

Response: We believe the approach adopted in the final Rule strikes the right balance between these concerns. It defers to State law or other applicable law and preserves the status quo to the greatest extent possible.

Comment: Health care providers generally opposed the changes to the parents and minors provisions claiming that they would eliminate protection of a minor's privacy, and therefore, would decrease the willingness of adolescents to obtain necessary health care for sensitive types of health care services. They also argued that the NPRM approach is inconsistent with State laws that give minors the right to consent to certain health care because the purpose of these laws is to provide minors with confidential health care.

Response: Issues related to parents' and minors' rights with respect to health care are best left for the States to decide. The standards regarding parents and minors are designed to defer to State law in this area. While we believe that there is a correlation between State laws that grant minors the authority to consent to treatment and confidentiality of the information related to such treatment, our research has not established that these laws bar parental access to such health information under all circumstances. Therefore, to act in a manner consistent with State law, the approach adopted in this Final Rule is more flexible than the standards adopted in December 2000, in order to assure that the Privacy Rule does not preclude a provider from granting access to a parent if this is permissible under State law. However, this new

standard would not permit activity that would be impermissible under State law.

Some State or other laws may state clearly that a covered entity must provide a parent access to the medical records of his or her minor child, even when the minor consents to the treatment without the parent. In this case, the covered entity must provide a parent access, subject to the access limitations in the Privacy Rule at § 164.524(a)(2) and (3). Other laws may state clearly that a covered entity must not provide a parent access to their minor child's medical records when the minor consents to the treatment without the parent. In this case, the covered entity would be precluded from granting access to the parent. If the State or other law clearly provides a covered entity with discretion to grant a parent access, then the covered entity may exercise such discretion, to the extent permitted under such other law.

If State law is silent or unclear on its face, then a covered entity would have to go through the same analysis as it would today to determine if such law permitted, required, or prohibited providing a parent with access to a minor's records. That analysis may involve review of case law, attorney general opinions, legislative history, etc. If such analysis showed that the State would permit an entity to provide a parent access to health information about a minor child, and under the Privacy Rule, the parent would not be the personal representative of the minor because of one of the limited exceptions in § 164.502(g)(3)(i), then the covered entity may exercise such discretion, based on the professional judgment of a licensed health care provider, to choose whether or not to provide the parent access to the medical records of his or her minor child. If, as the commenters suggest, a State consent law were interpreted to prohibit such access, then such access is prohibited under the Privacy Rule as well.

Comment: One commenter asserted that the Privacy Rule inappropriately erects barriers between parents and children. Specifically, the commenter stated that § 164.502(g)(5) delegates to private entities government power to decide whether a child may be subjected to abuse or could be endangered. The commenter also stated that the access provisions in § 164.502(g)(3) would erect barriers where State law is silent or unclear.

Response: The Department does not agree that the Privacy Rule erects barriers between a parent and a minor child because the relevant standards are intended to defer to State law. Health

care providers have responsibilities under other laws and professional standards to report child abuse to the appropriate authorities and to use professional discretion to protect the child's welfare in abuse situations. Similarly the Privacy Rule permits (but does not require) the provider to use professional discretion to act to protect a child she believes is being abused. If the Privacy Rule were to mandate that a provider grant a parent access to a medical record in abuse situations, as the commenter suggests, this would be a change from current law. In addition, the Privacy Rule does not allow a denial of parental access to medical records if State or other law would require such access.

Comment: Commenters continue to raise preemption issues. A few commenters called for preemption of all State law in this area. Others stated that there should be one standard, not 50 standards, controlling disclosure of protected health information about a minor to a parent and that the NPRM approach would burden regional and national health care providers. Others urged preemption of State laws that are less protective of a minor's privacy, consistent with the general preemption provisions.

Response: The Department does not want to interfere with a State's role in determining the appropriate rights of parents and their minor children. The claim that the Privacy Rule introduces 50 standards is inaccurate. These State standards exist today and are not created by the Privacy Rule. Our approach has been, and continues to be, to defer to State and other applicable law in this area.

Comment: One commenter requested the Privacy Rule state that good faith compliance with the Privacy Rule is an affirmative defense to enforcement of contrary laws ultimately determined to be more stringent than the Rule, or that it provide specific guidance on which State laws conflict with or are more stringent than the Privacy Rule.

Response: The Privacy Rule cannot dictate how States enforce their own privacy laws. Furthermore, guidance on whether or not a State law is preempted would not be binding on a State interpreting its own law.

Comment: Some commenters remain concerned that a parent will not get information about a child who receives care in an emergency without the consent of the parent and that the provisions in § 164.510(b) are not sufficient.

Response: As we have stated in previous guidance, a provider generally can discuss all the health information

C. HIPAA Final Rules, Privacy Standards, continued

about a minor child with his parent, because the parent usually will be the personal representative of the child. This is true, under the Privacy Rule, even if the parent did not provide consent to the treatment because of the emergency nature of the health care. A parent may be unable to obtain such information in limited circumstances, such as when the minor provided consent for the treatment in accordance with State law or the treating physician suspects abuse or neglect or reasonably believes that releasing the information to the parent will endanger the child.

Comment: A couple of commenters were concerned that the provisions regarding confidential communications conflict with the Fair Debt Collection Practices Act (FDCPA), which allows collection agencies to contact the party responsible for payment of the debt, be it the spouse or parent (of a minor) of the individual that incurred the debt, and share information that supports the incurrence and amount of the debt. They feared that the Privacy Rule would no longer allow collection agencies to continue this practice.

Response: Our analysis of the relevant provisions of the Privacy Rule and the FDCPA does not indicate any conflicts between the two laws. An entity that is subject to the FDCPA and the Privacy Rule (or that must act consistent with the Privacy Rule as a business associate of the covered entity) should be able to comply with both laws, because the FDCPA permits an entity to exercise discretion to disclose information about one individual to another.

The FDCPA allows debt collectors to communicate with the debtor's spouse or parent if the debtor is a minor. The provisions of the FDCPA are permissive rather than required.

Generally, the Privacy Rule permits covered entities to use the services of debt collectors as the use of such services to obtain payment for the provision of health care comes within the definition of "payment." The Privacy Rule generally does not identify to whom information can be disclosed when a covered entity is engaged in its own payment activities. Therefore, if a covered entity or a debt collector, as a business associate of a covered entity, needs to disclose protected health information to a spouse or a parent, the Privacy Rule generally would not prevent such disclosure. In these cases where the Privacy Rule would permit disclosure to a parent or spouse, there should be no concern with the interaction with the FDCPA.

However, there are some circumstances in which the Privacy Rule may prohibit a disclosure to a parent or a spouse for payment purposes. For example, under § 164.522(a), an individual has the right to request restrictions to the disclosure of health information for payment. A provider or health plan may choose whether or not to agree to the request. If the covered entity agreed to a restriction, the covered entity would be bound by that restriction and would not be permitted to disclose the individual's health information in violation of that agreement. Also, § 164.522(b) generally requires covered entities to accommodate reasonable requests by individuals to receive communications of protected health information by alternative means or at alternative locations. However, the covered entity may condition the accommodation on the individual providing information on how payment will be handled. In both of these cases, the covered entity has means for permitting disclosures as permitted by the FDCPA. Therefore, these provisions of the Privacy Rule need not limit options available under the FDCPA. However, if the agreed-to restrictions or accommodation for confidential communications prohibit disclosure to a parent or spouse of an individual, the covered entity, and the debt collector as a business associate of the covered entity, would be prohibited from disclosing such information under the Privacy Rule. In such case, because the FDCPA would provide discretion to make a disclosure, but the Privacy Rule would prohibit the disclosure, a covered entity or the debt collector as a business associate of a covered entity would have to exercise discretion granted under the FDCPA in a way that complies with the Privacy Rule. This means not making the disclosure.

C. Section 164.504—Uses and Disclosures: Organizational Requirements

1. Hybrid Entities

December 2000 Privacy Rule. The Privacy Rule, as published in December 2000, defined covered entities that primarily engage in activities that are not "covered functions," that is, functions that relate to the entity's operation as a health plan, health care provider, or health care clearinghouse, as hybrid entities. *See* 45 CFR 164.504(a). Examples of hybrid entities were: (1) corporations that are not in the health care industry, but that operate on-site health clinics that conduct the HIPAA standard transactions electronically; and (2) insurance carriers that have multiple lines of business that include both health insurance and other

insurance lines, such as general liability or property and casualty insurance.

Under the December 2000 Privacy Rule, a hybrid entity was required to define and designate those parts of the entity that engage in covered functions as one or more health care component(s). A hybrid entity also was required to include in the health care component(s) any other components of the entity that support the covered functions in the same way such support may be provided by a business associate (e.g., an auditing component). The health care component was to include such "business associate" functions for two reasons: (1) It is impracticable for the entity to contract with itself; and (2) having to obtain an authorization for disclosures to such support components would limit the ability of the hybrid entity to engage in necessary health care operations functions. In order to limit the burden on hybrid entities, most of the requirements of the Privacy Rule only applied to the health care component(s) of the entity and not to the parts of the entity that do not engage in covered functions.

The hybrid entity was required to create adequate separation, in the form of firewalls, between the health care component(s) and other components of the entity. Transfer of protected health information held by the health care component to other components of the hybrid entity was a disclosure under the Privacy Rule and was allowed only to the same extent such a disclosure was permitted to a separate entity.

In the preamble to the December 2000 Privacy Rule, the Department explained that the use of the term "primary" in the definition of a "hybrid entity" was not intended to operate with mathematical precision. The Department further explained that it intended a common sense evaluation of whether the covered entity mostly operates as a health plan, health care provider, or health care clearinghouse. If an entity's primary activity was a covered function, then the whole entity would have been a covered entity and the hybrid entity provisions would not have applied. However, if the covered entity primarily conducted non-health activities, it would have qualified as a hybrid entity and would have been required to comply with the Privacy Rule with respect to its health care component(s). *See* 65 FR 82502.

March 2002 NPRM. Since the publication of the final Rule, concerns were raised that the policy guidance in the preamble was insufficient so long as the Privacy Rule itself limited the hybrid entity provisions to entities that primarily conducted non-health related activities. In particular, concerns were

53204 Federal Register / Vol. 67, No. 157 / Wednesday, August 14, 2002 / Rules and Regulations

raised about whether entities, which have the health plan line of business as the primary business and an excepted benefits line, such as workers' compensation insurance, as a small portion of the business, qualified as hybrid entities. There were also concerns about how "primary" was to be defined, if it was not a mathematical calculation, and how an entity would know whether or not it was a hybrid entity based on the guidance in the preamble.

As a result of these comments, the Department proposed to delete the term "primary" from the definition of "hybrid entity" in § 164.504(a) and permit any covered entity that is a single legal entity and that performs both covered and non-covered functions to choose whether or not to be a hybrid entity for purposes of the Privacy Rule. Under the proposal, any covered entity could be a hybrid entity regardless of whether the non-covered functions represent the entity's primary functions, a substantial function, or even a small portion of the entity's activities. In order to be a hybrid entity under the proposal, a covered entity would have to designate its health care component(s). If the covered entity did not designate any health care component(s), the entire entity would be a covered entity and, therefore, subject to the Privacy Rule. Since the entire entity would be the covered entity, § 164.504(c)(2) requiring firewalls between covered and non-covered portions of hybrid entities would not apply.

The Department explained in the preamble to the proposal that there are advantages and disadvantages to being a hybrid entity. Whether or not the advantages outweigh the disadvantages would be a decision for each covered entity that qualified as a hybrid entity, taking into account factors such as how the entity was organized and the proportion of the entity that must be included in the health care component.

The Department also proposed to simplify the definition of "health care component" in § 164.504(a) to make clear that a health care component is whatever the covered entity designates as the health care component, consistent with the provisions regarding designation in proposed § 164.504(c)(3)(iii). The Department proposed to move the specific language regarding which components make up a health care component to the implementation specification that addresses designation of health care components at § 164.504(c)(3)(iii). At § 164.504(c)(3)(iii), the Department proposed that a health care component could include: (1) Components of the

covered entity that engage in covered functions, and (2) any component that engages in activities that would make such component a business associate of a component that performs covered functions, if the two components were separate legal entities. In addition, the Department proposed to make clear at § 164.504(c)(3)(iii) that a hybrid entity must designate as a health care component(s) any component that would meet the definition of "covered entity" if it were a separate legal entity.

There was some ambiguity in the December 2000 Privacy Rule as to whether a health care provider that does not conduct electronic transactions for which the Secretary has adopted standards (*i.e.*, a non-covered health care provider) and which is part of a larger covered entity was required to be included in the health care component. To clarify this issue, the proposal also would allow a hybrid entity the discretion to include in its health care component a non-covered health care provider component. Including a non-covered health care provider in the health care component would subject the non-covered provider to the Privacy Rule. Accordingly, the Department proposed a conforming change in § 164.504(c)(1)(ii) to make clear that a reference to a "covered health care provider" in the Privacy Rule could include the functions of a health care provider who does not engage in electronic transactions, if the covered entity chooses to include such functions in the health care component.

The proposal also would permit a hybrid entity to designate otherwise non-covered portions of its operations that provide services to the covered functions, such as parts of the legal or accounting divisions of the entity, as part of the health care component, so that protected health information could be shared with such functions of the entity without business associate agreements or individual authorizations. The proposal would not require that the covered entity designate entire divisions as in or out of the covered component. Rather, it would permit the covered entity to designate functions within such divisions, such as the functions of the accounting division that support health insurance activities, without including those functions that support life insurance activities. The Department proposed to delete as unnecessary and redundant the related language in paragraph (2)(ii) of the definition of "health care component" in the Privacy Rule that requires the "business associate" functions include the use of protected health information.

Overview of Public Comments. The following discussion provides an overview of the public comment received on this proposal. Additional comments received on this issue are discussed below in the section entitled, "Response to Other Public Comments."

The Department received relatively few comments on its proposal regarding hybrid entities. A number of comments supported the proposal, appreciative of the added flexibility it would afford covered entities in their compliance efforts. For example, some drug stores stated that the proposal would provide them with the flexibility to designate health care components, whereas under the December 2000 Rule, these entities would have been required to subject their entire business, including the "front end" of the store which is not associated with dispensing prescription drugs, to the Privacy Rule's requirements.

Some health plans and other insurers also expressed strong support for the proposal. These comments, however, seemed to be based on a misinterpretation of the uses and disclosures the proposal actually would permit. These commenters appear to assume that the proposal would allow information to flow freely between non-covered and covered functions in the same entity, if that entity chose not to be a hybrid entity. For example, commenters explained that they interpreted the proposal to mean that a multi-line insurer which does not elect hybrid entity status would be permitted to share protected health information between its covered lines and its otherwise non-covered lines. It was stated that such latitude would greatly enhance multi-line insurers' ability to detect and prevent fraudulent activities and eliminate barriers to sharing claims information between covered and non-covered lines of insurance where necessary to process a claim.

Some commenters opposed the Department's hybrid entity proposal, stating that the proposal would reduce the protections afforded under the Privacy Rule and would be subject to abuse. Commenters expressed concerns that the proposal would allow a covered entity with only a small health care component to avoid the extra protections of creating firewalls between the health care component and the rest of the organization. Moreover, one of the commenters stated that the proposal could allow a covered entity that is primarily performing health care functions to circumvent the requirements of the Rule for a large part of its operations by designating itself a hybrid and excluding from the health

C. HIPAA Final Rules, Privacy Standards, continued

Federal Register / Vol. 67, No. 157 / Wednesday, August 14, 2002 / Rules and Regulations   **53205**

care component a non-covered health care provider function, such as a free nurse advice line that does not bill electronically. In addition, it was stated that the ambiguous language in the proposal could potentially be construed as allowing a hybrid entity to designate only the business associate-like functions as the health care component, and exclude covered functions. The commenter urged the Department to clarify that a hybrid entity must, at a minimum, designate a component that performs covered functions as a health care component, and that a health care provider cannot avoid having its treatment component considered a health care component by relying on a billing department to conduct its standard electronic transactions. These commenters urged the Department to retain the existing policy by requiring those organizations whose primary functions are not health care to be hybrid entities and to institute firewall protections between their health care and other components.

Final Modifications. After consideration of the comments, the Department adopts in the final Rule the proposed approach to provide covered entities that otherwise qualify the discretion to decide whether to be a hybrid entity. To do so, the Department eliminates the term "primary" from the definition of "hybrid entity" at § 164.504(a). Any covered entity that otherwise qualifies (*i.e.*, is a single legal entity that performs both covered and non-covered functions) and that designates health care component(s) in accordance with § 164.504(c)(3)(iii) is a hybrid entity. A hybrid entity is required to create adequate separation, in the form of firewalls, between the health care component(s) and other components of the entity. Transfer of protected health information held by the health care component to other components of the hybrid entity continues to be a disclosure under the Privacy Rule, and, thus, allowed only to the same extent such a disclosure is permitted to a separate entity.

Most of the requirements of the Privacy Rule continue to apply only to the health care component(s) of a hybrid entity. Covered entities that choose not to designate health care component(s) are subject to the Privacy Rule in their entirety.

The final Rule regarding hybrid entities is intended to provide a covered entity with the flexibility to apply the Privacy Rule as best suited to the structure of its organization, while maintaining privacy protections for protected health information within the organization. In addition, the policy in

the final Rule simplifies the Privacy Rule and makes moot any questions about what "primary" means for purposes of determining whether an entity is a hybrid entity.

The final Rule adopts the proposal's simplified definition of "health care component," which makes clear that a health care component is what the covered entity designates as the health care component. The Department makes a conforming change in § 164.504(c)(2)(ii) to reflect the changes to the definition of "health care component." The final Rule at § 164.504(c)(3)(iii) requires a health care component to include a component that would meet the definition of a "covered entity" if it were a separate legal entity. The Department also modifies the language of the final Rule at § 164.504(c)(3)(iii) to clarify that only a component that performs covered functions, and a component to the extent that it performs covered functions or activities that would make such component a business associate of a component that performs covered functions if the two components were separate legal entities, may be included in the health care component. "Covered functions" are defined at § 164.501 as "those functions of a covered entity the performance of which makes the entity a health plan, health care provider, or health care clearinghouse."

As in the proposal, the Department provides a hybrid entity with some discretion as to what functions may be included in the health care component in two ways. First, the final Rule clarifies that a hybrid entity may include in its health care component a non-covered health care provider component. Accordingly, the Department adopts the proposed conforming change to § 164.504(c)(1)(ii) to make clear that a reference to a "covered health care provider" in the Privacy Rule may include the functions of a health care provider who does not engage in electronic transactions for which the Secretary has adopted standards, if the covered entity chooses to include such functions in the health care component. A hybrid entity that chooses to include a non-covered health care provider in its health care component is required to ensure that the non-covered health care provider, as well as the rest of the health care component, is in compliance with the Privacy Rule.

Second, the final Rule retains the proposed policy to provide hybrid entities with discretion as to whether or not to include business associate-like divisions within the health care component. It is not a violation of the

Privacy Rule to exclude such divisions from the health care component. However, a disclosure of protected health information from the health care component to such other division that is not part of the health care component is the same as a disclosure outside the covered entity. Because an entity cannot have a business associate contract with itself, such a disclosure likely will require individual authorization.

The Department clarifies, in response to comments, that a health care provider cannot avoid being a covered entity and, therefore, part of a health care component of a hybrid entity just by relying on a billing department to conduct standard transactions on its behalf. A health care provider is a covered entity if standard transactions are conducted on his behalf, regardless of whether the provider or a business associate (or billing department within a hybrid entity) actually conducts the transactions. In such a situation, however, designating relevant parts of the business associate division as part of the health care component would facilitate the conduct of health care operations and payment.

Also in response to comments, the Department clarifies that even if a covered entity does not choose to be a hybrid entity, and therefore is not required to erect firewalls around its health care functions, the entity still only is allowed to use protected health information as permitted by the Privacy Rule, for example, for treatment, payment, and health care operations. Additionally, the covered entity is still subject to minimum necessary restrictions under §§ 164.502 and 164.514(d), and, thus, must have policies and procedures that describe who within the entity may have access to the protected health information. Under these provisions, workforce members may be permitted access to protected health information only as necessary to carry out their duties with respect to the entity's covered functions. For example, the health insurance line of a multi-line insurer is not permitted to share protected health information with the life insurance line for purposes of determining eligibility for life insurance benefits or any other life insurance purposes absent an individual's written authorization. However, the health insurance line of a multi-line insurer may share protected health information with another line of business pursuant to § 164.512(a), if, for example, State law requires an insurer that receives a claim under one policy to share that information with other lines of insurance to determine if the event also may be payable under

C. HIPAA Final Rules, Privacy Standards, continued

53206 Federal Register / Vol. 67, No. 157 / Wednesday, August 14, 2002 / Rules and Regulations

another insurance policy. Furthermore, the health plan may share information with another line of business if necessary for the health plan's coordination of benefits activities, which would be a payment activity of the health plan.

Given the above restrictions on information flows within the covered entity, the Department disagrees with those commenters who raised concerns that the proposed policy would weaken the Rule by eliminating the formal requirement for "firewalls." Even if a covered entity does not designate health care component(s) and, therefore, does not have to establish firewalls to separate its health care function(s) from the non-covered functions, the Privacy Rule continues to restrict how protected health information may be used and shared within the entity and who gets access to the information.

Further, the Department does not believe that allowing a covered entity to exclude a non-covered health care provider component from its health care component will be subject to abuse. Excluding health care functions from the health care component has significant implications under the Rule. Specifically, the Privacy Rule treats the sharing of protected health information from a health care component to a non-covered component as a disclosure, subject to the same restrictions as a disclosure between two legally separate entities. For example, if a covered entity decides to exclude from its health care component a non-covered provider, the health care component is then restricted from disclosing protected health information to that provider for any of the non-covered provider's health care operations, absent an individual's authorization. *See* § 164.506(c). If, however, the non-covered health care provider function is not excluded, it would be part of the health care component and that information could be used for its operations without the individual's authorization.

Response to Other Public Comments

Comment: A number of academic medical centers expressed concern that the Privacy Rule prevents them from organizing for compliance in a manner that reflects the integration of operations between the medical school and affiliated faculty practice plans and teaching hospitals. These commenters stated that neither the proposal nor the existing Rule would permit many academic medical centers to designate themselves as either a hybrid or affiliated entity, since the components of each must belong to a single legal entity or share common ownership or

control. These commenters also explained that a typical medical school would not appear to qualify as an organized health care arrangement (OHCA) because it does not engage in any of the requisite joint activities, for example, quality assessment and improvement activities, on behalf of the covered entity. It was stated that it is essential that there not be impediments to the flow of information within an academic medical center. These commenters, therefore, urged that the Department add a definition of "academic medical center" to the Privacy Rule and modify the definition of "common control" to explicitly apply to the components of an academic medical center, so as to ensure that academic medical centers qualify as affiliated entities for purposes of the Rule.

Response: The Department does not believe that a modification to include a special rule for academic medical centers is warranted. The Privacy Rule's organizational requirements at § 164.504 for hybrid entities and affiliated entities, as well as the definition of "organized health care arrangement" in § 164.501, provide covered entities with much flexibility to apply the Rule's requirements as best suited to the structure of their businesses. However, in order to maintain privacy protections, the Privacy Rule places appropriate conditions on who may qualify for such organizational options, as well as how information may flow within such constructs. Additionally, if the commenter is suggesting that information should flow freely between the covered and non-covered functions within an academic medical center, the Department clarifies that the Privacy Rule restricts the sharing of protected health information between covered and non-covered functions, regardless of whether the information is shared within a single covered entity or a hybrid entity, or among affiliated covered entities or covered entities participating in an OHCA. Such uses and disclosures may only be made as permitted by the Rule.

Comment: A few commenters expressed concern with respect to governmental hybrid entities having to include business associate-like divisions within the health care component or else being required to obtain an individual's authorization for disclosures to such division. It was stated that this concept does not take into account the organizational structures of local governments and effectively forces such governmental hybrid entities to bring those components that perform business

associate type functions into their covered component. Additionally, a commenter stated that this places an undue burden on local government by essentially requiring that functions, such as auditor/controller or county counsel, be treated as fully covered by the Privacy Rule in order to minimize otherwise considerable risk. Commenters, therefore, urged that the Department allow a health care component to enter into a memorandum of understanding (MOU) or other agreement with the business associate division within the hybrid entity. Alternatively, it was suggested that a governmental hybrid entity be permitted to include in its notice of privacy practices the possibility that information may be shared with other divisions within the same government entity for specific purposes.

Response: The Department clarifies that a covered entity which chooses to include its business associate division within the health care component may only do so to the extent such division performs activities on behalf of, or provides services to, the health care component. That same division's activities with respect to non-covered activities may not be included. To clarify this point, the Department modified the proposed language in § 164.504(c)(3)(iii) to provide that a health care component may only include a component to the extent that it performs covered functions or activities that would make such component a business associate of a component that performs covered functions if the two components were separate legal entities. For example, employees within an accounting division may be included within the health care component to the extent that they provide services to such component. However, where these same employees also provide services to non-covered components of the entity, their activities with respect to the health care component must be adequately separated from their other non-covered functions.

While the Department does not believe that a MOU between governmental divisions within a hybrid entity may be necessary given the above clarification, the Department notes that a governmental hybrid entity may elect to have its health care component enter into a MOU with its business associate division, provided that such agreement is legally binding and meets the relevant requirements of § 164.504(e)(3) and (e)(4). Such agreement would eliminate the need for the health care component to include the business associate division or for obtaining the

C. HIPAA Final Rules, Privacy Standards, continued

individual's authorization to disclose to such division.

Additionally, the Department encourages covered entities to develop a notice of privacy practices that is as specific as possible, which may include, for a government hybrid entity, a statement that information may be shared with other divisions within the government entity as permitted by the Rule. However, the notice of privacy practices is not an adequate substitute for, as appropriate, a memorandum of understanding; designation of business associate functions as part of a health care component; or alternatively, conditioning disclosures to such business associate functions on individuals' authorizations.

Comment: One commenter requested a clarification that a pharmacy-convenience store, where the pharmacy itself is a separate enclosure under supervision of a licensed pharmacist, is not a hybrid entity.

Response: The Department clarifies that a pharmacy-convenience store, if a single legal entity, is permitted, but not required, to be a hybrid entity and designate the pharmacy as the health care component. Alternatively, such an entity may choose to be a covered entity in its entirety. However, if the pharmacy and the convenience store are separate legal entities, the convenience store is not a covered entity simply by virtue of sharing retail space with the covered pharmacy.

Comment: Another commenter stated that the Rule implies that individual providers, once covered, are covered for all circumstances even if they are employed by more than one entity—one sending transactions electronically but not the other—or if the individual provider changes functions or employment and no longer electronically transmits standard transactions. This commenter asked that either the Rule permit an individual provider to be a hybrid entity (recognizing that there are times when an individual provider may be engaging in standard transactions, and other times when he is not), or that the definition of a "covered entity" should be modified so that individual providers are themselves classified as covered entities only when they are working as individuals.

Response: A health care provider is not a covered entity based on his being a workforce member of a health care provider that conducts the standard transactions. Thus, a health care provider may maintain a separate uncovered practice (if he does not engage in standard transactions electronically in connection with that

practice), even though the provider may also practice at a hospital which may be a covered entity. However, the Rule does not permit an individual provider to use hybrid entity status to eliminate protections on information when he is not conducting standard transactions. If a health care provider conducts standard transactions electronically on his own behalf, then the protected health information maintained or transmitted by that provider is covered, regardless of whether the information is actually used in such transactions.

Comment: One commenter requested a clarification that employers are not hybrid entities simply because they may be the plan sponsor of a group health plan.

Response: The Department clarifies that an employer is not a hybrid entity simply because it is the plan sponsor of a group health plan. The employer/plan sponsor and group health plan are separate legal entities and, therefore, do not qualify as a hybrid entity. Further, disclosures from the group health plan to the plan sponsor are governed specifically by the requirements of § 164.504(f).

Comment: A few commenters asked the Department to permit a covered entity with multiple types of health care components to tailor notices to address the specific privacy practices within a component, rather than have just one generic notice for the entire covered entity.

Response: Covered entities are allowed to provide a separate notice for each separate health care component, and are encouraged to provide individuals with the most specific notice possible.

2. Group Health Plan Disclosures of Enrollment and Disenrollment Information to Plan Sponsors

December 2000 Privacy Rule. The Department recognized the legitimate need of plan sponsors and employers to access health information held by group health plans in order to carry out essential functions related to the group health plan. Therefore, the Privacy Rule at § 164.504(f) permits a group health plan, and health insurance issuers or HMOs with respect to the group health plan, to disclose protected health information to a plan sponsor provided that, among other requirements, the plan documents are amended appropriately to reflect and restrict the plan sponsor's uses and disclosures of such information. The Department further determined that there were two situations in which protected health information could be shared between the group health plan and the plan

sponsor without individual authorization or an amendment to the plan documents. First, § 164.504(f) permits the group health plan to share summary health information (as defined in § 164.504(a)) with the plan sponsor. Second, a group health plan is allowed to share enrollment or disenrollment information with the plan sponsor without amending the plan documents as required by § 164.504(f). As explained in the preamble to the December 2000 Privacy Rule, a plan sponsor is permitted to perform enrollment functions on behalf of its employees without meeting the requirements of § 164.504(f), as such functions are considered outside of the plan administration functions. However, the second exception was not stated in the regulation text.

March 2002 NPRM. The ability of group health plans to disclose enrollment or disenrollment information without amending the plan documents was addressed only in the preamble to the Privacy Rule. The absence of a specific provision in the regulation text caused many entities to conclude that plan documents would need to be amended for enrollment and disenrollment information to be exchanged between plans and plan sponsors. To remedy this misunderstanding and make its policy clear, the Department proposed to add an explicit exception at § 164.504(f)(1)(iii) to clarify that group health plans (or health insurance issuers or HMOs with respect to group health plans, as appropriate) are permitted to disclose enrollment or disenrollment information to a plan sponsor without meeting the plan document amendment and other related requirements.

Overview of Public Comments. The following discussion provides an overview of the public comment received on this proposal. Additional comments received on this issue are discussed below in the section entitled, "Response to Other Public Comments."

Commenters in general supported the proposed modification. Some supported the proposal because it was limited to information about whether an individual is participating or enrolled in a group health plan and would not permit the disclosure of any other protected health information. Others asserted that the modification is a reasonable approach because enrollment and disenrollment information is needed by plan sponsors for payroll and other employment reasons.

Final Modifications. The Department adopts the modification to § 164.504(f)(1)(iii) essentially as proposed. Thus, a group health plan, or

C. HIPAA Final Rules, Privacy Standards, continued

53208 Federal Register / Vol. 67, No. 157 / Wednesday, August 14, 2002 / Rules and Regulations

a health insurance issuer or HMO acting for a group health plan, may disclose to a plan sponsor information on whether the individual is participating in the group health plan, or is enrolled in or has disenrolled from a health insurance issuer or HMO offered by the plan. This disclosure can be made without amending the plan documents. In adopting the modification as a final Rule, the Department deletes the phrase "to the plan sponsor" that appeared at the end of the proposed new provision, as mere surplusage.

As a result of the modification, summary health information and enrollment and disenrollment information are treated consistently. Under § 164.504(f), as modified, group health plans can share summary health information and enrollment or disenrollment information with plan sponsors without having to amend the plan documents. Section 164.520(a) provides that a fully insured group health plan does not need to comply with the Privacy Rule's notice requirements if the only protected health information it creates or receives is summary health information and/or information about individuals' enrollment in, or disenrollment from, a health insurer or HMO offered by the group health plan. Similarly, in § 164.530(k), the Department exempts fully insured group health plans from many of the administrative requirements in that section if the only protected health information held by the group health plan is summary health information and/or information about individuals' enrollment in, or disenrollment from, a health insurer or HMO offered by the group health plan. Such consistency will simplify compliance with the Privacy Rule.

Response to Other Public Comments

Comment: One commenter stated that there needs to be protection for health information given to group health plans on enrollment forms. In particular, this commenter suggested that the Department include a definition of "enrollment" or "disenrollment" information that specifies that medical information, such as past or present medical conditions and doctor or hospital visits, is not enrollment information, but rather is individually identifiable health information, and therefore, subject to the Privacy Rule's protections.

Response: Individually identifiable health information received or created by the group health plan for enrollment purposes is protected health information under the Privacy Rule. The modification to § 164.504(f) being

adopted in this rulemaking does not affect this policy. The Privacy Rule does not define the information that may be transmitted for enrollment and disenrollment purposes. Rather, the Department in the Transactions Rule has adopted a standard transaction for enrollment and disenrollment in a health plan. That standard (ASC X12N 834, Benefit Enrollment and Maintenance, Version 4010, May 2000, Washington Publishing Company) specifies the required and situationally required data elements to be transmitted as part of such a transaction. While the standard enrollment and disenrollment transaction does not include any substantial clinical information, the information provided as part of the transaction may indicate whether or not tobacco use, substance abuse, or short, long-term, permanent, or total disability is relevant, when such information is available. However, the Department clarifies that, in disclosing or maintaining information about an individual's enrollment in, or disenrollment from, a health insurer or HMO offered by the group health plan, the group health plan may not include medical information about the individual above and beyond that which is required or situationally required by the standard transaction and still qualify for the exceptions for enrollment and disenrollment information allowed under the Rule.

Comment: Several commenters recommended that enrollment and disenrollment information specifically be excluded from the definition of "protected health information." They argued that this change would be warranted because enrollment and disenrollment information do not include health information. They further argued that such a change would help alleviate confusion surrounding the application of the Privacy Rule to employers.

Response: We disagree that enrollment and disenrollment information should be excluded from the definition of "protected health information." Enrollment and disenrollment information fall under the statutory definition of "individually identifiable health information," since it is received or created by a health plan, identifies an individual, and relates to the past, present, or future payment for the provision of health care to an individual. As such, the Department believes there is no statutory basis to exclude such information from the definition of "protected health information." The Department believes that the exception to the requirement for group health plans to amend plan

documents that has been added to the Privacy Rule for enrollment and disenrollment information balances the legitimate need that plan sponsors have for enrollment and disenrollment information against the individual's right to have such information kept private and confidential.

Comment: Given that, under § 164.504(f)(2), plan sponsors agree not to use or further disclose protected health information other than as permitted or required by plan documents or "required by law," one commenter requested that the definition of "required by law" set forth at § 164.501 should be revised to reflect that it applies not only to covered entities, but also to plan sponsors who are required to report under OSHA or similar laws.

Response: The Department agrees and has made a technical correction to the definition of "required by law" in § 164.501 to reflect that the definition applies to a requirement under law that compels any entity, not just a covered entity, to make a use or disclosure of protected health information.

D. Section 164.506—Uses and Disclosures for Treatment, Payment, and Health Care Operations

1. Consent

December 2000 Privacy Rule. Treatment and payment for health care are core functions of the health care industry, and uses and disclosures of individually identifiable health information for such purposes are critical to the effective operation of the health care system. Health care providers and health plans must also use individually identifiable health information for certain health care operations, such as administrative, financial, and legal activities, to run their businesses and to support the essential health care functions of treatment and payment. Equally important are health care operations designed to maintain and improve the quality of health care. In developing the Privacy Rule, the Department balanced the privacy implications of uses and disclosures for treatment, payment, and health care operations and the need for these core activities to continue. The Department considered the fact that many individuals expect that their health information will be used and disclosed as necessary to treat them, bill for treatment, and, to some extent, operate the covered entity's health care business. Given public expectations with respect to the use or disclosure of information for such activities and so as not to interfere with an individual's

C. HIPAA Final Rules, Privacy Standards, continued

Federal Register / Vol. 67, No. 157 / Wednesday, August 14, 2002 / Rules and Regulations **53209**

access to quality health care or the efficient payment for such health care, the Department's goal is, and has always been, to permit these activities to occur with little or no restriction.

Consistent with this goal, the Privacy Rule published in December 2000 generally provided covered entities with permission to use and disclose protected health information as necessary for treatment, payment, and health care operations. For certain health care providers that have direct treatment relationships with individuals, such as many physicians, hospitals, and pharmacies, the December 2000 Privacy Rule required such providers to obtain an individual's written consent prior to using or disclosing protected health information for these purposes. The Department designed consent as a one-time, general permission from the individual, which the individual would have had the right to revoke. A health care provider could have conditioned treatment on the receipt of consent. Other covered entities also could have chosen to obtain consent but would have been required to follow the consent standards if they opted to do so.

The consent requirement for health care providers with direct treatment relationships was a significant change from the Department's initial proposal published in November 1999. At that time, the Department proposed to permit all covered entities to use and disclose protected health information to carry out treatment, payment, and health care operations without any requirement that the covered entities obtain an individual's consent for such uses and disclosures, subject to a few limited exceptions. Further, the Department proposed to prohibit covered entities from obtaining an individual's consent for uses and disclosures of protected health information for these purposes, unless required by other applicable law.

The transition provisions of the Privacy Rule permit covered health care providers that were required to obtain consent to use and disclose protected health information they created or received prior to the compliance date of the Privacy Rule for treatment, payment, or health care operations if they had obtained consent, authorization, or other express legal permission to use or disclose such information for any of these purposes, even if such permission did not meet the consent requirements of the Privacy Rule.

March 2002 NPRM. The Department heard concerns about significant practical problems that resulted from the consent requirements in the Privacy

Rule. Covered entities and others provided numerous examples of obstacles that the consent provisions would pose to timely access to health care. These examples extended to various types of providers and various settings. The most troubling, pervasive problem was that health care providers would not have been able to use or disclose protected health information for treatment, payment, or health care operations purposes prior to their initial face-to-face contact with the patient, something which is routinely done today to provide patients with timely access to quality health care. A list of some of the more significant examples and concerns are as follows:

• Pharmacists would not have been able to fill a prescription, search for potential drug interactions, determine eligibility, or verify coverage before the individual arrived at the pharmacy to pick up the prescription if the individual had not already provided consent under the Privacy Rule.

• Hospitals would not have been able to use information from a referring physician to schedule and prepare for procedures before the individual presented at the hospital for such procedure, or the patient would have had to make a special trip to the hospital to sign the consent form.

• Providers who do not provide treatment in person may have been unable to provide care because they would have had difficulty obtaining prior written consent to use protected health information at the first service delivery.

• Emergency medical providers were concerned that, if a situation was urgent, they would have had to try to obtain consent to comply with the Privacy Rule, even if that would be inconsistent with appropriate practice of emergency medicine.

• Emergency medical providers were also concerned that the requirement that they attempt to obtain consent as soon as reasonably practicable after an emergency would have required significant efforts and administrative burden which might have been viewed as harassing by individuals, because these providers typically do not have ongoing relationships with individuals.

• Providers who did not meet one of the consent exceptions were concerned that they could have been put in the untenable position of having to decide whether to withhold treatment when an individual did not provide consent or proceed to use information to treat the individual in violation of the consent requirements.

• The right to revoke a consent would have required tracking consents, which

could have hampered treatment and resulted in large institutional providers deciding that it would be necessary to obtain consent at each patient encounter instead.

• The transition provisions would have resulted in significant operational problems, and the inability to access health records would have had an adverse effect on quality activities, because many providers currently are not required to obtain consent for treatment, payment, or health care operations.

• Providers that are required by law to treat were concerned about the mixed messages to patients and interference with the physician-patient relationship that would have resulted because they would have had to ask for consent to use or disclose protected health information for treatment, payment, or health care operations, but could have used or disclosed the information for such purposes even if the patient said "no."

As a result of the large number of treatment-related obstacles raised by various types of health care providers that would have been required to obtain consent, the Department became concerned that individual fixes would be too complex and could possibly overlook important problems. Instead, the Department proposed an approach designed to protect privacy interests by affording patients the opportunity to engage in important discussions regarding the use and disclosure of their health information through the strengthened notice requirement, while allowing activities that are essential to quality health care to occur unimpeded (see section III.H. of the preamble for a discussion of the strengthened notice requirements).

Specifically, the Department proposed to make the obtaining of consent to use and disclose protected health information for treatment, payment, or health care operations more flexible for all covered entities, including providers with direct treatment relationships. Under this proposal, health care providers with direct treatment relationships with individuals would no longer be required to obtain an individual's consent prior to using and disclosing information about him or her for treatment, payment, and health care operations. They, like other covered entities, would have regulatory permission for such uses and disclosures.

The NPRM included provisions to permit covered entities to obtain consent for uses and disclosures of protected health information for treatment, payment, or health care

C. HIPAA Final Rules, Privacy Standards, continued

operations, if they wished to do so. These provisions would grant providers complete discretion in designing this process. These proposed changes were partnered, however, by the proposal to strengthen the notice provisions to require direct treatment providers to make good faith efforts to obtain a written acknowledgment of receipt of the notice. The intent was to preserve the opportunity to raise questions about the entity's privacy policies that the consent requirements previously provided.

Overview of Public Comments. The following discussion provides an overview of the public comment received on this proposal. Additional comments received on this issue are discussed below in the section entitled, "Response to Other Public Comments."

The vast majority of commenters addressed the consent proposal. Most comments fell into three basic categories: (1) Many comments supported the NPRM approach to eliminate the consent requirement; (2) many comments urged the Department to require consent, but make targeted fixes to address workability issues; and (3) some comments urged the Department to strengthen the consent requirement.

The proposed approach of eliminating required consent and making obtaining of consent permissible, at the entity's discretion, was supported by many covered entities that asserted that it would provide the appropriate balance among access to quality health care, administrative burden, and patient privacy. Many argued that the appropriate privacy protections were preserved by strengthening the notice requirement. This approach was also supported by the NCVHS.

The comments received in response to the NPRM continued to raise the issues and obstacles described above, and others. For example, in addition to providing health care services to patients, hospices often provide psychological and emotional support to family members. These consultations often take place long distance and would likely be considered treatment. The consent requirement would make it difficult, or impossible in some circumstances, for hospices to provide these important services to grieving family members on a timely basis. Comments explained that the consent provisions in the Rule pose significant obstacles to oncologists as well. Cancer treatment is referral-based. Oncologists often obtain information from other doctors, hospital, labs, etc., speak with patients by telephone, identify treatment options, and develop

preliminary treatment plans, all before the initial patient visit. The prior consent requirement would prevent all of these important preliminary activities before the first patient visit, which would delay treatment in cases in which such delay cannot be tolerated.

Other commenters continued to strongly support a consent requirement, consistent with their views expressed during the comment period in March 2001. Some argued that the NPRM approach would eliminate an important consumer protection and that such a "radical" approach to fixing the workability issues was not required. They recommended a targeted approach to fixing each problem, and suggested ways to fix each unintended consequence of the consent requirement, in lieu of removing the requirement to obtain consent.

A few commenters argued for reinstating a consent requirement, but making it similar to the proposal for acknowledgment of notice by permitting flexibility and including a "good faith" standard. They also urged the Department to narrow the definition of health care operations and require that de-identified information be used where possible for health care operations.

Finally, a few commenters continued to assert that consent should be strengthened by applying it to more covered entities, requiring it to be obtained more frequently, or prohibiting the conditioning of treatment on the obtaining of consent.

Final Modifications. The Department continues to be concerned by the multitude of comments and examples demonstrating that the consent requirements would result in unintended consequences that would impede the provision of health care in many critical circumstances. We are also concerned that other such unintended consequences may exist which have yet to be brought to our attention. The Department would not have been able to address consent issues arising after publication of this Rule until at least a year had passed from this Rule's publication date due to statutory limitations on the timing of modifications. The Department believes in strong privacy protections for individually identifiable health information, but does not want to compromise timely access to quality health care. The Department also understands that the opportunity to discuss privacy practices and concerns is an important component of privacy, and that the confidential relationship between a patient and a health care provider includes the patient's ability to be involved in discussions and

decisions related to the use and disclosure of protected health information about him or her.

A review of the comments showed that almost all of the commenters that discussed consent acknowledged that there are unintended consequences of the consent requirement that would interfere with treatment. These comments point toward two potential approaches to fixing these problems. The Department could address these problems by adopting a single solution that would address most or all of the concerns, or could address these problems by adopting changes targeted to each specific problem that was brought to the attention of the Department. One of the goals in making changes to the Privacy Rule is to simplify, rather than add complexity to, the Rule. Another goal is to assure that the Privacy Rule does not hamper necessary treatment. For both of these reasons, the Department is concerned about adopting different changes for different issues related to consent and regulating to address specific examples that have been brought to its attention. Therefore, the options that the Department most seriously considered were those that would provide a global fix to the consent problems. Some commenters provided global options other than the proposed approach. However, none of these would have resolved the operational problems created by a mandatory consent.

The Department also reviewed State laws to understand how they approached uses and disclosures of health information for treatment, payment, or health care operations purposes. Of note was the California Confidentiality of Medical Information Act. Cal. Civ. Code § 56. This law permits health care providers and health plans to disclose health information for treatment, payment, and certain types of health care operations purposes without obtaining consent of the individual. The California HealthCare Foundation conducted a medical privacy and confidentiality survey in January 1999 that addressed consumer views on confidentiality of medical records. The results showed that, despite the California law that permitted disclosures of health information without an individual's consent, consumers in California did not have greater concerns about confidentiality than other health care consumers. This is true with respect to trust of providers and health plans to keep health information private and confidential and the level of access to health information that providers and health plans have.

C. HIPAA Final Rules, Privacy Standards, continued

The Department adopts the approach that was proposed in the NPRM, because it is the only one that resolves the operational problems that have been identified in a simple and uniform manner. First, this Rule strengthens the notice requirements to preserve the opportunity for individuals to discuss privacy practices and concerns with providers. (See section III.H. of the preamble for the related discussion of modifications to strengthen the notice requirements.) Second, the final Rule makes the obtaining of consent to use and disclose protected health information for treatment, payment, or health care operations optional on the part of all covered entities, including providers with direct treatment relationships. A health care provider that has a direct treatment relationship with an individual is not required by the Privacy Rule to obtain an individual's consent prior to using and disclosing information about him or her for treatment, payment, and health care operations. They, like other covered entities, have regulatory permission for such uses and disclosures. The fact that there is a State law that has been using a similar model for years provides us confidence that this is a workable approach.

Other rights provided by the Rule are not affected by this modification. Although covered entities will not be required to obtain an individual's consent, any uses or disclosures of protected health information for treatment, payment, or health care operations must still be consistent with the covered entity's notice of privacy practices. Also, the removal of the consent requirement applies only to consent for treatment, payment, and health care operations; it does not alter the requirement to obtain an authorization under § 164.508 for uses and disclosures of protected health information not otherwise permitted by the Privacy Rule or any other requirements for the use or disclosure of protected health information. The Department intends to enforce strictly the requirement for obtaining an individual's authorization, in accordance with § 164.508, for uses and disclosure of protected health information for purposes not otherwise permitted or required by the Privacy Rule. Furthermore, individuals retain the right to request restrictions, in accordance with § 164.522(a). This allows individuals and covered entities to enter into agreements to restrict uses and disclosures of protected health information for treatment, payment, and

health care operations that are enforceable under the Privacy Rule.

Although consent for use and disclosure of protected health information for treatment, payment, and health care operations is no longer mandated, this Final Rule allows covered entities to have a consent process if they wish to do so. The Department heard from many commenters that obtaining consent was an integral part of the ethical and other practice standards for many health care professionals. It, therefore, does not prohibit covered entities from obtaining consent.

This final Rule allows covered entities that choose to have a consent process complete discretion in designing that process. Prior comments have informed the Department that one consent process and one set of principles will likely be unworkable. Covered entities that choose to obtain consent may rely on industry practices to design a voluntary consent process that works best for their practice area and consumers, but they are not required to do so.

This final Rule effectuates these changes in the same manner as proposed by the NPRM. The consent provisions in § 164.506 are replaced with a new provision at § 164.506(a) that provides regulatory permission for covered entities to use or disclose protected health information for treatment, payment, and health care operations. A new provision is added at § 164.506(b) that permits covered entities to obtain consent if they choose to, and makes clear any such consent process does not override or alter the authorization requirements in § 164.508. Section 164.506(b) includes a small change from the proposed version to make it clearer that authorizations are still required by referring directly to authorizations under § 164.508.

Additionally, this final Rule includes a number of conforming modifications, identical to those proposed in the NPRM, to accommodate the new approach. The most substantive corresponding changes are at §§ 164.502 and 164.532. Section 164.502(a)(1) provides a list of the permissible uses and disclosures of protected health information, and refers to the corresponding section of the Privacy Rule for the detailed requirements. The provisions at §§ 164.502(a)(1)(ii) and (iii) that address uses and disclosures of protected health information for treatment, payment, and health care operations are collapsed into a single provision, and the language is modified to eliminate the consent requirement.

The references in § 164.532 to § 164.506 and to consent, authorization,

or other express legal permission obtained for uses and disclosures of protected health information for treatment, payment, and health care operations prior to the compliance date of the Privacy Rule are deleted. The proposal to permit a covered entity to use or disclose protected health information for these purposes without consent or authorization would apply to any protected health information held by a covered entity whether created or received before or after the compliance date. Therefore, transition provisions are not necessary.

This final Rule also includes conforming changes to the definition of "more stringent" in § 160.202; the text of § 164.500(b)(1)(v), §§ 164.508(a)(2)(i) and (b)(3)(i), and § 164.520(b)(1)(ii)(B); the introductory text of §§ 164.510 and 164.512, and the title of § 164.512 to eliminate references to required consent.

Response to Other Public Comments

Comment: There were three categories of commenters with respect to the Rule's general approach to consent—those that supported the changes proposed in the NPRM provisions, those that requested targeted changes to the consent requirement, and those that requested that the consent requirement be strengthened.

Many commenters supported the NPRM approach to consent, making consent to use or disclose protected health information for treatment, payment, and health care operations voluntary for all covered entities. These commenters said that this approach provided flexibility for covered entities to address consent in a way that is consistent with their practices. These commenters also stated that the NPRM approach assured that the Privacy Rule would not interfere with or delay necessary treatment.

Those that advocated retaining a consent requirement stated that the NPRM approach would undermine trust in the health care system and that requiring consent before using or disclosing protected health information shows respect for the patient's autonomy, underscores the need to inform the patient of the risks and benefits of sharing protected health information, and makes it possible for the patient to make an informed decision. Many of these commenters suggested that the consent requirement be retained and that the problems raised by consent be addressed through targeted changes or guidance for each issue.

Some suggestions targeted to specific problems were: (1) Fix the problems

C. HIPAA Final Rules, Privacy Standards, continued

53212   Federal Register / Vol. 67, No. 157 / Wednesday, August 14, 2002 / Rules and Regulations

related to filling prescriptions by treating pharmacists as providers with indirect treatment relationships or by deeming a prescription to serve as an implied consent; and (2) allow certain uses and disclosures prior to first patient encounter. Some of these commenters argued that certain issues could be addressed through guidance on other provisions in the Rule, rather than a change in the regulation. For example, they suggested that guidance could explain that physicians who take phone calls for one another are part of an organized health care arrangement, or could provide technical assistance about revocations on consent by identifying when a covered entity has taken action in reliance on a consent.

Other suggestions were more general. They included suggestions that the Department: (1) Substitute a good faith effort requirement for the current provisions; (2) provide regulatory permission for certain uses and disclosures of protected heath information prior to first service delivery; (3) permit oral consent with documentation; (4) retain a consent requirement for disclosures, but not uses; (5) retain a consent requirement for payment and operations, but not treatment uses and disclosures; (6) allow individuals to opt out of the consent requirement; (7) allow the consent to apply to activities of referred-to providers, and (8) retain the consent requirement but add flexibility, not exceptions.

The third group of commenters requested that the consent requirement be strengthened. Some requested that the Privacy Rule not permit conditioning of treatment or enrollment on consent for multiple uses and disclosures. Others requested that the consent requirement be extended to covered entities other than providers with direct treatment relationships, such as health plans. Some commenters also asked that the consent be time-limited or be required more frequently, such as at each service delivery.

Response: The Department recognizes that there are some benefits to the consent requirement and has considered all options to preserve the consent requirement while fixing the problems it raises. After examining each of these options, we do not believe that any would address all of the issues that were brought to the Department's attention during the comment process or would be the best approach for regulating this area. For example, the suggestion to treat pharmacists as indirect treatment providers would not be consistent with the current regulatory definition of that term and would not have addressed

other referral situations. This approach was also rejected by some pharmacists who view themselves as providing treatment directly to individuals. The suggestion to allow certain uses and disclosures prior to first patient encounter would not address concerns of tracking consents, use of historical data for quality purposes, or the concerns of emergency treatment providers.

The Department desired a global approach to resolving the problems raised by the prior consent requirement, so as not to add additional complexity to the Privacy Rule or apply different standards to different types of direct treatment providers. This approach is consistent with the basic goal of the Rule to provide flexibility as necessary for the standards to work for all sectors of the health care industry.

More global approaches suggested were carefully considered, but each had some flaw or failed to address all of the treatment-related concerns brought to our attention. For example, those who suggested that the Rule be modified to require a good faith effort to obtain consent at first service delivery failed to explain how that approach would provide additional protection than the approach we proposed. The Department also decided against eliminating the consent requirement only for uses and disclosures for treatment, or only for uses of protected health information but not for disclosures, because these options fall short of addressing all of the problems raised. Scheduling appointments and surgeries, and conducting many pre-admission activities, are health care operations activities, not treatment. Retaining the consent requirement for payment would be problematic because, in cases where a provider, such as a pharmacist or hospital, engages in a payment activity prior to face-to-face contact with the individual, it would prohibit the provider from contacting insurance companies to obtain pre-certification or to verify coverage.

Similarly, the suggestion to limit the prior consent requirement to disclosures and not to uses would not have addressed all of the problems raised by the consent requirements. Many of the basic activities that occur before the initial face-to-face meeting between a provider and an individual involve disclosures as well as uses. Like the previous approach, this approach also would prohibit pharmacists and hospitals from contacting insurance companies to obtain pre-certification or verify coverage if they did not have the individual's prior consent to disclose the protected health information for

payment. It also would prohibit a provider from contacting another provider to ask questions about the medical record and discuss the patient's condition, because this would be a disclosure and would require consent.

There was a substantial amount of support from commenters for the approach taken in the NPRM. The Department continues to believe that this approach makes the most sense and meets the goals of not interfering with access to quality health care and of providing a single standard that works for the entire health care industry. Therefore, the Department has adopted the approach proposed in the NPRM.

Comment: Some commenters asserted that eliminating the consent requirement would be a departure from current medical ethical standards that protect patient confidentiality and common law and State law remedies for breach of confidentiality that generally require or support patient consent prior to disclosing patient information for any reason. Another commenter was concerned that the removal of the consent requirement from the Privacy Rule will become the de facto industry standard and supplant professional ethical duties to obtain consent for the use of protected health information.

Response: The Privacy Rule provides a floor of privacy protection. State laws that are more stringent remain in force. In order not to interfere with such laws and ethical standards, this Rule permits covered entities to obtain consent. Nor is the Privacy Rule intended to serve as a "best practices" standard. Thus, professional standards that are more protective of privacy retain their vitality.

Comment: Some commenters requested that, if the Department adopts the NPRM approach to eliminate the consent requirement for uses and disclosures of protected health information for treatment, payment, or health care operations, the definition of "health care operations" should also be narrowed to protect individual expectations of privacy.

Response: We disagree. As stated in the preamble to the December 2000 Privacy Rule, the Department believes that narrowing the definition of "health care operations" will place serious burdens on covered entities and impair their ability to conduct legitimate business and management functions.

Comment: Some commenters requested that the regulation text state more specifically that a voluntary consent cannot substitute for an authorization when an authorization is otherwise required under the Privacy Rule.

C. HIPAA Final Rules, Privacy Standards, continued

Federal Register / Vol. 67, No. 157 / Wednesday, August 14, 2002 / Rules and Regulations   53213

Response: The Department agrees and modifies the regulation text, at § 164.506(b)(2), to make this clear. As stated in the preamble to the NPRM, the Department intends to enforce strictly the requirement for obtaining an individual's authorization, in accordance with § 164.508, for uses and disclosures of protected health information for purposes not otherwise permitted or required by the Privacy Rule. A consent obtained voluntarily would not be sufficient to permit a use or disclosure which, under the Privacy Rule, requires an authorization or is otherwise expressly conditioned under the Rule. For example, a consent under § 164.506 could not be obtained in lieu of an authorization required by § 164.508 or a waiver of authorization by an IRB or Privacy Board under § 164.512(i) to disclose protected health information for research purposes.

Comment: Some commenters requested that, if the Department decides to allow consent on a voluntary basis, the Privacy Rule include requirements for those covered entities that voluntarily choose to obtain consents.

Response: The goal of the NPRM approach was to enhance flexibility for covered entities by allowing them to design a consent process that best matches their needs. The Department learned over the past year that no single consent process works for all covered entities. In addition, the Department wants to encourage covered entities to adopt a consent process, and is concerned that by prescribing particular rules, it would discourage some covered entities from doing so.

Comment: Some commenters asserted that the consent requirement provides individuals with control because providers may not opt to withhold treatment if a patient refuses consent only for the use or disclosure of protected health information for health care operations.

Response: These commenters may not fully understand the consent requirements in the December 2000 Rule. That requirement did not allow separate consents for use of protected health information for treatment, payment, and health care operations. The only way to allow use of protected health information for treatment but not for health care operations purposes would have been to invoke the right to request restrictions (§ 164.522(a)); the provider could agree or not agree to restrict use and disclosure of protected health information for health care operations. That is also how the Rule will work with these modifications. The

Department is not modifying the right to request restrictions.

Comment: Some commenters were confused about the relationship between the proposed changes to the consent provisions and State law. Some were concerned that the Privacy Rule would override State consent laws which provide stronger protections for medical and psychotherapeutic privacy.

Response: The Privacy Rule does not weaken the operation of State laws that require consent to use or disclose health information. The Privacy Rule permits a covered entity to obtain consent to use or disclose health information, and, therefore, presents no barrier to the entity's ability to comply with State law requirements.

Comment: One commenter suggested that the consent requirement be retained to protect victims of domestic violence.

Response: The Department understands the concerns that the Privacy Rule not endanger victims of domestic violence, but we do not believe that eliminating the consent requirement will do so. The Department believes that the provisions that provide real protections to victims of domestic violence in how information is used or disclosed for treatment, payment, and health care operations, are provisions that allow an individual to object to disclosure of directory information and of protected health information to family members or friends involved in the individual's care (*see* § 164.510), that provide an individual the right to request restrictions (*see* § 164.522(a)), and that grant an individual the right to request confidential communications (*see* § 164.522(b)). These provisions are not affected by the changes in this final Rule.

Comment: One commenter asserted that written consent represents a signed agreement between the provider and patient regarding the manner in which covered entities will use and disclose health information in the future, and that the removal of this requirement would shift "ownership" of records from patients to doctors and corporate entities.

Response: The Department disagrees with this position. Our research indicates that a signed consent form is most typically treated as a waiver of rights by a patient and not as a binding agreement between a provider and a patient. Further, many States have laws assigning the ownership of records, apart from any consent requirements. The Privacy Rule does not address, and is not intended to affect, existing laws governing the ownership of health records.

Comment: A few commenters claimed that the signed notice of a provider's privacy policy is meaningless if the individual has no right to withhold consent and the NPRM approach would reinforce the fact that individuals have no say in how their health information is used or disclosed.

Response: The Department disagrees. The individual's options under the consent requirement established by the Privacy Rule published in December 2000 and the voluntary consent and strengthened notice provisions adopted by this Rule are the same. Under the previous Rule, a patient who disagreed with the covered entity's information practices as stated in the notice could withhold consent and not receive treatment, or could sign the consent form and obtain treatment despite concerns about the information practices. The patient could request that the provider restrict the use and/or disclosure of the information. Under the Rule as modified, a patient who disagrees with the covered entity's information practices as stated in the notice, can choose not to receive treatment from that provider, or can obtain treatment despite concerns about the information practices. The patient can request that the provider restrict the use and/or disclosure of the information. The result, for the patient, is the same.

Comment: One commenter requested clarification with respect to the effect of a revocation of voluntary consent and whether agreed-to restrictions must be honored.

Response: The final Rule is silent as to how a covered entity handles the revocation of a voluntary consent under § 164.506(b)(1). The Rule provides the covered entity that chooses to adopt a consent process discretion to design the process that works for that entity.

The change to the consent provision in the Privacy Rule does not affect the right of an individual under § 164.522(a) to request restrictions to a use or disclosure of protected health information. While a covered entity is not required to agree to such restrictions, it must act in accordance with any restriction it does agree to. Failure of a covered entity to act in accordance with an agreed-to restriction is a violation of the Rule.

Comment: Commenters asked the Department to rename consent to "consent for information use" to reduce confusion with consent for treatment.

Response: In order to clear up confusion between informed consent for treatment, which is addressed by State law, and consent to use or disclose protected health information under the

C. HIPAA Final Rules, Privacy Standards, continued

Privacy Rule, we changed the title of § 164.506(b) from "Consent permitted" to "Consent for uses and disclosures of information permitted." The Privacy Rule does not affect informed consent for treatment.

Comment: A few commenters requested that the Department modify the regulation to state that de-identified information should be used for health care operations where possible.

Response: The Department continues to encourage covered entities to use de-identified information wherever possible. As the Department has made this position clear in the preambles to both the December 2000 Privacy Rule and the March 2002 NPRM, as well as in this preamble, we do not believe that it is necessary to modify the regulation to include such language. Further, the minimum necessary requirements, under §§ 164.502(b)(2) and 164.514(d), already require a covered entity to make reasonable efforts to limit protected health information used for health care operations and other purposes to the minimum necessary to accomplish the intended purpose, which may, in some cases, be de-identified information.

Comment: One commenter requested that the Privacy Rule state that consent is not required for provider-to-provider communications.

Response: Prior to these final modifications, the consent requirements of the Privacy Rule would have required a provider to obtain written consent to disclose protected health information to another provider for treatment purposes—which could have interfered with an individual's ability to obtain timely access to quality care. This is one reason the Department has eliminated the consent requirement for treatment, payment, and health care operations. Providers will not need a patient's consent to consult with other providers about the treatment of a patient. However, if a provider is disclosing protected health information to another provider for purposes other than treatment, payment, or health care operations, an authorization may be required under § 164.508 (e.g., generally, disclosures for clinical trials would require an authorization).

Comment: One commenter asserted that, without a consent requirement, nothing will stop a health plan from demanding a patient's mental health records as a condition of payment for physical therapy.

Response: The Department does not agree that the former consent requirement is the relevant standard with respect to the activities of the health plan that concern the commenter. Rather, the Transactions Rule and the minimum necessary standard of the Privacy Rule prescribe and limit the health information that may be disclosed as part of payment transactions between health plans and health care providers. Although a health plan may request additional information to process a specific claim, in addition to the required and situational elements under the Transactions Rule, the request must comply with the Privacy Rule's minimum necessary requirements. In this example, the health plan can only request mental health records if they are reasonably necessary for the plan to process the physical therapy claim.

2. Disclosures for Treatment, Payment, or Health Care Operations of Another Entity

December 2000 Privacy Rule. The Privacy Rule permits a covered entity to use and disclose protected health information for treatment, payment, or health care operations. For treatment purposes, the Rule generally allows protected health information to be shared without restriction. The definition of "treatment" incorporates the necessary interaction of more than one entity. In particular, the definition of "treatment" includes the coordination and management of health care among health care providers or by a health care provider with a third party, consultations between health care providers, and referrals of a patient for health care from one health care provider to another. As a result, covered entities are permitted to disclose protected health information for treatment purposes regardless of to whom the disclosure is made, as well as to disclose protected health information for the treatment activities of another health care provider.

However, for payment and health care operations, the Privacy Rule, as published in December 2000, generally limited a covered entity's uses and disclosures of protected health information to those that were necessary for its own payment and health care operations activities. This limitation was explicitly stated in the December 2000 preamble discussions of the definitions of "payment" and "health care operations." 65 FR 82490, 82495. The Privacy Rule also provided that a covered entity must obtain authorization to disclose protected health information for the payment or health care operations of another entity. The Department intended these requirements to be consistent with individuals' privacy expectations. *See* 45 CFR 164.506(a)(5) and 164.508(e).

March 2002 NPRM. Since the publication of the December 2000 Rule, a number of commenters raised specific concerns with the restriction that a covered entity may not disclose protected health information for another entity's payment and health care operations activities, absent an authorization. These commenters presented a number of examples where such a restriction would impede the ability of certain entities to obtain reimbursement for health care, to conduct certain quality assurance or improvement activities, such as accreditation, or to monitor fraud and abuse.

With regard to payment, for example, the Department heard concerns of ambulance service providers who explained that they normally receive the information they need to obtain payment for their treatment services from the hospital emergency departments to which they transport their patients. They explained that it is usually not possible for the ambulance service provider to obtain such information directly from the individual, nor is it always practicable or feasible for the hospital to obtain the individual's authorization to provide payment information to the ambulance service provider. This disclosure of protected health information from the hospital to the ambulance service provider was not permitted under the December 2000 Privacy Rule without an authorization from the patient, because it was a disclosure by the hospital for the payment activities of the ambulance service provider.

Commenters also were concerned about situations in which covered entities outsource their billing, claims, and reimbursement functions to accounts receivable management companies. These collectors often attempt to recover payments from a patient on behalf of multiple health care providers. Commenters were concerned that the Privacy Rule would prevent these collectors, as business associates of multiple providers, from using a patient's demographic information received from one provider to facilitate collection for another provider's payment.

With regard to health care operations, the Department also received comments about the difficulty that the Privacy Rule would place on health plans trying to obtain information needed for quality assessment activities. Health plans informed the Department that they need to obtain individually identifiable health information from health care providers for the plans' quality-related activities, accreditation, and performance measures, such as Health Plan Employer Data and Information Set

C. HIPAA Final Rules, Privacy Standards, continued

(HEDIS). Commenters explained that the information provided to plans for payment purposes (e.g., claims or encounter information) may not be sufficient for quality assessment or accreditation purposes.

The NCVHS, in response to public testimony on this issue at its August 2001 hearing, also recommended that the Department amend the Privacy Rule to allow for uses and disclosures for quality-related activities among covered entities, without the individual's written authorization.

Based on these concerns, the Department proposed to modify § 164.506 to permit a covered entity to disclose protected health information for the payment activities of another covered entity or any health care provider, and also for certain types of health care operations of another covered entity. The proposal would broaden the uses and disclosures that are permitted without authorization as part of treatment, payment, and health care operations so as not to interfere inappropriately with access to quality and effective health care, while limiting this expansion in order to continue to protect the privacy expectations of the individual.

Specifically, the Department proposed the following. First, the Department proposed to add to § 164.506(c)(1) language stating that a covered entity may use or disclose protected health information for its own treatment, payment, or health care operations without prior permission.

Second, the Department proposed to include language in § 164.506(c)(2) to clarify its intent that a covered entity may share protected health information for the treatment activities of another health care provider. For example, a primary care provider who is a covered entity under the Privacy Rule may send a copy of an individual's medical record to a specialist who needs the information to treat the same individual, whether or not that specialist is also a covered entity. No authorization would be required.

Third, the Department proposed to include language in § 164.506(c)(3) to permit a covered entity to disclose protected health information to another covered entity or any health care provider for the payment activities of that entity. The Department recognized that not all health care providers who need protected health information to obtain payment are covered entities, and, therefore, proposed to allow disclosures of protected health information to both covered and non-covered health care providers. In addition, the Department proposed a

conforming change to delete the word "covered" in paragraph (1)(ii) of the definition of "payment," to permit disclosures to non-covered providers for their payment activities.

The Department also proposed to limit disclosures under this provision to those health plans that are covered by the Privacy Rule. However, the Department solicited comment on whether plans that are not covered by the Privacy Rule would be able to obtain the protected health information that they need for payment purposes.

Fourth, in § 164.506(c)(4), the Department proposed to permit a covered entity to disclose protected health information about an individual to another covered entity for specified health care operations purposes of the covered entity that receives the information, provided that both entities have a relationship with the individual. This proposed expansion was limited in a number of ways. The proposal would permit such disclosures only for the activities described in paragraphs (1) and (2) of the definition of "health care operations," as well as for health care fraud and abuse detection and compliance programs (as provided for in paragraph (4) of the definition of "health care operations"). The activities that fall into paragraphs (1) and (2) of the definition of "health care operations" include quality assessment and improvement activities, population-based activities relating to improving health or reducing health care costs, case management, conducting training programs, and accreditation, certification, licensing, or credentialing activities. The Department proposed this limitation because it recognized that "health care operations" is a broad term and that individuals are less aware of the business-related activities that are part of health care operations than they are of treatment- or payment-related activities. In addition, many commenters and the NCVHS focused their comments on covered entities' needs to share protected health information for quality-related health care operations activities. The proposed provision was intended to allow information to flow from one covered entity to another for activities important to providing quality and effective health care.

The proposal would have applied only to disclosures of protected health information to other covered entities. By limiting such disclosures to those entities that are required to comply with the Privacy Rule, the Department intended to ensure that the protected health information remained protected. The Department believed that this

would create the appropriate balance between meeting an individual's privacy expectations and meeting a covered entity's need for information for quality-related health care operations.

Further, such disclosures would be permitted only to the extent that each entity has, or had, a relationship with the individual who is the subject of the information being disclosed. Where the relationship between the individual and the covered entity has ended, a disclosure of protected health information about the individual would be allowed only if related to the past relationship. The Department believed that this limitation would be necessary in order to further protect the privacy expectations of the individual.

The proposal made clear that these provisions would not eliminate a covered entity's responsibility to apply the Privacy Rule's minimum necessary provisions to both the disclosure of and request for protected health information for payment and health care operations purposes. In addition, the proposal strongly encouraged the use of de-identified information, wherever feasible.

While the Department stated that it believed it had struck the right balance with respect to the proposed modification for disclosures for health care operations, the Department was aware that the proposal could pose barriers to disclosures for quality-related health care operations to health plans and health care providers that are not covered entities, or to entities that do not have a relationship with the individual. Therefore, the preamble referred commenters to the Department's request for comment on an approach that would permit for any health care operations purposes the disclosure of protected health information that does not contain direct identifiers, subject to a data use or similar agreement.

In addition, related to the above modifications and in response to comments evidencing confusion on this matter, the Department also proposed to clarify that covered entities participating in an organized health care arrangement (OHCA) may share protected health information for the health care operations of the OHCA (§ 164.506(c)(5)). The Department also proposed to remove the language regarding OHCAs from the definition of "health care operations" as unnecessary because such language now would appear in § 164.506(c)(5).

Overview of Public Comments. The following discussion provides an overview of the public comment received on this proposal. Additional

C. HIPAA Final Rules, Privacy Standards, continued

53216   Federal Register / Vol. 67, No. 157 / Wednesday, August 14, 2002 / Rules and Regulations

comments received on this issue are discussed below in the section entitled, "Response to Other Public Comments."

The Department received a number of comments on its proposal to permit a covered entity to disclose protected health information for the payment and health care operations activities of other entities.

Most of the commenters who addressed the Department's proposed clarification regarding treatment expressed support for the clarification. Also, the majority of commenters supported, either wholly or in part, the Department's proposal to expand the payment and health care operations disclosures that would be permitted.

Most commenters generally were supportive of the Department's proposed approach regarding disclosures for payment. A number of commenters stated that the proposed expansion is important to facilitate coordination of benefits for many patients who have multiple sources of payment for prescription drugs. One commenter, however, requested that the Department narrow its proposed language to address only those problems specifically described in the preamble, that is, payment issues faced by ambulance providers and collection agencies that are business associates of multiple health care providers. This commenter stated that, at the very least, covered entities should be required to obtain assurances from non-covered providers, prior to disclosure of protected health information, that the recipient will not use protected health information for any other purpose or disclose it to others. Another commenter remarked that the proposal to limit disclosures only to another covered entity or any health care provider may impede disclosures to reinsurers that are not covered entities.

While most commenters supported expanding disclosures for health care operations, many requested that the Department modify the proposal in a number of ways. For example, a number of health plans and others requested that the Department eliminate the condition that both covered entities have a relationship with the individual. Some of these commenters explained that such a restriction would impede some fraud and abuse activities, credentialing investigations, and quality assurance research and outcome studies. Some commenters asked that the Department clarify that the condition that both covered entities have a relationship with the individual would not be limited to a current relationship, but also would include a past relationship with the individual.

In addition, many commenters requested that the Department expand the proposed provision to allow for disclosures for any type of health care operation of another covered entity, or at least additional activities beyond those specified in the proposal. Some health plans commented that they may need information from a health care provider in order for the health plan to resolve member or internal grievances, provide customer service, arrange for legal services, or conduct medical review or auditing activities. A number of commenters requested that the proposal be expanded to allow for disclosures for another covered entity's underwriting or premium rating.

Some commenters also requested that the Department expand the provision to allow for disclosures to non-covered entities. In particular, a number of these commenters urged that the Department allow disclosures to non-covered insurers for fraud and abuse purposes. Some of these commenters specifically requested that the Department allow for disclosures to affiliated entities or non-health care components of the covered entity for purposes of investigating fraud and abuse. A few commenters requested that the Rule allow for disclosures to a non-covered health care provider for that provider's operations. For example, it was explained that an independent emergency services provider, who is not a covered entity and who often asks for outcome information on patients it has treated and transported to a facility because it wants to improve care, would be unable to obtain such information absent the individual's authorization.

Some commenters were generally opposed to the proposed expansion of the disclosures permitted under the Rule for health care operations purposes, viewing the proposal as a weakening of the Privacy Rule. One of these commenters urged the Department to implement a targeted solution allowing disclosures for only those activities specifically identified as problematic in the preamble, instead of allowing disclosures for all activities that fall within certain paragraphs within the definition of "health care operations."

Final Modifications. In this final Rule, the Department adopts its proposal to allow covered entities to disclose protected health information for the treatment, payment, and certain health care operations purposes of another entity. Specifically, the final Rule at § 164.506(c):

(1) States that a covered entity may use or disclose protected health information for its own treatment, payment, or health care operations.

(2) Clarifies that a covered entity may use or disclose protected health information for the treatment activities of any health care provider.

(3) Permits a covered entity to disclose protected health information to another covered entity or any health care provider for the payment activities of the entity that receives the information.

(4) Permits a covered entity to disclose protected health information to another covered entity for the health care operations activities of the entity that receives the information, if each entity either has or had a relationship with the individual who is the subject of the information, the protected health information pertains to such relationship, and the disclosure is:

(i) For a purpose listed in paragraphs (1) or (2) of the definition of "health care operations," which includes quality assessment and improvement activities, population-based activities relating to improving health or reducing health care costs, case management and care coordination, conducting training programs, and accreditation, licensing, or credentialing activities; or

(ii) For the purpose of health care fraud and abuse detection or compliance.

(5) Clarifies that a covered entity that participates in an organized health care arrangement may disclose protected health information about an individual to another covered entity that participates in the organized health care arrangement for any health care operations activities of the organized health care arrangement.

Based on the comments received, the Department believes that the above provisions strike the appropriate balance between meeting an individual's privacy expectations and meeting a covered entity's need for information for reimbursement and quality purposes. The Department also clarifies that disclosures pursuant to the above provisions may be made to or by a business associate of a covered entity.

In § 164.506(c)(2), in response to a comment, the Department deletes the word "another" before "health care provider" to eliminate any implication that the disclosing entity must also be a health care provider.

With respect to payment, the majority of commenters were supportive of the Department's proposal. In response to those commenters who expressed support for the proposal because it would facilitate coordination of benefits, the Department clarifies that the definition of "payment" in the

C. HIPAA Final Rules, Privacy Standards, continued

Federal Register / Vol. 67, No. 157 / Wednesday, August 14, 2002 / Rules and Regulations **53217**

Privacy Rule allows for uses and disclosures necessary for coordination of benefits. The new language may, however, reinforce that uses and disclosures for such purposes are permitted under the Rule.

The Department does not believe, as suggested by one commenter, that a targeted approach, one that would address only the problems raised by the ambulance providers and collection agencies, is a practical solution to these problems. The Department believes that these problems may apply in other situations. For example, an indirect treatment provider, such as a pathologist, may need to obtain health coverage information about an individual for billing purposes from the hospital to which the pathologist provided services. If the Department addressed only these discrete scenarios in this final modification, each additional similar problem that arises would require another rulemaking, which would, in and of itself, create a problem because the Department can change a standard only once per year. In addition, by creating special rules to address multiple, distinct circumstances, the Department would have created a substantially more complicated policy for covered entities to follow and implement.

The suggestion that the Department require a covered entity to obtain assurances from non-covered providers, prior to disclosure of protected health information for payment purposes, that the recipient will not use protected health information for any other purpose or disclose it to others, similarly would add a layer of complexity to payment disclosures. Such a requirement would encumber these communications and may interfere with the ability of non-covered health care providers to be paid for treatment they have provided. Moreover, the Privacy Rule requires a covered entity to apply the minimum necessary standard to disclosures for a non-covered provider's payment purposes. Thus, a non-covered provider will receive only the minimum information reasonably necessary for such purposes. Accordingly, the Department believes the final Rule appropriately and practically addresses the issue.

In response to the comment that the proposal may impede disclosures to reinsurers who are not covered entities, the Department clarifies that disclosures to obtain payment under a contract for reinsurance explicitly are permitted as part of the definition of "payment," regardless of whether the reinsurer is a covered entity. Similarly, disclosures for the purposes of ceding, securing, or placing a contract for reinsurance of risk relating to claims for health care are explicitly permitted as part of the definition of "health care operations," also without regard to whether the reinsurer is a covered entity. *See* the definitions of "payment" and "health care operations" in § 164.501.

With respect to disclosures for the health care operations of another covered entity, the Department continues to believe that the condition that both entities have a relationship with the individual is appropriate to balance an individual's privacy expectations with a covered entity's need for the information. The Department clarifies that a covered entity, prior to making a disclosure allowed under this requirement, is permitted to communicate with another covered entity as necessary to determine if this condition has been met. Additionally, in response to comments, the Department adds language to § 164.506(c)(4) to make clear that the condition that both covered entities have a relationship with the individual is not limited to a current relationship. Where the relationship between the covered entity and the individual has ended, a disclosure of protected health information about the individual is permitted to the extent the disclosure is related to the past relationship. For example, the final Rule would permit a health care provider to disclose protected health information to a health plan for HEDIS purposes, even if the individual no longer was covered by the health plan, provided that the period for which information is needed overlaps with the period for which the individual was enrolled in the health plan.

In response to commenters who were concerned that this condition would impede certain health care operations activities where the covered entity may not have a relationship with the individual, the Department notes that the new limited data set provisions in § 164.514(e) are intended to provide a mechanism for disclosures of protected health information for quality and other health care operations where the covered entity requesting the information does not have a relationship with the individual. Under those provisions, the final modifications permit a covered entity to disclose protected health information, with direct identifiers removed, for any health care operations activities of the entity requesting the information, subject to a data use agreement. Additionally, as clarified by § 164.506(c)(5), covered entities that participate in an OHCA may share protected health information for the health care operations of the OHCA, without the condition that each covered entity have a relationship with the individual who is the subject of the information. The Department believes that such provisions provide adequate avenues for covered entities to obtain the information they need for health care operations activities, without eliminating appropriate privacy protections and conditions on such disclosures.

The Department also was not persuaded by the comments that the proposal should be broadened to allow disclosures for other types of health care operations activities, such as resolution of internal grievances, customer service, or medical review or auditing activities. The Department believes that the provisions at § 164.506(c)(5), which permit covered entities that participate in an OHCA to share information for any health care operations activities of the OHCA, adequately provides for such disclosures. For example, a health plan and the health care providers in its network that participate as part of the same OHCA are permitted to share information for any of the activities listed in the definition of "health care operations." The Department understands the need for entities participating in these joint arrangements to have shared access to information for health care operations purposes and intended the OHCA provisions to provide for such access. Where such a joint arrangement does not exist and fully identifiable health information is needed, one covered entity may disclose protected health information for another covered entity's health care operations pursuant to an individual's authorization as required by § 164.508. In addition, as described above, a covered entity also may disclose protected health information as part of a limited data set, with direct identifiers removed, for such purposes, as permitted by § 164.514(e).

With respect to underwriting and premium rating, a few commenters raised similar concerns that the Department's proposal to expand the disclosures permitted under health care operations would not allow for the disclosures between a health insurance issuer and a group health plan, or the agent or broker as a business associate of the plan, needed to perform functions related to supplementing or replacing insurance coverage, such as to solicit bids from prospective issuers. The Department clarifies that, if more than summary health information is needed for this purpose, paragraphs (3), (4), and (5) of the definition of "organized health

C. HIPAA Final Rules, Privacy Standards, continued

care arrangement" may permit the disclosure. These provisions define the arrangements between group health plans and their health insurance issuers or HMOs as OHCAs, which are permitted to share information for each other's health care operations. Such disclosures also may be made to a broker or agent that is a business associate of the health plan. The Department clarifies that the OHCA provisions also permit the sharing of protected health information between such entities even when they no longer have a current relationship, that is, when a group health plan needs protected health information from a former issuer. The Department, therefore, does not believe that a broadening of the provisions under § 164.506(c)(4), to allow disclosures of protected health information for other types of health care operations activities, is warranted.

The final Rule also adopts the condition proposed in the NPRM that disclosures for these health care operations may be made only to another covered entity. The Department continues to consider such a condition necessary to appropriately balance an individual's privacy interests with entities' needs for the information. The Department was not convinced by the commenters who urged that this condition needed to be eliminated to allow for disclosures to non-covered health care providers or third parties. The Department believes that permitting disclosures of protected health information to a non-covered provider for that provider's treatment and payment purposes is warranted and appropriate so as not to impede such core activities. However, given that an individual's health information will no longer be protected when it is disclosed to a non-covered provider, the Department does not consider disclosures for a non-covered provider's health care operations to warrant similar consideration under the Rule. Moreover, this final Rule at § 164.514(e) permits a covered entity to disclose a limited data set, with direct identifiers removed, to a non-covered provider for any of the provider's health care operations purposes, without individual authorization.

Also, the Department believes that expanding the provision to allow disclosures to a third party for any of the third party's business operations would severely weaken the Privacy Rule and essentially negate the need for individual authorization. With respect to those commenters who urged the Department to permit disclosures to non-health care components of a hybrid

entity or to an affiliated entity for the purposes of investigating fraud and abuse, the Department's position is that disclosures to a non-health care component within a hybrid entity or to a non-covered affiliated entity present the same privacy risks as do disclosures to a non-covered entity. The Privacy Rule, therefore, permits such disclosures only to the same extent the disclosures are permitted to a separate entity. This policy is further explained in section III.C.1. regarding hybrid entities.

Lastly, the Department believes that the final Rule does in fact implement a targeted solution to the problems previously identified by commenters, by allowing disclosures for only quality-related and fraud and abuse activities. The Department does not believe further limiting such disclosures to only certain activities within paragraphs (1) and (2) of the definition of "health care operations" is practical or appropriate. The Department is aware of the important role that these quality-related activities play in ensuring that individuals have access to quality health care. Covered entities have a legitimate need for protected health information in order to conduct these quality activities, regardless of whether such information is used for HEDIS purposes or for training. Moreover, as described above, the final Rule retains a number of conditions on such disclosures that serve to protect an individual's privacy interests and expectations. In addition, the Privacy Rule requires that the minimum necessary standard be applied to both covered entities' requests for and disclosures of protected health information for such purposes.

Response to Other Public Comments

Comment: One commenter urged that the Department permit disclosures among participants in an OHCA only when their privacy notices (or any joint notice they issue) informs individuals of this possibility.

Response: The Privacy Rule requires the joint notice of an OHCA to reflect the fact that the notice covers more than one covered entity and that, if applicable, the covered entities participating in the OHCA will share protected health information with each other, as necessary to carry out treatment, payment, or health care operations relating to the OHCA. *See* § 164.520(d). Where the participants of an OHCA choose to have separate notices, such notices must reflect and describe in sufficient detail the particular uses and disclosures that each covered entity may make to place the

individual on notice. This detail should include disclosures to other members of an OHCA, where appropriate.

Comment: Another commenter requested clarification as to whether a covered entity (such as an HMO) is permitted to disclose protected health information for payment and health care operations both to the group health plan and to the plan's third party administrator or plan sponsor. The commenter stated that it was not clear from the proposal whether a covered entity could share protected health information directly with another covered entity's business associate.

Response: The Department clarifies that, if the Rule permits a covered entity to share protected health information with another covered entity, the covered entity is permitted to disclose protected health information directly to a business associate acting on behalf of that other covered entity. This is true with respect to all of the Rule's provisions. Also, an HMO may disclose protected health information to a group health plan, or a third party administrator that is a business associate of the plan, because the relationship between the HMO and the group health plan is defined as an OHCA for purposes of the Rule. See § 164.501, definition of "organized health care arrangement." The group health plan (or the HMO with respect to the group health plan) may disclose protected health information to a plan sponsor in accordance with § 164.504(f).

Comment: Several commenters requested that the Department expand the definition of "payment" to include disclosures to a responsible party. Additionally, these commenters urged that the Department permit covered entities (and their business associates) to use and disclose protected health information as permitted by other law, rather than only as required by law. These commenters were concerned that the Privacy Rule would impede the ability of first-party billing companies, collection agencies, and accounts receivable management companies to continue to bill and communicate, on behalf of a health care provider, with the responsible party on an account when that person is different from the individual to whom health care services were provided; report outstanding receivables owed by the responsible party on an account to a credit reporting agency; and perform collection litigation services.

Response: The Department does not believe a modification to the definition of "payment" is necessary. The Privacy Rule permits a covered entity, or a business associate acting on behalf of a covered entity (*e.g.*, a collection agency),

C. HIPAA Final Rules, Privacy Standards, continued

to disclose protected health information as necessary to obtain payment for health care, and does not limit to whom such a disclosure may be made. See the definition of "payment" in § 164.501. Therefore, a collection agency, as a business associate of a covered entity, is permitted to contact persons other than the individual to whom health care is provided as necessary to obtain payment for such services.

Regarding the commenters' concerns about collection or payment activities otherwise permitted by law, the Department clarifies that the Privacy Rule permits covered entities to use and disclose protected health information as required by other law, or as permitted by other law provided that such use or disclosure does not conflict with the Privacy Rule. For example, the Privacy Rule permits a collection agency, as a business associate of a covered health care provider, to use and disclose protected health information as necessary to obtain reimbursement for health care services, which could include disclosures of certain protected health information to a credit reporting agency, or as part of collection litigation. See the definition of "payment" in § 164.501.

The Department notes, however, that a covered entity, and its business associate through its contract, is required to reasonably limit the amount of information disclosed for such purposes to the minimum necessary, where applicable, as well as abide by any reasonable requests for confidential communications and any agreed-to restrictions as required by the Privacy Rule.

Comment: One commenter asked that the Department clarify that disclosure by an eye doctor to confirm a contact prescription received by a mail-order contact company is treatment.

Response: The Department agrees that disclosure of protected health information by an eye doctor to a distributor of contact lenses for the purpose of confirming a contact lens prescription is treatment and is permissible under § 164.506. In relevant part, treatment is defined by the Privacy Rule as "the provision, coordination, or management of health care and related services by one or more health care providers, including the coordination or management of health care by a health care provider with a third party * * *" Health care is defined, in part, as "care, services, or supplies related to the health of an individual. Health care includes * * * Sale or dispensing of a drug, device, equipment, or other item in accordance with a prescription." Therefore, the dispensing of contact

lenses based on a prescription is health care and the disclosure of protected health information by a provider to confirm a prescription falls within the provision, coordination, or management of health care and related services and is a treatment activity.

E. Uses and Disclosures for Which Authorization Is Required

1. Restructuring Authorization

December 2000 Privacy Rule. The Privacy Rule requires individual authorization for uses and disclosures of protected health information for purposes that are not otherwise permitted or required under the Rule. To ensure that authorizations are informed and voluntary, the Rule prohibits, with limited exceptions, covered entities from conditioning treatment, payment, or eligibility for benefits or enrollment in a health plan, on obtaining an authorization. The Rule also permits, with limited exceptions, individuals to revoke an authorization at any time. Additionally, the Rule sets out core elements that must be included in any authorization. These elements are intended to provide individuals with the information they need to make an informed decision about giving their authorization. This information includes specific details about the use or disclosure, and provides the individual fair notice about his or her rights with respect to the authorization and the potential for the information to be redisclosed. Additionally, the authorization must be written in plain language so individuals can read and understand its contents. The Privacy Rule required that authorizations provide individuals with additional information for specific circumstances under the following three sets of implementation specifications: In § 164.508(d), for authorizations requested by a covered entity for its own uses and disclosures; in § 164.508(e), for authorizations requested by a covered entity for another entity to disclose protected health information to the covered entity requesting the authorization to carry out treatment, payment, or health care operations; and in § 164.508(f), for authorizations requested by a covered entity for research that includes treatment of the individual.

March 2002 NPRM. Various issues were raised regarding the authorization requirements. Commenters claimed the authorization provisions were too complex and confusing. They alleged that the different sets of implementation specifications were not discrete, creating the potential for the

implementation specifications for specific circumstances to conflict with the required core elements. Some covered entities were confused about which authorization requirements they should implement in any given circumstance. Also, although the Department intended to permit insurers to obtain necessary protected health information during contestability periods under State law, the Rule did not provide an exception to the revocation provision when other law provides an insurer the right to contest an insurance policy.

To address these issues, the Department proposed to simplify the authorization provisions by consolidating the implementation specifications into a single set of criteria under § 164.508(c), thus eliminating paragraphs (d), (e), and (f) which contained separate implementation specifications. Under the proposal, paragraph (c)(1) would require all authorizations to contain the following core elements: (1) A description of the information to be used or disclosed, (2) the identification of the persons or class of persons authorized to make the use or disclosure of the protected health information, (3) the identification of the persons or class of persons to whom the covered entity is authorized to make the use or disclosure, (4) a description of each purpose of the use or disclosure, (5) an expiration date or event, (6) the individual's signature and date, and (7) if signed by a personal representative, a description of his or her authority to act for the individual. The proposal also included new language to clarify that when individuals initiate an authorization for their own purposes, the purpose may be described as "at the request of the individual."

In the NPRM, the Department proposed that § 164.508(c)(2) require authorizations to contain the following required notifications: (1) A statement that the individual may revoke the authorization in writing, and either a statement regarding the right to revoke and instructions on how to exercise such right or, to the extent this information is included in the covered entity's notice, a reference to the notice, (2) a statement that treatment, payment, enrollment, or eligibility for benefits may not be conditioned on obtaining the authorization if such conditioning is prohibited by the Privacy Rule, or, if conditioning is permitted by the Privacy Rule a statement about the consequences of refusing to sign the authorization, and (3) a statement about the potential for the protected health information to be redisclosed by the recipient.

C. HIPAA Final Rules, Privacy Standards, continued

53220 Federal Register / Vol. 67, No. 157 / Wednesday, August 14, 2002 / Rules and Regulations

Also under the proposal, covered entities would be required to obtain an authorization to use or disclose protected health information for marketing purposes, and to disclose in such authorizations any direct or indirect remuneration the covered entity would receive from a third party as a result of obtaining or disclosing the protected health information. The other proposed changes regarding marketing are discussed in section III.A.1. of the preamble.

The NPRM proposed a new exception to the revocation provision at § 164.508(b)(5)(ii) for authorizations obtained as a condition of obtaining insurance coverage when other law gives the insurer the right to contest the policy. Additionally, the Department proposed that the exception to permit conditioning payment of a claim on obtaining an authorization be deleted, since the proposed provision to permit the sharing of protected health information for the payment activities of another covered entity or a health care provider would eliminate the need for an authorization in such situations.

Finally, the Department proposed modifications at § 164.508(a)(2)(i)(A), (B), and (C), to clarify its intent that the proposed provisions for sharing protected health information for the treatment, payment, or health care operations of another entity would not apply to psychotherapy notes.

There were a number of proposed modifications concerning authorizations for research purposes. Those modifications are discussed in section III.E.2. of the preamble.

Overview of Public Comments. The following discussion provides an overview of the public comment received on this proposal. Additional comments received on this issue are discussed below in the section entitled, "Response to Other Public Comments."

There was overwhelming support for the proposed modifications. Overall, supporters were of the opinion that the consolidation and simplification would promote efficiency, simplify compliance, and reduce confusion. Many commenters claimed the changes would eliminate barriers to quality health care. Some commenters claimed the proposed modifications would make the authorization process easier for both providers and individuals, and one commenter said they would make authorizations easier to read and understand. A number of commenters stated the changes would not have adverse consequences for individuals, and one commenter noted the proposal would preserve the opportunity for

individuals to give a meaningful authorization.

However, some of the proponents suggested the Department go further to ease the administrative burden of obtaining authorizations. Some urged the Department to eliminate some of the required elements which they perceived as unnecessary to protect privacy, while others suggested that covered entities should decide which elements were relevant in a given situation. Some commenters urged the Department to retain the exception to the prohibition on conditioning payment of a claim on obtaining an authorization. These commenters expressed fear that the voluntary consent process and/or the right to request restrictions on uses and disclosures for treatment, payment, or health care operations might prevent covered entities from disclosing protected health information needed for payment purposes, or providers may be reluctant to cooperate in disclosures for payment purposes based on inadequately drafted notices.

Comments were divided on the proposed requirement to disclose remuneration in marketing authorizations. Recommendations ranged from requiring the disclosure of remuneration on all authorizations, to eliminating the requirement altogether.

Final Modifications. In the final modifications, the Department adopts the changes proposed in the NPRM. Since the modifications to the authorization provision are comprehensive, the Department is publishing this section in its entirety so that it will be easier to use and understand. Therefore, the preamble addresses all authorization requirements, and not just those that were modified.

In § 164.508(a), covered entities are required to obtain an authorization for uses and disclosures of protected health information, unless the use or disclosure is required or otherwise permitted by the Rule. Covered entities may use only authorizations that meet the requirements of § 164.508(b), and any such use or disclosure will be lawful only to the extent it is consistent with the terms of such authorization. Thus, a voluntary consent document will not constitute a valid permission to use or disclose protected health information for a purpose that requires an authorization under the Rule.

Although the requirements regarding uses and disclosures of psychotherapy notes are not changed substantively, the Department made minor changes to the language in paragraph (a)(2) to clarify that a covered entity may not use or disclose psychotherapy notes for

purposes of another covered entity's treatment, payment, or health care operations without obtaining the individual's authorization. However, covered entities may use and disclose psychotherapy notes, without obtaining individual authorization, to carry out its own limited treatment, payment, or health care operations as follows: (1) Use by the originator of the notes for treatment, (2) use or disclosure for the covered entity's own training programs for its mental health professionals, students, and trainees, and (3) use or disclosure by the covered entity to defend itself in a legal action or other proceeding brought by the individual.

Section 164.508(a)(3) requires covered entities to obtain an authorization to use or disclose protected health information for marketing purposes, with two exceptions. The authorization requirements for marketing and the comments received on these provisions are discussed in detail in section III.A.1. of the preamble.

If the marketing involves any direct or indirect remuneration to the covered entity from a third party, the authorization must state that fact. The comments on this requirement also are discussed in section III.A.1. of the preamble. However, a statement concerning remuneration is not a required notification for other authorizations. Such a statement was never required for all authorizations and the Department believes it would be most meaningful for consumers on authorizations for uses and disclosures of protected health information for marketing purposes. Some commenters urged the Department to require remuneration statements on research authorizations. The Department has not done so because the complexity of such arrangements would make it difficult to define what constitutes remuneration in the research context. Moreover, to require covered entities to disclose remuneration by a third party on authorizations for research would go beyond the requirements imposed in the December 2000 Rule, which did not require such a disclosure on authorizations obtained for the research of a third party. The Department believes that concerns regarding financial conflicts of interest that arise in research are not limited to privacy concerns, but also are important to the objectivity of research and to protecting human subjects from harm. Therefore, in the near future, the Department plans to issue guidance for the research community on this important topic.

Pursuant to § 164.508(b)(1), an authorization is not valid under the Rule unless it contains all of the

C. HIPAA Final Rules, Privacy Standards, continued

required core elements and notification statements, which are discussed below. Covered entities may include additional, non-required elements so long as they are not inconsistent with the required elements and statements. The language regarding defective authorizations in § 164.508(b)(2) is not changed substantively. However, some changes are made to conform this paragraph to modifications to other parts of the authorization provision, as well as other sections of the Rule. An authorization is not valid if it contains any of the following defects: (1) The expiration date has passed or the expiration event has occurred, and the covered entity is aware of the fact, (2) any of the required core elements or notification statements are omitted or incomplete, (3) the authorization violates the specifications regarding compounding or conditioning authorizations, or (4) the covered entity knows that material information in the authorization is false.

In § 164.508(b)(3) regarding compound authorizations, the requirements for authorizations for purposes other than research are not changed. That is, authorizations for use or disclosure of psychotherapy notes may be combined only with another authorization for the use or disclosure of psychotherapy notes. Other authorizations may be combined, unless a covered entity has conditioned the provision of treatment, payment, enrollment in a health plan, or eligibility for benefits on one of the authorizations. A covered entity generally may not combine an authorization with any other type of document, such as a notice of privacy practices or a written voluntary consent. However, there are exceptions for research authorizations, which are discussed in section III.E.2. of the preamble.

Section 164.508(b)(4) prohibits the conditioning of treatment, payment, enrollment in a health plan, or eligibility for benefits on obtaining an authorization, with a few exceptions. The exceptions to this requirement for research-related treatment, eligibility for benefits and enrollment in a health plan, and health care solely for creating protected health information for disclosure to a third party are not changed. Moreover, the Department eliminates the exception to the prohibition on conditioning payment of a claim on obtaining an authorization. Although some insurers urged that this conditioning authority be retained to provide them with more collection options, the Department believes this authorization is no longer necessary

because we are adding a new provision in § 164.506 that permits covered entities to disclose protected health information for the payment purposes of another covered entity or health care provider. Therefore, that exception has been eliminated.

Section 164.508(b)(5) provides individuals the right to revoke an authorization at any time in writing. The two exceptions to this right are retained, but with some modification. An individual may not revoke an authorization if the covered entity has acted in reliance on the authorization, or if the authorization was obtained as a condition of obtaining insurance coverage and other law gives the insurer the right to contest the claim or the policy itself. The Department adopts the proposed modification to the latter exception so that insurers can exercise the right to contest an insurance policy under other law. Public comment was generally supportive of this proposed modification.

Section 164.508(b)(6) requires covered entities to document and retain authorizations as required under § 164.530(j). This requirement is not changed.

The different sets of implementation criteria are consolidated into one set of criteria under § 164.508(c), thus eliminating the confusion and uncertainty associated with different requirements for specific circumstances. Covered entities may use one authorization form for all purposes. The Department adopts in paragraph (c)(1), the following core elements for a valid authorization: (1) A description of the information to be used or disclosed, (2) the identification of the persons or class of persons authorized to make the use or disclosure of the protected health information, (3) the identification of the persons or class of persons to whom the covered entity is authorized to make the use or disclosure, (4) a description of each purpose of the use or disclosure, (5) an expiration date or event, (6) the individual's signature and date, and (7) if signed by a personal representative, a description of his or her authority to act for the individual. An authorization that does not contain all of the core elements does not meet the requirements for a valid authorization. The Department intends for the authorization process to provide individuals with the opportunity to know and understand the circumstances surrounding a requested authorization.

To further protect the privacy interests of individuals, when individuals initiate an authorization for their own purposes, the purpose may be stated as "at the request of the

individual." Other changes to the core elements pertain to authorizations for research, and are discussed in section III.E.2. of the preamble.

Also, under § 164.508(c)(2), an authorization is not valid unless it contains all of the following: (1) A statement that the individual may revoke the authorization in writing, and either a statement regarding the right to revoke, and instructions on how to exercise such right or, to the extent this information is included in the covered entity's notice, a reference to the notice, (2) a statement that treatment, payment, enrollment, or eligibility for benefits may not be conditioned on obtaining the authorization if such conditioning is prohibited by the Privacy Rule or, if conditioning is permitted, a statement about the consequences of refusing to sign the authorization, and (3) a statement about the potential for the protected health information to be redisclosed by the recipient. Although the notification statements are not included in the paragraph on core elements an authorization is not valid unless it contains both the required core elements, and all of the required statements. This is the minimum information the Department believes is needed to ensure individuals are fully informed of their rights with respect to an authorization and to understand the consequences of authorizing the use or disclosure. The required statements must be written in a manner that is adequate to place the individual on notice of the substance of the statements.

In response to comments, the Department clarifies that the statement regarding the potential for redisclosure does not require an analysis of the risk for redisclosure, but may be a general statement that the health information may no longer be protected by the Privacy Rule once it is disclosed by the covered entity. Others objected to this statement because individuals might be hesitant to sign an authorization if they knew their protected health information could be redisclosed and no longer protected by the Rule. In response, the Department believes that individuals need to know about the consequences of authorizing the disclosure of their protected health information. As the commenter recognized, the potential for redisclosure may, indeed, be an important factor in an individual's decision to give or deny a requested authorization.

Others suggested that the statement regarding redisclosure should be omitted when an authorization is obtained only for a use, since such a statement would be confusing and

C. HIPAA Final Rules, Privacy Standards, continued

inappropriate when the covered entity maintains the information. Similarly, some commenters were concerned that the statement may be misleading where the recipient of the information, although not a covered entity, will keep the information confidential. In response, the Department clarifies that, while a general statement would suffice, a covered entity has the discretion to provide a more definitive statement where appropriate. Thus, the covered entity requesting an authorization for its own use of protected health information may provide assurances that the information will remain subject to the Privacy Rule. Similarly, if a third party, such as a researcher, is seeking an authorization for research, the statement may refer to the privacy protections that the researcher will provide for the data.

Under § 164.508(c)(3), authorizations must be written in plain language so that individuals can understand the information contained in the form, and thus be able to make an informed decision about whether to give the authorization. A few commenters urged the Department to keep the plain language requirement as a core element of a valid authorization. Under the December 2000 Rule, the plain language requirement was not a requisite for a valid authorization. Nevertheless, under both the December 2000 Rule and the final modifications, authorizations must be written in plain language. The fact that the plain language requirement is not a core element does not diminish its importance or effect, and the failure to meet this requirement is a violation of the Rule.

Finally, under § 164.508(c)(4), covered entities who seek an authorization are required to provide the individual with a copy of the signed authorization form.

Response to Other Public Comments

Comment: A number of commenters specifically expressed support of the proposed authorization requirement for marketing, and urged the Department to adopt the requirement. However, one commenter claimed that requiring authorizations for marketing would reduce hospitals' ability to market their programs and services effectively in order to compete in the marketplace, and that obtaining, storing, and maintaining marketing authorizations would be too burdensome.

Response: In light of the support in the comments, the Department has adopted the proposed requirement for an authorization before a covered entity may use or disclose protected health information for marketing. However, the commenter is mistaken that this

requirement will interfere with a hospital's ability to promote its own program and services within the community. First, such broad-based marketing is likely taking place without resort to protected health information, through dissemination of information about the hospital through community-wide mailing lists. Second, under the Privacy Rule, a communication is not marketing if a covered entity is describing its own products and services. Therefore, nothing in the Rule will inhibit a hospital from competing in the marketplace by communicating about its programs and services.

Comment: One commenter suggested that authorizations for marketing should clearly indicate that they are comprehensive and may contain sensitive protected health information.

Response: The Department treats all individually identifiable health information as sensitive and equally deserving of protections under the Privacy Rule. The Rule requires all authorizations to contain the specified core elements to ensure individuals are given the information they need to make an informed decision. One of the core elements for all authorizations is a clear description of the information that is authorized to be used or disclosed in specific and meaningful terms. The authorization process provides the individual with the opportunity to ask questions, negotiate how their information will be used and disclosed, and ultimately to control whether these uses and disclosures will be made.

Comment: Several commenters urged the Department to retain the existing structure of the implementation specifications, whereby the notification statements about the individual's right to revoke and the potential for redisclosure are "core elements." It was argued that this information is essential to an informed decision. One of the commenters claimed that moving them out of the core elements and only requiring a statement adequate to put the person on notice of the information would increase uncertainty, and that these two elements are too important to risk inadequate explanation.

Response: The Department agrees that the required notification statements are essential information that a person needs in order to make an informed decision about authorizing the use or disclosure of protected health information. Individuals need to know what rights they have with respect to an authorization, and how they can exercise those rights. However, separating the core elements and notification statements into two different subparagraphs does not

diminish the importance or effect of the notification statements. The Department clarifies that both the core elements and the notification statements are required, and both must be included for an authorization to be valid.

Comment: Several commenters urged the Department to eliminate unnecessary authorization contents. They argued the test should be whether the person needs the information to protect his or her privacy, and cited the disclosure of remuneration by a third party as an example of unnecessary content, alleging that the disclosure of remuneration is not relevant to protecting privacy. One commenter suggested that covered entities should be given the flexibility to decide which contents are applicable in a given situation.

Response: The Department believes the core elements are all essential information. Individuals need to know this information to make an informed decision about giving the authorization to use or disclose their protected health information. Therefore, the Department believes all of the core elements are necessary content in all situations. The Department does not agree that the remuneration statement required on an authorization for uses and disclosures of an individual's protected health information for marketing purposes is not relevant to protecting privacy. Individuals exercise control over the privacy of their protected health information by either giving or denying an authorization, and remuneration from a third party to the covered entity for obtaining an authorization for marketing is an important factor in making that choice.

Comment: One commenter suggested that covered entities should not be required to state on an authorization a person's authority to act on an individual's behalf, and they should be trusted to require such identification or proof of legal authority when the authorization is signed. The commenter stated that this requirement only increases administrative burden for covered entities.

Response: The Department does not agree. The authorization requirement is intended to give individuals some control over uses and disclosures of protected health information that are not otherwise permitted or required by the Rule. Therefore, the Rule requires that covered entities verify and document a person's authority to sign an authorization on an individual's behalf, since that person is exercising the individual's control of the information. Furthermore, the Department understands that it is a

C. HIPAA Final Rules, Privacy Standards, continued

Federal Register / Vol. 67, No. 157 / Wednesday, August 14, 2002 / Rules and Regulations   53223

current industry standard to verify and document a person's authority to sign any legal permission on another person's behalf. Thus, the requirement should not result in any undue administrative burden for covered entities.

Comment: One commenter suggested that the Department should require authorizations to include a complete list of entities that will use and share the information, and that the individual should be notified periodically of any changes to the list so that the individual can provide written authorization for the changes.

Response: It may not always be feasible or practical for covered entities to include a comprehensive list of persons authorized to use and share the information disclosed pursuant to an authorization. However, individuals may discuss this option with covered entities, and they may refuse to sign an authorization that does not meet their expectations. Also, subject to certain limitations, individuals may revoke an authorization at any time.

Comment: One commenter asked for clarification that a health plan may not condition a provider's participation in the health plan on seeking authorization for the disclosure of psychotherapy notes, arguing that this practice would coerce providers to request, and patients to provide, an authorization to disclose psychotherapy notes.

Response: The Privacy Rule does not permit a health plan to condition enrollment, eligibility for benefits, or payment of a claim on obtaining the individual's authorization to use or disclose psychotherapy notes. Nor may a health care provider condition treatment on an authorization for the use or disclosure of psychotherapy notes. In a situation such as the one described by the commenter, the Department would look closely at whether the health plan was attempting to accomplish indirectly that which the Rule prohibits. These prohibitions are to ensure that the individual's permission is wholly voluntary and informed with regard to such an authorization. To meet these standards, in the circumstances set forth in the comment, the Department would expect the provider subject to such a requirement by the health plan to explain to the individual in very clear terms that, while the provider is required to ask, the individual remains free to refuse to authorize the disclosure and that such refusal will have no effect on either the provision of treatment or the individual's coverage under, and payment of claims by, the health plan.

Comment: A few commenters suggested the Department should allow covered entities to combine an authorization with other documents, such as the notice acknowledgment, claiming it would reduce administrative burden and paperwork, as well as reduce patient confusion and waiting times, without compromising privacy protections.

Response: The Department disagrees that combining an authorization with other documents, such as the notice acknowledgment, would be less confusing for individuals. To the contrary, the Department believes that combining unrelated documents would be more confusing. However, the Rule does permit an authorization to be combined with other authorizations so long as the provision of treatment, payment, enrollment in a health plan or eligibility for benefits is not conditioned on obtaining any of the authorizations, and the authorization is not for the use or disclosure of psychotherapy notes.

Also, authorizations must contain the same information, whether it is a separate document or combined with another document; and the individual must be given the opportunity to read and discuss that information. Combining an authorization with routine paperwork diminishes individuals' ability to make a considered and informed judgment to permit the use or disclosure of their medical information for some other purpose.

Comment: One commenter stated that the requirement for covered entities to use only authorizations that are valid under the Rule must be an unintended result of the Rule, because covered entities would have to use only valid authorizations when requesting information from non-covered entities. The commenter did not believe the Department intended this requirement to apply with respect to non-covered entities, and gave the example of dental health plans obtaining protected health information in connection with paper claims submitted by dental offices. The commenter requested clarification that health plans may continue to use authorization forms currently in use for all claims submitted by non-covered entities.

Response: The commenter misapprehends the Rule's requirements. The requirements apply to uses and disclosure of protected health information by covered entities. In the example provided, where a health plan is requesting additional information in support of a claim for payment by a non-covered health care provider, the health plan is not required to use an authorization. The plan does not need the individual's authorization to use protected health information for payment purposes, and the non-covered health care provider is not subject to any of the Rule's requirements. Therefore, the exchange of information may occur as it does today. The Department notes that, based on the modifications regarding consent adopted in this rulemaking, neither a consent nor an authorization would be required in this example even if the health care provider was also a covered entity.

Comment: Several commenters urged the Department to add a transition provision to permit hospitals to use protected health information in already existing databases for marketing and outreach to the communities they serve. Commenters claimed that these databases are important assets that would take many years to rebuild, and hospitals may not have an already existing authorization or other express legal permission for such use of the information. They contended that, without a transition provision, these databases would become useless under the Rule. Commenters suggested the Department should adopt an "opt out" provision that would allow continued use of these databases to initially communicate with the persons listed in the database; at that time, they could obtain authorization for future communications, thus providing a smooth transition.

Response: Covered entities are provided a two-year period in which to come into compliance with the Privacy Rule. One of the purposes of the compliance period is to allow covered entities sufficient time to undertake actions such as those described in the comment (obtaining the legal permissions that would permit databases to continue to operate after the compliance date). An additional transition period for these activities has not been justified by the commenters. However, the Department notes that a covered entity is permitted to use the information in a database for communications that are either excepted from or that do not meet the definition of "marketing" in § 164.501, without individual authorization. For example, a hospital may use protected health information in an existing database to distribute information about the services it provides, or to distribute a newsletter with general health or wellness information that does not promote a particular product or service.

C. HIPAA Final Rules, Privacy Standards, continued

2. Research Authorizations

December 2000 Privacy Rule. The Privacy Rule requires covered entities to obtain an individual's voluntary and informed authorization before using or disclosing protected health information for any purpose that is not otherwise permitted or required under the Rule. Uses and disclosures of protected health information for research purposes are subject to the same authorization requirements as uses and disclosures for other purposes. However, for research that includes treatment of the individual, the December 2000 Privacy Rule prescribed special authorization requirements at § 164.508(f). The December 2000 Privacy Rule, at § 164.508(b)(5), also permitted individuals to revoke their authorization at any time, with limited exceptions. Further, the December 2000 Privacy Rule prohibited the combining of the authorization for the use or disclosure of existing protected health information with any other legal permission related to the research study.

March 2002 NPRM. Several of those who commented on the December 2000 Privacy Rule argued that certain authorization requirements in § 164.508 were unduly complex and burdensome as applied to research uses and disclosures. In particular, several commenters favored eliminating the Rule's specific provisions at § 164.508(f) for authorizations for uses and disclosures of protected health information for research that includes treatment of the individual. The Department also heard from several provider groups who argued in favor of permitting covered entities to combine all of the research authorizations required by the Privacy Rule with the informed consent to participate in the research. Commenters also noted that the Rule's requirement for an "expiration date or event that relates to the individual or the purpose of the use or disclosure" runs counter to the needs of research databases and repositories that are often retained indefinitely.

In response to these concerns, the Department proposed to a number of modifications to simplify the authorization requirements both generally, and in certain circumstances, as they specifically applied to uses and disclosures of protected health information for research. In particular, the Department proposed a single set of authorization requirements for all uses and disclosures, including those for research purposes. This proposal would eliminate the additional authorization requirements for the use and disclosure of protected health information created

for research that includes treatment of the individual. Consistent with this proposed change, the Department further proposed to modify the requirements prohibiting the conditioning of authorizations at § 164.508(b)(4)(i) to remove the reference to § 164.508(f).

In addition, the Department proposed that the Privacy Rule permit an authorization for the use or disclosure of protected health information to be combined with any other legal permission related to the research study, including another authorization or consent to participate in the research.

Finally, the Department proposed to provide explicitly that the statement, "end of a research study," or similar language be sufficient to meet the requirement for an expiration date in § 164.508(c)(1)(v). Additionally, the Department proposed that the statement "none" or similar language be sufficient to meet this provision if the authorization was for a covered entity to use or disclose protected health information for the creation or maintenance of a research database or repository.

Overview of Public Comments. The following discussion provides an overview of the public comment received on this proposal. Additional comments received on this issue are discussed below in the section entitled, "Response to Other Public Comments."

The vast majority of commenters were very supportive of the proposed revisions to the Rule's provisions for research authorizations. However, the Department did hear from several commenters that the Privacy Rule's requirement for an expiration date or event should be eliminated for all research uses and disclosures of protected health information, not just for uses and disclosures for the creation or maintenance of a research database or repository, as was proposed in the NPRM. These commenters were concerned that the Privacy Rule would prohibit important uses and disclosures of protected health information after the termination of a research project, such as the reporting of research results to the Food and Drug Administration (FDA) for an FDA investigational new drug application, unless the covered entity obtained another patient authorization. In addition, several of these commenters cited confusion in defining repositories and databases. Some of these commenters stated that an individual who authorizes information to be used for an indeterminate time most likely expects and intends for the information to be used and disclosed if needed well into the future, regardless of whether or

not the research involves the use or disclosure of protected health information for the creation or maintenance of a database or repository.

Several commenters responded to the Department's request for comments on how to appropriately limit uses and disclosures following revocation of an authorization, while preserving the integrity of the research. The NPRM attempted to clarify that "even though a revocation will prevent a covered entity from further disclosing protected health information for research purposes, the exception to this requirement is intended to allow for certain continued uses of information as appropriate to preserve the integrity of the research study." However, the NPRM further stated that "if covered entities were permitted to continue using or disclosing protected health information for the research project even after an individual had revoked his or her authorization, this would undermine the primary objective of the authorization requirements to be a voluntary, informed choice of the individual." Several commenters were concerned and confused by the NPRM's statements. In particular, the Department received comments urging that the regulation permit covered entities to use and disclose research data already obtained, even after an individual has withdrawn his or her authorization. These commenters suggested that once a subject has authorized the use and disclosure of protected health information for research and the covered entity has relied on the authorization, the covered entity must retain the ability to use or disclose the subject's pre-withdrawal information for purposes consistent with the overall research. One commenter argued that it would be inadequate for the reliance exception at § 164.508(b)(5) to be interpreted to permit continued uses of the individual's information as appropriate only to account for an individual's withdrawal from the study. In this commenter's opinion, most research would call for the continued use of protected health information obtained prior to an individual's revocation of their authorization to safeguard statistical validity and truly to preserve the integrity of human research.

Final Modifications. The Department agrees with the commenters that supported the NPRM's proposed simplification of authorizations for research uses and disclosures of protected health information and, therefore, adopts the modifications to these provisions as proposed in the NPRM. The final Rule requires a single

C. HIPAA Final Rules, Privacy Standards, continued

set of authorization requirements for all uses and disclosures, including those for research purposes, and permits an authorization for the use or disclosure of protected health information to be combined with any other legal permission related to the research study, including another authorization or consent to participate in the research.

In addition, in response to commenters' concerns that the Rule would prohibit important uses and disclosures of protected health information after the termination of a research project, the final Rule eliminates the requirement for an expiration date for all uses and disclosures of protected health information for research purposes, not only for the creation and maintenance of a research database or repository. The Department agrees that the line between research repositories and databases in particular, and research data collection in general, is sometimes arbitrary and unclear. If the authorization for research uses and disclosures of protected health information does not have an expiration date, the final Rule at § 164.508(c)(1)(v), requires that this fact be stated on the authorization form. Patients continue to control whether protected health information about them may be used or disclosed for research, since the authorization must include an expiration date or event, or a statement that the authorization will have no expiration date. In addition, patients will be permitted to revoke their authorization at any time during the research project, except as specified under § 164.508(b)(5). However, the Department notes that researchers may choose to include, and covered entities may choose to require, an expiration date when appropriate.

Although the final Rule does not modify the revocation provision at § 164.508(b)(5), in response to commenters' concerns, the Department clarifies that this provision permits covered entities to continue using and disclosing protected health information that was obtained prior to the time the individual revoked his or her authorization, as necessary to maintain the integrity of the research study. An individual may not revoke an authorization to the extent the covered entity has acted in reliance on the authorization. For research uses and disclosures, this reliance exception at § 164.508(b)(5)(i) permits the continued use and disclosure of protected health information already obtained pursuant to a valid authorization to the extent necessary to preserve the integrity of the research study. For example, the reliance exception would permit the

continued use and disclosure of protected health information to account for a subject's withdrawal from the research study, as necessary to incorporate the information as part of a marketing application submitted to the FDA, to conduct investigations of scientific misconduct, or to report adverse events. However, the reliance exception would not permit a covered entity to continue disclosing additional protected health information to a researcher or to use for its own research purposes information not already gathered at the time an individual withdraws his or her authorization. The Department believes that this clarification of the Rule will minimize the negative effects on research caused by participant withdrawal and will allow for important continued uses and disclosures to occur, while maintaining privacy protections for research subjects.

Response to Other Public Comments

Comment: In opposition to the March 2002 NPRM, one commenter suggested prohibiting the combining of authorization forms with an informed consent when the covered entity disclosing the protected health information is not otherwise participating in research. The commenter argued that the NPRM would allow covered entities to receive more information than necessary to fulfill a patient's authorization request, such as information about the particular type or purpose of the study itself, and could, thereby, violate the patient's privacy.

Response: The Department acknowledges the concern raised by these commenters; however, prohibiting the combination of authorization forms with an informed consent reduces the flexibility proposed in the March 2002 NPRM. Since the final modifications permit—but do not require—such combining of forms, the Department has decided to leave it to the discretion of researchers or the IRBs to determine whether the combining of authorization forms and consent forms for research would be appropriate for a particular research study.

Comment: Some commenters supported retaining the December 2000 Privacy Rule requirement that a description of the extent to which protected health information will be used or disclosed for treatment, payment, or health care operations be included in an authorization to use or disclose protected health information for a research study that includes treatment of individuals. These commenters argued that an individual's

ability to make informed decisions requires that he or she know how research information will and will not be used and disclosed.

Response: The Department agrees with the majority of the commenters who were in support of the March 2002 NPRM proposal to eliminate the additional authorization requirements for research that includes treatment, and has adopted these proposed modifications in the final Rule. Retaining the distinction between research that involves treatment and research that does not would require overly subjective decisions without providing commensurate privacy protections for individuals. However, the Department notes that it may sometimes be advisable for authorization forms to include a statement regarding how protected health information obtained for a research study will be used and disclosed for treatment, payment, and health care operations, if such information would assist individuals in making informed decisions about whether or not to provide their authorization for a research study.

Comment: One commenter argued that expiration dates should be included on authorizations and that extensions should be required for all research uses and disclosures made after the expiration date or event has passed.

Response: The Department disagrees. We have determined that an expiration date or event would not always be feasible or desirable for some research uses and disclosures of protected health information. By allowing for no expiration date, the final Rule permits without separate patient authorization important disclosures even after the "termination of the research project" that might otherwise be prohibited. However, the final Rule contains the requirement that the patient authorization specify if the authorization would not have an expiration date or event. Therefore, patients will have this information to make an informed decision about whether to sign the authorization.

Comment: Another commenter suggested permitting covered entities/researchers to continue using or disclosing protected health information even after a revocation of the initial authorization but only if an IRB or Privacy Board approved the continuation. This commenter argued that such review by an IRB or Privacy Board would protect privacy, while permitting continued uses and disclosures of protected health information for important purposes.

C. HIPAA Final Rules, Privacy Standards, continued

53226 Federal Register / Vol. 67, No. 157 / Wednesday, August 14, 2002 / Rules and Regulations

Response: As stated above, the Department agrees that it may sometimes be necessary to continue using and disclosing protected health information even after an individual has revoked his or her authorization in order to preserve the integrity of a research study. Therefore, the Department has clarified that the reliance exception at § 164.508(b)(5)(i) would permit the continued use and disclosure of protected health information already obtained pursuant to a valid authorization to the extent necessary to preserve the integrity of the research study. A requirement for documentation of IRB or Privacy Board review and approval of the continued use or disclosure of protected health information after an individual's authorization had been revoked could protect patient privacy. However, the Department believes that the additional burden on the IRB or Privacy Board could be substantial, and is not warranted at this time.

Comment: A commenter requested clarification that the "reliance exception" does not permit covered entities as researchers to continue analyzing data once an individual has revoked his or her authorization.

Response: As discussed above, the Department disagrees with this comment. Patient privacy must be balanced against other public goods, such as research and the risk of compromising such research projects if researchers could not continue to use such data. The Department determined that permitting continued uses and disclosures of protected health information already obtained to protect the integrity of research, even after an individual's authorization has been revoked, would pose minimal privacy risk to individuals without compromising research.

Comment: Several commenters suggested permitting the proposed authorization requirement for a "description of each purpose of the requested use or disclosure" at § 164.508 to be sufficiently broad to encompass future unspecified research. These commenters argued that this option would reduce the burden for covered entities and researchers by permitting covered entities to use or disclose protected health information for re-analysis without having to obtain an additional authorization from the individual. Some discussed the possibility that burden for patients would also be reduced because they would not have to provide additional authorizations. These commenters also argued that such a provision would more directly align the Rule with the

Common Rule, which permits broad informed consent for secondary studies if the IRB deems the original informed consent to be adequate.

Response: The Department disagrees with broadening the required "description of the purpose of the use or disclosure" because of the concern that patients would lack necessary information to make an informed decision. In addition, unlike the Common Rule, the Privacy Rule does not require IRB or Privacy Board review of research uses and disclosures made with individual authorization. Therefore, instead of IRBs or Privacy Boards reviewing the adequacy of existing patient authorizations, covered entities would be left to decide whether or not the initial authorization was broad enough to cover subsequent research analyses. Furthermore, it should be noted that patient authorization would not be required for such re-analysis if, with respect to the re-analysis, the covered entity obtains IRB or Privacy Board waiver of such authorization as required by § 164.512(i). For these reasons, the Department has decided to retain the requirement that each purpose of the requested use or disclosure described in the authorization form be research study specific. However, the Department understands that, in the past, some express legal permissions and informed consents have not been study-specific and sometimes authorize the use or disclosure of information for future unspecified research. Furthermore, some IRB-approved waivers of informed consent have been for future unspecified research. Therefore, the final Rule at § 164.532 permits covered entities to rely on an express legal permission, informed consent, or IRB-approved waiver of informed consent for future unspecified research, provided the legal permission, informed consent or IRB-approved waiver was obtained prior to the compliance date.

Comment: Several commenters suggested retaining the authorization element requiring a statement regarding "the potential for information disclosed pursuant to the authorization to be subject to redisclosure by the recipient and no longer protected by this Rule" but with one addition. This addition would state that "researchers could only use or disclose the protected health information for purposes approved by the IRB or as required by law or regulation." These commenters argued that this would be clearer to participants and would prevent the misconception that their information would not be protected by any confidentiality standards.

Response: The Department recognizes the concern of the commenters seeking to supplement the requirement, but points out that, although the final Rule will not require this addition, it is permissible to include such a statement in the authorization. In addition, since the Privacy Rule does not require IRB or Privacy Board review of research uses and disclosures made with patient authorization, the Department determined that adding the commenters' suggestion to the final Rule would be inappropriate. Section III.E.1. above provides further discussion of this provision.

F. Section 164.512—Uses and Disclosures for Which Authorization or Opportunity To Agree or Object Is Not Required

1. Uses and Disclosures Regarding FDA-Regulated Products and Activities

December 2000 Privacy Rule. The Privacy Rule permits covered entities to disclose protected health information without consent or authorization for public health purposes. Generally, these disclosures may be made to public health authorities, as well as to contractors and agents of public health authorities. However, in recognition of the essential role of drug and medical device manufacturers and other private persons in carrying out the Food and Drug Administration's (FDA) public health mission, the December 2000 Privacy Rule permitted covered entities to make such disclosures to a person who is subject to the jurisdiction of the FDA, but only for the following specified purposes: (1) To report adverse events, defects or problems, or biological product deviations with respect to products regulated by the FDA (if the disclosure is made to the person required or directed to report such information to the FDA); (2) to track products (if the disclosure is made to the person required or directed to report such information to the FDA); (3) for product recalls, repairs, or replacement; and (4) for conducting post-marketing surveillance to comply with FDA requirements or at the direction of the FDA.

March 2002 NPRM. The Department heard a number of concerns about the scope of the disclosures permitted for FDA-regulated products and activities and the failure of the Privacy Rule to reflect the breadth of the public health activities currently conducted by private sector entities subject to the jurisdiction of the FDA on a voluntary basis. These commenters claimed the Rule would constrain important public health surveillance and reporting activities by

C. HIPAA Final Rules, Privacy Standards, continued

Federal Register / Vol. 67, No. 157 / Wednesday, August 14, 2002 / Rules and Regulations   53227

impeding the flow of needed information to those subject to the jurisdiction of the FDA. For instance, there were concerns that the Rule would have a chilling effect on current voluntary reporting practices. The FDA gets the vast majority of information concerning problems with FDA-regulated products, including drugs, medical devices, biological products, and food indirectly through voluntary reports made by health care providers to the manufacturers. These reports are critically important to public health and safety. The December 2000 Rule permitted such disclosures only when made to a person "required or directed" to report the information to the FDA or to track the product. The manufacturer may or may not be required to report such problems to the FDA, and the covered entities who make these reports are not in a position to know whether the recipient of the information is so obligated. Consequently, many feared that this uncertainty would cause covered entities to discontinue their practices of voluntary reporting of adverse events related to FDA-regulated products or entities.

Some covered entities also expressed fears of the risk of liability should they inadvertently report the information to a person who is not subject to the jurisdiction of the FDA or to the wrong manufacturer. Hence, they urged the Department to provide a "good-faith" safe harbor to protect covered entities from enforcement actions arising from unintentional violations of the Privacy Rule.

A number of commenters, including some subject to the jurisdiction of the FDA, suggested that it is not necessary to disclose identifiable health information for some or all of these public health purposes, that identifiable health information is not reported to the FDA, and that information without direct identifiers (such as name, mailing address, phone number, social security number, and email address) is sufficient for post-marketing surveillance purposes.

The Rule is not intended to discourage or prevent adverse event reporting or otherwise disrupt the flow of essential information that the FDA and persons subject to the jurisdiction of the FDA need in order to carry out their important public health activities. Therefore, the Department proposed some modifications to the Rule to address these issues in the NPRM. Specifically, the Department proposed to remove from §§ 164.512(b)(1)(iii)(A) and (B) the phrase "if the disclosure is made to a person required or directed to report such information to the Food and

Drug Administration" and to remove from subparagraph (D) the phrase "to comply with requirements or at the direction of the Food and Drug Administration." In lieu of this language, the Department proposed to describe at the outset the public health purposes for which disclosures may be made. The proposed language read: "A person subject to the jurisdiction of the Food and Drug Administration (FDA) with respect to an FDA-regulated product or activity for which that person has responsibility, for the purpose of activities related to the quality, safety or effectiveness of such FDA-regulated product or activity."

The proposal retained the specific activities identified in paragraphs (A), (B), (C), and (D) as examples of common FDA purposes for which disclosures would be permitted, but eliminated the language that would have made this listing the only activities for which such disclosures would be allowed. These activities include reporting of adverse events and other product defects, the tracking of FDA-regulated products, enabling product recalls, repairs, or replacement, and conducting post-marketing surveillance. Additionally, the Department proposed to include "lookback" activities in paragraph (C), which are necessary for tracking blood and plasma products, as well as quarantining tainted blood or plasma and notifying recipients of such tainted products.

In addition to these specific changes, the Department solicited comments on whether a limited data set should be required or permitted for some or all public health purposes, or if a special rule should be developed for public health reporting. The Department also requested comments as to whether the proposed modifications would be sufficient, or if additional measures, such as a good-faith safe harbor, would be needed for covered entities to continue to report vital information concerning FDA-regulated products or activities on a voluntary basis.

Overview of Public Comments. The following discussion provides an overview of the public comment received on this proposal. Additional comments received on this issue are discussed below in the section entitled, "Response to Other Public Comments."

The proposed changes received wide support. The overwhelming majority of commenters urged the Department to adopt the proposed changes, claiming it would reduce the chilling effect that the Rule would otherwise have on current voluntary reporting practices, which are an important means of identifying adverse events, defects, and other

problems regarding FDA-regulated products. Several commenters further urged the Department to provide a good-faith safe harbor to allay providers' fears of inadvertently violating the Rule, stating that covered entities would otherwise be reluctant to risk liability to make these important public health disclosures.

A few commenters opposed the proposed changes, expressing concern that the scope of the proposal was too broad. They were particularly concerned that including activities related to "quality" or "effectiveness" would create a loophole for manufacturers to obtain and use protected health information for purposes the average person would consider unrelated to public health or safety, such as using information to market products to individuals. Some of these commenters said the Department should retain the exclusive list of purposes and activities for which such disclosures may be made, and some urged the Department to retain the "required or directed" language, as it creates an essential nexus to a government authority or requirement. It was also suggested that the chilling effect on reporting of adverse events could be counteracted by a more targeted approach. Commenters were also concerned that the proposal would permit disclosure of much more protected health information to non-covered entities that are not obligated by the Rule to protect the privacy of the information. Comments regarding use of a limited data set for public health disclosures are discussed in section III.G.1. of the preamble.

Final Modifications. In the final modifications, the Department adopts the language proposed in the NPRM. Section 164.512(b)(1)(iii), as modified, permits covered entities to disclose protected health information, without authorization, to a person subject to the jurisdiction of the FDA with respect to an FDA-regulated product or activity for which that person has responsibility, for the purpose of activities related to the quality, safety, or effectiveness of such FDA-regulated product or activity. Such purposes include, but are not limited to, the following activities and purposes listed in subparagraphs (A) through (D): (1) To collect or report adverse events (or similar activities regarding food or dietary supplements), product defects or problems (including problems with the use or labeling of a product), or biological product deviations, (2) to track FDA-regulated products, (3) to enable product recalls, repairs, or replacement, or for lookback (including locating and notifying persons who have

C. HIPAA Final Rules, Privacy Standards, continued

received products that have been withdrawn, recalled, or are the subject of lookback), and (4) to conduct post-marketing surveillance.

The Department believes these modifications are necessary to remove barriers that could prevent or chill the continued flow of vital information between health care providers and manufacturers of food, drugs, medical and other devices, and biological products. Health care providers have been making these disclosures to manufacturers for many years, and commenters opposed to the proposal did not cite any examples of abuses of information disclosed for such purposes. Furthermore, both the individuals who are the subjects of the information and the general public benefit from these disclosures, which are an important means of identifying and dealing with FDA-regulated products on the market that potentially pose a health or safety threat. For example, FDA learns a great deal about the safety of a drug after it is marketed as a result of voluntary adverse event reports made by covered entities to the product's manufacturer. The manufacturer is required to submit these safety reports to FDA, which uses the information to help make the product safer by, among other things, adding warnings or changing the product's directions for use. The modifications provide the necessary assurances to covered entities that such voluntary reporting may continue.

Although the list of permissible disclosures is no longer exclusive, the Department disagrees with commenters that asserted the modifications permit virtually unlimited disclosures for FDA purposes. As modified, such disclosures must still be made to a person subject to the jurisdiction of the FDA. The disclosure also must relate to FDA-regulated products or activities for which the person using or receiving the information has responsibility, and be made only for activities related to the safety, effectiveness, or quality of such FDA-regulated product or activity. These terms are terms of art with commonly accepted and understood meanings in the FDA context, meanings of which providers making such reports are aware. This limits the possibility that FDA-regulated manufacturers and entities will able to abuse this provision to obtain information to which they would otherwise not be entitled.

Moreover, § 164.512(b)(1) specifically limits permissible disclosures to those made for public health activities and purposes. While a disclosure related to the safety, quality or effectiveness of an FDA-regulated product is a permissible

disclosure, the disclosure also must be for a "public health" activity or purpose. For example, it is not permissible under § 164.512(b)(1)(iii) for a covered entity to disclose protected health information to a manufacturer to allow the manufacturer to evaluate the effectiveness of a marketing campaign for a prescription drug. In this example, although the disclosure may be related to the effectiveness of an FDA-regulated activity (the advertising of a prescription drug), the disclosure is made for the commercial purposes of the manufacturer rather than for a public health purpose.

A disclosure related to a "quality" defect of an FDA-regulated product is also permitted. For instance, the public health exception permits a covered entity to contact the manufacturer of a product to report drug packaging quality defects. However, this section does not permit all possible reports from a covered entity to a person subject to FDA jurisdiction about product quality. It would not be permissible for a provider to furnish a manufacturer with a list of patients who prefer a different flavored cough syrup over the flavor of the manufacturer's product. Such a disclosure generally would not be for a public health purpose. However, a disclosure related to the flavor of a product would be permitted under this section if the covered entity believed that a difference in the product's flavor indicated, for example, a possible manufacturing problem or suggested that the product had been tampered with in a way that could affect the product's safety.

The Department clarifies that the types of disclosures that covered entities are permitted to make to persons subject to FDA jurisdiction are those of the type that have been traditionally made over the years. These reports include, but are not limited to, those made for the purposes identified in paragraphs (A)–(D) of § 164.512(b)(1)(iii) of this final Rule.

Also, the minimum necessary standard applies to public health disclosures, including those made to persons subject to the jurisdiction of the FDA. There are many instances where a report about the quality, safety, or effectiveness of an FDA-regulated product can be made without disclosing protected health information. Such may be the case with many adverse drug events where it is important to know what happened but it may not be important to know to whom. However, in other circumstances, such as device tracking or blood lookback, it is essential for the manufacturer to have identifying patient information in order

to carry out its responsibilities under the Food, Drug, and Cosmetic Act. Therefore, identifiable health information can be disclosed for these purposes, consistent with the minimum necessary standard.

As the Department stated in the preamble of the NPRM, "a person" subject to the jurisdiction of the FDA does not mean that the disclosure must be made to a specific individual. The Food, Drug, and Cosmetic Act defines "person" to include an individual, partnership, corporation, and association. Therefore, covered entities may continue to disclose protected health information to the companies subject to FDA's jurisdiction that have responsibility for the product or activity. Covered entities may identify responsible companies by using information obtained from product labels or product labeling (written material about the product that accompanies the product) including sources of labeling, such as the Physician's Desk Reference.

The Department believes these modifications effectively balance the privacy interests of individuals with the interests of public health and safety. Since the vast majority of commenters were silent on the question of the potential need for a "good faith" exception, the Department believes that these modifications will be sufficient to preserve the current public health activities of persons subject to the jurisdiction of the FDA, without such a safe harbor. However, the Department will continue to evaluate the effect of the Rule to determine whether there is need for further modifications or guidance.

Response to Other Public Comments

Comment: A few commenters urged the Department to include foreign public health authorities in the Rule's definition of "public health authority." These commenters claimed that medical products are often distributed in multiple countries, and the associated public health issues are experienced globally. They further claimed that requiring covered entities to obtain the permission of a United States-based public health authority before disclosing protected health information to a foreign government public health authority will impede important communications.

Response: The Department notes that covered entities are permitted to disclose protected health information for public health purposes, at the direction of a public health authority, to an official of a foreign government agency that is acting in collaboration with a public health authority. The

C. HIPAA Final Rules, Privacy Standards, continued

Department does not have sufficient information at this time as to any potential impacts or workability issues that could arise from this language and, therefore, does not modify the Rule in this regard.

Comment: Some commenters, who opposed the proposal as a weakening of the Privacy Rule, suggested that the Department implement a more targeted approach to address only those issues raised in the preamble to the NPRM, such as voluntary adverse event reporting activities, rather than broadening the provision generally.

Response: The NPRM was intended to address a number of issues in addition to the concern that the December 2000 Privacy Rule would chill reporting of adverse events to entities from whom the FDA receives much of its adverse event information. For instance, the text of the December 2000 Privacy Rule did not expressly permit disclosure of protected health information to FDA-regulated entities for the purpose of enabling "lookback," which is an activity performed by the blood and plasma industry to identify and quarantine blood and blood products that may be at increased risk of transmitting certain blood-borne diseases, and which includes the notification of individuals who received possibly tainted products, permitting them to seek medical attention and counseling. The NPRM also was intended to simplify the public health reporting provision and to make it more readily understandable. Finally, the approach proposed in the NPRM, and adopted in this final Rule, is intended to add flexibility to the public health reporting provision of the December 2000 Rule, whose exclusive list of permissible disclosures was insufficiently flexible to assure that § 164.512(b)(1)(iii) will allow legitimate public health reporting activities that might arise in the future.

In addition, the Department clarifies that the reporting of adverse events is not restricted to the FDA or persons subject to the jurisdiction of the FDA. A covered entity may, under § 164.512(b), disclose protected health information to a public health authority that is authorized to receive or collect a report on an adverse event. In addition, to the extent an adverse event is required to be reported by law, the disclosure of protected health information for this purpose is also permitted under § 164.512(a). For example, a Federally funded researcher who is a covered health care provider under the Privacy Rule may disclose protected health information related to an adverse event to the National Institutes of Health

(NIH) if required to do so by NIH regulations. Even if not required to do so, the researcher may also disclose adverse events directly to NIH as a public health authority. To the extent that NIH has public health matters as part of its official mandate it qualifies as a public health authority under the Privacy Rule, and to the extent it is authorized by law to collect or receive reports about injury and other adverse events such collection would qualify as a public health activity.

2. Institutional Review Board (IRB) or Privacy Board Approval of a Waiver of Authorization

December 2000 Privacy Rule. The Privacy Rule builds upon existing Federal regulations governing the conduct of human subjects research. In particular, the Rule at § 164.512(i) establishes conditions under which covered entities can use and disclose protected health information for research purposes without individual authorization if the covered entity first obtains either of the following:

• Documentation of approval of a waiver of authorization from an Institutional Review Board (IRB) or a Privacy Board. The Privacy Rule specifies requirements that must be documented, including the Board's determination that eight defined waiver criteria had been met.

• Where a review of protected health information is conducted preparatory to research or where research is conducted solely on decedents' information, certain representations from the researcher, including that the use or disclosure is sought solely for such a purpose and that the protected health information is necessary for the purpose.

March 2002 NPRM. A number of commenters informed the Department that the eight waiver criteria in the December 2000 Privacy Rule were confusing, redundant, and internally inconsistent. These commenters urged the Department to simplify these provisions, noting that they would be especially burdensome and duplicative for research that was currently governed by the Common Rule. In response to these comments, the Department proposed the following modifications to the waiver criteria for all research uses and disclosures of protected health information, regardless of whether or not the research is subject to the Common Rule:

• The Department proposed to delete the criterion that "the alteration or waiver will not adversely affect the privacy rights and the welfare of the individuals," because it may conflict

with the criterion regarding the assessment of minimal privacy risk.

• In response to commenters' concerns about the overlap and potential inconsistency among several of the Privacy Rule's criteria, the Department proposed to turn the following three criteria into factors that must be considered as part of the IRB's or Privacy Board's assessment of minimal risk to privacy:

• There is an adequate plan to protect the identifiers from improper use and disclosure;

• There is an adequate plan to destroy the identifiers at the earliest opportunity consistent with the conduct of the research, unless there is a health or research justification for retaining the identifiers, or such retention is otherwise required by law; and

• There are adequate written assurances that the protected health information will not be reused or disclosed to any other person or entity, except as required by law, for authorized oversight of the research project, or for other research for which the use or disclosure of protected health information would be permitted by this subpart.

• In response to concerns that the following waiver criterion was unnecessarily duplicative of other provisions to protect patients' confidentiality interests, the Department proposed to eliminate the criterion that: "the privacy risks to individuals whose protected health information is to be used or disclosed are reasonable in relation to the anticipated benefits, if any, to the individual, and the importance of the knowledge that may reasonably be expected to result from the research."

In sum, the NPRM proposed that the following waiver criteria replace the waiver criteria in the December 2000 Privacy Rule at § 164.512(i)(2)(ii):

(1) The use or disclosure of protected health information involves no more than a minimal risk to the privacy of individuals, based on, at least, the presence of the following elements:

(a) An adequate plan to protect the identifiers from improper use and disclosure;

(b) An adequate plan to destroy the identifiers at the earliest opportunity consistent with conduct of the research, unless there is a health or research justification for retaining the identifiers or such retention is otherwise required by law; and

(c) Adequate written assurances that the protected health information will not be reused or disclosed to any other person or entity, except as required by law, for authorized oversight of the

C. HIPAA Final Rules, Privacy Standards, continued

53230   **Federal Register** / Vol. 67, No. 157 / Wednesday, August 14, 2002 / Rules and Regulations

research project, or for other research for which the use or disclosure of protected health information would be permitted by this subpart;

(2) The research could not practicably be conducted without the waiver or alteration; and

(3) The research could not practicably be conducted without access to and use of the protected health information.

Overview of Public Comments. The following discussion provides an overview of the public comment received on this proposal. Additional comments received on this issue are discussed below in the section entitled, "Response to Other Public Comments."

The overwhelming majority of commenters were supportive of the Department's proposed modifications to the Privacy Rule's waiver criteria. These commenters found that the proposed revisions adequately addressed earlier concerns that the waiver criteria in the December 2000 Rule were confusing, redundant, and internally inconsistent. However, a few commenters argued that some of the proposed criteria continued to be too subjective and urged that they be eliminated.

Final Modifications. The Department agrees with the majority of commenters that supported the proposed waiver criteria, and adopts the modifications as proposed in the NPRM. The criteria safeguard patient privacy, require attention to issues sometimes currently overlooked by IRBs, and are compatible with the Common Rule. Though IRBs and Privacy Boards may initially struggle to interpret the criteria, as a few commenters mentioned, the Department intends to issue guidance documents to address this concern. Furthermore, the Department notes that experience and guidance have enabled IRBs to successfully implement the Common Rule's waiver criteria, which also require subjective determinations.

This final Rule also contains a conforming modification in § 164.512(i)(2)(iii) to replace "(i)(2)(ii)(D)" with "(i)(2)(ii)(C)."

Response to Other Public Comments

Comment: It was suggested that the Department eliminate the March 2002 NPRM waiver criterion that requires IRBs or Privacy Boards to determine if there is an "adequate plan to protect identifiers from improper use and disclosure," in order to avoid the IRB having to make subjective decisions.

Response: The Department disagrees with the commenter that the waiver criterion adopted in this final Rule is too subjective for an IRB or a Privacy Board to use. First, the consideration of whether there is an adequate plan to

protect identifiers from improper use and disclosure is one of three factors that an IRB or Privacy Board must weigh in determining that the use or disclosure of protected health information for the research proposal involves no more than a minimal risk to the privacy of the individual. The Department does not believe that the minimal risk determination, which is based upon a similar waiver criterion in the Common Rule, is made unduly subjective by requiring the IRB to take into account the researcher's plans for maintaining the confidentiality of the information.

Second, as noted in the discussion of these provisions in the proposal, the Privacy Rule is intended to supplement and build upon the human subject protections already afforded by the Common Rule and the Food and Drug Administration's human subject protection regulations. One provision already in effect under these authorities is that, to approve a study, an IRB must determine that "when appropriate, there are adequate provisions to protect the privacy of subjects and to maintain the confidentiality of data." (Common Rule § __.111(a)(7), 21 CFR 56.111(a)(7).) The Department, therefore, believes that IRBs and Privacy Boards are accustomed to making the type of determinations required under the Privacy Rule.

Nonetheless, as stated above, the Department is prepared to respond to actual issues that may arise during the implementation of these provisions and to provide the guidance necessary to address concerns of IRBs, Privacy Boards, and researchers in this area.

Comment: A few commenters requested elimination of the waiver element at § 164.512(i)(2)(ii)(A)(2) that would require the IRB or Privacy Board to determine that "there is an adequate plan to destroy identifiers at the earliest opportunity consistent with the conduct of the research, unless there is a health or research justification for their retention or such retention is required by law." These commenters argued that this requirement may lead to premature destruction of the data, which may hinder investigations of defective data analysis or research misconduct.

Response: The waiver element at § 164.512(i)(2)(ii)(A)(2) accounts for these concerns by permitting the retention of identifiers if there is a health or research justification, or if such retention is required by law. It is expected that IRBs and Privacy Boards will consider the need for continued analysis of the data, research, and possible investigations of research misconduct when considering whether this waiver element has been met. In addition, destroying identifiers at the

earliest opportunity helps to ensure that the use or disclosure of protected health information will indeed pose no more than "minimal risk to the privacy of individuals." Requiring the researcher to justify the need to retain patient identifiers provides needed flexibility for research, while maintaining the goal of protecting individuals' privacy interests. If additional issues arise after implementation, the Department can most appropriately address them through guidance.

Comment: Commenters also requested clarification of the proposed waiver element at § 164.512(i)(2)(ii)(A)(3), that will require an IRB or Privacy Board to determine that there are "adequate written assurances that the protected health information would not be reused or disclosed to any other person or entity, except as required by law, for authorized oversight of the research project, or for other research for which the use or disclosure of protected health information would be permitted by this subpart." Specifically, the commenter's concern centered on what effect this criterion could have on retrospective studies involving data re-analysis.

Response: The Department clarifies that the Privacy Rule permits the use or disclosure of protected health information for retrospective research studies involving data re-analysis only if such use or disclosure is made either with patient authorization or a waiver of patient authorization as permitted by § 164.508 or § 164.512(i), respectively. If issues develop in the course of implementation, the Department intends to provide the guidance necessary to address these questions.

Comment: A few commenters suggested clarifying that recruitment for clinical trials by a covered entity using protected health information in the covered entity's possession is a health care operation function, not a marketing function. These commenters argued that a partial IRB or Privacy Board waiver of authorization for recruitment purposes would be too burdensome for the covered entity, and would prevent covered health care providers from communicating with their patients about the availability of clinical trials.

Response: Research recruitment is neither a marketing nor a health care operations activity. Under the Rule, a covered entity is permitted to disclose protected health information to the individual who is the subject of the information, regardless of the purpose of the disclosure. See § 164.502(a)(1)(i). Therefore, covered health care providers and patients may continue to discuss the option of enrolling in a clinical trial without patient authorization, and

C. HIPAA Final Rules, Privacy Standards, continued

Federal Register / Vol. 67, No. 157 / Wednesday, August 14, 2002 / Rules and Regulations   53231

without an IRB or Privacy Board waiver of patient authorization. However, where a covered entity wants to disclose an individual's information to a third party for purposes of recruitment in a research study, the covered entity first must obtain either authorization from that individual as required at § 164.508, or a waiver of authorization as permitted at § 164.512(i).

Comment: It was suggested that the Rule should permit covered health care providers to obtain an authorization allowing the use of protected health information for recruitment into clinical trials without specifying the person to whom the information would be disclosed and the exact information to be disclosed, but retaining the authorization requirements of specified duration and purpose, and adding a requirement for the minimum necessary use or disclosure.

Response: The Department understands that the Privacy Rule will alter some research recruitment but disagrees with the commenter's proposal to permit broad authorizations for recruitment into clinical trials. The Department decided not to adopt this suggestion because such a blanket authorization would not provide individuals with sufficient information to make an informed choice about whether to sign the authorization. In addition, adopting this change also would be inconsistent with Department's decision to eliminate the distinction in the Rule between research that includes treatment and research that does not.

Comment: It was suggested that the Department exempt from the Privacy Rule research that is already covered by the Common Rule and/or FDA's human subject protection regulations. Commenters stated that this would reduce the burden of complying with the Rule for covered entities and researchers already governed by human subject protection regulations, while requiring those not previously subject to compliance with human subject protection regulations to protect individuals' privacy.

Response: Many who commented on the December 2000 Privacy Rule argued for this option as well. The Department had previously considered, but chose not to adopt, this approach. Since the Common Rule and the FDA's human subject protection regulations contain only two requirements that specifically address confidentiality protections, the Privacy Rule will strengthen existing human subject privacy protections for research. More importantly, the Privacy Rule creates equal standards of privacy protection for research governed by the

existing regulations and research that is not.

Comment: It was argued that the waiver provision should be eliminated. The commenter argued that IRBs or Privacy Boards should not have the right to waive a person's privacy rights, and that individuals should have the right to authorize all uses and disclosures of protected health information about themselves.

Response: The Department disagrees that safeguarding individuals' privacy interests requires that individuals be permitted to authorize all uses and disclosures of protected health information about themselves. In developing the Privacy Rule, the Department carefully weighed individuals' privacy interests with the need for identifiable health information for certain public policy and national priority purposes. The Department believes that the Privacy Rule reflects an appropriate balance. For example, the Rule appropriately allows for the reporting of information necessary to ensure public health, such as information about a contagious disease that may be indicative of a bioterrorism event, without individual authorization. With respect to research, the Department strongly believes that continued improvements in our nation's health require that researchers be permitted access to protected health information without individual authorization in certain limited circumstances. However, we do believe that researchers' ability to use protected health information without a patient's authorization is a privilege that requires strong confidentiality protections to ensure that the information is not misused. The Department believes that the safeguards required by the final Rule achieve the appropriate balance between protecting individuals' privacy interests, while permitting researchers to access protected health information for important, and potentially life-saving, studies.

Comment: A few commenters stated that, if the Rule permits covered entities to release protected health information to sponsor-initiated registries related to quality, safety, or effectiveness of FDA-regulated products, then this permission should apply to academic institutes and non-profit organizations as well. Otherwise, the commenters argued, the Rule establishes a double standard for research registries created by FDA-regulated entities versus registries created by academic or non-profit sponsored entities.

Response: The provisions under § 164.512(b)(iii) are intended to allow the disclosure of information to FDA-

regulated entities for the limited purpose of conducting public health activities to ensure the qualify, safety, or effectiveness of FDA-regulated products, including drugs, medical devices, biological products, and food. Thus, the Department does not believe a modification to the research provisions is appropriate. The Privacy Rule permits covered entities to disclose protected health information to a registry for research purposes, including those sponsored by academic and non-profit organizations, if such disclosure: is required by law under § 164.512(a), is made pursuant to an IRB or Privacy Board waiver of authorization under § 164.512(i), is made pursuant to the individual's authorization as provided by § 164.508, or consists only of a limited data set as provided by § 164.514(e).

Comment: It was suggested that the Department modify the Rule's definition of "research" or the provision for preparatory research to explicitly permit the building and maintenance of research databases and repositories. The commenter further asserted that, under the Common Rule, "research" signifies an actual research protocol, and would not include a data or tissue compilation that is undertaken to facilitate future protocols. Therefore, since the Privacy Rule and the Common Rule have the same definition of "research," this commenter was concerned that the Privacy Rule would not permit a pre-research practice in which a covered entity compiles protected health information in a systematic way to either assist researchers in their reviews that are preparatory to research, or to conduct future research.

Response: The Department does not believe such a modification is necessary. Under the Common Rule, the Office for Human Research Protections (OHRP) has interpreted the definition of "research" to include the development of a repository or database for future research purposes. In fact, OHRP has issued guidance on this issue, which can be found at the following URL: *http://ohrp.osophs.dhhs.gov/humansubjects/guidance/reposit.htm.* The Department interprets the definition of "research" in the Privacy Rule to be consistent with what is considered research under the Common Rule. Thus, the development of research repositories and databases for future research are considered research for the purposes of the Privacy Rule.

Comment: A commenter suggested eliminating the minimum necessary requirement for uses and disclosures made pursuant to a waiver of authorization by an IRB or Privacy

C. HIPAA Final Rules, Privacy Standards, continued

53232 Federal Register / Vol. 67, No. 157 / Wednesday, August 14, 2002 / Rules and Regulations

Board. The commenter argued that this proposal would lessen covered entities' concern that they would be held responsible for an IRB or Privacy Board's inappropriate determination and would, thus, increase the likelihood that covered entities would rely on the requesting researcher's IRB or Privacy Board documentation that patient authorization could be waived as permitted at § 164.512(i). This commenter further argued that this proposal would discourage covered entities from imposing duplicate review by the covered entities' own IRB or Privacy Board, thereby decreasing burden for covered entities, researchers, IRBs, and Privacy Boards.

Response: Although the Secretary acknowledges the concern of these commenters, the Rule at § 164.514(d)(3)(iii)(D) already permits covered entities to reasonably rely on documentation from an external IRB or Privacy Board as meeting the minimum necessary requirement, provided the documentation complies with the applicable requirements of § 164.512(i). The Department understands that covered entities may elect to require duplicate IRB or Privacy Board reviews before disclosing protected health information to requesting researchers, but has determined that eliminating the minimum necessary requirement would pose inappropriate and unnecessary risk to individuals' privacy. For example, if the covered entity has knowledge that the documentation of IRB or Privacy Board approval was fraudulent with respect to the protected health information needed for a research study, the covered entity should not be permitted to rely on the IRB or Privacy Board's documentation as fulfilling the minimum necessary requirement. Therefore, in the revised Final Rule, the Department has retained the minimum necessary requirement for research uses and disclosures made pursuant to § 164.512(i).

G. Section 164.514—Other Requirements Relating to Uses and Disclosures of Protected Health Information

1. De-Identification of Protected Health Information

December 2000 Privacy Rule. At § 164.514(a)–(c), the Privacy Rule permits a covered entity to de-identify protected health information so that such information may be used and disclosed freely, without being subject to the Privacy Rule's protections. Health information is de-identified, or not individually identifiable, under the Privacy Rule, if it does not identify an individual and if the covered entity has no reasonable basis to believe that the information can be used to identify an individual. In order to meet this standard, the Privacy Rule provides two alternative methods for covered entities to de-identify protected health information.

First, a covered entity may demonstrate that it has met the standard if a person with appropriate knowledge and experience applying generally acceptable statistical and scientific principles and methods for rendering information not individually identifiable makes and documents a determination that there is a very small risk that the information could be used by others to identify a subject of the information. The preamble to the Privacy Rule refers to two government reports that provide guidance for applying these principles and methods, including describing types of techniques intended to reduce the risk of disclosure that should be considered by a professional when de-identifying health information. These techniques include removing all direct identifiers, reducing the number of variables on which a match might be made, and limiting the distribution of records through a "data use agreement" or "restricted access agreement" in which the recipient agrees to limits on who can use or receive the data.

Alternatively, covered entities may choose to use the Privacy Rule's safe harbor method for de-identification. Under the safe harbor method, covered entities must remove all of a list of 18 enumerated identifiers and have no actual knowledge that the information remaining could be used, alone or in combination, to identify a subject of the information. The identifiers that must be removed include direct identifiers, such as name, street address, social security number, as well as other identifiers, such as birth date, admission and discharge dates, and five-digit zip code. The safe harbor requires removal of geographic subdivisions smaller than a State, except for the initial three digits of a zip code if the geographic unit formed by combining all zip codes with the same initial three digits contains more than 20,000 people. In addition, age, if less than 90, gender, ethnicity, and other demographic information not listed may remain in the information. The safe harbor is intended to provide covered entities with a simple, definitive method that does not require much judgment by the covered entity to determine if the information is adequately de-identified.

The Privacy Rule also allows for the covered entity to assign a code or other means of record identification to allow de-identified information to be re-identified by the covered entity, if the code is not derived from, or related to, information about the subject of the information. For example, the code cannot be a derivation of the individual's social security number, nor can it be otherwise capable of being translated so as to identify the individual. The covered entity also may not use or disclose the code for any other purpose, and may not disclose the mechanism (*e.g.*, algorithm or other tool) for re-identification.

The Department is cognizant of the increasing capabilities and sophistication of electronic data matching used to link data elements from various sources and from which, therefore, individuals may be identified. Given this increasing risk to individuals' privacy, the Department included in the Privacy Rule the above stringent standards for determining when information may flow unprotected. The Department also wanted the standards to be flexible enough so the Privacy Rule would not be a disincentive for covered entities to use or disclose de-identified information wherever possible. The Privacy Rule, therefore, strives to balance the need to protect individuals' identities with the need to allow de-identified databases to be useful.

March 2002 NPRM. The Department heard a number of concerns regarding the de-identification standard in the Privacy Rule. These concerns generally were raised in the context of using and disclosing information for research, public health purposes, or for certain health care operations. In particular, concerns were expressed that the safe harbor method for de-identifying protected health information was so stringent that it required removal of many of the data elements that were essential to analyses for research and these other purposes. The comments, however, demonstrated little consensus as to which data elements were needed for such analyses and were largely silent regarding the feasibility of using the Privacy Rule's alternative statistical method to de-identify information.

Based on the comments received, the Department was not convinced of the need to modify the safe harbor standard for de-identified information. However, the Department was aware that a number of entities were confused by potentially conflicting provisions within the de-identification standard. These entities argued that, on the one hand, the Privacy Rule treats information as de-identified if all listed identifiers on the information are stripped, including

C. HIPAA Final Rules, Privacy Standards, continued

any unique, identifying number, characteristic, or code. Yet, the Privacy Rule permits a covered entity to assign a code or other record identification to the information so that it may be re-identified by the covered entity at some later date.

The Department did not intend such a re-identification code to be considered one of the unique, identifying numbers or codes that prevented the information from being de-identified. Therefore, the Department proposed a technical modification to the safe harbor provisions explicitly to except the re-identification code or other means of record identification permitted by § 164.514(c) from the listed identifiers (§ 164.514(b)(2)(i)(R)).

Overview of Public Comments. The following provides an overview of the public comment received on this proposal. Additional comments received on this issue are discussed below in the section entitled, "Response to Other Public Comments."

All commenters on our clarification of the safe harbor re-identification code not being an enumerated identifier supported our proposed regulatory clarification.

Final Modifications. Based on the Department's intent that the re-identification code not be considered one of the enumerated identifiers that must be excluded under the safe harbor for de-identification, and the public comment supporting this clarification, the Department adopts the provision as proposed. The re-identification code or other means of record identification permitted by § 164.514(c) is expressly excepted from the listed safe harbor identifiers at § 164.514(b)(2)(i)(R).

Response to Other Public Comments

Comment: One commenter asked if data can be linked inside the covered entity and a dummy identifier substituted for the actual identifier when the data is disclosed to the external researcher, with control of the dummy identifier remaining with the covered entity.

Response: The Privacy Rule does not restrict linkage of protected health information inside a covered entity. The model that the commenter describes for the dummy identifier is consistent with the re-identification code allowed under the Rule's safe harbor so long as the covered entity does not generate the dummy identifier using any individually identifiable information. For example, the dummy identifier cannot be derived from the individual's social security number, birth date, or hospital record number.

Comment: Several commenters who supported the creation of de-identified data for research based on removal of facial identifiers asked if a keyed-hash message authentication code (HMAC) can be used as a re-identification code even though it is derived from patient information, because it is not intended to re-identify the patient and it is not possible to identify the patient from the code. The commenters stated that use of the keyed-hash message authentication code would be valuable for research, public health and bio-terrorism detection purposes where there is a need to link clinical events on the same person occurring in different health care settings (e.g. to avoid double counting of cases or to observe long-term outcomes).

These commenters referenced Federal Information Processing Standard (FIPS) 198: "The Keyed-Hash Message Authentication Code." This standard describes a keyed-hash message authentication code (HMAC) as a mechanism for message authentication using cryptographic hash functions. The HMAC can be used with any iterative approved cryptographic hash function, in combination with a shared secret key. A hash function is an approved mathematical function that maps a string of arbitrary length (up to a pre-determined maximum size) to a fixed length string. It may be used to produce a checksum, called a hash value or message digest, for a potentially long string or message.

According to the commenters, the HMAC can only be breached when the key and the identifier from which the HMAC is derived and the de-identified information attached to this code are known to the public. It is common practice that the key is limited in time and scope (e.g. only for the purpose of a single research query) and that data not be accumulated with such codes (with the code needed for joining records being discarded after the de-identified data has been joined).

Response: The HMAC does not meet the conditions for use as a re-identification code for de-identified information. It is derived from individually identified information and it appears the key is shared with or provided by the recipient of the data in order for that recipient to be able to link information about the individual from multiple entities or over time. Since the HMAC allows identification of individuals by the recipient, disclosure of the HMAC violates the Rule. It is not solely the public's access to the key that matters for these purposes; the covered entity may not share the key to the re-identification code with anyone, including the recipient of the data,

regardless of whether the intent is to facilitate re-identification or not.

The HMAC methodology, however, may be used in the context of the limited data set, discussed below. The limited data set contains individually identifiable health information and is not a de-identified data set. Creation of a limited data set for research with a data use agreement, as specified in § 164.514(e), would not preclude inclusion of the keyed-hash message authentication code in the limited data set. The Department encourages inclusion of the additional safeguards mentioned by the commenters as part of the data use agreement whenever the HMAC is used.

Comment: One commenter requested that HHS update the safe harbor de-identification standard with prohibited 3-digit zip codes based on 2000 Census data.

Response: The Department stated in the preamble to the December 2000 Privacy Rule that it would monitor such data and the associated re-identification risks and adjust the safe harbor as necessary. Accordingly, the Department provides such updated information in response to the above comment. The Department notes that these three-digit zip codes are based on the five-digit zip Code Tabulation Areas created by the Census Bureau for the 2000 Census. This new methodology also is briefly described below, as it will likely be of interest to all users of data tabulated by zip code.

The Census Bureau will not be producing data files containing U.S. Postal Service zip codes either as part of the Census 2000 product series or as a post Census 2000 product. However, due to the public's interest in having statistics tabulated by zip code, the Census Bureau has created a new statistical area called the Zip Code Tabulation Area (ZCTA) for Census 2000. The ZCTAs were designed to overcome the operational difficulties of creating a well-defined zip code area by using Census blocks (and the addresses found in them) as the basis for the ZCTAs. In the past, there has been no correlation between zip codes and Census Bureau geography. Zip codes can cross State, place, county, census tract, block group and census block boundaries. The geographic entities the Census Bureau uses to tabulate data are relatively stable over time. For instance, census tracts are only defined every ten years. In contrast, zip codes can change more frequently. Because of the ill-defined nature of zip code boundaries, the Census Bureau has no file (crosswalk) showing the relationship

C. HIPAA Final Rules, Privacy Standards, continued

53234   Federal Register / Vol. 67, No. 157 / Wednesday, August 14, 2002 / Rules and Regulations

between US Census Bureau geography and US Postal Service zip codes.

ZCTAs are generalized area representations of U.S. Postal Service (USPS) zip code service areas. Simply put, each one is built by aggregating the Census 2000 blocks, whose addresses use a given zip code, into a ZCTA which gets that zip code assigned as its ZCTA code. They represent the majority USPS five-digit zip code found in a given area. For those areas where it is difficult to determine the prevailing five-digit zip code, the higher-level three-digit zip code is used for the ZCTA. For further information, go to: *http:// www.census.gov/geo/www/gazetteer/ places2k.html*.

Utilizing 2000 Census data, the following three-digit ZCTAs have a population of 20,000 or fewer persons. To produce a de-identified data set utilizing the safe harbor method, all records with three-digit zip codes corresponding to these three-digit ZCTAs must have the zip code changed to 000. The 17 restricted zip codes are: 036, 059, 063, 102, 203, 556, 692, 790, 821, 823, 830, 831, 878, 879, 884, 890, and 893.

2. Limited Data Sets

March 2002 NPRM. As noted above, the Department heard many concerns that the de-identification standard in the Privacy Rule could curtail important research, public health, and health care operations activities. Specific concerns were raised by State hospital associations regarding their current role in using patient information from area hospitals to conduct and disseminate analyses that are useful for hospitals in making decisions about quality and efficiency improvements. Similarly, researchers raised concerns that the impracticality of using de-identified data would significantly increase the workload of IRBs because waivers of individual authorization would need to be sought more frequently for research studies even though no direct identifiers were needed for the studies. Many of these activities and studies were also being pursued for public health purposes. Some commenters urged the Department to permit covered entities to disclose protected health information for research if the protected health information is facially de-identified, that is, stripped of direct identifiers, so long as the research entity provides assurances that it will not use or disclose the information for purposes other than research and will not identify or contact the individuals who are the subjects of the information.

In response to these concerns, the Department, in the NPRM, requested

comments on an alternative approach that would permit uses and disclosures of a limited data set which would not include direct identifiers but in which certain potentially identifying information would remain. The Department proposed limiting the use or disclosure of any such limited data set to research, public health, and health care operations purposes only.

From the de-identification safe harbor list of identifiers, we proposed the following as direct identifiers that would have to be removed from any limited data set: name, street address, telephone and fax numbers, e-mail address, social security number, certificate/license number, vehicle identifiers and serial numbers, URLs and IP addresses, and full face photos and any other comparable images. The proposed limited data set could include the following identifiable information: admission, discharge, and service dates; date of death; age (including age 90 or over); and five-digit zip code.

The Department solicited comment on whether one or more other geographic units smaller than State, such as city, county, precinct, neighborhood or other unit, would be needed in addition to, or be preferable to, the five-digit zip code. In addition, to address concerns raised by commenters regarding access to birth date for research or other studies relating to young children or infants, the Department clarified that the Privacy Rule de-identification safe harbor allows disclosure of the age of an individual, including age expressed in months, days, or hours. Given that the limited data set could include all ages, including age in months, days, or hours (if preferable), the Department requested comment on whether date of birth would be needed and, if so, whether the entire date would be needed, or just the month and year.

In addition, to further protect privacy, the Department proposed to condition the disclosure of the limited data set on covered entities obtaining from the recipients a data use or similar agreement, in which the recipient would agree to limit the use of the limited data set to the purposes specified in the Privacy Rule, to limit who can use or receive the data, and agree not to re-identify the data or contact the individuals.

Overview of Public Comments. The following discussion provides an overview of the public comment received on this proposal. Additional comments received on this issue are discussed below in the section entitled, "Response to Other Public Comments."

Almost all those who commented on this issue supported the basic premise

of the limited data set for research, public health, and health care operations. Many of these commenters used the opportunity to reiterate their opposition to the safe harbor and statistical de-identification methods, and some misinterpreted the limited data set proposal as creating another safe-harbor form of de-identified data. In general, commenters agreed with the list of direct identifiers proposed in the preamble of the NPRM; some recommended changes. The requirement of a data use agreement was similarly widely supported, although a few commenters viewed it as unnecessary and others offered additional terms which they argued would make the data use agreement more effective. Others questioned the enforceability of the data use agreements.

A few commenters argued that the limited data set would present a significant risk of identification of individuals because of the increased ability to use the other demographic variables (*e.g.,* race, gender) in such data sets to link to other publicly available data. Some of these commenters also argued that the development of computer-based solutions to support the statistical method of de-identification is advancing rapidly and can support, in some cases better than the limited data set, many of the needs for research, public health and health care operations. These commenters asserted that authorization of the limited data set approach would undermine incentives to further develop statistical techniques for de-identification that may be more protective of privacy.

Most commenters who supported the limited data set concept favored including the five-digit zip code, but also wanted other geographic units smaller than a State to be included in the limited data set. Examples of other geographic units that commenters argued are needed for research, public health or health care operational purposes were county, city, full zip code, census tract, and neighborhood. Various analytical needs were cited to support these positions, such as tracking the occurrence of a particular disease to the neighborhood level or using county level data for a needs assessment of physician specialties. A few commenters opposed inclusion of the 5-digit zip code in the limited data set, recommending that the current Rule, which requires data aggregation at the 3-digit zip code level, remain the standard.

Similarly, the majority of commenters addressing the issue supported inclusion of the full birth date in the

C. HIPAA Final Rules, Privacy Standards, continued

Federal Register / Vol. 67, No. 157 / Wednesday, August 14, 2002 / Rules and Regulations   **53235**

limited data set. These commenters asserted that the full birth date was needed for longitudinal studies, and similar research, to assure accuracy of data. Others stated that while they preferred access to the full birth date, their data needs would be satisfied by inclusion of at least the month and year of birth in the limited data set. A number of commenters also opposed inclusion of the date of birth in the limited data as unduly increasing the risk of identification of individuals.

Final Modifications. In view of the support in the public comments for the concept of a limited data set, the Department determines that adoption of standards for the use and disclosure of protected health information for this purpose is warranted. Therefore, the Department adds at § 164.514(e) a new standard and implementation specifications for a limited data set for research, public health, or health care operations purposes if the covered entity (1) uses or discloses only a "limited data set" as defined at § 164.514(e)(2), and (2) obtains from the recipient of the limited data set a "data use agreement" as defined at § 164.514(e)(4). In addition, the Department adds to the permissible uses and disclosures in § 164.502(a) express reference to the limited data set standards.

The implementation specifications do not delineate the data that can be released through a limited data set. Rather, the Rule specifies the direct identifiers that must be removed for a data set to qualify as a limited data set. As with the de-identification safe harbor provisions, the direct identifiers listed apply to protected health information about the individual or about relatives, employers, or household members of the individual. The direct identifiers include all of the facial identifiers proposed in the preamble to the NPRM: (1) Name; (2) street address (renamed postal address information, other than city, State and zip code); (3) telephone and fax numbers; (4) e-mail address; (5) social security number; (6) certificate/license numbers; (7) vehicle identifiers and serial numbers; (8) URLs and IP addresses; and (9) full face photos and any other comparable images. The public comment generally supported the removal of this facially identifying information.

In addition to these direct identifiers, the Department designates the following information as direct identifiers that must be removed before protected health information will be considered a limited data set: (1) Medical record numbers, health plan beneficiary numbers, and other account numbers;

(2) device identifiers and serial numbers; and (3) biometric identifiers, including finger and voice prints. Only a few commenters specifically stated a need for some or all of these identifiers as part of the limited data set. For example, one commenter wanted an (encrypted) medical record number to be included in the limited data set to support disease management planning and program development to meet community needs and quality management. Another commenter wanted the health plan beneficiary number included in the limited data set to permit researchers to ensure that results indicating sex, gender or ethnic differences were not influenced by the participant's health plan. And a few commenters wanted device identifiers and serial numbers included in the limited data set, to facilitate product recalls and patient safety initiatives. However, the Department has not been persuaded that the need for these identifiers outweighs the potential privacy risks to the individual by their release as part of a limited data set, particularly when the Rule makes other avenues available for the release of information that may directly identify an individual.

The Department does not include in the list of direct identifiers the "catch-all" category from the de-identification safe harbor of "any other unique identifying number, characteristic or code." While this requirement is essential to assure that the de-identification safe harbor does in fact produce a de-identified data set, it is difficult to define in advance in the context of a limited data set. Since our goal in establishing a limited data set is not to create de-identified information and since the data use agreement constrains further disclosure of the information, we determined that it would only add complexity to implementation of the limited data set with little added protection.

In response to wide public support, the Department does not designate as a direct identifier any dates related to the individual or any geographic subdivision other than street address. Therefore, as part of a limited data set, researchers and others involved in public health studies will have access to dates of admission and discharge, as well as dates of birth and death for the individual. We agree with commenters who asserted that birth date is critical for certain research, such as longitudinal studies where there is a need to track individuals across time and for certain infant-related research. Rather than adding complexity to the Rule by trying to carve out an exception

for these specific situations, and other justifiable uses, we rely on the minimum necessary requirement to keep the Rule simple while avoiding abuse. Birth date should only be disclosed where the researcher and covered entity agree that it is needed for the purpose of the research. Further, even though birth date may be included with a limited data set, the Department clarifies, as it did in the preamble to the proposed rulemaking, that the Privacy Rule allows the age of an individual to be expressed in years or in months, days, or hours as appropriate.

Moreover, the limited data set may include the five-digit zip code or any other geographic subdivision, such as State, county, city, precinct and their equivalent geocodes, except for street address. We substitute for street address the term postal address information, other than city, State and zip code in order to make clear that individual elements of postal address such as street name by itself are also direct identifiers. Commenters identified a variety of needs for various geographical codes (county, city, neighborhood, census tract, precinct) to support a range of essential research, public health and health care operations activities. Some of the examples provided included the need to analyze local geographic variations in disease burdens or in the provision of health services, conducting research looking at pathogens or patterns of health risks which may need to compare areas within a single zip code, or studies to examine data by county or neighborhood when looking for external causes of disease, as would be the case for illnesses and diseases such as bladder cancer that may have environmental links. The Department agrees with these commenters that a variety of geographical designations other than five-digit zip code are needed to permit useful and significant studies and other research to go forward unimpeded. So long as an appropriate data use agreement is in place, the Department does not believe that there is any greater privacy risk in including in the limited data set such geographic codes than in releasing the five-digit zip code.

Finally, the implementation specifications adopted at § 164.514(e) require a data use agreement between the covered entity and the recipient of the limited data set. The need for a data use agreement and the core elements of such an agreement were widely supported in the public comment. In the NPRM, we asked whether additional conditions should be added to the data use agreement. In response, a few commenters made specific

C. HIPAA Final Rules, Privacy Standards, continued

53236   **Federal Register** / Vol. 67, No. 157 / Wednesday, August 14, 2002 / Rules and Regulations

suggestions. These included prohibiting further disclosure of the limited data set except as required by law, prohibiting further disclosure without the written consent of the covered entity, requiring that the recipient safeguard the information received in the limited data set, prohibiting further disclosure unless the data has been de-identified utilizing the statistical or safe harbor methods of the Privacy Rule, and limiting use of the data to the purpose for which it was received.

In response to these comments, in the final Rule we specify that the covered entity must enter into a data use agreement with the intended recipient which establishes the permitted uses and disclosures of such information by the recipient, consistent with the purposes of research, public health, or health care operations, limits who can use or receive the data, and requires the recipient to agree not to re-identify the data or contact the individuals. In addition, the data use agreement must contain adequate assurances that the recipient use appropriate safeguards to prevent use or disclosure of the limited data set other than as permitted by the Rule and the data use agreement, or as required by law. These adequate assurances are similar to the existing requirements for business associate agreements.

Since the data use agreement already requires the recipient to limit who can use or receive the data, and to prevent uses and disclosures beyond those stated in the agreement, and since we could not anticipate all the possible scenarios under which a limited data set with a data use agreement would be created, the Department concluded that adding any of the other suggested restrictions would bring only marginal additional protection while potentially impeding some of the purposes intended for the limited data set. The Department believes the provisions of the data use agreement provide a firm foundation for protection of the information in the limited data set, but encourages and expects covered entities and data recipients to further strengthen their agreements to conform to current practices.

We do not specify the form of the data use agreement. Thus, private parties might choose to enter into a formal contract, while two government agencies might use a memorandum of understanding to specify the terms of the agreement. In the case of a covered entity that wants to create and use a limited data set for its own research purposes, the requirements of the data use agreement could be met by having affected workforce members sign an

agreement with the covered entity, comparable to confidentiality agreements that employees handling sensitive information frequently sign.

A few commenters questioned the enforceability of the data use agreements. The Department clarifies that, if the recipient breaches a data use agreement, HHS cannot take enforcement action directly against that recipient unless the recipient is a covered entity. Where the recipient is a covered entity, the final modifications provide that such covered entity is in noncompliance with the Rule if it violates a data use agreement. See § 164.514(e)(4)(iii)(B). Additionally, the Department clarifies that the disclosing covered entity is not liable for breaches of the data use agreement by the recipient of the limited data set. However, similar to business associate agreements, if a covered entity knows of a pattern of activity or practice of the data recipient that constitutes a material breach or violation of the data recipient's obligation under the data use agreement, then it must take reasonable steps to cure the breach or end the violation, as applicable, and, if unsuccessful, discontinue disclosure of protected health information to the recipient and report the problem to the Secretary. And the recipient is required to report to the covered entity any improper uses or disclosures of limited data set information of which it becomes aware. We also clarify that the data use agreement requirements apply to disclosures of the limited data set to agents and subcontractors of the original limited data set recipient.

In sum, we have created the limited data set option because we believe that this mechanism provides a way to allow important research, public health and health care operations activities to continue in a manner consistent with the privacy protections of the Rule. We agree with those commenters who stated that the limited data set is not de-identified information, as retention of geographical and date identifiers measurably increases the risk of identification of the individual through matching of data with other public (or private) data sets. However, we believe that the limitations on the specific uses of the limited data set, coupled with the requirements of the data use agreement, will provide sufficient protections for privacy and confidentiality of the data. The December 2000 Privacy Rule preamble on the statistical method for de-identification discussed the data use agreement as one of the techniques identified that can be used to reduce the risk of disclosure. A number of Federal agencies that distribute data sets for

research or other uses routinely employ data use agreements successfully to protect and otherwise restrict further use of the information.

We note that, while disclosures of protected health information for certain public health purposes is already allowed under § 164.512(b), the limited data set provision may permit disclosures for some public health activities not allowed under that section. These might include disease registries maintained by private organizations or universities or other types of studies undertaken by the private sector or non-profit organizations for public health purposes.

In response to comments, the Department clarifies that, when a covered entity discloses protected health information in a limited data set to a researcher who has entered into an appropriate data use agreement, the covered entity does not also need to have documentation from an IRB or a Privacy Board that individual authorization has been waived for the purposes of the research. However, the covered entity may not disclose any of the direct identifiers listed in § 164.514(e) without either the individual's authorization or documentation of an IRB or Privacy Board waiver of that authorization.

The Department further clarifies that there are other requirements in the Privacy Rule that apply to disclosure of a limited data set, just as they do to other disclosures. For example, any use, disclosure, or request for a limited data set must also adhere to the minimum necessary requirements of the Rule. The covered entity could accomplish this by, for example, requiring the data requestor, in the data use agreement, to specify not only the purposes of the limited data set, but also the particular data elements, or categories of data elements, requested. The covered entity may reasonably rely on a requested disclosure as the minimum necessary, consistent with the provisions of § 164.514(d)(3)(iii). As an example of the use of the minimum necessary standard, a covered entity who believes that another covered entity's request to include date of birth in the limited data set is not warranted is free to negotiate with the recipient about that requirement. If the entity requesting a limited data set including date of birth is not one on whose request a covered entity may reasonably rely under § 164.514(d)(3)(iii), and the covered entity believes inclusion of date of birth is not warranted, the covered entity must either negotiate a reasonably

C. HIPAA Final Rules, Privacy Standards, continued

Federal Register / Vol. 67, No. 157 / Wednesday, August 14, 2002 / Rules and Regulations   53237

necessary limited data set or not make a disclosure.

The Department amends § 164.514(e)(3)(ii) to make clear that a covered entity may engage a business associate to create a limited data set, in the same way it can use a business associate to create de-identified data. As with de-identified data, a business associate relationship arises even if the limited data set is not being created for the covered entity's own use. For instance, if a researcher needs county data, but the covered entity's data contains only the postal address of the individual, a business associate may be used to convert the covered entity's geographical information into that needed by the researcher. The covered entity may hire the intended recipient of the limited data set as a business associate for this purpose. That is, the covered entity may provide protected health information, including direct identifiers, to a business associate who is also the intended data recipient, to create a limited data set of the information responsive to the business associate's request.

Finally, the Department amends § 164.528 to make clear that the covered entity does not need to include disclosures of protected health information in limited data sets in any accounting of disclosures provided to the individual. Although the Department does not consider the limited data set to constitute de-identified information, all direct identifiers are removed from the limited data set and the recipient of the data agrees not to identify or contact the individual. The burden of accounting for these disclosures in these circumstances is not warranted, given that the data may not be used in any way to gain knowledge about a specific individual or to take action in relation to that individual.

Response to Other Public Comments

Comment: A small number of commenters argued that the development of computer-based solutions to support the statistical method of de-identification is advancing rapidly and can support, in some cases better than the limited data set, many of the needs for research, public health and health care operations. They also asserted that authorization of the limited data set approach will undermine incentives to further develop statistical techniques that will be more protective of privacy than the limited data set. They proposed imposing a sunset clause on the limited data set provision in order to promote use of de-identification tools.

Response: We agree that progress is being made in the development of electronic tools to de-identify protected health information. However, the information presented by commenters did not convince us that current techniques meet all the needs identified or are easy enough to use that they can have the broad application needed to support key research, public health and health care operations needs. Where de-identification can provide better outcomes than a limited data set, purveyors of such de-identification tools will have to demonstrate to covered entities the applicability and ease of use of their products. We do not believe a sunset provision on the limited data set authority is appropriate. Rather, as part of its ongoing review of the Privacy Rule in general, and the de-identification provisions in particular, the Office for Civil Rights will periodically assess the need for these provisions.

Comment: Some commenters said that if HHS clearly defines direct identifiers and facially identifiable information, there is no need for a data use agreement.

Response: We disagree. As previously noted, the resulting limited data set is not de-identified; it still contains individually identifiable health information. As a means to assure continued protection of the information once it leaves the control of the covered entity, we believe a data use agreement is essential.

Comment: Several commenters wanted to be able to have a single coordinated data use agreement between a State hospital association and its member hospitals where data collection is coordinated through the hospital association. In addition, there was concern that requiring a data use agreement and a business associate agreement in this circumstance would create an excessive and unnecessary burden.

Response: Nothing in the requirement for a data use agreement prevents a State hospital association and its member hospitals from being parties to a common data use agreement. Furthermore, that data use agreement can be combined with a business associate agreement into a single agreement that meets the requirements of both Privacy Rule provisions.

Comment: A few commenters argued that a data use agreement should not be required for data users getting a limited data set and performing data analysis as part of the Medicaid rebate validation process under which third-party data vendors, working for pharmaceutical companies, collect prescription claims data from State agencies and analyze the results for errors and discrepancies. They argued that State agencies often find entering into such contracts difficult and time consuming. Consequently, if States have to establish data use or similar agreements, then the Medicaid rebate validation process could be adversely impacted.

Response: We are not persuaded that there is a compelling reason to exempt this category of limited data set use from the requirements for a data use agreement, as compared to other important uses. The data use agreement is key to ensuring the integrity of the limited data set process and avoiding inappropriate further uses and disclosures.

Comment: One commenter stated that allowing disclosure of the limited data set without IRB or Privacy Board review would create a loophole in the Privacy Rule, with Federally funded research continuing to undergo IRB review while private research would not.

Response: The Rule continues to make no distinction between disclosure of protected health information to Federally and privately funded researchers. To obtain a limited data set from a covered entity, both Federally-funded and privately-funded researchers must enter into a data use agreement with the covered entity. One of the reasons for establishing the limited data set provisions is that the concept of "personally identifiable information" that triggers IRB review of research that is subject to the Common Rule does not coincide with the definition of "individually identifiable health information" in the Privacy Rule. The Department believes that the limited data set comes closer to the type of information not requiring IRB approval under the Common Rule than does the de-identified data set of the Privacy Rule. However, there is no uniform definition of "personally identifiable information" under the Common Rule; rather, as a matter of practice, it is currently set by each individual IRB.

Comment: A few commenters suggested expanding the allowable purposes for the limited data set. One commenter proposed including payment as an allowable purpose, in order to facilitate comparison of premiums charged to insured versus uninsured patients. A few commenters wanted to allow disclosures to journalists if the individual's name and social security number have been removed and if, in the context of the record or file, the identity of the patient has not been revealed. A few commenters suggested that there was no need to restrict the purpose at all as long

C. HIPAA Final Rules, Privacy Standards, continued

as there is a data use agreement. A couple of commenters wanted to extend the purpose to include creation or maintenance of research databases and repositories.

Response: If the comparison of premiums charged to different classes of patients is being performed as a health care operation of another entity, then a limited data set could be used for this purpose. It seems unlikely that this activity would occur in relation to a payment activity, so a change to include payment as a permissible purpose is not warranted. A "payment" activity must relate to payment for an individual and, thus, will need direct identifiers, and uses and disclosures of protected health information for such purposes is permitted under § 164.506.

With respect to disclosures to journalists, while recognizing the important role performed by newspapers and other media in reporting on public health issues and the health care system, we disagree that the purposes of the limited data set should be expanded to include journalists. A key element of the limited data set is that the recipient enter into a data use agreement that would limit access to the limited data set, prohibit any attempt to identify or contact any individual, and limit further use or disclosure of the limited data set. These limitations are inherently at odds with journalists' asserted need for access to patient information.

The suggestion to allow disclosure of a limited data set for any purpose if there is a data use agreement would undermine the purpose of the Privacy Rule to protect individually identifiable health information from unauthorized disclosures and would conflict with the requirement in the data use agreement to restrict further use to research, public health, health care operations purposes. The Department clarifies that research encompasses the establishment of research databases and repositories. Therefore, no change to the proposal is necessary.

Comment: One commenter said that HHS should not create a list of excluded direct identifiers; rather it should enunciate principles and leave it to researchers to apply the principles.

Response: The statistical method of de-identification is based on scientific principles and methods and leaves the application to the researcher and the covered entity. Unfortunately, many have viewed this approach as too complex or imprecise for broad use. To allow broad discretion in selection of variables in the creation of a limited data set would trigger the same concerns as the statistical method, because some

measure of reasonableness would have to be established. Commenters have consistently asked for precision so that they would not have to worry as to whether they were in compliance with the requirements of the Privacy Rule. The commenter's proposal runs counter to this desire for precision.

Comment: One commenter wanted prescription numbers allowed in a limited data set because they do not include any "facially identifiable information."

Response: Prescription numbers are medical record numbers in that they are used to track an individual's encounter with a health care provider and are uniquely associated with that individual. The fact that an individual receives a new prescription number for each prescription, even if it is randomly generated, is analogous to an individual receiving a separate medical record number for different hospital visits. Thus, a prescription number is an excluded direct identifier under the medical record number exclusion for the limited data set (and also must be excluded in the creation of de-identified data).

Comment: One commenter wanted clarification that a sponsor of a multi-employer group health plan could utilize the limited data set approach for the purpose of resolving claim appeals. That commenter also suggested that if the only information that a plan sponsor received was the limited data set, the group health plan should be able to give that information to the plan sponsor without amending plan documents. In lieu of the limited data set, this commenter wanted clarification that redacted information, as delineated in their comment, is a reasonable way to meet the minimum necessary standard if the plan sponsor has certified that the plan documents have been amended pursuant to the requirements of the Privacy Rule.

Response: Uses and disclosures of a limited data set is authorized only for public health, research, and health care operations purposes. A claims appeal is more likely to be a payment function, rather than a health care operation. It is also likely to require use of protected health information that includes direct identifiers. The Department disagrees with the commenter's suggestions that the Rule should allow group health plans to disclose a limited data set to a plan sponsor without amending the plan documents to describe such disclosures. Limited data sets are not de-identified information, and thus warrant this degree of protection. Therefore, only summary health information and the enrollment status of

the individual can be disclosed by the group health plan to the plan sponsor without amending the plan documents. The Privacy Rule does not specify what particular data elements constitute the minimum necessary for any particular purpose.

H. Section 164.520—Notice of Privacy Practices for Protected Health Information

December 2000 Privacy Rule. The Privacy Rule at § 164.520 requires most covered entities to provide individuals with adequate notice of the uses and disclosures of protected health information that may be made by the covered entity, and of the individual's rights and the covered entity's responsibilities with respect to protected health information. The Rule delineates specific requirements for the content of the notice, as well as for provision of the notice. The requirements for providing notice to individuals vary based on type of covered entity and method of service delivery. For example, a covered health care provider that has a direct treatment relationship with an individual must provide the notice no later than the date of first service delivery and, if the provider maintains a physical service delivery site, must post the notice in a clear and prominent location and have it available upon request for individuals to take with them. If the first service delivery to an individual is electronic, the covered provider must furnish electronic notice automatically and contemporaneously in response to the individual's first request for service. In addition, if a covered entity maintains a website, the notice must be available electronically through the web site.

March 2002 NPRM. The Department proposed to modify the notice requirements at § 164.520(c)(2) to require that a covered health care provider with a direct treatment relationship make a good faith effort to obtain an individual's written acknowledgment of receipt of the provider's notice of privacy practices. Other covered entities, such as health plans, would not be required to obtain this acknowledgment from individuals, but could do so if they chose.

The Department proposed to strengthen the notice requirements in order to preserve a valuable aspect of the consent process. The notice acknowledgment proposal was intended to create the "initial moment" between a covered health care provider and an individual, formerly a result of the consent requirement, when individuals may focus on information practices and privacy rights and discuss with the

C. HIPAA Final Rules, Privacy Standards, continued

provider any concerns related to the privacy of their protected health information. This "initial moment" also would provide an opportunity for an individual to make a request for additional restrictions on the use or disclosure of his or her protected health information or for additional confidential treatment of communications, as permitted under § 164.522.

With one exception for emergency treatment situations, the proposal would require that the good faith effort to obtain the written acknowledgment be made no later than the date of first service delivery, including service delivered electronically. To address potential operational difficulties with implementing these notice requirements in emergency treatment situations, the Department proposed in § 164.520(c)(2) to delay the requirement for provision of notice until reasonably practicable after the emergency treatment situation, and exempt health care providers with a direct treatment relationship with the individual from having to make a good faith effort to obtain the acknowledgment altogether in such situations.

Other than requiring that the acknowledgment be in writing, the proposal would not prescribe other details of the form of the acknowledgment or limit the manner in which a covered health care provider could obtain the acknowledgment.

The proposal also provided that, if the individual's acknowledgment of receipt of the notice could not be obtained, the covered health care provider would be required to document its good faith efforts to obtain the acknowledgment and the reason why the acknowledgment was not obtained. Failure by a covered entity to obtain an individual's acknowledgment, assuming it otherwise documented its good faith effort, would not be considered a violation of the Privacy Rule.

Overview of Public Comments. The following discussion provides an overview of the public comment received on this proposal. Additional comments received on this issue are discussed below in the section entitled, "Response to Other Public Comments."

In general, many commenters expressed support for the proposal to require that certain health care providers, as an alternative to obtaining prior consent, make a good faith effort to obtain a written acknowledgment from the individual of receipt of the notice. Commenters stated that even though the requirement would place some burden on certain health care providers, the proposed policy was a reasonable and workable alternative to the Rule's prior consent requirement. A number of these commenters conveyed support for the proposed flexibility of the requirement that would allow covered entities to implement the requirement in accordance with their own practices. Commenters urged that the Department not prescribe (other than that the acknowledgment be in writing) the form or content of the acknowledgment, or other requirements that would further burden the acknowledgment process. In addition, commenters viewed the proposed exception for emergency treatment situations as a practical policy.

A number of other commenters, while supportive of the Department's proposal to make the obtaining of consent optional for all covered entities, expressed concern over the administrative burden the proposed notice acknowledgment requirements would impose on certain health care providers. Some of these commenters viewed the notice acknowledgment as an unnecessary burden on providers that would not afford individuals with any additional privacy rights or protections. Thus, some commenters urged that the good faith acknowledgment not be adopted in the final Rule. As an alternative, it was suggested by some that covered entities instead be required to make a good faith effort to make the notice available to consumers.

Several commenters expressed concerns that the notice acknowledgment process would reestablish some of the same operational problems associated with the prior consent requirement. For example, commenters questioned how the requirement should be implemented when the provider's first contact with the patient is over the phone, electronically, or otherwise not face-to-face, such as with telemedicine. Accordingly, it was suggested that the good faith acknowledgment of the notice be required no later than the date of first face-to-face encounter with the patient rather than first service delivery to eliminate these perceived problems.

A few others urged that the proposed notice acknowledgment requirement be modified to allow for an individual's oral acknowledgment of the notice, so long as the provider maintained a record that the individual's acknowledgment was obtained.

Some commenters did not support the proposal's written notice acknowledgment as a suitable alternative to the consent requirement, stating that such a requirement would not provide individuals with comparable privacy protections or rights. It was stated that there are a number of fundamental differences between a consent and an acknowledgment of the notice. For example, one commenter argued that asking individuals to acknowledge receipt of the notice does not provide a comparable "initial moment" between the provider and the individual, especially when the individual is only asked to acknowledge receipt of the notice, and not whether they have read or understood it, or have questions. Further, commenters argued that the notice acknowledgment process would not be the same as seeking the individual's permission through a consent process. Some of these commenters urged that the Department retain the consent requirements and make appropriate modifications to fix the known operational problems associated with the requirement.

A few commenters urged that the Department strengthen the notice acknowledgment process. Some commenters suggested that the Department do so by eliminating the "good faith" aspect of the standard and simply requiring certain health care providers to obtain the written acknowledgment, with appropriate exceptions for emergencies and other situations where it may not be practical to do so. It was also suggested that the Department require providers to ensure that the consumer has an understanding of the information provided in the notice. One commenter suggested that this may be achieved by having individuals not only indicate whether they have received the notice, but also be asked on separate lines after each section of the notice whether they have read that section. Another commenter argued that consumers should be asked to sign something more meaningful than a notice acknowledgment, such as a "Summary of Consumer Rights," which clearly and briefly summarizes the ways in which their information may be used by covered entities, as well as the key rights consumers have under the Privacy Rule.

Final Modifications. After consideration of the public comment, the Department adopts in this final Rule at § 164.520(c)(2)(ii), the proposed requirement that a covered health care provider with a direct treatment relationship with an individual make a good faith effort to obtain the individual's written acknowledgment of receipt of the notice. Other covered entities, such as health plans, are not required to obtain this acknowledgment from individuals, but may do so if they choose. The Department agrees with

C. HIPAA Final Rules, Privacy Standards, continued

those commenters who stated that the notice acknowledgment process is a workable alternative to the prior consent process, retaining the beneficial aspects of the consent without impeding timely access to quality health care. The Department continues to believe strongly that promoting individuals' understanding of privacy practices is an essential component of providing notice to individuals. Through this requirement, the Department facilitates achieving this goal by retaining the opportunity for individuals to discuss privacy practices and concerns with their health care providers. Additionally, the requirement provides individuals with an opportunity to request any additional restrictions on uses and disclosures of their health information or confidential communications, as permitted by § 164.522.

As proposed in the NPRM, the final Rule requires, with one exception, that a covered direct treatment provider make a good faith effort to obtain the written acknowledgment no later than the date of first service delivery, including service delivered electronically, that is, at the time the notice is required to be provided. During emergency treatment situations, the final Rule at § 164.520(c)(2)(i)(B) delays the requirement for provision of the notice until reasonably practicable after the emergency situation, and at § 164.520(c)(2)(ii) exempts health care providers from having to make a good faith effort to obtain an individual's acknowledgment in such emergency situations. The Department agrees with commenters that such exceptions are practical and necessary to ensure that the notice and acknowledgment requirements do not impede an individual's timely access to quality health care.

The Department also agrees with commenters that the notice acknowledgment process must be flexible and provide covered entities with discretion in order to be workable. Therefore, the final modification adopts the flexibility proposed in the NPRM for the acknowledgment requirement. The Rule requires only that the acknowledgment be in writing, and does not prescribe other details such as the form that the acknowledgment must take or the process for obtaining the acknowledgment. For example, the final Rule does not require an individual's signature to be on the notice. Instead, a covered health provider is permitted, for example, to have the individual sign a separate sheet or list, or to simply initial a cover sheet of the notice to be retained by the provider. Alternatively, a

pharmacist is permitted to have the individual sign or initial an acknowledgment within the log book that patients already sign when they pick up prescriptions, so long as the individual is clearly informed on the log book of what they are acknowledging and the acknowledgment is not also used as a waiver or permission for something else (such as a waiver to consult with the pharmacist). For notice that is delivered electronically as part of first service delivery, the Department believes the provider's system should be capable of capturing the individual's acknowledgment of receipt electronically. In addition, those covered health care providers that choose to obtain consent from an individual may design one form that includes both a consent and the acknowledgment of receipt of the notice. Covered health care providers are provided discretion to design the acknowledgment process best suited to their practices.

While the Department believes that the notice acknowledgment process must remain flexible, the Department does not consider oral acknowledgment by the individual to be either a meaningful or appropriate manner by which a covered health care provider may implement these provisions. The notice acknowledgment process is intended to provide a formal opportunity for the individual to engage in a discussion with a health care provider about privacy. At the very least, the process is intended to draw the individual's attention to the importance of the notice. The Department believes these goals are better accomplished by requiring a written acknowledgment and, therefore, adopts such provision in this final modification.

Under the final modification, if an individual refuses to sign or otherwise fails to provide an acknowledgment, a covered health care provider is required to document its good faith efforts to obtain the acknowledgment and the reason why the acknowledgment was not obtained. Failure by a covered entity to obtain an individual's acknowledgment, assuming it otherwise documented its good faith effort, is not a violation of this Rule. Such reason for failure simply may be, for example, that the individual refused to sign the acknowledgment after being requested to do so. This provision also is intended to allow covered health care providers flexibility to deal with a variety of circumstances in which obtaining an acknowledgment is problematic. In response to commenters requests for examples of good faith efforts, the

Department intends to provide future guidance on this and other modifications.

A covered entity is required by § 164.530(j) to document compliance with these provisions by retaining copies of any written acknowledgments of receipt of the notice or, if not obtained, documentation of its good faith efforts to obtain such written acknowledgment.

The Department was not persuaded by those commenters who urged that the Department eliminate the proposed notice acknowledgment requirements because of concerns about burden. The Department believes that the final modification is simple and flexible enough so as not to impose a significant burden on covered health care providers. Covered entities are provided much discretion to design the notice acknowledgment process that works best for their business. Further, as described above, the Department believes that the notice acknowledgment requirements are important in that they retain the important aspects of the prior consent process that otherwise would be lost in the final modifications.

In response to commenters' operational concerns about the proposed notice acknowledgment requirements, the Department clarifies that the modification as proposed and now adopted as final is intended to be flexible enough to address the various types of relationships that covered health care providers may have with the individuals to whom they provide treatment, including those treatment situations that are not face-to-face. For example, a health care provider whose first treatment encounter with a patient is over the phone satisfies the notice provision requirements of the Rule by mailing the notice to the individual no later than the day of that service delivery. To satisfy the requirement that the provider also make a good faith effort to obtain the individual's acknowledgment of the notice, the provider may include a tear-off sheet or other document with the notice that requests such acknowledgment be mailed back to the provider. The Department would not consider the health care provider in violation of the Rule if the individual chooses not to mail back an acknowledgment. The Department clarifies, however, that where a health care provider's initial contact with the patient is simply to schedule an appointment, the notice provision and acknowledgment requirements may be satisfied at the time the individual arrives at the provider's facility for his or her

C. HIPAA Final Rules, Privacy Standards, continued

appointment. For service provided electronically, the Department believes that, just as a notice may be delivered electronically, a provider should be capable of capturing the individual's acknowledgment of receipt electronically in response to that transmission.

Finally, the Department does not agree with those commenters who argued that the proposed notice acknowledgment requirements are not an adequate alternative to the prior consent requirements, nor with those who argued that the proposed acknowledgment process should be strengthened if an individual's consent is no longer required. The Department believes that the notice acknowledgment process retains the important aspects of the consent process, such as creating an opportunity for a discussion between the individual and the provider of privacy issues, including the opportunity for the individual to request restrictions on how her information may be used and disclosed as permitted by § 164.522.

Additionally, the Department believes that requiring certain health care providers to obtain the individual's acknowledgment of receipt of the notice, rather than make a good faith effort to do so, would remove the flexibility of the standard and increase the burden substantially on covered entities. Such a modification, therefore, would have the potential to cause workability and operational problems similar to those caused by the prior consent requirements. Prescribing the form or content of the acknowledgment could have the same effect. The Department believes that the notice acknowledgment process must not negatively impact timely access to quality health care.

Also, the Department agrees that it will not be easy for every individual to understand fully the information in the notice, and acknowledges that the onus of ensuring that individuals have an understanding of the notice should not be placed solely on health care providers. The Rule ensures that individuals are provided with a notice in plain language but leaves it to each individual's discretion to review the notice and to initiate a discussion with the covered entity about the use and disclosure of his or her health information or the individual's rights. However, the Department continues to believe strongly that promoting individuals' understanding of privacy practices is an essential component of providing notice to individuals. The Department anticipates that many stakeholders, including the Department,

covered entities, consumer organizations, health educators, the mass media and journalists, and a host of other organizations and individuals, will be involved in educating individuals about privacy notices and practices.

Response to Other Public Comments

Comment: Several commenters requested clarification as to whether a health care provider is required to obtain from individuals a new acknowledgment of receipt of the notice if the facility changes its privacy policy.

Response: The Department clarifies that this is not required. To minimize burden on the covered direct treatment provider, the final modification intends the obtaining of the individual's acknowledgment to be consistent with the timing for provision of the notice to the individual, that is, no later than the date of first service delivery. Upon revision of the notice, the Privacy Rule requires only that the direct treatment provider make the notice available upon request on or after the effective date of the revision, and, if he maintains a physical service delivery site, to post the revised notice in a clear and prominent location in his facility. *See* § 164.520(c)(2)(iii). As the Rule does not require a health care provider to provide the revised notice directly to the individual, unless requested by the individual, a new written acknowledgment is not required at the time of revision of the notice.

Comment: A few commenters requested clarification as to how the Department intended the notice acknowledgment process to be implemented within an affiliated covered entity or an organized health care arrangement (OHCA).

Response: The requirement for an individual's written acknowledgment of the notice corresponds with the requirement that the notice be provided to the individual by certain health care providers at first service delivery, regardless of whether the notice itself is the joint notice of an OHCA, the notice of an affiliated covered entity, or the notice of one entity. With respect to an OHCA, the Privacy Rule permits covered entities that participate in an OHCA to satisfy the notice requirements through the use of a joint notice, provided that the relevant conditions of § 164.520(d) are met. Section 164.520(d)(3) further provides that provision of a joint notice to an individual by any one of the covered entities included in the joint notice satisfies the notice provision requirements at § 164.520(c) with respect to all others covered by the joint

notice. Thus, a health care provider with a direct treatment relationship with an individual that is participating in an OHCA only need make a good faith effort to obtain the individual's acknowledgment of the joint notice if that provider is the covered entity within the OHCA that is providing the joint notice to the individual. Where the joint notice is provided to the individual by a participating covered entity other than a provider with a direct treatment relationship with the individual, no acknowledgment need be obtained. However, covered entities that participate in an OHCA are not required to utilize a joint notice and may maintain separate notices. In such case, each covered health care provider with a direct treatment relationship within the OHCA must make a good faith effort to obtain the individual's acknowledgment of the notice he or she provides.

Similarly, an affiliated covered entity may have one single notice that covers all of its affiliates. Thus, if the affiliated covered entity's notice is provided to the individual by a health care provider with which the individual has a direct treatment relationship, the health care provider must make a good faith effort to obtain the individual's acknowledgment of receipt of the notice. Alternatively, where the affiliated entity's notice is provided to the individual by a participating entity other than a provider with a direct treatment relationship with the individual, no acknowledgment need be obtained. However, as with the OHCA, the Department clarifies that covered entities that are part of an affiliated covered entity may maintain separate notices if they choose to do so; if they do so, each provider with a direct treatment relationship with the individual must make a good faith effort to obtain the individual's acknowledgment of the notice he or she provides.

Comment: It was suggested that if a provider chooses to obtain consent, the provider should not also be required to obtain the individual's acknowledgment of the notice.

Response: For those covered entities that choose to obtain consent, the Rule does not prescribe any details of the form or manner in which the consent must be obtained. Given this discretion, the Department does not believe that all consents will provide the same benefits to the individual as those afforded by the notice acknowledgment process. The Rule, therefore, does not relieve a covered health care provider of his obligations with respect to obtaining an individual's acknowledgment of the

C. HIPAA Final Rules, Privacy Standards, continued

notice if that provider also obtains the individual's consent. However, the Rule provides those covered health care providers that choose to obtain consent from an individual the discretion to design one form that includes both a consent and the acknowledgment of receipt of the notice.

Comment: Some commenters asked that the Privacy Rule allow the written acknowledgment of the notice to be obtained electronically without regard to channel of delivery (electronically or on paper) of the notice.

Response: Generally, the Privacy Rule allows for electronic documents to qualify as written documents for purposes of meeting the Rule's requirements. This also applies with respect to the notice acknowledgment. For notice delivered electronically, the Department intends a return receipt or other transmission from the individual to suffice as the notice acknowledgment.

For notice delivered on paper in a face-to-face encounter with the provider, although it is unclear to the Department how exactly the provider may do so, the Rule does not preclude providers from obtaining the individual's written acknowledgment electronically. The Department cautions, however, that the notice acknowledgment process is intended to alert individuals to the importance of the notice and provide them the opportunity to discuss privacy issues with their providers. To ensure that individuals are aware of the importance of the notice, the Rule requires that the individual's acknowledgment be in writing. Thus, the Department would not consider a receptionist's notation in a computer system to be an individual's written acknowledgment.

Comment: One commenter expressed concern that the Rule did not define "emergency" as it applies to ambulance services given the Rule's exceptions to the notice requirements for such situations. This commenter also urged that the Rule's notice provisions at § 164.520(c)(2) with respect to emergency treatment situations be expanded also to apply to non-emergency trips of ambulance providers. The commenter explained that even in non-emergency circumstances, patients, especially the elderly, often suffer from incapacitating or stressful conditions when they need to be transferred by ambulance, at which time it may not be effective or appropriate to provide the notice and obtain the individual's acknowledgment of receipt of the notice.

Response: During emergency treatment situations, the final Rule at § 164.520(c)(2)(i)(B) delays the

requirement for provision of the notice until reasonably practicable after the emergency situation, and exempts health care providers from having to make a good faith effort to obtain an individual's acknowledgment. As the provisions are not intended to apply only to ambulance providers, the Department does not believe that defining emergency with respect to such providers is appropriate or necessary. Nor does the Department believe that expanding these provisions to cover non-emergency trips of ambulance providers is appropriate. The provisions are intended to provide exceptions for those situations where providing the notice and obtaining an individual's acknowledgment may not be feasible or practicable. Where such extenuating circumstances do not exist, the Department expects that covered health care providers are able to provide individuals with a notice and make a good faith effort to obtain their acknowledgment of receipt. Where an individual does not provide an acknowledgment, the Rule requires only that the provider document his good faith effort to obtain the acknowledgment.

Comment: A number of commenters requested clarification on how to implement the "good faith" standard and urged the Department to provide more specific guidance and examples. Some commenters expressed concern over the perceived liability that would arise from such a discretionary standard.

Response: Covered entities are provided much discretion to implement the notice acknowledgment process as best suited to their specific business practices. The standard is designed as a "good faith effort" standard because the Department understands that obtaining an individual's acknowledgment of the notice may not always be feasible or practical, in spite of a covered entity's efforts. Thus, the standard is intended to account for those difficult situations, including where an individual simply refuses to provide the written acknowledgment. Given the discretion covered health care providers have in implementing these standards and the various ways such providers interact with their patients, it is difficult for the Department to provide specific guidance in this area that is generally applicable to many covered health care providers. However, the Department intends to provide future guidance through frequently asked questions or other materials in response to specific scenarios that are raised by industry.

With respect to commenters' concerns regarding potential liability, the

Department's position is that a failure by a covered entity to obtain an individual's acknowledgment, assuming it otherwise documented its good faith effort (as required by § 164.520(c)(2)(ii)), will not be considered a violation of this Rule.

Comment: Many commenters generally urged that the Department modify the Rule to allow for a simpler, shorter, and, therefore, more readable notice. Some of the commenters explained that a shorter notice would assure that more individuals would take the time to read and be able to understand the information. Others suggested that a shorter notice would help to alleviate burden on the covered entity. A number of these commenters suggested that the Department allow for a shorter summary or 1-page notice to replace the prescriptive notice required by the Privacy Rule. It was recommended that such a notice could refer individuals to a more detailed notice, available on request, or to an HHS web site, for additional information about an individual's rights under the Privacy Rule. Others recommended that the Department allow for a layered notice that contains: (1) A short notice that briefly describes, for example, the entity's principal uses and disclosures of an individual's health information, as well as the individual's rights with respect to that information; and (2) a longer notice, layered beneath the short notice, that contains all the elements required by the Rule.

Certain other commenters urged that one way to make the notice shorter, as well as to alleviate burden on the covered entity, would be to eliminate the requirement that the notice explain the more stringent State privacy laws. Commenters stated that companies that operate in multiple States will have to develop and print up to 50 different notices, and then update and reissue those notices whenever a material change is made to the State law. These commenters recommended instead that the notice simply state that State law may provide additional protections.

A few commenters urged that the Department provide a model notice that covered entities could use in their implementation efforts.

Response: The Department does not modify the notice content provisions at § 164.520(b). The Department believes that the elements required by § 164.520(b) are important to fully inform the individual of the covered entity's privacy practices, as well as his or her rights. However, the Department agrees that such information must be provided in a clear, concise, and easy to

C. HIPAA Final Rules, Privacy Standards, continued

Federal Register / Vol. 67, No. 157 / Wednesday, August 14, 2002 / Rules and Regulations   53243

understand manner. Therefore, the Department clarifies that covered entities may utilize a "layered notice" to implement the Rule's provisions, so long as the elements required by § 164.520(b) are included in the document that is provided to the individual. For example, a covered entity may satisfy the notice provisions by providing the individual with both a short notice that briefly summarizes the individual's rights, as well as other information; and a longer notice, layered beneath the short notice, that contains all the elements required by the Privacy Rule. Covered entities, however, while encouraged to use a layered notice, are not required to do so. Nothing in the final modifications relieve a covered entity of its duty to provide the entire notice in plain language so the average reader can understand it. *See* § 164.520(b)(1).

In response to comments regarding a model notice, it would be difficult for the Department to develop a document that would be generally useful to many different types of covered entities. A covered entity's notice must reflect in sufficient detail the particular uses and disclosures that entity may make. Such uses and disclosures likely will be very different for each type of covered entity. Thus, a uniform, model notice could not capture the wide variation in information practices across covered entities. The Department intends, however, to issue further general guidance to help covered entities implement the notice provisions of the Rule.

Comment: A number of commenters also requested that the Department lessen the burden associated with distributing the notice. For example, some commenters asked that covered entities be permitted to satisfy the notice provision requirements by posting the notice at the facility or on a web site and by providing a copy only to those consumers who request one, or by placing copies on display where an interested consumer may take one.

Response: The Department's position that making the notice available to individuals, either on request, by posting it at a facility or on a web site, or by placing copies on display, does not substitute for physically providing the notice directly to individuals. Adequate notice of privacy practices is a fundamental right afforded individuals by the Rule. As such, the Department does not believe that the burden of obtaining such information should be placed on the individual. Covered entities are required to distribute the notice in the manner described under § 164.520(c).

Comment: A few commenters requested that the Department make clear that no special mailings are required to provide individuals with a covered entity's notice; rather, that the notice may be distributed as part of other mailings or distributions by the covered entity. For example, one commenter argued that the Rule should be flexible enough to allow for notices to be included in a health plan's Summary Plan Descriptions, Booklets, or an Enrollment Application. It was argued that the notice would receive greater attention, be more carefully reviewed and, thus, better understood if it were published in materials known to be widely read by members.

Response: The Department clarifies that no special or separate mailings are required to satisfy the notice distribution requirements. The Privacy Rule provides covered entities with discretion in this area. A health plan distributing its notice through the mail, in accordance with § 164.520(c)(1), may do so as part of another mailing to the individual. In addition, a covered entity that provides its notice to an individual by e-mail, in accordance with § 164.520(c)(3), may include additional materials in the e-mail. No separate e-mail is required. However, the Privacy Rule at § 164.508(b)(3) continues to prohibit a covered entity from combining the notice in a single document with an authorization.

Comment: Commenters also urged that the Rule permit, for group products, a health plan to send its notice to the administrator of the group product or the plan sponsor, who would then be responsible for distributing the notice to each enrollee/employee. One commenter claimed this distribution method is especially appropriate where there is no regular communication with the covered individuals, as in an employer-pay-all group medical or dental plan. According to the commenter, providing the notice to the employer makes sense because the employer picks the plan and should be aware of the plan's privacy practices when doing so.

Response: The Privacy Rule requires a health plan to distribute its notice to each individual covered by the plan. Health plans may arrange to have another entity, or person, for example, a group administrator or a plan sponsor, distribute the notice on their behalf. However, the Department cautions that if such other entity or person fails to distribute the notice to individuals, the health plan would be in violation of the Rule.

Comment: Another commenter asked that the Department eliminate the requirement that a covered entity must provide the notice to every dependent, rather than just the head of the household. This commenter argued that while it makes sense to provide the notice to an emancipated minor or to a minor who pursuant to State law has consented to treatment, it does not make sense to send the notice to a 2-year old child.

Response: The Privacy Rule provides that a health plan may satisfy the notice provision requirements by distributing the notice to the named insured of a policy under which coverage is provided to the named insured and one or more dependents. A health plan is not required to distribute the notice to each dependent. *See* § 164.520(c)(1)(iii).

Further, a covered health care provider with a direct treatment relationship with the individual is required only to provide the notice to the individual receiving treatment at first service delivery. Where a parent brings a 2-year old child in for treatment, the provider satisfies the notice distribution requirements by providing the notice only to the child's parent.

I. Section 164.528—Accounting of Disclosures of Protected Health Information

December 2000 Privacy Rule. Under the Privacy Rule at § 164.528, individuals have the right to receive an accounting of disclosures of protected health information made by the covered entity, with certain exceptions. These exceptions, or instances where a covered entity is not required to account for disclosures, include disclosures made by the covered entity to carry out treatment, payment, or health care operations, as well as disclosures to individuals of protected health information about them. The individual must request an accounting of disclosures.

The accounting is required to include the following: (1) Disclosures of protected health information that occurred during the six years prior to the date of the request for an accounting; and (2) for each disclosure: the date of the disclosure; the name of the entity or person who received the protected health information, and, if known, the address of such entity or person; a brief description of the protected health information disclosed; and a brief statement of the purpose of the disclosure that reasonably informs the individual of the basis for the disclosure, or in lieu of such a statement, a copy of the individual's written authorization pursuant to § 164.508 or a copy of a written request

C. HIPAA Final Rules, Privacy Standards, continued

53244 Federal Register / Vol. 67, No. 157 / Wednesday, August 14, 2002 / Rules and Regulations

for a disclosure under §§ 164.502(a)(2)(ii) or 164.512. For multiple disclosures of protected health information to the same person, the Privacy Rule allows covered entities to provide individuals with an accounting that contains only the following information: (1) For the first disclosure, a full accounting, with the elements described above; (2) the frequency, periodicity, or number of disclosures made during the accounting period; and (3) the date of the last such disclosure made during the accounting period.

March 2002 NPRM. In response to concerns about the high costs and administrative burdens associated with the requirement to account to individuals for the covered entity's disclosure of protected health information, the Department proposed to expand the exceptions to the standard at § 164.528(a)(1) to include disclosures made pursuant to an authorization as provided in § 164.508. Covered entities would no longer be required to account for any disclosures authorized by the individual in accordance with § 164.508. The Department proposed to alleviate burden in this way because, like disclosures of protected health information made directly to the individual—which are already excluded from the accounting provisions in § 164.528(a)(1)—disclosures made pursuant to an authorization are also known by the individual, in as much as the individual was required to sign the forms authorizing the disclosures.

In addition to the exception language at § 164.528(a)(1), the Department proposed two conforming amendments at §§ 164.528(b)(2)(iv) and (b)(3) to delete references in the accounting content requirements to disclosures made pursuant to an authorization.

Overview of Public Comments. The following discussion provides an overview of the public comment received on this proposal. Additional comments received on this issue are discussed below in the section entitled, "Response to Other Public Comments."

The majority of comments on the accounting proposal supported the elimination of the accounting for authorized disclosures. The commenters agreed that, on balance, since the individual had elected to authorize the disclosure in the first instance, and that election was fully informed and voluntary, subsequently accounting for the disclosure made pursuant to that authorization was not necessary.

Many of the commenters went on to suggest other ways in which the accounting requirement could be made less burdensome. For example, several commenters wanted some or all of the disclosures which are permitted at § 164.512 without individual consent or authorization to also be exempt from the accounting requirements. Others proposed alternative means of accounting for disclosures for research, particularly when such disclosures involve large numbers of records. These commenters argued that accounting for each individual record disclosed for a large research project would be burdensome and may deter covered entities from participating in such research. Rather than an individual accounting, the commenters suggested that the covered entity be required only to disclose a listing of all relevant protocols under which an individual's information may have been released during the accounting period, the timeframes during which disclosures were made under a protocol, and the name of the institution and researcher or investigator responsible for the protocol, together with contact information for the researcher. The National Committee on Vital Health Statistics, while not endorsing a protocol listing directly, recommended the Department consider alternatives to minimize the burden of the accounting requirements on research.

Finally, several commenters objected to the elimination of the accounting requirement for authorized disclosures. Some of these commenters expressed concern that the proposal would eliminate the requirement to account for the authorized disclosure of psychotherapy notes. Others were primarily concerned that the proposal would weaken the accounting rights of individuals. According to these commenters, informing the individual of disclosures was only part of the purpose of an accounting. Even with regard to authorized disclosures, an accounting could be important to verify that disclosures were in accord with the scope and purpose as stated in the authorization and to detect potentially fraudulent, altered, or otherwise improperly accepted authorizations. Since authorizations had to be maintained in any event, accounting for these disclosures represented minimal work for the covered entity.

Final Modifications. Based on the general support in the public comment, the Department adopts the modification to eliminate the accounting requirement for authorized disclosures. The authorization process itself adequately protects individual privacy by assuring that the individual's permission is given both knowingly and voluntarily. The Department agrees with the majority of commenters that felt accounting for authorized disclosures did not serve to add to the individual's knowledge about disclosures of protected health information. The Department does recognize the role of accounting requirements in the detection of altered or fraudulent authorizations. However, the Department considers the incidence of these types of abuses, and the likelihood of their detection through a request for an accounting, to be too remote to warrant the burden on all covered entities of including authorized disclosures in an accounting. As noted by some commenters, the covered entity must retain a copy of the authorization to document their disclosure of protected health information and that documentation would be available to help resolve an individual's complaint to either the covered entity or the Secretary.

Specific concern about the elimination of the accounting requirement for authorized disclosures was expressed by mental health professionals, who believed their patients should always have the right to monitor access to their personal information. The Department appreciates theses commenters' concern about the need for heightened protections and accountability with regard to psychotherapy notes. It is because of these concerns that the Rule requires, with limited exceptions, individual authorization for even routine uses and disclosures of psychotherapy notes by anyone other than the originator of the notes. The Department clarifies that nothing in modifications adopted in this rulemaking prevents a mental health professional from including authorized disclosures of psychotherapy notes in an accounting requested by their patients. Indeed, any covered entity may account to the individual for disclosures based on the individual's authorization. The modification adopted by the Department simply no longer requires such an accounting.

In response to comment on this proposal, as well as on the proposals to permit incidental disclosures and disclosures of protected health information, other than direct identifiers, as part of a limited data set, the Department has added two additional exclusions to the accounting requirements. Disclosures that are part of a limited data set and disclosures that are merely incidental to another permissible use or disclosure will not require an accounting. The limited data set does not contain any protected health information that directly identifies the individual and the individual is further protected from identification by the required data use

C. HIPAA Final Rules, Privacy Standards, continued

agreement. The Department believes that accounting for these disclosures would be too burdensome. Similarly, the Department believes that it is impracticable to account for incidental disclosures, which by their very nature, may be uncertain or unknown to the covered entity at the time they occur. Incidental disclosures are permitted as long as reasonable safeguards and minimum necessary standards have been observed for the underlying communication. Moreover, incidental disclosures may most often happen in the context of a communication that relates to treatment or health care operations. In that case, the underlying disclosure is not subject to an accounting and it would be arbitrary to require an accounting for a disclosure that was merely incidental to such a communication.

The Department however disagrees with commenters who requested that other public purpose disclosures not be subject to the accounting requirement. Although the Rule permits disclosure for a variety of public purposes, they are not routine disclosures of the individual's information. The accounting requirement was designed as a means for the individual to find out the non-routine purposes for which his or her protected health information was disclosed by the covered entity, so as to increase the individual's awareness of persons or entities other than the individual's health care provider or health plan in possession of this information. To eliminate some or all of these public purposes would defeat the core purpose of the accounting requirement.

The Department disagrees with commenters' proposal to exempt all research disclosures made pursuant to a waiver of authorization from the accounting requirement. Individuals have a right to know what information about them has been disclosed without their authorization, and for what purpose(s). However, the Department agrees that the Rule's accounting requirements could have the undesired effect of causing covered entities to halt disclosures of protected health information for research. Therefore, the Department adopts commenters' proposal to revise the accounting requirement at § 164.528 to permit covered entities to meet the requirement for research disclosures if they provide individuals with a list of all protocols for which the patient's protected health information may have been disclosed for research pursuant to a waiver of authorization under § 164.512(i), as well as the researcher's name and contact information. The Department agrees

with commenters that this option struck the appropriate balance between affirming individuals' right to know how information about them is disclosed, and ensuring that important research is not halted.

The Department considered and rejected a similar proposal by commenters when it adopted the Privacy Rule in December 2000. While recognizing the potential burden for research, the Department determined that the individual was entitled to the same level of specificity in an accounting for research disclosures as any other disclosure. At that time, however, the Department added the summary accounting procedures at § 164.528(b)(3) to address the burden issues of researchers and others in accounting for multiple disclosures to the same entity. In response to the Department's most recent request for comments, researchers and others explained that the summary accounting procedures do not address the burden of having to account for disclosures for research permitted by § 164.512(i). These research projects usually involve many records. It is the volume of records for each disclosure, not the repeated nature of the disclosures, that presents an administrative obstacle for research if each record must be individually tracked for the accounting. Similarly, the summary accounting procedures do not relieve the burden for covered entities that participate in many different studies on a routine basis. The Department, therefore, reconsidered the proposal to account for large research projects by providing a list of protocols in light of these comments.

Specifically, the Department adds a paragraph (4) to § 164.528(b) to provide for simplified accounting for research disclosures as follows:

(1) The research disclosure must be pursuant to § 164.512(i) and involve at least 50 records. Thus, the simplified accounting procedures may be used for research disclosures based on an IRB or Privacy Board waiver of individual authorization, the provision of access to the researcher to protected health information for purposes preparatory to research, or for research using only records of deceased individuals. The large number of records likely to be disclosed for these research purposes justifies the need for the simplified accounting procedures. The Department has determined that a research request for 50 or more records warrants use of these special procedures.

(2) For research protocols for which the individual's protected health information may have been disclosed during the accounting period, the

accounting must include the name of the study or protocol, a description of the purpose of the study and the type of protected health information sought, and the timeframe of disclosures in response to the request.

(3) When requested by the individual, the covered entity must provide assistance in contacting those researchers to whom it is likely that the individual's protected health information was actually disclosed.

Support for streamlining accounting for research disclosures came in comments and from NCVHS. The Department wants to encourage research and believes protections afforded information in hands of researcher, particularly research overseen by IRB or Privacy Board, provides assurance of continued confidentiality of information. The Department does not agree that the individual has no need to know that his or her information has been disclosed for a research purpose. Covered entities, of course, may account for research disclosures in the same manner as all other disclosures. Even when the covered entity elects to use the alternative of a protocol listing, the Department encourages covered entities to provide individuals with disclosure of the specific research study or protocol for which their protected health information was disclosed, and other specific information relating to such actual disclosures if they so choose. If the covered entity lists all protocols for which the individual's information may have been disclosed, the Department would further encourage that the covered entity list under separate headings, or on separate lists, all protocols relating to particular health issues or conditions, so that individuals may more readily identify the specific studies for which their protected health information is more likely to have been disclosed.

The Department intends to monitor the simplified accounting procedures for certain research disclosures to determine if they are effective in providing meaningful information to individuals about how their protected health information is disclosed for research purposes, while still reducing the administrative burden on covered entities participating in such research efforts. The Department may make adjustments to the accounting procedures for research in the future as necessary to ensure both goals are fully met.

Response to Other Public Comments

Comment: A few commenters opposed the proposal to eliminate the accounting requirement for all

C. HIPAA Final Rules, Privacy Standards, continued

authorized disclosures arguing that, absent a full accounting, the individual cannot meaningfully exercise the right to amend or to revoke the authorization. Others also felt that a comprehensive right to an accounting, with no exceptions, was better from an oversight and enforcement standpoint as it encouraged consistent documentation of disclosures. One commenter also pointed to an example of the potential for fraudulent authorizations by citing press accounts of a chain drug store that allegedly took customers signatures from a log that waived their right to consult with the pharmacist and attached those signatures to a form authorizing the receipt of marketing materials. Under the proposal, the commenter asserted, the chain drug store would not have to include such fraudulent authorizations as part of an accounting to the individual.

Response: The Department does not agree that the individual's right to amendment is materially affected by the accounting requirements for authorized disclosures. The covered entity that created the protected health information contained in a designated record set has the primary obligation to the individual to amend any erroneous or incomplete information. The individual does not necessarily have a right to amend information that is maintained by other entities that the individual has authorized to have his or her protected health information. Furthermore, the covered entity that has amended its own designated record set at the request of the individual is obligated to make reasonable efforts to notify other persons, including business associates, that are known to have the protected health information that was the subject of the amendment and that may rely on such information to the detriment of the individual. This obligation would arise with regard to persons to whom protected health information was disclosed with the individual's authorization. Therefore, the individual's amendment rights are not adversely affected by the modifications to the accounting requirements. Furthermore, nothing in the modification adversely affects the individual's right to revoke the authorization.

The Department agrees that oversight is facilitated by consistent documentation of disclosures. However, the Department must balance its oversight functions with the burden on entities to track all disclosures regardless of purpose. Based on this balancing, the Department has exempted routine disclosures, such as those for treatment, payment, and health care operations, and others for security reasons. The addition of authorized disclosures to the exemption from the accounting does not materially affect the Department's oversight function. Compliance with the Rule's authorization requirements can still be effectively monitored because covered entities are required to maintain signed authorizations as documentation of disclosures. Therefore, the Department believes that effective oversight, not the happenstance of discovery by an individual through the accounting requirement, is the best means to detect and prevent serious misdeeds such as those alleged in fraudulent authorizations.

Comment: A number of commenters recommended other types of disclosures for exemption from the accounting requirement. Many recommended elimination of the accounting requirement for public health disclosures arguing that the burden of the requirement may deter entities from making such disclosures and that because many are made directly to public health authorities by doctors and nurses, rather than from a central records component of the entity, public health disclosures are particularly difficult to track and document. Others suggested exempting from an accounting requirement any disclosure required by another law on the grounds that neither the individual nor the entity has any choice about such required disclosures. Still others wanted all disclosures to a governmental entity exempted as many such disclosures are required and often reports are routine or require lots of data. Some wanted disclosures to law enforcement or to insurers for claims investigations exempted from the accounting requirement to prevent interference with such investigatory efforts. Finally, a few commenters suggested that all of the disclosures permitted or required by the Privacy Rule should be excluded from the accounting requirement.

Response: Elimination of an accounting requirement for authorized disclosures is justified in large part by the individual's knowledge of and voluntary agreement to such disclosures. None of the above suggestions for exemption of other permitted disclosures can be similarly justified. The right to an accounting of disclosures serves an important function in informing the individual as to which information was sent to which recipients. While it is possible that informing individuals about the disclosures of their health information may on occasion discourage some worthwhile activity, the Department believes that the individual's right to know who is using their information and for what purposes takes precedence.

Comment: One commenter sought an exemption from the accounting requirement for disclosures to adult protective services when referrals are made for abuse, neglect, or domestic violence victims. For the same reasons that the Rule permits waiver of notification to the victim at the time of the referral based on considerations of the victim's safety, the regulation should not make such disclosures known after the fact through the accounting requirement.

Response: The Department appreciates the concerns expressed by the commenter for the safety and welfare of the victims of abuse, neglect, or domestic violence. In recognition of these concerns, the Department does give the covered entity discretion in notifying the victim and/or the individual's personal representative at the time of the disclosure. These concerns become more attenuated in the context of an accounting for disclosures, which must be requested by the individual and for which the covered entity has a longer timeframe to respond. Concern for the safety of victims of abuse or domestic violence should not result in stripping these individuals of the rights granted to others. If the individual is requesting the accounting, even after being warned of the potential dangers, the covered entity should honor that request. However, if the request is by the individual's personal representative and the covered entity has a reasonable belief that such person is the abuser or that providing the accounting to such person could endanger the individual, the covered entity continues to have the discretion in § 164.502(g)(5) to decline such a request.

Comment: One commenter suggested elimination of the accounting requirement in its entirety. The commenter argued that HIPAA does not require an accounting as the individual's right and the accounting does not provide any additional privacy protections to the individual's information.

Response: The Department disagrees with the commenter. HIPAA authorized the Secretary to identify rights of the individual with respect to protected health information and how those rights should be exercised. In absence of regulation, HIPAA also authorized the Secretary to effectuate these rights by regulation. As stated in the preamble to the December 2000 Privacy Rule, the standard adopted by the Secretary that provides individuals with a right to an

C. HIPAA Final Rules, Privacy Standards, continued

accounting of disclosures, is consistent with well-established privacy principles in other law and with industry standards and ethical guidelines, such as the Federal Privacy Act (5 U.S.C. 552a), the July 1977 Report of the Privacy Protection Study Commission, and NAIC Health Information Privacy Model Act. (*See* 65 FR 82739.)

Comment: A few commenters requested that the accounting period be shortened from six years to two years or three years.

Response: The Department selected six years as the time period for an accounting to be consistent with documentation retention requirements in the Rule. We note that the Rule exempts from the accounting disclosures made prior to the compliance date for Rule, or April 14, 2003. Therefore, it will not be until April 2009 that a full six year accounting period will occur. Also, the Rule permits individuals to request and the covered entity to provide for an accounting for less than full six year period. For example, an individual may be interested only in disclosures that occurred in the prior year or in a particular month. The Department will monitor the use of the accounting requirements after the compliance date and will evaluate the need for changes in the future if the six year period for the accounting proves to be unduly burdensome.

Comment: Commenters requested clarification of the need to account for disclosures to business associates, noting that while the regulation states that disclosures to and by a business associate are subject to an accounting, most such disclosures are for health care operations for which no accounting is required.

Response: The Department clarifies that the implementation specification in § 164.528(b)(1), that expressly includes in the content of an accounting disclosures to or by a business associate, must be read in conjunction with the basic standard for an accounting for disclosures in § 164.528(a). Indeed, the implementation specification expressly references the standard. Read together, the Rule does not require an accounting of any disclosure to or by a business associate that is for any exempt purpose, including disclosures for treatment, payment, and health care operations.

Comment: One commenter wanted health care providers to be able to charge reasonable fees to cover the retrieval and preparation costs of an accounting for disclosures.

Response: In granting individuals the right to an accounting, the Department had to balance the individual's right to know how and to whom protected health information is being disclosed and the financial and administrative burden on covered entities in responding to such requests. The balance struck by the Department with regard to cost was to grant the individual a right to an accounting once a year without charge. The covered entity may impose reasonable, cost-based fees for any subsequent requests during the one year period. The Department clarifies that the covered entity may recoup its reasonable retrieval and report preparation costs, as well as any mailing costs, incurred in responding to subsequent requests. The Rule requires that individuals be notified in advance of these fees and provided an opportunity to withdraw or amend its request for a subsequent accounting to avoid incurring excessive fees.

Comment: One commenter wanted clarification of the covered entity's responsibility to account for the disclosures of others. For example, the commenter wanted to know if the covered entity was responsible only for its own disclosures or did it also need to account for disclosures by every person that may subsequently handle the information.

Response: The Department clarifies in response to this comment that a covered entity is responsible to account to the individual for certain disclosures that it makes and for disclosures by its business associates. The covered entity is not responsible to account to the individual for any subsequent disclosures of the information by others that receive the information from the covered entity or its business associate.

J. Section 164.532—Transition Provisions

1. Research Transition

December 2000 Privacy Rule. The December 2000 Privacy Rule at § 164.532 contained different transition requirements for research being conducted with an individual's legal permission that included treatment, and for research being conducted with an individual's legal permission that did not include treatment. However, the Rule did not explicitly address transition provisions for research studies ongoing after the compliance date where the legal permission of the individual had not been sought.

March 2002 NPRM. Several commenters found the transition provisions for research to be confusing, and further noted that December 2000 Privacy Rule did not address research ongoing after the compliance date where the legal permission of the individual had not been sought. To address these concerns, the Department proposed several revisions to the Privacy Rule's transition provisions. In particular, the Department proposed that there be no distinction in the transition provisions between research that includes treatment and research that does not, and no distinction between the requirements for research conducted with a patient's legal permission and research conducted with an IRB-approved waiver of a patient's informed consent. In sum, the NPRM proposed that covered entities be permitted to use or disclose protected health information created or received for a specific research study before the compliance date (if there was no agreed-to restriction in accordance with § 164.522(a)), if the covered entity has obtained, prior to the compliance date, any one of the following: (1) An authorization or other express legal permission from an individual to use or disclose protected health information for the research study; (2) the informed consent of the individual to participate in the research study; or (3) a waiver, by an IRB of informed consent for the research study in accordance with the Common Rule or FDA's human subject protection regulations. However, even if the researcher obtained, from an IRB, a waiver of informed consent, an authorization would be required if informed consent is later obtained. This may occur if there is a temporary waiver of informed consent for emergency research under the Food and Drug Administration human subject protection regulations.

Overview of Public Comments. The following discussion provides an overview of the public comment received on this proposal. Additional comments received on this issue are discussed below in the section entitled, "Response to Other Public Comments."

Most commenters supported the proposed revisions to the Privacy Rule's transition provisions for research. However, a few commenters requested that the transition provisions be broadened to permit covered entities to rely on an express legal permission or informed consent approved by an IRB before the compliance date, even if the permission or consent had not been signed by the individual prior to the compliance date. Consequently, a researcher could use the same forms throughout their study, decreasing the chance of introducing error into the research through the use of multiple recruitment procedures, disruption to the research, and the burden for the IRBs and researchers. A few other

C. HIPAA Final Rules, Privacy Standards, continued

commenters suggested that covered entities be permitted to use and disclose protected health information with consent forms approved by an IRB prior to the compliance date until the next review by the IRB, as required by the Common Rule. They argued that this would result in all informed consent forms being in compliance with the Privacy Rule's authorization regulations within a one-year period, and it would avoid disruption to ongoing research, as well as a flood of consent form revision requests to the IRBs.

Final Modifications. The Department agrees with the majority of comments that supported the modifications to the transition provisions, and has therefore adopted the research transition modifications as proposed in the NPRM. The Department disagrees with the comments that suggest broadening the transition provisions to permit covered entities to rely on an express legal permission or informed consent that had not been signed by the individual before the compliance date. The Department understands that this provision may disrupt some ongoing research; however, the recruitment periods for some studies may continue long after the compliance date, and it would be unreasonable to grandfather-in existing informed consent documents indefinitely. While the commenter's suggestion to only grandfather-in such informed consent documents until the next review by the IRB would address this concern, the Privacy Rule does not require initial or continuing IRB or Privacy Board review of authorization forms or informed consent documents. Therefore, the Department does not adopt this change to its proposal.

However, the Department understands that some existing express legal permissions, informed consents, or IRB-approved waivers of informed consents are not study specific. Therefore, the final Rule permits covered entities to rely on an express legal permission, informed consent, or IRB-approved waiver of informed consent for future unspecified research, provided the legal permission, informed consent or IRB-approved waiver was obtained prior to the compliance date.

Response to Other Public Comments

Comment: A commenter requested that the transition provision be narrowed by requiring research that received a waiver of informed consent from an IRB prior to the compliance date but that begins after the compliance date be re-evaluated under the Privacy Rule's waiver criteria.

Response: The Department disagrees. Given that the Privacy Rule's waiver

criteria for an individual's authorization generally are consistent with the same types of considerations currently applied to a waiver of an individual's informed consent, this suggestion would impose unnecessary burdens on researchers, IRBs, and Privacy Boards, with respect to the few research studies that would fall in this category.

2. Business Associates

December 2000 Privacy Rule. The Privacy Rule at § 164.502(e) permits a covered entity to disclose protected health information to a business associate who performs a function or activity on behalf of, or provides a service to, the covered entity that involves the creation, use, or disclosure of, protected health information, provided that the covered entity obtains satisfactory assurances that the business associate will appropriately safeguard the information. The Department recognizes that most covered entities do not perform or carry out all of their health care activities and functions by themselves, but rather use the services of, or receive assistance from, a variety of other persons or entities. Given this framework, the Department intended these provisions to allow such business relationships to continue while ensuring that identifiable health information created or shared in the course of the relationships was protected.

The Privacy Rule requires that the satisfactory assurances obtained from the business associate be in the form of a written contract (or other written arrangement, as between governmental entities) between the covered entity and the business associate that contains the elements specified at § 164.504(e). For example, the agreement must identify the uses and disclosures of protected health information the business associate is permitted or required to make, as well as require the business associate to put in place appropriate safeguards to protect against a use or disclosure not permitted by the contract or agreement.

The Privacy Rule also provides that, where a covered entity knows of a material breach or violation by the business associate of the contract or agreement, the covered entity is required to take reasonable steps to cure the breach or end the violation, and if such steps are unsuccessful, to terminate the contract or arrangement. If termination of the contract or arrangement is not feasible, a covered entity is required to report the problem to the Secretary of HHS. A covered entity that violates the satisfactory assurances it provided as a business

associate of another covered entity is in noncompliance with the Privacy Rule.

The Privacy Rule's definition of "business associate" at § 160.103 includes the types of functions or activities, and list of services, that make a person or entity who engages in them a business associate, if such activity or service involves protected health information. For example, a third party administrator (TPA) is a business associate of a health plan to the extent the TPA assists the health plan with claims processing or another covered function. Similarly, accounting services performed by an outside consultant give rise to a business associate relationship when provision of the service entails access to the protected health information held by a covered entity.

The Privacy Rule excepts from the business associate standard certain uses or disclosures of protected health information. That is, in certain situations, a covered entity is not required to have a contract or other written agreement in place before disclosing protected health information to a business associate or allowing protected health information to be created by the business associate on its behalf. Specifically, the standard does not apply to: disclosures by a covered entity to a health care provider for treatment purposes; disclosures to the plan sponsor by a group health plan, or a health insurance issuer or HMO with respect to a group health plan, to the extent that the requirements of § 164.504(f) apply and are met; or to the collection and sharing of protected health information by a health plan that is a public benefits program and an agency other than the agency administering the health plan, where the other agency collects protected health information for, or determines eligibility or enrollment with respect to, the government program, and where such activity is authorized by law. See § 164.502(e)(1)(ii).

March 2002 NPRM. The Department heard concerns from many covered entities and others about the business associate provisions of the Privacy Rule. The majority expressed some concern over the anticipated administrative burden and cost to implement the business associate provisions. Some stated that many covered entities have existing contracts that are not set to terminate or expire until after the compliance date of the Privacy Rule. Others expressed specific concern that the two-year compliance period does not provide enough time to reopen and renegotiate what could be hundreds or more contracts for large covered entities. These entities went on to urge the

C. HIPAA Final Rules, Privacy Standards, continued

Federal Register / Vol. 67, No. 157 / Wednesday, August 14, 2002 / Rules and Regulations   **53249**

Department to grandfather in existing contracts until such contracts come up for renewal instead of requiring that all contracts be in compliance with the business associate provisions by the compliance date of the Privacy Rule.

In response to these concerns, the Department proposed to relieve some of the burden on covered entities in complying with the business associate provisions by both adding a transition provision to grandfather certain existing contracts for a specified period of time, as well as publishing sample contract language in the proposed Rule. The following discussion addresses the issue of the business associate transition provisions. A discussion of the business associate sample contract language is included in Part X of the preamble.

The Department proposed new transition provisions at § 164.532(d) and (e) to allow covered entities, other than small health plans, to continue to operate under certain existing contracts with business associates for up to one year beyond the April 14, 2003, compliance date of the Privacy Rule. The additional transition period would be available to a covered entity, other than a small health plan, if, prior to the effective date of the transition provision, the covered entity had an existing contract or other written arrangement with a business associate, and such contract or arrangement was not renewed or modified between the effective date of this provision and the Privacy Rule's compliance date of April 14, 2003. The proposed provisions were intended to allow those covered entities with contracts that qualified as described above to continue to disclose protected health information to the business associate, or allow the business associate to create or receive protected health information on its behalf, for up to one year beyond the Privacy Rule's compliance date, regardless of whether the contract meets the applicable contract requirements in the Privacy Rule. The Department proposed to deem such contracts to be compliant with the Privacy Rule until either the covered entity had renewed or modified the contract following the compliance date of the Privacy Rule (April 14, 2003), or April 14, 2004, whichever was sooner. In cases where a contract simply renewed automatically without any change in terms or other action by the parties (also known as "evergreen contracts"), the Department intended that such evergreen contracts would be eligible for the extension and that deemed compliance would not terminate when these contracts automatically rolled over.

These transition provisions would apply to covered entities only with respect to written contracts or other written arrangements as specified above, and not to oral contracts or other arrangements. In addition, the proposed transition provisions would not apply to small health plans, as defined in the Privacy Rule. Small health plans would be required to have all business associate contracts be in compliance with the Privacy Rule's applicable provisions, by the compliance deadline of April 14, 2004, for such covered entities.

In proposed § 164.532(e)(2), the Department provided that the new transition provisions would not relieve a covered entity of its responsibilities with respect to making protected health information available to the Secretary, including information held by a business associate, as necessary for the Secretary to determine compliance. Similarly, these provisions would not relieve a covered entity of its responsibilities with respect to an individual's rights to access or amend his or her protected health information held by a business associate, or receive an accounting of disclosures by a business associate, as provided for by the Privacy Rule's requirements at §§ 164.524, 164.526, and 164.528. Covered entities still would be required to fulfill individuals' rights with respect to their protected health information, including information held by a business associate of the covered entity. Covered entities would have to ensure, in whatever manner effective, the appropriate cooperation by their business associates in meeting these requirements.

The Department did not propose modifications to the standards and implementation specifications that apply to business associate relationships as set forth at §§ 164.502(e) and 164.504(e), respectively, of the Privacy Rule.

Overview of Public Comments. The following discussion provides an overview of the public comment received on this proposal. Additional comments received on this issue are discussed below in the section entitled, "Response to Other Public Comments."

Most commenters on this issue expressed general support for a transition period for business associate contracts. Of these commenters, however, many requested that the Department modify the proposal in a number of different ways. For example, a number of commenters urged the Department to modify which contracts qualify for the transition period, such as by making the transition period

available to contracts existing as of the compliance date of the Privacy Rule, rather than as of the effective date of the transition modification. Others requested that the Department apply the transition period to all business associate arrangements, even those arrangements for which there was no existing written contract.

Some commenters urged the Department to modify the end date of the transition period. A few of these commenters requested that the transition period apply to existing business associate contracts until they expired or were renewed, with no specified end date in the regulation. It was also suggested that the Department simply provide one extra year, until April 14, 2004, for compliance with the business associate contract provisions, without the provision that a renewal or modification of the contract would trigger an earlier transition period end date. A few commenters requested further guidance as to the types of actions the Department would or would not consider to be a "renewal or modification" of the contract.

Additionally, numerous commenters requested that the Department further clarify a covered entity's responsibilities with regard to their business associates during the transition period. Commenters expressed concerns with the proposal's requirement that the transition provisions would not have relieved a covered entity of its responsibilities with respect to an individual's rights to access or amend his or her protected health information held by business associates, or receive an accounting of disclosures by a business associate. Similarly, commenters raised concerns that the transition provisions would not have relieved a covered entity of its responsibilities to make information available to the Secretary, including information held by a business associate, as necessary for the Secretary to determine compliance. Commenters also expressed concerns about the fact that it appeared that covered entities still would have been required to obtain satisfactory assurances from a business associate that protected health information not be used improperly by the business associate, or that the covered entity still would have been required to mitigate any known harmful effects of a business associate's improper use or disclosure of protected health information during the transition period. It was stated that cooperation by a business associate with respect to the covered entity's obligations under the Rule would be difficult, if not

C. HIPAA Final Rules, Privacy Standards, continued

impossible, to secure without a formal agreement.

A few commenters opposed the proposal, one of whom raised concerns that the proposed transition period would encourage covered entities to enter into "stop gap" contracts instead of compliant business associate contracts. This commenter urged that the Department maintain the original compliance date for business associate contracts.

Final Modifications. In the final Rule, the Department adopts the transition period for certain business associate contracts as proposed in the NPRM. The final Rule's transition provisions at § 164.532(d) and (e) permit covered entities, other than small health plans, to continue to operate under certain existing contracts with business associates for up to one year beyond the April 14, 2003, compliance date of the Privacy Rule. The transition period is available to covered entities who have an existing contract (or other written arrangement) with a business associate prior to the effective date of this modification, provided that the contract is not renewed or modified prior to the April 14, 2003, compliance date of the Privacy Rule. (See the "Dates" section above for the effective date of this modification.) Covered entities with contracts that qualify are permitted to continue to operate under those contracts with their business associates until April 14, 2004, or until the contract is renewed or modified, whichever is sooner. During the transition period, such contracts are deemed to be compliant with the Privacy Rule regardless of whether the contract meets the Rule's applicable contract requirements at §§ 164.502(e) and 164.504(e).

The transition provisions are intended to address the concerns of covered entities that the two-year period between the effective date and compliance date of the Privacy Rule is insufficient to reopen and renegotiate all existing contracts for the purposes of bringing them into compliance with the Rule. These provisions also provide covered entities with added flexibility to incorporate the business associate contract requirements at the time they would otherwise modify or renew the existing contract.

Given the intended purpose of these provisions, the Department is not persuaded by the comments that it is necessary to modify the provision to make the transition period available to those contracts existing prior to the Rule's compliance date of April 14, 2003, rather than the effective date of the modification, or, even less so, to any

business associate arrangement regardless of whether a written contract currently exists.

A covered entity that does not have a written contract with a business associate prior to the effective date of this modification does not encounter the same burdens described by other commenters associated with having to reopen and renegotiate many existing contracts at once. The Department believes that such a covered entity should be able to enter into a compliant business associate contract by the compliance date of the Rule. Further, those covered entities whose business associate contracts come up for renewal or modification prior to the compliance date have the opportunity to bring such contracts into compliance by April 14, 2003. Thus, a covered entity that enters into a business associate contract after the effective date of this modification, or that has a contract that is renewed or modified prior to the compliance date of the Rule, is not eligible for the transition period and is required to have a business associate contract in place that meets the applicable requirements of §§ 164.502(e) and 164.504(e) by the Privacy Rule's compliance date of April 14, 2003. Further, as in the proposed Rule, the transition provisions apply only to written contracts or other written arrangements. Oral contracts or other arrangements are not eligible for the transition period. The Department clarifies, however, that nothing in these provisions requires a covered entity to come into compliance with the business associate contract provisions prior to April 14, 2003.

Similarly, in response to those commenters who requested that the Department permit existing contracts to be transitioned until April 14, 2004, regardless of whether such contracts are renewed or modified prior to that date, the Department considers a renewal or modification of the contract to be an appropriate, less burdensome opportunity to bring such contracts into compliance with the Privacy Rule. The Department, therefore, does not modify the proposal in such a way. Further, in response to commenters who requested that the Rule grandfather in existing business associate contracts until they expire or are renewed, with no specified end date in the regulation, the Department believes that limiting the transition period to one year beyond the Rule's compliance date is the proper balance between individuals' privacy interests and alleviating burden on the covered entity. All existing business associate contracts must be compliant with the Rule's business associate contract *provisions by April 14, 2004.*

As in the proposal, evergreen or other contracts that renew automatically without any change in terms or other action by the parties and that exist by the effective date of this modification are eligible for the transition period. The automatic renewal of such contracts itself does not terminate qualification for, or deemed compliance during, the transition period. Renewal or modification for the purposes of these transition provisions requires action by the parties involved. For example, the Department does not consider an automatic inflation adjustment to the price of a contract to be a renewal or modification for purposes of these provisions. Such an adjustment will not trigger the end of the transition period, nor make the contract ineligible for the transition period if the adjustment occurs before the compliance date of the Rule.

The transition provisions do not apply to "small health plans," as defined at § 160.103. Small health plans are required to have business associate contracts that are compliant with §§ 164.502(e) and 164.504(e) by the April 14, 2004, compliance date for such entities. As explained in the proposal, the Department believes that the additional year provided by the statute for these entities to comply with the Privacy Rule provides sufficient time for compliance with the Rule's business associate provisions. In addition, the sample contract provisions provided in the Appendix to the preamble will assist small health plans and other covered entities in their implementation of the Privacy Rule's business associate provisions by April 14, 2004.

Like the proposal, the final Rule at § 164.532(e)(2) provides that, during the transition period, covered entities are not relieved of their responsibilities to make information available to the Secretary, including information held by a business associate, as necessary for the Secretary to determine compliance by the covered entity. Similarly, the transition period does not relieve a covered entity of its responsibilities with respect to an individual's rights to access or amend his or her protected health information held by a business associate, or receive an accounting of disclosures by a business associate, as provided for by the Privacy Rule's requirements at §§ 164.524, 164.526, and 164.528. In addition, unlike the proposed Rule, the final Rule at § 164.532(e)(3) explicitly provides that with respect to those business associate contracts that qualify for the transition period as described above, a covered *entity is not relieved of its obligation*

C. HIPAA Final Rules, Privacy Standards, continued

under § 164.530(f) to mitigate, to the extent practicable, any harmful effect that is known to the covered entity of a use or disclosure of protected health information by its business associate in violation of the covered entity's policies and procedures or the requirements of this subpart, as required by § 164.530(f).

The Department does not believe that a covered entity should be relieved during the transition period of its responsibilities with respect to cooperating with the Secretary or fulfilling an individual's rights with respect to protected health information held by the business associate, or mitigating any harmful effects of an inappropriate use or disclosure by the business associate. The transition period is intended to alleviate some of the burden on covered entities, but not at the expense of individuals' privacy rights. Eliminating these privacy protections and rights would severely weaken the Rule with respect to those covered entities with contracts that qualify for the transition period.

Further, the Rule provides covered entities some discretion in implementing these requirements with respect to their business associates. For example, a covered entity does not need to provide an individual with access to protected health information held by a business associate if the only information the business associate holds is a duplicate of what the covered entity maintains and to which it has provided the individual access. Covered entities are required to ensure, in whatever manner deemed effective by the covered entity, the appropriate cooperation by their business associates in meeting these requirements.

In response to other concerns from commenters, the Department clarifies that a covered entity is not required to obtain satisfactory assurances (in any form), as required by § 164.502(e)(1), from a business associate to which the transition period applies. The transition period effectively deems such qualified contracts to fulfill the requirement for satisfactory assurances from the business associate.

The Department is aware that the transition provisions may encourage some covered entities to enter into contracts before the effective date of the modification solely to take advantage of the transition period, rather than encourage such entities to execute fully compliant business associate contracts. However, the Department believes that the provision appropriately limits the potential for such misuse by requiring that qualified contracts exist prior to the modification effective date rather than the Privacy Rule's compliance date.

Further, the transition provisions do not relieve the covered entity of its obligations with respect to protected health information held by the business associate and, therefore, ensures that an individual's rights, as provided for by the Rule, remain intact during the transition period.

Response to Other Public Comments

Comment: One commenter requested that the transition period also be applied to the requirement that a group health plan amend plan documents pursuant to § 164.504(f) before protected health information may be disclosed to the plan sponsor.

Response: The Department does not make such a modification. The intent of the business associate transition provisions is to alleviate burden on those covered entities with many existing contracts, where as a result, the two-year period between the effective date and compliance date of the Privacy Rule may be insufficient to reopen and renegotiate all such contracts for the purposes of bringing them into compliance with the Rule. The Privacy Rule does not require a business associate contract for disclosure of protected health information from a group health plan to a plan sponsor. Rather, the Rule permits a group health plan to disclose protected health information to a plan sponsor if, among other requirements, the plan documents are amended to appropriately reflect and restrict the plan sponsor's uses and disclosures of such information. As the group health plan should only have one set of plan documents that must be amended, the same burdens described above do not exist with respect to this activity. Thus, the Department expects that group health plans will be able to modify plan documents in accordance with the Rule by the Rule's compliance date.

Comment: Many commenters continued to recommend various modifications to the business associate standard, unrelated to the proposed modifications. For example, some commenters urged that the Department eliminate the business associate requirements entirely. Several commenters urged that the Department exempt covered entities from having to enter into contracts with business associates who are also covered entities under the Privacy Rule. Alternatively, one commenter suggested that the Department simplify the requirements by requiring a covered entity that is a business associate to specify in writing the uses and disclosures the covered entity is permitted to make as a business associate.

Other commenters requested that the Department allow business associates to self-certify or be certified by a third party or HHS as compliant with the Privacy Rule, as an alternative to the business associate contract requirement. Certain commenters urged the Department to modify the Rule to eliminate the need for a contract with accreditation organizations. Some commenters suggested that the Department do so by reclassifying private accreditation organizations acting under authority from a government agency as health oversight organizations, rather than as business associates.

Response: The proposed modifications regarding business associates were intended to address the concerns of commenters with respect to having insufficient time to reopen and renegotiate what could be thousands of contracts for some covered entities by the compliance date of the Privacy Rule. The proposed modifications did not address changes to the definition of, or requirements for, business associates generally. The Department has, in previous guidance, as well as in the preamble to the December 2000 Privacy Rule, explained its position with respect to most of the above concerns. However, the Department summarizes its position in response to such comments briefly below.

The Department recognizes that most covered entities acquire the services of a variety of other persons or entities to assist in carrying covered entities' health care activities. The business associate provisions are necessary to ensure that individually identifiable health information created or shared in the course of these relationships is protected. Further, without the business associate provisions, covered entities would be able to circumvent the requirements of the Privacy Rule simply by contracting out certain of its functions.

With respect to a contract between a covered entity and a business associate who is also a covered entity, the Department restates its position that a covered entity that is a business associate should be restricted from using or disclosing the protected health information it creates or receives as a business associate for any purposes other than those explicitly provided for in its contract. Further, to modify the provisions to require or permit a type of written assurance, other than a contract, by a covered entity would add unnecessary complexity to the Rule.

Additionally, the Department at this time does not believe that a business associate certification process would

C. HIPAA Final Rules, Privacy Standards, continued

provide the same kind of protections and guarantees with respect to a business associate's actions that are available to a covered entity through a contract under State law. With respect to certification by a third party, it is unclear whether such a process would allow for any meaningful enforcement (such as termination of a contract) for the actions of a business associate. Further, the Department could not require that a business associate be certified by a third party. Thus, the Privacy Rule still would have to allow for a contract between a covered entity and a business associate.

The Privacy Rule explicitly defines organizations that accredit covered entities as business associates. See the definition of "business associate" at § 160.103. The Department defined such organizations as business associates because, like other business associates, they provide a service to the covered entity during which much protected health information is shared. The Privacy Rule treats all organizations that provide accreditation services to covered entities alike. The Department has not been persuaded by the comments that those accreditation organizations acting under grant of authority from a government agency should be treated differently under the Rule and relieved of the conditions placed on other such relationships. However, the Department understands concerns regarding the burdens associated with the business associate contract requirements. The Department clarifies that the business associate provisions may be satisfied by standard or model contract forms which could require little or no modification for each covered entity. As an alternative to the business associate contract, these final modifications permit a covered entity to disclose a limited data set of protected health information, not including direct identifiers, for accreditation and other health care operations purposes subject to a data use agreement. See § 164.514(e).

Comment: A number of commenters continued to express concern over a covered entity's perceived liability with respect to the actions of its business associate. Some commenters requested further clarification that a covered entity is not responsible for or required to monitor the actions of its business associates. It also was suggested that such language expressly be included in the Rule's regulatory text. One commenter recommended that the Rule provide that business associates are directly liable for their own failure to comply with the Privacy Rule. Another commenter urged that the Department

eliminate a covered entity's obligation to mitigate any harmful effects caused by a business associate's improper use or disclosure of protected health information.

Response: The Privacy Rule does not require a covered entity to actively monitor the actions of its business associates nor is the covered entity responsible or liable for the actions of its business associates. Rather, the Rule only requires that, where a covered entity knows of a pattern of activity or practice that constitutes a material breach or violation of the business associate's obligations under the contract, the covered entity take steps to cure the breach or end the violation. See § 164.504(e)(1). The Department does not believe a regulatory modification is necessary in this area. The Department does not have the statutory authority to hold business associates, that are not also covered entities, liable under the Privacy Rule.

With respect to mitigation, the Department does not accept the commenter's suggestion. When protected health information is used or disclosed inappropriately, the harm to the individual is the same, regardless of whether the violation was caused by the covered entity or a by business associate. Further, this provision is not an absolute standard intended to require active monitoring of the business associate or mitigation of all harm caused by the business associate. Rather, the provision applies only if the covered entity has actual knowledge of the harm, and requires mitigation only "to the extent practicable" by the covered entity. See § 164.530(f).

Comment: Several commenters asked the Department to provide additional clarification as to who is and is not a business associate for purposes of the Rule. For example, commenters questioned whether researchers were business associates. Other commenters requested further clarification as to when a health care provider would be the business associate of another health care provider. One commenter asked the Department to clarify whether covered entities that engage in joint activities under an organized health care arrangement (OHCA) are required to have a business associate contract. Several commenters asked the Department to clarify that a business associate agreement is not required with organizations or persons where contact with protected health information would result inadvertently (if at all), for example, janitorial services.

Response: The Department provides the following guidance in response to commenters. Disclosures from a covered

entity to a researcher for research purposes as permitted by the Rule do not require a business associate contract. This remains true even in those instances where the covered entity has hired the researcher to perform research on the covered entity's own behalf because research is not a covered function or activity. However, the Rule does not prohibit a covered entity from entering into a business associate contract with a researcher if the covered entity wishes to do so. Notwithstanding the above, a covered entity must enter into a data use agreement, as required by § 164.514(e), prior to disclosing a limited data set for research purposes to a researcher.

With respect to business associate contracts between health care providers, the Privacy Rule explicitly excepts from the business associate requirements disclosures by a covered entity to a health care provider for treatment purposes. See § 164.502(e)(1). Therefore, any covered health care provider (or other covered entity) may share protected health information with a health care provider for treatment purposes without a business associate contract. The Department does not intend the Rule to interfere with the sharing of information among health care providers for treatment. However, this exception does not preclude one health care provider from establishing a business associate relationship with another health care provider for some other purpose. For example, a hospital may enlist the services of another health care provider to assist in the hospital's training of medical students. In this case, a business associate contract would be required before the hospital could allow the health care provider access to patient health information.

As to disclosures among covered entities who participate in an organized health care arrangement, the Department clarifies that no business associate contract is needed to the extent the disclosure relates to the joint activities of the OHCA.

The Department also clarifies that a business associate contract is not required with persons or organizations whose functions, activities, or services do not involve the use or disclosure of protected health information, and where any access to protected health information by such persons would be de minimus, if at all. For example, a health care provider is not required to enter into a business associate contract with its janitorial service because the performance of such service does not involve the use or disclosure of protected health information. In this case, where a janitor has contact with

C. HIPAA Final Rules, Privacy Standards, continued

Federal Register / Vol. 67, No. 157 / Wednesday, August 14, 2002 / Rules and Regulations 53253

protected health information incidentally, such disclosure is permissible under § 164.502(a)(1)(iii) provided reasonable safeguards are in place.

The Department is aware that similar questions still remain with respect to the business associate provisions of the Privacy Rule and intends to provide technical assistance and further clarifications as necessary to address these questions.

Comment: A few commenters urged that the Department modify the Privacy Rule's requirement for a covered entity to take reasonable steps to cure a breach or end a violation of its business associate contract by a business associate. One commenter recommended that the requirement be modified instead to require a covered entity who has knowledge of a breach to ask its business associate to cure the breach or end the violation. Another commenter argued that a covered entity only should be required to take reasonable steps to cure a breach or end a violation if the business associate or a patient reports to the privacy officer or other responsible employee of the covered entity that a misuse of protected health information has occurred.

Response: It is expected that a covered entity with evidence of a violation will ask its business associate, where appropriate, to cure the breach or end the violation. Further, the Department intends that whether a covered entity "knew" of a pattern or practice of the business associate in breach or violation of the contract will be consistent with common principles of law that dictate when knowledge can be attributed to a corporate entity. Regardless, a covered entity's training of its workforce, as required by § 164.530(b), should address the recognition and reporting of violations to the appropriate responsible persons with the entity.

Comment: Several commenters requested clarification as to whether a business associate is required to provide individuals with access to their protected health information as provided by § 164.524 or an accounting of disclosures as provided by § 164.528, or amend protected health information as required by § 164.526. Some commenters wanted clarification that the access and amendment provisions apply to the business associate only if the business associate maintains the original designated record set of the protected health information.

Response: Under the Rule, the covered entity is responsible for fulfilling all of an individual's rights, including the rights of access,

amendment, and accounting, as provided for by §§ 164.524, 164.526, and 164.528. With limited exceptions, a covered entity is required to provide an individual access to his or her protected health information in a designated record set. This includes information in a designated record set of a business associate, unless the information held by the business associate merely duplicates the information maintained by the covered entity. However, the Privacy Rule does not prevent the parties from agreeing through the business associate contract that the business associate will provide access to individuals, as may be appropriate where the business associate is the only holder of the, or part of the, designated record set.

As governed by § 164.526, a covered entity must amend protected health information about an individual in a designated record set, including any designated record sets (or copies thereof) held by a business associate. Therefore, the Rule requires covered entities to specify in the business associate contract that the business associate will make protected health information available for amendment and will incorporate amendments accordingly. The covered entity itself is responsible for addressing requests from individuals for amendment and coordinating such requests with its business associate. However, the Privacy Rule also does not prevent the parties from agreeing through the contract that the business associate will receive and address requests for amendment on behalf of the covered entity.

With respect to accounting, § 164.528 requires a covered entity to provide an accounting of certain disclosures, including certain disclosures by its business associate, to the individual upon request. The business associate contract must provide that the business associate will make such information available to the covered entity in order for the covered entity to fulfill its obligation to the individual. As with access and amendment, the parties can agree through the business associate contract that the business associate will provide the accounting to individuals, as may be appropriate given the protected health information held by, and the functions of, the business associate.

Comment: One commenter asked whether a business associate agreement in electronic form, with an electronic signature, would satisfy the Privacy Rule's business associate requirements.

Response: The Privacy Rule generally allows for electronic documents to

qualify as written documents for purposes of meeting the Rule's requirements. This also applies with respect to business associate agreements. However, currently, no standards exist under HIPAA for electronic signatures. Thus, in the absence of specific standards, covered entities should ensure any electronic signature used will result in a legally binding contract under applicable State or other law.

Comment: Certain commenters raised concerns with the Rule's classification of attorneys as business associates. A few of these commenters urged the Department to clarify that the Rule's requirement at § 164.504(e)(2)(ii)(H), which requires a contract to state the business associate must make information relating to the use or disclosure of protected health information available to the Secretary for purposes of determining the covered entity's compliance with the Rule, not apply to protected health information in possession of a covered entity's lawyer. Commenters argued that such a requirement threatens to impact attorney-client privilege. Others expressed concern over the requirement that the attorney, as a business associate, must return or destroy protected health information at termination of the contract. It was argued that such a requirement is inconsistent with many current obligations of legal counsel and is neither warranted nor useful.

Response: The Department does not modify the Rule in this regard. The Privacy Rule is not intended to interfere with attorney-client privilege. Nor does the Department anticipate that it will be necessary for the Secretary to have access to privileged material in order to resolve a complaint or investigate a violation of the Privacy Rule. However, the Department does not believe that it is appropriate to exempt attorneys from the business associate requirements.

With respect to the requirement for the return or destruction of protected health information, the Rule requires the return or destruction of all protected health information at termination of the contract only where feasible or permitted by law. Where such action is not feasible, the contract must state that the information will remain protected after the contract ends for as long as the information is maintained by the business associate, and that further uses and disclosures of the information will be limited to those purposes that make the return or destruction infeasible.

Comment: One commenter was concerned that the business associate provisions regarding the return or

C. HIPAA Final Rules, Privacy Standards, continued

destruction of protected health information upon termination of the business associate agreement conflict with various provisions of the Bank Secrecy Act, which require financial institutions to retain certain records for up to five years. The commenter further noted that there are many State banking regulations that require financial institutions to retain certain records for up to ten years. The commenter recommended that the Department clarify, in instances of conflict with the Privacy Rule, that financial institutions comply with Federal and State banking regulations.

Response: The Department does not believe there is a conflict between the Privacy Rule and the Bank Secrecy Act retention requirements or that the Privacy Rule would prevent a financial institution that is a business associate of a covered entity from complying with the Bank Secrecy Act. The Privacy Rule generally requires a business associate contract to provide that the business associate will return or destroy protected health information upon the termination of the contract; however, it does not require this if the return or destruction of protected health information is infeasible. Return or destruction would be considered "infeasible" if other law, such as the Bank Secrecy Act, requires the business associate to retain protected health information for a period of time beyond the termination of the business associate contract. The Privacy Rule would require that the business associate contract extend the protections of the contract and limit further uses and disclosures to those purposes that make the return or destruction of the information infeasible. In this case, the business associate would have to limit the use or disclosure of the protected health information to purposes of the Bank Secrecy Act or State banking regulations.

Comment: A commenter requested clarification concerning the economic impact on business associates of the cost-based copying fees allowed to be charged to individuals who request a copy of their medical record under the right of access provided by the Privacy Rule. See § 164.524. According to the commenter, many hospitals and other covered entities currently outsource their records reproduction function for fees that often include administrative costs over and above the costs of copying. In some cases, the fees may be set in accordance with State law. The Privacy Rule, at § 164.524(c)(4), however, permits only reasonable, cost-based copying fees to be charged to individuals seeking to obtain a copy of

their medical record under their right of access. The commenter was concerned that others seeking copies of all or part of the medical record, such as payers, attorneys, or entities that have the individual's authorization, would try to claim the limited copying fees provided in § 164.524(c)(4). The commenter asserted that such a result would drastically alter the economics of the outsourcing industry, driving outsourcing companies out of business, and raising costs for the health industry as a whole. A clarification that the fee structure in § 164.524(c)(4) applies only to individuals exercising their right of access was sought.

Response: The Department clarifies that the Rule, at § 164.524(c)(4), limits only the fees that may be charged to individuals, or to their personal representatives in accordance with § 164.502(g), when the request is to obtain a copy of protected health information about the individual in accordance with the right of access. The fee limitations in § 164.524(c)(4) do not apply to any other permissible disclosures by the covered entity, including disclosures that are permitted for treatment, payment or health care operations, disclosures that are based on an individual's authorization that is valid under § 164.508, or other disclosures permitted without the individual's authorization as specified in § 164.512.

The fee limitation in § 164.524(c)(4) is intended to assure that the right of access provided by the Privacy Rule is available to all individuals, and not just to those who can afford to do so. Based on the clarification provided, the Department does not anticipate that this provision will cause any significant disruption in the way that covered entities do business today. To the extent hospitals and other entities outsource this function because it is less expensive than doing it themselves, the fee limitation for individuals seeking access under § 164.524 will affect only a portion of this business; and, in these cases, hospitals should still find it economical to outsource these activities, even if they can only pass on a portion of the costs to the individual.

K. Technical Corrections and Other Clarifications

1. Definition of "Individually Identifiable Health Information"

Part 160 contains the definitions that are relevant to all of the Administrative Simplification provisions at Parts 160 through 164. Although the term "individually identifiable health information" is relevant to Parts 160

through 164, it is defined in § 164.501 of the Privacy Rule. To correct this technical error, the Department proposed to move the definition of individually identifiable health information from § 164.501 to § 160.103.

The limited comment on this proposal supported moving the definition into § 160.103, for the same reasons cited by the Department. Therefore, the Department in this final Rule deletes the definition of "individually identifiable health information" from § 164.501 of the Privacy Rule, and adds the definition to § 160.103.

2. Technical Corrections

The Privacy Rule contained some technical and typographical errors. Therefore, the Department is making the following corrections:

a. In § 160.102(b), beginning in the second line, "section 201(a)(5) of the Health Insurance Portability Act of 1996, (Pub. L. 104–191)," is replaced with "42 U.S.C. 1320a–7c(a)(5)."

b. In § 160.203(b), in the second line, "health information" is replaced with "individually identifiable health information."

c. In § 164.102, "implementation standards" is corrected to read "implementation specifications."

d. In § 164.501, in the definition of "protected health information", "Family Educational Right and Privacy Act" is corrected to read "Family Educational Rights and Privacy Act."

e. In § 164.508(b)(1)(ii), in the fifth line, the word "be" is deleted.

f. In § 164.508(b)(3)(iii), a comma is added after the words "psychotherapy notes."

g. In § 164.510(b)(3), in the third line, the word "for" is deleted.

h. In § 164.512(b)(1)(v)(A), in the fourth line, the word "a" is deleted.

i. In § 164.512(b)(1)(v)(C), in the eighth line, the word "and" is added after the semicolon.

j. In § 164.512(f)(3), paragraphs (ii) and (iii) are redesignated as (i) and (ii), respectively.

k. In § 164.512(g)(2), in the seventh line, the word "to" is added after the word "directors."

l. In § 164.512(i)(1)(iii)(A), in the second line, the word "is" after the word "sought" is deleted.

m. In § 164.514(d)(5), the word "discloses" is corrected to read "disclose."

n. In § 164.520(c), in the introductory text, "(c)(4)" is corrected to read "(c)(3)."

o. In § 164.522(a)(1)(v), in the sixth line, "§§ 164.502(a)(2)(i)" is corrected to read "§§ 164.502(a)(2)(ii)."

p. In § 164.530(i)(4)(ii)(A), in the second line, "the requirements" is

C. HIPAA Final Rules, Privacy Standards, continued

replaced with the word "specifications."

IV. Final Regulatory Impact Analysis

Federal law (5 U.S.C. 804(2), as added by section 251 of Pub. L. No. 104–21), specifies that a "major rule" is any rule that the Office of Management and Budget finds is likely to result in:

• An annual effect on the economy of $100 million or more;

• A major increase in costs or prices for consumers, individual industries, Federal, State, or local government agencies, or geographic regions; or

• Significant adverse effects in competition, employment, investment productivity, innovation, or on the ability of United States based enterprises to compete with foreign-based enterprises in domestic and export markets.

The impact of the modifications adopted in this rulemaking will have an annual effect on the economy of at least $100 million. Therefore, this Rule is a major rule as defined in 5 U.S.C. 804(2).

Executive Order 12866 directs agencies to assess all costs and benefits of available regulatory alternatives and, when regulation is necessary, to select regulatory approaches that maximize net benefits (including potential economic, environmental, public health and safety effects; distributive impacts; and equity). According to Executive Order 12866, a regulatory action is "significant" if it meets any one of a number of specified conditions, including having an annual effect on the economy of $100 million or more, adversely affecting in a material way a sector of the economy, competition, or jobs, or if it raises novel legal or policy issues. The purpose of the regulatory impact analysis is to assist decision-makers in understanding the potential ramifications of a regulation as it is being developed. The analysis is also intended to assist the public in understanding the general economic ramifications of the regulatory changes.

The December 2000 preamble to the Privacy Rule included a regulatory impact analysis (RIA), which estimated the cost of the Privacy Rule at $17.6 billion over ten years. 65 FR 82462, 82758. The modifications to the Privacy Rule adopted by this rulemaking are a result of comment by the industry and the public at large identifying a number of unintended consequences of the Privacy Rule that could adversely affect access to, or the quality of, health care delivery. These modifications should facilitate implementation and compliance with the Privacy Rule, and lower the costs and burdens associated with the Privacy Rule while maintaining the confidentiality of protected health information. The Department estimates the impact of the modifications adopted in this rulemaking will be a net reduction of costs associated with the Privacy Rule of at least $100 million over ten years.

The modifications affect five areas of the Privacy Rule that will have an economic impact: (1) consent; (2) notice; (3) marketing; (4) research; and (5) business associates. In addition, this rulemaking contains a number of changes that, though important, can be categorized as clarifications of intended policy. For example, the modifications permit certain uses and disclosures of protected health information that are incidental to an otherwise permitted use or disclosure. This change recognizes such practices as the need for physicians to talk to patients in semi-private hospital rooms or nurses to communicate with others in public areas, and avoids the costs covered entities might have incurred to reconfigure facilities as necessary to ensure absolute privacy for these common treatment-related communications. This and other modifications adopted in this rulemaking (other than those described below) clarify the intent of the standards in the Privacy Rule and, as such, do not change or alter the associated costs that were estimated for the Privacy Rule. Public comments have indicated that these provisions would be interpreted in a way that could significantly increase costs. However, because that was not the intent of the December 2000 Privacy Rule, the Department is not ascribing cost savings to the clarification of these provisions.

A. Summary of Costs and Benefits in the December 2000 Regulatory Impact Statement

The Privacy Rule was estimated to produce net costs of $17.6 billion, with net present value costs of $11.8 billion (2003 dollars) over ten years (2003–2012). The Department estimates the modifications in this proposal would lower the net cost of the Privacy Rule by approximately $100 million over ten years.

Measuring both the economic costs and benefits of health information privacy was recognized as a difficult task. The paucity of data and incomplete information on current industry privacy and information system practices made cost estimation a challenge. Benefits were difficult to measure because they are, for the most part, inherently intangible. Therefore, the regulatory impact analysis in the Privacy Rule focused on the key policy areas addressed by the privacy standards, some of which are affected by the modifications adopted in this rulemaking.

B. Proposed Modifications To Prevent Barriers to Access to or Quality of Health Care

The modifications adopted in this rulemaking are intended to address the possible adverse effects of the final privacy standards on an individual's access to, or the quality of, health care. The modifications touch on five of the key policy areas addressed by the final regulatory impact analysis, including consent, research, marketing, notice, and business associates.

The Department received few comments on this section of the March 2002 proposal. Most of the comments on the cost implications of the modifications indicated a general belief that the costs would be higher than the Department estimated. None of commenters, however, provided sufficient specific information concerning costs to permit the Department to adjust its estimates. The public comment on each of the key policy areas is summarized in the following sections. However, the estimated cost impact of each area has not changed.

1. Consent

Under the December 2000 Privacy Rule, a covered health care provider with a direct treatment relationship with an individual must have obtained the individual's prior written consent for use or disclosure of protected health information for treatment, payment, or health care operations, subject to a limited number of exceptions. Other covered health care providers and health plans may have obtained such a consent if they so chose. The initial cost of the consent requirement was estimated in December 2000 to be $42 million. Based on assumptions for growth in the number of patients, the total costs for ten years was estimated to be $103 million. *See* 65 FR 82771 (December 28, 2000).[2]

The modifications eliminate the consent requirement. The consent requirement posed many difficulties for an individual's access to health care, and was problematic for operations essential for the quality of the health

---

[2] The total cost for consent in the regulatory impact analysis showed an initial cost of $166 million and $227 million over ten years. Included in these total numbers is the cost of tracking patient requests to restrict the disclosure of their health information. This right is not changed in these modifications. The numbers here represent the costs associated with the consent functions that are proposed to be repealed.

C. HIPAA Final Rules, Privacy Standards, continued

care delivery system. However, any health care provider or health plan may choose to obtain an individual's consent for treatment, payment, and health care operations. The elimination of the consent requirement reduces the initial cost of the privacy standards by $42 million in the first year and by $103 million over ten years.

As explained in detail in section III.D.1. above, the Department received many comments supporting the proposed elimination of the consent requirement on the ground that it created unintended barriers to timely provision of care, particularly with respect to use and disclosure of health information prior to a health care provider's first face-to-face contact with the individual. These and other barriers discussed above would have entailed costs not anticipated in the economic analyses in the Privacy Rule. These comments also revealed that the consent requirements create administrative burdens, for example, with respect to tracking the status and revocation of consents, that were not foreseen and thus not included in that economic analysis. Therefore, while the estimated costs of the consent provisions over a ten-year period were $103 million, the comments suggest that the costs would likely be much higher. If these comments are accurate, the cost savings associated with retracting the consent provisions would, therefore, also be significantly higher than $103 million over a ten-year period.

Response to Public Comments

Comment: As discussed in section III.H. above, many commenters expressed support for the proposed requirement that certain health care providers make a good faith effort to obtain a written acknowledgment of receipt of the notice, as a workable alternative to the Rule's prior consent requirement. Many of these commenters conveyed support for the flexibility of the requirement, and most commenters agreed that eliminating the consent requirement would mean considerable savings.

Response: The Department received no public comment containing empirical, direct evidence on the estimates of financial impact that either supported or contradicted the Department's calculations. Therefore, our estimates remain unchanged.

Comment: Many other commenters confused the net savings associated with the Administrative Simplification provisions with cost savings associated with the Privacy Rule, and relied on this misinformation to argue in favor of retaining the consent provisions for

treatment, payment, and health care operations.

Response: These commenters were essentially propounding a policy choice and not making a comment on the validity of the estimates for cost savings associated with the elimination of the consent requirement. The comments did not include any reliable estimation that would cause the Department to reevaluate its savings estimate.

2. Notice

In eliminating the consent requirement, the Department preserves the opportunity for a covered health care provider with a direct treatment relationship with an individual to engage in a meaningful communication about the provider's privacy practices and the individual's rights by strengthening the notice requirements. Under the Privacy Rule, these health care providers are required to distribute to individuals their notice of privacy practices no later than the date of the first service delivery after the compliance date. The modifications do not change this distribution requirement, but add a new documentation requirement. A covered health care provider with a direct treatment relationship is required to make a good faith effort to obtain the individual's acknowledgment of receipt of the notice provided at the first service delivery. The form of the acknowledgment is not prescribed and can be as unintrusive as retaining a copy of the notice initialed by the individual. If the provider's good faith effort fails, documentation of the attempt is all that is required. Since the modification does not require any change in the form of the notice or its distribution, the ten-year cost estimate of $391 million for these areas in the Privacy Rule's impact analysis remains the same. *See* 65 FR 82770.

However, the additional effort by direct treatment providers in obtaining and documenting the individual's acknowledgment of receipt of the notice adds costs. This new requirement attaches only to the initial provision of notice by a direct treatment provider to an individual after the compliance date. Under the modification, providers have considerable flexibility on how to achieve this. Some providers could choose to obtain the required written acknowledgment on a separate piece of paper, while others could take different approaches, such as an initialed check-off sheet or a signature line on the notice itself with the provider keeping a copy.

In its December 2000 analysis, the Department estimated that the consent

cost would be $0.05 per page based on the fact that the consent had to be a stand alone document requiring a signature. This modification to the notice requirement provides greater flexibility and, therefore, greater opportunity to reduce costs compared to the consent requirement. Without knowing exactly how direct treatment providers will decide to exercise the flexibility provided, the Department cannot, with any precision, estimate the cost to implement this provision. In the NPRM, the Department estimated that the flexibility of the notice acknowledgment requirement would mean that the cost of the notice acknowledgment would be 20 percent less than the cost of the signed consent. The Department did not receive any comments on this estimate and, therefore, does not change it's estimate that the additional cost of the signature requirement, on average, is $0.03 per notice. Based on data obtained from the Medical Expenditure Panel Survey (MEPS), which estimate the number of patient visits in a year, the Department estimates that in the first year there would be 816 million notices distributed to which the new good faith acknowledgment requirement will attach. Over the next nine years, the Department estimates, again based on MEPS data, that there would be 5.3 billion visits to health care providers by new patients (established patients will not need to receive another copy of the notice). At $0.03 per document, the first year cost will be $24 million and the total cost over ten years will be $184 million.

Response to Public Comments

Comment: As discussed in section III.H. above, a number of other commenters expressed concern over the administrative and financial burden the requirement to obtain a good faith acknowledgment of the notice would impose.

Response: The Department received no public comment containing empirical, direct evidence on the estimates of financial impact that either supported or contradicted the Department's calculations. Therefore, our estimates remain unchanged.

Comment: One commenter requested that model language for the notice be developed as a means of reducing the costs associated with Privacy Rule compliance.

Response: As stated in section III.H. above, in the final Rule, the Department sought to retain the maximum flexibility by requiring only that the acknowledgment be in writing and does not prescribe other details of the form

C. HIPAA Final Rules, Privacy Standards, continued

that the acknowledgment must take or the process for obtaining the acknowledgment. This permits covered health care providers the discretion to design the acknowledgment process as best suited to their practices, including the option of obtaining an electronic acknowledgment regardless of whether the notice is provided electronically or on paper. Furthermore, there is no change to the substance of the notice and the commenter provided no empirical, direct benefit/cost data in support of their proposal.

Comment: The Department received comments expressing opposition to obtaining written acknowledgment of the receipt of the notice because it is too costly. Others commented that the acknowledgment increases the administrative burden as it would not replace a signed consent for uses and disclosures of health information when State law requires providers to obtain consent.

Response: The Department received no public comment containing empirical, direct evidence on the estimates of financial impact that either supported or contradicted the Department's calculations. Therefore, our estimates remain unchanged.

Comment: A number of commenters expressed concern over the perceived increase in liability that would arise from the discretionary standard of "good faith" efforts (i.e., risk of tort-based litigation for private right of action under State laws).

Response: The Department received no estimate of the impact of this perceived risk of liability. As no empirical, direct evidence on the estimates of financial impact that either supported or contradicted the Department's calculations was supplied, our estimates remain unchanged.

3. Business Associates

The Privacy Rule requires a covered entity to have a written contract, or other arrangement, that documents satisfactory assurances that a business associates will appropriately safeguard protected health information in order to disclose protected health information to the business associate. The regulatory impact analysis for the Privacy Rule provided cost estimates for two aspects of this requirement. In the Privacy Rule, $103 million in first-year costs was estimated for development of a standard business associate contract language. (There were additional costs associated with these requirements related to the technical implementation of new data transfer protocols, but these are not affected by the modification adopted here.) In addition, $197 million in first-

year costs and $697 million in total costs over ten years were estimated in the Privacy Rule for the review and oversight of existing business associate contracts.

The modifications do not change the standards for business associate contracts or the implementation specifications with respect to the covered entity's responsibilities for managing the contracts. However, the Department includes sample business associate contract language as part of the preamble to this rulemaking. This sample language is only suggested language and is not a complete contract. The sample language is designed to be adapted to the business arrangement between the covered entity and the business associate and to be incorporated into a contract drafted by the parties. Certain provisions of the sample language have been revised, as described in more detail below, based on the public comment received on the proposal. The December 2000 regulatory impact analysis assumed the development of such standard language by trade and professional associations. While this has occurred to some degree, the Department received strong public comment supporting the for sample contract language. The Department expects that trade and professional associations will continue to provide assistance to their members. However, the sample contract language in this rulemaking will simplify their efforts by providing a base from which they can develop language. The Department had estimated $103 million in initial year costs for this activity based on the assumption it would require one hour per non-hospital provider and two hours for hospitals and health plans to develop contract language and to tailor the language to the particular needs of the covered entity. The additional time for hospitals and health plans reflected the likelihood that these covered entities would have a more extensive number of business associate relationships. Because there will be less effort expended than originally estimated in the Privacy Rule, the Department estimates a reduction in contract development time by one-third because of the availability of the model language. Thus, the Department now estimates that this activity will take 40 minutes for non-hospital providers and 80 minutes for hospitals and health plans. The Department estimates that the savings from the proposed business associate contract language would be approximately $35 million in the first year. The changes being adopted to the

sample contract language do not affect these cost estimates.

The Department, in this rulemaking, also gives most covered entities additional time to conform written contracts to the privacy standards. Under the modification, a covered entity's written business associate contracts, existing at the time the modifications become effective, are deemed to comply with the privacy standards until such time as the contracts are renewed or modified, or until April 14, 2004, whichever is earlier. The effect of this proposal is to spread first-year costs over an additional year, with a corresponding postponement of the costs estimated for the out years. However, the Department has no reliable information as to the number of contracts potentially affected by the modification or the average delay that will occur. Therefore, the Department is uncertain about the extent of the cost savings attributable to this modification.

Response to Public Comments

Comment: While many commenters supported the business associate transition provisions as helpful to reducing the administrative burden and cost of compliance, commenters argued that the business associate provisions would still be very burdensome and costly to implement, especially for small and solo businesses.

Response: The Department acknowledges that there are compliance costs associated with the business associate standards. However, no commenters supplied empirical, direct evidence in support of or contradictory to the Department's estimates of the cost savings associated with the business associate transition provisions. Therefore, our estimates remain unchanged.

Comment: Some commenters disputed the estimated costs of complying with the business associate requirements based on the quantity of contracts (with suppliers, physicians, local agencies and national concerns), and the number of hours necessary to individually tailor and renegotiate all of these contracts.

Response: These comments address the underlying costs of the business associate requirements and do not address the reduction in costs afforded through the sample business associate agreement language. Moreover, no empirical, direct evidence, based on accomplished workload rather than extrapolations of singular events, were provided to contradict the Department's calculations. Therefore, our estimates remain unchanged.

C. HIPAA Final Rules, Privacy Standards, continued

53258 Federal Register/Vol. 67, No. 157/Wednesday, August 14, 2002/Rules and Regulations

4. Marketing

Under § 164.514(e) of the December 2000 Privacy Rule, certain health-related communications were subject to special conditions on marketing communications, if they also served to promote the use or sale of a product or service. These marketing conditions required that particular disclosures be made as part of the marketing materials sent to individuals. Absent these disclosures, protected health information could only be used or disclosed in connection with such marketing communications with the individual's authorization. The Department is aware that the Privacy Rule's § 164.514(e) conditions for health-related communications created a potential burden on covered entities to make difficult assessments regarding many of their communications. The modifications to the marketing provisions relieve the burden on covered entities by making most marketing subject to an authorization requirement (see § 164.508(a)(3)), making clear that necessary treatment and health care operations activities were not marketing, and eliminating the § 164.514(e) conditions on marketing communications.

In developing the December 2000 impact analysis for the Privacy Rule, the Department was unable to estimate the cost of the marketing provisions. There was too little data and too much variation in current practice to estimate how the Privacy Rule might affect marketing. The same remains true today. However, the modifications relieve burden on the covered entities in making communications for treatment and certain health care operations relative to the requirements in the Privacy Rule. Although the Department cannot provide a quantifiable estimate, the effect of these modifications is to lower the costs associated with the Privacy Rule.

Response to Public Comment

Comment: Many providers, especially mental health providers, opposed the changes to marketing and consent as they fear increased access to individually identifiable health information would cause patients to refrain from seeking treatment. By not seeking timely treatment, the medical conditions could worsen, and result in increased or additional costs to society.

Response: The commenters did not attempt to segment out the cost attributed to marketing alone. In fact, no empirical, direct evidence on the estimates of financial impact that either supported or contradicted the

Department's calculations was provided. Therefore, our estimates remain unchanged.

5. Research

In the final impact analysis of the December 2000 Privacy Rule, the Department estimated the total cost of the provisions requiring documentation of an Institutional Review Board (IRB) or Privacy Board waiver of individual authorization for the use or disclosure of protected health information for a research purpose as $40 million for the first year and $585 million for the ten-year period. The costs were estimated based on the time that an IRB or Privacy Board would need to consider a request for a waiver under the criteria provided in the Privacy Rule. *See* 65 FR 82770–82771 (December 28, 2000).

The modifications simplify and reduce the number of criteria required for an IRB or Privacy Board to approve a waiver of authorization to better conform to the Common Rule's waiver criteria for informed consent to participate in the research study. The Department estimates that the net effect of these modifications is to reduce the time necessary to assemble the waivers and for an IRB or Privacy Board to consider and act on waiver requests by one quarter. The Department estimates these simplifications would reduce the expected costs first year costs by $10 million and the ten year costs by $146 million, relative to the December 2000 Privacy Rule. Although the Department requested information to better assess this cost savings, the public comment period failed to produce any sound data. Therefore, the Department's estimates have not changed.

The Department adopts three other modifications to simplify the Privacy Rule requirements to relieve the potential administrative burden on research. First, the modifications permit a covered entity to use and disclose protected health information in the form of a limited data set for research, public health, and health care operations. A limited data set does not contain any direct identifiers of individuals, but may contain any other demographic or health information needed for research, public health or health care operations purposes. The covered entity must obtain a data use agreement from the recipient of a limited data set pursuant to which the recipient agrees to restrict use and disclosure of the limited data set and not to identify or contact any individual. With a data use agreement, a researcher may access a limited data set without obtaining individual authorization or having to go through an IRB or a Privacy Board for a waiver of

the authorization. (*See* discussion at III.G.2.) Second, the modifications simplify the accounting procedures for research disclosures by the covered entity by eliminating the need to account for disclosures which the individual has authorized or which are part of a limited data set, and by providing a simplified basis to account for a research disclosure involving 50 or more records. (*See* discussion at III.F.2.) Third, the modifications simplify the authorization process for research to facilitate the combining of the informed consent for participation in the research itself with an authorization required under the Privacy Rule. (*See* discussion at III.E.2.) Any cost savings attributed to the later two modifications would accrue primarily to the covered entity disclosing protected health information for research purposes and, therefore, would not affect the costs estimated here for the impact of the Privacy Rule on IRBs.

With regard to limited data sets, the Department anticipates that the modification will avoid IRBs having to review and approve researchers' requests for waiver of authorization for numerous studies that are undertaken today without IRB review and approval. For example, a researcher may not need IRB approval or waiver of informed consent to collect health information that is linked to the individual only by inclusion of the individual's zip code as this may not be personally identifying information under the Common Rule. However, this information would not be considered de-identified information under the Privacy Rule and it could not be disclosed to the researcher without the individual's authorization or an IRB waiver of that authorization. With the limited data set, research that does not require direct identifiers can continue to go on expeditiously without adding burden to IRBs and Privacy Boards. Similarly, limited data sets, similar to the Hospital Discharge Abstract data, will permit much useful information to be available for research, public health, and health care operations purposes.

Although there was broad support for limited data sets in the comments received by the Department, we do not have sufficient information to estimate the amount of research that currently occurs without IRB review or approval and which, but for the provision on limited data sets, would have had to involved the IRB to meet the use and disclosure requirements of the Privacy Rule. Nor did the comments supply information upon which the Department could reasonably rely in making a estimate of the cost savings. Therefore, the Department does not increase its

C. HIPAA Final Rules, Privacy Standards, continued

Federal Register/Vol. 67, No. 157/Wednesday, August 14, 2002/Rules and Regulations **53259**

estimated savings for research to reflect this modification, although we are confident that the overall impact of the Privacy Rule on research will be much lower based on the modifications adopted in this rulemaking.

Response to Public Comments

Comment: The Department received a number of comments that argued that the Privacy Rule would increase costs and workloads for researchers and research institutions. One commenter delineated these issues as: (1) An increased difficulty in recruiting research participants; (2) the need for increased IRB scrutiny (and the associated resource costs); and (3) the additional paperwork and documentation required.

Response: The Department recognized the impact of the final Privacy Rule on researchers and research institutions and provided a cost estimate for this impact as part of the Final Rule. Likewise, the NPRM offered modifications, such as more closely aligning the Privacy and Common Rule criteria, to ease the burden and, correspondingly, estimated cost savings of these proposed modifications. The specific comments appear to dispute the research cost estimates in the final Rule, as their delineated issues are not reflective of the modifications and cost savings specified in the NPRM. In any event, no reliable empirical, direct information on the estimates of financial impact that either supported or contradicted the Department's calculations was provided. Therefore, our estimates remain unchanged.

PRIVACY RULE MODIFICATIONS—TEN-YEAR COST ESTIMATES

Policy	Original cost	Modification	Change due to modification
Consent	$103 million	Provision removed	−$103 million.[1]
Notice	$391 million	Good faith effort to obtain acknowledgment of receipt.	+$184 million.
Marketing	Not scored due to lack of data	Fewer activities constitute marketing	Reduction in cost but magnitude cannot be estimated.
Business Associates	$103 million for contract modifications.	Model language provided	−$35 million.
Research	$585 million	Waiver requirements simplified	−$146 million.
Net Change			−$100 million.

[1] As noted above in the discussion on consent, while the estimated costs of the consent provisions were $103 million, comments have suggested that the costs were likely to be much higher. If these comments are accurate, the cost savings associated with retracting the consent provisions would, therefore, also be significantly higher than $103 million.

C. Costs to the Federal Government

The modifications adopted in this Rule will result in small savings to the Federal government relative to the costs that would have occurred under the Privacy Rule. Although there will be some increase in costs for the new requirements for obtaining acknowledgment for receipt of the notice, these costs are at least partially offset by the savings in the elimination of the consent. As discussed above, to the extent concerns are accurate that the costs for the consent provisions are much higher than estimated, the cost savings associated with the retraction of these provisions would, therefore, be significantly higher. The Department does not believe the Federal government engages in significant marketing as defined in the Privacy Rule. The Federal government will have business associates under the Privacy Rule, and, therefore, the sample language proposed in this rulemaking will be of benefit to Federal departments and agencies. The Department has not estimated the Federal government's portion of the $35 million savings it estimated for this change. Similarly, the Federal government, which conducts and sponsors a significant amount of research that is subject to IRBs, will realize some savings as a result of the research modifications in this rulemaking. The Department does not

have sufficient information, however, to estimate the Federal government's portion of the total $146 million savings with respect to research modifications.

D. Costs to State and Local Government

The modifications also may affect the costs to State and local governments. However, these effects likely will be small. As with the Federal government, State and local governments will have any costs of the additional notice requirement offset by the savings realized by the elimination of the consent requirement. As discussed above, to the extent concerns are accurate that the costs for the consent provisions are much higher than estimated, the cost savings associated with the retraction of these provisions would, therefore, be significantly higher. State and local governments could realize savings from the sample language for business associates and the changes in research, but the savings are likely to be small. The Department does not have sufficient information to estimate the State and local government's share of the net savings from the modifications.

E. Benefits

The benefits of various provisions of these modifications will be strong privacy protections for individuals coupled with increased access to quality health care, and ease of compliance

with privacy protections by covered entities. The changes will have the benefit of eliminating obstacles that could interfere with patient access to timely and high quality health care. The modifications will also improve quality health care by removing obstacles that may have interfered with research activities that form the basis of advancements in medical technology and provide greater understanding of disease. It is extremely difficult to quantify the benefits of enhanced privacy of medical records and elimination of obstacles to research and quality activities. This section provides examples of the qualitative benefits of these Privacy Rule modifications.

1. Strengthened Notice, Flexible Consent

The new requirement that a covered entity make a good faith attempt to obtain written acknowledgment of the notice of privacy practices will increase privacy protections to patients. The strengthened notice requirement will focus individuals on uses and disclosures of their health information, and assure that individuals have the opportunity to discuss privacy concerns with the health care providers with whom they have direct treatment relationships. Awareness of privacy practices should provide patients with a greater degree of comfort in discussing sensitive personal information with

53260 **Federal Register** / Vol. 67, No. 157 / Wednesday, August 14, 2002 / Rules and Regulations

their doctors. The strengthened notice standard was adopted in tandem with changes to make consent more flexible. The changes to the consent requirement have the benefit of removing significant barriers to health care. In many circumstances, the consent requirement would have resulted in delayed treatment and, in other circumstances, would have required patients to be greatly inconvenienced at a time when they needed care, by forcing additional trips simply to sign consent forms. These modifications have the benefit of removing barriers to access to health care that would have resulted from the consent requirement while preserving important privacy protections in the notice standard.

2. Research

Research is key to the continued availability of high quality health care. The modifications remove potential barriers to research. For example, the modifications streamline the criteria to be used by IRBs or Privacy Boards in approving a waiver of individual authorization for research that could not otherwise be done and ensure the criteria are compatible with similar waiver determinations under the Common Rule. Thus, administrative burdens on IRBs and Privacy Boards are eased, without diminishing the health information privacy and confidentiality standards for research. In addition, the research transition provisions have been modified to ensure that the Privacy Rule does not interfere with ongoing or future research for which an individual has granted permission to use his information. By permitting this research to continue, these modifications make sure that vast research resources continue to be usable for important research that result in development of new medical technology and increased quality of health care.

3. Sharing Information for Quality Activities and Public Health

Health plans and health care providers play a valuable role in assessing the quality of health care and improving health care outcomes. The modifications ensure access to health information needed by covered entities and others involved in quality activities. The increased sharing of information will help to limit medical error rates and to determine appropriate, high quality treatment for specific conditions by encouraging these issues to be studied and allowing benchmarking against similar entities. The modifications, in creating a limited data set, also encourages private entities to continue studies and research in

support of public health activities. These activities help reduce the spread and occurrence of diseases.

4. Availability of Information About Treatment Alternatives

Understanding treatment alternatives is an important factor in increasing an individual's involvement in his or her own treatment and making informed health care decisions. By streamlining the marketing requirements, the modifications make it easier for a covered entity to understand that they may share valuable information about treatment alternatives with their patients or enrollees, and the conditions for doing so. These modifications make sure that covered entities will be permitted to continue to share important treatment alternative information that gives patients knowledge about newer, less expensive, and/or more appropriate health care options.

F. Alternatives

In July 2001, the Department clarified the Privacy Rule in guidance, where feasible, to resolve some of the issues raised by commenters. Issues that could not adequately be addressed through guidance because of the need for a regulatory change are addressed in this rulemaking. The Department examined a number of alternatives to these modifications. One alternative was to not make any changes to the Privacy Rule, but this option was rejected for the reasons explained throughout the preamble. The Department also considered various alternatives to specific provisions in the development of this final Rule. These alternatives are generally discussed above, where appropriate.

V. Preliminary Regulatory Flexibility Analysis

The Department also examined the impact of this proposed Rule as required by the Small Business Regulatory Enforcement and Fairness Act (SBREFA) (5 U.S.C. 601, *et seq.*). SBREFA requires agencies to determine whether a rule will have a significant economic impact on a substantial number of small entities.

The law does not define the thresholds to use in implementing the law and the Small Business Administration discourages establishing quantitative criteria. However, the Department has long used two criteria—the number of entities affected and the impact on revenue and costs—for assessing whether a regulatory flexibility analysis is necessary. Department guidelines state that an

impact of three to five percent should be considered a significant economic impact. Based on these criteria, the Department has determined that a regulatory flexibility analysis is not required.

As described in the December 2000 Regulatory Flexibility Analysis for the Privacy Rule, most covered entities are small businesses—approximately 465,000. *See* Table A, 65 FR 82780 (December 28, 2000). Lessening the burden for small entities, consistent with the intent of protecting privacy, was an important consideration in developing these modifications. However, as discussed in the Final Regulatory Impact Analysis, above, the net affect of the modifications is an overall savings of approximately $100 million over ten years. Even if all of this savings were to accrue to small entities (an over estimation), the impact per small entity would be *de minimis*.

VI. Collection of Information Requirements

Under the Paperwork Reduction Act (PRA) of 1995, the Department is required to provide 30-day notice in the **Federal Register** and solicit public comment before a collection of information requirement is submitted to the Office of Management and Budget (OMB) for review and approval. In order to fairly evaluate whether an information collection should be approved by OMB, section 3506(c)(2)(A) of the PRA requires that the Department solicit comment on the following issues:

• The need for the information collection and its usefulness in carrying out the proper functions of the agency;

• The accuracy of the estimate of the information collection burden;

• The quality, utility, and clarity of the information to be collected; and

• Recommendations to minimize the information collection burden on the affected public, including automated collection techniques.

Section A below summarizes the proposed information collection requirements on which we explicitly seek, and will consider, public comment for 30 days. Due to the complexity of this regulation, and to avoid redundancy of effort, we are referring readers to Section V (Final Regulatory Impact Analysis published in the **Federal Register** on December 28, 2000), to review the detailed cost assumptions associated with these PRA requirements.

Section B below references the HIPAA Privacy Rule regulation sections published for 60-day public comment on November 3, 1999, and for 30-day public comment on December 28, 2000,

C. HIPAA Final Rules, Privacy Standards, continued

in compliance with the PRA public comment process. These earlier publications contained the information collection requirements for these sections as required by the PRA. The portions of the Privacy Rule, included by reference only in Section B, have not changed subsequent to the two public comment periods. Thus, the Department has fulfilled its statutory obligation to solicit public comment on the information collection requirements for these provisions. The information in Section B is pending OMB PRA approval, but is not reopened for comment. However, for clarity purposes, we will upon this publication submit to OMB for PRA review and approval the entire set of information collection requirements required referenced in §§ 160.204, 160.306, 160.310, 164.502, 164.504, 164.506, 164.508, 164.510, 164.512, 164.514, 164.520, 164.522, 164.524, 164.526, 164.528, and 164.530.

Section A

1. Section 164.506—Consent for Treatment, Payment, and Health Care Operations

Under the Privacy Rule, as issued in December 2000, a covered health care provider that has a direct treatment relationship with individuals would have had, except in certain circumstances, to obtain an individual's consent to use or disclose protected health information to carry out treatment, payment, and health care operations. The amended final Rule eliminates this requirement.

2. Section 164.520—Notice of Privacy Practices for Protected Health Information

The amended final Privacy Rule imposes a good faith effort on direct treatment providers to obtain an individual's acknowledgment of receipt of the entity's notice of privacy practices for protected health information, and to document such acknowledgment or, in the absence of such acknowledgment, the entity's good faith efforts to obtain it.

The underlying requirements for notice of privacy practices for protected health information are not changed. These requirements provide that, except in certain circumstances set forth in this section of the Rule, individuals have a right to adequate notice of the uses and disclosures of protected health information that may be made by the covered entity, and of the individual's rights and the covered entity's legal duties with respect to protected health information. To comply with this requirement a covered entity must provide a notice, written in plain language, that includes the elements set forth at § 164.520(b). For health plans, there will be an average of 160.2 million notices each year. We assume that the most efficient means of distribution for health plans will be to send them out annually as part of the materials they send to current and potential enrollees, even though it is not required by the regulation. The number of notices per health plan per year would be about 10,570. We further estimate that it will require each health plan, on average, only 10 seconds to disseminate each notice. The total annual burden associated with this requirement is calculated to be 267,000 hours.

Health care providers with direct treatment relationships would:
• Provide a copy of the notice to an individual at the time of first service delivery to the individual;
• Make the notice available at the service delivery site for individuals to request and take with them;
• Whenever the content of the notice is revised, make it available upon request and post it, if required by this section, in a location where it is reasonable to expect individuals seeking services from the provider to be able to read the notice.

The annual number of notices disseminated by all providers is 613 million. We further estimate that it will require each health care provider, on average, 10 seconds to disseminate each notice. This estimate is based upon the assumption that the required notice will be incorporated into and disseminated with other patient materials. The total annual burden associated with this requirement is calculated to be 1 million hours. However, the amended final Privacy Rule also imposes a good faith effort on direct treatment providers to obtain an individual's acknowledgment of receipt of the provider's notice, and to document such acknowledgment or, in the absence of such acknowledgment, the provider's good faith efforts to obtain it. The estimated burden for the acknowledgment of receipt of the notice is 10 seconds for each notice. This is based on the fact that the provider does not need to take elaborate steps to receive acknowledgment. Initialing a box on an existing form or some other simple means will suffice. With the annual estimate of 613,000,000 acknowledgment forms it is estimated that the acknowledgment burden is 1,000,000 hours.

A covered entity is also required to document compliance with the notice requirements by retaining copies of the versions of the notice issued by the covered entity, and a direct treatment provider is required to retain a copy of each individual's acknowledgment or documentation of the good faith effort as required by § 164.530(j).

3. Appendix to Preamble—Sample Business Associate Contract Provisions

The Department also solicits public comments on the collection of information requirements associated with the model business associate contract language displayed in the Appendix to this preamble Rule. The language displayed has been changed in response to comments on the language that was published with the Notice of Proposed Rulemaking on March 27, 2002. The Department provided the model business associate contract provisions in response to numerous requests for guidance. These provisions were designed to help covered entities more easily comply with the business associate contract requirements of the Privacy Rule. However, use of these model provisions is not required for compliance with the Privacy Rule. Nor is the model language a complete contract. Rather, the model language is designed to be adapted to the business arrangement between the covered entity and the business associate and to be incorporated into a contract drafted by the parties.

Section B

As referenced above, the Department has complied with the public comment process as it relates to the information collection requirements contained in the sections of regulation referenced below. The Department is referencing this information solely for the purposes of providing an overview of the regulation sections containing information collection requirements established by the final Privacy Rule.

Section 160.204—Process for Requesting Exception Determinations
Section 160.306—Complaints to the Secretary
Section 160.310—Responsibilities of Covered Entities
Section 164.502—Uses and Disclosures of Protected Health Information: General Rules
Section 164.504—Uses and Disclosures—Organizational Requirements
Section 164.508—Uses and Disclosures for Which Individual Authorization Is Required
Section 164.510—Uses and Disclosures Requiring an Opportunity for the Individual to Agree or to Object
Section 164.512—Uses and Disclosures for Which Consent, an Authorization, or Opportunity to Agree or Object is Not Required
Section 164.514—Other Procedural Requirements Relating to Uses and

C. HIPAA Final Rules, Privacy Standards, continued

53262 **Federal Register** / Vol. 67, No. 157 / Wednesday, August 14, 2002 / Rules and Regulations

Disclosures of Protected Health Information
Section 164.522—Rights to Request Privacy Protection for Protected Health Information
Section 164.524—Access of Individuals to Protected Health Information
Section 164.526—Amendment of Protected Health Information
Section 164.528—Accounting for Disclosures of Protected Health Information
Section 164.530—Administrative Requirements

C. Comments on Information Collection Requirements in Section A

The Department has submitted a copy of these modifications to the Privacy Rule to OMB for its review and approval of the information collection requirements summarized in Section A above. If you comment on any of the modifications to the information collection and record keeping requirements in §§ 164.506, 164.520, and/or the model business associate contract language please mail copies directly to the following:

Center for Medicaid and Medicare Services, Information Technology Investment Management Group, Division of CMS Enterprise Standards, Room C2–26–17, 7500 Security Boulevard, Baltimore, MD 21244–1850, ATTN: John Burke, HIPAA Privacy,
and
Office of Information and Regulatory Affairs, Office of Management and Budget, Room 10235, New Executive Office Building, Washington, DC 20503, ATTN: Brenda Aguilar, CMS Desk Officer.

VII. Unfunded Mandates

Section 202 of the Unfunded Mandates Reform Act of 1995 also requires that agencies assess anticipated costs and benefits before issuing any rule that may result in an expenditure by State, local, or tribal governments, in the aggregate, or by the private sector, of $110 million in a single year. A final cost-benefit analysis was published in the Privacy Rule of December 28, 2000 (65 FR 82462, 82794). In developing the final Privacy Rule, the Department adopted the least burdensome alternatives, consistent with achieving the Rule's goals. The Department does not believe that the amendments to the Privacy Rule would qualify as an unfunded mandate under the statute.

VIII. Environmental Impact

The Department has determined under 21 CFR 25.30(k) that this action is of a type that does not individually or cumulatively have a significant effect on the human environment. Therefore, neither an environmental assessment nor an environmental impact statement is required.

IX. Executive Order 13132: Federalism

Executive Order 13132 establishes certain requirements that an agency must meet when it promulgates a rule that imposes substantial direct requirement costs on State and local governments, preempts State law, or otherwise has Federalism implications. The Federalism implications of the Privacy Rule were assessed as required by Executive Order 13132 and published in the Privacy Rule of December 28, 2000 (65 FR 82462, 82797). The amendments with the most direct effect on Federalism principles concerns the clarifications regarding the rights of parents and minors under State law.

The amendments make clear the intent of the Department to defer to State law with respect to such rights. Therefore, the Department believes that the amended Privacy Rule would not significantly affect the rights, roles and responsibilities of States.

X. Sample Business Associate Contract Provisions—Appendix

March 2002 NPRM. In response to requests for guidance, the Department provided sample language for business associate contracts. The provisions were provided as an appendix to the preamble and were intended to serve as guidance for covered entities to assist in compliance with the business associate provisions of the Privacy Rule. The proposal was not a model contract, but rather was sample language that could be included in a contract.

Overview of Public Comment. The Department received a small number of comments addressing the sample business associate contract provisions. The comments fell into four general categories. Most commenters were pleased with the Department's guidance for business associate contracts and expressed appreciation for such guidance. There were some commenters that thought the language was insufficient and requested the Department create a complete model contract not just sample provisions. The third category of commenters thought the provisions went further than the requirements in the regulation and requested specific changes to the sample language. In addition, a few commenters requested that the Department withdraw the sample provisions asserting that they will eliminate the potential of negotiating or establishing a business associate contract that is tailored to the precise requirements of the particular relationship.

Final Modifications. This Rule continues to include sample business associate contract provisions as an appendix to the preamble, because the majority of commenters that addressed this subject found these provisions to be helpful guidance in their compliance efforts with the business associate contract requirements in the Privacy Rule.

The Department has made several changes to the language originally proposed in response to comment. Although these are only sample provisions, the changes, which are described below, should help to clear up some confusion.

First, the Department has changed the name from "model language" to "sample language" to clarify that the provisions are merely sample clauses, and that none are required to be in a business associate contract so long as the contract meets the requirements of the regulation. The sample language continues to indicate, using square brackets, those instances in which a provision or phrase in a provision applies only in certain circumstances or is optional.

The Department has made three modifications in the Obligations and Activities of the Business Associate provisions. First, there are modifications to clarify that the parties can negotiate appropriate terms regarding the time and manner of providing access to protected health information in a designated record set, providing information to account for disclosures of protected health information, and for making amendments to protected health information in a designated record set. Although the language clarifies that the terms are to be negotiated by the Parties, the agreement must permit the covered entity to comply with its obligations under the Privacy Rule.

Second, the Department has amended the sample language regarding review of business associate practices, books, and records to clarify that the contract must permit the Secretary, not the covered entity, to have access to such records, including protected health information, for purposes of determining the covered entity's compliance with the Privacy Rule. The sample language continues to include the option that parties additionally agree that the business associate shall disclose this information to the covered entity for compliance purposes to indicate that this is still an appropriate approach for this purpose. The modifications also clarify that parties can negotiate the time and manner of providing the covered entity with access to the business associate's internal practices, books, and records.

C. HIPAA Final Rules, Privacy Standards, continued

Finally, the Department has modified the sample language to clarify that business associates are only required to notify the covered entity of uses and disclosures of protected health information not provided for by the agreement of which it becomes aware in order to more closely align the sample contract provisions with the regulation text. The Department did not intend to imply a different standard than that included in the regulation.

The Department has modified the General Use and Disclosure sample language to clarify that there are two possible approaches, and that in each approach the use or disclosure of protected health information by a business associate shall be consistent with the minimum necessary policies and procedures of the covered entity.

The Department has adopted one change to the sample language under Specific Use and Disclosure that clarifies that a permitted specific use of protected health information by the business associate includes reporting violations of law to appropriate Federal and State authorities. This would permit a business associate to use or disclose protected health information in accordance with the standards in § 164.502(j)(1). We indicate that this is optional text, not required by the Privacy Rule. Because we have included this language as sample language, we have deleted discussion of this issue in the statement preceding the sample business associate contract provisions.

Under Obligations of Covered Entity, the Department has clarified that covered entities need only notify business associates of a restriction to the use or disclosure of protected health information in its notice of privacy practices to the extent that such restriction may affect the business associates' use or disclosure of protected health information. The other provisions requiring the covered entity to notify the business associate of restrictions to the use or disclosure of protected health information remain and have been modified to include similar limiting language.

In the Term and Termination provisions, the Department has added clarifying language that indicates that if neither termination nor cure are feasible, the covered entity shall report the violation to the Secretary. We have also clarified that the parties should negotiate how they will determine whether the return or destruction of protected health information is infeasible.

Finally, the Department has clarified the miscellaneous provision regarding interpretation to clarify that ambiguities shall be resolved to permit the covered entity's compliance with the Privacy Rule.

Each entity should carefully analyze each of the sample provisions to ensure that it is appropriate given the specific business associate relationship. Some of the modifications are intended to address some commenters concerns that the sample language is weighted too heavily in favor of the covered entity. Individual parties are reminded that all contract provisions are subject to negotiation, provided that they are consistent with the requirements in the Privacy Rule. The sample language is not intended to, and cannot, substitute for responsible legal advice.

Response to Other Public Comments

Comment: Several commenters noted that the sample language was missing certain required contractual elements, such as an effective date, insurance and indemnification clauses, procedures for amending the contract, as well as other provisions that may be implicated by the Privacy Rule, such as the Electronic Transactions Standards. Some of these commenters requested that the guidance be a complete model contract rather than sample contract provisions so that the covered entity would not need legal assistance.

Response: The Department intentionally did not make this guidance a complete model contract, but rather provided only those provisions specifically tied to requirements of the Privacy Rule. As stated above, this guidance does not substitute for legal advice. Other contract provisions may be dictated by State or other law or by the relationship between the parties. It is not feasible to provide sample contracts that would accommodate each situation. Parties are free to negotiate additional terms, including those that may be required by other laws or regulations.

Comment: Some commenters requested that use of the sample business associate contract language create a safe harbor for an entity that adopts them.

Response: The sample business associate contract provisions are not a safe harbor. Rather, the sample language is intended to provide guidance and assist covered entities in the effort required to enter into a business associate agreement. Use of the sample provisions or similar provisions, where appropriate, would be considered strong evidence of compliance with the business associate contract provisions of the Privacy Rule. However, contracts will necessarily vary based on State law and the relationship between the covered entity and the business associate.

Comment: Some commenters were concerned that the sample provision permitting a covered entity to have access to the practices, books, and records of the business associate would impose an audit requirement on the covered entity.

Response: The sample business associate contract provisions do not impose any additional requirements on covered entities. Only the regulation imposes requirements. Therefore, the inclusion of the provision that the business associate shall allow the covered entity access to the business associate practices, books, and records does not indicate that the Privacy Rule imposes an audit requirement on the covered entity. We have stated numerous times that the Privacy Rule does not require covered entities to monitor the activities of their business associates.

Comment: One commenter noted that the business associate should not be required, under the contract, to mitigate damages resulting from a violation.

Response: We disagree. In order for a covered entity to be able to act as it is required to under the Privacy Rule when a business associate is holding protected health information, the covered entity must require the same activities of the business associate through the contract.

Comment: One commenter noted that the Privacy Rule does not explicitly direct that a covered entity provide its notice of privacy practices to its business associates.

Response: We agree and have modified the language in the sample provision accordingly. However, in order for the business associate to act consistently with the privacy practices of the covered entity, which is required by the Privacy Rule, the parties may find it necessary to require disclosure of these policies. To the extent that parties can craft an alternate approach, they are free to do so.

Comment: One commenter indicated that traditional contract terms such as "term" and "termination" should not be included in the sample language if the Department's intention is to address only those terms required by the Rule.

Response: Because termination of the business associate agreement is specifically addressed in the Privacy Rule, we have retained these provisions in the sample language. As with all other provisions, parties are free to negotiate alternative Term and Termination provisions that meet their unique situations and concerns,

C. HIPAA Final Rules, Privacy Standards, continued

53264   Federal Register/Vol. 67, No. 157/Wednesday, August 14, 2002/Rules and Regulations

provided that they meet the requirements of the Privacy Rule.

Comment: Another commenter indicated that the sample language should not require the return or destruction of protected health information in the possession of subcontractors or agents of the business associate.

Response: We have retained this language as this is consistent with the Privacy Rule. Section 164.504(e)(2)(ii)(D) requires that the business associate contract include a provision that the business associate ensures that any agents, including subcontractors, agree to the same restrictions and conditions as the business associate. Generally, the contract must require the business associate to return or destroy protected health information; therefore, the contract also must require the business associate to have agents and subcontractors to do the same. This is reflected in the sample contract language.

Comment: One commenter requested that the sample language include a provision that the covered entity may impose monetary damages on a business associate for violation of its privacy policies.

Response: We have not included such a provision because the Privacy Rule does not address this issue. The Privacy Rule would not prohibit a monetary damages provision from being included in the contract. This, again, is a matter to be negotiated between covered entities and their business associates.

Comment: One commenter suggested that specific references to sections in the Rule be deleted and either replaced by a general statement that the contract shall be interpreted in a manner consistent with the Rule or supplemented with clarifying language with examples.

Response: We believe that using section reference is a valid and expeditious approach as it incorporates changes as modifications are made to the Privacy Rule. A business associate contract may take a different approach than using section references to the Privacy Rule.

Comment: One commenter asked that the sample business associate contract provisions be included in the Rule rather than published as an appendix to the preamble so that it will be in the Code of Federal Regulations.

Response: We have published the sample business associate contract provisions as an appendix to the preamble because they are meant as guidance. The sample language shall be available on the Office for Civil Rights web site at *www.hhs.gov/ocr/hipaa;* and may be updated or revised as necessary.

Appendix to the Preamble—Sample Business Associate Contract Provisions

Statement of Intent

The Department provides these sample business associate contract provisions in response to numerous requests for guidance. This is only sample language. These provisions are designed to help covered entities more easily comply with the business associate contract requirements of the Privacy Rule. However, use of these sample provisions is not required for compliance with the Privacy Rule. The language may be amended to more accurately reflect business arrangements between the covered entity and the business associate.

These or similar provisions may be incorporated into an agreement for the provision of services between the entities or they may be incorporated into a separate business associate agreement. These provisions only address concepts and requirements set forth in the Privacy Rule and alone are not sufficient to result in a binding contract under State law. They do not include many formalities and substantive provisions that are required or typically included in a valid contract. Reliance on this sample is not sufficient for compliance with State law and does not replace consultation with a lawyer or negotiations between the parties to the contract.

Furthermore, a covered entity may want to include other provisions that are related to the Privacy Rule but that are not required by the Privacy Rule. For example, a covered entity may want to add provisions in a business associate contract in order for the covered entity to be able to rely on the business associate to help the covered entity meet its obligations under the Privacy Rule. In addition, there may be permissible uses or disclosures by a business associate that are not specifically addressed in these sample provisions, for example having a business associate create a limited data set. These and other types of issues will need to be worked out between the parties.

Sample Business Associate Contract Provisions [3]

Definitions (Alternative Approaches)

Catch-all definition:

---

[3] Words or phrases contained in brackets are intended as either optional language or as instructions to the users of these sample provisions and are not intended to be included in the contractual provisions.

Terms used, but not otherwise defined, in this Agreement shall have the same meaning as those terms in the Privacy Rule.

Examples of specific definitions:

(a) *Business Associate.* "Business Associate" shall mean [Insert Name of Business Associate].

(b) *Covered Entity.* "Covered Entity" shall mean [Insert Name of Covered Entity].

(c) *Individual.* "Individual" shall have the same meaning as the term "individual" in 45 CFR 164.501 and shall include a person who qualifies as a personal representative in accordance with 45 CFR 164.502(g).

(d) *Privacy Rule.* "Privacy Rule" shall mean the Standards for Privacy of Individually Identifiable Health Information at 45 CFR part 160 and part 164, subparts A and E.

(e) *Protected Health Information.* "Protected Health Information" shall have the same meaning as the term "protected health information" in 45 CFR 164.501, limited to the information created or received by Business Associate from or on behalf of Covered Entity.

(f) *Required By Law.* "Required By Law" shall have the same meaning as the term "required by law" in 45 CFR 164.501.

(g) *Secretary.* "Secretary" shall mean the Secretary of the Department of Health and Human Services or his designee.

Obligations and Activities of Business Associate

(a) Business Associate agrees to not use or disclose Protected Health Information other than as permitted or required by the Agreement or as Required By Law.

(b) Business Associate agrees to use appropriate safeguards to prevent use or disclosure of the Protected Health Information other than as provided for by this Agreement.

(c) Business Associate agrees to mitigate, to the extent practicable, any harmful effect that is known to Business Associate of a use or disclosure of Protected Health Information by Business Associate in violation of the requirements of this Agreement. [This provision may be included if it is appropriate for the Covered Entity to pass on its duty to mitigate damages to a Business Associate.]

(d) Business Associate agrees to report to Covered Entity any use or disclosure of the Protected Health Information not provided for by this Agreement of which it becomes aware.

(e) Business Associate agrees to ensure that any agent, including a

C. HIPAA Final Rules, Privacy Standards, continued

subcontractor, to whom it provides Protected Health Information received from, or created or received by Business Associate on behalf of Covered Entity agrees to the same restrictions and conditions that apply through this Agreement to Business Associate with respect to such information.

(f) Business Associate agrees to provide access, at the request of Covered Entity, and in the time and manner [Insert negotiated terms], to Protected Health Information in a Designated Record Set, to Covered Entity or, as directed by Covered Entity, to an Individual in order to meet the requirements under 45 CFR 164.524. [Not necessary if business associate does not have protected health information in a designated record set.]

(g) Business Associate agrees to make any amendment(s) to Protected Health Information in a Designated Record Set that the Covered Entity directs or agrees to pursuant to 45 CFR 164.526 at the request of Covered Entity or an Individual, and in the time and manner [Insert negotiated terms]. [Not necessary if business associate does not have protected health information in a designated record set.]

(h) Business Associate agrees to make internal practices, books, and records, including policies and procedures and Protected Health Information, relating to the use and disclosure of Protected Health Information received from, or created or received by Business Associate on behalf of, Covered Entity available [to the Covered Entity, or] to the Secretary, in a time and manner [Insert negotiated terms] or designated by the Secretary, for purposes of the Secretary determining Covered Entity's compliance with the Privacy Rule.

(i) Business Associate agrees to document such disclosures of Protected Health Information and information related to such disclosures as would be required for Covered Entity to respond to a request by an Individual for an accounting of disclosures of Protected Health Information in accordance with 45 CFR 164.528.

(j) Business Associate agrees to provide to Covered Entity or an Individual, in time and manner [Insert negotiated terms], information collected in accordance with Section [Insert Section Number in Contract Where Provision (i) Appears] of this Agreement, to permit Covered Entity to respond to a request by an Individual for an accounting of disclosures of Protected Health Information in accordance with 45 CFR 164.528.

Permitted Uses and Disclosures by Business Associate

General Use and Disclosure Provisions [(a) and (b) are alternative approaches]

(a) *Specify purposes:*
Except as otherwise limited in this Agreement, Business Associate may use or disclose Protected Health Information on behalf of, or to provide services to, Covered Entity for the following purposes, if such use or disclosure of Protected Health Information would not violate the Privacy Rule if done by Covered Entity or the minimum necessary policies and procedures of the Covered Entity: [List Purposes].

(b) *Refer to underlying services agreement:*
Except as otherwise limited in this Agreement, Business Associate may use or disclose Protected Health Information to perform functions, activities, or services for, or on behalf of, Covered Entity as specified in [Insert Name of Services Agreement], provided that such use or disclosure would not violate the Privacy Rule if done by Covered Entity or the minimum necessary policies and procedures of the Covered Entity.

Specific Use and Disclosure Provisions [only necessary if parties wish to allow Business Associate to engage in such activities]

(a) Except as otherwise limited in this Agreement, Business Associate may use Protected Health Information for the proper management and administration of the Business Associate or to carry out the legal responsibilities of the Business Associate.

(b) Except as otherwise limited in this Agreement, Business Associate may disclose Protected Health Information for the proper management and administration of the Business Associate, provided that disclosures are Required By Law, or Business Associate obtains reasonable assurances from the person to whom the information is disclosed that it will remain confidential and used or further disclosed only as Required By Law or for the purpose for which it was disclosed to the person, and the person notifies the Business Associate of any instances of which it is aware in which the confidentiality of the information has been breached.

(c) Except as otherwise limited in this Agreement, Business Associate may use Protected Health Information to provide Data Aggregation services to Covered Entity as permitted by 42 CFR 164.504(e)(2)(i)(B).

(d) Business Associate may use Protected Health Information to report violations of law to appropriate Federal

and State authorities, consistent with § 164.502(j)(1).

Obligations of Covered Entity

Provisions for Covered Entity To Inform Business Associate of Privacy Practices and Restrictions [provisions dependent on business arrangement]

(a) Covered Entity shall notify Business Associate of any limitation(s) in its notice of privacy practices of Covered Entity in accordance with 45 CFR 164.520, to the extent that such limitation may affect Business Associate's use or disclosure of Protected Health Information.

(b) Covered Entity shall notify Business Associate of any changes in, or revocation of, permission by Individual to use or disclose Protected Health Information, to the extent that such changes may affect Business Associate's use or disclosure of Protected Health Information.

(c) Covered Entity shall notify Business Associate of any restriction to the use or disclosure of Protected Health Information that Covered Entity has agreed to in accordance with 45 CFR 164.522, to the extent that such restriction may affect Business Associate's use or disclosure of Protected Health Information.

Permissible Requests by Covered Entity

Covered Entity shall not request Business Associate to use or disclose Protected Health Information in any manner that would not be permissible under the Privacy Rule if done by Covered Entity. [Include an exception if the Business Associate will use or disclose protected health information for, and the contract includes provisions for, data aggregation or management and administrative activities of Business Associate].

Term and Termination

(a) *Term.* The Term of this Agreement shall be effective as of [Insert Effective Date], and shall terminate when all of the Protected Health Information provided by Covered Entity to Business Associate, or created or received by Business Associate on behalf of Covered Entity, is destroyed or returned to Covered Entity, or, if it is infeasible to return or destroy Protected Health Information, protections are extended to such information, in accordance with the termination provisions in this Section. [Term may differ.]

(b) *Termination for Cause.* Upon Covered Entity's knowledge of a material breach by Business Associate, Covered Entity shall either:
(1) Provide an opportunity for Business Associate to cure the breach or

53266   Federal Register / Vol. 67, No. 157 / Wednesday, August 14, 2002 / Rules and Regulations

end the violation and terminate this Agreement [and the ___ Agreement/ sections ___ of the ___ Agreement] if Business Associate does not cure the breach or end the violation within the time specified by Covered Entity;

(2) Immediately terminate this Agreement [and the ___ Agreement/ sections ___ of the ___ Agreement] if Business Associate has breached a material term of this Agreement and cure is not possible; or

(3) If neither termination nor cure are feasible, Covered Entity shall report the violation to the Secretary. [Bracketed language in this provision may be necessary if there is an underlying services agreement. Also, opportunity to cure is permitted, but not required by the Privacy Rule.]

(c) *Effect of Termination.*

(1) Except as provided in paragraph (2) of this section, upon termination of this Agreement, for any reason, Business Associate shall return or destroy all Protected Health Information received from Covered Entity, or created or received by Business Associate on behalf of Covered Entity. This provision shall apply to Protected Health Information that is in the possession of subcontractors or agents of Business Associate. Business Associate shall retain no copies of the Protected Health Information.

(2) In the event that Business Associate determines that returning or destroying the Protected Health Information is infeasible, Business Associate shall provide to Covered Entity notification of the conditions that make return or destruction infeasible. Upon [Insert negotiated terms] that return or destruction of Protected Health Information is infeasible, Business Associate shall extend the protections of this Agreement to such Protected Health Information and limit further uses and disclosures of such Protected Health Information to those purposes that make the return or destruction infeasible, for so long as Business Associate maintains such Protected Health Information.

Miscellaneous

(a) *Regulatory References.* A reference in this Agreement to a section in the Privacy Rule means the section as in effect or as amended.

(b) *Amendment.* The Parties agree to take such action as is necessary to amend this Agreement from time to time as is necessary for Covered Entity to comply with the requirements of the Privacy Rule and the Health Insurance Portability and Accountability Act of 1996, Pub. L. No. 104–191.

(c) *Survival.* The respective rights and obligations of Business Associate under

Section [Insert Section Number Related to "Effect of Termination"] of this Agreement shall survive the termination of this Agreement.

(d) *Interpretation.* Any ambiguity in this Agreement shall be resolved to permit Covered Entity to comply with the Privacy Rule.

List of Subjects

45 CFR Part 160

Electronic transactions, Employer benefit plan, Health, Health care, Health facilities, Health insurance, Health records, Medicaid, Medical research, Medicare, Privacy, Reporting and record keeping requirements.

45 CFR Part 164

Electronic transactions, Employer benefit plan, Health, Health care, Health facilities, Health insurance, Health records, Medicaid, Medical research, Medicare, Privacy, Reporting and record keeping requirements.

Dated: August 6, 2002.

Tommy G. Thompson,

Secretary.

For the reasons set forth in the preamble, the Department amends 45 CFR subtitle A, subchapter C, as follows:

PART 160—GENERAL ADMINISTRATIVE REQUIREMENTS

1. The authority citation for part 160 continues to read as follows:

Authority: Sec. 1171 through 1179 of the Social Security Act (42 U.S.C. 1320d–1329d–8), as added by sec. 262 of Pub. L. No. 104–191, 110 Stat. 2021–2031 and sec. 264 of Pub. L. No. 104–191 (42 U.S.C. 1320d–2(note)).

2. Amend § 160.102(b), by removing the phrase "section 201(a)(5) of the Health Insurance Portability Act of 1996, (Pub. L. No. 104–191)" and adding in its place the phrase "the Social Security Act, 42 U.S.C. 1320a–7c(a)(5)".

3. In § 160.103 add the definition of "individually identifiable health information" in alphabetical order to read as follows:

§ 160.103   Definitions.

* * * * *

Individually identifiable health information is information that is a subset of health information, including demographic information collected from an individual, and:

(1) Is created or received by a health care provider, health plan, employer, or health care clearinghouse; and

(2) Relates to the past, present, or future physical or mental health or

condition of an individual; the provision of health care to an individual; or the past, present, or future payment for the provision of health care to an individual; and

(i) That identifies the individual; or

(ii) With respect to which there is a reasonable basis to believe the information can be used to identify the individual.

* * * * *

4. In § 160.202 revise paragraphs (2) and (4) of the definition of "more stringent" to read as follows:

§ 160.202   Definitions.

* * * * *

More stringent means * * *

(2) With respect to the rights of an individual, who is the subject of the individually identifiable health information, regarding access to or amendment of individually identifiable health information, permits greater rights of access or amendment, as applicable.

* * * * *

(4) With respect to the form, substance, or the need for express legal permission from an individual, who is the subject of the individually identifiable health information, for use or disclosure of individually identifiable health information, provides requirements that narrow the scope or duration, increase the privacy protections afforded (such as by expanding the criteria for), or reduce the coercive effect of the circumstances surrounding the express legal permission, as applicable.

* * * * *

5. Amend § 160.203(b) by adding the words "individually identifiable" before the word "health".

PART 164—SECURITY AND PRIVACY

Subpart E—Privacy of Individually Identifiable Health Information

1. The authority citation for part 164 continues to read as follows:

Authority: 42 U.S.C. 1320d–2 and 1320d–4, sec. 264 of Pub. L. No. 104–191, 110 Stat. 2033–2034 (42 U.S.C. 1320d–2(note)).

2. Amend § 164.102 by removing the words "implementation standards" and adding in its place the words "implementation specifications."

3. In § 164.500, remove "consent," from paragraph (b)(1)(v).

4. Amend § 164.501 as follows:

a. In the definition of "health care operations" remove from the introductory text of the definition ", and any of the following activities of an

C. HIPAA Final Rules, Privacy Standards, continued

organized health care arrangement in which the covered entity participates" and revise paragraphs (6)(iv) and (v).

b. Remove the definition of "individually identifiable health information".

c. Revise the definition of "marketing".

d. In paragraph (1)(ii) of the definition of "payment," remove the word "covered".

e. Revise paragraph (2) of the definition of "protected health information".

f. Remove the words "a covered" and replace them with "an" in the definition of "required by law".

The revisions read as follows:

§ 164.501 Definitions.

*   *   *   *   *

Health care operations means *   *   *
(6) *   *   *

(iv) The sale, transfer, merger, or consolidation of all or part of the covered entity with another covered entity, or an entity that following such activity will become a covered entity and due diligence related to such activity; and

(v) Consistent with the applicable requirements of § 164.514, creating de-identified health information or a limited data set, and fundraising for the benefit of the covered entity.

*   *   *   *   *

Marketing means:

(1) To make a communication about a product or service that encourages recipients of the communication to purchase or use the product or service, unless the communication is made:

(i) To describe a health-related product or service (or payment for such product or service) that is provided by, or included in a plan of benefits of, the covered entity making the communication, including communications about: the entities participating in a health care provider network or health plan network; replacement of, or enhancements to, a health plan; and health-related products or services available only to a health plan enrollee that add value to, but are not part of, a plan of benefits.

(ii) For treatment of the individual; or

(iii) For case management or care coordination for the individual, or to direct or recommend alternative treatments, therapies, health care providers, or settings of care to the individual.

(2) An arrangement between a covered entity and any other entity whereby the covered entity discloses protected health information to the other entity, in exchange for direct or indirect remuneration, for the other entity or its

affiliate to make a communication about its own product or service that encourages recipients of the communication to purchase or use that product or service.

*   *   *   *   *

Protected health information means *   *   *

(2) *Protected health information* excludes individually identifiable health information in:

(i) Education records covered by the Family Educational Rights and Privacy Act, as amended, 20 U.S.C. 1232g;

(ii) Records described at 20 U.S.C. 1232g(a)(4)(B)(iv); and

(iii) Employment records held by a covered entity in its role as employer.

*   *   *   *   *

5. Amend § 164.502 as follows:

a. Revise paragraphs (a)(1)(ii), (iii), and (vi).

b. Revise paragraph (b)(2)(ii).

c. Redesignate paragraphs (b)(2)(iii) through (v) as paragraphs (b)(2)(iv) through (vi).

d. Add a new paragraph (b)(2)(iii).

e. Redesignate paragraphs (g)(3)(i) through (iii) as (g)(3)(i)(A) through (C) and redesignate paragraph (g)(3) as (g)(3)(i).

f. Add a new paragraph (g)(3)(ii).

The revisions and additions read as follows:

§ 164.502 Uses and disclosures of protected health information: general rules.

(a) Standard. *   *   *

(1) *Permitted uses and disclosures.*
*   *   *

(ii) For treatment, payment, or health care operations, as permitted by and in compliance with § 164.506;

(iii) Incident to a use or disclosure otherwise permitted or required by this subpart, provided that the covered entity has complied with the applicable requirements of § 164.502(b), § 164.514(d), and § 164.530(c) with respect to such otherwise permitted or required use or disclosure;

*   *   *   *   *

(vi) As permitted by and in compliance with this section, § 164.512, or § 164.514(e), (f), or (g).

*   *   *   *   *

(b) *Standard: Minimum necessary.*
*   *   *

(2) *Minimum necessary does not apply.* *   *   *

(ii) Uses or disclosures made to the individual, as permitted under paragraph (a)(1)(i) of this section or as required by paragraph (a)(2)(i) of this section;

(iii) Uses or disclosures made pursuant to an authorization under § 164.508;

*   *   *   *   *

(g)(1) *Standard: Personal representatives.* *   *   *

(3) *Implementation specification: unemancipated minors.* *   *   *

(i) *   *   *

(ii) Notwithstanding the provisions of paragraph (g)(3)(i) of this section:

(A) If, and to the extent, permitted or required by an applicable provision of State or other law, including applicable case law, a covered entity may disclose, or provide access in accordance with § 164.524 to, protected health information about an unemancipated minor to a parent, guardian, or other person acting *in loco parentis*;

(B) If, and to the extent, prohibited by an applicable provision of State or other law, including applicable case law, a covered entity may not disclose, or provide access in accordance with § 164.524 to, protected health information about an unemancipated minor to a parent, guardian, or other person acting *in loco parentis*; and

(C) Where the parent, guardian, or other person acting *in loco parentis*, is not the personal representative under paragraphs (g)(3)(i)(A), (B), or (C) of this section and where there is no applicable access provision under State or other law, including case law, a covered entity may provide or deny access under § 164.524 to a parent, guardian, or other person acting *in loco parentis*, if such action is consistent with State or other applicable law, provided that such decision must be made by a licensed health care professional, in the exercise of professional judgment.

*   *   *   *   *

6. Amend § 164.504 as follows:

a. In paragraph (a), revise the definitions of "health care component" and "hybrid entity".

b. Revise paragraph (c)(1)(ii).

c. Revise paragraph (c)(2)(ii).

d. Revise paragraph (c)(3)(iii).

e. Revise paragraph (f)(1)(i).

f. Add paragraph (f)(1)(iii).

The revisions and addition read as follows:

§ 164.504 Uses and disclosures: Organizational requirements.

(a) *Definitions.* *   *   *

Health care component means a component or combination of components of a hybrid entity designated by the hybrid entity in accordance with paragraph (c)(3)(iii) of this section.

Hybrid entity means a single legal entity:

(1) That is a covered entity;

(2) Whose business activities include both covered and non-covered functions; and

C. HIPAA Final Rules, Privacy Standards, continued

(3) That designates health care components in accordance with paragraph (c)(3)(iii) of this section.

* * * * *

(c)(1) *Implementation specification: Application of other provisions.* * * *

(ii) A reference in such provision to a "health plan," "covered health care provider," or "health care clearinghouse" refers to a health care component of the covered entity if such health care component performs the functions of a health plan, health care provider, or health care clearinghouse, as applicable; and

* * * * *

(2) *Implementation specifications: Safeguard requirements.* * * *

(ii) A component that is described by paragraph (c)(3)(iii)(B) of this section does not use or disclose protected health information that it creates or receives from or on behalf of the health care component in a way prohibited by this subpart; and

* * * * *

(3) *Implementation specifications: Responsibilities of the covered entity.* * * *

(iii) The covered entity is responsible for designating the components that are part of one or more health care components of the covered entity and documenting the designation as required by § 164.530(j), provided that, if the covered entity designates a health care component or components, it must include any component that would meet the definition of covered entity if it were a separate legal entity. Health care component(s) also may include a component only to the extent that it performs:

(A) Covered functions; or

(B) Activities that would make such component a business associate of a component that performs covered functions if the two components were separate legal entities.

* * * * *

(f)(1) *Standard: Requirements for group health plans.* (i) Except as provided under paragraph (f)(1)(ii) or (iii) of this section or as otherwise authorized under § 164.508, a group health plan, in order to disclose protected health information to the plan sponsor or to provide for or permit the disclosure of protected health information to the plan sponsor by a health insurance issuer or HMO with respect to the group health plan, must ensure that the plan documents restrict uses and disclosures of such information by the plan sponsor consistent with the requirements of this subpart.

* * * * *

(iii) The group health plan, or a health insurance issuer or HMO with respect to the group health plan, may disclose to the plan sponsor information on whether the individual is participating in the group health plan, or is enrolled in or has disenrolled from a health insurance issuer or HMO offered by the plan.

* * * * *

7. Revise § 164.506 to read as follows:

§ 164.506   Uses and disclosures to carry out treatment, payment, or health care operations.

(a) *Standard: Permitted uses and disclosures.* Except with respect to uses or disclosures that require an authorization under § 164.508(a)(2) and (3), a covered entity may use or disclose protected health information for treatment, payment, or health care operations as set forth in paragraph (c) of this section, provided that such use or disclosure is consistent with other applicable requirements of this subpart.

(b) *Standard: Consent for uses and disclosures permitted.* (1) A covered entity may obtain consent of the individual to use or disclose protected health information to carry out treatment, payment, or health care operations.

(2) Consent, under paragraph (b) of this section, shall not be effective to permit a use or disclosure of protected health information when an authorization, under § 164.508, is required or when another condition must be met for such use or disclosure to be permissible under this subpart.

(c) *Implementation specifications: Treatment, payment, or health care operations.*

(1) A covered entity may use or disclose protected health information for its own treatment, payment, or health care operations.

(2) A covered entity may disclose protected health information for treatment activities of a health care provider.

(3) A covered entity may disclose protected health information to another covered entity or a health care provider for the payment activities of the entity that receives the information.

(4) A covered entity may disclose protected health information to another covered entity for health care operations activities of the entity that receives the information, if each entity either has or had a relationship with the individual who is the subject of the protected health information being requested, the protected health information pertains to such relationship, and the disclosure is:

(i) For a purpose listed in paragraph (1) or (2) of the definition of health care operations; or

(ii) For the purpose of health care fraud and abuse detection or compliance.

(5) A covered entity that participates in an organized health care arrangement may disclose protected health information about an individual to another covered entity that participates in the organized health care arrangement for any health care operations activities of the organized health care arrangement.

8. Revise § 164.508 to read as follows:

§ 164.508   Uses and disclosures for which an authorization is required.

(a) *Standard: authorizations for uses and disclosures.*—(1) *Authorization required: general rule.* Except as otherwise permitted or required by this subchapter, a covered entity may not use or disclose protected health information without an authorization that is valid under this section. When a covered entity obtains or receives a valid authorization for its use or disclosure of protected health information, such use or disclosure must be consistent with such authorization.

(2) *Authorization required: psychotherapy notes.* Notwithstanding any provision of this subpart, other than the transition provisions in § 164.532, a covered entity must obtain an authorization for any use or disclosure of psychotherapy notes, except:

(i) To carry out the following treatment, payment, or health care operations:

(A) Use by the originator of the psychotherapy notes for treatment;

(B) Use or disclosure by the covered entity for its own training programs in which students, trainees, or practitioners in mental health learn under supervision to practice or improve their skills in group, joint, family, or individual counseling; or

(C) Use or disclosure by the covered entity to defend itself in a legal action or other proceeding brought by the individual; and

(ii) A use or disclosure that is required by § 164.502(a)(2)(ii) or permitted by § 164.512(a); § 164.512(d) with respect to the oversight of the originator of the psychotherapy notes; § 164.512(g)(1); or § 164.512(j)(1)(i).

(3) *Authorization required: Marketing.* (i) Notwithstanding any provision of this subpart, other than the transition provisions in § 164.532, a covered entity must obtain an authorization for any use or disclosure of protected health

C. HIPAA Final Rules, Privacy Standards, continued

information for marketing, except if the communication is in the form of:

(A) A face-to-face communication made by a covered entity to an individual; or

(B) A promotional gift of nominal value provided by the covered entity.

(ii) If the marketing involves direct or indirect remuneration to the covered entity from a third party, the authorization must state that such remuneration is involved.

(b) *Implementation specifications: general requirements.*—(1) *Valid authorizations.* (i) A valid authorization is a document that meets the requirements in paragraphs (a)(3)(ii), (c)(1), and (c)(2) of this section, as applicable.

(ii) A valid authorization may contain elements or information in addition to the elements required by this section, provided that such additional elements or information are not inconsistent with the elements required by this section.

(2) *Defective authorizations.* An authorization is not valid, if the document submitted has any of the following defects:

(i) The expiration date has passed or the expiration event is known by the covered entity to have occurred;

(ii) The authorization has not been filled out completely, with respect to an element described by paragraph (c) of this section, if applicable;

(iii) The authorization is known by the covered entity to have been revoked;

(iv) The authorization violates paragraph (b)(3) or (4) of this section, if applicable;

(v) Any material information in the authorization is known by the covered entity to be false.

(3) *Compound authorizations.* An authorization for use or disclosure of protected health information may not be combined with any other document to create a compound authorization, except as follows:

(i) An authorization for the use or disclosure of protected health information for a research study may be combined with any other type of written permission for the same research study, including another authorization for the use or disclosure of protected health information for such research or a consent to participate in such research;

(ii) An authorization for a use or disclosure of psychotherapy notes may only be combined with another authorization for a use or disclosure of psychotherapy notes;

(iii) An authorization under this section, other than an authorization for a use or disclosure of psychotherapy notes, may be combined with any other such authorization under this section,

except when a covered entity has conditioned the provision of treatment, payment, enrollment in the health plan, or eligibility for benefits under paragraph (b)(4) of this section on the provision of one of the authorizations.

(4) *Prohibition on conditioning of authorizations.* A covered entity may not condition the provision to an individual of treatment, payment, enrollment in the health plan, or eligibility for benefits on the provision of an authorization, except:

(i) A covered health care provider may condition the provision of research-related treatment on provision of an authorization for the use or disclosure of protected health information for such research under this section;

(ii) A health plan may condition enrollment in the health plan or eligibility for benefits on provision of an authorization requested by the health plan prior to an individual's enrollment in the health plan, if:

(A) The authorization sought is for the health plan's eligibility or enrollment determinations relating to the individual or for its underwriting or risk rating determinations; and

(B) The authorization is not for a use or disclosure of psychotherapy notes under paragraph (a)(2) of this section; and

(iii) A covered entity may condition the provision of health care that is solely for the purpose of creating protected health information for disclosure to a third party on provision of an authorization for the disclosure of the protected health information to such third party.

(5) *Revocation of authorizations.* An individual may revoke an authorization provided under this section at any time, provided that the revocation is in writing, except to the extent that:

(i) The covered entity has taken action in reliance thereon; or

(ii) If the authorization was obtained as a condition of obtaining insurance coverage, other law provides the insurer with the right to contest a claim under the policy or the policy itself.

(6) *Documentation.* A covered entity must document and retain any signed authorization under this section as required by § 164.530(j).

(c) *Implementation specifications: Core elements and requirements.*—(1) *Core elements.* A valid authorization under this section must contain at least the following elements:

(i) A description of the information to be used or disclosed that identifies the information in a specific and meaningful fashion.

(ii) The name or other specific identification of the person(s), or class

of persons, authorized to make the requested use or disclosure.

(iii) The name or other specific identification of the person(s), or class of persons, to whom the covered entity may make the requested use or disclosure.

(iv) A description of each purpose of the requested use or disclosure. The statement "at the request of the individual" is a sufficient description of the purpose when an individual initiates the authorization and does not, or elects not to, provide a statement of the purpose.

(v) An expiration date or an expiration event that relates to the individual or the purpose of the use or disclosure. The statement "end of the research study," "none," or similar language is sufficient if the authorization is for a use or disclosure of protected health information for research, including for the creation and maintenance of a research database or research repository.

(vi) Signature of the individual and date. If the authorization is signed by a personal representative of the individual, a description of such representative's authority to act for the individual must also be provided.

(2) *Required statements.* In addition to the core elements, the authorization must contain statements adequate to place the individual on notice of all of the following:

(i) The individual's right to revoke the authorization in writing, and either:

(A) The exceptions to the right to revoke and a description of how the individual may revoke the authorization; or

(B) To the extent that the information in paragraph (c)(2)(i)(A) of this section is included in the notice required by § 164.520, a reference to the covered entity's notice.

(ii) The ability or inability to condition treatment, payment, enrollment or eligibility for benefits on the authorization, by stating either:

(A) The covered entity may not condition treatment, payment, enrollment or eligibility for benefits on whether the individual signs the authorization when the prohibition on conditioning of authorizations in paragraph (b)(4) of this section applies; or

(B) The consequences to the individual of a refusal to sign the authorization when, in accordance with paragraph (b)(4) of this section, the covered entity can condition treatment, enrollment in the health plan, or eligibility for benefits on failure to obtain such authorization.

C. HIPAA Final Rules, Privacy Standards, continued

53270 Federal Register / Vol. 67, No. 157 / Wednesday, August 14, 2002 / Rules and Regulations

(iii) The potential for information disclosed pursuant to the authorization to be subject to redisclosure by the recipient and no longer be protected by this subpart.

(3) *Plain language requirement.* The authorization must be written in plain language.

(4) *Copy to the individual.* If a covered entity seeks an authorization from an individual for a use or disclosure of protected health information, the covered entity must provide the individual with a copy of the signed authorization.

9. Amend § 164.510 as follows:

a. Revise the first sentence of the introductory text.

b. Remove the word "for" from paragraph (b)(3).

The revision reads as follows:

§ 164.510 Uses and disclosures requiring an opportunity for the individual to agree or to object.

A covered entity may use or disclose protected health information, provided that the individual is informed in advance of the use or disclosure and has the opportunity to agree to or prohibit or restrict the use or disclosure, in accordance with the applicable requirements of this section. * * *

* * * * *

10. Amend § 164.512 as follows:

a. Revise the section heading and the first sentence of the introductory text.

b. Revise paragraph (b)(1)(iii).

c. In paragraph (b)(1)(v)(A) remove the word "a" before the word "health."

d. Add the word "and" after the semicolon at the end of paragraph (b)(1)(v)(C).

e. Redesignate paragraphs (f)(3)(ii) and (iii) as (f)(3)(i) and (ii).

f. In the second sentence of paragraph (g)(2) add the word "to" after the word "directors."

g. In paragraph (i)(1)(iii)(A) remove the word "is" after the word "disclosure."

h. Revise paragraph (i)(2)(ii).

i. In paragraph (i)(2)(iii) remove "(i)(2)(ii)(D)" and add in its place "(i)(2)(ii)(C)".

The revisions read as follows:

§ 164.512 Uses and disclosures for which an authorization or opportunity to agree or object is not required.

A covered entity may use or disclose protected health information without the written authorization of the individual, as described in § 164.508, or the opportunity for the individual to agree or object as described in § 164.510, in the situations covered by this section, subject to the applicable requirements of this section. * * *

* * * * *

(b) *Standard: uses and disclosures for public health activities.*

(1) *Permitted disclosures.* * * *

(iii) A person subject to the jurisdiction of the Food and Drug Administration (FDA) with respect to an FDA-regulated product or activity for which that person has responsibility, for the purpose of activities related to the quality, safety or effectiveness of such FDA-regulated product or activity. Such purposes include:

(A) To collect or report adverse events (or similar activities with respect to food or dietary supplements), product defects or problems (including problems with the use or labeling of a product), or biological product deviations;

(B) To track FDA-regulated products;

(C) To enable product recalls, repairs, or replacement, or lookback (including locating and notifying individuals who have received products that have been recalled, withdrawn, or are the subject of lookback); or

(D) To conduct post marketing surveillance;

* * * * *

(i) *Standard: Uses and disclosures for research purposes.* * * *

(2) *Documentation of waiver approval.* * * *

(ii) *Waiver criteria.* A statement that the IRB or privacy board has determined that the alteration or waiver, in whole or in part, of authorization satisfies the following criteria:

(A) The use or disclosure of protected health information involves no more than a minimal risk to the privacy of individuals, based on, at least, the presence of the following elements;

(1) An adequate plan to protect the identifiers from improper use and disclosure;

(2) An adequate plan to destroy the identifiers at the earliest opportunity consistent with conduct of the research, unless there is a health or research justification for retaining the identifiers or such retention is otherwise required by law; and

(3) Adequate written assurances that the protected health information will not be reused or disclosed to any other person or entity, except as required by law, for authorized oversight of the research study, or for other research for which the use or disclosure of protected health information would be permitted by this subpart;

(B) The research could not practicably be conducted without the waiver or alteration; and

(C) The research could not practicably be conducted without access to and use of the protected health information.

* * * * *

11. Amend § 164.514 as follows:

a. Revise paragraph (b)(2)(i)(R).

b. Revise paragraph (d)(1).

c. Revise paragraph (d)(4)(iii).

d. In paragraph (d)(5), remove the word "discloses" and add in its place the word "disclose".

e. Revise paragraph (e).

The revisions read as follows:

§ 164.514 Other requirements relating to uses and disclosures of protected health information.

* * * * *

(b) *Implementation specifications: Requirements for de-identification of protected health information.* * * *

(2)(i) * * *

(R) Any other unique identifying number, characteristic, or code, except as permitted by paragraph (c) of this section; and

* * * * *

(d)(1) *Standard: minimum necessary requirements.* In order to comply with § 164.502(b) and this section, a covered entity must meet the requirements of paragraphs (d)(2) through (d)(5) of this section with respect to a request for, or the use and disclosure of, protected health information.

* * * * *

(4) *Implementation specifications: Minimum necessary requests for protected health information.* * * *

(iii) For all other requests, a covered entity must:

(A) Develop criteria designed to limit the request for protected health information to the information reasonably necessary to accomplish the purpose for which the request is made; and

(B) Review requests for disclosure on an individual basis in accordance with such criteria.

* * * * *

(e) (1) *Standard: Limited data set.* A covered entity may use or disclose a limited data set that meets the requirements of paragraphs (e)(2) and (e)(3) of this section, if the covered entity enters into a data use agreement with the limited data set recipient, in accordance with paragraph (e)(4) of this section.

(2) *Implementation specification: Limited data set:* A limited data set is protected health information that excludes the following direct identifiers of the individual or of relatives, employers, or household members of the individual:

(i) Names;

(ii) Postal address information, other than town or city, State, and zip code;

(iii) Telephone numbers;

(iv) Fax numbers;

C. HIPAA Final Rules, Privacy Standards, continued

(v) Electronic mail addresses;
(vi) Social security numbers;
(vii) Medical record numbers;
(viii) Health plan beneficiary numbers;
(ix) Account numbers;
(x) Certificate/license numbers;
(xi) Vehicle identifiers and serial numbers, including license plate numbers;
(xii) Device identifiers and serial numbers;
(xiii) Web Universal Resource Locators (URLs);
(xiv) Internet Protocol (IP) address numbers;
(xv) Biometric identifiers, including finger and voice prints; and
(xvi) Full face photographic images and any comparable images.

(3) *Implementation specification: Permitted purposes for uses and disclosures.* (i) A covered entity may use or disclose a limited data set under paragraph (e)(1) of this section only for the purposes of research, public health, or health care operations.

(ii) A covered entity may use protected health information to create a limited data set that meets the requirements of paragraph (e)(2) of this section, or disclose protected health information only to a business associate for such purpose, whether or not the limited data set is to be used by the covered entity.

(4) *Implementation specifications: Data use agreement.—*(i) *Agreement required.* A covered entity may use or disclose a limited data set under paragraph (e)(1) of this section only if the covered entity obtains satisfactory assurance, in the form of a data use agreement that meets the requirements of this section, that the limited data set recipient will only use or disclose the protected health information for limited purposes.

(ii) *Contents.* A data use agreement between the covered entity and the limited data set recipient must:

(A) Establish the permitted uses and disclosures of such information by the limited data set recipient, consistent with paragraph (e)(3) of this section. The data use agreement may not authorize the limited data set recipient to use or further disclose the information in a manner that would violate the requirements of this subpart, if done by the covered entity;

(B) Establish who is permitted to use or receive the limited data set; and

(C) Provide that the limited data set recipient will:

(1) Not use or further disclose the information other than as permitted by the data use agreement or as otherwise required by law;

(2) Use appropriate safeguards to prevent use or disclosure of the information other than as provided for by the data use agreement;

(3) Report to the covered entity any use or disclosure of the information not provided for by its data use agreement of which it becomes aware;

(4) Ensure that any agents, including a subcontractor, to whom it provides the limited data set agrees to the same restrictions and conditions that apply to the limited data set recipient with respect to such information; and

(5) Not identify the information or contact the individuals.

(iii) *Compliance.* (A) A covered entity is not in compliance with the standards in paragraph (e) of this section if the covered entity knew of a pattern of activity or practice of the limited data set recipient that constituted a material breach or violation of the data use agreement, unless the covered entity took reasonable steps to cure the breach or end the violation, as applicable, and, if such steps were unsuccessful:

(1) Discontinued disclosure of protected health information to the recipient; and

(2) Reported the problem to the Secretary.

(B) A covered entity that is a limited data set recipient and violates a data use agreement will be in noncompliance with the standards, implementation specifications, and requirements of paragraph (e) of this section.

* * * * *

12. Amend § 164.520 as follows:

a. Remove the words "consent or" from paragraph (b)(1)(ii)(B).

b. In paragraph (c), introductory text, remove "(c)(4)" and add in its place "(c)(3)".

c. Revise paragraph (c)(2)(i).

d. Redesignate paragraphs (c)(2)(ii) and (iii) as (c)(2)(iii) and (iv).

e. Add new paragraph (c)(2)(ii).

f. Amend redesignated paragraph (c)(2)(iv) by removing "(c)(2)(ii)" and adding in its place "(c)(2)(iii)".

g. Amend paragraph (c)(3)(iii) by adding a sentence at the end.

h. Revise paragraph (e).

The revisions and addition read as follows:

§ 164.520 Notice of privacy practices for protected health information.

* * * * *

(c) *Implementation specifications: provision of notice.* * * *

(2) *Specific requirements for certain covered health care providers.* * * *

(i) Provide the notice:

(A) No later than the date of the first service delivery, including service delivered electronically, to such individual after the compliance date for the covered health care provider; or

(B) In an emergency treatment situation, as soon as reasonably practicable after the emergency treatment situation.

(ii) Except in an emergency treatment situation, make a good faith effort to obtain a written acknowledgment of receipt of the notice provided in accordance with paragraph (c)(2)(i) of this section, and if not obtained, document its good faith efforts to obtain such acknowledgment and the reason why the acknowledgment was not obtained;

* * * * *

(3) *Specific requirements for electronic notice.* * * *

(iii) * * * The requirements in paragraph (c)(2)(ii) of this section apply to electronic notice.

* * * * *

(e) *Implementation specifications: Documentation.* A covered entity must document compliance with the notice requirements, as required by § 164.530(j), by retaining copies of the notices issued by the covered entity and, if applicable, any written acknowledgments of receipt of the notice or documentation of good faith efforts to obtain such written acknowledgment, in accordance with paragraph (c)(2)(ii) of this section.

13. Amend § 164.522 by removing the reference to "164.502(a)(2)(i)" in paragraph (a)(1)(v), and adding in its place "164.502(a)(2)(ii)".

14. Amend § 164.528 as follows:

a. In paragraph (a)(1)(i), remove "§ 164.502" and add in its place "§ 164.506".

b. Remove the word "or" from paragraph (a)(1)(v).

c. Redesignate paragraph (a)(1)(vi) as (a)(1)(ix) and redesignate paragraphs (a)(1)(iii) through (v) as (a)(1)(v) through (vii).

d. Add paragraphs (a)(1)(iii), (iv), and (a)(1)(viii).

e. Revise paragraph (b)(2), introductory text.

f. Revise paragraph (b)(2)(iv).

g. Remove "or pursuant to a single authorization under § 164.508," from paragraph (b)(3), introductory text.

h. Add paragraph (b)(4).

The additions and revisions read as follows:

§ 164.528 Accounting of disclosures of protected health information.

(a) *Standard: Right to an accounting of disclosures of protected health information.*

(1) * * *

C. HIPAA Final Rules, Privacy Standards, continued

(iii) Incident to a use or disclosure otherwise permitted or required by this subpart, as provided in § 164.502;

(iv) Pursuant to an authorization as provided in § 164.508;

* * * * *

(viii) As part of a limited data set in accordance with § 164.514(e); or

* * * * *

(b) *Implementation specifications: Content of the accounting.* * * *

(2) Except as otherwise provided by paragraphs (b)(3) or (b)(4) of this section, the accounting must include for each disclosure:

* * * * *

(iv) A brief statement of the purpose of the disclosure that reasonably informs the individual of the basis for the disclosure or, in lieu of such statement, a copy of a written request for a disclosure under §§ 164.502(a)(2)(ii) or 164.512, if any.

* * * * *

(4)(i) If, during the period covered by the accounting, the covered entity has made disclosures of protected health information for a particular research purpose in accordance with § 164.512(i) for 50 or more individuals, the accounting may, with respect to such disclosures for which the protected health information about the individual may have been included, provide:

(A) The name of the protocol or other research activity;

(B) A description, in plain language, of the research protocol or other research activity, including the purpose of the research and the criteria for selecting particular records;

(C) A brief description of the type of protected health information that was disclosed;

(D) The date or period of time during which such disclosures occurred, or may have occurred, including the date of the last such disclosure during the accounting period;

(E) The name, address, and telephone number of the entity that sponsored the research and of the researcher to whom the information was disclosed; and

(F) A statement that the protected health information of the individual may or may not have been disclosed for a particular protocol or other research activity.

(ii) If the covered entity provides an accounting for research disclosures, in accordance with paragraph (b)(4) of this section, and if it is reasonably likely that the protected health information of the individual was disclosed for such research protocol or activity, the covered entity shall, at the request of the individual, assist in contacting the

entity that sponsored the research and the researcher.

* * * * *

15. Amend § 164.530 as follows:

a. Redesignate paragraph (c)(2) as (c)(2)(i).

b. Add paragraph (c)(2)(ii).

c. Remove the words "the requirements" from paragraph (i)(4)(ii)(A) and add in their place the word "specifications."

The addition reads as follows:

§ 164.530   Administrative requirements.

* * * * *

(c) *Standard: Safeguards.* * * *

(2) *Implementation specifications: Safeguards.* (i) * * *

(ii) A covered entity must reasonably safeguard protected health information to limit incidental uses or disclosures made pursuant to an otherwise permitted or required use or disclosure.

* * * * *

16. Revise § 164.532 to read as follows:

§ 164.532   Transition provisions.

(a) *Standard: Effect of prior authorizations.* Notwithstanding §§ 164.508 and 164.512(i), a covered entity may use or disclose protected health information, consistent with paragraphs (b) and (c) of this section, pursuant to an authorization or other express legal permission obtained from an individual permitting the use or disclosure of protected health information, informed consent of the individual to participate in research, or a waiver of informed consent by an IRB.

(b) *Implementation specification: Effect of prior authorization for purposes other than research.* Notwithstanding any provisions in § 164.508, a covered entity may use or disclose protected health information that it created or received prior to the applicable compliance date of this subpart pursuant to an authorization or other express legal permission obtained from an individual prior to the applicable compliance date of this subpart, provided that the authorization or other express legal permission specifically permits such use or disclosure and there is no agreed-to restriction in accordance with § 164.522(a).

(c) *Implementation specification: Effect of prior permission for research.* Notwithstanding any provisions in §§ 164.508 and 164.512(i), a covered entity may, to the extent allowed by one of the following permissions, use or disclose, for research, protected health information that it created or received either before or after the applicable

compliance date of this subpart, provided that there is no agreed-to restriction in accordance with § 164.522(a), and the covered entity has obtained, prior to the applicable compliance date, either:

(1) An authorization or other express legal permission from an individual to use or disclose protected health information for the research;

(2) The informed consent of the individual to participate in the research; or

(3) A waiver, by an IRB, of informed consent for the research, in accordance with 7 CFR 1c.116(d), 10 CFR 745.116(d), 14 CFR 1230.116(d), 15 CFR 27.116(d), 16 CFR 1028.116(d), 21 CFR 50.24, 22 CFR 225.116(d), 24 CFR 60.116(d), 28 CFR 46.116(d), 32 CFR 219.116(d), 34 CFR 97.116(d), 38 CFR 16.116(d), 40 CFR 26.116(d), 45 CFR 46.116(d), 45 CFR 690.116(d), or 49 CFR 11.116(d), provided that a covered entity must obtain authorization in accordance with § 164.508 if, after the compliance date, informed consent is sought from an individual participating in the research.

(d) *Standard: Effect of prior contracts or other arrangements with business associates.* Notwithstanding any other provisions of this subpart, a covered entity, other than a small health plan, may disclose protected health information to a business associate and may allow a business associate to create, receive, or use protected health information on its behalf pursuant to a written contract or other written arrangement with such business associate that does not comply with §§ 164.502(e) and 164.504(e) consistent with the requirements, and only for such time, set forth in paragraph (e) of this section.

(e) *Implementation specification: Deemed compliance.*— (1) *Qualification.* Notwithstanding other sections of this subpart, a covered entity, other than a small health plan, is deemed to be in compliance with the documentation and contract requirements of §§ 164.502(e) and 164.504(e), with respect to a particular business associate relationship, for the time period set forth in paragraph (e)(2) of this section, if:

(i) Prior to October 15, 2002, such covered entity has entered into and is operating pursuant to a written contract or other written arrangement with a business associate for such business associate to perform functions or activities or provide services that make the entity a business associate; and

(ii) The contract or other arrangement is not renewed or modified from

C. HIPAA Final Rules, Privacy Standards, continued

October 15, 2002, until the compliance date set forth in § 164.534.

(2) *Limited deemed compliance period.* A prior contract or other arrangement that meets the qualification requirements in paragraph (e) of this section, shall be deemed compliant until the earlier of:

(i) The date such contract or other arrangement is renewed or modified on or after the compliance date set forth in § 164.534; or

(ii) April 14, 2004.

(3) *Covered entity responsibilities.* Nothing in this section shall alter the requirements of a covered entity to

comply with part 160, subpart C of this subchapter and §§ 164.524, 164.526, 164.528, and 164.530(f) with respect to protected health information held by a business associate.

[FR Doc. 02–20554 Filed 8–9–02; 2:00 pm]

BILLING CODE 4153–01–P

D. HIPAA Final Rules, Portability

Summary The U.S. Department of Health and Human Services (DHHS), the IRS, and the DOL published final rules on the portability for group health plans and issuers of health insurance coverage on December 30, 2004. The rules are effective February 28, 2005, and apply for plan years beginning on or after July 1, 2005. Thus, for calendar year plans, the rules apply as of January 1, 2006.

**Thursday,
December 30, 2004**

Part III

**Department of the
Treasury**
Internal Revenue Service
26 CFR Parts 54 and 602
Department of Labor
Employee Benefits Security
Administration

29 CFR Part 2590
**Department of Health
and Human Services**
Centers for Medicare & Medicaid Services

45 CFR Parts 144 and 146

Final Regulations for Health Coverage
Portability; Final Rule
Notice of Proposed Rulemaking for
Health Coverage Portability and Request
for Information on Benefit-Specific
Waiting Periods Under HIPAA Titles I &
IV; Proposed Rules

D. HIPAA Final Rules, Portability, continued

78720   Federal Register / Vol. 69, No. 250 / Thursday, December 30, 2004 / Rules and Regulations

DEPARTMENT OF THE TREASURY

Internal Revenue Service

26 CFR Parts 54 and 602

[TD 9166]

RIN 1545–AX84

DEPARTMENT OF LABOR

Employee Benefits Security Administration

29 CFR Part 2590

RIN 1210–AA54

DEPARTMENT OF HEALTH AND HUMAN SERVICES

Centers for Medicare & Medicaid Services

45 CFR Parts 144 and 146

RIN 0938–AL43

Final Regulations for Health Coverage Portability for Group Health Plans and Group Health Insurance Issuers Under HIPAA Titles I & IV

AGENCIES: Internal Revenue Service, Department of the Treasury; Employee Benefits Security Administration, Department of Labor; Centers for Medicare & Medicaid Services, Department of Health and Human Services.

ACTION: Final regulation.

SUMMARY: This document contains final regulations governing portability requirements for group health plans and issuers of health insurance coverage offered in connection with a group health plan. The rules contained in this document implement changes made to the Internal Revenue Code, the Employee Retirement Income Security Act, and the Public Health Service Act enacted as part of the Health Insurance Portability and Accountability Act of 1996.

DATES: *Effective date.* These final regulations are effective February 28, 2005.

Applicability date. These final regulations apply for plan years beginning on or after July 1, 2005.

FOR FURTHER INFORMATION CONTACT: Dave Mlawsky, Centers for Medicare & Medicaid Services (CMS), Department of Health and Human Services, at 1–877–267–2323 ext. 61565; Amy Turner, Employee Benefits Security Administration, Department of Labor, at (202) 693–8335; or Russ Weinheimer, Internal Revenue Service, Department of the Treasury, at (202) 622–6080.

SUPPLEMENTARY INFORMATION:

Customer Service Information

To assist consumers and the regulated community, the Departments have issued questions and answers concerning HIPAA. Individuals interested in obtaining copies of Department of Labor publications concerning changes in health care law may call a toll free number, 1–866–444–EBSA (3272), or access the publications on-line at *www.dol.gov/ebsa*, the Department of Labor's Web site. These regulations as well as other information on the new health care laws are also available on the Department of Labor's interactive web pages, Health Elaws. In addition, CMS's publication entitled "Protecting Your Health Insurance Coverage" is available by calling 1–800–633–4227 or on the Department of Health and Human Services' Web site (*www.cms.hhs.gov/hipaa1*), which includes the interactive webpages, HIPAA Online. Copies of the HIPAA regulations, as well as notices and press releases related to HIPAA and other health care laws, are also available at the above-referenced Web sites.

A. Background

The Health Insurance Portability and Accountability Act of 1996 (HIPAA), Public Law 104–191, was enacted on August 21, 1996. HIPAA amended the Internal Revenue Code of 1986 (Code), the Employee Retirement Income Security Act of 1974 (ERISA), and the Public Health Service Act (PHS Act) to provide for, among other things, improved portability and continuity of health coverage. Interim final regulations implementing the HIPAA provisions were first made available to the public on April 1, 1997 (published in the Federal Register on April 8, 1997, 62 FR 16894) (April 1997 interim rules). On December 29, 1997, the Departments published in the Federal Register (62 FR 67688) a clarification of the April 1997 interim rules as they relate to excepted benefits. On October 25, 1999, the Departments published a notice in the Federal Register (64 FR 57520) soliciting additional comments on the portability requirements based on the experience of plans and issuers operating under the April 1997 interim rules.

After consideration of all the comments received on the portability provisions, the Departments are publishing these final regulations. These final regulations do not significantly modify the framework established in the April 1997 interim rules. Instead, these final regulations implement changes to improve the portability of health coverage while seeking to minimize burdens on group health plans and group health insurance issuers. These final regulations become applicable to plans and issuers on the first day of the plan year beginning on or after July 1, 2005. Each plan or issuer must continue to comply with the April 1997 interim rules until these final regulations become applicable to that plan or issuer. In addition, the Departments are publishing proposed regulations elsewhere in this issue of the Federal Register to address additional and discrete issues.

B. Overview of the Final Regulations

1. Definitions—26 CFR 54.9801–2, 29 CFR 2590–701–2, 45 CFR 144.103

This section of the final regulations provides most of the definitions used in the regulations implementing HIPAA. In addition to some minor restructuring of the April 1997 interim rules (*i.e.*, some definitions have been moved into other sections of the regulations), some additional terms have been added. Among the new terms is the definition of the term *dependent. Dependent* is defined as any individual who is or may become eligible for coverage under the terms of a group health plan because of a relationship to a participant. This is intended to clarify that for purposes of HIPAA the terms of the group health plan determine which individuals are eligible for coverage as a dependent under the plan. Thus, for example, the plan terms control the age (if any) at which and conditions under which a child of a participant ceases to be eligible for coverage as a dependent. Moreover, whether an individual is eligible for special enrollment as a dependent is determined in part based on the plan's definition of dependent.

2. Limitations on Preexisting Condition Exclusions—26 CFR 54.9801–3, 29 CFR 2590.701–3, 45 CFR 146.111

This section of the final regulations addresses HIPAA's limitations on a plan's or issuer's ability to impose a preexisting condition exclusion. Comments addressing this topic generally approved of the approach taken in the Departments' April 1997 interim rules. Accordingly, these final regulations do not modify significantly the April 1997 interim rules but instead add several clarifications to the general framework already established. Also, some comments reflect a misunderstanding of the notice requirements for plans and issuers that impose a preexisting condition exclusion. Thus, these final regulations are restructured to clarify these notice

D. HIPAA Final Rules, Portability, continued

obligations. In addition, an example in the regulations contains language that plans and issuers can use to satisfy the notice requirements.

Definition of a Preexisting Condition Exclusion

In these final regulations, a preexisting condition exclusion continues to be defined broadly. A preexisting condition exclusion is any limitation or exclusion of benefits relating to a condition based on the fact that the condition was present before the effective date of coverage, whether or not any medical advice, diagnosis, care, or treatment was recommended or received before that day. This definition has been moved to this section on limitations on preexisting condition exclusions to emphasize the difference between the broadness of the definition and the narrowness of permissible preexisting condition exclusions. The definition has also been modified slightly from the previous definition and clarifications of its application have been added.

If a plan exclusion satisfies the definition of a preexisting condition exclusion, it is subject to the rules of this section for preexisting condition exclusions. Under the April 1997 interim rules, whether an exclusion is a preexisting condition exclusion is determined by whether the plan provision restricts benefits for a condition because it was present before the "first day of coverage." These final regulations have replaced the term *first day of coverage* with *effective date of coverage under a group health plan or health insurance coverage*. In the case of a plan that changes health insurance issuers, "first day of coverage" can be read to mean only the first day of coverage under the plan and not the first day of coverage under the new issuer's policy or contract (because "first day of coverage" is thus defined for purposes of determining the enrollment date). This reading would mean that an exclusion of benefits based on the fact that a condition existed before the effective date of coverage in the health insurance of the succeeding issuer would not be a preexisting condition (because it would not apply based on the fact that a condition existed before the first day of coverage under the plan). The phrase "effective date of coverage under a group health plan or health insurance coverage" under the final regulations thus applies to coverage either under a plan or health insurance coverage. Therefore, a provision used by a succeeding issuer to deny benefits for a condition because it arose before the effective date of coverage under the new

policy would also fit the definition of a preexisting condition exclusion.

Since the April 1997 interim rules were published, several situations have repeatedly arisen in which a plan exclusion is not designated as a preexisting condition exclusion but nevertheless satisfies the definition of a preexisting condition exclusion. Examples have been added to illustrate some of these common plan provisions. These situations include a plan provision that provides coverage for accidental injury only if the injury occurred while covered under the plan, a plan provision that counts against a lifetime limit benefits received under prior health coverage, and a plan provision that denies benefits for pregnancy until 12 months after an individual generally becomes eligible for benefits under the plan.[1] The regulations also include a series of examples relating to exclusions for congenital conditions. These examples illustrate that a plan that generally provides benefits for a condition cannot exclude benefits for the condition in instances when it arises congenitally without complying with these limitations on preexisting condition exclusions. However, these limitations would not apply if a plan excludes benefits for all instances of a condition, even if all instances are likely to be congenital. Plans and policies that contain these types of preexisting condition exclusions that are not designated as such should be modified to comply with HIPAA's requirements for preexisting condition exclusions, or the exclusions should be deleted. In addition, because a preexisting condition exclusion discriminates against individuals based on one or more health factors, unless a preexisting condition exclusion complies with HIPAA's limitations on preexisting condition exclusions, the plan provision will also violate the HIPAA nondiscrimination provisions.[2]

General Rules Governing Preexisting Condition Exclusions

In addition to modifying the definition of a preexisting condition exclusion, these final regulations set

---

[1] Several comments (including those of several State insurance commissioner's offices) have asked the Departments to clarify that a preexisting condition exclusion would also include any waiting period or other temporary benefit exclusion (other than a waiting period on all benefits). The Departments are publishing separately in this issue of the Federal Register a Request for Information, which invites further comments on this issue of benefit-specific waiting periods.

[2] See 26 CFR 54.9802-1T(b)(3), 29 CFR 2590.702(b)(3), and 45 CFR 146.121(b)(3), published on January 8, 2001 at 66 FR 1378.

forth HIPAA's limitations on preexisting condition exclusions, as follows:

Six-Month Look-Back Rule

The final regulations retain the 6-month look-back rule set forth in the April 1997 interim rules. In addition, these regulations clarify that a plan or issuer can use a period shorter than 6 months for purposes of applying the 6-month look-back rule. Examples in these final regulations also clarify that if a doctor's recommendation for treatment occurs before the 6-month look-back period, an individual can be subject to a preexisting condition exclusion only if the individual receives the recommended treatment within the 6-month look-back period.

Maximum Length of Preexisting Condition Exclusion

The final regulations retain the rule set forth in the April 1997 interim rules that a preexisting condition exclusion is not permitted to extend for more than 12 months (18 months in the case of a late enrollee) after the enrollment date.

Reducing a Preexisting Condition Exclusion Period by Creditable Coverage

The final regulations retain the rule set forth in the April 1997 interim rules. Accordingly, under these final regulations, the period of any preexisting condition exclusion that would otherwise apply to an individual under a group health plan is reduced by the number of days of creditable coverage[3] the individual has as of the enrollment date (not including any days before a significant break in coverage). Some comments asked how this rule applies to individuals who currently have coverage under another plan (that is, the coverage has not yet ended). An example clarifies that a plan or issuer must count all days of creditable coverage prior to an individual's enrollment date, even if that coverage is still in effect.

Other Standards

The final regulations retain the statement that other legal standards may apply to group health coverage preexisting condition exclusions. In this connection, the Department of Labor's Veterans' Employment and Training Service (VETS) has commented that the Uniformed Services Employment and Reemployment Rights Act (USERRA) provides reemployment rights for persons who leave civilian employment to perform service in the uniformed

---

[3] For purposes of these regulations, the phrase "days of creditable coverage" has the same meaning as the phrase "aggregate of the periods of creditable coverage" as such phrase is used in the statute.

D. HIPAA Final Rules, Portability, continued

services and prohibits employer discrimination against any person on the basis of the person's military service, obligations, intent to join or certain other protected activities. In general, USERRA reemployment rights apply to persons who leave civilian employment to serve a single enlistment period in the active military or to employees who are members of the National Guard or Reserve and are required to perform intermittent military service or training. USERRA provides rights regarding both continuation of group health plan coverage by an employee who is absent to perform service in the uniformed services and reinstatement of group health plan coverage upon reemployment if the coverage was interrupted by the service. In response to this comment, the final regulations include a statement that USERRA can affect the application of a preexisting condition exclusion to certain individuals who are reinstated in a group health plan following active military service. For more information, a VETS directory and additional USERRA information is available at *www.dol.gov/vets.*

Enrollment Definitions

Both the 6-month look-back period and the maximum length of preexisting condition exclusion are measured with respect to an individual's enrollment date. The final regulations generally retain the enrollment definitions that were set forth in the April 1997 interim rules (including definitions of enrollment date, waiting period, and late enrollee). Under HIPAA, the April 1997 interim rules, and these final regulations, the enrollment date is the first day of coverage under the plan or, if there is a waiting period, the first day of the waiting period. These final regulations clarify that if an individual receiving benefits under a group health plan changes benefit package options, or if the plan changes group health insurance issuers, the individual's enrollment date remains the same.

The Departments received several comments reflecting confusion about the relationship between the preexisting condition exclusion rules and the definitions of enrollment date and waiting period. Accordingly, guidance concerning waiting periods previously located in the definitions section has been moved to this section of the regulations and expanded. In addition, the definition of waiting period has been modified with respect to individuals seeking individual market coverage. Specifically, these final rules clarify that if an individual seeks

coverage in the individual market, a waiting period begins on the date the individual submits a substantially complete application for coverage and ends on either the date coverage begins (if the application results in coverage), or the date on which the application is denied by the issuer or the date on which the offer of coverage lapses (if the application does not result in coverage). Under the statute, the April 1997 interim rules, and these final regulations, the effect of considering this period a waiting period is that the period is not counted when determining the length of any break in coverage. This rule modifies the rule contained in the April 1997 interim rules (which provided a waiting period only if the individual actually obtained coverage). The modification addresses situations where some individuals have been denied individual market policies or individuals declined coverage because, for example, the policies had an exorbitant premium.

Additional examples illustrate the interaction between a waiting period and the 6-month look-back period, the application of the 6-month look-back and maximum preexisting condition exclusion period rules to plans with more than one benefit package option at open season, and the interaction between these rules and other eligibility criteria under the plan.

Individuals and Conditions That Cannot Be Subject to a Preexisting Condition Exclusion

Under HIPAA, the April 1997 interim rules, and these final rules, a preexisting condition exclusion cannot be applied to pregnancy. Nor can a preexisting condition exclusion be applied to a newborn, adopted child, or child placed for adoption if the child is covered under a group health plan (or other creditable coverage) within 30 days after birth, adoption, or placement for adoption.

One comment noted that the rule for newborns in the April 1997 interim rules is expressed inconsistently. Some of those expressions are inconsistent with the rule for adopted children. Specifically, the rule for adopted children and one expression of the rule for newborns refers to eligibility being conditioned on being covered under any creditable coverage as of the last day of the 30-day period after birth, adoption, or placement for adoption. However, in other expressions of the rule for newborns, a reference is made to being covered under creditable coverage within 30 days after birth. These final regulations use one term consistently, referring to coverage within 30 days

after birth, adoption, or placement for adoption. This accords with the conference report. H.R. Conf. Rep. No. 736, 104th Cong. 2d Session 184–185 (1996). Consequently, if, for example, a child is covered within 30 days of birth, the child cannot be subject to a preexisting condition exclusion even if the child is no longer covered under the plan on the 30th day after birth (unless the child has a significant break in coverage).

Several comments noted that State laws applicable to health insurance issuers sometimes require that a mother's health coverage must provide benefits for health care expenses incurred for the child for a specified period following birth and cannot be recouped even if the child never enrolls in the plan under which the mother is covered. A new example clarifies that, in this situation, the child has creditable coverage within 30 days after birth and, therefore, no preexisting condition exclusion may be imposed on the child unless the child has a subsequent significant break in coverage.

Finally, HIPAA, the April 1997 interim rules, and these final regulations provide that a group health plan, and a health insurance issuer offering group health insurance coverage, may not impose a preexisting condition exclusion relating to a condition based solely on genetic information. Comments expressed concern that the definition of genetic information in the April 1997 interim rules was too broad and would prevent the application of a preexisting condition exclusion to conditions that would be otherwise permitted independent of any genetic information. Although these regulations have not changed the definition of genetic information, the regulations clarify that if an individual is diagnosed with a condition, even if the condition relates to genetic information, the plan may impose a preexisting condition exclusion with respect to the condition, subject to the other limitations of this section. This rule was located in the definition of medical condition in the April 1997 interim rules. Some comments indicated this rule was difficult to locate. Thus, it has been moved to this section, and an example illustrating the rule has been added.

First Notice of Preexisting Condition Exclusion—General Notice

Under these final regulations, as with the April 1997 interim rules, a group health plan imposing a preexisting condition exclusion, and a health insurance issuer offering group health insurance coverage under a plan imposing a preexisting condition

D. HIPAA Final Rules, Portability, continued

Federal Register / Vol. 69, No. 250 / Thursday, December 30, 2004 / Rules and Regulations   78723

exclusion, must provide a written general notice of preexisting condition exclusion before it can impose a preexisting condition exclusion.

After publication of the April 1997 interim rules, the Departments received questions about the operation of this requirement. The April 1997 interim rules provided that a plan or issuer could not impose a preexisting condition exclusion with respect to a participant or dependent before providing the general notice to the participant. Several comments asked whether plans and issuers could delay providing the general notice until a large claim was filed and then pend the claim until the general notice was sent. Other comments expressed concern that if plans do not notify individuals upon enrollment about the benefit exclusions that apply to their coverage, individuals will not be able to make informed decisions about their health care choices.

The Departments had contemplated under the April 1997 interim rules that individuals should be provided the information required in the general notice before they incurred claims that could be denied under a preexisting condition exclusion. These final regulations clarify the procedural requirements for the general notice of preexisting condition exclusion. Specifically, under the final regulations, the general notice of preexisting condition exclusion must be provided as part of any written application materials distributed by the plan or issuer for enrollment. If the plan or issuer does not distribute such materials, the notice must be provided by the earliest date following a request for enrollment that the plan or issuer, acting in a reasonable and prompt fashion, can provide the notice. Moreover, regarding the content of this general notice, the final regulations clarify precisely what is required when disclosing the existence and terms of the plan's preexisting condition exclusion. In addition, these final regulations require the notice to include the person to contact (including an address or telephone number) for obtaining additional information or assistance regarding the preexisting condition exclusion. An example in these final regulations sets forth sample language that plans and issuers can use when developing the general notice for their coverages.

Issuers that sell different policies to different plans should also be aware that when describing the existence and terms of the maximum preexisting condition exclusion period, the issuer must describe to individuals the actual maximum exclusion period under their policy. Therefore, if an issuer sells two policies, one with a 6-month and one with a 12-month maximum preexisting condition exclusion, the issuer could not send one notice to individuals under both policies indicating that the maximum preexisting condition exclusion is 12 months. Instead, the issuer is required to send one notice to participants under the policy with the 6-month preexisting condition exclusion (indicating that the maximum exclusion period is 6 months) and a different notice to participants under the policy with the 12-month preexisting condition exclusion (indicating that the maximum exclusion period is 12 months).

Determination of Creditable Coverage

These final regulations require a plan or issuer that imposes a preexisting condition exclusion to make a determination of creditable coverage within a reasonable time after receiving information regarding prior health coverage. This rule was included in the section of the April 1997 interim rules addressing certification and disclosure of previous coverage, and it has been moved to this section on preexisting condition exclusions unchanged. These final regulations clarify that a plan or issuer may not impose any limit on the amount of time that an individual has to present a certificate or other evidence of creditable coverage.[4]

Second Notice of Preexisting Condition Exclusion—Individual Notice

These final regulations retain the requirement to provide an individual a written notice of the length of preexisting condition exclusion that remains after offsetting for prior creditable coverage. These final regulations clarify that this individual notice is not required to identify any medical conditions specific to the individual that could be subject to the exclusion. Also, a plan or issuer is not required to provide this notice if the plan or issuer does not impose any preexisting condition exclusion on the individual or if the plan's preexisting condition exclusion is completely offset by the individual's prior creditable coverage. These final regulations add a new example that illustrates how the notice works and includes sample language that may be helpful to plans and issuers in developing this type of notice with respect to their coverage.

[4] Of course, after a claim has been denied under a preexisting condition exclusion, other laws, such as section 503 of ERISA, may set forth timing rules for an individual to appeal a denied claim.

Reconsideration

Consistent with the April 1997 interim rules, these final regulations do not prevent a plan or issuer from modifying an initial determination of creditable coverage if it determines that the individual did not have the claimed creditable coverage and if certain procedural requirements are met. The final regulations have been slightly reorganized and modified to make clearer that a plan or issuer is permitted to modify its initial determination if a notice of the new determination (that meets the requirements of the second, individual notice of preexisting condition exclusion, described above) is provided and, until the notice of the new determination is provided, the plan or issuer acts in a manner consistent with the initial determination for purposes of approving access to medical services (such as pre-surgery authorization).

3. Rules Relating to Creditable Coverage—26 CFR 54.9801–4, 29 CFR 2590.701–4, 45 CFR 146.113

This section of the final regulations describes the varieties of health coverage that constitute creditable coverage and sets forth rules for how to count creditable coverage for purposes of the rule requiring plans and issuers to offset the maximum length of a preexisting condition exclusion by prior creditable coverage.

Creditable Coverage

The rules in the final regulations describing the varieties of health coverage that constitute creditable coverage generally follow the April 1997 interim rules, with two modifications. The April 1997 interim rules contain ten categories of creditable coverage. After publication of the April 1997 interim rules, Congress created the State Children's Health Insurance Program (S–CHIP), which allows states to provide health coverage to eligible children through Medicaid expansion or private market mechanisms. This coverage meets the definition of creditable coverage as either Medicaid coverage, group health plan coverage, or health insurance coverage. In addition, Congress specifically provides[5] that S–CHIP coverage is creditable coverage under HIPAA. Therefore, these final regulations have added coverage under S–CHIP as an eleventh category of creditable coverage.

The second modification is to the definition of public health plan. This

[5] Section 2109 of the Social Security Act, enacted by section 4901 of the Balanced Budget Act of 1997, Pub. L. 105–33, 111 Stat. 567.

D. HIPAA Final Rules, Portability, continued

definition has been changed in two ways. The first change relates to the type of health coverage provided by a public health plan. The statute does not define the term. The April 1997 interim rules limit the definition of public health plans to certain plans provided through health *insurance* coverage. Some comments suggested it was unnecessary to restrict the definition to insured coverage and argued that the term public health plan should be expanded. These final regulations delete the word "insurance" from that requirement so that any health coverage provided by a governmental entity, regardless of whether it has the risk-shifting or risk-distributing effects of insurance, is a public health plan.

The second change to the definition of public health plan relates to the type of governmental entity that can establish or maintain a public health plan. Under the April 1997 interim rules, only health coverage provided under a plan established or maintained by a State, a county, or another political subdivision of a State can be a public health plan. This definition does not include a plan established or maintained by a foreign government or the U.S. government. The preamble to the April 1997 interim rules specifically solicited comments on whether public health systems of foreign countries should be considered public health plans.

Many comments addressed this issue, arguing both for and against including public health systems of foreign governments in the definition of public health plan. The comments in favor of inclusion argued that generally the health coverage provided through public health systems in foreign countries is more comprehensive than that received in this country. Some comments argued that the exclusion of foreign public health systems from the definition of public health plan arbitrarily penalizes individuals who maintain continuous health coverage through a foreign public health system. The comments against inclusion focused on the difficulty for a plan or issuer to verify whether someone had the coverage they claimed under a foreign public health system.

Under these final regulations, the definition of a public health plan includes health coverage provided under a plan established or maintained by a foreign country or a political subdivision. While this result can inconvenience plans and issuers, verifying this type of coverage may be no more inconvenient than verifying certain other types of coverage, such as group health coverage provided through foreign employers. In addition, this

result is much less inequitable than denying an individual coverage for a preexisting condition in a case in which the individual can provide reliable evidence of having coverage under the public health system of a foreign government. Under the rules for establishing creditable coverage in the absence of a certificate of creditable coverage, an individual is required to present at a minimum some corroborating evidence of the claimed creditable coverage and is required to cooperate with a plan's or issuer's efforts to verify coverage. Thus, in the case of an individual claiming coverage under the public health system of a foreign country, a plan or issuer could require some evidence of residency in the foreign country (or evidence that some other eligibility standard had been met) and the individual would have to cooperate with the plan's or issuer's efforts to verify that the individual had coverage under that country's health system.

Under the revised definition in these final regulations, health coverage provided under a plan established or maintained by the U.S. Government is also a public health plan.

Counting Creditable Coverage

The rules in the final regulations for how to count creditable coverage are adopted with stylistic and conforming changes from the April 1997 interim rules. In addition, a technical modification was added, as required by a statutory change made by the Trade Act of 2002 ("the Trade Act", Public Law 107–210, enacted on August 6, 2002). Under the Trade Act, workers whose employment is adversely affected by international trade may become entitled to receive trade adjustment assistance (TAA) and a 65% health coverage tax credit (HCTC). The Trade Act also amended COBRA continuation coverage provisions in ERISA, the Public Health Service Act, and the Internal Revenue Code, to provide a second opportunity to elect COBRA for individuals who are eventually determined to qualify for TAA, but who did not elect COBRA after their original loss of health coverage. Because this could result in a "significant break in coverage" for purposes of HIPAA, the Trade Act specifies that the period beginning with the loss of coverage, and ending on the first day of the second election period, for individuals who elect COBRA during this second election period, should be disregarded for purposes of the HIPAA pre-existing condition provisions. Accordingly, as required by the Trade Act, under these final rules the days between the date an

individual lost group health plan coverage and the first day of the second COBRA election period are not taken into account in determining whether a significant break in coverage has occurred. For more information on TAA, contact the Department of Labor's Employment and Training Administration at 877–US2–JOBS or at *www.doleta.gov/tradeact*. For more information on the HCTC, contact the IRS toll-free at 866–628–4282.

The existing examples relating to the tolling of the period for determining a significant break in coverage in the case of individuals seeking coverage in the individual market have also been modified to conform to the change in the definition of waiting period, which under these final regulations includes the period beginning when an individual submits a substantially complete application for coverage in the individual market and ends when the application is denied or when the offer of coverage lapses. In addition, here, as throughout these final regulations, references in the April 1997 interim rules to "plan or policy" have been revised so that the reference includes health insurance coverage not offered through a policy of insurance, such as health insurance coverage offered through a contract of a health maintenance organization.

Published elsewhere in this issue of the **Federal Register** is a proposed rule that provides that the period that determines whether a significant break in coverage has occurred (generally 63 days) is tolled in cases in which a certificate of creditable coverage is not provided on or before the day coverage ceases. In those cases, the significant-break-in-coverage period would be tolled until a certificate is provided or, if earlier, until 44 days after the coverage ceases.

These final regulations retain the methods in the April 1997 interim rules for counting creditable coverage, that is, the standard method and the alternative method. Comments requested that the alternative method be expanded so that a plan or issuer could elect to have it apply to categories in addition to the five categories prescribed in the April 1997 interim rules (mental health; substance abuse treatment; prescription drugs; dental care; and vision care). The types of categories described in the comments were significant differences in deductibles, cost-sharing, or out-of-pocket maximums between plans. One comment suggested that any comparison between plans on the basis of difference in deductibles or cost sharing was unworkable.

D. HIPAA Final Rules, Portability, continued

Federal Register / Vol. 69, No. 250 / Thursday, December 30, 2004 / Rules and Regulations   78725

It is the view of the Departments that a comparison between plans, and allowing one plan not to count creditable coverage (in whole or in part) under another plan, based solely on differences in deductibles or in some other cost-sharing mechanism or in all cost-sharing mechanisms, is an insufficient basis for determining the comparative value of benefits under the plans. A plan with a low deductible or low co-payments might also have an annual or per-incident limit on benefits so low as to make the plan with the higher deductible or higher cost sharing actually more valuable. Similarly, a plan with a higher deductible or coinsurance might also have a higher table of usual, customary, and reasonable costs, might be much more liberal in covering treatments considered experimental, and might provide a much broader base of benefits than the plan with the lower deductible or coinsurance. Because of the numerous ways that plans or issuers can limit the amount of benefits available under the plan, it is very complicated to compare the value of one plan or coverage with another. Singling out one or several of these features is insufficient for making a true comparison of the value of the benefits.

4 Evidence of Creditable Coverage—26 CFR 54.9801–5, 29 CFR 2590.701–5, 45 CFR 146.115

This section of the final regulations sets forth guidance regarding the certification requirements and other requirements for disclosure of information relating to prior creditable coverage. The provision of a certificate and certain other disclosures of information provided for in the statute, the April 1997 interim rules, and these final regulations are intended to enable an individual to establish prior creditable coverage for purposes of reducing or eliminating any preexisting condition exclusion imposed on the individual by any subsequent group health plan coverage. The Departments received generally favorable comments on the April 1997 interim rules from interested parties who submitted comments with regard to the certification requirements. For example, several comments praised the Departments' promulgation of a model certificate in the April 1997 interim

rules as a vehicle that helped reduce compliance burdens associated with the statutory requirements under HIPAA.

Form of Certificate

These final regulations retain the requirement that the certificate must generally be provided in writing. The April 1997 interim rules clarified that for this purpose a writing included any form approved by the Secretaries as a writing. These final regulations modify that standard to include any other medium approved by the Secretary. As with the April 1997 interim rules, these final regulations provide that where an individual requests that the certificate be sent to another plan or issuer instead of the individual, and the other plan or issuer agrees, the certification information may be provided by other means, such as by telephone.

Information in Certificate

The information required to be provided in a certificate under these final regulations is the same as required under the April 1997 interim rules with one addition. In response to recommendations made by the U.S. General Accounting Office (GAO)[6] and several comments, the Departments have modified the April 1997 interim rules to require that an educational statement be provided as part of a certificate of creditable coverage in order to inform consumers of their HIPAA rights. Some comments stated that such educational language was not necessary, but indicated that if the Departments adopted such an approach

---

[6] In the report entitled "PRIVATE HEALTH INSURANCE: Progress and Challenges in Implementing 1996 Federal Standards" (GAO/HEHS–99–100, May 12, 1999) the GAO recommended that the Departments revise the model certificate of creditable health plan coverage to more explicitly inform consumers of their new rights under HIPAA. At a minimum, the GAO recommended that the certificate of creditable coverage should inform consumers about appropriate contacts for additional information about HIPAA and highlight key provisions and restrictions, including (1) the limits on preexisting condition exclusion periods and the guaranteed renewability of all health coverage; (2) the reduction or elimination of preexisting condition exclusion periods for employees changing jobs; (3) the prohibition against excluding an individual from an employer health plan on the basis of health status; and (4) the guarantee of access to insurance products for certain individuals losing group health coverage and the restrictions placed on that guarantee.

they should provide language for compliance purposes. In response to the GAO recommendation, the Departments have amended the requirements for the certificate of creditable coverage in the final regulations to include the provision of an educational statement regarding certain HIPAA protections. Model educational language is provided in the model certificate (set forth below). This eliminates the burden on plans and issuers of developing language to satisfy this requirement.

Model Certificate

The first model certificate below has been authorized by the Secretary of each of the Departments. The model educational statement is set forth under the heading "Statement of HIPAA Portability Rights." Use of the model certificate by group health plans and group health insurance issuers will satisfy the requirements of paragraph (a)(3)(ii) of the regulations. The second model certificate below has been authorized by the Secretary of Health and Human Services. State Medicaid programs may use this version. Once these final regulations are applicable, use of the previously-published model certificate (published in the preamble to the April 1997 interim rules) will no longer satisfy paragraph (a)(3)(ii) of the regulations.

In addition to these model certificates, the Departments are publishing a different model certificate for group health plans and group health insurance issuers in the preamble to the proposed rules published elsewhere in this issue of the **Federal Register**. That model certificate includes in its educational statement an additional paragraph regarding coordination with rules under the Family and Medical Leave Act (FMLA). The Secretaries of the Departments authorize plans and issuers to use either model certificate in fulfillment of their obligations under paragraph (a)(3)(ii) of this section in the final regulations. State Medicaid programs may use either the model certificate below that is designated for Medicaid programs, or the model certificate in the proposed rules that is so designated and includes an additional paragraph on FMLA.

BILLING CODE 4830–01–P

D. HIPAA Final Rules, Portability, continued

78726   Federal Register / Vol. 69, No. 250 / Thursday, December 30, 2004 / Rules and Regulations

CERTIFICATE OF GROUP HEALTH PLAN COVERAGE

1. Date of this certificate: _____

2. Name of group health plan: _____
_____

3. Name of participant: _____

4. Identification number of participant: _____

5. Name of individuals to whom this certificate applies: _____
_____

6. Name, address, and telephone number of plan administrator or issuer responsible for providing this certificate: _____
_____

7. For further information, call: _____

8. If the individual(s) identified in line 5 has (have) at least 18 months of creditable coverage (disregarding periods of coverage before a 63-day break), check here and skip lines 9 and 10: ____

9. Date waiting period or affiliation period (if any) began:
_____

10. Date coverage began: _____

11. Date coverage ended (or if coverage has not ended, enter "continuing"): _____

[Note: separate certificates will be furnished if information is not identical for the participant and each beneficiary.]

Statement of HIPAA Portability Rights

IMPORTANT — KEEP THIS CERTIFICATE. This certificate is evidence of your coverage under this plan. Under a federal law known as HIPAA, you may need evidence of your coverage to reduce a preexisting condition exclusion period under another plan, to help you get special enrollment in another plan, or to get certain types of individual health coverage even if you have health problems.

Preexisting condition exclusions. Some group health plans restrict coverage for medical conditions present before an individual's enrollment. These restrictions are known as "preexisting condition exclusions." A preexisting condition exclusion can apply only to conditions for which medical advice, diagnosis, care, or treatment was recommended or received within the 6 months before your "enrollment date." Your enrollment date is your first day of coverage under the plan, or, if there is a waiting period, the first day of your waiting period (typically, your first day of work). In addition, a preexisting condition exclusion cannot last for more than 12 months after your enrollment date (18 months if you are a late enrollee). Finally, a preexisting condition exclusion cannot apply to pregnancy and cannot apply to a child who is enrolled in health coverage within 30 days after birth, adoption, or placement for adoption.

If a plan imposes a preexisting condition exclusion, the length of the exclusion must be reduced by the amount of your prior creditable coverage. Most health coverage is creditable coverage, including group health plan coverage, COBRA continuation coverage, coverage under an individual health policy, Medicare, Medicaid, State Children's Health Insurance Program (SCHIP), and coverage through high-risk pools and the Peace Corps. Not all forms of creditable coverage are required to provide certificates like this one. If you do not receive a certificate for past coverage, talk to your new plan administrator.

You can add up any creditable coverage you have, including the coverage shown on this certificate. However, if at any time you went for 63 days or more without any coverage (called a break in coverage) a plan may not have to count the coverage you had before the break.

D. HIPAA Final Rules, Portability, continued

Federal Register / Vol. 69, No. 250 / Thursday, December 30, 2004 / Rules and Regulations   78727

→ Therefore, once your coverage ends, you should try to obtain alternative coverage as soon as possible to avoid a 63-day break. You may use this certificate as evidence of your creditable coverage to reduce the length of any preexisting condition exclusion if you enroll in another plan.

Right to get special enrollment in another plan. Under HIPAA, if you lose your group health plan coverage, you may be able to get into another group health plan for which you are eligible (such as a spouse's plan), even if the plan generally does not accept late enrollees, if you request enrollment within 30 days. (Additional special enrollment rights are triggered by marriage, birth, adoption, and placement for adoption.)

→ Therefore, once your coverage ends, if you are eligible for coverage in another plan (such as a spouse's plan), you should request special enrollment as soon as possible.

Prohibition against discrimination based on a health factor. Under HIPAA, a group health plan may not keep you (or your dependents) out of the plan based on anything related to your health. Also, a group health plan may not charge you (or your dependents) more for coverage, based on health, than the amount charged a similarly situated individual.

Right to individual health coverage. Under HIPAA, if you are an "eligible individual," you have a right to buy certain individual health policies (or in some states, to buy coverage through a high-risk pool) without a preexisting condition exclusion. To be an eligible individual, you must meet the following requirements:

- You have had coverage for at least 18 months without a break in coverage of 63 days or more;
- Your most recent coverage was under a group health plan (which can be shown by this certificate);
- Your group coverage was not terminated because of fraud or nonpayment of premiums;
- You are not eligible for COBRA continuation coverage or you have exhausted your COBRA benefits (or continuation coverage under a similar state provision); and
- You are not eligible for another group health plan, Medicare, or Medicaid, and do not have any other health insurance coverage.

The right to buy individual coverage is the same whether you are laid off, fired, or quit your job.

→ Therefore, if you are interested in obtaining individual coverage and you meet the other criteria to be an eligible individual, you should apply for this coverage as soon as possible to avoid losing your eligible individual status due to a 63-day break.

State flexibility. This certificate describes minimum HIPAA protections under federal law. States may require insurers and HMOs to provide additional protections to individuals in that state.

For more information. If you have questions about your HIPAA rights, you may contact your state insurance department or the U.S. Department of Labor, Employee Benefits Security Administration (EBSA) toll-free at 1-866-444-3272 (for free HIPAA publications ask for publications concerning changes in health care laws). You may also contact the CMS publication hotline at 1-800-633-4227 (ask for "Protecting Your Health Insurance Coverage"). These publications and other useful information are also available on the Internet at: http://www.dol.gov/ebsa, the DOL's interactive web pages - Health Elaws, or http://www.cms.hhs.gov/hipaa1.

D. HIPAA Final Rules, Portability, continued

78728   Federal Register / Vol. 69, No. 250 / Thursday, December 30, 2004 / Rules and Regulations

CERTIFICATE OF MEDICAID COVERAGE

1. Date of this certificate: _____

2. Name of state Medicaid program: _____

3. Name of recipient: _____

4. Identification number of recipient: _____

5. Name of individuals to whom this certificate applies: _____

6. Name, address, and telephone number of state Medicaid agency responsible for providing this certificate: _____

7. For further information call: _____

8. If the individual(s) identified in line 5 has (have) at least 18 months of creditable coverage (disregarding periods of coverage before a 63-day break), check here and skip line 9. _____

9. Date coverage began: _____

10. Date coverage ended (or if coverage has not ended, enter "continuing"): _____

[Note: separate certificates will be furnished if information is not identical for the recipient and each dependent.]

Statement of HIPAA Portability Rights

IMPORTANT — KEEP THIS CERTIFICATE. This certificate is evidence of your coverage under this state Medicaid program. Under a federal law known as HIPAA, you may need evidence of your coverage to reduce a preexisting condition exclusion period under a group health plan, to help you get special enrollment in a group health plan, or to get certain types of individual health coverage even if you have health problems.

Preexisting condition exclusions. Some group health plans restrict coverage for medical conditions present before an individual's enrollment. These restrictions are known as "preexisting condition exclusions." A preexisting condition exclusion can apply only to conditions for which medical advice, diagnosis, care, or treatment was recommended or received within the 6 months before your "enrollment date." Your enrollment date is your first day of coverage under the plan, or, if there is a waiting period, the first day of your waiting period (typically, your first day of work). In addition, a preexisting condition exclusion cannot last for more than 12 months after your enrollment date (18 months if you are a late enrollee). Finally, a preexisting condition exclusion cannot apply to pregnancy and cannot apply to a child who is enrolled in health coverage within 30 days after birth, adoption, or placement for adoption.

If a plan imposes a preexisting condition exclusion, the length of the exclusion must be reduced by the amount of your prior creditable coverage. Most health coverage is creditable coverage, including group health plan coverage, COBRA continuation coverage, coverage under an individual health policy, Medicare, Medicaid, State Children's Health Insurance Program (SCHIP), and coverage through high-risk pools and the Peace Corps. Not all forms of creditable coverage are required to provide certificates like this one. If you do not receive a certificate for past coverage, talk to your new plan administrator.

You can add up any creditable coverage you have, including the coverage shown on this certificate. However, if at any time you went for 63 days or more without any coverage (called a break in coverage) a plan may not have to count the coverage you had before the break.

D. HIPAA Final Rules, Portability, continued

➜ Therefore, once your coverage ends, you should try to obtain alternative coverage as soon as possible to avoid a 63-day break. You may use this certificate as evidence of your creditable coverage to reduce the length of any preexisting condition exclusion if you enroll in a group health plan.

Right to get special enrollment in another plan. Under HIPAA, if you lose your group health plan coverage, you may be able to get into another group health plan for which you are eligible (such as a spouse's plan), even if the plan generally does not accept late enrollees, if you request enrollment within 30 days. (Additional special enrollment rights are triggered by marriage, birth, adoption, and placement for adoption.)

➜ Therefore, once your coverage in a group health plan ends, if you are eligible for coverage in another plan (such as a spouse's plan), you should request special enrollment as soon as possible.

Prohibition against discrimination based on a health factor. Under HIPAA, a group health plan may not keep you (or your dependents) out of the plan based on anything related to your health. Also, a group health plan may not charge you (or your dependents) more for coverage, based on health, than the amount charged a similarly situated individual.

Right to individual health coverage. Under HIPAA, if you are an "eligible individual," you have a right to buy certain individual health policies (or in some states, to buy coverage through a high-risk pool) without a preexisting condition exclusion. To be an eligible individual, you must meet the following requirements:

- You have had coverage for at least 18 months without a break in coverage of 63 days or more;
- Your most recent coverage was under a group health plan;
- Your group coverage was not terminated because of fraud or nonpayment of premiums;
- You are not eligible for COBRA continuation coverage or you have exhausted your COBRA benefits (or continuation coverage under a similar state provision); and
- You are not eligible for another group health plan, Medicare, or Medicaid, and do not have any other health insurance coverage.

The right to buy individual coverage is the same whether you are laid off, fired, or quit your job.

➜ Therefore, if you are interested in obtaining individual coverage and you meet the other criteria to be an eligible individual, you should apply for this coverage as soon as possible to avoid losing your eligible individual status due to a 63-day break.

State flexibility. This certificate describes minimum HIPAA protections under federal law. States may require insurers and HMOs to provide additional protections to individuals in that state.

For more information. If you have questions about your HIPAA rights, you may contact your state insurance department or the U.S. Department of Labor, Employee Benefits Security Administration (EBSA) toll-free at 1-866-444-3272 (for free HIPAA publications ask for publications concerning changes in health care laws). You may also contact the CMS publication hotline at 1-800-633-4227 (ask for "Protecting Your Health Insurance Coverage"). These publications and other useful information are also available on the Internet at: http://www.dol.gov/ebsa or http://www.cms.hhs.gov/hipaa1.

BILLING CODE 4830-01-C

D. HIPAA Final Rules, Portability, continued

78730 Federal Register / Vol. 69, No. 250 / Thursday, December 30, 2004 / Rules and Regulations

Procedure for Requesting Certificates

The April 1997 interim rules require plans and health insurance issuers to establish a procedure for individuals to request and receive certificates of creditable coverage. The Departments have received requests to clarify whether such procedures need to be in writing. These final regulations clarify that the procedures need to be in writing, helping to ensure that individuals are aware of their right to request a certificate and how to make the request.

In addition, the Departments have become aware that some plans and issuers believe they are not required to provide a certificate to individuals who request one while their coverage is still in effect. This requirement exists under the April 1997 interim rules. However, due to these questions being raised, the final regulations more explicitly state this requirement.

Dependent Coverage Information

Under HIPAA, plans and health insurance issuers are required to issue certificates of creditable coverage (automatically, and upon request) to dependents who are or were covered under a group health plan. In response to comments, and in order to allow entities responsible for issuing certificates adequate time to modify their data collection systems, the Departments established a transitional rule in the April 1997 interim rules for providing dependent coverage information. Under this transitional rule, a group health plan or health insurance issuer that, after having made reasonable efforts, could not provide a certificate of creditable coverage for a dependent could satisfy the requirements for providing a certificate to the dependent by providing the name of the participant covered by the group health plan or health insurance issuer and specifying that the type of coverage described in the certificate was for dependent coverage (for example, family coverage or employee-plus-spouse coverage). This transitional rule was effective through June 30, 1998.

Under these final regulations, the transitional rule is no longer in effect and dependents are entitled to receive individualized certificates of creditable coverage under the same circumstances as other individuals. As with the April 1997 interim rules, these final regulations permit a single certificate of creditable coverage to be provided with respect to both a participant and the participant's dependents if the information is identical for each individual. In addition, these final regulations retain the provisions of the April 1997 interim rules permitting the combining of information for families. As a result, in situations where coverage information is not identical for a participant and the participant's dependents, these final regulations allow certificates for all individuals to be provided on one form if the form provides all the required information for each individual and separately states the information that is not identical.

Special Rules for Certain Entities

Section 2791(a)(3) of the PHS Act provides that certain entities not otherwise subject to HIPAA's requirements are to comply with the statutory certification of coverage requirements that apply to group health plans, with respect to providing certificates of creditable coverage for Medicare, Medicaid, TRICARE, and medical care programs provided through the Indian Health Service or a tribal organization. These rules further establish that such entities are required to comply with the general statutory requirement to provide certificates. However, the Departments recognize that these programs operate in a different manner than do private employment-based group health plans, nonfederal governmental group health plans, and health insurance issuers. In addition, the populations served by these programs are unique. Therefore, it may be appropriate to allow these programs to implement the certification process in a manner that addresses these unique characteristics and better serves the individuals covered by these programs, including requiring different information elements (for example, see the above model certificate of creditable coverage for use by State Medicaid programs). HHS will coordinate with the appropriate entities responsible for issuing these certificates and will issue separate guidance to these entities on how they must comply with the certification requirements.

5. Special Enrollment Periods—26 CFR 54.9801–6, 29 CFR 2590.701–6, 45 CFR 146.117

Under HIPAA, the April 1997 interim rules, and these final regulations, a group health plan and a health insurance issuer offering group health insurance coverage are required to provide for special enrollment periods during which certain individuals are allowed to enroll (without having to wait until a late enrollment opportunity and regardless of whether the plan offers late enrollment). A special enrollment right can arise if a person with other health coverage loses eligibility for that coverage or employer contributions toward the other coverage cease, or if a person becomes a dependent through marriage, birth, adoption, or placement for adoption.

In order to qualify for special enrollment, an individual must be otherwise eligible for coverage under the plan. Being otherwise eligible for coverage means having met the plan's substantive eligibility requirements (such as satisfying any waiting period, being in an eligible job classification, or working full time), regardless of whether the individual previously satisfied the plan's procedural requirements for becoming enrolled (such as completing written application materials or providing them to the plan within a specified time frame) during any enrollment opportunity prior to special enrollment.

The special enrollment rules have been reorganized and clarified. As discussed below, the special enrollment rules have also been modified in response to comments.

Loss of Eligibility for Other Coverage

A special enrollment right resulting from loss of eligibility for other coverage is available to employees and their dependents who meet certain requirements. As under the April 1997 interim rules, the employee or dependent must otherwise be eligible for coverage under the terms of the plan. When coverage was previously declined, the employee or dependent must have been covered under another group health plan or must have had other health insurance coverage. The plan can require that, when coverage in the plan was previously declined, the employee must have declared in writing that the reason was other coverage, in which case the plan must at that time have provided notice of this requirement and the consequences of the employee's failure to provide the statement.

These regulations include an example that clarifies that the initial opportunity for enrollment (generally provided when employment begins) is not the only time when an individual with other health coverage may decline coverage for purposes of satisfying the prerequisites to special enrollment upon loss of other coverage. (Other examples discussed below also illustrate this principle.) An individual who initially did not enroll for coverage without having other health coverage might later be eligible for special enrollment. This could occur if, after subsequently enrolling in other coverage, the individual had an opportunity for late

D. HIPAA Final Rules, Portability, continued

Federal Register / Vol. 69, No. 250 / Thursday, December 30, 2004 / Rules and Regulations   78731

enrollment or special enrollment under the plan, but again chose not to enroll.

These final regulations, like the April 1997 interim rules, contain a list of situations when an individual loses eligibility for other coverage. While the list is not exhaustive, it has nonetheless been expanded in these final regulations to address situations that have prompted frequent questions. Thus, these regulations clarify that a loss of eligibility for coverage occurs, in the case of individual coverage provided through an HMO, when an individual no longer resides, lives, or works in the service area of the HMO (whether or not within the choice of the individual) and the HMO does not provide coverage for that reason. In the case of group coverage provided through an HMO, the same rule applies, provided that there is no other coverage under the plan available to the individual. For purposes of this rule, the HMO service area is typically defined by State law. In addition, the regulations clarify that a loss of eligibility for coverage occurs due to the cessation of dependent status. For example, a child who "ages out" of dependent coverage—who attains an age in excess of the maximum age for coverage of a dependent child—incurs a loss of eligibility for coverage for purposes of special enrollment.

The regulations also clarify that a loss of eligibility for coverage occurs when a plan no longer offers any benefits to a class of similarly situated individuals. Thus, if a plan terminated health coverage for all part-time workers, the part-time workers incur a loss of eligibility for coverage, even if the plan continues to provide coverage to other employees. An example in the final regulations also illustrates how the loss of eligibility rule applies to a plan that terminates a benefit package option. Similarly, if an issuer providing one of the options ceases to operate in the group market, thus terminating one of the options offered by the plan, the individuals formerly in the terminated option would incur a loss of eligibility for coverage for purposes of special enrollment, unless the plan otherwise provided a current right to enroll in alternative health coverage. In addition, the final regulations clarify that an employee who is already enrolled in a benefit package may enroll in another benefit package under the plan if a dependent of that employee has a special enrollment right in the plan because the dependent lost eligibility for other coverage.

These regulations clarify that a loss of eligibility for coverage is still considered to exist even if there are subsequent coverage opportunities. As under the April 1997 interim rules, an individual does not have to elect COBRA continuation coverage or exercise similar continuation rights in order to preserve the right to special enrollment. Moreover, a special enrollment right exists even if an individual who lost coverage elects COBRA continuation coverage. In that case, if an individual declines special enrollment, and instead elects and exhausts COBRA continuation coverage, the individual has a second special enrollment right upon exhausting the COBRA continuation coverage.

In addition, as under the statute and the April 1997 interim rules, even if there is no loss of eligibility for coverage, a special enrollment right can result when employer contributions towards other coverage terminate. This is the case even if an individual continues the other coverage by paying the amount previously paid by the employer.

Lifetime Benefit Limits

Comments asked how the special enrollment rules apply when an individual reaches a lifetime limit on all benefits under a plan. The regulations clarify that where an individual has a claim denied due to the operation of a lifetime limit on all benefits, there is a loss of eligibility for coverage for special enrollment purposes. In this regard, an individual has a special enrollment right when a claim that would exceed a lifetime limit on all benefits is incurred, and the right continues at least until 30 days after the earliest date that a claim is denied due to the operation of the lifetime limit. Accordingly, because individuals who are keeping track of claims in relation to a lifetime limit can request enrollment immediately (after the claim is incurred, but before it is denied by the plan), the period for requesting special enrollment can be longer than 30 days. (Timeframes for providing certificates of creditable coverage and determining when COBRA is exhausted for individuals who have reached a lifetime limit on all benefits are set forth elsewhere in these final regulations, under the certificate and the definition provisions, respectively.)

Tolling of the Special Enrollment Period

Proposed rules, published elsewhere in this issue of the Federal Register, would toll the beginning of the 30-day period for requesting special enrollment until a certificate of creditable coverage is provided to the person losing coverage, up to a maximum of 44 days of tolling. This tolling rule would be in the paragraph reserved for special enrollment procedures in these final regulations.

Dependent Special Enrollment

Comments asked for clarification of the interaction of coverage for children under a State Children's Health Insurance Program (S–CHIP) and special enrollment. In particular, it was asked whether a child would have a right to special enrollment in a group health plan if the child becomes eligible for benefits under S–CHIP and the child is otherwise eligible for dependent coverage under the plan. This situation would arise if a State creates a children's health program that provides payments to a parent to cover the increased cost of enrolling a dependent child in the parent's employer's group health. However, without a special enrollment right, the parent might not be able to take advantage of the program until the next late enrollment opportunity, if the plan allows late enrollment at all. The statutory language of HIPAA, however, only provides special enrollment if there is loss of eligibility for other coverage, loss of employer contributions, or addition of a new dependent to the employee's family. Becoming eligible under a health program such as S–CHIP does not fall under any of these categories.[7]

Under these final regulations, as under the April 1997 interim rules, the special enrollment of dependents is subject to the plan's general eligibility requirements. For example, a plan may require an employee to remain enrolled, or to special enroll, in order to special enroll the employee's dependent. However, a plan's general eligibility requirements cannot prevent the application of a special enrollment right. For example, a plan may not deny special enrollment to an otherwise eligible dependent merely because the individual became a dependent of the participant after the participant's first day of coverage under the plan.

Modification of Special Enrollment Procedures

Under proposed rules, published elsewhere in this issue of the Federal Register, more detailed procedures are described for how plans and issuers would have to enroll individuals requesting special enrollment.

---

[7] Nonetheless, in addition to the dependent special enrollment rights under HIPAA, for plans subject to ERISA, section 609 of ERISA imposes additional requirements on group health plans to provide benefits to certain children, including in cases where a qualified medical child support order applies, as well as in cases of adoption. HIPAA does not prevent States from imposing similar requirements on nonfederal governmental plans.

D. HIPAA Final Rules, Portability, continued

78732   Federal Register / Vol. 69, No. 250 / Thursday, December 30, 2004 / Rules and Regulations

When Coverage Begins Under Special Enrollment

Where the special enrollment right results from marriage or a loss of eligibility, coverage generally begins no later than the first day of the first calendar month after the date the plan or issuer receives the request for special enrollment. Where the special enrollment right results from a birth, coverage must begin on the date of birth. In the case of adoption or placement for adoption, coverage must begin no later than the date of such adoption or placement for adoption.

Clarification of Special Enrollment During a Late Enrollment Opportunity

The April 1997 interim rules provided a definition of the term *special enrollment date.* The purpose of the definition and accompanying examples was to illustrate that if an individual who qualified for special enrollment enrolled during a coinciding late enrollment opportunity, the individual could not be treated as a late enrollee. The final regulations eliminate the term *special enrollment date* and clarify this issue by providing that if an individual requests enrollment while the individual is entitled to special enrollment, the individual is a special enrollee, even if the request coincides with a late enrollment opportunity under the plan. Thus, the individual cannot be treated as a late enrollee.

Notice of Special Enrollment

The preamble to the April 1997 interim rules stated that a plan must provide a description of the special enrollment rights to anyone who declines coverage. However, the text of the April 1997 interim rules required the notice to be provided to all eligible employees. Even employees who enroll may need to avail themselves of their special enrollment rights in the future, either for a spouse or other dependent, or if they lose the present coverage. Thus, these regulations reiterate the requirement in the April 1997 interim rules that a plan must provide all employees (those who enroll as well as those who decline enrollment) with a notice of special enrollment at or before the time the employee is initially offered the opportunity to enroll in the plan. The regulation also provides model language that plans can use to satisfy this requirement.

Treatment of Special Enrollees

HIPAA provides that a late enrollee does not include an individual who enrolls when first eligible or who enrolls during a special enrollment period. These regulations further clarify that individuals who enroll during a special enrollment period must generally be treated the same as individuals who enroll when first eligible. That is, relative to similarly situated individuals who enroll when first eligible, special enrollees must be offered all the same benefit packages, cannot be required to pay more for coverage, and cannot be subject to a longer preexisting condition exclusion.

6. HMO Affiliation Period as an Alternative to a Preexisting Condition Exclusion—29 CFR 2590.701-7, 45 CFR 146.119

Under HIPAA, the April 1997 interim rules, and these final regulations, a group health plan that offers health insurance coverage through an HMO, or an HMO that offers health insurance coverage in connection with a group health plan, may impose an affiliation period under certain conditions. An affiliation period is a period of time that must expire before health insurance coverage provided by an HMO becomes effective and during which time the HMO is not required to provide benefits. Under these final regulations an affiliation period can be imposed if each of the following requirements is satisfied:

(1) No preexisting condition exclusion is imposed with respect to any coverage offered by the HMO in connection with the particular group health plan.

(2) No premium is charged to a participant or beneficiary for the affiliation period.

(3) The affiliation period for the HMO coverage is imposed consistent with the requirements of the HIPAA nondiscrimination provisions.

(4) The affiliation period does not exceed 2 months (or 3 months for a late enrollee).

(5) The affiliation period begins on the enrollment date (or, in the case of a late enrollee, the affiliation period begins on the day that would be the first day of coverage, but for the affiliation period).

(6) The affiliation period for enrollment in the HMO under a plan runs concurrently with any waiting period.

The requirements related to HMO affiliation periods contained in these final regulations clarify that a group health plan offering health insurance through an HMO or an HMO that offers health insurance coverage in connection with a group health plan may impose different affiliation periods, so long as the affiliation period complies with the requirements of the HIPAA nondiscrimination provisions. To illustrate this clarification, these final regulations contain an example where a group health plan that provides benefits through an HMO imposes an affiliation period with respect to salaried employees but does not impose an affiliation period with respect to hourly employees. This example illustrates that it is permissible to impose an affiliation period on salaried employees but not hourly employees, so long as treating these two groups differently complies with the requirements of the HIPAA nondiscrimination provisions.

The April 1997 interim rules and these final regulations specify that the affiliation period begins on the enrollment date (which is the first day of coverage under the plan, or if there is a waiting period for coverage under the plan, the first day of the waiting period), not when coverage under a particular benefit package option begins. Accordingly, an example in these final regulations illustrates that if a group health plan offers multiple benefit package options simultaneously, the HMO cannot impose an affiliation period on a plan participant who later switches to the HMO benefit package option, assuming the period of time that has elapsed since the enrollment date (during which the participant was covered under the first benefit package option) exceeds the duration of the HMO affiliation period. Moreover, these regulations clarify that, in the case of a late enrollee, the affiliation period begins on the day that would be the first day of coverage, but for the affiliation period.

The April 1997 interim rules and these final regulations allow an HMO to use alternative methods in lieu of an affiliation period to address adverse selection, as approved by the State insurance commissioner or other official designated to regulate HMOs. Because an affiliation period may be imposed only if no preexisting condition exclusion is imposed, an alternative to an affiliation period may not encompass an arrangement that is in the nature of a preexisting condition exclusion.

7. Interaction With the Family and Medical Leave Act—26 CFR 54.9801-7, 29 CFR 701-8, 45 CFR 146.120

This section has been reserved. For proposed rules on the interaction with the Family and Medical Leave Act, see the Departments' notice of proposed rulemaking, published elsewhere in this issue of the **Federal Register.**

8. Special Rules; Excepted Plans and Excepted Benefits—26 CFR 54.9831-1, 29 2590.732, 45 CFR 146.145

This section of the final regulations contains special rules that apply for

D. HIPAA Final Rules, Portability, continued

Federal Register/Vol. 69, No. 250/Thursday, December 30, 2004/Rules and Regulations 78733

Chapter 100 of the Code, Part 7 of Subtitle B of Title I of ERISA (Part 7 of ERISA), and Title XXVII of the PHS Act. For ease in applying these rules, the definition of *group health plan* has been moved from the definitions section to this section (and the reference to employees in that definition has been modified to clarify that the term includes both current and former employees). New rules have been added for defining limited scope dental and vision benefits and for determining the extent to which benefits provided under a health flexible spending arrangement are excepted benefits. Special rules for partnerships have also been clarified.

Determination of the Number of Plans

A paragraph has been reserved in the final regulation for determining the number of plans an employer or employee organization maintains. For proposed rules on this topic, see the Departments' notice of proposed rulemaking, published elsewhere in this issue of the **Federal Register**.

Coverage Provided by an Employer Through Two or More Individual Policies

If an employer provides coverage to its employees through two or more individual policies, the coverage may be considered coverage offered in connection with a group health plan and, therefore, subject to the group market provisions under HIPAA. A determination of whether there is a group health plan depends on the particular facts and circumstances surrounding the extent of the employer's involvement. For example, one significant factor in establishing whether there is a group health plan is the extent to which the employer makes contributions to health insurance premiums. The fact that health insurance coverage is provided through a contract regulated under State law as individual health insurance coverage does not necessarily prevent the coverage from being treated for HIPAA purposes as coverage sold in the group market. Similarly, the policy that provides the coverage does not have to be considered a "group" policy under State law in order for the group market requirements to apply. Further, the mere fact that an employer forwards employee payroll deductions to a health insurance issuer will not, alone, cause the coverage to become group health plan coverage. However, the employer need not be a party to the insurance policy, or arrange or pay for it directly, in order for its coverage to be considered group health plan coverage. For example, if an employer's actions

appear to endorse one or more policies offered by a health insurance issuer (or issuers), the coverage might be considered group health plan coverage.

General Exception for Certain Small Group Health Plans

Under HIPAA, the April 1997 interim rules, and these final regulations, the group market requirements do not apply to a group health plan or to group health insurance coverage offered in connection with a group health plan for any plan year if, on the first day of the plan year, the plan has fewer than two participants who are current employees. As noted in the preamble to the April 1997 interim rules, a State may apply some or all of the group market provisions in the PHS Act to health insurance issuers in connection with group health plans with fewer than two participants who are current employees on the first day of the plan year. In this case, to the extent the State applies its group market provisions to such insurance, the insurance would not be subject to the individual market requirements.

In the event a group health plan has two or more participants who are current employees on the first day of the plan year but the number of participants who are current employees drops below two during the plan year, under these final regulations the group market requirements continue to apply to the group health plan for the duration of the plan year.

To the extent a health insurance issuer offers group health insurance that is subject to HIPAA's group health insurance requirements, HIPAA generally prohibits the issuer from terminating or failing to offer to renew the insurance (see 45 CFR 146.152). With respect to very small employers, whether group health insurance is subject to the requirements of 45 CFR 146.152 is generally determined by whether the group health plan has two or more participants who are current employees on the first day of the plan year. If so, the issuer generally must provide such coverage throughout the plan year, and is prohibited from terminating coverage in the midst of that plan year merely because the number of current-employee participants drops below two.[8] However, an issuer is permitted to terminate an employer's coverage in the midst of a plan year if the employer fails to satisfy any valid plan participation requirements in the midst of that plan year (see 45 CFR

146.152(a)(3)), including instances where such failure causes the number of current-employee participants to drop below two.

Excepted Benefits

Under HIPAA, the April 1997 interim rules, and these final regulations, certain benefits are excepted from HIPAA in all circumstances, including coverage only for accident (including accidental death and dismemberment); disability income coverage; liability insurance, including general liability insurance and automotive liability insurance; coverage issued as a supplement to liability insurance; workers' compensation or similar coverage; automobile medical payment insurance; credit-only insurance (for example, mortgage insurance); and coverage for on-site medical clinics.

Limited Excepted Benefits

Under HIPAA, the April 1997 interim rules, and these final regulations, limited scope dental benefits, limited scope vision benefits, and long-term care benefits[9] are excepted if they are provided under a separate policy, certificate, or contract of insurance, or are otherwise not an integral part of a plan that is subject to these regulations. Benefits are not an integral part of such a plan if participants have the right not to elect coverage for the benefits, and if participants who elect such coverage must pay an additional premium or contribution for it. These regulations clarify that whether limited scope dental benefits, limited scope vision benefits, or long-term care benefits are provided through a plan that is subject to these regulations, or through a separate plan, is irrelevant to determining whether such benefits are an integral part of a plan that is subject to these regulations. Thus, if participants can decline coverage for the limited-scope benefits, and those electing such coverage must pay an additional premium or contribution, the limited scope benefits could be considered not to be an integral part of a plan that is subject to these regulations, even if such benefits are not provided through that plan.

Limited Scope Vision and Dental Benefits

These regulations define *limited scope dental benefits* as benefits

---

[8] See CMS Program Memorandum No. 99–03, *Group Size Issues Under Title XXVII of the Public Health Service Act*, September 1999.

[9] Long term care benefits are defined as benefits that are either subject to State long-term care insurance laws; that meet the qualifications of section 7702B(c)(1) or 7702B0(b) of the Internal Revenue Code; or are based on cognitive impairment or loss of functional capacity that is expected to be chronic.

D. HIPAA Final Rules, Portability, continued

substantially all of which are for treatment of the mouth (including any organ or structure within the mouth). These regulations also define *limited scope vision benefits* as benefits substantially all of which are for treatment of the eye. Thus, if benefits meet the definition of limited scope dental benefits or limited scope vision benefits, they will be excepted benefits if they satisfy the requirements set forth in these regulations.

These definitions were added in response to questions raised in comments about the prior guidance. The April 1997 interim rules did not define these terms. The preamble to the April 1997 interim rules suggested that the term *limited scope dental benefits* typically does not include medical services, such as those procedures associated with oral cancer or with a mouth injury that results in broken, displaced, or lost teeth. Similarly, the preamble to the April 1997 interim rules suggested that the term *limited scope vision benefits* does not include benefits for such ophthalmological services as treatment of an eye disease (such as glaucoma or a bacterial eye infection) or an eye injury. Comments indicated that typically most independent dental and vision coverages include benefits for these types of medical services. Accordingly, these regulations include definitions of limited scope dental benefits and limited scope vision benefits that reflect this market reality.

Health FSAs

Some comments asked about the extent to which health flexible spending arrangements (FSAs) are subject to these regulations. A health FSA generally is a benefit program that provides employees with coverage under which specified, incurred expenses may be reimbursed (subject to reimbursement maximums and any other reasonable conditions) and under which the maximum amount of reimbursement that is reasonably available to a participant for a period of coverage is not substantially in excess of the total premium (including both employee-paid and employer-paid portions of the premium) for the participant's coverage. Coverage and reimbursements provided to an individual under a group health plan that is a health FSA and that conforms to the generally applicable rules for accident or health plans qualify for the same tax-favored treatment that generally is extended to coverage and reimbursements under employer-provided accident or health plans. Health FSA reimbursements typically provide coverage for medical care expenses not otherwise covered by the

employer's primary group health plan. A health FSA is permitted to operate under a cafeteria plan described in section 125 of the Code. Pursuant to the rules of section 125, an employee can elect to reduce the employee's salary in order to pay for health FSA coverage without the employee having to include that portion of the salary in gross income. Commonly, the maximum benefit payable under a health FSA for any year is equal to the amount of the employee's salary reduction election for the year, plus any additional employer contribution for the year.

The April 1997 interim rules did not address the extent to which health FSAs qualify as excepted benefits. On December 29, 1997, a clarification to the April 1997 interim rules was published that specified the circumstances under which a health FSA qualifies as excepted benefits. (62 FR 67688) That clarification stated that benefits under a health FSA are treated as excepted benefits if the FSA meets certain requirements. Specifically, FSA benefits are treated as excepted benefits if the maximum benefit payable under the FSA for the employee for the year does not exceed two times the employee's salary reduction election under the FSA for the year (or, if greater, the amount of the employee's salary reduction election under the FSA for the year, plus $500). In addition, the employee must have other coverage available under a group health plan of the employer for the year, and that other coverage cannot be limited to benefits that are excepted benefits.

Based on section 9832(c)(2)(C) of the Code, section 733(c)(2)(C) of ERISA, and section 2791(c)(2)(C) of the PHS Act, these regulations adopt the December 29, 1997 guidance with some additional clarifications. Specifically, these regulations clarify that to be considered excepted benefits, a health FSA must meet the definition of a health FSA in section 106(c)(2) of the Code. Also, these regulations clarify that other group health plan coverage not limited to excepted benefits must be made available for the year to the class of participants by reason of their employment. Similarly, the maximum amount payable to any participant in the class for the year is the amount to consider when determining whether the maximum amount payable under the FSA for the year complies with the limit specified in the previous paragraph. Additionally, these regulations clarify that an employer credit under a health FSA that an employee can elect to receive as taxable income is considered an employee salary reduction election. However, if the employee cannot

receive the employer credit as taxable income (that is, the credit is lost unless the employee uses the amount for nontaxable benefits under a cafeteria plan), then the amount is not considered an employee salary reduction election.

Application to HSAs and HDHPs

Section 1201 of the Medicare Prescription Drug, Improvement, and Modernization Act of 2003, Public Law 108–173, added section 223 to the Internal Revenue Code to permit individuals to establish Health Savings Accounts (HSAs). HSAs are established to receive tax-favored contributions and amounts in an HSA may be used to pay or reimburse qualified medical expenses. Questions have arisen concerning the application of HIPAA to HSAs.

In order to establish and contribute to an HSA, an individual must be covered by a High Deductible Health Plan (HDHP). An HDHP is a health plan that satisfies certain requirements with respect to deductibles and out-of-pocket expenses. An HDHP may be a group health plan sponsored by an employer or individual health insurance coverage purchased in the individual market. There is no provision in the HIPAA rules that excludes an HDHP, by virtue of qualifying as an HDHP, from the respective HIPAA requirements for group health plans or individual health insurance coverage. Generally, employer-sponsored HDHPs are employee welfare benefit plans. See Department of Labor Field Assistance Bulletin 2004–01 (FAB 2004–01), issued on April 7, 2004. Because an employer-sponsored HDHP provides medical care, it is generally subject to the portability requirements of HIPAA and the applicable regulations.

FAB 2004–01 concluded that HSAs, in contrast to HDHPs, generally will not constitute employee welfare benefit plans. See Department of Labor Field Assistance Bulletin 2004–01 (FAB 2004–01), issued on April 7, 2004. Because HSAs are generally not employee welfare benefit plans, the HIPAA portability requirements under ERISA or the PHS Act generally will not apply.

Moreover, the HIPAA portability requirements generally are not relevant for purposes of HSAs. Due to the rules imposed by the Internal Revenue Code with respect to HSAs, employers or HSA trustees do not have discretion with respect to the coverage provided by an HSA, both with respect to what expenses qualify for reimbursement as well as which individuals' expenses are eligible. For example, expenses reimbursable by an HSA cannot

D. HIPAA Final Rules, Portability, continued

generally be restricted by the employer or HSA trustee. Under the statute and administrative guidance, any expense incurred after an HSA is established is eligible for reimbursement, without restriction by an employer contributing to the HSA or trustee of the HSA. Thus, as a practical matter, whether or not an expense relates to a preexisting condition cannot determine the reimbursement. As such HSAs by design cannot impose a preexisting condition exclusion. Similarly, due to comparability rules requiring uniform contributions to HSAs by employers, employers and trustees generally cannot use differing amounts of contributions to impose a preexisting condition exclusion.

The eligibility for tax-free reimbursement from an HSA is also determined by statute; namely, the qualified medical expenses of the HSA owner and the HSA owner's dependents incurred after the HSA is established may be reimbursed on a tax-free basis by the HSA. Special enrollment rules for dependent children or spouses are not relevant because once an HSA is established they are eligible for tax-free reimbursements immediately. With respect to special enrollment upon loss of coverage, the rules for employer contributions generally require that all employees who are eligible for HSA contributions and participating in the employer's HDHP receive comparable HSA contributions. Thus, the combination of the comparability rules and the application of the special enrollment rules to the HDHP will generally ensure compliance with respect to employer HSA contributions because once an employee is enrolled in an employer-provided HDHP due to the special enrollment rules, the employer must make comparable contributions to the employee's HSA.

Indemnity Insurance

Under HIPAA, the April 1997 interim rules, and these final regulations, hospital indemnity and other fixed-dollar indemnity insurance are excepted benefits if the benefits are provided under a separate policy, certificate, or contract of insurance; if there is no coordination of benefits between the provision of the benefits and an exclusion of benefits under any group health plan maintained by the same plan sponsor; and if the benefits are paid with respect to an event regardless of whether benefits are provided with respect to the event under any group health plan maintained by the same plan sponsor. These regulations clarify that, for hospital indemnity or other fixed-dollar indemnity insurance to

qualify as excepted benefits, such insurance must pay a fixed dollar amount per day (or other period), regardless of the amount of expenses incurred. An example clarifies that if a policy provides benefits only for hospital stays at a fixed percentage of hospital expenses up to a maximum amount per day, the benefits are not excepted benefits. This is the result even if, in practice, the policy pays the maximum for every day of hospitalization.

Supplemental Insurance

Under HIPAA, the April 1997 interim rules, and these final regulations, Medicare supplemental health insurance (as defined under section 1882(g)(1) of the Social Security Act); coverage supplemental to TRICARE; and similar coverage that is supplemental to a group health plan are excepted benefits if they are provided under a separate policy, certificate, or contract of insurance. These regulations clarify that, for coverage supplemental to a group health plan to qualify as excepted benefits, the coverage must be specifically designed to fill gaps in primary coverage, such as coinsurance or deductibles. Coverage that becomes secondary or supplemental only under a coordination-of-benefits provision in the insurance contract or plan documents does not qualify as excepted supplemental benefits.

Treatment of Partnerships

Any plan, fund, or program that is established or maintained by a partnership and that provides medical care to present or former partners or their dependents, and that otherwise would not be an employee welfare benefit plan, is considered an employee welfare benefit plan that is a group health plan under Part 7 of ERISA and Title XXVII of the PHS Act.[10] As such, the partnership is considered the employer with respect to any partner. Participants in the plan include individuals who are partners of the partnership. Additionally, with respect to group health plans maintained by self-employed individuals (under which one or more employees are participants), the self-employed individual is considered a participant if this individual is or may become eligible to receive a benefit under the plan or if the individual's beneficiaries may be so eligible. These regulations clarify that, for purposes of Part 7 of ERISA and Title XXVII of PHS Act, a

partner must be a bona fide partner in order to be considered an employee, and the partnership is considered the employer of a partner only if the partner is a bona fide partner. These final regulations also clarify that whether an individual is a bona fide partner is determined based on all the relevant facts and circumstances, including whether the individual performs services on behalf of the partnership.

Counting the Average Number of Employees

A paragraph has been reserved in the final rules for determining the average number of employees employed by an employer for a year. For proposed rules on this topic, see the Departments' notice of proposed rulemaking, published elsewhere in this issue of the **Federal Register**.

C. Economic Impact and Paperwork Burden

Summary—Department of Labor and Department of Health and Human Services

HIPAA's group market portability provisions, which include limitations on the scope and application of preexisting condition exclusions, and special enrollment rights, provide a minimum standard of protection designed to increase access to health coverage. The Departments crafted these final regulations to secure these protections, consistent with the intent of Congress, and to do so in a manner that is economically efficient.

The primary economic effects of HIPAA's portability provisions ensue directly from the statute. These regulations, by clarifying and securing HIPAA's statutory protections, will delineate and possibly expand HIPAA's effects at the margin.

Effects of the Statute

HIPAA's statutory group market portability provisions extend coverage to certain individuals and preexisting conditions not otherwise covered. This extension of coverage entails both benefits and costs. Individuals enjoying expanded coverage will realize benefits. In some instances these individuals will gain coverage for services they otherwise would have purchased out-of-pocket. In other instances the extension of coverage will induce individuals to consume more (or different) health care services, which in some cases may improve health outcomes. The dollar value of the extended coverage is estimated to be $515 million annually. Potential additional benefits from improved health outcomes are difficult

---

[10] Such a plan, fund, or program is also considered a group health plan under section 5000(b)(1) and Chapter 100 of the Code.

D. HIPAA Final Rules, Portability, continued

78736   Federal Register / Vol. 69, No. 250 / Thursday, December 30, 2004 / Rules and Regulations

to quantify (and the Departments have not attempted to do so), but may be large in aggregate, and will be large for at least some individuals whose health outcomes may be substantially improved. Another indirect benefit of HIPAA's portability provisions is a reduction in so-called "job lock"—a phenomenon in which individuals keep jobs they would prefer to leave to avoid losing coverage for preexisting conditions. If workers move into more productive jobs, the overall economy will benefit.

It should be noted that the benefits of HIPAA's portability provisions in any given year will be concentrated in a relatively small population that gains coverage under HIPAA for needed care that would otherwise not be covered. The number that might so benefit has been estimated at 100,000 individuals.

The direct costs of HIPAA's portability provisions generally include the cost of extending coverage to additional services, as well as certain attendant administrative costs. The cost of extended coverage is estimated at $515 million annually. The major administrative costs include the cost of providing certificates of creditable coverage, and possibly the cost of carrying out special enrollments and offsets of preexisting condition exclusion periods. The Departments did not attempt to fully estimate the administrative costs of the HIPAA statute but in crafting this regulation did attempt to constrain these costs.

The Departments believe that the cost of HIPAA is borne by covered workers. Cost can be shifted to workers through increases in employee premium shares or reductions (or smaller increases) in pay or other components of compensation, or by increases in deductibles or other cost sharing or other reductions in the richness of health benefits. Whereas the benefits of HIPAA are concentrated in a relatively small population, the costs are distributed broadly across plans and enrollees.

The Departments have considered whether the costs imposed by HIPAA's statutory portability provisions have had any major indirect negative effects, and concluded that such effects are possible but probably small.

Any mandate to increase the richness or availability of health insurance adds to the cost of insurance. It is possible that some small number of employers and employees already at the brink of affordability would drop coverage in response to the implementation of HIPAA. The Departments also note that the estimated $515 million cost associated with extensions of coverage

under HIPAA amounts to a small fraction of one percent of total expenditures by private group health plans. This suggests that the cost of HIPAA is a small, possibly negligible, factor in most employers' decisions to offer health coverage and workers' decisions to enroll. The Departments believe that the benefits of HIPAA's statutory group market portability provisions justify their cost. The Departments' full assessment of the costs and benefits of HIPAA's statutory provisions and their basis for that assessment is detailed later in the preamble.

Effects of the Final Regulations

By clarifying and securing HIPAA's statutory portability protections, these regulations will help ensure that HIPAA rights are fully realized. The result is likely to be a small increase at the margin in the direct and indirect economic effects of HIPAA's statutory portability provisions. The Departments believe that the regulation's benefits will justify its costs.

Additional economic benefits derive from the regulations' clarifications of HIPAA's portability requirements. By clarifying employees' rights and plan sponsors' obligations under HIPAA's portability provisions, the regulations will reduce uncertainty over health benefits, thereby fostering labor market efficiency and the establishment and continuation of group health plans by employers.

Many provisions of the final regulations closely resemble provisions included in the interim final regulations that the final regulations supplant. This regulatory action, however, adds or amends both certain provisions directed at the scope of HIPAA's portability protections and certain provisions establishing administrative requirements intended to safeguard those protections.

Scope of Protections

These final regulations are intended to secure and implement HIPAA's group market portability provisions under certain special circumstances. The final regulations therefore contain a number of provisions intended to clearly delimit the scope of HIPAA's portability protections. Most of these provisions closely resemble and will have the same effect as provisions of the interim final regulations. Others, however, clarify or expand at the margin the range of situations to which HIPAA's portability protections apply or in which a loss of eligibility may trigger special enrollment rights. These include the requirement that health coverage under

foreign government programs be treated as creditable coverage for purposes of limiting the application of preexisting condition exclusions; the extension of special enrollment rights to individuals who lose eligibility for coverage in connection with the application of lifetime benefit limits, movement out of an HMO's service area, or the termination of a health coverage option previously offered under a group health plan; and the establishment of a special enrollment right for a participant to change among available coverage options under a group health plan when adding one or more dependents in connection with marriage, adoption, or placement for adoption. Each of these provisions is expected to result in a small increase in the economic effects of HIPAA's statutory portability protections. The Departments have no basis to quantify these small increases. The potential size of affected sub populations is explored later in the preamble.

Administrative Requirements

In order to secure and implement HIPAA's group market special enrollment and portability provisions, both the HIPAA statute and these final regulations establish certain administrative requirements.

As noted above, the HIPAA statute generally requires plans and issuers to provide certifications of prior coverage to individuals leaving coverage. These regulations additionally require plans and issuers to notify individuals of their special enrollments rights, any preexisting condition exclusion provisions, and the applicability of such exclusions where individuals provide evidence of prior coverage that is of insufficient duration to fully offset exclusion periods. Plans will incur cost to comply with these administrative requirements. The Departments estimate the administrative cost to prepare and distribute certifications and notices to be $97 million per year. Nearly all of this, or $96 million, is attributable to the preparation and distribution of certifications as required under HIPAA's statutory provisions. These final regulations include numerous special provisions that serve to reduce plans' cost of providing certifications. A more strict interpretation of the statute would require plans to send an individual certificate to each affected enrollee. Such strict interpretation would result in plans sending 80.1 million certificates annually at cost of $157.6 million, which is $61.6 million more than the burden imposed by the final regulations.

D. HIPAA Final Rules, Portability, continued

Generally all of the major administrative requirements included in the final regulations were also included in the interim final regulations. The final regulations make minor additions to two requirements, however. They require plans to include educational statements in certificates of creditable coverage and to maintain in writing their procedures for requesting certificates. The cost of these additional requirements is expected to be small, and was not estimated separately from the overall cost of providing certificates.

Other changes included in these final regulations are likely to slightly reduce plans' cost to provide certain HIPAA-required notices. Included with the final regulation is new sample language for general and specific notices of preexisting condition exclusions, which may serve to reduce some plans' costs of providing these notices, and revised sample language for special enrollment rights notices. The final regulations also clarify the narrow scope of the requirement to notify certain affected participants of the specific application of preexisting condition exclusions. The Departments did not estimate the impact of these provisions separately from the overall cost of providing general and specific notices of preexisting condition exclusions and notices of special enrollment rights.

The Departments' full assessment of the costs and benefits of this regulation and their basis for that assessment is detailed later in this preamble.

Executive Order 12866—Department of Labor and Department of Health and Human Services

Under Executive Order 12866 (58 FR 551735, Oct. 4, 1993), the Departments must determine whether a regulatory action is "significant" and therefore subject to the requirements of the Executive Order and subject to review by the Office of Management and Budget (OMB). Under section 3(f), the order defines a "significant regulatory action" as an action that is likely to result in a rule: (1) Having an annual effect on the economy of $100 million or more, or adversely and materially affecting a sector of the economy, productivity, competition, jobs, the environment, public health or safety, or State, local or tribal governments or communities (also referred to as "economically significant"); (2) creating serious inconsistency or otherwise interfering with an action taken or planned by another agency; (3) materially altering the budgetary impacts of entitlement grants, user fees, or loan programs or the rights and obligations of recipients thereof; or (4)

raising novel legal or policy issues arising out of legal mandates, the President's priorities, or the principles set forth in the Executive Order.

Pursuant to the terms of the Executive Order, this action is "economically significant" and subject to OMB review under Section 3(f) of the Executive Order. Consistent with the Executive Order, the Departments have assessed the costs and benefits of this action. The Departments' assessment, and the analysis underlying that assessment, is detailed below. The Departments performed a comprehensive, unified analysis to estimate the costs and benefits attributable to the regulations for purposes of compliance with Executive Order 12866, the Regulatory Flexibility Act, and the Paperwork Reduction Act.

Statement of Need for Action

These final regulations are needed to clarify and interpret the HIPAA portability provisions (increased portability through limitation on preexisting condition exclusions) under Section 701 of the Employee Retirement Income Security Act of 1974 (ERISA), Section 2701 of the Public Health Service Act, and Section 9801 of the Internal Revenue Code of 1986. The provisions are needed to improve the availability and portability of health coverage by limiting preexisting condition exclusions and their use, and requiring that group health plans and group health insurance issuers allow individuals to enroll under certain circumstances (special enrollment). Additional guidance was required to clarify certain definitions, such as the definition of creditable coverage; to clarify the method of determining the proper length of a preexisting condition exclusion period for an individual; to describe the circumstances under which an individual must be allowed a special enrollment opportunity; and to describe notices that group health plans and group health insurance issuers must provide to individuals.

Economic Effects

The Departments believe that this regulation's benefits will justify its costs. This belief is grounded in the assessment of costs and benefit that is summarized earlier in the preamble and detailed below.

Regulatory Flexibility Act—Department of Labor and Department of Health and Human Services

The Regulatory Flexibility Act (5 U.S.C. 601 *et seq.*) (RFA) imposes certain requirements with respect to Federal rules that are subject to the

notice and comment requirements of section 553(b) of the Administrative Procedure Act (5 U.S.C. 551 *et seq.*) that are likely to have a significant economic impact on a substantial number of small entities. Unless an agency certifies that a rule will not have a significant economic impact on a substantial number of small entities, section 604 of the RFA requires the agency to present a final regulatory flexibility analysis at the time of the publication of the notice of final rulemaking describing the impact of the rule on small entities. Small entities include small businesses, organizations, and governmental jurisdictions.

Because these final rules are being issued without prior notices of proposed rulemaking, the RFA does not apply, and the Departments are not required to either certify that the rule will not have a significant impact on a substantial number of small entities or conduct a regulatory flexibility analysis. The Departments nonetheless crafted these regulations in careful consideration of their effects on small entities.

For purposes of this discussion, the Departments consider a small entity to be an employee benefit plan with fewer than 100 participants. The basis for this definition is found in section 104(a)(2) of ERISA, which permits the Secretary of Labor to prescribe simplified annual reports for pension plans which cover fewer than 100 participants. Under section 104(a)(3), the Secretary may also provide for simplified annual reporting and disclosure if the statutory requirements of part 1 of Title I of ERISA would otherwise be inappropriate for welfare benefit plans. Pursuant to the authority of section 104(a)(3), the Department of Labor has previously issued at 29 CFR 2520.104-20, 2520.104-21, 2520.104-41, 2520.104-46 and 2520.104b-10, certain simplified reporting provisions and limited exemptions from reporting and disclosure requirements for small plans, including unfunded or insured welfare plans covering fewer than 100 participants and which satisfy certain other requirements.

Further, while some small plans are maintained by large employers, most are maintained by small employers. Both small and large plans may enlist small third party service providers to perform administrative functions, but it is generally understood that third party service providers transfer their costs to their plan clients in the form of fees. Thus, the Departments believe that assessing the impact of this rule on small plans is an appropriate substitute for evaluating the effect on small entities. The definition of small entity

D. HIPAA Final Rules, Portability, continued

considered appropriate for this purpose differs, however, from a definition of small business based on size standards promulgated by the Small Business Administration (SBA) (13 CFR 121.201) pursuant to the Small Business Act (5 U.S.C. 631 et seq.). The Department of Labor solicited comments on the use of this standard for evaluating the effects of the interim final on small entities. No comments were received with respect to the standard.

The Departments believe that the benefits of this regulation will justify its costs. This belief is grounded in the assessment of costs and benefit that is summarized earlier in the preamble and detailed below in the "Basis for Assessment of Economic Impact" section. The direct financial value of coverage extensions pursuant to HIPAA's portability provisions are estimated to be approximately $180 million for small plans, or a small fraction of one percent of total small plan expenditures.[11]

In order to secure and implement HIPAA's portability provisions, the HIPAA statute and interim final regulations established certain administrative requirements, including requirements to provide certifications of creditable coverage and notices of special enrollment rights and preexisting condition exclusions. The Departments estimate the cost for small plans to prepare and distribute certifications and notices to be $13 million per year.[12] These costs will initially be borne by issuers who supply small group insurance products and by third-party administrators who provide services to small insured plans. These two types of entities will spread the costs across a much larger pool of small

---

[11] Computer runs using Medical Expenditure Survey Household Component (MEPS–HC) and the Robert Wood Johnson Employer Healthy Benefits Survey determined that the share of covered private-sector job leavers at small firms average 35 percent of all covered private sector job leavers. From this, we inferred that the financial burden borne by small plans is approximately 35 percent of the total expenditures by private-sector group health plans.

[12] As noted above, the total cost for certificates and notices is estimated to be $97 million. We estimate that 13 percent of individuals receiving certificates and notices receive them from small group health plans, and on that basis estimates that 13% of the total cost falls on such plans. As noted below, we estimate that out of a total of 54 million individuals who leave coverage under group health plans, individual health insurance policies or public programs, 20 million, or 44 percent, are leaving private-sector group plans. Assuming that the proportion of these that are leaving small plans is equal to the proportion of covered, private-sector job leavers who leave small firms (estimated to be 35 percent, as noted above), 13 percent of those leaving any type of coverage are leaving coverage under small group plans.

plans who will in turn transfer cost broadly to plan enrollees.

Special Analyses—Department of the Treasury

Notwithstanding the determinations of the Departments of Labor and of Health and Human Services, for purposes of the Department of the Treasury it has been determined that this Treasury decision is not a significant regulatory action. Pursuant to sections 603(a) and 605(b) of the Regulatory Flexibility Act, it is hereby certified that the collections of information referenced in this Treasury decision (see §§ 54.9801–3, 54.9801–4, 54.9801–5, and 54.9801–6) will not have a significant economic impact on a substantial number of small entities. Although a substantial number of small entities will be subject to the collection of information requirements in these regulations, the requirements will not have a significant economic impact on these entities. The average time required to complete a certification required under these regulations is estimated to be 4 to 5 minutes for all employers. This average is based on the assumption that most employers will automate the certification process. The paperwork requirements other than certifications that are contained in the regulations are estimated to impose less than 2% of the burden imposed by the certifications. Many small employers that maintain group health plans have their plans administered by an insurance company or third party administrators (TPAs). Most insurers and TPAs are expected to automate the certification process and therefore their average time to produce a certificate should be similar to the 4 to 5 minute average estimated for all employers. However, even for small employers that do not automate the certification process, the collection of information requirements in the regulation will not have a significant impact. Even if it is conservatively assumed that their average time to produce a certificate is 3 times as long as the highest estimate for all employers (i.e., 15 minutes per certificate) and that all of their employees are covered by their group health plan and that half of the employees receive a certificate each year, the average burden per employee is less than 8 minutes per year. This can be rounded up to 8 minutes to more than account for the additional burden imposed by the other paperwork requirements of the final regulations. Thus, for example, for an employer with 10 employees, the annual burden would be not more than 1 hour and 20 minutes per year. At an estimated cost of $18 per hour, this would result in a cost of not

more than $24 per year for the employer, which is not a significant economic impact. Because the collection of information requirements of this Treasury decision will not have a significant economic impact on a substantial number of small entities, a Regulatory Flexibility Analysis under the Regulatory Flexibility Act (5 U.S.C. chapter 6) is not required. Pursuant to section 7805(f) of the Code, the notice of proposed rulemaking preceding these regulations was submitted to the Small Business Administration for comment on its impact on small business.

Paperwork Reduction Act

Department of Labor

These final regulations include three separate collections of information as that term is defined in the Paperwork Reduction Act of 1995 (PRA 95), 44 U.S.C. 3502(3): the Notice of Enrollment Rights, Notice of Preexisting Condition Exclusion, and Certificate of Creditable Coverage. Each of these disclosures is currently approved by the Office of Management and Budget (OMB) through October 31, 2006 in accordance with PRA 95 under control numbers 1210–0101, 1210–0102, and 1210–0103.

Department of the Treasury

These final regulations include a collection of information as that term is defined in PRA 95: the Notice of Enrollment Rights, Notice of Preexisting Condition Exclusion, and Certificate of Creditable Coverage. Each of these disclosures is currently approved by OMB under control number 1545–1537.

An agency may not conduct or sponsor, and a person is not required to respond to, a collection of information unless it displays a valid control number assigned by the Office of Management and Budget.

Books or records relating to a collection of information must be retained as long as their contents may become material in the administration of any internal revenue law. Generally, tax returns and tax return information are confidential, as required by 26 U.S.C. 6103.

Department of Health and Human Services

These final regulations include three separate collections of information as that term is defined in PRA 95: the Notice of Enrollment Rights, Notice of Preexisting Condition Exclusion, and Certificate of Creditable Coverage. Each of these disclosures is currently approved by OMB through June 30, 2006 in accordance with PRA 95 under control number 0938–0702.

D. HIPAA Final Rules, Portability, continued

Small Business Regulatory Enforcement Fairness Act

This final rule is subject to the provisions of the Small Business Regulatory Enforcement Fairness Act of 1996 (5 U.S.C. 801 *et seq.*) and is being transmitted to Congress and the Comptroller General for review. The final rule, is a "major rule," as that term is defined in 5 U.S.C. 804, because it may result in (1) an annual effect on the economy of $100 million or more; (2) a major increase in costs or prices for consumers, individual industries, or federal, State or local government agencies, or geographic regions; or (3) significant adverse effects on competition, employment, investment, productivity, innovation, or on the ability of United States-based enterprises to compete with foreign-based enterprises in domestic or export markets.

Unfunded Mandates Reform Act

Section 202 of the Unfunded Mandates Reform Act of 1995 requires that agencies assess anticipated costs and benefits before issuing any rule that may result in an expenditure in any 1 year by State, local, or tribal governments, in the aggregate, or by the private sector, of $100 million. These final regulations have no such mandated consequential effect on State, local, or tribal governments, or on the private sector.

Federalism Statement Under Executive Order 13132—Department of Labor and Department of Health and Human Services

Executive Order 13132 outlines fundamental principles of federalism. It requires adherence to specific criteria by federal agencies in formulating and implementing policies that have "substantial direct effects" on the States, the relationship between the national government and States, or on the distribution of power and responsibilities among the various levels of government. Federal agencies promulgating regulations that have these federalism implications must consult with State and local officials, and describe the extent of their consultation and the nature of the concerns of State and local officials in the preamble to the regulation.

In the Departments' view, these final regulations have federalism implications because they may have substantial direct effects on the States, the relationship between the national government and States, or on the distribution of power and responsibilities among the various

levels of government. However, in the Departments' view, the federalism implications of these final regulations are substantially mitigated because, with respect to health insurance issuers, the vast majority of States have enacted laws which meet or exceed the federal HIPAA portability standards.

In general, through section 514, ERISA supersedes State laws to the extent that they relate to any covered employee benefit plan, and preserves State laws that regulate insurance, banking or securities. While ERISA prohibits States from regulating a plan as an insurance or investment company or bank, HIPAA added a new section to ERISA (as well as to the PHS Act) narrowly preempting State requirements for issuers of group health insurance coverage. Specifically, with respect to seven provisions of the HIPAA portability rules, States may impose stricter obligations on health insurance issuers.[13] Moreover, with respect to other requirements for health insurance issuers, States may continue to apply State law requirements except to the extent that such requirements prevent the application of HIPAA's portability, access, and renewability provisions.

In enacting these new preemption provisions, Congress intended to preempt State insurance requirements only to the extent that they prevent the application of the basic protections set forth in HIPAA. HIPAA's conference report States that the conferees intended the narrowest preemption of State laws with regard to health insurance issuers. H.R. Conf. Rep. No. 736, 104th Cong. 2d Session 205 (1996). State insurance laws that are more stringent than the federal requirements are unlikely to "prevent the application of" the HIPAA portability provisions, and be preempted. Accordingly, States have significant latitude to impose requirements on health insurance insurers that are more restrictive than the federal law.

Guidance conveying this interpretation of HIPAA's preemption provisions was published in the **Federal Register** on April 8, 1997. 62 FR 16904.

[13] States may shorten the six-month look-back period prior to the enrollment date; shorten the 12-month and 18-month maximum preexisting condition exclusion periods; increase the 63-day significant break in coverage period; increase the 30-day period for newborns, adopted children, and children placed for adoption to enroll in the plan with no preexisting condition exclusion; further limit the circumstances in which a preexisting condition exclusion may be applied (beyond the federal exceptions for certain newborns, adopted children, children placed for adoption, pregnancy, and genetic information in the absence of a diagnosis; require additional special enrollment periods; and reduced the HMO affiliation period to less than 2 months (3 months for late enrollees).

These final regulations clarify and implement the statute's minimum standards and do not significantly reduce the discretion given the States by the statute. Moreover, the Departments understand that the vast majority of States have requirements that meet or exceed the minimum requirements of the HIPAA portability provisions.

HIPAA provides that the States may enforce the provisions of HIPAA as they pertain to issuers, but that the Secretary of Health and Human Services must enforce any provisions that a State fails to substantially enforce. Currently, HHS enforces the HIPAA portability provisions in only one State in accordance with that State's specific request to do so. When exercising its responsibility to enforce the provisions of HIPAA, HHS works cooperatively with the State for the purpose of addressing the State's concerns and avoiding conflicts with the exercise of State authority. HHS has developed procedures to implement its enforcement responsibilities, and to afford the States the maximum opportunity to enforce HIPAA's requirements in the first instance. HHS's procedures address the handling of reports that States may not be substantially enforcing HIPAA's requirements, and the mechanism for allocating responsibility between the States and HHS. In compliance with Executive Order 13132's requirement that agencies examine closely any policies that may have federalism implications or limit the policymaking discretion of the States, DOL and HHS have engaged in numerous efforts to consult and work cooperatively with affected State and local officials.

For example, the Departments sought and received input from State insurance regulators and the National Association of Insurance Commissioners (NAIC). The NAIC is a non-profit corporation established by the insurance commissioners of the 50 States, the District of Columbia, and the four U.S. territories. In most States the Insurance Commissioner is appointed by the Governor, in approximately 14 States, the insurance commissioner is an elected official. Among other activities, it provides a forum for the development of uniform policy when uniformity is appropriate. Its members meet, discuss and offer solutions to mutual problems. The NAIC sponsors quarterly meetings to provide a forum for the exchange of ideas and in-depth consideration of insurance issues by regulators, industry representatives and consumers. CMS and the Department of Labor staff have consistently attended these quarterly meetings to listen to the concerns of the

D. HIPAA Final Rules, Portability, continued

78740   **Federal Register** / Vol. 69, No. 250 / Thursday, December 30, 2004 / Rules and Regulations

State Insurance Departments regarding HIPAA portability issues. In addition to the general discussions, committee meetings, and task groups, the NAIC sponsors the standing CMS/DOL meeting on HIPAA issues for members during the quarterly conferences. This meeting provides CMS and the Department of Labor with the opportunity to provide updates on regulations, bulletins, enforcement actions, and outreach efforts regarding HIPAA.

The Departments received written comments on the interim regulation from the NAIC and from ten States. In general, these comments raised technical issues that the Departments considered in conjunction with similar issues raised by other commenters. In a letter sent before issuance of the interim regulation, the NAIC expressed concerns that the Departments interpret the new preemption provisions of HIPAA narrowly so as to give the States flexibility to impose more stringent requirements. As discussed above, the Departments address this concern in the preamble to the interim regulation.

In addition, the Departments specifically consulted with the NAIC in developing these final regulations. Through the NAIC, the Departments sought and received the input of State insurance departments regarding certain insurance industry definitions, enrollment procedures and standard coverage terms. This input is generally reflected in the discussion of comments received and changes made in Section B—Overview of the Regulations of the preamble to these regulations.

The Departments have also cooperated with the States in several ongoing outreach initiatives, through which information on HIPAA is shared among federal regulators, State regulators and the regulated community. In particular, the Department of Labor has established a Health Benefits Education Campaign with more than 70 partners, including CMS, NAIC and many business and consumer groups. CMS has sponsored conferences with the States—the Consumer Outreach and Advocacy conferences in March 1999 and June 2000, and the Implementation and Enforcement of HIPAA National State-Federal Conferences in August 1999, 2000, 2001, 2002, and 2003. Furthermore, both the Department of Labor and CMS Web sites offer links to important State Web sites and other resources, facilitating coordination between the State and federal regulators and the regulated community.

Throughout the process of developing these regulations, to the extent feasible within the specific preemption

provisions of HIPAA, the Departments have attempted to balance the States' interests in regulating health insurance issuers, and the Congress' intent to provide uniform minimum protections to consumers in every State. By doing so, it is the Departments' view that they have complied with the requirements of Executive Order 13132.

Pursuant to the requirements set forth in Section 8(a) of Executive Order 13132, and by the signatures affixed to these final regulations, the Departments certify that the Employee Benefits Security Administration and the Centers for Medicare & Medicaid Services have complied with the requirements of Executive Order 13132 for the attached final regulation, Final Regulations for Health Coverage Portability for Group Health Plans and Group Health Insurance Issuers (RIN 1210–AA54 and RIN 0938–AL43), in a meaningful and timely manner.

Basis for Assessment of Economic Impact—Department of Labor and Department of Health and Human Services

As noted above, the primary economic effects of HIPAA's portability provisions ensue directly from the statute. These regulations, by clarifying and securing HIPAA's statutory protections, will delineate and possibly expand HIPAA's effects at the margin.

Effects of the Statute

In order to determine how many workers could benefit from crediting prior coverage against a new health plan's preexisting condition exclusion period, we examined the 18 million individuals who changed jobs in 2002. Of these, approximately 1 in 3 had health care coverage at those jobs and an additional 8 million dependents also received employer-sponsored health care coverage through these job changers. By allowing prior creditable coverage, 4 million job changers, who had at least 12 months of prior creditable coverage, were able to change jobs without the risk of a preexisting condition exclusions for them or their 5 million dependents. An additional 2 million workers who changed jobs and had some smaller amount of prior coverage, faced reduced waiting periods before receiving full coverage for them and their 3 million dependents.[14]

---

[14] We calculated these estimates using internal runs off the MEPS–HC. These runs gave the number of total job changers, total job changers that had employer-sponsored insurance (ESI), and whether this coverage had been for less than 12 months or not. Estimates for dependents were based off the ratio of policy-holders to total dependents from the March 2003 Current Population Survey (March

The most direct effect of HIPAA's statutory group market portability provisions is the extension of coverage to individuals and preexisting conditions not otherwise covered. This extension of coverage entails both benefits and costs. Individuals enjoying expanded coverage will realize benefits. In some instances these individuals will gain coverage for services they otherwise would have purchased out-of-pocket, thereby reaping a simple and direct financial benefit In other instances the extension of coverage will induce individuals to consume more (or different) health care services, reaping a benefit which has financial value, and which in some cases will produce additional indirect benefits both to the individual (improved health) and possibly to the economy at large (increased productivity).[15] The simple financial value of the direct benefits (essentially the dollar value of the extended coverage) is estimated to be $515 million.[16] The indirect benefits are

---

CPS). This approach to the question of how many people are impacted by increased portability parallels that of the September 1995 U.S. General Accounting Office (GAO), Report HEHS–95–257, "Health Insurance Portability: Reform Could Ensure Continued Coverage for up to 25 Million Americans," September 1995.

[15] For more detailed information, see Ellen O'Brien's article "Employer' Benefits from Workers' Health Insurance" Milbank Quarterly, Vol. 1 No. 1, 2003. She provides an extensive analysis of the literature on benefits accruing to employers from offering health benefits. She reports that researchers are beginning to calculate the costs to employers of unhealthy employees. Her work provides information on studies that have demonstrated that poor health may be related to lower productivity. For example, she discusses studies that have examined the effects on workplace productivity of specific health conditions and show that poor health reduces workers' productivity at work, and that effective health care treatments can reduce productivity losses and may even pay for themselves in terms of increased productivity.

[16] The estimate of $515 million is the 1999 projection published in the August 1, 1996 Congressional Budget Office (CBO) report, "Estimate of Costs of Private Sector Mandates;" Bill Number H.R. 3103, indexed. The index is derived from the average annual percent change from 1999 to 2004 in aggregate private health insurance expenditures, as reported in Table 3 of the "National Health Care Projections Tables" by the Centers for Medicare & Medicaid Services, Office of the Actuary. CBO estimated the direct cost to the private sector would total about $300 million in 1999. The specific items included in the estimate are: (1) Limiting the length of time employer-sponsored and group insurance plans could withhold coverage for pre-existing conditions, and (2) requiring that periods of continuous prior health plan coverage be credited against pre-existing condition exclusions of a new plan.

According to CBO, two-thirds of the cost reflects the provision to limit exclusions for pre-existing conditions. The key components of this estimate are: (1) The number of people who would have more of their medical expenses covered by insurance if exclusions were limited to one year or less, and (2) the average cost to insurers of that newly insured medical care. The provision

D. HIPAA Final Rules, Portability, continued

difficult to quantify (and the Departments have not attempted to do so), but may be large in aggregate, and will be large for at least some individuals whose health outcomes may be substantially improved.

Another indirect (though intended) benefit of HIPAA's portability provisions is a reduction in so-called "job lock." Job lock occurs when an individual stays in a job with health insurance that he or she would prefer to leave out of concern that he or she would lose coverage for care of his or her own or a covered dependent's preexisting condition[17].

No attempt is made here to quantify increases in labor force mobility attributable to reduced job lock under HIPAA. However, it is noted that at least two indirect economic effects are likely to follow such increased mobility. First, the cost of coverage for some preexisting conditions will be transferred from one plan or issuer to another.[18] Second, if,

as is likely, a result is movement of workers into more productive jobs, the overall economy will benefit.

It should be noted that the benefits of HIPAA's portability provisions in any given year will be concentrated in a relatively small population—generally, individuals who because of some combination of family health status and use of health services, job mobility, and plan provisions related to preexisting condition exclusions or enrollment opportunities, gain coverage under HIPAA for needed care that would otherwise not be covered.

According to CBO, any point in time, about 100,000 individuals would have a preexisting condition exclusion reduced for prior creditable coverage. An additional 45,000 would gain added coverage in the individual market.[19]

The direct costs of HIPAA's portability provisions generally include the cost of extending coverage to additional services, as well as certain attendant administrative costs. The cost of extended coverage is estimated at $515 million annually. The major administrative costs include the cost of providing certificates of creditable coverage, and possibly the cost of carrying out special enrollments and offsets of preexisting condition exclusion periods. The Departments did not attempt to fully estimate the administrative costs of the HIPAA statute but did, in crafting this regulation, attempt to constrain these costs, where possible, without compromising HIPAA's intent, as discussed below.

The Departments considered the probable incidence of these costs. The Departments believe that by and large the cost of HIPAA, like all of the cost of group health benefits, are borne by covered workers.[20] The most direct

ways this cost can be shifted to workers is through increases in employee premium shares or reductions (or smaller increases) in pay or other components of compensation. Other paths for shifting of HIPAA's cost to workers might include increases in deductibles or other cost sharing, or other reductions in the richness of health benefits.

Whereas the benefits of HIPAA are concentrated in a relatively small population, the costs are distributed broadly across plans and enrollees. The cost for affected large, self-insured or experience rated group plans is spread across all enrollees in the plan. The cost for small insured plans typically is spread across large populations of small plans and their enrollees, partly as a result of State laws that compress small group premium rates.

The Departments have considered whether the costs imposed by HIPAA's statutory portability provisions have had any major indirect negative effects, and concluded that such effects are possible but probably small.

Any mandate to increase the richness or availability of health insurance adds to the cost of insurance. It is possible that some small number of employers already at the brink of affordability would drop coverage in response to the implementation of HIPAA. The number of employers so affected is probably limited in part because as noted above, employers can shift HIPAA's cost to workers in various ways, including through increases in employee premium shares or cost sharing—though such increases might prompt some workers at the margin to decline coverage. Economic literature provides some estimates of the responsiveness of employers and workers to increases in the price of insurance.[21]

---

crediting prior coverage against current exclusions will account for a third of the cost. This estimate is based on two components: (1) The number of people who would receive some added coverage, and (2) the additional full-year cost of coverage, adjusted to reflect the estimated number of months of that coverage.

[17] Findings on the effect of health insurance coverage on job mobility have been mixed. A thorough assessment of the job lock literature in the past 10 years concluded that the most convincing evidence suggests that health insurance plays an important role in job mobility decisions, but is unclear as to its implications (see Gruber, Jonathan and Brigitte C. Madrian, 2002, Health Insurance, Labor Supply and Job Mobility: A Critical Review of the Literature, NBER Working Paper Series, No. 8817). A major concern in this literature has been to find an identification strategy able to overcome the potential correlation between the holding of employer-sponsored health insurance and other factors affecting job mobility independent from health insurance (see Anna Sanz de Galdeano, 2004. Health Insurance and Job Mobility: Evidence from Clinton's Second Mandate, Center for Studies in Economics and Finance Working Paper, No. 122). This is illustrated by the 2004 Health Confidence Survey which finds that 27 percent of the non-aged population reported that they or an immediate family member had experienced some form of job lock, but only 15 percent of those attributed the job-lock to a preexisting condition (see Ruth Helman & Paul Frostin, "Public Attitudes on the U.S. Health Care System: Findings from the Health Confidence Survey." Employee Benefits Research Institute, Issue Brief no. 275 (EBRI, November 2004)).

[18] This transfer generally implies offsetting costs and benefits. It is possible, however, that in some instances individuals' mobility will allow them to exploit opportunities for adverse selection by moving into a richer health plan (see Cutler, D. and Reber, S., 1998. Paying for health insurance: the tradeoff between competition and adverse selection. Quarterly Journal of Economics 113, 433–466, and Cutler, D. and Zeckhauser, R. 2000. The anatomy of health insurance, in Culyer, A., Newhouse, J.P. (Eds.), Handbook of Health Economics, Vol. 1A. Elsevier, Amsterdam, pp. 564–629. For a contrasting study see, Pauly, M.V., Mitchell, O. and Zeng, Y. 2004 "Death Spiral Or Euthanasia? The Demise Of Generous Group Health Insurance Coverage" NBER Working Paper No. 10464, for a discussion). Such movements would constitute

extensions of coverage with costs and benefits resembling those of direct extensions of coverage under HIPAA.

[19] Congressional Budget Office, "Estimate of Costs of Private Sector Mandates; Bill Number H.R. 3103, August 1, 1996.

[20] The voluntary nature of the employment-based health benefit system in conjunction with the open and dynamic character of labor markets make explicit as well as implicit negotiations on compensation a key determinant of the prevalence of employee benefits coverage. It is likely that 80% to 100% of the cost of employee benefits is borne by workers through reduced wages (see for example Jonathan Gruber and Alan B. Krueger, "The Incidence of Mandated Employer-Provided Insurance: Lessons from Workers Compensation Insurance," Tax Policy and Economy (1991); Jonathan Gruber, "The Incidence of Mandated Maternity Benefits," American Economic Review, Vol. 84 (June 1994), pp. 622–641; Lawrence H. Summers, "Some Simple Economics of Mandated Benefits," American Economic Review, Vol. 79, No. 2 (May 1989); Louise Sheiner, "Health Care Costs, Wages, and Aging," Federal Reserve Board of

Governors working paper, April 1999; and Edward Montgomery, Kathryn Shaw, and Mary Ellen Benedict, "Pensions and Wages: An Hedonic Price Theory Approach," International Economic Review, Vol. 33 No. 1, Feb. 1992). The prevalence of benefits is therefore largely dependent on the efficacy of this exchange. If workers perceive that there is the potential that value to adjust for this risk. This discount drives a wedge in the compensation negotiation, limiting its efficiency. With workers unwilling to bear the full cost of the benefit, fewer benefits will be provided. To the extent which workers perceive a federal regulation supported by enforcement authority to improve the security and quality of benefits, the differential between the employers' costs and workers' willingness to accept wage offsets is minimized.

[21] Research shows that while the share of employers offering insurance is generally stable and eligibility rates have only declined slightly over time, the overall increase in uninsured workers is due to the decline in worker take-up rates, which workers primarily attribute to cost. Research on

Continued

D. HIPAA Final Rules, Portability, continued

78742 Federal Register / Vol. 69, No. 250 / Thursday, December 30, 2004 / Rules and Regulations

The Departments note, however, that cost increases attributable to HIPAA are not price increases per se but reflect the cost to enrich benefits, implying that negative responses should be smaller than would be expected in connection with pure price increases. The Departments also note that the estimated $515 million cost associated with extensions of coverage under HIPAA amounts to a small fraction of one percent of total expenditures by private group health plans.[22] This compares with average annual group premium growth of 9.4 percent for family coverage between 1996 and 2002.[23] To the extent that such increases are small, they are likely to have a negligible effect on employers' decisions to provide health insurance and in workers' decisions to enroll.

Various other studies to date suggest that any negative indirect effects of HIPAA are relatively minor. In one study,[24] large employers and health benefit consultants reported few ongoing problems in adopting HIPAA's portability provisions. Many issuers interviewed for the report said that their plans tended to require few changes to comply with HIPAA. This is probably because many large employer plans had already incorporated portability protections, similar to those of HIPAA. A second study indicates that while the share of small firms (those with fewer than 200 workers) offering health insurance has increased slightly from 1996 to 2004, the share has drifted downward from its high of 68 percent

in the economic boom year of 2000.[25] In addition, in aggregate, employers covered a larger proportion of health care costs for family plans in 2002 than in 1996, with a slight decrease in the share of single plans over the same time period.[26]

The data above suggest that the HIPAA changes may have been less significant in the decision about health insurance coverage than overall economic conditions and labor market forces. In fact, there is no evidence that any indirect economic effect, positive or negative, can be readily attributed to the statute. Therefore, it appears that HIPAA has not placed an unreasonable burden on health plans.

There has been a significant decrease in the prevalence of preexisting condition exclusion clauses among large plans. A major employee benefits survey[27] reported that in 1996, 59 percent of the employees in small firms (less than 200 employees) were subject to pre-existing condition limitations. In 2002, the figure had dropped to 33 percent. If preexisting condition limitation exists for new employees, the average number of months to wait before coverage declined from 10.7 months in 1996 to 10.0 months in 2002. A discussion of results from a 1998 version of the same survey noted that, overall, 42 percent of employers reported making changes to their plans' preexisting condition clauses due to HIPAA. The Departments are not aware of any surveys that have consistently tracked the prevalence of preexisting condition exclusions in smaller plans (less than 200 employees) since 1996.

Another significant trend involves the use of waiting periods. According to a survey of employers with 200 or more employees, the average number of days that new enrollees must wait before health coverage takes effect increased from 40 days in 1996 to 58 days in 1998. Some attribute this increase indirectly to HIPAA, suggesting that some plans may be replacing the preexisting condition exclusion period with a longer waiting period.

Effects of the Final Regulations

By clarifying and securing HIPAA's statutory portability protections, these regulations will help ensure that HIPAA rights are fully realized. The result is likely to be a small increase at the

margin in the direct and indirect economic effects of HIPAA's statutory portability provisions.

Additional economic benefits derive from the regulations' clarifications of HIPAA's portability requirements. The regulations provide clarity through both their provisions and their examples of how those provisions apply in various circumstances. By clarifying employees' rights and plan sponsors' obligations under HIPAA's portability provisions, the regulations will reduce uncertainty and costly disputes over these rights and obligations. They will promote employers' and employees' common understanding of the value of group health plan benefits and confidence in the security and predictability of those benefits, thereby improving labor market efficiency and fostering the establishment and continuation of group health plans by employers.

Many provisions of the final regulations closely resemble provisions included in the interim final regulations that the final regulations supplant. The economic impact of this regulatory action therefore generally will be limited to the impact of provisions that were not so included. These include both provisions directed at the scope of HIPAA's portability protections and provisions establishing administrative requirements intended to safeguard those protections.

Scope of Protections

These final regulations are intended to secure and implement HIPAA's group market portability provisions under certain special circumstances. The final regulations therefore contain a number of provisions intended to clearly delimit the scope of HIPAA's portability protections. Most of these provisions closely resemble and will have the same effect as provisions of the interim final regulations. Others, however, clarify or expand at the margin the range of situations to which HIPAA's portability protections explicitly apply. These include the requirement that health coverage under foreign government programs be treated as creditable coverage for purposes of limiting the application of preexisting condition exclusions; the extension of special enrollment rights to individuals who lose eligibility for coverage in connection with the application of lifetime benefit limits, movement out of an HMO's service area, or the termination of a health coverage option previously offered under a group health plan; and the establishment of a special enrollment right for a participant to change among available coverage options under a group health plan when

---

elasticity of coverage, however, has focused on getting uninsured workers to adopt coverage (which appears to require large subsidies) rather than covered workers opting out of coverage. This makes it difficult to ascertain the loss in coverage that would result from a marginal increase in costs. (See, for example, David M. Cutler "Employee Costs and the Decline in Health Insurance Coverage" NBER Working Paper #9036, July 2002; Gruber, Jonathon and Ebonya Washington. "Subsidies to Employee Health Insurance Premiums and the Health Insurance Market" NBER Working Paper #9567, March 2003; and Cooper, PF and J. Vistnes. "Workers' Decisions to Take-up Offered Insurance Coverage: Assessing the Importance of Out-of-Pocket Costs" Med Care 2003, 41(7 Suppl): III35–43.) Finally, economic discussions on elasticity of insurance tend to view coverage as a discrete concept and does not consider that the value of coverage may have also changed.

[22] While these costs are expected in aggregate to be less than one percent of total expenditures by group health plans, the statute may disproportionately affect particular plans.

[23] This is the average annual rate of increase in total family premiums as reported in the Medical Expenditure Panel Survey, Insurance Component (MEPS-IC) public tables, 1996–2002.

[24] U.S. General Accounting Office, Report HEH-99–100, "Private Health Insurance: Progress and Challenges in Implementing 1996 Federal Standards," pp. 6–7, May 1999.

[25] Gabel, Jon R. et al. "Health Benefits in 2004: Four Years of Double Digit Premium Increases Take Their Toll on Coverage" Health Affairs, Volume 23, Number 5, September/October 2004.

[26] As reported in the MEPS-IC 1996–2002 public tables.

[27] Employee Health Benefits 2002 Study, Kaiser Family Foundation.

D. HIPAA Final Rules, Portability, continued

adding one or more dependents in connection with marriage, adoption, or placement for adoption. Each of these provisions is expected to result in a small increase in the economic effects of HIPAA's statutory portability protections.

The Departments lack any firm basis for quantifying the number of individuals likely to be affected by these provisions, and therefore were unable to quantify the resultant increase in transfers. However, given the special and narrow circumstances to which these provisions apply, the number of affected individuals, and therefore the increase in transfers under these regulations, is expected to be small. In reaching this conclusion, the Departments considered the following.

In 2002, an estimated 359,000 employer sponsored insurance enrollees had moved from abroad in the previous year.[28] It is not known what fraction of these had been covered under foreign government programs, or of those, what fraction joined group health plans that included preexisting condition exclusions while suffering from and requiring additional care for preexisting conditions. Comparing GAO's estimate of the number of individuals who could potentially benefit from HIPAA's portability protections (20 million or more individuals with prior creditable coverage who join new health plans in a given year) with CBO estimates of the number who might actually have added coverage for needed care (145,000) produces a ratio of about 1 percent. If this proportion holds for group health plan enrollees who moved to the U.S. from abroad, and if all such enrollees were previously covered under a foreign government program (an upper bound), then about 4,000 individuals annually might gain coverage for needed care under the final regulation's provision treating coverage under such programs as creditable coverage.[29]

The provision that clarifies the special enrollment rights of individuals who lose eligibility for coverage in connection with the movement out of an HMO's service area is expected mainly to benefit certain individuals with COBRA continuation coverage. The number of individuals affected in any given year is expected to be small. It is estimated that in 2002, fewer than 10,000 COBRA enrollees were covered by HMOs, moved across State or county lines, and were potentially eligible for

coverage under another family member's group plan.[30]

Lifetime benefit limits (LBL) are fairly common in-group health plans and are typically set at $1 million or more.[31] Based on tabulations made by an actuarial consulting firm,[32] in plans with LBLs of $1 million, annually about 27 per one million enrollees will exceed the benefit limits. In plans with a $500,000 LBL, the comparable figure is 181 per million enrollees; and in plans with a $2 million LBL, 5 per million enrollees. Combining these proportions with a distribution of LBLs by plan enrollment reported by a national employer survey, yields about 8,700 plan enrollees who will annually reach their plan's LBL. The Departments recognize that those individuals who do encounter such limits by definition have very high expenses, a large portion of which would be transferred to the group health plans into which they special enroll. It is possible, however, that a large share of such transfers would have occurred even without the provisions of these final regulations establishing a right to special enroll upon encountering lifetime limits. For example, the same individuals might have enrolled in these plans during open enrollment opportunities, either before or after encountering the limits. Alternatively, participants who have met their LBL might have left their jobs in order to create a special enrollment opportunity.

The Departments estimate that annually about 1 million families will be eligible for special enrollments due to marriage, 2 million due to births. About one-half of employees offered coverage at work have a choice of plan options.[33] Taken together, this suggests that the number of individuals gaining special enrollment rights to switch among options within group health plans when adding dependents may be large. However, it is unclear how many will elect to switch, or how many who do would have been so permitted even absent the applicable requirement of

these final regulations. More important, it is unclear whether merely switching among options will increase or decrease the transfer from the affected health plans to the affected individuals. In any event, individuals exercising this special enrollment right to switch options are not gaining coverage under any particular group health plan but are merely modifying that coverage.

Administrative Requirements

In order to secure and implement HIPAA's group market special enrollment and portability provisions, both the HIPAA statute and these final regulations establish certain administrative requirements. As noted above, the HIPAA statute generally requires plans and issuers to provide certifications of prior coverage to individuals leaving coverage. These regulations additionally require plans and issuers to notify individuals of their special enrollments rights, any preexisting condition exclusion provisions, and the applicability of such exclusions where individuals provide evidence of prior coverage that is of insufficient duration to fully offset exclusion periods. Plans will incur cost to comply with these administrative requirements. The Departments estimate the administrative cost to prepare and distribute certifications and notices to be $97 million per year.[34]

Nearly all of this, or $96 million, is attributable to the preparation and distribution of certifications as required under HIPAA's statutory provisions. These final regulations include numerous special provisions that serve to reduce plans' cost of providing certifications. These provisions serve to streamline and standardize certifications' content and format, minimize the number of duplicative certifications issued, and encourage the use of telephone calls and other modes of communication when they will suffice in lieu of written certifications. The provisions are designed to minimize certifications' cost while ensuring that individuals and plans (respectively) can efficiently and effectively demonstrate and verify prior coverage. Demonstration and verification of prior coverage enable individuals to secure and plans to

---

[28] Calculation from the 2003 March CPS.

[29] This number is 1 percent of the number of ESI holders in 2002 who moved from abroad the previous year.

[30] Estimates using the March 2003 CPS. It should be noted that CPS is a weighted survey and that the number of actual observations of individuals that were COBRA enrollees with HMO coverage, moved across counties and/or States and were eligible for coverage under another family member's group plan was extremely small. As a result, this estimate is extremely noisy.

[31] See, for example, U.S. Bureau of Labor Statistics. *Employee Benefits in Medium and Large Establishments, 2000* (Washington, DC: U.S. Government Printing Office, 2003).

[32] Milliman USA memorandum dated December 6, 2001.

[33] Sally Trude, "Who Has A Choice of Health Plans?" Center for Studying Health Systems Change, *Issue Brief: Findings from HSC*, No. 27, Feb. 2000.

[34] The Departments assumed that a clerical-level employee at a total labor cost (wages, fringe benefits, and overhead) of $17.24 per-hour would generate the certificates. The Departments further assumed that the average time required to complete a certification is 4 to 5 minutes for all employers. This average is based on the assumption that most employers will automate the certification process. The cost of printing/copying, an envelope and postage is assumed to be $0.53 per employee.

D. HIPAA Final Rules, Portability, continued

appropriately honor individuals' portability rights under HIPAA.

First, an intermediate issuer will not have to issue a certificate of creditable coverage when an individual changes options under the same health plan. In lieu of the certificate, the issuer could simply transmit to the plan information regarding individuals' effective date of coverage and the last date of coverage. An individual would retain the right to get a certificate automatically and upon request if he/she leaves the plan.

Second, telephonic certification will fulfill the requirement to send a certificate if the receiving plan, prior plan, and the participant mutually agree to that arrangement. The individual can get a written certificate upon request.

Third, in situations where the issuer and the plan contract for the issuer to complete the certificates, the plan would not remain liable even if the issuer failed to send the certificates.

Fourth, the period of coverage listed on automatic certificates will be only the last continuous period of coverage without any break. This is the most efficient and simplest method of record keeping for plans and issuers.

Fifth, the period of coverage contained in the on-request certification will be all periods of coverage ending within 24 months before the date of the request. Essentially, a plan may simply look back two years and send copies of any automatic certificates issued during that period.

Sixth, a single certificate of creditable coverage can be provided with respect to both a participant and the participant's dependent if the information is identical for each individual. In addition, certificates may contain combined information for families.

Seventh, plans and issuers are not required to furnish an individual an automatic certificate with respect to a dependent until they know or should know of the dependent's cessation of coverage under the plan.

The above reductions in burdens on plans and issuers may cause more frequent circumstances in which participants are required to demonstrate creditable coverage. In order to help offset some of the additional burdens that will be shifted to the participants, the regulations provide the following protections:

First, if an individual is required to demonstrate dependent status, the group health plan or issuer is required to treat the individual as having furnished a certificate showing the dependent status if the individual attests to such dependency and the period of dependent status, and the

individual cooperates with the plan's or issuer's efforts to verify the dependent status.

Second, if the accuracy of a certificate is contested or a certificate is unavailable when needed, individuals have the right to demonstrate creditable coverage through the presentation of relevant corroborating evidence of creditable coverage during the relevant time period and by cooperating with the plan's efforts to verify the individual's coverage.

Third, plans and issuers that impose preexisting condition exclusion periods must notify participants of this fact. They must also explain that prior creditable coverage can reduce the length of a preexisting condition exclusion period, and that the plan or issuer will assist in obtaining a certificate of creditable coverage from any prior plan or issuer, if necessary. An exclusion may not be imposed until this notice is given. This is beneficial to participants insofar as it forewarns them of potential claim denials and enables them to more easily exercise their right to protection from such denials under HIPAA's portability provisions.

Fourth, after an individual has presented evidence of creditable coverage, the plan or issuer must give the individual a written notice of the length of any preexisting condition exclusion that remains after offsetting for creditable coverage.

Fifth, certificates of creditable coverage now contain educational language that more explicitly informs consumers of their HIPAA rights.

As noted earlier in this preamble, GAO and others recommended that educational statements be added to certifications. The Departments have provided a suitable statement for use by plans, thereby eliminating any need for plans to develop their own. The cost of providing such statements is therefore expected to be minimal.

The administrative cost associated with provision of certifications under the HIPAA statute and these final regulations was estimated as follows.

The ongoing burden associated with the issuance of automatic certifications by group plans is estimated as a function of (1) the number of events that trigger such issuances; (2) the statutory and regulatory specifications for the content of the certificates; and (3) the assumed burden associated with the preparation and distribution of each certificate.

Certifications must be issued when an event, defined as the loss of health coverage by a participant or by a dependent, occurs. Survey tabulations indicate that there were 54.3 million

events in 2002.[35] Additionally, results from the March 1999 CPS indicate that about 3 percent of the events involve a dependent who lives at a different address than the participant. In such cases the plan is required to send out at least 2 separate certificates.

The model certificate illustrates how plans may incur a lesser burden when it is certified that prior periods of coverage were of at least 18 months duration; that is, in lieu of a specific date that coverage began and waiting/affiliation period information, such certifications may simply indicate that the prior period of coverage lasted at least 18 months. In contrast, certifications of shorter periods of prior coverage must contain the specific dates when coverage—and waiting/affiliation periods, if applicable—began.

Combining the options for the addresses with the time periods results in four categories of certifications: (1) One address and less than 18 months of prior creditable coverage (12 million annual events); (2) one address and 18 months or more of prior creditable coverage (42.3 million); (3) more than one address and prior creditable coverage of less than 18 months (.4 million); and (4) more than one address and 18 months or more of prior creditable coverage (1.3 million).

Consistent with the interim regulations, we assume that the per-certificate preparation effort requires 5 minutes for prior creditable coverage of less than 18 months and 4 minutes for creditable coverage that is greater than or equal to 18 months. The additional cost involved in sending certificates to multiple addresses for a given participant is assumed to be 50 percent of the cost of sending a certificate to one address.

The Departments assumed that the certificates would be generated by a clerical-level employee who costs the plans $17.24 per-hour in wages, benefits, and overhead [36]. The cost of printing/copying, envelope and postage is assumed to be $0.53 per envelope.

[35] This total is based on internal estimates. The ESI total (24.0 million and 20.4 private-sector and 3.6 public sector) was the sum of policy-holders who left jobs, according to the 2002 MEPS-HC, and their dependents, which were derived by multiplying this number by the CPS ratio of dependents to policy holders. Based on counts of the number of people with partial year coverage off the March 2003 CPS, we estimated the SCHIP and Medicaid total to be 14.9 million and the private individual market to be 15.4 million.

[36] The total labor cost is derived from wage and compensation data from the Bureau of Labor Statistics and includes an overhead componenet, which is a multiple of compensation based on the Government Cost Estimate.

D. HIPAA Final Rules, Portability, continued

The resulting annual burden is $96 million.

A more strict interpretation of the statute would require plans to send an individual certificate to each affected enrollee. Obviously, this requirement would significantly increase the administrative burden. Such strict interpretation would result in plans sending 80.1 million certificates annually at cost of $157.6 million, which is $61.6 million more than the burden imposed by the final regulations.

The final regulations require that plans, in response to requests made by or on behalf of individuals, provide certificates at any time while the individual is covered under the plan and for up to 24 months after coverage ceases. Such requests are most likely to be made by an individual who is unable to locate the certificate of creditable coverage from his/her prior health plan and is seeking to enroll in a group health plan that imposes preexisting condition exclusions or is seeking to reduce or eliminate any preexisting condition exclusions that may otherwise be applied by a source of individual coverage.

The Departments believe that the requested certificate burden is negligible for several reasons. First, as reported by a major health benefits survey [37] the proportion of enrollees that are in plans with preexisting condition exclusion has not changed from the 2000 share of 30 percent, which is down from the pre-HIPAA level of 60 percent. In addition, the educational statement contained within the certificate serves to highlight the importance of the document, thus encouraging its retention. Furthermore, the final rules permit individuals to establish and verify creditable coverage through other means. Finally, evidence of creditable coverage may be transmitted through means other than documentation, such as by a telephone call from the plan to a third party.

Apart from the provision of certifications of prior creditable coverage, the remaining $1 million in administrative expenses is attributable to notices of special enrollment rights and of the existence and application of preexisting condition exclusions, which are required under these final regulations. The Departments believe that these notices are necessary to ensure that individuals understand and can effectively exercise their special enrollment and portability rights under HIPAA, and that the benefits of ensuring

[37] Kaiser Family Foundation and Health Research and Educational Trust, Employer Health Benefits 2002 Annual Survey.

this outweigh the associated administrative cost.

The regulations provide that a plan must provide all employees with a notice describing special enrollment rights at or before the time the employee is initially offered the opportunity to enroll in the plan. The final regulations provide model language that can be used to satisfy the special enrollment notice requirement.

The Departments believe that the vast majority of plans have incorporated special enrollment language into their plan enrollment materials. Thus, the cost of the special enrollment notice is assumed to be a minor component of the overall cost of providing plan enrollment materials.

The number of employees who are hired annually by firms that offer health coverage and who are eligible for such coverage was developed by using the proportion of workers with less than one year of tenure as reported by the 2002 MEPS–HC. We find that 10.8 million employees will be newly hired and eligible for health coverage on an annual basis. We assume that the special enrollment notice is a component of plan enrollment materials and requires one-third of a sheet of paper. Using a printing/copying cost of $0.05 per page, we assume that the per-notice cost is $0.0167. The resulting burden is estimated to be $180,687.

The final regulations provide that every plan with a preexisting condition exclusion must provide in writing a general notice of such provisions to individuals eligible for enrollment under the plan. The regulations specify what is required of the plan when it discusses the amount and terms of its preexisting condition exclusion, including the person to contact for further information regarding the exclusions. In addition, the regulations clarify that issuers must describe the actual maximum exclusion period that is applicable to a specific plan. A regulatory example provides sample language that the plans can use to develop the general notice.

Based on results from the 2000 Kaiser/HRET Employer survey, we assume that 35 percent of plans with fewer than 100 participants, and 28 percent of plans with 100 or more participants, apply preexisting condition exclusions to new enrollees. If we apply these proportions to the number of new employees hired each year by employers that offer health coverage, we find that 3.1 million employees will annually receive the general notice.

As with the special enrollment notice, we assume that the general notice of

preexisting condition exclusions is a component of standard plan enrollment materials and also requires one-third of a sheet of paper. Assuming a printing/copying cost of $0.05 per page, the per-notice cost is $0.0167. The annual cost to distribute the notices is therefore estimated to be $51,852.

The regulations provide sample notice language, thus relieving the plans of the burden of developing their own forms.

Plans that impose preexisting condition exclusions must, in writing, notify participants who have failed to demonstrate sufficient prior coverage that the exclusions will affect them and indicate what the length of the preexisting condition exclusion period is, with respect to each individual. This notice is required only in situations in which the individual presents evidence of prior creditable coverage and its duration is less than the maximum length of the preexisting condition exclusion period. These final regulations clarify that the notice does not have to identify any medical conditions that are specific to the individual and subject to the exclusion.

Tabulations from the 2002 MEPS–HC indicate that, of those individuals in the private sector who changed jobs and hold insurance, 16 percent have prior creditable coverage of between 1 day and 12 months, which is the statutory preexisting condition exclusion maximum for individuals who enroll when first eligible. The comparable proportion for State and local governmental plans is 18 percent. Applying these proportion to the number of general preexisting exclusion notices required, yields 478,569 notices that will be prepared annually.

Because the notice must be customized to reflect each individual's applicable preexisting condition exclusion period, the per-notice time burden will be greater than that for the general notice of preexisting condition exclusions. Consistent with the interim final regulations, the Departments assume that the preparation of each notice will take two minutes of a clerical-level employee's time, plus $0.47 for printing, envelope, and postage, yielding a per-notice cost of $1.05. The resulting annual burden is estimated to be $582,497.

The estimated burden represents only the cost of producing and distributing the notices and does not include the expense involved in determining the adequacy of a participant's prior coverage, since such expense is considered to be part of the regular business practices necessary to comply with HIPAA's statutory portability protections.

D. HIPAA Final Rules, Portability, continued

78746 Federal Register / Vol. 69, No. 250 / Thursday, December 30, 2004 / Rules and Regulations

Generally all of the major administrative requirements included in the final regulations were also included in the interim final regulations. The final regulations make minor additions to two requirements, however. They require plans to include educational statements in certificates of creditable coverage and to maintain in writing their procedures for requesting certificates. The cost of these additional requirements is expected to be small, and was not estimated separately from the overall cost of providing certificates.

The requirement that certification request procedures be in writing is essentially a clarification of the interim final regulations' requirement that plans have such procedures. The Departments believe it is likely that most plans already maintain written procedures, and therefore expect the cost of this requirement to be small. The Departments did not estimate the cost of this requirement separately from the cost of providing certifications on request.

Other changes included in these final regulations are likely to slightly reduce plans' cost to provide certain HIPAA-required notices. Included with the final regulation is new sample language for general and specific notices of preexisting condition exclusions, which may serve to reduce some plans' costs of providing these notices, and revised sample language for special enrollment rights notices. The final regulations also clarify the narrow scope of the requirement to notify certain affected participants of the specific application of preexisting condition exclusions, thereby potentially relieving some plans of the burden associated with a more expansive interpretation of that requirement. The Departments did not estimate the impact of these provisions separately from the overall cost of providing general and specific notices of preexisting condition exclusions and notices of special enrollment rights.

Statutory Authority

The Department of the Treasury final rule is adopted pursuant to the authority contained in sections 7805 and 9833 of the Code (26 U.S.C. 7805, 9833).

The Department of Labor final rule is adopted pursuant to the authority contained in 29 U.S.C. 1027, 1059, 1135, 1161–1168, 1169, 1181–1183, 1181 note, 1185, 1185a, 1185b, 1191, 1191a, 1191b, and 1191c, sec. 101(g), Public Law 104–191, 101 Stat. 1936; sec. 401(b), Public Law 105–200, 112 Stat. 645 (42 U.S.C. 651 note); Secretary of Labor's Order 1–2003, 68 FR 5374 (Feb. 3, 2003).

The Department of HHS final rule is adopted pursuant to the authority

contained in sections 2701 through 2763, 2791, and 2792 of the PHS Act (42 U.S.C. 300gg through 300gg–63, 300gg–91, and 300gg–92), as added by HIPAA (Public Law 104–191, 110 Stat. 1936), and amended by MHPA and NMHPA (Public Law 104–204, 110 Stat. 2935), and WHCRA (Public Law 105–277, 112 Stat. 2681–436).

List of Subjects

26 CFR Part 54

Excise taxes, Health care, Health insurance, Pensions, Reporting and recordkeeping requirements.

26 CFR Part 602

Reporting and recordkeeping requirements.

29 CFR Part 2590

Continuation coverage, Disclosure, Employee benefit plans, Group health plans, Health care, Health insurance, Medical child support, Reporting and recordkeeping requirements.

45 CFR Parts 144 and 146

Health care, Health insurance, Reporting and recordkeeping requirements, and State regulation of health insurance.

Adoption of Amendments to the Regulations

Internal Revenue Service

26 CFR Chapter I

■ Accordingly, 26 CFR parts 54 and 602 are amended as follows:

PART 54—PENSION EXCISE TAXES

■ Paragraph 1. The authority citation for part 54 is amended by:
■ 1. Removing the citations for 54.9801–1T, 54.9801–2T, 54.9801–3T, 54.9801–4T, 54.9801–5T, 54.9801–6T, 54.9831–1T, and 54.9833–1T.
■ 2. Adding entries in numerical order for 54.9801–1, 54.9801–2, 54.9801–3, 54.9801–4, 54.9801–5, 54.9801–6, 54.9802–1, 54.9831–1, and 54.9833–1. The additions read as follows:

Authority: 26 U.S.C. 7805. * * *

Section 54.9801–1 also issued under 26 U.S.C. 9833.
Section 54.9801–2 also issued under 26 U.S.C. 9833.
Section 54.9801–3 also issued under 26 U.S.C. 9801(c)(4), 9801(e)(3), and 9833.
Section 54.9801–4 also issued under 26 U.S.C. 9801(c)(1)(I) and 9833.
Section 54.9801–5 also issued under 26 U.S.C. 9801(c)(4), 9801(e)(3), and 9833.
Section 54.9801–6 also issued under 26 U.S.C. 9833.
Section 54.9802–1 also issued under 26 U.S.C. 9833. * * *
Section 54.9831–1 also issued under 26 U.S.C. 9833.

Section 54.9833–1 also issued under 26 U.S.C. 9833.

■ Par. 2. Sections 54.9801–1T, 54.9801–2T, 54.9801–3T, 54.9801–4T, 54.9801–5T, 54.9801–6T, 54.9831–1T, and 54.9833–1T are removed.
■ Par. 3. Sections 54.9801–1, 54.9801–2, 54.9801–3, 54.9801–4, 54.9801–5, 54.9801–6, 54.9831–1, and 54.9833–1 are added to read as follows:

§ 54.9801–1 Basis and scope.

(a) *Statutory basis.* Sections 54.9801–1 through 54.9801–6, 54.9802–1, 54.9802–1T, 54.9811–1T, 54.9812–1T, 54.9831–1, and 54.9833–1 (portability sections) implement Chapter 100 of Subtitle K of the Internal Revenue Code of 1986.

(b) *Scope.* A group health plan may provide greater rights to participants and beneficiaries than those set forth in these portability sections. These portability sections set forth minimum requirements for group health plans concerning:

(1) Limitations on a preexisting condition exclusion period.

(2) Certificates and disclosure of previous coverage.

(3) Rules relating to creditable coverage.

(4) Special enrollment periods.

(5) Prohibition against discrimination on the basis of health factors.

(c) *Similar requirements under the Employee Retirement Income Security Act and the Public Health Service Act.* Sections 701, 702, 703, 711, 712, 732, and 733 of the Employee Retirement Income Security Act of 1974 and sections 2701, 2702, 2704, 2705, 2721, and 2791 of the Public Health Service Act impose requirements similar to those imposed under Chapter 100 of Subtitle K with respect to health insurance issuers offering group health insurance coverage. See 29 CFR part 2590 and 45 CFR parts 144, 146, and 148. See also part B of Title XXVII of the Public Health Service Act and 45 CFR part 148 for other rules applicable to health insurance offered in the individual market (defined in § 54.9801–2).

§ 54.9801–2 Definitions.

Unless otherwise provided, the definitions in this section govern in applying the provisions of §§ 54.9801–1 through 54.9801–6, 54.9802–1, 54.9802–1T, 54.9811–1T, 54.9812–1T, 54.9831–1, and 54.9833–1.

Affiliation period means a period of time that must expire before health insurance coverage provided by an HMO becomes effective, and during which the HMO is not required to provide benefits.

D. HIPAA Final Rules, Portability, continued

Federal Register / Vol. 69, No. 250 / Thursday, December 30, 2004 / Rules and Regulations 78747

COBRA definitions:

(1) *COBRA* means Title X of the Consolidated Omnibus Budget Reconciliation Act of 1985, as amended.

(2) *COBRA continuation coverage* means coverage, under a group health plan, that satisfies an applicable COBRA continuation provision.

(3) *COBRA continuation provision* means section 4980B (other than paragraph (f)(1) of section 4980B insofar as it relates to pediatric vaccines), sections 601–608 of ERISA, or Title XXII of the PHS Act.

(4) *Exhaustion of COBRA continuation coverage* means that an individual's COBRA continuation coverage ceases for any reason other than either failure of the individual to pay premiums on a timely basis, or for cause (such as making a fraudulent claim or an intentional misrepresentation of a material fact in connection with the plan). An individual is considered to have exhausted COBRA continuation coverage if such coverage ceases—

(i) Due to the failure of the employer or other responsible entity to remit premiums on a timely basis;

(ii) When the individual no longer resides, lives, or works in the service area of an HMO or similar program (whether or not within the choice of the individual) and there is no other COBRA continuation coverage available to the individual; or

(iii) When the individual incurs a claim that would meet or exceed a lifetime limit on all benefits and there is no other COBRA continuation coverage available to the individual.

Condition means a *medical condition*.

Creditable coverage means *creditable coverage* within the meaning of § 54.9801–4(a).

Dependent means any individual who is or may become eligible for coverage under the terms of a group health plan because of a relationship to a participant.

Employee Retirement Income Security Act of 1974 (ERISA) means the Employee Retirement Income Security Act of 1974, as amended (29 U.S.C. 1001 et seq.).

Enroll means to become covered for benefits under a group health plan (that is, when coverage becomes effective), without regard to when the individual may have completed or filed any forms that are required in order to become covered under the plan. For this purpose, an individual who has health coverage under a group health plan is enrolled in the plan regardless of whether the individual elects coverage, the individual is a dependent who becomes covered as a result of an election by a participant, or the individual becomes covered without an election.

Enrollment date definitions (enrollment date, first day of coverage, and waiting period) are set forth in § 54.9801–3(a)(3)(i), (ii), and (iii).

Excepted benefits means the benefits described as excepted in § 54.9831(c).

Genetic information means information about genes, gene products, and inherited characteristics that may derive from the individual or a family member. This includes information regarding carrier status and information derived from laboratory tests that identify mutations in specific genes or chromosomes, physical medical examinations, family histories, and direct analysis of genes or chromosomes.

Group health insurance coverage means health insurance coverage offered in connection with a group health plan.

Group health plan or *plan* means a group health plan within the meaning of § 54.9831(a).

Group market means the market for health insurance coverage offered in connection with a group health plan. (However, certain very small plans may be treated as being in the *individual market*, rather than the group market; see the definition of individual market in this section.)

Health insurance coverage means benefits consisting of medical care (provided directly, through insurance or reimbursement, or otherwise) under any hospital or medical service policy or certificate, hospital or medical service plan contract, or HMO contract offered by a health insurance issuer. Health insurance coverage includes group health insurance coverage, individual health insurance coverage, and short-term, limited-duration insurance. However, benefits described in § 54.9831(c)(2) are not treated as benefits consisting of medical care.

Health insurance issuer or *issuer* means an insurance company, insurance service, or insurance organization (including an HMO) that is required to be licensed to engage in the business of insurance in a State and that is subject to State law that regulates insurance (within the meaning of section 514(b)(2) of ERISA). Such term does not include a group health plan.

Health maintenance organization or *HMO* means—

(1) A federally qualified health maintenance organization (as defined in section 1301(a) of the PHS Act);

(2) An organization recognized under State law as a health maintenance organization; or

(3) A similar organization regulated under State law for solvency in the same manner and to the same extent as such a health maintenance organization.

Individual health insurance coverage means health insurance coverage offered to individuals in the individual market, but does not include short-term, limited-duration insurance. Individual health insurance coverage can include dependent coverage.

Individual market means the market for health insurance coverage offered to individuals other than in connection with a group health plan. Unless a State elects otherwise in accordance with section 2791(e)(1)(B)(ii) of the PHS Act, such term also includes coverage offered in connection with a group health plan that has fewer than two participants who are current employees on the first day of the plan year.

Issuer means a *health insurance issuer*.

Late enrollment definitions (late enrollee and late enrollment) are set forth in § 54.9801–3(a)(3)(v) and (vi).

Medical care has the meaning given such term by section 213(d), determined without regard to section 213(d)(1)(C) and so much of section 213(d)(1)(D) as relates to qualified long-term care insurance.

Medical condition or *condition* means any condition, whether physical or mental, including, but not limited to, any condition resulting from illness, injury (whether or not the injury is accidental), pregnancy, or congenital malformation. However, genetic information is not a condition.

Participant means *participant* within the meaning of section 3(7) of ERISA.

Placement, or being placed, for adoption means the assumption and retention of a legal obligation for total or partial support of a child by a person with whom the child has been placed in anticipation of the child's adoption. The child's placement for adoption with such person ends upon the termination of such legal obligation.

Plan year means the year that is designated as the plan year in the plan document of a group health plan, except that if the plan document does not designate a plan year or if there is no plan document, the plan year is—

(1) The deductible or limit year used under the plan;

(2) If the plan does not impose deductibles or limits on a yearly basis, then the plan year is the policy year;

(3) If the plan does not impose deductibles or limits on a yearly basis, and either the plan is not insured or the insurance policy is not renewed on an annual basis, then the plan year is the employer's taxable year; or

D. HIPAA Final Rules, Portability, continued

78748 Federal Register / Vol. 69, No. 250 / Thursday, December 30, 2004 / Rules and Regulations

(4) In any other case, the plan year is the calendar year.

Preexisting condition exclusion means *preexisting condition exclusion* within the meaning of § 54.9801–3(a)(1).

Public health plan means *public health plan* within the meaning of § 54.9801–4(a)(1)(ix).

Public Health Service Act (PHS Act) means the Public Health Service Act (42 U.S.C. 201, *et seq.*).

Short-term, limited-duration insurance means health insurance coverage provided pursuant to a contract with an issuer that has an expiration date specified in the contract (taking into account any extensions that may be elected by the policyholder without the issuer's consent) that is less than 12 months after the original effective date of the contract.

Significant break in coverage means a *significant break in coverage* within the meaning of § 54.9801–4(b)(2)(iii).

Special enrollment means enrollment in a group health plan under the rights described in § 54.9801–6 or in group health insurance coverage under the rights described in 29 CFR 2590.701–6 or 45 CFR 146.117.

State health benefits risk pool means a *State health benefits risk pool* within the meaning of § 54.9801–4(a)(1)(vii).

Waiting period means *waiting period* within the meaning of § 54.9801–3(a)(3)(iii).

§ 54.9801–3 Limitations on preexisting condition exclusion period.

(a) *Preexisting condition exclusion—* (1) *Defined—*(i) A *preexisting condition exclusion* means a limitation or exclusion of benefits relating to a condition based on the fact that the condition was present before the effective date of coverage under a group health plan or group health insurance coverage, whether or not any medical advice, diagnosis, care, or treatment was recommended or received before that day. A preexisting condition exclusion includes any exclusion applicable to an individual as a result of information relating to an individual's health status before the individual's effective date of coverage under a group health plan or group health insurance coverage, such as a condition identified as a result of a pre-enrollment questionnaire or physical examination given to the individual, or review of medical records relating to the pre-enrollment period.

(ii) *Examples.* The rules of this paragraph (a)(1) are illustrated by the following examples:

Example 1. (i) *Facts.* A group health plan provides benefits solely through an insurance policy offered by Issuer *S.* At the expiration of the policy, the plan switches coverage to a policy offered by Issuer *T.* Issuer *T*'s policy excludes benefits for any prosthesis if the body part was lost before the effective date of coverage under the policy.

(ii) *Conclusion.* In this *Example 1,* the exclusion of benefits for any prosthesis if the body part was lost before the effective date of coverage is a preexisting condition exclusion because it operates to exclude benefits for a condition based on the fact that the condition was present before the effective date of coverage under the policy. (Therefore, the exclusion of benefits is required to comply with the limitations on preexisting condition exclusions in this section. For an example illustrating the application of these limitations to a succeeding insurance policy, see *Example 3* of paragraph (a)(3)(iv) of this section.)

Example 2. (i) *Facts.* A group health plan provides coverage for cosmetic surgery in cases of accidental injury, but only if the injury occurred while the individual was covered under the plan.

(ii) *Conclusion.* In this *Example 2,* the plan provision excluding cosmetic surgery benefits for individuals injured before enrolling in the plan is a preexisting condition exclusion because it operates to exclude benefits relating to a condition based on the fact that the condition was present before the effective date of coverage. The plan provision, therefore, is subject to the limitations on preexisting condition exclusions in this section.

Example 3. (i) *Facts.* A group health plan provides coverage for the treatment of diabetes, generally not subject to any lifetime dollar limit. However, if an individual was diagnosed with diabetes before the effective date of coverage under the plan, diabetes coverage is subject to a lifetime limit of $10,000.

(ii) *Conclusion.* In this *Example 3,* the $10,000 lifetime limit is a preexisting condition exclusion because it limits benefits for a condition based on the fact that the condition was present before the effective date of coverage. The plan provision, therefore, is subject to the limitations on preexisting condition exclusions in this section.

Example 4. (i) *Facts.* A group health plan provides coverage for the treatment of acne, subject to a lifetime limit of $2,000. The plan counts against this $2,000 lifetime limit on acne treatment benefits provided under prior health coverage.

(ii) *Conclusion.* In this *Example 4,* counting benefits for a specific condition provided under prior health coverage against a lifetime limit for that condition is a preexisting condition exclusion because it operates to limit benefits for a condition based on the fact that the condition was present before the effective date of coverage. The plan provision, therefore, is subject to the limitations on preexisting condition exclusions in this section.

Example 5. (i) *Facts.* When an individual's coverage begins under a group health plan, the individual generally becomes eligible for all benefits. However, benefits for pregnancy are not available until the individual has been covered under the plan for 12 months.

(ii) *Conclusion.* In this *Example 5,* the requirement to be covered under the plan for 12 months to be eligible for pregnancy benefits is a subterfuge for a preexisting condition exclusion because it is designed to exclude benefits for a condition (pregnancy) that arose before the effective date of coverage. Because a plan is prohibited under paragraph (b)(5) of this section from imposing any preexisting condition exclusion on pregnancy, the plan provision is prohibited. However, if the plan provision included an exception for women who were pregnant before the effective date of coverage under the plan (so that the provision applied only to women who became pregnant on or after the effective date of coverage) the plan provision would not be a preexisting condition exclusion (and would not be prohibited by paragraph (b)(5) of this section).

Example 6. (i) *Facts.* A group health plan provides coverage for medically necessary items and services, generally including treatment of heart conditions. However, the plan does not cover those same items and services when used for treatment of congenital heart conditions.

(ii) *Conclusion.* In this *Example 6,* the exclusion of coverage for treatment of congenital heart conditions is a preexisting condition exclusion because it operates to exclude benefits relating to a condition based on the fact that the condition was present before the effective date of coverage. The plan provision, therefore, is subject to the limitations on preexisting condition exclusions in this section.

Example 7. (i) *Facts.* A group health plan generally provides coverage for medically necessary items and services. However, the plan excludes coverage for the treatment of cleft palate.

(ii) *Conclusion.* In this *Example 7,* the exclusion of coverage for treatment of cleft palate is not a preexisting condition exclusion because the exclusion applies regardless of when the condition arose relative to the effective date of coverage. The plan provision, therefore, is not subject to the limitations on preexisting condition exclusions in this section.

Example 8. (i) *Facts.* A group health plan provides coverage for treatment of cleft palate, but only if the individual being treated has been continuously covered under the plan from the date of birth.

(ii) *Conclusion.* In this *Example 8,* the exclusion of coverage for treatment of cleft palate for individuals who have not been covered under the plan from the date of birth operates to exclude benefits in relation to a condition based on the fact that the condition was present before the effective date of coverage. The plan provision, therefore, is subject to the limitations on preexisting condition exclusions in this section.

(2) *General rules.* Subject to paragraph (b) of this section (prohibiting the imposition of a preexisting condition exclusion with respect to certain individuals and conditions), a group health plan may impose, with respect to a participant or beneficiary, a preexisting condition exclusion only if the requirements of this paragraph (a)(2) are satisfied. (*See* section 701 of ERISA

D. HIPAA Final Rules, Portability, continued

and section 2701 of the PHS Act, under which these requirements are also imposed on a health insurance issuer offering group health insurance coverage.)

(i) *6-month look-back rule.* A preexisting condition exclusion must relate to a condition (whether physical or mental), regardless of the cause of the condition, for which medical advice, diagnosis, care, or treatment was recommended or received within the 6-month period (or such shorter period as applies under the plan) ending on the enrollment date.

(A) For purposes of this paragraph (a)(2)(i), medical advice, diagnosis, care, or treatment is taken into account only if it is recommended by, or received from, an individual licensed or similarly authorized to provide such services under State law and operating within the scope of practice authorized by State law.

(B) For purposes of this paragraph (a)(2)(i), the 6-month period ending on the enrollment date begins on the 6-month anniversary date preceding the enrollment date. For example, for an enrollment date of August 1, 1998, the 6-month period preceding the enrollment date is the period commencing on February 1, 1998 and continuing through July 31, 1998. As another example, for an enrollment date of August 30, 1998, the 6-month period preceding the enrollment date is the period commencing on February 28, 1998 and continuing through August 29, 1998.

(C) The rules of this paragraph (a)(2)(i) are illustrated by the following examples:

Example 1. (i) *Facts.* Individual A is diagnosed with a medical condition 8 months before A's enrollment date in Employer R's group health plan. A's doctor recommends that A take a prescription drug for 3 months, and A follows the recommendation.

(ii) *Conclusion.* In this *Example 1,* Employer R's plan may impose a preexisting condition exclusion with respect to A's condition because A received treatment during the 6-month period ending on A's enrollment date in Employer R's plan by taking the prescription medication during that period. However, if A did not take the prescription drug during the 6-month period, Employer R's plan would not be able to impose a preexisting condition exclusion with respect to that condition.

Example 2. (i) *Facts.* Individual B is treated for a medical condition 7 months before the enrollment date in Employer S's group health plan. As part of such treatment, B's physician recommends that a follow-up examination be given 2 months later. Despite this recommendation, B does not receive a follow-up examination, and no other medical advice, diagnosis, care, or treatment for that

condition is recommended to B or received by B during the 6-month period ending on B's enrollment date in Employer S's plan.

(ii) *Conclusion.* In this *Example 2,* Employer S's plan may not impose a preexisting condition exclusion with respect to the condition for which B received treatment 7 months prior to the enrollment date.

Example 3. (i) *Facts.* Same facts as *Example 2,* except that Employer S's plan learns of the condition and attaches a rider to B's certificate of coverage excluding coverage for the condition. Three months after enrollment, B's condition recurs, and Employer S's plan denies payment under the rider.

(ii) *Conclusion.* In this *Example 3,* the rider is a preexisting condition exclusion and Employer S's plan may not impose a preexisting condition exclusion with respect to the condition for which B received treatment 7 months prior to the enrollment date. (In addition, such a rider would violate the provisions of § 54.9802-1, even if B had received treatment for the condition within the 6-month period ending on the enrollment date.)

Example 4. (i) *Facts.* Individual C has asthma and is treated for that condition several times during the 6-month period before C's enrollment date in Employer T's plan. Three months after the enrollment date, C begins coverage under Employer T's plan. Two months later, C is hospitalized for asthma.

(ii) *Conclusion.* In this *Example 4,* Employer T's plan may impose a preexisting condition exclusion with respect to C's asthma because care relating to C's asthma was received during the 6-month period ending on C's enrollment date (which, under the rules of paragraph (a)(3)(i) of this section, is the first day of the waiting period).

Example 5. (i) *Facts.* Individual D, who is subject to a preexisting condition exclusion imposed by Employer U's plan, has diabetes, as well as retinal degeneration, a foot condition, and poor circulation (all of which are conditions that may be directly attributed to diabetes). D receives treatment for these conditions during the 6-month period ending on D's enrollment date in Employer U's plan. After enrolling in the plan, D stumbles and breaks a leg.

(ii) *Conclusion.* In this *Example 5,* the leg fracture is not a condition related to D's diabetes, retinal degeneration, foot condition, or poor circulation, even though they may have contributed to the accident. Therefore, benefits to treat the leg fracture cannot be subject to a preexisting condition exclusion. However, any additional medical services that may be needed because of D's preexisting diabetes, poor circulation, or retinal degeneration that would not be needed by another patient with a broken leg who does not have these conditions may be subject to the preexisting condition exclusion imposed under Employer U's plan.

(ii) *Maximum length of preexisting condition exclusion.* A preexisting condition exclusion is not permitted to extend for more than 12 months (18 months in the case of a late enrollee)

after the enrollment date. For example, for an enrollment date of August 1, 1998, the 12-month period after the enrollment date is the period commencing on August 1, 1998 and continuing through July 31, 1999; the 18-month period after the enrollment date is the period commencing on August 1, 1998 and continuing through January 31, 2000.

(iii) *Reducing a preexisting condition exclusion period by creditable coverage—*(A) The period of any preexisting condition exclusion that would otherwise apply to an individual under a group health plan is reduced by the number of days of creditable coverage the individual has as of the enrollment date, as counted under § 54.9801-4. Creditable coverage may be evidenced through a certificate of creditable coverage (required under § 54.9801-5(a)), or through other means in accordance with the rules of § 54.9801-5(c).

(B) The rules of this paragraph (a)(2)(iii) are illustrated by the following example:

Example. (i) *Facts.* Individual D works for Employer X and has been covered continuously under X's group health plan. D's spouse works for Employer Y. Y maintains a group health plan that imposes a 12-month preexisting condition exclusion (reduced by creditable coverage) on all new enrollees. D enrolls in Y's plan, but also stays covered under X's plan. D presents Y's plan with evidence of creditable coverage under X's plan.

(ii) *Conclusion.* In this *Example,* Y's plan must reduce the preexisting condition exclusion period that applies to D by the number of days of coverage that D had under X's plan as of D's enrollment date in Y's plan (even though D's coverage under X's plan was continuing as of that date).

(iv) *Other standards.* See § 54.9802-1 for other standards that may apply with respect to certain benefit limitations or restrictions under a group health plan. Other laws may also apply, such as the Uniformed Services Employment and Reemployment Rights Act (USERRA), which can affect the application of a preexisting condition exclusion to certain individuals who are reinstated in a group health plan following active military service.

(3) *Enrollment definitions—*(i) *Enrollment date* means the first day of coverage (as described in paragraph (a)(3)(ii) of this section) or, if there is a waiting period, the first day of the waiting period. If an individual receiving benefits under a group health plan changes benefit packages, or if the plan changes group health insurance issuers, the individual's enrollment date does not change.

D. HIPAA Final Rules, Portability, continued

(ii) *First day of coverage* means, in the case of an individual covered for benefits under a group health plan, the first day of coverage under the plan and, in the case of an individual covered by health insurance coverage in the individual market, the first day of coverage under the policy or contract.

(iii) *Waiting period* means the period that must pass before coverage for an employee or dependent who is otherwise eligible to enroll under the terms of a group health plan can become effective. If an employee or dependent enrolls as a late enrollee or special enrollee, any period before such late or special enrollment is not a waiting period. If an individual seeks coverage in the individual market, a waiting period begins on the date the individual submits a substantially complete application for coverage and ends on —

(A) If the application results in coverage, the date coverage begins;

(B) If the application does not result in coverage, the date on which the application is denied by the issuer or the date on which the offer of coverage lapses.

(iv) The rules of paragraphs (a)(3)(i), (ii), and (iii) of this section are illustrated by the following examples:

Example 1. (i) *Facts.* Employer V's group health plan provides for coverage to begin on the first day of the first payroll period following the date an employee is hired and completes the applicable enrollment forms, or on any subsequent January 1 after completion of the applicable enrollment forms. Employer V's plan imposes a preexisting condition exclusion for 12 months (reduced by the individual's creditable coverage) following an individual's enrollment date. Employee E is hired by Employer V on October 13, 1998, and on October 14, 1998 E completes and files all the forms necessary to enroll in the plan. E's coverage under the plan becomes effective on October 25, 1998 (which is the beginning of the first payroll period after E's date of hire).

(ii) *Conclusion.* In this *Example 1*, E's enrollment date is October 13, 1998 (which is the first day of the waiting period for E's enrollment and is also E's date of hire). Accordingly, with respect to E, the permissible 6-month period in paragraph (a)(2)(i) is the period from April 13, 1998 through October 12, 1998, the maximum permissible period during which Employer V's plan can apply a preexisting condition exclusion under paragraph (a)(2)(ii) is the period from October 13, 1998 through October 12, 1999, and this period must be reduced under paragraph (a)(2)(iii) by E's days of creditable coverage as of October 13, 1998.

Example 2. (i) *Facts.* A group health plan has two benefit package options, Option 1 and Option 2. Under each option a 12-month preexisting condition exclusion is imposed. Individual B is enrolled in Option 1 on the first day of employment with the employer maintaining the plan, remains enrolled in Option 1 for more than one year, and then decides to switch to Option 2 at open season.

(ii) *Conclusion.* In this *Example 2*, B cannot be subject to any preexisting condition exclusion under Option 2 because any preexisting condition exclusion period would have to begin on B's enrollment date, which is B's first day of coverage, rather than the date that B enrolled in Option 2. Therefore, the preexisting condition exclusion period expired before B switched to Option 2.

Example 3. (i) *Facts.* On May 13, 1997, Individual E is hired by an employer and enrolls in the employer's group health plan. The plan provides benefits solely through an insurance policy offered by Issuer S. On December 27, 1998, E's leg is injured in an accident and the leg is amputated. On January 1, 1999, the plan switches coverage to a policy offered by Issuer T. Issuer T's policy excludes benefits for any prosthesis if the body part was lost before the effective date of coverage under the policy.

(ii) *Conclusion.* In this *Example 3*, E's enrollment date is May 13, 1997, E's first day of coverage. Therefore, the permissible 6-month look-back period for the preexisting condition exclusion imposed under Issuer T's policy begins on November 13, 1996 and ends on May 12, 1997. In addition, the 12-month maximum permissible preexisting condition exclusion period begins on May 13, 1997 and ends on May 12, 1998. Accordingly, because no medical advice, diagnosis, care, or treatment was recommended to or received by E for the leg during the 6-month look-back period (even though medical care was provided within the 6-month period preceding the effective date of E's coverage under Issuer T's policy), the plan may not impose any preexisting condition exclusion with respect to E. Moreover, even if E had received treatment during the 6-month look-back period, the plan still would not be permitted to impose a preexisting condition exclusion because the 12-month maximum permissible preexisting condition exclusion period expired on May 12, 1998 (before the effective date of E's coverage under Issuer T's policy). See 29 CFR 2590.701–3(a)(3)(iv) *Example 3* and 45 CFR 146.111(a)(3)(iv) *Example 3* for a conclusion that Issuer T is similarly prohibited from imposing a preexisting condition exclusion with respect to E.

Example 4. (i) *Facts.* A group health plan limits eligibility for coverage to full-time employees of Employer Y. Coverage becomes effective on the first day of the month following the date the employee becomes eligible. Employee C begins working full-time for Employer Y on April 11. Prior to this date, C worked part-time for Y. C enrolls in the plan and coverage is effective May 1.

(ii) *Conclusion.* In this *Example 4*, C's enrollment date is April 11 and the period from April 11 through April 30 is a waiting period. The period while C was working part-time, and therefore not in an eligible class of employees, is not part of the waiting period.

Example 5. (i) *Facts.* To be eligible for coverage under a multiemployer group health plan in the current calendar quarter, the plan requires an individual to have worked 250 hours in covered employment during the previous quarter. If the hours requirement is satisfied, coverage becomes effective on the first day of the current calendar quarter. Employee D begins work on January 28 and does not work 250 hours in covered employment during the first quarter (ending March 31). D works at least 250 hours in the second quarter (ending June 30) and is enrolled in the plan with coverage effective July 1 (the first day of the third quarter).

(ii) *Conclusion.* In this *Example 5*, D's enrollment date is the first day of the quarter during which D satisfies the hours requirement, which is April 1. The period from April 1 through June 30 is a waiting period.

(v) *Late enrollee* means an individual whose enrollment in a plan is a late enrollment.

(vi) (A) *Late enrollment* means enrollment of an individual under a group health plan other than—

(1) On the earliest date on which coverage can become effective for the individual under the terms of the plan; or

(2) Through special enrollment. (For rules relating to special enrollment, see § 54.9801–6.)

(B) If an individual ceases to be eligible for coverage under the plan, and then subsequently becomes eligible for coverage under the plan, only the individual's most recent period of eligibility is taken into account in determining whether the individual is a late enrollee under the plan with respect to the most recent period of coverage. Similar rules apply if an individual again becomes eligible for coverage following a suspension of coverage that applied generally under the plan.

(vii) *Examples.* The rules of paragraphs (a)(3)(v) and (vi) of this section are illustrated by the following examples:

Example 1. (i) *Facts.* Employee F first becomes eligible to be covered by Employer W's group health plan on January 1, 1999 but elects not to enroll in the plan until a later annual open enrollment period, with coverage effective January 1, 2001. F has no special enrollment right at that time.

(ii) *Conclusion.* In this *Example 1*, F is a late enrollee with respect to F's coverage that became effective under the plan on January 1, 2001.

Example 2. (i) *Facts.* Same facts as *Example 1*, except that F terminates employment with Employer W on July 1, 1999 without having had any health insurance coverage under the plan. F is rehired by Employer W on January 1, 2000 and is eligible for and elects coverage under Employer W's plan effective on January 1, 2000.

(ii) *Conclusion.* In this *Example 2*, F would not be a late enrollee with respect to F's coverage that became effective on January 1, 2000.

D. HIPAA Final Rules, Portability, continued

Federal Register / Vol. 69, No. 250 / Thursday, December 30, 2004 / Rules and Regulations 78751

(b) *Exceptions pertaining to preexisting condition exclusions*—(1) *Newborns*—(i) *In general.* Subject to paragraph (b)(3) of this section, a group health plan may not impose any preexisting condition exclusion on a child who, within 30 days after birth, is covered under any creditable coverage. Accordingly, if a child is enrolled in a group health plan (or other creditable coverage) within 30 days after birth and subsequently enrolls in another group health plan without a significant break in coverage (as described in § 54.9801–4(b)(2)(iii)), the other plan may not impose any preexisting condition exclusion on the child.

(ii) *Examples.* The rules of this paragraph (b)(1) are illustrated by the following examples:

Example 1. (i) *Facts.* Individual *E*, who has no prior creditable coverage, begins working for Employer *W* and has accumulated 210 days of creditable coverage under Employer *W*'s group health plan on the date *E* gives birth to a child. Within 30 days after the birth, the child is enrolled in the plan. Ninety days after the birth, both *E* and the child terminate coverage under the plan. Both *E* and the child then experience a break in coverage of 45 days before *E* is hired by Employer *X* and the two are enrolled in Employer *X*'s group health plan.

(ii) *Conclusion.* In this *Example 1*, because *E*'s child is enrolled in Employer *W*'s plan within 30 days after birth, no preexisting condition exclusion may be imposed with respect to the child under Employer *W*'s plan. Likewise, Employer *X*'s plan may not impose any preexisting condition exclusion on *E*'s child because the child was covered under creditable coverage within 30 days after birth and had no significant break in coverage before enrolling in Employer *X*'s plan. On the other hand, because *E* had only 300 days of creditable coverage prior to *E*'s enrollment date in Employer *X*'s plan, Employer *X*'s plan may impose a preexisting condition exclusion on *E* for up to 65 days (66 days if the 12-month period after *E*'s enrollment date in *X*'s plan includes February 29).

Example 2. (i) *Facts.* Individual *F* is enrolled in a group health plan in which coverage is provided through a health insurance issuer. *F* gives birth. Under State law applicable to the health insurance issuer, health care expenses incurred for the child during the 30 days following birth are covered as part of *F*'s coverage. Although *F* may obtain coverage for the child beyond 30 days by timely requesting special enrollment and paying an additional premium, the issuer is prohibited under State law from recouping the cost of any expenses incurred for the child within the 30-day period if the child is not later enrolled.

(ii) *Conclusion.* In this *Example 2*, the child is covered under creditable coverage within 30 days after birth, regardless of whether the child enrolls as a special enrollee under the plan. Therefore, no preexisting condition exclusion may be imposed on the child unless the child has a significant break in coverage.

(2) *Adopted children.* Subject to paragraph (b)(3) of this section, a group health plan may not impose any preexisting condition exclusion on a child who is adopted or placed for adoption before attaining 18 years of age and who, within 30 days after the adoption or placement for adoption, is covered under any creditable coverage. Accordingly, if a child is enrolled in a group health plan (or other creditable coverage) within 30 days after adoption or placement for adoption and subsequently enrolls in another group health plan without a significant break in coverage (as described in § 54.9801–4(b)(2)(iii)), the other plan may not impose any preexisting condition exclusion on the child. This rule does not apply to coverage before the date of such adoption or placement for adoption.

(3) *Significant break in coverage.* Paragraphs (b)(1) and (2) of this section no longer apply to a child after a significant break in coverage. (See § 54.9801–4(b)(2)(iii) for rules relating to the determination of a significant break in coverage.)

(4) *Special enrollment.* For special enrollment rules relating to new dependents, see § 54.9801–6(b).

(5) *Pregnancy.* A group health plan may not impose a preexisting condition exclusion relating to pregnancy.

(6) *Genetic information*—(i) A group health plan may not impose a preexisting condition exclusion relating to a condition based solely on genetic information. However, if an individual is diagnosed with a condition, even if the condition relates to genetic information, the plan may impose a preexisting condition exclusion with respect to the condition, subject to the other limitations of this section.

(ii) The rules of this paragraph (b)(6) are illustrated by the following example:

Example. (i) *Facts.* Individual *A* enrolls in a group health plan that imposes a 12-month maximum preexisting condition exclusion. Three months before *A*'s enrollment, *A*'s doctor told *A* that, based on genetic information, *A* has a predisposition towards breast cancer. *A* was not diagnosed with breast cancer at any time prior to *A*'s enrollment date in the plan. Nine months after *A*'s enrollment date in the plan, *A* is diagnosed with breast cancer.

(ii) *Conclusion.* In this *Example*, the plan may not impose a preexisting condition exclusion with respect to *A*'s breast cancer because, prior to *A*'s enrollment date, *A* was not diagnosed with breast cancer.

(c) *General notice of preexisting condition exclusion.* A group health plan imposing a preexisting condition

exclusion must provide a written general notice of preexisting condition exclusion to participants under the plan and cannot impose a preexisting condition exclusion with respect to a participant or a dependent of the participant until such a notice is provided. (See 29 CFR 2590.701–3(c) and 45 CFR 146.111(c), which also impose this requirement on a health insurance issuer offering group health insurance coverage subject to a preexisting condition exclusion.)

(1) *Manner and timing.* A plan must provide the general notice of preexisting condition exclusion as part of any written application materials distributed by the plan for enrollment. If the plan does not distribute such materials, the notice must be provided by the earliest date following a request for enrollment that the plan, acting in a reasonable and prompt fashion, can provide the notice.

(2) *Content.* The general notice of preexisting condition exclusion must notify participants of the following:

(i) The existence and terms of any preexisting condition exclusion under the plan. This description includes the length of the plan's look-back period (which is not to exceed 6 months under paragraph (a)(2)(i) of this section); the maximum preexisting condition exclusion period under the plan (which cannot exceed 12 months (or 18 months for late enrollees) under paragraph (a)(2)(ii) of this section); and how the plan will reduce the maximum preexisting condition exclusion period by creditable coverage (described in paragraph (a)(2)(iii) of this section).

(ii) A description of the rights of individuals to demonstrate creditable coverage, and any applicable waiting periods, through a certificate of creditable coverage (as required by § 54.9801–5(a)) or through other means (as described in § 54.9801–5(c)). This must include a description of the right of the individual to request a certificate from a prior plan or issuer, if necessary, and a statement that the current plan will assist in obtaining a certificate from any prior plan or issuer, if necessary.

(iii) A person to contact (including an address or telephone number) for obtaining additional information or assistance regarding the preexisting condition exclusion.

(3) *Duplicate notices not required.* If a notice satisfying the requirements of this paragraph (c) is provided to an individual by another party, the plan's obligation to provide a general notice of preexisting condition exclusion with respect to that individual is satisfied. (See 29 CFR 2590.701–3(c)(3) and 45 CFR 146.111(c)(3), which provide that

D. HIPAA Final Rules, Portability, continued

the issuer's obligation is similarly satisfied.)

(4) *Example with sample language.* The rules of this paragraph (c) are illustrated by the following example, which includes sample language that plans can use as a basis for preparing their own notices to satisfy the requirements of this paragraph (c):

Example. (i) *Facts.* A group health plan makes coverage effective on the first day of the first calendar month after hire and on each January 1 following an open season. The plan imposes a 12-month maximum preexisting condition exclusion (18 months for late enrollees) and uses a 6-month lookback period. As part of the enrollment application materials, the plan provides the following statement:

This plan imposes a preexisting condition exclusion. This means that if you have a medical condition before coming to our plan, you might have to wait a certain period of time before the plan will provide coverage for that condition. This exclusion applies only to conditions for which medical advice, diagnosis, care, or treatment was recommended or received within a six-month period. Generally, this six-month period ends the day before your coverage becomes effective. However, if you were in a waiting period for coverage, the six-month period ends on the day before the waiting period begins. The preexisting condition exclusion does not apply to pregnancy nor to a child who is enrolled in the plan within 30 days after birth, adoption, or placement for adoption.

This exclusion may last up to 12 months (18 months if you are a late enrollee) from your first day of coverage, or, if you were in a waiting period, from the first day of your waiting period. However, you can reduce the length of this exclusion period by the number of days of your prior "creditable coverage." Most prior health coverage is creditable coverage and can be used to reduce the preexisting condition exclusion if you have not experienced a break in coverage of at least 63 days. To reduce the 12-month (or 18-month) exclusion period by your creditable coverage, you should give us a copy of any certificates of creditable coverage you have. If you do not have a certificate, but you do have prior health coverage, we will help you obtain one from your prior plan or issuer. There are also other ways that you can show you have creditable coverage. Please contact us if you need help demonstrating creditable coverage.

All questions about the preexisting condition exclusion and creditable coverage should be directed to Individual *B* at Address *M* or Telephone Number *N*.

(ii) *Conclusion.* In this *Example*, the plan satisfies the general notice requirement of this paragraph (c).

(d) *Determination of creditable coverage*—(1) *Determination within reasonable time.* If a group health plan receives creditable coverage information under § 54.9801–5, the plan is required, within a reasonable time following receipt of the information, to make a determination regarding the amount of the individual's creditable coverage and the length of any exclusion that remains. Whether this determination is made within a reasonable time depends on the relevant facts and circumstances. Relevant facts and circumstances include whether a plan's application of a preexisting condition exclusion would prevent an individual from having access to urgent medical care. (See 29 CFR 2590.701–3(d) and 45 CFR 146.111(d), which also impose this requirement on a health insurance issuer offering group health insurance coverage.)

(2) *No time limit on presenting evidence of creditable coverage.* A plan may not impose any limit on the amount of time that an individual has to present a certificate or other evidence of creditable coverage.

(3) *Example.* The rules of this paragraph (d) are illustrated by the following example:

Example. (i) *Facts.* A group health plan imposes a preexisting condition exclusion period of 12 months. After receiving the general notice of preexisting condition exclusion, Individual *H* develops an urgent health condition before receiving a certificate of creditable coverage from *H*'s prior group health plan. *H* attests to the period of prior coverage, presents corroborating documentation of the coverage period, and authorizes the plan to request a certificate on *H*'s behalf in accordance with the rules of § 54.9801–5.

(ii) *Conclusion.* In this *Example*, the plan must review the evidence presented by *H* and make a determination of creditable coverage within a reasonable time that is consistent with the urgency of *H*'s health condition. (This determination may be modified as permitted under paragraph (f) of this section.)

(e) *Individual notice of period of preexisting condition exclusion.* After an individual has presented evidence of creditable coverage and after the plan has made a determination of creditable coverage under paragraph (d) of this section, the plan must provide the individual a written notice of the length of preexisting condition exclusion that remains after offsetting for prior creditable coverage. This individual notice is not required to identify any medical conditions specific to the individual that could be subject to the exclusion. A plan is not required to provide this notice if the plan does not impose any preexisting condition exclusion on the individual or if the plan's preexisting condition exclusion is completely offset by the individual's prior creditable coverage. (See 29 CFR 2590.701–3(e) and 45 CFR 146.111(e), which also impose this requirement on a health insurance issuer offering group health insurance coverage.)

(1) *Manner and timing.* The individual notice must be provided by the earliest date following a determination that the plan, acting in a reasonable and prompt fashion, can provide the notice.

(2) *Content.* A plan must disclose—

(i) Its determination of any preexisting condition exclusion period that applies to the individual (including the last day on which the preexisting condition exclusion applies);

(ii) The basis for such determination, including the source and substance of any information on which the plan relied;

(iii) An explanation of the individual's right to submit additional evidence of creditable coverage; and

(iv) A description of any applicable appeal procedures established by the plan.

(3) *Duplicate notices not required.* If a notice satisfying the requirements of this paragraph (e) is provided to an individual by another party, the plan's obligation to provide this individual notice of preexisting condition exclusion with respect to that individual is satisfied. (See 29 CFR 2590.701–3(e)(3) and 45 CFR 146.111(e)(3), which provide that the issuer's obligation is similarly satisfied.)

(4) *Examples.* The rules of this paragraph (e) are illustrated by the following examples:

Example 1. (i) *Facts.* A group health plan imposes a preexisting condition exclusion period of 12 months. After receiving the general notice of preexisting condition exclusion, Individual *G* presents a certificate of creditable coverage indicating 240 days of creditable coverage. Within seven days of receipt of the certificate, the plan determines that *G* is subject to a preexisting condition exclusion of 125 days, the last day of which is March 5. Five days later, the plan notifies *G* that, based on the certificate *G* submitted, *G* is subject to a preexisting condition exclusion period of 125 days, ending on March 5. The notice also explains the opportunity to submit additional evidence of creditable coverage and the plan's appeal procedures. The notice does not identify any of *G*'s medical conditions that could be subject to the exclusion.

(ii) *Conclusion.* In this *Example 1*, the plan satisfies the requirements of this paragraph (e).

Example 2. (i) *Facts.* Same facts as in *Example 1*, except that the plan determines that *G* has 430 days of creditable coverage based on *G*'s certificate indicating 430 days of creditable coverage under *G*'s prior plan.

(ii) *Conclusion.* In this *Example 2*, the plan is not required to notify *G* that *G* will not be subject to a preexisting condition exclusion.

(f) *Reconsideration.* Nothing in this section prevents a plan from modifying

D. HIPAA Final Rules, Portability, continued

Federal Register / Vol. 69, No. 250 / Thursday, December 30, 2004 / Rules and Regulations 78753

an initial determination of creditable coverage if it determines that the individual did not have the claimed creditable coverage, provided that—

(1) A notice of the new determination (consistent with the requirements of paragraph (e) of this section) is provided to the individual; and

(2) Until the notice of the new determination is provided, the plan, for purposes of approving access to medical services (such as a pre-surgery authorization), acts in a manner consistent with the initial determination.

§ 54.9801–4 Rules relating to creditable coverage.

(a) *General rules*—(1) *Creditable coverage.* For purposes of this section, except as provided in paragraph (a)(2) of this section, the term *creditable coverage* means coverage of an individual under any of the following:

(i) A group health plan as defined in § 54.9831–1(a).

(ii) Health insurance coverage as defined in § 54.9801–2 (whether or not the entity offering the coverage is subject to Chapter 100 of Subtitle K, and without regard to whether the coverage is offered in the group market, the individual market, or otherwise).

(iii) Part A or B of Title XVIII of the Social Security Act (Medicare).

(iv) Title XIX of the Social Security Act (Medicaid), other than coverage consisting solely of benefits under section 1928 of the Social Security Act (the program for distribution of pediatric vaccines).

(v) Title 10 U.S.C. Chapter 55 (medical and dental care for members and certain former members of the uniformed services, and for their dependents; for purposes of Title 10 U.S.C. Chapter 55, *uniformed services* means the armed forces and the Commissioned Corps of the National Oceanic and Atmospheric Administration and of the Public Health Service).

(vi) A medical care program of the Indian Health Service or of a tribal organization.

(vii) A State health benefits risk pool. For purposes of this section, a *State health benefits risk pool* means—

(A) An organization qualifying under section 501(c)(26);

(B) A qualified high risk pool described in section 2744(c)(2) of the PHS Act; or

(C) Any other arrangement sponsored by a State, the membership composition of which is specified by the State and which is established and maintained primarily to provide health coverage for individuals who are residents of such

State and who, by reason of the existence or history of a medical condition—

(1) Are unable to acquire medical care coverage for such condition through insurance or from an HMO, or

(2) Are able to acquire such coverage only at a rate which is substantially in excess of the rate for such coverage through the membership organization.

(viii) A health plan offered under Title 5 U.S.C. Chapter 89 (the Federal Employees Health Benefits Program).

(ix) A public health plan. For purposes of this section, a public health plan means any plan established or maintained by a State, the U.S. government, a foreign country, or any political subdivision of a State, the U.S. government, or a foreign country that provides health coverage to individuals who are enrolled in the plan.

(x) A health benefit plan under section 5(e) of the Peace Corps Act (22 U.S.C. 2504(e)).

(xi) Title XXI of the Social Security Act (State Children's Health Insurance Program).

(2) *Excluded coverage.* Creditable coverage does not include coverage of solely excepted benefits (described in § 54.9831–1).

(3) *Methods of counting creditable coverage.* For purposes of reducing any preexisting condition exclusion period, as provided under § 54.9801–3(a)(2)(iii), the amount of an individual's creditable coverage generally is determined by using the standard method described in paragraph (b) of this section. A plan may use the alternative method under paragraph (c) of this section with respect to any or all of the categories of benefits described under paragraph (c)(3) of this section or may provide that a health insurance issuer offering health insurance coverage under the plan may use the alternative method of counting creditable coverage.

(b) *Standard method*—(1) *Specific benefits not considered.* Under the standard method, the amount of creditable coverage is determined without regard to the specific benefits included in the coverage.

(2) *Counting creditable coverage*—(i) *Based on days.* For purposes of reducing the preexisting condition exclusion period that applies to an individual, the amount of creditable coverage is determined by counting all the days on which the individual has one or more types of creditable coverage. Accordingly, if on a particular day an individual has creditable coverage from more than one source, all the creditable coverage on that day is counted as one day. Any days in a waiting period for coverage are not creditable coverage.

(ii) *Days not counted before significant break in coverage.* Days of creditable coverage that occur before a significant break in coverage are not required to be counted.

(iii) *Significant break in coverage defined*—A significant break in coverage means a period of 63 consecutive days during each of which an individual does not have any creditable coverage. (*See* section 731(b)(2)(iii) of ERISA and section 2723(b)(2)(iii) of the PHS Act, which exclude from preemption State insurance laws that require a break of more than 63 days before an individual has a significant break in coverage for purposes of State law.)

(iv) *Periods that toll a significant break.* Days in a waiting period and days in an affiliation period are not taken into account in determining whether a significant break in coverage has occurred. In addition, for an individual who elects COBRA continuation coverage during the second election period provided under the Trade Act of 2002, the days between the date the individual lost group health plan coverage and the first day of the second COBRA election period are not taken into account in determining whether a significant break in coverage has occurred.

(v) *Examples.* The rules of this paragraph (b)(2) are illustrated by the following examples:

Example 1. (i) *Facts.* Individual *A* has creditable coverage under Employer *P*'s plan for 18 months before coverage ceases. *A* is provided a certificate of creditable coverage on *A*'s last day of coverage. Sixty-four days after the last date of coverage under *P*'s plan, *a* is hired by Employer *Q* and enrolls in *Q*'s group health plan. *Q*'s plan has a 12-month preexisting condition exclusion.

(ii) *Conclusion.* In this *Example 1*, *A* has a break in coverage of 63 days. Because *A*'s break in coverage is a significant break in coverage, *Q*'s plan may disregard *A*'s prior coverage and *a* may be subject to a 12-month preexisting condition exclusion.

Example 2. (i) *Facts.* Same facts as *Example 1*, except that *A* is hired by *Q* and enrolls in *Q*'s plan on the 63rd day after the last date of coverage under *P*'s plan.

(ii) *Conclusion.* In this *Example 2*, *A* has a break in coverage of 62 days. Because *A*'s break in coverage is not a significant break in coverage, *Q*'s plan must count *A*'s prior creditable coverage for purposes of reducing the plan's preexisting condition exclusion period that applies to *A*.

Example 3. (i) *Facts.* Same facts as *Example 1*, except that *Q*'s plan provides benefits through an insurance policy that, as required by applicable State insurance laws, defines a significant break in coverage as 90 days.

(ii) *Conclusion.* In this *Example 3*, under State law, the issuer that provides group health insurance coverage to *Q*'s plan must count *A*'s period of creditable coverage prior

D. HIPAA Final Rules, Portability, continued

to the 63-day break. (However, if Q's plan was a self-insured plan, the coverage would not be subject to State law. Therefore, the health coverage would not be governed by the longer break rules and A's previous health coverage could be disregarded.)

Example 4. [Reserved]

Example 5. (i) *Facts.* Individual C has creditable coverage under Employer S's plan for 200 days before coverage ceases. C is provided a certificate of creditable coverage on C's last day of coverage. C then does not have any creditable coverage for 51 days before being hired by Employer T. T's plan has a 3-month waiting period. C works for T for 2 months and then terminates employment. Eleven days after terminating employment with T, C begins working for Employer U. U's plan has no waiting period, but has a 6-month preexisting condition exclusion.

(ii) *Conclusion.* In this *Example 5*, C does not have a significant break in coverage because, after disregarding the waiting period under T's plan, C had only a 62-day break in coverage (51 days plus 11 days). accordingly, C has 200 days of creditable coverage, and U's plan may not apply its 6-month preexisting condition exclusion with respect to C.

Example 6. [Reserved]

Example 7. (i) *Facts.* Individual E has creditable coverage under Employer X's plan. E is provided a certificate of creditable coverage on E's last day of coverage. On the 63rd day without coverage, E submits a substantially complete application for a health insurance policy in the individual market. E's application is accepted and coverage is made effective 10 days later.

(ii) *Conclusion.*

In this *Example 7*, because E applied for the policy before the end of the 63rd day, the period between the date of application and the first day of coverage is a waiting period and no significant break in coverage occurred even though the actual period without coverage was 73 days.

Example 8. (i) *Facts.* Same facts as *Example 7*, except that E's application for a policy in the individual market is denied.

(ii) *Conclusion.* In this *Example 8*, even though E did not obtain coverage following application, the period between the date of application and the date the coverage was denied is a waiting period. However, to avoid a significant break in coverage, no later than the day after the application for the policy is denied E would need to do one of the following: submit a substantially complete application for a different individual market policy; obtain coverage in the group market; or be in a waiting period for coverage in the group market.

(vi) *Other permissible counting methods*—(a) *Rule.* Notwithstanding any other provisions of this paragraph (b)(2), for purposes of reducing a preexisting condition exclusion period (but not for purposes of issuing a certificate under § 54.9801–5), a group health plan may determine the amount of creditable coverage in any other manner that is at least as favorable to the individual as the method set forth in

this paragraph (b)(2), subject to the requirements of other applicable law.

(B) *Example.* The rule of this paragraph (b)(2)(vi) is illustrated by the following example:

Example. (i) *Facts.* Individual F has coverage under Group Health Plan Y from January 3, 1997 through March 25, 1997. F then becomes covered by Group Health Plan Z. F's enrollment date in Plan Z is May 1, 1997. Plan Z has a 12-month preexisting condition exclusion.

(ii) *Conclusion.* In this *Example*, Plan Z may determine, in accordance with the rules prescribed in paragraphs (b)(2)(i), (ii), and (iii) of this section, that F has 82 days of creditable coverage (29 days in January, 28 days in February, and 25 days in March). Thus, the preexisting condition exclusion will no longer apply to F on February 8, 1998 (82 days before the 12-month anniversary of F's enrollment (May 1)). For administrative convenience, however, Plan Z may consider that the preexisting condition exclusion will no longer apply to F on the first day of the month (February 1).

(c) *Alternative method*—(1) *Specific benefits considered.* Under the alternative method, a group health plan determines the amount of creditable coverage based on coverage within any category of benefits described in paragraph (c)(3) of this section and not based on coverage for any other benefits. The plan may use the alternative method for any or all of the categories. The plan may apply a different preexisting condition exclusion period with respect to each category (and may apply a different preexisting condition exclusion period for benefits that are not within any category). The creditable coverage determined for a category of benefits applies only for purposes of reducing the preexisting condition exclusion period with respect to that category. An individual's creditable coverage for benefits that are not within any category for which the alternative method is being used is determined under the standard method of paragraph (b) of this section.

(2) *Uniform application.* A plan using the alternative method is required to apply it uniformly to all participants and beneficiaries under the plan. A plan that provides benefits (in part or in whole) through one or more policies or contracts of insurance will not fail the uniform application requirement of this paragraph (c)(2) if the alternative method is used (or not used) separately with respect to participants and beneficiaries under any policy or contact, provided that the alternative method is applied uniformly with respect to all coverage under that policy or contract. The use of the alternative method is required to be set forth in the plan.

(3) *Categories of benefits.* The alternative method for counting creditable coverage may be used for coverage for the following categories of benefits—

(i) Mental health;

(ii) Substance abuse treatment;

(iii) Prescription drugs;

(iv) Dental care; or

(v) Vision care.

(4) *Plan notice.* If the alternative method is used, the plan is required to—

(i) State prominently that the plan is using the alternative method of counting creditable coverage in disclosure statements concerning the plan, and State this to each enrollee at the time of enrollment under the plan; and

(ii) Include in these statements a description of the effect of using the alternative method, including an identification of the categories used.

(5) *Disclosure of information on previous benefits.* See § 54.9801–5(b) for special rules concerning disclosure of coverage to a plan (or issuer) using the alternative method of counting creditable coverage under this paragraph (c).

(6) *Counting creditable coverage*—(i) *In general.* Under the alternative method, the group health plan counts creditable coverage within a category if any level of benefits is provided within the category. Coverage under a reimbursement account or arrangement, such as a flexible spending arrangement (as defined in section 106(c)(2)), does not constitute coverage within any category.

(ii) *Special rules.* In counting an individual's creditable coverage under the alternative method, the group health plan first determines the amount of the individual's creditable coverage that may be counted under paragraph (b) of this section, up to a total of 365 days of the most recent creditable coverage (546 days for a late enrollee). The period over which this creditable coverage is determined is referred to as the determination period. Then, for the category specified under the alternative method, the plan counts within the category all days of coverage that occurred during the determination period (whether or not a significant break in coverage for that category occurs), and reduces the individual's preexisting condition exclusion period for that category by that number of days. The plan may determine the amount of creditable coverage in any other reasonable manner, uniformly applied, that is at least as favorable to the individual.

D. HIPAA Final Rules, Portability, continued

Federal Register / Vol. 69, No. 250 / Thursday, December 30, 2004 / Rules and Regulations   78755

(iii) *Example*. The rules of this paragraph (c)(6) are illustrated by the following example:

Example. (i) *Facts*. Individual *D* enrolls in Employer *V*'s plan on January 1, 2001. Coverage under the plan includes prescription drug benefits. On April 1, 2001, the plan ceases providing prescription drug benefits. *D*'s employment with Employer *V* ends on January 1, 2002, after *D* was covered under Employer *V*'s group health plan for 365 days. *D* enrolls in Employer *Y*'s plan on February 1, 2002 (*D*'s enrollment date). Employer *Y*'s plan uses the alternative method of counting creditable coverage and imposes a 12-month preexisting condition exclusion on prescription drug benefits.

(ii) *Conclusion*. In this *Example*, Employer *Y*'s plan may impose a 275-day preexisting condition exclusion with respect to *D* for prescription drug benefits because *D* had 90 days of creditable coverage relating to prescription drug benefits within *D*'s determination period.

§54.9801–5 Evidence of creditable coverage.

(a) *Certificate of creditable coverage*—(1) *Entities required to provide certificate*—(i) *In general*. A group health plan is required to furnish certificates of creditable coverage in accordance with this paragraph (a). (See section 701(e) of ERISA and section 2701(e) of the PHS Act, under which this obligation is also imposed on each health insurance issuer offering group health insurance coverage under the plan.)

(ii) *Duplicate certificates not required*. An entity required to provide a certificate under this paragraph (a) with respect to an individual satisfies that requirement if another party provides the certificate, but only to the extent that the certificate contains the information required in paragraph (a)(3) of this section. For example, a group health plan is deemed to have satisfied the certification requirement with respect to a participant or beneficiary if any other entity actually provides a certificate that includes the information required under paragraph (a)(3) of this section with respect to the participant or beneficiary.

(iii) *Special rule for group health plans*. To the extent coverage under a plan consists of group health insurance coverage, the plan satisfies the certification requirements under this paragraph (a) if any issuer offering the coverage is required to provide the certificates pursuant to an agreement between the plan and the issuer. For example, if there is an agreement between an issuer and an employer sponsoring a plan under which the issuer agrees to provide certificates for individuals covered under the plan, and the issuer fails to provide a certificate to

an individual when the plan would have been required to provide one under this paragraph (a), then the plan does not violate the certification requirements of this paragraph (a) (though the issuer would have violated the certification requirements pursuant to section 701(e) of ERISA and section 2701(e) of the PHS Act).

(iv) *Special rules relating to issuers providing coverage under a plan*—(A)(1) *Responsibility of issuer for coverage period*. See 29 CFR 2590.701–5 and 45 CFR 146.115, under which an issuer is not required to provide information regarding coverage provided to an individual by another party.

(2) *Example*. The rule referenced by this paragraph (a)(1)(iv)(A) is illustrated by the following example:

Example. (i) *Facts*. A plan offers coverage with an HMO option from one issuer and an indemnity option from a different issuer. The HMO has not entered into an agreement with the plan to provide certificates as permitted under paragraph (a)(1)(iii) of this section.

(ii) *Conclusion*. In this *Example*, if an employee switches from the indemnity option to the HMO option and later ceases to be covered under the plan, any certificate provided by the HMO is not required to provide information regarding the employee's coverage under the indemnity option.

(B)(1) *Cessation of issuer coverage prior to cessation of coverage under a plan*. If an individual's coverage under an issuer's policy or contract ceases before the individual's coverage under the plan ceases, the issuer is required (under section 701(e) of ERISA and section 2701(e) of the PHS Act) to provide sufficient information to the plan (or to another party designated by the plan) to enable the plan (or other party), after cessation of the individual's coverage under the plan, to provide a certificate that reflects the period of coverage under the policy or contract. By providing that information to the plan, the issuer satisfies its obligation to provide an automatic certificate for that period of creditable coverage with respect to the individual under paragraph (a)(2)(ii) of this section. The issuer, however, must still provide a certificate upon request as required under paragraph (a)(2)(iii) of this section. In addition, the issuer is required to cooperate with the plan in responding to any request made under paragraph (b)(2) of this section (relating to the alternative method of counting creditable coverage). Moreover, if the individual's coverage under the plan ceases at the time the individual's coverage under the issuer's policy or contract ceases, the issuer must still provide an automatic certificate under

paragraph (a)(2)(ii) of this section. If an individual's coverage under an issuer's policy or contract ceases on the effective date for changing enrollment options under the plan, the issuer may presume (absent information to the contrary) that the individual's coverage under the plan continues. Therefore, the issuer is required to provide information to the plan in accordance with this paragraph (a)(1)(iv)(B)(1) (and is not required to provide an automatic certificate under paragraph (a)(2)(ii) of this section).

(2) *Example*. The rule of this paragraph (a)(1)(iv)(B) is illustrated by the following example:

Example. (i) *Facts*. A group health plan provides coverage under an HMO option and an indemnity option through different issuers, and only allows employees to switch on each January 1. Neither the HMO nor the indemnity issuer has entered into an agreement with the plan to provide certificates as permitted under paragraph (a)(1)(iii) of this section.

(ii) *Conclusion*. In this *Example*, if an employee switches from the indemnity option to the HMO option on January 1, the indemnity issuer must provide the plan (or a person designated by the plan) with appropriate information with respect to the individual's coverage with the indemnity issuer. However, if the individual's coverage with the indemnity issuer ceases at a date other than January 1, the issuer is instead required to provide the individual with an automatic certificate.

(2) *Individuals for whom certificate must be provided; timing of issuance*—(i) *Individuals*. A certificate must be provided, without charge, for participants or dependents who are or were covered under a group health plan upon the occurrence of any of the events described in paragraph (a)(2)(ii) or (iii) of this section.

(ii) *Issuance of automatic certificates*. The certificates described in this paragraph (a)(2)(ii) are referred to as automatic certificates.

(A) *Qualified beneficiaries upon a qualifying event*. In the case of an individual who is a qualified beneficiary (as defined in section 4980B(g)(3)) entitled to elect COBRA continuation coverage, an automatic certificate is required to be provided at the time the individual would lose coverage under the plan in the absence of COBRA continuation coverage or alternative coverage elected instead of COBRA continuation coverage. A plan satisfies this requirement if it provides the automatic certificate no later than the time a notice is required to be furnished for a qualifying event under section 4980B(f)(6) (relating to notices required under COBRA).

(B) *Other individuals when coverage ceases*. In the case of an individual who

D. HIPAA Final Rules, Portability, continued

is not a qualified beneficiary entitled to elect COBRA continuation coverage, an automatic certificate must be provided at the time the individual ceases to be covered under the plan. A plan satisfies the requirement to provide an automatic certificate at the time the individual ceases to be covered if it provides the automatic certificate within a reasonable time after coverage ceases (or after the expiration of any grace period for nonpayment of premiums).

(1) The cessation of temporary continuation coverage (TCC) under Title 5 U.S.C. Chapter 89 (the Federal Employees Health Benefit Program) is a cessation of coverage upon which an automatic certificate must be provided.

(2) In the case of an individual who is entitled to elect to continue coverage under a State program similar to COBRA and who receives the automatic certificate not later than the time a notice is required to be furnished under the State program, the certificate is deemed to be provided within a reasonable time after coverage ceases under the plan.

(3) If an individual's coverage ceases due to the operation of a lifetime limit on all benefits, coverage is considered to cease for purposes of this paragraph (a)(2)(ii)(B) on the earliest date that a claim is denied due to the operation of the lifetime limit.

(C) *Qualified beneficiaries when COBRA ceases.* In the case of an individual who is a qualified beneficiary and has elected COBRA continuation coverage (or whose coverage has continued after the individual became entitled to elect COBRA continuation coverage), an automatic certificate is to be provided at the time the individual's coverage under the plan ceases. A plan satisfies this requirement if it provides the automatic certificate within a reasonable time after coverage ceases (or after the expiration of any grace period for nonpayment of premiums). An automatic certificate is required to be provided to such an individual regardless of whether the individual has previously received an automatic certificate under paragraph (a)(2)(ii)(A) of this section.

(iii) *Any individual upon request.* A certificate must be provided in response to a request made by, or on behalf of, an individual at any time while the individual is covered under a plan and up to 24 months after coverage ceases. Thus, for example, a plan in which an individual enrolls may, if authorized by the individual, request a certificate of the individual's creditable coverage on behalf of the individual from a plan in which the individual was formerly

enrolled. After the request is received, a plan or issuer is required to provide the certificate by the earliest date that the plan, acting in a reasonable and prompt fashion, can provide the certificate. A certificate is required to be provided under this paragraph (a)(2)(iii) even if the individual has previously received a certificate under this paragraph (a)(2)(iii) or an automatic certificate under paragraph (a)(2)(ii) of this section.

(iv) *Examples.* The rules of this paragraph (a)(2) are illustrated by the following examples:

Example 1. (i) *Facts.* Individual *A* terminates employment with Employer *Q*. *A* is a qualified beneficiary entitled to elect COBRA continuation coverage under Employer *Q's* group health plan. A notice of the rights provided under COBRA is typically furnished to qualified beneficiaries under the plan within 10 days after a covered employee terminates employment.

(ii) *Conclusion.* In this *Example 1*, the automatic certificate may be provided at the same time that *A* is provided the COBRA notice.

Example 2. (i) *Facts.* Same facts as *Example 1*, except that the automatic certificate for *A* is not completed by the time the COBRA notice is furnished to *A*.

(ii) *Conclusion.* In this *Example 2*, the automatic certificate may be provided after the COBRA notice but must be provided within the period permitted by law for the delivery of notices under COBRA.

Example 3. (i) *Facts.* Employer *R* maintains an insured group health plan. *R* has never had 20 employees and thus *R's* plan is not subject to the COBRA continuation provisions. However, *R* is in a State that has a State program similar to COBRA. *B* terminates employment with *R* and loses coverage under *R's* plan.

(ii) *Conclusion.* In this *Example 3*, the automatic certificate must be provided not later than the time a notice is required to be furnished under the State program.

Example 4. (i) *Facts.* Individual *C* terminates employment with Employer *S* and receives both a notice of *C's* rights under COBRA and an automatic certificate. *C* elects COBRA continuation coverage under Employer *S's* group health plan. After four months of COBRA continuation coverage and the expiration of a 30-day grace period, *S's* group health plan determines that *C's* COBRA continuation coverage has ceased due to a failure to make a timely payment for continuation coverage.

(ii) *Conclusion.* In this *Example 4*, the plan must provide an updated automatic certificate to *C* within a reasonable time after the end of the grace period.

Example 5. (i) *Facts.* Individual *D* is currently covered under the group health plan of Employer *T. D* requests a certificate, as permitted under paragraph (a)(2)(iii) of this section. Under the procedure for *T's* plan, certificates are mailed (by first class mail) 7 business days following receipt of the request. This date reflects the earliest date that the plan, acting in a reasonable and prompt fashion, can provide certificates.

(ii) *Conclusion.* In this *Example 5*, the plan's procedure satisfies paragraph (a)(2)(iii) of this section.

(3) *Form and content of certificate*—
(i) *Written certificate*—(A) *In general.* Except as provided in paragraph (a)(3)(i)(B) of this section, the certificate must be provided in writing (including any form approved by the Secretary as a writing).

(B) *Other permissible forms.* No written certificate is required to be provided under this paragraph (a) with respect to a particular event described in paragraph (a)(2)(ii) or (iii) of this section, if—

(1) An individual who is entitled to receive the certificate requests that the certificate be sent to another plan or issuer instead of to the individual;

(2) The plan or issuer that would otherwise receive the certificate agrees to accept the information in this paragraph (a)(3) through means other than a written certificate (such as by telephone); and

(3) The receiving plan or issuer receives the information from the sending plan or issuer through such means within the time required under paragraph (a)(2) of this section.

(ii) *Required information.* The certificate must include the following—
(A) The date the certificate is issued;

(B) The name of the group health plan that provided the coverage described in the certificate;

(C) The name of the participant or dependent with respect to whom the certificate applies, and any other information necessary for the plan providing the coverage specified in the certificate to identify the individual, such as the individual's identification number under the plan and the name of the participant if the certificate is for (or includes) a dependent;

(D) The name, address, and telephone number of the plan administrator or issuer required to provide the certificate;

(E) The telephone number to call for further information regarding the certificate (if different from paragraph (a)(3)(ii)(D) of this section);

(F) Either—
(1) A statement that an individual has at least 18 months (for this purpose, 546 days is deemed to be 18 months) of creditable coverage, disregarding days of creditable coverage before a significant break in coverage, or

(2) The date any waiting period (and affiliation period, if applicable) began and the date creditable coverage began;

(G) The date creditable coverage ended, unless the certificate indicates that creditable coverage is continuing as of the date of the certificate; and

D. HIPAA Final Rules, Portability, continued

(H) An educational statement regarding HIPAA, which explains:

(1) The restrictions on the ability of a plan or issuer to impose a preexisting condition exclusion (including an individual's ability to reduce a preexisting condition exclusion by creditable coverage);

(2) Special enrollment rights;

(3) The prohibitions against discrimination based on any health factor;

(4) The right to individual health coverage;

(5) The fact that State law may require issuers to provide additional protections to individuals in that State; and

(6) Where to get more information.

(iii) *Periods of coverage under the certificate.* If an automatic certificate is provided pursuant to paragraph (a)(2)(ii) of this section, the period that must be included on the certificate is the last period of continuous coverage ending on the date coverage ceased. If an individual requests a certificate pursuant to paragraph (a)(2)(iii) of this section, the certificate provided must include each period of continuous coverage ending within the 24-month period ending on the date of the request (or continuing on the date of the request). A separate certificate may be provided for each such period of continuous coverage.

(iv) *Combining information for families.* A certificate may provide information with respect to both a participant and the participant's dependents if the information is identical for each individual. If the information is not identical, certificates may be provided on one form if the form provides all the required information for each individual and separately states the information that is not identical.

(v) *Model certificate.* The requirements of paragraph (a)(3)(ii) of this section are satisfied if the plan provides a certificate in accordance with a model certificate authorized by the Secretary.

(vi) *Excepted benefits; categories of benefits.* No certificate is required to be furnished with respect to excepted benefits described in § 54.9831–1(c). In addition, the information in the certificate regarding coverage is not required to specify categories of benefits described in § 54.9801–4(c) (relating to the alternative method of counting creditable coverage). However, if excepted benefits are provided concurrently with other creditable coverage (so that the coverage does not consist solely of excepted benefits), information concerning the benefits may be required to be disclosed under paragraph (b) of this section.

(4) *Procedures—(i) Method of delivery.* The certificate is required to be provided to each individual described in paragraph (a)(2) of this section or an entity requesting the certificate on behalf of the individual. The certificate may be provided by first-class mail. If the certificate or certificates are provided to the participant and the participant's spouse at the participant's last known address, then the requirements of this paragraph (a)(4) are satisfied with respect to all individuals residing at that address. If a dependent's last known address is different than the participant's last known address, a separate certificate is required to be provided to the dependent at the dependent's last known address. If separate certificates are being provided by mail to individuals who reside at the same address, separate mailings of each certificate are not required.

(ii) *Procedure for requesting certificates.* A plan or issuer must establish a written procedure for individuals to request and receive certificates pursuant to paragraph (a)(2)(iii) of this section. The written procedure must include all contact information necessary to request a certificate (such as name and phone number or address).

(iii) *Designated recipients.* If an automatic certificate is required to be provided under paragraph (a)(2)(ii) of this section, and the individual entitled to receive the certificate designates another individual or entity to receive the certificate, the plan or issuer responsible for providing the certificate is permitted to provide the certificate to the designated individual or entity. If a certificate is required to be provided upon request under paragraph (a)(2)(iii) of this section and the individual entitled to receive the certificate designates another individual or entity to receive the certificate, the plan or issuer responsible for providing the certificate is required to provide the certificate to the designated individual or entity.

(5) *Special rules concerning dependent coverage—(i)(A) Reasonable efforts.* A plan is required to use reasonable efforts to determine any information needed for a certificate relating to dependent coverage. In any case in which an automatic certificate is required to be furnished with respect to a dependent under paragraph (a)(2)(ii) of this section, no individual certificate is required to be furnished until the plan knows (or making reasonable efforts should know) of the dependent's cessation of coverage under the plan.

(B) *Example.* The rules of this paragraph (a)(5)(i) are illustrated by the following example:

Example. (i) *Facts.* A group health plan covers employees and their dependents. The plan annually requests all employees to provide updated information regarding dependents, including the specific date on which an employee has a new dependent or on which a person ceases to be a dependent of the employee.

(ii) *Conclusion.* In this *Example,* the plan has satisfied the standard in this paragraph (a)(5)(i) of this section that it make reasonable efforts to determine the cessation of dependents' coverage and the related dependent coverage information.

(ii) *Special rules for demonstrating coverage.* If a certificate furnished by a plan or issuer does not provide the name of any dependent covered by the certificate, the procedures described in paragraph (c)(5) of this section may be used to demonstrate dependent status. In addition, these procedures may be used to demonstrate that a child was covered under any creditable coverage within 30 days after birth, adoption, or placement for adoption. See also § 54.9801–3(b), under which such a child cannot be subject to a preexisting condition exclusion.

(6) *Special certification rules for entities not subject to Chapter 100 of Subtitle K—(i) Issuers.* For rules requiring that issuers in the group and individual markets provide certificates consistent with the rules in this section, see section 701(e) of ERISA and sections 2701(e), 2721(b)(1)(B), and 2743 of the PHS Act.

(ii) *Other entities.* For special rules requiring that certain other entities not subject to Chapter 100 of Subtitle K provide certificates consistent with the rules in this section, see section 2791(a)(3) of the PHS Act applicable to entities described in sections 2701(c)(1)(C), (D), (E), and (F) of the PHS Act (relating to Medicare, Medicaid, TRICARE, and Indian Health Service), section 2721(b)(1)(A) of the PHS Act applicable to nonfederal governmental plans generally, and section 2721(b)(2)(C)(ii) of the PHS Act applicable to nonfederal governmental plans that elect to be excluded from the requirements of Subparts 1 through 3 of Part A of Title XXVII of the PHS Act.

(b) *Disclosure of coverage to a plan or issuer using the alternative method of counting creditable coverage—(1) In general.* After an individual provides a certificate of creditable coverage to a plan (or issuer) using the alternative method under § 54.9801–4(c), that plan (or issuer) (requesting entity) must request that the entity that issued the certificate (prior entity) disclose the

D. HIPAA Final Rules, Portability, continued

information set forth in paragraph (b)(2) of this section. The prior entity is required to disclose this information promptly.

(2) *Information to be disclosed.* The prior entity is required to identify to the requesting entity the categories of benefits with respect to which the requesting entity is using the alternative method of counting creditable coverage, and the requesting entity may identify specific information that the requesting entity reasonably needs in order to determine the individual's creditable coverage with respect to any such category.

(3) *Charge for providing information.* The prior entity may charge the requesting entity for the reasonable cost of disclosing such information.

(c) *Ability of an individual to demonstrate creditable coverage and waiting period information*—(1) *Purpose.* The rules in this paragraph (c) implement section 9801(c)(4), which permits individuals to demonstrate the duration of creditable coverage through means other than certificates, and section 9801(e)(3), which requires the Secretary to establish rules designed to prevent an individual's subsequent coverage under a group health plan or health insurance coverage from being adversely affected by an entity's failure to provide a certificate with respect to that individual.

(2) *In general.* If the accuracy of a certificate is contested or a certificate is unavailable when needed by an individual, the individual has the right to demonstrate creditable coverage (and waiting or affiliation periods) through the presentation of documents or other means. For example, the individual may make such a demonstration when—

(i) An entity has failed to provide a certificate within the required time;

(ii) The individual has creditable coverage provided by an entity that is not required to provide a certificate of the coverage pursuant to paragraph (a) of this section;

(iii) The individual has an urgent medical condition that necessitates a determination before the individual can deliver a certificate to the plan; or

(iv) The individual lost a certificate that the individual had previously received and is unable to obtain another certificate.

(3) *Evidence of creditable coverage*—(i) *Consideration of evidence*—(A) A plan is required to take into account all information that it obtains or that is presented on behalf of an individual to make a determination, based on the relevant facts and circumstances, whether an individual has creditable coverage. A plan shall treat the

individual as having furnished a certificate under paragraph (a) of this section if—

(1) The individual attests to the period of creditable coverage;

(2) The individual also presents relevant corroborating evidence of some creditable coverage during the period; and

(3) The individual cooperates with the plan's efforts to verify the individual's coverage.

(B) For purposes of this paragraph (c)(3)(i), cooperation includes providing (upon the plan's or issuer's request) a written authorization for the plan to request a certificate on behalf of the individual, and cooperating in efforts to determine the validity of the corroborating evidence and the dates of creditable coverage. While a plan may refuse to credit coverage where the individual fails to cooperate with the plan's or issuer's efforts to verify coverage, the plan may not consider an individual's inability to obtain a certificate to be evidence of the absence of creditable coverage.

(ii) *Documents.* Documents that corroborate creditable coverage (and waiting or affiliation periods) include explanations of benefits (EOBs) or other correspondence from a plan or issuer indicating coverage, pay stubs showing a payroll deduction for health coverage, a health insurance identification card, a certificate of coverage under a group health insurance policy, records from medical care providers indicating health coverage, third party statements verifying periods of coverage, and any other relevant documents that evidence periods of health coverage.

(iii) *Other evidence.* Creditable coverage (and waiting or affiliation periods) may also be corroborated through means other than documentation, such as by a telephone call from the plan or provider to a third party verifying creditable coverage.

(iv) *Example.* The rules of this paragraph (c)(3) are illustrated by the following example:

Example. (i) *Facts.* Individual *F* terminates employment with Employer *W* and, a month later, is hired by Employer *X*. *X*'s group health plan imposes a preexisting condition exclusion of 12 months on new enrollees under the plan and uses the standard method of determining creditable coverage. *F* fails to receive a certificate of prior coverage from the self-insured group health plan maintained by *F*'s prior employer, *W*, and requests a certificate. However, *F* (and *X*'s plan, on *F*'s behalf and with *F*'s cooperation) is unable to obtain a certificate from *W*'s plan. *F* attests that, to the best of *F*'s knowledge, *F* had at least 12 months of continuous coverage under *W*'s plan, and that the coverage ended no earlier than *F*'s

termination of employment from *W*. In addition, *F* presents evidence of coverage, such as an explanation of benefits for a claim that was made during the relevant period.

(ii) *Conclusion.* In this *Example*, based solely on these facts, *F* has demonstrated creditable coverage for the 12 months of coverage under *W*'s plan in the same manner as if *F* had presented a written certificate of creditable coverage.

(4) *Demonstrating categories of creditable coverage.* Procedures similar to those described in this paragraph (c) apply in order to determine the duration of an individual's creditable coverage with respect to any category under paragraph (b) of this section (relating to determining creditable coverage under the alternative method).

(5) *Demonstrating dependent status.* If, in the course of providing evidence (including a certificate) of creditable coverage, an individual is required to demonstrate dependent status, the group health plan or issuer is required to treat the individual as having furnished a certificate showing the dependent status if the individual attests to such dependency and the period of such status and the individual cooperates with the plan's or issuer's efforts to verify the dependent status.

§54.9801–6 Special enrollment periods.

(a) *Special enrollment for certain individuals who lose coverage*—(1) *In general.* A group health plan is required to permit current employees and dependents (as defined in §54.9801–2) who are described in paragraph (a)(2) of this section to enroll for coverage under the terms of the plan if the conditions in paragraph (a)(3) of this section are satisfied. The special enrollment rights under this paragraph (a) apply without regard to the dates on which an individual would otherwise be able to enroll under the plan. (See section 701(f)(1) of ERISA and section 2701(f)(1) of the PHS Act, under which this obligation is also imposed on a health insurance issuer offering group health insurance coverage.)

(2) *Individuals eligible for special enrollment*—(i) *When employee loses coverage.* A current employee and any dependents (including the employee's spouse) each are eligible for special enrollment in any benefit package under the plan (subject to plan eligibility rules conditioning dependent enrollment on enrollment of the employee) if—

(A) The employee and the dependents are otherwise eligible to enroll in the benefit package;

(B) When coverage under the plan was previously offered, the employee had coverage under any group health plan or health insurance coverage; and

D. HIPAA Final Rules, Portability, continued

(C) The employee satisfies the conditions of paragraph (a)(3)(i), (ii), or (iii) of this section and, if applicable, paragraph (a)(3)(iv) of this section.

(ii) *When dependent loses coverage*—(A) A dependent of a current employee (including the employee's spouse) and the employee each are eligible for special enrollment in any benefit package under the plan (subject to plan eligibility rules conditioning dependent enrollment on enrollment of the employee) if—

(*1*) The dependent and the employee are otherwise eligible to enroll in the benefit package;

(*2*) When coverage under the plan was previously offered, the dependent had coverage under any group health plan or health insurance coverage; and

(*3*) The dependent satisfies the conditions of paragraph (a)(3)(i), (ii), or (iii) of this section and, if applicable, paragraph (a)(3)(iv) of this section.

(B) However, the plan is not required to enroll any other dependent unless that dependent satisfies the criteria of this paragraph (a)(2)(ii), or the employee satisfies the criteria of paragraph (a)(2)(i) of this section.

(iii) *Examples.* The rules of this paragraph (a)(2) are illustrated by the following examples:

Example 1. (i) *Facts.* Individual A works for Employer X. A, A's spouse, and A's dependent children are eligible but not enrolled for coverage under X's group health plan. A's spouse works for Employer Y and at the time coverage was offered under X's plan, A was enrolled in coverage under Y's plan. Then, A loses eligibility for coverage under Y's plan.

(ii) *Conclusion.* In this *Example 1,* because A satisfies the conditions for special enrollment under paragraph (a)(2)(i) of this section, A, A's spouse, and A's dependent children are eligible for special enrollment under X's plan.

Example 2. (i) *Facts.* Individual A and A's spouse are eligible but not enrolled for coverage under Group Health Plan P maintained by A's employer. When A was first presented with an opportunity to enroll A and A's spouse, they did not have other coverage. Later, A and A's spouse enroll in Group Health Plan Q maintained by the employer of A's spouse. During a subsequent open enrollment period in P, A and A's spouse did not enroll because of their coverage under Q. They then lose eligibility for coverage under Q.

(ii) *Conclusion.* In this *Example 2,* because A and A's spouse were covered under Q when they did not enroll in P during open enrollment, they satisfy the conditions for special enrollment under paragraphs (a)(2)(i) and (ii) of this section. Consequently, A and A's spouse are eligible for special enrollment under P.

Example 3. (i) *Facts.* Individual B works for Employer X. B and B's spouse are eligible but not enrolled for coverage under X's group

health plan. B's spouse works for Employer Y and at the time coverage was offered under X's plan, B's spouse was enrolled in self-only coverage under Y's group health plan. Then, B's spouse loses eligibility for coverage under Y's plan.

(ii) *Conclusion.* In this *Example 3,* because B's spouse satisfies the conditions for special enrollment under paragraph (a)(2)(ii) of this section, both B and B's spouse are eligible for special enrollment under X's plan.

Example 4. (i) *Facts.* Individual A works for Employer X. X maintains a group health plan with two benefit packages—an HMO option and an indemnity option. Self-only and family coverage are available under both options. A enrolls for self-only coverage in the HMO option. A's spouse works for Employer Y and was enrolled for self-only coverage under Y's plan at the time coverage was offered under X's plan. Then, A's spouse loses coverage under Y's plan. A requests special enrollment for A and A's spouse under the plan's indemnity option.

(ii) *Conclusion.* In this *Example 4,* because A's spouse satisfies the conditions for special enrollment under paragraph (a)(2)(ii) of this section, both A and A's spouse can enroll in either benefit package under X's plan. Therefore, if A requests enrollment in accordance with the requirements of this section, the plan must allow A and A's spouse to enroll in the indemnity option.

(3) *Conditions for special enrollment*—(i) *Loss of eligibility for coverage.* In the case of an employee or dependent who has coverage that is not COBRA continuation coverage, the conditions of this paragraph (a)(3)(i) are satisfied at the time the coverage is terminated as a result of loss of eligibility (regardless of whether the individual is eligible for or elects COBRA continuation coverage). Loss of eligibility under this paragraph (a)(3)(i) does not include a loss due to the failure of the employee or dependent to pay premiums on a timely basis or termination of coverage for cause (such as making a fraudulent claim or an intentional misrepresentation of a material fact in connection with the plan). Loss of eligibility for coverage under this paragraph (a)(3)(i) includes (but is not limited to)—

(A) Loss of eligibility for coverage as a result of legal separation, divorce, cessation of dependent status (such as attaining the maximum age to be eligible as a dependent child under the plan), death of an employee, termination of employment, reduction in the number of hours of employment, and any loss of eligibility for coverage after a period that is measured by reference to any of the foregoing;

(B) In the case of coverage offered through an HMO, or other arrangement, in the individual market that does not provide benefits to individuals who no longer reside, live, or work in a service area, loss of coverage because an

individual no longer resides, lives, or works in the service area (whether or not within the choice of the individual);

(C) In the case of coverage offered through an HMO, or other arrangement, in the group market that does not provide benefits to individuals who no longer reside, live, or work in a service area, loss of coverage because an individual no longer resides, lives, or works in the service area (whether or not within the choice of the individual), and no other benefit package is available to the individual;

(D) A situation in which an individual incurs a claim that would meet or exceed a lifetime limit on all benefits; and

(E) A situation in which a plan no longer offers any benefits to the class of similarly situated individuals (as described in § 54.9802–1(d)) that includes the individual.

(ii) *Termination of employer contributions.* In the case of an employee or dependent who has coverage that is not COBRA continuation coverage, the conditions of this paragraph (a)(3)(ii) are satisfied at the time employer contributions towards the employee's or dependent's coverage terminate. Employer contributions include contributions by any current or former employer that was contributing to coverage for the employee or dependent.

(iii) *Exhaustion of COBRA continuation coverage.* In the case of an employee or dependent who has coverage that is COBRA continuation coverage, the conditions of this paragraph (a)(3)(iii) are satisfied at the time the COBRA continuation coverage is exhausted. For purposes of this paragraph (a)(3)(iii), an individual who satisfies the conditions for special enrollment of paragraph (a)(3)(i) of this section, does not enroll, and instead elects and exhausts COBRA continuation coverage satisfies the conditions of this paragraph (a)(3)(iii). (*Exhaustion of COBRA continuation coverage* is defined in § 54.9801–2.)

(iv) *Written statement.* A plan may require an employee declining coverage (for the employee or any dependent of the employee) to State in writing whether the coverage is being declined due to other health coverage only if, at or before the time the employee declines coverage, the employee is provided with notice of the requirement to provide the statement (and the consequences of the employee's failure to provide the statement). If a plan requires such a statement, and an employee does not provide it, the plan is not required to provide special enrollment to the employee or any dependent of the

D. HIPAA Final Rules, Portability, continued

employee under this paragraph (a)(3). A plan must treat an employee as having satisfied the plan requirement permitted under this paragraph (a)(3)(iv) if the employee provides a written statement that coverage was being declined because the employee or dependent had other coverage; a plan cannot require anything more for the employee to satisfy the plan's requirement to provide a written statement. (For example, the plan cannot require that the statement be notarized.)

(v) The rules of this paragraph (a)(3) are illustrated by the following examples:

Example 1. (i) *Facts.* Individual *D* enrolls in a group health plan maintained by Employer *Y*. At the time *D* enrolls, *Y* pays 70 percent of the cost of employee coverage and *D* pays the rest. *Y* announces that beginning January 1, *Y* will no longer make employer contributions towards the coverage. Employees may maintain coverage, however, if they pay the total cost of the coverage.

(ii) *Conclusion.* In this *Example 1,* employer contributions towards *D*'s coverage ceased on January 1 and the conditions of paragraph (a)(3)(ii) of this section are satisfied on this date (regardless of whether *D* elects to pay the total cost and continue coverage under *Y*'s plan).

Example 2. (i) *Facts.* A group health plan provides coverage through two options—Option 1 and Option 2. Employees can enroll in either option only within 30 days of hire or on January 1 of each year. Employee *A* is eligible for both options and enrolls in Option 1. Effective July 1 the plan terminates coverage under Option 1 and the plan does not create an immediate open enrollment opportunity into Option 2.

(ii) *Conclusion.* In this *Example 2, A* has experienced a loss of eligibility for coverage that satisfies paragraph (a)(3)(i) of this section, and has satisfied the other conditions for special enrollment under paragraph (a)(2)(i) of this section. Therefore, if *A* satisfies the other conditions of this paragraph (a), the plan must permit *A* to enroll in Option 2 as a special enrollee. (*A* may also be eligible to enroll in another group health plan, such as a plan maintained by the employer of *A*'s spouse, as a special enrollee.) The outcome would be the same if Option 1 was terminated by an issuer and the plan made no other coverage available to *A*.

Example 3. (i) *Facts.* Individual *C* is covered under a group health plan maintained by Employer *X*. While covered under *X*'s plan, *C* was eligible for but did not enroll in a plan maintained by Employer *Z*, the employer of *C*'s spouse. *C* terminates employment with *X* and loses eligibility for coverage under *X*'s plan. *C* has a special enrollment right to enroll in *Z*'s plan, but *C* instead elects COBRA continuation coverage under *X*'s plan. *C* exhausts COBRA continuation coverage under *X*'s plan and requests special enrollment in *Z*'s plan.

(ii) *Conclusion.* In this *Example 3, C* has satisfied the conditions for special enrollment under paragraph (a)(3)(iii) of this section, and has satisfied the other

conditions for special enrollment under paragraph (a)(2)(i) of this section. The special enrollment right that *C* had into *Z*'s plan immediately after the loss of eligibility for coverage under *X*'s plan was an offer of coverage under *Z*'s plan. When *C* later exhausts COBRA coverage under *X*'s plan, *C* has a second special enrollment right in *Z*'s plan.

(4) *Applying for special enrollment and effective date of coverage*—(i) A plan or issuer must allow an employee a period of at least 30 days after an event described in paragraph (a)(3) of this section (other than an event described in paragraph (a)(3)(i)(D)) to request enrollment (for the employee or the employee's dependent). In the case of an event described in paragraph (a)(3)(i)(D) of this section (relating to loss of eligibility for coverage due to the operation of a lifetime limit on all benefits), a plan or issuer must allow an employee a period of at least 30 days after a claim is denied due to the operation of a lifetime limit on all benefits.

(ii) Coverage must begin no later than the first day of the first calendar month beginning after the date the plan or issuer receives the request for special enrollment.

(b) *Special enrollment with respect to certain dependent beneficiaries*—(1) In general. A group health plan that makes coverage available with respect to dependents is required to permit individuals described in paragraph (b)(2) of this section to be enrolled for coverage in a benefit package under the terms of the plan. Paragraph (b)(3) of this section describes the required special enrollment period and the date by which coverage must begin. The special enrollment rights under this paragraph (b) apply without regard to the dates on which an individual would otherwise be able to enroll under the plan. (*See* 29 CFR 2590.701–6(b) and 45 CFR 146.117(b), under which this obligation is also imposed on a health insurance issuer offering group health insurance coverage.)

(2) *Individuals eligible for special enrollment.* An individual is described in this paragraph (b)(2) if the individual is otherwise eligible for coverage in a benefit package under the plan and if the individual is described in paragraph (b)(2)(i), (ii), (iii), (iv), (v), or (vi) of this section.

(i) *Current employee only.* A current employee is described in this paragraph (b)(2)(i) if a person becomes a dependent of the individual through marriage, birth, adoption, or placement for adoption.

(ii) *Spouse of a participant only.* An individual is described in this paragraph (b)(2)(ii) if either—

(A) The individual becomes the spouse of a participant; or

(B) The individual is a spouse of a participant and a child becomes a dependent of the participant through birth, adoption, or placement for adoption.

(iii) *Current employee and spouse.* A current employee and an individual who is or becomes a spouse of such an employee, are described in this paragraph (b)(2)(iii) if either—

(A) The employee and the spouse become married; or

(B) The employee and spouse are married and a child becomes a dependent of the employee through birth, adoption, or placement for adoption.

(iv) *Dependent of a participant only.* An individual is described in this paragraph (b)(2)(iv) if the individual is a dependent (as defined in § 54.9801–2) of a participant and the individual has become a dependent of the participant through marriage, birth, adoption, or placement for adoption.

(v) *Current employee and a new dependent.* A current employee and an individual who is a dependent of the employee, are described in this paragraph (b)(2)(v) if the individual becomes a dependent of the employee through marriage, birth, adoption, or placement for adoption.

(vi) *Current employee, spouse, and a new dependent.* A current employee, the employee's spouse, and the employee's dependent are described in this paragraph (b)(2)(vi) if the dependent becomes a dependent of the employee through marriage, birth, adoption, or placement for adoption.

(3) *Applying for special enrollment and effective date of coverage*—(i) *Request.* A plan must allow an individual a period of at least 30 days after the date of the marriage, birth, adoption, or placement for adoption (or, if dependent coverage is not generally made available at the time of the marriage, birth, adoption, or placement for adoption, a period of at least 30 days after the date the plan makes dependent coverage generally available) to request enrollment (for the individual or the individual's dependent).

(ii) *Reasonable procedures for special enrollment.* [Reserved]

(iii) *Date coverage must begin*—(A) *Marriage.* In the case of marriage, coverage must begin no later than the first day of the first calendar month beginning after the date the plan (or any issuer offering health insurance

D. HIPAA Final Rules, Portability, continued

coverage under the plan) receives the request for special enrollment.

(B) *Birth, adoption, or placement for adoption.* Coverage must begin in the case of a dependent's birth on the date of birth and in the case of a dependent's adoption or placement for adoption no later than the date of such adoption or placement for adoption (or, if dependent coverage is not made generally available at the time of the birth, adoption, or placement for adoption, the date the plan makes dependent coverage available).

(4) *Examples.* The rules of this paragraph (b) are illustrated by the following examples:

Example 1. (i) *Facts.* An employer maintains a group health plan that offers all employees employee-only coverage, employee-plus-spouse coverage, or family coverage. Under the terms of the plan, any employee may elect to enroll when first hired (with coverage beginning on the date of hire) or during an annual open enrollment period held each December (with coverage beginning the following January 1). Employee A is hired on September 3. A is married to B, and they have no children. On March 15 in the following year a child C is born to A and B. Before that date, A and B have not been enrolled in the plan.

(ii) *Conclusion.* In this *Example 1,* the conditions for special enrollment of an employee with a spouse and new dependent under paragraph (b)(2)(vi) of this section are satisfied. If A satisfies the conditions of paragraph (b)(3) of this section for requesting enrollment timely, the plan will satisfy this paragraph (b) if it allows A to enroll either with employee-only coverage, with employee-plus-spouse coverage (for A and B), or with family coverage (for A, B, and C). The plan must allow whatever coverage is chosen to begin on March 15, the date of C's birth.

Example 2. (i) *Facts.* Individual D works for Employer X. X maintains a group health plan with two benefit packages—an HMO option and an indemnity option. Self-only and family coverage are available under both options. D enrolls for self-only coverage in the HMO option. Then, a child, E, is placed for adoption with D. Within 30 days of the placement of E for adoption, D requests enrollment for D and E under the plan's indemnity option.

(ii) *Conclusion.* In this *Example 2,* D and E satisfy the conditions for special enrollment under paragraphs (b)(2)(v) and (b)(3) of this section. Therefore, the plan must allow D and E to enroll in the indemnity coverage, effective as of the date of the placement for adoption.

(c) *Notice of special enrollment.* At or before the time an employee is initially offered the opportunity to enroll in a group health plan, the plan must furnish the employee with a notice of special enrollment that complies with the requirements of this paragraph (c).

(1) *Description of special enrollment rights.* The notice of special enrollment

must include a description of special enrollment rights. The following model language may be used to satisfy this requirement:

If you are declining enrollment for yourself or your dependents (including your spouse) because of other health insurance or group health plan coverage, you may be able to enroll yourself and your dependents in this plan if you or your dependents lose eligibility for that other coverage (or if the employer stops contributing towards your or your dependents' other coverage). However, you must request enrollment within [insert "30 days" or any longer period that applies under the plan] after your or your dependents' other coverage ends (or after the employer stops contributing toward the other coverage).

In addition, if you have a new dependent as a result of marriage, birth, adoption, or placement for adoption, you may be able to enroll yourself and your dependents. However, you must request enrollment within [insert "30 days" or any longer period that applies under the plan] after the marriage, birth, adoption, or placement for adoption.

To request special enrollment or obtain more information, contact [insert the name, title, telephone number, and any additional contact information of the appropriate plan representative].

(2) *Additional information that may be required.* The notice of special enrollment must also include, if applicable, the notice described in paragraph (a)(3)(iv) of this section (the notice required to be furnished to an individual declining coverage if the plan requires the reason for declining coverage to be in writing).

(d) *Treatment of special enrollees—*(1) If an individual requests enrollment while the individual is entitled to special enrollment under either paragraph (a) or (b) of this section, the individual is a special enrollee, even if the request for enrollment coincides with a late enrollment opportunity under the plan. Therefore, the individual cannot be treated as a late enrollee.

(2) Special enrollees must be offered all the benefit packages available to similarly situated individuals who enroll when first eligible. For this purpose, any difference in benefits or cost-sharing requirements for different individuals constitutes a different benefit package. In addition, a special enrollee cannot be required to pay more for coverage than a similarly situated individual who enrolls in the same coverage when first eligible. The length of any preexisting condition exclusion that may be applied to a special enrollee cannot exceed the length of any preexisting condition exclusion that is applied to similarly situated individuals who enroll when first eligible. For rules

prohibiting the application of a preexisting condition exclusion to certain newborns, adopted children, and children placed for adoption, see § 54.9801–3(b).

(3) The rules of this section are illustrated by the following example:

Example 2. (i) *Facts.* Employer Y maintains a group health plan that has an enrollment period for late enrollees every November 1 through November 30 with coverage effective the following January 1. On October 18, Individual B loses coverage under another group health plan and satisfies the requirements of paragraphs (a)(2), (3), and (4) of this section. B submits a completed application for coverage on November 2.

(ii) *Conclusion.* In this *Example,* B is a special enrollee. Therefore, even though B's request for enrollment coincides with an open enrollment period, B's coverage is required to be made effective no later than December 1 (rather than the plan's January 1 effective date for late enrollees).

§ 54.9831–1 Special rules relating to group health plans.

(a) *Group health plan*—(1) *Defined.* A group health plan means a plan (including a self-insured plan) of, or contributed to by, an employer (including a self-employed person) or employee organization to provide health care (directly or otherwise) to the employees, former employees, the employer, others associated or formerly associated with the employer in a business relationship, or their families.

(2) *Determination of number of plans.* [Reserved]

(b) *General exception for certain small group health plans.* The requirements of §§ 54.9801–1 through 54.9801–6, 54.9802–1, 54.9802–1T, 54.9811–1T, 54.9812–1T, and 54.9833–1 do not apply to any group health plan for any plan year if, on the first day of the plan year, the plan has fewer than two participants who are current employees.

(c) *Excepted benefits*—(1) *In general.* The requirements of §§ 54.9801–1 through 54.9801–6, 54.9802–1, 54.9802–1T, 54.9811–1T, 54.9812–1T, and 54.9833–1 do not apply to any group health plan in relation to its provision of the benefits described in paragraph (c)(2), (3), (4), or (5) of this section (or any combination of these benefits).

(2) *Benefits excepted in all circumstances.* The following benefits are excepted in all circumstances—

(i) Coverage only for accident (including accidental death and dismemberment);

(ii) Disability income coverage;

(iii) Liability insurance, including general liability insurance and automobile liability insurance;

(iv) Coverage issued as a supplement to liability insurance;

78762 Federal Register / Vol. 69, No. 250 / Thursday, December 30, 2004 / Rules and Regulations

(v) Workers' compensation or similar coverage;

(vi) Automobile medical payment insurance;

(vii) Credit-only insurance (for example, mortgage insurance); and

(viii) Coverage for on-site medical clinics.

(3) *Limited excepted benefits*—(i) *In general.* Limited-scope dental benefits, limited-scope vision benefits, or long-term care benefits are excepted if they are provided under a separate policy, certificate, or contract of insurance, or are otherwise not an integral part of a group health plan as described in paragraph (c)(3)(ii) of this section. In addition, benefits provided under a health flexible spending arrangement are excepted benefits if they satisfy the requirements of paragraph (c)(3)(v) of this section.

(ii) *Not an integral part of a group health plan.* For purposes of this paragraph (c)(3), benefits are not an integral part of a group health plan (whether the benefits are provided through the same plan or a separate plan) only if the following two requirements are satisfied—

(A) Participants must have the right to elect not to receive coverage for the benefits; and

(B) If a participant elects to receive coverage for the benefits, the participant must pay an additional premium or contribution for that coverage.

(iii) *Limited scope*—(A) *Dental benefits.* Limited scope dental benefits are benefits substantially all of which are for treatment of the mouth (including any organ or structure within the mouth).

(B) *Vision benefits.* Limited scope vision benefits are benefits substantially all of which are for treatment of the eye.

(iv) *Long-term care.* Long-term care benefits are benefits that are either—

(A) Subject to State long-term care insurance laws;

(B) For qualified long-term care services, as defined in section 7702B(c)(1), or provided under a qualified long-term care insurance contract, as defined in section 7702B(b); or

(C) Based on cognitive impairment or a loss of functional capacity that is expected to be chronic.

(v) *Health flexible spending arrangements.* Benefits provided under a health flexible spending arrangement (as defined in section 106(c)(2)) are excepted for a class of participants only if they satisfy the following two requirements—

(A) Other group health plan coverage, not limited to excepted benefits, is made available for the year to the class of

participants by reason of their employment; and

(B) The arrangement is structured so that the maximum benefit payable to any participant in the class for a year cannot exceed two times the participant's salary reduction election under the arrangement for the year (or, if greater, cannot exceed $500 plus the amount of the participant's salary reduction election). For this purpose, any amount that an employee can elect to receive as taxable income but elects to apply to the health flexible spending arrangement is considered a salary reduction election (regardless of whether the amount is characterized as salary or as a credit under the arrangement).

(4) *Noncoordinated benefits*—(i) *Excepted benefits that are not coordinated.* Coverage for only a specified disease or illness (for example, cancer-only policies) or hospital indemnity or other fixed indemnity insurance is excepted only if it meets each of the conditions specified in paragraph (c)(4)(ii) of this section. To be hospital indemnity or other fixed indemnity insurance, the insurance must pay a fixed dollar amount per day (or per other period) of hospitalization or illness (for example, $100/day) regardless of the amount of expenses incurred.

(ii) *Conditions.* Benefits are described in paragraph (c)(4)(i) of this section only if—

(A) The benefits are provided under a separate policy, certificate, or contract of insurance;

(B) There is no coordination between the provision of the benefits and an exclusion of benefits under any group health plan maintained by the same plan sponsor; and

(C) The benefits are paid with respect to an event without regard to whether benefits are provided with respect to the event under any group health plan maintained by the same plan sponsor.

(iii) *Example.* The rules of this paragraph (c)(4) are illustrated by the following example:

Example. (i) *Facts.* An employer sponsors a group health plan that provides coverage through an insurance policy. The policy provides benefits only for hospital stays at a fixed percentage of hospital expenses up to a maximum of $100 a day.

(ii) *Conclusion.* In this *Example,* even though the benefits under the policy satisfy the conditions in paragraph (c)(4)(ii) of this section, because the policy pays a percentage of expenses incurred rather than a fixed dollar amount, the benefits under the policy are not excepted benefits under this paragraph (c)(4). This is the result even if, in practice, the policy pays the maximum of $100 for every day of hospitalization.

(5) *Supplemental benefits.* (i) The following benefits are excepted only if they are provided under a separate policy, certificate, or contract of insurance—

(A) Medicare supplemental health insurance (as defined under section 1882(g)(1) of the Social Security Act; also known as Medigap or MedSupp insurance);

(B) Coverage supplemental to the coverage provided under Chapter 55, Title 10 of the United States Code (also known as TRICARE supplemental programs); and

(C) Similar supplemental coverage provided to coverage under a group health plan. To be similar supplemental coverage, the coverage must be specifically designed to fill gaps in primary coverage, such as coinsurance or deductibles. Similar supplemental coverage does not include coverage that becomes secondary or supplemental only under a coordination-of-benefits provision.

(ii) The rules of this paragraph (c)(5) are illustrated by the following example:

Example. (i) *Facts.* An employer sponsors a group health plan that provides coverage for both active employees and retirees. The coverage for retirees supplements benefits provided by Medicare, but does not meet the requirements for a supplemental policy under section 1882(g)(1) of the Social Security Act.

(ii) *Conclusion.* In this *Example,* the coverage provided to retirees does not meet the definition of supplemental excepted benefits under this paragraph (c)(5) because the coverage is not Medicare supplemental insurance as defined under section 1882(g)(1) of the Social Security Act, is not a TRICARE supplemental program, and is not supplemental to coverage provided under a group health plan.

(d) *Treatment of partnerships.* For purposes of this part:

(1) *Treatment as a group health plan.* (See 29 CFR 2590.732(d)(1) and 45 CFR 146.145(d)(1), under which a plan providing medical care, maintained by a partnership, and usually not treated as an employee welfare benefit plan under ERISA is treated as a group health plan for purposes of Part 7 of Subtitle B of Title I of ERISA and Title XXVII of the PHS Act.)

(2) *Employment relationship.* In the case of a group health plan, the term *employer* also includes the partnership in relation to any bona fide partner. In addition, the term *employee* also includes any bona fide partner. Whether or not an individual is a bona fide partner is determined based on all the relevant facts and circumstances, including whether the individual performs services on behalf of the partnership.

D. HIPAA Final Rules, Portability, continued

(3) *Participants of group health plans.* In the case of a group health plan, the term *participant* also includes any individual described in paragraph (d)(3)(i) or (ii) of this section if the individual is, or may become, eligible to receive a benefit under the plan or the individual's beneficiaries may be eligible to receive any such benefit.

(i) In connection with a group health plan maintained by a partnership, the individual is a partner in relation to the partnership.

(ii) In connection with a group health plan maintained by a self-employed individual (under which one or more employees are participants), the individual is the self-employed individual.

(e) *Determining the average number of employees.* [Reserved]

§ 54.9833–1 Effective dates.

Sections 54.9801–1 through 54.9801–6, 54.9831–1, and this section are applicable for plan years beginning on or after July 1, 2005.

PART 602—OMB CONTROL NUMBERS UNDER THE PAPERWORK REDUCTION ACT

■ Par. 4. The authority citation for part 602 continues to read as follows:

Authority: 26 U.S.C. 7805.

■ Par. 5. In § 602.101, paragraph (b) is amended by:
■ a. Removing the entries in the table for §§ 54.9801–3T, 54.9801–4T, 54.9801–5T, and 54.9801–6T.
■ b. Adding the following entries in numerical order to the table:

§ 602.101 OMB Control numbers.

*　　*　　*　　*　　*

(b) * * *

CFR part or section where identified and described	Current OMB control No.
*　*　*　*　*	
54.9801–3	1545–1537
54.9801–4	1545–1537
54.9801–5	1545–1537
54.9801–6	1545–1537
*　*　*　*　*	

Mark E. Matthews,
Deputy Commissioner for Services and Enforcement, Internal Revenue Service.
Approved: July 14, 2004.
Gregory F. Jenner,
Acting Assistant Secretary of the Treasury.

Employee Benefits Security Administration

29 CFR Chapter XXV

■ For the reasons set forth above, Chapter XXV of Title 29 of the Code of Federal Regulations is amended as set forth below:

PART 2590—RULES AND REGULATIONS FOR GROUP HEALTH PLANS

■ 1. The authority citation for Part 2590 is revised to read as follows:

Authority: 29 U.S.C. 1027, 1059, 1135, 1161–1168, 1169, 1181–1183, 1181 note, 1185, 1185a, 1185b, 1191, 1191a, 1191b, and 1191c, sec. 101(g), Public Law 104–191, 101 Stat. 1936; sec. 401(b), Public Law 105–200, 112 Stat. 645 (42 U.S.C. 651 note); Secretary of Labor's Order 1–2003, 68 FR 5374 (Feb. 3, 2003).

■ 2. The heading for Subpart B is revised to read as follows:

Subpart B—Health Coverage Portability, Nondiscrimination, and Renewability

■ 3. Sections 2590.701–1, 2590.701–2, 2590.701–3, 2590.701–4, 2590.701–5, 2590.701–6, and 2590.701–7 are revised to read as follows:

§ 2590.701–1 Basis and scope.

(a) *Statutory basis.* This Subpart B implements Part 7 of Subtitle B of Title I of the Employee Retirement Income Security Act of 1974, as amended (hereinafter ERISA or the Act).

(b) *Scope.* A group health plan or health insurance issuer offering group health insurance coverage may provide greater rights to participants and beneficiaries than those set forth in this Subpart B. This Subpart B sets forth minimum requirements for group health plans and health insurance issuers offering group health insurance coverage concerning:

(1) Limitations on a preexisting condition exclusion period.

(2) Certificates and disclosure of previous coverage.

(3) Rules relating to counting creditable coverage.

(4) Special enrollment periods.

(5) Prohibition against discrimination on the basis of health factors.

(6) Use of an affiliation period by an HMO as an alternative to a preexisting condition exclusion.

§ 2590.701–2 Definitions.

Unless otherwise provided, the definitions in this section govern in applying the provisions of §§ 2590.701 through 2590.734.

Affiliation period means a period of time that must expire before health insurance coverage provided by an HMO becomes effective, and during which the HMO is not required to provide benefits.

COBRA definitions:

(1) *COBRA* means Title X of the Consolidated Omnibus Budget Reconciliation Act of 1985, as amended.

(2) *COBRA continuation coverage* means coverage, under a group health plan, that satisfies an applicable COBRA continuation provision.

(3) *COBRA continuation provision* means sections 601–608 of the Act, section 4980B of the Internal Revenue Code (other than paragraph (f)(1) of such section 4980B insofar as it relates to pediatric vaccines), or Title XXII of the PHS Act.

(4) *Exhaustion of COBRA continuation coverage* means that an individual's COBRA continuation coverage ceases for any reason other than either failure of the individual to pay premiums on a timely basis, or for cause (such as making a fraudulent claim or an intentional misrepresentation of a material fact in connection with the plan). An individual is considered to have exhausted COBRA continuation coverage if such coverage ceases—

(i) Due to the failure of the employer or other responsible entity to remit premiums on a timely basis;

(ii) When the individual no longer resides, lives, or works in the service area of an HMO or similar program (whether or not within the choice of the individual) and there is no other COBRA continuation coverage available to the individual; or

(iii) When the individual incurs a claim that would meet or exceed a lifetime limit on all benefits and there is no other COBRA continuation coverage available to the individual.

Condition means a *medical condition.*

Creditable coverage means *creditable coverage* within the meaning of § 2590.701–4(a).

Dependent means any individual who is or may become eligible for coverage under the terms of a group health plan because of a relationship to a participant.

Enroll means to become covered for benefits under a group health plan (that is, when coverage becomes effective), without regard to when the individual may have completed or filed any forms that are required in order to become covered under the plan. For this purpose, an individual who has health coverage under a group health plan is enrolled in the plan regardless of whether the individual elects coverage, the individual is a dependent who becomes covered as a result of an election by a participant, or the individual becomes covered without an election.

Enrollment date definitions (*enrollment date, first day of coverage,*

D. HIPAA Final Rules, Portability, continued

and *waiting period*) are set forth in § 2590.701–3(a)(3)(i), (ii), and (iii).

Excepted benefits means the benefits described as excepted in § 2590.732(c).

Genetic information means information about genes, gene products, and inherited characteristics that may derive from the individual or a family member. This includes information regarding carrier status and information derived from laboratory tests that identify mutations in specific genes or chromosomes, physical medical examinations, family histories, and direct analysis of genes or chromosomes.

Group health insurance coverage means health insurance coverage offered in connection with a group health plan.

Group health plan or *plan* means a group health plan within the meaning of § 2590.732(a).

Group market means the market for health insurance coverage offered in connection with a group health plan. (However, certain very small plans may be treated as being in the individual market, rather than the group market; see the definition of *individual market* in this section.)

Health insurance coverage means benefits consisting of medical care (provided directly, through insurance or reimbursement, or otherwise) under any hospital or medical service policy or certificate, hospital or medical service plan contract, or HMO contract offered by a health insurance issuer. Health insurance coverage includes group health insurance coverage, individual health insurance coverage, and short-term, limited-duration insurance.

Health insurance issuer or *issuer* means an insurance company, insurance service, or insurance organization (including an HMO) that is required to be licensed to engage in the business of insurance in a State and that is subject to State law that regulates insurance (within the meaning of section 514(b)(2) of the Act). Such term does not include a group health plan.

Health maintenance organization or *HMO* means—

(1) A federally qualified health maintenance organization (as defined in section 1301(a) of the PHS Act);

(2) An organization recognized under State law as a health maintenance organization; or

(3) A similar organization regulated under State law for solvency in the same manner and to the same extent as such a health maintenance organization.

Individual health insurance coverage means health insurance coverage offered to individuals in the individual market, but does not include short-term, limited-duration insurance. Individual health insurance coverage can include dependent coverage.

Individual market means the market for health insurance coverage offered to individuals other than in connection with a group health plan. Unless a State elects otherwise in accordance with section 2791(e)(1)(B)(ii) of the PHS Act, such term also includes coverage offered in connection with a group health plan that has fewer than two participants who are current employees on the first day of the plan year.

Internal Revenue Code means the Internal Revenue Code of 1986, as amended (Title 26, United States Code).

Issuer means a *health insurance issuer*.

Late enrollment definitions (*late enrollee* and *late enrollment*) are set forth in § 2590.701–3(a)(3)(v) and (vi).

Medical care means amounts paid for—

(1) The diagnosis, cure, mitigation, treatment, or prevention of disease, or amounts paid for the purpose of affecting any structure or function of the body;

(2) Transportation primarily for and essential to medical care referred to in paragraph (1) of this definition; and

(3) Insurance covering medical care referred to in paragraphs (1) and (2) of this definition.

Medical condition or *condition* means any condition, whether physical or mental, including, but not limited to, any condition resulting from illness, injury (whether or not the injury is accidental), pregnancy, or congenital malformation. However, genetic information is not a condition.

Participant means *participant* within the meaning of section 3(7) of the Act.

Placement, or *being placed*, for *adoption* means the assumption and retention of a legal obligation for total or partial support of a child by a person with whom the child has been placed in anticipation of the child's adoption. The child's placement for adoption with such person ends upon the termination of such legal obligation.

Plan year means the year that is designated as the plan year in the plan document of a group health plan, except that if the plan document does not designate a plan year or if there is no plan document, the plan year is—

(1) The deductible or limit year used under the plan;

(2) If the plan does not impose deductibles or limits on a yearly basis, then the plan year is the policy year;

(3) If the plan does not impose deductibles or limits on a yearly basis, and either the plan is not insured or the insurance policy is not renewed on an annual basis, then the plan year is the employer's taxable year; or

(4) In any other case, the plan year is the calendar year.

Preexisting condition exclusion means *preexisting condition exclusion* within the meaning of § 2590.701–3(a)(1).

Public health plan means *public health plan* within the meaning of § 2590.701–4(a)(1)(ix).

Public Health Service Act (PHS Act) means the Public Health Service Act (42 U.S.C. 201, *et seq.*).

Short-term, limited-duration insurance means health insurance coverage provided pursuant to a contract with an issuer that has an expiration date specified in the contract (taking into account any extensions that may be elected by the policyholder without the issuer's consent) that is less than 12 months after the original effective date of the contract.

Significant break in coverage means a *significant break in coverage* within the meaning of § 2590.701–4(b)(2)(iii).

Special enrollment means enrollment in a group health plan or group health insurance coverage under the rights described in § 2590.701–6.

State means each of the several States, the District of Columbia, Puerto Rico, the Virgin Islands, Guam, American Samoa, and the Northern Mariana Islands.

State health benefits risk pool means a *State health benefits risk pool* within the meaning of § 2590.701–4(a)(1)(vii).

Waiting period means *waiting period* within the meaning of § 2590.701–3(a)(3)(iii).

§ 2590.701–3 Limitations on preexisting condition exclusion period.

(a) *Preexisting condition exclusion*—

(1) *Defined*—(i) A *preexisting condition exclusion* means a limitation or exclusion of benefits relating to a condition based on the fact that the condition was present before the effective date of coverage under a group health plan or group health insurance coverage, whether or not any medical advice, diagnosis, care, or treatment was recommended or received before that day. A preexisting condition exclusion includes any exclusion applicable to an individual as a result of information relating to an individual's health status before the individual's effective date of coverage under a group health plan or group health insurance coverage, such as a condition identified as a result of a pre-enrollment questionnaire or physical examination given to the individual, or review of medical records relating to the pre-enrollment period.

(ii) *Examples.* The rules of this paragraph (a)(1) are illustrated by the following examples:

D. HIPAA Final Rules, Portability, continued

Example 1. (i) *Facts.* A group health plan provides benefits solely through an insurance policy offered by Issuer *S.* At the expiration of the policy, the plan switches coverage to a policy offered by Issuer *T.* Issuer *T*'s policy excludes benefits for any prosthesis if the body part was lost before the effective date of coverage under the policy.

(ii) *Conclusion.* In this *Example 1,* the exclusion of benefits for any prosthesis if the body part was lost before the effective date of coverage is a preexisting condition exclusion because it operates to exclude benefits for a condition based on the fact that the condition was present before the effective date of coverage under the policy. (Therefore, the exclusion of benefits is required to comply with the limitations on preexisting condition exclusions in this section. For an example illustrating the application of these limitations to a succeeding insurance policy, see *Example 3* of paragraph (a)(3)(iv) of this section.)

Example 2. (i) *Facts.* A group health plan provides coverage for cosmetic surgery in cases of accidental injury, but only if the injury occurred while the individual was covered under the plan.

(ii) *Conclusion.* In this *Example 2,* the plan provision excluding cosmetic surgery benefits for individuals injured before enrolling in the plan is a preexisting condition exclusion because it operates to exclude benefits relating to a condition based on the fact that the condition was present before the effective date of coverage. The plan provision, therefore, is subject to the limitations on preexisting condition exclusions in this section.

Example 3. (i) *Facts.* A group health plan provides coverage for the treatment of diabetes, generally not subject to any lifetime dollar limit. However, if an individual was diagnosed with diabetes before the effective date of coverage under the plan, diabetes coverage is subject to a lifetime limit of $10,000.

(ii) *Conclusion.* In this *Example 3,* the $10,000 lifetime limit is a preexisting condition exclusion because it limits benefits for a condition based on the fact that the condition was present before the effective date of coverage. The plan provision, therefore, is subject to the limitations on preexisting condition exclusions in this section.

Example 4. (i) *Facts.* A group health plan provides coverage for the treatment of acne, subject to a lifetime limit of $2,000. The plan counts against this $2,000 lifetime limit acne treatment benefits provided under prior health coverage.

(ii) *Conclusion.* In this *Example 4,* counting benefits for a specific condition provided under prior health coverage against a lifetime limit for that condition is a preexisting condition exclusion because it operates to limit benefits for a condition based on the fact that the condition was present before the effective date of coverage. The plan provision, therefore, is subject to the limitations on preexisting condition exclusions in this section.

Example 5. (i) *Facts.* When an individual's coverage begins under a group health plan, the individual generally becomes eligible for all benefits. However, benefits for pregnancy are not available until the individual has been covered under the plan for 12 months.

(ii) *Conclusion.* In this *Example 5,* the requirement to be covered under the plan for 12 months to be eligible for pregnancy benefits is a subterfuge for a preexisting condition exclusion because it is designed to exclude benefits for a condition (pregnancy) that arose before the effective date of coverage. Because a plan is prohibited under paragraph (b)(5) of this section from imposing any preexisting condition exclusion on pregnancy, the plan provision is prohibited. However, if the plan provision included an exception for women who were pregnant before the effective date of coverage under the plan (so that the provision applied only to women who became pregnant on or after the effective date of coverage) the plan provision would not be a preexisting condition exclusion (and would not be prohibited by paragraph (b)(5) of this section).

Example 6. (i) *Facts.* A group health plan provides coverage for medically necessary items and services, generally including treatment of heart conditions. However, the plan does not cover those same items and services when used for treatment of congenital heart conditions.

(ii) *Conclusion.* In this *Example 6,* the exclusion of coverage for treatment of congenital heart conditions is a preexisting condition exclusion because it operates to exclude benefits relating to a condition based on the fact that the condition was present before the effective date of coverage. The plan provision, therefore, is subject to the limitations on preexisting condition exclusions in this section.

Example 7. (i) *Facts.* A group health plan generally provides coverage for medically necessary items and services. However, the plan excludes coverage for the treatment of cleft palate.

(ii) *Conclusion.* In this *Example 7,* the exclusion of coverage for treatment of cleft palate is not a preexisting condition exclusion because the exclusion applies regardless of when the condition arose relative to the effective date of coverage. The plan provision, therefore, is not subject to the limitations on preexisting condition exclusions in this section.

Example 8. (i) *Facts.* A group health plan provides coverage for treatment of cleft palate, but only if the individual being treated has been continuously covered under the plan from the date of birth.

(ii) *Conclusion.* In this *Example 8,* the exclusion of coverage for treatment of cleft palate for individuals who have not been covered under the plan from the date of birth operates to exclude benefits in relation to a condition based on the fact that the condition was present before the effective date of coverage. The plan provision, therefore, is subject to the limitations on preexisting condition exclusions in this section.

(2) *General rules.* Subject to paragraph (b) of this section (prohibiting the imposition of a preexisting condition exclusion with respect to certain individuals and conditions), a group health plan, and a health insurance issuer offering group health insurance coverage, may impose, with respect to a participant or beneficiary, a preexisting condition exclusion only if the requirements of this paragraph (a)(2) are satisfied.

(i) *6-month look-back rule.* A preexisting condition exclusion must relate to a condition (whether physical or mental), regardless of the cause of the condition, for which medical advice, diagnosis, care, or treatment was recommended or received within the 6-month period (or such shorter period as applies under the plan) ending on the enrollment date.

(A) For purposes of this paragraph (a)(2)(i), medical advice, diagnosis, care, or treatment is taken into account only if it is recommended by, or received from, an individual licensed or similarly authorized to provide such services under State law and operating within the scope of practice authorized by State law.

(B) For purposes of this paragraph (a)(2)(i), the 6-month period ending on the enrollment date begins on the 6-month anniversary date preceding the enrollment date. For example, for an enrollment date of August 1, 1998, the 6-month period preceding the enrollment date is the period commencing on February 1, 1998 and continuing through July 31, 1998. As another example, for an enrollment date of August 30, 1998, the 6-month period preceding the enrollment date is the period commencing on February 28, 1998 and continuing through August 29, 1998.

(C) The rules of this paragraph (a)(2)(i) are illustrated by the following examples:

Example 1. (i) *Facts.* Individual *A* is diagnosed with a medical condition 8 months before *A*'s enrollment date in Employer *R*'s group health plan. *A*'s doctor recommends that *A* take a prescription drug for 3 months, and *A* follows the recommendation.

(ii) *Conclusion.* In this *Example 1,* Employer *R*'s plan may impose a preexisting condition exclusion with respect to *A*'s condition because *A* received treatment during the 6-month period ending on *A*'s enrollment date in Employer *R*'s plan by taking the prescription medication during that period. However, if *A* did not take the prescription drug during the 6-month period, Employer *R*'s plan would not be able to impose a preexisting condition exclusion with respect to that condition.

Example 2. (i) *Facts.* Individual *B* is treated for a medical condition 7 months before the enrollment date in Employer *S*'s group health plan. As part of such treatment, *B*'s physician recommends that a follow-up examination be given 2 months later. Despite this recommendation, *B* does not receive a

D. HIPAA Final Rules, Portability, continued

follow-up examination, and no other medical advice, diagnosis, care, or treatment for that condition is recommended to B or received by B during the 6-month period ending on B's enrollment date in Employer S's plan.

(ii) *Conclusion.* In this *Example 2*, Employer S's plan may not impose a preexisting condition exclusion with respect to the condition for which B received treatment 7 months prior to the enrollment date.

Example 3. (i) *Facts.* Same facts as Example 2, except that Employer S's plan learns of the condition and attaches a rider to B's certificate of coverage excluding coverage for the condition. Three months after enrollment, B's condition recurs, and Employer S's plan denies payment under the rider.

(ii) *Conclusion.* In this *Example 3*, the rider is a preexisting condition exclusion and Employer S's plan may not impose a preexisting condition exclusion with respect to the condition for which B received treatment 7 months prior to the enrollment date. (In addition, such a rider would violate the provisions of § 2590.702, even if B had received treatment for the condition within the 6-month period ending on the enrollment date.)

Example 4. (i) *Facts.* Individual C has asthma and is treated for that condition several times during the 6-month period before C's enrollment date in Employer T's plan. Three months after the enrollment date, C begins coverage under Employer T's plan. Two months later, C is hospitalized for asthma.

(ii) *Conclusion.* In this *Example 4*, Employer T's plan may impose a preexisting condition exclusion with respect to C's asthma because care relating to C's asthma was received during the 6-month period ending on C's enrollment date (which, under the rules of paragraph (a)(3)(i) of this section, is the first day of the waiting period).

Example 5. (i) *Facts.* Individual D, who is subject to a preexisting condition exclusion imposed by Employer U's plan, has diabetes, as well as retinal degeneration, a foot condition, and poor circulation (all of which are conditions that may be directly attributed to diabetes). D receives treatment for these conditions during the 6-month period ending on D's enrollment date in Employer U's plan. After enrolling in the plan, D stumbles and breaks a leg.

(ii) *Conclusion.* In this *Example 5*, the leg fracture is not a condition related to D's diabetes, retinal degeneration, foot condition, or poor circulation, even though they may have contributed to the accident. Therefore, benefits to treat the leg fracture cannot be subject to a preexisting condition exclusion. However, any additional medical services that may be needed because of D's preexisting diabetes, poor circulation, or retinal degeneration that would not be needed by another patient with a broken leg who does not have these conditions may be subject to the preexisting condition exclusion imposed under Employer U's plan.

(ii) *Maximum length of preexisting condition exclusion.* A preexisting condition exclusion is not permitted to extend for more than 12 months (18 months in the case of a late enrollee) after the enrollment date. For example, for an enrollment date of August 1, 1998, the 12-month period after the enrollment date is the period commencing on August 1, 1998 and continuing through July 31, 1999; the 18-month period after the enrollment date is the period commencing on August 1, 1998 and continuing through January 31, 2000.

(iii) *Reducing a preexisting condition exclusion period by creditable coverage*—(A) The period of any preexisting condition exclusion that would otherwise apply to an individual under a group health plan is reduced by the number of days of creditable coverage the individual has as of the enrollment date, as counted under § 2590.701–4. Creditable coverage may be evidenced through a certificate of creditable coverage (required under § 2590.701–5(a)), or through other means in accordance with the rules of § 2590.701–5(c).

(B) The rules of this paragraph (a)(2)(iii) are illustrated by the following example:

Example. (i) *Facts.* Individual D works for Employer X and has been covered continuously under X's group health plan. D's spouse works for Employer Y. Y maintains a group health plan that imposes a 12-month preexisting condition exclusion (reduced by creditable coverage) on all new enrollees. D enrolls in Y's plan, but also stays covered under X's plan. D presents Y's plan with evidence of creditable coverage under X's plan.

(ii) *Conclusion.* In this *Example*, Y's plan must reduce the preexisting condition exclusion period that applies to D by the number of days of coverage that D had under X's plan as of D's enrollment date in Y's plan (even though D's coverage under X's plan was continuing as of that date).

(iv) *Other standards.* See § 2590.702 for other standards in this Subpart B that may apply with respect to certain benefit limitations or restrictions under a group health plan. Other laws may also apply, such as the Uniformed Services Employment and Reemployment Rights Act (USERRA), which can affect the application of a preexisting condition exclusion to certain individuals who are reinstated in a group health plan following active military service.

(3) *Enrollment definitions*—(i) *Enrollment date* means the first day of coverage (as described in paragraph (a)(3)(ii) of this section) or, if there is a waiting period, the first day of the waiting period. If an individual receiving benefits under a group health plan changes benefit packages, or if the plan changes group health insurance issuers, the individual's enrollment date does not change.

(ii) *First day of coverage* means, in the case of an individual covered for benefits under a group health plan, the first day of coverage under the plan and, in the case of an individual covered by health insurance coverage in the individual market, the first day of coverage under the policy or contract.

(iii) *Waiting period* means the period that must pass before coverage for an employee or dependent who is otherwise eligible to enroll under the terms of a group health plan can become effective. If an employee or dependent enrolls as a late enrollee or special enrollee, any period before such late or special enrollment is not a waiting period. If an individual seeks coverage in the individual market, a waiting period begins on the date the individual submits a substantially complete application for coverage and ends on—

(A) If the application results in coverage, the date coverage begins;

(B) If the application does not result in coverage, the date on which the application is denied by the issuer or the date on which the offer of coverage lapses.

(iv) The rules of paragraphs (a)(3)(i), (ii), and (iii) of this section are illustrated by the following examples:

Example 1. (i) *Facts.* Employer V's group health plan provides for coverage to begin on the first day of the first payroll period following the date an employee is hired and completes the applicable enrollment forms, or on any subsequent January 1 after completion of the applicable enrollment forms. Employer V's plan imposes a preexisting condition exclusion for 12 months (reduced by the individual's creditable coverage) following an individual's enrollment date. Employee E is hired by Employer V on October 13, 1998 and on October 14, 1998 E completes and files all the forms necessary to enroll in the plan. E's coverage under the plan becomes effective on October 25, 1998 (which is the beginning of the first payroll period after E's date of hire).

(ii) *Conclusion.* In this *Example 1*, E's enrollment date is October 13, 1998 (which is the first day of the waiting period for E's enrollment and is also E's date of hire). Accordingly, with respect to E, the permissible 6-month period in paragraph (a)(2)(i) is the period from April 13, 1998 through October 12, 1998, the maximum permissible period during which Employer V's plan can apply a preexisting condition exclusion under paragraph (a)(2)(ii) is the period from October 13, 1998 through October 12, 1999, and this period must be reduced under paragraph (a)(2)(iii) by E's days of creditable coverage as of October 13, 1998.

Example 2. (i) *Facts.* A group health plan has two benefit package options, Option 1 and Option 2. Under each option a 12-month

D. HIPAA Final Rules, Portability, continued

preexisting condition exclusion is imposed. Individual *B* is enrolled in Option 1 on the first day of employment with the employer maintaining the plan, remains enrolled in Option 1 for more than one year, and then decides to switch to Option 2 at open season.

(ii) *Conclusion.* In this *Example 2, B* cannot be subject to any preexisting condition exclusion under Option 2 because any preexisting condition exclusion period would have to begin on *B*'s enrollment date, which is *B*'s first day of coverage, rather than the date that *B* enrolled in Option 2. Therefore, the preexisting condition exclusion period expired before *B* switched to Option 2.

Example 3. (i) *Facts.* On May 13, 1997, Individual *E* is hired by an employer and enrolls in the employer's group health plan. The plan provides benefits solely through an insurance policy offered by Issuer *S.* On December 27, 1998, *E*'s leg is injured in an accident and the leg is amputated. On January 1, 1999, the plan switches coverage to a policy offered by Issuer *T.* Issuer *T*'s policy excludes benefits for any prosthesis if the body part was lost before the effective date of coverage under the policy.

(ii) *Conclusion.* In this *Example 3, E*'s enrollment date is May 13, 1997, *E*'s first day of coverage. Therefore, the permissible 6-month look-back period for the preexisting condition exclusion imposed under Issuer *T*'s policy begins on November 13, 1996 and ends on May 12, 1997. In addition, the 12-month maximum permissible preexisting condition exclusion period begins on May 13, 1997 and ends on May 12, 1998. Accordingly, because no medical advice, diagnosis, care, or treatment was recommended to or received by *E* for the leg during the 6-month look-back period (even though medical care was provided within the 6-month period preceding the effective date of *E*'s coverage under Issuer *T*'s policy), Issuer *T* may not impose any preexisting condition exclusion with respect to *E.* Moreover, even if *E* had received treatment during the 6-month look-back period, Issuer *T* still would not be permitted to impose a preexisting condition exclusion because the 12-month maximum permissible preexisting condition exclusion period expired on May 12, 1998 (before the effective date of *E*'s coverage under Issuer *T*'s policy).

Example 4. (i) *Facts.* A group health plan limits eligibility for coverage to full-time employees of Employer *Y.* Coverage becomes effective on the first day of the month following the date the employee becomes eligible. Employee *C* begins working full-time for Employer *Y* on April 11. Prior to this date, *C* worked part-time for *Y. C* enrolls in the plan and coverage is effective May 1.

(ii) *Conclusion.* In this *Example 4, C*'s enrollment date is April 11 and the period from April 11 through April 30 is a waiting period. The period while *C* was working part-time, and therefore not in an eligible class of employees, is not part of the waiting period.

Example 5. (i) *Facts.* To be eligible for coverage under a multiemployer group health plan in the current calendar quarter, the plan requires an individual to have worked 250 hours in covered employment during the previous quarter. If the hours requirement is satisfied, coverage becomes effective on the first day of the current calendar quarter. Employee *D* begins work on January 28 and does not work 250 hours in covered employment during the first quarter (ending March 31). *D* works at least 250 hours in the second quarter (ending June 30) and is enrolled in the plan with coverage effective July 1 (the first day of the third quarter).

(ii) *Conclusion.* In this *Example 5, D*'s enrollment date is the first day of the quarter during which *D* satisfies the hours requirement, which is April 1. The period from April 1 through June 30 is a waiting period.

(v) *Late enrollee* means an individual whose enrollment in a plan is a late enrollment.

(vi) (A) *Late enrollment* means enrollment of an individual under a group health plan other than—

(*1*) On the earliest date on which coverage can become effective for the individual under the terms of the plan; or

(*2*) Through special enrollment. (For rules relating to special enrollment, see § 2590.701–6.)

(B) If an individual ceases to be eligible for coverage under the plan, and then subsequently becomes eligible for coverage under the plan, only the individual's most recent period of eligibility is taken into account in determining whether the individual is a late enrollee under the plan with respect to the most recent period of coverage. Similar rules apply if an individual again becomes eligible for coverage following a suspension of coverage that applied generally under the plan.

(vii) *Examples.* The rules of paragraphs (a)(3)(v) and (vi) of this section are illustrated by the following examples:

Example 1. (i) *Facts.* Employee *F* first becomes eligible to be covered by Employer *W*'s group health plan on January 1, 1999 but elects not to enroll in the plan until a later annual open enrollment period, with coverage effective January 1, 2001. *F* has no special enrollment right at that time.

(ii) *Conclusion.* In this *Example 1, F* is a late enrollee with respect to *F*'s coverage that became effective under the plan on January 1, 2001.

Example 2. (i) *Facts.* Same facts as *Example 1,* except that *F* terminates employment with Employer *W* on July 1, 1999 without having had any health insurance coverage under the plan. *F* is rehired by Employer *W* on January 1, 2000 and is eligible for and elects coverage under Employer *W*'s plan effective on January 1, 2000.

(ii) *Conclusion.* In this *Example 2, F* would not be a late enrollee with respect to *F*'s coverage that became effective on January 1, 2000.

(b) *Exceptions pertaining to preexisting condition exclusions*—(1)

Newborns—(i) *In general.* Subject to paragraph (b)(3) of this section, a group health plan, and a health insurance issuer offering group health insurance coverage, may not impose any preexisting condition exclusion on a child who, within 30 days after birth, is covered under any creditable coverage. Accordingly, if a child is enrolled in a group health plan (or other creditable coverage) within 30 days after birth and subsequently enrolls in another group health plan without a significant break in coverage (as described in § 2590.701–4(b)(2)(iii)), the other plan may not impose any preexisting condition exclusion on the child.

(ii) *Examples.* The rules of this paragraph (b)(1) are illustrated by the following examples:

Example 1. (i) *Facts.* Individual *E,* who has no prior creditable coverage, begins working for Employer *W* and has accumulated 210 days of creditable coverage under Employer *W*'s group health plan on the date *E* gives birth to a child. Within 30 days after the birth, the child is enrolled in the plan. Ninety days after the birth, both *E* and the child terminate coverage under the plan. Both *E* and the child then experience a break in coverage of 45 days before *E* is hired by Employer *X* and the two are enrolled in Employer *X*'s group health plan.

(ii) *Conclusion.* In this *Example 1,* because *E*'s child is enrolled in Employer *W*'s plan within 30 days after birth, no preexisting condition exclusion may be imposed with respect to the child under Employer *W*'s plan. Likewise, Employer *X*'s plan may not impose any preexisting condition exclusion on *E*'s child because the child was covered under creditable coverage within 30 days after birth and had no significant break in coverage before enrolling in Employer *X*'s plan. On the other hand, because *E* had only 300 days of creditable coverage prior to *E*'s enrollment date in Employer *X*'s plan, Employer *X*'s plan may impose a preexisting condition exclusion on *E* for up to 65 days (66 days if the 12-month period after *E*'s enrollment date in *X*'s plan includes February 29).

Example 2. (i) *Facts.* Individual *F* is enrolled in a group health plan in which coverage is provided through a health insurance issuer. *F* gives birth. Under State law applicable to the health insurance issuer, health care expenses incurred for the child during the 30 days following birth are covered as part of *F*'s coverage. Although *F* may obtain coverage for the child beyond 30 days by timely requesting special enrollment and paying an additional premium, the issuer is prohibited under State law from recouping the cost of any expenses incurred for the child within the 30-day period if the child is not later enrolled.

(ii) *Conclusion.* In this *Example 2,* the child is covered under creditable coverage within 30 days after birth, regardless of whether the child enrolls as a special enrollee under the plan. Therefore, no preexisting condition exclusion may be imposed on the child unless the child has a significant break in coverage.

D. HIPAA Final Rules, Portability, continued

78768 Federal Register / Vol. 69, No. 250 / Thursday, December 30, 2004 / Rules and Regulations

(2) *Adopted children.* Subject to paragraph (b)(3) of this section, a group health plan, and a health insurance issuer offering group health insurance coverage, may not impose any preexisting condition exclusion on a child who is adopted or placed for adoption before attaining 18 years of age and who, within 30 days after the adoption or placement for adoption, is covered under any creditable coverage. Accordingly, if a child is enrolled in a group health plan (or other creditable coverage) within 30 days after adoption or placement for adoption and subsequently enrolls in another group health plan without a significant break in coverage (as described in § 2590.701–4(b)(2)(iii)), the other plan may not impose any preexisting condition exclusion on the child. This rule does not apply to coverage before the date of such adoption or placement for adoption.

(3) *Significant break in coverage.* Paragraphs (b)(1) and (2) of this section no longer apply to a child after a significant break in coverage. (*See* § 2590.701–4(b)(2)(iii) for rules relating to the determination of a significant break in coverage.)

(4) *Special enrollment.* For special enrollment rules relating to new dependents, see § 2590.701–6(b).

(5) *Pregnancy.* A group health plan, and a health insurance issuer offering group health insurance coverage, may not impose a preexisting condition exclusion relating to pregnancy.

(6) *Genetic information*—(i) A group health plan, and a health insurance issuer offering group health insurance coverage, may not impose a preexisting condition exclusion relating to a condition based solely on genetic information. However, if an individual is diagnosed with a condition, even if the condition relates to genetic information, the plan may impose a preexisting condition exclusion with respect to the condition, subject to the other limitations of this section.

(ii) The rules of this paragraph (b)(6) are illustrated by the following example:

Example. (i) *Facts.* Individual *A* enrolls in a group health plan that imposes a 12-month maximum preexisting condition exclusion. Three months before *A*'s enrollment, *A*'s doctor told *A* that, based on genetic information, *A* has a predisposition towards breast cancer. *A* was not diagnosed with breast cancer at any time prior to *A*'s enrollment date in the plan. Nine months after *A*'s enrollment date in the plan, *A* is diagnosed with breast cancer.

(ii) *Conclusion.* In this *Example,* the plan may not impose a preexisting condition exclusion with respect to *A*'s breast cancer because, prior to *A*'s enrollment date, *A* was not diagnosed with breast cancer.

(c) *General notice of preexisting condition exclusion.* A group health plan imposing a preexisting condition exclusion, and a health insurance issuer offering group health insurance coverage subject to a preexisting condition exclusion, must provide a written general notice of preexisting condition exclusion to participants under the plan and cannot impose a preexisting condition exclusion with respect to a participant or a dependent of the participant until such a notice is provided.

(1) *Manner and timing.* A plan or issuer must provide the general notice of preexisting condition exclusion as part of any written application materials distributed by the plan or issuer for enrollment. If the plan or issuer does not distribute such materials, the notice must be provided by the earliest date following a request for enrollment that the plan or issuer, acting in a reasonable and prompt fashion, can provide the notice.

(2) *Content.* The general notice of preexisting condition exclusion must notify participants of the following:

(i) The existence and terms of any preexisting condition exclusion under the plan. This description includes the length of the plan's look-back period (which is not to exceed 6 months under paragraph (a)(2)(i) of this section); the maximum preexisting condition exclusion period under the plan (which cannot exceed 12 months (or 18-months for late enrollees) under paragraph (a)(2)(ii) of this section); and how the plan will reduce the maximum preexisting condition exclusion period by creditable coverage (described in paragraph (a)(2)(iii) of this section).

(ii) A description of the rights of individuals to demonstrate creditable coverage, and any applicable waiting periods, through a certificate of creditable coverage (as required by § 2590.701–5(a)) or through other means (as described in § 2590.701–5(c)). This must include a description of the right of the individual to request a certificate from a prior plan or issuer, if necessary, and a statement that the current plan or issuer will assist in obtaining a certificate from any prior plan or issuer, if necessary.

(iii) A person to contact (including an address or telephone number) for obtaining additional information or assistance regarding the preexisting condition exclusion.

(3) *Duplicate notices not required.* If a notice satisfying the requirements of this paragraph (c) is provided to an individual, the obligation to provide a general notice of preexisting condition exclusion with respect to that

individual is satisfied for both the plan and the issuer.

(4) *Example with sample language.* The rules of this paragraph (c) are illustrated by the following example, which includes sample language that plans and issuers can use as a basis for preparing their own notices to satisfy the requirements of this paragraph (c):

Example. (i) *Facts.* A group health plan makes coverage effective on the first day of the first calendar month after hire and on each January 1 following an open season. The plan imposes a 12-month maximum preexisting condition exclusion (18 months for late enrollees) and uses a 6-month look-back period. As part of the enrollment application materials, the plan provides the following statement:

This plan imposes a preexisting condition exclusion. This means that if you have a medical condition before coming to our plan, you might have to wait a certain period of time before the plan will provide coverage for that condition. This exclusion applies only to conditions for which medical advice, diagnosis, care, or treatment was recommended or received within a six-month period. Generally, this six-month period ends the day before your coverage becomes effective. However, if you were in a waiting period for coverage, the six-month period ends on the day before the waiting period begins. The preexisting condition exclusion does not apply to pregnancy nor to a child who is enrolled in the plan within 30 days after birth, adoption, or placement for adoption.

This exclusion may last up to 12 months (18 months if you are a late enrollee) from your first day of coverage, or, if you were in a waiting period, from the first day of your waiting period. However, you can reduce the length of this exclusion period by the number of days of your prior "creditable coverage." Most prior health coverage is creditable coverage and can be used to reduce the preexisting condition exclusion if you have not experienced a break in coverage of at least 63 days. To reduce the 12-month (or 18-month) exclusion period by your creditable coverage, you should give us a copy of any certificates of creditable coverage you have. If you do not have a certificate, but you do have prior health coverage, we will help you obtain one from your prior plan or issuer. There are also other ways that you can show you have creditable coverage. Please contact us if you need help demonstrating creditable coverage.

All questions about the preexisting condition exclusion and creditable coverage should be directed to Individual *B* at Address *M* or Telephone Number *N.*

(ii) *Conclusion.* In this *Example,* the plan satisfies the general notice requirement of this paragraph (c), and thus also satisfies this requirement for any issuer providing the coverage.

(d) *Determination of creditable coverage*—(1) *Determination within reasonable time.* If a group health plan or health insurance issuer offering group health insurance coverage receives

D. HIPAA Final Rules, Portability, continued

creditable coverage information under § 2590.701–5, the plan or issuer is required, within a reasonable time following receipt of the information, to make a determination regarding the amount of the individual's creditable coverage and the length of any exclusion that remains. Whether this determination is made within a reasonable time depends on the relevant facts and circumstances. Relevant facts and circumstances include whether a plan's application of a preexisting condition exclusion would prevent an individual from having access to urgent medical care.

(2) *No time limit on presenting evidence of creditable coverage.* A plan or issuer may not impose any limit on the amount of time that an individual has to present a certificate or other evidence of creditable coverage.

(3) *Example.* The rules of this paragraph (d) are illustrated by the following example:

Example. (i) Facts. A group health plan imposes a preexisting condition exclusion period of 12 months. After receiving the general notice of preexisting condition exclusion, Individual H develops an urgent health condition before receiving a certificate of creditable coverage from H's prior group health plan. H attests to the period of prior coverage, presents corroborating documentation of the coverage period, and authorizes the plan to request a certificate on H's behalf in accordance with the rules of § 2590.701–5.

(ii) *Conclusion.* In this *Example*, the plan must review the evidence presented by H and make a determination of creditable coverage within a reasonable time that is consistent with the urgency of H's health condition. (This determination may be modified as permitted under paragraph (f) of this section.)

(e) *Individual notice of period of preexisting condition exclusion.* After an individual has presented evidence of creditable coverage and after the plan or issuer has made a determination of creditable coverage under paragraph (d) of this section, the plan or issuer must provide the individual a written notice of the length of preexisting condition exclusion that remains after offsetting for prior creditable coverage. This individual notice is not required to identify any medical conditions specific to the individual that could be subject to the exclusion. A plan or issuer is not required to provide this notice if the plan or issuer does not impose any preexisting condition exclusion on the individual or if the plan's preexisting condition exclusion is completely offset by the individual's prior creditable coverage.

(1) *Manner and timing.* The individual notice must be provided by the earliest date following a

determination that the plan or issuer, acting in a reasonable and prompt fashion, can provide the notice.

(2) *Content.* A plan or issuer must disclose—

(i) Its determination of any preexisting condition exclusion period that applies to the individual (including the last day on which the preexisting condition exclusion applies);

(ii) The basis for such determination, including the source and substance of any information on which the plan or issuer relied;

(iii) An explanation of the individual's right to submit additional evidence of creditable coverage; and

(iv) A description of any applicable appeal procedures established by the plan or issuer.

(3) *Duplicate notices not required.* If a notice satisfying the requirements of this paragraph (e) is provided to an individual, the obligation to provide this individual notice of preexisting condition exclusion with respect to that individual is satisfied for both the plan and the issuer.

(4) *Examples.* The rules of this paragraph (e) are illustrated by the following examples:

Example 1. (i) Facts. A group health plan imposes a preexisting condition exclusion period of 12 months. After receiving the general notice of preexisting condition exclusion, Individual G presents a certificate of creditable coverage indicating 240 days of creditable coverage. Within seven days of receipt of the certificate, the plan determines that G is subject to a preexisting condition exclusion of 125 days, the last day of which is March 5. Five days later, the plan notifies G that, based on the certificate G submitted, G is subject to a preexisting condition exclusion period of 125 days, ending on March 5. The notice also explains the opportunity to submit additional evidence of creditable coverage and the plan's appeal procedures. The notice does not identify any of G's medical conditions that could be subject to the exclusion.

(ii) *Conclusion.* In this *Example 1*, the plan satisfies the requirements of this paragraph (e).

Example 2. (i) Facts. Same facts as in *Example 1*, except that the plan determines that G has 430 days of creditable coverage based on G's certificate indicating 430 days of creditable coverage under G's prior plan.

(ii) *Conclusion.* In this *Example 2*, the plan is not required to notify G that G will not be subject to a preexisting condition exclusion.

(f) *Reconsideration.* Nothing in this section prevents a plan or issuer from modifying an initial determination of creditable coverage if it determines that the individual did not have the claimed creditable coverage, provided that—

(1) A notice of the new determination (consistent with the requirements of paragraph (e) of this section) is provided to the individual; and

(2) Until the notice of the new determination is provided, the plan or issuer, for purposes of approving access to medical services (such as a pre-surgery authorization), acts in a manner consistent with the initial determination.

§ 2590.701–4   Rules relating to creditable coverage.

(a) *General rules*—(1) *Creditable coverage.* For purposes of this section, except as provided in paragraph (a)(2) of this section, the term *creditable coverage* means coverage of an individual under any of the following:

(i) A group health plan as defined in § 2590.732(a).

(ii) Health insurance coverage as defined in § 2590.701–2 (whether or not the entity offering the coverage is subject to Part 7 of Subtitle B of Title I of the Act, and without regard to whether the coverage is offered in the group market, the individual market, or otherwise).

(iii) Part A or B of Title XVIII of the Social Security Act (Medicare).

(iv) Title XIX of the Social Security Act (Medicaid), other than coverage consisting solely of benefits under section 1928 of the Social Security Act (the program for distribution of pediatric vaccines).

(v) Title 10 U.S.C. Chapter 55 (medical and dental care for members and certain former members of the uniformed services, and for their dependents; for purposes of Title 10 U.S.C. Chapter 55, *uniformed services* means the armed forces and the Commissioned Corps of the National Oceanic and Atmospheric Administration and of the Public Health Service).

(vi) A medical care program of the Indian Health Service or of a tribal organization.

(vii) A State health benefits risk pool. For purposes of this section, a *State health benefits risk pool* means—

(A) An organization qualifying under section 501(c)(26) of the Internal Revenue Code;

(B) A qualified high risk pool described in section 2744(c)(2) of the PHS Act; or

(C) Any other arrangement sponsored by a State, the membership composition of which is specified by the State and which is established and maintained primarily to provide health coverage for individuals who are residents of such State and who, by reason of the existence or history of a medical condition—

(1) Are unable to acquire medical care coverage for such condition through insurance or from an HMO, or

D. HIPAA Final Rules, Portability, continued

(2) Are able to acquire such coverage only at a rate which is substantially in excess of the rate for such coverage through the membership organization.

(viii) A health plan offered under Title 5 U.S.C. Chapter 89 (the Federal Employees Health Benefits Program).

(ix) A public health plan. For purposes of this section, a *public health plan* means any plan established or maintained by a State, the U.S. government, a foreign country, or any political subdivision of a State, the U.S. government, or a foreign country that provides health coverage to individuals who are enrolled in the plan.

(x) A health benefit plan under section 5(e) of the Peace Corps Act (22 U.S.C. 2504(e)).

(xi) Title XXI of the Social Security Act (State Children's Health Insurance Program).

(2) *Excluded coverage.* Creditable coverage does not include coverage of solely excepted benefits (described in § 2590.732).

(3) *Methods of counting creditable coverage.* For purposes of reducing any preexisting condition exclusion period, as provided under § 2590.701–3(a)(2)(iii), the amount of an individual's creditable coverage generally is determined by using the standard method described in paragraph (b) of this section. A plan or issuer may use the alternative method under paragraph (c) of this section with respect to any or all of the categories of benefits described under paragraph (c)(3) of this section.

(b) *Standard method*—(1) *Specific benefits not considered.* Under the standard method, the amount of creditable coverage is determined without regard to the specific benefits included in the coverage.

(2) *Counting creditable coverage*—(i) *Based on days.* For purposes of reducing the preexisting condition exclusion period that applies to an individual, the amount of creditable coverage is determined by counting all the days on which the individual has one or more types of creditable coverage. Accordingly, if on a particular day an individual has creditable coverage from more than one source, all the creditable coverage on that day is counted as one day. Any days in a waiting period for coverage are not creditable coverage.

(ii) *Days not counted before significant break in coverage.* Days of creditable coverage that occur before a significant break in coverage are not required to be counted.

(iii) *Significant break in coverage defined*—A significant break in coverage means a period of 63 consecutive days during each of which an individual does

not have any creditable coverage. (*See also* § 2590.731(c)(2)(iii) regarding the applicability to issuers of State insurance laws that require a break of more than 63 days before an individual has a significant break in coverage for purposes of State insurance law.)

(iv) *Periods that toll a significant break.* Days in a waiting period and days in an affiliation period are not taken into account in determining whether a significant break in coverage has occurred. In addition, for an individual who elects COBRA continuation coverage during the second election period provided under the Trade Act of 2002, the days between the date the individual lost group health plan coverage and the first day of the second COBRA election period are not taken into account in determining whether a significant break in coverage has occurred.

(v) *Examples.* The rules of this paragraph (b)(2) are illustrated by the following examples:

Example 1. (i) *Facts.* Individual A has creditable coverage under Employer P's plan for 18 months before coverage ceases. A is provided a certificate of creditable coverage on A's last day of coverage. Sixty-four days after the last date of coverage under P's plan, A is hired by Employer Q and enrolls in Q's group health plan. Q's plan has a 12-month preexisting condition exclusion.

(ii) *Conclusion.* In this *Example 1,* A has a break in coverage of 63 days. Because A's break in coverage is a significant break in coverage, Q's plan may disregard A's prior coverage and A may be subject to a 12-month preexisting condition exclusion.

Example 2. (i) *Facts.* Same facts as *Example 1,* except that A is hired by Q and enrolls in Q's plan on the 63rd day after the last date of coverage under P's plan.

(ii) *Conclusion.* In this *Example 2,* A has a break in coverage of 62 days. Because A's break in coverage is not a significant break in coverage, Q's plan must count A's prior creditable coverage for purposes of reducing the plan's preexisting condition exclusion period that applies to A.

Example 3. (i) *Facts.* Same facts as *Example 1,* except that Q's plan provides benefits through an insurance policy that, as required by applicable State insurance laws, defines a significant break in coverage as 90 days.

(ii) *Conclusion.* In this *Example 3,* under State law, the issuer that provides group health insurance coverage to Q's plan must count A's period of creditable coverage prior to the 63-day break. (However, if Q's plan was a self-insured plan, the coverage would not be subject to State law. Therefore, the health coverage would not be governed by the longer break rules and A's previous health coverage could be disregarded.)

Example 4. —[Reserved]

Example 5. (i) *Facts.* Individual C has creditable coverage under Employer S's plan for 200 days before coverage ceases. C is provided a certificate of creditable coverage

on C's last day of coverage. C then does not have any creditable coverage for 51 days before being hired by Employer T. T's plan has a 3-month waiting period. C works for T for 2 months and then terminates employment. Eleven days after terminating employment with T, C begins working for Employer U. U's plan has no waiting period, but has a 6-month preexisting condition exclusion.

(ii) *Conclusion.* In this *Example 5,* C does not have a significant break in coverage because, after disregarding the waiting period under T's plan, C had only a 62-day break in coverage (51 days plus 11 days). Accordingly, C has 200 days of creditable coverage, and U's plan may not apply its 6-month preexisting condition exclusion with respect to C.

Example 6. —[Reserved]

Example 7. (i) *Facts.* Individual E has creditable coverage under Employer X's plan. E is provided a certificate of creditable coverage on E's last day of coverage. On the 63rd day without coverage, E submits a substantially complete application for a health insurance policy in the individual market. E's application is accepted and coverage is made effective 10 days later.

(ii) *Conclusion.* In this *Example 7,* because E applied for the policy before the end of the 63rd day, the period between the date of application and the first day of coverage is a waiting period and no significant break in coverage occurred even though the actual period without coverage was 73 days.

Example 8. (i) *Facts.* Same facts as *Example 7,* except that E's application for a policy in the individual market is denied.

(ii) *Conclusion.* In this *Example 8,* even though E did not obtain coverage following application, the period between the date of application and the date the coverage was denied is a waiting period. However, to avoid a significant break in coverage, no later than the day after the application for the policy is denied E would need to do one of the following: submit a substantially complete application for a different individual market policy; obtain coverage in the group market; or be in a waiting period for coverage in the group market.

(vi) *Other permissible counting methods*—(A) *Rule.* Notwithstanding any other provisions of this paragraph (b)(2), for purposes of reducing a preexisting condition exclusion period (but not for purposes of issuing a certificate under § 2590.701–5), a group health plan, and a health insurance issuer offering group health insurance coverage, may determine the amount of creditable coverage in any other manner that is at least as favorable to the individual as the method set forth in this paragraph (b)(2), subject to the requirements of other applicable law.

(B) *Example.* The rule of this paragraph (b)(2)(vi) is illustrated by the following example:

Example. (i) *Facts.* Individual F has coverage under Group Health Plan Y from January 3, 1997 through March 25, 1997. F

D. HIPAA Final Rules, Portability, continued

then becomes covered by Group Health Plan Z. F's enrollment date in Plan Z is May 1, 1997. Plan Z has a 12-month preexisting condition exclusion.

(ii) *Conclusion.* In this *Example,* Plan Z may determine, in accordance with the rules prescribed in paragraphs (b)(2)(i), (ii), and (iii) of this section, that F has 82 days of creditable coverage (29 days in January, 28 days in February, and 25 days in March). Thus, the preexisting condition exclusion will no longer apply to F on February 8, 1998 (82 days before the 12-month anniversary of F's enrollment (May 1)). For administrative convenience, however, Plan Z may consider that the preexisting condition exclusion will no longer apply to F on the first day of the month (February 1).

(c) *Alternative method—*(1) *Specific benefits considered.* Under the alternative method, a group health plan, or a health insurance issuer offering group health insurance coverage, determines the amount of creditable coverage based on coverage within any category of benefits described in paragraph (c)(3) of this section and not based on coverage for any other benefits. The plan or issuer may use the alternative method for any or all of the categories. The plan or issuer may apply a different preexisting condition exclusion period with respect to each category (and may apply a different preexisting condition exclusion period for benefits that are not within any category). The creditable coverage determined for a category of benefits applies only for purposes of reducing the preexisting condition exclusion period with respect to that category. An individual's creditable coverage for benefits that are not within any category for which the alternative method is being used is determined under the standard method of paragraph (b) of this section.

(2) *Uniform application.* A plan or issuer using the alternative method is required to apply it uniformly to all participants and beneficiaries under the plan or health insurance coverage. The use of the alternative method is required to be set forth in the plan.

(3) *Categories of benefits.* The alternative method for counting creditable coverage may be used for coverage for the following categories of benefits—

(i) Mental health;

(ii) Substance abuse treatment;

(iii) Prescription drugs;

(iv) Dental care; or

(v) Vision care.

(4) *Plan notice.* If the alternative method is used, the plan is required to—

(i) State prominently that the plan is using the alternative method of counting creditable coverage in disclosure statements concerning the plan, and State this to each enrollee at the time of enrollment under the plan; and

(ii) Include in these statements a description of the effect of using the alternative method, including an identification of the categories used.

(5) *Disclosure of information on previous benefits.* See § 2590.701–5(b) for special rules concerning disclosure of coverage to a plan, or issuer, using the alternative method of counting creditable coverage under this paragraph (c).

(6) *Counting creditable coverage—*(i) *In general.* Under the alternative method, the group health plan or issuer counts creditable coverage within a category if any level of benefits is provided within the category. Coverage under a reimbursement account or arrangement, such as a flexible spending arrangement (as defined in section 106(c)(2) of the Internal Revenue Code), does not constitute coverage within any category.

(ii) *Special rules.* In counting an individual's creditable coverage under the alternative method, the group health plan, or issuer, first determines the amount of the individual's creditable coverage that may be counted under paragraph (b) of this section, up to a total of 365 days of the most recent creditable coverage (546 days for a late enrollee). The period over which this creditable coverage is determined is referred to as the determination period. Then, for the category specified under the alternative method, the plan or issuer counts within the category all days of coverage that occurred during the determination period (whether or not a significant break in coverage for that category occurs), and reduces the individual's preexisting condition exclusion period for that category by that number of days. The plan or issuer may determine the amount of creditable coverage in any other reasonable manner, uniformly applied, that is at least as favorable to the individual.

(iii) *Example.* The rules of this paragraph (c)(6) are illustrated by the following example:

Example. (i) *Facts.* Individual D enrolls in Employer V's plan on January 1, 2001. Coverage under the plan includes prescription drug benefits. On April 1, 2001, the plan ceases providing prescription drug benefits. D's employment with Employer V ends on January 1, 2002, after D was covered under Employer V's group health plan for 365 days. D enrolls in Employer Y's plan on February 1, 2002 (D's enrollment date). Employer Y's plan uses the alternative method of counting creditable coverage and imposes a 12-month preexisting condition exclusion on prescription drug benefits.

(ii) *Conclusion.* In this *Example,* Employer Y's plan may impose a 275-day preexisting condition exclusion with respect to D for prescription drug benefits because D had 90 days of creditable coverage relating to prescription drug benefits within D's determination period.

§ 2590.701–5 Evidence of creditable coverage.

(a) *Certificate of creditable coverage—*(1) *Entities required to provide certificate—*(i) *In general.* A group health plan, and each health insurance issuer offering group health insurance coverage under a group health plan, is required to furnish certificates of creditable coverage in accordance with this paragraph (a).

(ii) *Duplicate certificates not required.* An entity required to provide a certificate under this paragraph (a) with respect to an individual satisfies that requirement if another party provides the certificate, but only to the extent that the certificate contains the information required in paragraph (a)(3) of this section. For example, in the case of a group health plan funded through an insurance policy, the issuer satisfies the certification requirement with respect to an individual if the plan actually provides a certificate that includes all the information required under paragraph (a)(3) of this section with respect to the individual.

(iii) *Special rule for group health plans.* To the extent coverage under a plan consists of group health insurance coverage, the plan satisfies the certification requirements under this paragraph (a) if any issuer offering the coverage is required to provide the certificates pursuant to an agreement between the plan and the issuer. For example, if there is an agreement between an issuer and a plan sponsor under which the issuer agrees to provide certificates for individuals covered under the plan, and the issuer fails to provide a certificate to an individual when the plan would have been required to provide one under this paragraph (a), then the issuer, but not the plan, violates the certification requirements of this paragraph (a).

(iv) *Special rules for issuers—*(A)(1) *Responsibility of issuer for coverage period.* An issuer is not required to provide information regarding coverage provided to an individual by another party.

(2) *Example.* The rule of this paragraph (a)(1)(iv)(A) is illustrated by the following example:

Example. (i) *Facts.* A plan offers coverage with an HMO option from one issuer and an indemnity option from a different issuer. The HMO has not entered into an agreement with

D. HIPAA Final Rules, Portability, continued

the plan to provide certificates as permitted under paragraph (a)(1)(iii) of this section.

(ii) *Conclusion.* In this *Example*, if an employee switches from the indemnity option to the HMO option and later ceases to be covered under the plan, any certificate provided by the HMO is not required to provide information regarding the employee's coverage under the indemnity option.

(B)(1) *Cessation of issuer coverage prior to cessation of coverage under a plan.* If an individual's coverage under an issuer's policy or contract ceases before the individual's coverage under the plan ceases, the issuer is required to provide sufficient information to the plan (or to another party designated by the plan) to enable the plan (or other party), after cessation of the individual's coverage under the plan, to provide a certificate that reflects the period of coverage under the policy or contract. By providing that information to the plan, the issuer satisfies its obligation to provide an automatic certificate for that period of creditable coverage with respect to the individual under paragraph (a)(2)(ii) of this section. The issuer, however, must still provide a certificate upon request as required under paragraph (a)(2)(iii) of this section. In addition, the issuer is required to cooperate with the plan in responding to any request made under paragraph (b)(2) of this section (relating to the alternative method of counting creditable coverage). Moreover, if the individual's coverage under the plan ceases at the time the individual's coverage under the issuer's policy or contract ceases, the issuer must still provide an automatic certificate under paragraph (a)(2)(ii) of this section. If an individual's coverage under an issuer's policy or contract ceases on the effective date for changing enrollment options under the plan, the issuer may presume (absent information to the contrary) that the individual's coverage under the plan continues. Therefore, the issuer is required to provide information to the plan in accordance with this paragraph (a)(1)(iv)(B)(1) (and is not required to provide an automatic certificate under paragraph (a)(2)(ii) of this section).

(2) *Example.* The rule of this paragraph (a)(1)(iv)(B) is illustrated by the following example:

Example. (i) *Facts.* A group health plan provides coverage under an HMO option and an indemnity option through different issuers, and only allows employees to switch on each January 1. Neither the HMO nor the indemnity issuer has entered into an agreement with the plan to provide certificates as permitted under paragraph (a)(1)(iii) of this section.

(ii) *Conclusion.* In this *Example,* if an employee switches from the indemnity

option to the HMO option on January 1, the indemnity issuer must provide the plan (or a person designated by the plan) with appropriate information with respect to the individual's coverage with the indemnity issuer. However, if the individual's coverage with the indemnity issuer ceases at a date other than January 1, the issuer is instead required to provide the individual with an automatic certificate.

(2) *Individuals for whom certificate must be provided; timing of issuance—* (i) *Individuals.* A certificate must be provided, without charge, for participants or dependents who are or were covered under a group health plan upon the occurrence of any of the events described in paragraph (a)(2)(ii) or (iii) of this section.

(ii) *Issuance of automatic certificates.* The certificates described in this paragraph (a)(2)(ii) are referred to as automatic certificates.

(A) *Qualified beneficiaries upon a qualifying event.* In the case of an individual who is a qualified beneficiary (as defined in section 607(3) of the Act) entitled to elect COBRA continuation coverage, an automatic certificate is required to be provided at the time the individual would lose coverage under the plan in the absence of COBRA continuation coverage or alternative coverage elected instead of COBRA continuation coverage. A plan or issuer satisfies this requirement if it provides the automatic certificate no later than the time a notice is required to be furnished for a qualifying event under section 606 of the Act (relating to notices required under COBRA).

(B) *Other individuals when coverage ceases.* In the case of an individual who is not a qualified beneficiary entitled to elect COBRA continuation coverage, an automatic certificate must be provided at the time the individual ceases to be covered under the plan. A plan or issuer satisfies the requirement to provide an automatic certificate at the time the individual ceases to be covered if it provides the automatic certificate within a reasonable time after coverage ceases (or after the expiration of any grace period for nonpayment of premiums).

(1) The cessation of temporary continuation coverage (TCC) under Title 5 U.S.C. Chapter 89 (the Federal Employees Health Benefit Program) is a cessation of coverage upon which an automatic certificate must be provided.

(2) In the case of an individual who is entitled to elect to continue coverage under a State program similar to COBRA and who receives the automatic certificate not later than the time a notice is required to be furnished under the State program, the certificate is

deemed to be provided within a reasonable time after coverage ceases under the plan.

(3) If an individual's coverage ceases due to the operation of a lifetime limit on all benefits, coverage is considered to cease for purposes of this paragraph (a)(2)(ii)(B) on the earliest date that a claim is denied due to the operation of the lifetime limit.

(C) *Qualified beneficiaries when COBRA ceases.* In the case of an individual who is a qualified beneficiary and has elected COBRA continuation coverage (or whose coverage has continued after the individual became entitled to elect COBRA continuation coverage), an automatic certificate is to be provided at the time the individual's coverage under the plan ceases. A plan, or issuer, satisfies this requirement if it provides the automatic certificate within a reasonable time after coverage ceases (or after the expiration of any grace period for nonpayment of premiums). An automatic certificate is required to be provided to such an individual regardless of whether the individual has previously received an automatic certificate under paragraph (a)(2)(ii)(A) of this section.

(iii) *Any individual upon request.* A certificate must be provided in response to a request made by, or on behalf of, an individual at any time while the individual is covered under a plan and up to 24 months after coverage ceases. Thus, for example, a plan in which an individual enrolls may, if authorized by the individual, request a certificate of the individual's creditable coverage on behalf of the individual from a plan in which the individual was formerly enrolled. After the request is received, a plan or issuer is required to provide the certificate by the earliest date that the plan or issuer, acting in a reasonable and prompt fashion, can provide the certificate. A certificate is required to be provided under this paragraph (a)(2)(iii) even if the individual has previously received a certificate under this paragraph (a)(2)(iii) or an automatic certificate under paragraph (a)(2)(ii) of this section.

(iv) *Examples.* The rules of this paragraph (a)(2) are illustrated by the following examples:

Example 1. (i) *Facts.* Individual A terminates employment with Employer Q. A is a qualified beneficiary entitled to elect COBRA continuation coverage under Employer Q's group health plan. A notice of the rights provided under COBRA is typically furnished to qualified beneficiaries under the plan within 10 days after a covered employee terminates employment.

D. HIPAA Final Rules, Portability, continued

Federal Register / Vol. 69, No. 250 / Thursday, December 30, 2004 / Rules and Regulations   78773

(ii) *Conclusion.* In this *Example 1*, the automatic certificate may be provided at the same time that *A* is provided the COBRA notice.

Example 2. (i) *Facts.* Same facts as *Example 1*, except that the automatic certificate for *A* is not completed by the time the COBRA notice is furnished to *A*.

(ii) *Conclusion.* In this *Example 2*, the automatic certificate may be provided after the COBRA notice but must be provided within the period permitted by law for the delivery of notices under COBRA.

Example 3. (i) *Facts.* Employer *R* maintains an insured group health plan. *R* has never had 20 employees and thus *R*'s plan is not subject to the COBRA continuation provisions. However, *R* is in a State that has a State program similar to COBRA. *B* terminates employment with *R* and loses coverage under *R*'s plan.

(ii) *Conclusion.* In this *Example 3*, the automatic certificate must be provided not later than the time a notice is required to be furnished under the State program.

Example 4. (i) *Facts.* Individual *C* terminates employment with Employer *S* and receives both a notice of *C*'s rights under COBRA and an automatic certificate. *C* elects COBRA continuation coverage under Employer *S*'s group health plan. After four months of COBRA continuation coverage and the expiration of a 30-day grace period, *S*'s group health plan determines that *C*'s COBRA continuation coverage has ceased due to a failure to make a timely payment for continuation coverage.

(ii) *Conclusion.* In this *Example 4*, the plan must provide an updated automatic certificate to *C* within a reasonable time after the end of the grace period.

Example 5. (i) *Facts.* Individual *D* is currently covered under the group health plan of Employer *T*. *D* requests a certificate, as permitted under paragraph (a)(2)(iii) of this section. Under the procedure for *T*'s plan, certificates are mailed (by first class mail) 7 business days following receipt of the request. This date reflects the earliest date that the plan, acting in a reasonable and prompt fashion, can provide certificates.

(ii) *Conclusion.* In this *Example 5*, the plan's procedure satisfies paragraph (a)(2)(iii) of this section.

(3) *Form and content of certificate*—(i) *Written certificate*—(A) *In general.* Except as provided in paragraph (a)(3)(i)(B) of this section, the certificate must be provided in writing (or any other medium approved by the Secretary).

(B) *Other permissible forms.* No written certificate is required to be provided under this paragraph (a) with respect to a particular event described in paragraph (a)(2)(ii) or (iii) of this section, if—

(1) An individual who is entitled to receive the certificate requests that the certificate be sent to another plan or issuer instead of to the individual;

(2) The plan or issuer that would otherwise receive the certificate agrees to accept the information in this paragraph (a)(3) through means other than a written certificate (such as by telephone); and

(3) The receiving plan or issuer receives the information from the sending plan or issuer through such means within the time required under paragraph (a)(2) of this section.

(ii) *Required information.* The certificate must include the following—

(A) The date the certificate is issued;

(B) The name of the group health plan that provided the coverage described in the certificate;

(C) The name of the participant or dependent with respect to whom the certificate applies, and any other information necessary for the plan providing the coverage specified in the certificate to identify the individual, such as the individual's identification number under the plan and the name of the participant if the certificate is for (or includes) a dependent;

(D) The name, address, and telephone number of the plan administrator or issuer required to provide the certificate;

(E) The telephone number to call for further information regarding the certificate (if different from paragraph (a)(3)(ii)(D) of this section);

(F) Either—

(1) A statement that an individual has at least 18 months (for this purpose, 546 days is deemed to be 18 months) of creditable coverage, disregarding days of creditable coverage before a significant break in coverage, or

(2) The date any waiting period (and affiliation period, if applicable) began and the date creditable coverage began;

(G) The date creditable coverage ended, unless the certificate indicates that creditable coverage is continuing as of the date of the certificate; and

(H) An educational statement regarding HIPAA, which explains:

(1) The restrictions on the ability of a plan or issuer to impose a preexisting condition exclusion (including an individual's ability to reduce a preexisting condition exclusion by creditable coverage);

(2) Special enrollment rights;

(3) The prohibitions against discrimination based on any health factor;

(4) The right to individual health coverage;

(5) The fact that state law may require issuers to provide additional protections to individuals in that State; and

(6) Where to get more information.

(iii) *Periods of coverage under the certificate.* If an automatic certificate is provided pursuant to paragraph (a)(2)(ii) of this section, the period that must be included on the certificate is the last period of continuous coverage ending on the date coverage ceased. If an individual requests a certificate pursuant to paragraph (a)(2)(iii) of this section, the certificate provided must include each period of continuous coverage ending within the 24-month period ending on the date of the request (or continuing on the date of the request). A separate certificate may be provided for each such period of continuous coverage.

(iv) *Combining information for families.* A certificate may provide information with respect to both a participant and the participant's dependents if the information is identical for each individual. If the information is not identical, certificates may be provided on one form if the form provides all the required information for each individual and separately States the information that is not identical.

(v) *Model certificate.* The requirements of paragraph (a)(3)(ii) of this section are satisfied if the plan or issuer provides a certificate in accordance with a model certificate authorized by the Secretary.

(vi) *Excepted benefits; categories of benefits.* No certificate is required to be furnished with respect to excepted benefits described in § 2590.732(c). In addition, the information in the certificate regarding coverage is not required to specify categories of benefits described in § 2590.701–4(c) (relating to the alternative method of counting creditable coverage). However, if excepted benefits are provided concurrently with other creditable coverage (so that the coverage does not consist solely of excepted benefits), information concerning the benefits may be required to be disclosed under paragraph (b) of this section.

(4) *Procedures*—(i) *Method of delivery.* The certificate is required to be provided to each individual described in paragraph (a)(2) of this section or an entity requesting the certificate on behalf of the individual. The certificate may be provided by first-class mail. (*See also* § 2520.104b–1, which permits plans to make disclosures under the Act—including the furnishing of certificates—through electronic means if certain standards are met.) If the certificate or certificates are provided to the participant and the participant's spouse at the participant's last known address, then the requirements of this paragraph (a)(4) are satisfied with respect to all individuals residing at that address. If a dependent's last known address is different than the participant's last known address, a separate certificate is required to be provided to the dependent at the

D. HIPAA Final Rules, Portability, continued

dependent's last known address. If separate certificates are being provided by mail to individuals who reside at the same address, separate mailings of each certificate are not required.

(ii) *Procedure for requesting certificates.* A plan or issuer must establish a written procedure for individuals to request and receive certificates pursuant to paragraph (a)(2)(iii) of this section. The written procedure must include all contact information necessary to request a certificate (such as name and phone number or address).

(iii) *Designated recipients.* If an automatic certificate is required to be provided under paragraph (a)(2)(ii) of this section, and the individual entitled to receive the certificate designates another individual or entity to receive the certificate, the plan or issuer responsible for providing the certificate is permitted to provide the certificate to the designated individual or entity. If a certificate is required to be provided upon request under paragraph (a)(2)(iii) of this section and the individual entitled to receive the certificate designates another individual or entity to receive the certificate, the plan or issuer responsible for providing the certificate is required to provide the certificate to the designated individual or entity.

(5) *Special rules concerning dependent coverage*—(i)(A) *Reasonable efforts.* A plan or issuer is required to use reasonable efforts to determine any information needed for a certificate relating to dependent coverage. In any case in which an automatic certificate is required to be furnished with respect to a dependent under paragraph (a)(2)(ii) of this section, no individual certificate is required to be furnished until the plan or issuer knows (or making reasonable efforts should know) of the dependent's cessation of coverage under the plan.

(B) *Example.* The rules of this paragraph (a)(5)(i) are illustrated by the following example:

Example. (i) *Facts.* A group health plan covers employees and their dependents. The plan annually requests all employees to provide updated information regarding dependents, including the specific date on which an employee has a new dependent or on which a person ceases to be a dependent of the employee.

(ii) *Conclusion.* In this *Example,* the plan has satisfied the standard in this paragraph (a)(5)(i) of this section that it make reasonable efforts to determine the cessation of dependents' coverage and the related dependent coverage information.

(ii) *Special rules for demonstrating coverage.* If a certificate furnished by a

plan or issuer does not provide the name of any dependent covered by the certificate, the procedures described in paragraph (c)(5) of this section may be used to demonstrate dependent status. In addition, these procedures may be used to demonstrate that a child was covered under any creditable coverage within 30 days after birth, adoption, or placement for adoption. *See also* § 2590.701–3(b), under which such a child cannot be subject to a preexisting condition exclusion.

(6) *Special certification rules for entities not subject to Part 7 of Subtitle B of Title I of the Act*—(i) *Issuers.* For special rules requiring that issuers not subject to Part 7 of Subtitle B of Title I of the Act provide certificates consistent with the rules in this section, including issuers offering coverage with respect to creditable coverage described in sections 701(c)(1)(G), (I), and (J) of the Act (coverage under a State health benefits risk pool, a public health plan, and a health benefit plan under section 5(e) of the Peace Corps Act), see sections 2743 and 2721(b)(1)(B) of the PHS Act (requiring certificates by issuers in the individual market, and issuers offering health insurance coverage in connection with a group health plan, including a church plan or a governmental plan (such as the Federal Employees Health Benefits Program (FEHBP)). (However, this section does not require a certificate to be provided with respect to short-term, limited-duration insurance, as described in the definition of *individual health insurance coverage* in § 2590.701–2, that is not provided by a group health plan or issuer offering health insurance coverage in connection with a group health plan.)

(ii) *Other entities.* For special rules requiring that certain other entities not subject to Part 7 of Subtitle B of Title I of the Act provide certificates consistent with the rules in this section, see section 2791(a)(3) of the PHS Act applicable to entities described in sections 2701(c)(1)(C), (D), (E), and (F) of the PHS Act (relating to Medicare, Medicaid, TRICARE, and Indian Health Service), section 2721(b)(1)(A) of the PHS Act applicable to nonfederal governmental plans generally, section 2721(b)(2)(C)(ii) of the PHS Act applicable to nonfederal governmental plans that elect to be excluded from the requirements of Subparts 1 through 3 of Part A of Title XXVII of the PHS Act, and section 9832(a) of the Internal Revenue Code applicable to group health plans, which includes church plans (as defined in section 414(e) of the Internal Revenue Code).

(b) *Disclosure of coverage to a plan or issuer using the alternative method of*

counting creditable coverage—(1) *In general.* After an individual provides a certificate of creditable coverage to a plan or issuer using the alternative method under § 2590.701–4(c), that plan or issuer (requesting entity) must request that the entity that issued the certificate (prior entity) disclose the information set forth in paragraph (b)(2) of this section. The prior entity is required to disclose this information promptly.

(2) *Information to be disclosed.* The prior entity is required to identify to the requesting entity the categories of benefits with respect to which the requesting entity is using the alternative method of counting creditable coverage, and the requesting entity may identify specific information that the requesting entity reasonably needs in order to determine the individual's creditable coverage with respect to any such category.

(3) *Charge for providing information.* The prior entity may charge the requesting entity for the reasonable cost of disclosing such information.

(c) *Ability of an individual to demonstrate creditable coverage and waiting period information*—(1) *Purpose.* The rules in this paragraph (c) implement section 701(c)(4) of the Act, which permits individuals to demonstrate the duration of creditable coverage through means other than certificates, and section 701(e)(3) of the Act, which requires the Secretary to establish rules designed to prevent an individual's subsequent coverage under a group health plan or health insurance coverage from being adversely affected by an entity's failure to provide a certificate with respect to that individual.

(2) *In general.* If the accuracy of a certificate is contested or a certificate is unavailable when needed by an individual, the individual has the right to demonstrate creditable coverage (and waiting or affiliation periods) through the presentation of documents or other means. For example, the individual may make such a demonstration when—

(i) An entity has failed to provide a certificate within the required time;

(ii) The individual has creditable coverage provided by an entity that is not required to provide a certificate of the coverage pursuant to paragraph (a) of this section;

(iii) The individual has an urgent medical condition that necessitates a determination before the individual can deliver a certificate to the plan; or

(iv) The individual lost a certificate that the individual had previously received and is unable to obtain another certificate.

D. HIPAA Final Rules, Portability, continued

(3) *Evidence of creditable coverage—* (i) *Consideration of evidence*—(A) A plan or issuer is required to take into account all information that it obtains or that is presented on behalf of an individual to make a determination, based on the relevant facts and circumstances, whether an individual has creditable coverage. A plan or issuer shall treat the individual as having furnished a certificate under paragraph (a) of this section if—

(1) The individual attests to the period of creditable coverage;

(2) The individual also presents relevant corroborating evidence of some creditable coverage during the period; and

(3) The individual cooperates with the plan's or issuer's efforts to verify the individual's coverage.

(B) For purposes of this paragraph (c)(3)(i), cooperation includes providing (upon the plan's or issuer's request) a written authorization for the plan or issuer to request a certificate on behalf of the individual, and cooperating in efforts to determine the validity of the corroborating evidence and the dates of creditable coverage. While a plan or issuer may refuse to credit coverage where the individual fails to cooperate with the plan's or issuer's efforts to verify coverage, the plan or issuer may not consider an individual's inability to obtain a certificate to be evidence of the absence of creditable coverage.

(ii) *Documents.* Documents that corroborate creditable coverage (and waiting or affiliation periods) include explanations of benefits (EOBs) or other correspondence from a plan or issuer indicating coverage, pay stubs showing a payroll deduction for health coverage, a health insurance identification card, a certificate of coverage under a group health policy, records from medical care providers indicating health coverage, third party statements verifying periods of coverage, and any other relevant documents that evidence periods of health coverage.

(iii) *Other evidence.* Creditable coverage (and waiting or affiliation periods) may also be corroborated through means other than documentation, such as by a telephone call from the plan or provider to a third party verifying creditable coverage.

(iv) *Example.* The rules of this paragraph (c)(3) are illustrated by the following example:

Example. (i) *Facts.* Individual F terminates employment with Employer W and, a month later, is hired by Employer X. X's group health plan imposes a preexisting condition exclusion of 12 months on new enrollees under the plan and uses the standard method of determining creditable coverage. F fails to receive a certificate of prior coverage from the self-insured group health plan maintained by F's prior employer, W, and requests a certificate. However, F (and X's plan, on F's behalf and with F's cooperation) is unable to obtain a certificate from W's plan. F attests that, to the best of F's knowledge, F had at least 12 months of continuous coverage under W's plan, and that the coverage ended no earlier than F's termination of employment from W. In addition, F presents evidence of coverage, such as an explanation of benefits for a claim that was made during the relevant period.

(ii) *Conclusion.* In this *Example,* based solely on these facts, F has demonstrated creditable coverage for the 12 months of coverage under W's plan in the same manner as if F had presented a written certificate of creditable coverage.

(4) *Demonstrating categories of creditable coverage.* Procedures similar to those described in this paragraph (c) apply in order to determine the duration of an individual's creditable coverage with respect to any category under paragraph (b) of this section (relating to determining creditable coverage under the alternative method).

(5) *Demonstrating dependent status.* If, in the course of providing evidence (including a certificate) of creditable coverage, an individual is required to demonstrate dependent status, the group health plan or issuer is required to treat the individual as having furnished a certificate showing the dependent status if the individual attests to such dependency and the period of such status and the individual cooperates with the plan's or issuer's efforts to verify the dependent status.

§ 2590.701–6 Special enrollment periods.

(a) *Special enrollment for certain individuals who lose coverage*—(1) *In general.* A group health plan, and a health insurance issuer offering health insurance coverage in connection with a group health plan, is required to permit current employees and dependents (as defined in § 2590.701–2) who are described in paragraph (a)(2) of this section to enroll for coverage under the terms of the plan if the conditions in paragraph (a)(3) of this section are satisfied. The special enrollment rights under this paragraph (a) apply without regard to the dates on which an individual would otherwise be able to enroll under the plan.

(2) *Individuals eligible for special enrollment*—(i) *When employee loses coverage.* A current employee and any dependents (including the employee's spouse) each are eligible for special enrollment in any benefit package under the plan (subject to plan eligibility rules conditioning dependent enrollment on enrollment of the employee) if—

(A) The employee and the dependents are otherwise eligible to enroll in the benefit package;

(B) When coverage under the plan was previously offered, the employee had coverage under any group health plan or health insurance coverage; and

(C) The employee satisfies the conditions of paragraph (a)(3)(i), (ii), or (iii) of this section and, if applicable, paragraph (a)(3)(iv) of this section.

(ii) *When dependent loses coverage*— (A) A dependent of a current employee (including the employee's spouse) and the employee each are eligible for special enrollment in any benefit package under the plan (subject to plan eligibility rules conditioning dependent enrollment on enrollment of the employee) if—

(1) The dependent and the employee are otherwise eligible to enroll in the benefit package;

(2) When coverage under the plan was previously offered, the dependent had coverage under any group health plan or health insurance coverage; and

(3) The dependent satisfies the conditions of paragraph (a)(3)(i), (ii), or (iii) of this section and, if applicable, paragraph (a)(3)(iv) of this section.

(B) However, the plan or issuer is not required to enroll any other dependent unless that dependent satisfies the criteria of this paragraph (a)(2)(ii), or the employee satisfies the criteria of paragraph (a)(2)(i) of this section.

(iii) *Examples.* The rules of this paragraph (a)(2) are illustrated by the following examples:

Example 1. (i) *Facts.* Individual A works for Employer X. A, A's spouse, and A's dependent children are eligible but not enrolled for coverage under X's group health plan. A's spouse works for Employer Y and at the time coverage was offered under X's plan, A was enrolled in coverage under Y's plan. Then, A loses eligibility for coverage under Y's plan.

(ii) *Conclusion.* In this *Example 1,* because A satisfies the conditions for special enrollment under paragraph (a)(2)(i) of this section, A, A's spouse, and A's dependent children are eligible for special enrollment under X's plan.

Example 2. (i) *Facts.* Individual A and A's spouse are eligible but not enrolled for coverage under Group Health Plan P maintained by A's employer. When A was first presented with an opportunity to enroll A and A's spouse, they did not have other coverage. Later, A and A's spouse enroll in Group Health Plan Q maintained by the employer of A's spouse. During a subsequent open enrollment period in P, A and A's spouse did not enroll because of their coverage under Q. They then lose eligibility for coverage under Q.

(ii) *Conclusion.* In this *Example 2,* because A and A's spouse were covered under Q when they did not enroll in P during open

D. HIPAA Final Rules, Portability, continued

enrollment, they satisfy the conditions for special enrollment under paragraphs (a)(2)(i) and (ii) of this section. Consequently, A and A's spouse are eligible for special enrollment under P.

Example 3. (i) Facts. Individual B works for Employer X. B and B's spouse are eligible but not enrolled for coverage under X's group health plan. B's spouse works for Employer Y and at the time coverage was offered under X's plan, B's spouse was enrolled in self-only coverage under Y's group health plan. Then, B's spouse loses eligibility for coverage under Y's plan.

(ii) *Conclusion.* In this *Example 3,* because B's spouse satisfies the conditions for special enrollment under paragraph (a)(2)(ii) of this section, both B and B's spouse are eligible for special enrollment under X's plan.

Example 4. (i) Facts. Individual A works for Employer X. X maintains a group health plan with two benefit packages—an HMO option and an indemnity option. Self-only and family coverage are available under both options. A enrolls for self-only coverage in the HMO option. A's spouse works for Employer Y and was enrolled for self-only coverage under Y's plan at the time coverage was offered under X's plan. Then, A's spouse loses coverage under Y's plan. A requests special enrollment for A and A's spouse under the plan's indemnity option.

(ii) *Conclusion.* In this *Example 4,* because A's spouse satisfies the conditions for special enrollment under paragraph (a)(2)(ii) of this section, both A and A's spouse can enroll in either benefit package under X's plan. Therefore, if A requests enrollment in accordance with the requirements of this section, the plan must allow A and A's spouse to enroll in the indemnity option.

(3) *Conditions for special enrollment—(i) Loss of eligibility for coverage.* In the case of an employee or dependent who has coverage that is not COBRA continuation coverage, the conditions of this paragraph (a)(3)(i) are satisfied at the time the coverage is terminated as a result of loss of eligibility (regardless of whether the individual is eligible for or elects COBRA continuation coverage). Loss of eligibility under this paragraph (a)(3)(i) does not include a loss due to the failure of the employee or dependent to pay premiums on a timely basis or termination of coverage for cause (such as making a fraudulent claim or an intentional misrepresentation of a material fact in connection with the plan). Loss of eligibility for coverage under this paragraph (a)(3)(i) includes (but is not limited to)—

(A) Loss of eligibility for coverage as a result of legal separation, divorce, cessation of dependent status (such as attaining the maximum age to be eligible as a dependent child under the plan), death of an employee, termination of employment, reduction in the number of hours of employment, and any loss of eligibility for coverage after a period

that is measured by reference to any of the foregoing;

(B) In the case of coverage offered through an HMO, or other arrangement, in the individual market that does not provide benefits to individuals who no longer reside, live, or work in a service area, loss of coverage because an individual no longer resides, lives, or works in the service area (whether or not within the choice of the individual);

(C) In the case of coverage offered through an HMO, or other arrangement, in the group market that does not provide benefits to individuals who no longer reside, live, or work in a service area, loss of coverage because an individual no longer resides, lives, or works in the service area (whether or not within the choice of the individual), and no other benefit package is available to the individual;

(D) A situation in which an individual incurs a claim that would meet or exceed a lifetime limit on all benefits; and

(E) A situation in which a plan no longer offers any benefits to the class of similarly situated individuals (as described in § 2590.702(d)) that includes the individual.

(ii) *Termination of employer contributions.* In the case of an employee or dependent who has coverage that is not COBRA continuation coverage, the conditions of this paragraph (a)(3)(ii) are satisfied at the time employer contributions towards the employee's or dependent's coverage terminate. Employer contributions include contributions by any current or former employer that was contributing to coverage for the employee or dependent.

(iii) *Exhaustion of COBRA continuation coverage.* In the case of an employee or dependent who has coverage that is COBRA continuation coverage, the conditions of this paragraph (a)(3)(iii) are satisfied at the time the COBRA continuation coverage is exhausted. For purposes of this paragraph (a)(3)(iii), an individual who satisfies the conditions for special enrollment of paragraph (a)(3)(i) of this section, does not enroll, and instead elects and exhausts COBRA continuation coverage satisfies the conditions of this paragraph (a)(3)(iii). (*Exhaustion of COBRA continuation coverage* is defined in § 2590.701–2.)

(iv) *Written statement.* A plan may require an employee declining coverage (for the employee or any dependent of the employee) to State in writing whether the coverage is being declined due to other health coverage only if, at or before the time the employee declines coverage, the employee is provided with

notice of the requirement to provide the statement (and the consequences of the employee's failure to provide the statement). If a plan requires such a statement, and an employee does not provide it, the plan is not required to provide special enrollment to the employee or any dependent of the employee under this paragraph (a)(3). A plan must treat an employee as having satisfied the plan requirement permitted under this paragraph (a)(3)(iv) if the employee provides a written statement that coverage was being declined because the employee or dependent had other coverage; a plan cannot require anything more for the employee to satisfy the plan's requirement to provide a written statement. (For example, the plan cannot require that the statement be notarized.)

(v) The rules of this paragraph (a)(3) are illustrated by the following examples:

Example 1. (i) Facts. Individual D enrolls in a group health plan maintained by Employer Y. At the time D enrolls, Y pays 70 percent of the cost of employee coverage and D pays the rest. Y announces that beginning January 1, Y will no longer make employer contributions towards the coverage. Employees may maintain coverage, however, if they pay the total cost of the coverage.

(ii) *Conclusion.* In this *Example 1,* employer contributions towards D's coverage ceased on January 1 and the conditions of paragraph (a)(3)(ii) of this section are satisfied on this date (regardless of whether D elects to pay the total cost and continue coverage under Y's plan).

Example 2. (i) Facts. A group health plan provides coverage through two options—Option 1 and Option 2. Employees can enroll in either option only within 30 days of hire or on January 1 of each year. Employee A is eligible for both options and enrolls in Option 1. Effective July 1 the plan terminates coverage under Option 1 and the plan does not create an immediate open enrollment opportunity into Option 2.

(ii) *Conclusion.* In this *Example 2,* A has experienced a loss of eligibility for coverage that satisfies paragraph (a)(3)(i) of this section, and has satisfied the other conditions for special enrollment under paragraph (a)(2)(i) of this section. Therefore, if A satisfies the other conditions of this paragraph (a), the plan must permit A to enroll in Option 2 as a special enrollee. (A may also be eligible to enroll in another group health plan, such as a plan maintained by the employer of A's spouse, as a special enrollee.) The outcome would be the same if Option 1 was terminated by an issuer and the plan made no other coverage available to A.

Example 3. (i) Facts. Individual C is covered under a group health plan maintained by Employer X. While covered under X's plan, C was eligible for but did not enroll in a plan maintained by Employer Z, the employer of C's spouse. C terminates employment with X and loses eligibility for coverage under X's plan. C has a special

D. HIPAA Final Rules, Portability, continued

enrollment right to enroll in Z's plan, but C instead elects COBRA continuation coverage under X's plan. C exhausts COBRA continuation coverage under X's plan and requests special enrollment in Z's plan.

(ii) *Conclusion.* In this *Example 3,* C has satisfied the conditions for special enrollment under paragraph (a)(3)(iii) of this section, and has satisfied the other conditions for special enrollment under paragraph (a)(2)(i) of this section. The special enrollment right that C had into Z's plan immediately after the loss of eligibility for coverage under X's plan was an offer of coverage under Z's plan. When C later exhausts COBRA coverage under X's plan, C has a second special enrollment right in Z's plan.

(4) *Applying for special enrollment and effective date of coverage*—(i) A plan or issuer must allow an employee a period of at least 30 days after an event described in paragraph (a)(3) of this section (other than an event described in paragraph (a)(3)(i)(D)) to request enrollment (for the employee or the employee's dependent). In the case of an event described in paragraph (a)(3)(i)(D) of this section (relating to loss of eligibility for coverage due to the operation of a lifetime limit on all benefits), a plan or issuer must allow an employee a period of at least 30 days after a claim is denied due to the operation of a lifetime limit on all benefits.

(ii) Coverage must begin no later than the first day of the first calendar month beginning after the date the plan or issuer receives the request for special enrollment.

(b) *Special enrollment with respect to certain dependent beneficiaries*—(1) *In general.* A group health plan, and a health insurance issuer offering health insurance coverage in connection with a group health plan, that makes coverage available with respect to dependents is required to permit individuals described in paragraph (b)(2) of this section to be enrolled for coverage in a benefit package under the terms of the plan. Paragraph (b)(3) of this section describes the required special enrollment period and the date by which coverage must begin. The special enrollment rights under this paragraph (b) apply without regard to the dates on which an individual would otherwise be able to enroll under the plan.

(2) *Individuals eligible for special enrollment.* An individual is described in this paragraph (b)(2) if the individual is otherwise eligible for coverage in a benefit package under the plan and if the individual is described in paragraph (b)(2)(i), (ii), (iii), (iv), (v), or (vi) of this section.

(i) *Current employee only.* A current employee is described in this paragraph

(b)(2)(i) if a person becomes a dependent of the individual through marriage, birth, adoption, or placement for adoption.

(ii) *Spouse of a participant only.* An individual is described in this paragraph (b)(2)(ii) if either —
(A) The individual becomes the spouse of a participant; or
(B) The individual is a spouse of a participant and a child becomes a dependent of the participant through birth, adoption, or placement for adoption.

(iii) *Current employee and spouse.* A current employee and an individual who is or becomes a spouse of such an employee, are described in this paragraph (b)(2)(iii) if either—
(A) The employee and the spouse become married; or
(B) The employee and spouse are married and a child becomes a dependent of the employee through birth, adoption, or placement for adoption.

(iv) *Dependent of a participant only.* An individual is described in this paragraph (b)(2)(iv) if the individual is a dependent (as defined in § 2590.701–2) of a participant and the individual has become a dependent of the participant through marriage, birth, adoption, or placement for adoption.

(v) *Current employee and a new dependent.* A current employee and an individual who is a dependent of the employee, are described in this paragraph (b)(2)(v) if the individual becomes a dependent of the employee through marriage, birth, adoption, or placement for adoption.

(vi) *Current employee, spouse, and a new dependent.* A current employee, the employee's spouse, and the employee's dependent are described in this paragraph (b)(2)(vi) if the dependent becomes a dependent of the employee through marriage, birth, adoption, or placement for adoption.

(3) *Applying for special enrollment and effective date of coverage*—(i) *Request.* A plan or issuer must allow an individual a period of at least 30 days after the date of the marriage, birth, adoption, or placement for adoption (or, if dependent coverage is not generally made available at the time of the marriage, birth, adoption, or placement for adoption, a period of at least 30 days after the date the plan makes dependent coverage generally available) to request enrollment (for the individual or the individual's dependent).

(ii) *Reasonable procedures for special enrollment.* [Reserved]

(iii) *Date coverage must begin*—(A) *Marriage.* In the case of marriage, coverage must begin no later than the

first day of the first calendar month beginning after the date the plan or issuer receives the request for special enrollment.

(B) *Birth, adoption, or placement for adoption.* Coverage must begin in the case of a dependent's birth on the date of birth and in the case of a dependent's adoption or placement for adoption no later than the date of such adoption or placement for adoption (or, if dependent coverage is not made generally available at the time of the birth, adoption, or placement for adoption, the date the plan makes dependent coverage available).

(4) *Examples.* The rules of this paragraph (b) are illustrated by the following examples:

Example 1. (i) *Facts.* An employer maintains a group health plan that offers all employees employee-only coverage, employee-plus-spouse coverage, or family coverage. Under the terms of the plan, any employee may elect to enroll when first hired (with coverage beginning on the date of hire) or during an annual open enrollment period held each December (with coverage beginning the following January 1). Employee A is hired on September 3. A is married to B, and they have no children. On March 15 in the following year a child C is born to A and B. Before that date, A and B have not been enrolled in the plan.

(ii) *Conclusion.* In this *Example 1,* the conditions for special enrollment of an employee with a spouse and new dependent under paragraph (b)(2)(vi) of this section are satisfied. If A satisfies the conditions of paragraph (b)(3) of this section for requesting enrollment timely, the plan will satisfy this paragraph (b) if it allows A to enroll either with employee-only coverage, with employee-plus-spouse coverage (for A and B), or with family coverage (for A, B, and C). The plan must allow whatever coverage is chosen to begin on March 15, the date of C's birth.

Example 2. (i) *Facts.* Individual D works for Employer X. X maintains a group health plan with two benefit packages—an HMO option and an indemnity option. Self-only and family coverage are available under both options. D enrolls for self-only coverage in the HMO option. Then, a child, E, is placed for adoption with D. Within 30 days of the placement of E for adoption, D requests enrollment for D and E under the plan's indemnity option.

(ii) *Conclusion.* In this *Example 2,* D and E satisfy the conditions for special enrollment under paragraphs (b)(2)(v) and (b)(3) of this section. Therefore, the plan must allow D and E to enroll in the indemnity coverage, effective as of the date of the placement for adoption.

(c) *Notice of special enrollment.* At or before the time an employee is initially offered the opportunity to enroll in a group health plan, the plan must furnish the employee with a notice of special enrollment that complies with the requirements of this paragraph (c).

D. HIPAA Final Rules, Portability, continued

(1) *Description of special enrollment rights.* The notice of special enrollment must include a description of special enrollment rights. The following model language may be used to satisfy this requirement:

If you are declining enrollment for yourself or your dependents (including your spouse) because of other health insurance or group health plan coverage, you may be able to enroll yourself and your dependents in this plan if you or your dependents lose eligibility for that other coverage (or if the employer stops contributing towards your or your dependents' other coverage). However, you must request enrollment within [insert "30 days" or any longer period that applies under the plan] after your or your dependents' other coverage ends (or after the employer stops contributing toward the other coverage).

In addition, if you have a new dependent as a result of marriage, birth, adoption, or placement for adoption, you may be able to enroll yourself and your dependents. However, you must request enrollment within [insert "30 days" or any longer period that applies under the plan] after the marriage, birth, adoption, or placement for adoption.

To request special enrollment or obtain more information, contact [insert the name, title, telephone number, and any additional contact information of the appropriate plan representative].

(2) *Additional information that may be required.* The notice of special enrollment must also include, if applicable, the notice described in paragraph (a)(3)(iv) of this section (the notice required to be furnished to an individual declining coverage if the plan requires the reason for declining coverage to be in writing).

(d) *Treatment of special enrollees*—(1) If an individual requests enrollment while the individual is entitled to special enrollment under either paragraph (a) or (b) of this section, the individual is a special enrollee, even if the request for enrollment coincides with a late enrollment opportunity under the plan. Therefore, the individual cannot be treated as a late enrollee.

(2) Special enrollees must be offered all the benefit packages available to similarly situated individuals who enroll when first eligible. For this purpose, any difference in benefits or cost-sharing requirements for different individuals constitutes a different benefit package. In addition, a special enrollee cannot be required to pay more for coverage than a similarly situated individual who enrolls in the same coverage when first eligible. The length of any preexisting condition exclusion that may be applied to a special enrollee cannot exceed the length of any preexisting condition exclusion that is

applied to similarly situated individuals who enroll when first eligible. For rules prohibiting the application of a preexisting condition exclusion to certain newborns, adopted children, and children placed for adoption, see § 2590.701–3(b).

(3) The rules of this section are illustrated by the following example:

Example. (i) *Facts.* Employer Y maintains a group health plan that has an enrollment period for late enrollees every November 1 through November 30 with coverage effective the following January 1. On October 18, Individual B loses coverage under another group health plan and satisfies the requirements of paragraphs (a)(2), (3), and (4) of this section. B submits a completed application for coverage on November 2.

(ii) *Conclusion.* In this *Example,* B is a special enrollee. Therefore, even though B's request for enrollment coincides with an open enrollment period, B's coverage is required to be made effective no later than December 1 (rather than the plan's January 1 effective date for late enrollees).

§ 2590.701–7 HMO affiliation period as an alternative to a preexisting condition exclusion.

(a) *In general.* A group health plan offering health insurance coverage through an HMO, or an HMO that offers health insurance coverage in connection with a group health plan, may impose an affiliation period only if each of the following requirements is satisfied—

(1) No preexisting condition exclusion is imposed with respect to any coverage offered by the HMO in connection with the particular group health plan.

(2) No premium is charged to a participant or beneficiary for the affiliation period.

(3) The affiliation period for the HMO coverage is imposed consistent with the requirements of § 2590.702 (prohibiting discrimination based on a health factor).

(4) The affiliation period does not exceed 2 months (or 3 months in the case of a late enrollee).

(5) The affiliation period begins on the enrollment date, or in the case of a late enrollee, the affiliation period begins on the day that would be the first day of coverage but for the affiliation period.

(6) The affiliation period for enrollment in the HMO under a plan runs concurrently with any waiting period.

(b) *Examples.* The rules of paragraph (a) of this section are illustrated by the following examples:

Example 1. (i) *Facts.* An employer sponsors a group health plan. Benefits under the plan are provided through an HMO, which imposes a two-month affiliation period. In order to be eligible under the plan, employees must have worked for the

employer for six months. Individual A begins working for the employer on February 1.

(ii) *Conclusion.* In this *Example 1,* Individual A's enrollment date is February 1 (see § 2590.701–3(a)(2)), and both the waiting period and the affiliation period begin on this date and run concurrently. Therefore, the affiliation period ends on March 31, the waiting period ends on July 31, and A is eligible to have coverage begin on August 1.

Example 2. (i) *Facts.* A group health plan has two benefit package options, a fee-for-service option and an HMO option. The HMO imposes a 1-month affiliation period. Individual B is enrolled in the fee-for-service option for more than one month and then decides to switch to the HMO option at open season.

(ii) *Conclusion.* In this *Example 2,* the HMO may not impose the affiliation period with respect to B because any affiliation period would have to begin on B's enrollment date in the plan rather than the date that B enrolled in the HMO option. Therefore, the affiliation period would have expired before B switched to the HMO option.

Example 3. (i) *Facts.* An employer sponsors a group health plan that provides benefits through an HMO. The plan imposes a two-month affiliation period with respect to salaried employees, but it does not impose an affiliation period with respect to hourly employees.

(ii) *Conclusion.* In this *Example 3,* the plan may impose the affiliation period with respect to salaried employees without imposing any affiliation period with respect to hourly employees (unless, under the circumstances, treating salaried and hourly employees differently does not comply with the requirements of § 2590.702).

(c) *Alternatives to affiliation period.* An HMO may use alternative methods in lieu of an affiliation period to address adverse selection, as approved by the State insurance commissioner or other official designated to regulate HMOs. However, an arrangement that is in the nature of a preexisting condition exclusion cannot be an alternative to an affiliation period. Nothing in this part requires a State to receive proposals for or approve alternatives to affiliation periods.

■ 4. Section 2590.701–8 is added and reserved to read as follows:

§ 2590.701–8 Interaction with the Family and Medical Leave Act. [Reserved]

■ 5. Revise the heading of subpart D to read as follows:

Subpart D—General Provisions Related to Subparts B and C

■ 6. Sections 2590.731, 2590.732 and 2590.736 are revised to read as follows:

§ 2590.731 Preemption; State flexibility; construction.

(a) *Continued applicability of State law with respect to health insurance issuers.* Subject to paragraph (b) of this

D. HIPAA Final Rules, Portability, continued

Federal Register / Vol. 69, No. 250 / Thursday, December 30, 2004 / Rules and Regulations   78779

section and except as provided in paragraph (c) of this section, part 7 of subtitle B of Title I of the Act is not to be construed to supersede any provision of State law which establishes, implements, or continues in effect any standard or requirement solely relating to health insurance issuers in connection with group health insurance coverage except to the extent that such standard or requirement prevents the application of a requirement of this part.

(b) *Continued preemption with respect to group health plans.* Nothing in part 7 of subtitle B of Title I of the Act affects or modifies the provisions of section 514 of the Act with respect to group health plans.

(c) *Special rules*—(1) *In general.* Subject to paragraph (c)(2) of this section, the provisions of part 7 of subtitle B of Title I of the Act relating to health insurance coverage offered by a health insurance issuer supersede any provision of State law which establishes, implements, or continues in effect a standard or requirement applicable to imposition of a preexisting condition exclusion specifically governed by section 701 which differs from the standards or requirements specified in such section.

(2) *Exceptions.* Only in relation to health insurance coverage offered by a health insurance issuer, the provisions of this part do not supersede any provision of State law to the extent that such provision—

(i) Shortens the period of time from the "6-month period" described in section 701(a)(1) of the Act and § 2590.701–3(a)(1)(i) (for purposes of identifying a preexisting condition);

(ii) Shortens the period of time from the "12 months" and "18 months" described in section 701(a)(2) of the Act and § 2590.701–3(a)(1)(ii) (for purposes of applying a preexisting condition exclusion period);

(iii) Provides for a greater number of days than the "63-day period" described in sections 701(c)(2)(A) and (d)(4)(A) of the Act and §§ 2590.701–3(a)(1)(iii) and 2590.701–4 (for purposes of applying the break in coverage rules);

(iv) Provides for a greater number of days than the "30-day period" described in sections 701(b)(2) and (d)(1) of the Act and § 2590.701–3(b) (for purposes of the enrollment period and preexisting condition exclusion periods for certain newborns and children that are adopted or placed for adoption);

(v) Prohibits the imposition of any preexisting condition exclusion in cases not described in section 701(d) of the Act or expands the exceptions described therein;

(vi) Requires special enrollment periods in addition to those required under section 701(f) of the Act; or

(vii) Reduces the maximum period permitted in an affiliation period under section 701(g)(1)(B) of the Act.

(d) *Definitions*—(1) *State law.* For purposes of this section the term *State law* includes all laws, decisions, rules, regulations, or other State action having the effect of law, of any State. *A law of the United States applicable only to the District of Columbia is treated as a State law rather than a law of the United States.*

(2) *State.* For purposes of this section the term *State* includes a State (as defined in § 2590.701–2), any political subdivisions of a State, or any agency or instrumentality of either.

§ 2590.732 Special rules relating to group health plans.

(a) *Group health plan*—(1) *Defined.* A group health plan means an employee welfare benefit plan to the extent that the plan provides medical care (including items and services paid for as medical care) to employees (including both current and former employees) or their dependents (as defined under the terms of the plan) directly or through insurance, reimbursement, or otherwise.

(2) *Determination of number of plans.* [Reserved]

(b) *General exception for certain small group health plans.* The requirements of this part, other than § 2590.711, do not apply to any group health plan (and group health insurance coverage) for any plan year if, on the first day of the plan year, the plan has fewer than two participants who are current employees.

(c) *Excepted benefits*—(1) *In general.* The requirements of this Part do not apply to any group health plan (or any group health insurance coverage) in relation to its provision of the benefits described in paragraph (c)(2), (3), (4), or (5) of this section (or any combination of these benefits).

(2) *Benefits excepted in all circumstances.* The following benefits are excepted in all circumstances—

(i) Coverage only for accident (including accidental death and dismemberment);

(ii) Disability income coverage;

(iii) Liability insurance, including general liability insurance and automobile liability insurance;

(iv) Coverage issued as a supplement to liability insurance;

(v) Workers' compensation or similar coverage;

(vi) Automobile medical payment insurance;

(vii) Credit-only insurance (for example, mortgage insurance); and

(viii) Coverage for on-site medical clinics.

(3) *Limited excepted benefits*—(i) *In general.* Limited-scope dental benefits, limited-scope vision benefits, or long-term care benefits are excepted if they are provided under a separate policy, certificate, or contract of insurance, or are otherwise not an integral part of a group health plan as described in paragraph (c)(3)(ii) of this section. In addition, benefits provided under a health flexible spending arrangement are excepted benefits if they satisfy the requirements of paragraph (c)(3)(v) of this section.

(ii) *Not an integral part of a group health plan.* For purposes of this paragraph (c)(3), benefits are not an integral part of a group health plan (whether the benefits are provided through the same plan or a separate plan) only if the following two requirements are satisfied—

(A) Participants must have the right to elect not to receive coverage for the benefits; and

(B) If a participant elects to receive coverage for the benefits, the participant must pay an additional premium or contribution for that coverage.

(iii) *Limited scope*—(A) *Dental benefits.* Limited scope dental benefits are benefits substantially all of which are for treatment of the mouth (including any organ or structure within the mouth).

(B) *Vision benefits.* Limited scope vision benefits are benefits substantially all of which are for treatment of the eye.

(iv) *Long-term care.* Long-term care benefits are benefits that are either—

(A) Subject to State long-term care insurance laws;

(B) For qualified long-term care services, as defined in section 7702B(c)(1) of the Internal Revenue Code, or provided under a qualified long-term care insurance contract, as defined in section 7702B(b) of the Internal Revenue Code; or

(C) Based on cognitive impairment or a loss of functional capacity that is expected to be chronic.

(v) *Health flexible spending arrangements.* Benefits provided under a health flexible spending arrangement (as defined in section 106(c)(2) of the Internal Revenue Code) are excepted for a class of participants only if they satisfy the following two requirements—

(A) Other group health plan coverage, not limited to excepted benefits, is made available for the year to the class of participants by reason of their employment; and

(B) The arrangement is structured so that the maximum benefit payable to any participant in the class for a year

D. HIPAA Final Rules, Portability, continued

cannot exceed two times the participant's salary reduction election under the arrangement for the year (or, if greater, cannot exceed $500 plus the amount of the participant's salary reduction election). For this purpose, any amount that an employee can elect to receive as taxable income but elects to apply to the health flexible spending arrangement is considered a salary reduction election (regardless of whether the amount is characterized as salary or as a credit under the arrangement).

(4) *Noncoordinated benefits*—(i) *Excepted benefits that are not coordinated.* Coverage for only a specified disease or illness (for example, cancer-only policies) or hospital indemnity or other fixed indemnity insurance is excepted only if it meets each of the conditions specified in paragraph (c)(4)(ii) of this section. To be hospital indemnity or other fixed indemnity insurance, the insurance must pay a fixed dollar amount per day (or per other period) of hospitalization or illness (for example, $100/day) regardless of the amount of expenses incurred.

(ii) *Conditions.* Benefits are described in paragraph (c)(4)(i) of this section only if—

(A) The benefits are provided under a separate policy, certificate, or contract of insurance;

(B) There is no coordination between the provision of the benefits and an exclusion of benefits under any group health plan maintained by the same plan sponsor; and

(C) The benefits are paid with respect to an event without regard to whether benefits are provided with respect to the event under any group health plan maintained by the same plan sponsor.

(iii) *Example.* The rules of this paragraph (c)(4) are illustrated by the following example:

Example. (i) *Facts.* An employer sponsors a group health plan that provides coverage through an insurance policy. The policy provides benefits only for hospital stays at a fixed percentage of hospital expenses up to a maximum of $100 a day.

(ii) *Conclusion.* In this *Example*, even though the benefits under the policy satisfy the conditions in paragraph (c)(4)(ii) of this section, because the policy pays a percentage of expenses incurred rather than a fixed dollar amount, the benefits under the policy are not excepted benefits under this paragraph (c)(4). This is the result even if, in practice, the policy pays the maximum of $100 for every day of hospitalization.

(5) *Supplemental benefits.* (i) The following benefits are excepted only if they are provided under a separate policy, certificate, or contract of insurance—

(A) Medicare supplemental health insurance (as defined under section 1882(g)(1) of the Social Security Act; also known as Medigap or MedSupp insurance);

(B) Coverage supplemental to the coverage provided under Chapter 55, Title 10 of the United States Code (also known as TRICARE supplemental programs); and

(C) Similar supplemental coverage provided to coverage under a group health plan. To be similar supplemental coverage, the coverage must be specifically designed to fill gaps in primary coverage, such as coinsurance or deductibles. Similar supplemental coverage does not include coverage that becomes secondary or supplemental only under a coordination-of-benefits provision.

(ii) The rules of this paragraph (c)(5) are illustrated by the following example:

Example. (i) *Facts.* An employer sponsors a group health plan that provides coverage for both active employees and retirees. The coverage for retirees supplements benefits provided by Medicare, but does not meet the requirements for a supplemental policy under section 1882(g)(1) of the Social Security Act.

(ii) *Conclusion.* In this *Example*, the coverage provided to retirees does not meet the definition of supplemental excepted benefits under this paragraph (c)(5) because the coverage is not Medicare supplemental insurance as defined under section 1882(g)(1) of the Social Security Act, is not a TRICARE supplemental program, and is not supplemental to coverage provided under a group health plan.

(d) *Treatment of partnerships.* For purposes of this part:

(1) *Treatment as a group health plan.* Any plan, fund, or program that would not be (but for this paragraph (d)) an employee welfare benefit plan and that is established or maintained by a partnership, to the extent that the plan, fund, or program provides medical care (including items and services paid for as medical care) to present or former partners in the partnership or to their dependents (as defined under the terms of the plan, fund, or program), directly or through insurance, reimbursement, or otherwise, is treated (subject to paragraph (d)(2)) as an employee welfare benefit plan that is a group health plan.

(2) *Employment relationship.* In the case of a group health plan, the term *employer* also includes the partnership in relation to any bona fide partner. In addition, the term *employee* also includes any bona fide partner. Whether or not an individual is a bona fide partner is determined based on all the relevant facts and circumstances, including whether the individual

performs services on behalf of the partnership.

(3) *Participants of group health plans.* In the case of a group health plan, the term participant also includes any individual described in paragraph (d)(3)(i) or (ii) of this section if the individual is, or may become, eligible to receive a benefit under the plan or the individual's beneficiaries may be eligible to receive any such benefit.

(i) In connection with a group health plan maintained by a partnership, the individual is a partner in relation to the partnership.

(ii) In connection with a group health plan maintained by a self-employed individual (under which one or more employees are participants), the individual is the self-employed individual.

(e) *Determining the average number of employees.* [Reserved]

§ 2590.736 Applicability dates.

Sections 2590.701–1 through 2590.701–8 and 2590.731 through 2590.736 are applicable for plan years beginning on or after July 1, 2005. Until the applicability date for this regulation, plans and issuers are required to continue to comply with the corresponding sections of 29 CFR part 2590, contained in the 29 CFR, parts 1927 to end, edition revised as of July 1, 2004.

Signed at Washington, DC, this 1st day of December, 2004.

Ann L. Combs,

Assistant Secretary, Employee Benefits Security Administration, U.S. Department of Labor.

Department of Health and Human Services

45 CFR Subtitle A

■ For the reasons set forth in the preamble, the Department of Health and Human Services amends 45 CFR Part 144 and Part 146 as follows:

PART 144—REQUIREMENTS RELATING TO HEALTH INSURANCE COVERAGE

■ A. Part 144 is amended as set forth below:

■ 1. The authority citation for Part 144 is revised to read as follows:

Authority: Secs. 2701 through 2763, 2791, and 2792 of the Public Health Service Act, 42 U.S.C. 300gg through 300gg-63, 300gg-91, 30gg-92 as amended by HIPAA (Public Law 104–191, 110 Stat. 1936), MHPA (Public Law 104–204, 110 Stat. 2944, as amended by Public Law 107–116, 115 Stat. 2177), NMHPA (Public Law 104–204, 110 Stat. 2935), WHCRA (Public Law 105–277, 112 Stat. 2681–436), and section 103(c)(4) of HIPAA.

D. HIPAA Final Rules, Portability, continued

■ 2. Section 144.103 is revised to read as follows:

§144.103 Definitions.

For purposes of parts 146 (group market), 148 (individual market), and 150 (enforcement) of this subchapter, the following definitions apply unless otherwise provided:

Affiliation period means a period of time that must expire before health insurance coverage provided by an HMO becomes effective, and during which the HMO is not required to provide benefits.

Applicable State authority means, with respect to a health insurance issuer in a State, the State insurance commissioner or official or officials designated by the State to enforce the requirements of 45 CFR parts 146 and 148 for the State involved with respect to the issuer.

Beneficiary has the meaning given the term under section 3(8) of the Employee Retirement Income Security Act of 1974 (ERISA), which States, "a person designated by a participant, or by the terms of an employee benefit plan, who is or may become entitled to a benefit" under the plan.

Bona fide association means, with respect to health insurance coverage offered in a State, an association that meets the following conditions:

(1) Has been actively in existence for at least 5 years.

(2) Has been formed and maintained in good faith for purposes other than obtaining insurance.

(3) Does not condition membership in the association on any health status-related factor relating to an individual (including an employee of an employer or a dependent of any employee).

(4) Makes health insurance coverage offered through the association available to all members regardless of any health status-related factor relating to the members (or individuals eligible for coverage through a member).

(5) Does not make health insurance coverage offered through the association available other than in connection with a member of the association.

(6) Meets any additional requirements that may be imposed under State law.

Church plan means a Church plan within the meaning of section 3(33) of ERISA.

COBRA definitions:

(1) *COBRA* means Title X of the Consolidated Omnibus Budget Reconciliation Act of 1985, as amended.

(2) *COBRA continuation coverage* means coverage, under a group health plan, that satisfies an applicable COBRA continuation provision.

(3) *COBRA continuation provision* means sections 601–608 of the Employee Retirement Income Security Act, section 4980B of the Internal Revenue Code of 1986 (other than paragraph (f)(1) of such section 4980B insofar as it relates to pediatric vaccines), or Title XXII of the PHS Act.

(4) *Continuation coverage* means coverage under a COBRA continuation provision or a similar State program. Coverage provided by a plan that is subject to a COBRA continuation provision or similar State program, but that does not satisfy all the requirements of that provision or program, will be deemed to be continuation coverage if it allows an individual to elect to continue coverage for a period of at least 18 months. Continuation coverage does not include coverage under a conversion policy required to be offered to an individual upon exhaustion of continuation coverage, nor does it include continuation coverage under the Federal Employees Health Benefits Program.

(5) *Exhaustion of COBRA continuation coverage* means that an individual's COBRA continuation coverage ceases for any reason other than either failure of the individual to pay premiums on a timely basis, or for cause (such as making a fraudulent claim or an intentional misrepresentation of a material fact in connection with the plan). An individual is considered to have exhausted COBRA continuation coverage if such coverage ceases—

(i) Due to the failure of the employer or other responsible entity to remit premiums on a timely basis;

(ii) When the individual no longer resides, lives, or works in the service area of an HMO or similar program (whether or not within the choice of the individual) and there is no other COBRA continuation coverage available to the individual; or

(iii) When the individual incurs a claim that would meet or exceed a lifetime limit on all benefits and there is no other COBRA continuation coverage available to the individual.

(6) *Exhaustion of continuation coverage* means that an individual's continuation coverage ceases for any reason other than either failure of the individual to pay premiums on a timely basis, or for cause (such as making a fraudulent claim or an intentional misrepresentation of a material fact in connection with the plan). An individual is considered to have exhausted continuation coverage if—

(i) Coverage ceases due to the failure of the employer or other responsible entity to remit premiums on a timely basis;

(ii) When the individual no longer resides, lives or works in a service area of an HMO or similar program (whether or not within the choice of the individual) and there is no other continuation coverage available to the individual; or

(iii) When the individual incurs a claim that would meet or exceed a lifetime limit on all benefits and there is no other continuation coverage available to the individual.

Condition means a medical condition.

Creditable coverage has the meaning given the term in 45 CFR 146.113(a).

Dependent means any individual who is or may become eligible for coverage under the terms of a group health plan because of a relationship to a participant.

Eligible individual, for purposes of—

(1) The group market provisions in 45 CFR part 146, subpart E, is defined in 45 CFR 146.150(b); and

(2) The individual market provisions in 45 CFR part 148, is defined in 45 CFR 148.103.

Employee has the meaning given the term under section 3(6) of ERISA, which States, "any individual employed by an employer."

Employer has the meaning given the term under section 3(5) of ERISA, which States, "any person acting directly as an employer, or indirectly in the interest of an employer, in relation to an employee benefit plan; and includes a group or association of employers acting for an employer in such capacity."

Enroll means to become covered for benefits under a group health plan (that is, when coverage becomes effective), without regard to when the individual may have completed or filed any forms that are required in order to become covered under the plan. For this purpose, an individual who has health coverage under a group health plan is enrolled in the plan regardless of whether the individual elects coverage, the individual is a dependent who becomes covered as a result of an election by a participant, or the individual becomes covered without an election.

Enrollment date definitions (*enrollment date, first day of coverage,* and *waiting period*) are set forth in 45 CFR 146.111(a)(3)(i) through (iii).

ERISA stands for the Employee Retirement Income Security Act of 1974, as amended (29 U.S.C. 1001 et seq.).

Excepted benefits, consistent for purposes of the—

(1) Group market provisions in 45 CFR part 146 subpart D, is defined in 45 CFR 146.145(c); and

D. HIPAA Final Rules, Portability, continued

78782   Federal Register / Vol. 69, No. 250 / Thursday, December 30, 2004 / Rules and Regulations

(2) Individual market provisions in 45 CFR part 148, is defined in 45 CFR 148.220.

Federal governmental plan means a governmental plan established or maintained for its employees by the Government of the United States or by any agency or instrumentality of such Government.

Genetic information means information about genes, gene products, and inherited characteristics that may derive from the individual or a family member. This includes information regarding carrier status and information derived from laboratory tests that identify mutations in specific genes or chromosomes, physical medical examinations, family histories, and direct analysis of genes or chromosomes.

Governmental plan means a governmental plan within the meaning of section 3(32) of ERISA.

Group health insurance coverage means health insurance coverage offered in connection with a group health plan.

Group health plan or *plan* means a group health plan within the meaning of 45 CFR 146.145(a).

Group market means the market for health insurance coverage offered in connection with a group health plan. (However, certain very small plans may be treated as being in the individual market, rather than the group market; see the definition of *individual market* in this section.)

Health insurance coverage means benefits consisting of medical care (provided directly, through insurance or reimbursement, or otherwise) under any hospital or medical service policy or certificate, hospital or medical service plan contract, or HMO contract offered by a health insurance issuer. Health insurance coverage includes group health insurance coverage, individual health insurance coverage, and short-term, limited-duration insurance.

Health insurance issuer or *issuer* means an insurance company, insurance service, or insurance organization (including an HMO) that is required to be licensed to engage in the business of insurance in a State and that is subject to State law that regulates insurance (within the meaning of section 514(b)(2) of ERISA). This term does not include a group health plan.

Health maintenance organization or *HMO* means—

(1) A Federally qualified health maintenance organization (as defined in section 1301(a) of the PHS Act);

(2) An organization recognized under State law as a health maintenance organization; or

(3) A similar organization regulated under State law for solvency in the same manner and to the same extent as such a health maintenance organization.

Health status-related factor is any factor identified as a health factor in 45 CFR 146.121(a).

Individual health insurance coverage means health insurance coverage offered to individuals in the individual market, but does not include short-term, limited-duration insurance. Individual health insurance coverage can include dependent coverage.

Individual market means the market for health insurance coverage offered to individuals other than in connection with a group health plan. Unless a State elects otherwise in accordance with section 2791(e)(1)(B)(ii) of the PHS Act, such term also includes coverage offered in connection with a group health plan that has fewer than two participants who are current employees on the first day of the plan year.

Internal Revenue Code means the Internal Revenue Code of 1986, as amended (Title 26, United States Code).

Issuer means a *health insurance issuer.*

Large employer means, in connection with a group health plan with respect to a calendar year and a plan year, an employer who employed an average of at least 51 employees on business days during the preceding calendar year and who employs at least 2 employees on the first day of the plan year, unless otherwise provided under State law.

Large group market means the health insurance market under which individuals obtain health insurance coverage (directly or through any arrangement) on behalf of themselves (and their dependents) through a group health plan maintained by a large employer, unless otherwise provided under State law.

Late enrollment definitions (*late enrollee* and *late enrollment*) are set forth in 45 CFR 146.111(a)(3)(v) and (vi).

Medical care means amounts paid for—

(1) The diagnosis, cure, mitigation, treatment, or prevention of disease, or amounts paid for the purpose of affecting any structure or function of the body;

(2) Transportation primarily for and essential to medical care referred to in paragraph (1) of this definition; and

(3) Insurance covering medical care referred to in paragraphs (1) and (2) of this definition.

Medical condition or *condition* means any condition, whether physical or mental, including, but not limited to, any condition resulting from illness, injury (whether or not the injury is accidental), pregnancy, or congenital malformation. However, genetic information is not a condition.

Network plan means health insurance coverage of a health insurance issuer under which the financing and delivery of medical care (including items and services paid for as medical care) are provided, in whole or in part, through a defined set of providers under contract with the issuer.

Non-Federal governmental plan means a governmental plan that is not a Federal governmental plan.

Participant has the meaning given the term under section 3(7) of ERISA, which States, "any employee or former employee of an employer, or any member or former member of an employee organization, who is or may become eligible to receive a benefit of any type from an employee benefit plan which covers employees of such employer or members of such organization, or whose beneficiaries may be eligible to receive any such benefit."

PHS Act stands for the Public Health Service Act (42 U.S.C. 201 *et seq.*).

Placement, or being placed, for adoption means the assumption and retention of a legal obligation for total or partial support of a child by a person with whom the child has been placed in anticipation of the child's adoption. The child's placement for adoption with such person ends upon the termination of such legal obligation.

Plan sponsor has the meaning given the term under section 3(16)(B) of ERISA, which states, "(i) the employer in the case of an employee benefit plan established or maintained by a single employer, (ii) the employee organization in the case of a plan established or maintained by an employee organization, or (iii) in the case of a plan established or maintained by two or more employers or jointly by one or more employers and one or more employee organizations, the association, committee, joint board of trustees, or other similar group of representatives of the parties who establish or maintain the plan."

Plan year means the year that is designated as the plan year in the plan document of a group health plan, except that if the plan document does not designate a plan year or if there is no plan document, the plan year is—

(1) The deductible or limit year used under the plan;

(2) If the plan does not impose deductibles or limits on a yearly basis, then the plan year is the policy year;

(3) If the plan does not impose deductibles or limits on a yearly basis, and either the plan is not insured or the

D. HIPAA Final Rules, Portability, continued

insurance policy is not renewed on an annual basis, then the plan year is the employer's taxable year; or

(4) In any other case, the plan year is the calendar year.

Preexisting condition exclusion has the meaning given the term in 45 CFR 146.111(a)(1), with respect to group health plans and group health insurance coverage. With respect to individual market health insurance issuers or other entities providing coverage to federally eligible individuals pursuant to 45 CFR part 148, preexisting condition exclusion means a limitation or exclusion of benefits relating to a condition based on the fact that the condition was present before the first day of coverage, whether or not any medical advice, diagnosis, care, or treatment was recommended or received before that day. A preexisting condition exclusion includes any exclusion applicable to an individual as a result of information that is obtained relating to an individual's health status before the individual's first day of coverage, such as a condition identified as a result of a pre-enrollment questionnaire or physical examination given to the individual, or review of medical records relating to the pre-enrollment period.

Public health plan has the meaning given the term in 45 CFR 146.113(a)(1)(ix).

Short-term, limited-duration insurance means health insurance coverage provided pursuant to a contract with an issuer that has an expiration date specified in the contract (taking into account any extensions that may be elected by the policyholder without the issuer's consent) that is less than 12 months after the original effective date of the contract.

Significant break in coverage has the meaning given the term in 45 CFR 146.113(b)(2)(iii).

Small employer means, in connection with a group health plan with respect to a calendar year and a plan year, an employer who employed an average of at least 2 but not more than 50 employees on business days during the preceding calendar year and who employs at least 2 employees on the first day of the plan year, unless otherwise provided under State law.

Small group market means the health insurance market under which individuals obtain health insurance coverage (directly or through any arrangement) on behalf of themselves (and their dependents) through a group health plan maintained by a small employer.

Special enrollment means enrollment in a group health plan or group health

insurance coverage under the rights described in 45 CFR 146.117.

State means each of the several States, the District of Columbia, Puerto Rico, the Virgin Islands, Guam, American Samoa, and the Northern Mariana Islands.

State health benefits risk pool has the meaning given the term in 45 CFR § 146.113(a)(1)(vii).

Waiting period has the meaning given the term in 45 CFR 146.111(a)(3)(iii).

PART 146—REQUIREMENTS FOR THE GROUP HEALTH INSURANCE MARKET

■ B. Part 146 is amended as set forth below:

■ 1. The authority citation for Part 146 is revised to read as follows:

Authority: Secs. 2701 through 2763, 2791, and 2792 of the Public Health Service Act, 42 U.S.C. 300gg through 300gg-63, 300gg-91, 30gg-92 as amended by HIPAA (Public Law 104-191, 110 Stat. 1936), MHPA (Public Law 104-204, 110 Stat. 2944, as amended by Public Law 107-116, 115 Stat. 2177), NMHPA (Public Law 104-204, 110 Stat. 2935), WHCRA (Public Law 105-277, 112 Stat. 2681-436), and section 103(c)(4) of HIPAA.

■ 2. Revise § 146.111 to read as follows:

§ 146.111 Limitations on preexisting condition exclusion period.

(a) *Preexisting condition exclusion*—(1) *Defined.*—(i) A *preexisting condition exclusion* means a limitation or exclusion of benefits relating to a condition based on the fact that the condition was present before the effective date of coverage under a group health plan or group health insurance coverage, whether or not any medical advice, diagnosis, care, or treatment was recommended or received before that day. A preexisting condition exclusion includes any exclusion applicable to an individual as a result of information relating to an individual's health status before the individual's effective date of coverage under a group health plan or group health insurance coverage, such as a condition identified as a result of a pre-enrollment questionnaire or physical examination given to the individual, or review of medical records relating to the pre-enrollment period.

(ii) *Examples.* The rules of this paragraph (a)(1) are illustrated by the following examples:

Example 1. (i) *Facts.* A group health plan provides benefits solely through an insurance policy offered by Issuer S. At the expiration of the policy, the plan switches coverage to a policy offered by Issuer T. Issuer T's policy excludes benefits for any prosthesis if the body part was lost before the effective date of coverage under the policy.

(ii) *Conclusion.* In this *Example 1,* the exclusion of benefits for any prosthesis if the body part was lost before the effective date of coverage is a preexisting condition exclusion because it operates to exclude benefits for a condition based on the fact that the condition was present before the effective date of coverage under the policy. (Therefore, the exclusion of benefits is required to comply with the limitations on preexisting condition exclusions in this section. For an example illustrating the application of these limitations to a succeeding insurance policy, see *Example 3* of paragraph (a)(3)(iv) of this section.)

Example 2. (i) *Facts.* A group health plan provides coverage for cosmetic surgery in cases of accidental injury, but only if the injury occurred while the individual was covered under the plan.

(ii) *Conclusion.* In this *Example 2,* the plan provision excluding cosmetic surgery benefits for individuals injured before enrolling in the plan is a preexisting condition exclusion because it operates to exclude benefits relating to a condition based on the fact that the condition was present before the effective date of coverage. The plan provision, therefore, is subject to the limitations on preexisting condition exclusions in this section.

Example 3. (i) *Facts.* A group health plan provides coverage for the treatment of diabetes, generally not subject to any lifetime dollar limit. However, if an individual was diagnosed with diabetes before the effective date of coverage under the plan, diabetes coverage is subject to a lifetime limit of $10,000.

(ii) *Conclusion.* In this *Example 3,* the $10,000 lifetime limit is a preexisting condition exclusion because it limits benefits for a condition based on the fact that the condition was present before the effective date of coverage. The plan provision, therefore, is subject to the limitations on preexisting condition exclusions in this section.

Example 4. (i) *Facts.* A group health plan provides coverage for the treatment of acne, subject to a lifetime limit of $2,000. The plan counts against this $2,000 lifetime limit acne treatment benefits provided under prior health coverage.

(ii) *Conclusion.* In this *Example 4,* counting benefits for a specific condition provided under prior health coverage against a lifetime limit for that condition is a preexisting condition exclusion because it operates to limit benefits for a condition based on the fact that the condition was present before the effective date of coverage. The plan provision, therefore, is subject to the limitations on preexisting condition exclusions in this section.

Example 5. (i) *Facts.* When an individual's coverage begins under a group health plan, the individual generally becomes eligible for all benefits. However, benefits for pregnancy are not available until the individual has been covered under the plan for 12 months.

(ii) *Conclusion.* In this *Example 5,* the requirement to be covered under the plan for 12 months to be eligible for pregnancy benefits is a subterfuge for a preexisting condition exclusion because it is designed to

D. HIPAA Final Rules, Portability, continued

exclude benefits for a condition (pregnancy) that arose before the effective date of coverage. Because a plan is prohibited under paragraph (b)(5) of this section from imposing any preexisting condition exclusion on pregnancy, the plan provision is prohibited. However, if the plan provision included an exception for women who were pregnant before the effective date of coverage under the plan (so that the provision applied only to women who became pregnant on or after the effective date of coverage) the plan provision would not be a preexisting condition exclusion (and would not be prohibited by paragraph (b)(5) of this section).

Example 6. (i) *Facts.* A group health plan provides coverage for medically necessary items and services, generally including treatment of heart conditions. However, the plan does not cover those same items and services when used for treatment of congenital heart conditions.

(ii) *Conclusion.* In this *Example 6,* the exclusion of coverage for treatment of congenital heart conditions is a preexisting condition exclusion because it operates to exclude benefits relating to a condition based on the fact that the condition was present before the effective date of coverage. The plan provision, therefore, is subject to the limitations on preexisting condition exclusions in this section.

Example 7. (i) *Facts.* A group health plan generally provides coverage for medically necessary items and services. However, the plan excludes coverage for the treatment of cleft palate.

(ii) *Conclusion.* In this *Example 7,* the exclusion of coverage for treatment of cleft palate is not a preexisting condition exclusion because the exclusion applies regardless of when the condition arose relative to the effective date of coverage. The plan provision, therefore, is not subject to the limitations on preexisting condition exclusions in this section.

Example 8. (i) *Facts.* A group health plan provides coverage for treatment of cleft palate, but only if the individual being treated has been continuously covered under the plan from the date of birth.

(ii) *Conclusion.* In this *Example 8,* the exclusion of coverage for treatment of cleft palate for individuals who have not been covered under the plan from the date of birth operates to exclude benefits in relation to a condition based on the fact that the condition was present before the effective date of coverage. The plan provision, therefore, is subject to the limitations on preexisting condition exclusions in this section.

(2) *General rules.* Subject to paragraph (b) of this section (prohibiting the imposition of a preexisting condition exclusion with respect to certain individuals and conditions), a group health plan, and a health insurance issuer offering group health insurance coverage, may impose, with respect to a participant or beneficiary, a preexisting condition exclusion only if the requirements of this paragraph (a)(2) are satisfied.

(i) *6-month look-back rule.* A preexisting condition exclusion must relate to a condition (whether physical or mental), regardless of the cause of the condition, for which medical advice, diagnosis, care, or treatment was recommended or received within the 6-month period (or such shorter period as applies under the plan) ending on the enrollment date.

(A) For purposes of this paragraph (a)(2)(i), medical advice, diagnosis, care, or treatment is taken into account only if it is recommended by, or received from, an individual licensed or similarly authorized to provide such services under State law and operating within the scope of practice authorized by State law.

(B) For purposes of this paragraph (a)(2)(i), the 6-month period ending on the enrollment date begins on the 6-month anniversary date preceding the enrollment date. For example, for an enrollment date of August 1, 1998, the 6-month period preceding the enrollment date is the period commencing on February 1, 1998 and continuing through July 31, 1998. As another example, for an enrollment date of August 30, 1998, the 6-month period preceding the enrollment date is the period commencing on February 28, 1998 and continuing through August 29, 1998.

(C) The rules of this paragraph (a)(2)(i) are illustrated by the following examples:

Example 1. (i) *Facts.* Individual *A* is diagnosed with a medical condition 8 months before *A's* enrollment date in Employer *R's* group health plan. *A's* doctor recommends that *A* take a prescription drug for 3 months, and *A* follows the recommendation.

(ii) *Conclusion.* In this *Example 1,* Employer *R's* plan may impose a preexisting condition exclusion with respect to *A's* condition because *A* received treatment during the 6-month period ending on *A's* enrollment date in Employer *R's* plan by taking the prescription medication during that period. However, if *A* did not take the prescription drug during the 6-month period, Employer *R's* plan would not be able to impose a preexisting condition exclusion with respect to that condition.

Example 2. (i) *Facts.* Individual *B* is treated for a medical condition 7 months before the enrollment date in Employer *S's* group health plan. As part of such treatment, *B's* physician recommends that a follow-up examination be given 2 months later. Despite this recommendation, *B* does not receive a follow-up examination, and no other medical advice, diagnosis, care, or treatment for that condition is recommended to *B* or received by *B* during the 6-month period ending on *B's* enrollment date in Employer *S's* plan.

(ii) *Conclusion.* In this *Example 2,* Employer *S's* plan may not impose a preexisting condition exclusion with respect to the condition for which *B* received treatment 7 months prior to the enrollment date.

Example 3. (i) *Facts.* Same facts as *Example 2,* except that Employer *S's* plan learns of the condition and attaches a rider to *B's* certificate of coverage excluding coverage for the condition. Three months after enrollment, *B's* condition recurs, and Employer *S's* plan denies payment under the rider.

(ii) *Conclusion.* In this *Example 3,* the rider is a preexisting condition exclusion and Employer *S's* plan may not impose a preexisting condition exclusion with respect to the condition for which *B* received treatment 7 months prior to the enrollment date. (In addition, such a rider would violate the provisions of § 146.121, even if *B* had received treatment for the condition within the 6-month period ending on the enrollment date.)

Example 4. (i) *Facts.* Individual *C* has asthma and is treated for that condition several times during the 6-month period before *C's* enrollment date in Employer *T's* plan. Three months after the enrollment date, *C* begins coverage under Employer *T's* plan. Two months later, *C* is hospitalized for asthma.

(ii) *Conclusion.* In this *Example 4,* Employer *T's* plan may impose a preexisting condition exclusion with respect to *C's* asthma because care relating to *C's* asthma was received during the 6-month period ending on *C's* enrollment date (which, under the rules of paragraph (a)(3)(i) of this section, is the first day of the waiting period).

Example 5. (i) *Facts.* Individual *D,* who is subject to a preexisting condition exclusion imposed by Employer *U's* plan, has diabetes, as well as retinal degeneration, a foot condition, and poor circulation (all of which are conditions that may be directly attributed to diabetes). *D* receives treatment for these conditions during the 6-month period ending on *D's* enrollment date in Employer *U's* plan. After enrolling in the plan, *D* stumbles and breaks a leg.

(ii) *Conclusion.* In this *Example 5,* the leg fracture is not a condition related to *D's* diabetes, retinal degeneration, foot condition, or poor circulation, even though they may have contributed to the accident. Therefore, benefits to treat the leg fracture cannot be subject to a preexisting condition exclusion. However, any additional medical services that may be needed because of *D's* preexisting diabetes, poor circulation, or retinal degeneration that would not be needed by another patient with a broken leg who does not have these conditions may be subject to the preexisting condition exclusion imposed under Employer *U's* plan.

(ii) *Maximum length of preexisting condition exclusion.* A preexisting condition exclusion is not permitted to extend for more than 12 months (18 months in the case of a late enrollee) after the enrollment date. For example, for an enrollment date of August 1, 1998, the 12-month period after the enrollment date is the period commencing on August 1, 1998 and continuing through July 31, 1999; the

D. HIPAA Final Rules, Portability, continued

18-month period after the enrollment date is the period commencing on August 1, 1998 and continuing through January 31, 2000.

(iii) *Reducing a preexisting condition exclusion period by creditable coverage*—(A) The period of any preexisting condition exclusion that would otherwise apply to an individual under a group health plan is reduced by the number of days of creditable coverage the individual has as of the enrollment date, as counted under § 146.113. Creditable coverage may be evidenced through a certificate of creditable coverage (required under § 146.115(a)), or through other means in accordance with the rules of § 146.115(c).

(B) The rules of this paragraph (a)(2)(iii) are illustrated by the following example:

Example. (i) *Facts.* Individual *D* works for Employer *X* and has been covered continuously under *X*'s group health plan. *D*'s spouse works for Employer *Y*. *Y* maintains a group health plan that imposes a 12-month preexisting condition exclusion (reduced by creditable coverage) on all new enrollees. *D* enrolls in *Y*'s plan, but also stays covered under *X*'s plan. *D* presents *Y*'s plan with evidence of creditable coverage under *X*'s plan.

(ii) *Conclusion.* In this *Example*, *Y*'s plan must reduce the preexisting condition exclusion period that applies to *D* by the number of days of coverage that *D* had under *X*'s plan as of *D*'s enrollment date in *Y*'s plan (even though *D*'s coverage under *X*'s plan was continuing as of that date).

(iv) *Other standards.* See § 146.121 for other standards in this Subpart A that may apply with respect to certain benefit limitations or restrictions under a group health plan. Other laws may also apply, such as the Uniformed Services Employment and Reemployment Rights Act (USERRA), which can affect the application of a preexisting condition exclusion to certain individuals who are reinstated in a group health plan following active military service.

(3) *Enrollment definitions*—(i) *Enrollment date* means the first day of coverage (as described in paragraph (a)(3)(ii) of this section) or, if there is a waiting period, the first day of the waiting period. If an individual receiving benefits under a group health plan changes benefit packages, or if the plan changes group health insurance issuers, the individual's enrollment date does not change.

(ii) *First day of coverage* means, in the case of an individual covered for benefits under a group health plan, the first day of coverage under the plan and, in the case of an individual covered by health insurance coverage in the individual market, the first day of coverage under the policy or contract.

(iii) *Waiting period* means the period that must pass before coverage for an employee or dependent who is otherwise eligible to enroll under the terms of a group health plan can become effective. If an employee or dependent enrolls as a late enrollee or special enrollee, any period before such late or special enrollment is not a waiting period. If an individual seeks coverage in the individual market, a waiting period begins on the date the individual submits a substantially complete application for coverage and ends on—

(A) If the application results in coverage, the date coverage begins;

(B) If the application does not result in coverage, the date on which the application is denied by the issuer or the date on which the offer of coverage lapses.

(iv) The rules of paragraphs (a)(3)(i), (ii), and (iii) of this section are illustrated by the following examples:

Example 1. (i) *Facts.* Employer *V*'s group health plan provides for coverage to begin on the first day of the first payroll period following the date an employee is hired and completes the applicable enrollment forms, or on any subsequent January 1 after completion of the applicable enrollment forms. Employer *V*'s plan imposes a preexisting condition exclusion for 12 months (reduced by the individual's creditable coverage) following an individual's enrollment date. Employee *E* is hired by Employer *V* on October 13, 1998 and on October 14, 1998 *E* completes and files all the forms necessary to enroll in the plan. *E*'s coverage under the plan becomes effective on October 25, 1998 (which is the beginning of the first payroll period after *E*'s date of hire).

(ii) *Conclusion.* In this *Example 1*, *E*'s enrollment date is October 13, 1998 (which is the first day of the waiting period for *E*'s enrollment and is also *E*'s date of hire). Accordingly, with respect to *E*, the permissible 6-month period in paragraph (a)(2)(i) is the period from April 13, 1998 through October 13, 1998, the maximum permissible period during which Employer *V*'s plan can apply a preexisting condition exclusion under paragraph (a)(2)(iii) is the period from October 13, 1998 through October 12, 1999, and this period must be reduced under paragraph (a)(2)(iii) by *E*'s days of creditable coverage as of October 13, 1998.

Example 2. (i) *Facts.* A group health plan has two benefit package options, Option 1 and Option 2. Under each option a 12-month preexisting condition exclusion is imposed. Individual *B* is enrolled in Option 1 on the first day of employment with the employer maintaining the plan, remains enrolled in Option 1 for more than one year, and then decides to switch to Option 2 at open season.

(ii) *Conclusion.* In this *Example 2*, *B* cannot be subject to any preexisting condition exclusion under Option 2 because

any preexisting condition exclusion period would have to begin on *B*'s enrollment date, which is *B*'s first day of coverage, rather than the date that *B* enrolled in Option 2. Therefore, the preexisting condition exclusion period expired before *B* switched to Option 2.

Example 3. (i) *Facts.* On May 13, 1997, Individual *E* is hired by an employer and enrolls in the employer's group health plan. The plan provides benefits solely through an insurance policy offered by Issuer *S*. On December 27, 1998, *E*'s leg is injured in an accident and the leg is amputated. On January 1, 1999, the plan switches coverage to a policy offered by Issuer *T*. Issuer *T*'s policy excludes benefits for any prosthesis if the body part was lost before the effective date of coverage under the policy.

(ii) *Conclusion.* In this *Example 3*, *E*'s enrollment date is May 13, 1997, *E*'s first day of coverage. Therefore, the permissible 6-month look-back period for the preexisting condition exclusion imposed under Issuer *T*'s policy begins on November 13, 1996 and ends on May 12, 1997. In addition, the 12-month maximum permissible preexisting condition exclusion period begins on May 13, 1997 and ends on May 12, 1998. Accordingly, because no medical advice, diagnosis, care, or treatment was recommended to or received by *E* for the leg during the 6-month look-back period (even though medical care was provided within the 6-month period preceding the effective date of *E*'s coverage under Issuer *T*'s policy), Issuer *T* may not impose any preexisting condition exclusion with respect to *E*. Moreover, even if *E* had received treatment during the 6-month look-back period, Issuer *T* still would not be permitted to impose a preexisting condition exclusion because the 12-month maximum permissible preexisting condition exclusion period expired on May 12, 1998 (before the effective date of *E*'s coverage under Issuer *T*'s policy).

Example 4. (i) *Facts.* A group health plan limits eligibility for coverage to full-time employees of Employer *Y*. Coverage becomes effective on the first day of the month following the date the employee becomes eligible. Employee *C* begins working full-time for Employer *Y* on April 11. Prior to this date, *C* worked part-time for *Y*. *C* enrolls in the plan and coverage is effective May 1.

(ii) *Conclusion.* In this *Example 4*, *C*'s enrollment date is April 11 and the period from April 11 through April 30 is a waiting period. The period while *C* was working part-time, and therefore not in an eligible class of employees, is not part of the waiting period.

Example 5. (i) *Facts.* To be eligible for coverage under a multiemployer group health plan in the current calendar quarter, the plan requires an individual to have worked 250 hours in covered employment during the previous quarter. If the hours requirement is satisfied, coverage becomes effective on the first day of the current calendar quarter. Employee *D* begins work on January 28 and does not work 250 hours in covered employment during the first quarter (ending March 31). *D* works at least 250 hours in the second quarter (ending June 30) and is enrolled in the plan with coverage effective July 1 (the first day of the third quarter).

D. HIPAA Final Rules, Portability, continued

(ii) *Conclusion.* In this *Example 5, D's* enrollment date is the first day of the quarter during which *D* satisfies the hours requirement, which is April 1. The period from April 1 through June 30 is a waiting period.

(v) *Late enrollee* means an individual whose enrollment in a plan is a late enrollment.

(vi) (A) *Late enrollment* means enrollment of an individual under a group health plan other than—

(*1*) On the earliest date on which coverage can become effective for the individual under the terms of the plan; or

(*2*) Through special enrollment. (For rules relating to special enrollment, see § 146.117.)

(B) If an individual ceases to be eligible for coverage under the plan, and then subsequently becomes eligible for coverage under the plan, only the individual's most recent period of eligibility is taken into account in determining whether the individual is a late enrollee under the plan with respect to the most recent period of coverage. Similar rules apply if an individual again becomes eligible for coverage following a suspension of coverage that applied generally under the plan.

(vii) *Examples.* The rules of paragraphs (a)(3)(v) and (vi) of this section are illustrated by the following examples:

Example 1. (i) *Facts.* Employee *F* first becomes eligible to be covered by Employer *W's* group health plan on January 1, 1999 but elects not to enroll in the plan until a later annual open enrollment period, with coverage effective January 1, 2001. *F* has no special enrollment right at that time.

(ii) *Conclusion.* In this *Example 1, F* is a late enrollee with respect to *F's* coverage that became effective under the plan on January 1, 2001.

Example 2. (i) *Facts.* Same facts as *Example 1,* except that *F* terminates employment with Employer *W* on July 1, 1999 without having had any health insurance coverage under the plan. *F* is rehired by Employer *W* on January 1, 2000 and is eligible for and elects coverage under Employer *W's* plan effective on January 1, 2000.

(ii) *Conclusion.* In this *Example 2, F* would not be a late enrollee with respect to *F's* coverage that became effective on January 1, 2000.

(b) *Exceptions pertaining to preexisting condition exclusions*—(1) *Newborns*—(i) *In general.* Subject to paragraph (b)(3) of this section, a group health plan, and a health insurance issuer offering group health insurance coverage, may not impose any preexisting condition exclusion on a child who, within 30 days after birth, is covered under any creditable coverage.

Accordingly, if a child is enrolled in a group health plan (or other creditable coverage) within 30 days after birth and subsequently enrolls in another group health plan without a significant break in coverage (as described in § 146.113(b)(2)(iii)), the other plan may not impose any preexisting condition exclusion on the child.

(ii) *Examples.* The rules of this paragraph (b)(1) are illustrated by the following examples:

Example 1. (i) *Facts.* Individual *E,* who has no prior creditable coverage, begins working for Employer *W* and has accumulated 210 days of creditable coverage under Employer *W's* group health plan on the date *E* gives birth to a child. Within 30 days after the birth, the child is enrolled in the plan. Ninety days after the birth, both *E* and the child terminate coverage under the plan. Both *E* and the child then experience a break in coverage of 45 days before *E* is hired by Employer *X* and the two are enrolled in Employer *X's* group health plan.

(ii) *Conclusion.* In this *Example 1,* because *E's* child is enrolled in Employer *W's* plan within 30 days after birth, no preexisting condition exclusion may be imposed with respect to the child under Employer *W's* plan. Likewise, Employer *X's* plan may not impose any preexisting condition exclusion on *E's* child because the child was covered under creditable coverage within 30 days after birth and had no significant break in coverage before enrolling in Employer *X's* plan. On the other hand, because *E* had only 300 days of creditable coverage prior to *E's* enrollment date in Employer *X's* plan, Employer *X's* plan may impose a preexisting condition exclusion on *E* for up to 65 days (66 days if the 12-month period after *E's* enrollment date in *X's* plan includes February 29).

Example 2. (i) *Facts.* Individual *F* is enrolled in a group health plan in which coverage is provided through a health insurance issuer. *F* gives birth. Under State law applicable to the health insurance issuer, health care expenses incurred for the child during the 30 days following birth are covered as part of *F's* coverage. Although *F* may obtain coverage for the child beyond 30 days by timely requesting special enrollment and paying an additional premium, the issuer is prohibited under State law from recouping the cost of any expenses incurred for the child within the 30-day period if the child is not later enrolled.

(ii) *Conclusion.* In this *Example 2,* the child is covered under creditable coverage within 30 days after birth, regardless of whether the child enrolls as a special enrollee under the plan. Therefore, no preexisting condition exclusion may be imposed on the child unless the child has a significant break in coverage.

(2) *Adopted children.* Subject to paragraph (b)(3) of this section, a group health plan, and a health insurance issuer offering group health insurance coverage, may not impose any preexisting condition exclusion on a

child who is adopted or placed for adoption before attaining 18 years of age and who, within 30 days after the adoption or placement for adoption, is covered under any creditable coverage. Accordingly, if a child is enrolled in a group health plan (or other creditable coverage) within 30 days after adoption or placement for adoption and subsequently enrolls in another group health plan without a significant break in coverage (as described in § 146.113(b)(2)(iii)), the other plan may not impose any preexisting condition exclusion on the child. This rule does not apply to coverage before the date of such adoption or placement for adoption.

(3) *Significant break in coverage.* Paragraphs (b)(1) and (2) of this section no longer apply to a child after a significant break in coverage. (*See* § 146.113(b)(2)(iii) for rules relating to the determination of a significant break in coverage.)

(4) *Special enrollment.* For special enrollment rules relating to new dependents, see § 146.117(b).

(5) *Pregnancy.* A group health plan, and a health insurance issuer offering group health insurance coverage, may not impose a preexisting condition exclusion relating to pregnancy.

(6) *Genetic information*—(i) A group health plan, and a health insurance issuer offering group health insurance coverage, may not impose a preexisting condition exclusion relating to a condition based solely on genetic information. However, if an individual is diagnosed with a condition, even if the condition relates to genetic information, the plan may impose a preexisting condition exclusion with respect to the condition, subject to the other limitations of this section.

(ii) The rules of this paragraph (b)(6) are illustrated by the following example:

Example. (i) *Facts.* Individual *A* enrolls in a group health plan that imposes a 12-month maximum preexisting condition exclusion. Three months before *A's* enrollment, *A's* doctor told *A* that, based on genetic information, *A* has a predisposition towards breast cancer. *A* was not diagnosed with breast cancer at any time prior to *A's* enrollment date in the plan. Nine months after *A's* enrollment date in the plan, *A* is diagnosed with breast cancer.

(ii) *Conclusion.* In this *Example,* the plan may not impose a preexisting condition exclusion with respect to *A's* breast cancer because, prior to *A's* enrollment date, *A* was not diagnosed with breast cancer.

(c) *General notice of preexisting condition exclusion.* A group health plan imposing a preexisting condition exclusion, and a health insurance issuer offering group health insurance

D. HIPAA Final Rules, Portability, continued

Federal Register / Vol. 69, No. 250 / Thursday, December 30, 2004 / Rules and Regulations   78787

coverage subject to a preexisting condition exclusion, must provide a written general notice of preexisting condition exclusion to participants under the plan and cannot impose a preexisting condition exclusion with respect to a participant or a dependent of the participant until such a notice is provided.

(1) *Manner and timing.* A plan or issuer must provide the general notice of preexisting condition exclusion as part of any written application materials distributed by the plan or issuer for enrollment. If the plan or issuer does not distribute such materials, the notice must be provided by the earliest date following a request for enrollment that the plan or issuer, acting in a reasonable and prompt fashion, can provide the notice.

(2) *Content.* The general notice of preexisting condition exclusion must notify participants of the following:

(i) The existence and terms of any preexisting condition exclusion under the plan. This description includes the length of the plan's look-back period [which is not to exceed 6 months under paragraph (a)(2)(i) of this section); the maximum preexisting condition exclusion period under the plan (which cannot exceed 12 months (or 18-months for late enrollees) under paragraph (a)(2)(ii) of this section); and how the plan will reduce the maximum preexisting condition exclusion period by creditable coverage (described in paragraph (a)(2)(iii) of this section).

(ii) A description of the rights of individuals to demonstrate creditable coverage, and any applicable waiting periods, through a certificate of creditable coverage (as required by § 146.115(a)) or through other means (as described in § 146.115(c)). This must include a description of the right of the individual to request a certificate from a prior plan or issuer, if necessary, and a statement that the current plan or issuer will assist in obtaining a certificate from any prior plan or issuer, if necessary.

(iii) A person to contact (including an address or telephone number) for obtaining additional information or assistance regarding the preexisting condition exclusion.

(3) *Duplicate notices not required.* If a notice satisfying the requirements of this paragraph (c) is provided to an individual, the obligation to provide a general notice of preexisting condition exclusion with respect to that individual is satisfied for both the plan and the issuer.

(4) *Example with sample language.* The rules of this paragraph (c) are illustrated by the following example, which includes sample language that plans and issuers can use as a basis for preparing their own notices to satisfy the requirements of this paragraph (c):

Example. (i) *Facts.* A group health plan makes coverage effective on the first day of the first calendar month after hire and on each January 1 following an open season. The plan imposes a 12-month maximum preexisting condition exclusion (18 months for late enrollees) and uses a 6-month look-back period. As part of the enrollment application materials, the plan provides the following statement:

This plan imposes a preexisting condition exclusion. This means that if you have a medical condition before coming to our plan, you might have to wait a certain period of time before the plan will provide coverage for that condition. This exclusion applies only to conditions for which medical advice, diagnosis, care, or treatment was recommended or received within a six-month period. Generally, this six-month period ends the day before your coverage becomes effective. However, if you were in a waiting period for coverage, the six-month period ends on the day before the waiting period begins. The preexisting condition exclusion does not apply to pregnancy nor to a child who is enrolled in the plan within 30 days after birth, adoption, or placement for adoption.

This exclusion may last up to 12 months (18 months if you are a late enrollee) from your first day of coverage, or, if you were in a waiting period, from the first day of your waiting period. However, you can reduce the length of this exclusion period by the number of days of your prior "creditable coverage." Most prior health coverage is creditable coverage and can be used to reduce the preexisting condition exclusion if you have not experienced a break in coverage of at least 63 days. To reduce the 12-month (or 18-month) exclusion period by your creditable coverage, you should give us a copy of any certificates of creditable coverage you have. If you do not have a certificate, but you do have prior health coverage, we will help you obtain one from your prior plan or issuer. There are also other ways that you can show you have creditable coverage. Please contact us if you need help demonstrating creditable coverage.

All questions about the preexisting condition exclusion and creditable coverage should be directed to Individual *B* at Address *M* or Telephone Number *N.*

(ii) *Conclusion.* In this *Example,* the plan satisfies the general notice requirement of this paragraph (c), and thus also satisfies this requirement for any issuer providing the coverage.

(d) *Determination of creditable coverage*—(1) *Determination within reasonable time.* If a group health plan or health insurance issuer offering group health insurance coverage receives creditable coverage information under § 146.115, the plan or issuer is required, within a reasonable time following receipt of the information, to make a determination regarding the amount of the individual's creditable coverage and the length of any exclusion that remains. Whether this determination is made within a reasonable time depends on the relevant facts and circumstances. Relevant facts and circumstances include whether a plan's application of a preexisting condition exclusion would prevent an individual from having access to urgent medical care.

(2) *No time limit on presenting evidence of creditable coverage.* A plan or issuer may not impose any limit on the amount of time that an individual has to present a certificate or other evidence of creditable coverage.

(3) *Example.* The rules of this paragraph (d) are illustrated by the following example:

Example. (i) *Facts.* A group health plan imposes a preexisting condition exclusion period of 12 months. After receiving the general notice of preexisting condition exclusion, Individual *H* develops an urgent health condition before receiving a certificate of creditable coverage from *H's* prior group health plan. *H* attests to the period of prior coverage, presents corroborating documentation of the coverage period, and authorizes the plan to request a certificate on *H's* behalf in accordance with the rules of § 146.115.

(ii) *Conclusion.* In this *Example,* the plan must review the evidence presented by *H* and make a determination of creditable coverage within a reasonable time that is consistent with the urgency of *H's* health condition. (This determination may be modified as permitted under paragraph (f) of this section.)

(e) *Individual notice of period of preexisting condition exclusion.* After an individual has presented evidence of creditable coverage and after the plan or issuer has made a determination of creditable coverage under paragraph (d) of this section, the plan or issuer must provide the individual a written notice of the length of preexisting condition exclusion that remains after offsetting for prior creditable coverage. This individual notice is not required to identify any medical conditions specific to the individual that could be subject to the exclusion. A plan or issuer is not required to provide this notice if the plan or issuer does not impose any preexisting condition exclusion on the individual or if the plan's preexisting condition exclusion is completely offset by the individual's prior creditable coverage.

(1) *Manner and timing.* The individual notice must be provided by the earliest date following a determination that the plan or issuer, acting in a reasonable and prompt fashion, can provide the notice.

(2) *Content.* A plan or issuer must disclose—

D. HIPAA Final Rules, Portability, continued

(i) Its determination of any preexisting condition exclusion period that applies to the individual (including the last day on which the preexisting condition exclusion applies);

(ii) The basis for such determination, including the source and substance of any information on which the plan or issuer relied;

(iii) An explanation of the individual's right to submit additional evidence of creditable coverage; and

(iv) A description of any applicable appeal procedures established by the plan or issuer.

(3) *Duplicate notices not required.* If a notice satisfying the requirements of this paragraph (e) is provided to an individual, the obligation to provide this individual notice of preexisting condition exclusion with respect to that individual is satisfied for both the plan and the issuer.

(4) *Examples.* The rules of this paragraph (e) are illustrated by the following examples:

Example 1. (i) *Facts.* A group health plan imposes a preexisting condition exclusion period on 12 months. After receiving the general notice of preexisting condition exclusion, Individual *G* presents a certificate of creditable coverage indicating 240 days of creditable coverage. Within seven days of receipt of the certificate, the plan determines that *G* is subject to a preexisting condition exclusion of 125 days, the last day of which is March 5. Five days later, the plan notifies *G* that, based on the certificate *G* submitted, *G* is subject to a preexisting condition exclusion period of 125 days, ending on March 5. The notice also explains the opportunity to submit additional evidence of creditable coverage and the plan's appeal procedures. The notice does not identify any of *G's* medical conditions that could be subject to the exclusion.

(ii) *Conclusion.* In this *Example 1*, the plan satisfies the requirements of this paragraph (e).

Example 2. (i) *Facts.* Same facts as in *Example 1*, except that the plan determines that *G* has 430 days of creditable coverage based on *G's* certificate indicating 430 days of creditable coverage under *G's* prior plan.

(ii) *Conclusion.* In this *Example 2*, the plan is not required to notify *G* that *G* will not be subject to a preexisting condition exclusion.

(f) *Reconsideration.* Nothing in this section prevents a plan or issuer from modifying an initial determination of creditable coverage if it determines that the individual did not have the claimed creditable coverage, provided that —

(1) A notice of the new determination (consistent with the requirements of paragraph (e) of this section) is provided to the individual; and

(2) Until the notice of the new determination is provided, the plan or issuer, for purposes of approving access to medical services (such as a pre-

surgery authorization), acts in a manner consistent with the initial determination.

■ 3. Revise § 146.113 to read as follows:

§ 146.113 Rules relating to creditable coverage.

(a) *General rules*—(1) *Creditable coverage.* For purposes of this section, except as provided in paragraph (a)(2) of this section, the term *creditable coverage* means coverage of an individual under any of the following:

(i) A group health plan as defined in § 146.145(a).

(ii) Health insurance coverage as defined in § 144.103 of this chapter (whether or not the entity offering the coverage is subject to the requirements of this part and 45 CFR part 148 and without regard to whether the coverage is offered in the group market, the individual market, or otherwise).

(iii) Part A or B of Title XVIII of the Social Security Act (Medicare).

(iv) Title XIX of the Social Security Act (Medicaid), other than coverage consisting solely of benefits under section 1928 of the Social Security Act (the program for distribution of pediatric vaccines).

(v) Title 10 U.S.C. Chapter 55 (medical and dental care for members and certain former members of the uniformed services, and for their dependents; for purposes of Title 10 U.S.C. Chapter 55, *uniformed services* means the armed forces and the Commissioned Corps of the National Oceanic and Atmospheric Administration and of the Public Health Service).

(vi) A medical care program of the Indian Health Service or of a tribal organization.

(vii) A State health benefits risk pool. For purposes of this section, a *State health benefits risk pool* means—

(A) An organization qualifying under section 501(c)(26) of the Internal Revenue Code;

(B) A qualified high risk pool described in section 2744(c)(2) of the PHS Act; or

(C) Any other arrangement sponsored by a State, the membership composition of which is specified by the State and which is established and maintained primarily to provide health coverage for individuals who are residents of such State and who, by reason of the existence or history of a medical condition—

(*1*) Are unable to acquire medical care coverage for such condition through insurance or from an HMO, or

(*2*) Are able to acquire such coverage only at a rate which is substantially in excess of the rate for such coverage through the membership organization.

(viii) A health plan offered under Title 5 U.S.C. Chapter 89 (the Federal Employees Health Benefits Program).

(ix) A public health plan. For purposes of this section, a *public health plan* means any plan established or maintained by a State, the U.S. government, a foreign country, or any political subdivision of a State, the U.S. government, or a foreign country that provides health coverage to individuals who are enrolled in the plan.

(x) A health benefit plan under section 5(e) of the Peace Corps Act (22 U.S.C. 2504(e)).

(xi) Title XXI of the Social Security Act (State Children's Health Insurance Program).

(2) *Excluded coverage.* Creditable coverage does not include coverage of solely excepted benefits (described in § 146.145).

(3) *Methods of counting creditable coverage.* For purposes of reducing any preexisting condition exclusion period, as provided under § 146.111(a)(2)(iii), the amount of an individual's creditable coverage generally is determined by using the standard method described in paragraph (b) of this section. A plan or issuer may use the alternative method under paragraph (c) of this section with respect to any or all of the categories of benefits described under paragraph (c)(3) of this section.

(b) *Standard method*—(1) *Specific benefits not considered.* Under the standard method, the amount of creditable coverage is determined without regard to the specific benefits included in the coverage.

(2) *Counting creditable coverage*—(i) *Based on days.* For purposes of reducing the preexisting condition exclusion period that applies to an individual, the amount of creditable coverage is determined by counting all the days on which the individual has one or more types of creditable coverage. Accordingly, if on a particular day an individual has creditable coverage from more than one source, all the creditable coverage on that day is counted as one day. Any days in a waiting period for coverage are not creditable coverage.

(ii) *Days not counted before significant break in coverage.* Days of creditable coverage that occur before a significant break in coverage are not required to be counted.

(iii) *Significant break in coverage defined*—A significant break in coverage means a period of 63 consecutive days during each of which an individual does not have any creditable coverage. (See also § 146.143(c)(2)(iii) regarding the applicability to issuers of State insurance laws that require a break of more than 63 days before an individual

D. HIPAA Final Rules, Portability, continued

Federal Register / Vol. 69, No. 250 / Thursday, December 30, 2004 / Rules and Regulations   78789

has a significant break in coverage for purposes of State insurance law.)

(iv) *Periods that toll a significant break.* Days in a waiting period and days in an affiliation period are not taken into account in determining whether a significant break in coverage has occurred. In addition, for an individual who elects COBRA continuation coverage during the second election period provided under the Trade Act of 2002, the days between the date the individual lost group health plan coverage and the first day of the second COBRA election period are not taken into account in determining whether a significant break in coverage has occurred.

(v) *Examples.* The rules of this paragraph (b)(2) are illustrated by the following examples:

Example 1. (i) *Facts.* Individual *A* has creditable coverage under Employer *P*'s plan for 18 months before coverage ceases. *A* is provided a certificate of creditable coverage on *A*'s last day of coverage. Sixty-four days after the last date of coverage under *P*'s plan, *A* is hired by Employer *Q* and enrolls in *Q*'s group health plan. *Q*'s plan has a 12-month preexisting condition exclusion.

(ii) *Conclusion.* In this *Example 1*, *A* has a break in coverage of 63 days. Because *A*'s break in coverage is a significant break in coverage, *Q*'s plan may disregard *A*'s prior coverage and *A* may be subject to a 12-month preexisting condition exclusion.

Example 2. (i) *Facts.* Same facts as *Example 1*, except that *A* is hired by *Q* and enrolls in *Q*'s plan on the 63rd day after the last date of coverage under *P*'s plan.

(ii) *Conclusion.* In this *Example 2*, *A* has a break in coverage of 62 days. Because *A*'s break in coverage is not a significant break in coverage, *Q*'s plan must count *A*'s prior creditable coverage for purposes of reducing the plan's preexisting condition exclusion period that applies to *A*.

Example 3. (i) *Facts.* Same facts as *Example 1*, except that *Q*'s plan provides benefits through an insurance policy that, as required by applicable State insurance laws, defines a significant break in coverage as 90 days.

(ii) *Conclusion.* In this *Example 3*, under State law, the issuer that provides group health insurance coverage to *Q*'s plan must count *A*'s period of creditable coverage prior to the 63-day break. (However, if *Q*'s plan was a self-insured plan, the coverage would not be subject to State law. Therefore, the health coverage would not be governed by the longer break rules and *A*'s previous health coverage could be disregarded.)

Example 4. —[Reserved]

Example 5. (i) *Facts.* Individual *C* has creditable coverage under Employer *S*'s plan for 200 days before coverage ceases. *C* is provided a certificate of creditable coverage on *C*'s last day of coverage. *C* then does not have any creditable coverage for 51 days before being hired by Employer *T*. *T*'s plan has a 3-month waiting period. *C* works for *T* for 2 months and then terminates

employment. Eleven days after terminating employment with *T*, *C* begins working for Employer *U*. *U*'s plan has no waiting period, but has a 6-month preexisting condition exclusion.

(ii) *Conclusion.* In this *Example 5*, *C* does not have a significant break in coverage because, after disregarding the waiting period under *T*'s plan, *C* had only a 62-day break in coverage (51 days plus 11 days). Accordingly, *C* has 200 days of creditable coverage, and *U*'s plan may not apply its 6-month preexisting condition exclusion with respect to *C*.

Example 6. —[Reserved]

Example 7. (i) *Facts.* Individual *E* has creditable coverage under Employer *X*'s plan. *E* is provided a certificate of creditable coverage on *E*'s last day of coverage. On the 63rd day without coverage, *E* submits a substantially complete application for a health insurance policy in the individual market. *E*'s application is accepted and coverage is made effective 10 days later.

(ii) *Conclusion.* In this *Example 7*, because *E* applied for the policy before the end of the 63rd day, the period between the date of application and the first day of coverage is a waiting period and no significant break in coverage occurred even though the actual period without coverage was 73 days.

Example 8. (i) *Facts.* Same facts as *Example 7*, except that *E*'s application for a policy in the individual market is denied.

(ii) *Conclusion.* In this *Example 8*, even though *E* did not obtain coverage following application, the period between the date of application and the date the coverage was denied is a waiting period. However, to avoid a significant break in coverage, no later than the day after the application for the policy is denied *E* would need to do one of the following: submit a substantially complete application for a different individual market policy; obtain coverage in the group market; or be in a waiting period for coverage in the group market.

(vi) *Other permissible counting methods*—(A) *Rule.* Notwithstanding any other provisions of this paragraph (b)(2), for purposes of reducing a preexisting condition exclusion period (but not for purposes of issuing a certificate under § 146.115), a group health plan, and a health insurance issuer offering group health insurance coverage, may determine the amount of creditable coverage in any other manner that is at least as favorable to the individual as the method set forth in this paragraph (b)(2), subject to the requirements of other applicable law.

(B) *Example.* The rule of this paragraph (b)(2)(vi) is illustrated by the following example:

Example. (i) *Facts.* Individual *F* has coverage under Group Health Plan *Y* from January 3, 1997 through March 25, 1997. *F* then becomes covered by Group Health Plan *Z*. *F*'s enrollment date in Plan *Z* is May 1, 1997. Plan *Z* has a 12-month preexisting condition exclusion.

(ii) *Conclusion.* In this *Example*, Plan *Z* may determine, in accordance with the rules

prescribed in paragraphs (b)(2)(i), (ii), and (iii) of this section, that *F* has 82 days of creditable coverage (29 days in January, 28 days in February, and 25 days in March). Thus, the preexisting condition exclusion will no longer apply to *F* on February 8, 1998 (82 days before the 12-month anniversary of *F*'s enrollment (May 1)). For administrative convenience, however, Plan *Z* may consider that the preexisting condition exclusion will no longer apply to *F* on the first day of the month (February 1).

(c) *Alternative method*—(1) *Specific benefits considered.* Under the alternative method, a group health plan, or a health insurance issuer offering group health insurance coverage, determines the amount of creditable coverage based on coverage within any category of benefits described in paragraph (c)(3) of this section and not based on coverage for any other benefits. The plan or issuer may use the alternative method for any or all of the categories. The plan or issuer may apply a different preexisting condition exclusion period with respect to each category (and may apply a different preexisting condition exclusion period for benefits that are not within any category). The creditable coverage determined for a category of benefits applies only for purposes of reducing the preexisting condition exclusion period with respect to that category. An individual's creditable coverage for benefits that are not within any category for which the alternative method is being used is determined under the standard method of paragraph (b) of this section.

(2) *Uniform application.* A plan or issuer using the alternative method is required to apply it uniformly to all participants and beneficiaries under the plan or health insurance coverage. The use of the alternative method is required to be set forth in the plan.

(3) *Categories of benefits.* The alternative method for counting creditable coverage may be used for coverage for the following categories of benefits—

(i) Mental health;

(ii) Substance abuse treatment;

(iii) Prescription drugs;

(iv) Dental care; or

(v) Vision care.

(4) *Plan notice.* If the alternative method is used, the plan is required to—

(i) State prominently that the plan is using the alternative method of counting creditable coverage in disclosure statements concerning the plan, and state this to each enrollee at the time of enrollment under the plan; and

(ii) Include in these statements a description of the effect of using the

D. HIPAA Final Rules, Portability, continued

alternative method, including an identification of the categories used.

(5) *Issuer notice.* With respect to health insurance coverage offered by an issuer in the small or large group market, if the insurance coverage uses the alternative method, the issuer states prominently in any disclosure statement concerning the coverage, that the issuer is using the alternative method, and includes in such statements a description of the effect of using the alternative method. This applies separately to each type of coverage offered by the health insurance issuer.

(6) *Disclosure of information on previous benefits.* See § 146.115(b) for special rules concerning disclosure of coverage to a plan, or issuer, using the alternative method of counting creditable coverage under this paragraph (c).

(7) *Counting creditable coverage—(i) In general.* Under the alternative method, the group health plan or issuer counts creditable coverage within a category if any level of benefits is provided within the category. Coverage under a reimbursement account or arrangement, such as a flexible spending arrangement (as defined in section 106(c)(2) of the Internal Revenue Code), does not constitute coverage within any category.

(ii) *Special rules.* In counting an individual's creditable coverage under the alternative method, the group health plan, or issuer, first determines the amount of the individual's creditable coverage that may be counted under paragraph (b) of this section, up to a total of 365 days of the most recent creditable coverage (546 days for a late enrollee). The period over which this creditable coverage is determined is referred to as the determination period. Then, for the category specified under the alternative method, the plan or issuer counts within the category all days of coverage that occurred during the determination period (whether or not a significant break in coverage for that category occurs), and reduces the individual's preexisting condition exclusion period for that category by that number of days. The plan or issuer may determine the amount of creditable coverage in any other reasonable manner, uniformly applied, that is at least as favorable to the individual.

(iii) *Example.* The rules of this paragraph (c)(7) are illustrated by the following example:

Example. (i) *Facts.* Individual *D* enrolls in Employer *V*'s plan on January 1, 2001. Coverage under the plan includes prescription drug benefits. On April 1, 2001, the plan ceases providing prescription drug benefits. *D*'s employment with Employer *V*

ends on January 1, 2002, after *D* was covered under Employer *V*'s group health plan for 365 days. *D* enrolls in Employer *Y*'s plan on February 1, 2002 (*D*'s enrollment date). Employer *Y*'s plan uses the alternative method of counting creditable coverage and imposes a 12-month preexisting condition exclusion on prescription drug benefits.

(ii) *Conclusion.* In this *Example,* Employer *Y*'s plan may impose a 275-day preexisting condition exclusion with respect to *D* for prescription drug benefits because *D* had 90 days of creditable coverage relating to prescription drug benefits within *D*'s determination period.

■ 4. Revise § 146.115 to read as follows:

§ 146.115 Certification and disclosure of previous coverage.

(a) *Certificate of creditable coverage—* (1) *Entities required to provide certificate—(i) In General.* A group health plan, and each health insurance issuer offering group health insurance coverage under a group health plan, is required to furnish certificates of creditable coverage in accordance with this paragraph (a).

(ii) *Duplicate certificates not required.* An entity required to provide a certificate under this paragraph (a) with respect to an individual satisfies that requirement if another party provides the certificate, but only to the extent that the certificate contains the information required in paragraph (a)(3) of this section. For example, in the case of a group health plan funded through an insurance policy, the issuer satisfies the certification requirement with respect to an individual if the plan actually provides a certificate that includes all the information required under paragraph (a)(3) of this section with respect to the individual.

(iii) *Special rule for group health plans.* To the extent coverage under a plan consists of group health insurance coverage, the plan satisfies the certification requirements under this paragraph (a) if any issuer offering the coverage is required to provide the certificates pursuant to an agreement between the plan and the issuer. For example, if there is an agreement between an issuer and a plan sponsor under which the issuer agrees to provide certificates for individuals covered under the plan, and the issuer fails to provide a certificate to an individual when the plan would have been required to provide one under this paragraph (a), then the issuer, but not the plan, violates the certification requirements of this paragraph (a).

(iv) *Special rules for issuers—*(A)(*1*) *Responsibility of issuer for coverage period.* An issuer is not required to provide information regarding coverage

provided to an individual by another party.

(*2*) *Example.* The rule of this paragraph (a)(1)(iv)(A) is illustrated by the following example:

Example. (i) *Facts.* A plan offers coverage with an HMO option from one issuer and an indemnity option from a different issuer. The HMO has not entered into an agreement with the plan to provide certificates as permitted under paragraph (a)(1)(iii) of this section.

(ii) *Conclusion.* In this *Example,* if an employee switches from the indemnity option to the HMO option and later ceases to be covered under the plan, any certificate provided by the HMO is not required to provide information regarding the employee's coverage under the indemnity option.

(B)(*1*) *Cessation of issuer coverage prior to cessation of coverage under a plan.* If an individual's coverage under an issuer's policy or contract ceases before the individual's coverage under the plan ceases, the issuer is required to provide sufficient information to the plan (or to another party designated by the plan) to enable the plan (or other party), after cessation of the individual's coverage under the plan, to provide a certificate that reflects the period of coverage under the policy or contract. By providing that information to the plan, the issuer satisfies its obligation to provide an automatic certificate for that period of creditable coverage with respect to the individual under paragraph (a)(2)(ii) of this section. The issuer, however, must still provide a certificate upon request as required under paragraph (a)(2)(iii) of this section. In addition, the issuer is required to cooperate with the plan in responding to any request made under paragraph (b)(2) of this section (relating to the alternative method of counting creditable coverage). Moreover, if the individual's coverage under the plan ceases at the time the individual's coverage under the issuer's policy or contract ceases, the issuer must still provide an automatic certificate under paragraph (a)(2)(ii) of this section. If an individual's coverage under an issuer's policy or contract ceases on the effective date for changing enrollment options under the plan, the issuer may presume (absent information to the contrary) that the individual's coverage under the plan continues. Therefore, the issuer is required to provide information to the plan in accordance with this paragraph (a)(1)(iv)(B)(*1*) (and is not required to provide an automatic certificate under paragraph (a)(2)(ii) of this section).

(*2*) *Example.* The rule of this paragraph (a)(1)(iv)(B) is illustrated by the following example:

D. HIPAA Final Rules, Portability, continued

Example. (i) *Facts.* A group health plan provides coverage under an HMO option and an indemnity option through different issuers, and only allows employees to switch on each January 1. Neither the HMO nor the indemnity issuer has entered into an agreement with the plan to provide certificates as permitted under paragraph (a)(1)(iii) of this section.

(ii) *Conclusion.* In this *Example,* if an employee switches from the indemnity option to the HMO option on January 1, the indemnity issuer must provide the plan (or a person designated by the plan) with appropriate information with respect to the individual's coverage with the indemnity issuer. However, if the individual's coverage with the indemnity issuer ceases at a date other than January 1, the issuer is instead required to provide the individual with an automatic certificate.

(2) *Individuals for whom certificate must be provided; timing of issuance*—(i) *Individuals.* A certificate must be provided, without charge, for participants or dependents who are or were covered under a group health plan upon the occurrence of any of the events described in paragraph (a)(2)(ii) or (iii) of this section.

(ii) *Issuance of automatic certificates.* The certificates described in this paragraph (a)(2)(ii) are referred to as automatic certificates.

(A) *Qualified beneficiaries upon a qualifying event.* In the case of an individual who is a qualified beneficiary (as defined in section 607(3) of ERISA, section 4980(B)(g)(1) of the Internal Revenue Code, or section 2208 of the PHS Act) entitled to elect COBRA continuation coverage, an automatic certificate is required to be provided at the time the individual would lose coverage under the plan in the absence of COBRA continuation coverage or alternative coverage elected instead of COBRA continuation coverage. A plan or issuer satisfies this requirement if it provides the automatic certificate no later than the time a notice is required to be furnished for a qualifying event under section 606 of ERISA, section 4980(B)(f)(6) of the Internal Revenue Code, and section 2206 of the PHS Act (relating to notices required under COBRA).

(B) *Other individuals when coverage ceases.* In the case of an individual who is not a qualified beneficiary entitled to elect COBRA continuation coverage, an automatic certificate must be provided at the time the individual ceases to be covered under the plan. A plan or issuer satisfies the requirement to provide an automatic certificate at the time the individual ceases to be covered if it provides the automatic certificate within a reasonable time after coverage ceases (or after the expiration of any

grace period for nonpayment of premiums).

(1) The cessation of temporary continuation coverage (TCC) under Title 5 U.S.C. Chapter 89 (the Federal Employees Health Benefit Program) is a cessation of coverage upon which an automatic certificate must be provided.

(2) In the case of an individual who is entitled to elect to continue coverage under a State program similar to COBRA and who receives the automatic certificate not later than the time a notice is required to be furnished under the State program, the certificate is deemed to be provided within a reasonable time after coverage ceases under the plan.

(3) If an individual's coverage ceases due to the operation of a lifetime limit on all benefits, coverage is considered to cease for purposes of this paragraph (a)(2)(ii)(B) on the earliest date that a claim is denied due to the operation of the lifetime limit.

(C) *Qualified beneficiaries when COBRA ceases.* In the case of an individual who is a qualified beneficiary and has elected COBRA continuation coverage (or whose coverage has continued after the individual became entitled to elect COBRA continuation coverage), an automatic certificate is to be provided at the time the individual's coverage under the plan ceases. A plan, or issuer, satisfies this requirement if it provides the automatic certificate within a reasonable time after coverage ceases (or after the expiration of any grace period for nonpayment of premiums). An automatic certificate is required to be provided to such an individual would regardless of whether the individual has previously received an automatic certificate under paragraph (a)(2)(ii)(A) of this section.

(iii) *Any individual upon request.* A certificate must be provided in response to a request made by, or on behalf of, an individual at any time while the individual is covered under a plan and up to 24 months after coverage ceases. Thus, for example, a plan in which an individual enrolls may, if authorized by the individual, request a certificate of the individual's creditable coverage on behalf of the individual from a plan in which the individual was formerly enrolled. After the request is received, a plan or issuer is required to provide the certificate by the earliest date that the plan or issuer, acting in a reasonable and prompt fashion, can provide the certificate. A certificate is required to be provided under this paragraph (a)(2)(iii) even if the individual has previously received a certificate under this paragraph (a)(2)(iii) or an automatic

certificate under paragraph (a)(2)(ii) of this section.

(iv) *Examples.* The rules of this paragraph (a)(2) are illustrated by the following examples:

Example 1. (i) *Facts.* Individual A terminates employment with Employer Q. A is a qualified beneficiary entitled to elect COBRA continuation coverage under Employer Q's group health plan. A notice of the rights provided under COBRA is typically furnished to qualified beneficiaries under the plan within 10 days after a covered employee terminates employment.

(ii) *Conclusion.* In this *Example 1,* the automatic certificate may be provided at the same time that A is provided the COBRA notice.

Example 2. (i) *Facts.* Same facts as *Example 1,* except that the automatic certificate for A is not completed by the time the COBRA notice is furnished to A.

(ii) *Conclusion.* In this *Example 2,* the automatic certificate may be provided after the COBRA notice but must be provided within the period permitted by law for the delivery of notices under COBRA.

Example 3. (i) *Facts.* Employer R maintains an insured group health plan. R has never had 20 employees and thus R's plan is not subject to the COBRA continuation provisions. However, R is in a State that has a State program similar to COBRA. B terminates employment with R and loses coverage under R's plan.

(ii) *Conclusion.* In this *Example 3,* the automatic certificate must be provided not later than the time a notice is required to be furnished under the State program.

Example 4. (i) *Facts.* Individual C terminates employment with Employer S and receives both a notice of C's rights under COBRA and an automatic certificate. C elects COBRA continuation coverage under Employer S's group health plan. After four months of COBRA continuation coverage and the expiration of a 30-day grace period, S's group health plan determines that C's COBRA continuation coverage has ceased due to a failure to make a timely payment for continuation coverage.

(ii) *Conclusion.* In this *Example 4,* the plan must provide an updated automatic certificate to C within a reasonable time after the end of the grace period.

Example 5. (i) *Facts.* Individual D is currently covered under the group health plan of Employer T. D requests a certificate, as permitted under paragraph (a)(2)(iii) of this section. Under the procedure for T's plan, certificates are mailed (by first class mail) 7 business days following receipt of the request. This date reflects the earliest date that the plan, acting in a reasonable and prompt fashion, can provide certificates.

(ii) *Conclusion.* In this *Example 5,* the plan's procedure satisfies paragraph (a)(2)(iii) of this section.

(3) *Form and content of certificate*—(i) *Written certificate*—(A) *In General.* Except as provided in paragraph (a)(3)(i)(B) of this section, the certificate must be provided in writing (or any

D. HIPAA Final Rules, Portability, continued

other medium approved by the Secretary).

(B) *Other permissible forms.* No written certificate is required to be provided under this paragraph (a) with respect to a particular event described in paragraph (a)(2)(ii) or (iii) of this section, if—

(1) An individual who is entitled to receive the certificate requests that the certificate be sent to another plan or issuer instead of to the individual;

(2) The plan or issuer that would otherwise receive the certificate agrees to accept the information in this paragraph (a)(3) through means other than a written certificate (such as by telephone); and

(3) The receiving plan or issuer receives the information from the sending plan or issuer through such means within the time required under paragraph (a)(2) of this section.

(ii) *Required information.* The certificate must include the following—

(A) The date the certificate is issued;

(B) The name of the group health plan that provided the coverage described in the certificate;

(C) The name of the participant or dependent with respect to whom the certificate applies, and any other information necessary for the plan providing the coverage specified in the certificate to identify the individual, such as the individual's identification number under the plan and the name of the participant if the certificate is for (or includes) a dependent;

(D) The name, address, and telephone number of the plan administrator or issuer required to provide the certificate;

(E) The telephone number to call for further information regarding the certificate (if different from paragraph (a)(3)(ii)(D) of this section);

(F) Either—

(1) A statement that an individual has at least 18 months (for this purpose, 546 days is deemed to be 18 months) of creditable coverage, disregarding days of creditable coverage before a significant break in coverage, or

(2) The date any waiting period (and affiliation period, if applicable) began and the date creditable coverage began;

(G) The date creditable coverage ended, unless the certificate indicates that creditable coverage is continuing as of the date of the certificate; and

(H) An educational statement regarding HIPAA, which explains:

(1) The restrictions on the ability of a plan or issuer to impose a preexisting condition exclusion (including an individual's ability to reduce a preexisting condition exclusion by creditable coverage);

(2) Special enrollment rights;

(3) The prohibitions against discrimination based on any health factor;

(4) The right to individual health coverage;

(5) The fact that State law may require issuers to provide additional protections to individuals in that State; and

(6) Where to get more information.

(iii) *Periods of coverage under the certificate.* If an automatic certificate is provided pursuant to paragraph (a)(2)(ii) of this section, the period that must be included on the certificate is the last period of continuous coverage ending on the date coverage ceased. If an individual requests a certificate pursuant to paragraph (a)(2)(iii) of this section, the certificate provided must include each period of continuous coverage ending within the 24-month period ending on the date of the request (or continuing on the date of the request). A separate certificate may be provided for each such period of continuous coverage.

(iv) *Combining information for families.* A certificate may provide information with respect to both a participant and the participant's dependents if the information is identical for each individual. If the information is not identical, certificates may be provided on one form if the form provides all the required information for each individual and separately states the information that is not identical.

(v) *Model certificate.* The requirements of paragraph (a)(3)(ii) of this section are satisfied if the plan or issuer provides a certificate in accordance with a model certificate authorized by the Secretary.

(vi) *Excepted benefits; categories of benefits.* No certificate is required to be furnished with respect to excepted benefits described in § 146.145(c). In addition, the information in the certificate regarding coverage is not required to specify categories of benefits described in § 146.113(c) (relating to the alternative method of counting creditable coverage). However, if excepted benefits are provided concurrently with other creditable coverage (so that the coverage does not consist solely of excepted benefits), information concerning the benefits may be required to be disclosed under paragraph (b) of this section.

(4) *Procedures—*(i) *Method of delivery.* The certificate is required to be provided to each individual described in paragraph (a)(2) of this section or an entity requesting the certificate on behalf of the individual. The certificate may be provided by first-class mail. If the certificate or certificates are

provided to the participant and the participant's spouse at the participant's last known address, then the requirements of this paragraph (a)(4) are satisfied with respect to all individuals residing at that address. If a dependent's last known address is different than the participant's last known address, a separate certificate is required to be provided to the dependent at the dependent's last known address. If separate certificates are being provided by mail to individuals who reside at the same address, separate mailings of each certificate are not required.

(ii) *Procedure for requesting certificates.* A plan or issuer must establish a written procedure for individuals to request and receive certificates pursuant to paragraph (a)(2)(iii) of this section. The written procedure must include all contact information necessary to request a certificate (such as name and phone number or address).

(iii) *Designated recipients.* If an automatic certificate is required to be provided under paragraph (a)(2)(ii) of this section, and the individual entitled to receive the certificate designates another individual or entity to receive the certificate, the plan or issuer responsible for providing the certificate is permitted to provide the certificate to the designated individual or entity. If a certificate is required to be provided upon request under paragraph (a)(2)(iii) of this section and the individual entitled to receive the certificate designates another individual or entity to receive the certificate, the plan or issuer responsible for providing the certificate is required to provide the certificate to the designated individual or entity.

(5) *Special rules concerning dependent coverage—*(i)(A) *Reasonable efforts.* A plan or issuer is required to use reasonable efforts to determine any information needed for a certificate relating to dependent coverage. In any case in which an automatic certificate is required to be furnished with respect to a dependent under paragraph (a)(2)(ii) of this section, no individual certificate is required to be furnished until the plan or issuer knows (or making reasonable efforts should know) of the dependent's cessation of coverage under the plan.

(B) *Example.* The rules of this paragraph (a)(5)(i) are illustrated by the following example:

Example. (i) *Facts.* A group health plan covers employees and their dependents. The plan annually requests all employees to provide updated information regarding dependents, including the specific date on which an employee has a new dependent or

D. HIPAA Final Rules, Portability, continued

on which a person ceases to be a dependent of the employee.

(ii) *Conclusion.* In this *Example,* the plan has satisfied the standard in this paragraph (a)(5)(i) of this section that it make reasonable efforts to determine the cessation of dependents' coverage and the related dependent coverage information.

(ii) *Special rules for demonstrating coverage.* If a certificate furnished by a plan or issuer does not provide the name of any dependent covered by the certificate, the procedures described in paragraph (c)(5) of this section may be used to demonstrate dependent status. In addition, these procedures may be used to demonstrate that a child was covered under any creditable coverage within 30 days after birth, adoption, or placement for adoption. See also § 146.111(b), under which such a child cannot be subject to a preexisting condition exclusion.

(6) *Special certification rules—*(i) *Issuers.* Issuers of group and individual health insurance are required to provide certificates of any creditable coverage they provide in the group or individual health insurance market, even if the coverage is provided in connection with an entity or program that is not itself required to provide a certificate because it is not subject to the group market provisions of this part, part 7 of subtitle B of title I of ERISA, or chapter 100 of subtitle K of the Internal Revenue Code. This would include coverage provided in connection with any of the following:

(A) Creditable coverage described in sections 2701(c)(1)(G), (I) and (J) of the PHS Act (coverage under a State health benefits risk pool, a public health plan, and a health benefit plan under section 5(e) of the Peace Corps Act).

(B) Coverage subject to section 2721(b)(1)(B) of the PHS Act (requiring certificates by issuers offering health insurance coverage in connection with any group health plan, including a church plan or a governmental plan (including the Federal Employees Health Benefits Program).

(C) Coverage subject to section 2743 of the PHS Act applicable to health insurance issuers in the individual market. (However, this section does not require a certificate to be provided with respect to short-term limited duration insurance, which is excluded from the definition of "individual health insurance coverage" in 45 CFR 144.103 that is not provided in connection with a group health plan, as described in paragraph (a)(6)(i)(B) of this section.)

(ii) *Other entities.* For special rules requiring that certain other entities, not subject to this part, provide certificates consistent with the rules of this section, see section 2791(a)(3) of the PHS Act

applicable to entities described in sections 2701(c)(1)(C), (D), (E), and (F) of the PHS Act (relating to Medicare, Medicaid, TRICARE, and Indian Health Service), section 2721(b)(1)(A) of the PHS Act applicable to non-Federal governmental plans generally, section 2721(b)(2)(C)(ii) of the PHS Act applicable to non-Federal governmental plans that elect to be excluded from the requirements of subparts 1 through 3 of part A of title XXVII of the PHS Act, and section 9805(a) of the Internal Revenue Code applicable to group health plans, which includes church plans (as defined in section 414(e) of the Internal Revenue Code).

(b) *Disclosure of coverage to a plan or issuer using the alternative method of counting creditable coverage—*(1) *In general.* After an individual provides a certificate of creditable coverage to a plan or issuer using the alternative method under § 146.113(c), that plan or issuer (requesting entity) must request that the entity that issued the certificate (prior entity) disclose the information set forth in paragraph (b)(2) of this section. The prior entity is required to disclose this information promptly.

(2) *Information to be disclosed.* The prior entity is required to identify to the requesting entity the categories of benefits with respect to which the requesting entity is using the alternative method of counting creditable coverage, and the requesting entity may identify specific information that the requesting entity reasonably needs in order to determine the individual's creditable coverage with respect to any such category.

(3) *Charge for providing information.* The prior entity may charge the requesting entity for the reasonable cost of disclosing such information.

(c) *Ability of an individual to demonstrate creditable coverage and waiting period information—*(1) *Purpose.* The rules in this paragraph (c) implement section 2701(c)(4) of the PHS Act, which permits individuals to demonstrate the duration of creditable coverage through means other than certificates, and section 2701(e)(3) of the PHS Act, which requires the Secretary to establish rules designed to prevent an individual's subsequent coverage under a group health plan or health insurance coverage from being adversely affected by an entity's failure to provide a certificate with respect to that individual.

(2) *In general.* If the accuracy of a certificate is contested or a certificate is unavailable when needed by an individual, the individual has the right to demonstrate creditable coverage (and waiting or affiliation periods) through

the presentation of documents or other means. For example, the individual may make such a demonstration when—

(i) An entity has failed to provide a certificate within the required time;

(ii) The individual has creditable coverage provided by an entity that is not required to provide a certificate of the coverage pursuant to paragraph (a) of this section;

(iii) The individual has an urgent medical condition that necessitates a determination before the individual can deliver a certificate to the plan; or

(iv) The individual lost a certificate that the individual had previously received and is unable to obtain another certificate.

(3) *Evidence of creditable coverage—* (i) *Consideration of evidence—*(A) A plan or issuer is required to take into account all information that it obtains or that is presented on behalf of an individual to make a determination, based on the relevant facts and circumstances, whether an individual has creditable coverage. A plan or issuer shall treat the individual as having furnished a certificate under paragraph (a) of this section if—

(1) The individual attests to the period of creditable coverage;

(2) The individual also presents relevant corroborating evidence of some creditable coverage during the period; and

(3) The individual cooperates with the plan's or issuer's efforts to verify the individual's coverage.

(B) For purposes of this paragraph (c)(3)(i), cooperation includes providing (upon the plan's or issuer's request) a written authorization for the plan or issuer to request a certificate on behalf of the individual, and cooperating in efforts to determine the validity of the corroborating evidence and the dates of creditable coverage. While a plan or issuer may refuse to credit coverage where the individual fails to cooperate with the plan's or issuer's efforts to verify coverage, the plan or issuer may not consider an individual's inability to obtain a certificate to be evidence of the absence of creditable coverage.

(ii) *Documents.* Documents that corroborate creditable coverage (and waiting or affiliation periods) include explanations of benefits (EOBs) or other correspondence from a plan or issuer indicating coverage, pay stubs showing a payroll deduction for health coverage, a health insurance identification card, a certificate of coverage under a group health policy, records from medical care providers indicating health coverage, third party statements verifying periods of coverage, and any other relevant

D. HIPAA Final Rules, Portability, continued

documents that evidence periods of health coverage.

(iii) *Other evidence.* Creditable coverage (and waiting or affiliation periods) may also be corroborated through means other than documentation, such as by a telephone call from the plan or provider to a third party verifying creditable coverage.

(iv) *Example.* The rules of this paragraph (c)(3) are illustrated by the following example:

Example. (i) *Facts.* Individual *F* terminates employment with Employer *W* and, a month later, is hired by Employer *X. X*'s group health plan imposes a preexisting condition exclusion of 12 months on new enrollees under the plan and uses the standard method of determining creditable coverage. *F* fails to receive a certificate of prior coverage from the self-insured group health plan maintained by *F*'s prior employer, *W,* and requests a certificate. However, *F* (and *X*'s plan, on *F*'s behalf and with *F*'s cooperation) is unable to obtain a certificate from *W*'s plan. *F* attests that, to the best of *F*'s knowledge, *F* had at least 12 months of continuous coverage under *W*'s plan, and that the coverage ended no earlier than *F*'s termination of employment from *W.* In addition, *F* presents evidence of coverage, such as an explanation of benefits for a claim that was made during the relevant period.

(ii) *Conclusion.* In this *Example,* based solely on these facts, *F* has demonstrated creditable coverage for the 12 months of coverage under *W*'s plan in the same manner as if *F* had presented a written certificate of creditable coverage.

(4) *Demonstrating categories of creditable coverage.* Procedures similar to those described in this paragraph (c) apply in order to determine the duration of an individual's creditable coverage with respect to any category under paragraph (b) of this section (relating to determining creditable coverage under the alternative method).

(5) *Demonstrating dependent status.* If, in the course of providing evidence (including a certificate) of creditable coverage, an individual is required to demonstrate dependent status, the group health plan or issuer is required to treat the individual as having furnished a certificate showing the dependent status if the individual attests to such dependency and the period of such status and the individual cooperates with the plan's or issuer's efforts to verify the dependent status.

■ 5. Revise § 146.117 to read as follows:

§ 146.117 Special enrollment periods.

(a) *Special enrollment for certain individuals who lose coverage*—(1) *In General.* A group health plan, and a health insurance issuer offering health insurance coverage in connection with a group health plan, is required to permit current employees and dependents (as

defined in § 144.103 of this chapter) who are described in paragraph (a)(2) of this section to enroll for coverage under the terms of the plan if the conditions in paragraph (a)(3) of this section are satisfied. The special enrollment rights under this paragraph (a) apply without regard to the dates on which an individual would otherwise be able to enroll under the plan.

(2) *Individuals eligible for special enrollment*—(i) *When employee loses coverage.* A current employee and any dependents (including the employee's spouse) each are eligible for special enrollment in any benefit package under the plan (subject to plan eligibility rules conditioning dependent enrollment on enrollment of the employee) if—

(A) The employee and the dependents are otherwise eligible to enroll in the benefit package;

(B) When coverage under the plan was previously offered, the employee had coverage under any group health plan or health insurance coverage; and

(C) The employee satisfies the conditions of paragraph (a)(3)(i), (ii), or (iii) of this section and, if applicable, paragraph (a)(3)(iv) of this section.

(ii) *When dependent loses coverage*—(A) A dependent of a current employee (including the employee's spouse) and the employee each are eligible for special enrollment in any benefit package under the plan (subject to plan eligibility rules conditioning dependent enrollment on enrollment of the employee) if—

(1) The dependent and the employee are otherwise eligible to enroll in the benefit package;

(2) When coverage under the plan was previously offered, the dependent had coverage under any group health plan or health insurance coverage; and

(3) The dependent satisfies the conditions of paragraph (a)(3)(i), (ii), or (iii) of this section and, if applicable, paragraph (a)(3)(iv) of this section.

(B) However, the plan or issuer is not required to enroll any other dependent unless that dependent satisfies the criteria of this paragraph (a)(2)(ii), or the employee satisfies the criteria of paragraph (a)(2)(i) of this section.

(iii) *Examples.* The rules of this paragraph (a)(2) are illustrated by the following examples:

Example 1. (i) *Facts.* Individual *A* works for Employer *X. A, A*'s spouse, and *A*'s dependent children are eligible but not enrolled for coverage under *X*'s group health plan. *A*'s spouse works for Employer *Y* and at the time coverage was offered under *X*'s plan, *A* was enrolled in coverage under *Y*'s plan. Then, *A* loses eligibility for coverage under *Y*'s plan.

(ii) *Conclusion.* In this *Example 1,* because *A* satisfies the conditions for special

enrollment under paragraph (a)(2)(i) of this section, *A, A*'s spouse, and *A*'s dependent children are eligible for special enrollment under *X*'s plan.

Example 2. (i) *Facts.* Individual *A* and *A*'s spouse are eligible but not enrolled for coverage under Group Health Plan *P* maintained by *A*'s employer. When *A* was first presented with an opportunity to enroll *A* and *A*'s spouse, they did not have other coverage. Later, *A* and *A*'s spouse enroll in Group Health Plan *Q* maintained by the employer of *A*'s spouse. During a subsequent open enrollment period in *P, A* and *A*'s spouse did not enroll because of their coverage under *Q.* They then lose eligibility for coverage under *Q.*

(ii) *Conclusion.* In this *Example 2,* because *A* and *A*'s spouse were covered under *Q* when they did not enroll in *P* during open enrollment, they satisfy the conditions for special enrollment under paragraphs (a)(2)(i) and (ii) of this section. Consequently, *A* and *A*'s spouse are eligible for special enrollment under *P.*

Example 3. (i) *Facts.* Individual *B* works for Employer *X. B* and *B*'s spouse are eligible but not enrolled for coverage under *X*'s group health plan. *B*'s spouse works for Employer *Y* and at the time coverage was offered under *X*'s plan, *B*'s spouse was enrolled in self-only coverage under *Y*'s group health plan. Then, *B*'s spouse loses eligibility for coverage under *Y*'s plan.

(ii) *Conclusion.* In this *Example 3,* because *B*'s spouse satisfies the conditions for special enrollment under paragraph (a)(2)(ii) of this section, both *B* and *B*'s spouse are eligible for special enrollment under *X*'s plan.

Example 4. (i) *Facts.* Individual *A* works for Employer *X. X* maintains a group health plan with two benefit packages—an HMO option and an indemnity option. Self-only and family coverage are available under both options. *A* enrolls for self-only coverage in the HMO option. *A*'s spouse works for Employer *Y* and was enrolled for self-only coverage under *Y*'s plan at the time coverage was offered under *X*'s plan. Then, *A*'s spouse loses coverage under *Y*'s plan. *A* requests special enrollment for *A* and *A*'s spouse under the plan's indemnity option.

(ii) *Conclusion.* In this *Example 4,* because *A*'s spouse satisfies the conditions for special enrollment under paragraph (a)(2)(ii) of this section, both *A* and *A*'s spouse can enroll in either benefit package under *X*'s plan. Therefore, if *A* requests enrollment in accordance with the requirements of this section, the plan must allow *A* and *A*'s spouse to enroll in the indemnity option.

(3) *Conditions for special enrollment*—(i) *Loss of eligibility for coverage.* In the case of an employee or dependent who has coverage that is not COBRA continuation coverage, the conditions of this paragraph (a)(3)(i) are satisfied at the time the coverage is terminated as a result of loss of eligibility (regardless of whether the individual is eligible for or elects COBRA continuation coverage). Loss of eligibility under this paragraph (a)(3)(i) does not include a loss due to the failure

D. HIPAA Final Rules, Portability, continued

Federal Register / Vol. 69, No. 250 / Thursday, December 30, 2004 / Rules and Regulations   78795

of the employee or dependent to pay premiums on a timely basis or termination of coverage for cause (such as making a fraudulent claim or an intentional misrepresentation of a material fact in connection with the plan). Loss of eligibility for coverage under this paragraph (a)(3)(i) includes (but is not limited to)—

(A) Loss of eligibility for coverage as a result of legal separation, divorce, cessation of dependent status (such as attaining the maximum age to be eligible as a dependent child under the plan), death of an employee, termination of employment, reduction in the number of hours of employment, and any loss of eligibility for coverage after a period that is measured by reference to any of the foregoing;

(B) In the case of coverage offered through an HMO, or other arrangement, in the individual market that does not provide benefits to individuals who no longer reside, live, or work in a service area, loss of coverage because an individual no longer resides, lives, or works in the service area (whether or not within the choice of the individual);

(C) In the case of coverage offered through an HMO, or other arrangement, in the group market that does not provide benefits to individuals who no longer reside, live, or work in a service area, loss of coverage because an individual no longer resides, lives, or works in the service area (whether or not within the choice of the individual), and no other benefit package is available to the individual;

(D) A situation in which an individual incurs a claim that would meet or exceed a lifetime limit on all benefits; and

(E) A situation in which a plan no longer offers any benefits to the class of similarly situated individuals (as described in § 146.121(d)) that includes the individual.

(ii) *Termination of employer contributions.* In the case of an employee or dependent who has coverage that is not COBRA continuation coverage, the conditions of this paragraph (a)(3)(ii) are satisfied at the time employer contributions towards the employee's or dependent's coverage terminate. Employer contributions include contributions by any current or former employer that was contributing to coverage for the employee or dependent.

(iii) *Exhaustion of COBRA continuation coverage.* In the case of an employee or dependent who has coverage that is COBRA continuation coverage, the conditions of this paragraph (a)(3)(iii) are satisfied at the time the COBRA continuation coverage

is exhausted. For purposes of this paragraph (a)(3)(iii), an individual who satisfies the conditions for special enrollment of paragraph (a)(3)(i) of this section, does not enroll, and instead elects and exhausts COBRA continuation coverage satisfies the conditions of this paragraph (a)(3)(iii). (*Exhaustion of COBRA continuation coverage* is defined in § 144.103 of this chapter.)

(iv) *Written statement.* A plan may require an employee declining coverage (for the employee or any dependent of the employee) to state in writing whether the coverage is being declined due to other health coverage only if, at or before the time the employee declines coverage, the employee is provided with notice of the requirement to provide the statement (and the consequences of the employee's failure to provide the statement). If a plan requires such a statement, and an employee does not provide it, the plan is not required to provide special enrollment to the employee or any dependent of the employee under this paragraph (a)(3). A plan must treat an employee as having satisfied the plan requirement permitted under this paragraph (a)(3)(iv) if the employee provides a written statement that coverage was being declined because the employee or dependent had other coverage; a plan cannot require anything more for the employee to satisfy the plan's requirement to provide a written statement. (For example, the plan cannot require that the statement be notarized.)

(v) The rules of this paragraph (a)(3) are illustrated by the following examples:

Example 1. (i) *Facts.* Individual D enrolls in a group health plan maintained by Employer Y. At the time D enrolls, Y pays 70 percent of the cost of employee coverage and D pays the rest. Y announces that beginning January 1, Y will no longer make employer contributions towards the coverage. Employees may maintain coverage, however, if they pay the total cost of the coverage.

(ii) *Conclusion.* In this *Example 1,* employer contributions towards D's coverage ceased on January 1 and the conditions of paragraph (a)(3)(ii) of this section are satisfied on this date (regardless of whether D elects to pay the total cost and continue coverage under Y's plan).

Example 2. (i) *Facts.* A group health plan provides coverage through two options— Option 1 and Option 2. Employees can enroll in either option only within 30 days of hire or on January 1 of each year. Employee A is eligible for both options and enrolls in Option 1. Effective July 1 the plan terminates coverage under Option 1 and the plan does not create an immediate open enrollment opportunity into Option 2.

(ii) *Conclusion.* In this *Example 2,* A has experienced a loss of eligibility for coverage

that satisfies paragraph (a)(3)(i) of this section, and has satisfied the other conditions for special enrollment under paragraph (a)(2)(i) of this section. Therefore, if A satisfies the other conditions of this paragraph (a), the plan must permit A to enroll in Option 2 as a special enrollee. (A may also be eligible to enroll in another group health plan, such as a plan maintained by the employer of A's spouse, as a special enrollee.) The outcome would be the same if Option 1 was terminated by an issuer and the plan made no other coverage available to A.

Example 3. (i) *Facts.* Individual C is covered under a group health plan maintained by Employer X. While covered under X's plan, C was eligible for but did not enroll in a plan maintained by Employer Z, the employer of C's spouse. C terminates employment with X and loses eligibility for coverage under X's plan. C has a special enrollment right to enroll in Z's plan, but C instead elects COBRA continuation coverage under X's plan. C exhausts COBRA continuation coverage under X's plan and requests special enrollment in Z's plan.

(ii) *Conclusion.* In this *Example 3,* C has satisfied the conditions for special enrollment under paragraph (a)(3)(iii) of this section, and has satisfied the other conditions for special enrollment under paragraph (a)(2)(i) of this section. The special enrollment right that C had into Z's plan immediately after the loss of eligibility for coverage under X's plan was an offer of coverage under Z's plan. When C later exhausts COBRA coverage under X's plan, C has a second special enrollment right in Z's plan.

(4) *Applying for special enrollment and effective date of coverage*—(i) A plan or issuer must allow an employee a period of at least 30 days after an event described in paragraph (a)(3) of this section (other than an event described in paragraph (a)(3)(i)(D)) to request enrollment (for the employee or the employee's dependent). In the case of an event described in paragraph (a)(3)(i)(D) of this section (relating to loss of eligibility for coverage due to the operation of a lifetime limit on all benefits), a plan or issuer must allow an employee a period of at least 30 days after a claim is denied due to the operation of a lifetime limit on all benefits.

(ii) Coverage must begin no later than the first day of the first calendar month beginning after the date the plan or issuer receives the request for special enrollment.

(b) *Special enrollment with respect to certain dependent beneficiaries*—(1) *General.* A group health plan, and a health insurance issuer offering health insurance coverage in connection with a group health plan, that makes coverage available with respect to dependents is required to permit individuals described in paragraph (b)(2) of this section to be enrolled for coverage in a benefit

D. HIPAA Final Rules, Portability, continued

package under the terms of the plan. Paragraph (b)(3) of this section describes the required special enrollment period and the date by which coverage must begin. The special enrollment rights under this paragraph (b) apply without regard to the dates on which an individual would otherwise be able to enroll under the plan.

(2) *Individuals eligible for special enrollment.* An individual is described in this paragraph (b)(2) if the individual is otherwise eligible for coverage in a benefit package under the plan and if the individual is described in paragraph (b)(2)(i), (ii), (iii), (iv), (v), or (vi) of this section.

(i) *Current employee only.* A current employee is described in this paragraph (b)(2)(i) if a person becomes a dependent of the individual through marriage, birth, adoption, or placement for adoption.

(ii) *Spouse of a participant only.* An individual is described in this paragraph (b)(2)(ii) if either—

(A) The individual becomes the spouse of a participant; or

(B) The individual is a spouse of a participant and a child becomes a dependent of the participant through birth, adoption, or placement for adoption.

(iii) *Current employee and spouse.* A current employee and an individual who is or becomes a spouse of such an employee, are described in this paragraph (b)(2)(iii) if either—

(A) The employee and the spouse become married; or

(B) The employee and spouse are married and a child becomes a dependent of the employee through birth, adoption, or placement for adoption.

(iv) *Dependent of a participant only.* An individual is described in this paragraph (b)(2)(iv) if the individual is a dependent (as defined in § 144.103 of this chapter) of a participant and the individual has become a dependent of the participant through marriage, birth, adoption, or placement for adoption.

(v) *Current employee and a new dependent.* A current employee and an individual who is a dependent of the employee, are described in this paragraph (b)(2)(v) if the individual becomes a dependent of the employee through marriage, birth, adoption, or placement for adoption.

(vi) *Current employee, spouse, and a new dependent.* A current employee, the employee's spouse, and the employee's dependent are described in this paragraph (b)(2)(vi) if the dependent becomes a dependent of the employee through marriage, birth, adoption, or placement for adoption.

(3) *Applying for special enrollment and effective date of coverage*—(i) *Request.* A plan or issuer must allow an individual a period of at least 30 days after the date of the marriage, birth, adoption, or placement for adoption (or, if dependent coverage is not generally made available at the time of the marriage, birth, adoption, or placement for adoption, a period of at least 30 days after the date the plan makes dependent coverage generally available) to request enrollment (for the individual or the individual's dependent).

(ii) *Reasonable procedures for special enrollment.* [Reserved]

(iii) *Date coverage must begin*—(A) *Marriage.* In the case of marriage, coverage must begin no later than the first day of the first calendar month beginning after the date the plan or issuer receives the request for special enrollment.

(B) *Birth, adoption, or placement for adoption.* Coverage must begin in the case of a dependent's birth on the date of birth and in the case of a dependent's adoption or placement for adoption no later than the date of such adoption or placement for adoption (or, if dependent coverage is not made generally available at the time of the birth, adoption, or placement for adoption, the date the plan makes dependent coverage available).

(4) *Examples.* The rules of this paragraph (b) are illustrated by the following examples:

Example 1. (i) *Facts.* An employer maintains a group health plan that offers all employees employee-only coverage, employee-plus-spouse coverage, or family coverage. Under the terms of the plan, any employee may elect to enroll when first hired (with coverage beginning on the date of hire) or during an annual open enrollment period held each December (with coverage beginning the following January 1). Employee *A* is hired on September 3. *A* is married to *B*, and they have no children. On March 15 in the following year a child *C* is born to *A* and *B*. Before that date, *A* and *B* have not been enrolled in the plan.

(ii) *Conclusion.* In this *Example 1*, the conditions for special enrollment of an employee with a spouse and new dependent under paragraph (b)(2)(vi) of this section are satisfied. If *A* satisfies the conditions of paragraph (b)(3) of this section for requesting enrollment timely, the plan will satisfy this paragraph (b) if it allows *A* to enroll either with employee-only coverage, with employee-plus-spouse coverage (for *A* and *B*), or with family coverage (for *A*, *B*, and *C*). The plan must allow whatever coverage is chosen to begin on March 15, the date of *C*'s birth.

Example 2. (i) *Facts.* Individual *D* works for Employer *X*. *X* maintains a group health plan with two benefit packages—an HMO option and an indemnity option. Self-only and family coverage are available under both options. *D* enrolls for self-only coverage in

the HMO option. Then, a child, *E*, is placed for adoption with *D*. Within 30 days of the placement of *E* for adoption, *D* requests enrollment for *D* and *E* under the plan's indemnity option.

(ii) *Conclusion.* In this *Example 2*, *D* and *E* satisfy the conditions for special enrollment under paragraphs (b)(2)(v) and (b)(3) of this section. Therefore, the plan must allow *D* and *E* to enroll in the indemnity coverage, effective as of the date of the placement for adoption.

(c) *Notice of special enrollment.* At or before the time an employee is initially offered the opportunity to enroll in a group health plan, the plan must furnish the employee with a notice of special enrollment that complies with the requirements of this paragraph (c).

(1) *Description of special enrollment rights.* The notice of special enrollment must include a description of special enrollment rights. The following model language may be used to satisfy this requirement:

If you are declining enrollment for yourself or your dependents (including your spouse) because of other health insurance or group health plan coverage, you may be able to enroll yourself and your dependents in this plan if you or your dependents lose eligibility for that other coverage (or if the employer stops contributing towards your or your dependents' other coverage). However, you must request enrollment within [insert "30 days" or any longer period that applies under the plan] after your or your dependents' other coverage ends (or after the employer stops contributing toward the other coverage).

In addition, if you have a new dependent as a result of marriage, birth, adoption, or placement for adoption, you may be able to enroll yourself and your dependents. However, you must request enrollment within [insert "30 days" or any longer period that applies under the plan] after the marriage, birth, adoption, or placement for adoption.

To request special enrollment or obtain more information, contact [insert the name, title, telephone number, and any additional contact information of the appropriate plan representative].

(2) *Additional information that may be required.* The notice of special enrollment must also include, if applicable, the notice described in paragraph (a)(3)(iv) of this section (the notice required to be furnished to an individual declining coverage if the plan requires the reason for declining coverage to be in writing).

(d) *Treatment of special enrollees*—(1) If an individual requests enrollment while the individual is entitled to special enrollment under either paragraph (a) or (b) of this section, the individual is a special enrollee, even if the request for enrollment coincides with a late enrollment opportunity under the plan. Therefore, the

D. HIPAA Final Rules, Portability, continued

individual cannot be treated as a late enrollee.

(2) Special enrollees must be offered all the benefit packages available to similarly situated individuals who enroll when first eligible. For this purpose, any difference in benefits or cost-sharing requirements for different individuals constitutes a different benefit package. In addition, a special enrollee cannot be required to pay more for coverage than a similarly situated individual who enrolls in the same coverage when first eligible. The length of any preexisting condition exclusion that may be applied to a special enrollee cannot exceed the length of any preexisting condition exclusion that is applied to similarly situated individuals who enroll when first eligible. For rules prohibiting the application of a preexisting condition exclusion to certain newborns, adopted children, and children placed for adoption, see § 146.111(b).

(3) The rules of this section are illustrated by the following example:

Example. (i) *Facts.* Employer Y maintains a group health plan that has an enrollment period for late enrollees every November 1 through November 30 with coverage effective the following January 1. On October 18, Individual *B* loses coverage under another group health plan and satisfies the requirements of paragraphs (a)(2), (3), and (4) of this section. *B* submits a completed application for coverage on November 2.

(ii) *Conclusion.* In this *Example*, *B* is a special enrollee. Therefore, even though *B's* request for enrollment coincides with an open enrollment period, *B's* coverage is required to be made effective no later than December 1 (rather than the plan's January 1 effective date for late enrollees).

■ 6. Revise § 146.119 to read as follows:

§ 146.119 HMO affiliation period as an alternative to a preexisting condition exclusion.

(a) *In general.* A group health plan offering health insurance coverage through an HMO, or an HMO that offers health insurance coverage in connection with a group health plan, may impose an affiliation period only if each of the following requirements is satisfied—

(1) No preexisting condition exclusion is imposed with respect to any coverage offered by the HMO in connection with the particular group health plan.

(2) No premium is charged to a participant or beneficiary for the affiliation period.

(3) The affiliation period for the HMO coverage is imposed consistent with the requirements of § 146.121 (prohibiting discrimination based on a health factor).

(4) The affiliation period does not exceed 2 months (or 3 months in the case of a late enrollee).

(5) The affiliation period begins on the enrollment date, or in the case of a late enrollee, the affiliation period begins on the day that would be the first day of coverage but for the affiliation period.

(6) The affiliation period for enrollment in the HMO under a plan runs concurrently with any waiting period.

(b) *Examples.* The rules of paragraph (a) of this section are illustrated by the following examples:

Example 1. (i) *Facts.* An employer sponsors a group health plan. Benefits under the plan are provided through an HMO, which imposes a two-month affiliation period. In order to be eligible under the plan, employees must have worked for the employer for six months. Individual *A* begins working for the employer on February 1.

(ii) *Conclusion.* In this *Example 1*, Individual *A's* enrollment date is February 1 (see § 146.111(a)(2)), and both the waiting period and the affiliation period begin on this date and run concurrently. Therefore, the affiliation period ends on March 31, the waiting period ends on July 31, and *A* is eligible to have coverage begin on August 1.

Example 2. (i) *Facts.* A group health plan has two benefit package options, a fee-for-service option and an HMO option. The HMO imposes a 1-month affiliation period. Individual *B* is enrolled in the fee-for-service option for more than one month and then decides to switch to the HMO option at open season.

(ii) *Conclusion.* In this *Example 2*, the HMO may not impose the affiliation period with respect to *B* because any affiliation period would have to begin on *B's* enrollment date in the plan rather than the date that *B* enrolled in the HMO option. Therefore, the affiliation period would have expired before *B* switched to the HMO option.

Example 3. (i) *Facts.* An employer sponsors a group health plan that provides benefits through an HMO. The plan imposes a two-month affiliation period with respect to salaried employees, but it does not impose an affiliation period with respect to hourly employees.

(ii) *Conclusion.* In this *Example 3*, the plan may impose the affiliation period with respect to salaried employees without imposing any affiliation period with respect to hourly employees (unless, under the circumstances, treating salaried and hourly employees differently does not comply with the requirements of § 146.121).

(c) *Alternatives to affiliation period.* An HMO may use alternative methods in lieu of an affiliation period to address adverse selection, as approved by the State insurance commissioner or other official designated to regulate HMOs. However, an arrangement that is in the nature of a preexisting condition exclusion cannot be an alternative to an affiliation period. Nothing in this part requires a State to receive proposals for

or approve alternatives to affiliation periods.

■ 7. Add and reserve § 146.120 to read as follows:

§ 146.120 Interaction with the Family and Medical Leave Act [Reserved]

■ 8. Revise § 146.125 to read as follows:

§ 146.125 Applicability dates.

Sections 146.111 through 146.119, § 146.143, and § 146.145 are applicable for plan years beginning on or after July 1, 2005. Until the applicability date for this regulation, plans and issuers are required to continue to comply with the corresponding sections of 45 CFR parts 144 and 146, contained in the 45 CFR, parts 1 to 199, edition revised as of October 1, 2004.

■ 9. Revise § 146.143 to read as follows:

§ 146.143 Preemption; State flexibility; construction.

(a) *Continued applicability of State law with respect to health insurance issuers.* Subject to paragraph (b) of this section and except as provided in paragraph (c) of this section, part A of title XXVII of the PHS Act is not to be construed to supersede any provision of State law which establishes, implements, or continues in effect any standard or requirement solely relating to health insurance issuers in connection with group health insurance coverage except to the extent that such standard or requirement prevents the application of a requirement of this part.

(b) *Continued preemption with respect to group health plans.* Nothing in part A of title XXVII of the PHS Act affects or modifies the provisions of section 514 of the Act with respect to group health plans.

(c) *Special rules*—(1) *In general.* Subject to paragraph (c)(2) of this section, the provisions of part A of title XXVII of the PHS Act relating to health insurance coverage offered by a health insurance issuer supersede any provision of State law which establishes, implements, or continues in effect a standard or requirement applicable to imposition of a preexisting condition exclusion specifically governed by section 2701 of the PHS Act which differs from the standards or requirements specified in section 2701 of the PHS Act.

(2) *Exceptions.* Only in relation to health insurance coverage offered by a health insurance issuer, the provisions of this part do not supersede any provision of State law to the extent that such provision—

(i) Shortens the period of time from the "6-month period" described in section 2701(a)(1) of the PHS Act and

D. HIPAA Final Rules, Portability, continued

§ 146.111(a)(1)(i) (for purposes of identifying a preexisting condition);

(ii) Shortens the period of time from the "12 months" and "18 months" described in section 2701(a)(2) of the PHS Act and § 146.111(a)(1)(ii) (for purposes of applying a preexisting condition exclusion period);

(iii) Provides for a greater number of days than the "63-day period" described in sections 2701(c)(2)(A) and (d)(4)(A) of the PHS Act and §§ 146.111(a)(1)(iii) and 146.113 (for purposes of applying the break in coverage rules);

(iv) Provides for a greater number of days than the "30-day period" described in sections 2701(b)(2) and (d)(1) of the PHS Act and § 146.111(b) (for purposes of the enrollment period and preexisting condition exclusion periods for certain newborns and children that are adopted or placed for adoption);

(v) Prohibits the imposition of any preexisting condition exclusion in cases not described in section 2701(d) of the PHS Act or expands the exceptions described therein;

(vi) Requires special enrollment periods in addition to those required under section 2701(f) of the PHS Act; or

(vii) Reduces the maximum period permitted in an affiliation period under section 2701(g)(1)(B) of the PHS Act.

(d) *Definitions*—(1) *State law.* For purposes of this section the term *State law* includes all laws, decisions, rules, regulations, or other State action having the effect of law, of any State. A law of the United States applicable only to the District of Columbia is treated as a State law rather than a law of the United States.

(2) *State.* For purposes of this section the term *State* includes a State (as defined in § 144.103), any political subdivisions of a State, or any agency or instrumentality of either.

■ 10. Revise § 146.145 to read as follows:

§ 146.145 Special rules relating to group health plans.

(a) *Group health plan*—(1) *Definition.* A group health plan means an employee welfare benefit plan to the extent that the plan provides medical care (including items and services paid for as medical care) to employees (including both current and former employees) or their dependents (as defined under the terms of the plan) directly or through insurance, reimbursement, or otherwise.

(2) *Determination of number of plans.* [Reserved]

(b) *General exception for certain small group health plans.* The requirements of this part, other than § 146.130, do not apply to any group health plan (and group health insurance coverage) for any plan year if, on the first day of the

plan year, the plan has fewer than two participants who are current employees.

(c) *Excepted benefits*—(1) *In general.* The requirements of subparts B and C of this part do not apply to any group health plan (or any group health insurance coverage) in relation to its provision of the benefits described in paragraph (c)(2), (3), (4), or (5) of this section (or any combination of these benefits).

(2) *Benefits excepted in all circumstances.* The following benefits are excepted in all circumstances—

(i) Coverage only for accident (including accidental death and dismemberment);

(ii) Disability income coverage;

(iii) Liability insurance, including general liability insurance and automobile liability insurance;

(iv) Coverage issued as a supplement to liability insurance;

(v) Workers' compensation or similar coverage;

(vi) Automobile medical payment insurance;

(vii) Credit-only insurance (for example, mortgage insurance); and

(viii) Coverage for on-site medical clinics.

(3) *Limited excepted benefits*—(i) *In general.* Limited-scope dental benefits, limited-scope vision benefits, or long-term care benefits are excepted if they are provided under a separate policy, certificate, or contract of insurance, or are otherwise not an integral part of a group health plan as described in paragraph (c)(3)(ii) of this section. In addition, benefits provided under a health flexible spending arrangement are excepted benefits if they satisfy the requirements of paragraph (c)(3)(v) of this section.

(ii) *Not an integral part of a group health plan.* For purposes of this paragraph (c)(3), benefits are not an integral part of a group health plan (whether the benefits are provided through the same plan or a separate plan) only if the following two requirements are satisfied—

(A) Participants must have the right to elect not to receive coverage for the benefits; and

(B) If a participant elects to receive coverage for the benefits, the participant must pay an additional premium or contribution for that coverage.

(iii) *Limited scope*—(A) *Dental benefits.* Limited scope dental benefits are benefits substantially all of which are for treatment of the mouth (including any organ or structure within the mouth).

(B) *Vision benefits.* Limited scope vision benefits are benefits substantially all of which are for treatment of the eye.

(iv) *Long-term care.* Long-term care benefits are benefits that are either—

(A) Subject to State long-term care insurance laws;

(B) For qualified long-term care services, as defined in section 7702B(c)(1) of the Internal Revenue Code, or provided under a qualified long-term care insurance contract, as defined in section 7702B(b) of the Internal Revenue Code; or

(C) Based on cognitive impairment or a loss of functional capacity that is expected to be chronic.

(v) *Health flexible spending arrangements.* Benefits provided under a health flexible spending arrangement (as defined in section 106(c)(2) of the Internal Revenue Code) are excepted for a class of participants only if they satisfy the following two requirements—

(A) Other group health plan coverage, not limited to excepted benefits, is made available for the year to the class of participants by reason of their employment; and

(B) The arrangement is structured so that the maximum benefit payable to any participant in the class for a year cannot exceed two times the participant's salary reduction election under the arrangement for the year (or, if greater, cannot exceed $500 plus the amount of the participant's salary reduction election). For this purpose, any amount that an employee can elect to receive as taxable income but elects to apply to the health flexible spending arrangement is considered a salary reduction election (regardless of whether the amount is characterized as salary or as a credit under the arrangement).

(4) *Noncoordinated benefits*—(i) *Excepted benefits that are not coordinated.* Coverage for only a specified disease or illness (for example, cancer-only policies) or hospital indemnity or other fixed indemnity insurance is excepted only if it meets each of the conditions specified in paragraph (c)(4)(ii) of this section. To be hospital indemnity or other fixed indemnity insurance, the insurance must pay a fixed dollar amount per day (or per other period) of hospitalization or illness (for example, $100/day) regardless of the amount of expenses incurred.

(ii) *Conditions.* Benefits are described in paragraph (c)(4)(i) of this section only if—

(A) The benefits are provided under a separate policy, certificate, or contract of insurance;

(B) There is no coordination between the provision of the benefits and an exclusion of benefits under any group

D. HIPAA Final Rules, Portability, continued

Federal Register / Vol. 69, No. 250 / Thursday, December 30, 2004 / Rules and Regulations   78799

health plan maintained by the same plan sponsor; and

(C) The benefits are paid with respect to an event without regard to whether benefits are provided with respect to the event under any group health plan maintained by the same plan sponsor.

(iii) *Example.* The rules of this paragraph (c)(4) are illustrated by the following example:

Example. (i) *Facts.* An employer sponsors a group health plan that provides coverage through an insurance policy. The policy provides benefits only for hospital stays at a fixed percentage of hospital expenses up to a maximum of $100 a day.

(ii) *Conclusion.* In this *Example,* even though the benefits under the policy satisfy the conditions in paragraph (c)(4)(ii) of this section, because the policy pays a percentage of expenses incurred rather than a fixed dollar amount, the benefits under the policy are not excepted benefits under this paragraph (c)(4). This is the result even if, in practice, the policy pays the maximum of $100 for every day of hospitalization.

(5) *Supplemental benefits.* (i) The following benefits are excepted only if they are provided under a separate policy, certificate, or contract of insurance—

(A) Medicare supplemental health insurance (as defined under section 1882(g)(1) of the Social Security Act; also known as Medigap or MedSupp insurance);

(B) Coverage supplemental to the coverage provided under Chapter 55, Title 10 of the United States Code (also known as TRICARE supplemental programs); and

(C) Similar supplemental coverage provided to coverage under a group health plan. To be similar supplemental coverage, the coverage must be specifically designed to fill gaps in primary coverage, such as coinsurance or deductibles. Similar supplemental coverage does not include coverage that becomes secondary or supplemental only under a coordination-of-benefits provision.

(ii) The rules of this paragraph (c)(5) are illustrated by the following example:

Example. (i) *Facts.* An employer sponsors a group health plan that provides coverage for both active employees and retirees. The coverage for retirees supplements benefits provided by Medicare, but does not meet the requirements for a supplemental policy under section 1882(g)(1) of the Social Security Act.

(ii) *Conclusion.* In this *Example,* the coverage provided to retirees does not meet the definition of supplemental excepted benefits under this paragraph (c)(5) because the coverage is not Medicare supplemental insurance as defined under section 1882(g)(1) of the Social Security Act, is not a TRICARE supplemental program, and is not supplemental to coverage provided under a group health plan.

(d) *Treatment of partnerships.* For purposes of this part:

(1) *Treatment as a group health plan.* Any plan, fund, or program that would not be (but for this paragraph (d)) an employee welfare benefit plan and that is established or maintained by a partnership, to the extent that the plan, fund, or program provides medical care (including items and services paid for as medical care) to present or former partners in the partnership or to their dependents (as defined under the terms of the plan, fund, or program), directly or through insurance, reimbursement, or otherwise, is treated (subject to paragraph (d)(2) of this section) as an employee welfare benefit plan that is a group health plan.

(2) *Employment relationship.* In the case of a group health plan, the term *employer* also includes the partnership in relation to any bona fide partner. In addition, the term *employee* also includes any bona fide partner. Whether or not an individual is a bona fide partner is determined based on all the relevant facts and circumstances, including whether the individual performs services on behalf of the partnership.

(3) *Participants of group health plans.* In the case of a group health plan, the term *participant* also includes any individual described in paragraph (d)(3)(i) or (ii) of this section if the individual is, or may become, eligible to receive a benefit under the plan or the individual's beneficiaries may be eligible to receive any such benefit.

(i) In connection with a group health plan maintained by a partnership, the individual is a partner in relation to the partnership.

(ii) In connection with a group health plan maintained by a self-employed individual (under which one or more employees are participants), the individual is the self-employed individual.

(e) *Determining the average number of employees.* [Reserved]

Dated: November 24, 2004.

Mark B. McClellan,

Administrator, Centers for Medicare & Medicaid Services.

Dated: December 2, 2004.

Tommy G. Thompson,

Secretary, Department of Health and Human Services.

[FR Doc. 04–28112 Filed 12–29–04; 8:45 am]

BILLING CODE 4830–01–P; 4510–29–P; 4120–01–P

E. HIPAA Final Rules, Administrative Simplification Enforcement

Summary   The Department of Health and Human Services published final rules to impose civil money penalties on entities that violate the administrative simplification rules under HIPAA. The rules, published on February 16, 2006, are effective on March 16, 2006.

Thursday,
February 16, 2006

Part III

Department of Health and Human Services

Office of the Secretary

---

45 CFR Parts 160 and 164
HIPAA Administrative Simplification:
Enforcement; Final Rule

E. HIPAA Final Rules, Administrative Simplification Enforcement, continued

8390   Federal Register / Vol. 71, No. 32 / Thursday, February 16, 2006 / Rules and Regulations

DEPARTMENT OF HEALTH AND HUMAN SERVICES

Office of the Secretary

45 CFR Parts 160 and 164

RIN 0991–AB29

HIPAA Administrative Simplification: Enforcement

AGENCY: Office of the Secretary, HHS.

ACTION: Final rule.

SUMMARY: The Secretary of Health and Human Services is adopting rules for the imposition of civil money penalties on entities that violate rules adopted by the Secretary to implement the Administrative Simplification provisions of the Health Insurance Portability and Accountability Act of 1996, Public Law 104–191 (HIPAA). The final rule amends the existing rules relating to the investigation of noncompliance to make them apply to all of the HIPAA Administrative Simplification rules, rather than exclusively to the privacy standards. It also amends the existing rules relating to the process for imposition of civil money penalties. Among other matters, the final rule clarifies and elaborates upon the investigation process, bases for liability, determination of the penalty amount, grounds for waiver, conduct of the hearing, and the appeal process.

DATES: This final rule is effective on March 16, 2006.

FOR FURTHER INFORMATION CONTACT: Carol C. Conrad, (202) 690–1840.

SUPPLEMENTARY INFORMATION: On April 18, 2005, the Department of Health and Human Services (HHS) published a Notice of Proposed Rulemaking (proposed rule) proposing to revise the existing rules relating to compliance with, and enforcement of, the Administrative Simplification regulations (HIPAA rules) adopted by the Secretary of Health and Human Services (Secretary) under subtitle F of Title II of HIPAA (HIPAA provisions). 70 FR 20224. The proposed rule also proposed the adoption of new provisions relating to the imposition of civil money penalties on covered entities that violate a HIPAA provision or HIPAA rule. The comment period on the proposed rule closed on June 17, 2005. Forty-nine comments, principally from health care organizations, were received during the comment period.

In this final rule, HHS revises existing rules that relate to compliance with, and enforcement of, the HIPAA rules. These rules are codified at 45 CFR part 160, subparts C and E. In addition, this final rule adds a new subpart D to part 160. The new subpart D contains additional rules relating to the imposition by the Secretary of civil money penalties on covered entities that violate the HIPAA rules. The full set of rules to be codified at subparts C, D, and E of 45 CFR part 160 is collectively referred to in this final rule as the "Enforcement Rule." Finally, HHS makes minor and conforming changes to subpart A of part 160 and subpart E of part 164.

The statutory and regulatory background of the final rule is set out below. A description of the provisions of the proposed rule, the public comments, and HHS's responses to the comments follows. The preamble concludes with HHS's analyses of impact and other issues under applicable law.

I. Background

A. Statutory Background

Subtitle F of Title II of HIPAA, entitled "Administrative Simplification," requires the Secretary to adopt national standards for certain information-related activities of the health care industry. Under section 1173 of the Social Security Act (Act), 42 U.S.C. 1320d–2, the Secretary is required to adopt national standards for certain financial and administrative transactions, code sets, the security of health information, and certain unique health identifiers. In addition, section 264 of HIPAA, 42 U.S.C. 1320d–2 note, requires the Secretary to promulgate standards to protect the privacy of certain health information. Under section 1172(a) of the Act, 42 U.S.C. 1320d–1(a), the provisions of Subtitle F apply only to—

The following persons:
(1) A health plan.
(2) A health care clearinghouse.
(3) A health care provider who transmits any health information in electronic form in connection with a transaction referred to in section 1173(a)(1).

These entities are collectively known as "covered entities." [1]

HIPAA requires certain consultations with industry as a predicate to the issuance of the HIPAA standards and provides that most covered entities have

---

[1] An additional category of covered entities was added by the Medicare Prescription Drug, Improvement, and Modernization Act of 2003 (Pub. L. 108–173) (MMA). As added by MMA, section 1860D–31(h)(6)(A) of the Act, 42 U.S.C. 1395w–141(h)(6)(A), provides that a prescription drug card sponsor is a covered entity for purposes of applying part C of title XI and all regulatory provisions promulgated thereunder, including regulations (relating to privacy) adopted pursuant to the authority of the Secretary under section 264(c) of the Health Insurance Portability and Accountability Act of 1996 (42 U.S.C. 1320d–2 note).

up to 2 years (small health plans have up to 3 years) to come into compliance with the standards, once adopted. Act, sections 1172(c) (42 U.S.C. 1320d–1(c)), 1175(b) (42 U.S.C. 1320d–4(b)). The statute establishes civil money penalties and criminal penalties for violations. Act, sections 1176 (42 U.S.C. 1320d–5), 1177 (42 U.S.C. 1320d–6). HHS enforces the civil money penalties, while the U.S. Department of Justice enforces the criminal penalties.

HIPAA's civil money penalty provision, section 1176(a) of the Act, 42 U.S.C. 1320d–5(a), authorizes the Secretary to impose a civil money penalty, as follows:

(1) IN GENERAL. Except as provided in subsection (b), the Secretary shall impose on any person who violates a provision of this part [42 U.S.C. 1320d, et seq.] a penalty of not more than $100 for each such violation, except that the total amount imposed on the person for all violations of an identical requirement or prohibition during a calendar year may not exceed $25,000.

(2) PROCEDURES. The provisions of section 1128A [42 U.S.C. 1320a–7a] (other than subsections (a) and (b) and the second sentence of subsection (f)) shall apply to the imposition of a civil money penalty under this subsection in the same manner as such provisions apply to the imposition of a penalty under such section 1128A.

For simplicity, we refer throughout this preamble to this provision, the related provisions at section 1128A of the Act, and other related provisions of the Act, by their Social Security Act citations, rather than by their U.S. Code citations.

Subsection (b) of section 1176 sets out limitations on the Secretary's authority to impose civil money penalties and also provides authority for waiving such penalties. Under section 1176(b)(1), a civil money penalty may not be imposed with respect to an act that "constitutes an offense punishable" under the related criminal penalty provision, section 1177 of the Act. Under section 1176(b)(2), a civil money penalty may not be imposed "if it is established to the satisfaction of the Secretary that the person liable for the penalty did not know, and by exercising reasonable diligence would not have known, that such person violated the provision." Under section 1176(b)(3), a civil money penalty may not be imposed if the failure to comply was due "to reasonable cause and not to willful neglect" and is corrected within a certain time. Finally, under section 1176(b)(4), a civil money penalty may be reduced or entirely waived "to the extent that the payment of such penalty would be excessive relative to the compliance failure involved."

As noted above, section 1176(a) incorporates by reference certain

E. HIPAA Final Rules, Administrative Simplification Enforcement, continued

Federal Register / Vol. 71, No. 32 / Thursday, February 16, 2006 / Rules and Regulations   **8391**

provisions of section 1128A of the Act. Those provisions, as relevant here, establish a number of requirements with respect to the imposition of civil money penalties. Under section 1128A(c)(1), the Secretary may not initiate a civil money penalty action "later than six years after the date" of the occurrence that forms the basis for the civil money penalty. Under section 1128A(c)(2), a person upon whom the Secretary seeks to impose a civil money penalty must be given written notice and an opportunity for a determination to be made "on the record after a hearing at which the person is entitled to be represented by counsel, to present witnesses, and to cross-examine witnesses against the person." Section 1128A also provides, at subsections (c), (e), and (j), respectively, requirements for: Service of the notice and authority for sanctions which the hearing officer may impose for misconduct in connection with the civil money penalty proceeding; judicial review of the Secretary's determination in the United States Court of Appeals for the circuit in which the person resides or maintains his/its principal place of business; and the issuance and enforcement of subpoenas by the Secretary. In addition, section 1128A of the Act contains provisions relating to liability for civil money penalties and what measures must be taken once they are imposed. For example, section 1128A(d) provides that the Secretary must take into account certain factors "in determining the amount * * * of any penalty"; section 1128A(h) makes certain notifications once a civil money penalty is imposed; and section 1128A(*l*) makes a principal liable for penalties "for the actions of the principal's agent acting within the scope of the agency." These provisions are discussed more fully below.

B. Regulatory Background

As noted above, section 1173 of the Act and section 264 of HIPAA require the Secretary to adopt a number of national standards to facilitate the exchange, and protect the privacy and security, of certain health information. The Secretary has already adopted many of these HIPAA standards by regulation. These regulations consist of the following: Health Insurance Reform: Standards for Electronic Transactions (Transactions Rule); Standards for Privacy of Individually Identifiable Health Information (Privacy Rule); Health Insurance Reform: Standard Unique Employer Identifier (EIN Rule); Health Insurance Reform: Security Standards (Security Rule); and HIPAA Administrative Simplification: Standard Unique Health Identifier for Health Care

Providers (NPI Rule). Proposed standards for certain claims attachments were published on September 23, 2005 (70 FR 55990) and proposed standards for health plan identifiers are under development. The history of these and related rules is described in a proposed rule published on April 18, 2005 at 70 FR 20225–20226.

An interim final rule promulgating procedural requirements for imposition of civil money penalties, Civil Money Penalties: Procedures for Investigations, Imposition of Penalties, and Hearings (April 17, 2003 interim final rule), was published on April 17, 2003 (68 FR 18895), and was effective on May 19, 2003, with a sunset date of September 16, 2004 (as corrected at 68 FR 22453, April 28, 2003). The April 17, 2003 interim final rule adopted a new subpart E of part 160. The sunset date of the April 17, 2003 interim final rule was extended to September 16, 2005 on September 15, 2004 (69 FR 55515) and was further extended to March 16, 2006 on September 14, 2005 (70 FR 54293).

The authority for administering and enforcing compliance with the Privacy Rule has been delegated to the HHS Office for Civil Rights (OCR). 65 FR 82381 (December 28, 2000). The authority for administering and enforcing compliance with the non-privacy HIPAA rules has been delegated to the HHS Centers for Medicare & Medicaid Services (CMS). 68 FR 60694 (October 23, 2003).

II. Overview of the Proposed and Final Rules

A. The Proposed Rule

In the proposed rule, we proposed to bring together and adopt rules governing the implementation of the civil money penalty authority of section 1176 of the Act for all of the HIPAA rules. As previously noted, parts of the Enforcement Rule are already in place: subpart C of part 160 establishes certain investigative procedures for the Privacy Rule, and subpart E establishes interim procedures for investigations and for the imposition, and challenges to the imposition, of civil money penalties for all of the HIPAA rules. The proposed rule would complete the Enforcement Rule by (1) making subpart C applicable to all of the HIPAA rules; (2) adopting on a permanent basis most of the provisions of subpart E; and (3) addressing, among other issues, our policies for determining violations and calculating civil money penalties, how we will address the statutory limitations on the imposition of civil money penalties, and various procedural issues, such as provisions for appellate

review within HHS of a hearing decision, burden of proof, and notification of other agencies of the imposition of a civil money penalty.

Several fundamental considerations shaped the proposed rule. First, there is one statutory provision for imposing civil money penalties on covered entities that violate the HIPAA rules; thus, the proposed rule sought to establish a uniform enforcement and compliance policy for all of the HIPAA rules to minimize the potential for confusion and burden and maximize the potential for fairness and consistency in enforcement. Second, the proposed rule sought to facilitate the movement from noncompliance to compliance by covered entities by extending to all of the HIPAA rules the regulatory commitment to promoting and encouraging voluntary compliance with the HIPAA rules that currently applies to the Privacy Rule, subpart C of part 160. Third, the proposed rule sought to minimize confusion with the procedures for investigations and hearings by building upon pre-existing Departmental procedures for investigations and hearings under section 1128A of the Act—the civil money penalty regulations of the Office of the Inspector General, which are codified at 42 CFR parts 1003, 1005, and 1006 (OIG regulations). Fourth, the proposed rule was intended to be clear and easy to understand. Finally, the proposed rule sought to provide the Secretary with reasonable discretion, particularly in areas where the exercise of judgment is called for by the statute or rules, and to avoid being overly prescriptive in areas where it would be helpful to gain experience with the practical impact of the HIPAA rules, to avoid unintended adverse effects.

We proposed to amend subpart A of part 160, which contains general provisions, to include a definition of "person." With respect to subpart C of part 160, we proposed to incorporate several provisions currently found in subpart E and to make subpart C applicable to the non-privacy HIPAA rules. We also proposed to add to part 160 a new subpart D, which would establish rules relating to the imposition of civil money penalties, including those which apply whether or not there is a hearing. We also proposed to incorporate into subpart D several provisions currently found in subpart E. Proposed subpart E addressed the pre-hearing and hearing phases of the enforcement process. Many of the provisions of proposed subpart E were adopted by the April 17, 2003 interim final rule; we did not propose to change them substantively, although we

E. HIPAA Final Rules, Administrative Simplification Enforcement, continued

8392 Federal Register / Vol. 71, No. 32 / Thursday, February 16, 2006 / Rules and Regulations

proposed to renumber them. Finally, a conforming change to the privacy standards in subpart E of part 164 was proposed.

B. The Final Rule

While the final rule adopts most of the provisions of the proposed rule without change, several significant changes to certain provisions of the proposed rule have been made in response to comments. We do not list variables in the final rule, as was proposed, to count the number of violations of an identical requirement or prohibition; rather, the final rule clarifies that the method for determining the number of such violations is grounded in the substantive requirement or prohibition violated. In addition, the ALJ will be able to review the number of violations determined as part of his or her review of the proposed civil money penalty. The provision for joint and several liability of the members of an affiliated covered entity is retained, unless it is established that another member of the affiliated covered entity was responsible for the violation. While we continue to treat section 1176(b)(1) as an affirmative defense, we provide that it may be raised at any time. We retain the provision for statistical sampling, but we provide that, where statistical sampling is used, HHS must provide a copy of the study on which its statistical findings are based with the notice of proposed determination. As a corollary, we provide that a respondent who intends to introduce evidence of its statistical expert at the hearing must provide the study prepared by its expert to HHS at least 30 days prior to the scheduled hearing. We also provide that a respondent will have 90, rather than 60, days in which to file its request for hearing. Other changes made by the final rule are described below.

The Enforcement Rule does not adopt standards, as that term is defined and interpreted under Subtitle F of Title II of HIPAA. Thus, the requirement for industry consultations in section 1172(c) of the Act does not apply. For the same reason, the statute's time frames for compliance, set forth in section 1175 of the Act, do not apply to the Enforcement Rule. Accordingly, the Enforcement Rule is effective on March 16, 2006.

III. Section-by-Section Description of the Final Rule and Response to Comments

We received 49 comments on the proposed rule. Many of these comments were from associations or interest

groups involved in the health care industry. We also received comments from covered entities, a state agency, a law school class, and a number of individuals.

While the comments addressed most of the provisions of the proposed rule, the following 14 sections of the proposed rule received no comment: proposed §§ 160.400, 160.418, 160.500, 160.502, 160.506, 160.510, 160.514, 160.524, 160.526, 160.528, 160.530, 160.532, 160.544, and 160.550. We have, accordingly, not changed these sections in the final rule from what was proposed, and we do not discuss them below. The basis and purpose of sections that are unchanged from the proposed rule and are not discussed below are set out in the proposed rule published on April 18, 2005 at 70 FR 20240–20247 and, in certain cases, in the interim final rule published on April 17, 2003 at 68 FR 18895–18901.

A number of comments also expressed support for particular provisions. In most cases, we do not discuss these comments, with which we generally agree, below. Finally, certain comments raised issues concerning other HIPAA rules, such as allegations that a particular entity had violated the Privacy Rule or that particular provisions of a HIPAA rule create a hardship. Such issues are outside the scope of this rulemaking and, accordingly, are not addressed here.

A. Subpart A

Subpart A of the final rule adopts a new definition of the term "person." This definition is placed in § 160.103, which contains definitions that apply to all of the HIPAA rules. Thus, the new definition of "person" applies to all of the HIPAA rules.

Proposed rule: We proposed to amend § 160.103 to add a definition of the term "person" to replace the definition of that term adopted by the April 17, 2003 interim final rule. We proposed to define the term "person" as "a natural person, trust or estate, partnership, corporation, professional association or corporation, or other entity, public or private." As more fully explained at 70 FR 20227–20228, the proposed definition clarified, consistent with the HIPAA provisions, that the term includes States and other public entities.

Final rule: The final rule adopts the provisions of the proposed rule.

Comment: We received one comment on this section, endorsing its application to all of the HIPAA rules.

Response: The definition of "person" in the final rule remains the same as proposed.

B. Subpart C—Compliance and Investigations

We amend subpart C to make the compliance and investigation provisions of the subpart—which at present apply only to the Privacy Rule—apply to all of the HIPAA rules. In addition, we include in subpart C the definitions that apply to subparts C, D, and E. We move to subpart C from subpart E the provisions relating to investigational subpoenas and inquiries. We also add to subpart C provisions prohibiting intimidation or retaliation that are currently found in the Privacy Rule but not in the other HIPAA rules. We change the title of this subpart to reflect the focus of this subpart within the larger Enforcement Rule. Aside from a change to § 160.306 and certain minor and conforming changes to §§ 160.300, 160.312, 160.314, and 160.316, we do not change the substance of the existing provisions of subpart C.

1. Section 160.300—Applicability

Proposed rule: We proposed to amend § 160.300 (along with § 160.304— Principles for achieving compliance; § 160.306—Complaints to the Secretary; § 160.308—Compliance reviews; and § 160.310—Responsibilities of covered entities) to make the provisions of · subpart C applicable to all of the HIPAA rules, instead of applicable only to the Privacy Rule. The proposed rule would accomplish this by changing the present references in these sections from "subpart E of part 164" to the more inclusive, defined term, "administrative simplification provision" or "administrative simplification provisions," as appropriate. As explained at 70 FR 20228, the purpose of this proposed change was to simplify and make uniform the compliance and enforcement process for the HIPAA rules.

Final rule: The final rule streamlines the provisions of the proposed rule by substituting the term "provisions" for the references to standards, requirements, and implementation specifications in § 160.300.

Comment: A number of comments endorsed the approach of having uniform compliance and enforcement provisions for the HIPAA rules, and no comments disagreed with this approach.

Response: The final rule retains the policy of the proposed rule, consistent with the expression of support for this approach in the public comment, but streamlines the language of the section.

Comment: A couple of comments asked whether "affiliated entities" were the same as "hybrid entities," in terms of applying the rule.

E. HIPAA Final Rules, Administrative Simplification Enforcement, continued

Response: As described at § 164.105(b)(2)(i)(A), an affiliated covered entity consists of "[l]egally separate covered entities [that] designate themselves (including any health care component of such covered entity) as a single affiliated covered entity * * * [where] all of the covered entities designated are under common ownership or control." Thus, an affiliated covered entity is comprised of more than one covered entity. By contrast, a hybrid entity is defined at § 164.103 as "a single legal entity: (1) That is a covered entity; (2) Whose business activities include both covered and non-covered functions; and (3) That designates health care components in accordance with [the regulation]." The Privacy and Security Rules apply to any covered entity in either arrangement. The issue of liability for a particular violation with respect to covered entities in an affiliated covered entity is discussed in connection with § 160.402(b) below.

2. Section 160.302—Definitions

Proposed rule: We proposed to move to § 160.302 three definitions that were adopted in the April 17, 2003 interim final rule at § 160.502: "ALJ" (Administrative Law Judge), "civil money penalty or penalty", and "respondent." We also proposed to add to § 160.302 two terms which are used throughout subparts C, D, and E: "administrative simplification provision" and "violation" or "to violate." We proposed to define the term "administrative simplification provision" in § 160.302 to mean any requirement or prohibition established by the HIPAA provisions or HIPAA rules: "* * * any requirement or prohibition established by: (1) 42 U.S.C. 1320d–1320d–4, 1320d–7, and 1320d–8; (2) Section 264 of Public Law 104–191; or (3) This subchapter." We proposed to define a "violation" (or "to violate") to mean a "failure to comply with an administrative simplification provision." As more fully explained at 70 FR 20228–20229, both definitions derive directly from the statutory language, and both definitions function consistently and fairly across the various HIPAA rules.

Final rule: The final rule adopts the provisions of the proposed rule.

a. "Administrative Simplification Provision"

Comment: One comment expressed general support for the definitions. Another comment stated that the definition of "administrative simplification provision" should be revised to include only standards. The

comment argued that this approach would be more consistent with the statute, which provides that covered entities must comply with standards, not requirements, prohibitions, or other restrictions set forth in the HIPAA rules.

Response: No change is made to the definition of "administrative simplification provision." With respect to the second comment above, we do not agree that the definition of this term should be limited to standards. As discussed at 70 FR 20229, limiting the elements of the HIPAA rules that could be violated to those designated as standards would have the effect of, among other things, insulating from enforcement explicit statutory requirements and prohibitions (e.g., the prohibitions at section 1175(a) of the Act, which the statute terms "requirements" and which the Transactions Rule treats as requirements but not standards). We do not agree that Congress intended such an effect. We note, moreover, that the statute explicitly provides for the adoption of implementation specifications. See section 1172(d) of the Act. Furthermore, we disagree with the contention that the statute does not contemplate that violations may be tied to requirements and prohibitions: section 1176(a)(1) speaks of "violations of an identical requirement or prohibition."

Comment: Several comments argued that this definition could lead to multiple violations from a single act and lead to more liability than covered entities could reasonably expect. It also was argued that this definition would render almost meaningless the statutory $25,000 cap on liability for violations of an identical provision in a calendar year.

Response: No examples were supplied to illustrate the concern as to how this definition would increase the anticipated liability of covered entities, so we can only respond generally. The prohibition in § 160.404(b)(2) on counting overlapping requirements twice should minimize any such effect. As for violations that might be implicated in a single act and not be insulated by § 160.404(b)(2), we see no reason why they should not be considered as separate violations, since covered entities must comply with all applicable requirements and prohibitions of the HIPAA provisions and rules. Also, the definition does not render the statutory cap meaningless; rather, the "requirement or prohibition" language of the definition is taken directly from the part of section 1176(a) that establishes the $25,000 statutory cap ("the total amount imposed on the person for all violations of an identical

requirement or prohibition for a calendar year may not exceed $25,000"). Furthermore, for the reasons explained in the preamble to the proposed rule, none of the other possible formulations of what constitutes a "provision of this part" works uniformly and fairly across the HIPAA rules. Thus, we retain the definition of "administrative simplification provision" as proposed.

b. "Violation" or "Violate"

Comment: One comment asked how the definition of "violation" would work with the addressable components of the Security Rule.

Response: With respect to the issue of how this term would apply to the addressable implementation specifications of the Security Rule, we provide the following guidance. Under § 164.306(d)(3)(ii), a covered entity must implement an addressable implementation specification if doing so is "reasonable and appropriate." Where that condition is met, the addressable implementation specification is a requirement, and failure to implement the addressable implementation specification would, accordingly, constitute a violation. Where that condition is not met, the covered entity must document why it would not be reasonable and appropriate to implement the implementation specification and implement "an equivalent alternative measure if reasonable and appropriate." In this latter situation, creating the documentation referred to is a requirement, and implementing an alternative measure is also a requirement, if doing so is reasonable and appropriate in the covered entity's circumstances; failure to take either required action would, accordingly, constitute a violation.

3. Section 160.304—Principles for Achieving Compliance

Proposed rule: We proposed to amend § 160.304 to make it applicable to all of the HIPAA rules; otherwise, we proposed to leave the rule substantively unchanged. Section 160.304 provides that the Secretary will, to the extent practicable, seek the cooperation of covered entities in obtaining compliance. Section 160.304 also provides that the Secretary may provide technical assistance to help covered entities voluntarily comply with the HIPAA rules.

Final rule: The final rule adopts the provisions of the proposed rule.

Comment: Many comments supported HHS's approach to voluntary compliance and the use of a complaint-based process to identify and correct

E. HIPAA Final Rules, Administrative Simplification Enforcement, continued

8394   Federal Register / Vol. 71, No. 32 / Thursday, February 16, 2006 / Rules and Regulations

noncompliance, on the grounds that it is the most efficient and effective way of obtaining compliance and realizing the benefits of the HIPAA rules. In addition, some contended that, given the confusion of many covered entities with many of the rules' requirements, it is an appropriate approach. However, one comment criticized HHS's reliance on voluntary compliance and informal resolution of complaints on the ground that the statute contemplates that violations of the HIPAA rules should be pursued in the same manner as fraud and abuse cases, that is, through the formal, adversarial process provided for by section 1128A(c). Another comment stated that HHS's reliance on voluntary compliance has led to lax enforcement and that reliance on a complaint-based system is a fundamentally flawed approach, particularly with respect to enforcement of the Privacy Rule, because HHS has provided insufficient education to consumers, and it is impossible for consumers to complain about a law about which they know very little. Several comments urged that OCR and CMS continue to provide educational materials and guidance to help covered entities comply with the HIPAA rules and to educate consumers about their rights under the Privacy Rule.

Response: We agree that encouraging voluntary compliance is the most effective and quickest way of obtaining compliance in most cases. We do not agree that encouraging voluntary compliance and seeking informal resolution of complaints in individual cases constitutes lax enforcement or that such an approach is inconsistent with our statutory obligations. Our experience to date with privacy complaints illustrates the effectiveness of our enforcement approach. As of October 31, 2005, OCR had received and initiated reviews of over 16,000 privacy complaints from health care consumers and others across the country. These complaints are widespread and diverse, not only geographically, but also with respect to the type of entity complained against, as well as the Privacy Rule issues raised by the complaints. Complaints are filed against all sizes and types of covered entities, from solo practitioners to hospitals and pharmacy chains, and from health insurance issuers to group health plans, for example. In addition, the complaints implicate a full range of Privacy Rule issues, from uses and disclosures of protected health information to individual rights to administrative requirements. The variation and expansiveness of the complaints

provide HHS with a much broader approach to compliance than would a compliance review system, which likely would need to be targeted to larger institutions and/or a smaller set of concerns. Further, our experience with these cases—68 percent have been resolved or otherwise closed to date—indicates that generally we are receiving good cooperation from covered entities in quickly addressing compliance problems. Such resolutions bring the benefits of the HIPAA rules to consumers far more quickly than would a formalized, adversarial process, which would also be time-consuming and costly for both sides.

We also do not agree that the statute contemplates only a formalized, adversarial process; rather, it only requires such a process where a proposed civil money penalty is contested. It is important to note, moreover, that section 1176 contemplates that we would work with covered entities to help them achieve compliance, even when there is an allegation that the covered entity is in violation of the rules. Section 1176 provides that a civil money penalty may not be imposed if the failure to comply was due to reasonable cause and not willful neglect and is corrected within a certain period of time after the covered entity knew or should have known of the compliance failure, and that the Secretary may, in some circumstances, provide technical assistance to the covered entity during that period. Further, an approach that is primarily complaint-based does not limit our ability to perform compliance reviews when appropriate, and this has, in fact, occurred. We will continue to review the effectiveness of our enforcement approach and revise it, if needed. Notwithstanding our above approach, however, we will resort to civil money penalties, as needed, for matters that cannot be resolved by informal means.

Further, we disagree that persons affected by the Privacy Rule and the other HIPAA rules are unaware of their rights, as evidenced by the large number of complaints that HHS has received from consumers and covered and other entities. HHS has an ongoing program of providing information to the public and guidance to covered entities through the Internet, public speaking and educational events, and toll-free call-in lines. The millions of hits to our Web sites—*http://www.hhs.gov/ocr/hipaa* for the Privacy Rule and *http://www.cms.gov/hipaa/hipaa2* for the other HIPAA rules—suggest that covered entities and the public are increasingly aware of the application of the HIPAA rules to their business

activities and lives, respectively, and are able to access the information we have made available. In addition, the American Health Information Management Association issued the results of their latest compliance survey in a report entitled "The State of HIPAA Privacy and Security Compliance, April 2005," which indicated, with respect to the Privacy Rule, that over two-thirds of all hospital and health system patients had some or a complete understanding of their rights and the facility's responsibilities. Nonetheless, while such evidence is encouraging, we recognize that HHS must remain active in providing outreach and public education. We are committed to doing so, and thus, continue to develop educational material for consumers and industry guidance for covered entities.

Comment: One comment suggested that the Secretary commit to providing technical assistance to covered entities.

Response: We do not agree that the provision of technical assistance should be mandated. The statute (at section 1176(b)(3)(B)(ii)) makes the provision of technical assistance discretionary if the Secretary determines that the compliance failure was due to the covered entity's inability to comply. While OCR and CMS provide technical assistance in many cases, it is not necessary in all instances to provide such assistance in order to obtain compliance. Thus, it is inappropriate to mandate the provision of technical assistance.

Comment: One comment suggested amending § 160.304(b) to require ongoing reporting of complaints and resolutions to the healthcare industry. The goal in requiring reporting would be to educate covered entities regarding complaints that are found to be actual violations and encourage them to review their compliance. The comment stated that the current reports made by OCR to the National Committee on Vital and Health Statistics are not helpful since they only report the volume of complaints, not the nature of the complaints or whether a violation occurred.

Response: We do not believe mandatory reporting of complaints and resolutions is necessary. Both CMS and OCR currently have the ability to report to the public, including the healthcare industry, about complaints and their resolutions, and do so in summary form. We continue to present summaries of actions on complaints in various fora, including in public presentations, testimony, and in written documents. Our enforcement experience also informs our development of FAQs and guidance documents to explain certain

E. HIPAA Final Rules, Administrative Simplification Enforcement, continued

provisions and how to comply with them. In any event, covered entities should use their own internal complaint processes and experience to assess and improve their compliance and ability to serve the needs of their customers.

Comment: One comment suggested that the informal resolution process should allow HHS to render opinions on a covered entity's interpretation of the HIPAA rules. The comment expressed concern that a covered entity would not be able to resolve a compliance issue during the informal resolution process if it made a good faith, but incorrect, interpretation of a HIPAA rule. The comment suggested allowing HHS to render an opinion on the entity's interpretation to facilitate the informal resolution of compliance problems.

Response: As a general matter, we do not issue advisory opinions, but the informal resolution process will provide covered entities with information about HHS's interpretation of the HIPAA rules. Covered entities may also find guidance as to the proper interpretation of a HIPAA rule in the FAQs posted on the HHS website and technical assistance offered to the covered entities by HHS. Covered entities may also submit questions to HHS for consideration with respect to future FAQs and guidance.

4. Section 160.306—Complaints to the Secretary

Proposed rule: Section 160.306 provides for investigations of covered entities by the Secretary. It also outlines the procedure and requirements for filing a complaint against a covered entity. For example, it provides that a complaint must name the person that is the subject of the complaint and describe the acts or omissions believed to be violations. It also requires that complaints be filed within 180 days of when the complainant knew or should have known that the act or omission occurred, unless this time limit is waived for good cause. The proposed rule would have amended this section to apply it to all of the HIPAA rules, rather than exclusively to the Privacy Rule, but otherwise proposed no substantive changes to the section.

Final rule: The final rule adopts the provisions of the proposed rule, except that proposed § 160.306(c) is revised to require the Secretary to describe the basis of the complaint in the first written communication with the covered entity about the complaint.

Comment: One comment asked for clarification on when a complaint will be considered to have been timely filed in situations when a complainant should have known of the violation,

thus triggering the 180-day time period for filing a complaint.

Response: Deciding whether or not a complaint was properly filed within the 180-day period will need to be determined in each case. For example, an individual who is informed through an accounting of disclosures that his or her health information was impermissibly disclosed would be considered to know of the violation at the time the individual receives the accounting. In any event, however, the 180-day period can be waived for good cause shown.

Comment: Two comments suggested that HHS be required to inform a covered entity of the specific basis for an investigation or compliance review. These comments suggested the best way to accomplish this goal would be to send a copy of the complaint to the covered entity. The comments stated that, without specific information as to the basis of the complaint, a covered entity will not be able to properly respond to the agency's request for information.

Response: Both CMS and OCR currently provide the basis for an investigation in the first written communication with a covered entity about a complaint. This policy will continue to be followed, and the final rule is revised to require it. It should be noted that provision of a description of the basis for the complaint does not circumscribe the investigation, if the investigation subsequently uncovers other compliance issues with respect to the covered entity.

We disagree that sending a copy of the complaint is necessary for a covered entity to adequately respond to the Secretary's inquiries. As noted above, covered entities receive a description of the basis for the complaint. Other information contained in the complaint, such as the complainant's identity, is not always relevant to the investigation. In some cases, in fact, it may be necessary to withhold such information to, for example, protect the complainant's privacy. In instances where it is necessary to provide the complainant's identity in order for the covered entity to properly respond to the investigation, the complainant is so informed before this information is released to the covered entity.

Comment: One comment suggested that the rule be revised to require that a complaint include the name of the covered entity that is the subject of the complaint.

Response: The rule, both as proposed and as adopted below, already requires that a complaint "name the person that

is the subject of the complaint." See § 160.306(b)(2).

Comment: In one comment, a covered entity complained that it had expended a great deal of time and money defending itself against what turned out to be a false allegation and asked that HHS put more effort into gathering detailed information from complainants and helping covered entities respond to complaints. Another comment criticized the rule for providing no way of sanctioning a person bringing a negligent or malicious complaint.

Response: We understand that it may take time and effort to establish that an allegation is unfounded. When complaints are received, we make every effort to determine if the complaint is legitimate, so as not to place undue burdens on covered entities. Further, covered entities are encouraged promptly to contact the OCR or CMS investigators handling their complaints to discuss the allegations once notice of an investigation is received by the covered entity. Doing so should help a covered entity avoid the expenditure of unnecessary time and funds on defending itself against baseless complaints. The statute provides no basis for our penalizing a person for bringing a negligent or malicious complaint, although remedies may exist at common law. However, as discussed below in connection with § 160.316, lack of good faith would typically be a matter that is looked at in the course of investigating a complaint.

Comment: One comment suggested that only individuals or personal representatives should have standing to file a complaint. The comment takes the position that one covered entity should not be able to bring a complaint against another.

Response: We disagree. The purpose of the complaint process is to bring violations to the attention of HHS, so that any noncompliance with the HIPAA rules may be corrected. Particularly with respect to the Transactions Rule, the persons or entities that are likely to be disadvantaged by the noncompliance of a covered entity are other covered entities. It would, accordingly, be inconsistent with the purpose of the complaint process to exclude such entities from it.

Comment: Two comments suggested that HHS be required to notify covered entities of a complaint within a specified time-frame.

Response: OCR and CMS make every effort to notify covered entities of complaints on a timely basis. However, we do not include a specific deadline for notifying covered entities of

E. HIPAA Final Rules, Administrative Simplification Enforcement, continued

8396   Federal Register / Vol. 71, No. 32 / Thursday, February 16, 2006 / Rules and Regulations

complaints in the rule. The time needed to determine whether a complaint states issues that should be investigated can vary greatly, while fluctuations in the volume of complaints and other workload demands may also make meeting a specific deadline problematic.

Comment: One comment suggested that § 160.306(a)(2) should be amended to require that "uses or disclosures" be described in the complaint rather than "acts or omissions."

Response: The suggested change would not be appropriate. The provisions of this rule apply to all of the HIPAA rules, not just the Privacy Rule; the other HIPAA rules regulate actions other than uses and disclosures of protected health information. Moreover, even under the Privacy Rule, a violation may occur where no impermissible use or disclosure of protected health information has occurred. Failure to comply with a notice requirement under § 164.520 is an example of a violation that does not involve a use or disclosure of protected health information.

Comment: One comment suggested that the Secretary should be required to investigate all complaints and that failure to do so is inconsistent with section 1176(a) of the Act, which compels the Secretary to impose penalties for violations unless a statutory limitation applies. Imposing a deadline for beginning investigations was also suggested.

Response: The decision to investigate a complaint is based on the facts presented. Not all complaints need to be investigated. For example, in our experience, a substantial percentage of privacy complaints allege facts that fall outside of OCR's jurisdiction under HIPAA—e.g., an action prior to the compliance date of the Privacy Rule or an action by an entity not covered by the Rule. Revising the rule to require the Secretary to investigate all complaints would be counterproductive and lead to an inefficient allocation of enforcement resources. Similarly, imposing a deadline for beginning an investigation is unrealistic: Some investigations may turn out to be more time-consuming than anticipated, delaying the start of other investigations. It is necessary to provide OCR and CMS with the flexibility to deal with variations in circumstances and resource constraints.

5. Section 160.308—Compliance Reviews

Proposed rule: The proposed rule provided that the Secretary may conduct compliance reviews to determine whether covered entities are complying with the applicable administrative simplification provisions.

Final rule: The final rule adopts the provisions of the proposed rule.

Comment: Several comments asked HHS to outline the circumstances under which a compliance review would be undertaken or asked that the compliance review provision be eliminated from the rule. One comment suggested that compliance reviews be limited to evidence-based reviews. These comments expressed concern that the rule does not specifically define when a compliance review will be undertaken.

Response: Compliance reviews are conducted at the discretion of the Secretary. Outlining specific instances in which a compliance review will be conducted could have the counterproductive effect of skewing compliance efforts toward those aspects of compliance that had been identified as likely to result in a compliance review. It also does not seem advisable to limit, by rule, the circumstances under which such reviews may be conducted at this early stage of the enforcement program, when our knowledge of the types of violations that may arise is necessarily limited. We also do not agree that the provision for compliance reviews should be eliminated. There are situations where instances of potential noncompliance come to HHS's attention outside of the complaint process (e.g., where media reports suggest that a violation has occurred), and HHS must have clear authority to investigate such situations.

Comment: A number of comments suggested that HHS detail the compliance review process and rules for notification of covered entities when they are being reviewed.

Response: The rule already contains procedures to be followed, and requirements to be met, that apply to compliance reviews. See §§ 160.304, 160.310, 160.312, 160.314, and 160.316. It is unnecessary to establish procedures comparable to the complaint filing procedures of § 160.306 for compliance reviews, since they are initiated by HHS. The concerns expressed by most of the comments on this topic—that HHS would undertake a compliance review without notice to the covered entity and without specifying the basis for, or the focus of, the review—are misplaced. Section 160.312 requires HHS to attempt to resolve violations found in a compliance review by informal means and to inform the covered entity in writing if a compliance review is or is not resolved by informal means. Failing to notify the covered entity of a compliance review or the basis for such a review is not consistent with our practice generally and would be unlikely to yield much information of use, resulting in an ineffective use of the covered entity's and the agency's resources.

Comment: One comment suggests that compliance reviews should be mandatory and should be initiated within a specified time period.

Response: The rule, as proposed and adopted, does not preclude establishing a compliance review program or schedule, but it does not require it either. One purpose of compliance reviews is to permit investigation when allegations or situations warranting investigation come to our attention outside of the complaint process. The necessity for a compliance review in a particular case or a program of scheduled compliance reviews is inherently unpredictable, and it is important to retain the administrative flexibility to address such situations. Mandating compliance reviews on a fixed basis or schedule would be an inefficient allocation of limited enforcement resources and would hamper the agency's ability to target resources at actual noncompliance problems as they arise.

Comment: One comment suggested that the rule contain provisions outlining the coordination and cooperation between CMS and OCR when a compliance review under more than one rule occurs.

Response: As with complaint-based investigations, CMS and OCR will coordinate and allocate responsibility for compliance reviews based upon the HIPAA provisions involved and the facts of the case. We do not consider it advisable to specify detailed rules in this regard, as the allocation of function and responsibility will depend on the facts of each case and the resources available at the time.

6. Section 160.310—Responsibilities of Covered Entities

Proposed rule: Section 160.310 addresses the responsibilities of a covered entity, such as providing records and compliance reports to the Secretary and cooperating during a compliance review or complaint investigation. Section 160.310(c) provides that a covered entity must permit HHS to have access during normal business hours to its facilities, books, records, and other information necessary to determine compliance, but provides that if the Secretary determines that "exigent circumstances exist, such as when documents may be hidden or destroyed," the covered entity must permit access at any time without

E. HIPAA Final Rules, Administrative Simplification Enforcement, continued

notice. Section 160.310 also requires that the Secretary may not disclose protected health information obtained by the Secretary in the course of an investigation or compliance review except when necessary to ascertaining or enforcing compliance or as otherwise required by law. The proposed rule would amend this section to apply it to all of the HIPAA rules, rather than exclusively to the Privacy Rule, but otherwise proposed no substantive changes to the section.

Final rule: The final rule adopts the provisions of the proposed rule.

Comment: A couple of comments asked HHS either to further define "exigent circumstances," such as by limiting it to situations involving national security or by inserting specific examples of exigent circumstances in § 160.310(c)(1). One comment suggested that the rule be revised to require that the Secretary's determination that "exigent circumstances" exist be a "reasonable" one.

Response: The determination of what constitutes "exigent circumstances" will inevitably be fact-dependent. Specific language defining "exigent circumstances" is unnecessary, as the rule already provides a clarifying example and the principle underlying the provision is reasonably universal. We note that limiting the provision to situations where matters of national security are involved would most likely not cover the types of situations the provision is intended to cover—situations in which it is likely that the covered entity will seek to conceal or destroy evidence of noncompliance that HHS needs to carry out its statutory obligation to enforce the HIPAA rules.

Comment: Two comments asked for further guidance and notice of record retention requirements and another comment expressed concerns with the record retention requirements of the Privacy Rule.

Response: Record retention requirements applicable to the Privacy and Security Rules are spelled out in those rules; see, § 164.530(j) and § 164.316(b), respectively. We do not address these record retention requirements here, as this topic lies outside the scope of this rule.

The other HIPAA rules do not contain explicit record retention requirements, as such. However, it is likely that the documentation that would be relevant to showing compliance with those rules—such as health plan instructions to providers, software documentation, contracts, and systems processes—is kept as part of normal business practices. Covered entities should consider any other applicable laws,

such as state law, in making such decisions.

7. Section 160.312—Secretarial Action Regarding Complaints and Compliance Reviews

Proposed rule: We proposed to revise § 160.312(a) to require that, where noncompliance is indicated, the Secretary would seek to reach by informal means a resolution of the matter that is satisfactory to the Secretary. Informal means could include demonstrated compliance, or a completed corrective action plan or other agreement. We proposed to revise § 160.312(a)(2) to require, where noncompliance is indicated and the matter is resolved by informal means, that HHS notify the covered entity in writing and, if the matter arose from a complaint, the complainant. Where noncompliance is indicated and the matter is not resolved by informal means, proposed § 160.312(a)(3)(i) would require the Secretary to so inform the covered entity and provide the covered entity an opportunity to submit, within 30 days of receipt of such notification, written evidence of any mitigating factors or affirmative defenses. To avoid confusion with the notice of proposed determination process provided for at proposed § 160.420, proposed § 160.312(a)(3)(ii) provided that, where the matter is not resolved by informal means and the Secretary finds that imposition of a civil money penalty is warranted, the formal finding would be contained in the notice of proposed determination issued under proposed § 160.420. We proposed to leave § 160.312(b) substantively unchanged.

Final rule: The final rule adopts the provisions of the proposed rule.

Comment: One comment suggested that covered entities should be able to appeal the Secretary's findings during the informal resolution process and that the Secretary's decision to resolve a matter informally should not preclude the respondent from questioning the Secretary's interpretation or application of the rule in question.

Response: The purpose of the informal resolution process described in § 160.312 is to bring closure at an early stage to a matter where compliance is in issue and, thus, to obviate the need to issue a notice of proposed determination. Section 160.312 recognizes, however, that informal resolutions will not always be achieved. Where the agency and the covered entity are not able to resolve the matter informally, HHS (through OCR and/or CMS) will make a finding of noncompliance pursuant to § 160.420,

which the covered entity may then challenge through the applicable procedures of subparts D and E. Nothing in the rule compels the covered entity to challenge the finding of noncompliance under § 160.420, but if the covered entity wishes to challenge such a finding, including the agency's interpretation or application of a rule, it must do so through the procedural avenue provided by subparts D and E. These procedures implement the requirement of section 1128A(c) of the Act that the Secretary may not make an adverse determination against a person until the person has been given written notice and an opportunity for a hearing on the record on the adverse determination.

Comment: One comment asked how informal resolution is possible, given HHS's position that, where a violation is found, a CMP must be imposed. Another comment expressed concern that the informal resolution process would allow covered entities to skirt penalties and the consequences of noncompliance with the HIPAA rules and suggested that the Secretary should not be compelled to reach a resolution through informal processes.

Response: These comments misunderstand our position as to the mandatory nature of the statute. The Secretary must impose a civil money penalty where a formal determination of a violation is made. However, many opportunities exist prior to this determination that allow the Secretary to exercise his discretion to not impose a penalty. This issue is discussed more fully in connection with § 160.402 below.

The second comment above also misconstrues § 160.312. Nothing in that section compels OCR or CMS to resolve matters informally. Indeed, § 160.312(a)(3) describes the actions to be taken "[i]f the matter is not resolved by informal means * * *".

Comment: One comment suggested that HHS and the covered entity should be required to put the informal resolution in writing.

Response: Both § 160.312(a)(2) and § 160.312(b) require that the resolutions contemplated in those sections be "in writing." CMS and OCR currently document informal resolutions.

Comment: One comment suggested that the 30-day time period for a covered entity to submit to the Secretary evidence of mitigating factors or affirmative defenses should be extended.

Response: Thirty days should be sufficient for a covered entity to submit such evidence. The opportunity to provide additional evidence comes at

E. HIPAA Final Rules, Administrative Simplification Enforcement, continued

the end of investigation, and the covered entity should be gathering any evidence of mitigating factors or affirmative defenses during the investigation. In addition, the covered entity will have the opportunity to present such evidence to the ALJ if it chooses to appeal the Secretary's findings. Accordingly, we do not change this provision.

Comment: One comment suggested that a deadline should be imposed for HHS to notify the covered entity of its findings after an investigation.

Response: The time needed to finalize the agency's findings will depend on the complexity of the case, its outcome, and workload considerations. As these factors are inherently variable and unpredictable, we do not believe it would be advisable to impose fixed deadlines for taking the actions described in § 160.312.

Comment: One comment requested clarification of proposed § 160.312(a)(3)(ii), with respect to what action is referred to and the associated time frame.

Response: The action referred to is HHS's notification of the covered entity of its finding of noncompliance when it determines that the matter cannot be resolved informally. Section 160.312(a)(3)(ii) provides that, if HHS decides to impose a civil money penalty, it will send a notice of proposed determination to the covered entity pursuant to § 160.420. Thus, the intent of this provision is to clarify that, once OCR and/or CMS, as applicable, has determined that a violation has occurred, the matter cannot be resolved informally in a manner that is satisfactory to OCR and/or CMS, and a civil money penalty should be imposed, the agency's next step is to provide the formal notice required by section 1128A(c)(1), which in this rule is the notice of proposed determination under § 160.420. The rule imposes no specific deadline on the agency for sending this notice. However, it should be noted that if the notice is not sent within six years of the violation, pursuit of the civil money penalty would be precluded by section 1128A(c)(1), which is implemented in this rule by § 160.414.

Comment: One comment requested that § 160.312(a)(3) be revised to afford complainants the opportunity to express, in writing, the impact of the violation.

Response: The suggested change is unnecessary, since nothing in the rule precludes a complainant from providing such information to the agency at any point in the process. Complainants frequently describe, in their complaints or in the course of OCR's or CMS's initial contacts with the complainants, the impact of the alleged violation. HHS also may request such information from the complainant where, for example, it bears on the amount of the penalty to be imposed.

8. Section 160.314—Investigational Subpoenas and Inquiries

Proposed rule: The text of proposed § 160.314 was adopted by the April 17, 2003 interim final rule as § 160.504. We proposed to move this section to subpart C, consistent with our overall approach of organizing subparts C, D, and E to reflect the stages of the enforcement process. We proposed to include in the introductory language of proposed § 160.314(a) a sentence which states that, for the purposes of paragraph (a), a person other than a natural person is termed an "entity." We proposed not to modify § 160.314(b)(1), (2) and (8) from the provisions of the April 17, 2003 interim final rule at paragraphs (b)(1)–(3) of § 160.504. However, we proposed to add new paragraphs (3) through (7) and (9) to § 160.314(b) and also to add a new paragraph (c). The proposed new paragraphs at §§ 160.314(b)(3)–(b)(7) would permit representatives of HHS to attend and ask questions at the inquiry, give a witness the opportunity to clarify his answers on the record after being questioned by HHS, require any objections or claims of privilege to be asserted on the record, and permit HHS to seek enforcement of the subpoena through the federal district court if a witness refuses to answer non-privileged questions or produce requested documents or items. Further, proposed § 160.314(c) provided that, consistent with § 160.310, testimony and other evidence obtained in an investigational inquiry may be used by HHS in any of its activities and may be used or offered into evidence in any administrative or judicial proceeding. Together, these additions would clarify the manner in which investigational inquiries will be conducted, and how testimony given, and evidence obtained, during such an investigation may be used.

Final rule: The final rule adopts the provisions of the proposed rule, except that paragraph (a) is revised to clarify that investigational subpoenas may issue when a compliance review is conducted.

Comment: A few comments requested that this section provide for the protection of privileged documents when subpoenaed by the Secretary. Comments also suggested that covered entities should have the ability to challenge a subpoena issued by the Secretary.

Response: The rule, as proposed and adopted, provides a process for a subpoenaed witness to challenge the subpoena and/or assert privilege. Under section 205(e) of the Act, made applicable by section 1128A(j)(1) of the Act, the federal district court in which a person charged with contumacy or refusal to obey a subpoena resides or transacts business has jurisdiction upon application of HHS. As provided in § 160.314(a)(5), HHS may seek to enforce the subpoena in such cases through action in the relevant federal district court, which would presumably hear the basis for the witness's refusal to obey or claim of privilege in connection with a motion to quash under Fed. R. Civ. P. 45(c)(3). (28 U.S.C. Appendix).

Comment: Several comments requested that the scope of the subpoenas issued by the Secretary be limited to the investigation and that the Secretary not be allowed to pursue open-ended inquiries.

Response: Section 205(d) of the Act, which is made applicable by section 1128A(j)(1), provides that a subpoena may issue for "the production of any evidence that relates to any matter under investigation or in question before [the Secretary]." Moreover, the federal courts subject the exercise of an agency's administrative subpoena authority to a reasonableness analysis. In *U.S.* v. *Powell,* 397 U.S. 481 (1964), the holding of which was extended to all administrative subpoena authorities in *Securities and Exchange Commission* v. *Jerry T. O'Brien, Inc.,* 467 U.S. 735, 741–42 (1984), the U.S. Supreme Court articulated a standard for the judicial review of administrative subpoenas that requires that the investigation be conducted pursuant to a legitimate purpose and that the information requested under the subpoena is relevant to that purpose. HHS is required to comply with this standard in the exercise of the subpoena authority under this section.

Comment: One comment asked that covered entities be given notice of investigational inquiries directed at them.

Response: In general, we would expect that an investigational subpoena would be used where a covered entity has failed to respond to HHS's requests for information in the course of an investigation conducted under § 160.306. In such a case, the covered entity will have been previously notified of the investigation pursuant to § 160.306(c). Similarly, a subpoena would typically be issued in connection with a compliance review under § 160.308 where the covered entity had

E. HIPAA Final Rules, Administrative Simplification Enforcement, continued

failed to respond to HHS's prior requests for information. Thus, we do not expect the element of surprise to be present, which appears to be the concern underlying these comments. We clarify in § 160.314(a) that this section also applies to compliance reviews.

Comment: One comment suggested that § 160.314(a) be revised to state that the admissibility of written statements obtained by HHS during an investigational inquiry is subject to 45 CFR 160.518 and 160.538.

Response: We do not consider the suggested language necessary. Sections 160.518 and 160.538 apply to the exchange and admission of written statements. Should OCR or CMS seek to have written statements obtained during an investigation admitted into evidence, those statements would be subject to the requirements of §§ 160.518 and 160.538.

Comment: One comment asked for clarification as to who may amend a transcript and whether the Secretary has the discretion to limit a witness's amendment of his or her testimony transcript.

Response: Under § 160.314(b)(9), both sides may propose corrections to the transcript, and any proposed corrections are attached to the transcript; the transcript itself is not altered. Section 160.314(b)(9)(i) provides that, if a witness is provided with a copy of the transcript, the witness may submit written proposed corrections to the transcript, or, if the witness is afforded only the opportunity to inspect the transcript, the witness may propose corrections to the transcript at the time of inspection. In either case, the witness's proposed corrections are attached to the transcript. Similarly, under § 160.314(b)(9)(ii), the Secretary's proposed corrections are attached to the transcript. The purpose of the proposed corrections is to make the transcript "true and accurate." See § 160.314(b)(9)(i). Under this process, then, HHS would not be changing the witness's proposed corrections; HHS would, at most, be proposing different corrections.

Comment: One comment suggested that § 160.314 be revised to require HHS to provide for the same protection of protected health information that is required of covered entities when HHS receives protected health information during an investigation.

Response: Section 160.310(c)(3) explicitly protects the confidentiality of protected health information received by HHS "in connection with an investigation or compliance review under this subpart." Although these protections are not the same as those

required of covered entities with respect to protected health information, in some respects they are more stringent, given the limited circumstances for which the information may be disclosed under this provision. Because § 160.314 is now part of the subpart, the restriction of § 160.310(c)(3) applies to protected health information received during an investigational inquiry. See § 160.314(c), which provides that testimony and other evidence obtained in an investigational inquiry may only be used "[c]onsistent with § 160.310(c)(3) * * *".

Comment: One comment asked for clarification of the "good cause" limitation on a witness's ability to inspect the official transcript of their testimony.

Response: This provision derives from the Administrative Procedure Act, which requires, at 5 U.S.C. 555(c), that "[a] person compelled to submit data or evidence is entitled to retain or, on payment of lawfully prescribed costs, procure a copy or transcript thereof, except that in a nonpublic investigatory proceeding the witness may for good cause be limited to inspection of the official transcript of his testimony." The "good cause" language of this provision has been explained as follows:

The * * * grant[] to agencies of the right to inhibit access to testimony in nonpublic investigatory proceedings were in recognition that such investigations, "like those of a grand jury, might be thwarted in certain cases if not kept secret, and that if witnesses were given a copy of their transcript, suspected violators would be in a better position to tailor their own testimony to that of the previous testimony, and to threaten witness about to testify with economic or other reprisals."

LaMorte v. *Mansfield,* 438 F.2d 448, 451 (2d Cir. 1971) (quoting *Commercial Capital Corp.* v. *S.E.C.,* 360 F.2d 856, 858 (7th Cir. 1966)).

Comment: Several comments suggested that evidence obtained during an investigation by HHS should be used only within the scope of that investigation, not for other matters, as provided for by § 160.314(c).

Response: Section 160.314(c) mirrors the OIG rule. The concept that HHS may use evidence obtained in an investigation for matters outside the scope of the investigation is not novel. While we would expect to be careful in using such information for other purposes, we are legally obligated to take appropriate action if we obtain clear evidence of wrongdoing.

9. Section 160.316—Refraining From Intimidation or Retaliation

Proposed rule: Proposed § 160.316, which was taken from § 164.530(g)(2) of the Privacy Rule, would prohibit covered entities from threatening, intimidating, coercing, discriminating against, or taking any other retaliatory action against individuals or other persons (including other covered entities) who complain to HHS or otherwise assist or cooperate in the enforcement processes created by this rule. The intent of this addition to subpart C was to make these non-retaliation provisions applicable to all of the HIPAA rules, not just the Privacy Rule. A conforming change to § 164.530(g) of the Privacy Rule was proposed, to cross-reference proposed § 160.316.

Final rule: The final rule adopts the provisions of the proposed rule, except that the verb "harass" is inserted in the introductory language of this section. The related revision to § 164.530(g) is adopted without change.

Comment: Two comments asked HHS to strengthen the prohibition on retaliation and intimidation. The comments express concern that the current provision is not a sufficient deterrence to covered entities, particularly payers. One comment suggested that the language be revised to read in pertinent part as follows: "A covered entity may not threaten * * * including not threaten to reduce or eliminate payment, intimidate, coerce, harass, discriminate against, or take any other retaliatory action against any individual or other person * * * including suspending or terminating participation in a Medicaid program and/or in any other program or network or reducing or eliminating payment for * * *". Another comment suggested that persons who engage in prohibited retaliation or intimidation should be considered to have "knowingly" violated the statute and be subject to criminal penalties under section 1177 of the Act.

Response: We agree with the comment that the actions covered in the suggested language would constitute intimidation or retaliation under the appropriate facts, but we think that such claims may be made under the existing language. However, while harassment is encompassed by the phrase "other retaliatory action" in this section, since harassment is a form of pressure that is sufficiently different from, and as objectionable as, the other intimidating or retaliatory acts that are specifically mentioned, we clarify the section by including it in the text of the regulation;

E. HIPAA Final Rules, Administrative Simplification Enforcement, continued

8400 Federal Register / Vol. 71, No. 32 / Thursday, February 16, 2006 / Rules and Regulations

the text of the final rule is revised accordingly.

The statute does not make retaliation or intimidation the subject of a criminal penalty under section 1177, and we cannot expand the scope of the criminal provision by regulation. Accordingly, we do not adopt this suggestion.

Comment: One comment suggested amending the section to require that a complaint be filed in good faith under § 160.306 and that the same change be made to the remaining language in proposed § 164.530(g). The comment stated that covered entities should not be prohibited from firing employees who file false complaints and that covered health care providers should not be prohibited from terminating the provider-patient relationship where the patient files a false complaint.

Response: The good faith of a complainant is currently evaluated by OCR to the extent it bears upon determining whether a compliance failure appears to have occurred and the extent to which the complaint should be investigated. We do not read the rule as prohibiting the firing of an employee or the termination of a provider-patient relationship where other legitimate grounds for such action exist; whether such grounds exist would be a matter to be ascertained in the course of the investigation.

Comment: Two comments asked HHS to provide examples of retaliation and/ or outline procedures or criteria for how the occurrence of retaliation will be investigated and determined. One comment asked that the rule stipulate that an act be considered to be one of retaliation or intimidation only if it occurred after the filing of a complaint.

Response: Complaints regarding retaliation or intimidation will be handled in the same manner as investigations regarding other possible violations of the HIPAA rule, as § 160.316 is considered an administrative simplification provision for the purposes of imposing a civil money penalty. Because such situations are likely to be quite varied and factually complex, we are reluctant to preclude consideration of events prior to the filing of a complaint that may be relevant to a claim of retaliation or intimidation. We, thus, retain the language as proposed.

C. Subpart D—Imposition of Civil Money Penalties

Subpart D of the final rule addresses the issuance of a notice of proposed determination to impose a civil money penalty and other actions that are relevant thereafter, whether or not a hearing is requested following the issuance of the notice of proposed determination. It also contains provisions on identifying violations, calculating civil money penalties for such violations, and establishing affirmative defenses to the imposition of civil money penalties. It, thus, implements the provisions of section 1176, as well as related provisions of section 1128A. As noted above, many provisions of subpart D are based in large part upon the OIG regulations, but we adapt the language of the OIG regulations to reflect issues presented by, or the authority underlying, the HIPAA rules.

1. Section 160.402—Basis for a Civil Money Penalty

Section 160.402 sets forth the rules concerning the basis for liability for a civil money penalty. It includes the rules for determining liability if more than one covered entity is responsible for a violation and where an agent of a covered entity is responsible for a violation.

a. Section 160.402(a)—General Rule

Proposed rule: Proposed § 160.402(a) would require the Secretary to impose a civil money penalty on any covered entity which the Secretary determines has violated an administrative simplification provision, unless the covered entity establishes that an affirmative defense, as provided for by § 160.410, exists. This provision is based on the language in section 1176(a) that "* * * the Secretary shall impose on any person who violates a provision of this part a penalty * * *". A "provision of this part" is considered to be a requirement or prohibition of the HIPAA statute or rules. See the discussion of "administrative simplification provision" under § 160.302 above.

Final rule: The final rule adopts the provisions of the proposed rule.

Comment: A number of comments suggested that the words "the Secretary will impose a civil money penalty * * *" are too strict. Some comments expressed concern that this language could jeopardize HHS's ability to resolve a matter informally; other comments questioned how this language was consistent with the provisions for voluntary compliance (§ 160.304), informal resolution (§ 160.312), and settlement (§ 160.416). Most of these comments suggested that the rule give the Secretary discretion to impose a civil money penalty instead of making it mandatory.

Response: Section 160.402(a) states the general rule of section 1176(a): If the Secretary determines that a covered entity has violated an administrative simplification provision, he will impose a civil money penalty unless a basis for not imposing a penalty under section 1176(b) exists. The use of the words "shall impose" in section 1176(a) is more than the mere conveyance of authority to the Secretary to exercise his discretion where he has made a formal determination that a covered entity has violated an administrative simplification provision. Under the procedures set forth in this final rule, the formal determination is proposed in a notice of proposed determination under § 160.420. A covered entity may request administrative review by an administrative law judge of this determination. If the covered entity does not so request, the proposed determination becomes final.

Many opportunities will precede a determination of a violation, however, that will permit the Secretary to exercise his discretion to not impose a penalty. As set forth in § 160.304, the principle for achieving compliance is to seek voluntary compliance by covered entities. To implement this principle in complaints and compliance reviews, § 160.312 provides that the Secretary will attempt to reach resolution by informal means prior to proposing a determination under § 160.420 that a covered entity has violated an administrative simplification provision. If resolution satisfactory to the Secretary is reached by informal means, the Secretary may exercise his discretion to close the matter without formally proposing a determination under § 160.420. The Secretary is also authorized by section 1128A(f) of the Act, which is incorporated by reference in section 1176, to exercise discretion to settle any matter. Thus, under §§ 160.416 and 160.514, settlements of civil money penalties which have been proposed or are being challenged through the administrative hearing process are possible. The Secretary also has discretion to waive civil money penalties, in whole or in part, in certain cases under § 160.412.

The general rule stated in § 160.402(a) that the Secretary will impose a civil money penalty upon a covered entity if the Secretary determines that the covered entity has violated an administrative simplification provision is not at odds with the Secretary's authority to exercise his discretion pursuant to §§ 160.304, 160.312, 160.412, 160.416, and 160.514. However, these exercises of Secretarial discretion require actions by covered entities. When a covered entity acts, or fails to act, in ways that do not allow the exercise of Secretarial discretion not to

E. HIPAA Final Rules, Administrative Simplification Enforcement, continued

impose a penalty, the Secretary will impose a civil money penalty upon the covered entity if the Secretary determines that the covered entity has violated an administrative simplification provision.

Comment: One comment complained that § 160.402(a) does not allow for early termination of frivolous complaints. The comment stated that covered entities are locked into paying a civil money penalty or initiating an expensive and elaborate defense to the complaint.

Response: It is our expectation that complaints that are frivolous will be resolved at an early stage of the informal resolution process under § 160.312. A covered entity can facilitate this process by cooperating with the OCR or CMS investigators on a timely basis.

Comment: One comment suggested that § 160.402(a) be revised to require HHS to issue a finding that informal resolution is not sufficient and that a civil money penalty is necessary.

Response: The provision suggested would be redundant. The notice of proposed determination under § 160.420 essentially fulfills this function, in that it must state the grounds upon which the Secretary has decided to impose the penalty.

b. Section 160.402(b)—Violations by More Than One Covered Entity

Proposed rule: Proposed § 160.402(b) provided that, except with respect to covered entities that are members of an affiliated covered entity, if the Secretary determines that more than one covered entity was responsible for violating an administrative simplification provision, the Secretary will impose a civil money penalty against each such covered entity. Based on the statutory language in section 1176(a), which states that the Secretary "* * * shall impose a penalty * * *" when there is a determination that an entity has violated a HIPAA provision, this provision would apply to any two or more covered entities (other than members of an affiliated covered entity, discussed below), including, but not limited to, those that are part of a joint arrangement, such as an organized health care arrangement. The preamble to the proposed rule noted that the determination of whether or not an entity is responsible for the violation would be based on the facts and that, while simply being part of a joint arrangement would not, in and of itself, make a covered entity responsible for a violation by another entity in the joint arrangement, it could be a factor considered in the analysis. See 70 FR 20231.

Proposed § 160.402(b)(2) provided that each covered entity that is a member of an affiliated covered entity would be jointly and severally liable for a civil money penalty for a violation by the affiliated covered entity. An affiliated covered entity is a group of covered entities under common ownership or control, which have elected to be treated as if they were one covered entity for purposes of compliance with the Security and Privacy Rules. *See* § 164.105(b).

Final rule: The final rule provides that a member of an affiliated covered entity is jointly and severally liable for a violation by the affiliated covered entity, unless it is established that another member of the affiliated covered entity was responsible for the violation.

Comment: Proposed § 160.402(b) was opposed by many on the ground that it was unfair to make one covered entity liable for a violation committed by another covered entity. A number of comments stated that this provision was particularly unfair, when coupled with the requirement of proposed § 160.426 that the public be notified of civil money penalties imposed, in that a covered entity that was not responsible for the violation in question could bear the reputational injury associated with such notification, due to the operation of proposed § 160.402(b). One comment pointed out that violations may not be system-wide, but may be limited to one member of the affiliated covered entity; in such a situation, it would not be fair to penalize the other members of the affiliated covered entity.

Response: We agree with these comments to a certain extent and have changed the final rule accordingly. We agree that, if responsibility for a violation can be shown to lie with one member of an affiliated covered entity, that member should be held liable for the violation. Thus, we have provided that a covered entity member of an affiliated covered entity may avoid liability if it is established that another member was responsible for the violation. We suspect that in most cases, which member was responsible for the violation will be clear—for example, if four of five members of a covered entity distributed privacy notices but the fifth member did not, the violations of the notice distribution requirement of § 164.520 would be attributed to the fifth member. In such cases, the objections to publication described above are beside the point, because liability follows responsibility.

However, we do not agree that the inability to assign specific responsibility for a violation to one or more members of an affiliated covered entity should shield all of its members from liability. We doubt that such situations will arise

often, but they may arise where the affiliated covered entity has failed to take a required act—for example, where the affiliated covered entity has failed to appoint a privacy officer. In such a case, all of the members of the affiliated covered entity bear a share of the responsibility for the failure to act, since any of them could have presumably taken action to bring the group, as a whole, into compliance. It is, thus, not unreasonable that all members of the affiliated covered entity should be jointly and severally liable for the consequent penalty. Moreover, absent joint and several liability, each member of the affiliated covered entity would be separately liable for the penalty for the violation, *e.g.*, the failure to appoint a privacy officer. Thus, the removal of joint and several liability may result in greater liability for the members of an affiliated covered entity in some cases.

Comment: Several comments argued that there is no statutory authority for holding the members of an affiliated covered entity jointly and severally liable, in that the statute requires that the penalty "shall be imposed on any person who violates a provision * * *" and, thus, does not authorize imposition of a penalty on a person who has not violated a provision of the statute or rules. One comment argued that proposed § 160.402(b) would violate the due process clause by imposing liability on entities not responsible for a violation.

Response: These objections are misplaced. Where, as will usually be the case, responsibility for the violation is evident and the responsible party is charged with the violation, they are obviously not relevant. In the case of other violations, where the responsibility for the violation is shared by the members of the affiliated covered entity, as in where the affiliated covered entity fails to take required actions, they are likewise not relevant. Since each covered entity member of the affiliated covered entity is responsible for complying with the rule in question, responsibility for the failure to act may be properly imputed to each member. Moreover, since an affiliated covered entity is a type of joint undertaking, it is reasonable to impute responsibility to the members of the affiliated covered entity, as is typically done with joint ventures.

Comment: Several comments argued that proposed § 160.402(b) uses a legal fiction of the Privacy and Security Rules to create liability where liability would not otherwise exist and substitutes this fiction for the corporate form and structure that establish the basis for enterprise liability under U.S. law.

E. HIPAA Final Rules, Administrative Simplification Enforcement, continued

8402 Federal Register / Vol. 71, No. 32 / Thursday, February 16, 2006 / Rules and Regulations

Another comment stated that this section is inconsistent with the provision of the HIPAA rules (§ 160.105(b)) that defines an affiliated covered entity as an entity comprised of "legally separate" entities.

Response: We disagree. The affiliated covered entity concept is more than a legal fiction. It is an operational approach to discharging certain compliance responsibilities. When covered entities create an affiliated covered entity, they mutually agree to conduct their business in a certain manner and hold themselves out to the world as a joint undertaking. While the Privacy and Security Rules do not prescribe detailed requirements for how an affiliated covered entity must be organized, the level of cooperation such an undertaking necessitates, the requirement for designation, and the requirement of common ownership or control mean that the participating members will have entered into an agreement of some sort, whether formal or informal. We, thus, think that it is properly viewed as a joint venture.

The fact that an affiliated covered entity is composed of "legally separate" entities is beside the point. Joint and several liability, as a concept, is imposed on legally separate entities. See, *e.g.*, Black's Law Dictionary (8th ed. 2004), liability.

Comment: A number of comments argued that the provision for joint and several liability would discourage covered entities from setting up affiliated covered entities. One comment stated that proposed § 160.402(b) represents a change in position by HHS, in that the preamble to the Privacy Rule, on which many covered entities relied, stated that covered entities that formed an affiliated covered entity are "separately subject to liability under this rule."

Response: Section 160.402(b), as adopted, should allay the concerns expressed by these comments with respect to the potential exposure to liability for the members of affiliated covered entities. We think that, in most cases, which member of an affiliated covered entity is responsible for a violation will be obvious; where this is the case, HHS would seek to impose the civil money penalties on that member. Even if it is not obvious from the violation itself who the responsible party is, a covered entity may adduce evidence to establish that responsibility for the violation lies elsewhere, and, if this is shown, avoid liability. In any event, the establishment of an affiliated covered entity is not mandated by either the Privacy Rule or the Security Rule. Rather, establishing an affiliated

covered entity is a business decision to be made by the covered entities involved. The affiliated covered entity arrangement carries with it certain benefits for the member entities; any increased exposure to potential liability under this rule, assuming there is one, should be part of the business calculus.

In addition, we do not agree that § 160.402(b) is inconsistent with the position taken in the preamble to the Privacy Rule. Our prior statement was intended to provide notice that liability for violations by an affiliated covered entity would devolve onto the member covered entities of an affiliated covered entity, rather than being attributed to the affiliated covered entity itself, so that member covered entities could not avoid liability by arguing that the affiliated covered entity had committed the violation in question. It was not intended to indicate the bases upon which that liability would be determined, which is the purpose of § 160.402(b).

Comment: A couple of comments supported the policy of holding the members of an affiliated covered entity jointly and severally liable. One comment supported holding all covered entities in an affiliated covered entity liable for the violations of one as an efficient mechanism for highlighting the seriousness of violations of the HIPAA rules.

Response: For the reasons set forth above, we have not adopted this policy in the final rule, insofar as responsibility for a violation can be determined.

Comment: Two comments requested clarification of the maximum amount of the penalty that will be assessed against an affiliated covered entity when one of its members has been found noncompliant.

Response: Where responsibility for a violation is allocated to individual covered entities, each covered entity determined to be responsible for the violation would be liable for violations of an identical requirement or prohibition in a calendar year up to the statutory maximum of $25,000. If responsibility for particular violations cannot be determined, so that the members of the affiliated covered entity are jointly and severally liable for the violation, the maximum that would be imposed for violations of an identical requirement or prohibition in a calendar year would be $25,000.

Comment: Several comments requested clarification of the statement in the preamble to the proposed rule that membership in an organized health care arrangement "could be a factor considered in the analysis" in

determining the liability of a member of such arrangement for a violation. Of particular concern was the potential liability of a hospital for the actions of physicians with privileges; one comment noted that the hospital exercises little control over medical staff in such situations. One comment requested that the final rule clarify that membership in an organized health care arrangement would not increase a covered entity's exposure to liability.

Response: As we noted in the preamble to the proposed rule, the members of an organized health care arrangement would be individually—not jointly and severally—liable for any violation of the HIPAA rules. What our preamble statement intended to indicate was that HHS might have to look carefully at how the organized health care arrangement operated in determining which member(s) of the organized health care arrangement was responsible for a particular violation, if that was not clear at the outset.

c. Section 160.402(c)—Violations Attributed to a Covered Entity

Proposed rule: Proposed § 160.402(c) provided that a covered entity can be held liable for a civil money penalty based on the actions of any agent, including a workforce member, acting within the scope of the agency. This provision derives from section 1128A(*l*) of the Act, which is made applicable to HIPAA by section 1176(a)(2) of the Act. Section 1128A(*l*) states that "a principal is liable for penalties * * * under this section for the actions of the principal's agents acting within the scope of the agency." Under the proposed rule, a covered entity could be liable for a civil money penalty for a violation by any agent acting within the scope of the agency, including a workforce member. ("Workforce" is defined at § 160.103 as "employees, volunteers, trainees, or other persons whose conduct in the performance of work for a covered entity is under the direct control of such entity, whether or not they are paid by the covered entity.") The proposed rule excepted covered entities from liability for actions of a business associate agent that violate the HIPAA rules, if the covered entity was in compliance with the HIPAA rules governing business associates at §§ 164.308(b) and 164.502(e). Proposed § 160.402(c) also provided that the Federal common law of agency would apply to determine agency issues under this provision.

Final rule: The final rule adopts the provisions of the proposed rule.

Comment: A number of comments supported the provision of proposed § 160.402(c) relating to business

E. HIPAA Final Rules, Administrative Simplification Enforcement, continued

associates and requested that it be retained in the final rule.

Response: We agree and have done so.

Comment: One comment requested clarification of the liability of a covered entity for a violation committed by a non-covered entity who is not a business associate or workforce member, such as researchers, medical device vendors, and non-covered providers who have treatment privileges and access to protected health information at a covered entity's facility. The comment argued that, depending on the circumstances, such persons may or may not be considered agents.

Response: In general, a "violation" cannot occur, if the act in question is not done by a covered entity or its agent, because only covered entities are subject to the HIPAA rules. For example, if a permitted or required disclosure of protected health information is made by a covered entity to a person or entity that is not a workforce member or business associate, the covered entity would not generally be responsible for that person's or entity's subsequent use or disclosure of the information. Thus, if a hospital that is a covered entity discloses protected health information to a non-covered health care provider with privileges for treatment of a patient, the hospital would not be liable for a subsequent use or disclosure by that provider, as long as the hospital is not also involved in that use or disclosure. If the provider is an agent of the hospital, however, the hospital's liability will be determined in accordance with § 160.402(c).

Comment: We requested comment in the proposed rule on whether there are categories of workforce members whom it would be inappropriate to treat as agents under § 160.402(c). A number of comments suggested that independent contractors, volunteers, and students under the supervision of an academic institution be excluded from the definition of an agent for whose acts the covered entity could be liable, provided that the covered entity has given the requisite training to such persons. The comments indicated that generally covered entities have less control over such persons than they have over employees.

Response: Whether a person is sufficiently under the control of a covered entity and acting within the scope of the agency has to be determined on the facts of each situation, but § 160.402(c) creates a presumption that a workforce member is an agent of the covered entity for the member's conduct under the HIPAA rules, such as using and disclosing protected health information. With

regard to whether an independent contractor is a member of the covered entity's workforce, the question would be whether the covered entity had direct control over the independent contractor in the performance of its work for the covered entity. See § 160.103 (definition of "workforce"). If the covered entity does not have direct control over such persons, they do not fall within the definition of "workforce." Where persons, such as independent contractors, who are not under the direct control of the covered entity perform a function or activity that involves the use or disclosure of individually identifiable health information or a function or activity regulated by this subchapter on behalf of a covered entity, such persons would fall within the definition of "business associate," and the covered entity would be required to comply with the business associate provisions of the Privacy and Security Rules with regard to such persons. Because of the direct control requirement in the definition of workforce, we think it is appropriate for a covered entity to be liable for a violative act of an independent contractor who is a member of the workforce, that is, who is under the direct control of the covered entity.

With respect to volunteers and trainees, we note that, while covered entities may have less control over these persons, they do control their performance of activities that are governed by the HIPAA rules, such as access to protected health information. In regard to privacy, a covered entity is required to train these categories of workforce members as necessary and appropriate for these volunteers and trainees to carry out their functions within the covered entity. 45 CFR 164.530(b). This requirement allows a covered entity to adapt its training to a volunteer's or trainee's scope of duties. For example, a volunteer who files laboratory results in a medical record will require training that is different and more extensive than the training given to a volunteer in the lobby gift shop of a hospital. Section 160.402(c) is consistent with these distinctions. The acts of volunteers and trainees will be examined on a case-by-case basis to determine if they are acting as agents within the scope of their agency. Thus, we think that it is appropriate to treat volunteers and trainees as persons for whose acts a covered entity may be liable, if they act as agents for the covered entity and violate the HIPAA rules within the scope of their agency.

Comment: One comment recommended that the rule be revised to make covered entities liable for

violations committed by business associates. The comment suggested that, if a covered entity is not liable for the actions of its business associates, covered entities will outsource the handling of protected health information to avoid liability.

Response: We included the business associate exception in proposed § 160.402(c)(1)–(3) to make this rule consistent with the business associate provisions in the Privacy and Security Rules. Changing the business associate provisions in the Privacy and Security Rules is outside the scope of this rulemaking. (See the extensive discussion about business associates in the Privacy Rule and Security Rule preambles at 65 FR 82503–82507 and 82640–82645, 67 FR 53251–53253, and 68 FR 8358–8361). The satisfactory assurances that are required in written contracts or arrangements between covered entities and their business associates are intended to protect the confidentiality of protected health information handled by business associates. If a covered entity fails to comply with the business associate provisions in the Privacy and Security Rules, such as by not entering into the requisite contracts or arrangements, or by not taking reasonable steps to cure a breach or end a violation that is known to the covered entity, the covered entity may be liable for the actions of a business associate agent. We, therefore, decline to follow the recommendation.

Comment: Two comments suggested that HHS limit its use of the Federal common law of agency because its application may make a covered entity liable for the actions of a person, such as an independent contractor, for whom the covered entity is not liable under state law.

Response: As we stated above, covered entities must comply with the business associate provisions of the Privacy and Security Rules for independent contractors who are not under the direct control of the covered entity and who perform a function or activity that involves the use or disclosure of individually identifiable health information or a function or activity regulated by "this subchapter" (*i.e.*, the HIPAA rules) on behalf of a covered entity. If a covered entity complies with the business associate provisions, the exception from liability in § 160.402(c) will be applicable. The purpose of establishing the Federal common law of agency to determine when a covered entity is vicariously liable for the acts of its agents is to achieve nationwide uniformity in the implementation of the HIPAA rules by covered entities and nationwide

E. HIPAA Final Rules, Administrative Simplification Enforcement, continued

8404   Federal Register / Vol. 71, No. 32 / Thursday, February 16, 2006 / Rules and Regulations

consistency in the enforcement of these rules by HHS. The comments reinforced our conclusion that reliance on state law could introduce inconsistency in the implementation of the HIPAA rules by covered entities in different states. Thus, we retain the Federal common law of agency as the standard by which agency questions in specific cases will be determined.

Comment: Two comments requested clarification of how this section will apply to insurance agents, brokers, and consultants.

Response: Insurance agents, brokers, and consultants who are not members of the covered entity's workforce but with whom the covered entity shares protected health information will generally fall within the definition of "business associate" at § 160.103. A covered entity that complies with the business associate provisions of the Privacy and Security Rules would not be liable for a violation of those rules by the business associate pursuant to the liability exception in § 160.402(c). It is also possible that the insurance agent, broker, or consultant may be the covered entity's agent in some, but not all, of his or her activities. An agent or broker may be working on behalf of an employer to arrange insurance coverage for its employees and not on behalf of the health insurance issuer that is a covered entity. In cases where the liability exception for business associates is not available or not met, the determination of whether an insurance agent, broker, or consultant is an agent of a covered entity and was acting within the scope of the agency will be made based on the facts of each situation.

Comment: One comment argued that covered entities should not be liable for acts of employees outside the scope of their employment. Another comment suggested that covered entities should not be liable for the actions of agents who have been informed of the covered entity's HIPAA compliance policies, yet act contrary to them. Another suggested that a covered entity should not be liable for the acts of agents who, although authorized to disclose protected health information, disclose it for purposes of sale or with intent to do harm.

Response: Section 160.402(c), as proposed and adopted, provides that a covered entity is liable for the acts of an agent acting "within the scope of the agency." This provision necessarily implies that a covered entity is not liable for its agent's acts outside the scope of the agency (as determined under the federal common law of agency). With regard to the comments

that suggest that unauthorized conduct by an agent is outside the scope of the agency, the Federal common law of agency will be applied to the facts of each case to determine whether the covered entity is liable for the conduct, even though it was unauthorized.

Comment: Two comments expressed concern with the role of a Privacy Officer and his or her liability under this part and the covered entity's liability for the actions of a Privacy Officer who is a business associate. One comment suggested that the Privacy Officer should not incur any additional liability merely by being designated the Privacy Officer. The other comment requested clarification as to a covered entity's liability when the covered entity directly controls a Privacy Officer, if the Privacy Officer is a business associate.

Response: As stated above, the facts of each case will determine the liability of covered entities for wrongful conduct of its agents under the HIPAA rules. As a general matter, we think that a Privacy Officer is an officer of a covered entity for the purposes of the Privacy Rule and, thus, will likely be the covered entity's agent. As stated in § 160.402, a covered entity is liable for the acts of its agent acting within the scope of its agency and, thus, is liable for any penalties that result from those acts. However, if a Privacy Officer is a business associate of the covered entity, the liability exception in § 160.402(c) may apply. A covered entity that *is* in compliance with the business associate provisions of the Privacy and Security Rules will not be liable for a violation of those rules by the business associate.

2. Section 160.404—Amount of a Civil Money Penalty

Proposed rule: Under proposed § 160.404(a), the penalty amount would be determined through the method provided for in proposed § 160.406, using the factors set forth in proposed § 160.408, and subject to the statutory caps reflected in proposed § 160.404(b) and any reduction under proposed § 160.412. The proposed regulation would not establish minimum penalties. Proposed § 160.404 would follow the language of the statute and establish the maximum penalties for a violation and for violations of an identical requirement or prohibition during a calendar year, as set forth in the statute—up to $100 per violation and up to $25,000 for violations of an identical requirement or prohibition in a calendar year. Proposed § 160.404(b) provided that the term "calendar year" means the period from January 1 through the following December 31.

Under proposed § 160.404(b)(2), a violation of a more specific requirement or prohibition, such as one contained within an implementation specification, could not also be counted, for purposes of determining civil money penalties, as an automatic violation of a broader requirement or prohibition that entirely encompasses the more specific one. That is, the Secretary could impose a civil money penalty for violation of either the general or the specific requirement, but not both. Proposed § 160.404(b)(2) would not apply where a covered entity's action results in violations of multiple, differing requirements or prohibitions within the same HIPAA rule or in violations of more than one HIPAA rule. Proposed § 160.404(b)(2) also would not preclude assessing civil money penalties for multiple violations of an identical requirement or prohibition, up to the statutory cap.

Final rule: The final rule adopts the provisions of the proposed rule. Changes to the provisions referenced in this section are discussed in connection with those provisions.

Comment: While most comments that addressed proposed § 160.404(b)(2) supported it, several comments suggested that a single set of facts or single activity should not result in the finding of more than one violation, even of different subparts. According to the comments, covered entities should not be assessed penalties for violating more than one provision if all violations arise out of the same facts or incident. One comment suggested that penalties should not be doubly assessed for overlapping provisions in other subparts unless gross misconduct or willful negligence was involved.

Response: We do not count an act that violates overlapping provisions of a subpart as more than one violation because provisions that are duplicative in a subpart were written that way as a drafting convenience and were not intended to establish separate legal obligations. This rationale, however, does not apply where the legal obligations are found in different subparts. Further, the different subparts implement different statutory standards and, thus, impose separate legal obligations. For example, where a covered entity re-sells its used computers without scrubbing the hard drives that contain protected health information, this act may violate several separate legal obligations under the Security and Privacy Rules: (1) The media re-use requirement of § 164.310(d)(2)(ii); (2) the safeguards requirement of § 164.530(c); and (3) to the extent that the protected health

E. HIPAA Final Rules, Administrative Simplification Enforcement, continued

information on the drives is accessible by persons to whom it could not permissibly be disclosed. §§ 164.308(a)(4)(i) and 164.502(a). In such a situation, the act has violated requirements or prohibitions of different rules promulgated pursuant to different provisions of the statute, and it is appropriate that such violations be treated separately. Thus, we decline to extend § 160.404(b)(2) as suggested.

Further, the same facts may evidence noncompliance with more than one non-overlapping provision of a subpart and, thus, may result in multiple violations for which a penalty may be assessed. For example, a covered entity that makes an impermissible use of protected health information may also, by virtue of the impermissible use, have violated the Privacy Rule's minimum necessary and/or reasonable safeguard provisions.

We also note that, in some cases, a violation of one requirement or prohibition may produce consequential violations, and such cases would not come within § 160.404(b)(2). For example, § 164.308(a) requires covered entities to conduct security risk analyses. The security risk analysis is the foundation of the covered entity's security risk management plan and is one of the bases which it must take into account in deciding not to implement addressable implementation specifications under the Security Rule. If a covered entity does not do a security risk analysis, it has no basis for not implementing the addressable implementation specifications under the Security Rule, and any failure to implement such specifications could, thus, be considered a violation. Thus, while the failure to conduct the security risk analysis would be a violation, albeit a continuing one, of just one provision, it would necessarily result in other violations, to the extent the covered entity failed to implement the addressable implementation specifications of the Security Rule.

Comment: One comment suggested that the costs incurred by the covered entity as a result of the violation should be considered in calculating the amount of the penalty.

Response: We do not adopt this suggestion for several reasons. First, we are not certain what costs the comment is suggesting be considered—the costs associated with committing the violation, the costs associated with correcting the violation, or both. Second, the factors to be considered in determining the amount of the penalty for a violation are set out at section 1128A(d) and are implemented in this rule by § 160.408. "Costs incurred by

the covered entity as a result of the violation" is not a concept that fits squarely within any of the statutory factors. Third, to the extent consideration of such costs is reasonable, it would seem to be relevant only to the criterion for waiver under § 160.412 ("the extent that payment of the penalty would be excessive relative to the violation"); insofar as that criterion weighs the seriousness of the effect of the violation, costs associated with correcting the violation might in certain circumstances be a relevant factor to be considered.

3. Section 160.406—Number of Violations

Proposed rule: Proposed § 160.406 would establish the general rule that the Secretary will determine the number of violations of an identical requirement or prohibition by a covered entity by applying any of the variables of action, person, or time, as follows: (1) The number of times the covered entity failed to engage in required conduct or engaged in a prohibited act; (2) the number of persons involved in, or affected by, the violation; or (3) the duration of the violation, counted in days. Paragraph (a) of this section would require the Secretary to determine the appropriate variable or variables for counting the number of violations based on the specific facts and circumstances related to the violation, and take into consideration the underlying purpose of the particular HIPAA rule that is violated. More than one variable could be used to determine the number of violations (for example, the number of people affected multiplied by the time (number of days) over which the violation occurred). The Secretary would have discretion in determining which variable or variables were appropriate for determining the number of violations. The preamble to the proposed rule noted that, under this proposal, the policy for determining which variable(s) to use for which type of violation would be developed in the context of specific cases rather than established by regulation and that subsequent cases would be decided consistently with prior similar cases.

Final rule: The final rule eliminates the provision for variables and provides that the number of violations of an identical requirement or prohibition (termed "identical violations") will be determined based on the nature of the covered entity's obligation to act or not act under the provision violated, such as its obligation to act in a certain manner, or within a certain time, or with respect to certain persons. With respect to continuing violations, a separate

violation will be deemed to occur on each day such a violation continues.

Comment: While two comments supported the proposal, many comments challenged the variable approach of proposed § 160.406 to determining the number of violations. In particular, several comments expressed concern over the broad discretion provided to the Secretary to determine the number of violations, particularly in light of the fact that the proposed rule would have prohibited the ALJ from reviewing the Secretary's choice of variable(s). Further, some comments were concerned that the Secretary could use multiple variables to determine the number of violations. It was argued that the proposed approach was unfair in that it (1) did not allow covered entities to predict the amount of a civil money penalty that would result from a violation, and (2) could maximize the penalty to the statutory cap in virtually any case, which could result in very harsh penalties for relatively minor offenses. Other comments argued that the variable approach was inconsistent with the policy of proposed § 160.404(b)(2), prohibiting the double counting of overlapping regulatory requirements, or was inconsistent with HHS's general approach to voluntary compliance. It was suggested, for example, that HHS instead could establish one particular calculation method for each HIPAA rule or specify the types of violations for which HHS would use a particular method.

Comments also criticized the variable approach as inconsistent with the definition of "violation," arguing that the person and time variables have no logical relationship to a failure to comply, and thus, would not be appropriate for counting violations. Specifically, it was argued that since a "violation" is defined as a failure to comply with a requirement or prohibition, by definition a violation is a failure to take a required action or a failure to refrain from doing a prohibited act, and, thus, is not defined by the period of time during which such action or inaction occurs or by the number of people who may be affected by it. Further, several comments argued that the action/inaction variable was the only one that was consistent with the statute, so that penalizing covered entities by using other variables would be penalizing them for violations that, by definition, do not exist, which would be inconsistent with Congressional intent, as expressed in section 1176(a), and inappropriate as a matter of public policy. It was also argued that the time and person variables look at qualitative issues and attempt to measure the

E. HIPAA Final Rules, Administrative Simplification Enforcement, continued

importance of an act or omission; they do not measure where an act is quantitatively extensive—i.e., repeated or prolonged. It was argued that qualitative considerations are treated, under the statute, as aggravating or mitigating factors, not as questions of the quantity of violations, as is done under the variable approach.

Response: It was not our intent to suggest that the variables we proposed would be employed in a manner unrelated to the nature of the underlying violation, as assumed by many of the comments. However, since we agree that the manner in which the number of identical violations should be determined will depend on the nature of the provision violated, and the provision for variables was confusing and susceptible to misinterpretation, we have eliminated the explicit requirement to use the person, time, and action variables. The final rule instead makes clear that the Secretary will determine the number of identical violations based on the nature of the obligation of the covered entity to act (or not act) under the provision violated. While we agree, in principle, that the definition of "violation" looks to an action or a failure to act as the essence of a violation, defining what particular act or failure to act constitutes the specific violation in question will necessarily require looking at the substantive provision involved and determining what the covered entity was legally obligated to do. We do not agree, in this regard, that the elements of "people" and "time" are always irrelevant to a failure to comply or that consideration of these elements would result in double counting of violations. Rather, the precise nature of the covered entity's obligation will, as discussed below, in many cases be a function of to whom the obligation is owed or the manner in which it must be performed or other elements. Thus, we include in the regulation examples of elements that should be considered, as appropriate, in construing a provision to determine a covered entity's obligation thereunder. We believe that this approach, under which the number of violations is grounded in the language of the provision violated, is wholly consistent with the statutory scheme.

In many cases, applying this principle should not be difficult. For example, the Privacy Rule requires that covered entities have contracts or other arrangements in place with its business associates to assure the privacy of protected health information, and specifies what must (and may not) be included in the contract or other arrangement to do so. See § 164.504(e).

Two such provisions are that the contract may not authorize the business associate to use or further disclose the information in a manner that would violate the Privacy Rule, if done by the covered entity, and that the contract must provide that the business associate will use appropriate safeguards to prevent use or disclosure of the information other than as provided for by the contract. See § 164.504(e)(2)(i) and 164.504(e)(2)(ii)(B). If a covered entity enters into five contracts with business associates that authorize the business associates to use protected health information in a manner not permitted by the Privacy Rule and that do not require the business associates to use appropriate safeguards to protect the information, the covered entity will have committed five violations of each of the two separate requirements. Similarly, the Transactions Rule prohibits covered entities from entering into trading partner agreements that would change the use of a data element in a standard or add data elements not contained in the standard. See § 162.915(a), (b). If a health plan were, by trading partner agreement, to require 200 providers to use a data element in a given transaction in a manner that was inconsistent with the standard, and also required the use of another data element that was not part of the standard, we would view each inconsistent requirement in the trading partner agreement as a separate violation. The regulation prohibits the adoption of certain terms in trading partner agreements, so each noncompliant term in each agreement would constitute a separate violation, resulting in 200 violations of each of these requirements.

With respect to the transactions standards themselves, however, we anticipate defining the requirement violated to be the requirement to conduct a standard transaction. While one could view each required data element in a transaction as a separate requirement, because the Implementation Guide for each transaction is incorporated by reference into the regulation, one could also view the underlying Implementation Guides as functioning simply to describe what constitutes compliance in a particular case, rather than establishing separate compliance requirements. While we believe that either interpretation of the Transactions Rule is permissible, we expect to take the latter view of the Rule, to facilitate the predictability of determining violations under that Rule. Thus, we would count each noncompliant transaction as a single violation, regardless of the number of

missing data elements. For example, if a health plan is found to have conducted 200 eligibility transactions which are missing several required data elements, the health plan would have committed 200 violations of one identical requirement (i.e., the requirement at § 162.923(a) to conduct a covered transaction as a standard (i.e., compliant) transaction).

In some cases, determining how many times a provision has been violated will be a function of the number of individuals or other entities affected, because the covered entity's obligation is to act in a certain manner with respect to certain persons. We include the term "persons" in the list of examples in § 160.406 to make clear that such consideration may be appropriate. It may include not only individuals, but also other covered entities, their workforce members, or trading partners, where the obligation in question relates to such types of persons. For example, assume that a covered entity impermissibly allows a workforce member to access the protected health information of 20 patients whose information is stored on a computer file. The question is whether this set of facts constitutes one violation or 20 violations of § 164.502(a), which prohibits impermissible uses or disclosures of protected health information. Since the covered entity has an obligation with respect to each patient to protect his or her protected health information, the sharing of the 20 patients' protected health information with the employee constitutes a separate impermissible use, or violation, of § 164.502(a) with respect to each patient.

Some provisions embody a requirement or prohibition that is of an ongoing nature or for which timeliness is an element of compliance. We characterize violations of such a requirement or prohibition as continuing violations. In such cases, the covered entity's obligation to act continues over time, and, if it fails to take the required action, that failure to comply also continues over time. Thus, there needs to be a way of determining how such compliance failures are measured. We have decided to count such failures in days, as each day represents a new opportunity to correct the compliance failure. Accordingly, we have included, in the second sentence of § 160.406, language that establishes that continuing violations will be counted by days for purposes of determining how many violations of an identical requirement or prohibition occurred.

E. HIPAA Final Rules, Administrative Simplification Enforcement, continued

Federal Register / Vol. 71, No. 32 / Thursday, February 16, 2006 / Rules and Regulations **8407**

For example, the Security Rule requires covered entities to implement many types of policies and procedures. Under § 164.308(a)(4)(i), for example, a covered entity is required to implement policies and procedures for authorizing access to electronic protected health information that are consistent with the applicable requirements of the Privacy Rule. The implementation of such policies and procedures is an ongoing obligation and, thus, any failure to adopt them is a continuing violation. As another example, a covered entity generally is required by § 164.524 to act on a request by an individual for access to his or her protected health information no later than 30 days after the request is received. Thus, each day beyond the 30-day period a covered entity fails to provide such access would be a separate violation.

In contrast, situations in which the violation is a discrete act would not be continuing violations. The transaction example above illustrates violations that are discrete acts. Similarly, where a health plan violates § 162.925(a)(2) by rejecting transactions because they are standard transactions, each rejection would constitute a discrete act. The example above of the workforce member who impermissibly accesses protected health information likewise is an example of violations that are discrete acts.

As explained above, determining the number of violations in a particular case will depend, necessarily, on the precise provision violated and a covered entity's obligations thereunder. The examples above should assist covered entities in understanding their potential liability. These examples also illustrate that determining the number of violations may implicate a number of elements depending on the underlying provision violated, such as whether a covered entity had an obligation with respect to each person, or the amount of time that had elapsed with respect to a continuing violation, or a combination of these or other elements. While the final rule does not adopt the variable approach of the proposed rule, it does not preclude consideration of multiple elements in determining what constitutes the violation and, thus, the number of violations.

Comment: Several comments challenged the preamble statement that future cases would be decided consistently with prior similar cases. One comment suggested that giving HHS discretion to determine the variables used in counting violations, yet saying that future cases will be consistent with past use of variable in similar violations, creates conflict.

Other comments asked whether and how a covered entity would be able to challenge the selection of variable(s) based on the variables used in similar cases, if the facts of prior cases were not publicized, so that covered entities could determine how prior violations had been counted. Thus, comments requested that tracking of decided cases and the use of variables for each provision be assigned to a central entity within HHS, or that this information be made available to covered entities via the HHS Web sites.

Response: With respect to the comments regarding the preamble statement in the proposed rule that future cases would be decided consistently with prior similar cases, we clarify that the number of violations of a particular provision will be determined in a similar manner each time a case presents a violation of that particular provision, with due regard to the individual facts and circumstances of the case. In addition, as discussed below, the final rule eliminates the prohibition on ALJ review of the Secretary's choice of variable. Thus, under the final rule, the ALJ may review the Secretary's method of determining the number of violations for consistency or other purposes. With respect to a covered entity's ability to challenge the Secretary's method of determining the number of violations, HHS will make available for public inspection and copying final decisions imposing civil money penalties and may publish such decisions on its HIPAA Web sites. (This is discussed below in connection with § 160.426.) Thus, covered entities will be able to ascertain the application of the penalty provisions where penalties are imposed.

Comment: One comment suggested that there be a limit on the number of violations determined based upon the monetary impact the fine will have on the covered entity.

Response: A change is not necessary, as the statute and regulation already provide two points at which the financial impact of a civil money penalty on a covered entity may be considered—in connection with (1) the statutory factors (section 1128A(d), implemented in this rule by § 160.408) and (2) waiver (section 1176(b)(4), implemented in this rule by § 160.412).

Comment: Two comments suggested that the Secretary should consider whether or not the covered entity has enacted and completed a corrective action plan when determining the number of violations.

Response: Completion of a corrective action plan does not relate to determining the number of occurrences of a violation, so we do not include it as part of § 160.406. However, HHS would consider any such action prior to imposition of a civil money penalty for purposes of determining whether there is a basis for informal resolution of the complaint. In addition, this fact is taken into account in determining whether the penalty should be imposed at all, insofar as it pertains to the "reasonable cause" defense under section 1176(b)(3) and § 160.410(b)(3), since an element of that defense is whether the "failure to comply" has been corrected.

4. Section 160.408—Factors Considered in Determining the Amount of a Civil Money Penalty

Proposed rule: Section 1176(a)(2) states that, with some exceptions, the provisions of section 1128A of the Act shall apply to the imposition of a civil money penalty under section 1176 "in the same manner as" such provisions apply to the imposition of a civil money penalty under section 1128A. Section 1128A(d) requires that—

In determining the amount of * * * any penalty, * * * the Secretary shall take into account—

(1) The nature of the claims and the circumstances under which they were presented,

(2) The degree of culpability, history of prior offenses and financial condition of the person presenting the claims, and

(3) Such other matters as justice may require.

While the factors listed in section 1128A(d) were drafted to apply to violations involving claims for payment under federally funded health programs, HIPAA violations usually will not concern claims. Thus, we proposed to tailor the section 1128A(d) factors to the HIPAA rules and break them into their component elements for ease of understanding and application, as follows: (1) The nature of the violation; (2) the circumstances under which the violation occurred; (3) degree of culpability; (4) history of prior offenses; (5) financial condition of the covered entity; and (6) such other matters as justice may require. Proposed § 160.408 provided detailed factors, within the categories stated above, to consider in determining the amount of a civil money penalty. However, the proposed rule would not label any of these factors as aggravating or mitigating. Rather, proposed § 160.408 listed factors that could be considered either as aggravating or mitigating in determining the amount of the civil money penalty. The proposed approach would allow the Secretary to choose whether to consider a particular factor and how to consider each factor as appropriate in each

E. HIPAA Final Rules, Administrative Simplification Enforcement, continued

situation to avoid unfair or inappropriate results. It also would leave to the Secretary's discretion the decision regarding when aggravating and mitigating factors will be taken into account in determining the amount of the civil money penalty.

Final rule: The final rule adopts the provisions of the proposed rule, with a minor clarification. Section 160.408(d) is revised to clarify that the prior history to be considered relates to prior compliance with, and violations of, the administrative simplification provisions.

Comment: A number of comments supported the provision for mitigating factors and urged that it be retained in the final rule.

Response: We agree and have done so. See § 160.408 below.

Comment: A number of comments raised concerns or recommendations related to a covered entity's history of compliance. For example, several urged that HHS consider as a factor whether the covered entity has initiated correction action, and whether such action was performed independently and prior to contact from HHS. Some comments also requested that HHS consider any evidence of a covered entity's good faith attempts to comply with the administrative simplification requirements or that HHS take into consideration a history of prior controls. One comment stated that the phrase "history of prior offenses" in proposed § 160.408(d) was vague and requested that HHS revise the provision to clarify that it refers only to prior violations by a covered entity of the HIPAA rules, and not to prior offenses unrelated to the HIPAA rules. Another comment expressed concern with the provision at proposed § 160.408(d)(4), which would allow HHS to consider as a factor in determining the amount of a civil money penalty how the covered entity has responded to prior complaints, as well as the preamble statement that such factor could include complaints raised by individuals directly to the covered entity. The comment argued that the manner in which a covered entity responded to previous complaints about matters unrelated to the violation at issue, or to complaints raised by individuals, may be irrelevant and unfairly prejudicial.

Response: With respect to corrective action by a covered entity, HHS would consider any such action prior to imposition of a civil money penalty for purposes of determining whether there is a basis for informal resolution of a complaint. In addition, corrective actions of the covered entity are taken into account in determining whether the covered entity has established an affirmative defense to the violation as provided for under § 160.410(b)(3). Nonetheless, where the corrective action is taken in response to a complaint from an individual, the final rule at § 160.408(d)(4) provides the Secretary with authority to consider such corrective action as a factor in determining a civil money penalty.

With respect to a covered entity's good faith attempt to comply with the HIPAA provisions and rules, we agree that such actions could be mitigating factors depending on the circumstances and, thus, have revised the rule to clarify that a covered entity's history of prior compliance generally may be considered, which could include, as appropriate, prior violations, as well as prior compliance efforts. In addition, we agree that § 160.408(d) should apply only to violations of the HIPAA rules, and not to offenses of other provisions of law. Accordingly, we have revised the language of § 160.408(d) to substitute the term "violations"—which is defined at § 160.302 as a failure to comply with an administrative simplification provision—for the term "offenses" in the proposed rule.

Finally, we disagree that only those prior violations that are relevant to the issue at hand should be considered. While greater attention may be given to those violations that are similar in nature to the violation at issue, a covered entity's history of HIPAA compliance generally is relevant to determining whether the amount of a civil money penalty should be increased or decreased.

Comment: One comment urged that the size of the covered entity not be used as a factor in determining the amount of a civil money penalty, arguing that larger covered entities should not be subject to greater penalties for violations identical to those of smaller entities. The comment stated that, depending on the way the number of violations is calculated, larger covered entities are already subject to greater risk since more patients potentially could be affected by one act or omission. Another comment asked what financial information would be required of a respondent to make a showing of its financial condition and whether, given that section 1128A provides that the Secretary shall take into account financial condition, the burden is on HHS to do so even if the respondent does not. Another comment asked how the financial condition of a covered entity is to be assessed.

Response: With respect to the first comment, no change is made in the final rule. The size of the covered entity is relevant in considering, under § 160.408(e)(1), whether a covered entity experienced financial difficulties affecting its ability to comply, and under § 160.408(e)(2), whether the imposition of a civil money penalty would jeopardize a covered entity's ability to provide or pay for health care. In response to the second comment, the showing that a covered entity must make of its financial condition will vary depending on the circumstances. However, a respondent may provide whatever information it believes relevant to such a determination should it desire that HHS consider the entity's financial condition as a mitigating factor. Should a respondent fail to raise financial condition as a mitigating factor (or any other mitigating factor), however, HHS is under no obligation to raise the issue. See § 160.534(b)(1)(ii).

With respect to how financial condition is assessed, the Departmental Appeals Board (Board) has considered this issue in other cases litigated under section 1128A. The Board has said that an inquiry into a provider's financial condition should be focused on whether the provider can pay the civil money penalty without being put out of business. See Milpitas Care Center, DAB No. 1864 (2003). In Capitol Hill Community Rehabilitation and Specialty Care Center, DAB CR 469 (1997), aff'd, DAB No. 1629 (1997), the Board construed a regulation (42 CFR 488.438(f)(2)) that lists a facility's "financial condition" as one of the factors that must be considered in deciding the amounts of civil money penalties. The Board stated that, while the term "financial condition" is not defined in the regulations, the plain meaning of the term is that a facility's "financial condition" is its overall financial health. Thus, the relevant question to be considered in deciding whether a facility's financial condition would permit it to pay civil money penalties is whether the penalty amounts would jeopardize the facility's ability to survive as a business entity.

Comment: One comment argued that proposed § 160.408 should establish that HHS can only consider mitigating factors to determine the amount of the civil money penalty and not as a basis for waiving the penalty altogether. The comment stated that proposed § 160.410 already establishes circumstances under which HHS may not impose a fine, and it would be unreasonable to extend those circumstances.

Response: The final rule does not expand the circumstances under which the Secretary is prohibited from imposing, or may waive, a civil money penalty under §§ 160.410 and 160.412,

E. HIPAA Final Rules, Administrative Simplification Enforcement, continued

respectively. The factors in § 160.408 may be applied to determine, as appropriate, whether to increase or decrease the amount of a civil money penalty.

Comment: One comment expressed concern that the overlap of certain variables in proposed § 160.406 with factors in proposed § 160.408 (e.g., the variable for the duration of the violation counted in days versus the factor for the time period during which the violation occurred) could result in compounding the penalty.

Response: We disagree that providing for both counting continuing violations in days and taking time into account under § 160.408 is inappropriate. The provision for counting continuing violations in days relates to determining how many times violation of an identical provision occurred; the provision for considering the time period of the violation is one element, among others, that may constitute a mitigating or aggravating factor in determining the amount of a civil money penalty. While it is true that length of time will tend to operate in the same direction (*i.e.*, to reduce or enlarge the penalty) with respect to each of these elements of the penalty calculation, these two elements are different in nature, and time is relevant to both.

Comment: One comment that supported the list of factors in proposed § 160.408 nonetheless recommended that we better describe the factors in the preamble. Another comment requested examples of what may be included in the factor of "[s]uch other matters as justice may require" proposed at § 160.408(f).

Response: With respect to the first comment, the factors themselves are particularized and, thus, are fairly self-explanatory. However, where questions about the factors were raised in the public comments, we have provided further guidance in our responses in this preamble. With respect to the "such matters as justice may require" factor, many different circumstances have been cited for consideration in prior cases in other areas in which this factor applies. For example, ALJs have been asked to consider the following types of circumstances under this factor: the respondent's trustworthiness, the respondent's lack of veracity and remorse, measurable damages to the government, indirect or intangible damages to the government, the effect of the penalty on respondent's rehabilitation, and unprompted diligence in correcting violations.

5. Section 160.410—Affirmative Defenses to the Imposition of a Civil Money Penalty

Section 160.410 implements sections 1176(b)(1)–(3) of the Act. These sections specify certain limitations on when civil money penalties may be imposed. Paragraphs (1), (2), and (3) of section 1176(b) each state that, if the conditions described in those paragraphs are met, a penalty may not be imposed under subsection (a) of section 1176. Under section 1176(b)(1), a civil money penalty may not be imposed with respect to an act if the act constitutes a criminal offense punishable under section 1177 of the Act. Under section 1176(b)(2), a civil money penalty may not be imposed if it is established to the satisfaction of the Secretary that the person who would be liable for the penalty did not know, and by exercising reasonable diligence would not have known, that such person violated the provision. Under section 1176(b)(3), a civil money penalty may not be imposed if the failure to comply was due to reasonable cause and not to willful neglect and is corrected within a certain period. The period of time to correct a failure to comply may be extended as determined appropriate by the Secretary based on the nature and extent of the failure to comply.

Proposed rule: Proposed § 160.410 would characterize the limitations under section 1176(b)(1), (2), and (3) as "affirmative defenses," to make clear that they must be raised in the first instance by the respondent. In order not to preclude the raising of affirmative defenses that could legitimately be raised, the introductory text of proposed § 160.410 would permit a respondent to offer affirmative defenses other than those provided in section 1176(b).

Under proposed § 160.410(a), several terms relevant to the affirmative defenses would be defined: "Reasonable cause," "reasonable diligence," and "willful neglect." "Reasonable cause" would be defined as "circumstances that make it unreasonable for the covered entity, despite the exercise of ordinary business care and prudence, to comply with the administrative simplification provision violated." "Reasonable diligence" would be defined as "the business care and prudence expected from a person seeking to satisfy a legal requirement under similar circumstances." "Willful neglect" would be defined as "conscious, intentional failure or reckless indifference to the obligation to comply with the administrative simplification provision violated."

Proposed § 160.410(b)(1) simply referred to section 1177.[2] Proposed § 160.410(b)(2) generally tracked the statutory language, but also provided that whether or not a covered entity possesses the requisite knowledge to make this affirmative defense inapplicable would be "determined by the federal common law of agency." The text of proposed § 160.410(b)(3) used the defined term "reasonable diligence" and, thus, would build on the analysis conducted under proposed § 160.410(b)(2). Proposed § 160.410(b)(3)(ii)(B) would follow the statutory language and would permit the Secretary to use the full discretion provided by the statute in extending the statutory cure period.

Final rule: The final rule adopts the provisions of the proposed rule. A related change is made to § 160.504(c), as discussed below.

a. Section 160.410(b)—General Rule

Comment: One comment asked whether a covered entity could challenge in a hearing the reasonableness of the Secretary's finding that an affirmative defense has not been sufficiently established.

Response: A respondent may challenge in a hearing the finding in a notice of proposed determination that an affirmative defense has not been established. See § 160.534(b)(1)(i), which provides that the respondent bears the burden of proof with respect to affirmative defenses.

Comment: Two comments noted that the preamble to the proposed rule (70 FR 20237) would allow a covered entity to raise affirmative defenses in addition to those listed under § 160.410(b), but that the text of the proposed rule would not allow for additional defenses. They asked that the final rule be revised to allow a covered entity to present affirmative defenses not expressly listed in § 160.410(b). One comment contended, however, that § 160.410 would allow covered entities too many opportunities to avoid a penalty.

Response: The introductory text of § 160.410(b) permits other affirmative defenses to be raised by using the phrase "including the following." While we do not delineate what additional affirmative defenses might be raised, the "[e]xcept as provided in subsection (b)"

---

[2] Section 1177(a) provides that a person who knowingly and in violation of this part uses or causes to be used a unique health identifier, obtains individually identifiable health information relating to an individual, or discloses individually identifiable health information relating to another person shall be punished as provided in subsection (b). Section 1177(b) sets out three levels of penalties that vary depending on the circumstances under which the offense was committed.

E. HIPAA Final Rules, Administrative Simplification Enforcement, continued

language of section 1176(a)(1) suggests that they are limited. Nonetheless, the statute clearly contemplates at least one defense other than the limitations set out at section 1176(b)—the statute of limitations provision at section 1128A(h). Statutes of limitations defenses are typically treated as affirmative defenses, see Fed. R. Civ. P. 8(c). (28 U.S.C. Appendix). Thus, we believe that provision for other affirmative defenses that may be fairly implied from the HIPAA provisions or section 1128A must be made and, accordingly, have done so.

We do not eliminate the affirmative defenses that may be raised and that are provided for by § 160.410, as suggested by the final comment above. We have no authority to eliminate a limitation that the statute imposes on our authority to impose civil money penalties, whether or not it has the effect complained of.

Comment: One comment suggested that § 160.410(b) should be revised to state that the Secretary "shall not" impose a civil money penalty. The comment stated that if a covered entity establishes an affirmative defense, the Secretary should not have discretion to impose a penalty as indicated by the current wording "may not impose."

Response: We do not make the suggested change, because the present wording accomplishes what the comment urges. The phrase "may not impose" means, in this context, "is not permitted to impose." We do not change the language here, as it is consistent with the usage in the HIPAA rules generally, and we do not wish to suggest an inconsistency or a different meaning for similar prohibitions in other HIPAA rules.

b. Section 160.410(b)(1)—"Criminal Offense" Affirmative Defense

Comment: Several comments expressed concern that covered entities are being forced to incriminate themselves if they raise the affirmative defense under § 160.410(b)(1) in the request for hearing under § 160.504. These comments stated that covered entities should be able to raise this defense after a case has been referred to the Department of Justice, on the theory that section 1176(b)(1) operates as a jurisdictional bar to the imposition of a civil money penalty. One comment cited the Memorandum for Alex M. Azar II and Timothy J. Coleman from Stephen G. Bradbury, Re: Scope of Criminal Enforcement Under 42 U.S.C. 1320d–6 (June 1, 2005) (Justice Memorandum). The Justice Memorandum is available at *http://www.usdoj.gov/olc/hipaa_final.htm*. The comment cited the Justice

Memorandum for the proposition that this section of the statute operates as an absolute bar to imposition of a civil money penalty, rather than as an affirmative defense. Several comments argued that the burden of establishing that the limitation of section 1176(b)(1) applied should be on HHS, not on the respondent, as a matter of fairness.

Response: We continue to be of the view that the statute is structured to make the limitation of section 1176(b)(1) a defense that must be raised by the respondent. The fact that meeting the condition described in this subsection operates to bar the imposition of a civil money penalty does not distinguish it from the limitations provided for by sections 1176(b)(2) and 1176(b)(3), and those sections of the statute clearly are defenses which the respondent should raise. Moreover, the burden of establishing that section 1176(b)(1) applied could never be on HHS, as that would require HHS to carry the burden of proving a fact that would defeat its claim; it is the respondent, not HHS, who, in the context of the hearing, will be the proponent of the claim that the act for which a civil money penalty is sought is a criminal offense.

However, we recognize that section 1176(b)(1) could potentially present a situation of some difficulty for a respondent, where the Department of Justice is considering a referral related to the violations on which the civil money penalty action has been brought. While the requirement that civil money penalties be authorized by the Department of Justice before they are brought should prevent such situations from arising, we cannot assume that they will never arise. Accordingly, we provide that, unlike the other affirmative defenses, which are waived if not raised in the request for hearing, this affirmative defense may be raised at any time during the administrative proceedings, to permit respondents to better manage such legal risks, should they ever arise. Provision for this is made in § 160.504(c), and a conforming change is made to § 160.548(e).

Comment: One comment stated that the fact of referral to the Department of Justice should constitute conclusive evidence that the act is one "punishable" under section 1177, even if the Department of Justice declines to prosecute (so that the act is not "punished" under section 1177).

Response: We do not agree. Referral to the Department of Justice constitutes, at most, our preliminary assessment that the act in question may be subject to criminal prosecution. The Department of Justice may not agree with our

preliminary assessment and may return the case to us for administrative action.

Comment: One comment requested that knowledge under section 1177 be defined.

Response: "Knowingly" is the term used in section 1177 of the Act ("A person who knowingly and in violation of this part * * *"). According to the Office of Legal Counsel of the United States Department of Justice, "'the term 'knowingly' merely requires proof of knowledge of the facts that constitute the offense.'" Justice Memorandum, at 11, quoting *U.S. v. Bryan*, 524 U.S. 184, 193 (1998).

c. Section 160.410(b)(2)—"Lack of Knowledge" Affirmative Defense

Comment: One comment asks HHS to clarify the definition of knowledge required for a civil money penalty to be imposed.

Response: Under section 1176(b)(2), a civil money penalty may not be imposed for a violation "if it is established to the satisfaction of the Secretary that the person liable for the penalty did not know * * * that such person violated the provision." As we observed at 70 FR 20237—

This language on its face suggests that the knowledge involved must be knowledge that a "violation" has occurred, not just knowledge of the facts constituting the violation. * * * We, thus, interpret this knowledge requirement to mean that the covered entity must have knowledge that a violation has occurred, not just knowledge of the facts underlying the violation.

Comment: One comment asked whether, if a covered entity were found not to be liable because the knowledge of an agent could not be imputed to it, the individual committing the violation would be held liable for the penalty.

Response: The Enforcement Rule provides that only a covered entity is liable for a civil money penalty under section 1176. See § 160.402(a) and the definition of "respondent" at § 160.302.

Comment: One comment contended that the phrase "to the satisfaction of the Secretary" should be stricken from proposed § 160.410(b)(2). The comment stated that this phrase would preclude the covered entity from raising an argument before the ALJ that the Secretary did not properly consider their affirmative defenses before imposing a penalty. Another comment asked whether this phrase makes the finding totally discretionary and, thus, unreviewable by the ALJ.

Response: This language is statutory, as may be seen at section 1176(b)(2), set out above. Further, as discussed above, a respondent may raise affirmative defenses in a hearing. Where so raised,

E. HIPAA Final Rules, Administrative Simplification Enforcement, continued

Federal Register / Vol. 71, No. 32 / Thursday, February 16, 2006 / Rules and Regulations   8411

the ALJ's decision as to whether the covered entity lacked knowledge would become the decision of the Secretary, unless reversed on subsequent appeal.

Comment: One comment asked, with respect to imputing knowledge to the covered entity, who would be considered to be a "responsible officer or manager" and whether a Privacy Officer is considered a "responsible officer or manager."

Response: With respect to who would be considered to be a responsible officer or manager and whether a Privacy Officer would be considered a responsible officer or manager, see the discussion above under § 160.402(c).

Comment: One comment asked whether, if a Privacy Officer mitigates or corrects a violation, that action would satisfy the requirement that a responsible officer or manager be made aware of the violation.

Response: We are unsure what the precise concern of this comment is, as the issue of knowledge typically would arise in the context of the "lack of knowledge" affirmative defense. That defense requires, for its application, that the covered entity not have actual or constructive knowledge of the violation. If the violation has been corrected, as the comment suggests, one would normally presume that the covered entity knew of the violation, making the lack of knowledge defense unavailable. Under the scenario posed by the comment, as we understand it, the issue would be whether the elements of the "reasonable cause" affirmative defense were present.

d. Section 160.410(b)(3)—"Reasonable Cause" Affirmative Defense

Comment: One comment asked that the word "corrected" in § 160.410(b)(3)(ii) be changed to "mitigated," because not all violations can be fully corrected.

Response: We agree with the comment that not all violations of the HIPAA rules can be fully corrected, in the sense of being undone or fully remediated. However, we do not agree that the term "corrected," which is the term used by the statute, need be read so narrowly. Rather, the statute speaks of the "failure to comply" being corrected. Thus, the term "corrected," as used in the statute, could include correction of a covered entity's noncompliant procedure by making the procedure compliant. In any event, since the term "corrected" is the term used in the statute, we employ it in the rule below.

Comment: One comment requested clarification as to how a covered entity could ask for an extension of time to

cure a violation under § 160.410(b)(3)(ii)(B).

Response: The covered entity should make this request in writing to, as applicable, CMS or OCR. The request should state when the violation will be corrected and the reasons that support the need for additional time.

Comment: One comment asked that the 30-day cure period be extended by an additional 30 days.

Response: The initial cure period is, by statute, 30 days. However, section 1176(b)(3)(B)(i) permits the Secretary to extend the initial cure period "as determined appropriate by the Secretary based on the nature and extent of the failure to comply." Section 160.410(b)(3)(ii)(B) adopts, and does not expand upon, this statutory language. Thus, HHS could extend the cure period for an additional 30 days (or some greater or lesser period), if it were determined appropriate to do so.

6. Section 160.412—Waiver

Section 1176(b)(4) of the Act provides for waiver of a civil money penalty in certain circumstances. Section 1176(b)(4) provides that, if the failure to comply is "due to reasonable cause and not to willful neglect," a penalty that has not already been waived under section 1176(b)(3) "may be waived to the extent that the payment of such penalty would be excessive relative to the compliance failure involved." If there is reasonable cause and no willful neglect and the violation has been timely corrected, the imposition of the civil money penalty would be precluded by section 1176(b)(3). Therefore, waiver under this section would be available only where there was reasonable cause for the violation and no willful neglect, but the violation was not timely corrected.

Proposed rule: Proposed § 160.412 did not propose to elaborate on the statute in any material way. This provision would provide the Secretary with the flexibility to utilize the discretion provided by the statutory language as necessary.

Final rule: The final rule adopts the provisions of the proposed rule.

Comment: One comment suggested that this section be removed entirely. The comment stated that section 1176(b)(4) authorizes, but does not compel, the Secretary to allow for waiver of civil money penalties. The comment argued that waiver is an unnecessary avenue for covered entities to avoid penalties, as the statute and the proposed rule would provide so many other avenues by which a covered entity could avoid being penalized for violations.

Response: As was more fully discussed at 70 FR 20239, the statute, in our view, creates a statutory right for covered entities to request a waiver, where a violation is due to reasonable cause and not willful neglect, but has not been corrected within the statutory cure period (including any extensions thereof). While the grant of a waiver is within the agency's discretion, the statute clearly contemplates that covered entities may request a waiver in such circumstances and that HHS must consider the request. Accordingly, we do not make the change suggested.

7. Section 160.414—Limitations

Proposed rule: Proposed § 160.414 was adopted by the April 17, 2003 interim final rule as § 160.522. We proposed to move this section, which sets forth the six-year limitation period provided for in section 1128A(c)(1), from subpart E to subpart D, because this provision applies generally to the imposition of civil money penalties and is not dependent on whether a hearing is requested. We also proposed to change the language of this provision so that the date of the occurrence of the violation is the date from which the limitation is determined.

Final rule: The final rule adopts the provisions of the proposed rule.

Comment: One comment requested clarification of record retention requirements and their interaction with the time limitation on bringing an enforcement action.

Response: The issue raised by this comment is discussed in connection with § 160.310 above.

Comment: One comment suggested shortening the time period to two years in the interest of accomplishing compliance faster and making record-keeping less burdensome for covered entities.

Response: The six-year limitations period of § 160.414 is provided for by statute (section 1128A(c)(1) of the Act), and, thus, is not within our power to change by regulation. Insofar as this comment suggests changing the record retention requirements of the Privacy and Security Rules, the requested change is outside the scope of this rulemaking.

8. Section 160.416—Authority To Settle

Proposed rule: Proposed § 160.416 was adopted by the April 17, 2003 interim final rule as § 160.510. We proposed to move this section, which addresses the authority of the Secretary to settle any issue or case or to compromise any penalty imposed on a covered entity, from subpart E to subpart D, because this provision

E. HIPAA Final Rules, Administrative Simplification Enforcement, continued

applies generally to the imposition of civil money penalties, and is not dependent on whether a hearing is requested. No change was proposed to the text of the provision.

Final rule: The final rule adopts the provisions of the proposed rule.

Comment: One comment expressed concern that this provision does not provide for alternative dispute resolution. The comment urged HHS to remain committed to the informal resolution process.

Response: We provide in the rule that HHS will attempt to resolve compliance issues informally, for the reasons discussed above and in the preamble to the proposed rule. Where this process is insufficient to resolve the matter, the statute requires provision of a formal hearing process, if a hearing is requested. We note that under their current procedures, the ALJ and/or the Departmental Appeals Board routinely afford parties the opportunity to engage in alternative dispute resolution.

Comment: Two comments suggested removing § 160.416 from the final rule, on the ground that it is inappropriate to give the Secretary this authority without oversight.

Response: We do not adopt this suggestion. The statute explicitly gives the Secretary the authority to compromise penalties, which would typically be done through settlement of the case. See section 1128A(f).

9. Section 160.420—Notice of Proposed Determination

Proposed rule: The text of proposed § 160.420 was adopted by the April 17, 2003 interim final rule as § 160.514. We proposed to move this section from subpart E, which sets out the procedures and rights of the parties to a hearing, to subpart D, because the notice provided for in this section must be given whenever a civil money penalty is proposed, regardless of whether a hearing is requested. No changes, other than conforming changes, were proposed to paragraphs (a)(1) and (a)(3), (a)(4), or to paragraph (b). We proposed to revise paragraph (a)(2) by adding that, in the event the Secretary employs statistical sampling techniques under § 160.536, the sample relied upon and the methodology employed must be generally described in the notice of proposed determination. A new paragraph (a)(5) would require the notice to describe any circumstances described in § 160.408 that were considered in determining the amount of the proposed penalty; this provision would correspond to § 1003.109(a)(5) of the OIG regulations. Paragraph (a)(5) of § 160.514 of the April 17, 2003 interim

final rule would be renumbered as § 160.420(a)(6).

Final rule: We adopt the section as proposed, except that, where HHS bases the proposed penalty in part on statistical sampling, a copy of the report of the agency's statistical expert, rather than just a description of the study and the sampling technique used, must be provided with the notice of proposed determination.

Comment: One comment requested clarification as to whether the notice of proposed determination serves as the notice required by the statute.

Response: Yes, the notice provided for by § 160.420—the notice of proposed determination—implements the requirement for notice of section 1128A(c)(1).

Comment: One comment recommended that the final rule retain § 160.420(a)(5) to ensure that covered entities have sufficient information as to why the penalty was imposed.

Response: This has been done. See § 160.420(a)(5) below.

Comment: Several comments requested that the rule specify that the notice of proposed determination will be sent to the covered entity's Privacy Officer or another designated officer.

Response: This issue is discussed below in connection with § 160.504.

Comment: Several comments stated that, if HHS bases its proposed penalty on statistical sampling, the notice of proposed determination should include a copy of the study relied upon, so that a covered entity has adequate notice and time to prepare its defense.

Response: We agree and have made the requested change.

10. Section 160.422—Failure To Request a Hearing

Proposed rule: The text of proposed § 160.422 was adopted by the April 17, 2003 interim final rule as § 160.516. We proposed to add language ("and the matter is not settled pursuant to § 160.416") to recognize that the Secretary and the respondent may agree to a settlement after the Secretary has issued a notice of proposed determination. We also proposed that the penalty be final upon receipt of the penalty notice, to make clear when subsequent actions, such as collection, may commence.

Final rule: The final rule adopts the provisions of the proposed rule.

Comment: Several comments suggested that a provision should be added allowing the time frame to request a hearing to be extended when the notice of proposed determination is not received by the appropriate person within the covered entity.

Response: This issue is discussed in connection with § 160.504 below.

11. Section 160.424—Collection of Penalty

Proposed rule: The text of § 160.424 was adopted by the April 17, 2003 interim final rule as § 160.518. We proposed to move this section, which addresses how a final penalty is collected, from subpart E to subpart D, because this provision applies generally to the imposition of civil money penalties and is not dependent upon whether a hearing is requested. The rule provides that once a proposed penalty becomes final, it will be collected by the Secretary, unless compromised. The Secretary may bring a collection action in the Federal district court for the district in which the respondent resides, is found, or is located. The penalty amount, as finally determined, may be collected by means of offset from Federal funds or state funds owing to the respondent. Matters that were, or could have been, raised in a hearing or in an appeal to the U.S. Circuit Court of Appeals may not be raised as a defense to the collection action.

Final rule: The final rule adopts the provisions of the proposed rule.

Comment: One comment asked what interest rate will accrue, if a penalty is not paid promptly by the covered entity.

Response: Under the Federal Claims Collection rules, interest is calculated as provided by 31 U.S.C. 3717. See 31 CFR 901.9.

Comment: One comment asked whether, if a penalty is assessed against a hybrid entity, the part of the entity responsible for the violation would pay the penalty or the entire hybrid entity would pay the penalty.

Response: As noted above, a hybrid entity is, by definition, a single legal entity. Where a penalty is assessed against a covered entity that has designated itself as a hybrid entity, the legal entity that is the covered entity is responsible for payment of the penalty. How the covered entity allocates the penalty payment as a matter of internal accounting is a business decision of the covered entity.

Comment: One comment asked whether, if an agency with the same structure as a Medicaid agency is assessed a penalty, federal dollars can be withheld in lieu of payment of the penalty.

Response: Yes. Section 1128A(f) provides for setoff of penalty amounts against Federal or state agency funds then or later owing to the person penalized.

Comment: One comment suggests that the Secretary does not have the

E. HIPAA Final Rules, Administrative Simp. Enforcement, continued

Federal Register / Vol. 71, No. 32 / Thursday, February 16, 2006 / Rules and Regulations

authority to preclude issues from being raised in a civil action in federal court. The comment suggests removing § 160.424(d) from the final rule.

Response: Section 160.424(d) merely states the well-recognized principle that, where an administrative remedy exists, a plaintiff must exhaust that remedy as a precondition to raising the issue in question in court.

12. Section 160.426—Notification of the Public and Other Agencies

Proposed rule: We proposed to require notification of the public generally whenever a proposed penalty became final, in order to make the information available to anyone who must make decisions with respect to covered entities. The regulatory language would provide for notification in such manner as the Secretary deems appropriate, which would include posting to an HHS Web site and/or the periodic publication of a notice in the **Federal Register**.

Final rule: The final rule adopts the provisions of the proposed rule.

Comment: Several comments argued that the provision for notification of the public in proposed § 160.426 would extend beyond the scope of the Secretary's statutory authority under section 1128A(h), since section 1128A(h) specifies only that certain types of organizations and agencies to be notified. They urged that the requirement be eliminated.

Response: We disagree that the requirement for public notification is unauthorized. It is true that § 160.426 establishes the means by which HHS may carry out its obligation to notify various agencies and organizations under section 1128A(h). However, the basis for the public notice portion of § 160.426 lies not in section 1128A(h), as the comments assumed, but in the Freedom of Information Act (FOIA), 5 U.S.C. 552.

FOIA requires final opinions and orders made in adjudication cases to be made available for public inspection and copying. *See* 5 U.S.C. 552(a)(2)(A). The adjudicatory process [3] set forth in the Enforcement Rule begins with the service upon the respondent of a notice of proposed determination under § 160.420. This proposed penalty becomes final if the respondent fails to contest it in the time and manner provided in § 160.504(b). If the respondent does contest the proposed

penalty, the final agency order is the decision of the ALJ, or the Board, as the case may be. While it is true that section 1128A(h) does not require that such notice be given to the public, neither does it prohibit such wider dissemination of that information, and nothing in section 1128A(h) suggests that it modifies the Secretary's obligations under FOIA. FOIA requires making final orders or opinions available for public inspection and copying by "computer telecommunication * * * or other electronic means," which would encompass putting them up on the Department's Web site, and further provides that, absent actual and timely notice, in order for the Department to rely upon final opinions that affect a member of the public or to cite them as precedent against a party, the opinions or orders must be indexed and made available electronically. *See* 5 U.S.C. 552(a)(2).

Comment: Many comments objected to the requirement for public notice. Comments argued that since final decisions of the Departmental Appeals Board are available under FOIA, there is no need for further notice to the public. Further, it was stated that many HIPAA violations, particularly of the Transactions Rule, are very technical in nature and the public may be unable to understand the nature of such violations. Accordingly, public notification may injure the reputation of covered entities and cause them to lose business, while the reputational injury attendant on public notification may be wholly disproportionate to the violations involved. Also, comments argued that entities that are members of an affiliated covered entity and that are held liable for the actions of others under § 160.402(b) may be unfairly labeled as noncompliant. Finally, comments stated that covered entities may have to expend additional resources to fight complaints, because the public notification provision would give competitors an incentive to use the complaint process to gain an unfair business advantage.

Response: Final decisions of the ALJs and the Departmental Appeals Board are made public via the Board's Web site. *See http://www.hhs.gov/dab/search.html.* Such postings, however, would not include penalties that become final because a request for hearing was not filed under § 160.422. Notices of proposed determination under § 160.420 that become final because a hearing has not been timely requested, would likewise be made available for such public inspection and copying as final orders. By making the

entire final opinion or order available the public, the facts underlying the penalty determination and the law applied to those facts will be apparent. Given that information, the public may discern the nature and extent of the violation as well as the basis for imposition of the civil money penalty on the covered entity. Finally, the process established for the review and investigation of complaints should identify those without merit, or over which HHS has no jurisdiction under the HIPAA provisions, but, in any event, we doubt that the notification provisions of this section will increase the likelihood that complaints will be filed.

Comment: One comment suggested that, rather than mandating the provision of notice to the public, the rule should give the Secretary discretion to determine when public notification is prudent, as doing so may not be appropriate in all instances—for example, where there is an ongoing investigation or a technical failure is involved. A number of comments urged HHS to publish violations of HIPAA without the name of the covered entity. They argued that this approach would enable covered entities to understand how OCR and CMS apply the HIPAA rules in particular circumstances and would, thus, encourage voluntary compliance.

Response: As noted, under FOIA, we must make final orders and opinions available for public inspection and copying. FOIA permits the Secretary to withhold information whose release could, for instance, reasonably be expected to interfere with prospective or ongoing law enforcement proceedings, but such exemption does not apply where, as in the case of such final opinions and orders, they are made after the conclusion of such proceedings. *See* 5 U.S.C. 552(b)(7)(A). While FOIA permits the deletion of identifying details to prevent a clearly unwarranted invasion of personal privacy, identifying the name(s) of the covered entities against whom penalties are imposed would not be such an invasion of personal privacy.

Comment: One comment suggested that the rule be revised to require covered entities to notify the Secretary and potentially affected individuals when there is a suspected breach of the Privacy Rule. The comment also suggested that HHS make available a list of violations organized by entity, including the number of persons affected by each violation. One comment asked that all final decisions of the ALJ or the Board, including those to not assess a penalty, be made public.

---

[3] Under the Administrative Procedure Act, "adjudication means agency process for the formulation of an order." 5 U.S.C. 551(7). An "order" means the whole or part of a final disposition * * * of an agency in a matter other than rule making * * *". 5 U.S.C. 551(6).

. HIPAA Final Rules, Administrative Simplification Enforcement, continued

so that covered entities could present a better defense in the future based on past decisions to not impose a penalty in a similar situation. Another comment supported the proposal to notify the public of final penalties, on the ground that the public should be aware of violations, particularly of the Privacy Rule. Another comment suggested that complainants should be notified when a penalty is imposed.

Response: As noted, final opinions or orders imposing penalties will be made available to the public for inspection and copying. Given that this information will be public, we do not accept the other comments above.

Comment: One comment stated that the public notification rule should not apply to, or include, matters referred to the Department of Justice. Another comment asked that HHS confirm that the public notification provision would not apply to informal resolutions.

Response: In neither of the above situations has a final order on a penalty proposed under § 160.420 been entered. Consequently, neither situation would come within the public notification requirement of § 160.426.

Comment: Several comments expressed concern that publication of a penalty could occur prematurely, before all of the covered entity's appeals had been exhausted. They requested clarification as to when a penalty is considered final for purposes of notification. A couple of comments stated that the penalty should be considered to be final, for purposes of the public notification, when all court appeals have been exhausted.

Response: A civil money penalty is considered to be final, for purposes of notification, when it is a final agency action—*i.e.*, the time for administrative appeal has run or the adverse administrative finding has otherwise become final. The final opinion or order that is subject to the notification provisions of this section is the notice of proposed determination, if a request for hearing is not timely filed, the decision of the ALJ, if that is not appealed, or the final decision of the Board.

D. Subpart E—Procedures for Hearings

As previously explained, the provisions of section 1128A of the Act apply to the imposition of a civil money penalty under section 1176 "in the same manner as" they apply to the imposition of civil money penalties under section 1128A itself. The provisions of subpart E are, as a consequence, based in large part upon, and are in many respects the same as, the OIG regulations implementing section 1128A. We adapt,

re-order, or combine the language of the OIG regulations in a number of places for clarity of presentation or to reflect concepts unique to the HIPAA provisions or rules. To avoid confusion, we also employ certain language usages in order to be consistent with the usages in the other HIPAA rules (for example, for mandatory duties, "must" or "will" instead of "shall" is used; for discretionary duties, "may" instead of "has the authority to" is used).

Subpart E, as adopted by the April 17, 2003 interim final rule, adopted provisions relating to investigational inquiries and subpoenas and certain definitions that have now been moved to subpart C. It also adopted a number of provisions that relate to all civil money penalties that have now been moved to subpart D. Subpart E, as revised below, addresses only the administrative hearing phase of the enforcement process.

General comment: Several comments argued that the proposed Enforcement Rule, as a whole, would give the government an unfair advantage and seriously compromise the ability of covered entities to defend themselves before an ALJ and on an appeal to the Board. It was argued that the following provisions, in combination, would "stack the deck" in the government's favor:

(1) The severely restricted ability of covered entities to rebut the statistical sampling report; (2) the "extraordinary circumstances" standard for failure to timely exchange exhibits and witness statements; (3) the inability to depose prior to the hearing or question at the hearing the government's statistical sampling expert; (4) the ability of the * * * ALJ * * * to admit prior evidence of witnesses which were not subject to cross examination by the covered entity; (5) the requirements regarding hearing requests; (6) the limited nature of discovery and the lack of obligation to share exculpatory evidence; (7) the ALJ's discretion about applying the Federal Rules of Evidence; (8) the very broad harmless error rule which significantly restricts a covered entity's appeal rights; and (9) the limited authority of the ALJ and correspondingly broad discretion provided to the Secretary.

Response: While we also discuss the above provisions individually, we provide the following general response. We do not agree that the proposed rule would have given HHS an unfair advantage or compromised the ability of covered entities to defend themselves. Most of the provisions cited should operate even-handedly, providing no greater advantage to the government than to the respondent. For example, the limitation on depositions will also mean that the governmental party cannot depose any statistical expert of the

respondent; similarly, the other limitations on discovery should operate similarly for both parties, as should the ALJ's discretion with respect to the application of the Federal Rules of Evidence and the application of the harmless error rule.

In any event, we have changed several of the provisions cited. We have required the government's statistical study to be provided with the notice of proposed determination, we have clarified the conditions for the admission of written statements, and we have eliminated the restriction on the ALJ's authority to review the method by which the number of violations is determined. We believe that the final rule strikes an appropriate balance and should ensure that neither party has a procedural advantage.

1. Section 160.504—Hearing Before an ALJ

Proposed rule: The proposed rule proposed few changes to this section, which was § 160.526 of the April 17, 2003 interim final rule. Section 160.526(a)(2) of the April 17, 2003 interim final rule stated that the Departmental party in a hearing is "the Secretary." The term "Secretary" is defined at § 160.103 of the HIPAA rules as "the Secretary of Health and Human Services or any other officer or employee of HHS to whom the authority involved has been delegated." However, in light of the multiple roles of the Secretary in the context of a hearing (OCR and/or CMS would be a party, while the ALJ or the Board would be the adjudicator), we proposed to clarify in § 160.504(a)(2) which part of HHS acts as the "party" in the hearing. Because which component of HHS will be the "party" in a particular case will depend on which rule is alleged to have been violated, and because a particular case could involve more than one HIPAA rule, we proposed to define the Secretarial party generically, by reference to the component with the delegated enforcement authority. Under the proposed provision, the Secretarial party could consist of more than one officer or employee, so that it is possible for both CMS and OCR to be the Secretarial party in a particular case.

Proposed § 160.504(b) provided that the request for a hearing must be mailed within 60 days, via certified mail, return receipt requested, to the address specified in the notice of proposed determination. The last sentence of proposed § 160.504(b) provided that the date of receipt of the notice of proposed determination is presumed to be five days after the date of the notice unless the respondent makes a reasonable

E. HIPAA Final Rules, Administrative Simpli..
Enforcement, continued

showing to the contrary. This showing may be made even where the notice is sent by mail and is not precluded by the computation of time rule of proposed § 160.526(c), establishing a five-day allowance for mailing.

Proposed § 160.504(c) would require that the request for hearing clearly and directly admit, deny, or explain each of the findings of fact contained in the notice of proposed determination with respect to which the respondent has knowledge and must also state the circumstances or arguments that the respondent alleges constitute the grounds for any defense and the factual and legal basis for opposing the penalty. Proposed § 160.504(d)(1) would require the ALJ to dismiss a hearing request where "[t]he respondent's hearing request is not filed as required by paragraphs (b) and (c) of this section." Proposed §§ 160.504(d)(2)–(4) would require dismissal where the hearing request was, respectively, withdrawn, abandoned, or raised no issue that could properly be addressed in a hearing.

Final rule: Section 160.504 below revises the proposed rule in several respects. The proposed 60-day time limit for filing a request for hearing is extended to 90 days. See § 160.504(b). Section 160.504(c) provides that an affirmative defense under § 160.410(b)(1) may be raised at any time. Section 160.504(d)(1) provides that a dismissal on the grounds stated in that paragraph may only be made on motion of the Secretary, and the ground for dismissal under paragraph (b) is limited to the respondent's failure to comply with the timely filing requirement of paragraph (b).

Comment: A number of comments objected to the 60-day time limit of proposed § 160.504(b) as unreasonably short and unfair, given the detailed showing the covered entity is required to provide in its request for hearing and the severe consequences, under proposed § 160.504(d)(1), of failing to meet this requirement. A couple of comments also objected that this provision is not necessary and does not follow the OIG regulation in this respect. Comments suggested several changes: (1) That the required specificity of the request for hearing be eliminated, (2) that the time for response be lengthened, and/or (3) that there be a provision to excuse an untimely request for hearing based on good cause.

Response: We accommodate the concerns raised in the public comment by extending the period for filing a request for hearing from 60 to 90 days. We note that, as so revised, the rule does not parallel the analogous

provision of the OIG regulations (42 CFR 1005.2(c)) in two respects: (1) It requires more specificity in the hearing request; and (2) it provides the respondent more time in which to file the hearing request. We are of the view, however, that the compromise in § 160.504(b), as revised, will promote the conduct of the hearing in an efficient manner by clarifying at an early stage of the process the issues in dispute and the basis for those disputes. We retain the requirement of proposed § 160.504(c) that the request for hearing clearly and directly admit, deny, or explain each of the findings of fact and state the circumstances or arguments that the respondent alleges constitute the grounds for any defense and the factual and legal basis for opposing the penalty. (However, the respondent need not provide its statistical study, assuming it has one, until 30 days before the scheduled hearing. See § 160.518.) This requirement will facilitate narrowing and refining the issues in dispute, thereby expediting the conduct of the hearing.

Comment: One comment suggested that, if the 60-day time period for response were retained, HHS be required to send a reminder on the 45th day.

Response: We do not adopt this suggestion. The need for the suggested change is obviated by our decision to extend the 60-day period.

Comment: Several comments suggested that the rule does not properly take into account the possibility of notices being delivered to the wrong official in a covered entity or getting lost in a covered entity's internal mail system. They recommended that the rule specify the official(s) in the covered entity to whom the notice of proposed determination must be sent, so that the covered entity does not lose time needed to prepare its defense. A few comments suggested that the notice of proposed determination be sent to the Privacy Officer. It was suggested that the covered entity be able to show good cause for failing to respond in a timely manner in such cases, or that the 60-day time period be tolled.

Response: We do not think it is necessary or feasible to identify the person(s) to whom the notice of proposed determination should be addressed. Fed. R. Civ. P. 4 (28 U.S.C. Appendix), which applies under section 1128A(c), establishes who may be served and applies without need for further regulatory action. Because the size and other organizational circumstances of covered entities vary greatly, a rule that further limited or defined who must be served would most

likely be inappropriate for some covered entities. Further, it is likely that a notice of proposed determination would be issued after significant prior contact with the covered entity, so we anticipate that our investigators would be able to ascertain which officer would be the appropriate recipient of the notice.

In any event, a respondent can raise the issues of concern raised by the comments—e.g., failure to reach the appropriate official or the official to whom the notice of proposed determination was addressed due to problems in the entity's mail system—under § 160.504(b). Under that section, if the respondent makes "a reasonable showing" to the ALJ that the mailed notice of proposed determination was not properly received by the covered entity or by a proper official within the covered entity, the ALJ can extend the 90-day period to the extent he or she considers appropriate.

Comment: One comment asked whether findings of fact that are not contested or about which the claim is made of insufficient knowledge to respond in the hearing request are deemed admitted.

Response: Section 160.504(c) provides respondents with two choices with respect to denying findings of fact: (1) The respondent may deny them; or (2) the respondent may claim a lack of knowledge, in which case the finding in question is "deemed denied." Since the regulation deems a finding of fact denied only where lack of knowledge is claimed, if the respondent has neither denied nor asserted lack of knowledge with respect to the finding, the finding must be deemed admitted.

Comment: One comment stated that dismissal of a hearing request on the grounds described in proposed § 160.504(d)(1)–(3) should be made permissive, not mandatory, and § 160.504(d)(4) (dismissal where the respondent fails to state an issue that may properly be addressed in a hearing) should be eliminated, to ensure that covered entities are provided a fair opportunity to request a hearing and develop an appropriate defense.

Response: We revise proposed § 160.504(d)(1) to require dismissal on the ground of failure to comply with paragraph (b) to be limited to failure to comply with the requirement of the paragraph for timely filing of the request for hearing. We revise proposed § 160.504(d)(1) to provide that dismissal on this ground may occur only if the Secretary moves for dismissal on this ground. If the Secretarial party—OCR, CMS, or both—does not believe that the hearing should be dismissed due to the insufficiency of the respondent's request

E. HIPAA Final Rules, Administrative Simplification Enforcement, continued

for hearing, and so does not challenge the timeliness or sufficiency of the request for hearing under paragraph (b) or (c), respectively, the hearing should go forward. The revision to paragraph (d)(1) would permit this to occur.

Like its counterparts in other rules issued pursuant to section 1128A, § 160.504(d)(1)–(3) mandates dismissal so that the limited resources of the government and of respondents are not expended on hearing requests that fail to comply with the straightforward requirements of this section or that have been withdrawn or abandoned by the respondent. We believe that considerations of economy and efficiency require the dismissal of cases that fall within the descriptions of these subsections. However, in response to the comments, we have added a requirement to § 160.504(d)(1) that the Secretary must file a motion for dismissal of a hearing request rather than permit an automatic dismissal by the ALJ. The filing of such a motion will require the Secretary to enunciate the reasons a hearing request is deficient under paragraphs (b) and (c) of this section and allow the respondent the opportunity to answer those charges. We do not add such a requirement to § 160.504(d)(2)–(3), because we think that the ALJ should have authority to dismiss such cases for reasons of withdrawal or abandonment by the respondent without being requested to do so by the Secretary.

Section 160.504(d)(4) provides the administrative review channel leading to judicial review of claims that may not be reviewed administratively, such as constitutional claims. This subsection is necessary so that there is no confusion about how respondents can efficiently exhaust the administrative process for such claims. We, thus, decline to eliminate this subsection.

2. Section 160.508—Authority of the ALJ

Proposed rule: The text of proposed § 160.508 was adopted by the April 17, 2003 interim final rule as § 160.530. No changes to paragraphs (a) and (b) were proposed. We proposed to revise paragraph (c) by adding paragraphs (c)(1) and (c)(5) to the list of limitations on the authority of the ALJ. Proposed paragraph (c)(1) would require the ALJ to follow Federal statutes, regulations, and Secretarial delegations of authority, and to give deference to published guidance to the extent not inconsistent with statute or regulation; the preamble to the proposed rule indicated that by "published guidance" we meant guidance that has been publicly disseminated, including posting on the

CMS or OCR Web site. Proposed paragraph (c)(5) would clarify that ALJs may not review the Secretary's exercise of discretion whether to grant an extension or to provide technical assistance under section 1176(b)(3)(B) of the Act or the Secretary's exercise of discretion in the choice of variable(s) under proposed § 160.406.

Final rule: The final rule adopts the provisions of the proposed rule, except for proposed § 160.508(c)(5)(ii), which is eliminated. A conforming change is made to § 160.508(c)(5).

a. Section 160.508(b)

Comment: One comment stated that this provision should be amended to add a provision requiring that a requested hearing be conducted within a time certain, not to exceed 90 days from receipt of the request for a hearing. Another comment suggested that the ALJ should notify a respondent of the date and time for the hearing no later than 90 days after the request for hearing is filed.

Response: It would not be reasonable or appropriate to impose a fixed deadline by which hearings must be scheduled, and we decline to do so. In a complicated case, the time for discovery and pre-hearing motions may take more than 90 days, and, thus, imposing such a deadline may circumscribe the parties' ability to prepare their cases. Moreover, the ALJs have other cases on their dockets, and we cannot assume that they will in all cases be able to begin a hearing on a civil money penalty within 90 days. The scheduling of the hearing is best left to the ALJs, in consultation with the parties.

b. Section 160.508(c)

Comment: A number of comments opposed proposed § 160.508(c), on the ground that it would significantly limit the ALJ's authority to rule on pertinent issues. They stated that it was questionable under this section whether the ALJ would have the authority to review the determination of the number of violations, or imposition of joint and several liability, since they may be addressed in published guidance to which the ALJ must give deference. It was suggested that this limitation would be a problem under proposed § 160.424(d), since those are issues that a respondent would be unable to raise at the administrative level.

Response: We do not agree. We believe that it is of importance to covered entities that ALJ and Board decisions, as components of HHS, be consistent with one another and with the published compliance guidance

HHS provides to covered entities. Accordingly, we require ALJs and the Board to follow guidance which has been publicly disseminated, unless the ALJ or Board finds the guidance to be inconsistent with statute or regulation. In the examples cited, any published guidance related to the determination of the number of violations, or when joint and several liability is appropriate must be consistent with applicable statute and regulation, matters upon which the ALJ may rule. See section 1176 and §§ 160.402(b)(2), 160.406, and 160.508. While deference to such published guidance is required of the ALJs and DAB, as components of HHS, similar deference is not necessarily afforded such guidance in any judicial review of an adverse final agency determination sought by a respondent. Section 160.424(d) should not present a problem, since challenges related to published guidance may be raised during administrative and judicial reviews of the proposed penalty.

Comment: One comment stated that ALJs should be allowed to consider affirmative defenses during a hearing, even if they relate to issues committed to the Secretary's discretion. The comment argued that an inability to raise affirmative defenses before the ALJ might impact a covered entity's ability to subsequently pursue legal remedies under § 160.424(d).

Response: We agree that the ALJ is allowed to consider affirmative defenses during a hearing. See the discussion of § 160.410 above.

Comment: A couple of comments agreed that ALJs should have the authority to evaluate whether there was a violation in the first place and asked that this provision be retained in the final rule.

Response: We agree and have done so.

c. Section 160.508(c)(1)

Comment: One comment asked, if a guidance in effect at the time a violation occurred were changed before the date of the hearing, which version of the guidance the ALJ would have to follow.

Response: The guidance in effect at the time the violation occurred would govern.

Comment: One comment expressed concern with § 160.508(c)(1), insofar as it would include in "published guidance" FAQs published on the CMS and OCR Web sites. According to the comment, FAQs have never been designated in the HIPAA regulations as having the force of regulations themselves. According to the comment, many covered entities are not aware of these postings and the industry is unaware that they will have the same

E. HIPAA Final Rules, Administrative Simplificatio Enforcement, continued

force and effect as regulations. The comment further stated that if FAQs are to have the force of regulation, then the questions and responses should be organized for such use, and the HIPAA regulation should specifically designate that covered entities will be held accountable for compliance with these responses or "published guidance." Another comment suggested that proposed § 160.508(c)(1) should be revised to require the ALJ to give consideration to published guidance and consider whether the covered entity reasonably relied on such guidance, as is done in the regulations relating to hearings by the Provider Reimbursement Review Board (PRRB), citing to 42 CFR 405.1867.

Response: The "published guidances", including FAQs, inform covered entities of the approach HHS is taking in the enforcement of the HIPAA rules. The guidances do not have the force and effect of a regulation, as the comment suggests, and are not controlling upon the courts, as would be the case with a regulation. As previously explained, HHS seeks to provide consistent compliance guidance to covered entities and, to the extent possible, to render decisions in the adjudicative process that are both consistent with other adjudicated cases and with the policy decisions of the Secretary expressed in HHS rules and guidances. The consistency sought within HHS is achieved by requiring the ALJ and the Board, which are components of HHS, to defer to such published guidances, if they are consistent with statute and regulation. This is consistent with, and recognizes the effect of, the existing delegations of authority by the Secretary, which delegate to the programs the Secretary's authority to establish policy. Requiring that only consideration be given to such published guidances, as in PRRB hearings, rather than deference, would not achieve the desired result.

Comment: One comment argued that proposed § 160.508(c)(1) should be changed to add "and does not establish requirements in addition to those specified in the applicable statute or regulation," on the ground that covered entities should not be penalized for not complying with requirements that exceed the plain language of the statute.

Response: It is not clear what the comment is suggesting, but if the comment is suggesting that guidance merely parrot what is in the statute and regulations, guidance would be both unnecessary and unhelpful. If, however, the comment is suggesting that guidance not exceed any explicit limits imposed by the statute or regulations, the

language is likewise unnecessary, as the current language would permit the ALJ or the Board to disregard guidance that was not consistent with statute or regulations.

d. Section 160.508(c)(5)

Comment: Proposed § 160.508(c)(5)(ii) would have made the Secretary's selection of the variable under § 160.406 unreviewable by the ALJ. It was criticized by several commenters as unfair and inconsistent with the statute on the grounds that the whole purpose of the hearing before an ALJ is to review the Secretary's assessment of a penalty. It was argued that, if a covered entity has a reasonable argument as to why the use of variables or a particular variable was not appropriate, it should be allowed to present the argument during the ALJ hearing to which it is entitled by statute. It was also argued that, since proposed § 160.406 would include a factual determination of the number of times a covered entity may have failed to engage in required conduct, or may have engaged in a prohibited act, each of the parties should be authorized to address, and the ALJ to consider at a hearing, that factual determination. One comment asked whether, even if the ALJ lacks authority to directly question the variable(s) selected, a challenge to the variable could be made through a claim that "justice required" selection of a different variable.

Response: Section 1128A(c)(2) establishes the right to a hearing on the record for any person who has been given an adverse determination by the Secretary. In a proceeding under section 1176, the adverse determination by the Secretary is the civil money penalty proposed in the notice of proposed determination under § 160.420. Upon review of the comments regarding proposed § 160.508(c)(5)(ii), we agree that the count of violations is an integral part of a civil money penalty and should be reviewable by the ALJ. Thus, we have deleted proposed subparagraph (ii) from § 160.508(c)(5) in the final rule. As a conforming change, we have integrated subparagraph (i) into the text of § 160.508(c)(5).

3. Section 160.512—Prehearing Conferences

Proposed rule: Proposed § 160.512 would adopt § 160.534, as added by the April 17, 2003 interim final rule, with two changes. Proposed § 160.512 would revise paragraph (a) to establish a minimum amount of notice (not less than 14 business days) that must be provided to the parties in the scheduling of prehearing conferences. Proposed § 160.512 would also revise

paragraph (b)(11) to include the issue of the protection of individually identifiable health information as a matter that may be discussed at the prehearing conference, if appropriate.

Final rule: The final rule adopts the provisions of the proposed rule.

Comment: One comment recommended that a provision be added to § 160.512 to require the ALJ to schedule a prehearing conference within 30 days of a request for a hearing, unless both parties agree to a later date.

Response: The scheduling of a prehearing conference will depend, in part, on the scheduling of the hearing. For the reasons discussed under § 160.508(b) above, we do not agree that it is advisable to so circumscribe the ALJ's flexibility to set the hearing calendar.

Comment: A couple of comments objected that the time frame for notice of a pre-hearing conference provided for by proposed § 160.512 is inadequate to permit all necessary parties involved to prepare a response. One comment stated that the rule should extend the time frame to 25 business days, while the other suggested that the rule should require at least a 30-day notice of a pre-hearing conference.

Response: Section 160.512 does not prescribe 14 days as the amount of notice of a pre-hearing conference that must be given; rather, it simply establishes 14 days as the minimum amount of notice that is "reasonable." In our experience, 14 days should in most cases be sufficient for the parties to prepare for the conference adequately; however, nothing in the rule prohibits a party from requesting a longer period of time to prepare for a pre-hearing conference or the ALJ from granting such a request.

4. Section 160.516—Discovery

Proposed rule: Proposed § 160.516 would adopt § 160.538 of the April 17, 2003 interim final rule. As relevant here, proposed § 160.516 would permit requests for production of documents, but would not permit other forms of discovery, such as interrogatories, requests for admission, and depositions. Proposed paragraph (d) states that this section "may not be construed to require the disclosure of interview reports or statements obtained by any party, or on behalf of any party, of persons who will not be called as witnesses by that party, or analyses and summaries prepared in conjunction with the investigation or litigation of the case, or any otherwise privileged documents."

E. HIPAA Final Rules, Administrative Simplification Enforcement, continued

Final rule: The final rule adopts the provisions of the proposed rule.

Comment: Several comments recommended that proposed § 160.516 should be revised to allow requests for admissions, depositions, and written interrogatories in the discovery process. It was argued that permitting these forms of discovery would ensure that covered entities are able to mount a proper defense. It also was asserted that expert testimony will be necessary to establish both the alleged violation(s) and any affirmative defenses. Allowing such discovery would, it was asserted, help to produce a record, make appeals less likely, and potentially decrease the length of administrative hearings.

Response: We believe that the level of detail provided to a covered entity in the notice of proposed determination (including, where applicable, a copy of HHS's statistical expert's study), coupled with a right to request the production of documents for copying and inspection, provides the covered entity with the information reasonably required to mount its challenge to the proposed civil money penalty or to determine whether an affirmative defense applies. The additional discovery mentioned in the comments would result in delays and costs. Experience with the OIG regulation at 42 CFR 1005.7, which likewise does not authorize other types of discovery, has demonstrated that the discovery provided for is appropriate and sufficient.

Comment: Several comments argued that, at a minimum, depositions should be permitted at least with regard to expert witnesses, including the government's statistical expert. They asserted that, because depositions would not be permitted, covered entities would lose another potential opportunity to question the government's statistician in an effort to understand and defend against the conclusion and assumptions made in establishing the proposed civil money penalty, which would be prejudicial to the covered entity.

Response: We do not agree that depositions are necessary. Under § 160.420(a)(2), as adopted in this final rule, the study of HHS's statistical expert must be provided to the respondent with the notice of proposed determination.

Comment: A couple of comments criticized the proposed rule for not requiring that OCR and/or CMS hand over potentially exculpatory information to the entity being investigated. The obligation to provide exculpatory evidence should include handing over exculpatory interview reports or statements obtained by the government of persons who will not be called as witnesses by that party. It was recommended that this obligation be added to the final rule.

Response: The obligation to provide exculpatory evidence to an accused, which applies in criminal proceedings, is inapplicable in a HIPAA administrative simplification enforcement case.

Comment: One comment contended that § 160.516 should be revised to treat personal health information as privileged information not subject to discovery, since hearings are open to the public under proposed § 160.534.

Response: A covered entity concerned with potential public access to protected health information may raise the issue before the ALJ and seek a protective order under § 160.512(b)(11). Depending on the circumstances, an ALJ may require the information to be de-identified or direct identifiers to be stripped to protect the privacy of individuals or order other protections routinely afforded to similarly confidential information within the litigation forum, such as protective orders on the use of the information in public portions of the proceedings. In addition, the ALJ may, for good cause shown, order appropriate redactions made to the record after hearing. *See* § 160.542(d).

5. Section 160.518—Exchange of Witness Lists, Witness Statements, and Exhibits

Proposed rule: Proposed § 160.518 would carry forward § 160.540, as adopted by the April 17, 2003 interim final rule, with one substantive change. It would revise paragraph (a) to provide time limits within which the exchange of witness lists, statements, and exhibits must occur prior to a hearing. Under proposed § 160.518(a), these items must be exchanged not more than 60, but not less than 15, days prior to the scheduled hearing.

Final rule: The final rule revises this provision to require that, where a respondent retains a statistical expert for the purpose of challenging the Secretary's statistical sampling, a report by the respondent's expert be provided to the Secretarial party not less than 30 days prior to the hearing.

Comment: Several comments criticized the time frames of proposed § 160.518 as problematic in light of the anticipated use of statistical sampling. They argued that, if HHS uses statistical sampling to determine the number of violations and to establish its prima facie case against a covered entity, the covered entity must have a fair opportunity to rebut this evidence. That fair opportunity should permit the addition of rebuttal witnesses, statements and exhibits after the 15-day period and/or requiring the government to provide more detailed information to the covered entity regarding its statistical sampling calculations, methodology and assumptions at a time that is sufficiently prior to the 15-day deadline. The comments requested that the time frames listed in the regulation be increased to allow a covered entity adequate time to prepare for a hearing. Specifically, the comments urged that witness lists, statements, and exhibits for a hearing be exchanged by the parties not more than 60 days and not less than 30 days before a scheduled hearing date.

Response: We have accommodated the concern that the details of HHS's statistical study will not be made available early enough in the proceeding to allow a fair opportunity for rebuttal by requiring in § 160.420(a)(2) that a copy of the study be given to the respondent with the notice of proposed determination. Accordingly, under such circumstances, there should not be a problem identifying who respondent should call as a rebuttal witness within the time frames set out in this section.

We revise § 160.518(a) to require the respondent to provide to HHS a copy of the report of its statistical expert not less than 30 days before the scheduled hearing. This will give the Secretarial party adequate time to prepare the statistical part of its case and is reasonable in light of the fact that the respondent is given HHS's statistical study at the commencement of the proceeding.

Comment: With respect to proposed § 160.518(b)(2), one comment asked what would constitute extraordinary circumstances. The comment stated that this standard seems unnecessarily high and that "good cause" would be a more reasonable and fairer standard, given the need for covered entities to rebut the evidence of a statistical expert whose information they will not receive until the exchange of witnesses and exhibits.

Response: The decision concerning what is sufficient to convince the ALJ that extraordinary circumstances exist will be case-specific. The justification for lowering the standard no longer applies, given our change to § 160.420. Accordingly, we retain the "extraordinary circumstances" standard to emphasize the importance of observing the time frame for the exchange of such information.

E. HIPAA Final Rules, Administrative Simplification Enforcement, continued

6. Section 160.520—Subpoenas for Attendance at Hearing

Proposed rule: Proposed § 160.520 would carry forward § 160.542, as adopted by the April 17, 2003 interim final rule, mainly unchanged. Proposed § 160.520 would clarify that when a subpoena is served on HHS, the Secretary may comply with the subpoena by designating any knowledgeable representative to testify. Proposed § 160.520(d) would require a party seeking a subpoena to file a written motion not less than 30 days before the scheduled hearing, unless otherwise allowed by the ALJ for good cause shown; the paragraph specified what such a motion must contain.

Final rule: The final rule adopts the provisions of the proposed rule.

Comment: One comment asked that the language in proposed § 160.520(c) be modified to provide that, if a respondent subpoenas a particular employee or official with specific knowledge of the case at hand, the identified employee or official would be required to testify. While acknowledging that it was reasonable for HHS to be able to substitute a witness if a respondent subpoenas an employee or official with no knowledge of the case (such as the Secretary), the comment argued that HHS should not have such discretion if the employee or official who is subpoenaed has specific knowledge of the case.

Response: We retain the provision as proposed, because it is necessary to permit the smooth conduct of government business. We do not agree that the provision will damage a respondent's ability to litigate his case, as the provision requires that, although the Secretary may designate an HHS representative, the person so designated must be "knowledgeable." That person may be the employee or official upon whom the subpoena was first served, if the Secretary determines that such person is the appropriate witness, possessed of the requisite knowledge to testify upon the issues which are the subject of the subpoena.

Comment: One comment stated concerns with the interplay of proposed § 160.538 with proposed § 160.520(d). Under proposed § 160.538(b), if a party seeks to admit the testimony of a witness in the form of a written statement, that statement must be provided to the other party "in a manner that allows sufficient time for the other party to subpoena the witness for cross-examination at the hearing." Under proposed § 160.520(d), "a party seeking a subpoena must file a written motion not less than 30 days before the

date fixed for the hearing, unless otherwise allowed by the ALJ for good cause shown." The comment argued that a party that wanted to subpoena a person whose written statement was being offered by the opposing party should not have the burden of showing good cause for moving for a subpoena less than 30 days before the hearing date. Instead, the party seeking to admit the written statement should be required to provide that statement to the other party more than 30 days before the hearing, so that the other party will have an opportunity to subpoena that witness under the procedures established by these regulations.

Response: We believe that the rules adequately provide for such a contingency, and so do not revise § 160.520 as requested. The party that seeks to introduce testimony, other than expert testimony, in the form of a written statement must provide the other party with a copy of the statement and the address of the witness in sufficient time to allow that other party to subpoena that witness for cross examination. Since § 160.520(d) requires that motions seeking a subpoena be filed not less than 30 days before the hearing, the witness statement and address should be provided in sufficient time to allow a timely motion to be made. In the event that such statement and/or address is not provided in sufficient time to allow for a timely motion, good cause for permitting the motion for subpoena to be made on fewer than 30 days notice would exist.

7. Section 160.522—Fees

Proposed rule: The proposed rule proposed in § 160.522 to carry forward unchanged § 160.544 of the April 17, 2003 interim final rule. The provision requires the party subpoenaing a witness to pay the cost of fees and mileage. Where the respondent is the party subpoenaing the witness, the check for such fees and mileage must accompany the subpoena when served, but the check is not required to accompany the subpoena where the party subpoenaing the witness is the Secretary.

Final rule: The final rule adopts the provisions of the proposed rule.

Comment: One comment requested clarification of this provision. Observing that proposed § 160.522 would require a check for specific fees to accompany the subpoena except when HHS issues such a subpoena, the comment questioned whether this meant that HHS would be required to reimburse someone they subpoenaed or whether the HHS reimbursement would come at a later

date. Further, if it was the case that HHS was not required to reimburse such fees, the comment asked why this is the case, since any other party would be required to reimburse those fees.

Response: HHS is required to, and will, pay to a subpoenaed witness the fees provided for in this section. The payment, however, need not accompany the subpoena. Instead, the party seeking to admit the witness, the respondent would bear the burden of proof with respect to: (1) Any affirmative defense, including those set out in section 1176(b) of the Act, as implemented by proposed § 160.410; (2) any challenge to the amount or scope of a proposed penalty under section 1128A(d), as implemented by proposed §§ 160.404–160.408, including mitigating factors; and (3) any contention that a proposed penalty should be reduced or waived under section 1176(b)(4), as implemented by § 160.412. The Secretary would have the burden of proof with respect to all other issues, including issues of liability and the factors considered as aggravating factors under proposed § 160.408 in determining the amount of penalties to be imposed. The burden of persuasion would be judged by a preponderance of the evidence (*i.e.*, it is more likely than not that the position advocated is true).

We also proposed a new § 160.534(d), which would provide that any party may present items or information, during its case in chief, that were discovered after the date of the notice of proposed determination or request for a hearing, as applicable. The admissibility of such proffered evidence would be governed generally by the provisions of proposed § 160.540, and be subject to the 15-day rule for the exchange of trial exhibits, witness lists and statements set out at proposed § 160.518(a). If any such evidence is offered by the Secretary, it would not be admissible, unless relevant and material to the findings of fact set forth in the notice of proposed determination, including circumstances that may increase such penalty. If any such evidence is offered by the respondent, it would not be admissible unless relevant and material to a

E. HIPAA Final Rules, Administrative Simplification Enforcement, continued

specific admission, denial, or explanation of a finding of fact, or to a specific circumstance or argument expressly stated in the respondent's request for hearing that are alleged to constitute grounds for any defense or the factual and legal basis for opposing or reducing the penalty.

Final rule: The final rule adopts the provisions of the proposed rule.

Comment: One comment recommended that proposed § 160.534(b)(1)(ii) (placing the burden of proof on the respondent with respect to any challenge to the amount of a proposed penalty pursuant to § 160.404–160.408, including mitigating factors) be deleted. It was argued that due process requires that HHS sustain the burden of going forward with evidence proving the amount of a proposed penalty and the burden of persuasion. It was also noted that this section would place on the respondent the burden of proof with respect to an issue that is unreviewable under proposed § 160.508(c)(5)—the selection of variables under § 160.406.

Response: We disagree that § 160.534(b)(1)(ii) violates the due process clause. Rather, it is consistent with the normal allocation of the burden of proof, in which the proponent of a fact or argument has the burden of proving it. Our change to § 160.508(c)(5) renders the remainder of the comment moot.

Comment: One comment suggested that § 160.534(c) be revised to require the ALJ, upon the request of either party, to close a public hearing that could result in disclosure of privacy or security information that should not be made public and seal the records.

Response: We agree that protecting protected health information is important and is an issue about which all parties and the ALJ should be concerned. However, administrative hearings are, in general, required to be open to the public. See, e.g., Detroit Free Press v. Ashcroft, 303 F.3d 681, 700 (6th Cir. 2002) (stating that INS deportation hearings and similar administrative proceedings are traditionally open to the public). An ALJ has means by which he can protect the privacy of protected health information to be introduced into evidence, if he determines that this should be done, including requiring redaction of identifying information and closing part of the hearing. In our view, the ALJ will be in the best position to balance the competing interests of the public's right to information and the privacy interests associated with any protected health information. Accordingly, we do not mandate closure of the hearing on request.

9. Section 160.536—Statistical Sampling

Proposed rule: Proposed § 160.536 would permit the Secretary to introduce the results of a statistical sampling study as evidence of the number of violations under proposed § 160.406(b), or, where appropriate, any factor considered in determining the amount of the civil money penalty under proposed § 160.408. If the estimation is based upon an appropriate sampling and employs valid statistical methods, it would constitute prima facie evidence of the number of violations or amount of the penalty sought that is a part of the Secretary's burden of proof. Such a showing would cause the burden of going forward to shift to the respondent, although the burden of persuasion would remain with the Secretary.

Final rule: The final rule adopts the provisions of the proposed rule.

Comment: Several comments argued that the proposed rule would significantly limit a covered entity's ability to challenge HHS's statistical evidence. Although proposed § 160.420(a)(2) would require HHS, in the notice of proposed determination, to describe the sampling technique used by the Secretary, it is unclear what constitutes a "brief" description, and a brief description will most likely be insufficient to provide the covered entity with enough information to mount an adequate challenge. Because the covered entity may not receive a copy of the actual statistical study until 15 days before the hearing, it would have a very short period of time in which to review, investigate, critique, and/or rebut the statistical study. Because proposed § 160.516 would prohibit the taking of depositions, there would be no way to subject the HHS's statistical expert to adverse examination until the hearing, if then. The comments requested that proposed § 160.536 be deleted or, alternatively, the rule be revised to permit depositions of HHS's statistical expert and require HHS to give covered entities more detail of the technique utilized in sufficient time to allow entities to provide a meaningful defense and rebuttal.

Response: We recognize the concern that to make an effective challenge to the Secretary's introduction of the results of a statistical study, a covered entity should be provided with the details of that study early in the proceeding. Accordingly, we have revised proposed § 160.420(a)(2) to require HHS to provide a copy of the study relied upon to the respondent with the notice of proposed determination. Further, we have revised proposed § 160.504(b) to enlarge the

time within which a respondent seeking a hearing before an ALJ must mail its request for hearing from 60 to 90 days. We do not agree that depositions, which are expensive and time consuming, are required; the statistical study relied upon will be given to respondent with the notice of proposed determination, allowing an adequate amount of time to prepare any opposition thereto.

Comment: Several comments contended that permitting proof of violations by statistical sampling violates basic notions of due process and fundamental fairness, in that either a violation is provable or it is not. The comments raised the following specific objections on this ground. Statistical sampling merely estimates the number of violations that could have occurred and should not be used as a "short cut" for appropriate investigation and review. The determination of any variable used to calculate the number of violations should be based on an objective standard. The proposed approach would not treat all covered entities the same. The following example was provided to illustrate this latter concern. Suppose that a dentist had 3,000 patients of record, and that seven percent of those patients, or 210, did not receive a Notice of Privacy Practices. Suppose that a sample of 100 of the 3,000 patients was examined by HHS, and it was determined that 15 did not receive a notice. A statistical inference from this sample would estimate that 600, or 15 percent of all patients of record, did not receive a notice, even though in fact only 210 had not received a notice. Under § 160.536, the provider could be charged for 600 violations. While, on average, the sampling approach would yield the correct estimate of all providers, it would not necessarily be correct for any specific provider, which would be unfair to the individual providers involved.

Response: The use of sampling and statistical methods is recognized under Fed. R. Evid. 702 and under 42 CFR 1003.133 of the OIG rules, upon which the language of this section is based. The respondent may challenge whether the estimation offered by the Secretary is based upon a valid sample and employs valid statistical methods or may otherwise rebut the statistical evidence submitted. In the example cited by the comment, the respondent also could rebut the results with evidence that the actual number of violations is less than the estimate derived from the statistical sample.

With respect to the concerns regarding the fairness and appropriateness of using statistical

E. HIPAA Final Rules, Administrative Simplification Enforcement, continued

sampling to determine the number of violations, HHS will use sampling methods which follow recognized scientific guidelines for statistical validity and precision. These methods would be applicable to all types of covered entities and will objectively measure the number of violations by a covered entity or the number of occurrences of a particular aggravating circumstance. Because of the wide range of possible violations, however, we cannot at this time present specific sampling designs or levels of acceptable precision. However, the methodology employed will be documented and made available in the statistical sampling study provided with the notice of proposed determination.

Comment: Several comments argued that the use of statistical sampling is inappropriate to determine violations of the HIPAA rules. A couple of comments argued that, because of the many variables and discretionary considerations that can go into determining that a violation has occurred, and because many complaints or investigations will relate to individual circumstances, using statistical sampling to determine the number of violations is not appropriate. Another comment gave as an example of this problem Privacy Rule violations involving disclosure of protected health information beyond the "minimum necessary;" it asserted that the number of such violations cannot be adequately assessed through a statistical sample. Use of statistical sampling in such a case could preclude a covered entity from asserting its fact-based affirmative defenses. It was argued that statistical sampling is appropriate for use in estimating averages, but is not appropriate for determining the number of violations by a specific covered entity.

Response: As noted above, statistical sampling is recognized under the Federal Rules of Evidence and other HHS regulations. See, *e.g.*, 42 CFR 1003.133. The results, if based upon an appropriate sampling and computed by valid statistical methods, are only prima facie evidence of the number of violations or the existence of factors material to the proposed civil money penalty. The respondent may challenge the adequacy or size of the sample or the statistical methods employed, and may offer other evidence to rebut the results derived through the statistical methodology.

We do not agree that statistical methods are, per se, inappropriate for determining the number of violations that have occurred. For example, suppose that a health plan with a large

volume of electronic claims is found to have required providers to include on such claims a data element which is not part of the standard. A sample of the claims would be selected, and the percentage of claims found to be in violation of the standard would be computed from the sample and projected to the universe of claims for the year to establish the total number of violations of the standard in the calendar year. Of course, HHS's statistical methods would have to pass muster, and a respondent could challenge the statistical results, on normal statistical grounds, *e.g.*, that the sample size was insufficient, that the sample was not representative, and so on.

Comment: Several comments contended that, by allowing statistical sampling to be introduced at a hearing, proposed § 160.536 directly contradicts the language of § 160.508, which does not allow an ALJ to review issues under the Secretary's discretion, which includes calculating the number of violations. Other comments stated that, in the event that statistical sampling is used by HHS to determine the number of violations, it should be subject to ALJ review and that insulating it from review would increase the potential for abuse exponentially.

Response: Proposed § 160.508(c) has been revised to permit the ALJ to review the Secretary's calculation of the number of violations of an identical administrative simplification provision under § 160.406. If statistical sampling is employed to determine the number of violations, the results are subject to challenge before the ALJ.

Comment: The provision of proposed § 160.536 limiting statistical studies to those "based upon an appropriate sampling and computed by valid statistical methods" was criticized. It was noted that no criteria for validity are given, even though the comments by the agency specifically acknowledge the danger of extrapolating from small sample sizes. It also was argued that the appropriateness and validity of such sampling techniques are left to the discretion of the Secretary, who will employ criteria known only to the Secretary. It was recommended that statistical sampling not be permitted without clearer guidelines or more flexibility to challenge the study at an early stage, before significant investment of resources.

Response: By requiring that appropriate sampling and valid statistical methods be employed, HHS is mirroring the standard by which the reliability of such expert testimony is assessed under Fed. R. Evid. 702. If

statistical sampling is employed to determine the number of violations of an administrative simplification provision in a calendar year, such determination is subject to review by the ALJ. With respect to a respondent's ability to challenge the study at an earlier stage, under § 160.420(a)(2), a copy of the study relied upon will be provided to the respondent with the notice of proposed determination.

10. Section 160.538—Witnesses

Proposed rule: Proposed § 160.538 would carry forward unchanged § 160.556, as adopted by the April 17, 2003 interim final rule. As relevant here, paragraph (b) provides that, at the discretion of the ALJ and subject to certain conditions, testimony of witnesses other than the testimony of expert witnesses may be admitted in the form of a written statement and the ALJ may, at his discretion, admit prior sworn testimony of experts that has been subject to adverse examination.

Final rule: The final rule adopts the provisions of the proposed rule, except that the fourth sentence of proposed § 160.538(b) is placed before the second sentence of proposed § 160.538(b).

Comment: One comment stated that it was unclear whether the government's statistician could even be required to testify; rather, it appeared that the government could rely solely on the expert's prior testimony in other cases and/or the expert's report. Because depositions are not allowed, this provision must mean that testimony from experts in other cases may be used. It was argued that this would be prejudicial, because the covered entity will not have had an opportunity to subject the testimony to adverse examination and the facts of different cases would likely not be identical. Therefore, the expert testimony in one case may not be appropriate for use in a different case. It was recommended that this section be revised to require, at the covered entity's request, the testimony at the hearing of the government's statistical expert and prohibit the use of prior sworn testimony of experts unless from the specific case at issue.

Response: HHS expects that its statistical expert will testify at the hearing. Moreover, the respondent may move the ALJ to subpoena HHS's statistical expert to appear and testify at the hearing. See § 160.520.

Comment: One comment stated that, when §§ 160.538 and 160.516(b) are read together, they would permit an expert's testimony, taken under oath in a different case, to be admitted into

E. HIPAA Final Rules, Administrative Simplification Enforcement, continued

evidence, leaving the respondent with no chance to question the expert.

Response: We recognize the concern raised, which we believe arises out of an inadvertent transposition of a sentence in the text of proposed § 160.538(b). We intended that the subsection's text mirror that of the OIG regulation at 45 CFR 1005.16(b) by ending with the following: "Any such written statement must be provided to the other party, along with the last known address of the witness, in a manner that allows sufficient time for the other party to subpoena the witness for cross-examination at the hearing. Prior written statements of witnesses proposed to testify at the hearing must be exchanged as provided in § 160.518." We have corrected this error. As the rule now reads, the prior sworn testimony of an expert will be treated like any other witness's statement that a party proposes to offer in lieu of testimony at the hearing: a copy must be provided to the other party along with the witness's address in sufficient time to permit such other party to subpoena and question that witness at the hearing.

11. Section 160.540—Evidence

Proposed rule: Proposed § 160.540 would carry forward unchanged § 160.558, which was adopted by the April 17, 2003 interim final rule. Paragraph (b) of this section provides that the ALJ is not bound by the Federal Rules of Evidence, except as provided in the subpart.

Final rule: The final rule adopts the provisions of the proposed rule.

Comment: One comment argued that proposed § 160.540(b) should be revised. The comment stated that the optional use of the Federal Rules of Evidence is insufficient and would not allow entities to know what evidence will be admissible at the hearing or what rules of evidence will apply. At a minimum, it was argued, the use of hearsay should be prohibited except pursuant to the hearsay exceptions of the Federal Rules of Evidence.

Response: The Administrative Procedure Act does not require HHS to apply the Federal Rules of Evidence to limit the discretion of ALJs to admit evidence at hearings. See 5 U.S.C. 556(d). To be admissible, evidence need only be relevant, material, reliable, and probative. However, the ALJ may apply the Federal Rules of Evidence, where appropriate. Examples of situations where use of the Federal Rules of Evidence might be appropriate would include to exclude unreliable evidence, to weigh the probative value of evidence against the risks attending its admission, to determine whether a Federal

privilege exists, or to determine whether the evidence relates to an offered compromise and settlement, which would be inadmissible under Fed. R. Evid. 408.

Comment: One comment argued that proposed § 160.540(g) should be deleted. It was argued that this provision is inconsistent with the six-year time limit in § 160.414, in that it permits admission at the hearing of "crimes, wrongs or acts" without limit as to when they may have occurred. The comment stated that acts or other behaviors that are not the subject of civil money penalties are not relevant factors in determining the penalties that should be imposed, nor are they proof that the prohibited activity occurred. The Secretary is not required in a civil administrative proceeding to prove intent or mens rea.

Response: We believe that evidence of prior bad acts, admitted for the purposes listed (which are consistent with Fed. R. Evid. 404(b)) may be relevant and material in particular cases and, thus, should not be categorically excluded, as suggested. For instance, such evidence may be relevant and material to proving a covered entity's knowledge of the violation or aggravating circumstances affecting the amount of the civil money penalty imposed. In the latter case, for example, the evidence would be admitted to prove the aggravating circumstances and not the actual violations at issue; thus, the statute of limitations would not apply with respect to the bad acts. (We note, however, that prior bad acts unrelated to the covered entity's compliance with the HIPAA provisions or rules would not be admissible to prove aggravating circumstances under § 160.408(d).)

Comment: Another comment argued that proposed § 160.540(g) should be deleted, but if retained, such evidence should be reviewable under the other criteria for admissibility of proposed § 160.540, and HHS should be required to provide advance notice of its intent to present such evidence.

Response: Evidence of prior bad acts would be subject to the same criteria for admissibility as other evidence offered at the hearing—for instance, whether the probative value of such evidence is substantially outweighed by its potential for prejudice. Such evidence is also subject to the rules regarding notice that apply to other evidence; see, *e.g.,* §§ 160.420(a)(5), 160.516, and 160.518.

12. Section 160.542—The Record

Proposed rule: This section would carry forward unchanged § 160.560, adopted by the April 17, 2003 interim final rule. Since the section provides

that the record of the proceedings be transcribed, we proposed to add to paragraph (a) of this section a requirement that the cost of transcription of the record be borne equally by the parties, in the interest of fairness.

Final rule: The final rule adopts the provisions of the proposed rule, except that paragraph (a) is revised to clarify that if a party requests a copy of the transcript of the hearing proceedings it must pay the cost of such transcript, unless such payment is waived by the ALJ or the Board for good cause shown.

Comment: One comment recommended that this fee be assessed at the end of the investigation and assumed by the responsible party based on the outcome of the investigation. Another comment requested that HHS bear the cost of the court reporter's appearance (as opposed to the cost of copies).

Response: We acknowledge that the language of proposed paragraph (a) suggested that there is a fee or cost for a court reporter's appearance, in addition to the cost of obtaining a copy of the transcript of the hearing proceedings. As there is no such additional cost, we have revised paragraph (a) to state that a party that requests a copy of the transcript of hearing is required to pay the cost of preparing such transcript. We have also added a provision that will permit the ALJ or the Board, for good cause shown, to waive the cost of obtaining the transcript.

13. Section 160.546—ALJ Decision

Proposed rule: The proposed rule proposed that the ALJ decision would be the initial decision of the Secretary, rather than the final decision of the Secretary as set forth in § 160.564(d) of the April 17, 2003 interim final rule. Thus, we proposed to revise paragraph (d) to provide that the decision of the ALJ will be final and binding on the parties 60 days from the date of service of the ALJ decision, unless it is timely appealed by either party.

Final rule: The final rule adopts the provisions of the proposed rule.

Comment: One comment requested that the section be revised to provide that the ALJ could not increase a penalty beyond the statutory cap of section 1176(a)(1).

Response: The ALJ is bound by both the statute and the regulations, which both explicitly address this issue. Section 1176(a)(1) states that "the total amount imposed on the person for all violations of an identical requirement or prohibition during a calendar year may not exceed $25,000." Section

E. HIPAA Final Rules, Administrative Simplification Enforcement, continued

160.404(b)(1)(ii) states that the Secretary may not impose a civil money penalty in excess of $25,000 for identical violations during a calendar year.

In light of these explicit provisions, we do not agree that the suggested change is necessary.

14. Section 160.548—Appeal of the ALJ Decision

Proposed rule: Proposed § 160.548 would provide that any party may appeal the initial decision of the ALJ to the Board within 30 days of the date of service of the ALJ initial decision, unless extended for good cause. The appealing party must file a written brief specifying its exceptions to the initial decision. The opposing party may file an opposition brief, which is limited to the exceptions raised in the brief accompanying notice of appeal and any relevant issues not addressed in said exceptions and must be filed within 30 days of receiving the appealing party's notice of appeal and brief. The appealing party may, if permitted by the Board, file a reply brief. These briefs may be the only means that the parties will have to present their case to the Board, since there is no right to appear personally before the Board. The proposed rule provided that if a party demonstrates that additional evidence is material and relevant and there are reasonable grounds why such evidence was not introduced at the ALJ hearing, the Board may remand the case to the ALJ for consideration of the additional evidence. In an appeal to the Board, the standard of review on a disputed issue of fact would be whether the ALJ's initial decision is supported by substantial evidence on the record as a whole; on a disputed issue of law, the standard of review is whether the ALJ's initial decision is erroneous. The Board could decline review, affirm, increase, reduce, or reverse any penalty, or remand a penalty determination to the ALJ.

Under proposed § 160.548(i), the Board must serve its decision on the parties within 60 days after final briefs are filed. The decision of the Board becomes the final decision of the Secretary 60 days after service of the decision, except where the decision is to remand to the ALJ or a party requests reconsideration before the decision becomes final. Proposed § 160.548(j) provides that a party may request reconsideration of the Board's decision, provides a reconsideration process, and provides that the Board's reconsideration decision becomes final on service. The decision of the Board constitutes the final decision of the Secretary from which a petition for judicial review may be filed by a respondent aggrieved by the Board's decision. Proposed § 160.548(k) provides for a petition for judicial review of a final decision of the Secretary.

Final rule: The final rule adopts the provisions of the proposed rule, except that paragraph (e) is revised to make it consistent with the revision to § 160.504(c). The revision would permit the Board to consider an affirmative defense under § 160.410(b)(1) that is raised for the first time before the Board. Thus, under paragraph (f) of this section, the Board could, but would not be required to, remand the case to the ALJ for consideration of any evidence adduced with respect to such defense.

Comment: One comment was received on this section. It requested that the section be revised to provide that the Board could not increase a penalty beyond the statutory cap of section 1176(a)(1).

Response: We do not agree that such a provision is necessary, for the reasons discussed in the preceding section.

15. Section 160.552—Harmless Error

Proposed rule: Proposed § 160.552 proposed to adopt the "harmless error" rule that applies to civil litigation in Federal courts. The provision would provide, in general, that the ALJ and the Board at every stage of the proceeding will disregard any error or defect in the proceeding that does not affect the substantial rights of the parties.

Final rule: The final rule adopts the provisions of the proposed rule.

Comment: One comment asked for further guidance on, and clarification of, this provision. Another comment stated that the provision was far too broad, particularly given the limited discovery available to covered entities. Concern was expressed that the rule would severely limit a covered entity's ability to appeal an adverse ruling.

Response: The proposed rule was modeled after Fed. R. Civ. P. 61 and 42 CFR 1005.23 of the OIG regulations. It is a common provision in procedural rules that govern civil and administrative adjudications and is intended to promote efficiency in the resolution of disputes. If a respondent seeks an appeal because of an error that affects the party's substantive rights or the case's outcome, this section would not be applicable. Thus, we do not agree that it would severely limit a covered entity's ability to appeal an adverse ruling, and we adopt the section as proposed.

IV. Impact Statement and Other Required Analyses

Comment: Only one comment was received on the impact and other required analyses of the proposed rule (see 70 FR 20247–49). The comment asserted that HHS was declaring itself exempt from complying with the Paperwork Reduction Act, the Regulatory Flexibility Act, the Unfunded Mandates Reform Act of 1995, the Small Business Regulatory Enforcement and Fairness Act, and Executive Order 13132, and that an effort to compute vigorously the range of potential effects is needed to assure agency accountability.

Response: The comment misstates the position HHS took in the proposed rules concerning these laws. HHS does not consider itself, or the Enforcement Rule, exempt from these laws. However, each of these laws covers only certain types of rules and agency actions. For the reasons stated in the proposed rule and summarized below, those laws do not apply to the particular actions taken with respect to this rule. The comment provides no substantive grounds for altering our prior conclusions with respect to these laws.

A. Paperwork Reduction Act

We reviewed this final rule to determine whether it raises issues that would subject it to the Paperwork Reduction Act (PRA). Since the final rule comes within the exemption of 5 CFR 1320.4(a), as it deals entirely with administrative investigations and actions against specific individuals or entities, it need not be reviewed by the Office of Management and Budget under the authority of the PRA.

B. Executive Order 12866; Regulatory Flexibility Act; Unfunded Mandates Reform Act of 1995; Small Business Regulatory Enforcement Fairness Act of 1996; Executive Order 13132

We have examined the impacts of this final rule as required by Executive Order 12866 (September 1993, Regulatory Planning and Review), the Regulatory Flexibility Act (RFA) (September 16, 1980, Pub. L. 96–354), the Unfunded Mandates Reform Act of 1995 (Pub. L. 104–4), the Small Business Regulatory Enforcement and Fairness Act, 5 U.S.C. 801, et seq., and Executive Order 13132.

1. Executive Order 12866

Executive Order 12866 (as amended by Executive Order 13258, which merely reassigns responsibility of duties) directs agencies to assess all costs and benefits of available regulatory alternatives and, if regulation is

E. HIPAA Final Rules, Administrative Simplification Enforcement, continued

necessary, to select regulatory approaches that maximize net benefits (including potential economic, environmental, public health and safety effects, distributive impacts, and equity). Executive Order 12866 defines, at section 3(f), several categories of "significant regulatory actions." One category is "economically significant" rules, which are defined in section 3(f)(1) of the Order as rules that may "have an annual effect on the economy of $100 million or more, or adversely affect in a material way the economy, productivity, competition, jobs, the environment, public health or safety, or State, local, or tribal governments or communities." Another category, under section 3(f)(4) of the Order, consists of rules that are "significant regulatory actions" because they "raise novel legal or policy issues arising out of legal mandates, the President's priorities, or the principles set forth in this Executive Order." Executive Order 12866 requires a full economic impact analysis only for "economically significant" rules under section 3(f)(1). For the reasons stated at 70 FR 20248–49, we have concluded that this rule should be treated as a "significant regulatory action" within the meaning of section 3(f)(4) of Executive Order 12866, but that the impact of this rule is not such that it reaches the economically significant threshold under section 3(f)(1) of the Order.

We note, with regard to our prior analysis, that our ongoing experiences with HIPAA complaints bears out our experience to July 2004, which was discussed at 70 FR 20248. As of October 31, 2005, OCR had received and initiated review of over 16,000 complaints and had closed 68 percent of the complaints; at the same time, CMS had received and initiated review of 413 complaints and closed 67 percent of the complaints. Thus, we continue to be of the view that the costs attributable to the provisions of this rule will, in most cases that are opened, be low. We likewise continue to believe, for the reasons stated at 70 FR 20249, that the value of the benefits brought by the HIPAA provisions are sufficient to warrant appropriate enforcement efforts and that the benefits of these protections far outweigh the costs of this enforcement regulation.

Thus, in most cases, if covered entities comply with the various HIPAA rules, they should not incur any significant additional costs as a result of the Enforcement Rule. This is based on the fact the costs intrinsic to most of the HIPAA rules and operating directions against which compliance is evaluated have been scored independently of this

rule, and those requirements are not changed by this rule. We recognize that the specific requirements against which compliance is evaluated are not yet well known and may evolve with experience under HIPAA, but we expect that covered entities have both the ability and expectation to maintain compliance, especially given our commitment to encouraging and facilitating voluntary compliance. While not straightforward to project, it seems likely that the number of times in which the full civil money penalty enforcement process will be invoked will be extremely small, based on the evidence to date.

2. Other Analyses

We also examined the impact of this rule as required by the Regulatory Flexibility Act (RFA). The RFA requires agencies to determine whether a rule will have a significant economic impact on a substantial number of small entities. For purposes of the RFA, small entities include small businesses, nonprofit organizations, and government jurisdictions; for health care entities, the size standard for a "small" entity ranges from $6 million to $29 million in revenues in any one year. For the reasons discussed at 70 FR 20249, the Secretary certifies that this rule will not have a significant economic impact on a substantial number of small entities.

Section 202 of the Unfunded Mandates Reform Act of 1995, 2 U.S.C. 1531 *et seq.*, also requires that agencies assess anticipated costs and benefits before issuing any rule that may result in expenditure in any one year by State, local, or tribal governments, in the aggregate, or by the private sector, of $100 million, adjusted for inflation. The Small Business Regulatory Enforcement Fairness Act of 1996 (SBREFA), 5 U.S.C. 801, *et seq.*, requires that rules that will have an impact on the economy of $100 million or more per annum be submitted for Congressional review. For the reasons discussed above and at 70 FR 20248–49, this rule will not impose a burden large enough to require a section 202 statement under the Unfunded Mandates Reform Act of 1995 or Congressional review under SBREFA.

Executive Order 13132 establishes certain requirements that an agency must meet when it adopts a final rule that imposes substantial direct requirement costs on State and local governments, preempts State law, or otherwise has Federalism implications. This final rule does not have "Federalism implications, " as it will not have "substantial direct effects on the States, on the relationship between

the national government and the States, or on the distribution of power and responsibilities among the various levels of government," nor, for the reasons previously explained, will it have substantial economic effects would not be substantial, while any preemption of State law that could occur would be a function of the underlying HIPAA rules, not this rule. Therefore, the Enforcement Rule is not subject to Executive Order 13132 (Federalism).

Dated: December 20, 2005.

Michael O. Leavitt,
Secretary.

List of Subjects

45 CFR Part 160

Administrative practice and procedure, Computer technology, Electronic transactions, Employer benefit plan, Health, Health care, Health facilities, Health insurance, Health records, Hospitals, Investigations, Medicaid, Medical research, Medicare, Penalties, Privacy, Reporting and record keeping requirements, Security.

45 CFR Part 164

Administrative practice and procedure, Electronic information system, Electronic transactions, Employer benefit plan, Health, Health care, Health facilities, Health Insurance, Health records, Hospitals, Medicaid, Medical research, Medicare, Privacy, Reporting and record keeping requirements, Security.

■ For the reasons set forth in the preamble, the Department of Health and Human Services amends 45 CFR subtitle A, subchapter C, parts 160 and 164, as set forth below.

PART 160—GENERAL ADMINISTRATIVE REQUIREMENTS

■ 1. The authority citation for part 160 is revised to read as follows:

Authority: 42 U.S.C. 1302(a), 42 U.S.C. 1320d—1320d–8, sec. 264 of Pub. L.104–191, 110 Stat. 2033–2034 (42 U.S.C. 1320d–2 (note)), and 5 U.S.C. 552.

■ 2. Add to § 160.103 in alphabetical order the definition of "Person" to read as follows:

§ 160.103   Definitions.

*   *   *   *   *

"Person" means a natural person, trust or estate, partnership, corporation, professional association or corporation, or other entity, public or private.

*   *   *   *   *

■ 3. Revise subpart C to read as follows:

E. HIPAA Final Rules, Administrative Simplification Enforcement, continued

Federal Register / Vol. 71, No. 32 / Thursday, February 16, 2006 / Rules and Regulations   8425

Subpart C—Compliance and Investigations

§ 160.300 Applicability.

This subpart applies to actions by the Secretary, covered entities, and others with respect to ascertaining the compliance by covered entities with, and the enforcement of, the applicable provisions of this part 160 and parts 162 and 164 of this subchapter.

§ 160.302 Definitions.

As used in this subpart and subparts D and E of this part, the following terms have the following meanings:

Administrative simplification provision means any requirement or prohibition established by:

(1) 42 U.S.C. 1320d—1320d–4, 1320d–7, and 1320d–8;

(2) Section 264 of Pub. L. 104–191; or

(3) This subchapter.

ALJ means Administrative Law Judge.

Civil money penalty or *penalty* means the amount determined under § 160.404 of this part and includes the plural of these terms.

Respondent means a covered entity upon which the Secretary has imposed, or proposes to impose, a civil money penalty.

Violation or *violate* means, as the context may require, failure to comply with an administrative simplification provision.

§ 160.304 Principles for achieving compliance.

(a) *Cooperation.* The Secretary will, to the extent practicable, seek the cooperation of covered entities in obtaining compliance with the applicable administrative simplification provisions.

(b) *Assistance.* The Secretary may provide technical assistance to covered entities to help them comply voluntarily with the applicable administrative simplification provisions.

§ 160.306 Complaints to the Secretary.

(a) *Right to file a complaint.* A person who believes a covered entity is not complying with the administrative simplification provisions may file a complaint with the Secretary.

(b) *Requirements for filing complaints.* Complaints under this section must meet the following requirements:

(1) A complaint must be filed in writing, either on paper or electronically.

(2) A complaint must name the person that is the subject of the complaint and describe the acts or omissions believed to be in violation of the applicable administrative simplification provision(s).

(3) A complaint must be filed within 180 days of when the complainant knew or should have known that the act or omission complained of occurred, unless this time limit is waived by the Secretary for good cause shown.

(4) The Secretary may prescribe additional procedures for the filing of complaints, as well as the place and manner of filing, by notice in the **Federal Register.**

(c) *Investigation.* The Secretary may investigate complaints filed under this section. Such investigation may include a review of the pertinent policies, procedures, or practices of the covered entity and of the circumstances regarding any alleged violation. At the time of initial written communication with the covered entity about the complaint, the Secretary will describe the act(s) and/or omission(s) that are the basis of the complaint.

§ 160.308 Compliance reviews.

The Secretary may conduct compliance reviews to determine whether covered entities are complying with the applicable administrative simplification provisions.

§ 160.310 Responsibilities of covered entities.

(a) *Provide records and compliance reports.* A covered entity must keep such records and submit such compliance reports, in such time and manner and containing such information, as the Secretary may determine to be necessary to enable the Secretary to ascertain whether the covered entity has complied or is complying with the applicable administrative simplification provisions.

(b) *Cooperate with complaint investigations and compliance reviews.* A covered entity must cooperate with the Secretary, if the Secretary undertakes an investigation or compliance review of the policies, procedures, or practices of the covered entity to determine whether it is complying with the applicable administrative simplification provisions.

(c) *Permit access to information.* (1) A covered entity must permit access by the Secretary during normal business hours to its facilities, books, records, accounts, and other sources of information, including protected health information, that are pertinent to ascertaining compliance with the applicable administrative simplification provisions. If the Secretary determines that exigent circumstances exist, such as when documents may be hidden or destroyed, a covered entity must permit access by the Secretary at any time and without notice.

(2) If any information required of a covered entity under this section is in the exclusive possession of any other agency, institution, or person and the other agency, institution, or person fails or refuses to furnish the information, the covered entity must so certify and set forth what efforts it has made to obtain the information.

(3) Protected health information obtained by the Secretary in connection with an investigation or compliance review under this subpart will not be disclosed by the Secretary, except if necessary for ascertaining or enforcing compliance with the applicable administrative simplification provisions, or if otherwise required by law.

§ 160.312 Secretarial action regarding complaints and compliance reviews.

(a) *Resolution when noncompliance is indicated.* (1) If an investigation of a complaint pursuant to § 160.306 or a compliance review pursuant to § 160.308 indicates noncompliance, the Secretary will attempt to reach a resolution of the matter satisfactory to the Secretary by informal means. Informal means may include demonstrated compliance or a completed corrective action plan or other agreement.

(2) If the matter is resolved by informal means, the Secretary will so inform the covered entity and, if the matter arose from a complaint, the complainant, in writing.

(3) If the matter is not resolved by informal means, the Secretary will—

(i) So inform the covered entity and provide the covered entity an opportunity to submit written evidence of any mitigating factors or affirmative defenses for consideration under §§ 160.408 and 160.410 of this part. The covered entity must submit any such evidence to the Secretary within 30 days (computed in the same manner as prescribed under § 160.526 of this part) of receipt of such notification; and

(ii) If, following action pursuant to paragraph (a)(3)(i) of this section, the

E. HIPAA Final Rules, Administrative Simplification Enforcement, continued

8426 Federal Register / Vol. 71, No. 32 / Thursday, February 16, 2006 / Rules and Regulations

Secretary finds that a civil money penalty should be imposed, inform the covered entity of such finding in a notice of proposed determination in accordance with § 160.420 of this part.

(b) *Resolution when no violation is found.* If, after an investigation pursuant to § 160.306 or a compliance review pursuant to § 160.308, the Secretary determines that further action is not warranted, the Secretary will so inform the covered entity and, if the matter arose from a complaint, the complainant, in writing.

§ 160.314 Investigational subpoenas and inquiries.

(a) The Secretary may issue subpoenas in accordance with 42 U.S.C. 405(d) and (e), 1320a–7a(j), and 1320d–5 to require the attendance and testimony of witnesses and the production of any other evidence during an investigation or compliance review pursuant to this part. For purposes of this paragraph, a person other than a natural person is termed an "entity."

(1) A subpoena issued under this paragraph must—

(i) State the name of the person (including the entity, if applicable) to whom the subpoena is addressed;

(ii) State the statutory authority for the subpoena;

(iii) Indicate the date, time, and place that the testimony will take place;

(iv) Include a reasonably specific description of any documents or items required to be produced; and

(v) If the subpoena is addressed to an entity, describe with reasonable particularity the subject matter on which testimony is required. In that event, the entity must designate one or more natural persons who will testify on its behalf, and must state as to each such person that person's name and address and the matters on which he or she will testify. The designated person must testify as to matters known or reasonably available to the entity.

(2) A subpoena under this section must be served by—

(i) Delivering a copy to the natural person named in the subpoena or to the entity named in the subpoena at its last principal place of business; or

(ii) Registered or certified mail addressed to the natural person at his or her last known dwelling place or to the entity at its last known principal place of business.

(3) A verified return by the natural person serving the subpoena setting forth the manner of service or, in the case of service by registered or certified mail, the signed return post office receipt, constitutes proof of service.

(4) Witnesses are entitled to the same fees and mileage as witnesses in the district courts of the United States (28 U.S.C. 1821 and 1825). Fees need not be paid at the time the subpoena is served.

(5) A subpoena under this section is enforceable through the district court of the United States for the district where the subpoenaed natural person resides or is found or where the entity transacts business.

(b) Investigational inquiries are non-public investigational proceedings conducted by the Secretary.

(1) Testimony at investigational inquiries will be taken under oath or affirmation.

(2) Attendance of non-witnesses is discretionary with the Secretary, except that a witness is entitled to be accompanied, represented, and advised by an attorney.

(3) Representatives of the Secretary are entitled to attend and ask questions.

(4) A witness will have the opportunity to clarify his or her answers on the record following questioning by the Secretary.

(5) Any claim of privilege must be asserted by the witness on the record.

(6) Objections must be asserted on the record. Errors of any kind that might be corrected if promptly presented will be deemed to be waived unless reasonable objection is made at the investigational inquiry. Except where the objection is on the grounds of privilege, the question will be answered on the record, subject to objection.

(7) If a witness refuses to answer any question not privileged or to produce requested documents or items, or engages in conduct likely to delay or obstruct the investigational inquiry, the Secretary may seek enforcement of the subpoena under paragraph (a)(5) of this section.

(8) The proceedings will be recorded and transcribed. The witness is entitled to a copy of the transcript, upon payment of prescribed costs, except that, for good cause, the witness may be limited to inspection of the official transcript of his or her testimony.

(9)(i) The transcript will be submitted to the witness for signature.

(A) Where the witness will be provided a copy of the transcript, the transcript will be submitted to the witness for signature. The witness may submit to the Secretary written proposed corrections to the transcript, with such corrections attached to the transcript. If the witness does not return a signed copy of the transcript or proposed corrections within 30 days (computed in the same manner as prescribed under § 160.526 of this part) of its being submitted to him or her for signature, the witness will be deemed to have agreed that the transcript is true and accurate.

(B) Where, as provided in paragraph (b)(8) of this section, the witness is limited to inspecting the transcript, the witness will have the opportunity at the time of inspection to propose corrections to the transcript, with corrections attached to the transcript. The witness will also have the opportunity to sign the transcript. If the witness does not sign the transcript or offer corrections within 30 days (computed in the same manner as prescribed under § 160.526 of this part) of receipt of notice of the opportunity to inspect the transcript, the witness will be deemed to have agreed that the transcript is true and accurate.

(ii) The Secretary's proposed corrections to the record of transcript will be attached to the transcript.

(c) Consistent with § 160.310(c)(3), testimony and other evidence obtained in an investigational inquiry may be used by HHS in any of its activities and may be used or offered into evidence in any administrative or judicial proceeding.

§ 160.316 Refraining from intimidation or retaliation.

A covered entity may not threaten, intimidate, coerce, harass, discriminate against, or take any other retaliatory action against any individual or other person for—

(a) Filing of a complaint under § 160.306;

(b) Testifying, assisting, or participating in an investigation, compliance review, proceeding, or hearing under this part; or

(c) Opposing any act or practice made unlawful by this subchapter, provided the individual or person has a good faith belief that the practice opposed is unlawful, and the manner of opposition is reasonable and does not involve a disclosure of protected health information in violation of subpart E of part 164 of this subchapter.

■ 4. Add a new subpart D to read as follows:

Subpart D—Imposition of Civil Money Penalties

E. HIPAA Final Rules, Administrative Simplification Enforcement, continued

160.420 Notice of proposed determination.
160.422 Failure to request a hearing.
160.424 Collection of penalty.
160.426 Notification of the public and other agencies.

§ 160.400 Applicability.

This subpart applies to the imposition of a civil money penalty by the Secretary under 42 U.S.C. 1320d–5.

§ 160.402 Basis for a civil money penalty.

(a) *General rule.* Subject to § 160.410, the Secretary will impose a civil money penalty upon a covered entity if the Secretary determines that the covered entity has violated an administrative simplification provision.

(b) *Violation by more than one covered entity.* (1) Except as provided in paragraph (b)(2) of this section, if the Secretary determines that more than one covered entity was responsible for a violation, the Secretary will impose a civil money penalty against each such covered entity.

(2) A covered entity that is a member of an affiliated covered entity, in accordance with § 164.105(b) of this subchapter, is jointly and severally liable for a civil money penalty for a violation of part 164 of this subchapter based on an act or omission of the affiliated covered entity, unless it is established that another member of the affiliated covered entity was responsible for the violation.

(c) *Violation attributed to a covered entity.* A covered entity is liable, in accordance with the federal common law of agency, for a civil money penalty for a violation based on the act or omission of any agent of the covered entity, including a workforce member, acting within the scope of the agency, unless—

(1) The agent is a business associate of the covered entity;

(2) The covered entity has complied, with respect to such business associate, with the applicable requirements of §§ 164.308(b) and 164.502(e) of this subchapter; and

(3) The covered entity did not—

(i) Know of a pattern of activity or practice of the business associate, and

(ii) Fail to act as required by §§ 164.314(a)(1)(ii) and 164.504(e)(1)(ii) of this subchapter, as applicable.

§ 160.404 Amount of a civil money penalty.

(a) The amount of a civil money penalty will be determined in accordance with paragraph (b) of this section and §§ 160.406, 160.408, and 160.412.

(b) The amount of a civil money penalty that may be imposed is subject to the following limitations:

(1) The Secretary may not impose a civil money penalty—

(i) In the amount of more than $100 for each violation; or

(ii) In excess of $25,000 for identical violations during a calendar year (January 1 through the following December 31).

(2) If a requirement or prohibition in one administrative simplification provision is repeated in a more general form in another administrative simplification provision in the same subpart, a civil money penalty may be imposed for a violation of only one of these administrative simplification provisions.

§ 160.406 Violations of an identical requirement or prohibition.

The Secretary will determine the number of violations of an administrative simplification provision based on the nature of the covered entity's obligation to act or not act under the provision that is violated, such as its obligation to act in a certain manner, or within a certain time, or to act or not act with respect to certain persons. In the case of continuing violation of a provision, a separate violation occurs each day the covered entity is in violation of the provision.

§ 160.408 Factors considered in determining the amount of a civil money penalty.

In determining the amount of any civil money penalty, the Secretary may consider as aggravating or mitigating factors, as appropriate, any of the following:

(a) The nature of the violation, in light of the purpose of the rule violated.

(b) The circumstances, including the consequences, of the violation, including but not limited to:

(1) The time period during which the violation(s) occurred;

(2) Whether the violation caused physical harm;

(3) Whether the violation hindered or facilitated an individual's ability to obtain health care; and

(4) Whether the violation resulted in financial harm.

(c) The degree of culpability of the covered entity, including but not limited to:

(1) Whether the violation was intentional; and

(2) Whether the violation was beyond the direct control of the covered entity.

(d) Any history of prior compliance with the administrative simplification provisions, including violations, by the covered entity, including but not limited to:

(1) Whether the current violation is the same or similar to prior violation(s);

(2) Whether and to what extent the covered entity has attempted to correct previous violations;

(3) How the covered entity has responded to technical assistance from the Secretary provided in the context of a compliance effort; and

(4) How the covered entity has responded to prior complaints.

(e) The financial condition of the covered entity, including but not limited to:

(1) Whether the covered entity had financial difficulties that affected its ability to comply;

(2) Whether the imposition of a civil money penalty would jeopardize the ability of the covered entity to continue to provide, or to pay for, health care; and

(3) The size of the covered entity.

(f) Such other matters as justice may require.

§ 160.410 Affirmative defenses.

(a) As used in this section, the following terms have the following meanings:

Reasonable cause means circumstances that would make it unreasonable for the covered entity, despite the exercise of ordinary business care and prudence, to comply with the administrative simplification provision violated.

Reasonable diligence means the business care and prudence expected from a person seeking to satisfy a legal requirement under similar circumstances.

Willful neglect means conscious, intentional failure or reckless indifference to the obligation to comply with the administrative simplification provision violated.

(b) The Secretary may not impose a civil money penalty on a covered entity for a violation if the covered entity establishes that an affirmative defense exists with respect to the violation, including the following:

(1) The violation is an act punishable under 42 U.S.C. 1320d–6;

(2) The covered entity establishes, to the satisfaction of the Secretary, that it did not have knowledge of the violation, determined in accordance with the federal common law of agency, and, by exercising reasonable diligence, would not have known that the violation occurred; or

(3) The violation is—

(i) Due to reasonable cause and not willful neglect; and

(ii) Corrected during either:

(A) The 30-day period beginning on the date the covered entity liable for the penalty knew, or by exercising reasonable diligence would have known, that the violation occurred; or

E. HIPAA Final Rules, Administrative Simplification Enforcement, continued

(B) Such additional period as the Secretary determines to be appropriate based on the nature and extent of the failure to comply.

§ 160.412 Waiver.

For violations described in § 160.410(b)(3)(i) that are not corrected within the period described in § 160.410(b)(3)(ii), the Secretary may waive the civil money penalty, in whole or in part, to the extent that payment of the penalty would be excessive relative to the violation.

§ 160.414 Limitations.

No action under this subpart may be entertained unless commenced by the Secretary, in accordance with § 160.420, within 6 years from the date of the occurrence of the violation.

§ 160.416 Authority to settle.

Nothing in this subpart limits the authority of the Secretary to settle any issue or case or to compromise any penalty.

§ 160.418 Penalty not exclusive.

Except as otherwise provided by 42 U.S.C. 1320d-5(b)(1), a penalty imposed under this part is in addition to any other penalty prescribed by law.

§ 160.420 Notice of proposed determination.

(a) If a penalty is proposed in accordance with this part, the Secretary must deliver, or send by certified mail with return receipt requested, to the respondent, written notice of the Secretary's intent to impose a penalty. This notice of proposed determination must include—

(1) Reference to the statutory basis for the penalty;

(2) A description of the findings of fact regarding the violations with respect to which the penalty is proposed (except that, in any case where the Secretary is relying upon a statistical sampling study in accordance with § 160.536 of this part, the notice must provide a copy of the study relied upon by the Secretary);

(3) The reason(s) why the violation(s) subject(s) the respondent to a penalty;

(4) The amount of the proposed penalty;

(5) Any circumstances described in § 160.408 that were considered in determining the amount of the proposed penalty; and

(6) Instructions for responding to the notice, including a statement of the respondent's right to a hearing, a statement that failure to request a hearing within 90 days permits the imposition of the proposed penalty without the right to a hearing under

§ 160.504 or a right of appeal under § 160.548 of this part, and the address to which the hearing request must be sent.

(b) The respondent may request a hearing before an ALJ on the proposed penalty by filing a request in accordance with § 160.504 of this part.

§ 160.422 Failure to request a hearing.

If the respondent does not request a hearing within the time prescribed by § 160.504 of this part and the matter is not settled pursuant to § 160.416, the Secretary will impose the proposed penalty or any lesser penalty permitted by 42 U.S.C. 1320d-5. The Secretary will notify the respondent by certified mail, return receipt requested, of any penalty that has been imposed and of the means by which the respondent may satisfy the penalty, and the penalty is final on receipt of the notice. The respondent has no right to appeal a penalty under § 160.548 of this part with respect to which the respondent has not timely requested a hearing.

§ 160.424 Collection of penalty.

(a) Once a determination of the Secretary to impose a penalty has become final, the penalty will be collected by the Secretary, subject to the first sentence of 42 U.S.C. 1320a-7a(f).

(b) The penalty may be recovered in a civil action brought in the United States district court for the district where the respondent resides, is found, or is located.

(c) The amount of a penalty, when finally determined, or the amount agreed upon in compromise, may be deducted from any sum then or later owing by the United States, or by a State agency, to the respondent.

(d) Matters that were raised or that could have been raised in a hearing before an ALJ, or in an appeal under 42 U.S.C. 1320a-7a(e), may not be raised as a defense in a civil action by the United States to collect a penalty under this part.

§ 160.426 Notification of the public and other agencies.

Whenever a proposed penalty becomes final, the Secretary will notify, in such manner as the Secretary deems appropriate, the public and the following organizations and entities thereof and the reason it was imposed: the appropriate State or local medical or professional organization, the appropriate State agency or agencies administering or supervising the administration of State health care programs (as defined in 42 U.S.C. 1320a-7(h)), the appropriate utilization and quality control peer review

organization, and the appropriate State or local licensing agency or organization (including the agency specified in 42 U.S.C. 1395aa(a), 1396a(a)(33)).

■ 5. Revise subpart E of this part to read as follows:

Subpart E—Procedures for Hearings

§ 160.500 Applicability.

This subpart applies to hearings conducted relating to the imposition of a civil money penalty by the Secretary under 42 U.S.C. 1320d-5.

§ 160.502 Definitions.

As used in this subpart, the following term has the following meaning:

Board means the members of the HHS Departmental Appeals Board, in the Office of the Secretary, who issue decisions in panels of three.

§ 160.504 Hearing before an ALJ.

(a) A respondent may request a hearing before an ALJ. The parties to the hearing proceeding consist of—

(1) The respondent; and

(2) The officer(s) or employee(s) of HHS to whom the enforcement authority involved has been delegated.

(b) The request for a hearing must be made in writing signed by the respondent or by the respondent's attorney and sent by certified mail, return receipt requested, to the address specified in the notice of proposed determination. The request for a hearing must be mailed within 90 days after notice of the proposed determination is received by the respondent. For purposes of this section, the

E. HIPAA Final Rules, Administrative Simplification Enforcement, continued

Federal Register / Vol. 71, No. 32 / Thursday, February 16, 2006 / Rules and Regulations   8429

respondent's date of receipt of the notice of proposed determination is presumed to be 5 days after the date of the notice unless the respondent makes a reasonable showing to the contrary to the ALJ.

(c) The request for a hearing must clearly and directly admit, deny, or explain each of the findings of fact contained in the notice of proposed determination with regard to which the respondent has any knowledge. If the respondent has no knowledge of a particular finding of fact and so states, the finding shall be deemed denied. The request for a hearing must also state the circumstances or arguments that the respondent alleges constitute the grounds for any defense and the factual and legal basis for opposing the penalty, except that a respondent may raise an affirmative defense under § 160.410(b)(1) at any time.

(d) The ALJ must dismiss a hearing request where—

(1) On motion of the Secretary, the ALJ determines that the respondent's hearing request is not timely filed as required by paragraphs (b) or does not meet the requirements of paragraph (c) of this section;

(2) The respondent withdraws the request for a hearing;

(3) The respondent abandons the request for a hearing; or

(4) The respondent's hearing request fails to raise any issue that may properly be addressed in a hearing.

§ 160.506   Rights of the parties.

(a) Except as otherwise limited by this subpart, each party may—

(1) Be accompanied, represented, and advised by an attorney;

(2) Participate in any conference held by the ALJ;

(3) Conduct discovery of documents as permitted by this subpart;

(4) Agree to stipulations of fact or law that will be made part of the record;

(5) Present evidence relevant to the issues at the hearing;

(6) Present and cross-examine witnesses;

(7) Present oral arguments at the hearing as permitted by the ALJ; and

(8) Submit written briefs and proposed findings of fact and conclusions of law after the hearing.

(b) A party may appear in person or by a representative. Natural persons who appear as an attorney or other representative must conform to the standards of conduct and ethics required of practitioners before the courts of the United States.

(c) Fees for any services performed on behalf of a party by an attorney are not subject to the provisions of 42 U.S.C. 406, which authorizes the Secretary to specify or limit their fees.

§ 160.508   Authority of the ALJ.

(a) The ALJ must conduct a fair and impartial hearing, avoid delay, maintain order, and ensure that a record of the proceeding is made.

(b) The ALJ may—

(1) Set and change the date, time and place of the hearing upon reasonable notice to the parties;

(2) Continue or recess the hearing in whole or in part for a reasonable period of time;

(3) Hold conferences to identify or simplify the issues, or to consider other matters that may aid in the expeditious disposition of the proceeding;

(4) Administer oaths and affirmations;

(5) Issue subpoenas requiring the attendance of witnesses at hearings and the production of documents at or in relation to hearings;

(6) Rule on motions and other procedural matters;

(7) Regulate the scope and timing of documentary discovery as permitted by this subpart;

(8) Regulate the course of the hearing and the conduct of representatives, parties, and witnesses;

(9) Examine witnesses;

(10) Receive, rule on, exclude, or limit evidence;

(11) Upon motion of a party, take official notice of facts;

(12) Conduct any conference, argument or hearing in person or, upon agreement of the parties, by telephone; and

(13) Upon motion of a party, decide cases, in whole or in part, by summary judgment where there is no disputed issue of material fact. A summary judgment decision constitutes a hearing on the record for the purposes of this subpart.

(c) The ALJ—

(1) May not find invalid or refuse to follow Federal statutes, regulations, or Secretarial delegations of authority and must give deference to published guidance to the extent not inconsistent with statute or regulation;

(2) May not enter an order in the nature of a directed verdict;

(3) May not compel settlement negotiations;

(4) May not enjoin any act of the Secretary; or

(5) May not review the exercise of discretion by the Secretary with respect to whether to grant an extension under § 160.410(b)(3)(ii)(B) of this part or to provide technical assistance under 42 U.S.C. 1320d–5(b)(3)(B).

§ 160.510   Ex parte contacts.

No party or person (except employees of the ALJ's office) may communicate in any way with the ALJ on any matter at issue in a case, unless on notice and opportunity for both parties to participate. This provision does not prohibit a party or person from inquiring about the status of a case or asking routine questions concerning administrative functions or procedures.

§ 160.512   Prehearing conferences.

(a) The ALJ must schedule at least one prehearing conference, and may schedule additional prehearing conferences as appropriate, upon reasonable notice, which may not be less than 14 business days, to the parties.

(b) The ALJ may use prehearing conferences to discuss the following—

(1) Simplification of the issues;

(2) The necessity or desirability of amendments to the pleadings, including the need for a more definite statement;

(3) Stipulations and admissions of fact or as to the contents and authenticity of documents;

(4) Whether the parties can agree to submission of the case on a stipulated record;

(5) Whether a party chooses to waive appearance at an oral hearing and to submit only documentary evidence (subject to the objection of the other party) and written argument;

(6) Limitation of the number of witnesses;

(7) Scheduling dates for the exchange of witness lists and of proposed exhibits;

(8) Discovery of documents as permitted by this subpart;

(9) The time and place for the hearing;

(10) The potential for the settlement of the case by the parties; and

(11) Other matters as may tend to encourage the fair, just and expeditious disposition of the proceedings, including the protection of privacy of individually identifiable health information that may be submitted into evidence or otherwise used in the proceeding, if appropriate.

(c) The ALJ must issue an order containing the matters agreed upon by the parties or ordered by the ALJ at a prehearing conference.

§ 160.514   Authority to settle.

The Secretary has exclusive authority to settle any issue or case without the consent of the ALJ.

§ 160.516   Discovery.

(a) A party may make a request to another party for production of documents for inspection and copying

E. HIPAA Final Rules, Administrative Simplification Enforcement, continued

that are relevant and material to the issues before the ALJ.

(b) For the purpose of this section, the term "documents" includes information, reports, answers, records, accounts, papers and other data and documentary evidence. Nothing contained in this section may be interpreted to require the creation of a document, except that requested data stored in an electronic data storage system must be produced in a form accessible to the requesting party.

(c) Requests for documents, requests for admissions, written interrogatories, depositions and any forms of discovery, other than those permitted under paragraph (a) of this section, are not authorized.

(d) This section may not be construed to require the disclosure of interview reports or statements obtained by any party, or on behalf of any party, of persons who will not be called as witnesses by that party, or analyses and summaries prepared in conjunction with the investigation or litigation of the case, or any otherwise privileged documents.

(e)(1) When a request for production of documents has been received, within 30 days the party receiving that request must either fully respond to the request, or state that the request is being objected to and the reasons for that objection. If objection is made to part of an item or category, the part must be specified. Upon receiving any objections, the party seeking production may then, within 30 days or any other time frame set by the ALJ, file a motion for an order compelling discovery. The party receiving a request for production may also file a motion for protective order any time before the date the production is due.

(2) The ALJ may grant a motion for protective order or deny a motion for an order compelling discovery if the ALJ finds that the discovery sought—

(i) Is irrelevant;
(ii) Is unduly costly or burdensome;
(iii) Will unduly delay the proceeding; or
(iv) Seeks privileged information.

(3) The ALJ may extend any of the time frames set forth in paragraph (e)(1) of this section.

(4) The burden of showing that discovery should be allowed is on the party seeking discovery.

§ 160.518 Exchange of witness lists, witness statements, and exhibits.

(a) The parties must exchange witness lists, copies of prior written statements of proposed witnesses, and copies of proposed hearing exhibits, including copies of any written statements that the

party intends to offer in lieu of live testimony in accordance with § 160.538, not more than 60, and not less than 15, days before the scheduled hearing, except that if a respondent intends to introduce the evidence of a statistical expert, the respondent must provide the Secretarial party with a copy of the statistical expert's report not less than 30 days before the scheduled hearing.

(b)(1) If, at any time, a party objects to the proposed admission of evidence not exchanged in accordance with paragraph (a) of this section, the ALJ must determine whether the failure to comply with paragraph (a) of this section should result in the exclusion of that evidence.

(2) Unless the ALJ finds that extraordinary circumstances justified the failure timely to exchange the information listed under paragraph (a) of this section, the ALJ must exclude from the party's case-in-chief—

(i) The testimony of any witness whose name does not appear on the witness list; and
(ii) Any exhibit not provided to the opposing party as specified in paragraph (a) of this section.

(3) If the ALJ finds that extraordinary circumstances existed, the ALJ must then determine whether the admission of that evidence would cause substantial prejudice to the objecting party.

(i) If the ALJ finds that there is no substantial prejudice, the evidence may be admitted.
(ii) If the ALJ finds that there is substantial prejudice, the ALJ may exclude the evidence, or, if he or she does not exclude the evidence, must postpone the hearing for such time as is necessary for the objecting party to prepare and respond to the evidence, unless the objecting party waives postponement.

(c) Unless the other party objects within a reasonable period of time before the hearing, documents exchanged in accordance with paragraph (a) of this section will be deemed to be authentic for the purpose of admissibility at the hearing.

§ 160.520 Subpoenas for attendance at hearing.

(a) A party wishing to procure the appearance and testimony of any person at the hearing may make a motion requesting the ALJ to issue a subpoena if the appearance and testimony are reasonably necessary for the presentation of a party's case.

(b) A subpoena requiring the attendance of a person in accordance with paragraph (a) of this section may also require the person (whether or not the person is a party) to produce

relevant and material evidence at or before the hearing.

(c) When a subpoena is served by a respondent on a particular employee or official or particular office of HHS, the Secretary may comply by designating any knowledgeable HHS representative to appear and testify.

(d) A party seeking a subpoena must file a written motion not less than 30 days before the date fixed for the hearing, unless otherwise allowed by the ALJ for good cause shown. That motion must—

(1) Specify any evidence to be produced;
(2) Designate the witnesses; and
(3) Describe the address and location with sufficient particularity to permit those witnesses to be found.

(e) The subpoena must specify the time and place at which the witness is to appear and any evidence the witness is to produce.

(f) Within 15 days after the written motion requesting issuance of a subpoena is served, any party may file an opposition or other response.

(g) If the motion requesting issuance of a subpoena is granted, the party seeking the subpoena must serve it by delivery to the person named, or by certified mail addressed to that person at the person's last dwelling place or principal place of business.

(h) The person to whom the subpoena is directed may file with the ALJ a motion to quash the subpoena within 10 days after service.

(i) The exclusive remedy for contumacy by, or refusal to obey a subpoena duly served upon, any person is specified in 42 U.S.C. 405(e).

§ 160.522 Fees.

The party requesting a subpoena must pay the cost of the fees and mileage of any witness subpoenaed in the amounts that would be payable to a witness in a proceeding in United States District Court. A check for witness fees and mileage must accompany the subpoena when served, except that, when a subpoena is issued on behalf of the Secretary, a check for witness fees and mileage need not accompany the subpoena.

§ 160.524 Form, filing, and service of papers.

(a) *Forms*. (1) Unless the ALJ directs the parties to do otherwise, documents filed with the ALJ must include an original and two copies.

(2) Every pleading and paper filed in the proceeding must contain a caption setting forth the title of the action, the case number, and a designation of the paper, such as motion to quash subpoena.

E. HIPAA Final Rules, Administrative Simplification Enforcement, continued

(3) Every pleading and paper must be signed by and must contain the address and telephone number of the party or the person on whose behalf the paper was filed, or his or her representative.

(4) Papers are considered filed when they are mailed.

(b) *Service.* A party filing a document with the ALJ or the Board must, at the time of filing, serve a copy of the document on the other party. Service upon any party of any document must be made by delivering a copy, or placing a copy of the document in the United States mail, postage prepaid and addressed, or with a private delivery service, to the party's last known address. When a party is represented by an attorney, service must be made upon the attorney in lieu of the party.

(c) *Proof of service.* A certificate of the natural person serving the document by personal delivery or by mail, setting forth the manner of service, constitutes proof of service.

§ 160.526 Computation of time.

(a) In computing any period of time under this subpart or in an order issued thereunder, the time begins with the day following the act, event or default, and includes the last day of the period unless it is a Saturday, Sunday, or legal holiday observed by the Federal Government, in which event it includes the next business day.

(b) When the period of time allowed is less than 7 days, intermediate Saturdays, Sundays, and legal holidays observed by the Federal Government must be excluded from the computation.

(c) Where a document has been served or issued by placing it in the mail, an additional 5 days must be added to the time permitted for any response. This paragraph does not apply to requests for hearing under § 160.504.

§ 160.528 Motions.

(a) An application to the ALJ for an order or ruling must be by motion. Motions must state the relief sought, the authority relied upon and the facts alleged, and must be filed with the ALJ and served on all other parties.

(b) Except for motions made during a prehearing conference or at the hearing, all motions must be in writing. The ALJ may require that oral motions be reduced to writing.

(c) Within 10 days after a written motion is served, or such other time as may be fixed by the ALJ, any party may file a response to the motion.

(d) The ALJ may not grant a written motion before the time for filing responses has expired, except upon consent of the parties or following a hearing on the motion, but may overrule

or deny the motion without awaiting a response.

(e) The ALJ must make a reasonable effort to dispose of all outstanding motions before the beginning of the hearing.

§ 160.530 Sanctions.

The ALJ may sanction a person, including any party or attorney, for failing to comply with an order or procedure, for failing to defend an action or for other misconduct that interferes with the speedy, orderly or fair conduct of the hearing. The sanctions must reasonably relate to the severity and nature of the failure or misconduct. The sanctions may include—

(a) In the case of refusal to provide or permit discovery under the terms of this part, drawing negative factual inferences or treating the refusal as an admission by deeming the matter, or certain facts, to be established;

(b) Prohibiting a party from introducing certain evidence or otherwise supporting a particular claim or defense;

(c) Striking pleadings, in whole or in part;

(d) Staying the proceedings;

(e) Dismissal of the action;

(f) Entering a decision by default;

(g) Ordering the party or attorney to pay the attorney's fees and other costs caused by the failure or misconduct; and

(h) Refusing to consider any motion or other action that is not filed in a timely manner.

§ 160.532 Collateral estoppel.

When a final determination that the respondent violated an administrative simplification provision has been rendered in any proceeding in which the respondent was a party and had an opportunity to be heard, the respondent is bound by that determination in any proceeding under this part.

§ 160.534 The hearing.

(a) The ALJ must conduct a hearing on the record in order to determine whether the respondent should be found liable under this part.

(b) (1) The respondent has the burden of going forward and the burden of persuasion with respect to any:

(i) Affirmative defense pursuant to § 160.410 of this part;

(ii) Challenge to the amount of a proposed penalty pursuant to §§ 160.404–160.408 of this part, including any factors raised as mitigating factors; or

(iii) Claim that a proposed penalty should be reduced or waived pursuant to § 160.412 of this part.

(2) The Secretary has the burden of going forward and the burden of persuasion with respect to all other issues, including issues of liability and the existence of any factors considered as aggravating factors in determining the amount of the proposed penalty.

(3) The burden of persuasion will be judged by a preponderance of the evidence.

(c) The hearing must be open to the public unless otherwise ordered by the ALJ for good cause shown.

(d)(1) Subject to the 15-day rule under § 160.518(a) and the admissibility of evidence under § 160.540, either party may introduce, during its case in chief, items or information that arose or became known after the date of the issuance of the notice of proposed determination or the request for hearing, as applicable. Such items and information may not be admitted into evidence, if introduced—

(i) By the Secretary, unless they are material and relevant to the acts or omissions with respect to which the penalty is proposed in the notice of proposed determination pursuant to § 160.420 of this part, including circumstances that may increase penalties; or

(ii) By the respondent, unless they are material and relevant to an admission, denial or explanation of a finding of fact in the notice of proposed determination under § 160.420 of this part, or to a specific circumstance or argument expressly stated in the request for hearing under § 160.504, including circumstances that may reduce penalties.

(2) After both parties have presented their cases, evidence may be admitted in rebuttal even if not previously exchanged in accordance with § 160.518.

§ 160.536 Statistical sampling.

(a) In meeting the burden of proof set forth in § 160.534, the Secretary may introduce the results of a statistical sampling study as evidence of the number of violations under § 160.406 of this part, or the factors considered in determining the amount of the civil money penalty under § 160.408 of this part. Such statistical sampling study, if based upon an appropriate sampling and computed by valid statistical methods, constitutes prima facie evidence of the number of violations and the existence of factors material to the proposed civil money penalty as described in §§ 160.406 and 160.408.

(b) Once the Secretary has made a prima facie case, as described in paragraph (a) of this section, the burden of going forward shifts to the respondent

E. HIPAA Final Rules, Administrative Simplification Enforcement, continued

to produce evidence reasonably calculated to rebut the findings of the statistical sampling study. The Secretary will then be given the opportunity to rebut this evidence.

§ 160.538 Witnesses.

(a) Except as provided in paragraph (b) of this section, testimony at the hearing must be given orally by witnesses under oath or affirmation.

(b) At the discretion of the ALJ, testimony of witnesses other than the testimony of expert witnesses may be admitted in the form of a written statement. The ALJ may, at his or her discretion, admit prior sworn testimony of experts that has been subject to adverse examination, such as a deposition or trial testimony. Any such written statement must be provided to the other party, along with the last known address of the witness, in a manner that allows sufficient time for the other party to subpoena the witness for cross-examination at the hearing. Prior written statements of witnesses proposed to testify at the hearing must be exchanged as provided in § 160.518.

(c) The ALJ must exercise reasonable control over the mode and order of interrogating witnesses and presenting evidence so as to:

(1) Make the interrogation and presentation effective for the ascertainment of the truth;

(2) Avoid repetition or needless consumption of time; and

(3) Protect witnesses from harassment or undue embarrassment.

(d) The ALJ must permit the parties to conduct cross-examination of witnesses as may be required for a full and true disclosure of the facts.

(e) The ALJ may order witnesses excluded so that they cannot hear the testimony of other witnesses, except that the ALJ may not order to be excluded—

(1) A party who is a natural person;

(2) In the case of a party that is not a natural person, the officer or employee of the party appearing for the entity pro se or designated as the party's representative; or

(3) A natural person whose presence is shown by a party to be essential to the presentation of its case, including a person engaged in assisting the attorney for the Secretary.

§ 160.540 Evidence.

(a) The ALJ must determine the admissibility of evidence.

(b) Except as provided in this subpart, the ALJ is not bound by the Federal Rules of Evidence. However, the ALJ may apply the Federal Rules of Evidence where appropriate, for example, to exclude unreliable evidence.

(c) The ALJ must exclude irrelevant or immaterial evidence.

(d) Although relevant, evidence may be excluded if its probative value is substantially outweighed by the danger of unfair prejudice, confusion of the issues, or by considerations of undue delay or needless presentation of cumulative evidence.

(e) Although relevant, evidence must be excluded if it is privileged under Federal law.

(f) Evidence concerning offers of compromise or settlement are inadmissible to the extent provided in Rule 408 of the Federal Rules of Evidence.

(g) Evidence of crimes, wrongs, or acts other than those at issue in the instant case is admissible in order to show motive, opportunity, intent, knowledge, preparation, identity, lack of mistake, or existence of a scheme. This evidence is admissible regardless of whether the crimes, wrongs, or acts occurred during the statute of limitations period applicable to the acts or omissions that constitute the basis for liability in the case and regardless of whether they were referenced in the Secretary's notice of proposed determination under § 160.420 of this part.

(h) The ALJ must permit the parties to introduce rebuttal witnesses and evidence.

(i) All documents and other evidence offered or taken for the record must be open to examination by both parties, unless otherwise ordered by the ALJ for good cause shown.

§ 160.542 The record.

(a) The hearing must be recorded and transcribed. Transcripts may be obtained following the hearing from the ALJ. A party that requests a transcript of hearing proceedings must pay the cost of preparing the transcript unless, for good cause shown by the party, the payment is waived by the ALJ or the Board, as appropriate.

(b) The transcript of the testimony, exhibits, and other evidence admitted at the hearing, and all papers and requests filed in the proceeding constitute the record for decision by the ALJ and the Secretary.

(c) The record may be inspected and copied (upon payment of a reasonable fee) by any person, unless otherwise ordered by the ALJ for good cause shown.

(d) For good cause, the ALJ may order appropriate redactions made to the record.

§ 160.544 Post hearing briefs.

The ALJ may require the parties to file post-hearing briefs. In any event, any party may file a post-hearing brief. The ALJ must fix the time for filing the briefs. The time for filing may not exceed 60 days from the date the parties receive the transcript of the hearing or, if applicable, the stipulated record. The briefs may be accompanied by proposed findings of fact and conclusions of law. The ALJ may permit the parties to file reply briefs.

§ 160.546 ALJ's decision.

(a) The ALJ must issue a decision, based only on the record, which must contain findings of fact and conclusions of law.

(b) The ALJ may affirm, increase, or reduce the penalties imposed by the Secretary.

(c) The ALJ must issue the decision to both parties within 60 days after the time for submission of post-hearing briefs and reply briefs, if permitted, has expired. If the ALJ fails to meet the deadline contained in this paragraph, he or she must notify the parties of the reason for the delay and set a new deadline.

(d) Unless the decision of the ALJ is timely appealed as provided for in § 160.548, the decision of the ALJ will be final and binding on the parties 60 days from the date of service of the ALJ's decision.

§ 160.548 Appeal of the ALJ's decision.

(a) Any party may appeal the decision of the ALJ to the Board by filing a notice of appeal with the Board within 30 days of the date of service of the ALJ decision. The Board may extend the initial 30 day period for a period of time not to exceed 30 days if a party files with the Board a request for an extension within the initial 30 day period and shows good cause.

(b) If a party files a timely notice of appeal with the Board, the ALJ must forward the record of the proceeding to the Board.

(c) A notice of appeal must be accompanied by a written brief specifying exceptions to the initial decision and reasons supporting the exceptions. Any party may file a brief in opposition to the exceptions, which may raise any relevant issue not addressed in the exceptions, within 30 days of receiving the notice of appeal and the accompanying brief. The Board may permit the parties to file reply briefs.

(d) There is no right to appear personally before the Board or to appeal to the Board any interlocutory ruling by the ALJ.

E. HIPAA Final Rules, Administrative Simplification Enforcement, continued

(e) Except for an affirmative defense under § 160.410(b)(1) of this part, the Board may not consider any issue not raised in the parties' briefs, nor any issue in the briefs that could have been raised before the ALJ but was not.

(f) If any party demonstrates to the satisfaction of the Board that additional evidence not presented at such hearing is relevant and material and that there were reasonable grounds for the failure to adduce such evidence at the hearing, the Board may remand the matter to the ALJ for consideration of such additional evidence.

(g) The Board may decline to review the case, or may affirm, increase, reduce, reverse or remand any penalty determined by the ALJ.

(h) The standard of review on a disputed issue of fact is whether the initial decision of the ALJ is supported by substantial evidence on the whole record. The standard of review on a disputed issue of law is whether the decision is erroneous.

(i) Within 60 days after the time for submission of briefs and reply briefs, if permitted, has expired, the Board must serve on each party to the appeal a copy of the Board's decision and a statement describing the right of any respondent who is penalized to seek judicial review.

(j)(1) The Board's decision under paragraph (i) of this section, including a decision to decline review of the initial decision, becomes the final decision of the Secretary 60 days after the date of service of the Board's decision, except with respect to a decision to remand to the ALJ or if reconsideration is requested under this paragraph.

(2) The Board will reconsider its decision only if it determines that the decision contains a clear error of fact or error of law. New evidence will not be a basis for reconsideration unless the party demonstrates that the evidence is newly discovered and was not previously available.

(3) A party may file a motion for reconsideration with the Board before the date the decision becomes final under paragraph (j)(1) of this section. A motion for reconsideration must be accompanied by a written brief specifying any alleged error of fact or law and, if the party is relying on additional evidence, explaining why the evidence was not previously available. Any party may file a brief in opposition within 15 days of receiving the motion for reconsideration and the accompanying brief unless this time limit is extended by the Board for good cause shown. Reply briefs are not permitted.

(4) The Board must rule on the motion for reconsideration not later than 30 days from the date the opposition brief is due. If the Board denies the motion, the decision issued under paragraph (i) of this section becomes the final decision of the Secretary on the date of service of the ruling. If the Board grants the motion, the Board will issue a reconsidered decision, after such procedures as the Board determines necessary to address the effect of any error. The Board's decision on reconsideration becomes the final decision of the Secretary on the date of service of the decision, except with respect to a decision to remand to the ALJ.

(5) If service of a ruling or decision issued under this section is by mail, the date of service will be deemed to be 5 days from the date of mailing.

(k)(1) A respondent's petition for judicial review must be filed within 60 days of the date on which the decision of the Board becomes the final decision of the Secretary under paragraph (j) of this section.

(2) In compliance with 28 U.S.C. 2112(a), a copy of any petition for judicial review filed in any U.S. Court of Appeals challenging the final decision of the Secretary must be sent by certified mail, return receipt requested, to the General Counsel of HHS. The petition copy must be a copy showing that it has been time-stamped by the clerk of the court when the original was filed with the court.

(3) If the General Counsel of HHS received two or more petitions within 10 days after the final decision of the Secretary, the General Counsel will notify the U.S. Judicial Panel on Multidistrict Litigation of any petitions that were received within the 10 day period.

§ 160.550   Stay of the Secretary's decision.

(a) Pending judicial review, the respondent may file a request for stay of the effective date of any penalty with the ALJ. The request must be accompanied by a copy of the notice of appeal filed with the Federal court. The filing of the request automatically stays the effective date of the penalty until such time as the ALJ rules upon the request.

(b) The ALJ may not grant a respondent's request for stay of any penalty unless the respondent posts a bond or provides other adequate security.

(c) The ALJ must rule upon a respondent's request for stay within 10 days of receipt.

§ 160.552   Harmless error.

No error in either the admission or the exclusion of evidence, and no error or defect in any ruling or order or in any act done or omitted by the ALJ or by any of the parties is ground for vacating, modifying or otherwise disturbing an otherwise appropriate ruling or order or act, unless refusal to take such action appears to the ALJ or the Board inconsistent with substantial justice. The ALJ and the Board at every stage of the proceeding must disregard any error or defect in the proceeding that does not affect the substantial rights of the parties.

PART 164—SECURITY AND PRIVACY

■ 1. The authority citation for part 164 is revised to read as follows:

Authority: 42 U.S.C. 1320d–1320d–8 and sec. 264, Pub. L. No. 104–191, 110 Stat. 2033–2034 (42 U.S.C. 1320d–2 (note)).

■ 2. In § 164.530, revise paragraph (g) to read as follows:

§ 164.530   Administrative requirements.

*   *   *   *   *

(g) *Standard: refraining from intimidating or retaliatory acts.* A covered entity—

(1) May not intimidate, threaten, coerce, discriminate against, or take other retaliatory action against any individual for the exercise by the individual of any right established, or for participation in any process provided for by this subpart, including the filing of a complaint under this section; and

(2) Must refrain from intimidation and retaliation as provided in § 160.316 of this subchapter.

*   *   *   *   *

[FR Doc. 06–1376 Filed 2–10–06; 2:59 pm]
BILLING CODE 4153–01–P

F. HIPAA Final Rules, Nondiscrimination and Wellness Benefits

Summary   The Department of the Treasury, the Department of Labor, and the Department of Health and Human Services jointly published final rules on nondiscrimination and wellness benefits on December 13, 2006. The final rules are effective for plan years beginning on or after July 1, 2007. Thus the effective date for calendar year plans is January 1, 2008.

F. HIPAA Final Rules, Nondiscrimination and Wellness Benefits, continued

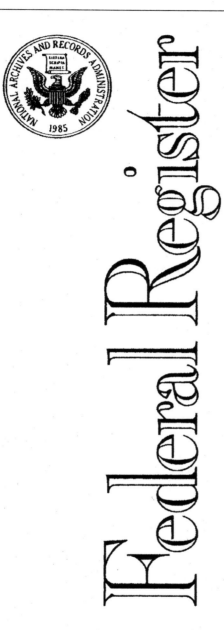

Wednesday,
December 13, 2006

Part III

Department of the Treasury
Internal Revenue Service
26 CFR Part 54

Department of Labor
Employee Benefits Security Administration

29 CFR Part 2590

Department of Health and Human Services
Centers for Medicare & Medicaid Services

45 CFR Part 146

Nondiscrimination and Wellness Programs in Health Coverage in the Group Market; Final Rules

F. HIPAA Final Rules, Nondiscrimination and Wellness Benefits, continued

75014   Federal Register / Vol. 71, No. 239 / Wednesday, December 13, 2006 / Rules and Regulations

DEPARTMENT OF THE TREASURY

Internal Revenue Service

26 CFR Part 54

[TD 9298]

RIN 1545–AY32

DEPARTMENT OF LABOR

Employee Benefits Security Administration

29 CFR Part 2590

RIN 1210–AA77

DEPARTMENT OF HEALTH AND HUMAN SERVICES

Centers for Medicare & Medicaid Services

45 CFR Part 146

RIN 0938–AI08

Nondiscrimination and Wellness Programs in Health Coverage in the Group Market

AGENCIES: Internal Revenue Service, Department of the Treasury; Employee Benefits Security Administration, Department of Labor; Centers for Medicare & Medicaid Services, Department of Health and Human Services.

ACTION: Final rules.

SUMMARY: This document contains final rules governing the provisions prohibiting discrimination based on a health factor for group health plans and issuers of health insurance coverage offered in connection with a group health plan. The rules contained in this document implement changes made to the Internal Revenue Code of 1986 (Code), the Employee Retirement Income Security Act of 1974 (ERISA), and the Public Health Service (PHS Act) enacted as part of the Health Insurance Portability and Accountability Act of 1996 (HIPAA).

DATES: *Effective date.* These final regulations are effective February 12, 2007.

Applicability dates. These final regulations apply for plan years beginning on or after July 1, 2007.

FOR FURTHER INFORMATION CONTACT: Russ Weinheimer, Internal Revenue Service, Department of the Treasury, at (202) 622–6080; Amy Turner or Elena Lynett, Employee Benefits Security Administration, Department of Labor, at (202) 693–8335; or Karen Levin or Adam Shaw, Centers for Medicare &

Medicaid Services, Department of Health and Human Services, at (877) 267–2323 extension 65445 and 61091, respectively.

Customer Service Information: Individuals interested in obtaining copies of Department of Labor publications concerning health care laws may request copies by calling the Department of Labor (DOL), Employee Benefits Security Administration (EBSA) Toll-Free Hotline at 1–866–444–EBSA (3272) or may request a copy of the Department of Health and Human Services (HHS), Centers for Medicare & Medicaid Services (CMS) publication entitled "Protecting Your Health Insurance Coverage" by calling 1–800–633–4227. These regulations as well as other information on HIPAA's nondiscrimination rules and other health care laws are also available on the Department of Labor's Web site (*http://www.dol.gov/ebsa*), including the interactive web pages Health Elaws.

SUPPLEMENTARY INFORMATION:

I. Background

The Health Insurance Portability and Accountability Act of 1996 (HIPAA), Public Law 104–191 (110 Stat. 1936), was enacted on August 21, 1996. HIPAA amended the Internal Revenue Code of 1986 (Code), the Employee Retirement Income Security Act of 1974 (ERISA), and the Public Health Service Act (PHS Act) to provide for, among other things, improved portability and continuity of health coverage. HIPAA added section 9802 of the Code, section 702 of ERISA, and section 2702 of the PHS Act, which prohibit discrimination in health coverage based on a health factor. Interim final rules implementing the HIPAA provisions were published in the Federal Register on April 8, 1997 (62 FR 16894) (1997 interim rules). On December 29, 1997, the Department of Labor, the Department of Health and Human Services, and the Department of the Treasury (the Departments) published a clarification of the April 1997 interim rules as they relate to individuals who were denied coverage before the effective date of HIPAA on the basis of any health factor (62 FR 67689).

On January 8, 2001, the Departments published interim final regulations (2001 interim rules) on many issues under the HIPAA nondiscrimination provisions (66 FR 1378) and proposed regulations on wellness programs under those nondiscrimination provisions (66 FR 1421). These regulations being published today in the Federal Register finalize both the 2001 interim rules and the proposed rules.

II. Overview of the Regulations

Section 9802 of the Code, section 702 of ERISA, and section 2702 of the PHS Act (the HIPAA nondiscrimination provisions) establish rules generally prohibiting group health plans and group health insurance issuers from discriminating against individual participants or beneficiaries based on any health factor of such participants or beneficiaries. The 2001 interim rules —

• Explained the application of these provisions to benefits;

• Clarified the relationship between the HIPAA nondiscrimination provisions and the HIPAA preexisting condition exclusion limitations;

• Explained the application of these provisions to premiums;

• Described similarly situated individuals;

• Explained the application of these provisions to actively-at-work and nonconfinement clauses; and

• Clarified that more favorable treatment of individuals with medical needs generally is permitted.

In general, these final regulations do not change the 2001 interim rules or the proposed rules on wellness programs. However, these regulations do not republish the expired transitional rules regarding individuals who were denied coverage based on a health factor prior to the applicability date of the 2001 interim rules. (These regulations do republish, and slightly modify, the special transitional rule for self-funded nonfederal governmental plans that had denied any individual coverage due to the plan's election to opt out of the nondiscrimination requirements under 45 CFR 146.180, in cases where the plan sponsor subsequently chooses to bring the plan into compliance with those requirements). These regulations clarify how the source-of-injury rules apply to the timing of a diagnosis of a medical condition and add an example to illustrate how the benefits rules apply to the carryover feature of health 0reimbursement arrangements (HRAs). For wellness programs, the final regulations clarify some ambiguities in the proposed rules, make some changes in terminology and organization, and add a description of wellness programs not required to satisfy additional standards.

Application to Benefits

Under the 2001 interim rules and these regulations, a plan or issuer is not required to provide coverage for any particular benefit to any group of similarly situated individuals. However, benefits provided must be uniformly available to all similarly situated

F. HIPAA Final Rules, Nondiscrimination and Wellness Benefits, continued

individuals. Likewise, any restriction on a benefit or benefits must apply uniformly to all similarly situated individuals and must not be directed at individual participants or beneficiaries based on any health factor of the participants or beneficiaries (determined based on all the relevant facts and circumstances).

With respect to these benefit rules, the Departments received many inquiries about HRAs and one comment about nondiscrimination requirements under other laws. Under HRAs, employees are reimbursed for medical expenses up to a maximum amount for a period, based on the employer's contribution to the plan. These plans may or may not be funded. Another common feature is that the plans typically allow amounts remaining available at the end of the period to be used to reimburse medical expenses in later periods. Because the maximum reimbursement available under a plan to an employee in any single period may vary based on the claims experience of the employee, concerns have arisen about the application of the HIPAA nondiscrimination rules to these plans.

To address these concerns, these final regulations include an example under which the carryforward of unused employer-provided medical care reimbursement amounts to later years does not violate the HIPAA nondiscrimination requirements, even though the maximum reimbursement amount for a year varies among employees within the same group of similarly situated individuals based on prior claims experience. In the example, an employer sponsors a group health plan under which medical care expenses are reimbursed up to an annual maximum amount. The maximum reimbursement amount with respect to an employee for a year is a uniform amount multiplied by the number of years the employee has participated in the plan, reduced by the total reimbursements for prior years. Because employees who have participated in the plan for the same length of time are eligible for the same total benefit over that length of time, the example concludes that the arrangement does not violate the HIPAA nondiscrimination requirements.

The Equal Employment Opportunity Commission (EEOC) asked the Departments to clarify that certain plan practices or provisions permitted under the benefits paragraphs of the 2001 interim rules may violate the Americans with Disabilities Act of 1990 (ADA) or Title VII of the Civil Rights Act of 1964 (Title VII). Specifically, the 2001 interim rules allow plans to exclude or limit

benefits for certain types of conditions or treatments. The EEOC commented that, if such a benefit limit were applied to AIDS, it would be a disability-based distinction that violates the ADA (unless it is permitted under section 501(c) of the ADA). In addition, the EEOC commented that an exclusion from coverage of prescription contraceptives, but not of other preventive treatments, would violate Title VII because prescription contraceptives are used exclusively by women.

Paragraph (h) of the 2001 interim rules and these final regulations is entitled "No effect on other laws." This section clarifies that compliance with the nondiscrimination rules is not determinative of compliance with any other provision of ERISA, or any other State or Federal law, including the ADA. Moreover, in paragraph (b) of the 2001 interim rules and these final regulations, the general rule governing the application of the nondiscrimination rules to benefits clarifies that whether any plan provision or practice with respect to benefits complies with these rules does not affect whether the provision or practice is permitted under any other provision of the Code, ERISA, or the PHS Act, the Americans with Disabilities Act, or any other law, whether State or Federal.

Many other laws may regulate plans and issuers in their provision of benefits to participants and beneficiaries. These laws include the ADA, Title VII, the Family and Medical Leave Act, ERISA's fiduciary provisions, and State law. The Departments have not attempted to summarize the requirements of those laws in the HIPAA nondiscrimination rules. Instead, these rules clarify the application of the HIPAA nondiscrimination rules to group health plans, which may permit certain practices that other laws prohibit. Nonetheless, to avoid misleading plans and issuers as to the permissibility of any plan provision under other laws, the Departments included, in both paragraph (h) and paragraph (b) of the regulations, references to the potential applicability of other laws. Employers, plans, issuers, and other service providers should consider the applicability of these laws to their coverage and contact legal counsel or other government agencies such as the EEOC and State insurance departments if they have questions under those laws.

Source-of-Injury Exclusions

Some plans and issuers, while generally providing coverage for the treatment of an injury, deny benefits if the injury arose from a specified cause

or activity. These kinds of exclusions are known as source-of-injury exclusions. Under the 2001 interim rules, if a plan or issuer provides benefits for a particular injury, it may not deny benefits otherwise provided for treatment of the injury due to the fact that the injury results from a medical condition or an act of domestic violence. Two examples in the 2001 interim rules illustrate the application of this rule, to injuries resulting from an attempted suicide due to depression and to injuries resulting from bungee jumping.

These final regulations retain the provisions in the 2001 interim rules and add a clarification. Some people have inquired if a suicide exclusion can apply if an individual had not been diagnosed with a medical condition such as depression before the suicide attempt. These final regulations clarify that benefits may not be denied for injuries resulting from a medical condition even if the medical condition was not diagnosed before the injury.

Some comments expressed concern that the discussion of the source-of-injury rule in the 2001 interim rules might be used to support the use of vague language to identify plan benefit exclusions, especially to identify source-of-injury exclusions. Requirements for plan benefit descriptions are generally outside of the scope of these regulations. Nonetheless, Department of Labor regulations at 29 CFR 2520.102–2(b) provide, "The format of the summary plan description must not have the effect of misleading, misinforming or failing to inform participants and beneficiaries. Any description of exception, limitations, reductions, and other restrictions of plan benefits shall not be minimized, rendered obscure or otherwise made to appear unimportant * * * The advantages and disadvantages of the plan shall be presented without either exaggerating the benefits or minimizing the limitations." State laws governing group insurance or nonfederal governmental plans may provide additional protections.

The Departments received thousands of comments protesting that the source-of-injury provisions in the 2001 interim rules would generally permit plans or issuers to exclude benefits for the treatment of injuries sustained in the activities listed in the conference report to HIPAA (motorcycling, snowmobiling, all-terrain vehicle riding, horseback riding, skiing, and other similar activities). Many comments requested that the source-of-injury rule be amended to provide that a source-of-injury exclusion could not apply if the

F. HIPAA Final Rules, Nondiscrimination and Wellness Benefits, continued

75016   Federal Register / Vol. 71, No. 239 / Wednesday, December 13, 2006 / Rules and Regulations

injury resulted from (in addition to an act of domestic violence or a medical condition) participation in legal recreational activities such as those listed in the conference report. Some comments expressed the concern that the rule in the 2001 interim rules would cause plans and issuers to begin excluding benefits for treatment of injuries sustained in these kinds of activities.

One comment generally supported the position in the 2001 interim rules. That comment expressed the belief that Congress intended with this issue, as with many other issues, to continue its longstanding deference to the States on the regulation of benefit design under health insurance. The comment also noted that the source-of-injury rule in the 2001 interim rules would not change the practice of plans or issuers with regard to the activities listed in the conference report and that the practice of plans and issuers in this regard would continue to be governed, as they had been before HIPAA, by market conditions and the States.

The Departments have not added the list of activities from the conference report to the source-of-injury rule in the final regulations. The statute itself is unclear about how benefits in general are affected by the nondiscrimination requirements and is silent with respect to source-of-injury exclusions in particular. The legislative history provides that the inclusion of evidence of insurability in the list of health factors is intended to ensure, among other things, that individuals are not excluded from health care coverage due to their participation in the activities listed in the conference report. This language is unclear because the term "health care coverage" could mean only eligibility to enroll for coverage under the plan, so that people who participate in the activities listed in the conference report could not be kept out of the plan but could be denied benefits for injuries sustained in those activities. Alternatively, it could mean eligibility both to enroll for coverage and for benefits, so that people who participate in those activities could not be kept out of the plan or denied benefits for injuries sustained in those activities. Without any indication in the statute and without a clear indication in the legislative history about this issue, and in light of the overall scheme of the statute, the Departments have made no changes to the regulations.

Moreover, to the extent not prohibited by State law, plans and issuers have been free to impose source-of-injury exclusions since before HIPAA. There is no reason to believe that plans and

issuers will begin to impose source-of-injury exclusions with respect to the conference report activities merely because such exclusions are not prohibited under the 2001 interim rules and these final regulations.

Relationship of Prohibition on Nonconfinement Clauses to State Extension-of-Benefits Laws

Questions have arisen about the relationship of the prohibition on nonconfinement clauses in the 2001 interim rules to State extension-of-benefits laws. Plan provisions that deny an individual benefits based on the individual's confinement to a hospital or other health care institution at the time coverage would otherwise become effective are often called nonconfinement clauses. The 2001 interim rules prohibit such nonconfinement clauses. At the same time, many States require issuers to provide benefits beyond the date on which coverage under the policy would otherwise have ended to individuals who continue to be hospitalized beyond that date. Example 2 in the 2001 interim rules illustrated that a current issuer cannot impose a nonconfinement clause that restricts benefits for an individual based on whether that individual is entitled to continued benefits from a prior issuer pursuant to a State law requirement. The final sentence in Example 2 provided that HIPAA does not affect the prior issuer's obligation under State law and does not affect any State law governing coordination of benefits.

Under the laws of some States, a prior issuer has the obligation to provide health benefits to an individual confined to a hospital beyond the nominal end of the policy only if the hospitalization is not covered by a succeeding issuer. Because HIPAA requires a succeeding issuer to provide benefits that it would otherwise provide if not for the nonconfinement clause, in such a case State law would not require the prior issuer to provide benefits for a confinement beyond the nominal end of the policy. In this context, the statement in the final sentence of Example 2—that HIPAA does not affect the prior issuer's obligation under State law—could be read to conflict with the text of the rule and the main point of Example 2 that the succeeding issuer must cover the confinement.

There has been some dispute about how this potential ambiguity should be resolved. One interpretation is that the succeeding issuer can never impose a nonconfinement clause, and if this has the effect under State law of not requiring the prior issuer to provide

benefits beyond the nominal end of the policy, then the prior issuer is not obligated to provide the extended benefits. This interpretation is consistent with the text of the nonconfinement rule and the main point of Example 2, though it could be read to conflict with the last sentence in Example 2.

Another interpretation proposed by some is that, consistent with the last sentence of Example 2, the obligation of a prior issuer is never affected by the HIPAA prohibition against nonconfinement clauses. Under this interpretation, if a State law conditions a prior issuer's obligation on there being no succeeding issuer with the obligation, then in order to leave the prior issuer's obligation unaffected under State law, the succeeding issuer could apply a nonconfinement clause and the HIPAA prohibition would not apply. This interpretation elevates a minor clarification at the end of an example to supersede not only the main point of the example but also the express text of the rule the example illustrates. This proposed interpretation is clearly contrary to the intent of the 2001 interim rules.

To avoid other interpretations, these final rules have replaced the final sentence of Example 2 in the 2001 interim rules with three sentences. The new language clarifies that: State law cannot change the succeeding issuer's obligation under HIPAA; a prior issuer may also have an obligation; and in a case in which a succeeding issuer has an obligation under HIPAA and a prior issuer has an obligation under State law to provide benefits for a confinement, any State laws designed to prevent more than 100 percent reimbursement, such as State coordination-of-benefits laws, continue to apply. Thus, under HIPAA a succeeding issuer cannot deny benefits to an individual on the basis of a nonconfinement clause. If this requirement under HIPAA has the effect under State law of removing a prior issuer's obligation to provide benefits, then the prior issuer is not obligated to provide benefits for the confinement. If under State law this requirement under HIPAA has the effect of obligating both the prior issuer and the succeeding issuer to provide benefits, then any State coordination-of-benefits law that is used to determine the order of payment and to prevent more than 100 percent reimbursement continues to apply.

Actively-at-Work Rules and Employer Leave Policies

The final regulations make no changes to the 2001 interim rules relating to actively-at-work provisions. Actively-at-

F. HIPAA Final Rules, Nondiscrimination and Wellness Benefits, continued

work clauses are generally prohibited, unless individuals who are absent from work due to any health factor are treated, for purposes of health coverage, as if they are actively at work. Nonetheless, a plan or issuer may distinguish between groups of similarly situated individuals (provided the distinction is not directed at individual participants or beneficiaries based on a health factor). Examples in the regulations illustrate that a plan or issuer may condition coverage on an individual's meeting the plan's requirement of working full-time (such as a minimum of 250 hours in a three-month period or 30 hours per week).

Several members of the regulated community have asked the Departments to clarify the applicability of the actively-at-work rules to various plan provisions that require an individual to perform a minimum amount of service per week in order to be eligible for coverage. It is the Departments' experience that much of the complexity in applying these rules derives from the myriad variations in the operation of employers' leave policies. The Departments believe that the 2001 interim rules provide adequate principles for applying the actively-at-work provisions to different types of eligibility provisions. In order to comply with these rules, a plan or issuer should apply the plan's service requirements consistently to all similarly situated employees eligible for coverage under the plan without regard to whether an employee is seeking eligibility to enroll in the plan or continued eligibility to remain in the plan. Accordingly, if a plan imposes a 30-hour-per-week requirement and treats employees on paid leave (including sick leave and vacation leave) who are already in the plan as if they are actively-at-work, the plan generally is required to credit time on paid leave towards satisfying the 30-hour-per-week requirement for employees seeking enrollment in the plan. Similarly, if a plan allowed employees to continue eligibility under the plan while on paid leave and for an additional period of 30 days while on unpaid leave, the plan is generally required to credit these same periods for employees seeking enrollment in the plan.[1] To help ensure consistency in application, plans and issuers may wish to clarify, in writing, how employees on various types of leave are treated for purposes of interpreting a service requirement. Without clear plan rules, plans and issuers might slip into

inconsistent applications of their rules, which could lead to violations of the actively-at-work provisions.

Wellness Programs

The HIPAA nondiscrimination provisions do not prevent a plan or issuer from establishing discounts or rebates or modifying otherwise applicable copayments or deductibles in return for adherence to programs of health promotion and disease prevention. The 1997 interim rules refer to these programs as "bona fide wellness programs." In the preamble to the 1997 interim rules, the Departments invited comments on whether additional guidance was needed concerning, among other things, the permissible standards for determining bona fide wellness programs. The Departments also stated their intent to issue further regulations on the nondiscrimination requirements and that in no event would the Departments take any enforcement action against a plan or issuer that had sought to comply in good faith with section 9802 of the Code, section 702 of ERISA, and section 2702 of the PHS Act before the publication of additional guidance. The preambles to the 2001 interim final and proposed rules noted that the period for nonenforcement in cases of good faith compliance with the HIPAA nondiscrimination provisions generally ended on the applicability date of those regulations but continued with respect to wellness programs until the issuance of further guidance. Accordingly, the nonenforcement policy of the Departments ends upon the applicability date of these final regulations for cases in which a plan or issuer fails to comply with the regulations but complies in good faith with an otherwise reasonable interpretation of the statute.

The HIPAA nondiscrimination provisions generally prohibit a plan or issuer from charging similarly situated individuals different premiums or contributions based on a health factor. These final regulations also generally prohibit a plan or issuer from requiring similarly situated individuals to satisfy differing deductible, copayment, or other cost-sharing requirements. However, the HIPAA nondiscrimination provisions do not prevent a plan or issuer from establishing premium discounts or rebates or modifying otherwise applicable copayments or deductibles in return for adherence to programs of health promotion and disease prevention. Thus, there is an exception to the general rule prohibiting discrimination based on a health factor if the reward, such as a premium

discount or waiver of a cost-sharing requirement, is based on participation in a program of health promotion or disease prevention.

Both the 1997 interim rules and the 2001 proposed regulations refer to programs of health promotion and disease prevention allowed under this exception as "bona fide wellness programs." These regulations generally adopt the provisions in the 2001 proposed rules. However, as more fully explained below, the final regulations no longer use the term "bona fide" in connection with wellness programs, add a description of wellness programs that do not have to satisfy additional requirements in order to comply with the nondiscrimination requirements, reorganize the four requirements from the proposed rules into five requirements, provide that the reward for a wellness program—coupled with the reward for other wellness programs with respect to the plan that require satisfaction of a standard related to a health factor—must not exceed 20% of the total cost of coverage under the plan, and add examples and make other changes to more accurately describe how the requirements apply.

The term "wellness program". Comments suggested that the use of the term "bona fide" with respect to wellness programs was confusing because, under the proposed rules, some wellness programs that are not "bona fide" within the narrow meaning of that term in the proposed rules nonetheless satisfy the HIPAA nondiscrimination requirements. To address this concern, these final regulations do not use the term "bona fide wellness program." Instead the final regulations treat all programs of health promotion or disease prevention as wellness programs and specify which of those wellness programs must satisfy additional standards to comply with the nondiscrimination requirements.

Programs not subject to additional standards. The preamble to the 2001 proposed rules described a number of wellness programs that comply with the HIPAA nondiscrimination requirements without having to satisfy any additional standards. However, the text of the regulation did not make such a distinction. The Departments have received many comments and inquiries about whether programs like those described in the 2001 preamble would have to satisfy the additional standards in the proposed rules. As a result, a paragraph has been added to the final regulations defining and illustrating programs that comply with the nondiscrimination requirements without having to satisfy any additional

---

[1] These nondiscrimination rules do not address the applicability of the Family and Medical Leave Act to employers or group health coverage.

F. HIPAA Final Rules, Nondiscrimination and Wellness Benefits, continued

75018   Federal Register / Vol. 71, No. 239 / Wednesday, December 13, 2006 / Rules and Regulations

standards (assuming participation in the program is made available to all similarly situated individuals). Such programs are those under which none of the conditions for obtaining a reward is based on an individual satisfying a standard related to a health factor or under which no reward is offered. The final regulations include the following list to illustrate the wide range of programs that would not have to satisfy any additional standards to comply with the nondiscrimination requirements:

• A program that reimburses all or part of the cost for memberships in a fitness center.

• A diagnostic testing program that provides a reward for participation and does not base any part of the reward on outcomes.

• A program that encourages preventive care through the waiver of the copayment or deductible requirement under a group health plan for the costs of, for example, prenatal care or well-baby visits.

• A program that reimburses employees for the costs of smoking cessation programs without regard to whether the employee quits smoking.

• A program that provides a reward to employees for attending a monthly health education seminar.

Only programs under which any of the conditions for obtaining a reward is based on an individual satisfying a standard related to a health factor must meet the five additional requirements described in paragraph (f)(2) of these regulations in order to comply with the nondiscrimination requirements.

Limit on the reward. As under the proposed rules, the total reward that may be given to an individual under the plan for all wellness programs is limited. A reward can be in the form of a discount or rebate of a premium or contribution, a waiver of all or part of a cost-sharing mechanism (such as deductibles, copayments, or coinsurance), the absence of a surcharge, or the value of a benefit that would otherwise not be provided under the plan. Under the proposed rule, the reward for the wellness program, coupled with the reward for other wellness programs with respect to the plan that require satisfaction of a standard related to a health factor, must not exceed a specified percentage of the cost of employee-only coverage under the plan. The cost of employee-only coverage is determined based on the total amount of employer and employee contributions for the benefit package under which the employee is receiving coverage.

Comments indicated that in some circumstances dependents are permitted to participate in the wellness program in addition to the employee and that in those circumstances the reward should be higher to reflect dependent participation in the program. These final regulations provide that if, in addition to employees, any class of dependents (such as spouses or spouses and dependent children) may participate in the wellness program, the limit on the reward is based on the cost of the coverage category in which the employee and any dependents are enrolled.

The proposed regulations specified three alternative percentages: 10, 15, and 20. The final regulations provide that the amount of the reward may not exceed 20 percent of the cost of coverage. The proposed regulations solicited comments on the appropriate percentage. The percentage limit is designed to avoid a reward or penalty being so large as to have the effect of denying coverage or creating too heavy a financial penalty on individuals who do not satisfy an initial wellness program standard that is related to a health factor. Comments from one employer and two national insurance industry associations requested that the level of the percentage for rewards should provide plans and issuers maximum flexibility for designing wellness programs. Comments suggested that plans and issuers have a greater opportunity to encourage healthy behaviors through programs of health promotion and disease prevention if they are allowed flexibility in designing such programs. The 20 percent limit on the size of the reward in the final regulations allows plans and issuers to maintain flexibility in their ability to design wellness programs, while avoiding rewards or penalties so large as to deny coverage or create too heavy a financial penalty on individuals who do not satisfy an initial wellness program standard that is related to a health factor.

Reasonably-designed and at-least-once-per-year requirements. In the 2001 proposed rules, the second of four requirements was that the program must be reasonably designed to promote good health or prevent disease. The regulations also provided that a program did not meet this standard unless it gave individuals eligible for the program the opportunity to qualify for the reward at least once per year.

One comment suggested a safe harbor under which a wellness program that allows individuals to qualify at least once a year for the reward under the program would satisfy the "reasonably designed" standard without regard to other attributes of the program. The Departments have not adopted this suggestion. The "reasonably designed" standard is a broad standard. A wide range of factors could affect the reasonableness of the design of a wellness program, not just the frequency with which a participant could qualify for the reward. For example, a program might not be reasonably designed to promote good health or prevent disease if it imposed, as a condition to obtaining the reward, an overly burdensome time commitment or a requirement to engage in illegal behavior. The once-per-year requirement was included in the proposed rules merely as a bright-line standard for determining the minimum frequency that is consistent with a reasonable design for promoting good health or preventing disease. Thus, this second requirement of the proposed rules has been divided into two requirements in the final rules (the second and the third requirements). This division was made to emphasize that a program that must satisfy the additional standards in order to comply with the nondiscrimination requirements must allow eligible individuals to qualify for the reward at least once per year and must also be otherwise reasonably designed to promote health or prevent disease.

Comments also expressed other concerns about the "reasonably designed" requirement. While acknowledging that this standard provides significant flexibility, these comments were concerned that this flexible approach might also require substantial resources in evaluating all the facts and circumstances of a proposed program to determine whether it was reasonable in its design.

The "reasonably designed" requirement is intended to be an easy standard to satisfy. To make this clear, the final regulations have added language providing that if a program has a reasonable chance of improving the health of participants and it is not overly burdensome, is not a subterfuge for discriminating based on a health factor, and is not highly suspect in the method chosen to promote health or prevent disease, it satisfies this standard. There does not need to be a scientific record that the method promotes wellness to satisfy this standard. The standard is intended to allow experimentation in diverse ways of promoting wellness. For example, a plan or issuer could satisfy this standard by providing rewards to individuals who participated in a course of aromatherapy. The requirement of reasonableness in this standard prohibits bizarre, extreme, or illegal requirements in a wellness program.

F. HIPAA Final Rules, Nondiscrimination and Wellness Benefits, continued

Federal Register / Vol. 71, No. 239 / Wednesday, December 13, 2006 / Rules and Regulations 75019

One comment requested that the final regulations set forth one or more safe harbors that would demonstrate compliance with the "reasonably designed" standard. The examples in the proposed and final regulations present a range of wellness programs that are well within the borders of what is considered reasonably designed to promote health and prevent disease. The examples serve as safe harbors, so that a plan or issuer could adopt a program identical to one described as satisfying the wellness program requirements in the examples and be assured of satisfying the requirements in the regulations. Wellness programs similar to the examples also would satisfy the "reasonably designed" requirement. The Departments, though, do not want plans or issuers to feel constrained by the relatively narrow range of programs described by the examples but want plans and issuers to feel free to consider innovative programs for motivating individuals to make efforts to improve their health.

Reasonable alternative standard. Under the 2001 proposed rules and these final regulations, a wellness program that provides a reward requiring satisfaction of a standard related to a health factor must provide a reasonable alternative standard for obtaining the reward for certain individuals. This alternative standard must be available for individuals for whom, for that period, it is unreasonably difficult due to a medical condition to satisfy the otherwise applicable standard, or for whom, for that period, it is medically inadvisable to attempt to satisfy the otherwise applicable standard. A program does not need to establish the specific reasonable alternative standard before the program commences. It is sufficient to determine a reasonable alternative standard once a participant informs the plan that it is unreasonably difficult for the participant due to a medical condition to satisfy the general standard (or that it is medically inadvisable for the participant to attempt to achieve the general standard) under the program.

Some comments suggested that the requirement to devise and offer such a reasonable alternative standard potentially creates a significant burden on plans and issuers. Comments also suggested that the Departments should define a "safe harbor" for what constitutes a reasonable alternative standard, and that plans and issuers should be permitted to establish a single alternative standard, rather than having to tailor a standard for each individual for whom a reasonable alternative standard must be offered.

The Departments understand that, in devising wellness programs, plans and issuers strive to improve the health of participating individuals in a way that is not administratively burdensome or expensive. Under the proposed and final rules, it is permissible for a plan or issuer to devise a reasonable alternative standard by lowering the threshold of the existing health-factor-related standard, substituting a different standard, or waiving the standard. (For the alternative standard to be reasonable, the individual must be able to satisfy it without regard to any health factor.) To address the concern regarding the potential burden of this requirement, the final regulations explicitly provide that a plan or issuer can waive the health-factor-related standard for all individuals for whom a reasonable alternative standard must be offered. Additionally, the final regulations include an example demonstrating that a reasonable alternative standard could include following the recommendations of an individual's physician regarding the health factor at issue. Thus, a plan or issuer need not assume the burden of designing a discrete alternative standard for each individual for whom an alternative standard must be offered. An example also illustrates that if an alternative standard is health-factor-related (*i.e.,* walking three days a week for 20 minutes a day), the wellness program must provide an additional *alternative* standard (*i.e.,* following the individual's physician's recommendations regarding the health factor at issue) to the appropriate individuals.

The 2001 proposed rules included an example illustrating a smoking cessation program. Comments expressed concern that, under the proposed regulations, individuals addicted to nicotine who comply with a reasonable alternative standard year after year would always be entitled to the reward even if they did not quit using tobacco. Comments questioned whether this result is consistent with the goal of promoting wellness. The final regulations retain the example from the proposed rules. Comments noted that overcoming an addiction sometimes requires a cycle of failure and renewed effort. For those individuals for whom it remains unreasonably difficult due to an addiction, a reasonable alternative standard must continue to be offered. Plans and issuers can accommodate this health factor by continuing to offer the same or a new reasonable alternative standard. For example, a plan or issuer using a smoking cessation class might

use different classes from year to year or might change from using a class to providing nicotine replacement therapy. These final regulations provide an additional example of a reasonable alternative standard of viewing, over a period of 12 months, a 12-hour video series on health problems associated with tobacco use.

Concern has been expressed that individuals might claim that it would be unreasonably difficult or medically inadvisable to meet the wellness program standard, when in fact the individual could meet the standard. The final rules clarify that plans may seek verification, such as a statement from a physician, that a health factor makes it unreasonably difficult or medically inadvisable for an individual to meet a standard.

Disclosure requirements. The fifth requirement for a wellness program that provides a reward requiring satisfaction of a standard related to a health factor is that all plan materials describing the terms of the program must disclose the availability of a reasonable alternative standard. This requirement is unchanged from the proposed rules. The 2001 proposed rules and these final regulations include the same model language that can be used to satisfy this requirement; examples also illustrate substantially similar language that would satisfy the requirement.

The final regulations retain the two clarifications of this requirement. First, plan materials are not required to describe specific reasonable alternative standards. It is sufficient to disclose that some reasonable alternative standard will be made available. Second, any plan materials that describe the general standard would also have to disclose the availability of a reasonable alternative standard. However, if the program is merely mentioned (and does not describe the general standard), disclosure of the availability of a reasonable alternative standard is not required.

Special Rule for Self-Funded Nonfederal Governmental Plans Exempted Under 45 CFR 146.180

The sponsor of a self-funded nonfederal governmental plan may elect under section 2721(b)(2) of the PHS Act and 45 CFR 146.180 to exempt its group health plan from the nondiscrimination requirements of section 2702 of the PHS Act and 45 CFR 146.121. Under the interim final nondiscrimination rules, if the plan sponsor subsequently chooses to bring the plan into compliance with the nondiscrimination requirements, the plan must provide notice to that effect to individuals who were denied

F. HIPAA Final Rules, Nondiscrimination and Wellness Benefits, continued

enrollment based on one or more health factors, and afford those individuals an opportunity, that continues for at least 30 days, to enroll in the plan. (An individual is considered to have been denied coverage if he or she failed to apply for coverage because, given an exemption election under 45 CFR 146.180, it was reasonable to believe that an application for coverage would have been denied based on a health factor). The notice must specify the effective date of compliance, and inform the individual regarding any enrollment restrictions that may apply under the terms of the plan once the plan comes into compliance. The plan may not treat the individual as a late enrollee or a special enrollee. These final regulations retain this transitional rule, and state that the plan must permit coverage to be effective as of the first day of plan coverage for which an exemption election under 45 CFR 146.180 (with regard to the nondiscrimination requirements) is no longer in effect. (These final regulations delete the reference giving the plan the option of having the coverage start July 1, 2001, because that option implicated the expired transitional rules regarding individuals who were denied coverage based on a health factor prior to the applicability of the 2001 interim rules. As previously stated, those transitional rules have not been republished in these final regulations.) Additionally, the examples illustrating how the special rule for nonfederal governmental plans operates have been revised slightly.

Applicability Date

These regulations apply for plan years beginning on or after July 1, 2007. Until the applicability date for this regulation, plans and issuers are required to comply with the corresponding sections of the regulations previously published in the **Federal Register** (66 FR 1378) and other applicable regulations.

III. Economic Impact and Paperwork Burden

Summary—Department of Labor and Department of Health and Human Services

HIPAA's nondiscrimination provisions generally prohibit group health plans and group health insurance issuers from discriminating against individuals in eligibility or premiums on the basis of health factors. The Departments have crafted these regulations to secure the protections from discrimination as intended by Congress in as economically efficient a manner as possible, and believe that the economic benefits of the regulations justify their costs.

The primary economic benefits associated with securing HIPAA's nondiscrimination provisions derive from increased access to affordable group health plan coverage for individuals with health problems. Increased access benefits both newly-covered individuals and society at large. It fosters expanded health coverage, timelier and more complete medical care, better health outcomes, and improved productivity and quality of life. This is especially true for the individuals most affected by HIPAA's nondiscrimination provisions—those with adverse health conditions. Denied health coverage, individuals in poorer health are more likely to suffer economic hardship, to forego badly needed care for financial reasons, and to suffer adverse health outcomes as a result. For them, gaining health coverage is more likely to mean gaining economic security, receiving timely, quality care, and living healthier, more productive lives. Similarly, participation by these individuals in wellness programs fosters better health outcomes, increases productivity and quality of life, and has the same outcome in terms of overall gains in economic security. The wellness provisions of these regulations will result in fewer instances in which wellness programs shift costs to high-risk individuals, and more instances in which these individuals succeed at improving health habits and health.

Additional economic benefits derive directly from the improved clarity provided by the regulations. The regulations will reduce uncertainty and costly disputes and promote confidence in health benefits' value, thereby improving labor market efficiency and fostering the establishment and continuation of group health plans and their wellness program provisions.

The Departments estimate that the dollar value of the expanded coverage attributable to HIPAA's nondiscrimination provisions is approximately $850 million annually. The Departments believe that the cost of HIPAA's nondiscrimination provisions is borne by covered workers. Costs can be shifted to workers through increases in employee premium shares or reductions (or smaller increases) in pay or other components of compensation, by increases in deductibles or other cost sharing, or by reducing the richness of health benefits. Whereas the benefits of the nondiscrimination provisions are concentrated in a relatively small population, the costs are distributed broadly across plans and enrollees.

The proposed rules on wellness programs impose certain requirements on wellness programs providing rewards that would otherwise discriminate based on a health factor in order to ensure that the exception for wellness programs does not eviscerate the general rule contained in HIPAA's nondiscrimination provisions. Costs associated with the wellness program provisions are justified by the benefits received by those individuals now able, through alternative standards, to participate in such programs. Because the new provisions limit rewards for wellness programs that require an individual to satisfy a standard related to a health factor to 20 percent of the cost of single coverage (with additional provisions related to rewards that apply also to classes of dependents), some rewards will be reduced and this reduction might compel some individuals to decline coverage. The number of individuals affected, however, is thought to be small. Moreover, the Departments estimate that the cost of the reduction in rewards that would exceed the limit will amount to only $6 million. Establishing reasonable alternative standards, which should increase coverage for those now eligible for discounts as well as their participation in programs designed to promote health or prevent disease, is expected to cost between $2 million to $9 million. The total costs should therefore fall within a range between $8 million and $15 million annually.

New economic costs may be also incurred in connection with the wellness provisions if reductions in rewards result in the reduction of wellness programs' effectiveness, but this effect is expected to be very small. Other new economic costs may be incurred by plan sponsors to make available reasonable alternative standards where required. The Departments are unable to estimate these costs due to the variety of options available to plan sponsors for bringing wellness programs into compliance with these rules.

Executive Order 12866—Department of Labor and Department of Health and Human Services

Under Executive Order 12866, the Departments must determine whether a regulatory action is "significant" and therefore subject to the requirements of the Executive Order and subject to review by the Office of Management and Budget (OMB). Under section 3(f), the order defines a "significant regulatory action" as an action that is likely to result in a rule (1) having an annual effect on the economy of $100 million

F. HIPAA Final Rules, Nondiscrimination and Wellness Benefits, continued

or more, or adversely and materially affecting a sector of the economy, productivity, competition, jobs, the environment, public health or safety, or State, local or tribal governments or communities (also referred to as "economically significant"); (2) creating serious inconsistency or otherwise interfering with an action taken or planned by another agency; (3) materially altering the budgetary impacts of entitlement grants, user fees, or loan programs or the rights and obligations of recipients thereof; or (4) raising novel legal or policy issues arising out of legal mandates, the President's priorities, or the principles set forth in the Executive Order.

Pursuant to the terms of the Executive Order, this action is "economically significant" and subject to OMB review under Section 3(f) of the Executive Order. Consistent with the Executive Order, the Departments have assessed the costs and benefits of this regulatory action. The Departments performed a comprehensive, unified analysis to estimate the costs and benefits attributable to the final regulations for purposes of compliance with the Executive Order 12866, the Regulatory Flexibility Act, and the Paperwork Reduction Act. The Departments' analyses and underlying assumptions are detailed below. The Departments believe that the benefits of the final regulations justify their costs.

Regulatory Flexibility Act—Department of Labor and Department of Health and Human Services

The Regulatory Flexibility Act (5 U.S.C. 601 *et seq.*) (RFA) imposes certain requirements with respect to federal rules that are subject to the notice and comment requirements of section 553(b) of the Administrative Procedure Act (5 U.S.C. 551 *et seq.*) and likely to have a significant economic impact on a substantial number of small entities. Unless an agency certifies that a final rule will not have a significant economic impact on a substantial number of small entities, section 604 of the RFA requires that the agency present a final regulatory flexibility analysis (FRFA) at the time of the publication of the notice of final rulemaking describing the impact of the rule on small entities. Small entities include small businesses, organizations, and governmental jurisdictions.

Because the 2001 interim rules were issued as final rules and not as a notice of proposed rulemaking, the RFA did not apply and the Departments were not required to either certify that the rule would not have a significant impact on a substantial number of small entities or

conduct a regulatory flexibility analysis. The Departments nonetheless crafted those regulations in careful consideration of effects on small entities, and conducted an analysis of the likely impact of the rules on small entities. This analysis was detailed in the preamble to the interim final rule.

The Departments also conducted an initial regulatory flexibility analysis in connection with the proposed regulations on wellness programs and present here a FRFA with respect to the final regulations on wellness programs pursuant to section 604 of the RFA. For purposes of their unified FRFA, the Departments adhered to EBSA's proposed definition of small entities. The Departments consider a small entity to be an employee benefit plan with fewer than 100 participants. The basis of this definition is found in section 104(a)(2) of ERISA, which permits the Secretary of Labor to prescribe simplified annual reports for pension plans that cover fewer than 100 participants. The Departments believe that assessing the impact of this final rule on small plans is an appropriate substitute for evaluating the effect on small entities as that term is defined in the RFA. This definition of small entity differs, however, from the definition of small business based on standards promulgated by the Small Business Administration (13 CFR 121.201) pursuant to the Small Business Act (15 U.S.C. 631 *et seq.*). Because of this difference, the Departments requested comments on the appropriateness of this size standard for evaluating the impact of the proposed regulations on small entities. No comments were received.

The Departments estimate that 35,000 plans with fewer than 100 participants vary employee premium contributions or cost-sharing across similarly situated individuals based on health factors.[2] While this represents just one percent of all small plans, the Departments believe that because of the large number of plans, this may constitute a substantial number of small entities. The Departments also note that at least some premium rewards may be large. Premium discounts associated with

wellness programs are believed to range as high as $920 per affected participant per year. Therefore, the Departments believe that the impact of this regulation on at least some small entities may be significant.

Under these final regulations on wellness programs, such programs are not subject to additional requirements if none of the conditions for obtaining a reward is based on an individual satisfying a standard that is related to a health factor (or if a wellness program does not provide a reward).

Where a condition for obtaining a reward is based on an individual satisfying a standard related to a health factor, the wellness program will not violate the nondiscrimination provisions if additional requirements are met. The first requirement limits the maximum allowable reward or total of rewards to a maximum of 20 percent of the cost of employee-only coverage under the plan (with additional provisions related to rewards that apply also to classes of dependents). The magnitude of the limit is intended to offer plans maximum flexibility while avoiding the effect of denying coverage or creating an excessive financial penalty for individuals who cannot satisfy the initial standard based on a health factor.

The Departments estimate that 4,000 small plans and 22,000 small plan participants will be affected by this limit.[3] These plans can comply with this requirement by reducing the discount to the regulated maximum. This will result in an increase in premiums (or decrease in cost-sharing) by about $1.3 million on aggregate for those participants receiving qualified premium discounts[4] This constitutes an ongoing, annual cost of $338 on average per affected plan. The regulation does not limit small plans' flexibility to shift this cost to all participants in the form

---

[2] Based on tabulations of the 2003 Medical Expenditure Panel Survey Insurance Component (MEPS-IC) and 1997 Survey of Government Finances (SGF), the Departments estimate that roughly 2.4 million small health plans exist. Of these, 1.2 percent of these plans are believed to vary premiums (as suggested in a 1993 study by the Robert Woods Johnson Foundation) while .5 percent are thought to vary benefits (as suggested in, Spec Summary. United States Salaried Managed Health/Health Promotion Initiatives, 2003–2004, Hewitt Associates, July, 2003.). Assuming that half of those that vary premiums also vary benefits, the Departments conclude that 1.5 percent of all small plans are potentially affected by the statute.

[3] Simulations run by the Departments suggest that 10.7 percent of all plans exceed the capped premium discount. For the purposes of this analysis, it was assumed that the affected plans were proportionally distributed between large and small plans. However, it is likely that larger plans would have more generous welfare programs and therefore, this estimate is likely an upper bound.

[4] Estimate is based on the 2003–04 Hewitt Study and various measures of the general health of the labor force suggest that roughly 30 percent of health plan participants will not qualify for the discount. While plans exceeding the capped discount could meet the statutes requirements by transferring the excess amount, on average $57, to the non-qualifying participants, given current trends in the health insurance industry, it is considered more likely that plans would instead lower the amount of the discount given to the 70 percent of participants that qualify. This transfer would roughly total $1.3 million dollars.

F. HIPAA Final Rules, Nondiscrimination and Wellness Benefits, continued

of small premium increases or benefit cuts.

The second requirement provides that wellness programs must be reasonably designed to promote health or prevent disease. Comments received by the Departments and available literature on employee wellness programs suggest that existing wellness programs generally satisfy this requirement. The requirement therefore is not expected to compel small plans to modify existing wellness programs.

The third requirement is that the program give individuals eligible for the program the opportunity to qualify for the reward at least once per year. This provision was included within the terms of the requirements for reasonable design in the proposed regulations. The Departments did not anticipate that a cost would arise from the requirements related to reasonable design when taken together, but requested comments on their assumptions. Because no comments were received, the Departments have not attributed a cost to this provision of the final rule.

The fourth requirement provides that rewards under wellness programs must be available to all similarly situated individuals. Rewards are not available to similarly situated individuals unless a program allows a reasonable alternative standard or waiver of the applicable standard, if it is unreasonably difficult due to a medical condition or medically inadvisable to attempt to satisfy the otherwise applicable standard. The Departments believe that some small plans' wellness programs do not currently satisfy this requirement and will have to be modified.

The Departments estimate that 3,000 small plans' wellness programs include initial standards that may be unreasonably difficult due to a medical condition or medically inadvisable for some participants to meet.[5] These plans are estimated to include 4,000 participants for whom the standard is in fact unreasonably difficult due to a medical condition or medically inadvisable to meet.[6] Satisfaction of alternative standards by these participants will result in cost increases for plans as these individuals qualify for discounts or avoid surcharges. If all of

these participants request and then satisfy an alternative standard, the cost would amount to about $2 million annually. If one-half request alternative standards and one-half of those meet them, the cost would be $0.5 million.[7]

In addition to the costs associated with new participants qualifying for discounts through alternative standards, small plans may also incur new economic costs by simply providing alternative standards. However, plans can satisfy this requirement by providing inexpensive alternative standards and have the flexibility to select whatever reasonable alternative standard is most desirable or cost effective. Plans not wishing to provide alternative standards also have the option of eliminating health status-based variation in employee premiums or waiving standards for individuals for whom the program standard is unreasonably difficult due to a medical condition or medically inadvisable to meet. The Departments expect that the economic cost to provide alternatives combined with the associated cost of granting discounts or waiving surcharges will not exceed the cost associated with granting discounts or waiving surcharges for all participants who qualify for an alternative. Those costs are estimated here at $0.5 million to $2 million, or about $160 to $650 per affected plan. Plans have the flexibility to pass back some or all of this cost to all participants in the form of small premium increases or benefit cuts.

The fifth requirement provides that plan materials describing wellness program standards disclose the availability of reasonable alternative standards. This requirement will affect the approximately 4,000 small plans that condition rewards on satisfaction of a standard. These plans will incur economic costs to revise affected plan materials. The estimated 1,000 to 4,000 small plan participants who will succeed at satisfying these alternative standards will benefit from these disclosures. The disclosures need not specify what alternatives are available unless the plan describes the initial standard in writing and the regulation provides sample language that can be used to satisfy this requirement. Legal requirements other than this regulation generally require plans and issuers to maintain accurate materials describing

plans. Plans and issuers generally update such materials on a regular basis as part of their normal business practices. This requirement is expected to represent a negligible fraction of the ongoing, normal cost of updating plans' materials. This analysis therefore attributes no cost to this requirement.

Paperwork Reduction Act—Department of Labor and Department of the Treasury

The 2001 interim rules included an information collection request (ICR) related to the notice of the opportunity to enroll in a plan where coverage had been denied based on a health factor before the effective date of HIPAA. That ICR was approved under OMB control numbers 1210–0120 and 1545–1728, and was subsequently withdrawn from OMB inventory because the notice, if applicable, was to have been provided only once.

The proposed regulations on wellness programs did not include an information collection request. Like the proposed regulations, the final regulations include a requirement that, if a plan's wellness program requires individuals to meet a standard related to a health factor in order to qualify for a reward and if the plan materials describe this standard, the materials must also disclose the availability of a reasonable alternative standard. If plan materials merely mention that a program is available, the disclosure relating to alternatives is not required. The regulations include samples of disclosures that could be used to satisfy the requirements of the final regulations.

In concluding that the proposed rules did not include an information collection request, the Departments reasoned that much of the information required was likely already provided as a result of state and local mandates or the usual business practices of group health plans and group health insurance issuers in connection with the offer and promotion of health care coverage. In addition, the sample disclosures would enable group health plans to make any modifications necessary with minimal effort.

Finally, although neither the proposed or final regulations include a new information collection request, the regulations might have been interpreted to require a revision to an existing collection of information. Administrators of group health plans covered under Title I of ERISA are generally required to make certain disclosures about the terms of a plan and material changes in terms through a Summary Plan Description (SPD) or

---

[5] The 2003–04 Hewitt Survey finds that 9 percent of its respondents require participants to achieve a certain health standard to be eligible for discounts. Based on assumptions about the general health of the labor force, approximately 2.3 percent of health plan participants may and 1.5 percent will find these standards difficult to achieve.

[6] Many small plans are very small, having fewer than 10 participants. Hence, many small plans will include no participant for whom either of these standards apply.

[7] Simulations run by the Departments find that the average premium discount for all health plans after the cap is enforced will be approximately $450 dollars. This average is then applied to the upper and lower bounds of those able to pass the alternative standards in small health plans in order to determine the upper and lower bound of the transfer cost.

F. HIPAA Final Rules, Nondiscrimination and Wellness Benefits, continued

Summary of Material Modifications (SMM) pursuant to sections 101(a) and 102(a) of ERISA and related regulations. The ICR related to the SPD and SMM is currently approved under OMB control number 1210–0039. While these materials may in some cases require revisions to comply with the final regulations, the associated burden is expected to be negligible, and is in fact already accounted for in connection with the SPD and SMM ICR by a burden estimation methodology that anticipates ongoing revisions. Therefore, any change to the existing information collection request arising from these final regulations is not substantive or material. Accordingly, no application for approval of a revision to the existing ICR has been made to OMB in connection with these final regulations.

Paperwork Reduction Act—Department of Health and Human Services

Collection of Information Requirements

Under the Paperwork Reduction Act of 1995, we are required to provide notice in the **Federal Register** and solicit public comment before a collection of information requirement is submitted to the Office of Management and Budget (OMB) for review and approval. In order to fairly evaluate whether an information collection should be approved by OMB, section 3506(c)(2)(A) of the Paperwork Reduction Act of 1995 requires that we solicit comment on the following issues:

• The need for the information collection and its usefulness in carrying out the proper functions of our agency.
• The accuracy of our estimate of the information collection burden.
• The quality, utility, and clarity of the information to be collected.
• Recommendations to minimize the information collection burden on the affected public, including automated techniques.

Department regulations in 45 CFR 146.121(i)(4) require that if coverage has been denied to any individual because the sponsor of a self-funded nonfederal governmental plan has elected under 45 CFR Part 146 to exempt the plan from the requirements of this section, and the plan sponsor subsequently chooses to bring the plan into compliance, the plan must: notify the individual that the plan will be coming into compliance; afford the individual an opportunity to enroll that continues for at least 30 days, specify the effective date of compliance; and inform the individual regarding any enrollment restrictions that may apply once the plan is in compliance.

The burden associated with this requirement was approved by The

Office of Management and Budget (OMB) under OMB control number 0938–0827, with a current expiration date of April 30, 2009.

In addition, CMS–2078–P, published in the **Federal Register** on January 8, 2001 (66 FR 1421) describes the bona fide wellness programs and specifies their criteria. Section 146.121(f)(1)(iv) further stipulates that the plan or issuer disclose in all plan materials describing the terms of the program the availability of a reasonable alternative standard to qualify for the reward under a wellness program. However, in plan materials that merely mention that a program is available, without describing its terms, the disclosure is not required.

The burden associated with this requirement was approved by OMB control number 0938–0819, with a current expiration date of April 30, 2009.

Special Analyses—Department of the Treasury

Notwithstanding the determinations of the Departments of Labor and of Health and Human Services, for purposes of the Department of the Treasury it has been determined that this Treasury decision is not a significant regulatory action. Therefore, a regulatory assessment is not required. It has also been determined that section 553(b) of the Administrative Procedure Act (5 U.S.C. chapter 5) does not apply to these regulations, and, because these regulations do not impose a collection of information on small entities, a Regulatory Flexibility Analysis under the Regulatory Flexibility Act (5 U.S.C. chapter 6) is not required. Pursuant to section 7805(f) of the Code, the notice of proposed rulemaking preceding these regulations was submitted to the Small Business Administration for comment on its impact on small business.

Congressional Review Act

These final regulations are subject to the Congressional Review Act provisions of the Small Business Regulatory Enforcement Fairness Act of 1996 (5 U.S.C. 801 *et seq.*) and have been transmitted to Congress and the Comptroller General for review. These regulations, however, constitute a "major rule," as that term is defined in 5 U.S.C. 804, because they are likely to result in (1) an annual effect on the economy of $100 million or more; (2) a major increase in costs or prices for consumers, individual industries, or federal, State or local government agencies, or geographic regions; or (3) significant adverse effects on competition, employment, investment, productivity, innovation, or on the

ability of United States-based enterprises to compete with foreign-based enterprises in domestic or export markets.

Unfunded Mandates Reform Act

For purposes of the Unfunded Mandates Reform Act of 1995 (Pub. L. 104–4), as well as Executive Order 12875, these final regulations do not include any federal mandate that may result in expenditures by state, local, or tribal governments, nor does it include mandates which may impose an annual burden of $100 million or more on the private sector.

Federalism Statement—Department of Labor and Department of Health and Human Services

Executive Order 13132 outlines fundamental principles of federalism, and requires the adherence to specific criteria by federal agencies in the process of their formulation and implementation of policies that have "substantial direct effects" on the States, the relationship between the national government and States, or on the distribution of power and responsibilities among the various levels of government. Federal agencies promulgating regulations that have these federalism implications must consult with State and local officials, and describe the extent of their consultation and the nature of the concerns of State and local officials in the preamble to the regulation.

In the Departments' view, these final regulations have federalism implications, because they have substantial direct effects on the States, the relationship between the national government and States, or on the distribution of power and responsibilities among various levels of government. However, in the Departments' view, the federalism implications of these final regulations are substantially mitigated because, with respect to health insurance issuers, the vast majority of States have enacted laws, which meet or exceed the federal HIPAA standards prohibiting discrimination based on health factors.

In general, through section 514, ERISA supersedes State laws to the extent that they relate to any covered employee benefit plan, and preserves State laws that regulate insurance, banking, or securities. While ERISA prohibits States from regulating a plan as an insurance or investment company or bank, HIPAA added a new preemption provision to ERISA (as well as to the PHS Act) narrowly preempting State requirements for group health insurance coverage. With respect to the

F. HIPAA Final Rules, Nondiscrimination and Wellness Benefits, continued

HIPAA nondiscrimination provisions, States may continue to apply State law requirements except to the extent that such requirements prevent the application of the portability, access, and renewability requirements of HIPAA, which include HIPAA's nondiscrimination requirements provisions that are the subject of this rulemaking.

In enacting these new preemption provisions, Congress intended to preempt State insurance requirements only to the extent that those requirements prevent the application of the basic protections set forth in HIPAA. HIPAA's Conference Report states that the conferees intended the narrowest preemption of State laws with regard to health insurance issuers. H.R. Conf. Rep. No. 736, 104th Cong. 2d Session 205 (1996). State insurance laws that are more stringent than the federal requirements are unlikely to "prevent the application of" the HIPAA nondiscrimination provisions, and be preempted. Accordingly, States have significant latitude to impose requirements on health insurance issuers that are more restrictive than the federal law.

Guidance conveying this interpretation was published in the **Federal Register** on April 8, 1997. (62 FR 16904) and on December 30, 2004 (62 FR 78720). These final regulations clarify and implement the statute's minimum standards and do not significantly reduce the discretion given the States by the statute. Moreover, the Departments understand that the vast majority of States have requirements that meet or exceed the minimum requirements of the HIPAA nondiscrimination provisions.

HIPAA provides that the States may enforce the provisions of HIPAA as they pertain to issuers, but that the Secretary of Health and Human Services must enforce any provisions that a State fails to substantially enforce. To date, HHS has had occasion to enforce the HIPAA nondiscrimination provisions in only two States and currently enforces the nondiscrimination provisions in only one State in accordance with that State's specific request to do so. When exercising its responsibility to enforce provisions of HIPAA, HHS works cooperatively with the State for the purpose of addressing the State's concerns and avoiding conflicts with the exercise of State authority.[8] HHS has

developed procedures to implement its enforcement responsibilities, and to afford the States the maximum opportunity to enforce HIPAA's requirements in the first instance. HHS's procedures address the handling of reports that States may not be enforcing HIPAA's requirements, and the mechanism for allocating enforcement responsibility between the States and HHS. In compliance with Executive Order 13132's requirement that agencies examine closely any policies that may have federalism implications or limit the policy making discretion of the States, DOL and HHS have engaged in numerous efforts to consult with and work cooperatively with affected State and local officials.

For example, the Departments sought and received input from State insurance regulators and the National Association of Insurance Commissioners (NAIC). The NAIC is a non-profit corporation established by the insurance commissioners of the 50 States, the District of Columbia, and the four U.S. territories. In most States the Insurance Commissioner is appointed by the Governor, in approximately 14 States the insurance commissioner is an elected official. Among other activities, it provides a forum for the development of uniform policy when uniformity is appropriate. Its members meet, discuss, and offer solutions to mutual problems. The NAIC sponsors quarterly meetings to provide a forum for the exchange of ideas, and in-depth consideration of insurance issues by regulators, industry representatives, and consumers. CMS and Department of Labor staff have attended the quarterly meetings consistently to listen to the concerns of the State Insurance Departments regarding HIPAA issues, including the nondiscrimination provisions. In addition to the general discussions, committee meetings and task groups, the NAIC sponsors the standing CMS/DOL meeting on HIPAA issues for members during the quarterly conferences. This meeting provides CMS and the Department of Labor with the opportunity to provide updates on regulations, bulletins, enforcement actions and outreach efforts regarding HIPAA.

In addition, the Departments specifically consulted with the NAIC in developing these final regulations. Through the NAIC, the Departments sought and received the input of State insurance departments regarding certain insurance rating practices and late

enrollment issues. The Departments employed the States' insights on insurance rating practices in developing the provisions prohibiting "list-billing," and their experience with late enrollment in crafting the regulatory provision clarifying the relationship between the nondiscrimination provisions and late enrollment. Specifically, the regulations clarify that while late enrollment, if offered by a plan, must be available to all similarly situated individuals regardless of any health factor, an individual's status as a late enrollee is not itself within the scope of any health factor.

The Departments have also cooperated with the States in several ongoing outreach initiatives, through which information on HIPAA is shared among federal regulators, State regulators, and the regulated community. In particular, the Department of Labor has established a Health Benefits Education Campaign with more than 70 partners, including CMS, the NAIC and many business and consumer groups. CMS has sponsored conferences with the States—the Consumer Outreach and Advocacy conferences in March 1999 and June 2000 and the Implementation and Enforcement of HIPAA National State-federal Conferences in August 1999, 2000, 2001, 2002, and 2003. Furthermore, both the Department of Labor and CMS Web sites offer links to important State Web sites and other resources, facilitating coordination between the State and federal regulators and the regulated community.

Throughout the process of developing these regulations, to the extent feasible within the specific preemption provisions of HIPAA, the Departments have attempted to balance the States' interests in regulating health insurance issuers, and Congress's intent to provide uniform minimum protections to consumers in every State. By doing so, it is the Departments' view that they have complied with the requirements of Executive Order 13132.

Pursuant to the requirements set forth in section 8(a) of Executive Order 13132, and by the signatures affixed to these regulations, the Departments certify that the Employee Benefits Security Administration and the Centers for Medicare & Medicaid Services have complied with the requirements of Executive Order 13132 for the attached final regulation, Final Rules for Nondiscrimination in Health Coverage in the Group Market (RIN 1210–AA77 and RIN 0938–AI08), in a meaningful and timely manner.

---

[8] This authority applies to insurance issued with respect to group health plans generally, including plans covering employees of church organizations. Thus, this discussion of federalism applies to all group health insurance coverage that is subject to the PHS Act, including those church plans that provide coverage through a health insurance issuer (but not to church plans that do not provide coverage through a health insurance issuer).

F. HIPAA Final Rules, Nondiscrimination and Wellness Benefits, continued

Unified Analysis of Costs and Benefits

1. Introduction

HIPAA's nondiscrimination provisions generally prohibit group health plans and group health insurance issuers from discriminating against individuals on the basis of health factors. The primary effect and intent of the provision is to increase access to affordable group health coverage for individuals with health problems. This effect, and the economic costs and benefits attendant to it, primarily flows from the statutory provisions of HIPAA that this regulation implements. However, the statute alone leaves room for varying interpretations of exactly which practices are prohibited or permitted at the margin. These regulations draw on the Departments' authority to clarify and interpret HIPAA's statutory nondiscrimination provisions in order to secure the protections intended by Congress for plan participants and beneficiaries. The Departments crafted them to satisfy this mandate in as economically efficient a manner as possible, and believe that the economic benefits of the regulations justify their costs. The analysis underlying this conclusion takes into account both the effect of the statute and the impact of the discretion exercised in the regulations.

The nondiscrimination provisions of the HIPAA statute and of these regulations generally apply to both group health plans and group health insurance issuers. Economic theory predicts that issuers will pass their costs of compliance back to plans, and that plans may pass some or all of issuers' and their own costs of compliance to participants. This analysis is carried out in light of this prediction.

These final regulations are needed to clarify and interpret the HIPAA nondiscrimination provisions under section 702 of ERISA, section 2702 of the PHS Act, and section 9802 of the Code, and to ensure that group health plans and group health insurance issuers do not discriminate against individual participants or beneficiaries based on any health factors with respect to health care coverage and premiums. The 2001 interim rules provided additional guidance to explain the application of the statute to benefits, to clarify the relationship between the HIPAA nondiscrimination provisions and the HIPAA preexisting condition exclusion limitations, to explain the applications of these provisions to premiums, to describe similarly situated individuals, to explain the application of the provisions to actively-at-work and nonconfinement clauses, to clarify that

more favorable treatment of individuals with medical needs generally is permitted, and to describe plans' and issuers' obligations with respect to plan amendments.[9] These final regulations clarify the relationship between the source-of-injury rules and the timing of a diagnosis of a medical condition and add an example to illustrate how the benefits rules apply to the carryover feature of HRAs.

The proposed rules on wellness programs were issued in order to ensure that the exception for wellness programs would not contravene HIPAA's nondiscrimination provisions. With respect to wellness programs, these final regulations clarify some ambiguities in the proposed rules, make some changes in terminology and organization, and add a description of wellness programs not required to satisfy additional standards. The final rules also set the maximum reward for wellness programs that require satisfaction of a standard at 20 percent of the cost of single coverage (with additional provisions related to rewards that apply also to classes of dependents), where the proposed rules had stated the limit in terms of a range of percentages.

Because the 2001 interim rules and proposed regulations on wellness programs were originally issued as separate rulemaking actions, the Departments estimated their economic impacts separately. The costs and benefits of the statutory nondiscrimination provisions and the 2001 interim rules are again described separately from the wellness program provisions here, due to both differing baselines for the measurement of impact, and to reliance on different types of information and assumptions in the analyses.

2. Costs and Benefits of HIPAA's Nondiscrimination Provisions

The Departments have evaluated the impacts of HIPAA's nondiscrimination provisions. The nondiscrimination provisions of the 2001 interim final rules were estimated to result in costs of about $20 million to amend plans, revise plan informational materials, and notify employees previously denied coverage on the basis of a health factor of enrollment opportunities. Because these costs were associated with one-time activities that were required to be completed by the applicability date of the 2001 interim rules, these costs have been fully defrayed.

The primary statutory economic benefits associated with the HIPAA nondiscrimination provisions derive from increased access to affordable group health plan coverage for individuals whose health factors had previously restricted their participation in such plans. Expanding access entails both benefits and costs. Newly-covered individuals, who previously had to purchase similar services out-of-pocket, reap a simple and direct financial gain. In addition, these individuals may be induced to consume more (or different) health care services, reaping a benefit which has financial value, and which in some cases will produce additional indirect benefits both to the individual (improved health) and possibly to the economy at large.[10]

---

[9] The Departments' estimate of the economic impact of the 2001 interim final regulations was published at 66 FR 1393 (January 8, 2001). These one-time costs were already absorbed by plans and issuers and are not discussed in this analysis. In fact, the only notice requirement in the 2001 interim final regulations was deleted from the final regulations because the time period for compliance has passed, with one small exception. Certain self-insured, nonfederal governmental plans that had opted out of the HIPAA nondiscrimination provisions under Section 2721(b)(2) of the PHS Act and that have since decided to opt back in may be required to send a notice to individuals previously denied coverage due to a health factor. However, to date, only approximately 550 such plans have notified CMS that they are opting-out of the HIPAA nondiscrimination provisions and CMS does not receive information regarding a plan's decision to opt back in. The Departments estimate that the number of plans having done this is very small and, therefore, estimate that the impact of the notice provision on such plans is too small to calculate.

[10] Individuals without health insurance are less likely to get preventive care and less likely to have a regular source of care. A lack of health insurance generally increases the likelihood that needed medical treatment will be forgone or delayed. Forgoing or delaying care increases the risk of adverse health outcomes. These adverse outcomes in turn generate higher medical costs, which are often shifted to public funding sources (and therefore to taxpayers) or to other payers. They also erode productivity and the quality of life. Improved access to affordable group health coverage for individuals with health problems under HIPAA's nondiscrimination provisions will lead to more insurance coverage, timelier and fuller medical care, better health outcomes, and improved productivity and quality of life. This is especially true for the individuals most affected by HIPAA's nondiscrimination provisions—those with adverse health conditions. Denied insurance, individuals in poorer health are more likely to suffer economic hardship, to forgo badly needed care for financial reasons, and to suffer adverse health outcomes as a result. For them, gaining insurance is more likely to mean gaining economic security, receiving timely, quality care, and living healthier, more productive lives. For an extensive discussion of the consequences of uninsurance, see: "The Uninsured and their Access to Health Care" (2004). *The Kaiser Commission on Medicaid and the Uninsured*, November; "Insuring America's Health", (2004). *Institute of Medicine*, "Health Policy and the Uninsured" (2004) edited by Catherine G. McLaughlin. Washington, DC: Urban Institute Press; Miller, Wilhelmine et al (2004) "Covering the Uninsured: What is it Worth," *Health Affairs*, March: w157–w167.

F. HIPAA Final Rules, Nondiscrimination and Wellness Benefits, continued

Inclusion of these newly-covered individuals, though, will increase both premiums and claims costs incurred by group health plans. Economic theory predicts that these costs will ultimately be shifted to all plan participants or employees, either through an increased share of insurance costs, or lowered compensation.[11] If the number of newly-covered individuals is small relative to the total number of plan participants and costs are distributed evenly, then the increased burden for each individual should be minimal. However, it is unclear how previously-covered individuals will respond to subsequent changes in their benefits package and if their response will have unforeseen economic costs.[12] The

[11] The voluntary nature of the employment-based health benefit system in conjunction with the open and dynamic character of labor markets make explicit as well as implicit negotiations on compensation a key determinant of the prevalence of employee benefits coverage. It is likely that 80% to 100% of the cost of employee benefits is borne by workers through reduced wages (see for example Jonathan Gruber and Alan B. Krueger, "The Incidence of Mandated Employer-Provided Insurance: Lessons from Workers Compensation Insurance," *Tax Policy and Economy* (1991); Jonathan Gruber, "The Incidence of Mandated Maternity Benefits," *American Economic Review*, Vol. 84 (June 1994), pp. 622–641; Lawrence H. Summers, "Some Simple Economics of Mandated Benefits," *American Economic Review*, Vol. 79, No. 2 (May 1989); Louise Sheiner, "Health Care Costs, Wages, and Aging," Federal Reserve Board of Governors working paper, April 1999; and Edward Montgomery, Kathryn Shaw, and Mary Ellen Benedict. "Pensions and Wages: An Hedonic Price Theory Approach," *International Economic Review*, Vol. 33 No. 1, Feb. 1992.). The prevalence of benefits is therefore largely dependent on the efficacy of this exchange. If workers perceive that there is the potential for inappropriate denial of benefits they will discount their value to adjust for this risk. This discount drives a wedge in the compensation negotiation, limiting its efficiency. With workers unwilling to bear the full cost of the benefit, fewer benefits will be provided. The extent to which workers perceive a federal regulation supported by enforcement authority to improve the security and quality of benefits, the differential between the employers costs and workers willingness top accept wage offsets is minimized.

[12] Research shows that while the share of employers offering insurance is generally stable and eligibility rates have only declined slightly over time, the overall increase in uninsured workers is due to the decline in worker take-up rates, which workers primarily attribute to cost. Research on elasticity of coverage, however, has focused on getting uninsured workers to adopt coverage (which appears to require large subsidies) rather than covered workers opting out of coverage. This makes it difficult to ascertain the loss in coverage that would result from a marginal increase in costs. (See, for example, David M. Cutler "Employee Costs and the Decline in Health Insurance Coverage" NBER Working Paper #9036. July 2002; Gruber, Jonathon and Ebonya Washington. "Subsidies to Employee Health Insurance Premiums and the Health Insurance Market" NBER Working Paper #9567. March 2003; and Cooper, PF and J. Vistnes. "Workers' Decisions to Take-up Offered Insurance Coverage: Assessing the Importance of Out-of-Pocket Costs" Med Care 2003, 41(7 Suppl): III35–43.) Finally, economic discussions on elasticity of

HIPAA nondiscrimination cost is estimated to be substantial. Annual group health plan costs average approximately $7,100 per-participant,[13] and it is likely that average costs would be higher for individuals who had been denied coverage due to health factors. Prior to HIPAA's enactment, less than one-tenth of one percent of employees, or roughly 120,000 in today's labor market, were denied employment-based coverage annually because of health factors.[14] A simple assessment suggests that the total cost of coverage for such employees could be $850 million. However, this estimated statutory transfer is small relative to the overall cost of employment-based health coverage. Group health plans will spend over $620 billion this year to cover approximately 174 million employees and their dependents.[15] Estimated costs under HIPAA's nondiscrimination provisions represent a very small fraction of one percent of total group health plan expenditures.

3. Costs and Benefits of Finalizing the 2001 Interim Rules

Prohibiting Discrimination

Many of the provisions of these regulations serve to specify more precisely than the statute alone exactly what practices are prohibited by HIPAA as unlawful discrimination in eligibility or employee premiums among similarly situated employees. For example, under the regulations, eligibility generally may not be restricted based on an individual's participation in risky activities, confinement to an institution, or absence from work on an individual's enrollment date due to illness. The regulations provide that various plan

[13] Departments' tabulations using the 2005 Kaiser Family Foundation's Employer Health Benefits Annual Survey. Average employee premium is a weighted average of premiums for single, family, and employee-plus-one health plans. The estimate for Employee-Plus-One health premiums was derived using the 2003 MEPS-IC, as was the share of employees in each type of plans. Participants are defined as the workers or primary policy holders.

[14] Departments' tabulations off the February 1997 Current Population Survey (CPS), Contingent Worker Supplement. The estimate was projected to reflect current labor market conditions by assuming the same share of the employed, civilian force would be affected and using the 2004 CPS table, "Employment status of the civilian noninstitutional population, 1940 to date."

[15] The Departments' estimate is based on the Office of the Actuary at the Centers for Medicare and Medicaid Services (CMS) projected measure of total personal health expenditures by private health insurance in 2004. This total ($707.0 billion) is then multiplied by the share of privately insured individuals covered by employer-sponsored health insurance in 2004 as estimated by the 2005 March CPS (88 percent).

insurance tend to view coverage as a discrete concept and does not consider that the value of coverage may have also changed.

features including waiting periods and eligibility for certain benefits constitute rules for eligibility which may not vary across similarly situated individuals based on health factors. They also provide that plans may not reclassify employees based on health factors in order to create separate groups of similarly situated individuals among which discrimination would be permitted.

All of these provisions have the effect of clarifying and ensuring certain participants' right to freedom from discrimination in eligibility and premium amounts, thereby securing their access to affordable group health plan coverage. The costs and benefits attributable to these provisions resemble those attendant to HIPAA's statutory nondiscrimination provisions. Securing participants' access to affordable group coverage provides economic benefits by reducing the numbers of uninsured and thereby improving health outcomes. The regulations entail a shifting of costs from the employees whose rights are secured (and/or from other parties who would otherwise pay for their health care) to plan sponsors (or to other plan participants if sponsors pass those costs back to them).

The Departments lack any basis on which to distinguish these benefits and costs from those of the statute itself. It is unclear how many plans were engaging in the discriminatory practices targeted for prohibition by these regulatory provisions. Because these provisions operate largely at the margin of the statutory requirements, it is likely that the effects of these provisions were far smaller than the similar statutory effects. The Departments are confident, however, that by securing employees' access to affordable coverage at the margin, the regulations, like the statute, have yielded benefits that justify costs.

Clarifying Requirements

Additional economic benefits derive directly from the improved clarity provided by the regulations. The regulation provides clarity through both its provisions and its examples of how those provisions apply in various circumstances. By clarifying employees' rights and plan sponsors' obligations under HIPAA's nondiscrimination provisions, the regulations reduce uncertainty and costly disputes over these rights and obligations. Greater clarity promotes employers' and employees' common understanding of the value of group health plan benefits and confidence in the security and predictability of those benefits, thereby improving labor market efficiency and fostering the establishment and

F. HIPAA Final Rules, Nondiscrimination and Wellness Benefits, continued

continuation of group health plans by employers.

Impact of the Final Rules

As noted earlier in this preamble, the Departments have not modified the 2001 interim rules in any way that would impact the original cost estimates or the magnitude of the statutory transfers. Accordingly, no impact is attributable to these final regulations when measured against the baseline of the interim final rules. The provisions of the 2001 interim rules offer the appropriate baseline for this measurement because these rules were generally applicable for plan years beginning on or after July 1, 2001.

4. Costs and Benefits of the Rules Applicable to Wellness Programs

By contrast with the nondiscrimination regulatory provisions issued as interim final rules, the provisions relating to wellness programs were issued as proposed rules. This final regulation will not become effective until its applicability date.

Under the final regulation, health plans generally may vary employee premium contributions or benefit levels across similarly situated individuals based on a health factor only in connection with wellness programs. The final regulation establishes five requirements for wellness programs that vary premiums or benefits based on participation in the program and condition a reward involving premiums or benefits on satisfaction of a standard related to a health factor. These requirements will, therefore, apply to only a subset of all wellness programs.

Available literature, together with comments received by the Departments, demonstrate that well-designed wellness programs can deliver benefits well in excess of their costs. For example, the U.S. Centers for Disease Control and Prevention estimate that implementing proven clinical smoking cessation interventions can save one year of life for each $2,587 invested.[16] In addition to reduced mortality, benefits of effective wellness programs can include reduced absenteeism, improved productivity, and reduced medical costs.[17] The requirements of the

final regulation were crafted to accommodate and not impair such beneficial programs, while combating discrimination in eligibility and premiums for similarly situated individuals as intended by Congress.

Estimation of the economic impacts of the requirements is difficult because data on affected plans' current practices are incomplete, and because plans' approaches to compliance with the requirements and the effects of those approaches will vary and cannot be predicted. Nonetheless, the Departments endeavored to consider the impacts fully and to develop estimates based on reasonable assumptions.

The Departments estimate that 1.6 percent of large plans and 1.2 percent of small plans currently vary employee premium contributions across similarly situated individuals due to participation in a wellness program that provides rewards based on satisfaction of a standard related to a health factor.[18] This amounts to 30,000 plans covering 1.1 million participants. According to survey data reported by Hewitt Associates,[19] just less than one-half as many plans vary benefit levels across similarly situated individuals as vary premiums. This amounts to 13,000 plans covering 460,000 participants. The Departments considered the effect of each of the five requirements on these plans. For purposes of its estimates, the Departments assumed that one-half of the plans in the latter group are also included in the former, thereby estimating that 37,000 plans covering 1.3 million participants will be subject to the five requirements for wellness programs.

Limit on Reward

Under the first requirement, any reward, whether applicable to employee premiums or benefit levels, must not exceed 20 percent of the total premium for employee-only coverage under the

plan (with additional provisions related to rewards that apply also to classes of dependents). This percentage is the highest of the three alternative percentages suggested in the proposed rule, and the award limit used for purposes of the analysis of the proposed rule, which was 15 percent—the midpoint of the three alternative percentages suggested in the proposal. The estimates here also reflect increases in average annual premiums and the numbers of plans and participants since publication of the proposed rules.

The Departments lack representative data on the magnitude of the rewards applied by affected plans today. One consultant practicing in this area suggested that wellness incentive premium discounts ranged from about 3 percent to 23 percent, with an average of about 11 percent.[20] This suggests that most affected plans, including some whose discounts are somewhat larger than average, already comply with the first requirement and will not need to reduce the size of the rewards they apply. It appears likely, however, that perhaps a few thousand plans covering approximately one hundred thousand participants will need to reduce the size of their rewards in order to comply with the first requirement.

The Departments considered the potential economic effects of requiring these plans to reduce the size of their rewards. These effects are likely to include a shifting of costs between plan sponsors and participants, as well as new economic costs and benefits. Shifts in costs will arise as plans reduce rewards where necessary. Plan sponsors can exercise substantial control over the size and direction of these shifts. Limiting the size of rewards restricts only the differential treatment between participants who satisfy wellness program standards and those who do not. It does not, for example, restrict plans sponsors' flexibility to determine the overall respective employer and employee shares of base premiums. Possible outcomes include a shifting of costs to plan sponsors from participants who satisfy wellness program standards, from plan sponsors to participants who do not satisfy the standards, from participants who satisfy the standards to those who do not, or some combination of these.

---

[16] Cromwell, J., W. J. Bartosch, M. C. Fiore, V. Hasselblad and T. Baker. "Cost-Effectiveness of the Clinical Practice Recommendations in the AHCPR Guideline for Smoking Cessation." *Journal of the American Medical Association,* vol. 278 (December 3, 1997): 1759–66.

[17] The benefits of employer wellness programs are well documented. One study found the annual per participant savings to be $613 while private companies have reported returns of as much as $4.50 in lowered medical expenses for every dollar spent on health programs. (See for example, Gregg

M. State et al. "Quantifiable Impact of the Contract for Health Wellness: Health Behaviors, Health Care Costs, Disability and Workers' Compensation." *Journal of Occupational and Environmental Medicine* (2003), vol. 45 (2):109–117; Morgan O'Rourke & Laura Sullivan, "A Health Return on Employee Investment" *Risk Management* (2003), vol. 50 (11): 34–38; American Association of Health Plans and Health Insurance Association of America "The Cost Savings of Disease Management Programs: Report on a Study of Health Plans." November, 2003; Rachel Christensen, "Employment-Based Health Promotion and Wellness Programs" EBRI Notes (2001), vol. 22 (7): 1–6; and Steven G. Aldana "Financial Impact of Wellness Programs: A Comprehensive Review of the Literature," *American Journal of Health Promotions* (2001), vol. 15 (5): 296–320.)

[18] Estimates are based on a 1993 survey of employers by the Robert Wood Johnson Foundation. More recent estimates are unavailable.

[19] Hewitt Associates. July 2003.

[20] This estimate was made in 1998, shortly after the 1997 interim final rule was published. Since then, it appears that wellness programs advocates have been advising health plans to offer premium discounts in the range of 5 to 11 percent, well below the proposed ceiling. For a full discussion, see Larry Chapman's, "Increasing Participation in Wellness Programs," *National Wellness Institute Members "Ask the Expert,"* July/August 2004.

F. HIPAA Final Rules, Nondiscrimination and Wellness Benefits, continued

The Departments developed a very rough estimate of the total amount of costs that might derive from this requirement. The Departments' estimate assumes that (1) all rewards take the form of employee premium discounts; (2) discounts are distributed evenly within both the low-to-average range and the average-to-high range, and are distributed across these ranges such that their mean equals the assumed average; and (3) 70 percent of participants qualify for the discount. The 4,000 affected plans could satisfy this requirement by reducing the premium discount for the 100,000 participants who successfully complete a certified wellness program. When applied to the 2005 average annual employee-only premium of $4,024,[21] discounts range from $115 to $920, with an average of $460. The maximum allowable discount based on 20 percent of current premium is $805. Reducing all discounts greater than $805 to that amount will result in an average annual reduction of about $57. Applying this reduction to the 100,000 participants assumed to be covered by 4,000 plans affected by the limit results in an estimate of the aggregate cost at $6 million.

New economic costs and benefits may arise if changes in the size of rewards result in changes in participant behavior. Net economic welfare might be lost if some wellness programs' effectiveness is eroded, but the magnitude and incidence of such effects is expected to be negligible. Consider a wellness program that discounts premiums for participants who take part in an exercise program. It is plausible that, at the margin, a few participants who would take part in order to obtain an existing discount will not take part to obtain a somewhat lower discount. This effect is expected to be negligible, however. Reductions in discounts are likely to average about $57 annually, which is very small when spread over biweekly pay periods. Moreover, the final regulation limits only rewards applied to similarly situated individuals in the context of a group health plan. It does not restrict plan sponsors from encouraging healthy lifestyles in other ways, such as by varying life insurance premiums.

On the other hand, net economic welfare likely will be gained in instances where large premium differentials would otherwise have served to discourage enrollment in

health plans by employees who did not satisfy wellness program requirements. The Departments believe that the net economic gains from prohibiting rewards so large that they could discourage enrollment based on health factors justify any net losses that might derive from the negligible reduction of some employees' incentive to participate in wellness programs.

Reasonable Design

Under the second requirement, the program must be reasonably designed to promote health or prevent disease. The Departments believe that a program that is not so designed would not provide economic benefits, but would serve merely to shift costs from plan sponsors to targeted individuals based on health factors. Comments received by the Departments and available literature on employee wellness programs, however, suggest that existing wellness programs generally satisfy this requirement. As was stated in the analysis of the proposed rule, this requirement therefore is not expected to compel plans to modify existing wellness programs or entail additional economic costs.

Annual Opportunity To Qualify

Although this requirement was included in the proposal within the requirement for reasonable design, it has been reorganized as a separate provision in these final regulations. At the time of the proposal, the Departments assumed that most plans satisfied the requirements for reasonable design, such that they would not be required to modify existing programs. Accordingly, no cost was attributed to the reasonable design requirements when taken together. The Departments did request comments on this assumption, but received no additional information in response. Accordingly, the Departments have not attributed a cost to this provision of the final regulations.

Uniform Availability

The fourth requirement provides that where rewards are conditioned on satisfaction of a standard related to a health factor, rewards must be available to all similarly situated individuals. A reward is not available to all similarly situated individuals unless the program allows for a reasonable alternative standard if the otherwise applicable initial standard is unreasonably difficult to achieve due to a medical condition or medically inadvisable for the individual to meet. In particular, the program must offer any such individual the opportunity to satisfy a reasonable alternative standard. Comments

received by the Departments and available literature on employee wellness programs suggest that some wellness programs do not currently satisfy this requirement and will have to be modified. The Departments estimate that among employers that provide incentives for employees to participate in wellness programs, nine percent require employees to achieve a low risk behavior to qualify for the incentive, 53 percent require a pledge of compliance, and 55 percent require participation in a program.[22] Depending on the nature of the wellness program, it might be unreasonably difficult due to a medical condition or medically inadvisable for at least some plan participants to achieve the behavior or to comply with or participate in the program.

The Departments identified three broad types of economic impact that might arise from this requirement. First, affected plans will incur some economic cost to make available reasonable alternative standards. Second, additional economic costs and benefits may arise depending on the nature of alternatives provided, individuals' use of these alternatives, and any changes in the affected individuals' behavioral and health outcomes. Third, some costs may be shifted from individuals who would fail to satisfy programs' initial standards, but who will satisfy reasonable alternative standards once available (and thereby qualify for associated rewards), to plan sponsors (or to other participants in their plans if plan sponsors elect to pass these costs back to all participants).

The Departments note that some plans that offer rewards to similarly situated individuals based on their ability to meet a standard related to a health factor (and are therefore subject to the requirement) may not need to provide alternative standards. The requirement provides that alternative standards need not be specified or provided until a participant for whom it is unreasonably difficult due to a medical condition or medically inadvisable to satisfy the initial standard seeks such an alternative. Some wellness programs' initial standards may be such that no participant would ever find them unreasonably difficult to satisfy due to a medical condition or medically inadvisable to attempt. The Departments estimate that 3,000 potentially affected plans have initial wellness program standards that might be unreasonably difficult for some participants to satisfy due to a medical condition or medically

---

[21] Average based on the Kaiser Family Foundation/Health Research and Education Trust *Survey of Employer-Sponsored Health Benefits,* 2005.

[22] Hewitt Associates, July, 2003. The sum of these shares exceeds 100 percent due to some employers using multiple criteria to determine compliance.

F. HIPAA Final Rules, Nondiscrimination and Wellness Benefits, continued

inadvisable to attempt.[23] Moreover, because alternatives need not be made available until they are sought by qualified plan participants, it might be possible for some plans to go for years without needing to make available an alternative standard. This could be particularly likely for small plans.[24]

The Departments estimate that as many as 27 percent of participants in plans with rewards that are based on meeting a standard related to a health factor, or 344,000 individuals, might fail to satisfy wellness programs' initial standards because they are unreasonably difficult due to a medical condition or medically inadvisable to meet.[25] Of these, only about 30,000 are in the 3,000 plans assumed to apply standards that might be unreasonably difficult due to a medical condition or medically inadvisable for some plan participants to satisfy. The standards would in fact be unreasonably difficult or medically inadvisable to satisfy for some subset of these individuals— roughly two-thirds, or 19,000 by the Departments' estimate.[26] Of these, it is

assumed that between 5,000 and 19,000 of those individuals that seek alternative standards are able to satisfy them.[27]

The cost associated with establishing alternative standards is unknown. However, the regulation does not prescribe a particular type of alternative standard that must be provided. Instead, it permits plan sponsors flexibility to provide any reasonable alternative, or to waive the standard, for individuals for whom the initial standard is unreasonably difficult due to a medical condition or medically inadvisable to meet. The Departments expect that plan sponsors will select alternatives that entail the minimum net costs possible. Plan sponsors may select low-cost alternatives, such as requiring an individual for whom it would be unreasonably difficult to quit smoking (and thereby qualify for a non-smoker discount) to attend a smoking cessation program that is available at little or no cost in the community, or to watch educational videos or review educational literature. Plan sponsors presumably will select higher-cost alternatives only if they thereby derive offsetting benefits, such as a higher smoking cessation success rate.

Although there is considerable uncertainty in these estimates, it seems reasonable to assume that the net cost sponsors will incur in the provision of alternatives, including new economic costs and benefits, will not exceed the cost of providing discounts (or waiving surcharges) for all plan participants who qualify for alternatives, which is estimated at between $2 million and $9 million.[28] Other economic costs and benefits might arise where alternative standards are made available. For example, some individuals might

receive a discount for satisfying alternative standards that turn out to be less beneficial to overall health than the initial standard might have been, resulting in a net loss of economic welfare. In other cases, the satisfaction of an alternative standard might produce the desired health improvement, which would represent a net gain in economic welfare.

Although outcomes are uncertain, the Departments note that plan sponsors have strong motivation to identify and provide alternative standards that have positive net economic effects. They will be disinclined to provide alternatives that worsen behavioral and health outcomes, or that make financial rewards available absent meaningful efforts by participants to improve their health habits and health. Instead they will be inclined to provide alternatives that sustain or reinforce plan participants' incentive to improve their health habits and health, and/or that help participants make such improvements. It therefore seems likely that gains in economic welfare from this requirement will equal or justify losses. The Departments anticipate that the requirement to provide reasonable alternative standards will reduce instances where wellness programs serve only to shift costs to higher risk individuals and increase instances where programs succeed at helping individuals with higher health risks improve their health habits and health.

Disclosure Regarding Reasonable Alternative Standards

The fifth requirement provides that plan materials describing wellness program standards that are related to a health factor must disclose the availability of reasonable alternative standards. Under some wellness programs, an individual must satisfy a standard related to a health factor in order to qualify for the reward.

Plans offering wellness programs under which an individual must satisfy a standard related to a health factor in order to qualify for the reward must disclose in all plan materials describing the terms of the program the availability of a reasonable alternative standard. The regulations provide sample language for this disclosure. An actual description of the alternative standard is not required in such materials. In plan materials that merely mention that a wellness program is available but do not describe its terms, this disclosure of the availability of an alternative standard is not required. The Departments generally account elsewhere for plans' cost of updating such materials to reflect changes in plan provisions as required

---

[23] Estimate is based on both the share of plans in the 2003-04 Hewitt survey stating that certain health factors or lifestyle choices affect employees' benefit coverage and the share of employers requiring employees to achieve a lower-risk behavior to earn incentives. These measures are then combined with the number of workers in the civilian labor force (from 2003 estimates of the Bureau of Labor Statistics (BLS) suffering from these maladies (as provided by the Centers for Disease Control (CDC) 2004 *Health* and the National Center for Statistics and Analysis (NCSA) 2004 estimates of seatbelt use), by demographic group.

[24] The most common standards that would be implemented by this provision of the wellness program rules pertain to smoking, blood pressure, and cholesterol levels, according to the Hewitt survey. Based on data from the CDC, NCSA and BLS, the Departments estimate that among plans with five participants, about one-fourth will not contain any smokers, one-third will not contain participants with high blood pressure and two-fifths will not contain any with high cholesterol. Approximately 97 percent of all plans with potentially difficult initial wellness program standards have fewer than 100 participants.

[25] This estimate is considerably lower than that offered in the proposal due to a difference in the format of the data reported in the 2001 and 2003 Hewitt surveys, and the Departments' original adjustment for data reported in the 2001 survey as, "not provided." The Departments believe in light of the 2003 data that the adjustments thought to be appropriate at the time overestimated the number of plans with standards that might be unreasonably difficult or medically inadvisable to meet, resulting in more instances in which alternative standards might be established and met, and greater magnitudes of transfers for individuals who would newly attain rewards. The Departments have revised their assumptions to account for a smaller number of plans with standards unreasonably difficult or medically inadvisable to meet, and a correspondingly larger number of participants who will already have been satisfying these standards. Accordingly, this results in a reduction of the estimates of transfers in connection with establishing reasonable alternative standards.

[26] Having previously determined the share of the working class population suffering from various

maladies using CDC, NCSA and BLS estimates and how, according to the Hewitt survey, these conditions are factored into wellness programs, the Departments were able to estimate that 26.8 percent of plan participants may initially fail to satisfy program standards. Since the Hewitt study went on to state that 9 percent of employers surveyed required participants to meet the standard in order to receive premium discounts, it was then concluded that 2.3 percent may have difficulty meeting the standards and 1.5 percent will have difficulty meeting the standards.

[27] No independent estimates of the those satisfying alternative standards were available, so the Departments created an upper bound which assumes all individuals for whom the standards are unreasonably difficult seek and satisfy an alternative standard, and a lower bound which assumes half of those for whom the standards are unreasonably difficult seek an alternative, and half of those are able to satisfy it.

[28] These estimates are the product of the range of numbers of individuals who might newly attain rewards and the average premium reward. It is likely that many plan sponsors will find more cost-effective ways to satisfy this requirement, and that the true net cost to them will therefore be smaller than this.

F. HIPAA Final Rules, Nondiscrimination and Wellness Benefits, continued

under various disclosure requirements and as is part of usual business practice. This particular requirement is expected to represent a negligible fraction of the ongoing cost of updating plans' materials, and is not separately accounted for here.

Statutory Authority

The Department of the Treasury final rule is adopted pursuant to the authority contained in sections 7805 and 9833 of the Code (26 U.S.C. 7805, 9833).

The Department of Labor final rule is adopted pursuant to the authority contained in sections 29 U.S.C. 1027, 1059, 1135, 1161–1168, 1169, 1181–1183, 1181 note, 1185, 1185a, 1185b, 1191, 1191a, 1191b, and 1191c, sec. 101(g), Public Law 104–191, 110 Stat. 1936; sec. 401(b), Public Law 105–200, 112 Stat. 645 (42 U.S.C. 651 note); Secretary of Labor's Order 1–2003, 68 FR 5374 (Feb. 3, 2003).

The Department of Health and Human Services final rule is adopted pursuant to the authority contained in sections 2701 through 2763, 2791, and 2792 of the PHS Act (42 U.S.C. 300gg through 300gg–63, 300gg–91, and 300gg–92), as added by HIPAA (Pub. L. 104–191, 110 Stat. 1936), and amended by the Mental Health Parity Act (MHPA) and the Newborns' and Mothers' Health Protection Act (NMHPA) (Pub. L. 104–204, 110 Stat. 2935), and the Women's Health and Cancer Rights Act (WHCRA) (Pub. L. 105–277, 112 Stat. 2681–436).

List of Subjects

26 CFR Part 54

Excise taxes, Health care, Health insurance, Pensions, Reporting and recordkeeping requirements.

29 CFR Part 2590

Continuation coverage, Disclosure, Employee benefit plans, Group health plans, Health care, Health insurance, Medical child support, Reporting and recordkeeping requirements.

45 CFR Part 146

Health care, Health insurance, Reporting and recordkeeping requirements, and State regulation of health insurance.

Adoption of Amendments to the Regulations

Internal Revenue Service

26 CFR Chapter I

■ Accordingly, 26 CFR Part 54 is amended as follows:

PART 54—PENSION EXCISE TAXES

■ Paragraph 1. The authority citation for part 54 is amended by removing the citation for § 54.9802–1T to read, in part, as follows:

> Authority: 26 U.S.C. 7805. * * *

§ 54.9802–1T [Removed]

■ Par. 2. Section 54.9802–1T is removed.

■ Par. 3. Section 54.9802–1 is revised to read as follows:

§ 54.9802–1 Prohibiting discrimination against participants and beneficiaries based on a health factor.

(a) *Health factors.* (1) The term *health factor* means, in relation to an individual, any of the following health status-related factors:

(i) Health status;

(ii) Medical condition (including both physical and mental illnesses), as defined in § 54.9801–2;

(iii) Claims experience;

(iv) Receipt of health care;

(v) Medical history;

(vi) Genetic information, as defined in § 54.9801–2;

(vii) Evidence of insurability; or

(viii) Disability.

(2) Evidence of insurability includes—

(i) Conditions arising out of acts of domestic violence; and

(ii) Participation in activities such as motorcycling, snowmobiling, all-terrain vehicle riding, horseback riding, skiing, and other similar activities.

(3) The decision whether health coverage is elected for an individual (including the time chosen to enroll, such as under special enrollment or late enrollment) is not, itself, within the scope of any health factor. (However, under § 54.9801–6, a plan must treat special enrollees the same as similarly situated individuals who are enrolled when first eligible.)

(b) *Prohibited discrimination in rules for eligibility*—(1) *In general*—(i) A group health plan may not establish any rule for eligibility (including continued eligibility) of any individual to enroll for benefits under the terms of the plan that discriminates based on any health factor that relates to that individual or a dependent of that individual. This rule is subject to the provisions of paragraph (b)(2) of this section (explaining how this rule applies to benefits), paragraph (b)(3) of this section (allowing plans to impose certain preexisting condition exclusions), paragraph (d) of this section (containing rules for establishing groups of similarly situated individuals), paragraph (e) of this section (relating to nonconfinement, actively-at-work, and other service requirements), paragraph (f) of this section (relating to wellness programs), and paragraph (g) of this section

(permitting favorable treatment of individuals with adverse health factors).

(ii) For purposes of this section, rules for eligibility include, but are not limited to, rules relating to—

(A) Enrollment;

(B) The effective date of coverage;

(C) Waiting (or affiliation) periods;

(D) Late and special enrollment;

(E) Eligibility for benefit packages (including rules for individuals to change their selection among benefit packages);

(F) Benefits (including rules relating to covered benefits, benefit restrictions, and cost-sharing mechanisms such as coinsurance, copayments, and deductibles), as described in paragraphs (b)(2) and (3) of this section;

(G) Continued eligibility; and

(H) Terminating coverage (including disenrollment) of any individual under the plan.

(iii) The rules of this paragraph (b)(1) are illustrated by the following examples:

Example 1. (i) *Facts.* An employer sponsors a group health plan that is available to all employees who enroll within the first 30 days of their employment. However, employees who do not enroll within the first 30 days cannot enroll later unless they pass a physical examination.

(ii) *Conclusion.* In this *Example 1*, the requirement to pass a physical examination in order to enroll in the plan is a rule for eligibility that discriminates based on one or more health factors and thus violates this paragraph (b)(1).

Example 2. (i) *Facts.* Under an employer's group health plan, employees who enroll during the first 30 days of employment (and during special enrollment periods) may choose between two benefit packages: An indemnity option and an HMO option. However, employees who enroll during late enrollment are permitted to enroll only in the HMO option and only if they provide evidence of good health.

(ii) *Conclusion.* In this *Example 2*, the requirement to provide evidence of good health in order to be eligible for late enrollment in the HMO option is a rule for eligibility that discriminates based on one or more health factors and thus violates this paragraph (b)(1). However, if the plan did not require evidence of good health but limited late enrollees to the HMO option, the plan's rules for eligibility would not discriminate based on any health factor, and thus would not violate this paragraph (b)(1), because the time an individual chooses to enroll is not, itself, within the scope of any health factor.

Example 3. (i) *Facts.* Under an employer's group health plan, all employees generally may enroll within the first 30 days of employment. However, individuals who participate in certain recreational activities, including motorcycling, are excluded from coverage.

(ii) *Conclusion.* In this *Example 3*, excluding from the plan individuals who participate in recreational activities, such as

F. HIPAA Final Rules, Nondiscrimination and Wellness Benefits, continued

motorcycling, is a rule for eligibility that discriminates based on one or more health factors and thus violates this paragraph (b)(1).

Example 4. (i) *Facts.* A group health plan applies for a group health policy offered by an issuer. As part of the application, the issuer receives health information about individuals to be covered under the plan. Individual *A* is an employee of the employer maintaining the plan. *A* and *A's* dependents have a history of high health claims. Based on the information about *A* and *A's* dependents, the issuer excludes *A* and *A's* dependents from the group policy it offers to the employer.

(ii) *Conclusion.* See *Example 4* in 29 CFR 2590.702(b)(1) and 45 CFR 146.121(b)(1) for a conclusion that the exclusion by the issuer of *A* and *A's* dependents from coverage is a rule for eligibility that discriminates based on one or more health factors and violates rules under 29 CFR 2590.702(b)(1) and 45 CFR 146.121(b)(1) similar to the rules under this paragraph (b)(1). (If the employer is a small employer under 45 CFR 144.103 (generally, an employer with 50 or fewer employees), the issuer also may violate 45 CFR 146.150, which requires issuers to offer all the policies they sell in the small group market on a guaranteed available basis to all small employers and to accept every eligible individual in every small employer group.) If the plan provides coverage through this policy and does not provide equivalent coverage for *A* and *A's* dependents through other means, the plan violates this paragraph (b)(1).

(2) *Application to benefits—*(i) *General rule—*(A) Under this section, a group health plan is not required to provide coverage for any particular benefit to any group of similarly situated individuals.

(B) However, benefits provided under a plan must be uniformly available to all similarly situated individuals (as described in paragraph (d) of this section). Likewise, any restriction on a benefit or benefits must apply uniformly to all similarly situated individuals and must not be directed at individual participants or beneficiaries based on any health factor of the participants or beneficiaries (determined based on all the relevant facts and circumstances). Thus, for example, a plan may limit or exclude benefits in relation to a specific disease or condition, limit or exclude benefits for certain types of treatments or drugs, or limit or exclude benefits based on a determination of whether the benefits are experimental or not medically necessary, but only if the benefit limitation or exclusion applies uniformly to all similarly situated individuals and is not directed at individual participants or beneficiaries based on any health factor of the participants or beneficiaries. In addition, a plan may impose annual, lifetime, or other limits on benefits and

may require the satisfaction of a deductible, copayment, coinsurance, or other cost-sharing requirement in order to obtain a benefit if the limit or cost-sharing requirement applies uniformly to all similarly situated individuals and is not directed at individual participants or beneficiaries based on any health factor of the participants or beneficiaries. In the case of a cost-sharing requirement, see also paragraph (b)(2)(ii) of this section, which permits variances in the application of a cost-sharing mechanism made available under a wellness program. (Whether any plan provision or practice with respect to benefits complies with this paragraph (b)(2)(i) does not affect whether the provision or practice is permitted under ERISA, the Americans with Disabilities Act, or any other law, whether State or Federal.)

(C) For purposes of this paragraph (b)(2)(i), a plan amendment applicable to all individuals in one or more groups of similarly situated individuals under the plan and made effective no earlier than the first day of the first plan year after the amendment is adopted is not considered to be directed at any individual participants or beneficiaries.

(D) The rules of this paragraph (b)(2)(i) are illustrated by the following examples:

Example 1. (i) *Facts.* A group health plan applies a $500,000 lifetime limit on all benefits to each participant or beneficiary covered under the plan. The limit is not directed at individual participants or beneficiaries.

(ii) *Conclusion.* In this *Example 1,* the limit does not violate this paragraph (b)(2)(i) because $500,000 of benefits are available uniformly to each participant and beneficiary under the plan and because the limit is applied uniformly to all participants and beneficiaries and is not directed at individual participants or beneficiaries.

Example 2. (i) *Facts.* A group health plan has a $2 million lifetime limit on all benefits (and no other lifetime limits) for participants covered under the plan. Participant *B* files a claim for the treatment of AIDS. At the next corporate board meeting of the plan sponsor, the claim is discussed. Shortly thereafter, the plan is modified to impose a $10,000 lifetime limit on benefits for the treatment of AIDS, effective before the beginning of the next plan year.

(ii) *Conclusion.* The facts of this *Example 2* strongly suggest that the plan modification is directed at *B* based on *B's* claim. Absent outweighing evidence to the contrary, the plan violates this paragraph (b)(2)(i).

Example 3. (i) A group health plan applies for a group health policy offered by an issuer. Individual *C* is covered under the plan and has an adverse health condition. As part of the application, the issuer receives health information about the individuals to be covered, including information about *C's* adverse health condition. The policy form

offered by the issuer generally provides benefits for the adverse health condition that *C* has, but in this case the issuer offers the plan a policy modified by a rider that excludes benefits for *C* for that condition. The exclusionary rider is made effective the first day of the next plan year.

(ii) *Conclusion.* See *Example 3* in 29 CFR 2590.702(b)(2)(i) and 45 CFR 146.121(b)(2)(i) for a conclusion that the issuer violates rules under 29 CFR 2590.702(b)(2)(i) and 45 CFR 146.121(b)(2)(i) similar to the rules under this paragraph (b)(2)(i) because benefits for *C's* condition are available to other individuals in the group of similarly situated individuals that includes *C* but are not available to *C.* Thus, the benefits are not uniformly available to all similarly situated individuals. Even though the exclusionary rider is made effective the first day of the next plan year, because the rider does not apply to all similarly situated individuals, the issuer violates the rules under 29 CFR 2590.702(b)(2)(i) and 45 CFR 146.121(b)(2)(i). If the plan provides coverage through this policy and does not provide equivalent coverage for *C* through other means, the plan violates this paragraph (b)(2)(i).

Example 4. (i) *Facts.* A group health plan has a $2,000 lifetime limit for the treatment of temporomandibular joint syndrome (TMJ). The limit is applied uniformly to all similarly situated individuals and is not directed at individual participants or beneficiaries.

(ii) *Conclusion.* In this *Example 4,* the limit does not violate this paragraph (b)(2)(i) because $2,000 of benefits for the treatment of TMJ are available uniformly to all similarly situated individuals and a plan may limit benefits covered in relation to a specific disease or condition if the limit applies uniformly to all similarly situated individuals and is not directed at individual participants or beneficiaries. * * * (This example does not address whether the plan provision is permissible under the Americans with Disabilities Act or any other applicable law.)

Example 5. (i) *Facts.* A group health plan applies a $2 million lifetime limit on all benefits. However, the $2 million lifetime limit is reduced to $10,000 for any participant or beneficiary covered under the plan who has a congenital heart defect.

(ii) *Conclusion.* In this *Example 5,* the lower lifetime limit for participants and beneficiaries with a congenital heart defect violates this paragraph (b)(2)(i) because benefits under the plan are not uniformly available to all similarly situated individuals and the plan's lifetime limit on benefits does not apply uniformly to all similarly situated individuals.

Example 6. (i) *Facts.* A group health plan limits benefits for prescription drugs to those listed on a drug formulary. The limit is applied uniformly to all similarly situated individuals and is not directed at individual participants or beneficiaries.

(ii) *Conclusion.* In this *Example 6,* the exclusion from coverage of drugs not listed on the drug formulary does not violate this paragraph (b)(2)(i) because benefits for prescription drugs listed on the formulary are uniformly available to all similarly situated individuals and because the exclusion of

F. HIPAA Final Rules, Nondiscrimination and Wellness Benefits, continued

drugs not listed on the formulary applies uniformly to all similarly situated individuals and is not directed at individual participants or beneficiaries.

Example 7. (i) *Facts.* Under a group health plan, doctor visits are generally subject to a $250 annual deductible and 20 percent coinsurance requirement. However, prenatal doctor visits are not subject to any deductible or coinsurance requirement. These rules are applied uniformly to all similarly situated individuals and are not directed at individual participants or beneficiaries.

(ii) *Conclusion.* In this *Example 7,* imposing different deductible and coinsurance requirements for prenatal doctor visits and other visits does not violate this paragraph (b)(2)(i) because a plan may establish different deductibles or coinsurance requirements for different services if the deductible or coinsurance requirement is applied uniformly to all similarly situated individuals and is not directed at individual participants or beneficiaries.

Example 8. (i) *Facts.* An employer sponsors a group health plan that is available to all current employees. Under the plan, the medical care expenses of each employee (and the employee's dependents) are reimbursed up to an annual maximum amount. The maximum reimbursement amount with respect to an employee for a year is $1500 multiplied by the number of years the employee has participated in the plan, reduced by the total reimbursements for prior years.

(ii) *Conclusion.* In this *Example 8,* the variable annual limit does not violate this paragraph (b)(2)(i). Although the maximum reimbursement amount for a year varies among employees within the same group of similarly situated individuals based on prior claims experience, employees who have participated in the plan for the same length of time are eligible for the same total benefit over that length of time (and the restriction on the maximum reimbursement amount is not directed at any individual participants or beneficiaries based on any health factor).

(ii) *Exception for wellness programs.* A group health plan may vary benefits, including cost-sharing mechanisms (such as a deductible, copayment, or coinsurance), based on whether an individual has met the standards of a wellness program that satisfies the requirements of paragraph (f) of this section.

(iii) *Specific rule relating to source-of-injury exclusions*—(A) If a group health plan generally provides benefits for a type of injury, the plan may not deny benefits otherwise provided for treatment of the injury if the injury results from an act of domestic violence or a medical condition (including both physical and mental health conditions). This rule applies in the case of an injury resulting from a medical condition even if the condition is not diagnosed before the injury.

(B) The rules of this paragraph (b)(2)(iii) are illustrated by the following examples:

Example 1. (i) *Facts.* A group health plan generally provides medical/surgical benefits, including benefits for hospital stays, that are medically necessary. However, the plan excludes benefits for self-inflicted injuries or injuries sustained in connection with attempted suicide. Because of depression, Individual *D* attempts suicide. As a result, *D* sustains injuries and is hospitalized for treatment of the injuries. Under the exclusion, the plan denies *D* benefits for treatment of the injuries.

(ii) *Conclusion.* In this *Example 1,* the suicide attempt is the result of a medical condition (depression). Accordingly, the denial of benefits for the treatments of *D*'s injuries violates the requirements of this paragraph (b)(2)(iii) because the plan provision excludes benefits for treatment of an injury resulting from a medical condition.

Example 2. (i) *Facts.* A group health plan provides benefits for head injuries generally. The plan also has a general exclusion for any injury sustained while participating in any of a number of recreational activities, including bungee jumping. However, this exclusion does not apply to any injury that results from a medical condition (nor from domestic violence). Participant *E* sustains a head injury while bungee jumping. The injury did not result from a medical condition (nor from domestic violence). Accordingly, the plan denies benefits for *E*'s head injury.

(ii) *Conclusion.* In this *Example 2,* the plan provision that denies benefits based on the source of an injury does not restrict benefits based on an act of domestic violence or any medical condition. Therefore, the provision is permissible under this paragraph (b)(2)(iii) and does not violate this section. (However, if the plan did not allow *E* to enroll in the plan (or applied different rules for eligibility to *E*) because *E* frequently participates in bungee jumping, the plan would violate paragraph (b)(1) of this section.)

(3) *Relationship to § 54.9801–3.* (i) A preexisting condition exclusion is permitted under this section if it—

(A) Complies with § 54.9801–3;

(B) Applies uniformly to all similarly situated individuals (as described in paragraph (d) of this section); and

(C) Is not directed at individual participants or beneficiaries based on any health factor of the participants or beneficiaries. For purposes of this paragraph (b)(3)(i)(C), a plan amendment relating to a preexisting condition exclusion applicable to all individuals in one or more groups of similarly situated individuals under the plan and made effective no earlier than the first day of the first plan year after the amendment is adopted is not considered to be directed at any individual participants or beneficiaries.

(ii) The rules of this paragraph (b)(3) are illustrated by the following examples:

Example 1. (i) *Facts.* A group health plan imposes a preexisting condition exclusion on all individuals enrolled in the plan. The exclusion applies to conditions for which medical advice, diagnosis, care, or treatment was recommended or received within the six-month period ending on an individual's enrollment date. In addition, the exclusion generally extends for 12 months after an individual's enrollment date, but this 12-month period is offset by the number of days of an individual's creditable coverage in accordance with § 54.9801–3. There is nothing to indicate that the exclusion is directed at individual participants or beneficiaries.

(ii) *Conclusion.* In this *Example 1,* even though the plan's preexisting condition exclusion discriminates against individuals based on one or more health factors, the preexisting condition exclusion does not violate this section because it applies uniformly to all similarly situated individuals, is not directed at individual participants or beneficiaries, and complies with § 54.9801–3 (that is, the requirements relating to the six-month look-back period, the 12-month (or 18-month) maximum exclusion period, and the creditable coverage offset).

Example 2. (i) *Facts.* A group health plan excludes coverage for conditions with respect to which medical advice, diagnosis, care, or treatment was recommended or received within the six-month period ending on an individual's enrollment date. Under the plan, the preexisting condition exclusion generally extends for 12 months, offset by creditable coverage. However, if an individual has no claims in the first six months following enrollment, the remainder of the exclusion period is waived.

(ii) *Conclusion.* In this *Example 2,* the plan's preexisting condition exclusions violate this section because they do not meet the requirements of this paragraph (b)(3); specifically, they do not apply uniformly to all similarly situated individuals. The plan provisions do not apply uniformly to all similarly situated individuals because individuals who have medical claims during the first six months following enrollment are not treated the same as similarly situated individuals with no claims during that period. (Under paragraph (d) of this section, the groups cannot be treated as two separate groups of similarly situated individuals because the distinction is based on a health factor.)

(c) *Prohibited discrimination in premiums or contributions*—(1) *In general*—(i) A group health plan may not require an individual, as a condition of enrollment or continued enrollment under the plan, to pay a premium or contribution that is greater than the premium or contribution for a similarly situated individual (described in paragraph (d) of this section) enrolled in the plan based on any health factor that relates to the individual or a dependent of the individual.

(ii) Discounts, rebates, payments in kind, and any other premium differential mechanisms are taken into account in determining an individual's premium or contribution rate. (For rules relating to cost-sharing mechanisms, see

F. HIPAA Final Rules, Nondiscrimination and Wellness Benefits, continued

paragraph (b)(2) of this section (addressing benefits).)

(2) *Rules relating to premium rates—* (i) *Group rating based on health factors not restricted under this section.* Nothing in this section restricts the aggregate amount that an employer may be charged for coverage under a group health plan.

(ii) *List billing based on a health factor prohibited.* However, a group health plan may not quote or charge an employer (or an individual) a different premium for an individual in a group of similarly situated individuals based on a health factor. (But see paragraph (g) of this section permitting favorable treatment of individuals with adverse health factors.)

(iii) *Examples.* The rules of this paragraph (c)(2) are illustrated by the following examples:

Example 1. (i) *Facts.* An employer sponsors a group health plan and purchases coverage from a health insurance issuer. In order to determine the premium rate for the upcoming plan year, the issuer reviews the claims experience of individuals covered under the plan. The issuer finds that Individual *F* had significantly higher claims experience than similarly situated individuals in the plan. The issuer quotes the plan a higher per-participant rate because of *F*'s claims experience.

(ii) *Conclusion.* See *Example 1* in 29 CFR 2590.702(c)(2) and 45 CFR 146.121(c)(2) for a conclusion that the issuer does not violate the provisions of 29 CFR 2590.702(c)(2) and 45 CFR 146.121(c)(2) similar to the provisions of this paragraph (c)(2) because the issuer blends the rate so that the employer is not quoted a higher rate for *F* than for a similarly situated individual based on *F*'s claims experience.

Example 2. (i) *Facts.* Same facts as *Example 1,* except that the issuer quotes the employer a higher premium rate for *F,* because of *F*'s claims experience, than for a similarly situated individual.

(ii) *Conclusion.* See *Example 2* in 29 CFR 2590.702(c)(2) and 45 CFR 146.121(c)(2) for a conclusion that the issuer violates provisions of 29 CFR 2590.702(c)(2) and 45 CFR 146.121(c)(2) similar to the provisions of this paragraph (c)(2). Moreover, even if the plan purchased the policy based on the quote but did not require a higher participant contribution for *F* than for a similarly situated individual, see *Example 2* in 29 CFR 2590.702(c)(2) and 45 CFR 146.121(c)(2) for a conclusion that the issuer would still violate 29 CFR 2590.702(c)(2) and 45 CFR 146.121(c)(2) (but in such a case the plan would not violate this paragraph (c)(2)).

(3) *Exception for wellness programs.* Notwithstanding paragraphs (c)(1) and (2) of this section, a plan may vary the amount of premium or contribution it requires similarly situated individuals to pay based on whether an individual has met the standards of a wellness program that satisfies the requirements of paragraph (f) of this section.

(d) *Similarly situated individuals.* The requirements of this section apply only within a group of individuals who are treated as similarly situated individuals. A plan may treat participants as a group of similarly situated individuals separate from beneficiaries. In addition, participants may be treated as two or more distinct groups of similarly situated individuals and beneficiaries may be treated as two or more distinct groups of similarly situated individuals in accordance with the rules of this paragraph (d). Moreover, if individuals have a choice of two or more benefit packages, individuals choosing one benefit package may be treated as one or more groups of similarly situated individuals distinct from individuals choosing another benefit package.

(1) *Participants.* Subject to paragraph (d)(3) of this section, a plan may treat participants as two or more distinct groups of similarly situated individuals if the distinction between or among the groups of participants is based on a bona fide employment-based classification consistent with the employer's usual business practice. Whether an employment-based classification is bona fide is determined on the basis of all the relevant facts and circumstances. Relevant facts and circumstances include whether the employer uses the classification for purposes independent of qualification for health coverage (for example, determining eligibility for other employee benefits or determining other terms of employment). Subject to paragraph (d)(3) of this section, examples of classifications that, based on all the relevant facts and circumstances, may be bona fide include full-time versus part-time status, different geographic location, membership in a collective bargaining unit, date of hire, length of service, current employee versus former employee status, and different occupations. However, a classification based on any health factor is not a bona fide employment-based classification, unless the requirements of paragraph (g) of this section are satisfied (permitting favorable treatment of individuals with adverse health factors).

(2) *Beneficiaries*—(i) Subject to paragraph (d)(3) of this section, a plan may treat beneficiaries as two or more distinct groups of similarly situated individuals if the distinction between or among the groups of beneficiaries is based on any of the following factors:

(A) A bona fide employment-based classification of the participant through whom the beneficiary is receiving coverage;

(B) Relationship to the participant (for example, as a spouse or as a dependent child);

(C) Marital status;

(D) With respect to children of a participant, age or student status; or

(E) Any other factor if the factor is not a health factor.

(ii) Paragraph (d)(2)(i) of this section does not prevent more favorable treatment of individuals with adverse health factors in accordance with paragraph (g) of this section.

(3) *Discrimination directed at individuals.* Notwithstanding paragraphs (d)(1) and (2) of this section, if the creation or modification of an employment or coverage classification is directed at individual participants or beneficiaries based on any health factor of the participants or beneficiaries, the classification is not permitted under this paragraph (d), unless it is permitted under paragraph (g) of this section (permitting favorable treatment of individuals with adverse health factors). Thus, if an employer modified an employment-based classification to single out, based on a health factor, individual participants and beneficiaries and deny them health coverage, the new classification would not be permitted under this section.

(4) *Examples.* The rules of this paragraph (d) are illustrated by the following examples:

Example 1. (i) *Facts.* An employer sponsors a group health plan for full-time employees only. Under the plan (consistent with the employer's usual business practice), employees who normally work at least 30 hours per week are considered to be working full-time. Other employees are considered to be working part-time. There is no evidence to suggest that the classification is directed at individual participants or beneficiaries.

(ii) *Conclusion.* In this *Example 1,* treating the full-time and part-time employees as two separate groups of similarly situated individuals is permitted under this paragraph (d) because the classification is bona fide and is not directed at individual participants or beneficiaries.

Example 2. (i) *Facts.* Under a group health plan, coverage is made available to employees, their spouses, and their dependent children. However, coverage is made available to a dependent child only if the dependent child is under age 19 (or under age 25 if the child is continuously enrolled full-time in an institution of higher learning (full-time students)). There is no evidence to suggest that these classifications are directed at individual participants or beneficiaries.

(ii) *Conclusion.* In this *Example 2,* treating spouses and dependent children differently by imposing an age limitation on dependent children, but not on spouses, is permitted under this paragraph (d). Specifically, the distinction between spouses and dependent children is permitted under paragraph (d)(2)

F. HIPAA Final Rules, Nondiscrimination and Wellness Benefits, continued

75034 Federal Register / Vol. 71, No. 239 / Wednesday, December 13, 2006 / Rules and Regulations

of this section and is not prohibited under paragraph (d)(3) of this section because it is not directed at individual participants or beneficiaries. It is also permissible to treat dependent children who are under age 19 (or full-time students under age 25) as a group of similarly situated individuals separate from those who are age 25 or older (or age 19 or older if they are not full-time students) because the classification is permitted under paragraph (d)(2) of this section and is not directed at individual participants or beneficiaries.

Example 3. (i) *Facts.* A university sponsors a group health plan that provides one health benefit package to faculty and another health benefit package to other staff. Faculty and staff are treated differently with respect to other employee benefits such as retirement benefits and leaves of absence. There is no evidence to suggest that the distinction is directed at individual participants or beneficiaries.

(ii) *Conclusion.* In this *Example 3,* the classification is permitted under this paragraph (d) because there is a distinction based on a bona fide employment-based classification consistent with the employer's usual business practice and the distinction is not directed at individual participants and beneficiaries.

Example 4. (i) *Facts.* An employer sponsors a group health plan that is available to all current employees. Former employees may also be eligible, but only if they complete a specified number of years of service, are enrolled under the plan at the time of termination of employment, and are continuously enrolled from that date. There is no evidence to suggest that these distinctions are directed at individual participants or beneficiaries.

(ii) *Conclusion.* In this *Example 4,* imposing additional eligibility requirements on former employees is permitted because a classification that distinguishes between current and former employees is a bona fide employment-based classification that is permitted under this paragraph (d), provided that it is not directed at individual participants or beneficiaries. In addition, it is permissible to distinguish between former employees who satisfy the service requirement and those who do not, provided that the distinction is not directed at individual participants or beneficiaries. (However, former employees who do not satisfy the eligibility criteria may, nonetheless, be eligible for continued coverage pursuant to a COBRA continuation provision or similar State law.)

Example 5. (i) *Facts.* An employer sponsors a group health plan that provides the same benefit package to all seven employees of the employer. Six of the seven employees have the same job title and responsibilities, but Employee G has a different job title and different responsibilities. After G files an expensive claim for benefits under the plan, coverage under the plan is modified so that employees with G's job title receive a different benefit package that includes a lower lifetime dollar limit than in the benefit package made available to the other six employees.

(ii) *Conclusion.* Under the facts of this *Example 5,* changing the coverage

classification for G based on the existing employment classification for G is not permitted under this paragraph (d) because the creation of the new coverage classification for G is directed at G based on one or more health factors.

(e) *Nonconfinement and actively-at-work provisions—*(1) *Nonconfinement provisions—*(i) *General rule.* Under the rules of paragraphs (b) and (c) of this section, a plan may not establish a rule for eligibility (as described in paragraph (b)(1)(ii) of this section) or set any individual's premium or contribution rate based on whether an individual is confined to a hospital or other health care institution. In addition, under the rules of paragraphs (b) and (c) of this section, a plan may not establish a rule for eligibility or set any individual's premium or contribution rate based on an individual's ability to engage in normal life activities, except to the extent permitted under paragraphs (e)(2)(ii) and (3) of this section (permitting plans, under certain circumstances, to distinguish among employees based on the performance of services).

(ii) *Examples.* The rules of this paragraph (e)(1) are illustrated by the following examples:

Example 1. (i) *Facts.* Under a group health plan, coverage for employees and their dependents generally becomes effective on the first day of employment. However, coverage for a dependent who is confined to a hospital or other health care institution does not become effective until the confinement ends.

(ii) *Conclusion.* In this *Example 1,* the plan violates this paragraph (e)(1) because the plan delays the effective date of coverage for dependents based on confinement to a hospital or other health care institution.

Example 2. (i) *Facts.* In previous years, a group health plan has provided coverage through a group health insurance policy offered by Issuer M. However, for the current year, the plan provides coverage through a group health insurance policy offered by Issuer N. Under Issuer N's policy, items and services provided in connection with the confinement of a dependent to a hospital or other health care institution are not covered if the confinement is covered under an extension of benefits clause from a previous health insurance issuer.

(ii) *Conclusion.* See *Example 2* in 29 CFR 2590.702(e)(1) and 45 CFR 146.121(e)(1) for a conclusion that Issuer N violates provisions of 29 CFR 2590.702(e)(1) and 45 CFR 146.121(e)(1) similar to the provisions of this paragraph (e)(1) because the group health insurance coverage restricts benefits based on whether a dependent is confined to a hospital or other health care institution that is covered under an extension of benefits from a previous issuer. See *Example 2* in 29 CFR 2590.702(e)(1) and 45 CFR 146.121(e)(1) for the additional conclusions that under State law Issuer M may also be responsible

for providing benefits to such a dependent; and that in a case in which Issuer N has an obligation under 29 CFR 2590.702(e)(1) or 45 CFR 146.121(e)(1) to provide benefits and Issuer M has an obligation under State law to provide benefits, any State laws designed to prevent more than 100% reimbursement, such as State coordination-of-benefits laws, continue to apply.

(2) *Actively-at-work and continuous service provisions—*(i) *General rule—*(A) Under the rules of paragraphs (b) and (c) of this section and subject to the exception for the first day of work described in paragraph (e)(2)(ii) of this section, a plan may not establish a rule for eligibility (as described in paragraph (b)(1)(ii) of this section) or set any individual's premium or contribution rate based on whether an individual is actively at work (including whether an individual is continuously employed), unless absence from work due to any health factor (such as being absent from work on sick leave) is treated, for purposes of the plan, as being actively at work.

(B) The rules of this paragraph (e)(2)(i) are illustrated by the following examples:

Example 1. (i) *Facts.* Under a group health plan, an employee generally becomes eligible to enroll 30 days after the first day of employment. However, if the employee is not actively at work on the first day after the end of the 30-day period, then eligibility for enrollment is delayed until the first day the employee is actively at work.

(ii) *Conclusion.* In this *Example 1,* the plan violates this paragraph (e)(2) (and thus also violates paragraph (b) of this section). However, the plan would not violate paragraph (e)(2) or (b) of this section if, under the plan, an absence due to any health factor is considered being actively at work.

Example 2. (i) *Facts.* Under a group health plan, coverage for an employee becomes effective after 90 days of continuous service; that is, if an employee is absent from work (for any reason) before completing 90 days of service, the beginning of the 90-day period is measured from the day the employee returns to work (without any credit for service before the absence).

(ii) *Conclusion.* In this *Example 2,* the plan violates this paragraph (e)(2) (and thus also paragraph (b) of this section) because the 90-day continuous service requirement is a rule for eligibility based on whether an individual is actively at work. However, the plan would not violate this paragraph (e)(2) or paragraph (b) of this section if, under the plan, an absence due to any health factor is not considered an absence for purposes of measuring 90 days of continuous service.

(ii) *Exception for the first day of work—*(A) Notwithstanding the general rule in paragraph (e)(2)(i) of this section, a plan may establish a rule for eligibility that requires an individual to begin work for the employer sponsoring the plan (or, in the case of a multiemployer

F. HIPAA Final Rules, Nondiscrimination and Wellness Benefits, continued

plan, to begin a job in covered employment) before coverage becomes effective, provided that such a rule for eligibility applies regardless of the reason for the absence.

(B) The rules of this paragraph (e)(2)(ii) are illustrated by the following examples:

Example 1. (i) *Facts.* Under the eligibility provision of a group health plan, coverage for new employees becomes effective on the first day that the employee reports to work. Individual *H* is scheduled to begin work on August 3. However, *H* is unable to begin work on that day because of illness. *H* begins working on August 4, and *H's* coverage is effective on August 4.

(ii) *Conclusion.* In this *Example 1*, the plan provision does not violate this section. However, if coverage for individuals who do not report to work on the first day they were scheduled to work for a reason unrelated to a health factor (such as vacation or bereavement) becomes effective on the first day they were scheduled to work, then the plan would violate this section.

Example 2. (i) *Facts.* Under a group health plan, coverage for new employees becomes effective on the first day of the month following the employee's first day of work, regardless of whether the employee is actively at work on the first day of the month. Individual *J* is scheduled to begin work on March 24. However, *J* is unable to begin work on March 24 because of illness. *J* begins working on April 7 and *J's* coverage is effective May 1.

(ii) *Conclusion.* In this *Example 2*, the plan provision does not violate this section. However, as in *Example 1*, if coverage for individuals absent from work for reasons unrelated to a health factor became effective despite their absence, then the plan would violate this section.

(3) *Relationship to plan provisions defining similarly situated individuals—* (i) Notwithstanding the rules of paragraphs (e)(1) and (2) of this section, a plan may establish rules for eligibility or set any individual's premium or contribution rate in accordance with the rules relating to similarly situated individuals in paragraph (d) of this section. Accordingly, a plan may distinguish in rules for eligibility under the plan between full-time and part-time employees, between permanent and temporary or seasonal employees, between current and former employees, and between employees currently performing services and employees no longer performing services for the employer, subject to paragraph (d) of this section. However, other Federal or State laws (including the COBRA continuation provisions and the Family and Medical Leave Act of 1993) may require an employee or the employee's dependents to be offered coverage and set limits on the premium or contribution rate even though the employee is not performing services.

(ii) The rules of this paragraph (e)(3) are illustrated by the following examples:

Example 1. (i) *Facts.* Under a group health plan, employees are eligible for coverage if they perform services for the employer for 30 or more hours per week or if they are on paid leave (such as vacation, sick, or bereavement leave). Employees on unpaid leave are treated as a separate group of similarly situated individuals in accordance with the rules of paragraph (d) of this section.

(ii) *Conclusion.* In this *Example 1*, the plan provisions do not violate this section. However, if the plan treated individuals performing services for the employer for 30 or more hours per week, individuals on vacation leave, and individuals on bereavement leave as a group of similarly situated individuals separate from individuals on sick leave, the plan would violate this paragraph (e) (and thus also would violate paragraph (b) of this section) because groups of similarly situated individuals cannot be established based on a health factor (including the taking of sick leave) under paragraph (d) of this section.

Example 2. (i) *Facts.* To be eligible for coverage under a bona fide collectively bargained group health plan in the current calendar quarter, the plan requires an individual to have worked 250 hours in covered employment during the three-month period that ends one month before the beginning of the current calendar quarter. The distinction between employees working at least 250 hours and those working less than 250 hours in the earlier three-month period is not directed at individual participants or beneficiaries based on any health factor of the participants or beneficiaries.

(ii) *Conclusion.* In this *Example 2*, the plan provision does not violate this section because, under the rules for similarly situated individuals allowing full-time employees to be treated differently than part-time employees, employees who work at least 250 hours in a three-month period can be treated differently than employees who fail to work 250 hours in that period. The result would be the same if the plan permitted individuals to apply excess hours from previous periods to satisfy the requirement for the current quarter.

Example 3. (i) *Facts.* Under a group health plan, coverage of an employee is terminated when the individual's employment is terminated, in accordance with the rules of paragraph (d) of this section. Employee *B* has been covered under the plan. *B* experiences a disabling illness that prevents *B* from working. *B* takes a leave of absence under the Family and Medical Leave Act of 1993. At the end of such leave, *B* terminates employment and consequently loses coverage under the plan. (This termination of coverage is without regard to whatever rights the employee (or members of the employee's family) may have for COBRA continuation coverage.)

(ii) *Conclusion.* In this *Example 3*, the plan provision terminating *B's* coverage upon *B's* termination of employment does not violate this section.

Example 4. (i) *Facts.* Under a group health plan, coverage of an employee is terminated when the employee ceases to perform services for the employer sponsoring the plan, in accordance with the rules of paragraph (d) of this section. Employee *C* is laid off for three months. When the layoff begins, *C's* coverage under the plan is terminated. (This termination of coverage is without regard to whatever rights the employee (or members of the employee's family) may have for COBRA continuation coverage.)

(ii) *Conclusion.* In this *Example 4*, the plan provision terminating *C's* coverage upon the cessation of *C's* performance of services does not violate this section.

(f) *Wellness programs.* A wellness program is any program designed to promote health or prevent disease. Paragraphs (b)(2)(ii) and (c)(3) of this section provide exceptions to the general prohibitions against discrimination based on a health factor for plan provisions that vary benefits (including cost-sharing mechanisms) or the premium or contribution for similarly situated individuals in connection with a wellness program that satisfies the requirements of this paragraph (f). If none of the conditions for obtaining a reward under a wellness program is based on an individual satisfying a standard that is related to a health factor, paragraph (f)(1) of this section clarifies that the wellness program does not violate this section if participation in the program is made available to all similarly situated individuals. If any of the conditions for obtaining a reward under a wellness program is based on an individual satisfying a standard that is related to a health factor, the wellness program does not violate this section if the requirements of paragraph (f)(2) of this section are met.

(1) *Wellness programs not subject to requirements.* If none of the conditions for obtaining a reward under a wellness program is based on an individual satisfying a standard that are related to a health factor (or if a wellness program does not provide a reward), the wellness program does not violate this section, if participation in the program is made available to all similarly situated individuals. Thus, for example, the following programs need not satisfy the requirements of paragraph (f)(2) of this section, if participation in the program is made available to all similarly situated individuals:

(i) A program that reimburses all or part of the cost for memberships in a fitness center.

(ii) A diagnostic testing program that provides a reward for participation and does not base any part of the reward on outcomes.

F. HIPAA Final Rules, Nondiscrimination and Wellness Benefits, continued

(iii) A program that encourages preventive care through the waiver of the copayment or deductible requirement under a group health plan for the costs of, for example, prenatal care or well-baby visits.

(iv) A program that reimburses employees for the costs of smoking cessation programs without regard to whether the employee quits smoking.

(v) A program that provides a reward to employees for attending a monthly health education seminar.

(2) *Wellness programs subject to requirements.* If any of the conditions for obtaining a reward under a wellness program is based on an individual satisfying a standard that is related to a health factor, the wellness program does not violate this section if the requirements of this paragraph (f)(2) are met.

(i) The reward for the wellness program, coupled with the reward for other wellness programs with respect to the plan that require satisfaction of a standard related to a health factor, must not exceed 20 percent of the cost of employee-only coverage under the plan. However, if, in addition to employees, any class of dependents (such as spouses or spouses and dependent children) may participate in the wellness program, the reward must not exceed 20 percent of the cost of the coverage in which an employee and any dependents are enrolled. For purposes of this paragraph (f)(2), the cost of coverage is determined based on the total amount of employer and employee contributions for the benefit package under which the employee is (or the employee and any dependents are) receiving coverage. A reward can be in the form of a discount or rebate of a premium or contribution, a waiver of all or part of a cost-sharing mechanism (such as deductibles, copayments, or coinsurance), the absence of a surcharge, or the value of a benefit that would otherwise not be provided under the plan.

(ii) The program must be reasonably designed to promote health or prevent disease. A program satisfies this standard if it has a reasonable chance of improving the health of or preventing disease in participating individuals and it is not overly burdensome, is not a subterfuge for discriminating based on a health factor, and is not highly suspect in the method chosen to promote health or prevent disease.

(iii) The program must give individuals eligible for the program the opportunity to qualify for the reward under the program at least once per year.

(iv) The reward under the program must be available to all similarly situated individuals.

(A) A reward is not available to all similarly situated individuals for a period unless the program allows—

(1) A reasonable alternative standard (or waiver of the otherwise applicable standard) for obtaining the reward for any individual for whom, for that period, it is unreasonably difficult due to a medical condition to satisfy the otherwise applicable standard; and

(2) A reasonable alternative standard (or waiver of the otherwise applicable standard) for obtaining the reward for any individual for whom, for that period, it is medically inadvisable to attempt to satisfy the otherwise applicable standard.

(B) A plan or issuer may seek verification, such as a statement from an individual's physician, that a health factor makes it unreasonably difficult or medically inadvisable for the individual to satisfy or attempt to satisfy the otherwise applicable standard.

(v)(A) The plan must disclose in all plan materials describing the terms of the program the availability of a reasonable alternative standard (or the possibility of waiver of the otherwise applicable standard) required under paragraph (f)(2)(iv) of this section. However, if plan materials merely mention that a program is available, without describing its terms, this disclosure is not required.

(B) The following language, or substantially similar language, can be used to satisfy the requirement of this paragraph (f)(2)(v): "If it is unreasonably difficult due to a medical condition for you to achieve the standards for the reward under this program, or if it is medically inadvisable for you to attempt to achieve the standards for the reward under this program, call us at [insert telephone number] and we will work with you to develop another way to qualify for the reward." In addition, other examples of language that would satisfy this requirement are set forth in *Examples 3, 4,* and *5* of paragraph (f)(3) of this section.

(3) *Examples.* The rules of paragraph (f)(2) of this section are illustrated by the following examples:

Example 1. (i) *Facts.* An employer sponsors a group health plan. The annual premium for employee-only coverage is $3,600 (of which the employer pays $2,700 per year and the employee pays $900 per year). The annual premium for family coverage is $9,000 (of which the employer pays $4,500 per year and the employee pays $4,500 per year). The plan offers a wellness program with an annual premium rebate of $360. The program is available only to employees.

(ii) *Conclusion.* In this *Example 1,* the program satisfies the requirements of paragraph (f)(2)(i) of this section because the reward for the wellness program, $360, does not exceed 20 percent of the total annual cost of employee-only coverage, $720. ($3,600 × 20% = $720.) If any class of dependents is allowed to participate in the program and the employee is enrolled in family coverage, the plan could offer the employee a reward of up to 20 percent of the cost of family coverage, $1,800. ($9,000 × 20% = $1,800.)

Example 2. (i) *Facts.* A group health plan gives an annual premium discount of 20 percent of the cost of employee-only coverage to participants who adhere to a wellness program. The wellness program consists solely of giving an annual cholesterol test to participants. Those participants who achieve a count under 200 receive the premium discount for the year.

(ii) *Conclusion.* In this *Example 2,* the program fails to satisfy the requirement of being available to all similarly situated individuals because some participants may be unable to achieve a cholesterol count of under 200 and the plan does not make available a reasonable alternative standard or waive the cholesterol standard. (In addition, plan materials describing the program are required to disclose the availability of a reasonable alternative standard (or the possibility of waiver of the otherwise applicable standard) for obtaining the premium discount. Thus, the premium discount violates paragraph (c) of this section because it may require an individual to pay a higher premium based on a health factor of the individual than is required of a similarly situated individual under the plan.

Example 3. (i) *Facts.* Same facts as *Example 2,* except that the plan provides that if it is unreasonably difficult due to a medical condition for a participant to achieve the targeted cholesterol count (or if it is medically inadvisable for a participant to attempt to achieve the targeted cholesterol count) within a 60-day period, the plan will make available a reasonable alternative standard that takes the relevant medical condition into account. In addition, all plan materials describing the terms of the program include the following statement: "If it is unreasonably difficult due to a medical condition for you to achieve a cholesterol count under 200, or if it is medically inadvisable for you to attempt to achieve a count under 200, call us at the number below and we will work with you to develop another way to get the discount." Individual D begins a diet and exercise program but is unable to achieve a cholesterol count under 200 within the prescribed period. D's doctor determines D requires prescription medication to achieve a medically advisable cholesterol count. In addition, the doctor determines that D must be monitored through periodic blood tests to continually reevaluate D's health status. The plan accommodates D by making the discount available to D, but only if D follows the advice of D's doctor's regarding medication and blood tests.

(ii) *Conclusion.* In this *Example 3,* the program is a wellness program because it satisfies the five requirements of paragraph (f)(2) of this section. First, the program

F. HIPAA Final Rules, Nondiscrimination and Wellness Benefits, continued

complies with the limits on rewards under a program. Second, it is reasonably designed to promote health or prevent disease. Third, individuals eligible for the program are given the opportunity to qualify for the reward at least once per year. Fourth, the reward under the program is available to all similarly situated individuals because it accommodates individuals for whom it is unreasonably difficult due to a medical condition to achieve the targeted count (or for whom it is medically inadvisable to attempt to achieve the targeted count) in the prescribed period by providing a reasonable alternative standard. Fifth, the plan discloses in all materials describing the terms of the program the availability of a reasonable alternative standard. Thus, the premium discount does not violate this section.

Example 4. (i) *Facts.* A group health plan will waive the $250 annual deductible (which is less than 20 percent of the annual cost of employee-only coverage under the plan) for the following year for participants who have a body mass index between 19 and 26, determined shortly before the beginning of the year. However, any participant for whom it is unreasonably difficult due to a medical condition to attain this standard (and any participant for whom it is medically inadvisable to attempt to achieve this standard) during the plan year is given the same discount if the participant walks for 20 minutes three days a week. Any participant for whom it is unreasonably difficult due to a medical condition to attain either standard (and any participant for whom it is medically inadvisable to attempt to achieve either standard) during the year is given the same discount if the individual satisfies an alternative standard that is reasonable in the burden it imposes and is reasonable taking into consideration the individual's medical situation. All plan materials describing the terms of the wellness program include the following statement: "If it is unreasonably difficult due to a medical condition for you to achieve a body mass index between 19 and 26 (or if it is medically inadvisable for you to attempt to achieve this body mass index) this year, your deductible will be waived if you walk for 20 minutes three days a week. If you cannot follow the walking program, call us at the number above and we will work with you to develop another way to have your deductible waived." Due to a medical condition, Individual E is unable to achieve a BMI of between 19 and 26 and is also unable to follow the walking program. E proposes a program based on the *recommendations of E's physician.* The plan agrees to make the discount available to E if E follows the physician's recommendations.

(ii) *Conclusion.* In this *Example 4,* the program satisfies the five requirements of paragraph (f)(2) of this section. First, the program complies with the limits on rewards under a program. Second, it is reasonably designed to promote health or prevent disease. Third, individuals eligible for the program are given the opportunity to qualify for the reward at least once per year. Fourth, the reward under the program is available to all similarly situated individuals because it generally accommodates individuals for whom it is unreasonably difficult due to a

medical condition to achieve (or for whom it is medically inadvisable to attempt to achieve) the targeted body mass index by providing a reasonable alternative standard (walking) and it accommodates individuals for whom it is unreasonably difficult due to a medical condition (or for whom it is medically inadvisable to attempt) to walk by providing an alternative standard that is reasonable for the individual. Fifth, the plan discloses in all materials describing the terms of the program the availability of a reasonable alternative standard for every individual. Thus, the waiver of the deductible does not violate this section.

Example 5. (i) *Facts.* In conjunction with an annual open enrollment period, a group health plan provides a form for participants to certify that they have not used tobacco products in the preceding twelve months. Participants who do not provide the certification are assessed a surcharge that is 20 percent of the cost of employee-only coverage. However, all plan materials describing the terms of the wellness program include the following statement: "If it is unreasonably difficult due to a health factor for you to meet the requirements under this program (or if it is medically inadvisable for you to attempt to meet the requirements of this program), we will make available a reasonable alternative standard for you to avoid this surcharge." It is unreasonably difficult for Individual F to stop smoking cigarettes due to an addiction to nicotine (a medical condition). The plan accommodates F by requiring F to participate in a smoking cessation program to avoid the surcharge. F can avoid the surcharge for as long as F participates in the program, regardless of whether F stops smoking (as long as F continues to be addicted to nicotine).

(ii) *Conclusion.* In this *Example 5,* the premium surcharge is permissible as a wellness program because it satisfies the five requirements of paragraph (f)(2) of this section. First, the program complies with the limits on rewards under a program. Second, it is reasonably designed to promote health or prevent disease. Third, individuals eligible for the program are given the opportunity to qualify for the reward at least once per year. Fourth, the reward under the program is available to all similarly situated individuals because it accommodates individuals for whom it is unreasonably difficult due to a medical condition (or for whom it is medically inadvisable to attempt) to quit using tobacco products by providing a reasonable alternative standard. Fifth, the plan discloses in all materials describing the terms of the program the availability of a reasonable alternative standard. Thus, the premium surcharge does not violate this section.

Example 6. (i) *Facts.* Same facts as *Example 5,* except the plan accommodates F by requiring F to view, over a period of 12 months, a 12-hour video series on health problems associated with tobacco use. F can avoid the surcharge by complying with this requirement.

(ii) *Conclusion.* In this *Example 6,* the requirement to watch the series of video tapes is a reasonable alternative method for avoiding the surcharge.

(g) *More favorable treatment of individuals with adverse health factors permitted—*(1) *In rules for eligibility—*(i) Nothing in this section prevents a group health plan from establishing more favorable rules for eligibility (described in paragraph (b)(1) of this section) for individuals with an adverse health factor, such as disability, than for individuals without the adverse health factor. Moreover, nothing in this section prevents a plan from charging a higher premium or contribution with respect to individuals with an adverse health factor if they would not be eligible for the coverage were it not for the adverse health factor. (However, other laws, including State insurance laws, may set or limit premium rates; these laws are not affected by this section.)

(ii) The rules of this paragraph (g)(1) are illustrated by the following examples:

Example 1. (i) *Facts.* An employer sponsors a group health plan that generally is available to employees, spouses of employees, and dependent children until age 23. However, dependent children who are disabled are eligible for coverage beyond age 23.

(ii) *Conclusion.* In this *Example 1,* the plan provision allowing coverage for disabled dependent children beyond age 23 satisfies this paragraph (g)(1) (and thus does not violate this section).

Example 2. (i) *Facts.* An employer sponsors a group health plan, which is generally available to employees (and members of the employee's family) until the last day of the month in which the employee ceases to perform services for the employer. The plan generally charges employees $50 per month for employee-only coverage and $125 per month for family coverage. However, an employee who ceases to perform services for the employer by reason of disability may remain covered under the plan until the last day of the month that is 12 months after the month in which the employee ceased to perform services for the employer. During this extended period of coverage, the plan charges the employee $100 per month for employee-only coverage and $250 per month for family coverage. (This extended period of coverage is without regard to whatever rights the employee (or members of the employee's family) may have for COBRA continuation coverage.)

(ii) *Conclusion.* In this *Example 2,* the plan provision allowing extended coverage for disabled employees and their families satisfies this paragraph (g)(1) (and thus does not violate this section). In addition, the plan is permitted, under this paragraph (g)(1), to charge the disabled employees a higher premium during the extended period of coverage.

Example 3. (i) *Facts.* To comply with the requirements of a COBRA continuation provision, a group health plan generally makes COBRA continuation coverage available for a maximum period of 18 months in connection with a termination of employment but makes the coverage

F. HIPAA Final Rules, Nondiscrimination and Wellness Benefits, continued

75038   Federal Register / Vol. 71, No. 239 / Wednesday, December 13, 2006 / Rules and Regulations

available for a maximum period of 29 months to certain disabled individuals and certain members of the disabled individual's family. Although the plan generally requires payment of 102 percent of the applicable premium for the first 18 months of COBRA continuation coverage, the plan requires payment of 150 percent of the applicable premium for the disabled individual's COBRA continuation coverage during the disability extension if the disabled individual would not be entitled to COBRA continuation coverage but for the disability.

(ii) *Conclusion.* In this *Example 3*, the plan provision allowing extended COBRA continuation coverage for disabled individuals satisfies this paragraph (g)(1) (and thus does not violate this section). In addition, the plan is permitted, under this paragraph (g)(1), to charge the disabled individuals a higher premium for the extended coverage if the individuals would not be eligible for COBRA continuation coverage were it not for the disability. (Similarly, if the plan provided an extended period of coverage for disabled individuals pursuant to State law or plan provision rather than pursuant to a COBRA continuation coverage provision, the plan could likewise charge the disabled individuals a higher premium for the extended coverage.)

(2) *In premiums or contributions*—(i) Nothing in this section prevents a group health plan from charging individuals a premium or contribution that is less than the premium (or contribution) for similarly situated individuals if the lower charge is based on an adverse health factor, such as disability.

(ii) The rules of this paragraph (g)(2) are illustrated by the following example:

Example. (i) *Facts.* Under a group health plan, employees are generally required to pay $50 per month for employee-only coverage and $125 per month for family coverage under the plan. However, employees who are disabled receive coverage (whether employee-only or family coverage) under the plan free of charge.

(ii) *Conclusion.* In this *Example*, the plan provision waiving premium payment for disabled employees is permitted under this paragraph (g)(2) (and thus does not violate this section).

(h) *No effect on other laws.* Compliance with this section is not determinative of compliance with any provision of ERISA (including the COBRA continuation provisions) or any other State or Federal law, such as the Americans with Disabilities Act. Therefore, although the rules of this section would not prohibit a plan from treating one group of similarly situated individuals differently from another (such as providing different benefit packages to current and former employees), other Federal or State laws may require that two separate groups of similarly situated individuals be treated the same for certain purposes (such as making the same benefit package

available to COBRA qualified beneficiaries as is made available to active employees). In addition, although this section generally does not impose new disclosure obligations on plans, this section does not affect any other laws, including those that require accurate disclosures and prohibit intentional misrepresentation.

(i) *Applicability dates.* This section applies for plan years beginning on or after July 1, 2007.

Mark E. Matthews,

Deputy Commissioner for Services and Enforcement, Internal Revenue Service.

    Approved: June 22, 2006.

Eric Solomon,

Acting Deputy Assistant Secretary of the Treasury (Tax Policy).

Employee Benefits Security Administration

29 CFR Chapter XXV

■ For the reasons set forth above, 29 CFR Part 2590 is amended as follows:

PART 2590—RULES AND REGULATIONS FOR GROUP HEALTH PLANS

■ 1. The authority citation for Part 2590 continues to read as follows:

Authority: 29 U.S.C. 1027, 1059, 1135, 1161–1168, 1169, 1181–1183, 1181 note, 1185, 1185a, 1185b, 1191, 1191a, 1191b, and 1191c, sec. 101(g), Public Law 104–191, 110 Stat. 1936; sec. 401(b), Public Law 105–200, 112 Stat. 645 (42 U.S.C. 651 note); Secretary of Labor's Order 1–2003, 68 FR 5374 (Feb. 3, 2003).

■ 2. Section 2590.702 is revised to read as follows:

§ 2590.702 Prohibiting discrimination against participants and beneficiaries based on a health factor.

(a) *Health factors.* (1) The term *health factor* means, in relation to an individual, any of the following health status-related factors:

(i) Health status;

(ii) Medical condition (including both physical and mental illnesses), as defined in § 2590.701–2;

(iii) Claims experience;

(iv) Receipt of health care;

(v) Medical history;

(vi) Genetic information, as defined in § 2590.701–2;

(vii) Evidence of insurability; or

(viii) Disability.

(2) Evidence of insurability includes—

(i) Conditions arising out of acts of domestic violence; and

(ii) Participation in activities such as motorcycling, snowmobiling, all-terrain vehicle riding, horseback riding, skiing, and other similar activities.

(3) The decision whether health coverage is elected for an individual (including the time chosen to enroll, such as under special enrollment or late enrollment) is not, itself, within the scope of any health factor. (However, under § 2590.701–6, a plan or issuer must treat special enrollees the same as similarly situated individuals who are enrolled when first eligible.)

(b) *Prohibited discrimination in rules for eligibility*—(1) *In general*—(i) A group health plan, and a health insurance issuer offering health insurance coverage in connection with a group health plan, may not establish any rule for eligibility (including continued eligibility) of any individual to enroll for benefits under the terms of the plan or group health insurance coverage that discriminates based on any health factor that relates to that individual or a dependent of that individual. This rule is subject to the provisions of paragraph (b)(2) of this section (explaining how this rule applies to benefits), paragraph (b)(3) of this section (allowing plans to impose certain preexisting condition exclusions), paragraph (d) of this section (containing rules for establishing groups of similarly situated individuals), paragraph (e) of this section (relating to nonconfinement, actively-at-work, and other service requirements), paragraph (f) of this section (relating to wellness programs), and paragraph (g) of this section (permitting favorable treatment of individuals with adverse health factors).

(ii) For purposes of this section, rules for eligibility include, but are not limited to, rules relating to—

(A) Enrollment;

(B) The effective date of coverage;

(C) Waiting (or affiliation) periods;

(D) Late and special enrollment;

(E) Eligibility for benefit packages (including rules for individuals to change their selection among benefit packages);

(F) Benefits (including rules relating to covered benefits, benefit restrictions, and cost-sharing mechanisms such as coinsurance, copayments, and deductibles), as described in paragraphs (b)(2) and (3) of this section;

(G) Continued eligibility; and

(H) Terminating coverage (including disenrollment) of any individual under the plan.

(iii) The rules of this paragraph (b)(1) are illustrated by the following examples:

Example 1. (i) *Facts.* An employer sponsors a group health plan that is available to all employees who enroll within the first 30 days of their employment. However, employees who do not enroll within the first

F. HIPAA Final Rules, Nondiscrimination and Wellness Benefits, continued

Federal Register / Vol. 71, No. 239 / Wednesday, December 13, 2006 / Rules and Regulations **75039**

30 days cannot enroll later unless they pass a physical examination.

(ii) *Conclusion.* In this *Example 1*, the requirement to pass a physical examination in order to enroll in the plan is a rule for eligibility that discriminates based on one or more health factors and thus violates this paragraph (b)(1).

Example 2. (i) *Facts.* Under an employer's group health plan, employees who enroll during the first 30 days of employment (and during special enrollment periods) may choose between two benefit packages: an indemnity option and an HMO option. However, employees who enroll during late enrollment are permitted to enroll only in the HMO option and only if they provide evidence of good health.

(ii) *Conclusion.* In this *Example 2*, the requirement to provide evidence of good health in order to be eligible for late enrollment in the HMO option is a rule for eligibility that discriminates based on one or more health factors and thus violates this paragraph (b)(1). However, if the plan did not require evidence of good health but limited late enrollees to the HMO option, the plan's rules for eligibility would not discriminate based on any health factor, and thus would not violate this paragraph (b)(1), because the time an individual chooses to enroll is not, itself, within the scope of any health factor.

Example 3. (i) *Facts.* Under an employer's group health plan, all employees generally may enroll within the first 30 days of employment. However, individuals who participate in certain recreational activities, including motorcycling, are excluded from coverage.

(ii) *Conclusion.* In this *Example 3*, excluding from the plan individuals who participate in recreational activities, such as motorcycling, is a rule for eligibility that discriminates based on one more health factors and thus violates this paragraph (b)(1).

Example 4. (i) *Facts.* A group health plan applies for a group health policy offered by an issuer. As part of the application, the issuer receives health information about individuals to be covered under the plan. Individual *A* is an employee of the employer maintaining the plan. *A* and *A*'s dependents have a history of high health claims. Based on the information about *A* and *A*'s dependents, the issuer excludes *A* and *A*'s dependents from the group policy it offers to the employer.

(ii) *Conclusion.* In this *Example 4*, the issuer's exclusion of *A* and *A*'s dependents from coverage is a rule for eligibility that discriminates based on one or more health factors, and thus violates this paragraph (b)(1). (If the employer is a small employer under 45 CFR 144.103 (generally, an employer with 50 or fewer employees), the issuer also may violate 45 CFR 146.150, which requires issuers to offer all the policies they sell in the small group market on a guaranteed available basis to all small employers and to accept every eligible individual in every small employer group.) If the plan provides coverage through this policy and does not provide equivalent coverage for *A* and *A*'s dependents through other means, the plan will also violate this paragraph (b)(1).

(2) *Application to benefits*—(i) *General rule*—(A) Under this section, a group health plan or group health insurance issuer is not required to provide coverage for any particular benefit to any group of similarly situated individuals.

(B) However, benefits provided under a plan or through group health insurance coverage must be uniformly available to all similarly situated individuals (as described in paragraph (d) of this section). Likewise, any restriction on a benefit or benefits must apply uniformly to all similarly situated individuals and must not be directed at individual participants or beneficiaries based on any health factor of the participants or beneficiaries (determined based on all the relevant facts and circumstances). Thus, for example, a plan or issuer may limit or exclude benefits in relation to a specific disease or condition, limit or exclude benefits for certain types of treatments or drugs, or limit or exclude benefits based on a determination of whether the benefits are experimental or not medically necessary, but only if the benefit limitation or exclusion applies uniformly to all similarly situated individuals and is not directed at individual participants or beneficiaries based on any health factor of the participants or beneficiaries. In addition, a plan or issuer may impose annual, lifetime, or other limits on benefits and may require the satisfaction of a deductible, copayment, coinsurance, or other cost-sharing requirement in order to obtain a benefit if the limit or cost-sharing requirement applies uniformly to all similarly situated individuals and is not directed at individual participants or beneficiaries based on any health factor of the participants or beneficiaries. In the case of a cost-sharing requirement, see also paragraph (b)(2)(ii) of this section, which permits variances in the application of a cost-sharing mechanism made available under a wellness program. (Whether any plan provision or practice with respect to benefits complies with this paragraph (b)(2)(i) does not affect whether the provision or practice is permitted under any other provision of the Act, the Americans with Disabilities Act, or any other law, whether State or Federal.)

(C) For purposes of this paragraph (b)(2)(i), a plan amendment applicable to all individuals in one or more groups of similarly situated individuals under the plan and made effective no earlier than the first day of the first plan year after the amendment is adopted is not considered to be directed at any individual participants or beneficiaries.

(D) The rules of this paragraph (b)(2)(i) are illustrated by the following examples:

Example 1. (i) *Facts.* A group health plan applies a $500,000 lifetime limit on all benefits to each participant or beneficiary covered under the plan. The limit is not directed at individual participants or beneficiaries.

(ii) *Conclusion.* In this *Example 1*, the limit does not violate this paragraph (b)(2)(i) because $500,000 of benefits are available uniformly to each participant and beneficiary under the plan and because the limit is applied uniformly to all participants and beneficiaries and is not directed at individual participants or beneficiaries.

Example 2. (i) *Facts.* A group health plan has a $2 million lifetime limit on all benefits (and no other lifetime limits) for participants covered under the plan. Participant *B* files a claim for the treatment of AIDS. At the next corporate board meeting of the plan sponsor, the claim is discussed. Shortly thereafter, the plan is modified to impose a $10,000 lifetime limit on benefits for the treatment of AIDS, effective before the beginning of the next plan year.

(ii) *Conclusion.* The facts of this *Example 2* strongly suggest that the plan modification is directed at *B* based on *B*'s claim. Absent outweighing evidence to the contrary, the plan violates this paragraph (b)(2)(i).

Example 3. (i) *Facts.* A group health plan applies for a group health policy offered by an issuer. Individual *C* is covered under the plan and has an adverse health condition. As part of the application, the issuer receives health information about the individuals to be covered, including information about *C*'s adverse health condition. The policy form offered by the issuer generally provides benefits for the adverse health condition that *C* has, but in this case the issuer offers the plan a policy modified by a rider that excludes benefits for *C* for that condition. The exclusionary rider is made effective the first day of the next plan year.

(ii) *Conclusion.* In this *Example 3*, the issuer violates this paragraph (b)(2)(i) because benefits for *C*'s condition are available to other individuals in the group of similarly situated individuals that includes *C* but are not available to *C*. Thus, the benefits are not uniformly available to all similarly situated individuals. Even though the exclusionary rider is made effective the first day of the next plan year, because the rider does not apply to all similarly situated individuals, the issuer violates this paragraph (b)(2)(i).

Example 4. (i) *Facts.* A group health plan has a $2,000 lifetime limit for the treatment of temporomandibular joint syndrome (TMJ). The limit is applied uniformly to all similarly situated individuals and is not directed at individual participants or beneficiaries.

(ii) *Conclusion.* In this *Example 4*, the limit does not violate this paragraph (b)(2)(i) because $2,000 of benefits for the treatment of TMJ are available uniformly to all similarly situated individuals and a plan may limit benefits covered in relation to a specific disease or condition if the limit applies uniformly to all similarly situated

F. HIPAA Final Rules, Nondiscrimination and Wellness Benefits, continued

individuals and is not directed at individual participants or beneficiaries. (This example does not address whether the plan provision is permissible under the Americans with Disabilities Act or any other applicable law.)

Example 5. (i) *Facts.* A group health plan applies a $2 million lifetime limit on all benefits. However, the $2 million lifetime limit is reduced to $10,000 for any participant or beneficiary covered under the plan who has a congenital heart defect.

(ii) *Conclusion.* In this *Example 5,* the lower lifetime limit for participants and beneficiaries with a congenital heart defect violates this paragraph (b)(2)(i) because benefits under the plan are not uniformly available to all similarly situated individuals and the plan's lifetime limit on benefits does not apply uniformly to all similarly situated individuals.

Example 6. (i) *Facts.* A group health plan limits benefits for prescription drugs to those listed on a drug formulary. The limit is applied uniformly to all similarly situated individuals and is not directed at individual participants or beneficiaries.

(ii) *Conclusion.* In this *Example 6,* the exclusion from coverage of drugs not listed on the drug formulary does not violate this paragraph (b)(2)(i) because benefits for prescription drugs listed on the formulary are uniformly available to all similarly situated individuals and because the exclusion of drugs not listed on the formulary applies uniformly to all similarly situated individuals and is not directed at individual participants or beneficiaries.

Example 7. (i) *Facts.* Under a group health plan, doctor visits are generally subject to a $250 annual deductible and 20 percent coinsurance requirement. However, prenatal doctor visits are not subject to any deductible or coinsurance requirement. These rules are applied uniformly to all similarly situated individuals and are not directed at individual participants or beneficiaries.

(ii) *Conclusion.* In this *Example 7,* imposing different deductible and coinsurance requirements for prenatal doctor visits and other visits does not violate this paragraph (b)(2)(i) because a plan may establish different deductibles or coinsurance requirements for different services if the deductible or coinsurance requirement is applied uniformly to all similarly situated individuals and is not directed at individual participants or beneficiaries.

Example 8. (i) *Facts.* An employer sponsors a group health plan that is available to all current employees. Under the plan, the medical care expenses of each employee (and the employee's dependents) are reimbursed up to an annual maximum amount. The maximum reimbursement amount with respect to an employee for a year is $1500 multiplied by the number of years the employee has participated in the plan, reduced by the total reimbursements for prior years.

(ii) *Conclusion.* In this *Example 8,* the variable annual limit does not violate this paragraph (b)(2)(i). Although the maximum reimbursement amount for a year varies among employees within the same group of similarly situated individuals based on prior claims experience, employees who have participated in the plan for the same length of time are eligible for the same total benefit over that length of time (and the restriction on the maximum reimbursement amount is not directed at any individual participants or beneficiaries based on any health factor).

(ii) *Exception for wellness programs.* A group health plan or group health insurance issuer may vary benefits, including cost-sharing mechanisms (such as a deductible, copayment, or coinsurance), based on whether an individual has met the standards of a wellness program that satisfies the requirements of paragraph (f) of this section.

(iii) *Specific rule relating to source-of-injury exclusions*—(A) If a group health plan or group health insurance coverage generally provides benefits for a type of injury, the plan or issuer may not deny benefits otherwise provided for treatment of the injury if the injury results from an act of domestic violence or a medical condition (including both physical and mental health conditions). This rule applies in the case of an injury resulting from a medical condition even if the condition is not diagnosed before the injury.

(B) The rules of this paragraph (b)(2)(iii) are illustrated by the following examples:

Example 1. (i) *Facts.* A group health plan generally provides medical/surgical benefits, including benefits for hospital stays, that are medically necessary. However, the plan excludes benefits for self-inflicted injuries or injuries sustained in connection with attempted suicide. Because of depression, Individual *D* attempts suicide. As a result, *D* sustains injuries and is hospitalized for treatment of the injuries. Under the exclusion, the plan denies *D* benefits for treatment of the injuries.

(ii) *Conclusion.* In this *Example 1,* the suicide attempt is the result of a medical condition (depression). Accordingly, the denial of benefits for the treatments of *D*'s injuries violates the requirements of this paragraph (b)(2)(iii) because the plan provision excludes benefits for treatment of an injury resulting from a medical condition.

Example 2. (i) *Facts.* A group health plan provides benefits for head injuries generally. The plan also has a general exclusion for any injury sustained while participating in any of a number of recreational activities, including bungee jumping. However, this exclusion does not apply to any injury that results from a medical condition (nor from domestic violence). Participant *E* sustains a head injury while bungee jumping. The injury did not result from a medical condition (nor from domestic violence). Accordingly, the plan denies benefits for *E*'s head injury.

(ii) *Conclusion.* In this *Example 2,* the plan provision that denies benefits based on the source of an injury does not restrict benefits based on an act of domestic violence or any medical condition. Therefore, the provision is permissible under this paragraph (b)(2)(iii) and does not violate this section. (However, if the plan did not allow *E* to enroll in the plan (or applied different rules for eligibility to *E*) because *E* frequently participates in bungee jumping, the plan would violate paragraph (b)(1) of this section.)

(3) *Relationship to § 2590.701–3.* (i) A preexisting condition exclusion is permitted under this section if it —

(A) Complies with § 2590.701–3;

(B) Applies uniformly to all similarly situated individuals (as described in paragraph (d) of this section); and

(C) Is not directed at individual participants or beneficiaries based on any health factor of the participants or beneficiaries. For purposes of this paragraph (b)(3)(i)(C), a plan amendment relating to a preexisting condition exclusion applicable to all individuals in one or more groups of similarly situated individuals under the plan and made effective no earlier than the first day of the first plan year after the amendment is adopted is not considered to be directed at any individual participants or beneficiaries.

(ii) The rules of this paragraph (b)(3) are illustrated by the following examples:

Example 1. (i) *Facts.* A group health plan imposes a preexisting condition exclusion on all individuals enrolled in the plan. The exclusion applies to conditions for which medical advice, diagnosis, care, or treatment was recommended or received within the six-month period ending on an individual's enrollment date. In addition, the exclusion generally extends for 12 months after an individual's enrollment date, but this 12-month period is offset by the number of days of an individual's creditable coverage in accordance with § 2590.701–3. There is nothing to indicate that the exclusion is directed at individual participants or beneficiaries.

(ii) *Conclusion.* In this *Example 1,* even though the plan's preexisting condition exclusion discriminates against individuals based on one or more health factors, the preexisting condition exclusion does not violate this section because it applies uniformly to all similarly situated individuals, is not directed at individual participants or beneficiaries, and complies with § 2590.701–3 (that is, the requirements relating to the six-month look-back period, the 12-month (or 18-month) maximum exclusion period, and the creditable coverage offset).

Example 2. (i) *Facts.* A group health plan excludes coverage for conditions with respect to which medical advice, diagnosis, care, or treatment was recommended or received within the six-month period ending on an individual's enrollment date. Under the plan, the preexisting condition exclusion generally extends for 12 months, offset by creditable coverage. However, if an individual has no claims in the first six months following enrollment, the remainder of the exclusion period is waived.

F. HIPAA Final Rules, Nondiscrimination and Wellness Benefits, continued

(ii) *Conclusion.* In this *Example 2,* the plan's preexisting condition exclusions violate this section because they do not meet the requirements of this paragraph (b)(3); specifically, they do not apply uniformly to all similarly situated individuals. The plan provisions do not apply uniformly to all similarly situated individuals because individuals who have medical claims during the first six months following enrollment are not treated the same as similarly situated individuals with no claims during that period. (Under paragraph (d) of this section, the groups cannot be treated as two separate groups of similarly situated individuals because the distinction is based on a health factor.)

(c) *Prohibited discrimination in premiums or contributions*—(1) *In general*—(i) A group health plan, and a health insurance issuer offering health insurance coverage in connection with a group health plan, may not require an individual, as a condition of enrollment or continued enrollment under the plan or group health insurance coverage, to pay a premium or contribution that is greater than the premium or contribution for a similarly situated individual (described in paragraph (d) of this section) enrolled in the plan or group health insurance coverage based on any health factor that relates to the individual or a dependent of the individual.

(ii) Discounts, rebates, payments in kind, and any other premium differential mechanisms are taken into account in determining an individual's premium or contribution rate. (For rules relating to cost-sharing mechanisms, see paragraph (b)(2) of this section (addressing benefits).)

(2) *Rules relating to premium rates*—(i) *Group rating based on health factors not restricted under this section.* Nothing in this section restricts the aggregate amount that an employer may be charged for coverage under a group health plan.

(ii) *List billing based on a health factor prohibited.* However, a group health insurance issuer, or a group health plan, may not quote or charge an employer (or an individual) a different premium for an individual in a group of similarly situated individuals based on a health factor. (But see paragraph (g) of this section permitting favorable treatment of individuals with adverse health factors.)

(iii) *Examples.* The rules of this paragraph (c)(2) are illustrated by the following examples:

Example 1. (i) *Facts.* An employer sponsors a group health plan and purchases coverage from a health insurance issuer. In order to determine the premium rate for the upcoming plan year, the issuer reviews the claims experience of individuals covered under the plan. The issuer finds that Individual *F* had significantly higher claims experience than similarly situated individuals in the plan. The issuer quotes the plan a higher per-participant rate because of *F*'s claims experience.

(ii) *Conclusion.* In this *Example 1,* the issuer does not violate the provisions of this paragraph (c)(2) because the issuer blends the rate so that the employer is not quoted a higher rate for *F* than for a similarly situated individual based on *F*'s claims experience.

Example 2. (i) *Facts.* Same facts as *Example 1,* except that the issuer quotes the employer a higher premium rate for *F,* because of *F*'s claims experience, than for a similarly situated individual.

(ii) *Conclusion.* In this *Example 2,* the issuer violates this paragraph (c)(2). Moreover, even if the plan purchased the policy based on the quote but did not require a higher participant contribution for *F* than for a similarly situated individual, the issuer would still violate this paragraph (c)(2) (but in such a case the plan would not violate this paragraph (c)(2)).

(3) *Exception for wellness programs.* Notwithstanding paragraphs (c)(1) and (2) of this section, a plan or issuer may vary the amount of premium or contribution it requires similarly situated individuals to pay based on whether an individual has met the standards of a wellness program that satisfies the requirements of paragraph (f) of this section.

(d) *Similarly situated individuals.* The requirements of this section apply only within a group of individuals who are treated as similarly situated individuals. A plan or issuer may treat participants as a group of similarly situated individuals separate from beneficiaries. In addition, participants may be treated as two or more distinct groups of similarly situated individuals and beneficiaries may be treated as two or more distinct groups of similarly situated individuals in accordance with the rules of this paragraph (d). Moreover, if individuals have a choice of two or more benefit packages, individuals choosing one benefit package may be treated as one or more groups of similarly situated individuals distinct from individuals choosing another benefit package.

(1) *Participants.* Subject to paragraph (d)(3) of this section, a plan or issuer may treat participants as two or more distinct groups of similarly situated individuals if the distinction between or among the groups of participants is based on a bona fide employment-based classification consistent with the employer's usual business practice. Whether an employment-based classification is bona fide is determined on the basis of all the relevant facts and circumstances. Relevant facts and circumstances include whether the employer uses the classification for purposes independent of qualification for health coverage (for example, determining eligibility for other employee benefits or determining other terms of employment). Subject to paragraph (d)(3) of this section, examples of classifications that, based on all the relevant facts and circumstances, may be bona fide include full-time versus part-time status, different geographic location, membership in a collective bargaining unit, date of hire, length of service, current employee versus former employee status, and different occupations. However, a classification based on any health factor is not a bona fide employment-based classification, unless the requirements of paragraph (g) of this section are satisfied (permitting favorable treatment of individuals with adverse health factors).

(2) *Beneficiaries*—(i) Subject to paragraph (d)(3) of this section, a plan or issuer may treat beneficiaries as two or more distinct groups of similarly situated individuals if the distinction between or among the groups of beneficiaries is based on any of the following factors:

(A) A bona fide employment-based classification of the participant through whom the beneficiary is receiving coverage;

(B) Relationship to the participant (for example, as a spouse or as a dependent child);

(C) Marital status;

(D) With respect to children of a participant, age or student status; or

(E) Any other factor if the factor is not a health factor.

(ii) Paragraph (d)(2)(i) of this section does not prevent more favorable treatment of individuals with adverse health factors in accordance with paragraph (g) of this section.

(3) *Discrimination directed at individuals.* Notwithstanding paragraphs (d)(1) and (2) of this section, if the creation or modification of an employment or coverage classification is directed at individual participants or beneficiaries based on any health factor of the participants or beneficiaries, the classification is not permitted under this paragraph (d), unless it is permitted under paragraph (g) of this section (permitting favorable treatment of individuals with adverse health factors). Thus, if an employer modified an employment-based classification to single out, based on a health factor, individual participants and beneficiaries and deny them health coverage, the new classification would not be permitted under this section.

F. HIPAA Final Rules, Nondiscrimination and Wellness Benefits, continued

(4) *Examples.* The rules of this paragraph (d) are illustrated by the following examples:

Example 1. (i) *Facts.* An employer sponsors a group health plan for full-time employees only. Under the plan (consistent with the employer's usual business practice), employees who normally work at least 30 hours per week are considered to be working full-time. Other employees are considered to be working part-time. There is no evidence to suggest that the classification is directed at individual participants or beneficiaries.

(ii) *Conclusion.* In this *Example 1,* treating the full-time and part-time employees as two separate groups of similarly situated individuals is permitted under this paragraph (d) because the classification is bona fide and is not directed at individual participants or beneficiaries.

Example 2. (i) *Facts.* Under a group health plan, coverage is made available to employees, their spouses, and their dependent children. However, coverage is made available to a dependent child only if the dependent child is under age 19 (or under age 25 if the child is continuously enrolled full-time in an institution of higher learning (full-time students)). There is no evidence to suggest that these classifications are directed at individual participants or beneficiaries.

(ii) *Conclusion.* In this *Example 2,* treating spouses and dependent children differently by imposing an age limitation on dependent children, but not on spouses, is permitted under this paragraph (d). Specifically, the distinction between spouses and dependent children is permitted under paragraph (d)(2) of this section and is not prohibited under paragraph (d)(3) of this section because it is not directed at individual participants or beneficiaries. It is also permissible to treat dependent children who are under age 19 (or full-time students under age 25) as a group of similarly situated individuals separate from those who are age 25 or older (or age 19 or older if they are not full-time students) because the classification is permitted under paragraph (d)(2) of this section and is not directed at individual participants or beneficiaries.

Example 3. (i) *Facts.* A university sponsors a group health plan that provides one health benefit package to faculty and another health benefit package to other staff. Faculty and staff are treated differently with respect to other employee benefits such as retirement benefits and leaves of absence. There is no evidence to suggest that the distinction is directed at individual participants or beneficiaries.

(ii) *Conclusion.* In this *Example 3,* the classification is permitted under this paragraph (d) because there is a distinction based on a bona fide employment-based classification consistent with the employer's usual business practice and the distinction is not directed at individual participants and beneficiaries.

Example 4. (i) *Facts.* An employer sponsors a group health plan that is available to all current employees. Former employees may also be eligible, but only if they complete a specified number of years of service, are enrolled under the plan at the time of termination of employment, and are continuously enrolled from that date. There is no evidence to suggest that these distinctions are directed at individual participants or beneficiaries.

(ii) *Conclusion.* In this *Example 4,* imposing additional eligibility requirements on former employees is permitted because a classification that distinguishes between current and former employees is a bona fide employment-based classification that is permitted under this paragraph (d), provided that it is not directed at individual participants or beneficiaries. In addition, it is permissible to distinguish between former employees who satisfy the service requirement and those who do not, provided that the distinction is not directed at individual participants or beneficiaries. (However, former employees who do not satisfy the eligibility criteria may, nonetheless, be eligible for continued coverage pursuant to a COBRA continuation provision or similar State law.)

Example 5. (i) *Facts.* An employer sponsors a group health plan that provides the same benefit package to all seven employees of the employer. Six of the seven employees have the same job title and responsibilities, but Employee *G* has a different job title and different responsibilities. After *G* files an expensive claim for benefits under the plan, coverage under the plan is modified so that employees with *G*'s job title receive a different benefit package that includes a lower lifetime dollar limit than in the benefit package made available to the other six employees.

(ii) *Conclusion.* Under the facts of this *Example 5,* changing the coverage classification for *G* based on the existing employment classification for *G* is not permitted under this paragraph (d) because the creation of the new coverage classification for *G* is directed at *G* based on one or more health factors.

(e) *Nonconfinement and actively-at-work provisions*—(1) *Nonconfinement provisions*—(i) *General rule.* Under the rules of paragraphs (b) and (c) of this section, a plan or issuer may not establish a rule for eligibility (as described in paragraph (b)(1)(ii) of this section) or set any individual's premium or contribution rate based on whether an individual is confined to a hospital or other health care institution. In addition, under the rules of paragraphs (b) and (c) of this section, a plan or issuer may not establish a rule for eligibility or set any individual's premium or contribution rate based on an individual's ability to engage in normal life activities, except to the extent permitted under paragraphs (e)(2)(ii) and (3) of this section (permitting plans and issuers, under certain circumstances, to distinguish among employees based on the performance of services).

(ii) *Examples.* The rules of this paragraph (e)(1) are illustrated by the following examples:

Example 1. (i) *Facts.* Under a group health plan, coverage for employees and their dependents generally becomes effective on the first day of employment. However, coverage for a dependent who is confined to a hospital or other health care institution does not become effective until the confinement ends.

(ii) *Conclusion.* In this *Example 1,* the plan violates this paragraph (e)(1) because the plan delays the effective date of coverage for dependents based on confinement to a hospital or other health care institution.

Example 2. (i) *Facts.* In previous years, a group health plan has provided coverage through a group health insurance policy offered by Issuer *M.* However, for the current year, the plan provides coverage through a group health insurance policy offered by Issuer *N.* Under Issuer *N*'s policy, items and services provided in connection with the confinement of a dependent to a hospital or other health care institution are not covered if the confinement is covered under an extension of benefits clause from a previous health insurance issuer.

(ii) *Conclusion.* In this *Example 2,* Issuer *N* violates this paragraph (e)(1) because the group health insurance coverage restricts benefits (a rule for eligibility under paragraph (b)(1)) based on whether a dependent is confined to a hospital or other health care institution that is covered under an extension of benefits clause from a previous issuer. State law cannot change the obligation of Issuer *N* under this section. However, under State law Issuer *M* may also be responsible for providing benefits to such a dependent. In a case in which Issuer *N* has an obligation under this section to provide benefits and Issuer *M* has an obligation under State law to provide benefits, any State laws designed to prevent more than 100% reimbursement, such as State coordination-of-benefits laws, continue to apply.

(2) *Actively-at-work and continuous service provisions*—(i) *General rule*—(A) Under the rules of paragraphs (b) and (c) of this section and subject to the exception for the first day of work described in paragraph (e)(2)(ii) of this section, a plan or issuer may not establish a rule for eligibility (as described in paragraph (b)(1)(ii) of this section) or set any individual's premium or contribution rate based on whether an individual is actively at work (including whether an individual is continuously employed), unless absence from work due to any health factor (such as being absent from work on sick leave) is treated, for purposes of the plan or health insurance coverage, as being actively at work.

(B) The rules of this paragraph (e)(2)(i) are illustrated by the following examples:

Example 1. (i) *Facts.* Under a group health plan, an employee generally becomes eligible to enroll 30 days after the first day of employment. However, if the employee is not actively at work on the first day after the end of the 30-day period, then eligibility for

F. HIPAA Final Rules, Nondiscrimination and Wellness Benefits, continued

enrollment is delayed until the first day the employee is actively at work.

(ii) *Conclusion*. In this *Example 1*, the plan violates this paragraph (e)(2) (and thus also violates paragraph (b) of this section). However, the plan would not violate paragraph (e)(2) or (b) of this section if, under the plan, an absence due to any health factor is considered being actively at work.

Example 2. (i) *Facts*. Under a group health plan, coverage for an employee becomes effective after 90 days of continuous service; that is, if an employee is absent from work (for any reason) before completing 90 days of service, the beginning of the 90-day period is measured from the day the employee returns to work (without any credit for service before the absence).

(ii) *Conclusion*. In this *Example 2*, the plan violates this paragraph (e)(2) (and thus also paragraph (b) of this section) because the 90-day continuous service requirement is a rule for eligibility based on whether an individual is actively at work. However, the plan would not violate this paragraph (e)(2) or paragraph (b) of this section if, under the plan, an absence due to any health factor is not considered an absence for purposes of measuring 90 days of continuous service.

(ii) *Exception for the first day of work*—(A) Notwithstanding the general rule in paragraph (e)(2)(i) of this section, a plan or issuer may establish a rule for eligibility that requires an individual to begin work for the employer sponsoring the plan (or, in the case of a multiemployer plan, to begin a job in covered employment) before coverage becomes effective, provided that such a rule for eligibility applies regardless of the reason for the absence.

(B) The rules of this paragraph (e)(2)(ii) are illustrated by the following examples:

Example 1. (i) *Facts*. Under the eligibility provision of a group health plan, coverage for new employees becomes effective on the first day that the employee reports to work. Individual *H* is scheduled to begin work on August 3. However, *H* is unable to begin work on that day because of illness. *H* begins working on August 4, and *H*'s coverage is effective on August 4.

(ii) *Conclusion*. In this *Example 1*, the plan provision does not violate this section. However, if coverage for individuals who do not report to work on the first day they were scheduled to work for a reason unrelated to a health factor (such as vacation or bereavement) becomes effective on the first day they were scheduled to work, then the plan would violate this section.

Example 2. (i) *Facts*. Under a group health plan, coverage for new employees becomes effective on the first day of the month following the employee's first day of work, regardless of whether the employee is actively at work on the first day of the month. Individual *J* is scheduled to begin work on March 24. However, *J* is unable to begin work on March 24 because of illness. *J* begins working on April 7 and *J*'s coverage is effective May 1.

(ii) *Conclusion*. In this *Example 2*, the plan provision does not violate this section. However, as in *Example 1*, if coverage for individuals absent from work for reasons unrelated to a health factor became effective despite their absence, then the plan would violate this section.

(3) *Relationship to plan provisions defining similarly situated individuals*—(i) Notwithstanding the rules of paragraphs (e)(1) and (2) of this section, a plan or issuer may establish rules for eligibility or set any individual's premium or contribution rate in accordance with the rules relating to similarly situated individuals in paragraph (d) of this section. Accordingly, a plan or issuer may distinguish in rules for eligibility under the plan between full-time and part-time employees, between permanent and temporary or seasonal employees, between current and former employees, and between employees currently performing services and employees no longer performing services for the employer, subject to paragraph (d) of this section. However, other Federal or State laws (including the COBRA continuation provisions and the Family and Medical Leave Act of 1993) may require an employee or the employee's dependents to be offered coverage and set limits on the premium or contribution rate even though the employee is not performing services.

(ii) The rules of this paragraph (e)(3) are illustrated by the following examples:

Example 1. (i) *Facts*. Under a group health plan, employees are eligible for coverage if they perform services for the employer for 30 or more hours per week or if they are on paid leave (such as vacation, sick, or bereavement leave). Employees on unpaid leave are treated as a separate group of similarly situated individuals in accordance with the rules of paragraph (d) of this section.

(ii) *Conclusion*. In this *Example 1*, the plan provisions do not violate this section. However, if the plan treated individuals performing services for the employer for 30 or more hours per week, individuals on vacation leave, and individuals on bereavement leave as a group of similarly situated individuals separate from individuals on sick leave, the plan would violate this paragraph (e) (and thus also would violate paragraph (b) of this section) because groups of similarly situated individuals cannot be established based on a health factor (including the taking of sick leave) under paragraph (d) of this section.

Example 2. (i) *Facts*. To be eligible for coverage under a bona fide collectively bargained group health plan in the current calendar quarter, the plan requires an individual to have worked 250 hours in covered employment during the three-month period that ends one month before the beginning of the current calendar quarter. The distinction between employees working

at least 250 hours and those working less than 250 hours in the earlier three-month period is not directed at individual participants or beneficiaries based on any health factor of the participants or beneficiaries.

(ii) *Conclusion*. In this *Example 2*, the plan provision does not violate this section because, under the rules for similarly situated individuals allowing full-time employees to be treated differently than part-time employees, employees who work at least 250 hours in a three-month period can be treated differently than employees who fail to work 250 hours in that period. The result would be the same if the plan permitted individuals to apply excess hours from previous periods to satisfy the requirement for the current quarter.

Example 3. (i) *Facts*. Under a group health plan, coverage of an employee is terminated when the individual's employment is terminated, in accordance with the rules of paragraph (d) of this section. Employee *B* has been covered under the plan. *B* experiences a disabling illness that prevents *B* from working. *B* takes a leave of absence under the Family and Medical Leave Act of 1993. At the end of such leave, *B* terminates employment and consequently loses coverage under the plan. (This termination of coverage is without regard to whatever rights the employee (or members of the employee's family) may have for COBRA continuation coverage.)

(ii) *Conclusion*. In this *Example 3*, the plan provision terminating *B*'s coverage upon *B*'s termination of employment does not violate this section.

Example 4. (i) *Facts*. Under a group health plan, coverage of an employee is terminated when the employee ceases to perform services for the employer sponsoring the plan, in accordance with the rules of paragraph (d) of this section. Employee *C* is laid off for three months. When the layoff begins, *C*'s coverage under the plan is terminated. (This termination of coverage is without regard to whatever rights the employee (or members of the employee's family) may have for COBRA continuation coverage.)

(ii) *Conclusion*. In this *Example 4*, the plan provision terminating *C*'s coverage upon the cessation of *C*'s performance of services does not violate this section.

(f) *Wellness programs*. A wellness program is any program designed to promote health or prevent disease. Paragraphs (b)(2)(ii) and (c)(3) of this section provide exceptions to the general prohibitions against discrimination based on a health factor for plan provisions that vary benefits (including cost-sharing mechanisms) or the premium or contribution for similarly situated individuals in connection with a wellness program that satisfies the requirements of this paragraph (f). If none of the conditions for obtaining a reward under a wellness program is based on an individual satisfying a standard that is related to a health factor, paragraph (f)(1) of this

F. HIPAA Final Rules, Nondiscrimination and Wellness Benefits, continued

75044   Federal Register / Vol. 71, No. 239 / Wednesday, December 13, 2006 / Rules and Regulations

section clarifies that the wellness program does not violate this section if participation in the program is made available to all similarly situated individuals. If any of the conditions for obtaining a reward under a wellness program is based on an individual satisfying a standard that is related to a health factor, the wellness program does not violate this section if the requirements of paragraph (f)(2) of this section are met.

(1) *Wellness programs not subject to requirements.* If none of the conditions for obtaining a reward under a wellness program are based on an individual satisfying a standard that is related to a health factor (or if a wellness program does not provide a reward), the wellness program does not violate this section, if participation in the program is made available to all similarly situated individuals. Thus, for example, the following programs need not satisfy the requirements of paragraph (f)(2) of this section, if participation in the program is made available to all similarly situated individuals:

(i) A program that reimburses all or part of the cost for memberships in a fitness center.

(ii) A diagnostic testing program that provides a reward for participation and does not base any part of the reward on outcomes.

(iii) A program that encourages preventive care through the waiver of the copayment or deductible requirement under a group health plan for the costs of, for example, prenatal care or well-baby visits.

(iv) A program that reimburses employees for the costs of smoking cessation programs without regard to whether the employee quits smoking.

(v) A program that provides a reward to employees for attending a monthly health education seminar.

(2) *Wellness programs subject to requirements.* If any of the conditions for obtaining a reward under a wellness program is based on an individual satisfying a standard that is related to a health factor, the wellness program does not violate this section if the requirements of this paragraph (f)(2) are met.

(i) The reward for the wellness program, coupled with the reward for other wellness programs with respect to the plan that require satisfaction of a standard related to a health factor, must not exceed 20 percent of the cost of employee-only coverage under the plan. However, if, in addition to employees, any class of dependents (such as spouses or spouses and dependent children) may participate in the wellness program, the reward must not

exceed 20 percent of the cost of the coverage in which an employee and any dependents are enrolled. For purposes of this paragraph (f)(2), the cost of coverage is determined based on the total amount of employer and employee contributions for the benefit package under which the employee is (or the employee and any dependents are) receiving coverage. A reward can be in the form of a discount or rebate of a premium or contribution, a waiver of all or part of a cost-sharing mechanism (such as deductibles, copayments, or coinsurance), the absence of a surcharge, or the value of a benefit that would otherwise not be provided under the plan.

(ii) The program must be reasonably designed to promote health or prevent disease. A program satisfies this standard if it has a reasonable chance of improving the health of or preventing disease in participating individuals and it is not overly burdensome, is not a subterfuge for discriminating based on a health factor, and is not highly suspect in the method chosen to promote health or prevent disease.

(iii) The program must give individuals eligible for the program the opportunity to qualify for the reward under the program at least once per year.

(iv) The reward under the program must be available to all similarly situated individuals.

(A) A reward is not available to all similarly situated individuals for a period unless the program allows—

(1) A reasonable alternative standard (or waiver of the otherwise applicable standard) for obtaining the reward for any individual for whom, for that period, it is unreasonably difficult due to a medical condition to satisfy the otherwise applicable standard; and

(2) A reasonable alternative standard (or waiver of the otherwise applicable standard) for obtaining the reward for any individual for whom, for that period, it is medically inadvisable to attempt to satisfy the otherwise applicable standard.

(B) A plan or issuer may seek verification, such as a statement from an individual's physician, that a health factor makes it unreasonably difficult or medically inadvisable for the individual to satisfy or attempt to satisfy the otherwise applicable standard.

(v)(A) The plan or issuer must disclose in all plan materials describing the terms of the program the availability of a reasonable alternative standard (or the possibility of waiver of the otherwise applicable standard) required under paragraph (f)(2)(iv) of this section. However, if plan materials merely

mention that a program is available, without describing its terms, this disclosure is not required.

(B) The following language, or substantially similar language, can be used to satisfy the requirement of this paragraph (f)(2)(v): "If it is unreasonably difficult due to a medical condition for you to achieve the standards for the reward under this program, or if it is medically inadvisable for you to attempt to achieve the standards for the reward under this program, call us at [insert telephone number] and we will work with you to develop another way to qualify for the reward." In addition, other examples of language that would satisfy this requirement are set forth in *Examples 3, 4,* and *5* of paragraph (f)(3) of this section.

(3) *Examples.* The rules of paragraph (f)(2) of this section are illustrated by the following examples:

Example 1. (i) *Facts.* An employer sponsors a group health plan. The annual premium for employee-only coverage is $3,600 (of which the employer pays $2,700 per year and the employee pays $900 per year). The annual premium for family coverage is $9,000 (of which the employer pays $4,500 per year and the employee pays $4,500 per year). The plan offers a wellness program with an annual premium rebate of $360. The program is available only to employees.

(ii) *Conclusion.* In this *Example 1,* the program satisfies the requirements of paragraph (f)(2)(i) of this section because the reward for the wellness program, $360, does not exceed 20 percent of the total annual cost of employee-only coverage, $720. ($3,600 × 20% = $720.) If any class of dependents is allowed to participate in the program and the employee is enrolled in family coverage, the plan could offer the employee a reward of up to 20 percent of the cost of family coverage, $1,800. ($9,000 × 20% = $1,800.)

Example 2. (i) *Facts.* A group health plan gives an annual premium discount of 20 percent of the cost of employee-only coverage to participants who adhere to a wellness program. The wellness program consists solely of giving an annual cholesterol test to participants. Those participants who achieve a count under 200 receive the premium discount for the year.

(ii) *Conclusion.* In this *Example 2,* the program fails to satisfy the requirement of being available to all similarly situated individuals because some participants may be unable to achieve a cholesterol count of under 200 and the plan does not make available a reasonable alternative standard or waive the cholesterol standard. (In addition, plan materials describing the program are required to disclose the availability of a reasonable alternative standard (or the possibility of waiver of the otherwise applicable standard) for obtaining the premium discount. Thus, the premium discount violates paragraph (c) of this section because it may require an individual to pay a higher premium based on a health factor of the individual than is required of a similarly situated individual under the plan.

F. HIPAA Final Rules, Nondiscrimination and Wellness Benefits, continued

Example 3. (i) *Facts.* Same facts as *Example 2,* except that the plan provides that if it is unreasonably difficult due to a medical condition for a participant to achieve the targeted cholesterol count (or if it is medically inadvisable for a participant to attempt to achieve the targeted cholesterol count) within a 60-day period, the plan will make available a reasonable alternative standard that takes the relevant medical condition into account. In addition, all plan materials describing the terms of the program include the following statement: "If it is unreasonably difficult due to a medical condition for you to achieve a cholesterol count under 200, or if it is medically inadvisable for you to attempt to achieve a count under 200, call us at the number below and we will work with you to develop another way to get the discount." Individual *D* begins a diet and exercise program but is unable to achieve a cholesterol count under 200 within the prescribed period. *D*'s doctor determines *D* requires prescription medication to achieve a medically advisable cholesterol count. In addition, the doctor determines that *D* must be monitored through periodic blood tests to continually reevaluate *D*'s health status. The plan accommodates *D* by making the discount available to *D*, but only if *D* follows the advice of *D*'s doctor's regarding medication and blood tests.

(ii) *Conclusion.* In this *Example 3,* the program is a wellness program because it satisfies the five requirements of paragraph (f)(2) of this section. First, the program complies with the limits on rewards under a program. Second, it is reasonably designed to promote health or prevent disease. Third, individuals eligible for the program are given the opportunity to qualify for the reward at least once per year. Fourth, the reward under the program is available to all similarly situated individuals because it accommodates individuals for whom it is unreasonably difficult due to a medical condition to achieve the targeted count (or for whom it is medically inadvisable to attempt to achieve the targeted count) in the prescribed period by providing a reasonable alternative standard. Fifth, the plan discloses in all materials describing the terms of the program the availability of a reasonable alternative standard. Thus, the premium discount does not violate this section.

Example 4. (i) *Facts.* A group health plan will waive the $250 annual deductible (which is less than 20 percent of the annual cost of employee-only coverage under the plan) for the following year for participants who have a body mass index between 19 and 26, determined shortly before the beginning of the year. However, any participant for whom it is unreasonably difficult due to a medical condition to attain this standard (and any participant for whom it is medically inadvisable to attempt to achieve this standard) during the plan year is given the same discount if the participant walks for 20 minutes three days a week. Any participant for whom it is unreasonably difficult due to a medical condition to attain either standard (and any participant for whom it is medically inadvisable to attempt to achieve either standard) during the year is given the same discount if the individual satisfies an

alternative standard that is reasonable in the burden it imposes and is reasonable taking into consideration the individual's medical situation. All plan materials describing the terms of the wellness program include the following statement: "If it is unreasonably difficult due to a medical condition for you to achieve a body mass index between 19 and 26 (or if it is medically inadvisable for you to attempt to achieve this body mass index) this year, your deductible will be waived if you walk for 20 minutes three days a week. If you cannot follow the walking program, call us at the number above and we will work with you to develop another way to have your deductible waived." Due to a medical condition, Individual *E* is unable to achieve a BMI of between 19 and 26 and is also unable to follow the walking program. *E* proposes a program based on the recommendations of *E*'s physician. The plan agrees to make the discount available to *E* if *E* follows the physician's recommendations.

(ii) *Conclusion.* In this *Example 4,* the program satisfies the five requirements of paragraph (f)(2) of this section. First, the program complies with the limits on rewards under a program. Second, it is reasonably designed to promote health or prevent disease. Third, individuals eligible for the program are given the opportunity to qualify for the reward at least once per year. Fourth, the reward under the program is available to all similarly situated individuals because it generally accommodates individuals for whom it is unreasonably difficult due to a medical condition to achieve (or for whom it is medically inadvisable to attempt to achieve) the targeted body mass index by providing a reasonable alternative standard (walking) and it accommodates individuals for whom it is unreasonably difficult due to a medical condition (or for whom it is medically inadvisable to attempt) to walk by providing an alternative standard that is reasonable for the individual. Fifth, the plan discloses in all materials describing the terms of the program the availability of a reasonable alternative standard for every individual. Thus, the waiver of the deductible does not violate this section.

Example 5. (i) *Facts.* In conjunction with an annual open enrollment period, a group health plan provides a form for participants to certify that they have not used tobacco products in the preceding twelve months. Participants who do not provide the certification are assessed a surcharge that is 20 percent of the cost of employee-only coverage. However, all plan materials describing the terms of the wellness program include the following statement: "If it is unreasonably difficult due to a health factor for you to meet the requirements under this program (or if it is medically inadvisable for you to attempt to meet the requirements of this program), we will make available a reasonable alternative standard for you to avoid this surcharge." It is unreasonably difficult for Individual *F* to stop smoking cigarettes due to an addiction to nicotine (a medical condition). The plan accommodates *F* by requiring *F* to participate in a smoking cessation program. *F* can avoid the surcharge for as long as *F* participates in the program, regardless of

whether *F* stops smoking (as long as *F* continues to be addicted to nicotine).

(ii) *Conclusion.* In this *Example 5,* the premium surcharge is permissible as a wellness program because it satisfies the five requirements of paragraph (f)(2) of this section. First, the program complies with the limits on rewards under a program. Second, it is reasonably designed to promote health or prevent disease. Third, individuals eligible for the program are given the opportunity to qualify for the reward at least once per year. Fourth, the reward under the program is available to all similarly situated individuals because it accommodates individuals for whom it is unreasonably difficult due to a medical condition (or for whom it is medically inadvisable to attempt) to quit using tobacco products by providing a reasonable alternative standard. Fifth, the plan discloses in all materials describing the terms of the program the availability of a reasonable alternative standard. Thus, the premium surcharge does not violate this section.

Example 6. (i) *Facts.* Same facts as *Example 5,* except the plan accommodates *F* by requiring *F* to view, over a period of 12 months, a 12-hour video series on health problems associated with tobacco use. *F* can avoid the surcharge by complying with this requirement.

(ii) *Conclusion.* In this *Example 6,* the requirement to watch the series of video tapes is a reasonable alternative method for avoiding the surcharge.

(g) *More favorable treatment of individuals with adverse health factors permitted*—(1) *In rules for eligibility*—(i) Nothing in this section prevents a group health plan or group health insurance issuer from establishing more favorable rules for eligibility (described in paragraph (b)(1) of this section) for individuals with an adverse health factor, such as disability, than for individuals without the adverse health factor. Moreover, nothing in this section prevents a plan or issuer from charging a higher premium or contribution with respect to individuals with an adverse health factor if they would not be eligible for the coverage were it not for the adverse health factor. (However, other laws, including State insurance laws, may set or limit premium rates; these laws are not affected by this section.)

(ii) The rules of this paragraph (g)(1) are illustrated by the following examples:

Example 1. (i) *Facts.* An employer sponsors a group health plan that generally is available to employees, spouses of employees, and dependent children until age 23. However, dependent children who are disabled are eligible for coverage beyond age 23.

(ii) *Conclusion.* In this *Example 1,* the plan provision allowing coverage for disabled dependent children beyond age 23 satisfies this paragraph (g)(1) (and thus does not violate this section).

F. HIPAA Final Rules, Nondiscrimination and Wellness Benefits, continued

Example 2. (i) *Facts.* An employer sponsors a group health plan, which is generally available to employees (and members of the employee's family) until the last day of the month in which the employee ceases to perform services for the employer. The plan generally charges employees $50 per month for employee-only coverage and $125 per month for family coverage. However, an employee who ceases to perform services for the employer by reason of disability may remain covered under the plan until the last day of the month that is 12 months after the month in which the employee ceased to perform services for the employer. During this extended period of coverage, the plan charges the employee $100 per month for employee-only coverage and $250 per month for family coverage. (This extended period of coverage is without regard to whatever rights the employee (or members of the employee's family) may have for COBRA continuation coverage.)

(ii) *Conclusion.* In this *Example 2,* the plan provision allowing extended coverage for disabled employees and their families satisfies this paragraph (g)(1) (and thus does not violate this section). In addition, the plan is permitted, under this paragraph (g)(1), to charge the disabled employees a higher premium during the extended period of coverage.

Example 3. (i) *Facts.* To comply with the requirements of a COBRA continuation provision, a group health plan generally makes COBRA continuation coverage available for a maximum period of 18 months in connection with a termination of employment but makes the coverage available for a maximum period of 29 months to certain disabled individuals and certain members of the disabled individual's family. Although the plan generally requires payment of 102 percent of the applicable premium for the first 18 months of COBRA continuation coverage, the plan requires payment of 150 percent of the applicable premium for the disabled individual's COBRA continuation coverage during the disability extension if the disabled individual would not be entitled to COBRA continuation coverage but for the disability.

(ii) *Conclusion.* In this *Example 3,* the plan provision allowing extended COBRA continuation coverage for disabled individuals satisfies this paragraph (g)(1) (and thus does not violate this section). In addition, the plan is permitted, under this paragraph (g)(1), to charge the disabled individuals a higher premium for the extended coverage if the individuals would not be eligible for COBRA continuation coverage were it not for the disability. (Similarly, if the plan provided an extended period of coverage for disabled individuals pursuant to State law or plan provision rather than pursuant to a COBRA continuation coverage provision, the plan could likewise charge the disabled individuals a higher premium for the extended coverage.)

(2) *In premiums or contributions*—(i) Nothing in this section prevents a group health plan or group health insurance issuer from charging individuals a premium or contribution that is less

than the premium (or contribution) for similarly situated individuals if the lower charge is based on an adverse health factor, such as disability.

(ii) The rules of this paragraph (g)(2) are illustrated by the following example:

Example. (i) *Facts.* Under a group health plan, employees are generally required to pay $50 per month for employee-only coverage and $125 per month for family coverage under the plan. However, employees who are disabled receive coverage (whether employee-only or family coverage) under the plan free of charge.

(ii) *Conclusion.* In this *Example,* the plan provision waiving premium payment for disabled employees is permitted under this paragraph (g)(2) (and thus does not violate this section).

(h) *No effect on other laws.* Compliance with this section is not determinative of compliance with any other provision of the Act (including the COBRA continuation provisions) or any other State or Federal law, such as the Americans with Disabilities Act. Therefore, although the rules of this section would not prohibit a plan or issuer from treating one group of similarly situated individuals differently from another (such as providing different benefit packages to current and former employees), other Federal or State laws may require that two separate groups of similarly situated individuals be treated the same for certain purposes (such as making the same benefit package available to COBRA qualified beneficiaries as is made available to active employees). In addition, although this section generally does not impose new disclosure obligations on plans and issuers, this section does not affect any other laws, including those that require accurate disclosures and prohibit intentional misrepresentation.

(i) *Applicability dates.* This section applies for plan years beginning on or after July 1, 2007.

Signed at Washington, DC this 1st day of December, 2006.

Bradford P. Campbell,

Acting Assistant Secretary, Employee Benefits Security Administration, U.S. Department of Labor.

■ For the reasons set forth above, 45 CFR part 146 is amended as follows:

PART 146—REQUIREMENTS FOR THE GROUP HEALTH INSURANCE MARKET

■ 1. Paragraph (b)(1)(vi) is added to § 146.101 as follows:

§ 146.101   Basis and scope

*   *   *   *   *

(b) *   *   *

(1) *   *   *

(vi) Prohibiting discrimination against participants and beneficiaries based on a health factor.

*   *   *   *   *

■ 2. Section 146.121 is revised to read as follows:

§ 146.121   Prohibiting discrimination against participants and beneficiaries based on a health factor.

(a) *Health factors.* (1) The term *health factor* means, in relation to an individual, any of the following health status-related factors:

(i) Health status;

(ii) Medical condition (including both physical and mental illnesses), as defined in § 144.103 of this chapter;

(iii) Claims experience;

(iv) Receipt of health care;

(v) Medical history;

(vi) Genetic information, as defined in § 144.103 of this chapter;

(vii) Evidence of insurability; or

(viii) Disability.

(2) Evidence of insurability includes—

(i) Conditions arising out of acts of domestic violence; and

(ii) Participation in activities such as motorcycling, snowmobiling, all-terrain vehicle riding, horseback riding, skiing, and other similar activities.

(3) The decision whether health coverage is elected for an individual (including the time chosen to enroll, such as under special enrollment or late enrollment) is not, itself, within the scope of any health factor. (However, under § 146.117, a plan or issuer must treat special enrollees the same as similarly situated individuals who are enrolled when first eligible.)

(b) *Prohibited discrimination in rules for eligibility*—(1) *In general*—(i) A group health plan, and a health insurance issuer offering health insurance coverage in connection with a group health plan, may not establish any rule for eligibility (including continued eligibility) of any individual to enroll for benefits under the terms of the plan or group health insurance coverage that discriminates based on any health factor that relates to that individual or a dependent of that individual. This rule is subject to the provisions of paragraph (b)(2) of this section (explaining how this rule applies to benefits), paragraph (b)(3) of this section (allowing plans to impose certain preexisting condition exclusions), paragraph (d) of this section (containing rules for establishing groups of similarly situated individuals), paragraph (e) of this section (relating to nonconfinement, actively-at-work, and other service requirements), paragraph

F. HIPAA Final Rules, Nondiscrimination and Wellness Benefits, continued

Federal Register / Vol. 71, No. 239 / Wednesday, December 13, 2006 / Rules and Regulations **75047**

(f) of this section (relating to wellness programs), and paragraph (g) of this section (permitting favorable treatment of individuals with adverse health factors).

(ii) For purposes of this section, rules for eligibility include, but are not limited to, rules relating to—

(A) Enrollment;

(B) The effective date of coverage;

(C) Waiting (or affiliation) periods;

(D) Late and special enrollment;

(E) Eligibility for benefit packages (including rules for individuals to change their selection among benefit packages);

(F) Benefits (including rules relating to covered benefits, benefit restrictions, and cost-sharing mechanisms such as coinsurance, copayments, and deductibles), as described in paragraphs (b)(2) and (b)(3) of this section;

(G) Continued eligibility; and

(H) Terminating coverage (including disenrollment) of any individual under the plan.

(iii) The rules of this paragraph (b)(1) are illustrated by the following examples:

Example 1. (i) *Facts.* An employer sponsors a group health plan that is available to all employees who enroll within the first 30 days of their employment. However, employees who do not enroll within the first 30 days cannot enroll later unless they pass a physical examination.

(ii) *Conclusion.* In this *Example 1,* the requirement to pass a physical examination in order to enroll in the plan is a rule for eligibility that discriminates based on one or more health factors and thus violates this paragraph (b)(1).

Example 2. (i) *Facts.* Under an employer's group health plan, employees who enroll during the first 30 days of employment (and during special enrollment periods) may choose between two benefit packages: an indemnity option and an HMO option. However, employees who enroll during late enrollment are permitted to enroll only in the HMO option and only if they provide evidence of good health.

(ii) *Conclusion.* In this *Example 2,* the requirement to provide evidence of good health in order to be eligible for late enrollment in the HMO option is a rule for eligibility that discriminates based on one or more health factors and thus violates this paragraph (b)(1). However, if the plan did not require evidence of good health but limited late enrollees to the HMO option, the plan's rules for eligibility would not discriminate based on any health factor, and thus would not violate this paragraph (b)(1), because the time an individual chooses to enroll is not, itself, within the scope of any health factor.

Example 3. (i) *Facts.* Under an employer's group health plan, all employees generally may enroll within the first 30 days of employment. However, individuals who participate in certain recreational activities, including motorcycling, are excluded from coverage.

(ii) *Conclusion.* In this *Example 3,* excluding from the plan individuals who participate in recreational activities, such as motorcycling, is a rule for eligibility that discriminates based on one or more health factors and thus violates this paragraph (b)(1).

Example 4. (i) *Facts.* A group health plan applies for a group health policy offered by an issuer. As part of the application, the issuer receives health information about individuals to be covered under the plan. Individual *A* is an employee of the employer maintaining the plan. *A* and *A's* dependents have a history of high health claims. Based on the information about *A* and *A's* dependents, the issuer excludes *A* and *A's* dependents from the group policy it offers to the employer.

(ii) *Conclusion.* In this *Example 4,* the issuer's exclusion of *A* and *A's* dependents from coverage is a rule for eligibility that discriminates based on one or more health factors, and thus violates this paragraph (b)(1). (If the employer is a small employer under 45 CFR 144.103 (generally, an employer with 50 or fewer employees), the issuer also may violate 45 CFR 146.150, which requires issuers to offer all the policies they sell in the small group market on a guaranteed available basis to all small employers and to accept every eligible individual in every small employer group.) If the plan provides coverage through this policy and does not provide equivalent coverage for *A* and *A's* dependents through other means, the plan will also violate this paragraph (b)(1).

(2) *Application to benefits*—(i) *General rule*—(A) Under this section, a group health plan or group health insurance issuer is not required to provide coverage for any particular benefit to any group of similarly situated individuals.

(B) However, benefits provided under a plan or through group health insurance coverage must be uniformly available to all similarly situated individuals (as described in paragraph (d) of this section). Likewise, any restriction on a benefit or benefits must apply uniformly to all similarly situated individuals and must not be directed at individual participants or beneficiaries based on any health factor of the participants or beneficiaries (determined based on all the relevant facts and circumstances). Thus, for example, a plan or issuer may limit or exclude benefits in relation to a specific disease or condition, limit or exclude benefits for certain types of treatments or drugs, or limit or exclude benefits based on a determination of whether the benefits are experimental or not medically necessary, but only if the benefit limitation or exclusion applies uniformly to all similarly situated individuals and is not directed at individual participants or beneficiaries based on any health factor of the

participants or beneficiaries. In addition, a plan or issuer may impose annual, lifetime, or other limits on benefits and may require the satisfaction of a deductible, copayment, coinsurance, or other cost-sharing requirement in order to obtain a benefit if the limit or cost-sharing requirement applies uniformly to all similarly situated individuals and is not directed at individual participants or beneficiaries based on any health factor of the participants or beneficiaries. In the case of a cost-sharing requirement, see also paragraph (b)(2)(ii) of this section, which permits variances in the application of a cost-sharing mechanism made available under a wellness program. (Whether any plan provision or practice with respect to benefits complies with this paragraph (b)(2)(i) does not affect whether the provision or practice is permitted under any other provision of ERISA, the Americans with Disabilities Act, or any other law, whether State or Federal.)

(C) For purposes of this paragraph (b)(2)(i), a plan amendment applicable to all individuals in one or more groups of similarly situated individuals under the plan and made effective no earlier than the first day of the first plan year after the amendment is adopted is not considered to be directed at any individual participants or beneficiaries.

(D) The rules of this paragraph (b)(2)(i) are illustrated by the following examples:

Example 1. (i) *Facts.* A group health plan applies a $500,000 lifetime limit on all benefits to each participant or beneficiary covered under the plan. The limit is not directed at individual participants or beneficiaries.

(ii) *Conclusion.* In this *Example 1,* the limit does not violate this paragraph (b)(2)(i) because $500,000 of benefits are available uniformly to each participant and beneficiary under the plan and because the limit is applied uniformly to all participants and beneficiaries and is not directed at individual participants or beneficiaries.

Example 2. (i) *Facts.* A group health plan has a $2 million lifetime limit on all benefits (and no other lifetime limits) for participants covered under the plan. Participant *B* files a claim for the treatment of AIDS. At the next corporate board meeting of the plan sponsor, the claim is discussed. Shortly thereafter, the plan is modified to impose a $10,000 lifetime limit on benefits for the treatment of AIDS, effective before the beginning of the next plan year.

(ii) *Conclusion.* The facts of this *Example 2* strongly suggest that the plan modification is directed at *B* based on *B's* claim. Absent outweighing evidence to the contrary, the plan violates this paragraph (b)(2)(i).

Example 3. (i) A group health plan applies for a group health policy offered by an issuer. Individual *C* is covered under the plan and has an adverse health condition. As part of

F. HIPAA Final Rules, Nondiscrimination and Wellness Benefits, continued

the application, the issuer receives health information about the individuals to be covered, including information about C's adverse health condition. The policy form offered by the issuer generally provides benefits for the adverse health condition that C has, but in this case the issuer offers the plan a policy modified by a rider that excludes benefits for C for that condition. The exclusionary rider is made effective the first day of the next plan year.

(ii) *Conclusion.* In this *Example 3,* the issuer violates this paragraph (b)(2)(i) because benefits for C's condition are available to other individuals in the group of similarly situated individuals that includes C but are not available to C. Thus, the benefits are not uniformly available to all similarly situated individuals. Even though the exclusionary rider is made effective the first day of the next plan year, because the rider does not apply to all similarly situated individuals, the issuer violates this paragraph (b)(2)(i).

Example 4. (i) *Facts.* A group health plan has a $2,000 lifetime limit for the treatment of temporomandibular joint syndrome (TMJ). The limit is applied uniformly to all similarly situated individuals and is not directed at individual participants or beneficiaries.

(ii) *Conclusion.* In this *Example 4,* the limit does not violate this paragraph (b)(2)(i) because $2,000 of benefits for the treatment of TMJ are available uniformly to all similarly situated individuals and a plan may limit benefits covered in relation to a specific disease or condition if the limit applies uniformly to all similarly situated individuals and is not directed at individual participants or beneficiaries. (This example does not address whether the plan provision is permissible under the Americans with Disabilities Act or any other applicable law.)

Example 5. (i) *Facts.* A group health plan applies a $2 million lifetime limit on all benefits. However, the $2 million lifetime limit is reduced to $10,000 for any participant or beneficiary covered under the plan who has a congenital heart defect.

(ii) *Conclusion.* In this *Example 5,* the lower lifetime limit for participants and beneficiaries with a congenital heart defect violates this paragraph (b)(2)(i) because benefits under the plan are not uniformly available to all similarly situated individuals and the plan's lifetime limit on benefits does not apply uniformly to all similarly situated individuals.

Example 6. (i) *Facts.* A group health plan limits benefits for prescription drugs to those listed on a drug formulary. The limit is applied uniformly to all similarly situated individuals and is not directed at individual participants or beneficiaries.

(ii) *Conclusion.* In this *Example 6,* the exclusion from coverage of drugs not listed on the drug formulary does not violate this paragraph (b)(2)(i) because benefits for prescription drugs listed on the formulary are uniformly available to all similarly situated individuals and because the exclusion of drugs not listed on the formulary applies uniformly to all similarly situated individuals and is not directed at individual participants or beneficiaries.

Example 7. (i) *Facts.* Under a group health plan, doctor visits are generally subject to a $250 annual deductible and 20 percent coinsurance requirement. However, prenatal doctor visits are not subject to any deductible or coinsurance requirement. These rules are applied uniformly to all similarly situated individuals and are not directed at individual participants or beneficiaries.

(ii) *Conclusion.* In this *Example 7,* imposing different deductible and coinsurance requirements for prenatal doctor visits and other visits does not violate this paragraph (b)(2)(i) because a plan may establish different deductibles or coinsurance requirements for different services if the deductible or coinsurance requirement is applied uniformly to all similarly situated individuals and is not directed at individual participants or beneficiaries.

Example 8. (i) *Facts.* An employer sponsors a group health plan that is available to all current employees. Under the plan, the medical care expenses of each employee (and the employee's dependents) are reimbursed up to an annual maximum amount. The maximum reimbursement amount with respect to an employee for a year is $1500 multiplied by the number of years the employee has participated in the plan, reduced by the total reimbursements for prior years.

(ii) *Conclusion.* In this *Example 8,* the variable annual limit does not violate this paragraph (b)(2)(i). Although the maximum reimbursement amount for a year varies among employees within the same group of similarly situated individuals based on prior claims experience, employees who have participated in the plan for the same length of time are eligible for the same total benefit over that length of time (and the restriction on the maximum reimbursement amount is not directed at any individual participants or beneficiaries based on any health factor).

(ii) *Exception for wellness programs.* A group health plan or group health insurance issuer may vary benefits, including cost-sharing mechanisms (such as a deductible, copayment, or coinsurance), based on whether an individual has met the standards of a wellness program that satisfies the requirements of paragraph (f) of this section.

(iii) *Specific rule relating to source-of-injury exclusions*—(A) If a group health plan or group health insurance coverage generally provides benefits for a type of injury, the plan or issuer may not deny benefits otherwise provided for treatment of the injury if the injury results from an act of domestic violence or a medical condition (including both physical and mental health conditions). This rule applies in the case of an injury resulting from a medical condition even if the condition is not diagnosed before the injury.

(B) The rules of this paragraph (b)(2)(iii) are illustrated by the following examples:

Example 1. (i) *Facts.* A group health plan generally provides medical/surgical benefits, including benefits for hospital stays, that are medically necessary. However, the plan excludes benefits for self-inflicted injuries or injuries sustained in connection with attempted suicide. Because of depression, Individual D attempts suicide. As a result, D sustains injuries and is hospitalized for treatment of the injuries. Under the exclusion, the plan denies D benefits for treatment of the injuries.

(ii) *Conclusion.* In this Example 1, the suicide attempt is the result of a medical condition (depression). Accordingly, the denial of benefits for the treatments of D's injuries violates the requirements of this paragraph (b)(2)(iii) because the plan provision excludes benefits for treatment of an injury resulting from a medical condition.

Example 2. (i) *Facts.* A group health plan provides benefits for head injuries generally. The plan also has a general exclusion for any injury sustained while participating in any of a number of recreational activities, including bungee jumping. However, this exclusion does not apply to any injury that results from a medical condition (nor from domestic violence). Participant E sustains a head injury while bungee jumping. The injury did not result from a medical condition (nor from domestic violence). Accordingly, the plan denies benefits for E's head injury.

(ii) *Conclusion.* In this *Example 2,* the plan provision that denies benefits based on the source of an injury does not restrict benefits based on an act of domestic violence or any medical condition. Therefore, the provision is permissible under this paragraph (b)(2)(iii) and does not violate this section. (However, if the plan did not allow E to enroll in the plan (or applied different rules for eligibility to E) because E frequently participates in bungee jumping, the plan would violate paragraph (b)(1) of this section.)

(3) *Relationship to § 146.111.* (i) A preexisting condition exclusion is permitted under this section if it —

(A) Complies with § 146.111;

(B) Applies uniformly to all similarly situated individuals (as described in paragraph (d) of this section); and

(C) Is not directed at individual participants or beneficiaries based on any health factor of the participants or beneficiaries. For purposes of this paragraph (b)(3)(i)(C), a plan amendment relating to a preexisting condition exclusion applicable to all individuals in one or more groups of similarly situated individuals under the plan and made effective no earlier than the first day of the first plan year after the amendment is adopted is not considered to be directed at any individual participants or beneficiaries.

(ii) The rules of this paragraph (b)(3) are illustrated by the following examples:

Example 1. (i) *Facts.* A group health plan imposes a preexisting condition exclusion on all individuals enrolled in the plan. The exclusion applies to conditions for which medical advice, diagnosis, care, or treatment was recommended or received within the six-

F. HIPAA Final Rules, Nondiscrimination and Wellness Benefits, continued

month period ending on an individual's enrollment date. In addition, the exclusion generally extends for 12 months after an individual's enrollment date, but this 12-month period is offset by the number of days of an individual's creditable coverage in accordance with § 146.111. There is nothing to indicate that the exclusion is directed at individual participants or beneficiaries.

(ii) *Conclusion*. In this *Example 1*, even though the plan's preexisting condition exclusion discriminates against individuals based on one or more health factors, the preexisting condition exclusion does not violate this section because it applies uniformly to all similarly situated individuals, is not directed at individual participants or beneficiaries, and complies with § 146.111 (that is, the requirements relating to the six-month look-back period, the 12-month (or 18-month) maximum exclusion period, and the creditable coverage offset).

Example 2. (i) *Facts*. A group health plan excludes coverage for conditions with respect to which medical advice, diagnosis, care, or treatment was recommended or received within the six-month period ending on an individual's enrollment date. Under the plan, the preexisting condition exclusion generally extends for 12 months, offset by creditable coverage. However, if an individual has no claims in the first six months following enrollment, the remainder of the exclusion period is waived.

(ii) *Conclusion*. In this *Example 2*, the plan's preexisting condition exclusions violate this section because they do not meet the requirements of this paragraph (b)(3); specifically, they do not apply uniformly to all similarly situated individuals. The plan provisions do not apply uniformly to all similarly situated individuals because individuals who have medical claims during the first six months following enrollment are not treated the same as similarly situated individuals with no claims during that period. (Under paragraph (d) of this section, the groups cannot be treated as two separate groups of similarly situated individuals because the distinction is based on a health factor.)

(c) *Prohibited discrimination in premiums or contributions*—(1) *In general*—(i) A group health plan, and a health insurance issuer offering health insurance coverage in connection with a group health plan, may not require an individual, as a condition of enrollment or continued enrollment under the plan or group health insurance coverage, to pay a premium or contribution that is greater than the premium or contribution for a similarly situated individual (described in paragraph (d) of this section) enrolled in the plan or group health insurance coverage based on any health factor that relates to the individual or a dependent of the individual.

(ii) *Discounts, rebates, payments in kind, and any other premium differential mechanisms are taken into*

account in determining an individual's premium or contribution rate. (For rules relating to cost-sharing mechanisms, see paragraph (b)(2) of this section (addressing benefits).)

(2) *Rules relating to premium rates*—(i) *Group rating based on health factors not restricted under this section.* Nothing in this section restricts the aggregate amount that an employer may be charged for coverage under a group health plan.

(ii) *List billing based on a health factor prohibited.* However, a group health insurance issuer, or a group health plan, may not quote or charge an employer (or an individual) a different premium for an individual in a group of similarly situated individuals based on a health factor. (But see paragraph (g) of this section permitting favorable treatment of individuals with adverse health factors.)

(iii) *Examples.* The rules of this paragraph (c)(2) are illustrated by the following examples:

Example 1. (i) *Facts.* An employer sponsors a group health plan and purchases coverage from a health insurance issuer. In order to determine the premium rate for the upcoming plan year, the issuer reviews the claims experience of individuals covered under the plan. The issuer finds that Individual F had significantly higher claims experience than similarly situated individuals in the plan. The issuer quotes the plan a higher per-participant rate because of F's claims experience.

(ii) *Conclusion.* In this *Example 1*, the issuer does not violate the provisions of this paragraph (c)(2) because the issuer blends the rate so that the employer is not quoted a higher rate for F than for a similarly situated individual based on F's claims experience.

Example 2. (i) *Facts.* Same facts as *Example 1*, except that the issuer quotes the employer a higher premium rate for F, because of F's claims experience, than for a similarly situated individual.

(ii) *Conclusion.* In this *Example 2*, the issuer violates this paragraph (c)(2). Moreover, even if the plan purchased the policy based on the quote but did not require a higher participant contribution for F than for a similarly situated individual, the issuer would still violate this paragraph (c)(2) (but in such a case the plan would not violate this paragraph (c)(2)).

(3) *Exception for wellness programs.* Notwithstanding paragraphs (c)(1) and (c)(2) of this section, a plan or issuer may vary the amount of premium or contribution it requires similarly situated individuals to pay based on whether an individual has met the standards of a wellness program that satisfies the requirements of paragraph (f) of this section.

(d) *Similarly situated individuals.* The requirements of this section apply only within a group of individuals who are

treated as similarly situated individuals. A plan or issuer may treat participants as a group of similarly situated individuals separate from beneficiaries. In addition, participants may be treated as two or more distinct groups of similarly situated individuals and beneficiaries may be treated as two or more distinct groups of similarly situated individuals in accordance with the rules of this paragraph (d). Moreover, if individuals have a choice of two or more benefit packages, individuals choosing one benefit package may be treated as one or more groups of similarly situated individuals distinct from individuals choosing another benefit package.

(1) *Participants.* Subject to paragraph (d)(3) of this section, a plan or issuer may treat participants as two or more distinct groups of similarly situated individuals if the distinction between or among the groups of participants is based on a bona fide employment-based classification consistent with the employer's usual business practice. Whether an employment-based classification is bona fide is determined on the basis of all the relevant facts and circumstances. Relevant facts and circumstances include whether the employer uses the classification for purposes independent of qualification for health coverage (for example, determining eligibility for other employee benefits or determining other terms of employment). Subject to paragraph (d)(3) of this section, examples of classifications that, based on all the relevant facts and circumstances, may be bona fide include full-time versus part-time status, different geographic location, membership in a collective bargaining unit, date of hire, length of service, current employee versus former employee status, and different occupations. However, a classification based on any health factor is not a bona fide employment-based classification, unless the requirements of paragraph (g) of this section are satisfied (permitting favorable treatment of individuals with adverse health factors).

(2) *Beneficiaries*—(i) Subject to paragraph (d)(3) of this section, a plan or issuer may treat beneficiaries as two or more distinct groups of similarly situated individuals if the distinction between or among the groups of beneficiaries is based on any of the following factors:

(A) A bona fide employment-based classification of the participant through whom the beneficiary is receiving coverage;

F. HIPAA Final Rules, Nondiscrimination and Wellness Benefits, continued

(B) Relationship to the participant (for example, as a spouse or as a dependent child);

(C) Marital status;

(D) With respect to children of a participant, age or student status; or

(E) Any other factor if the factor is not a health factor.

(ii) Paragraph (d)(2)(i) of this section does not prevent more favorable treatment of individuals with adverse health factors in accordance with paragraph (g) of this section.

(3) *Discrimination directed at individuals.* Notwithstanding paragraphs (d)(1) and (d)(2) of this section, if the creation or modification of an employment or coverage classification is directed at individual participants or beneficiaries based on any health factor of the participants or beneficiaries, the classification is not permitted under this paragraph (d), unless it is permitted under paragraph (g) of this section (permitting favorable treatment of individuals with adverse health factors). Thus, if an employer modified an employment-based classification to single out, based on a health factor, individual participants and beneficiaries and deny them health coverage, the new classification would not be permitted under this section.

(4) *Examples.* The rules of this paragraph (d) are illustrated by the following examples:

Example 1. (i) *Facts.* An employer sponsors a group health plan for full-time employees only. Under the plan (consistent with the employer's usual business practice), employees who normally work at least 30 hours per week are considered to be working full-time. Other employees are considered to be working part-time. There is no evidence to suggest that the classification is directed at individual participants or beneficiaries.

(ii) *Conclusion.* In this *Example 1,* treating the full-time and part-time employees as two separate groups of similarly situated individuals is permitted under this paragraph (d) because the classification is bona fide and is not directed at individual participants or beneficiaries.

Example 2. (i) *Facts.* Under a group health plan, coverage is made available to employees, their spouses, and their dependent children. However, coverage is made available to a dependent child only if the dependent child is under age 19 (or under age 25 if the child is continuously enrolled full-time in an institution of higher learning (full-time students)). There is no evidence to suggest that these classifications are directed at individual participants or beneficiaries.

(ii) *Conclusion.* In this *Example 2,* treating spouses and dependent children differently by imposing an age limitation on dependent children, but not on spouses, is permitted under this paragraph (d)(2). Specifically, the distinction between spouses and dependent children is permitted under paragraph (d)(2)

of this section and is not prohibited under paragraph (d)(3) of this section because it is not directed at individual participants or beneficiaries. It is also permissible to treat dependent children who are under age 19 (or full-time students under age 25) as a group of similarly situated individuals separate from those who are age 25 or older (or age 19 or older if they are not full-time students) because the classification is permitted under paragraph (d)(2) of this section and is not directed at individual participants or beneficiaries.

Example 3. (i) *Facts.* A university sponsors a group health plan that provides one health benefit package to faculty and another health benefit package to other staff. Faculty and staff are treated differently with respect to other employee benefits such as retirement benefits and leaves of absence. There is no evidence to suggest that the distinction is directed at individual participants or beneficiaries.

(ii) *Conclusion.* In this *Example 3,* the classification is permitted under this paragraph (d) because there is a distinction based on a bona fide employment-based classification consistent with the employer's usual business practice and the distinction is not directed at individual participants and beneficiaries.

Example 4. (i) *Facts.* An employer sponsors a group health plan that is available to all current employees. Former employees may also be eligible, but only if they complete a specified number of years of service, are enrolled under the plan at the time of termination of employment, and are continuously enrolled from that date. There is no evidence to suggest that these distinctions are directed at individual participants or beneficiaries.

(ii) *Conclusion.* In this *Example 4,* imposing additional eligibility requirements on former employees is permitted because a classification that distinguishes between current and former employees is a bona fide employment-based classification that is permitted under this paragraph (d), provided that it is not directed at individual participants or beneficiaries. In addition, it is permissible to distinguish between former employees who satisfy the service requirement and those who do not, provided that the distinction is not directed at individual participants or beneficiaries. (However, former employees who do not satisfy the eligibility criteria may, nonetheless, be eligible for continued coverage pursuant to a COBRA continuation provision or similar State law.)

Example 5. (i) *Facts.* An employer sponsors a group health plan that provides the same benefit package to all seven employees of the employer. Six of the seven employees have the same job title and responsibilities, but Employee C has a different job title and different responsibilities. After G files an expensive claim for benefits under the plan, coverage under the plan is modified so that employees with C's job title receive a different benefit package that includes a lower lifetime dollar limit than in the benefit package made available to the other six employees.

(ii) *Conclusion.* Under the facts of this *Example 5,* changing the coverage

classification for G based on the existing employment classification for G is not permitted under this paragraph (d) because the creation of the new coverage classification for G is directed at G based on one or more health factors.

(e) *Nonconfinement and actively-at-work provisions—*(1) *Nonconfinement provisions—*(i) *General rule.* Under the rules of paragraphs (b) and (c) of this section, a plan or issuer may not establish a rule for eligibility (as described in paragraph (b)(1)(ii) of this section) or set any individual's premium or contribution rate based on whether an individual is confined to a hospital or other health care institution. In addition, under the rules of paragraphs (b) and (c) of this section, a plan or issuer may not establish a rule for eligibility or set any individual's premium or contribution rate based on an individual's ability to engage in normal life activities, except to the extent permitted under paragraphs (e)(2)(ii) and (e)(3) of this section (permitting plans and issuers, under certain circumstances, to distinguish among employees based on the performance of services).

(ii) *Examples.* The rules of this paragraph (e)(1) are illustrated by the following examples:

Example 1. (i) *Facts.* Under a group health plan, coverage for employees and their dependents generally becomes effective on the first day of employment. However, coverage for a dependent who is confined to a hospital or other health care institution does not become effective until the confinement ends.

(ii) *Conclusion.* In this *Example 1,* the plan violates this paragraph (e)(1) because the plan delays the effective date of coverage for dependents based on confinement to a hospital or other health care institution.

Example 2. (i) *Facts.* In previous years, a group health plan has provided coverage through a group health insurance policy offered by Issuer M. However, for the current year, the plan provides coverage through a group health insurance policy offered by Issuer N. Under Issuer N's policy, items and services provided in connection with the confinement of a dependent to a hospital or other health care institution are not covered if the confinement is covered under an extension of benefits clause from a previous health insurance issuer.

(ii) *Conclusion.* In this *Example 2,* Issuer N violates this paragraph (e)(1) because the group health insurance coverage restricts benefits (a rule for eligibility under paragraph (b)(1)) based on whether a dependent is confined to a hospital or other health care institution that is covered under an extension of benefits clause from a previous issuer. State law cannot change the obligation of Issuer N under this section. However, under State law Issuer M may also be responsible for providing benefits to such a dependent. In a case in which Issuer N has an obligation

F. HIPAA Final Rules, Nondiscrimination and Wellness Benefits, continued

under this section to provide benefits and Issuer *M* has an obligation under State law to provide benefits, any State laws designed to prevent more than 100% reimbursement, such as State coordination-of-benefits laws, continue to apply.

(2) *Actively-at-work and continuous service provisions*—(i) *General rule*—(A) Under the rules of paragraphs (b) and (c) of this section and subject to the exception for the first day of work described in paragraph (e)(2)(ii) of this section, a plan or issuer may not establish a rule for eligibility (as described in paragraph (b)(1)(ii) of this section) or set any individual's premium or contribution rate based on whether an individual is actively at work (including whether an individual is continuously employed), unless absence from work due to any health factor (such as being absent from work on sick leave) is treated, for purposes of the plan or health insurance coverage, as being actively at work.

(B) The rules of this paragraph (e)(2)(i) are illustrated by the following examples:

Example 1. (i) *Facts.* Under a group health plan, an employee generally becomes eligible to enroll 30 days after the first day of employment. However, if the employee is not actively at work on the first day after the end of the 30-day period, then eligibility for enrollment is delayed until the first day the employee is actively at work.

(ii) *Conclusion.* In this *Example 1*, the plan violates this paragraph (e)(2) (and thus also violates paragraph (b) of this section). However, the plan would not violate paragraph (e)(2) or (b) of this section if, under the plan, an absence due to any health factor is considered being actively at work.

Example 2. (i) *Facts.* Under a group health plan, coverage for an employee becomes effective after 90 days of continuous service; that is, if an employee is absent from work (for any reason) before completing 90 days of service, the beginning of the 90-day period is measured from the day the employee returns to work (without any credit for service before the absence).

(ii) *Conclusion.* In this *Example 2*, the plan violates this paragraph (e)(2) (and thus also paragraph (b) of this section) because the 90-day continuous service requirement is a rule for eligibility based on whether an individual is actively at work. However, the plan would not violate this paragraph (e)(2) or paragraph (b) of this section if, under the plan, an absence due to any health factor is not considered an absence for purposes of measuring 90 days of continuous service.

(ii) *Exception for the first day of work*—(A) Notwithstanding the general rule in paragraph (e)(2)(i) of this section, a plan or issuer may establish a rule for eligibility that requires an individual to

begin work for the employer sponsoring the plan (or, in the case of a multiemployer plan, to begin a job in covered employment) before coverage becomes effective, provided that such a rule for eligibility applies regardless of the reason for the absence.

(B) The rules of this paragraph (e)(2)(ii) are illustrated by the following examples:

Example 1. (i) *Facts.* Under the eligibility provision of a group health plan, coverage for new employees becomes effective on the first day that the employee reports to work. Individual *H* is scheduled to begin work on August 3. However, *H* is unable to begin work on that day because of illness. *H* begins working on August 4, and *H*'s coverage is effective on August 4.

(ii) *Conclusion.* In this *Example 1*, the plan provision does not violate this section. However, if coverage for individuals who do not report to work on the first day they were scheduled to work for a reason unrelated to a health factor (such as vacation or bereavement) becomes effective on the first day they were scheduled to work, then the plan would violate this section.

Example 2. (i) *Facts.* Under a group health plan, coverage for new employees becomes effective on the first day of the month following the employee's first day of work, regardless of whether the employee is actively at work on the first day of the month. Individual *J* is scheduled to begin work on March 24. However, *J* is unable to begin work on March 24 because of illness. *J* begins working on April 7 and *J*'s coverage is effective May 1.

(ii) *Conclusion.* In this *Example 2*, the plan provision does not violate this section. However, as in *Example 1*, if coverage for individuals absent from work for reasons unrelated to a health factor became effective despite their absence, then the plan would violate this section.

(3) *Relationship to plan provisions defining similarly situated individuals*—(i) Notwithstanding the rules of paragraphs (e)(1) and (e)(2) of this section, a plan or issuer may establish rules for eligibility or set any individual's premium or contribution rate in accordance with the rules relating to similarly situated individuals in paragraph (d) of this section. Accordingly, a plan or issuer may distinguish in rules for eligibility under the plan between full-time and part-time employees, between permanent and temporary or seasonal employees, between current and former employees, and between employees currently performing services and employees no longer performing services for the employer, subject to paragraph (d) of this section. However, other Federal or State laws (including the COBRA continuation provisions and the Family and Medical Leave Act of 1993) may require an employee or the employee's

dependents to be offered coverage and set limits on the premium or contribution rate even though the employee is not performing services.

(ii) The rules of this paragraph (e)(3) are illustrated by the following examples:

Example 1. (i) *Facts.* Under a group health plan, employees are eligible for coverage if they perform services for the employer for 30 or more hours per week or if they are on paid leave (such as vacation, sick, or bereavement leave). Employees on unpaid leave are treated as a separate group of similarly situated individuals in accordance with the rules of paragraph (d) of this section.

(ii) *Conclusion.* In this *Example 1*, the plan provisions do not violate this section. However, if the plan treated individuals performing services for the employer for 30 or more hours per week, individuals on vacation leave, and individuals on bereavement leave as a group of similarly situated individuals separate from individuals on sick leave, the plan would violate this paragraph (e) (and thus also would violate paragraph (b) of this section) because groups of similarly situated individuals cannot be established based on a health factor (including the taking of sick leave) under paragraph (d) of this section.

Example 2. (i) *Facts.* To be eligible for coverage under a bona fide collectively bargained group health plan in the current calendar quarter, the plan requires an individual to have worked 250 hours in covered employment during the three-month period that ends one month before the beginning of the current calendar quarter. The distinction between employees working at least 250 hours and those working less than 250 hours in the earlier three-month period is not directed at individual participants or beneficiaries based on any health factor of the participants or beneficiaries.

(ii) *Conclusion.* In this *Example 2*, the plan provision does not violate this section because, under the rules for similarly situated individuals allowing full-time employees to be treated differently than part-time employees, employees who work at least 250 hours in a three-month period can be treated differently than employees who fail to work 250 hours in that period. The result would be the same if the plan permitted individuals to apply excess hours from previous periods to satisfy the requirement for the current quarter.

Example 3. (i) *Facts.* Under a group health plan, coverage of an employee is terminated when the individual's employment is terminated, in accordance with the rules of paragraph (d) of this section. Employee *B* has been covered under the plan. *B* experiences a disabling illness that prevents *B* from working. *B* takes a leave of absence under the Family and Medical Leave Act of 1993. At the end of such leave, *B* terminates employment and consequently loses coverage under the plan. (This termination of coverage is without regard to whatever rights the employee (or members of the employee's family) may have for COBRA continuation coverage.)

F. HIPAA Final Rules, Nondiscrimination and Wellness Benefits, continued

(ii) *Conclusion.* In this *Example 3*, the plan provision terminating *B*'s coverage upon *B*'s termination of employment does not violate this section.

Example 4. (i) *Facts.* Under a group health plan, coverage of an employee is terminated when the employee ceases to perform services for the employer sponsoring the plan, in accordance with the rules of paragraph (d) of this section. Employee *C* is laid off for three months. When the layoff begins, *C*'s coverage under the plan is terminated. (This termination of coverage is without regard to whatever rights the employee (or members of the employee's family) may have for COBRA continuation coverage.)

(ii) *Conclusion.* In this *Example 4*, the plan provision terminating *C*'s coverage upon the cessation of *C*'s performance of services does not violate this section.

(f) *Wellness programs.* A wellness program is any program designed to promote health or prevent disease. Paragraphs (b)(2)(ii) and (c)(3) of this section provide exceptions to the general prohibitions against discrimination based on a health factor for plan provisions that vary benefits (including cost-sharing mechanisms) or the premium or contribution for similarly situated individuals in connection with a wellness program that satisfies the requirements of this paragraph (f). If none of the conditions for obtaining a reward under a wellness program is based on an individual satisfying a standard that is related to a health factor, paragraph (f)(1) of this section clarifies that the wellness program does not violate this section if participation in the program is made available to all similarly situated individuals. If any of the conditions for obtaining a reward under a wellness program is based on an individual satisfying a standard that is related to a health factor, the wellness program does not violate this section if the requirements of paragraph (f)(2) of this section are met.

(1) *Wellness programs not subject to requirements.* If none of the conditions for obtaining a reward under a wellness program are based on an individual satisfying a standard that is related to a health factor (or if a wellness program does not provide a reward), the wellness program does not violate this section, if participation in the program is made available to all similarly situated individuals. Thus, for example, the following programs need not satisfy the requirements of paragraph (f)(2) of this section, if participation in the program is made available to all similarly situated individuals:

(i) A program that reimburses all or part of the cost for memberships in a fitness center.

(ii) A diagnostic testing program that provides a reward for participation and does not base any part of the reward on outcomes.

(iii) A program that encourages preventive care through the waiver of the copayment or deductible requirement under a group health plan for the costs of, for example, prenatal care or well-baby visits.

(iv) A program that reimburses employees for the costs of smoking cessation programs without regard to whether the employee quits smoking.

(v) A program that provides a reward to employees for attending a monthly health education seminar.

(2) *Wellness programs subject to requirements.* If any of the conditions for obtaining a reward under a wellness program is based on an individual satisfying a standard that is related to a health factor, the wellness program does not violate this section if the requirements of this paragraph (f)(2) are met.

(i) The reward for the wellness program, coupled with the reward for other wellness programs with respect to the plan that require satisfaction of a standard related to a health factor, must not exceed 20 percent of the cost of employee-only coverage under the plan. However, if, in addition to employees, any class of dependents (such as spouses or spouses and dependent children) may participate in the wellness program, the reward must not exceed 20 percent of the cost of the coverage in which an employee and any dependents are enrolled. For purposes of this paragraph (f)(2), the cost of coverage is determined based on the total amount of employer and employee contributions for the benefit package under which the employee is (or the employee and any dependents are) receiving coverage. A reward can be in the form of a discount or rebate of a premium or contribution, a waiver of all or part of a cost-sharing mechanism (such as deductibles, copayments, or coinsurance), the absence of a surcharge, or the value of a benefit that would otherwise not be provided under the plan.

(ii) The program must be reasonably designed to promote health or prevent disease. A program satisfies this standard if it has a reasonable chance of improving the health of or preventing disease in participating individuals and it is not overly burdensome, is not a subterfuge for discriminating based on a health factor, and is not highly suspect in the method chosen to promote health or prevent disease.

(iii) The program must give individuals eligible for the program the

opportunity to qualify for the reward under the program at least once per year.

(iv) The reward under the program must be available to all similarly situated individuals. (A) A reward is not available to all similarly situated individuals for a period unless the program allows —

(1) A reasonable alternative standard (or waiver of the otherwise applicable standard) for obtaining the reward for any individual for whom, for that period, it is unreasonably difficult due to a medical condition to satisfy the otherwise applicable standard; and

(2) A reasonable alternative standard (or waiver of the otherwise applicable standard) for obtaining the reward for any individual for whom, for that period, it is medically inadvisable to attempt to satisfy the otherwise applicable standard.

(B) A plan or issuer may seek verification, such as a statement from an individual's physician, that a health factor makes it unreasonably difficult or medically inadvisable for the individual to satisfy or attempt to satisfy the otherwise applicable standard.

(v)(A) The plan or issuer must disclose in all plan materials describing the terms of the program the availability of a reasonable alternative standard (or the possibility of waiver of the otherwise applicable standard) required under paragraph (f)(2)(iv) of this section. However, if plan materials merely mention that a program is available, without describing its terms, this disclosure is not required.

(B) The following language, or substantially similar language, can be used to satisfy the requirement of this paragraph (f)(2)(v): "If it is unreasonably difficult due to a medical condition for you to achieve the standards for the reward under this program, or if it is medically inadvisable for you to attempt to achieve the standards for the reward under this program, call us at [insert telephone number] and we will work with you to develop another way to qualify for the reward." In addition, other examples of language that would satisfy this requirement are set forth in Examples 3, 4, and 5 of paragraph (f)(3) of this section.

(3) *Examples.* The rules of paragraph (f)(2) of this section are illustrated by the following examples:

Example 1. (i) *Facts.* An employer sponsors a group health plan. The annual premium for employee-only coverage is $3,600 (of which the employer pays $2,700 per year and the employee pays $900 per year). The annual premium for family coverage is $9,000 (of which the employer pays $4,500 per year and the employee pays $4,500 per year). The plan

F. HIPAA Final Rules, Nondiscrimination and Wellness Benefits, continued

offers a wellness program with an annual premium rebate of $360. The program is available only to employees.

(ii) *Conclusion.* In this *Example 1*, the program satisfies the requirements of paragraph (f)(2)(i) of this section because the reward for the wellness program, $360, does not exceed 20 percent of the total annual cost of employee-only coverage, $720. ($3,600 × 20% = $720.) If any class of dependents is allowed to participate in the program and the employee is enrolled in family coverage, the plan could offer the employee a reward of up to 20 percent of the cost of family coverage, $1,800. ($9,000 × 20% = $1,800.)

Example 2. (i) *Facts.* A group health plan gives an annual premium discount of 20 percent of the cost of employee-only coverage to participants who adhere to a wellness program. The wellness program consists solely of giving an annual cholesterol test to participants. Those participants who achieve a count under 200 receive the premium discount for the year.

(ii) *Conclusion.* In this *Example 2,* the program fails to satisfy the requirement of being available to all similarly situated individuals because some participants may be unable to achieve a cholesterol count of under 200 and the plan does not make available a reasonable alternative standard or waive the cholesterol standard. (In addition, plan materials describing the program are required to disclose the availability of a reasonable alternative standard (or the possibility of waiver of the otherwise applicable standard) for obtaining the premium discount. Thus, the premium discount violates paragraph (c) of this section because it may require an individual to pay a higher premium based on a health factor of the individual than is required of a similarly situated individual under the plan.

Example 3. (i) *Facts.* Same facts as *Example 2,* except that the plan provides that if it is unreasonably difficult due to a medical condition for a participant to achieve the targeted cholesterol count (or if it is medically inadvisable for a participant to attempt to achieve the targeted cholesterol count) within a 60-day period, the plan will make available a reasonable alternative standard that takes the relevant medical condition into account. In addition, all plan materials describing the terms of the program include the following statement: "If it is unreasonably difficult due to a medical condition for you to achieve a cholesterol count under 200, or if it is medically inadvisable for you to attempt to achieve a count under 200, call us at the number below and we will work with you to develop another way to get the discount." Individual D begins a diet and exercise program but is unable to achieve a cholesterol count under 200 within the prescribed period. D's doctor determines D requires prescription medication to achieve a medically advisable cholesterol count. In addition, the doctor determines that D must be monitored through periodic blood tests to continually reevaluate D's health status. The plan accommodates D by making the discount available to D, but only if D follows the advice of D's doctor regarding medication and blood tests.

(ii) *Conclusion.* In this *Example 3*, the program is a wellness program because it

satisfies the five requirements of paragraph (f)(2) of this section. First, the program complies with the limits on rewards under a program. Second, it is reasonably designed to promote health or prevent disease. Third, individuals eligible for the program are given the opportunity to qualify for the reward at least once per year. Fourth, the reward under the program is available to all similarly situated individuals because it accommodates individuals for whom it is unreasonably difficult due to a medical condition to achieve the targeted count (or for whom it is medically inadvisable to attempt to achieve the targeted count) in the prescribed period by providing a reasonable alternative standard. Fifth, the plan discloses in all materials describing the terms of the program the availability of a reasonable alternative standard. Thus, the premium discount does not violate this section.

Example 4. (i) *Facts.* A group health plan will waive the $250 annual deductible (which is less than 20 percent of the annual cost of employee-only coverage under the plan) for the following year for participants who have a body mass index between 19 and 26, determined shortly before the beginning of the year. However, any participant for whom it is unreasonably difficult due to a medical condition to attain this standard (and any participant for whom it is medically inadvisable to attempt to achieve this standard) during the plan year is given the same discount if the participant walks for 20 minutes three days a week. Any participant for whom it is unreasonably difficult due to a medical condition to attain either standard (and any participant for whom it is medically inadvisable to attempt to achieve either standard) during the year is given the same discount if the individual satisfies an alternative standard that is reasonable in the burden it imposes and is reasonable taking into consideration the individual's medical situation. All plan materials describing the terms of the wellness program include the following statement: "If it is unreasonably difficult due to a medical condition for you to achieve a body mass index between 19 and 26 (or if it is medically inadvisable for you to attempt to achieve this body mass index) this year, your deductible will be waived if you walk for 20 minutes three days a week. If you cannot follow the walking program, call us at the number above and we will work with you to develop another way to have your deductible waived." Due to a medical condition, Individual E is unable to achieve a BMI of between 19 and 26 and is also unable to follow the walking program. E proposes a program based on the recommendations of E's physician. The plan agrees to make the discount available to E if E follows the physician's recommendations.

(ii) *Conclusion.* In this *Example 4*, the program satisfies the five requirements of paragraph (f)(2) of this section. First, the program complies with the limits on rewards under a program. Second, it is reasonably designed to promote health or prevent disease. Third, individuals eligible for the program are given the opportunity to qualify for the reward at least once per year. Fourth, the reward under the program is available to all similarly situated individuals because it

generally accommodates individuals for whom it is unreasonably difficult due to a medical condition to achieve (or for whom it is medically inadvisable to attempt to achieve) the targeted body mass index by providing a reasonable alternative standard (walking) and it accommodates individuals for whom it is unreasonably difficult due to a medical condition (or for whom it is medically inadvisable to attempt) to walk by providing an alternative standard that is reasonable for the individual. Fifth, the plan discloses in all materials describing the terms of the program the availability of a reasonable alternative standard for every individual. Thus, the waiver of the deductible does not violate this section.

Example 5. (i) *Facts.* In conjunction with an annual open enrollment period, a group health plan provides a form for participants to certify that they have not used tobacco products in the preceding twelve months. Participants who do not provide the certification are assessed a surcharge that is 20 percent of the cost of employee-only coverage. However, all plan materials describing the terms of the wellness program include the following statement: "If it is unreasonably difficult due to a health factor for you to meet the requirements under this program (or if it is medically inadvisable for you to attempt to meet the requirements of this program), we will make available a reasonable alternative standard for you to avoid this surcharge." It is unreasonably difficult for Individual F to stop smoking cigarettes due to an addiction to nicotine (a medical condition). The plan accommodates F by requiring F to participate in a smoking cessation program to avoid the surcharge. F can avoid the surcharge for as long as F participates in the program, regardless of whether F stops smoking (as long as F continues to be addicted to nicotine).

(ii) *Conclusion.* In this *Example 5*, the premium surcharge is permissible as a wellness program because it satisfies the five requirements of paragraph (f)(2) of this section. First, the program complies with the limits on rewards under a program. Second, it is reasonably designed to promote health or prevent disease. Third, individuals eligible for the program are given the opportunity to qualify for the reward at least once per year. Fourth, the reward under the program is available to all similarly situated individuals because it accommodates individuals for whom it is unreasonably difficult due to a medical condition (or for whom it is medically inadvisable to attempt) to quit using tobacco products by providing a reasonable alternative standard. Fifth, the plan discloses in all materials describing the terms of the program the availability of a reasonable alternative standard. Thus, the premium surcharge does not violate this section.

Example 6. (i) *Facts.* Same facts as *Example 5,* except the plan accommodates F by requiring F to view, over a period of 12 months, a 12-hour video series on health problems associated with tobacco use. F can avoid the surcharge by complying with this requirement.

(ii) *Conclusion.* In this *Example 6*, the requirement to watch the series of video

F. HIPAA Final Rules, Nondiscrimination and Wellness Benefits, continued

75054   Federal Register / Vol. 71, No. 239 / Wednesday, December 13, 2006 / Rules and Regulations

tapes is a reasonable alternative method for avoiding the surcharge.

(g) *More favorable treatment of individuals with adverse health factors permitted*—(1) In rules for eligibility— (i) Nothing in this section prevents a group health plan or group health insurance issuer from establishing more favorable rules for eligibility (described in paragraph (b)(1) of this section) for individuals with an adverse health factor, such as disability, than for individuals without the adverse health factor. Moreover, nothing in this section prevents a plan or issuer from charging a higher premium or contribution with respect to individuals with an adverse health factor if they would not be eligible for the coverage were it not for the adverse health factor. (However, other laws, including State insurance laws, may set or limit premium rates; these laws are not affected by this section.)

(ii) The rules of this paragraph (g)(1) are illustrated by the following examples:

Example 1. (i) *Facts.* An employer sponsors a group health plan that generally is available to employees, spouses of employees, and dependent children until age 23. However, dependent children who are disabled are eligible for coverage beyond age 23.

(ii) *Conclusion.* In this *Example 1*, the plan provision allowing coverage for disabled dependent children beyond age 23 satisfies this paragraph (g)(1) (and thus does not violate this section).

Example 2. (i) *Facts.* An employer sponsors a group health plan, which is generally available to employees (and members of the employee's family) until the last day of the month in which the employee ceases to perform services for the employer. The plan generally charges employees $50 per month for employee-only coverage and $125 per month for family coverage. However, an employee who ceases to perform services for the employer by reason of disability may remain covered under the plan until the last day of the month that is 12 months after the month in which the employee ceased to perform services for the employer. During this extended period of coverage, the plan charges the employee $100 per month for employee-only coverage and $250 per month for family coverage. (This extended period of coverage is without regard to whatever rights the employee (or members of the employee's family) may have for COBRA continuation coverage.)

(ii) *Conclusion.* In this *Example 2*, the plan provision allowing extended coverage for disabled employees and their families satisfies this paragraph (g)(1) (and thus does not violate this section). In addition, the plan is permitted, under this paragraph (g)(1), to charge the disabled employees a higher premium during the extended period of coverage.

Example 3. (i) *Facts.* To comply with the requirements of a COBRA continuation provision, a group health plan generally

makes COBRA continuation coverage available for a maximum period of 18 months in connection with a termination of employment but makes the coverage available for a maximum period of 29 months to certain disabled individuals and certain members of the disabled individual's family. Although the plan generally requires payment of 102 percent of the applicable premium for the first 18 months of COBRA continuation coverage, the plan requires payment of 150 percent of the applicable premium for the disabled individual's COBRA continuation coverage during the disability extension if the disabled individual would not be entitled to COBRA continuation coverage but for the disability.

(ii) *Conclusion.* In this *Example 3*, the plan provision allowing extended COBRA continuation coverage for disabled individuals satisfies this paragraph (g)(1) (and thus does not violate this section). In addition, the plan is permitted, under this paragraph (g)(1), to charge the disabled individuals a higher premium for the extended coverage if the individuals would not be eligible for COBRA continuation coverage were it not for the disability. (Similarly, if the plan provided an extended period of coverage for disabled individuals pursuant to State law or plan provision rather than pursuant to a COBRA continuation coverage provision, the plan could likewise charge the disabled individuals a higher premium for the extended coverage.)

(2) *In premiums or contributions*—(i) Nothing in this section prevents a group health plan or group health insurance issuer from charging individuals a premium or contribution that is less than the premium (or contribution) for similarly situated individuals if the lower charge is based on an adverse health factor, such as disability.

(ii) The rules of this paragraph (g)(2) are illustrated by the following example:

Example. (i) *Facts.* Under a group health plan, employees are generally required to pay $50 per month for employee-only coverage and $125 per month for family coverage under the plan. However, employees who are disabled receive coverage (whether employee-only or family coverage) under the plan free of charge.

(ii) *Conclusion.* In this *Example*, the plan provision waiving premium payment for disabled employees is permitted under this paragraph (g)(2) (and thus does not violate this section).

(h) *No effect on other laws.* Compliance with this section is not determinative of compliance with any other provision of the PHS Act (including the COBRA continuation provisions) or any other State or Federal law, such as the Americans with Disabilities Act. Therefore, although the rules of this section would not prohibit a plan or issuer from treating one group of similarly situated individuals differently from another (such as providing different benefit packages to

current and former employees), other Federal or State laws may require that two separate groups of similarly situated individuals be treated the same for certain purposes (such as making the same benefit package available to COBRA qualified beneficiaries as is made available to active employees). In addition, although this section generally does not impose new disclosure obligations on plans and issuers, this section does not affect any other laws, including those that require accurate disclosures and prohibit intentional misrepresentation.

(i) *Applicability dates.* (1) *Generally.* This section applies for plan years beginning on or after July 1, 2007.

(2) *Special rule for self-funded nonfederal governmental plans exempted under 45 CFR 146.180*—(i) If coverage has been denied to any individual because the sponsor of a self-funded nonfederal governmental plan has elected under § 146.180 to exempt the plan from the requirements of this section, and the plan sponsor subsequently chooses to bring the plan into compliance with the requirements of this section, the plan—

(A) Must notify the individual that the plan will be coming into compliance with the requirements of this section, specify the effective date of compliance, and inform the individual regarding any enrollment restrictions that may apply under the terms of the plan once the plan is in compliance with this section (as a matter of administrative convenience, the notice may be disseminated to all employees);

(B) Must give the individual an opportunity to enroll that continues for at least 30 days;

(C) Must permit coverage to be effective as of the first day of plan coverage for which an exemption election under § 146.180 of this part (with regard to this section) is no longer in effect; and

(D) May not treat the individual as a late enrollee or a special enrollee.

(ii) For purposes of this paragraph (i)(2), an individual is considered to have been denied coverage if the individual failed to apply for coverage because, given an exemption election under § 146.180 of this part, it was reasonable to believe that an application for coverage would have been denied based on a health factor.

(iii) The rules of this paragraph (i)(2) are illustrated by the following examples:

Example 1. (i) *Facts.* Individual D was hired by a nonfederal governmental employer in June 1999. The employer maintains a self-funded group health plan with a plan year beginning on October 1. The plan sponsor

F. HIPAA Final Rules, Nondiscrimination and Wellness Benefits, continued

elected under § 146.180 of this part to exempt the plan from the requirements of this section for the plan year beginning October 1, 2005, and renewed the exemption election for the plan year beginning October 1, 2006. Under the terms of the plan while the exemption was in effect, employees and their dependents were allowed to enroll when the employee was first hired without regard to any health factor. If an individual declines to enroll when first eligible, the individual could enroll effective October 1 of any plan year if the individual could pass a physical examination. The evidence-of-good-health requirement for late enrollees, absent an exemption election under § 146.180 of this part, would have been in violation of this section. D chose not to enroll for coverage when first hired. In February of 2006, D was treated for skin cancer but did not apply for coverage under the plan for the plan year beginning October 1, 2006, because D assumed D could not meet the evidence-of-good-health requirement. With the plan year beginning October 1, 2007 the plan sponsor chose not to renew its exemption election and brought the plan into compliance with this section. The plan notifies individual D (and all other employees) that it will be coming into compliance with the requirements of this section. The notice specifies that the effective date of compliance will be October 1, 2007, explains the applicable enrollment restrictions that will apply under the plan, states that individuals will have at least 30 days to enroll, and explains that coverage for those who choose to enroll will be effective as of October 1, 2007. Individual D timely requests enrollment in the plan, and coverage commences under the plan on October 1, 2007.

(ii) *Conclusion.* In this *Example 1*, the plan complies with this paragraph (i)(2).

Example 2. (i) *Facts.* Individual E was hired by a nonfederal governmental employer in February 1999. The employer maintains a self-funded group health plan with a plan year beginning on September 1. The plan sponsor elected under § 146.180 of this part to exempt the plan from the requirements of this section and "§ 146.111 (limitations on preexisting condition exclusion periods) for the plan year beginning September 1, 2002, and renews the exemption election for the plan years beginning September 1, 2003, September 1, 2004, September 1, 2005, and September 1, 2006. Under the terms of the plan while the exemption was in effect, employees and their dependents were allowed to enroll when the employee was first hired without regard to any health factor. If an individual declined to enroll when first eligible, the individual could enroll effective September 1 of any plan year if the individual could pass a physical examination. Also under the terms of the plan, all enrollees were subject to a 12-month preexisting condition exclusion period, regardless of whether they had creditable coverage. E chose not to enroll for coverage when first hired. In June of 2006, E is diagnosed as having multiple sclerosis (MS). With the plan year beginning September 1, 2007, the plan sponsor chooses to bring the plan into compliance with this section, but

renews its exemption election with regard to limitations on preexisting condition exclusion periods. The plan notifies E of her opportunity to enroll, without a physical examination, effective September 1, 2007. The plan gives E 30 days to enroll. E is subject to a 12-month preexisting condition exclusion period with respect to any treatment E receives that is related to E's MS, without regard to any prior creditable coverage E may have. Beginning September 1, 2008, the plan will cover treatment of E's MS.

(ii) *Conclusion.* In this *Example 2*, the plan complies with the requirements of this section. (The plan is not required to comply with the requirements of § 146.111 because the plan continues to be exempted from those requirements in accordance with the plan sponsor's election under § 146.180.)

Editorial Note: This document was received at the Office of the Federal Register on December 1, 2006.

Dated: July 16, 2004.

Mark B. McClellan,

Administrator, Centers for Medicare & Medicaid Services.

Dated: November 28, 2005.

Michael O. Leavitt,

Secretary, Department of Health and Human Services.

[FR Doc. 06–9557 Filed 12–12–06; 8:45 am]

BILLING CODE 4830–01–P; 4510–29–P; 4120–01–P

DEPARTMENT OF THE TREASURY

Internal Revenue Service

26 CFR Part 54

[TD 9299]

RIN 1545–AY33

Exception to the HIPAA Nondiscrimination Requirements for Certain Grandfathered Church Plans

AGENCY: Internal Revenue Service (IRS), Treasury.

ACTION: Final regulations.

SUMMARY: This document contains final regulations that provide guidance under section 9802(c) of the Internal Revenue Code relating to the exception for certain grandfathered church plans from the nondiscrimination requirements applicable to group health plans under section 9802(a) and (b). Final regulations relating to the nondiscrimination requirements under section 9802(a) and (b) are being published elsewhere in this issue of the **Federal Register.** The regulations will generally affect sponsors of and participants in certain self-funded church plans that are group health plans, and the regulations provide plan sponsors and plan administrators with

guidance necessary to comply with the law.

DATES: *Effective Date:* These regulations are effective February 12, 2007.

Applicability Date: These regulations apply for plan years beginning on or after July 1, 2007.

FOR FURTHER INFORMATION CONTACT: Russ Weinheimer at 202–622–6080 (not a toll-free number).

SUPPLEMENTARY INFORMATION:

Background

This document contains amendments to the Miscellaneous Excise Tax Regulations (26 CFR part 54) relating to the exception for certain grandfathered church plans from the nondiscrimination requirements applicable to group health plans. The nondiscrimination requirements applicable to group health plans were added to the Internal Revenue Code (Code), in section 9802, by the Health Insurance Portability and Accountability Act of 1996 (HIPAA), Public Law 104–191 (110 Stat. 1936). HIPAA also added similar nondiscrimination provisions applicable to group health plans and health insurance issuers (such as health insurance companies and health maintenance organizations) under the Employee Retirement Income Security Act of 1974 (ERISA), administered by the U.S. Department of Labor, and the Public Health Service Act (PHS Act), administered by the U.S. Department of Health and Human Services.

Final regulations relating to the HIPAA nondiscrimination requirements in paragraphs (a) and (b) of section 9802 of the Code are being published elsewhere in this issue of the **Federal Register.** Those regulations are similar to, and have been developed in coordination with, final regulations also being published today by the Departments of Labor and of Health and Human Services. Guidance under the HIPAA nondiscrimination requirements is summarized in a joint preamble to the final regulations.

The exception for certain grandfathered church plans was added to section 9802, in subsection (c), by section 1532 of the Taxpayer Relief Act of 1997, Public Law 105–34 (111 Stat. 788). A notice of proposed rulemaking on the exception for certain grandfathered church plans and a request for comments (REG–114083–00) was published in the **Federal Register** of January 8, 2001. Two written comments were received. After consideration of the comments, the proposed regulations are adopted as amended by this Treasury decision.

G. American Recovery and Reinvestment Act of 2009, Privacy

Summary

The American Recovery and Reinvestment Act of 2009, was signed into law by President Obama on February 17, 2009, and included the following provision on Privacy.

Subtitle D—Privacy

SEC. 13400. DEFINITIONS.

In this subtitle, except as specified otherwise:

(1) BREACH.—

(A) IN GENERAL.—The term "breach" means the unauthorized acquisition, access, use, or disclosure of protected health information which compromises the security or privacy of such information, except where an unauthorized person to whom such information is disclosed would not reasonably have been able to retain such information.

(B) EXCEPTIONS.—The term "breach" does not include—

(i) any unintentional acquisition, access, or use of protected health information by an employee or individual acting under the authority of a covered entity or business associate if—

(I) such acquisition, access, or use was made in good faith and within the course and scope of the employment or other professional relationship of such employee or individual, respectively, with the covered entity or business associate; and

(II) such information is not further acquired, accessed, used, or disclosed by any person; or

(ii) any inadvertent disclosure from an individual who is otherwise authorized to access protected health information at a facility operated by a covered entity or business associate to another similarly situated individual at same facility; and

(iii) any such information received as a result of such disclosure is not further acquired, accessed, used, or disclosed without authorization by any person.

(2) BUSINESS ASSOCIATE.—The term "business associate" has the meaning given such term in section 160.103 of title 45, Code of Federal Regulations.

(3) COVERED ENTITY.—The term "covered entity" has the meaning given such term in section 160.103 of title 45, Code of Federal Regulations.

(4) DISCLOSE.—The terms "disclose" and "disclosure" have the meaning given the term "disclosure" in section 160.103 of title 45, Code of Federal Regulations.

(5) ELECTRONIC HEALTH RECORD.—The term "electronic health record" means an electronic record of health-related information on an individual that is created, gathered, managed, and consulted by authorized health care clinicians and staff.

(6) HEALTH CARE OPERATIONS.—The term "health care operation" has the meaning given such term in section 164.501 of title 45, Code of Federal Regulations.

(7) HEALTH CARE PROVIDER.—The term "health care provider" has the meaning given such term in section 160.103 of title 45, Code of Federal Regulations.

(8) HEALTH PLAN.—The term "health plan" has the meaning given such term in section 160.103 of title 45, Code of Federal Regulations.

(9) NATIONAL COORDINATOR.—The term "National Coordinator" means the head of the Office of the National Coordinator for Health Information Technology established under section 3001(a) of the Public Health Service Act, as added by section 13101.

(10) PAYMENT.—The term "payment" has the meaning given such term in section 164.501 of title 45, Code of Federal Regulations.

(11) PERSONAL HEALTH RECORD.—The term "personal health record" means an electronic record of PHR identifiable health information (as defined in section 13407(f)(2)) on an individual that can be drawn from multiple sources and that is managed, shared, and controlled by or primarily for the individual.

(12) PROTECTED HEALTH INFORMATION.—The term "protected health information" has the meaning given such term in section 160.103 of title 45, Code of Federal Regulations.

(13) SECRETARY.—The term "Secretary" means the Secretary of Health and Human Services.

(14) SECURITY.—The term "security" has the meaning given such term in section 164.304 of title 45, Code of Federal Regulations.

(15) STATE.—The term "State" means each of the several States, the District of Columbia, Puerto Rico, the Virgin Islands, Guam, American Samoa, and the Northern Mariana Islands.

(16) TREATMENT.—The term "treatment" has the meaning given such term in section 164.501 of title 45, Code of Federal Regulations.

(17) USE.—The term "use" has the meaning given such term in section 160.103 of title 45, Code of Federal Regulations.

(18) VENDOR OF PERSONAL HEALTH RECORDS.—The term "vendor of personal health records" means an entity, other than a covered entity (as defined in paragraph (3)), that offers or maintains a personal health record.

PART 1—IMPROVED PRIVACY PROVISIONS AND SECURITY PROVISIONS

SEC. 13401. APPLICATION OF SECURITY PROVISIONS AND PENALTIES TO BUSINESS ASSOCIATES OF COVERED ENTITIES; ANNUAL GUIDANCE ON SECURITY PROVISIONS.

(a) APPLICATION OF SECURITY PROVISIONS.—Sections 164.308, 164.310, 164.312, and 164.316 of title 45, Code of Federal Regulations, shall apply to a business associate of a covered entity in the same manner that such sections apply to the covered entity. The additional requirements of this title that relate to security and that are made applicable with respect to covered entities shall also be applicable to such a business associate and shall be incorporated into the business associate agreement between the business associate and the covered entity.

(b) APPLICATION OF CIVIL AND CRIMINAL PENALTIES.—In the case of a business associate that violates any security provision specified in subsection (a), sections 1176 and 1177 of the Social Security Act (42 U.S.C. 1320d–5, 1320d–6) shall apply to the business associate with respect to such violation in the same manner such sections apply to a covered entity that violates such security provision.

(c) ANNUAL GUIDANCE.—For the first year beginning after the date of the enactment of this Act and annually thereafter, the Secretary of Health and Human Services shall, after consultation with stakeholders, annually issue guidance on the most effective and appropriate technical safeguards for use in carrying out the sections referred to in subsection (a) and the security standards in subpart C of part 164 of title 45, Code of Federal Regulations, including the use of standards developed under section 3002(b)(2)(B)(vi) of the Public Health Service Act, as added by section 13101 of this Act, as such provisions are in effect as of the date before the enactment of this Act.

SEC. 13402. NOTIFICATION IN THE CASE OF BREACH.

(a) IN GENERAL.—A covered entity that accesses, maintains, retains, modifies, records, stores, destroys, or otherwise holds, uses, or discloses unsecured protected health information (as defined in subsection (h)(1)) shall, in the case of a breach of such information that is discovered by the covered entity, notify each individual whose unsecured protected health information has been, or is reasonably believed by the covered entity to have been, accessed, acquired, or disclosed as a result of such breach.

(b) NOTIFICATION OF COVERED ENTITY BY BUSINESS ASSOCIATE.—A business associate of a covered entity that accesses, maintains, retains, modifies, records, stores, destroys, or otherwise holds, uses, or discloses unsecured protected health information shall, following the discovery of a breach of such information, notify the covered entity of such breach. Such notice shall include the identification of each individual whose unsecured protected health information has been, or is reasonably believed by the business associate to have been, accessed, acquired, or disclosed during such breach.

(c) BREACHES TREATED AS DISCOVERED.—For purposes of this section, a breach shall be treated as discovered by a covered entity or by a business associate as of the first day on which such breach is known to such entity or associate, respectively, (including any person, other than the individual committing the breach, that is an employee, officer, or other agent of such entity or associate, respectively) or should reasonably have been known to such entity or associate (or person) to have occurred.

(d) TIMELINESS OF NOTIFICATION.—

(1) IN GENERAL.—Subject to subsection (g), all notifications required under this section shall be made without unreasonable delay and in no case later than 60 calendar days after the discovery of a breach by the covered entity involved (or business associate involved in the case of a notification required under subsection (b)).

(2) BURDEN OF PROOF.—The covered entity involved (or business associate involved in the case of a notification required under subsection (b)), shall have the burden of demonstrating that all notifications were made as required under this part, including evidence demonstrating the necessity of any delay.

(e) METHODS OF NOTICE.—

(1) INDIVIDUAL NOTICE.—Notice required under this section to be provided to an individual, with respect to a breach, shall be provided promptly and in the following form:

(A) Written notification by first-class mail to the individual (or the next of kin of the individual if the individual is deceased) at the last known address of the individual or the next of kin, respectively, or, if specified as a preference by the individual, by electronic mail. The notification may be provided in one or more mailings as information is available.

(B) In the case in which there is insufficient, or out-of-date contact information (including a phone number, email address, or any other form of appropriate communication) that precludes direct written (or, if specified by the individual under subparagraph (A), electronic) notification to the individual, a substitute form of notice shall be provided, including, in the case that there are 10 or more individuals for which there is insufficient or out-of-date contact information, a conspicuous posting for a period determined by the Secretary on the home page of the Web site of the covered entity involved or notice in major print or broadcast media, including major media in geographic areas where the individuals affected by the breach likely reside. Such a notice in media or web posting will include a toll-free phone number where an individual can learn whether or not the individual's unsecured protected health information is possibly included in the breach.

(C) In any case deemed by the covered entity involved to require urgency because of possible imminent misuse of unsecured protected health information, the covered entity, in addition to notice provided under subparagraph (A), may provide information to individuals by telephone or other means, as appropriate.

(2) MEDIA NOTICE.—Notice shall be provided to prominent media outlets serving a State or jurisdiction, following the discovery of a breach described in subsection (a), if the unsecured protected health information of more than 500 residents of such State or jurisdiction is, or is reasonably believed to have been, accessed, acquired, or disclosed during such breach.

(3) NOTICE TO SECRETARY.—Notice shall be provided to the Secretary by covered entities of unsecured protected health information that has been acquired or disclosed in a breach. If the breach was with respect to 500 or more individuals than such notice must be provided immediately. If the breach was with respect to less than 500 individuals, the covered entity may maintain a log of any such breach occurring and annually submit such a log to the Secretary documenting such breaches occurring during the year involved.

(4) POSTING ON HHS PUBLIC WEBSITE.—The Secretary shall make available to the public on the Internet website of the Department of Health and Human Services a list that identifies each covered entity involved in a breach described in subsection (a) in which the unsecured protected health information of more than 500 individuals is acquired or disclosed.

(f) CONTENT OF NOTIFICATION.—Regardless of the method by which notice is provided to individuals under this section, notice of a breach shall include, to the extent possible, the following:

(1) A brief description of what happened, including the date of the breach and the date of the discovery of the breach, if known.

(2) A description of the types of unsecured protected health information that were involved in the breach (such as full name, Social Security number, date of birth, home address, account number, or disability code).

(3) The steps individuals should take to protect themselves from potential harm resulting from the breach.

(4) A brief description of what the covered entity involved is doing to investigate the breach, to mitigate losses, and to protect against any further breaches.

(5) Contact procedures for individuals to ask questions or learn additional information, which shall include a toll-free telephone number, an e-mail address, Web site, or postal address.

(g) DELAY OF NOTIFICATION AUTHORIZED FOR LAW ENFORCEMENT PURPOSES.—If a law enforcement official determines that a notification, notice, or posting required under this section would impede a criminal investigation or cause damage to national security, such notification, notice, or posting shall be delayed in the same manner as provided under section 164.528(a)(2) of title 45, Code of Federal Regulations, in the case of a disclosure covered under such section.

(h) UNSECURED PROTECTED HEALTH INFORMATION.—

(1) DEFINITION.—

(A) IN GENERAL.—Subject to subparagraph (B), for purposes of this section, the term "unsecured protected health information" means protected health information that is not secured through the use of a technology or methodology specified by the Secretary in the guidance issued under paragraph (2).

(B) EXCEPTION IN CASE TIMELY GUIDANCE NOT ISSUED.— In the case that the Secretary does not issue guidance under paragraph (2) by the date specified in such paragraph, for purposes of this section, the term "unsecured protected health information" shall mean protected health information that is not secured by a technology standard that renders protected health information unusable, unreadable, or indecipherable to unauthorized individuals and is developed or endorsed by a standards developing organization that is accredited by the American National Standards Institute.

(2) GUIDANCE.—For purposes of paragraph (1) and section 13407(f)(3), not later than the date that is 60 days after the date of the enactment of this Act, the Secretary shall, after consultation with stakeholders, issue (and annually update) guidance specifying the technologies and methodologies that render protected health information unusable, unreadable, or indecipherable to unauthorized individuals, including the use of standards developed under section 3002(b)(2)(B)(vi) of the Public Health Service Act, as added by section 13101 of this Act.

(i) REPORT TO CONGRESS ON BREACHES.—

(1) IN GENERAL.—Not later than 12 months after the date of the enactment of this Act and annually thereafter, the Secretary shall prepare and submit to the Committee on Finance and the Committee on Health, Education, Labor, and Pensions of the Senate and the Committee on Ways and Means and the Committee on Energy and Commerce of the House of Representatives a report containing the information described in paragraph (2) regarding breaches for which notice was provided to the Secretary under subsection (e)(3).

(2) INFORMATION.—The information described in this paragraph regarding breaches specified in paragraph (1) shall include—

(A) the number and nature of such breaches; and

(B) actions taken in response to such breaches.

(j) REGULATIONS; EFFECTIVE DATE.—To carry out this section, the Secretary of Health and Human Services shall promulgate interim final regulations by not later than the date that is 180 days after the date of the enactment of this title. The provisions of this section shall apply to breaches that are discovered on or after the date that is 30 days after the date of publication of such interim final regulations.

SEC. 13403. EDUCATION ON HEALTH INFORMATION PRIVACY.

(a) REGIONAL OFFICE PRIVACY ADVISORS.—Not later than 6 months after the date of the enactment of this Act, the Secretary shall designate an individual in each regional office of the Department of Health and Human Services to offer guidance and education to covered entities, business associates, and individuals on their rights and responsibilities related to Federal privacy and security requirements for protected health information.

(b) EDUCATION INITIATIVE ON USES OF HEALTH INFORMATION.—Not later than 12 months after the date of the enactment of this Act, the Office for Civil Rights within the Department of Health and Human Services shall develop and maintain a multi-faceted national education initiative to enhance public transparency regarding the uses of protected health information, including programs to educate individuals about the potential uses of their protected health information, the effects of such uses, and the rights of individuals with respect to such uses. Such programs shall be conducted in a variety of languages and present information in a clear and understandable manner.

SEC. 13404. APPLICATION OF PRIVACY PROVISIONS AND PENALTIES TO BUSINESS ASSOCIATES OF COVERED ENTITIES.

(a) APPLICATION OF CONTRACT REQUIREMENTS.—In the case of a business associate of a covered entity that obtains or creates protected health information pursuant to a written contract (or other written arrangement) described in section 164.502(e)(2) of title 45, Code of Federal Regulations, with such covered entity, the business associate may use and disclose such protected health information only if such use or disclosure, respectively, is in compliance with each applicable requirement of section 164.504(e) of such title. The additional requirements of this subtitle that relate to privacy and that are made applicable with respect to covered entities shall also be applicable to such a business associate and shall be incorporated into the business associate agreement between the business associate and the covered entity.

(b) APPLICATION OF KNOWLEDGE ELEMENTS ASSOCIATED WITH CONTRACTS.—Section 164.504(e)(1)(ii) of title 45, Code of Federal Regulations, shall apply to a business associate described in subsection (a), with respect to compliance with such subsection, in the same manner that such section applies to a covered entity, with respect to compliance with the standards in sections 164.502(e) and 164.504(e) of such title, except that in applying such section 164.504(e)(1)(ii) each reference to the business associate, with respect to a contract, shall be treated as a reference to the covered entity involved in such contract.

(c) APPLICATION OF CIVIL AND CRIMINAL PENALTIES.—In the case of a business associate that violates any provision of subsection (a) or (b), the provisions of sections 1176 and 1177 of the Social Security Act (42 U.S.C. 1320d–5, 1320d–6) shall apply to the business associate with respect to such violation in the same manner as such provisions apply to a person who violates a provision of part C of title XI of such Act.

SEC. 13405. RESTRICTIONS ON CERTAIN DISCLOSURES AND SALES OF HEALTH INFORMATION; ACCOUNTING OF CERTAIN PROTECTED HEALTH INFORMATION DISCLOSURES; ACCESS TO CERTAIN INFORMATION IN ELECTRONIC FORMAT.

(a) REQUESTED RESTRICTIONS ON CERTAIN DISCLOSURES OF HEALTH INFORMATION.—In the case that an individual requests under paragraph (a)(1)(i)(A) of section 164.522 of title 45, Code of Federal Regulations, that a covered entity restrict the disclosure of the protected health information of the individual, notwithstanding paragraph (a)(1)(ii) of such section, the covered entity must comply with the requested restriction if—

(1) except as otherwise required by law, the disclosure is to a health plan for purposes of carrying out payment or health care operations (and is not for purposes of carrying out treatment); and

(2) the protected health information pertains solely to a health care item or service for which the health care provider involved has been paid out of pocket in full.

(b) DISCLOSURES REQUIRED TO BE LIMITED TO THE LIMITED DATA SET OR THE MINIMUM NECESSARY.—

(1) IN GENERAL.—

(A) IN GENERAL.—Subject to subparagraph (B), a covered entity shall be treated as being in compliance with section 164.502(b)(1) of title 45, Code of Federal Regulations, with respect to the use, disclosure, or request of protected health information described in such section, only if the covered entity limits such protected health information, to the extent practicable, to the limited data set (as defined in section 164.514(e)(2) of such title) or, if needed by such entity, to the minimum necessary to accomplish the intended purpose of such use, disclosure, or request, respectively.

(B) GUIDANCE.—Not later than 18 months after the date of the enactment of this section, the Secretary shall issue guidance on what constitutes "minimum necessary" for purposes of subpart E of part 164 of title 45, Code of Federal Regulation. In issuing such guidance the Secretary shall take into consideration the guidance under section 13424(c) and the information necessary to improve patient outcomes and to detect, prevent, and manage chronic disease.

(C) SUNSET.—Subparagraph (A) shall not apply on and after the effective date on which the Secretary issues the guidance under subparagraph (B).

(2) DETERMINATION OF MINIMUM NECESSARY.—For purposes of paragraph (1), in the case of the disclosure of protected health information, the covered entity or business associate disclosing such information shall determine what constitutes the minimum necessary to accomplish the intended purpose of such disclosure.

(3) APPLICATION OF EXCEPTIONS.—The exceptions described in section 164.502(b)(2) of title 45, Code of Federal Regulations, shall apply to the requirement under paragraph (1) as of the effective date described in section 13423 in the same manner that such exceptions apply to section 164.502(b)(1) of such title before such date.

(4) RULE OF CONSTRUCTION.—Nothing in this subsection shall be construed as affecting the use, disclosure, or request of protected health information that has been de-identified.

(c) ACCOUNTING OF CERTAIN PROTECTED HEALTH INFORMATION DISCLOSURES REQUIRED IF COVERED ENTITY USES ELECTRONIC HEALTH RECORD.—

"(1) IN GENERAL.—In applying section 164.528 of title 45, Code of Federal Regulations, in the case that a covered entity uses or maintains an electronic health record with respect to protected health information—

"(A) the exception under paragraph (a)(1)(i) of such section shall not apply to disclosures through an electronic health record made by such entity of such information; and

"(B) an individual shall have a right to receive an accounting of disclosures described in such paragraph of such information made by such covered entity during only the three years prior to the date on which the accounting is requested.

"(2) REGULATIONS.—The Secretary shall promulgate regulations on what information shall be collected about each disclosure referred to in paragraph (1), not later than 6 months after the date on which the Secretary adopts standards on accounting for disclosure described in the section

3002(b)(2)(B)(iv) of the Public Health Service Act, as added by section 13101. Such regulations shall only require such information to be collected through an electronic health record in a manner that takes into account the interests of the individuals in learning the circumstances under which their protected health information is being disclosed and takes into account the administrative burden of accounting for such disclosures.

"(3) PROCESS.—In response to an request from an individual for an accounting, a covered entity shall elect to provide either an—

"(A) accounting, as specified under paragraph (1), for disclosures of protected health information that are made by such covered entity and by a business associate acting on behalf of the covered entity; or

"(B) accounting, as specified under paragraph (1), for disclosures that are made by such covered entity and provide a list of all business associates acting on behalf of the covered entity, including contact information for such associates (such as mailing address, phone, and email address).

A business associate included on a list under subparagraph (B) shall provide an accounting of disclosures (as required under paragraph (1) for a covered entity) made by the business associate upon a request made by an individual directly to the business associate for such an accounting.

"(4) EFFECTIVE DATE.—

"(A) CURRENT USERS OF ELECTRONIC RECORDS.—In the case of a covered entity insofar as it acquired an electronic health record as of January 1, 2009, paragraph (1) shall apply to disclosures, with respect to protected health information, made by the covered entity from such a record on and after January 1, 2014.

"(B) OTHERS.—In the case of a covered entity insofar as it acquires an electronic health record after January 1, 2009, paragraph (1) shall apply to disclosures, with respect to protected health information, made by the covered entity from such record on and after the later of the following:

"(i) January 1, 2011; or

"(ii) the date that it acquires an electronic health record.

"(C) LATER DATE.—The Secretary may set an effective date that is later that the date specified under subparagraph (A) or (B) if the Secretary determines that such later date is necessary, but in no case may the date specified under—

"(i) subparagraph (A) be later than 2016; or

"(ii) subparagraph (B) be later than 2013."

(d) PROHIBITION ON SALE OF ELECTRONIC HEALTH RECORDS OR PROTECTED HEALTH INFORMATION.—

(1) IN GENERAL.—Except as provided in paragraph (2), a covered entity or business associate shall not directly or indirectly receive remuneration in exchange for any protected health information of an individual unless the covered entity obtained from the individual, in accordance with section 164.508 of title 45, Code of Federal Regulations, a valid authorization that includes, in accordance with such section, a specification

of whether the protected health information can be further exchanged for remuneration by the entity receiving protected health information of that individual.

(2) EXCEPTIONS.—Paragraph (1) shall not apply in the following cases:

(A) The purpose of the exchange is for public health activities (as described in section 164.512(b) of title 45, Code of Federal Regulations).

(B) The purpose of the exchange is for research (as described in sections 164.501 and 164.512(i) of title 45, Code of Federal Regulations) and the price charged reflects the costs of preparation and transmittal of the data for such purpose.

(C) The purpose of the exchange is for the treatment of the individual, subject to any regulation that the Secretary may promulgate to prevent protected health information from inappropriate access, use, or disclosure.

(D) The purpose of the exchange is the health care operation specifically described in subparagraph (iv) of paragraph (6) of the definition of healthcare operations in section 164.501 of title 45, Code of Federal Regulations.

(E) The purpose of the exchange is for remuneration that is provided by a covered entity to a business associate for activities involving the exchange of protected health information that the business associate undertakes on behalf of and at the specific request of the covered entity pursuant to a business associate agreement.

(F) The purpose of the exchange is to provide an individual with a copy of the individual's protected health information pursuant to section 164.524 of title 45, Code of Federal Regulations.

(G) The purpose of the exchange is otherwise determined by the Secretary in regulations to be similarly necessary and appropriate as the exceptions provided in subparagraphs (A) through (F).

(3) REGULATIONS.—Not later than 18 months after the date of enactment of this title, the Secretary shall promulgate regulations to carry out this subsection. In promulgating such regulations, the Secretary—

(A) shall evaluate the impact of restricting the exception described in paragraph (2)(A) to require that the price charged for the purposes described in such paragraph reflects the costs of the preparation and transmittal of the data for such purpose, on research or public health activities, including those conducted by or for the use of the Food and Drug Administration; and

(B) may further restrict the exception described in paragraph (2)(A) to require that the price charged for the purposes described in such paragraph reflects the costs of the preparation and transmittal of the data for such purpose, if the Secretary finds that such further restriction will not impede such research or public health activities.

(4) EFFECTIVE DATE.—Paragraph (1) shall apply to exchanges occurring on or after the date that is 6 months after the date of the promulgation of final regulations implementing this subsection.

G. American Recovery and Reinvestment Act of 2009, Privacy, continued

(e) ACCESS TO CERTAIN INFORMATION IN ELECTRONIC FORMAT.—In applying section 164.524 of title 45, Code of Federal Regulations, in the case that a covered entity uses or maintains an electronic health record with respect to protected health information of an individual—

(1) the individual shall have a right to obtain from such covered entity a copy of such information in an electronic format and, if the individual chooses, to direct the covered entity to transmit such copy directly to an entity or person designated by the individual, provided that any such choice is clear, conspicuous, and specific; and

(2) notwithstanding paragraph (c)(4) of such section, any fee that the covered entity may impose for providing such individual with a copy of such information (or a summary or explanation of such information) if such copy (or summary or explanation) is in an electronic form shall not be greater than the entity's labor costs in responding to the request for the copy (or summary or explanation).

SEC. 13406. CONDITIONS ON CERTAIN CONTACTS AS PART OF HEALTH CARE OPERATIONS.

(a) MARKETING.—

(1) IN GENERAL.—A communication by a covered entity or business associate that is about a product or service and that encourages recipients of the communication to purchase or use the product or service shall not be considered a health care operation for purposes of subpart E of part 164 of title 45, Code of Federal Regulations, unless the communication is made as described in subparagraph (i), (ii), or (iii) of paragraph (1) of the definition of marketing in section 164.501 of such title.

(2) PAYMENT FOR CERTAIN COMMUNICATIONS.—A communication by a covered entity or business associate that is described in subparagraph (i), (ii), or (iii) of paragraph (1) of the definition of marketing in section 164.501 of title 45, Code of Federal Regulations, shall not be considered a health care operation for purposes of subpart E of part 164 of title 45, Code of Federal Regulations if the covered entity receives or has received direct or indirect payment in exchange for making such communication, except where—

(A)(i) such communication describes only a drug or biologic that is currently being prescribed for the recipient of the communication; and

(ii) any payment received by such covered entity in exchange for making a communication described in clause (i) is reasonable in amount;

(B) each of the following conditions apply—

(i) the communication is made by the covered entity; and

(ii) the covered entity making such communication obtains from the recipient of the communication, in accordance with section 164.508 of title 45, Code of Federal Regulations, a valid authorization (as described in paragraph (b) of such section) with respect to such communication; or

(C) each of the following conditions apply—

(i) the communication is made by a business associate on behalf of the covered entity; and

(ii) the communication is consistent with the written contract (or other written arrangement described in section 164.502(e)(2) of such title) between such business associate and covered entity.

(3) REASONABLE IN AMOUNT DEFINED.—For purposes of paragraph (2), the term "reasonable in amount" shall have the meaning given such term by the Secretary by regulation.

(4) DIRECT OR INDIRECT PAYMENT.—For purposes of paragraph (2), the term "direct or indirect payment" shall not include any payment for treatment (as defined in section 164.501 of title 45, Code of Federal Regulations) of an individual.

(b) OPPORTUNITY TO OPT OUT OF FUNDRAISING.—The Secretary shall by rule provide that any written fundraising communication that is a healthcare operation as defined under section 164.501 of title 45, Code of Federal Regulations, shall, in a clear and conspicuous manner, provide an opportunity for the recipient of the communications to elect not to receive any further such communication. When an individual elects not to receive any further such communication, such election shall be treated as a revocation of authorization under section 164.508 of title 45, Code of Federal Regulations.

(c) EFFECTIVE DATE.—This section shall apply to written communications occurring on or after the effective date specified under section 13423.

SEC. 13407. TEMPORARY BREACH NOTIFICATION REQUIREMENT FOR VENDORS OF PERSONAL HEALTH RECORDS AND OTHER NON-HIPAA COVERED ENTITIES.

(a) IN GENERAL.—In accordance with subsection (c), each vendor of personal health records, following the discovery of a breach of security of unsecured PHR identifiable health information that is in a personal health record maintained or offered by such vendor, and each entity described in clause (ii), (iii), or (iv) of section 13424(b)(1)(A), following the discovery of a breach of security of such information that is obtained through a product or service provided by such entity, shall—

(1) notify each individual who is a citizen or resident of the United States whose unsecured PHR identifiable health information was acquired by an unauthorized person as a result of such a breach of security; and

(2) notify the Federal Trade Commission.

(b) NOTIFICATION BY THIRD PARTY SERVICE PROVIDERS.—A third party service provider that provides services to a vendor of personal health records or to an entity described in clause (ii), (iii). or (iv) of section 13424(b)(1)(A) in connection with the offering or maintenance of a personal health record or a related product or service and that accesses, maintains, retains, modifies, records, stores, destroys, or otherwise holds, uses, or discloses unsecured PHR identifiable health information in such a record as a result of such services shall, following the discovery of a breach of security of such information, notify such vendor or entity, respectively, of such breach. Such notice shall include the identification of each individual whose unsecured PHR identifiable health information has been, or is reasonably believed to have been, accessed, acquired, or disclosed during such breach.

(c) APPLICATION OF REQUIREMENTS FOR TIMELINESS, METHOD, AND CONTENT OF NOTIFICATIONS.—Subsections (c), (d), (e), and (f) of section 13402 shall apply to a notification required under subsection (a) and a vendor of personal health records, an entity described in subsection (a) and a third party service provider described in subsection (b), with respect to a breach of security under subsection (a) of unsecured PHR identifiable health information in such records maintained or offered by such vendor, in a manner specified by the Federal Trade Commission.

(d) NOTIFICATION OF THE SECRETARY.—Upon receipt of a notification of a breach of security under subsection (a)(2), the Federal Trade Commission shall notify the Secretary of such breach.

(e) ENFORCEMENT.—A violation of subsection (a) or (b) shall be treated as an unfair and deceptive act or practice in violation of a regulation under section 18(a)(1)(B) of the Federal Trade Commission Act (15 U.S.C. 57a(a)(1)(B)) regarding unfair or deceptive acts or practices.

(f) DEFINITIONS.—For purposes of this section:

(1) BREACH OF SECURITY.—The term "breach of security" means, with respect to unsecured PHR identifiable health information of an individual in a personal health record, acquisition of such information without the authorization of the individual.

(2) PHR IDENTIFIABLE HEALTH INFORMATION.—The term "PHR identifiable health information" means individually identifiable health information, as defined in section 1171(6) of the Social Security Act (42 U.S.C. 1320d(6)), and includes, with respect to an individual, information—

(A) that is provided by or on behalf of the individual; and

(B) that identifies the individual or with respect to which there is a reasonable basis to believe that the information can be used to identify the individual.

(3) UNSECURED PHR IDENTIFIABLE HEALTH INFORMATION.—

(A) IN GENERAL.—Subject to subparagraph (B), the term "unsecured PHR identifiable health information" means PHR identifiable health information that is not protected through the use of a technology or methodology specified by the Secretary in the guidance issued under section 13402(h)(2).

(B) EXCEPTION IN CASE TIMELY GUIDANCE NOT ISSUED.— In the case that the Secretary does not issue guidance under section 13402(h)(2) by the date specified in such section, for purposes of this section, the term "unsecured PHR identifiable health information" shall mean PHR identifiable health information that is not secured by a technology standard that renders protected health information unusable, unreadable, or indecipherable to unauthorized individuals and that is developed or endorsed by a standards developing organization that is accredited by the American National Standards Institute.

(g) REGULATIONS; EFFECTIVE DATE; SUNSET.—

(1) REGULATIONS; EFFECTIVE DATE.—To carry out this section, the Federal Trade Commission shall promulgate interim final regulations by not later than the date that is 180 days

after the date of the enactment of this section. The provisions of this section shall apply to breaches of security that are discovered on or after the date that is 30 days after the date of publication of such interim final regulations.

(2) SUNSET.—If Congress enacts new legislation establishing requirements for notification in the case of a breach of security, that apply to entities that are not covered entities or business associates, the provisions of this section shall not apply to breaches of security discovered on or after the effective date of regulations implementing such legislation.

SEC. 13408. BUSINESS ASSOCIATE CONTRACTS REQUIRED FOR CERTAIN ENTITIES.

Each organization, with respect to a covered entity, that provides data transmission of protected health information to such entity (or its business associate) and that requires access on a routine basis to such protected health information, such as a Health Information Exchange Organization, Regional Health Information Organization, E-prescribing Gateway, or each vendor that contracts with a covered entity to allow that covered entity to offer a personal health record to patients as part of its electronic health record, is required to enter into a written contract (or other written arrangement) described in section 164.502(e)(2) of title 45, Code of Federal Regulations and a written contract (or other arrangement) described in section 164.308(b) of such title, with such entity and shall be treated as a business associate of the covered entity for purposes of the provisions of this subtitle and subparts C and E of part 164 of title 45, Code of Federal Regulations, as such provisions are in effect as of the date of enactment of this title.

SEC. 13409. CLARIFICATION OF APPLICATION OF WRONGFUL DISCLOSURES CRIMINAL PENALTIES.

Section 1177(a) of the Social Security Act (42 U.S.C. 1320d–6(a)) is amended by adding at the end the following new sentence: "For purposes of the previous sentence, a person (including an employee or other individual) shall be considered to have obtained or disclosed individually identifiable health information in violation of this part if the information is maintained by a covered entity (as defined in the HIPAA privacy regulation described in section 1180(b)(3)) and the individual obtained or disclosed such information without authorization.".

SEC. 13410. IMPROVED ENFORCEMENT.

(a) IN GENERAL.—

(1) NONCOMPLIANCE DUE TO WILLFUL NEGLECT.—Section 1176 of the Social Security Act (42 U.S.C. 1320d–5) is amended—

(A) in subsection (b)(1), by striking "the act constitutes an offense punishable under section 1177" and inserting "a penalty has been imposed under section 1177 with respect to such act"; and

(B) by adding at the end the following new subsection:

"(c) NONCOMPLIANCE DUE TO WILLFUL NEGLECT.—

"(1) IN GENERAL.—A violation of a provision of this part due to willful neglect is a violation for which the Secretary is required to impose a penalty under subsection (a)(1).

"(2) REQUIRED INVESTIGATION.—For purposes of paragraph (1), the Secretary shall formally investigate any complaint of a violation of a provision of this part if a preliminary investigation of the facts of the complaint indicate such a possible violation due to willful neglect.".

(2) ENFORCEMENT UNDER SOCIAL SECURITY ACT.—Any violation by a covered entity under thus subtitle is subject to enforcement and penalties under section 1176 and 1177 of the Social Security Act.

(b) EFFECTIVE DATE; REGULATIONS.—

(1) The amendments made by subsection (a) shall apply to penalties imposed on or after the date that is 24 months after the date of the enactment of this title.

(2) Not later than 18 months after the date of the enactment of this title, the Secretary of Health and Human Services shall promulgate regulations to implement such amendments.

(c) DISTRIBUTION OF CERTAIN CIVIL MONETARY PENALTIES COLLECTED.—

(1) IN GENERAL.—Subject to the regulation promulgated pursuant to paragraph (3), any civil monetary penalty or monetary settlement collected with respect to an offense punishable under this subtitle or section 1176 of the Social Security Act (42 U.S.C. 1320d–5) insofar as such section relates to privacy or security shall be transferred to the Office for Civil Rights of the Department of Health and Human Services to be used for purposes of enforcing the provisions of this subtitle and subparts C and E of part 164 of title 45, Code of Federal Regulations, as such provisions are in effect as of the date of enactment of this Act.

(2) GAO REPORT.—Not later than 18 months after the date of the enactment of this title, the Comptroller General shall submit to the Secretary a report including recommendations for a methodology under which an individual who is harmed by an act that constitutes an offense referred to in paragraph (1) may receive a percentage of any civil monetary penalty or monetary settlement collected with respect to such offense.

(3) ESTABLISHMENT OF METHODOLOGY TO DISTRIBUTE PERCENTAGE OF CMPS COLLECTED TO HARMED INDIVIDUALS.— Not later than 3 years after the date of the enactment of this title, the Secretary shall establish by regulation and based on the recommendations submitted under paragraph (2), a methodology under which an individual who is harmed by an act that constitutes an offense referred to in paragraph (1) may receive a percentage of any civil monetary penalty or monetary settlement collected with respect to such offense.

(4) APPLICATION OF METHODOLOGY.—The methodology under paragraph (3) shall be applied with respect to civil monetary penalties or monetary settlements imposed on or after the effective date of the regulation.

(d) TIERED INCREASE IN AMOUNT OF CIVIL MONETARY PENALTIES.—

(1) IN GENERAL.—Section 1176(a)(1) of the Social Security Act (42 U.S.C. 1320d–5(a)(1)) is amended by striking "who violates a provision of this part a penalty of not more than" and all that follows and inserting the following: "who violates a provision of this part—

"(A) in the case of a violation of such provision in which it is established that the person did not know (and by exercising reasonable diligence would not have known) that such person violated such provision, a penalty for each such violation of an amount that is at least the amount described in paragraph (3)(A) but not to exceed the amount described in paragraph (3)(D);

"(B) in the case of a violation of such provision in which it is established that the violation was due to reasonable cause and not to willful neglect, a penalty for each such violation of an amount that is at least the amount described in paragraph (3)(B) but not to exceed the amount described in paragraph (3)(D); and

"(C) in the case of a violation of such provision in which it is established that the violation was due to willful neglect—

"(i) if the violation is corrected as described in subsection (b)(3)(A), a penalty in an amount that is at least the amount described in paragraph (3)(C) but not to exceed the amount described in paragraph (3)(D); and

"(ii) if the violation is not corrected as described in such subsection, a penalty in an amount that is at least the amount described in paragraph (3)(D). In determining the amount of a penalty under this section for a violation, the Secretary shall base such determination on the nature and extent of the violation and the nature and extent of the harm resulting from such violation.".

(2) TIERS OF PENALTIES DESCRIBED.—Section 1176(a) of such Act (42 U.S.C. 1320d–5(a)) is further amended by adding at the end the following new paragraph:

"(3) TIERS OF PENALTIES DESCRIBED.—For purposes of paragraph (1), with respect to a violation by a person of a provision of this part—

"(A) the amount described in this subparagraph is $100 for each such violation, except that the total amount imposed on the person for all such violations of an identical requirement or prohibition during a calendar year may not exceed $25,000;

"(B) the amount described in this subparagraph is $1,000 for each such violation, except that the total amount imposed on the person for all such violations of an identical requirement or prohibition during a calendar year may not exceed $100,000;

"(C) the amount described in this subparagraph is $10,000 for each such violation, except that the total amount imposed on the person for all such violations of an identical requirement or prohibition during a calendar year may not exceed $250,000; and

"(D) the amount described in this subparagraph is $50,000 for each such violation, except that the total amount imposed on the person for all such violations of an identical requirement or prohibition during a calendar year may not exceed $1,500,000.".

(3) CONFORMING AMENDMENTS.—Section 1176(b) of such Act (42 U.S.C. 1320d–5(b)) is amended—

(A) by striking paragraph (2) and redesignating paragraphs (3) and (4) as paragraphs (2) and (3), respectively; and

(B) in paragraph (2), as so redesignated—
(i) in subparagraph (A), by striking "in subparagraph (B), a penalty may not be imposed under subsection (a) if" and all that follows through "the failure to comply is corrected" and inserting "in subparagraph (B) or subsection (a)(1)(C), a penalty may not be imposed under subsection (a) if the failure to comply is corrected"; and
(ii) in subparagraph (B), by striking "(A)(ii)" and inserting "(A)" each place it appears.
(4) EFFECTIVE DATE.—The amendments made by this subsection shall apply to violations occurring after the date of the enactment of this title.
(e) ENFORCEMENT THROUGH STATE ATTORNEYS GENERAL.—
(1) IN GENERAL.—Section 1176 of the Social Security Act (42 U.S.C. 1320d–5) is amended by adding at the end the following new subsection:
"(d) ENFORCEMENT BY STATE ATTORNEYS GENERAL.—
"(1) CIVIL ACTION.—Except as provided in subsection (b), in any case in which the attorney general of a State has reason to believe that an interest of one or more of the residents of that State has been or is threatened or adversely affected by any person who violates a provision of this part, the attorney general of the State, as parens patriae, may bring a civil action on behalf of such residents of the State in a district court of the United States of appropriate jurisdiction—
"(A) to enjoin further such violation by the defendant; or
"(B) to obtain damages on behalf of such residents of the State, in an amount equal to the amount determined under paragraph (2).
"(2) STATUTORY DAMAGES.—
"(A) IN GENERAL.—For purposes of paragraph (1)(B), the amount determined under this paragraph is the amount calculated by multiplying the number of violations by up to $100. For purposes of the preceding sentence, in the case of a continuing violation, the number of violations shall be determined consistent with the HIPAA privacy regulations (as defined in section 1180(b)(3)) for violations of subsection (a).
"(B) LIMITATION.—The total amount of damages imposed on the person for all violations of an identical requirement or prohibition during a calendar year may not exceed $25,000.
"(C) REDUCTION OF DAMAGES.—In assessing damages under subparagraph (A), the court may consider the factors the Secretary may consider in determining the amount of a civil money penalty under subsection (a) under the HIPAA privacy regulations.
"(3) ATTORNEY FEES.—In the case of any successful action under paragraph (1), the court, in its discretion, may award the costs of the action and reasonable attorney fees to the State.
"(4) NOTICE TO SECRETARY.—The State shall serve prior written notice of any action under paragraph (1) upon the Secretary and provide the Secretary with a copy of its complaint, except in any case in which such prior notice is not

feasible, in which case the State shall serve such notice immediately upon instituting such action. The Secretary shall have the right—

"(A) to intervene in the action;

"(B) upon so intervening, to be heard on all matters arising therein; and

"(C) to file petitions for appeal.

"(5) CONSTRUCTION.—For purposes of bringing any civil action under paragraph (1), nothing in this section shall be construed to prevent an attorney general of a State from exercising the powers conferred on the attorney general by the laws of that State.

"(6) VENUE; SERVICE OF PROCESS.—

"(A) VENUE.—Any action brought under paragraph (1) may be brought in the district court of the United States that meets applicable requirements relating to venue under section 1391 of title 28, United States Code.

"(B) SERVICE OF PROCESS.—In an action brought under paragraph (1), process may be served in any district in which the defendant—

"(i) is an inhabitant; or

"(ii) maintains a physical place of business.

"(7) LIMITATION ON STATE ACTION WHILE FEDERAL ACTION IS PENDING.—If the Secretary has instituted an action against a person under subsection (a) with respect to a specific violation of this part, no State attorney general may bring an action under this subsection against the person with respect to such violation during the pendency of that action.

"(8) APPLICATION OF CMP STATUTE OF LIMITATION.—A civil action may not be instituted with respect to a violation of this part unless an action to impose a civil money penalty may be instituted under subsection (a) with respect to such violation consistent with the second sentence of section 1128A(c)(1).".

(2) CONFORMING AMENDMENTS.—Subsection (b) of such section, as amended by subsection (d)(3), is amended—

(A) in paragraph (1), by striking "A penalty may not be imposed under subsection (a)" and inserting "No penalty may be imposed under subsection (a) and no damages obtained under subsection (d)";

(B) in paragraph (2)(A)—

(i) after "subsection (a)(1)(C),", by striking "a penalty may not be imposed under subsection (a)" and inserting "no penalty may be imposed under subsection (a) and no damages obtained under subsection (d)"; and

(ii) in clause (ii), by inserting "or damages" after "the penalty";

(C) in paragraph (2)(B)(i), by striking "The period" and inserting "With respect to the imposition of a penalty by the Secretary under subsection (a), the period"; and

(D) in paragraph (3), by inserting "and any damages under subsection (d)" after "any penalty under subsection (a)".

(3) EFFECTIVE DATE.—The amendments made by this subsection shall apply to violations occurring after the date of the enactment of this Act.

(f) ALLOWING CONTINUED USE OF CORRECTIVE ACTION.—Such section is further amended by adding at the end the following new subsection:

"(e) ALLOWING CONTINUED USE OF CORRECTIVE ACTION.— Nothing in this section shall be construed as preventing the Office for Civil Rights of the Department of Health and Human Services from continuing, in its discretion, to use corrective action without a penalty in cases where the person did not know (and by exercising reasonable diligence would not have known) of the violation involved.".

SEC. 13411. AUDITS.

The Secretary shall provide for periodic audits to ensure that covered entities and business associates that are subject to the requirements of this subtitle and subparts C and E of part 164 of title 45, Code of Federal Regulations, as such provisions are in effect as of the date of enactment of this Act, comply with such requirements.

PART 2—RELATIONSHIP TO OTHER LAWS; REGULATORY REFERENCES; EFFECTIVE DATE; REPORTS

SEC. 13421. RELATIONSHIP TO OTHER LAWS.

(a) APPLICATION OF HIPAA STATE PREEMPTION.—Section 1178 of the Social Security Act (42 U.S.C. 1320d–7) shall apply to a provision or requirement under this subtitle in the same manner that such section applies to a provision or requirement under part C of title XI of such Act or a standard or implementation specification adopted or established under sections 1172 through 1174 of such Act.

(b) HEALTH INSURANCE PORTABILITY AND ACCOUNTABILITY ACT.—The standards governing the privacy and security of individually identifiable health information promulgated by the Secretary under sections 262(a) and 264 of the Health Insurance Portability and Accountability Act of 1996 shall remain in effect to the extent that they are consistent with this subtitle. The Secretary shall by rule amend such Federal regulations as required to make such regulations consistent with this subtitle.

(c) CONSTRUCTION.—Nothing in this subtitle shall constitute a waiver of any privilege otherwise applicable to an individual with respect to the protected health information of such individual.

SEC. 13422. REGULATORY REFERENCES.

Each reference in this subtitle to a provision of the Code of Federal Regulations refers to such provision as in effect on the date of the enactment of this title (or to the most recent update of such provision).

SEC. 13423. EFFECTIVE DATE.

Except as otherwise specifically provided, the provisions of part I shall take effect on the date that is 12 months after the date of the enactment of this title.

SEC. 13424. STUDIES, REPORTS, GUIDANCE.

(a) REPORT ON COMPLIANCE.—

(1) IN GENERAL.—For the first year beginning after the date of the enactment of this Act and annually thereafter, the Secretary shall prepare and submit to the Committee on Health, Education, Labor, and Pensions of the Senate and the Committee on Ways and Means and the Committee on Energy and Commerce of the House of Representatives a report concerning complaints of alleged violations of law, including the provisions of this subtitle as well as the provisions of subparts C and E of part 164 of title 45, Code of Federal Regulations, (as such provisions are in effect as of the date of enactment of this Act) relating to privacy and security of health information that are received by the Secretary during the year for which the report is being prepared. Each such report shall include, with respect to such complaints received during the year—

(A) the number of such complaints;

(B) the number of such complaints resolved informally, a summary of the types of such complaints so resolved, and the number of covered entities that received technical assistance from the Secretary during such year in order to achieve compliance with such provisions and the types of such technical assistance provided;

(C) the number of such complaints that have resulted in the imposition of civil monetary penalties or have been resolved through monetary settlements, including the nature of the complaints involved and the amount paid in each penalty or settlement;

(D) the number of compliance reviews conducted and the outcome of each such review;

(E) the number of subpoenas or inquiries issued;

(F) the Secretary's plan for improving compliance with and enforcement of such provisions for the following year; and

(G) the number of audits performed and a summary of audit findings pursuant to section 13411.

(2) AVAILABILITY TO PUBLIC.—Each report under paragraph (1) shall be made available to the public on the Internet website of the Department of Health and Human Services.

(b) STUDY AND REPORT ON APPLICATION OF PRIVACY AND SECURITY REQUIREMENTS TO NON-HIPAA COVERED ENTITIES.—

(1) STUDY.—Not later than one year after the date of the enactment of this title, the Secretary, in consultation with the Federal Trade Commission, shall conduct a study, and submit a report under paragraph (2), on privacy and security requirements for entities that are not covered entities or business associates as of the date of the enactment of this title, including—

(A) requirements relating to security, privacy, and notification in the case of a breach of security or privacy (including the applicability of an exemption to notification in the case of individually identifiable health information that has been rendered unusable, unreadable, or indecipherable through technologies or methodologies recognized by appropriate professional organization or standard setting bodies to provide effective security for the information) that should be applied to—

(i) vendors of personal health records;

(ii) entities that offer products or services through the website of a vendor of personal health records;

(iii) entities that are not covered entities and that offer products or services through the websites of covered entities that offer individuals personal health records;

(iv) entities that are not covered entities and that access information in a personal health record or send information to a personal health record; and

(v) third party service providers used by a vendor or entity described in clause (i), (ii), (iii), or (iv) to assist in providing personal health record products or services;

(B) a determination of which Federal government agency is best equipped to enforce such requirements recommended to be applied to such vendors, entities, and service providers under subparagraph (A); and

(C) a timeframe for implementing regulations based on such findings.

(2) REPORT.—The Secretary shall submit to the Committee on Finance, the Committee on Health, Education, Labor, and Pensions, and the Committee on Commerce of the Senate and the Committee on Ways and Means and the Committee on Energy and Commerce of the House of Representatives a report on the findings of the study under paragraph (1) and shall include in such report recommendations on the privacy and security requirements described in such paragraph.

(c) GUIDANCE ON IMPLEMENTATION SPECIFICATION TO DE-IDENTIFY PROTECTED HEALTH INFORMATION.—Not later than 12 months after the date of the enactment of this title, the Secretary shall, in consultation with stakeholders, issue guidance on how best to implement the requirements for the de-identification of protected health information under section 164.514(b) of title 45, Code of Federal Regulations.

(d) GAO REPORT ON TREATMENT DISCLOSURES.—Not later than one year after the date of the enactment of this title, the Comptroller General of the United States shall submit to the Committee on Health, Education, Labor, and Pensions of the Senate and the Committee on Ways and Means and the Committee on Energy and Commerce of the House of Representatives a report on the best practices related to the disclosure among health care providers of protected health information of an individual for purposes of treatment of such individual. Such report shall include an examination of the best practices implemented by States and by other entities, such as health information exchanges and regional health information organizations, an examination of the extent to which such best practices are successful with respect to the quality of the resulting health care provided to the individual and with respect to the ability of the health care provider to manage such best practices, and an examination of the use of electronic informed consent for disclosing protected health information for treatment, payment, and health care operations.

(e) REPORT REQUIRED.—Not later than 5 years after the date of enactment of this section, the Government Accountability Office shall submit to Congress and the Secretary of Health and Human Services a report on the impact of any of the provisions of this

Act on health insurance premiums, overall health care costs, adoption of electronic health records by providers, and reduction in medical errors and other quality improvements.

(f) STUDY.—The Secretary shall study the definition of "psychotherapy notes" in section 164.501 of title 45, Code of Federal Regulations, with regard to including test data that is related to direct responses, scores, items, forms, protocols, manuals, or other materials that are part of a mental health evaluation, as determined by the mental health professional providing treatment or evaluation in such definitions and may, based on such study, issue regulations to revise such definition.

H. Health Breach Notification, Proposed Rules

Summary

The Federal Trade Commission published these proposed rules requiring vendors of personal health records and related entities to notify individuals when the security of their individual identifiable health information is breached.

H. Health Breach Notification, Proposed Rules, continued

17914 Federal Register / Vol. 74, No. 74 / Monday, April 20, 2009 / Proposed Rules

Issued in Fort Worth, TX, on April 6, 2009.

Anthony D. Roetzel,

Manager, Operations Support Group, ATO Central Service Center.

[FR Doc. E9–9050 Filed 4–17–09; 8:45 am]

BILLING CODE 4901–13–P

FEDERAL TRADE COMMISSION

16 CFR Part 318

[RIN 3084–AB17]

Health Breach Notification Rule

AGENCY: Federal Trade Commission (FTC).

ACTION: Notice of proposed rulemaking; request for public comment.

SUMMARY: Under the American Recovery and Reinvestment Act of 2009 (the "Recovery Act" or "the Act"), the Federal Trade Commission ("FTC") or ("Commission") must issue rules requiring vendors of personal health records and related entities to notify individuals when the security of their individually identifiable health information is breached. Accordingly, the FTC seeks comment on a proposed rule.

DATES: Comments must be received on or before June 1, 2009.

ADDRESSES: Interested parties are invited to submit written comments electronically or in paper form. Comments should refer to "Health Breach Notification Rulemaking, Project No. R911002" to facilitate the organization of comments. Please note that your comment—including your name and your state—will be placed on the public record of this proceeding, including on the publicly accessible FTC website, at (*http://www.ftc.gov/os/ publiccomments.shtm*).

Because comments will be made public, they should not include any sensitive personal information, such as an individual's Social Security number; date of birth; driver's license number; state identification number, or foreign country equivalent; passport number; financial account number; or credit or debit card number. Comments also should not include any sensitive health information, such as medical records or other individually identifiable health information. In addition, comments should not include any "[t]rade secret or any commercial or financial information which is obtained from any person and which is privileged or confidential * * *," as provided in Section 6(f) of the FTC Act, 15 U.S.C. 46(f), and FTC Rule 4.10(a)(2), 16 CFR 4.10(a)(2). Comments containing material for

which confidential treatment is requested must be filed in paper form, must be clearly labeled "Confidential," and must comply with FTC Rule 4.9(c), 16 CFR 4.9(c).[1]

Because paper mail addressed to the FTC is subject to delay due to heightened security screening, please consider submitting your comments in electronic form. Comments filed in electronic form should be submitted by using the weblink (*https:// secure.commentworks.com/ftc- healthbreachnotification*), and following the instructions on the web-based form. To ensure that the Commission considers an electronic comment, you must file it on the web-based form at the weblink (*https:// secure.commentworks.com/ftc- healthbreachnotification*). If this Notice appears at (*http://www.regulations.gov/ search/index.jsp*), you also may file an electronic comment through that website. The Commission will consider all comments that regulations.gov forwards to it. You also may visit the FTC website at *http://www.ftc.gov* to read the Notice and the news release describing it.

A comment filed in paper form should include the "Health Breach Notification Rulemaking, Project No. R911002" reference both in the text and on the envelope, and should be mailed or delivered to the following address: Federal Trade Commission/Office of the Secretary, Room H–135 (Annex M), 600 Pennsylvania Avenue, NW., Washington, DC 20580. The FTC is requesting that any comment filed in paper form be sent by courier or overnight service, if possible, because U.S. postal mail in the Washington area and at the Commission is subject to delay due to heightened security precautions.

The FTC Act and other laws the Commission administers permit the collection of public comments to consider and use in this proceeding as appropriate. The Commission will consider all timely and responsive public comments that it receives, whether filed in paper or electronic form. Comments received will be available to the public on the FTC website, to the extent practicable, at (*http://www.ftc.gov/os/ publiccomments.shtm*). As a matter of

discretion, the Commission makes every effort to remove home contact information for individuals from the public comments it receives before placing those comments on the FTC website. More information, including routine uses permitted by the Privacy Act, may be found in the FTC's privacy policy, at (*http://www.ftc.gov/ftc/ privacy.shtm*).

Comments on any proposed filing, recordkeeping, or disclosure requirements that are subject to paperwork burden review under the Paperwork Reduction Act should additionally be submitted to: Office of Information and Regulatory Affairs, Office of Management and Budget ("OMB"), Attention: Desk Officer for Federal Trade Commission. Comments should be submitted via facsimile to (202) 395–5167 because U.S. postal mail at the OMB is subject to delays due to heightened security precautions.

FOR FURTHER INFORMATION CONTACT: Cora Tung Han or Maneesha Mithal, Attorneys, Division of Privacy and Identity Protection, Bureau of Consumer Protection, Federal Trade Commission, 600 Pennsylvania Avenue, NW., Washington, DC 20580, (202) 326–2252.

SUPPLEMENTARY INFORMATION:

Table of Contents

I. Background
II. Section-by-Section Analysis of the Proposed Rule
III. Paperwork Reduction Act
IV. Regulatory Flexibility Act
V. Proposed Rule

I. Background

On February 17, 2009, President Obama signed the American Recovery and Reinvestment Act of 2009 (the "Recovery Act" or "the Act") into law.[2] The Act includes provisions to advance the use of health information technology and, at the same time, strengthen privacy and security protections for health information.

Among other things, the Recovery Act recognizes that there are new types of web-based entities that collect consumers' health information. These entities include vendors of personal health records and online applications that interact with such personal health records. Some of these entities are not subject to the privacy and security requirements of the Health Insurance Portability and Accountability Act ("HIPAA").[3] For such entities, the Recovery Act requires the Department of Health and Human Services ("HHS") to

---

[1] *See also* FTC Rule 4.2(d), 16 CFR 4.2(d). The comment must be accompanied by an explicit request for confidential treatment, including the factual and legal basis for the request, and must identify the specific portions of the comment to be withheld from the public record. The request will be granted or denied by the Commission's General Counsel, consistent with applicable law and the public interest. *See* FTC Rule 4.9(c). 16 CFR 4.9(c).

[2] American Recovery & Reinvestment Act of 2009, Pub. L. 111–5, __ Stat. __.

[3] Health Insurance Portability & Accountability Act, Pub. L. 104–191, 110 Stat. 1936 (1996).

H. Health Breach Notification, Proposed Rules, continued

study, in consultation with the FTC, potential privacy, security, and breach notification requirements and submit a report to Congress containing recommendations within one year of enactment of the Recovery Act. Until Congress enacts new legislation implementing any recommendations contained in the HHS/FTC report, the Recovery Act contains temporary requirements, to be enforced by the FTC, that such entities notify customers in the event of a security breach.[4] The proposed rule implements these requirements.

The Recovery Act also directs HHS to promulgate interim final regulations requiring (1) HIPAA-covered entities, such as hospitals, doctors' offices, and health insurance plans, to notify individuals in the event of a security breach and (2) business associates of HIPAA-covered entities to notify such covered entities in the event of a security breach. To the extent that FTC-regulated entities engage in activities as business associates of HIPAA-covered entities, such entities will be subject only to HHS' rule requirements and not the FTC's rule requirements, as explained below. In addition, the Commission notes that many of the breach notification requirements applicable to FTC-regulated entities are the same as the breach notification requirements applicable to HHS-regulated entities. Indeed, section 13407 of the Recovery Act states that the statutory requirements for timeliness, method, and content of breach notifications contained in section 13402 (the section applicable to HHS-regulated entities) shall apply to FTC-regulated entities "in a manner specified by the Federal Trade Commission." Thus, the FTC is consulting with HHS to harmonize its proposed rule with HHS' proposed rule.

II. Section-by-Section Analysis of the Proposed Rule

The Commission proposes to issue the Health Breach Notification Rule as a new Part 318 of 16 CFR. The following is a section-by-section analysis of the proposed rule.

Proposed Section 318.1: Purpose and Scope

Proposed section 318.1 serves three purposes. First, it states the relevant statutory authority for the proposed rule. Second, it identifies the entities to which the proposed rule would apply:

vendors of personal health records, PHR[5] related entities, and third party service providers. Third, proposed section 318.1 clarifies that the proposed rule does not apply to HIPAA-covered entities or to an entity's activities as a business associate of a HIPAA-covered entity.

The Commission also notes that the proposed rule applies to entities beyond the FTC's traditional jurisdiction under Section 5 of the FTC Act, since the Recovery Act does not limit the FTC's enforcement authority to its enforcement jurisdiction under Section 5. Indeed, section 13407 of the Recovery Act expressly applies to "vendors of personal health records and other non-HIPAA covered entities," without regard to whether such entities fall within the FTC's enforcement jurisdiction. Thus, the proposed rule would apply to entities such as non-profit entities that offer personal health records or related products and services, as well as non-profit third party service providers.

With respect to the scope of the proposed rule, the Commission seeks comment on (1) the nature of entities to which its proposed rule would apply; (2) the particular products and services they offer; (3) the extent to which vendors of personal health records, PHR related entities, and third party service providers may be HIPAA-covered entities or business associates of HIPAA-covered entities; (4) whether some vendors of personal health records may have a dual role as a business associate of a HIPAA-covered entity and a direct provider of personal health records to the public; and (5) circumstances in which such a dual role might lead to consumers' receiving multiple breach notices or receiving breach notices from an unexpected entity, and whether and how the rule should address such circumstances.

Proposed Section 318.2: Definitions

This section defines terms used in the Health Breach Notification Rule.

Breach of Security

The first sentence of proposed paragraph (a) defines "breach of security" as the acquisition of unsecured PHR identifiable health information of an individual in a personal health record without the authorization of the individual. This sentence is identical to the definition of "breach of security" in section 13407(f)(1) of the Recovery Act.

In some cases, it will be fairly easy to determine whether unsecured PHR

identifiable health information has been acquired without authorization. Examples of such cases include the theft of a laptop containing unsecured personal health records; the theft of hard copies of such records; the unauthorized downloading or transfer of such records by an employee; and the electronic break-in and remote copying of such records by a hacker.

In other cases, there may be unauthorized access to data, but it is unclear, without further investigation, whether the data also has been acquired. Unauthorized persons may have *access* to information if it is available to them. The term *acquisition*, however, suggests that the information is not only available to unauthorized persons, but in fact has been obtained by them.

For example, if an entity's access log shows that an unauthorized employee obtained access to information by opening an online database of personal health records, there clearly has been access to the data, but it is not clear whether the data also has been acquired. Consider the following possible scenarios:

(1) the employee viewed the records to find health information about a particular public figure and sold the information to a national gossip magazine;

(2) the employee viewed the records to obtain information about his or her friends;

(3) the employee inadvertently accessed the database, realized that it was not the one he or she intended to view, and logged off without reading, using, or disclosing anything.

In scenario (3), the Commission believes that no acquisition has taken place; thus, breach notification is not required. Unauthorized acquisition has, however, occurred in scenarios (1) and (2).

In the types of situations described above, where there has been unauthorized access to unsecured PHR identifiable health information, the Commission believes that the entity that experienced the breach is in the best position to determine whether unauthorized acquisition has taken place. Thus, the proposed rule creates a presumption that unauthorized persons have acquired information if they have access to it, thus creating the obligation to provide breach notification. This presumption can be rebutted with reliable evidence showing that the information was not or could not reasonably have been acquired. Such evidence can be obtained by, among other things, conducting appropriate interviews of employees, contractors, or other third parties; reviewing access

---

[4] Section 13407(g)(1) of the Recovery Act requires the FTC to promulgate, within 180 days of its enactment, regulations on the breach of security notification provisions applicable to its regulated entities.

[5] PHR means personal health record.

H. Health Breach Notification, Proposed Rules, continued

logs and sign-in sheets; and/or examining forensic evidence.

For example, if an entity's employee loses a laptop containing unsecured health information in a public place, the information would be accessible to unauthorized persons, giving rise to a presumption that unauthorized acquisition has occurred. The entity can rebut this presumption by showing that the laptop was recovered, and that forensic analysis revealed that files were never opened, altered, transferred, or otherwise compromised.

Accordingly, the Commission proposes to add a second sentence to the definition of breach of security as follows: "Unauthorized acquisition will be presumed to include unauthorized access to unsecured PHR identifiable health information unless the vendor of personal health records, PHR related entity, or third party service provider that experienced the breach has reliable evidence showing that there has not been, or could not reasonably have been, any unauthorized acquisition of such information."

Business Associate

Proposed paragraph (b) defines "business associate" to mean a business associate under HIPAA, as defined in 45 CFR 160.103. That regulation, in relevant part, defines a business associate as an entity that (1) provides certain functions or activities on behalf of a HIPAA-covered entity or (2) provides "legal, actuarial, accounting, consulting, data aggregation, management, administrative, accreditation, or financial services to or for" a HIPAA-covered entity.

HIPAA-Covered Entity

Proposed paragraph (c) defines "HIPAA-covered entity" to mean a covered entity under HIPAA, as defined in 45 CFR 160.103. That regulation provides that a HIPAA-covered entity is a health care provider that conducts certain transactions in electronic form, a health care clearinghouse (which provides certain data processing services for health information), or a health plan.

Personal Health Record

Proposed paragraph (d) defines a "personal health record" as an "electronic record of PHR identifiable health information on an individual that can be drawn from multiple sources and that is managed, shared, and controlled by or primarily for the individual." This language is substantively identical to the definition of personal health record

in section 13400(11) of the Recovery Act.[6]

PHR Identifiable Health Information

Proposed paragraph (e) defines "PHR identifiable health information" as "individually identifiable health information, as defined in section 1171(6) of the Social Security Act (42 U.S.C. 1320d(6)),[7] and with respect to an individual, information (1) that is provided by or on behalf of the individual; and (2) that identifies the individual or with respect to which there is a reasonable basis to believe that the information can be used to identify the individual." This definition is substantively identical to section 13407(f)(2) of the Recovery Act.

The Commission notes three points with respect to this definition. First, because the definition of "PHR identifiable health information" includes information that relates to the "past, present, or future payment for the provision of health care to an individual," the proposed rule covers breaches of such information. Thus, for example, the proposed rule would cover a security breach of a database containing names and credit card information, even if no other information was included.

Second, because the definition includes information that relates to "the health or condition" of the individual, it would include *the fact of* having an account with a vendor of personal health records or related entity, where the products or services offered by such vendor or related entity relate to particular health conditions. For example, the theft of an unsecured customer list of a vendor of personal health records or related entity directed to AIDS patients or people with mental illness would require a breach

notification, even if no specific health information is contained in that list.

Third, if there is no reasonable basis to believe that information can be used to identify an individual, the information is not "PHR identifiable health information," and a breach notification need not be provided. For example, if a breach involves information that has been "de-identified" under HHS rules implementing HIPAA, the Commission will deem that information to fall outside the scope of "PHR identifiable health information" and therefore not covered by the proposed rule. The HHS rules specify two ways to de-identify information: (1) If there has been a formal determination by a qualified statistician that information has been de-identified; or (2) if specific identifiers about the individual, the individual's relatives, household members, and employers are removed, and the covered entity has no actual knowledge that the remaining information could be used to identify the individual.[8] There may be additional instances where, even though the standard for de-identification under 45 CFR 164.514(b) is not met, there is no reasonable basis to believe that information is individually identifiable. The Commission requests examples of such instances.

PHR Related Entity

Proposed paragraph (f) defines the term "PHR related entity" to cover the three types of entities set forth in clauses (ii), (iii), and (iv) of section 13424(b)(1)(A) of the Recovery Act.[9] First, the definition includes entities that are not HIPAA-covered entities and that offer products or services through the website of a vendor of personal health records. This definition is substantively identical to the statutory language but also clarifies that HIPAA-covered entities are excluded. This clarification is consistent with the coverage of section 13424, which requires a study and report on the "Application of Privacy and Security Requirements to Non-HIPAA Covered Entities."

Examples of entities that could fall within this category include a web-based application that helps consumers manage medications; a website offering

---

[6] Where this Notice characterizes an element of the proposed rule as "substantively identical" to a corresponding provision in the Recovery Act, the difference between the two texts is minor and not substantive, and the relevant text of both the rule and statute is intended to have the same meaning. For example, the Recovery Act's definition of "personal health record" states that it is an "electronic record of PHR identifiable health information (as defined in section 13407(f)(2))…" The proposed rule definition drops the cross-reference, but is identical in all other respects. In other places, the rule may change a plural to a singular or vice versa; substitute terminology such as "HIPAA-covered entity" for "covered entity"; spell out a shorthand notation in the statute; or make similar non-substantive changes.

[7] This provision defines "individually identifiable health information" as information that "(1) is created or received by a health care provider, health plan, employer, or health care clearinghouse; and (2) relates to the past, present, or future physical or mental health or condition of an individual, the provision of health care to an individual, or the past, present, or future payment for the provision of health care to an individual."

[8] 45 CFR 164.514(b); *see also* U.S. Department of Health and Human Services, OCR Privacy Brief: Summary of the HIPAA Privacy Rule, (*www.hhs.gov/ocr/privacy/hipaa/understanding/summary/privacysummary.pdf*).

[9] At the outset, proposed paragraph (f) clarifies that the term excludes HIPAA-covered entities, as well as other entities to the extent that they engage in activities as a business associate of a HIPAA-covered entity.

H. Health Breach Notification, Proposed Rules, continued

an online personalized health checklist; and a brick-and-mortar company advertising dietary supplements online. Consumers interact with entities in this category by clicking on the appropriate link on the website of a vendor of personal health records.

Second, PHR related entities include entities that are not HIPAA-covered entities and that offer products or services through the websites of HIPAA-covered entities that offer individuals personal health records. This language is substantively identical to section 13424(b)(1)(A)(iii) of the Recovery Act. This category differs from the first category in that it covers entities whose applications are offered through the websites of HIPAA-covered entities, as opposed to non-HIPAA covered entities. Entities may fall in both categories if they offer their applications through both HIPAA-covered websites and non-HIPAA covered websites.

Third, PHR related entities include non-HIPAA covered entities "that access information in a personal health record or send information to a personal health record." This language is substantively identical to section 13424(b)(1)(A)(iv) of the Recovery Act. This category could include online applications through which individuals, for example, connect their blood pressure cuffs, blood glucose monitors, or other devices so that the results could be tracked through their personal health records. It could also include an online medication or weight tracking program that pulls information from a personal health record.

Third Party Service Provider

Proposed paragraph (g) defines the term "third party service provider" as "an entity that (1) provides services to a vendor of personal health records in connection with the offering or maintenance of a personal health record or to a PHR related entity in connection with a product or service offered by that entity, and (2) accesses, maintains, retains, modifies, records, stores, destroys, or otherwise holds, uses, or discloses unsecured PHR identifiable health information as a result of such services." Because the term third party service provider is not defined in the Recovery Act, the Commission based its proposed definition on the description of third party service providers in section 13407(b) of the Act. Third party service providers include, for example, entities that provide billing or data storage services to vendors of personal health records or PHR related entities.

Unsecured

Proposed paragraph (h) defines the term "unsecured" as "not protected through the use of a technology or methodology specified by the Secretary of Health and Human Services in the guidance issued under section 13402(h)(2) of the American Recovery and Reinvestment Act of 2009." If such guidance is not issued by the date specified in such section (i.e., by 60 days after enactment of the Act and annually thereafter), the term unsecured means "not secured by a technology standard that renders PHR identifiable information unusable, unreadable, or indecipherable to unauthorized individuals and that is developed or endorsed by a standards developing organization that is accredited by the American National Standards Institute." The proposed definition is substantively identical to the definition of "unsecured PHR identifiable health information" in the Recovery Act.

Vendor of Personal Health Records

Proposed paragraph (i) defines the term "vendor of personal health records" to mean "an entity, other than a HIPAA-covered entity or an entity to the extent that it engages in activities as a business associate of a HIPAA-covered entity, that offers or maintains a personal health record." This proposed definition is substantively identical to the statutory definition contained in section 13400(18) of the Recovery Act, but also clarifies that a vendor of personal health records does not include entities' activities as a business associate of a HIPAA-covered entity.

Proposed Section 318.3: Breach Notification Requirement

Proposed paragraph 318.3(a) requires vendors of personal health records and PHR related entities, upon discovery of a breach of security, to notify U.S. citizens and residents whose information was acquired in the breach and to notify the FTC. This provision is substantively identical to section 13407(a) of the Recovery Act.

Proposed paragraph 318.3(b) requires third party service providers to both vendors of personal health records and PHR related entities to provide notification to such vendors and entities following the discovery of a breach. The purpose of this requirement is to ensure that the vendor or entity receiving the breach notification is aware of the breach, so that it can in turn provide its customers with a breach notice. To further this purpose, proposed paragraph 318.3(b) requires that the third party service provider's

notification shall include "the identification of each individual" whose information "has been, or is reasonably believed to have been acquired during such breach."

The proposed paragraph is substantively identical to section 13407(b) of the Recovery Act,[10] but adds language requiring entities to provide notice to a senior official of the vendor or PHR related entity and to obtain acknowledgment from such official that he or she has received the notice. The purpose of this requirement is to avoid the situation in which lower-level employees of two entities might have discussions about a breach that never reach senior management. It is also designed to avoid the problem of lost e-mails or voicemails.

Finally, proposed section 318.3(c) provides that a breach "shall be treated as discovered as of the first day on which such breach is known to a vendor of personal health records, PHR related entity, or third party service provider, respectively, (including any person, other than the individual committing the breach, that is an employee, officer, or other agent of such vendor of personal health records, PHR related entity, or third party service provider, respectively) or should reasonably have been known to such vendor of personal health records, PHR related entity, or third party service provider (or person) to have occurred." This proposed paragraph is substantively identical to section 13402(c) of the Recovery Act.[11]

Regarding the "reasonably should have been known" standard, the Commission expects entities that collect and store unsecured PHR identifiable health information to maintain reasonable security measures, including breach detection measures, which should assist them in discovering breaches in a timely manner. If an entity fails to maintain such measures, and

---

[10] As noted above, although the Recovery Act does not define the term "third party service provider," the proposed rule sets forth a definition based on the language in section 13407(b) describing such entities. Thus, it is not necessary to repeat the descriptive language in this section of the proposed rule.

In addition, the proposed rule requires notification to individuals whose information was "acquired," while the Recovery Act uses the terms "accessed, acquired, or disclosed." This change is intended to harmonize the proposed rule with the other provisions of the Act making clear that the standard for FTC-regulated entities, including third party service providers, is "acquired." Indeed, the statute requires third party service providers to notify individuals upon a "breach of security," which is defined only as unauthorized acquisition.

[11] Section 13407(c) of the Recovery Act states that the standard for when breaches are discovered for HIPAA-covered entities also shall apply to FTC-regulated entities "in a manner specified by the Federal Trade Commission."

H. Health Breach Notification, Proposed Rules, continued

thus fails to discover a breach, such failure could constitute a violation of the proposed rule because the entity "reasonably" should have known about the breach. The Commission recognizes, however, that certain breaches may be very difficult to detect, and that an entity with strong breach detection measures may nevertheless fail to discover a breach. In such circumstances, the failure to discover the breach would not constitute a violation of the proposed rule.[12]

Proposed Section 318.4: Timeliness of Notification[13]

Proposed section 318.4(a) requires breach notifications to individuals and the media to be made "without unreasonable delay" and in no case later than 60 calendar days after discovery of the breach. This language is substantively identical to section 13402(d)(1) of the Recovery Act, except that the Commission has clarified that the timing requirement for notice to consumers is different from the requirement for notice to the FTC. Proposed section 318.4(b) states that vendors of personal health records, PHR related entities, and third party service providers have the burden of proving that they provided the appropriate breach notifications. Finally, proposed section 318.4(c) allows breach notification to be delayed upon appropriate request of a law enforcement official. The proposed burden of proof and law enforcement provisions are substantively identical to sections 13402(d)(2) and 13402(g) of the Recovery Act.[14]

The Commission notes that the standard for timely notification is "without unreasonable delay," with the 60-day period serving as an outer limit. Thus, in some cases, it may be an "unreasonable delay" to wait until the 60th day to provide notification. For

example, if a vendor of personal health records or PHR related entity learns of a breach, gathers all necessary information, and has systems in place to provide notification within 30 days, it would be unreasonable to wait until the 60th day to send the notice. There may also be circumstances where a vendor of personal health records or PHR related entity discovers that its third party service provider has suffered a breach (e.g., through a customer or whistleblower) before the service provider notifies the vendor or entity that the breach has occurred. In such circumstances, the vendor or entity should treat this breach as "discovered" for purposes of providing timely notification, and should not wait until receiving notice from the service provider to begin taking steps to address the breach.

Proposed Section 318.5: Methods of Notice[15]

Proposed section 318.5 addresses the methods of notice to individuals, the Commission, and the media in the event of a breach of security of unsecured PHR identifiable health information. The goal of this proposed section is to ensure prompt and effective notice.

Individual Notice

Proposed paragraph (a) addresses notice to individuals. It contains four main requirements. First, proposed paragraph (a)(1) states that individuals must be given notice by first-class mail or, if the individual provides express affirmative consent, by e-mail. This language is identical to section 13402(e)(1)(A) of the Recovery Act, except that it interprets the statutory phrase "specified as a preference by the individual" to mean that the individual must provide "express affirmative consent" to receive breach notices by e-mail. Entities may obtain such consent by asking individuals, when they create an account, whether they would prefer to receive important notices about privacy by first-class mail or e-mail.[16]

The Commission recognizes that the relationship between a vendor of personal health records or PHR related entity and the individual takes place online. Thus, e-mail notice may be particularly well-suited to the relationship. In addition, vendors of

personal health records and PHR related entities may not want to collect mailing addresses from consumers, and consumers may not want to provide them. Under the proposed rule, these entities need not collect such mailing addresses, as long as they obtain consumers' express affirmative consent to receive notices by e-mail. The Commission recognizes that some e-mail notifications may be screened by consumers' spam filters and requests comment on how to address this issue.

Second, as provided in section 13402(e)(1)(C) of the Recovery Act, proposed paragraph (a)(2) allows a vendor of personal health records or PHR related entity to provide notice by telephone or other appropriate means, in addition to the notice provided in paragraph (a)(1), if there is possible imminent misuse of unsecured PHR identifiable health information.

Third, proposed paragraph (a)(3) states that if, after making reasonable efforts to contact an individual through his or her preferred method of communication, the vendor of personal health records or PHR related entity learns that such method is insufficient or out-of-date, the vendor or related entity shall attempt to provide the individual with a substitute form of actual notice, which may include written notice through the individual's less-preferred method, a telephone call, or other appropriate means. This provision gives effect to section 13402(e)(1)(B) of the Recovery Act, which requires a substitute form of notice in the case of insufficient or out-of-date contact information, but adds clarifying language requiring reasonable efforts to provide the preferred form of notice before substitute notice can be used. Examples of reasonable efforts include: (1) where e-mail is the consumer's preferred method, attempting to e-mail the notice and receiving a return message stating that the e-mail could not be delivered; (2) where first class mail is the consumer's preferred method, attempting to mail such notice and having it returned as undeliverable; (3) in the case of incomplete contact information, searching internal records and, if needed, undertaking additional reasonable efforts to obtain complete and accurate contact information from other sources. The proposed rule also adds language stating that methods of substitute notice may include written notice by the consumer's less preferred method or telephone.

Finally, the proposed rule states that if ten or more individuals cannot be reached, the vendor of personal health records or PHR related entity must

---

[12] The Commission enforces a variety of laws requiring entities to provide reasonable and appropriate security for the data that they collect from consumers. *See, e.g.,* Federal Trade Commission Act, 5 U.S.C. 45; Fair Credit Reporting Act, 15 U.S.C. 1681–1681x; Gramm-Leach-Bliley Act, 15 U.S.C. 6801(b), and Standards for Safeguarding Customer Information, 16 CFR Part 314 ("Safeguards Rule"), *available at (http://www.ftc.gov/os/2002/05/67fr36585.pdf.)* The Commission has also disseminated educational materials encouraging companies to provide security for consumer data and providing guidance regarding practical ways to do so.

[13] Section 13407(c) of the Recovery Act states that the requirements for timeliness of notification applicable to HIPAA-covered entities also shall apply to FTC-regulated entities "in a manner specified by the Federal Trade Commission."

[14] Section 13402(d)(1) of the Recovery Act sets forth the standard for timeliness of notification, but notes that this standard is subject to the exception for law enforcement set forth in section 13402(g).

[15] Section 13407(c) of the Recovery Act states that the requirements for methods of breach notification applicable to HIPAA-covered entities also shall apply to FTC-regulated entities "in a manner specified by the Federal Trade Commission."

[16] The Commission does not regard pre-checked boxes or disclosures that are buried in a privacy policy or terms of service agreement to be sufficient to obtain consumers' "express affirmative consent."

H. Health Breach Notification, Proposed Rules, continued

provide substitute notice in one of two forms. First, it can provide notice through the home page of its website. Second, it can provide notice in major print or broadcast media. The language in the proposed rule is substantively identical to section 13402(e)(1)(B) of the Recovery Act, but adds certain clarifying language, as noted below.

As to the first method of substitute notice, the Recovery Act states that the posting should appear for a period determined by the Commission and be "conspicuous." The Commission believes that six months is an appropriate time period for posting of the notice and has so specified in the proposed rule. Requiring a six month posting will ensure that individuals who intermittently check their accounts obtain notice, without being unduly burdensome for businesses.

To ensure conspicuousness, if an entity intends to use a hyperlink on the home page to convey the breach notice, the hyperlink should be (1) prominent so that it is noticeable to consumers, given the size, color and graphic treatment of the hyperlink in relation to other parts of the page; and (2) worded to convey the nature and importance of the information to which it leads. For example, "click here" would not be an appropriate hyperlink; a prominent "click here for an important notice about a security breach that may affect you" would be.[17]

Regarding the requirement that the notice be posted on the home page, the Commission notes that individuals who already have accounts with vendors of personal health records may be directed to a first or "landing" page that is different from the home page to which non-account holders are directed. The Commission thus construes "home page" to include both the home page for new visitors and the landing page for existing account holders. In general, the Commission anticipates that, because PHRs generally involve an online relationship, web posting would be a particularly well-suited method of substitute notice to individuals.

The alternative form of substitute notice described in this paragraph is media notice "in major print or broadcast media, including major media in geographic areas where individuals affected by the breach likely reside, which shall be reasonably calculated to reach individuals affected by the breach." This language is substantively identical to section 13402(e)(1)(B) of the Recovery Act, but also adds a clause

requiring that such notice "be reasonably calculated to reach the individuals affected." Indeed, because this notice is intended to serve as a substitute for notice to particular individuals, it should be reasonably calculated to reach those individuals.

The appropriate scope of substitute media notice will depend on several factors, including the number of individuals for whom no contact information can be obtained, the location of those individuals, and the reach of the particular media used. For example, if a vendor of personal health records experiences a breach in which a hacker obtains the health records of millions of individuals nationwide, and the vendor has no contact information for these individuals, the notice should run multiple times in national print publications and on national network and cable television. In contrast, if an online weight management application loses a customer list and can reach all but 20 individuals in a particular city, it could run a more limited number of advertisements in appropriate local media.

Further, a notice can only be "reasonably calculated to reach the individuals affected" if it is clear and conspicuous. Thus, the notices should be stated in plain language, be prominent, and run multiple times. The Commission requests further comment on the standards that should apply to substitute media notice.

As set forth in section 13402(e)(1)(B) of the Recovery Act, the proposed rule also provides that notice under paragraph (3), whether on the home page of the website or by media notice, must include a toll-free phone number where an individual can learn whether his or her unsecured PHR identifiable health information may be included in the breach. As to this requirement, the Commission notes that entities should have reasonable procedures in place to verify that they are providing the requested information only to the individual and not to an unauthorized person. For example, entities could provide the requested information pertaining to the consumer pursuant to the "preferred method" designated in paragraph (a)(1).

Notice to Media

Proposed paragraph (b) requires media notice "to prominent media outlets serving a State or jurisdiction" if there has been a breach of security of unsecured PHR identifiable health information of 500 or more residents of

the state or jurisdiction.[18] This media notice differs from the substitute media notice described in paragraph 318.5 in that it is directed "to" the media and is intended to supplement, but not substitute for, individual notice. The proposed paragraph is substantively identical to section 13402(e)(2) of the Recovery Act, but adds a requirement that the notice include the information set forth in proposed section 318.6.

This media notice should, at a minimum, include the dissemination of a press release to media outlets in the area(s) affected by the breach. For example, if a breach affects consumers from a particular state or locality, the press release could be sent to the relevant division or department (e.g., health, technology, or business) of a number of state or local print publications, network and cable new shows, and radio stations. The Commission requests further comment on the standards and criteria that should apply in determining the adequacy of media notice.

Notice to the Commission

Proposed paragraph (c) addresses notice to the Commission. Under the proposed paragraph, vendors of personal health records and PHR related entities must provide notice to the Commission as soon as possible and in no case later than five business days if the breach involves the unsecured PHR identifiable health information of 500 or more individuals. If the breach involves the unsecured PHR identifiable health information of fewer than 500 individuals, vendors of personal health records and PHR related entities may, in lieu of immediate notice, maintain a breach log and submit such a log annually to the Commission. The proposed paragraph is substantively identical to section 13402(e)(3) of the Recovery Act, but clarifies the Act's requirements as follows.

First, the paragraph interprets the term "immediately" to mean "as soon as possible, and in no case later than five business days." The Commission believes that this period of time satisfies the requirement for immediacy, while still being sufficient for the breached entity to learn enough about the breach to provide meaningful notice to the Commission.[19]

---

[17] See "Dot Com Disclosures: Information about Online Advertising," (http://www.ftc.gov/bcp/edu/pubs/business/ecommerce/bus41.pdf).

[18] Although section 13402(e)(2) of the Recovery Act requires notice to media for breaches involving "more than 500" residents, section 13402(e)(3) requires notice to the government for breaches with respect to "500 or more" individuals. For consistency, the proposed rule uses "500 or more" for both kinds of notice.

[19] The Commission recognizes that the breached entity may not learn all relevant information about

Continued

H. Health Breach Notification, Proposed Rules, continued

Second, the paragraph states that the "annual log" to be submitted to the Commission for breaches involving fewer than 500 individuals shall be due one year from the date of the entity's first breach.[20] The Commission believes that specifying a date for submitting the log will assist entities in complying with the proposed rule.

Third, the paragraph references a form that the Commission plans to develop, to be posted on the Commission's website, *www.ftc.gov*, and to be used by entities to provide both the immediate and the annual required notice to the Commission under the proposed rule.[21] Among other things, the form will request information similar to that required to be included in a notice to individuals under section 318.6.

Proposed Section 318.6: Content of Notice[22]

Proposed section 318.6 addresses the content of the notice to individuals. It requires that the notice include a description of how the breach occurred; a description of the types of unsecured PHR identifiable health information that were involved in the breach; the steps individuals should take to protect themselves from potential harm; a description of what the vendor of personal health records or PHR related entity involved is doing to investigate the breach, to mitigate any losses, and to protect against any further breaches; and contact procedures for individuals to ask questions or learn additional information. The language in the proposed rule is substantively identical to the language of section 13402(f) of the Recovery Act. The Commission notes two points with respect to this section.

First, to ensure that notices do not raise concerns about phishing, those sending notices should not include any requests for personal or financial information.[23]

Second, the proposed rule requires that the notice identify steps individuals

should take to protect themselves from potential harm. The Commission recognizes that these steps will differ depending on the circumstances of the breach and the type of PHR identifiable health information involved. In some instances—for example, if health insurance account information is compromised—there is a possibility that data will be misused. In such cases, the entity could suggest steps including, but not limited to, requesting and reviewing copies of medical files for potential errors; monitoring explanation of benefit forms for potential errors; contacting insurers to notify them of possible medical identity theft; following up with providers if medical bills do not arrive on time to ensure that an identity thief has not changed the billing address; and, in appropriate cases, trying to change health insurance account numbers.

If the breach also involves Social Security numbers, the entity should suggest additional steps such as placing a fraud alert on credit reports; obtaining and reviewing copies of credit reports for signs of identity theft; calling the local police or sheriff's office in the event suspicious activity is detected; and if appropriate, obtaining a credit freeze.[24] In the case of a breach involving financial account numbers, the entity also should direct consumers to monitor their accounts for suspicious activity and contact their financial institution about closing any compromised accounts. In appropriate cases, the entity also could refer consumers to the FTC's identity theft website, *www.ftc.gov/idtheft*.

In other instances, the likely harm will be personal embarrassment. In such cases, any steps that an individual may choose to take will likely be personal to that individual, and the entity may not be in a position to advise the consumer.

Proposed Sections 318.7, 318.8, and 318.9

Proposed sections 318.7, 318.8, and 318.9 are substantively identical to the statutory provisions on enforcement, effective date, and sunset. Proposed section 318.9 clarifies that the sunsetting of the rule is triggered when Congress enacts new legislation affecting entities subject to the FTC rule.

III. Communications by Outside Parties to Commissioners or Their Advisors

Written communications and summaries or transcripts of oral

communications respecting the merits of this proceeding from any outside party to any Commissioner or Commissioner's advisor will be placed on the public record. *See* 16 CFR 1.26(b)(5).

IV. Paperwork Reduction Act

The Commission is submitting this proposed rule and a Supporting Statement to the Office of Management and Budget for review under the Paperwork Reduction Act ("PRA") (44 U.S.C. 3501–3521). The breach notification requirements discussed above constitute "collections of information" for purposes of the PRA. *See* 5 CFR 1320.3(c). Accordingly, staff has estimated the paperwork burden for these requirements as set forth below.

In the event of a data breach, the proposed rule would require covered firms to investigate and, if certain conditions are met, notify consumers and the Commission. The paperwork burden of these requirements will depend on a variety of factors, including the number of covered firms; the percentage of such firms that will experience a breach requiring further investigation and, if necessary, the sending of breach notices; and the number of consumers notified.

Based on input from industry sources, staff estimates that approximately 200 vendors of personal health records and 500 PHR related entities will be covered by the Commission's proposed rule. Thus, a total of 700 entities may be required to notify consumers and the Commission in the event that they experience a breach. Approximately 200 third party service providers also will be subject to the rule, and thus required to notify vendors of personal health records or PHR related entities in the event of a breach. Thus, a total of approximately 900 entities will be subject to the proposed rule's breach notification requirements.

Staff estimates that these entities, cumulatively, will experience 11 breaches per year for which notification may be required. Because there is insufficient data at this time about the number and incidence of breaches in the PHR industry, staff used available data relating to breaches incurred by private sector businesses in order to calculate a breach incidence rate. Staff then applied this rate to the estimated total number of entities that will be subject to the proposed rule. According to one recent research paper, private sector businesses across multiple industries experienced a total of approximately 50 breaches per year

---

the breach within five business days, such as number of consumers affected or extent of the information breached. Nonetheless, the entity should tell the Commission all that it knows and should provide additional information as it becomes available.

[20] No annual log needs to be provided for years in which no breaches occur.

[21] The Commission also will provide notice of breaches to the Secretary of HHS, as required by section 13407(d) of the Recovery Act.

[22] Section 13407(c) of the Recovery Act states that the requirements for contents of breach notification applicable to HIPAA-covered entities also shall apply to FTC-regulated entities "in a manner specified by the Federal Trade Commission."

[23] Phishing is the act of sending an electronic message under false pretenses to induce unsuspecting victims to reveal personal and financial information.

[24] In general, once a consumer initiates a credit freeze with a consumer reporting agency, the freeze prevents the agency from releasing a credit report about that consumer unless the consumer removes the freeze.

H. Health Breach Notification, Proposed Rules, continued

Federal Register/Vol. 74, No. 74/Monday, April 20, 2009/Proposed Rules   **17921**

during the years 2002 through 2007.[25] Dividing 50 breaches by the estimated number of firms that would be subject to a breach (4,187)[26] yields an estimated breach incidence rate of 1.2% per year. Applying this incidence rate to the estimated 900 vendors of personal health records, PHR related entities, and third party service providers yields an estimate of 11 breaches per year that may require notification of consumers and the Commission.

To determine the annual paperwork burden, staff has developed estimates for three categories of potential costs: (1) The costs of determining what information has been breached, identifying the affected customers, preparing the breach notice, and making the required report to the Commission; (2) the cost of notifying consumers; and (3) the cost of setting up a toll-free number, if needed.

First, in order to determine what information has been breached, identify the affected customers, prepare the breach notice, and make the required report to the Commission, staff estimates that covered firms will require per breach, on average, 100 hours of employee labor at a cost of $4,652,[27] and the services of a forensic expert at an estimated cost of $2,930.[28] Thus, the cost estimate for each breach will be $7,582. This estimate does not include the cost of equipment or other tangible assets of the breached firms, because they likely will use the equipment and other assets they have for ordinary business purposes. Based on the estimate that there will be 11 breaches per year, the annual cost burden for affected entities to perform these tasks will be $83,402 (11 breaches × $7,582 each).

Second, the cost of breach notifications will depend on the number of consumers contacted. Based on a recent survey, 11.6 percent of adults reported receiving a breach notification during a one-year period.[29] Staff estimates that for the prospective 3-year PRA clearance, the average customer base of all vendors of personal health records and PHR related entities will be approximately two million per year. Accordingly, staff estimates that an average of 232,000 consumers per year will receive a breach notification.

Given the online relationship between consumers and vendors of personal health records and PHR related entities, most notifications will be made by email and the cost of such notifications will be de minimis.[30]

In some cases, however, vendors of personal health records and PHR related entities will need to notify individuals by postal mail, either because these individuals have asked for such notification, or because the email addresses of these individuals are not current or not working. Staff estimates that the cost of notifying an individual by postal mail is approximately $2.30 per letter.[31] Assuming that vendors of personal health records and PHR related entities will need to notify by postal mail 10 percent of their customers whose information is breached, the estimated cost of this notification will be $53,360 per year.

In addition, vendors of personal health records and PHR related entities sometimes may need to notify consumers by posting a message on their home page, or by providing media notice. Based on a recent study on data breach costs, staff estimates the cost of providing notice via website posting to be 6 cents per breached record, and the cost of providing notice via published media to be 3 cents per breached record.[32] Applied to the above-stated estimate of 232,000 consumers per year receiving breach notification, the estimated total annual cost of website notice will be $13,920, and the estimated total annual cost of media notice will be $6,960, yielding an estimated total annual cost for all forms of notice to consumers of $74,240.

Finally, the cost of a toll-free number will depend on the cost associated with T1 lines sufficient to handle the projected call volume, the cost of obtaining a toll-free telephone number and queue messaging (a service that provides rudimentary call routing), the cost of processing each call, and the telecommunication charges associated with each call. Because the proposed rule may require entities to notify consumers by posting a message on their homepage for a period of six months, staff estimated the cost of a toll-free line for a six-month period. Based on industry research, staff projects that in order to accommodate a sufficient number of incoming calls for that period, affected entities may need two T1 lines at a cost of $18,000.[33] Staff further estimates that the cost of obtaining a dedicated toll-free line and queue messaging will be $3,017,[34] and that processing an estimated 5,000 calls for the first month per breach will require an average of 1,917 hours of employee labor at a cost of $27,468.[35] Staff estimates that affected entities will need to offer the toll-free number for an additional five months, during which time staff projects that entities will

---

[25] Sasha Romanosky, Rahul Telang & Alessandro Acquisti. "Do Data Breach Disclosure Laws Reduce Identity Theft?" Seventh Workshop on the Economics of Information Security, June 2008. The authors tallied the breaches reported to the website Attrition.org during the time period 2002 to 2007 and counted a total of 773 breaches for a range of entities, including businesses, governments, health providers, and educational institutions. Staff used the volume of breaches reported for businesses (246 over a 5 year period, or approximately 50 per year) because that class of data is most compatible with other data staff used to calculate the incidence of breaches.

[26] Staff focused on firms that routinely collect information on a sizeable number of consumers, thereby rendering them attractive targets for data thieves. To do so, staff focused first on retail businesses and eliminated retailers with annual revenue under $1,000,000. The 2002 Economic Census reports that, in that year, there were 418,713 retailers with revenue of $1,000,000 or more. To apply 50 breaches to such a large population, however, would yield a very small incidence rate. In an abundance of caution, to estimate more conservatively the incidence of breach, staff then assumed that only one percent of these firms had security vulnerabilities that would render them breach targets, thus yielding the total of 4,187.

[27] Hourly wages throughout this notice are based on http://www.bls.gov/ncs/ncswage2007.htm (National Compensation Survey: Occupational Earnings in the United States 2007, U.S. Department of Labor released August 2008, Bulletin 2704, Table 3 ("Full-time civilian workers," mean and median hourly wages).

The breakdown of labor hours and costs is as follows: 50 hours of computer and information systems managerial time at $52.56 per hour; 12 hours of marketing managerial time at $53.00 per hour; 33 hours of computer programmer time at $33.77 per hour; and 5 hours of legal staff time at 54.69 per hour.

[28] Staff estimates that breached entities will use 30 hours of a forensic expert's time. Staff applied the wages of a network systems and data communications analyst ($32.56), tripled it to reflect profits and overhead for an outside consultant ($97.68), and multiplied it by 30 hours to yield $2,930.

[29] Ponemon Institute, "National Survey on Data Security Breach Notification," 2005. Staff believes that this estimate is likely high given the importance of data security to the PHR industry and the likelihood that data encryption will be a strong selling point to consumers.

[30] See National Do Not Email Registry, A Report to Congress, June 2004 n.93, available at www.ftc.gov/reports/dneregistry/report.pdf.

[31] Robin Sidel and Mitchell Pacelle, "Credit-Card Breach Tests Banking Industry's Defenses," Wall Street Journal, June 21, 2005, p.C1. Sidel and Pacelle reported that industry sources estimated the cost per letter to be about $2.00 in 2005. Allowing for inflation, staff estimates the cost to average about $2.30 per letter over the next three years of prospective PRA clearance sought from OMB.

[32] Ponemon Institute, 2006 Annual Study: Cost of a Data Breach, Understanding Financial Impact, Customer Turnover, and Preventative Solutions, Table 2.

[33] According to industry research, the cost of a single T1 line is $1,500 per month.

[34] Staff estimates that installation of a toll-free number and queue messaging will require 40 hours of a technician's time. Staff applied the wages of a telecommunications technician ($25.14), tripled it to reflect profits and overhead of a telecommunications firm ($75.42), and multiplied it by 40 hours to yield $3,017.

[35] The breakdown of labor hours and costs is as follows: 667 hours of telephone operator time (8 minutes per call × 5,000 calls) at $14.87 per hour and 1,250 hours of information processor time (15 minutes per call × 5,000 calls) at $14.04 per hour.

H. Health Breach Notification, Proposed Rules, continued

receive an additional 5,000 calls per breach,[36] yielding an estimated total processing cost of $54,936. In addition, according to industry research, the telecommunication charges associated with the toll-free line will be approximately $2,500.[37] Adding these costs together, staff estimates that the cost per breach for the toll-free line will be $78,453. Based on the above rate of 11 breaches per year, the annual cost burden for affected entities will be $862,983 (11 x $78,453).

In sum, the estimated annual cost burden associated with the breach notification requirements is $1,020,625: $83,402 (costs associated with investigating breaches, drafting notifications of breaches, and notifying the Commission) + $74,240 (costs associated with notifying consumers) + $862,983 (costs associated with establishing toll-free numbers). Staff notes that this estimate likely overstates the costs imposed by the proposed rule because: (1) it assumes that all breaches will require notification, whereas many breaches (e.g., those involving data that is "not unsecured") will not require notification; (2) it assumes that all covered entities will be required to take all of the steps required above; and (3) staff made conservative assumptions in developing many of the underlying estimates.

The Commission invites comments on: (1) whether the proposed collection of information is necessary for the proper performance of the functions of the FTC, including whether the information will have practical utility; (2) the accuracy of the FTC's estimate of the burden of the proposed collection of information; (3) ways to enhance the quality, utility, and clarity of the information to be collected; and (4) ways to minimize the burden of collecting information on those who respond, including through the use of appropriate automated, electronic, mechanical, or other technological collection techniques or other forms of information technology, e.g., permitting electronic submission of responses.

V. Regulatory Flexibility Act

The Regulatory Flexibility Act (RFA), 5 U.S.C. 604(a), requires an agency either to provide an Initial Regulatory Flexibility Analysis with a proposed rule, or certify that the proposed rule

will not have a significant economic impact on a substantial number of small entities. The FTC does not expect that this rule, if adopted, would have a significant economic impact on a substantial number of small entities. First, most of the burdens flow from the mandates of the Act, not from the specific provisions of the proposed rule. Second, the rule will apply to entities that, in many instances, already have obligations to provide notification of data breaches under certain state laws covering medical breaches. Third, once a notice is created, the costs of sending it should be minimal because the Commission anticipates that most consumers will elect to receive notification by e-mail. Nevertheless, to obtain more information about the impact of the proposed rule on small entities, the Commission has decided to publish the following initial regulatory flexibility analysis pursuant to the Regulatory Flexibility Act, 5 U.S.C. 601-612, as amended, and request public comment on the impact on small businesses of its proposed rule.

A. Description of the Reasons That Action by the Agency Is Being Considered

Section 13407 of the American Recovery and Reinvestment Act requires the Commission to promulgate this rule not later than six months after the date of enactment of the Act, or August 18, 2009.

B. Statement of the Objectives of, and Legal Basis for, the Proposed Rule

To implement the requirement that certain entities that handle health information provide notice to individuals whose individually identifiable health information has been breached. The legal basis for the proposed rule is Section 13407 of the American Recovery and Reinvestment Act.

C. Description and Estimate of the Number of Small Entities to Which the Proposed Rule Will Apply

The proposed rule will apply to vendors of personal health records, PHR related entities, and third party service providers. As discussed in the section on Paperwork Reduction Act above, FTC staff estimates that the proposed rule will apply to approximately 900 entities. Determining a precise estimate of which of these entities are small entities, or describing those entities further, is not readily feasible. The Commission invites comment and information on this issue.

D. Projected Reporting, Recordkeeping and Other Compliance Requirements

The Recovery Act and proposed rule impose certain reporting requirements within the meaning of the Paperwork Reduction Act. The Commission is seeking clearance from the Office of Management & Budget (OMB) for these requirements, and the Commission's Supporting Statement submitted as part of that process is being made available on the public record of this rulemaking.

Specifically, the Act and proposed rule require vendors of personal health records and PHR related entities to provide notice to consumers and the Commission in the event of a breach of unsecured PHR identifiable health information. The Act and proposed rule also require third party service providers to provide notice to vendors of personal health records and PHR related entities in the event of such a breach.

If a breach occurs, each entity covered by Act and proposed rule will expend costs to determine the extent of the breach and the individuals affected. If the entity is a vendor of personal health records or PHR related entity, additional costs will include the costs of preparing a breach notice, notifying the Commission, compiling a list of consumers to whom a breach notice must be sent, and sending a breach notice. Such entities may incur additional costs in locating consumers who cannot be reached, and in certain cases, posting a breach notice on a website, notifying consumers through media advertisements, or sending breach notices through press releases to media outlets.

In-house costs may include technical costs to determine the extent of breaches; investigative costs of conducting interviews and gathering information; administrative costs of compiling address lists; professional/legal costs of drafting the notice; and potentially, costs for postage, web posting, and/or advertising. Costs may also include the purchase of services of a forensic expert.

As noted in the Paperwork Reduction Act analysis above, the estimated annual cost burden for all entities subject to the proposed rule will be approximately $1,020,625. The Commission seeks further comment on the costs and burdens of small entities in complying with the requirements of the proposed rule.

E. Other Duplicative, Overlapping, or Conflicting Federal Rules

The FTC has not identified any other federal statutes, rules, or policies

---

[36] Staff anticipates that the greatest influx of calls will be in the first month, and that it will be equivalent to the volume of calls over the remaining five months.

[37] Staff estimates a cost per call of 25¢ (5¢ per minute/per call × 5 minutes per call). Assuming 10,000 calls for each breach, the total estimated telecommunications charges are $2,500.

H. Health Breach Notification, Proposed Rules, continued

currently in effect that would conflict with the proposed rule. As noted above, there is a potential for overlap with forthcoming HHS rules governing breach notification for HIPAA-covered entities. The Commission is consulting with HHS on this potential overlap. The Commission invites comment and information on this overlap, along with any other potentially duplicative, overlapping, or conflicting federal statutes, rules, or policies.

F. Description of Any Significant Alternatives to the Proposed Rule

In drafting the proposed rule, the Commission has made every effort to avoid unduly burdensome requirements for entities. In particular, the Commission believes that the alternative of providing notice to consumers electronically will assist small entities by significantly reducing the costs of sending breach notices.

The Commission is not aware of alternative methods of compliance that will reduce the impact of the proposed rule on small entities, while also comporting with the Recovery Act. The statutory requirements are specific as to the timing, method, and content of notice, as well as the effective date of the final rule that results from this Notice of Proposed Rulemaking. Accordingly, the Commission seeks comment and information on ways in which the rule could be modified to reduce any costs or burdens for small entities consistent with the Recovery Act's mandated requirements.

VI. Proposed Rule

List of Subjects in 16 CFR Part 318

Consumer protection, Data protection, Health records, Privacy, Trade practices.

Accordingly, for the reasons set forth in the preamble, the Commission proposes to add a new Part 318 of title 16 to the Code of Federal Regulations to read as follows:

PART 318—HEALTH BREACH NOTIFICATION RULE

Sec.
318.1   Purpose and scope.
318.2   Definitions.
318.3   Breach notification requirement.
318.4   Timeliness of notification.
318.5   Method of notice.
318.6   Content of notice.
318.7   Enforcement.
318.8   Effective date.
318.9   Sunset.

Authority: Pub. L. 111-5.

§ 318.1 Purpose and scope.

This part, which shall be called the "Health Breach Notification Rule," implements Section 13407 of the American Recovery and Reinvestment Act of 2009. It applies to vendors of personal health records, PHR related entities, and third party service providers. It does not apply to HIPAA-covered entities, or to any other entity to the extent that it engages in activities as a business associate of a HIPAA-covered entity.

§ 318.2 Definitions.

(a) *Breach of security* means, with respect to unsecured PHR identifiable health information of an individual in a personal health record, acquisition of such information without the authorization of the individual. Unauthorized acquisition will be presumed to include unauthorized access to unsecured PHR identifiable health information unless the vendor of personal health records, PHR related entity, or third party service provider that experienced the breach has reliable evidence showing that there has not been, or could not reasonably have been, any unauthorized acquisition of such information.

(b) *Business associate* means a business associate under the Health Insurance Portability and Accountability Act, Pub. L. 104–191, 110 Stat. 1936, as defined in 45 CFR 160.103.

(c) *HIPAA-covered entity* means a covered entity under the Health Insurance Portability and Accountability Act, Pub. L. 104–191, 110 Stat. 1936, as defined in 45 CFR 160.103.

(d) *Personal health record* means an electronic record of PHR identifiable health information on an individual that can be drawn from multiple sources and that is managed, shared, and controlled by or primarily for the individual.

(e) *PHR identifiable health information* means "individually identifiable health information," as defined in section 1171(6) of the Social Security Act (42 U.S.C. 1320d(6)), and, with respect to an individual, information:

(1) That is provided by or on behalf of the individual; and

(2) That identifies the individual or with respect to which there is a reasonable basis to believe that the information can be used to identify the individual.

(f) *PHR related entity* means an entity, other than a HIPAA-covered entity or an entity to the extent that it engages in activities as a business associate of a HIPAA-covered entity, that:

(1) Offers products or services through the website of a vendor of personal health records;

(2) Offers products or services through the websites of HIPAA-covered entities that offer individuals personal health records; or

(3) Accesses information in a personal health record or sends information to a personal health record.

(g) *Third party service provider* means an entity that:

(1) Provides services to a vendor of personal health records in connection with the offering or maintenance of a personal health record or to a PHR related entity in connection with a product or service offered by that entity; and

(2) Accesses, maintains, retains, modifies, records, stores, destroys, or otherwise holds, uses, or discloses unsecured PHR identifiable health information as a result of such services.

(h) *Unsecured* means PHR identifiable information that is not protected through the use of a technology or methodology specified by the Secretary of Health and Human Services in the guidance issued under section 13402(h)(2) of the American Reinvestment and Recovery Act of 2009. If such guidance is not issued by the date specified in section 13402(h)(2), the term "unsecured" shall mean not secured by a technology standard that renders PHR identifiable health information unusable, unreadable, or indecipherable to unauthorized individuals and that is developed or endorsed by a standards developing organization that is accredited by the American National Standards Institute.

(i) *Vendor of personal health records* means an entity, other than a HIPAA-covered entity or an entity to the extent that it engages in activities as a business associate of a HIPAA-covered entity, that offers or maintains a personal health record.

§ 318.3 Breach notification requirement.

(a) *In general.* In accordance with §§ 318.4, 318.5, and 318.6, each vendor of personal health records, following the discovery of a breach of security of unsecured PHR identifiable health information that is in a personal health record maintained or offered by such vendor, and each PHR related entity, following the discovery of a breach of security of such information that is obtained through a product or service provided by such entity, shall—

(1) Notify each individual who is a citizen or resident of the United States whose unsecured PHR identifiable health information was acquired by an unauthorized person as a result of such breach of security; and

(2) Notify the Federal Trade Commission.

H. Health Breach Notification, Proposed Rules, continued

(b) *Third party service providers.* A third party service provider shall, following the discovery of a breach of security, provide notice of the breach to a senior official at the vendor of personal health records or PHR related entity to which it provides services, and obtain acknowledgment from such official that such notice was received. Such notification shall include the identification of each individual whose unsecured PHR identifiable health information has been, or is reasonably believed to have been, acquired during such breach.

(c) *Breaches treated as discovered.* A breach of security shall be treated as discovered as of the first day on which such breach is known to a vendor of personal health records, PHR related entity, or third party service provider, respectively, (including any person, other than the individual committing the breach, that is an employee, officer, or other agent of such vendor of personal health records, PHR related entity, or third party service provider, respectively) or should reasonably have been known to such vendor of personal health records, PHR related entity, or third party service provider (or person) to have occurred.

§318.4   Timeliness of notification.

(a) *In general.* Except as provided in paragraph (c) of this section and §318.5(c), all notifications required under §§318.3(a) and 318.3(b) shall be made without unreasonable delay and in no case later than 60 calendar days after the discovery of a breach of security.

(b) *Burden of proof.* The vendor of personal health records, PHR related entity, and third party service provider involved shall have the burden of demonstrating that all notifications were made as required under this part, including evidence demonstrating the necessity of any delay.

(c) *Law enforcement exception.* If a law enforcement official determines that a notification, notice, or posting required under this part would impede a criminal investigation or cause damage to national security, such notification, notice, or posting shall be delayed. This paragraph shall be implemented in the same manner as provided under § 164.528(a)(2) of title 45, Code of Federal Regulations, in the case of a disclosure covered under such section.

§318.5   Method of notice.

(a) *Individual notice.* A vendor of personal health records or PHR related entity that experiences a breach of security shall provide notice of such

breach to an individual promptly, as described in § 318.4, and in the following form:

(1) Written notice by first-class mail to the individual (or the next of kin of the individual if the individual is deceased) at the last known address of the individual or the next of kin, respectively, or, if the individual provides express affirmative consent, by electronic mail. The notice may be provided in one or more mailings as information is available.

(2) In any case deemed by the vendor of personal health records or PHR related entity to require urgency because of possible imminent misuse of unsecured PHR identifiable health information, that entity may provide information to individuals by telephone or other means, as appropriate, in addition to notice provided under paragraph (a)(1) of this section.

(3) If, after making reasonable efforts to contact the individual through his or her preferred form of communication under paragraph (a)(1) of this section, the vendor of personal health records or PHR related entity finds that such preferred form of communication is insufficient or out-of-date, the vendor of personal health records or PHR related entity shall attempt to provide the individual with a substitute form of actual notice, which may include written notice by the consumer's less preferred method or telephone.

(4)(i) If ten or more individuals cannot be reached by the methods specified in paragraphs (a)(1)through (3) of this section, the vendor of personal health records or PHR related entity involved shall provide notice:

(A) Through a conspicuous posting for a period of six months on the home page of its website; or

(B) In major print or broadcast media, including major media in geographic areas where the individuals affected by the breach likely reside, which shall be reasonably calculated to reach the individuals affected by the breach.

(ii) Such a notice in media or web posting shall include a toll-free phone number where an individual can learn whether or not the individual's unsecured PHR identifiable health information may be included in the breach.

(b) *Notice to media.* A vendor of personal health records or PHR related entity shall provide notice to prominent media outlets serving a State or jurisdiction, following the discovery of a breach of security, if the unsecured PHR identifiable health information of 500 or more residents of such State or jurisdiction is, or is reasonably believed to have been, acquired during such

breach. Such notice shall include, at a minimum, the information contained in § 318.6.

(c) *Notice to FTC.* Vendors of personal health records and PHR related entities shall provide notice to the Federal Trade Commission following the discovery of a breach of security. If the breach involves the unsecured PHR identifiable health information of 500 or more individuals, then such notice shall be provided as soon as possible and in no case later than five business days following the date of discovery of the breach. If the breach involved the unsecured PHR identifiable health information of fewer than 500 individuals, the vendor of personal health records or PHR related entity may maintain a log of any such breach occurring over the ensuing twelve months and submit the log to the Federal Trade Commission documenting breaches from the preceding year. All notices pursuant to this paragraph shall be provided according to instructions at the Federal Trade Commission's website.

§318.6   Content of notice.

Regardless of the method by which notice is provided to individuals under section 318.5, notice of a breach of security shall include, to the extent possible, the following:

(a) A brief description of how the breach occurred, including the date of the breach and the date of the discovery of the breach, if known;

(b) A description of the types of unsecured PHR identifiable health information that were involved in the breach (such as full name, Social Security number, date of birth, home address, account number, or disability code);

(c) Steps individuals should take to protect themselves from potential harm resulting from the breach;

(d) A brief description of what the entity that suffered the breach is doing to investigate the breach, to mitigate losses, and to protect against any further breaches; and

(e) Contact procedures for individuals to ask questions or learn additional information, which shall include a toll-free telephone number, an e-mail address, website, or postal address.

§318.7   Enforcement.

A violation of § 318.3 of this part shall be treated as an unfair or deceptive act or practice in violation of a regulation under section 18(a)(1)(B) of the Federal Trade Commission Act (15 U.S.C. 57a(a)(1)(B)) regarding unfair or deceptive acts or practices.

H. Health Breach Notification, Proposed Rules, continued

§318.8 Effective date.

This part shall apply to breaches of security that are discovered on or after September 18, 2009.

§318.9 Sunset.

If new legislation is enacted establishing requirements for notification in the case of a breach of security that apply to entities covered by this part, the provisions of this part shall not apply to breaches of security discovered on or after the effective date of regulations implementing such legislation.

By direction of the Commission.

Donald S. Clark,
Secretary.

[FR Doc. E9–8882 Filed 4–17–09; 8:45 am]
[BILLING CODE 6750–01–S]

SECURITIES AND EXCHANGE COMMISSION

17 CFR Part 248

[Release Nos. 34–59769, IA–2866, IC–28697; File No. S7–09–07]

RIN 3235–AJO6

Interagency Proposal for Model Privacy Form Under the Gramm-Leach-Bliley Act

AGENCY: Securities and Exchange Commission.

ACTION: Proposed rule; reopening of comment period.

SUMMARY: The Securities and Exchange Commission ("Commission") is reopening the period for public comment on proposed amendments to Regulation S–P, which implements the privacy provisions of the Gramm-Leach-Bliley Act ("GLB Act"), originally published in the **Federal Register** on March 29, 2007. The proposed amendments would, if adopted, create a safe harbor for a model form that financial institutions may use to provide disclosures in initial and annual privacy notices required under Regulation S–P.

DATES: Comments should be received on or before May 20, 2009.

ADDRESSES: Comments may be submitted by any of the following methods:

Electronic Comments

• Use the Commission's Internet comment form (*http://www.sec.gov/rules/proposed.shtml*); or

• Send an e-mail to *rule-comments@sec.gov.* Please include File Number S7–09–07 on the subject line; or

• Use the Federal eRulemaking Portal (*http://www.regulations.gov*). Follow the instructions for submitting comments.

Paper Comments

• Send paper comments in triplicate to Elizabeth M. Murphy, Secretary, Securities and Exchange Commission, 100 F Street, NE., Washington, DC 20549–1090.

All submissions should refer to File Number S7–09–07. This file number should be included on the subject line if e-mail is used. To help us process and review your comments more efficiently, please use only one method. The Commission will post all comments on the Commission's Internet Web site (*http://www.sec.gov/rules/proposed.shtml*). Comments are also available for public inspection and copying in the Commission's Public Reference Room, 100 F Street, NE., Washington, DC 20549, on official business days between the hours of 10 a.m. and 3 p.m. All comments received will be posted without change; we do not edit personal identifying information from submissions. You should submit only information that you wish to make available publicly.

FOR FURTHER INFORMATION CONTACT: Paula Jenson, Deputy Chief Counsel, or Brice Prince, Special Counsel, Office of Chief Counsel, Division of Trading and Markets, (202) 551–5550; or Penelope Saltzman, Assistant Director, or Thoreau Bartmann, Senior Counsel, Office of Regulatory Policy, Division of Investment Management, (202) 551–6792, Securities and Exchange Commission, 100 F Street, NE., Washington, DC 20549.

SUPPLEMENTARY INFORMATION: The Commission is reopening the period for public comment on proposed rule amendments,[1] which were proposed pursuant to the Financial Services Regulatory Relief Act of 2006 (the "Act"), enacted on October 13, 2006.[2] The proposal was published on March 29, 2007, and the comment period closed on May 29, 2007. Section 728 of the Act added subsection (e) to section 503 of the GLB Act, which directs the Commission, together with seven other federal agencies[3] (collectively the

"Agencies") responsible for implementing Title V, Subtitle A of the GLB Act, to "jointly develop a model form which may be used, at the option of the financial institution, for the provision of disclosures under this section."[4] The proposed amendments would, if adopted, create a safe harbor for a model privacy notice form that financial institutions may use to provide disclosures required under the privacy rules[5] adopted by the Agencies pursuant to section 504 of the GLB Act.[6]

In connection with the development of the model form, an outside consultant, Macro International ("Macro") was retained to conduct quantitative testing to evaluate the effectiveness of four different types of privacy notices, including a slightly revised version of the proposed model privacy notice form.[7] Macro tested the notices on approximately 1,000 consumers at five retail shopping mall locations around the country. Each of the four notices used for testing was printed in a double-sided format, using the front and back sides of an 8½ x 11-inch piece of white paper. We have placed in the comment file for the proposed rule (available at *http://www.sec.gov/comments/s7-09-07/s70907.shtml* and at *http://www.ftc.gov/privacy/privacyinitiatives/financial_rule_inrp.html*) the following documents from the testing: (i) The test data collected and provided by Macro together with the codebook that relates to the data; (ii) the report provided by Macro, which includes a summary of the methodology used in collecting the data, the interview protocol, and the four test notices; and (iii) a report describing the results of the test data prepared by Dr. Alan Levy and Dr. Manoj Hastak.[8]

We are reopening the comment period before final action is taken on the proposal in order to provide all persons who are interested in this matter an opportunity to comment on these

---

Governors of the Federal Reserve System ("Board"), Federal Trade Commission ("FTC"), National Credit Union Administration ("NCUA"), Office of the Comptroller of the Currency ("OCC"), and Office of Thrift Supervision ("OTS").

[4] *See supra* note 2, adding 15 U.S.C. 6803(e). The Act stipulates that the model form shall be a safe harbor for financial institutions that elect to use it.

[5] For the Agencies' privacy rules *see* 12 CFR Part 40 (OCC); 12 CFR Part 216 (Board); 12 CFR Part 332 (FDIC); 12 CFR Part 573 (OTS); 12 CFR Part 716 (NCUA); 16 CFR Part 313 (FTC); 17 CFR Part 160 (CFTC); 17 CFR Part 248 (Commission).

[6] Codified at 15 U.S.C. 6804.

[7] As described in the Interagency Proposal, the consumer research project on privacy notices was launched in 2004. Interagency Proposal *supra* note 1, at Section I.B.

[8] Dr. Levy and Dr. Hastak are consultants to the model privacy notice research project.

---

[1] *See* Interagency Proposal for Model Privacy Form Under the Gramm-Leach-Bliley Act, Securities Exchange Act Release No. 55497, Investment Company Act Release No. 27755 (Mar. 20, 2007) [72 FR 14940 (Mar. 29, 2007)] ("Interagency Proposal") and (72 FR 16875 (Apr. 5, 2007)] (correction notice).

[2] Public Law 109–351 (Oct. 13, 2006), 120 Stat. 1966.

[3] The seven other agencies are the: Commodity Futures Trading Commission ("CFTC"), Federal Deposit Insurance Corporation ("FDIC"), Board of

Chapter 13

Other Major Health Plan Reform

Introduction   In addition to HIPAA, five other important laws affecting health plans have been enacted:

- The Consolidated Omnibus Budget Reconciliation Act of 1985 (COBRA)
- The Mental Health Parity Act of 1996 (MHPA)
- The Newborns' and Mothers' Health Protection Act of 1996 (NMHPA)
- The Women's Health and Cancer Rights Act of 1998 (WHCRA)
- The Children's Health Insurance Program Reauthorization Act of 2009

Additionally, many states are beginning to consider wide reforms in health laws that mandate health coverage for all residents.

This chapter provides an overview of these laws.

In this chapter   This chapter has five sections:

A. Consolidated Omnibus Budget Reconciliation Act

Introduction

The Consolidated Omnibus Budget Reconciliation Act (COBRA) was signed into law on April 7, 1986. The main purpose of COBRA is to require most employers maintaining group health plans to give employees and their dependents the opportunity to continue health coverage at affordable group rates in cases where they would otherwise lose coverage because of certain qualifying events. In general, the cost to the employee or dependent cannot exceed 102 percent of the cost for coverage.

For details regarding COBRA's requirements, refer to the *Quick Guide to COBRA Compliance.*

Eligibility for COBRA

Qualified beneficiaries eligible to elect COBRA coverage are:

- A covered employee, spouse, and dependent children who lose coverage as a result of a qualifying event
- Children born to or placed for adoption with a covered employee who has COBRA coverage

Qualifying events

Qualifying events are:

- A covered employee's reduction in work hours or termination of employment for any reason except gross misconduct
- A covered employee's death
- A covered employee's divorce or legal separation from a spouse
- A covered employee's entitlement to Medicare under title XVIII of the Social Security Act
- A covered dependent's loss of dependent status under the terms of the group health plan
- An employer's commencement of a Title 11 bankruptcy proceeding that causes a retiree (or spouse or child of a retiree) a substantial loss or elimination of coverage within one year of the filing

Election period

In general, qualified beneficiaries have 60 days to elect COBRA coverage. The 60-day election period generally begins the date the qualified beneficiary loses coverage, of if later, the date the beneficiary is notified of his or her right to elect COBRA coverage.

A. Consolidated Omnibus Budget Reconciliation Act, continued

Notice requirements

COBRA imposes several notice requirements, including:

- General notice to all plan participants explaining the right to elect COBRA within 90 days after coverage begins
- Notice that a qualifying event has occurred within 30 days of the event
- Election notice detailing a qualified beneficiary's right to elect COBRA coverage within 14 days of being notified of an event

Employers are required to provide notice of all qualifying events except in the case of a covered employee's divorce or legal separation or a child's loss of dependent status under the terms of the plan. In such cases, the qualified beneficiary must provide notice of the event.

Plan administrators must provide the election notice. As a practical matter, employers are frequently the named plan administrator.

COBRA payments

In general, qualified beneficiaries must pay the full cost of COBRA coverage plus a 2 percent administrative fee. A qualified beneficiary has 45 days from the date of his or her election to make the first payment for COBRA coverage. Thereafter, the qualified beneficiary has a 30-day grace period in which to pay for coverage.

COBRA premium subsidy requirements

The American Recovery and Reinvestment Act of 2009 (ARRA) made significant changes to COBRA. ARRA provides assistance for certain involuntarily terminated employees and their families who elect COBRA. These individuals are eligible for premium assistance in the form of a 65 percent reduction in their COBRA premium otherwise payable.

ARRA requires that those eligible for premium assistance be treated as having paid for coverage if they pay 35 percent of the COBRA premium. The employer is reimbursed the other 65 percent through a credit against payroll taxes.

ARRA applies to eligible employees who are involuntarily terminated from employment during the period September 1, 2008 through December 31, 2009.

B. Mental Health Parity Act

Overview

The Mental Health Parity Act (MHPA), as signed into law on September 26, 1996, required parity with respect to the application of annual and aggregate lifetime benefits to certain mental health benefits.

The Paul Wellstone and Pete Domenici Mental Health Parity and Addiction Equity Act of 2008 (MHPAEA), which was signed into law on October 3 as part of the Emergency Economic Stabilization Act, made significant changes to the MHPA.

General rules

In general, MHPA bars group health plans, insurance companies, and health maintenance organizations (HMOs) offering *mental health benefits* from setting annual or aggregate lifetime benefits on mental health benefits that are lower than the limits for *medical and surgical benefits*.[1] If a plan does not impose any annual or lifetime limits on medical and surgical benefits, then it cannot impose any annual or lifetime limits on mental health benefits.

The MHPAEA expands parity to include deductibles, co-pays, out-of-pocket maximums, coinsurance, covered hospital days, and covered out-patient visits.[2] Specifically, the MHPAEA requires a group health plan that provides both medical and surgical benefits and mental health or substance use disorder benefits to ensure **all** of the following:

- Financial requirements (e.g., deductibles and co-pays) are no more restrictive for mental health or substance use disorder benefits than they are for medical and surgical benefits.
- No separate cost sharing requirements apply to mental health or substance use disorder benefits.
- Treatment limitations are no more restrictive for mental health or substance use disorder benefits than they are for medical and surgical benefits.
- No separate treatment limitations apply to mental health or substance use disorder benefits.

In addition, the MHPAEA:

- Requires that the plan administrator make the criteria for medical necessity determinations and the reason for claims denials under the plan with respect to mental health or substance use disorder benefits to be made available.

---

[1] ERISA § 712(a)(1) and (2), PHSA 42 U.S.C.S. § 300gg-5(a)(1) and (2).
[2] Mental Health Parity and Addiction Equity Act of 2008 (MHPAEA), Title V, Subtitle B, Section 512, Summary

B. Mental Health Parity Act, continued

General rules (continued)	• Requires a plan to provide out-of-network coverage for mental health or substance use disorder benefits if the plan provides out-of-network coverage for medical or surgical benefits.
Aggregate lifetime limit, defined	An **aggregate lifetime limit** is the limit on the total amount of benefits that may be paid under a plan for a covered individual or other coverage unit.[3]
Annual limit, defined	An **annual limit** is the limit on the total amount of benefits that may be paid in a 12-month period under the plan for an individual or other coverage unit.[4]
Mental health benefits, defined	**Mental health benefits** are mental health services benefits as defined by the plan.[5]

---

[3] ERISA § 712(e)(1), PHSA 42 U.S.C.S. § 300gg-5(e)(1).
[4] ERISA § 712(e)(2), PHSA 42 U.S.C.S. § 300gg-5(e)(2).
[5] ERISA § 712(e)(4), PHSA 42 U.S.C.S. § 300gg-5(e)(4).

B. Mental Health Parity Act, continued

Medical and surgical benefits, defined

Medical and surgical benefits are medical and surgical services benefits as defined under the terms of the plan.[6] They do not include mental health benefits.

Mental health benefits not required

MHPA does not require employers or plans to provide mental health benefits.[7] That is, its provisions apply only to plans that actually offer medical and surgical benefits and mental health or substance abuse disorder benefits.

Exemptions

The MHPAEA requirements do not apply to:[8]

- Small employers (i.e., companies with 50 or fewer employees).
- A group health plan where application of the MHPAEA results in an actual increase in the total cost of coverage for medical, surgical, mental health, and substance abuse disorder benefits of greater than 2 percent for the first plan year and 1 percent for each plan year thereafter.

With regard to the exemption based on cost, the determination of increases in actual costs under a plan has to be made and certified by a qualified and licensed actuary. In addition, the determination cannot be made until after the plan has complied with the new requirements for the first six months of the plan year.

---

[6] ERISA § 712(e)(3), PHSA 42 U.S.C.S. § 300gg-5(e)(3).
[7] ERISA § 712(b)(1), PHSA 42 U.S.C.S. § 300gg-5(b)(1).
[8] MHPAEA, Title V, Subtitle B, Section 512, Summary.

B. Mental Health Parity Act, continued

Effective date

The MHPA requirements applied to group health plans for plan years beginning on or after January 1, 1998. As originally enacted, the MHPA requirements were to cease to apply to benefits for services furnished on or after September 30, 2001.[9] However, over the years, several amendments occurred to extend the sunset provision well beyond 2001.

In general, the provisions enacted under the MHPAEA take effect with the first plan year beginning after the MHPAEA was enacted. Thus, for calendar year plan years, the effective date is January 1, 2010.[10]

[9] ERISA §712(f), PHSA 42 U.S.C.S. §300gg-5(f)
[10] MHPAEA, Title V, Subtitle B, Section 512, Summary.

C. Newborns' and Mothers' Health Protection Act

Overview

The Newborns' and Mothers' Health Protection Act (NMHPA), signed into law on September 26, 1996, protects newborns and mothers by requiring that they be allowed to stay in a hospital for a certain length of time.

Length of stay requirements

Under NMHPA, group health plans, insurance companies, and HMOs offering health coverage for hospital stays in connection with the birth of a child must provide health coverage for a minimum period of time.[11] For normal vaginal deliveries, that time is 48 hours. For cesarean deliveries, the minimum period is 96 hours.

Exception

NMHPA does not apply to any case in which the mother, in consultation with the health provider, decides to leave the hospital before the period required by NMHPA ends.[12]

In addition, NMHPA does not require a mother to

- Give birth in a hospital or
- Stay in a hospital for a fixed period of time following the birth of her child.[13]

Prohibitions

A group health plan, a health insurer, and an HMO may not[14]

- Deny a mother and her newborn eligibility or continued eligibility to enroll in or to renew coverage under the plan to avoid the NMHPA requirements;
- Give money or rebates to mothers to encourage them to accept less than the minimum protection of NMHPA;
- Penalize or reduce or limit the reimbursement of an attending provider who provides care according to NMHPA;

---

[11] ERISA § 711(a)(1), PHSA 42 U.S.C.S. § 300gg-4(a)(1).
[12] ERISA § 711(a)(2), PHSA 42 U.S.C.S. § 300gg-4(a)(2).
[13] ERISA § 711(c)(1), PHSA 42 U.S.C.S. § 300gg-4(c)(1).
[14] ERISA § 711(b), PHSA 42 U.S.C.S. § 300gg-4(b).

C. Newborns' and Mothers' Health Protection Act, continued

Prohibitions (continued)

- Give incentives (monetary or otherwise) to an attending provider to provide a mother and newborn with care that is inconsistent with the NMHPA provisions; or
- Restrict benefits for any part of a period within a hospital length of stay in a manner that is less favorable than the benefits provided for any preceding portion of the stay.

What NMHPA does not require

NMHPA does not require employers, group health plans, health insurers, or HMOs to provide coverage for hospital stays for childbirth.[15] That is, NMHPA applies only to those who choose to provide the coverage.

NMHPA does not prevent a group health plan or insurer from imposing plan deductibles, co-insurance, or other cost-sharing in relation to benefits for hospital stays for childbirth.[16] However, the co-insurance or other cost-sharing for any portion of a period of a hospital stay cannot be greater than the co-insurance or other cost-sharing for any preceding portion of the hospital stay.

In addition, NMHPA does not prevent a group health plan or health insurer from negotiating with the provider on the level and type of reimbursement for care provided according to the NMHPA.[17]

Notice requirement

The imposition of the NMHPA requirements is considered a material modification to the terms of a plan.[18] The plan, therefore, must notify participants of the material change. NMHPA requires plans to notify participants no later than 60 days after the first day of the first plan year in which the requirements apply.

---

[15] ERISA § 711(c)(2), PHSA 42 U.S.C.S. § 300gg-4(c)(2).
[16] ERISA § 711(c)(3), PHSA 42 U.S.C.S. § 300gg-4(c)(3).
[17] ERISA § 711(e), PHSA 42 U.S.C.S. § 300gg-4(e).
[18] ERISA § 711(d), PHSA 42 U.S.C.S. § 300gg-4(d).

C. Newborns' and Mothers' Health Protection Act, continued

Preemption

State law preempts the NMHPA requirements in the following circumstances:[19]

- State law provides for at least a 48-hour hospital stay following a normal vaginal delivery and at least a 96-hour hospital stay following a cesarean delivery.
- State law requires that maternity and pediatric care be provided in accordance with the guidelines established by the American College of Obstetricians and Gynecologists, the American Academy of Pediatrics, or other established medical associations.
- State law requires that when maternity coverage is provided, the attending provider, in consultation with the mother, determine the length of hospital stay.

The rules concerning the continued applicability of state law with respect to health insurers do not supersede any state law described above.[20]

Effective date

The NMHPA requirements apply to group health plans and insurers for plan years beginning on or after January 1, 1998.

---

[19] ERISA § 711(f)(1), PHSA 42 U.S.C.S. § 300gg-4(f)(1).
[20] ERISA § 711(f)(2), PHSA 42 U.S.C.S. § 300gg-4(f)(2).

D. Women's Health and Cancer Rights Act

Overview

The Women's Health and Cancer Rights Act (WHCRA) was signed into law on October 21, 1998. This law requires group health plans, insurance companies, and HMOs that offer coverage for mastectomies to also provide coverage for reconstructive surgery in connection with mastectomies.[21]

Reconstructive surgery coverage

Coverage for reconstructive surgery must include:

- Reconstruction of the breast on which the mastectomy was performed,[22]
- Surgery and reconstruction of the other breast to produce a symmetrical appearance,[23] and
- Prostheses and treatment of any physical complications at all stages of the mastectomy, including lymphedemas.[24]

Group health plans (including HMOs) may impose deductibles or co-insurance if they are consistent with those established for other benefits under the plan.[25]

Covered plans

WHCRA applies to all group health plans, insurers, and HMOs that provide coverage for mastectomies.[26]

Effective date

The WHCRA requirements apply to group health plans for plan years beginning on or after October 21, 1998.[27]

---

[21] ERISA § 713(a), PHSA 42 U.S.C.S. § 2706.
[22] ERISA § 713(a)(1).
[23] ERISA § 713(a)(2).
[24] ERISA § 713(a)(3).
[25] *Id.*
[26] ERISA § 713(a).
[27] WHCRA § 902(c)(1).

D. Women's Health and Cancer Rights Act, continued

Collectively bargained plans

A special rule regarding the effective date applies to collectively bargained plans. The rule states that if a plan maintained pursuant to one or more collective bargaining agreements is amended to conform to the WHCRA requirements, the amendment cannot be treated as a termination of the agreement.[28]

Preemption

WHCRA does not preempt any state law that was in effect on the date it was enacted (October 21, 1998) as long as the state law requires at least the reconstructive breast surgery coverage that is required by WHCRA.[29]

Notice requirements

WHCRA imposes the following two notice requirements:[30]

1. A one-time initial notice that a plan had to furnish no later than January 1, 1999, describing the benefits that WHCRA requires;
2. A second notice describing the benefits that WHCRA requires, which must be furnished upon enrollment and annually.

Content requirements

Both the one-time initial notice and the second notice must include the following information:[31]

- The benefits that WHCRA requires the plan to provide.
- A statement that coverage will be provided to a participant or beneficiary who receives mastectomy benefits and elects breast reconstruction in a manner determined jointly by the attending physician and patient for reconstruction of the breast on which the mastectomy was performed, surgery and reconstruction of the other breast to produce a symmetrical appearance, and prostheses and treatment of physical complications at all stages of the mastectomy, including lymph edemas.
- A description of any deductibles and co-insurance that apply.

---

[28] WHCRA § 902(c)(2).
[29] ERISA § 713(e)(1).
[30] ERISA § 713(b).
[31] *The Women's Health and Cancer Rights Act of 1998: Questions and Answers.*

E. Children's Health Insurance Program Reauthorization Act

Overview	The Children's Health Insurance Program Reauthorization Act (CHIPRA) was signed into law by President Obama on February 4, 2009. CHIPRA extends and expands the State Children's Health Insurance Program (CHIP), which was established under the Social Security Act in 1997 to provide health coverage to eligible children in low income families.
	Among other things, CHIPRA allows states to subsidize premiums for certain employer-sponsored group health plans for eligible children and their families as an alternative to enrollment in a CHIP plan. This option was designed to reduce the number of people who drop private coverage to enroll in public health programs.[32] In addition, CHIPRA imposes new requirements on employers sponsoring group health plans, including special enrollment rights and notice requirements and penalties for noncompliance.

State Option to Subsidize Premiums

State option to subsidize premiums	Under CHIPRA, states have the option of offering a **premium assistance subsidy** for **qualified employer sponsored coverage** to all targeted low- income children who are eligible for child health assistance. However, for the subsidy to be provided to a targeted low-income child, the child or the child's parent must voluntarily elect to receive the subsidy. A state cannot require a child or parent's child to elect the subsidy as a condition of receiving child health assistance.[33]

---

[32] U.S. Senate Committee on Finance, The Children's Health Insurance Program Reauthorization Act Frequently Asked Questions.

[33] CHIPRA, Title III, Subtitle A, Sec. 301(a)(1)(A).

E. Children's Health Insurance Program Reauthorization Act, continued

Qualified employer-sponsored coverage

Qualified employer-sponsored coverage is group health insurance coverage offered by an employer that meets the following requirements:[34]

- The coverage qualifies as "creditable coverage" under HIPAA.
- The employer contributes at least 40 percent of the premium for the coverage.
- The coverage satisfies the eligibility nondiscrimination rules under section 105 of the Internal Revenue Code.

Qualified employer-sponsored coverage does not include benefits provided through a health flexible spending account plan or a high deductible health plan without regard to whether the plan includes a health savings account.

Premium assistance subsidy

In general, a ***premium assistance subsidy*** for a targeted low-income child equals the difference between the employee contribution required under the employer plan for:[35]

- Employee only coverage, and
- coverage for both the employee and the child, less
- any applicable premium cost-sharing required by the state child health plan, which is subject to certain limits including the requirement to count the total amount of the employee contribution required for enrollment toward the aggregate cost-sharing limit.

In addition, CHIPRA amended Medicaid to require that in the case of a child or parent participating in a premium assistance subsidy for qualified employer-sponsored coverage, the state pay not only the premiums for enrollment, but also the deductibles, coinsurance, co-payments, and any other cost sharing obligations for items and services covered by the state plan.[36]

---

[34] CHIPRA, Title III, Subtitle A, Sec. 301(a)(1)(B).
[35] CHIPRA, Title III, Subtitle A, Sec. 301(a)(1)(C).
[36] CHIPRA, Title III, Subtitle A, Sec. 301(b).

E. Children's Health Insurance Program Reauthorization Act, continued

How premium subsidy provided

A state has the option of providing a premium assistance subsidy by reimbursing an employee for out-of-pocket expenses, or by paying the subsidy directly to the employer on behalf of an employee, provided the employer does not opt-out of receiving subsidies from a state.[37]

An employer may notify a state that it elects to opt-out of receiving direct payments of a premium assistance subsidy. If the employer opts out, the employer must withhold the total amount of the employee contribution required for coverage for the employee and the child under the employer plan and the state must pay the premium assistance subsidy directly to the employee.

Parent opt-out

A state must set up a process that allows a parent of a targeted low-income child receiving a premium subsidy to dis-enroll the child from the employer's health plan and instead enroll the child in a state health plan.[38] When a parent opts to dis-enroll in the employer's plan, the change in coverage is effective on the first day of any month for which the child is eligible for assistance. The state must also ensure that the process provides for continuity of coverage for the child.

Premium assistance subsidy for parents

Some states also provide health benefits coverage to parents of children who qualify for health assistance. If so, the state can elect to offer a premium assistance subsidy to a parent in the same manner as the state offers a subsidy for the child, except that the amount of the premium assistance subsidy is increased to take into account the coverage for the parent.[39] The same is true of states providing coverage for families.

Employer-family premium assistance option

An additional option that states have for providing premium assistance is to establish an employer-family premium assistance pool for employers with less than 250 employees who have at least one pregnant employee eligible for health assistance or a member of a family with at least one targeted low-income child.[40] Enrollment in coverage is then made available through the pool. If a state elects this option, it must provide at least two private health plans.

---

[37] CHIPRA, Title III, Subtitle A, Sec. 301(a)(1)(C).
[38] CHIPRA, Title III, Subtitle A, Sec. 301(a)(1)(G).
[39] CHIPRA, Title III, Subtitle A, Sec. 301(a)(1)(H).
[40] CHIPRA, Title III, Subtitle A, Sec. 301(a)(1)(I).

E. Children's Health Insurance Program Reauthorization Act, continued

Special Enrollment Period, Notice Requirements, and Penalties for Noncompliance

Special enrollment period

Under CHIPRA, a group health plan must allow employees and dependents who are eligible, but not enrolled, to enroll in an employer's health plan if the employee or dependent loses his or her Medicaid or state child health plan coverage within 60 days after the date the employee or dependent becomes: [41]

- Ineligible for Medicaid or state child health plan coverage, or
- Eligible for a CHIPRA premium subsidy.

Notice requirements

If an employer maintains a group health plan in a state that provides premium assistance for group health plan coverage, the employer must provide each employee a written notice describing the potential opportunities available in the state in which the employee resides for premium assistance. To comply with this requirement, employers may use any model notice developed by the applicable state. In addition, employers may provide the model notice with other materials used to notify the employee of health plan eligibility or open enrollment or with the summary plan description. [42]

In addition to the above notice requirement, plan administrators must disclose to a state, upon request, information about the benefits available under the group health plan in sufficient specificity to permit the state to determine the cost-effectiveness of the premium assistance.[43]

Penalties for non-compliance

Employers who fail to comply with the new CHIPRA requirements can result in penalties of up to $100 per day from the date of the employer's failure to meet the notice requirements. Each violation with respect to any single employee is treated as a separate violation.

---

[41] CHIPRA, Title III, Subtitle b, Sec. 311(a).
[42] CHIPRA, Title III, Subtitle b, Sec. 311(a).
[43] CHIPRA, Title III, Subtitle b, Sec. 311(a).

E. Children's Health Insurance Program Reauthorization Act, continued

Penalties for non-compliance (continued)

In addition, plan administrators who fail to provide timely benefits information to a state is subject to a $100 per day penalty. Each violation with respect to any single employee is treated as a separate violation.[44]

Effective date

The effective date for the premium assistance and special enrollment requirements is April 1, 2009.

---

[44] CHIPRA, Title III, Subtitle b, Sec. 311(a).

Index

A

Index

C

Index

Index

E

F

Index

G

H

I

Index

Index

Index

Index

Index

Q

R

S

Index

Index

T

U

V

W